August 24–27, 2014
Edmonton, AB, Canada

Association for
Computing Machinery

Advancing Computing as a Science & Profession

PACT'14

Proceedings of the 23rd International Conference on
Parallel Architectures and Compilation Techniques

Sponsored by:

ACM SIGARCH, IEEE Computer Society and IFIP

Supported by:

Intel, EMC², IBM and Google

Association for
Computing Machinery

Advancing Computing as a Science & Profession

The Association for Computing Machinery
2 Penn Plaza, Suite 701
New York, New York 10121-0701

ISBN: 978-1-4503-2809-8 (Digital)

ISBN: 978-1-4503-3262-0 (Print)

Additional copies may be ordered prepaid from:

ACM Order Department
PO Box 30777
New York, NY 10087-0777, USA

Phone: 1-800-342-6626 (USA and Canada)
+1-212-626-0500 (Global)
Fax: +1-212-944-1318
E-mail: acmhelp@acm.org
Hours of Operation: 8:30 am – 4:30 pm ET

Printed in the USA

General Chair's Welcome

It is my great pleasure to welcome you to PACT 2014 in Edmonton. Our goal is for you to experience the University of Alberta campus life, the city of Edmonton and to gain some perspective on why a large city got established in this place given the very cold weather that we experience for a long stretch of the year. Most people understand that the First Nations have adapted and lived in this cold environment for a long time. There are three very important phases to the development of modern Edmonton. The first Europeans came because of the thirst in Europe for fur to make top hats and other fur attire. The settlers came next looking for new land, followed by the establishment of the railroad to the West. More recently, natural resources extraction, in the form of oil sands and natural gas, has fueled the development of Edmonton.

We will take advantage of the PACT tradition of a social event to give you a sense of the rich history of this place. We chose the Fort Edmonton Park, a living history museum, and the historical Fairmount Hotel Macdonald as the spots to illustrate this history. The social program is completed with a taste of modern Edmonton through a visit to the Alberta Art Gallery of Alberta before the banquet. We hope that, as you stand in front of the historical Hotel Macdonald, you will try to imagine that building standing there surrounded only by much smaller buildings. That luxurious hotel was one of a series of "railway hotels" that were built in the West to accommodate guests who would travel by rail from the East.

The actual conference program will take place in the Centennial Centre for Interdisciplinary Sciences located in the North end of the main quad of the University of Alberta main campus. The Department of Computing Science is housed in Athabasca Hall, which is the central red-brick building on the West side of the quad. Again you may try to imagine Athabasca Hall standing alone on a field as it was the very first building of the University of Alberta a little over 100 years ago — if you enter Athabasca Hall and walk straight across the hallway you will find the Heritage lounge, a quiet space for studying where you will see pictures of the building in its early days.

The Workshops and Tutorials will take place in the Edmonton Clinic Health Academy which is located across the street from the University of Alberta Hospital. This modern building was recently completed and was conceived as a home for integrated education and training in the area of medical sciences. PACT will also feature an ACM Student Research Competition (SRC) and a poster section, which will take place during a reception on Monday evening. I would like to thank the Program Chair, Workshop/Tutorial chair, SRC Chair, Program Committee members, external reviewers, authors, volunteers, publicity chairs, steering committee members, workshop and tutorial organizers, and all others that have worked diligently to make PACT 2014 a success. Thanks go to Melanie Calvert for overseeing all the logistics with such great care. And I would like to specially thank the participants for making their way to Edmonton to take part in PACT 2014. I hope you have a great conference and a great experience in Edmonton.

José Nelson Amaral
PACT'14 General Chair
Edmonton, AB, Canada

Message from the Program Chair

It is an honor to introduce the technical program for the 23rd International Conference on Parallel Architectures and Compilation Techniques (PACT 2014). This symposium is one of the leading venues for new ideas and results in the area of parallel computing. This year's program includes 37 papers, 17 posters, keynotes from Klara Nahrstedt (University of Illinois) and Bob Blainey (IBM), a day of workshops and tutorials, and the ACM Student Research Competition.

PACT 2014 received 144 paper submissions. I assigned each paper to at least 4 Program Committee (PC) members and 1 External Program Committee (EPC) member to review. To ensure the highest reviewing standards, the PC and EPC members were selected among the most recognized researchers in our field. Given that I had 51 PC members, each PC member had to review 11-12 papers personally. Overall, I believe that all of the PC and EPC members showed a very high degree of professionalism and fairness in their reviews.

After all the reviews were collected, a Rebuttal Period allowed the authors to respond to the reviews. Then, PC and EPC members read the 5 reviews and the authors' response for the papers they had read, and engaged in a week-long discussion with other reviewers of the same paper(s) via email. At the end of this process, each PC and EPC member had to explicitly assign a grade to each of the papers she/he had reviewed. The papers' average grade was used to order the discussion of papers at the PC meeting. The whole review process was double blind.

The PC meeting was held on May 10th, 2014, at the Chicago O'Hare Hilton. 46 PC members attended physically, while most of the others participated over the phone. The meeting started at 8am and lasted until 7:30pm. Before a paper was discussed, all conflicted PC members left the room and the authors' names were revealed. Then, the four PC members who had read the paper tried to reach a unanimous decision on the paper's outcome. If they could not, the whole PC voted. PC papers were discussed together with the other papers. The outcome of papers was not revealed to conflicted PC members until after the meeting. Over the course of the day, we discussed over 75 papers. We accepted 37 papers (25.7% acceptance rate) and 17 posters. To improve the quality of the program, several of the accepted papers were shepherded.

I need to thank many people. First, I thank the authors who submitted their work, irrespective of whether their paper was accepted or not — they are the lifeblood of the conference. I thank the 51 PC members, who selflessly contributed with many days of their working time. Thanks to Wonsun Ahn and Nima Honarmand who, as Submission Chairs, ensured that the submission and reviewing process went smoothly. Thanks to the 56 EPC members, who donated some of their time to the conference. Thanks to Dean Tullsen, who handled the review of the papers I had conflicts with. Thanks to Klara Nahrstedt and Bob Blainey, our two keynote speakers. Thanks to other key individuals who contributed to the technical program: Albert Cohen (Poster Chair), Andreas Moshovos (Workshops and Tutorials Chair), and Tarek Abdelrahman (ACM Student Research Competition Chair). Thank you to our outstanding organizing committee, led by Nelson Amaral, and formed by very dedicated individuals. Finally, I thank the PACT Steering Committee lead by Kemal Ebcioglu for their advice.

Most importantly, I thank you, the attendees. I hope that you find this conference interesting.

Josep Torrellas
University of Illinois at Urbana-Champaign

Table of Contents

Session 5A1: Compiler Frameworks

Session 5A2: Scheduling

Session 6A: Cache Hierarchies (II)

Session 6B: Performance Tools and I/O

Session 7: GPUs (II)

Poster Session

The 23rd International Conference on Parallel Architectures and Compilation Techniques Organization

General Chair:	J. Nelson Amaral, University of Alberta, Canada
Program Chair:	Josep Torrellas, University of Illinois, USA
Submission Chairs:	Nima Honarmand, University of Illinois, USA Wonsun Ahn, University of Illinois, USA
Publication Chair:	Xiaoming Li, University of Delaware, USA
Poster Co-Chairs:	Albert Cohen, INRIA, France Tarek Abdelrahman, University of Toronto, Canada
Workshops + Tutorials Chair:	Andreas Moshovos, University of Toronto, Canada
Finance Chair:	Mike MacGregor, University of Alberta, Canada
Student Travel and Awards:	Youtao Zhang, University of Pittsburgh, USA
Registration Chair:	Ehab Elmallah, University of Alberta, Canada
Steering Committee Chair:	Kemal Ebcioglu, Global Supercomputing, USA
Steering Committee:	Erik Altman, IBM, USA François Bodin, Irisa/CAPS Entreprise, France Sangyeun Cho, Samsung/University of Pittsburgh, South Korea/USA Michel Cosnard, Inria, France Luiz DeRose, Cray, USA Skevos Evripidou, University of Cyprus, Cyprus Chris Fensch, University of Edinburgh, Scotland Guang Gao, University of Delaware, USA Jean Luc Gaudiot, University of California, USA David Lilja, University of Minnesota, USA Bilha Mendelson, Consultant Michael O'Boyle, University of Edinburgh, Scotland Yale Patt, University of Texas at Austin, USA Lawrence Rauchweger, Texas A&M University, USA Valentina Salapura, IBM, USA Vivek Sarkar, Rice University, USA André Seznec, Inria Rennes, France Gabriel Silberman, Dell, USA Mateo Valero, UPC Barcelona, Spain Pen-Chung Yew, University of Minnesota, USA

Program Committee:

Wonsun Ahn, University of Illinois at Urbana-Champaign, USA
Saman Amarasinghe, MIT, USA
Nancy Amato, Texas A&M University, USA
Alper Buyuktosunoglu, IBM, USA
Albert Cohen, INRIA, France
Chita Das, Pennsylvania State University, USA
Chen Ding, University of Rochester, USA
Evelyn Duesterwald, IBM, USA
Jose Flich, Universitat Politecnica de Valencia, Spain
Phillip Gibbons, Intel, USA
R. Govindarajan, Indian Institute of Science, India
Yinhe Han, ICT Chinese Academy of Sciences, China
Michael Huang, University of Rochester, USA
Jaehyuk Huh, KAIST, Korea
Koji Inoue, Kyushu University, Japan
Francois Irigoin, MINES ParisTech, France
Ravi Iyer, Intel, USA
Natalie Enright Jerger, University of Toronto, Canada
Russ Joseph, Northwestern University, USA
Ulya Karpuzcu, University of Minnesota, USA
George Karypis, University of Minnesota, USA
John Kim, KAIST, Korea
Nam Sung Kim, University of Wisconsin, Madison, USA
Jaejin Lee, Seoul National University, Korea
Scott Mahlke, University of Michigan, USA
Rami Melhem, University of Pittsburgh, USA
Pablo Montesinos, Qualcomm, USA
Andreas Moshovos, University of Toronto, Canada
Abdullah Muzahid, University of Texas San Antonio, USA
Angeles Navarro, Universidad de Malaga, Spain
Nacho Navarro, Universitat Politecnica de Catalunya, Spain
Kunle Olukotun, Stanford University, USA
David Padua, University of Illinois at Urbana-Champaign, USA
Gilles Pokam, Intel, USA
Daniel Quinlan, Lawrence Livermore National Laboratory, USA
Lawrence Rauchwerger, Texas A&M University, USA
Glenn Reinman, University of California Los Angeles, USA
Saday Sadayappan, Ohio State University, USA
Daniel Sanchez, MIT, USA
Martin Schulz, Lawrence Livermore National Laboratory, USA
Xipeng Shen, College of William & Mary, USA
Daniel Sorin, Duke University, USA
Vijayalakshmi Srinivasan, IBM, USA

Program Committee (continued):

Per Stenstrom, Chalmers University of Technology, Sweden
Karin Strauss, Microsoft Research & University of Washington, USA
Zehra Sura, IBM, USA
Dean Tullsen, University of California San Diego, USA
Osman Unsal, Barcelona Supercomputing Center, Spain
Youfeng Wu, Intel, USA
Pen-Chung Yew, University of Minnesota, USA
Xiaodong Zhang, Ohio State University, USA

PACT'14 Additional Reviewers

Wonsun Ahn, University of Illinois at Urbana-Champaign, USA
Saman Amarasinghe, MIT, USA
Nancy Amato, Texas A&M University, USA
Alper Buyuktosunoglu, IBM, USA
Albert Cohen, INRIA, France
Chita Das, Pennsylvania State University, USA
Chen Ding, University of Rochester, USA
Evelyn Duesterwald, IBM, USA
Jose Flich, Universitat Politecnica de Valencia, Spain
Phillip Gibbons, Intel, USA
R. Govindarajan, Indian Institute of Science, India
Yinhe Han, ICT Chinese Academy of Sciences, China
Michael Huang, University of Rochester, USA
Jaehyuk Huh, KAIST, Korea
Koji Inoue, Kyushu University, Japan
Francois Irigoin, MINES ParisTech, France
Ravi Iyer, Intel, USA
Natalie Enright, University of Toronto, Canada
Russ Joseph, Northwestern University, USA
Ulya Karpuzcu, University of Minnesota, USA
George Karypis, University of Minnesota, USA
John Kim, KAIST, Korea
Nam Sung, University of Wisconsin, Madison, USA
Jaejin Lee, Seoul National University, Korea
Scott Mahlke, University of Michigan, USA
Rami Melhem, University of Pittsburgh, USA
Pablo Montesinos, Qualcomm, USA
Andreas Moshovos, University of Toronto, Canada
Abdullah Muzahid, University of Texas San Antonio, USA
Angeles Navarro, Universidad de Malaga, Spain
Nacho Navarro, Universitat Politecnica de Catalunya, Spain
Kunle Olukotun, Stanford University, USA
David Padua, University of Illinois at Urbana-Champaign, USA
Gilles Pokam, Intel, USA
Daniel Quinlan, Lawrence Livermore National Laboratory, USA
Lawrence Rauchwerger, Texas A&M University, USA
Glenn Reinman, University of California Los Angeles, USA
Saday Sadayappan, Ohio State University, USA
Daniel Sanchez, MIT, USA
Martin Schulz, Lawrence Livermore National Laboratory, USA
Xipeng Shen, College of William & Mary, USA
Daniel Sorin, Duke University, USA
Vijayalakshmi Srinivasan, IBM, USA
Per Stenstrom, Chalmers University of Technology, Sweden
Karin Strauss, Microsoft Research and University of Washington, USA
Zehra Sura, IBM, USA
Dean Tullsen, University of California San Diego, USA
Osman Unsal, Barcelona Supercomputing Center, Spain
Youfeng Wu, Intel, USA
Pen-Chung Yew, University of Minnesota, USA
Xiaodong Zhang, Ohio State University, USA
David Albonesi, Cornell University, USA
Erik Altman, IBM, USA
Ke Bai, Arizona State University, USA
Luis Ceze, University of Washington, USA
Sangyeun Cho, Samsung/University of Pittsburgh, USA
Joe Devietti, University of Pennsylvania, USA
Hadi Esmaeilzadeh, Georgia Institute of Technology, USA
Skevos Evripidou, University of Cyprus, Cyprus
Franz Franchetti, Carnegie Mellon University, USA
Marc Gonzalez, Universitat Politecnica de Catalunya, Spain
Erik Hagersten, Uppsala University, Sweden
Nikos Hardavellas, Northwestern University, USA
James Hoe, Carnegie Mellon University, USA
Yu Hu, ICT Chinese Academy of Sciences, China
Hillery Hunter, IBM, USA
Engin Ipek, University of Rochester, USA
Alex Jones, University of Pittsburgh, USA
Stefanos Kaxiras, Uppsala University, Sweden
Jangwoo Kim, POSTECH, Korea
Omer Khan, University of Connecticut, USA
Michihiro Koibuchi, National Institute of Informatics, Japan
Masaaki Kondo, The University of Tokyo, Japan
Josep Lluis, Universitat Politecnica de Catalunya, Spain

The 23rd International Conference on Parallel Architectures and Compilation Techniques Sponsors & Supporters

Sponsors: SIGARCH, IEEE Computer Society, ifip

Supporters: intel, EMC² where information lives, IBM, Google

Keynote

Internet of Mobile Things: Challenges and Opportunities

Klara Nahrstedt
University of Illinois at Urbana-Champaign, USA
klara@illinois.edu

Abstract

The Internet of Things (IoT) concept has been around for some time and applications such as transportation, health-care, education, travel, smart grid, retail, are and will be major benefactors of this concept. However, only recently, due to technological advances in sensor devices and rich wireless connectivity, Internet of Things at scale is becoming reality. For example, Cisco's Internet of Things Group predicts over 50 billion connected sensory devices by 2020.

In this talk, we will discuss the Internet of Mobile Things (IoMT) since several game-changing technological advances happened on 'mobile things' such as mobile phones, trains, and cars, where rich sets of sensors, connected via diverse sets of wireless Internet technologies, are changing and influencing how people communicate, move, and download and distribute information. In this space, challenges come from the needs to determine (1) contextual information such as location, duration of contact, density of devices, utilizing networked sensory information; (2) higher level knowledge such as users' activity detection, mood detection, applications usage pattern detection and user interactions on 'mobile things', utilizing contextual information; and (3) adaptive and real-time parallel and distributed architectures that integrate context, activity, mood, usage patterns into mobile application services on mobile 'things'. Solving these challenges will provide enormous opportunities to improve the utility of mobile 'things', optimizing scarce resources on mobile 'things' such as energy, memory, and bandwidth.

ACM Classification: C.2 COMPUTER-COMMUNICATION NETWORKS, C.2.1 Network Architecture and Design, Distributed Networks, Wireless Communication, C.3 SPECIAL-PURPOSE AND APPLICATION-BASED SYSTEMS, Real-time and embedded systems

Author Keywords: Internet of Things, Mobile Computing, Context Management, Activity Detection, Adaptive Parallel and Distributed Architectures and Systems.

Bio

Klara Nahrstedt is the Ralph and Catherine Fisher Professor in the Computer Science Department, and Acting Director of Coordinated Science Laboratory in the College of Engineering at the University of Illinois at Urbana-Champaign. Her research interests are directed toward 3D teleimmersive systems, mobile systems, Quality of Service (QoS) and resource management, Quality of Experience in multimedia systems, and real-time security in mission-critical systems. She is the co-author of widely used multimedia books `Multimedia: Computing, Communications and Applications' published by Prentice Hall, and 'Multimedia Systems' published by Springer Verlag. She is the recipient of the IEEE Communication Society Leonard Abraham Award for Research Achievements, University Scholar, Humboldt Award, IEEE Computer Society Technical Achievement Award, and the former chair of the ACM Special Interest Group in Multimedia. She was the general chair of ACM Multimedia 2006, general chair of ACM NOSSDAV 2007 and the general chair of IEEE Percom 2009.

Klara Nahrstedt received her Diploma in Mathematics from Humboldt University, Berlin, Germany in numerical analysis in 1985. In 1995 she received her PhD from the University of Pennsylvania in the Department of Computer and Information Science. She is ACM Fellow, IEEE Fellow, and Member of the Leopoldina German National Academy of Sciences.

PACT'14, August 24–27, 2014, Edmonton, AB, Canada.
ACM 978-1-4503-2809-8/14/08.
http://dx.doi.org/10.1145/2628071.2635931

Virtues and Limitations of Commodity Hardware Transactional Memory

Nuno Diegues, Paolo Romano, Luís Rodrigues
INESC-ID, Instituto Superior Técnico, Universidade de Lisboa
{nmld, paolo.romano, ler}@tecnico.ulisboa.pt

ABSTRACT

Over the last years Transactional Memory (TM) gained growing popularity as a simpler, attractive alternative to classic lock-based synchronization schemes. Recently, the TM landscape has been profoundly changed by the integration of Hardware TM (HTM) in Intel commodity processors, raising a number of questions on the future of TM.

We seek answers to these questions by conducting the largest study on TM to date, comparing different locking techniques, hardware and software TMs, as well as different combinations of these mechanisms, from the dual perspective of performance and power consumption.

Our study sheds a mix of light and shadows on currently available commodity HTM: on one hand, we identify workloads in which HTM clearly outperforms any alternative synchronization mechanism; on the other hand, we show that current HTM implementations suffer of restrictions that narrow the scope in which these can be more effective than state of the art software solutions. Thanks to the results of our study, we identify a number of compelling research problems in the areas of TM design, compilers and self-tuning.

Categories and Subject Descriptors

D.1.3 [**Software**]: Programming Techniques - Concurrent Programming

Keywords

Empirical Study; Synchronization Techniques; Transactional Memory; Performance; Energy Efficiency

1. INTRODUCTION

The advent of multi-core architectures has brought concurrent programming to the forefront of software development. For many years, locking has represented the *de-facto* standard approach to synchronization in concurrent applications. However, the inherent complexity and error-proneness of fine-grained locking [32] has motivated intense research on alternative methodologies aimed at making parallel programming accessible to the mass of software developers.

Transactional Memory (TM) [27] is one of the most prominent proposals in this sense. With the TM abstraction, programmers are required only to identify which code blocks should run atomically, and not how concurrent accesses to shared state should be synchronized (as with locks). The TM is then responsible for guaranteeing correctness by aborting transactions that would generate unsafe histories.

Over the last decade a large body of TM research focused on software-based implementations (STM) (e.g. [13, 17]). Unlike hardware implementations, however, STM requires software instrumentation of read and write memory accesses to trace conflicts between concurrent transactions. This instrumentation can, in certain scenarios, introduce large overheads and hinder performance with respect to conventional fine-grained locking [5]. HTM support is thus desirable, but its absence from commodity processors caused most research to be evaluated solely on simulators (e.g. [25]) — the only notorious exception being the Rock processor [12], which was never commercialized. Recently, the maturing of TM research led to a breakthrough that changed drastically this scenario: two major market players, IBM and Intel, introduced HTM support in their latest processors [37, 3, 36], targeting, respectively, HPC and commodity systems. This represents a significant milestone for TM, mainly due to the predictable widespread availability of Intel Haswell processors, which bring HTM support to millions of systems ranging from high-end servers to common laptops.

The advent of HTM in commodity processors raises a number of questions concerning the future of TM and concurrent programming: how competitive are available HTMs when compared with state of the art STMs? Will the performance of HTM be sufficiently alluring to turn TM into a mainstream programming paradigm? What role will STM play now that HTM is so widely available? How limiting are the architectural restrictions of existing HTM designs?

In this paper we seek an answer to these questions by conducting the largest study on TM-based synchronization to date. We compare, from the twofold perspective of performance and energy-efficiency, a range of synchronization mechanisms: 6 lock based approaches with different granularities; 4 state of the art STMs; Intel TSX's implementation of HTM; and 2 Hybrid TMs (HyTM) that use STM and HTM mechanisms in synergy. We study highly heterogeneous applications, encompassing 1) STAMP, a *de-facto* standard suite of benchmarks for TM, 2) Memcached [35], a popular in-memory caching system that was recently ported

PACT'14, August 24–27, 2014, Edmonton, AB, Canada.
Copyright 2014 ACM 978-1-4503-2809-8/14/08 ...$15.00.
http://dx.doi.org/10.1145/2628071.2628080 .

to use TM, and 3) concurrent data structures that are widely used as building blocks of parallel applications (yet, hard to parallelize efficiently). The results of our study allow us to draw two main conclusions:

Lights and shadows for HTM: Approaches based on TSX yielded outstanding performance in workloads characterized by small transactions, such as concurrent data structures and Memcached, but only with two of the STAMP benchmarks. TSX performance is strongly dependent on the access patterns to L1 cache, and long running transactions can lead to frequent cache capacity exceptions and spurious aborts. When transaction-intensity is medium, TSX is only the best choice for a limited degree of parallelism, and it is generally better on the energy side than on the performance side. The impact of its hardware limitations are highlighted by several STAMP benchmarks that generate long transactions, and in which TSX is outperformed by both locking and STM solutions. On the other hand, TSX shines as a synchronization primitive for concurrent data structures, for which it is by far the best choice in all considered workloads, with speed-ups up to 3.3× over the best alternative scheme.

STM is still competitive: Our study also shows that STM is quite competitive as an all-around solution across benchmarks, workloads, and parallelism degrees. Although STM was initially proposed as a prototyping alternative to actual hardware implementations of TM, its evolution throughout a decade of intense research has resulted in several highly-optimized mechanisms, which achieve performance comparable to that of fine-grained locking. This does not mean that STMs embody a perfect solution; instead, this result highlights the current limitations of HTM support, which make of STM still the most robust solution to date.

Further, the results of our study unveil a number of critical issues related with HTM performance and allow for identifying several research problems, whose timely solution could significantly enhance the chances for HTM to turn into a mainstream paradigm for concurrent programming:

HyTMs: a missed opportunity? The outcome of our study for what concerns the efficiency of HyTMs, when employed in conjunction with Intel's TSX, is rather grim. The mechanisms currently adopted to support the simultaneous coexistence of HTM and STM induce high overheads in terms of additional spurious aborts. Our study highlights that these costs make HyTM generally less efficient than solutions based purely on STM or TSX+locking. This motivates further research in the design of architectural supports (e.g., non-transactional memory accesses from transactions) capable of exploiting the potential synergies of HyTMs.

Complexity of HTM tuning. HTM performance can be significantly affected by the settings of several parameters and mechanisms. Without proper tuning, TSX suffer average throughput losses of 72% and of 89% in power consumption. Also, the optimal configuration of these parameters can vary significantly, depending on the characteristics of the workload. These findings urge for novel approaches capable of removing from the shoulders of programmers the burden of manually tuning HTM, by delegating this task to run-time or compiler based solutions.

Relevance of selective instrumentation. Both TSX and GCC library for STM trace every memory access performed within a transaction. We show that this can cause significant increases of the transaction footprint's size, amplifying the instrumentation overheads in STM, and the chances of incurring in capacity exceptions in HTM. These results motivate research on cross-layer mechanisms operating at the compiler and at the hardware level, aimed to achieve selective instrumentation in a way that is both convenient for the programmer and efficiently implementable in hardware.

The rest of the paper is structured as follows. Section 2 discusses related work. Section 3 overviews the synchronization mechanisms considered in the study. Section 4 describes our methodology, after which Section 5 presents preliminary experiments aimed at tuning properly TSX. We then present our study in Sections 6-7. In Section 8 we identify several research questions suggested by the findings of our study. Finally, Section 9 concludes the paper.

2. RELATED WORK

Transactional Memory was initially proposed as an extension to multi-processors' cache coherence protocols [27]. Due to the difficulty of rapid prototyping in hardware environments, researchers resorted to STMs to advance the state of the art [18, 17, 16, 14]. Simultaneously, hardware-based implementations have also been proposed, whose designs were validated using simulators [25].

The concern for both performance and power consumption metrics has been only marginally explored in the scope of TM, and mostly relying on simulation studies that did not target Intel's architecture (whose internals are only partially disclosed). In both [21, 20] the authors assess the behaviour of different HTM implementations via simulation (the latter focusing on embedded systems). The approach was also taken by [2], where the power consumption of one STM was studied via simulation. More recently, [22] studied both power consumption and performance in a non-simulated environment. Yet, this work considered a restricted set of synchronization alternatives focusing mainly on one STM.

As already mentioned, both Intel [37] and IBM [3, 36] have integrated HTM in their processors. IBM processors target high performance computing infra-structures that are not expected to be used in commodity systems. In this work, we focus on the former (by Intel), for which our results show aspects and insights that were not highlighted by Intel's paper [37]. Before the recent release of Intel Haswell processors, researchers had already proposed some theoretical improvements to best-effort HTMs [1, 30]. We integrate these mechanisms in our HTM-based runtimes, and evaluate them for the first time using an actual HTM implementation.

Traditional lock-based synchronization techniques have been thoroughly studied throughout decades. In [19], the authors show that the power consumption of locking primitives can be improved by exploring a trade-off between processor deep sleeping states, frequency downsizing and busy waiting. We highlight a recent work [10], which studied the impact in performance of different lock designs and hardware architectures (without however considering TM).

Our work is also related to the body of literature on performance modeling of TMs, which have relied on methodologies such as analytical modeling [11, 26], as well as machine learning [34]. These proposals were applied to self-tune various TM parameters, and our results clearly indicate the potentiality and importance of this line of research also in the scope of HTM.

3. SYNCHRONIZATION MECHANISMS CONSIDERED IN THE STUDY

In this comparative study we considered the several synchronization mechanisms listed in Table 1:

Locks — Decades of research on lock-based synchronization have resulted in a plethora of different implementations, many times trading off subtle changes with great impact in performance. We consider 6 different lock implementations [10] and both coarse and fine-grained strategies. Contrarily to the other approaches we used, fine-grained locking requires a *per-application* lock allocation strategy, which is a non-generalizable and error-prone task [32].

STM — With STM, reads and writes to shared memory (inside atomic blocks) are instrumented to detect conflicts between transactions. This instrumentation induces overheads that can have a detrimental impact on the efficiency of STMs. Yet, much research has been devoted over the last years to reduce STM's overheads. For our study we selected four state of the art STMs, which are representative of different choices in the design space of TM. These include an STM optimized for validations at commit-time (TL2 [13]); to maximize performance at low thread counts (NOrec [7]); in high contention scenarios (SwissTM [17]); and to minimize instrumentation costs (TinySTM [18]).

HTM — HTM implements a concurrency control scheme in hardware, avoiding the overheads of STM instrumentation. In our study we consider Intel TSX's implementation of HTM, which is integrated in the family of Intel commodity processors (Haswell). One fundamental design principle of TSX (and in general of HTM) is its best-effort nature: one cannot depend exclusively on TSX to synchronize accesses to data, since a transaction is not guaranteed to commit, even in absence of contention. Briefly, TSX uses the L1 cache to buffer transactional writes, and relies on the cache coherence protocol to detect conflicts. A plausible reason for a transaction to fail in hardware is because its data footprint exceeds the L1 capacity. Hardware transactions are also subject to abort due to reasons like page faults and system calls.

As a result, a fallback software synchronization mechanism must be provided to ensure progress in case a transaction cannot be committed with HTM. The software fallback mechanism must co-operate with the hardware in order to ensure correctness. As we shall see, the mechanisms used to coordinate the execution of the fallback mechanism have a crucial impact on the performance of TSX. The simplest approach, as suggested by Intel's optimization manual, is to use a single lock to protect atomic blocks (we call it TSX-GL). When a hardware transaction aborts, it has the alternative to acquire the global lock instead. To ensure a correct interplay with the fallback, hardware transactions must read the lock as free to guarantee correctness; the transactional semantics will guarantee that the transaction commits only when there is no ongoing fallback execution.

An obvious extension of this idea is to use fine-grained locks (TSX-FL). As the TM abstraction is motivated by the need of relieving programmers from the complexity of designing locking schemes, the usage of fine-grained locks as a fallback for HTM sounds somewhat contradictory. However, this choice allows us to assess to what extent a simplistic fallback (using a single lock) can hinder parallelism. Also, fine-grained locks may be automatically crafted, to some extent, by using recent techniques based on static analysis [29].

Table 1: Mechanisms used for synchronization in our study.

Mechanism	Description
Locks	Coarse/fine-grained locking [10]: TTAS, Spin, RW (pthreads), MCS, CLH, Ticket
STMs	TL2 [13], TinySTM [18], SwissTM [17], NOrec [7]
HTMs	TSX-GL [37] (global lock), TSX-FL (fine locks)
HyTMs	TSX-TL2 [30], TSX-NOrec [8]

HyTM — Another mechanism proposed in the literature is to use an STM as fallback for HTM, also known as Hybrid TM (HyTM). Its main advantage is to allow concurrent execution of hardware transactions and software ones, used in the fallback. However, during their concurrent execution, both software and hardware transactions have to play along in order to preserve correctness. In our study we considered two state of the art Hybrid TM proposals [30, 8], which are evaluated for the first time on a commodity HTM. We exploit the idea of reduced hardware transactions: normally transactions execute mainly in hardware, with a pure software fallback; the idea of these HyTMs is to have an intermediary mode where the software fallback still relies partially on hardware speculations to boost performance, namely during the commit in the fallback.

4. METHODOLOGY AND TESTBED

We consider in our study several parallel applications using atomic blocks for synchronization. First we use the STAMP suite, a popular set of benchmarks for TM [4], encompassing 8 applications representative of various domains that generate highly heterogeneous workload domains. We excluded the Bayes application given its non-deterministic executions, and used standard parameters for each application. STAMP contains manually instrumented reads and writes inside atomic blocks to invoke the STM-based synchronization. Naturally, this is not relevant for the case of pure HTM approaches. We shall additionally present results for compiler based instrumentation in Section 8.

We also consider a red-black tree and a hashmap, as examples of concurrent data structures, which represent important building blocks of parallel applications and that have two interesting characteristics: they are very hard to parallelize efficiently using locking schemes, and are challenging for STMs given that they generate extremely short transactions that suffer from relatively large instrumentation overheads. Finally, we also used a recent TM-based porting of the popular Memcached [35], an in-memory cache, widely used for instance at Facebook [31].

Each experiment is the average of 20 executions. We use the geometric mean whenever we show an average of normalized results. We often show speedup results, which are relative to the performance of sequential, non-instrumented executions, unless stated otherwise. The reported measurements of power consumption were obtained via the Intel RAPL [9] facility and are restricted to the processor and memory subsystems. Recent studies ([23, 24]) show that the model used by Intel RAPL estimates quite accurately the power consumption, when compared to a power meter attached to the machine.

Our machine is equipped with an Intel Haswell Xeon E3-1275 3.5GHz processor and 32GB RAM. This choice is dictated by the requirement of using a processor equipped with TSX, which is limited for now to 4 cores (and 8 hyper-threads). We always pin threads to physical cores in a round-robin fashion; for instance, 4 threads will be allocated uniformly, one per core. As a result, hyper-threading is only used when 5 or more threads are used. We used GCC 4.8.1 with all compiler optimizations enabled and Ubuntu 12.04.

5. TUNING TSX FALLBACK PATH

Before comparing the considered synchronization mechanisms, we conduct a set of preliminary experiments evaluating several alternative configurations of the coupling between TSX and its fallback. As we shall see, this can have significant impact on TSX's efficiency. The settings identified thanks to this preliminary study will be adopted in the remainder of the paper to ensure that the comparison is performed using an appropriately tuned HTM.

We begin in Section 5.1 by comparing the performance and energy efficiency when using six locks implementations to implement the fallback mechanism of TSX. This shall allow us to narrow down the multitude of combinations of TSX and lock implementations assessed in our study. Next, in Section 5.2, we optimize TSX-GL with a recently proposed technique [1] aimed at reducing spurious hardware aborts. This shall provide some insights about its actual practical effectiveness, as it was never evaluated before. Lastly, we investigate when it is best to give up on hardware and trigger the fallback path, in Section 5.3.

5.1 The Impact of Locks on the Fallback

The simpler way to use TSX is by relying on very coarse-grained locks on the fallback, or simply a single one. We considered the six lock listed in Table 1, to be used in the fallback. These implementations are representative of different design choices, and our goal is to understand if there is some implementation that consistently performs above the average across all parallelism degrees and benchmarks.

Table 2 shows the performance of TSX given the backing lock implementation used in the fallback path. We show the average overhead with respect to the best performing lock in each experiment, considering both time to complete the benchmark as well as power consumed. The reported overhead is the average across all STAMP benchmarks and thread counts (1 to 8). Using this metric, we can see that the Ticket, MCS and CLH locks perform best.

For each benchmark and thread count, we additionally sorted the considered lock implementations according to either their performance or power consumption, determining in this way their rank for that benchmark/configuration. This shows that no lock implementation is always the best or worse. However, we can see that the Ticket lock is consistently ranked higher, for which reason we shall rely on it from now on whenever we require locking (both standalone, or in the fallback of TSX).

5.2 Improving the Single-lock Fallback

The recommended fallback mechanism for TSX relies on a global lock (as explained in Section 3). In this section we evaluate for the first time on TSX the efficiency of an alternative technique proposed to reduce the situations under which best-effort HTMs have to follow this pessimistic fallback path [1].

The idea is that it may not be safe for transactions to execute speculatively in hardware if, at the same time, some transaction is executing pessimistically after acquiring the global lock. A pessimistic execution cannot restart, and hence its accesses must be consistent when faced with concurrency. For this reason, TSX's usage guide points out that the lock has to be read as being free during the course of a hardware transaction. Then any transaction that activates the fallback path has to first acquire the lock, and cause every hardware transaction to abort. This can cause a chain effect, also known as *lemming effect* [12], where the aborted hardware transactions also try to acquire the lock, preventing hardware speculation from ever resuming.

In [1], the authors use an auxiliary lock to prevent the lemming effect. The idea is to guard the global lock acquisition by another lock. Aborted hardware transactions have to acquire this auxiliary lock before restarting speculation, which effectively serializes them. However, this auxiliary lock is not added to the read-set of hardware transactions, which avoids aborting concurrent hardware transactions. If this procedure is attempted some times before actually giving up and acquiring the global lock, then the chain reaction effect can be avoided: the auxiliary lock serves as a manager preventing hardware aborts from continuously acquiring the fallback lock and preventing hardware speculations.

In Table 3 we compare TSX using the auxiliary lock against a single-lock (TSX-GL). For this, we report values for time, energy, and Energy Delay Product (EDP), normalized with respect to TSX-GL (analogously to traditional speedup metrics). We report the average across either benchmarks or threads. Naturally, we can see that there is no difference with 1 thread because there is no concurrency and hence no problem resuming speculative execution. But beyond that, and in particular at larger concurrency levels, this technique

Table 2: Overhead (%) of each lock (as fallback of TSX) with respect to the optimal choice in each execution.

-	Performance		Power	
Lock	Overhead (%)	Rank	Overhead (%)	Rank
Ticket	1.0	1.75	1.1	1.75
MCS	2.4	2.62	1.2	2.25
CLH	2.9	3.62	2.4	3.38
RW	14.2	4.89	17.4	3.88
TTAS	15.2	5.00	17.4	4.88
Spin	16.4	5.00	17.5	4.88

Table 3: Normalized performance of auxiliary lock [1] over TSX-GL across benchmarks and threads (higher is better).

Avg across Benchmarks				Avg across Threads			
	time	energy	edp		time	energy	edp
genome	1.58	1.6	2.54	1	1.00	1.00	1.01
intruder	1.80	1.95	3.52	2	1.08	1.06	1.14
kmeans	1.20	1.17	1.40	3	1.14	1.12	1.28
labyrinth	1.01	1.01	1.01	4	1.29	1.26	1.62
ssca2	1.00	1.00	1.00	5	1.26	1.25	1.57
vacation	1.52	1.48	2.25	6	1.26	1.23	1.55
yada	0.96	0.96	0.92	8	1.26	1.23	1.55

helps consistently to improve the EDP. Some benchmarks do not show any difference because there are very little aborts (SSCA2) or TSX is not able to execute speculatively most of the time (Labyrinth). Yada's workload is conflict-intensive, for which reason the non-optimized approach is slightly better due to its inherent pessimism in following the fallback path — that pays off since the high conflict probability limits the effectiveness of optimistic transactions.

5.3 Retry Policy for the Fallback

Given that TSX must always have a fallback due to its best-effort nature, an important decision is when to trigger that path. Upon a transaction abort, TSX provides an error code that informs about the reason of the abort. An abort due to a capacity exception is typically a good reason to trigger the fallback path. However, hardware transactions may abort for various micro-architectural conditions that are less deterministically prone to happen upon transaction re-execution, and even capacity exceptions may not always be deterministic. Also, of course, transactions may abort due to data contention. In these situations one may aggressively trigger the fallback, or opt to insist on using HTM.

As we will shall discuss in more detail in Section 8, the optimal choice of the retry policy can vary significantly across workloads and degrees of parallelism. As it is impractical to assume that the retry policy is ad-hoc tuned by programmers for each and single workload/application, we set the number of retries to 5, which is the configuration reported to deliver best all-around performance with TSX [37, 28] (a result that we have confirmed with TSX-GL on our testbed). For the HyTMs, 4 times was found to be the best number of retries on average.

6. STAMP BENCHMARK SUITE

In this section we rely on the STAMP benchmark suite to assess the efficiency of all the synchronization mechanisms listed in Section 3, namely HTM, STMs, HyTMs, and locking. In the following, we shall always include the TSX optimizations discussed in the previous section.

We start by summarizing our results in Table 4. There, we list the STAMP benchmarks sorted by two important characteristics of their workloads: the contention level between transactions, and the percentage of the workload that is transactional. We then identify the mechanism that takes the least time to complete and which one consumes the least power, given the averaged results across threads.

This summarized perspective allows to highlight an interesting fact. It is possible to distinguish three categories in which TSX behaves differently, according to the transaction's characteristics. Kmeans and SSCA2 represent workloads with small transactions, medium frequency and low contention; here, TSX-GL performs consistently better than the alternatives across all threads. Intruder and Vacation exhibit medium profiles for what concerns the time spent in transactions and contention; in these cases, TSX-GL results in the best performing solution using up to 4, resp. 2, threads, and the most energy efficient up to 5, resp. 4, threads. Finally, the other benchmarks spend almost all the time in transactions, encompassing both low and high contention scenarios. In these settings, TinySTM emerges as the most robust solution, both from the perspective of energy and performance.

This analysis allows to draw a set of guidelines to select which synchronization to use, at least when considering applications having analogous characteristics to those included in the STAMP suite. TSX-GL is desirable when transactions are small, generate low/medium contention, and the application does not spend all the time executing transactions. When contention increases, or the frequency of transactions is high, TSX-GL is competitive up to a medium degree of parallelism. In the remaining cases, STM is often the best choice, even when compared with fine-grained locking. The considered HyTMs perform poorly compared to the alternatives, never clearly outperforming the competing schemes in any benchmark. In Sections 6.1-6.2 we present our experiments with STAMP. We will consider additional benchmarks and fine-grained locks in Section 7.

6.1 Performance Study

In Fig. 1 we show, for each benchmark and while varying the parallelism level, the speedup of all the considered synchronization schemes (with the exception of schemes based on fine-grained locking, which shall be presented in Section 7) with respect to a sequential, non-instrumented execution, and the power consumption during the execution (in Kilo Joules). This allows us to discuss in detail the differences between the mechanisms in different workloads.

Kmeans: This benchmark yields the biggest gap in performance between a TSX variant and STMs. Namely, TSX-GL reaches 3.5× speedup over a sequential execution, beating every other alternative both performance-wise and in terms of energy-efficiency. An interesting trend concerning energy-efficiency is that the power consumption with TSX (and, to some extent, also for all other synchronization schemes but GL) tends to slightly decrease as the parallelism level grows, which is a symptom of efficient utilization of the available architecture resources achievable using TM-based solutions. If we consider TSX-TL2 and TSX-NOrec, they are still com-

Table 4: Summary of results according to the workload characterization of the STAMP suite (xt = number of threads).

	Time in Tx (%)	Contention	Best Performing	Least Power Consumption
kmeans	low (7)	low	TSX-GL	TSX-GL
ssca2	low (17)	low	TSX-GL	TSX-GL
intruder	medium (33)	high	TSX-GL ≤ 4t; TinySTM ≥ 5t	TSX-GL ≤ 5t; TinySTM ≥ 6t
vacation	high (89)	low	TSX-GL ≤ 2t; TinySTM ≥ 3t	TSX-GL ≤ 4t; TinySTM ≥ 5t
genome	high (97)	low	TinySTM	TinySTM
yada	high (99)	medium	SwissTM	TinySTM
labyrinth	high (100)	high	STMs (except TL2)	STMs (except TL2)

petitive and better than the corresponding STMs, but they are far from TSX-GL in both metrics. It is worth noticing that the small and rare atomic blocks of this benchmark allow the GL approach to scale up to 3 threads. This explains the considerable success of TSX-GL in this benchmark, as a transaction that resorts to the GL is still able to run concurrently with other threads that are not under an atomic block at that time.

SSCA2: This benchmark shows a similar trend between TSX variants, but with the significant difference that all STM approaches scale better as the degree of parallelism increases. Here, TSX-GL is only slightly better than the best STM, and this is consistent across all the thread counts. Also interestingly, TSX-TL2 improves little and fares rather bad on the energy side. This, however, is not the case for TL2 or TSX on their own, and as such is an artefact of the hybrid implementation integration. Finally, the reduced time within atomic blocks still allows the GL approach to scale up to 2 threads, which justifies the advantage of TSX-GL. However, this effect is smaller than in Kmeans, which also matches the fact that TSX-GL achieves less improvements over other approaches.

Intruder: Here TSX-NOrec (and TSX-GL to some extent) are competitive and even better (until 5 threads) than the best STMs (except for TL2). Since TL2 performs poorly in this benchmark, this also drags TSX-TL2 behind in both metrics. Interestingly, both TL2 and TSX-TL2 improve slightly performance with more threads, but TL2 consumes more power whereas TSX-TL2 slightly decreases it.

Vacation: Once again we see that the performance of TSX-TL2 is quite disappointing, as indeed TL2 itself performs poorly in this scenario. As we shall see throughout this study, TL2 is by far the worst STM among those considered, which is a result of having a similar algorithmic and synchronization complexity to that of SwissTM and TinySTM, while detecting conflicts lazily at commit-time. This results in TL2 doing useless work more often, whereas SwissTM and TinySTM restart the speculation faster when reacting to conflicts. On the other hand, NOrec is simpler, both in algorithmic as well as synchronization terms, reducing its instrumentation overheads and maximizing its performance at low thread counts. With regard to the other approaches, TSX-GL and TSX-NOrec are competitive with STMs until 4 threads. At higher parallelism degrees, their performance degrades due to contention on L1 caches caused by hyper-threading. Analogous results are achieved for what regards power consumption. It is interesting to note that TSX-GL performs worse than TSX-NOrec at 8 threads, but the two consume approximately the same power. This is a result of the power savings that are achievable with the lock acquisition in TSX-GL.

Genome: In the three last benchmarks we have either transaction-heavy or high-contention workloads, characterized by large transaction foot-prints. These conditions are clearly a much more favourable playground for STMs. In this case, we see a clear (and consistent across benchmarks) distinction between TL2 and NOrec, as these two lag behind in both metrics particularly at higher thread counts. Interestingly, we can see that TSX-TL2 performs best among the TSX variants at a higher concurrency degree, which is a singularity among all benchmarks. This benchmark also shows a clear trend when the 5th thread is used: all approaches stabilize (or even decrease) performance at that point, due to hyper-threading. Interestingly, this effect is not so noticeable on the energy side, as STM approaches are still able to reduce the power consumed as parallelism increases. This highlights an interesting trade-off of hyper-threading: it allows sub-linear speed-ups only, but it also consumes little additional power. This fact is favourable to STMs, as TSX approaches generate more transactional aborts when hyper-threading is used, due the higher contention on the L1 cache.

Yada: This benchmark shows one scenario where TSX-GL performs poorly, with slowdowns above 3 threads. HyTMs follow closely their fallback STMs' performance, as TSX is not able to succeed. This is also a case where TinySTM and SwissTM perform better than the other two STMs. This benchmark presents no surprises in the energy-efficiency, whose trends are highly correlated with the performance.

Labyrinth: Here we see STMs performing best and very alike each other. TSX-GL does not improve with thread count, simply because most transactions exceed the hardware cache capacity and, as such, eventually follow the fallback path which is a sequential bottleneck given the GL. For this reason, TSX-TL2 and TSX-NOrec obtain some improvements, exactly because the fallback allows for concurrency, contrarily to the global lock on TSX-GL. This scenario highlights, however, that HyTMs are capped by either TSX or the fallback STM — as such, it is dubious whether they are practical (at least when used with TSX), or if it

Table 5: Transactional abort rate (%). For STM we show the lowest and highest values obtained (across all considered STMs).

	benchmark	*kmeans*	*ssca2*	*intruder*	*vacation*	*genome*	*yada*	*labyrinth*
1 thread	STM	0 - 0	0 - 0	0 - 0	0 - 0	0 - 0	0 - 0	0 - 0
	TSX-GL	0	0	7	49	11	46	95
	TSX-TL2	0	0	36	94	35	19	53
	TSX-NOrec	0	0	4	40	6	19	53
4 threads	STM	10 - 34	0 - 0	0 - 0	0 - 6	1 - 51	5 - 58	4 - 13
	TSX-GL	26	0	22	69	31	48	100
	TSX-TL2	50	74	74	100	45	84	60
	TSX-NOrec	31	46	29	66	17	31	55
8 threads	STM	25 - 54	0 - 0	3 - 57	0 - 10	0 - 1	7 - 65	8 - 23
	TSX-GL	42	1	33	72	48	47	100
	TSX-TL2	60	99	92	100	53	92	69
	TSX-NOrec	44	88	62	99	69	39	60

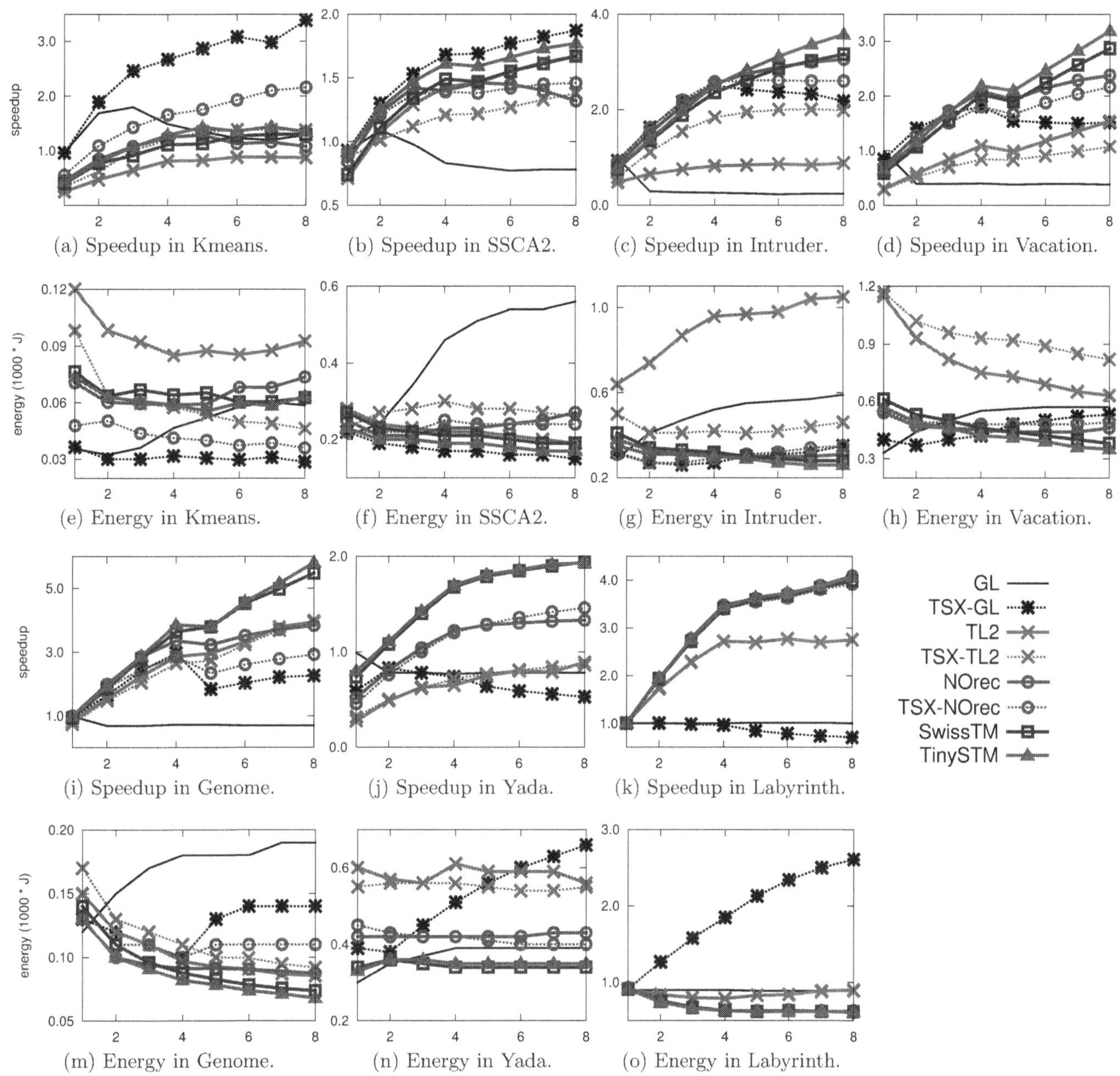

(a) Speedup in Kmeans. (b) Speedup in SSCA2. (c) Speedup in Intruder. (d) Speedup in Vacation.

(e) Energy in Kmeans. (f) Energy in SSCA2. (g) Energy in Intruder. (h) Energy in Vacation.

(i) Speedup in Genome. (j) Speedup in Yada. (k) Speedup in Labyrinth.

(m) Energy in Genome. (n) Energy in Yada. (o) Energy in Labyrinth.

Figure 1: Speedup (relative to non-instrumented sequential execution) and Energy Consumption (in Kilo Joules) when varying the number of threads (horizontal axis) in all the STAMP benchmarks

would be preferable to adaptively employ the most promising technique (TSX-GL or an STM) based on the workload.

6.2 Insights on TM Efficiency

In this section we shed some additional light on the factors dictating the trends observed in the experiments. To this end, in Table 5 we report the average abort rate across benchmarks and threads for each speculative mechanism. This represents the percentage of speculations that do not complete. Since there are four STMs under evaluation, we show the minimum and maximum abort rates among them — typically the smallest abort rate belongs to TinySTM and SwissTM, whereas TL2 yields the maximum abort rate.

Once again, we structure the table considering the different categories of workloads. As we move right (more contended or transaction-intensive workloads) and down (higher degree of parallelism), TSX approaches increase abort rates, which causes the loss of efficiency shown in the previous section. These results highlight that TSX has non-negligible aborts in many occasions where STMs abort very little.

In Fig. 2 we consider four different benchmarks, representative of scenarios that allow to derive insights on the efficiency of the considered TSX variants. In those plots we present a breakdown of the reasons motivating transactional aborts, for each TSX mechanism. We distinguish aborts caused by exceeding the capacity of L1 cache; micro-

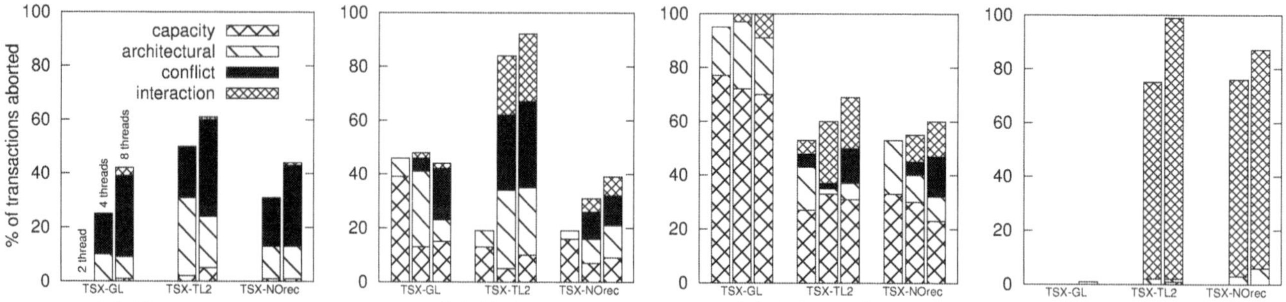

(a) Kmeans. (b) Yada. (c) Labyrinth. (d) SSCA2.

Figure 2: Breakdown of reasons causing transactional aborts for TSX variants.

architectural instructions or states forbidden by TSX, such as some system calls; data contention resulting in conflicts; and interaction between TSX and the fallback paths, such as checking if the GL is free in TSX-GL or more complex logic in the case of HyTMs.

Kmeans' breakdown shows that, as expected, as concurrency increases, also abort rates increase due mainly to data conflicts. It is worth mentioning that Kmeans is the benchmark with the least average aborts for TSX variants. Half of the aborts are due to conflicts, whereas the rest is motivated by a non-negligible percentage of aborts due to architectural instructions. This is something intrinsic to TSX, which is common throughout different benchmarks. The fact that these aborts occur less often in this benchmark allows TSX to obtain the most favourable results among all benchmarks.

In Yada and Labyrinth, instead, the workloads are much more transaction-intensive with non-negligible conflict rates. On top of this, the capacity of L1 caches is often exceeded by the hardware transactions (this is particularly visible in Labyrinth, where this phenomena dominates the aborts). This explains why the TSX variants followed up closely the performance of their fallbacks (with some constant overhead). HyTMs have a reduced abort rate because the fallback's software transactions are also taken into account in these statistics, on top of the hardware transactions — since software transactions have little aborts due to the uncontended workload, they amortize the overall abort rate. In TSX-GL, instead, the fallback executes non-speculatively due to the global lock, so we only count statistics for the hardware transactions there.

Finally, SSCA2 shows a completely different scenario, in which TSX-GL generates almost no aborts (in line with STMs' behaviour), whereas HyTMs have enormous abort rates, dominated by the interaction with the fallback path.

This motivates to better understand the usage of the fallback path in the HyTMs. Table 6 shows the percentage of transactions that were executed in the fallback (i.e., not purely in hardware). We also show the percentage of transactions in the fallback that are able to execute in a fast mode, i.e., a mode in which the transaction executes in software but the commit is boosted by using a reduced hardware transaction [30] (as explained in Section 3). For every table cell we show the percentage corresponding to 1 and 8 threads. Overall, the percentages vary linearly from 1 to 8 threads, for which reason we omit the intermediate values.

We start by highlighting in SSCA2 how both HyTMs are able to execute purely in hardware with 1 thread (they trigger the fallback < 1% of the transactions). However, a higher thread count typically results in executing in the fallback mode almost all the time, which matches the idea conveyed by Fig. 2(d). In particular, for this benchmark, the ability to rely on hardware to speed up the software fallback path is reduced from above 90% to 14% or even less.

These results for HyTMs show that TSX-TL2 triggers the fallback more often, and is able to execute in the fast mode less frequently than TSX-NOrec. This justifies the advantage of TSX-NOrec, which fared better across all benchmarks in Section 6: TSX-NOrec executes the fallback software transactions in fast mode for most of the time. The reason is that the much simpler design of NOrec allows for a much easier integration with TSX in a HyTM.

Ideally one may want to also rely on more scalable STMs, like TinySTM or SwissTM, in the fallback of TSX. However, due to the higher complexity of their algorithms, coupling them efficiently with HTM is a challenging task, and, in fact, we are not aware of any proposal in this sense in literature.

Finally, it has been pointed out in [8] that, in order to support efficient HyTMs, it is desirable to have hardware support for selective non-transactional memory accesses in the scope of transactions. Such a feature is not currently supported in TSX, whereas its inclusion was, e.g., planned in AMD's HTM proposal [6] (which was never commercialized). Hence, an interesting research direction suggested by this study is to investigate the impact of supporting non-transactional accesses, not only in terms of performance and energy, but also in terms of architectural intrusiveness.

Table 6: Rate (%) of triggering the fallback on HyTMs and of executing it in fast mode. Intervals of values are shown, ranging from 1 (lower) to 8 threads (upper bound).

	TSX-TL2		TSX-NOrec	
	fallback	Fast	fallback	Fast
kmeans	< 1 - 77	92 - 32	< 1 - 78	100 - 23
ssca2	< 1 - 99	91 - 2	< 1 - 86	95 - 14
intruder	33 - 88	98 - 39	3 - 55	100 - 52
vacation	94 - 100	43 - 3	38 - 99	100 - 89
genome	50 - 100	97 - 71	6 - 67	100 - 94
yada	18 - 78	50 - 34	17 - 32	99 - 82
labyrinth	58 - 100	14 - 2	54 - 98	10 - 3

7. BENCHMARKS USING FINE-GRAINED LOCKING

Most of the STAMP benchmarks have an irregular nature, which makes it very challenging to derive fine-grained locking schemes. In this section we focus on benchmarks for which it is possible to use (possibly very complex) fine-grained locking approaches. We start, in Section 7.1, by focusing on a subset of three STAMP benchmarks, for which we could craft an ad-hoc fine grained locking strategy. We then present results for Memcached in Section 7.2 and for two concurrent data structures in Section 7.3.

7.1 Fine-grained Locking in STAMP

As already mentioned, implementing a fine-grained locking strategy is a complex task for most of the STAMP benchmarks. We were, however, able to devise fine-grained locking strategies for three of the STAMP benchmarks, whose results we report in Fig. 3. Besides fine-grained locks (FL), we also show results for TSX-FL, which combines hardware transactions with a fallback path that relies on FL. Naturally, the combination of both schemes in TSX-FL requires hardware transactions to read all necessary locks as being free. We then compare these two approaches with TSX-GL and TinySTM, which were the best mechanisms in our previous experiments, and remove the others to improve the readability of the plots.

TSX-FL presents one advantage over TSX-GL, in that the fallback path allows for threads to proceed in parallel if they require different locks (which is highly likely if there is little data contention). However, this has the drawback that more locks have to be checked (during speculative executions) or acquired (during the fallback executions). Hence, there is a clear trade-off that is subtle and difficult to manage.

Recall that Kmeans and SSCA2 were the two benchmarks with workload characteristics more amenable to TSX-GL. This is justified by the low frequency of activation of the fallback path. As such, TSX-GL incurs minimal overhead thanks to the hardware speculation and to the avoidance of any software-based instrumentation. Therefore, it is not a surprise that fine-grained locking is of no advantage in this scenario: each lock acquisition represents a synchronization point, whereas for TSX-GL there exists only explicit synchronization at the hardware level when a transaction attempts to commit. Note, however, that FL is consistently better than the best STM (TinySTM). This fact is even more relevant from the energy perspective, where the gap between FL and TinySTM is larger. Since the TSX fallback is not triggered often, then TSX-FL goes through the additional verifications over more locks that are useless most of the time (to ensure a correct integration of the fallback with hardware transactions), which explains its lower performance in this kind of workload.

In SSCA2 we see a different behaviour as both TSX variants perform quite similarly. This is explained by the fact that the fine-grained scheme is not very efficient: its locks are relatively coarse, which induces unnecessary serialization. This has the side-effect of making TSX-FL competitive with TSX-GL, because both have a similar effort in checking the locks in the speculative executions to ensure correct integration with the fallback. Notice how the FL scheme still performs better than GL, which is a consequence of the higher degrees of parallelism achievable by reducing lock granularity. This confirms an expectable trade-off concerning lock granularity: the more fine-grained, the best the fallback performs; however this can have an impact on the performance of the speculative executions as we saw for Kmeans.

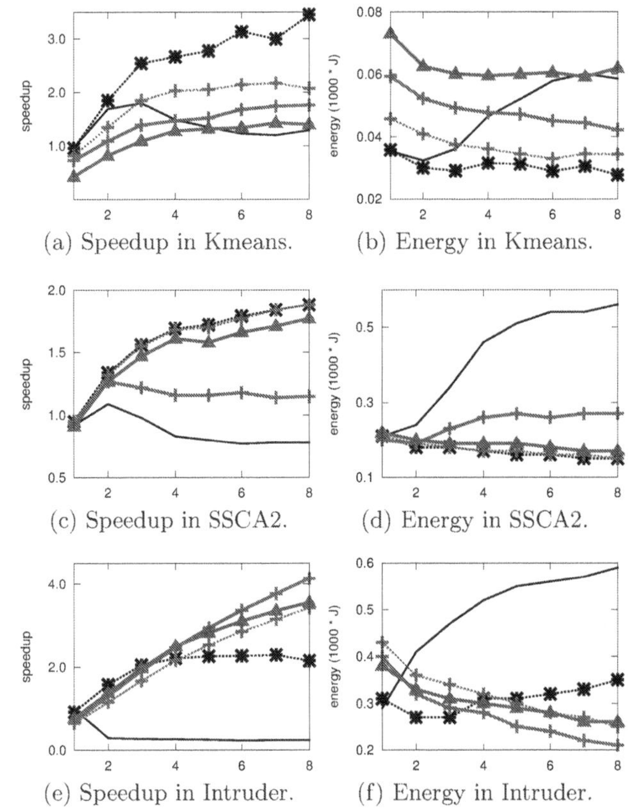

(a) Speedup in Kmeans. (b) Energy in Kmeans.

(c) Speedup in SSCA2. (d) Energy in SSCA2.

(e) Speedup in Intruder. (f) Energy in Intruder.

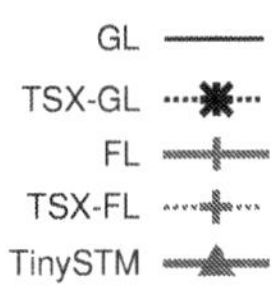

Strategy	10^3* Operations/sec
GL	223
TSX-GL	467
FL	501
TSX-FL	481
TinySTM	329

(h) Throughput in Memcached.

Figure 3: Experiment similar to that in Fig. 1, but instead using fine-grained locking and Memcached.

Finally, Intruder spends a large fraction of time within atomic blocks. As already discussed, this workload is more advantageous for STMs than for TSX. It is not surprising to see that TSX-GL is no longer the most competitive choice (although it still fares best until 3 threads). The interesting fact is that this kind of workload is more beneficial for FL. With more threads, TinySTM degrades its scalability, and is surpassed by FL. From an energy perspective, it is even clearer that FL is the best choice comparing to TinySTM, as it is almost always consuming less energy. TSX-FL suffers from the overheads of checking additional locks, until 3 threads, for which reason it is not as good as TSX-GL. However, at that point TSX triggers the fallback more often, which justifies the use of fine locks and allows TSX-FL to perform substantially better than TSX-GL. On the energy side, TSX-FL is closer to TinySTM, following the trend of STMs that often fare worse on the energy side to obtain comparative levels of performance to the other approaches.

7.2 Memcached

Memcached is a popular distributed object caching system [31]. In this study, we rely on a recent TM-based porting [35], and use the original Memcached as the basis for FL. We used the memslap tool, configuring the workload with 95% gets and 5% puts, 8 threads and a concurrency of 256.

In Memcached it is not really possible to measure, for reference purposes, the performance of a sequential execution, because there is always concurrency due to the existence of a pool of maintenance threads. Hence, we present the peak throughput obtained using the maximum number of available hardware threads (see Fig. 3(h)). The results show that FL has the best performance, but TSX-GL is only 7% behind. This is a significant achievement as the effort to devise such fine-grained locks is considerably higher than using TSX-GL. Also, since FL is quite optimized, it is expectable that TSX-FL is not able to extract any further parallelism. Interestingly, with this benchmark, TinySTM is not competitive because the instrumentation overheads are amplified by the short and uncontended transactions.

7.3 Concurrent Data Structures

We now consider two concurrent data structures, namely a red-black tree and a hashmap, which represent particularly relevant use cases for TM given the complexity of designing efficient fine-grained locking strategies for these scenarios.

Fig. 4 shows two different scenarios: we consider a small hashmap (512 buckets) with only 10% transactions performing writes (the rest are lookup operations), and a large red-black tree (1 million items) with 90% transactions performing updates. In the former case, TSX-GL achieves perfect linear scalability, which is a consequence of its negligible overheads and of the very reduced abort rate. With larger transactions, the gains achievable by TSX tend to diminish, although it still remains a very competitive solutions.

Table 4(e) shows a spectrum of workloads in red-black tree, by considering the normalized EDP of TSX-GL against the best alternative in each experiment. For this, we vary the size of the tree and the percentage of write transactions. The trend is clear in this table: TSX behaves best with light workloads, and looses advantage when transactions become larger or write-intensive. This confirms the results of the analysis that we performed for STAMP, given that, also in this case, TSX shines most when atomic blocks have little duration and the workload is not fully transactional.

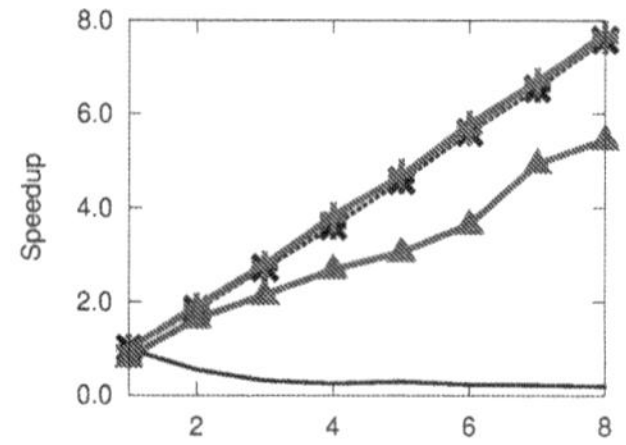

(a) Hashmap 10% writes.

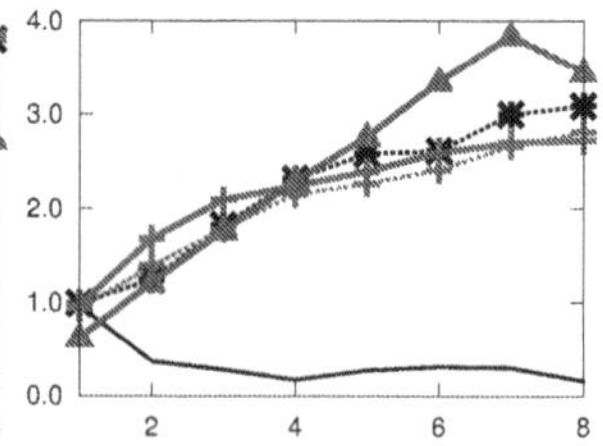

(b) RB Tree 90% writes.

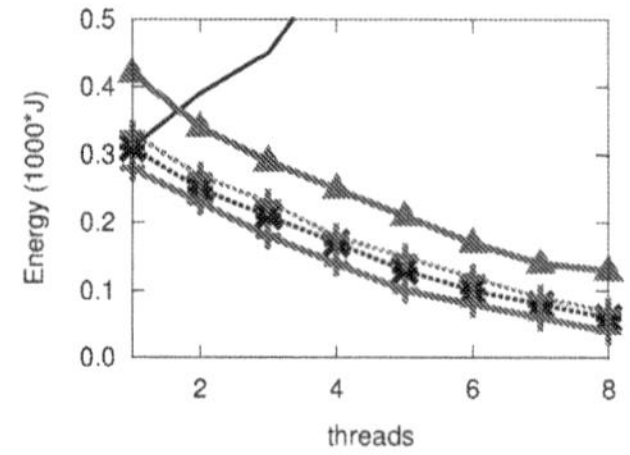

(c) Hashmap 10% writes.

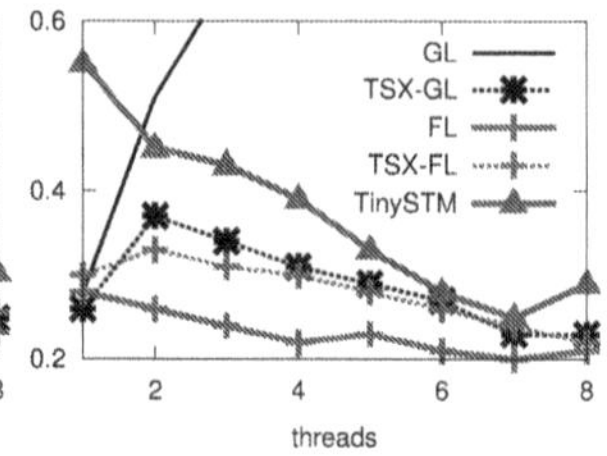

(d) RB Tree 90% writes.

size and % of writes	10%	50%	90%
2^7 elements	3.30	1.79	1.21
2^{14} elements	2.96	1.58	1.11
2^{21} elements	1.86	1.33	1.06

(e) Normalized EDP of the best alternative to TSX-GL in Red-black Tree (higher is favourable to TSX-GL).

Figure 4: Data Structures varying contention level.

8. RESEARCH DIRECTIONS SUGGESTED BY OUR STUDY

We now identify some relevant research directions that emerged from the analysis of our experimental study:

• The overall performance of the tested HyTM solutions is quite disappointing. These findings contradict the simulation results published in several previous works, e.g., [30]. Our analysis suggest that the root cause of the problem is related to the inefficiency of the mechanisms used to couple hardware and software transactions, which is generating a large number of spurious aborts. However, further research is due in order to understand what can be done to address such a problem. An interesting research question, in this sense, is whether the availability of support for enabling non-transactional memory accesses while executing hardware-assisted atomic blocks could indeed allow for more efficient interplay between HTM and STM (which has been assumed by other works in the area of HyTM, e.g. [33]). A related research question is how to support such a feature while minimizing the disruptiveness of the changes required at the hardware level — an aspect that cannot be overlooked given the complexity of modern processor architectures.

• As mentioned in Section 5.3, the performance of TSX is significantly affected by the retry policy (e.g., the settings of the number of retries upon abort, and the choice of how to react to capacity aborts). While in our study we used the configuration that performed best on average, as shown in Table 7, significant speedups (up to 80%) with regard to the configuration used in our study can be achieved by ad-hoc tuning the retry policy for the specific workload — even more could be achieved by considering the specific concurrency degree as well. Unfortunately, this is a tedious and error prone task that is not desirable to delegate to programmers. Hence, these findings highlight the relevance of devising solutions for adaptively tuning these parameters in an automated manner. The key challenge is how to do it with minimal overhead, given that the cost imposed by self-tuning approaches targeting STMs (based on complex machine-learning [34] or analytical models [11]) is going to be strongly amplified in HTM settings because there exists no instrumentation as in STMs. In the light of these findings, we have concurrently obtained some initial results with regard to this research direction [15].

• Our study has used (selective) manual instrumentation when considering both STMs and HyTMs, i.e. only the relevant subset of memory locations accessed in atomic blocks have been traced. As an alternative, one could rely on the compiler to automatically instrument atomic blocks with calls to the TM runtime. The plots in Fig. 5, which were

Table 7: **Improvement of configuring TSX-GL for each workload compared to the single configuration used in our study.**

Speedup %	*kmeans*	*ssca2*	*intruder*	*vacation*	*genome*	*yada*	*labyrinth*
4 threads	12	7	20	36	12	13	2
8 threads	5	8	80	21	2	55	39

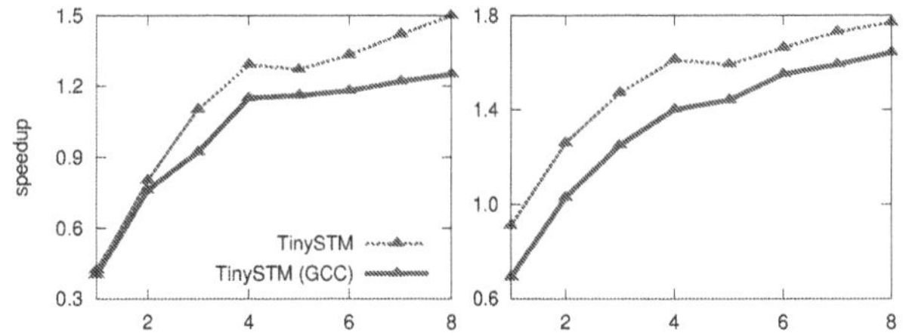

(a) Kmeans. (b) SSCA2.

Figure 5: Impact of GCC instrumentation.

obtained using the C++ TM extension integrated in GCC 4.8.2, show that non-selective instrumentations can impact performance by approximately 20% when using TinySTM. This is a consequence of the increase of the transaction footprint (up to 3x larger with SSCA2) caused by the "blind' instrumentation performed by GCC.

Not only these results unveil the possibility of optimizations in existing compiler's support for STM, but also provide an additional compelling motivation to incorporate support for selective instrumentation in HTM. Indeed, we have shown that capacity exceptions are one of the key sources of aborts with HTM. Hence, techniques capable of achieving noticeable reductions of the transactions' footprint are expected to strongly benefit HTM's performance. These considerations open interesting research avenues investigating cross-layer mechanisms operating at the compiler and architectural level, and aimed at supporting selective instrumentation in a way that is both convenient for the programmer (i.e., possibly fully transparent) and sufficiently non-intrusive to simplify integration in existing architectures.

9. CONCLUSIONS

This paper analyzed extensively the performance and energy efficiency of several state of the art TM systems. We compared different TM solutions (software, hardware and combinations thereof) among each other and against lock based systems. Our study demonstrates that the recent HTM implementation by Intel can strongly outperform any other synchronization alternative in a set of relevant workloads. On the other hand, it also identified some critical limitations of Intel TSX, and highlighted the robustness of state of the art STMs. These software implementations achieve performance competitive with fine-grained locking, and outperform HTM in workloads encompassing long and contention-prone transactions.

Furthermore we have shown that the performance of Hybrid TM, when used in combination with TSX, is normally quite disappointing; we determined that the root cause of this surprising result lies in the inefficiency of the mechanisms used to couple software and hardware transactions. Finally, our study allowed to identify a set of compelling research questions, which, we believe, should be timely addressed to increase the chances of turning HTM into a mainstream paradigm for parallel programming.

Acknowledgements: We thank Konrad Lai, Ravi Rajwar and Richard Yoo from Intel for the insightful discussions about TSX during the conduct of this research.

This work was supported by funds from Fundação para a Ciência e Tecnologia under PEst-OE/EEI/LA0021/2013 and by GreenTM EXPL/EEI-ESS/0361/2013.

10. REFERENCES

[1] Y. Afek, A. Levy, and A. Morrison. Programming with hardware lock elision. In *Proc. of Principles and Practice of Parallel Programming*, PPoPP, pages 295–296, 2013.

[2] A. Baldassin, F. Klein, G. Araujo, R. Azevedo, and P. Centoducatte. Characterizing the Energy Consumption of Software Transactional Memory. *IEEE Comput. Archit. Lett.*, 8(2):56–59, July 2009.

[3] H. Cain et al. Robust architectural support for transactional memory in the power architecture. In *Proc. of International Symposium on Computer Architecture*, ISCA, pages 225–236, 2013.

[4] C. Cao Minh, J. Chung, C. Kozyrakis, and K. Olukotun. STAMP: Stanford Transactional Applications for Multi-Processing. In *Proc. of International Symposium on Workload Characterization*, IISWC, pages 35–46, 2008.

[5] C. Cascaval et al. Software Transactional Memory: Why Is It Only a Research Toy? *Queue*, 6(5):40:46–40:58, Sept. 2008.

[6] D. Christie et al. Evaluation of AMD's Advanced Synchronization Facility Within a Complete Transactional Memory Stack. In *Proc. of EuroSys*, pages 27–40, 2010.

[7] L. Dalessandro, M. Spear, and M. Scott. NOrec: streamlining STM by abolishing ownership records. In *Proc. of Principles and Practice of Parallel Programming*, PPoPP, pages 67–78, 2010.

[8] L. Dalessandro et al. Hybrid NOrec: a case study in the effectiveness of best effort hardware transactional memory. In *Proc. of Architectural Support for Programming Languages and Operating Systems*, ASPLOS, pages 39–52, 2011.

[9] H. David, E. Gorbatov, U. Hanebutte, R. Khanna, and C. Le. RAPL: memory power estimation and capping. In *Proc. of International Symposium on Low power Electronics and Design*, ISLPED, pages 189–194, 2010.

[10] T. David, R. Guerraoui, and V. Trigonakis. Everything you always wanted to know about synchronization but were afraid to ask. In *Proc. of Symposium on Operating Systems Principles*, SOSP, pages 33–48, 2013.

[11] P. Di Sanzo, B. Ciciani, R. Palmieri, F. Quaglia, and P. Romano. On the analytical modeling of concurrency control algorithms for software transactional memories: The case of commit-time-locking. *Perform. Eval.*, 69(5):187–205, May 2012.

[12] D. Dice, Y. Lev, M. Moir, and D. Nussbaum. Early Experience with a Commercial Hardware Transactional Memory Implementation. In *Proc. of Architectural Support for Programming Languages and Operating Systems*, ASPLOS, pages 157–168, 2012.

[13] D. Dice, O. Shalev, and N. Shavit. Transactional locking II. In *Proc. of International Symposium on Distributed Computing*, DISC, pages 194–208, 2006.

[14] N. Diegues and J. Cachopo. Practical Parallel Nesting for Software Transactional Memory. In *Proceedings of International Symposium on Distributed Computing*, DISC, pages 149–163, 2013.

[15] N. Diegues and P. Romano. Self-Tuning Intel Transactional Synchronization Extensions. In *Proc. of International Conference on Autonomic Computing*, ICAC, 2014.

[16] N. Diegues and P. Romano. Time-Warp: Lightweight Abort Minimization in Transactional Memory. In *Proc. of Principles and Practice of Parallel Programming*, PPoPP, pages 167–178, 2014.

[17] A. Dragojević, R. Guerraoui, and M. Kapalka. Stretching transactional memory. In *Proc. of Programming Language Design and Implementation*, PLDI, pages 155–165, 2009.

[18] P. Felber, C. Fetzer, and T. Riegel. Dynamic performance tuning of word-based software transactional memory. In *Proc. of Principles and Practice of Parallel Programming*, PPoPP, pages 237–246, 2008.

[19] C. Ferri, R. I. Bahar, M. Loghi, and M. Poncino. Energy-optimal Synchronization Primitives for Single-chip Multi-processors. In *Proc. of Great Lakes Symposium on VLSI*, GLSVLSI, pages 141–144, 2009.

[20] C. Ferri, S. Wood, T. Moreshet, R. Iris Bahar, and M. Herlihy. Embedded-TM: Energy and complexity-effective hardware transactional memory for embedded multicore systems. *J. Parallel Distrib. Comput.*, 70(10):1042–1052, Oct. 2010.

[21] E. Gaona, R. Titos, J. Fernandez, and M. Acacio. On the design of energy-efficient hardware transactional memory systems. *Concurrency and Computation: Practice and Experience*, 25(6):862–880, 2013.

[22] A. Gautham, K. Korgaonkar, P. Slpsk, S. Balachandran, and K. Veezhinathan. The implications of shared data synchronization techniques on multi-core energy efficiency. In *Proc. of Power-Aware Computing and Systems*, HotPower, pages 1–6, 2012.

[23] D. Hackenberg et al. Power measurement techniques on standard compute nodes: A quantitative comparison. In *Proc. of the International Symposium on Performance Analysis of Systems and Software*, ISPASS, pages 194–204, 2013.

[24] M. Hähnel, B. Döbel, M. Völp, and H. Härtig. Measuring Energy Consumption for Short Code Paths Using RAPL. *SIGMETRICS Performance Evaluation Review*, 40(3):13–17, Jan. 2012.

[25] L. Hammond et al. Transactional Memory Coherence and Consistency. In *Proc. of International Symposium on Computer Architecture*, ISCA, pages 102–113, 2004.

[26] A. Heindl and G. Pokam. An Analytic Framework for Performance Modeling of Software Transactional Memory. *Comput. Netw.*, 53(8):1202–1214, June 2009.

[27] M. Herlihy and J. E. B. Moss. Transactional memory: architectural support for lock-free data structures. In *Proc. of the International Symposium on Computer Architecture*, ISCA, pages 289–300, 1993.

[28] T. Karnagel et al. Improving In-Memory Database Index Performance with Intel TSX. In *Proc. of International Symposium on High Performance Computer Architecture*, HPCA, 2014.

[29] S. Mannarswamy, D. Chakrabarti, K. Rajan, and S. Saraswati. Compiler aided selective lock assignment for improving the performance of software transactional memory. In *Proc. of Principles and Practice of Parallel Programming*, PPoPP, pages 37–46, 2010.

[30] A. Matveev and N. Shavit. Reduced hardware transactions: a new approach to hybrid transactional memory. In *Proc. of the Symposium on Parallelism in Algorithms and Architectures*, SPAA, pages 11–22, 2013.

[31] R. Nishtala et al. Scaling Memcache at Facebook. In *Proc. of Conference on Networked Systems Design and Implementation*, NSDI, pages 385–398, 2013.

[32] V. Pankratius and A.-R. Adl-Tabatabai. A Study of Transactional Memory vs. Locks in Practice. In *Proc. of Symposium on Parallelism in Algorithms and Architectures*, SPAA, pages 43–52, 2011.

[33] T. Riegel, P. Marlier, M. Nowack, P. Felber, and C. Fetzer. Optimizing Hybrid Transactional Memory: The Importance of Nonspeculative Operations. In *Proc. of the Symposium on Parallelism in Algorithms and Architectures*, SPAA, pages 53–64, 2011.

[34] D. Rughetti, P. Di Sanzo, B. Ciciani, and F. Quaglia. Machine Learning-Based Self-Adjusting Concurrency in Software Transactional Memory Systems. In *Proc. of Modeling, Analysis Simulation of Computer and Telecommunication Systems*, MASCOTS, pages 278–285, 2012.

[35] M. Spear, T. Vyas, and Y. Ruan, Wenjia Liu. Transactionalizing Legacy Code: An Experience Report Using GCC and Memcached. In *Proceedings of Conference on Architectural Support for Programming Languages and Operating Systems*, ASPLOS, pages 398–412, 2014.

[36] A. Wang et al. Evaluation of Blue Gene/Q hardware support for transactional memories. In *Proc. of Parallel Architectures and Compilation Techniques*, PACT, pages 127–136, 2012.

[37] R. Yoo, C. Hughes, K. Lai, and R. Rajwar. Performance Evaluation of Intel Transactional Synchronization Extensions for High-Performance Computing. In *Proc. of High Performance Computing, Networking, Storage, and Analysis*, SC, pages 1–11, 2013.

Cooperative Cache Scrubbing

Jennifer B. Sartor
Ghent University
Belgium

Wim Heirman
Intel ExaScience Lab*
Belgium

Stephen M. Blackburn
Australian National University
Australia

Lieven Eeckhout
Ghent University
Belgium

Kathryn S. McKinley
Microsoft Research
Washington, USA

ABSTRACT

Managing the limited resources of power and memory bandwidth while improving performance on multicore hardware is challenging. In particular, more cores demand more memory bandwidth, and multi-threaded applications increasingly stress memory systems, leading to more energy consumption. However, we demonstrate that not all memory traffic is necessary. For modern Java programs, 10 to 60% of DRAM writes are *useless*, because the data on these lines are *dead* - the program is guaranteed to never read them again. Furthermore, reading memory only to immediately zero initialize it wastes bandwidth. We propose a software/hardware cooperative solution: the memory manager communicates dead and zero lines with cache *scrubbing* instructions. We show how scrubbing instructions satisfy MESI cache coherence protocol invariants and demonstrate them in a Java Virtual Machine and multicore simulator. Scrubbing reduces average DRAM traffic by 59%, total DRAM energy by 14%, and dynamic DRAM energy by 57% on a range of configurations. Cooperative software/hardware cache scrubbing reduces memory bandwidth and improves energy efficiency, two critical problems in modern systems.

Categories and Subject Descriptors

C.0 [**Computer Systems Organization**]: General—*Hardware/software interfaces, instruction set design*; D.3.4 [**Programming Languages**]: Processors—*Memory management (garbage collection), optimization, runtimes*

1. INTRODUCTION

Historically, improvements in processor speeds have outpaced improvements in memory speeds and current trends exacerbate this memory wall. For example, as multicore processors add cores, they rarely include commensurate memory or bandwidth [43]. Today, the memory wall translates into a power wall. More cores need bigger memories to store all of their data, which requires more power. The limits on total power due to packaging and temperature constrain system design and consequently, the fraction of total system power consumed by main memory is expected to grow. For some large commercial servers, memory power already dominates total system power [31].

Software trends exacerbate memory bandwidth problems. Evolving applications have seemingly insatiable memory needs with increasingly larger working set sizes and irregular memory access patterns. Recent studies of managed and native programs on multicore processors show that memory bandwidth limits performance and scaling [21, 43, 55]. Two factors in managed languages pose both opportunities and challenges for memory bandwidth optimization: (1) rapid object allocation and (2) zero initialization.

(1) Many applications rapidly allocate short-lived objects, relying on garbage collection or region memory managers to clean up. This programming style creates an object stream with excellent temporal locality, which the allocator exploits to create spatial locality [5, 6, 7]. Unfortunately, short-lived streams displace useful long-lived objects, leave dead objects on dirty cache lines, and increase bandwidth pressure. The memory system must write dirty lines back to memory as they are evicted, but many writes are *useless* because they contain dead objects that the program is guaranteed to never read again. Our measurements of Java benchmarks show that 10 to 60% of write backs are useless!

(2) Managed languages and safe C variants require zero initialization of all fresh allocation. With the widely used fetch-on-write cache policy, writes of zeroes produce useless reads from memory that fetch cache lines, only to immediately over-write them with zeroes. Prior work shows memory traffic due to zeroing ranges between 10 and 45% [54].

While prodigious object allocation and zero initialization present challenges to the memory system, they also offer an opportunity. Because the memory manager identifies dead objects and zero initializes memory, software can communicate this semantic information to hardware to better manage caches, avoid useless traffic to memory, and save energy.

These observations motivate software/hardware cooperative cache *scrubbing*. We leverage standard high-performance generational garbage collectors, which allocate new objects in a region and periodically copy out all live objects, at which point the collector guarantees that any remaining objects are *dead* – the program will never read from the region before writing to it. However, any memory manager that identifies dead cache-line sized blocks, including widely used region allocators in C programs [4], can

*Wim Heirman was a post-doctoral researcher at Ghent University while this work was being done.

PACT'14, August 24–27, 2014, Edmonton, AB, Canada.

http://dx.doi.org/10.1145/2628071.2628083.

use scrubbing to eliminate writes to DRAM. The memory manager communicates dead regions to hardware. We explore three cache scrubbing instructions: *clinvalidate* invalidates the cache-line, *clundirty* unsets the dirty bit, and *clclean* unsets the dirty bit and moves the cache line to the set's least-recently-used (LRU) position. While *clinvalidate* is similar to PowerPC's discontinued *dcbi* instruction [20], and ARM's privileged cache invalidation instruction [3], *clundirty* and *clclean* are new contributions. We also use *clzero*, which is based on existing cache zeroing instructions [20, 32, 47] to eliminate read traffic. We extend the widely used MESI cache coherence protocol to handle these instructions and show how they maintain MESI invariants [14, 20, 22, 24, 37, 41]. After each collection, the memory manager issues one of the three scrubbing instructions for each dead cache line. During application execution, the memory manager zero initializes memory regions with *clzero*.

To evaluate cache scrubbing, we modify Jikes RVM [2, 7], a Java Virtual Machine (JVM), and the Sniper multicore simulator [11] and execute 11 single and multi-threaded Java applications. Because memory systems hide write latencies relatively well, simulated performance improvements are modest, but consistent: 4.6% on average across a range of configurations. However, scrubbing dramatically improves the efficiency of the memory system. Scrubbing and zeroing together reduce DRAM traffic by 59%, total DRAM energy by 14%, and dynamic DRAM energy by 57%, on average. Across the three scrubbing instructions, we find that *clclean*, which suppresses the write back and puts the cache line in the LRU position, performs best.

While we focus on managed languages, prior work by Isen et al. identifies and reduces useless write backs in explicitly managed sequential C programs [23]. They require a map of the live/free status of blocks of allocated memory, which hardware stores after software communicates the information. Their approach is not practical since (1) it requires a 100 KB hardware lookup table and a mark bit on every cache line, (2) it exacerbates limitations of the C memory model on undefined references, and (3) the separate map breaks cache coherence on multicore processors.

Our paper proposes a practical approach to save memory bandwidth and energy on multicore processors. While we leverage region allocation semantics, any memory manager that identifies dead cache lines can save traffic with cache scrubbing instructions. Our instructions require only small changes to the widely used MESI coherence protocol [20, 22] for multicore hardware. In summary, our contributions are:

- We identify an enormous opportunity to eliminate memory traffic in managed languages and region allocators.
- We design a practical cooperative software/hardware approach with the necessary modifications to the MESI cache coherence protocol to scrub cache lines.
- We quantify how cooperative scrubbing, used together with zeroing instructions, significantly reduces memory traffic and DRAM energy.
- We develop a novel multicore architectural simulation technology to simulate multi-threaded Java workloads on multicore hardware in reasonable amounts of time.

By exploiting the semantics of programming languages, software and hardware can cooperate to tackle some of the hardest bottlenecks in modern computer systems related to energy, power, and memory bandwidth.

2. BACKGROUND AND MOTIVATION

We first present background on the bandwidth bottleneck and memory management. We then characterize the opportunity due to useless write backs. In our Java benchmarks, from 10 to 60% of write backs are useless, i.e., the garbage collector has determined that the data is dead before the cache writes it back. We then describe why existing cache hint instructions are insufficient to solve this problem.

2.1 Bandwidth and Allocation Wall

Much prior research shows that bandwidth is increasingly a performance bottleneck as chip-multiprocessor machines scale up the number of cores, both in hardware and software [10, 21, 35, 40, 43, 55]. Rogers et al. show that the *bandwidth wall* between off-chip memory and on-chip cores is a performance bottleneck and can severely limit core scaling [43]. Molka et al. perform a detailed study on the Nehalem microarchitecture [40], showing that on the quad-core Intel X5570 processor, memory read bandwidth does not scale beyond two cores, while write bandwidth does not scale beyond one core.

On the software side, Zhao et al. show that allocation-intensive Java programs pose an *allocation wall* which quickly saturates memory bandwidth, limiting application scaling and performance [55]. Languages with region allocators and garbage collection encourage rapid allocation of short-lived objects, which sometimes interact poorly with cache memory designs. Scrubbing addresses this issue by communicating language semantics down to hardware.

2.2 Memory Management

The best performing memory managers for explicit and managed languages have converged on a similar regime. Explicit memory managers use region allocators when possible [4, 21] and high-performance garbage collectors use generational collectors with a copying nursery [5, 55]. Both allocate contiguously into large regions of memory, putting objects allocated together in time adjacent in memory, creating spatial locality based on the program's temporal locality [5]. Region allocation is only applicable when all the objects in the region die together, but this case is relatively frequent [4, 21], especially in transactional workloads, such as web services.

A standard copying generational garbage collector puts all fresh allocation into the *nursery*, i.e., a large region of contiguous memory. When the region is full, the collector copies out the survivors into the old space. Most managed programs follow the weak generational hypothesis, i.e., most objects die young [33, 48]. Therefore, frequent nursery collections copy small amounts of live objects, yet yield a large free region for subsequent fresh allocation.

Safe C dialects and managed languages, such as Java, PHP, JavaScript, and C#, require the runtime to zero initialize all fresh allocation. Prior work shows that zeroing incurs time overheads of 3 to 5% on average and produces 10 to 45% of memory traffic [54].

Sizing nurseries. Memory management is a time-space tradeoff. Smaller nurseries and heap sizes induce more frequent collections and higher collection costs, but consume less memory. In particular, small nursery sizes repeatedly incur fixed per-collection costs (e.g., scanning the thread stacks and coordinating application threads). Applications that allocate a lot, or have many threads, or have high nursery survival rates, need large nursery sizes to minimize garbage collection time. Prior work established that large nurseries offer the best performance on average, with the advantage tapering off at nursery sizes twice the size of the last-level

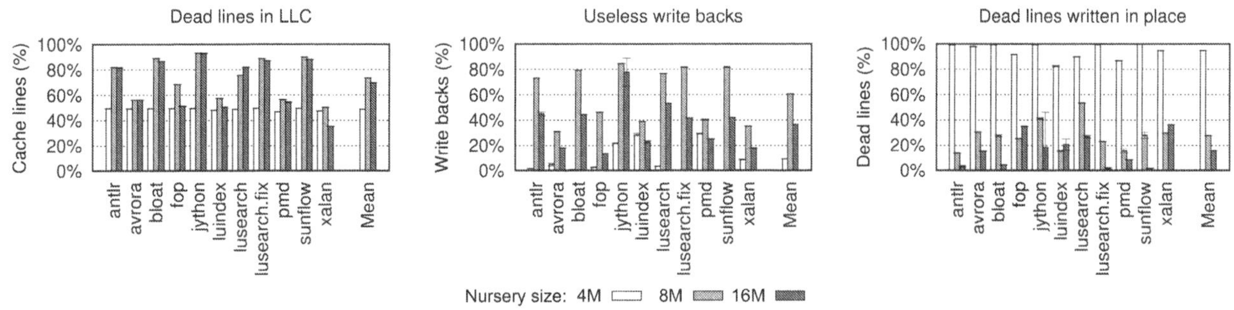

Figure 1: Dead data in last-level cache after nursery collections. (a) Percent of last-level cache lines that are dead. (b) Percent of write backs that are useless. (c) Percent of dead lines in last-level cache that are written in cache. ***Dirty cache lines are often dead and many dead lines are uselessly written to memory.***

cache [5, 55]. We confirmed this result on modern hardware and applications by running the DaCapo Java benchmarks [8], using the default generational Immix garbage collector in Jikes RVM [2, 7]. We found that a nursery size of 16 MB offered close to optimal performance on a Bloomfield processor with 8 MB of last-level cache, with 8 MB and 4 MB nurseries showing average overall slowdowns of 3 to 8%.

Since nursery sizes are adjustable and, in part, sized to coordinate with memory systems for responsiveness, in the remainder of this paper we explore a range of practical nursery sizes (4, 8, and 16 MB) that pivot around the last-level cache size (8 MB), which we keep constant.

2.3 Useless Write Backs

Allocation in both garbage collected and region allocation settings produce an *object stream*, a small irregular window of temporal and spatial reuse [6]. Object streams march linearly through the cache, displace other useful data, and have a short window of use. When the cache later evicts these lines, they are dirty and must be written to memory. Because these objects and their cache lines are mostly short-lived, the objects on the line are often dead; i.e., the program never reads them again.

A lot of this write traffic is useless, wasting bandwidth and energy. To explore this opportunity, we executed single and multithreaded DaCapo Java benchmarks [8], using the default generational Immix garbage collector in Jikes RVM [2, 7]. We execute them with the Sniper simulator [11], which models a multicore processor with four cores, inclusive caches, and a shared 8 MB L3 cache. (Section 4 has more methodological details.) After each nursery collection, the memory manager communicates the address range of the dead nursery to the simulator. The simulator marks resident cache lines in this range as dead. When the program subsequently writes a new object on a dead line, the simulator unmarks the line.

Figure 1 presents 'dead lines in last-level cache', the average fraction of the last-level cache that contains dead lines immediately after each nursery collection. 'Useless write backs' shows the fraction of all lines written to DRAM that exclusively contain dead objects and are thus useless. 'Dead lines written in place' shows the fraction of lines marked dead, but later written while in cache when the application allocates new objects on these lines.

Figure 1 shows that at the end of each collection, the last-level cache is dominated by dead lines (49 to 73% on average), and the fraction is a function of the nursery size.

A small nursery (4 MB) that fits in cache performs collections more often, degrading total time. However, because dead lines remain cache resident, this nursery size has very few useless write backs and around 95% of subsequent writes to these lines hit in the cache. Larger nurseries (8 and 16 MB) generate a substantial number of useless write backs (61% and 36% on average). Since the program takes longer to reuse a given line, the cache evicts more dead lines. Likewise, larger nurseries are less likely to write (28% and 16%) to the dead lines while they are still cache resident.

For 8 MB and 16 MB nursery sizes, over 70% of the last-level cache contains dead lines and the cache generates many useless write backs. For instance, over 75% of write backs are useless for bloat, jython, lusearch, lusearch.fix, and sunflow with an 8 MB nursery and can be eliminated. However, even in these cases, over 23% of the lines marked dead are written while still cache resident. These writes to dead lines in cache motivate using a scrubbing instruction that does not preemptively evict all dead cache lines, which will result in subsequent useless memory fetches, but instead motivates delaying the decision to evict based on program cache demand. In summary, there is a significant opportunity for saving traffic and improving memory efficiency.

2.4 Cache Hint Instructions

Scrubbing is, in part, inspired by prior instruction-set architectures (ISAs). For instance, the PowerPC ISA [20] contains a data cache block flush (*dcbf*) instruction, which writes a line back to memory. Prior to 2005, it contained a supervisor-level data cache block invalidate (*dcbi*), which invalidated a cache line and suppressed write backs. However, *dcbi* was never included in multicore processors. The ARM ISA also includes supervisor-level instructions to invalidate a cache line and clean a cache line, but the latter does not avoid the write back [3]. Section 3.1 describes how to implement user-level cache line invalidate instructions that avoid writing back data, including required changes to the cache coherence protocol for multicore processors.

The Intel Xeon Phi's ISA [22] introduces two instructions, *clevict0* and *clevict1*, which suggest cache lines to evict from the L1 and L2 cache, respectively. These instructions are local hints. The intent of these instructions is to remove lines from the cache that are no longer needed, but, like *dcbf*, they do not suppress write backs.

The current PowerPC ISA also includes a data cache block zero (*dcbz*) instruction that forgoes fetching from memory to zero a cache line directly, eliminating the default fetch on write [20, 47]. However, none of IBM's J9, Oracle HotSpot, or Jikes RVM uses it to perform zero initialization. Azul Systems, which built custom hundreds-of-core hardware for Java applications, used a cache line zero (CLZ) instruction to zero in place without fetching in order to save bandwidth. Azul states that CLZ avoided the fencing overhead of *dcbz* [13]. Our contribution is showing that zeroing works well and synergistically with scrubbing instructions.

Scrub Instructions	Description
clinvalidate(addr)	Set cache line state to invalid, no write back
clundirty(addr)	Unset cache line dirty bit
clclean(addr)	Unset dirty bit and move to LRU position

Zero Instruction	Description
clzeroX(addr)	Allocate and zero cache line in level X

Table 1: Each scrubbing and zeroing instruction takes an address and operates on one cache line.

3. COOPERATIVE SCRUBBING

This section describes cache scrubbing instructions that eliminate write backs to relieve off-chip memory bandwidth pressure, including the required changes to the cache coherence protocol and how we maintain its invariants. We then describe our software approach for inserting scrub instructions in any region allocator and, in particular, in a copying generational garbage collector.

3.1 ISA Modifications

Scrubbing instructions. We propose simple yet powerful instructions in which software conveys to hardware that the data in the specified cache line is dead, and that its contents can safely be discarded. Table 1 summarizes these instructions. The scrubbing variants differ in the expected distance until the program will next write the cache line to explore the space. The immediate or eventual eviction of the cache line will forgo the write back to main memory, saving off-chip *write* bandwidth.

The *clinvalidate* (cache line invalidate) instruction immediately invalidates the respective cache line from the cache. A subsequent access to the line will trigger a memory fetch, assuming the widely implemented fetch-on-write allocation policy. This instruction will be effective when the program does not write the line for a long time.

The *clundirty* (cache line unset dirty bit) instruction keeps the line in cache but clears its dirty bit. If the program writes to the line soon, it is still in cache and will not require a read and fetch from memory. If the line is evicted from the cache, *clundirty* eliminates the useless write to main memory.

The *clclean* instruction clears the dirty bit and moves the line into the LRU position, making the line the preferred candidate for replacement. This instruction is a flexible middle ground between *clinvalidate* and *clundirty*. If the program writes the line again soon, it will still be in cache. If instead the program needs capacity for other lines, the hardware will evict this line and forego a useless write back to main memory. Section 5.1 shows that this flexibility pays off: *clclean* is the most effective of the three at reducing main memory traffic.

Zeroing instructions. The semantics of many languages guarantee zero initialization of newly allocated memory, which can waste *read* memory bandwidth. Typical cache policies, fetch-on-write and write-allocate, cause the memory system to read data from main memory in large blocks, only to overwrite it with zeroes immediately, thus consuming unnecessary read bandwidth. As discussed in Section 2.4, the PowerPC ISA and others already include a data cache block zero instruction which forgoes fetching from memory and allocates a cache line filled with zeroes in the L1 cache. In this paper, we explore variants of existing zeroing instructions, and show that they are synergistic with scrubbing instructions. We evaluate *clzero1*, *clzero2* and *clzero3*, which allocate cache lines in the L1, L2 and L3 cache, respectively, to optimize for block size and expected reuse distance.

3.2 Cache Coherence

Each scrubbing or zeroing instruction operates on a single cache line and updates cache status bits and coherence states. With respect to memory consistency, both scrubbing and zeroing instructions potentially change memory contents. The processor core therefore treats them as writes with respect to ordering and serialization. Zeroing instructions target a specific level of cache, as defined by the instruction. We perform scrubbing instructions at the last level of cache, L3, and rely on existing mechanisms to propagate invalidations to the L1 and L2 caches sharing each L3. In our implementation, the software issues many scrubbing instructions in a row and thus the hardware can perform them in parallel.

Scrubbing instructions do not affect program correctness, and hardware may ignore them. The hardware is free to return undefined values if the software violates scrubbing instruction guarantees. In a memory-safe language, the garbage collector guarantees that the program will never read a dead line before writing it and communicates this fact to hardware. The correctness of memory-safe languages and region allocators depends on this guarantee.

Scrubbing instructions require minor changes to cache coherence protocols. We describe changes to a MESI protocol with inclusive last-level caches and then show how these changes do not violate key protocol invariants proved in prior work [14, 24, 37, 41]. Many multicore processors use MESI or close variants, such as MESIF (Intel [22]) or MERSI (IBMs PowerPC [20]).

Each letter in the MESI protocol name stands for a cache-line state: Modified, Exclusive, Shared, and Invalid. A finite state machine describes the transitions between states on bus and processor actions. Table 2 shows the transitions that occur in the MESI protocol at the last-level cache in response to each scrubbing or zeroing instruction. Each row shows the initial state and each column header shows the instruction. Given the current state (row) and the scrubbing instruction (column), the row-column intersection shows the resulting state and actions.

Scrubbing instructions. Scrubbing instructions operate at the last-level cache of the core that issues the scrubbing instruction. On systems with multiple last-level caches, such as multi-socket systems and cache-coherent multiprocessors, scrubbing instructions do not generate off-chip coherence traffic since all transitions happen locally. As shown in Table 2, starting from the M (modified) state, the *clinvalidate* instruction transitions cache lines in the last-level cache to I (invalid), as would a bus write request. Remember that a line in the M state in one last-level cache is not present in any other last-level cache. With inclusive caching, the protocol invalidates other cache levels that replicate this line, suppressing all write backs to memory. The *clclean* and *clundirty* instructions transition lines from M to E (exclusive), suppress the write, and invalidate other cache levels that contain this line. We choose to invalidate lines in the other cache levels (as opposed to undirtying them) because this uses existing hardware mechanisms. We did explore undirtying lines in the other cache levels and found no significant performance difference.

Starting from the E and S states, *clinvalidate* transitions the line to I (invalid) and invalidates copies of the line in the other levels of the cache hierarchy. The *clundirty* and *clclean* instructions do not change the state from E or S, but do trigger invalidations of the line in other cache levels. From all M, E, or S states, *clclean* modifies

State		*clinvalidate*	*clundirty*/*clclean*	*clzero*	BusInvalidate
M	modified	invalidate L1/L2 (no WB) → I	invalidate L1/L2 (no WB) → E (*clclean*: → LRU)	—	invalidate L1/L2 (no WB) → I
E	exclusive	invalidate L1/L2 → I	invalidate L1/L2 (*clclean*: → LRU)	→ M	invalidate L1/L2 → I
S	shared	invalidate L1/L2 → I	invalidate L1/L2 (*clclean*: → LRU)	BusInvalidate → M	invalidate L1/L2 → I
I	invalid	—	—	BusInvalidate → M	—

Table 2: Coherence state transitions for scrubbing instructions in the last-level cache.

the LRU position of the line, a cache-local property. *Clinvalidate*, *clundirty*, and *clclean* do nothing if the line is invalid.

Our simulator implements this protocol and scrubbing in the context of a multi-socket multicore system with snooping coherence and a single shared inclusive last-level cache per processor socket. However, scrubbing instructions will work with non-inclusive cache hierarchies by using their snoop filter, but fleshing out this design is left for future work.

Zeroing instructions. Zeroing instructions operate at the specific cache level encoded in the instruction. If the cache block is in a modified or exclusive state, the lines are instantiated with zeros, and an exclusive line transitions to M. Otherwise (from an S or I state), the access is propagated to the next-level caches, through to the last-level cache, using a special zeroing request. At the last-level cache, the protocol delivers a *BusInvalidate* message off-chip to the coherence network to obtain exclusive access, which is similar to the existing *BusRdX* request but elides the write back from other last-level caches if the line is in a modified state. This step prevents dirty but soon to be overwritten data from being sent across the off-chip coherence network. If the cache line started in the S or I states, it transitions to the M state upon a *clzero* instruction.

Maintaining protocol invariants. Proofs of the multiprocessor cache coherence protocols establish properties such as deadlock freedom, the fact that requests for cache lines are satisfied correctly, and consistency of cache line contents between caches and memory [14, 24, 37, 41]. We assume a proof of existing MESI invariants and show the effect of each of our instructions. We focus on the following key invariants for cache line states and contents.

1. Given a line in the M state in one cache, the line will be in the I state or not present in other caches.
2. Given a line in the E state in one cache, the line will be in I state or not present in other caches.
3. If a line is in the S state in one cache, the line will be in the S or I state or not present in other caches.
4. If a line is in the I state in one cache (or not present), the line may be in any other state in other caches.
5. When a cache requests a line, another cache will satisfy the request if it contains the line in the M state. Otherwise, memory will satisfy the request.

The simplest case is the *clzero* instruction. All five invariants are easily established, since *clzero* is the same as any other write. Invariants 2, 3, and 5 are trivially maintained. For invariants 1 and 4, when the protocol finds and invalidates copies of the line in other caches (taking invalidation and bus actions to re-establishing invariants 1 and 4), it suppresses fetches from both caches and memory. A subsequent request for the line will use this copy, since it is in the M state.

The *clinvalidate* instruction easily maintains these key five invariants. Transitioning any line in the M, E, and S states to I trivially maintains the first four invariants. Invariant 5 is maintained because in all cases, no cache contains a valid copy (M, E, or S state) of the line. For the purposes of validation, it is as if the system writes the original data to memory.

The *clundirty/clclean* instructions are the most subtle because they transition a line from M to E. Since invariant 1 holds before this transition, invariant 2 must hold afterward. Invariants 1, 3, and 4 are unaffected in this case. In the case where the line starts in the E, S, or I state, the line stays in the same state and, as such, maintains all five invariants.

Optimizations of invariant 5 where caches may satisfy read requests for data they have in the E or S state are affected because the cache and main memory may contain different data values due to scrubbing. However, the correctness of the programming language implementation *guarantees* that the application cannot generate any such subsequent read for the line after a scrubbing instruction. However for the purposes of completeness, if such a read were to occur, the response is undefined.

3.3 Security Implications of Scrubbing

Our premise for the correctness of the application is that the programming language implementation only uses scrubbing instructions on data that is in fact never subsequently read. If the application were somehow to violate this guarantee, it will read an undefined value. Such misuse does not constitute a security violation because the application is never made privy to another process' data. However, without correct support from the OS, scrubbing can open up an attack. When process *A* gives up a physical page, the OS may subsequently make it available to process *B*. Before making the page available to *B*, the OS will initialize the page, either zeroing it, when *B* requests a fresh page, or populating the page when *B* pages in from a swap. In either case, unless the OS ensures that the writes that it performs are propagated to main memory, *B* may use *clinvalidate*, discarding the data written by the OS, before reading from the page to reveal *A*'s data. The OS can avoid this problem by using a non-temporal store instruction, which invalidates all copies of the relevant cache line throughout the memory hierarchy, and writes the data straight into main memory — effectively destroying all remaining copies of the previous owner's data. To ensure that scrubbing instructions are only used in the presence of safe OS support, the instructions are disabled by default, and the OS only enables them by issuing a privileged instruction or setting a bit in a model-specific register. If disabled, the system safely ignores scrubbing instructions, requiring no change to existing operating systems.

3.4 Software Responsibilities

This section describes modifications to the memory manager to enable it to eliminate useless reads and writes to main memory using scrubbing instructions. A region allocator or a garbage collector may only reclaim memory if it determines that the region is dead and the program will never read from the region again. We implement scrubbing in a stop-the-world high-performance generational Immix collector [7]. At the end of each nursery collection, the collector has copied all reachable objects from the nursery region to the mature space. The collector thus guarantees that the entire nursery is dead. We modify the collector to iterate over the entire nursery's contiguous address range, calling a scrubbing instruction (*clinvalidate*, *clundirty*, or *clclean*) for each cache-line-sized block. We also modify the memory manager to issue our zeroing instructions to zero initialize regions during regular program execution, replacing the store instructions normally used. Our memory manager manages memory, and in particular the nursery, in 32 KB regions, zeroing a region on demand when the program first allocates into it. We modify the allocator to iterate over each cache-line-sized block in the 32 KB region, calling *clzero2* to initialize each line without fetching from memory. We evaluated zeroing at all three cache levels, but found L2 to be most effective because of the granularity of zeroing.

We also explored instructions that perform invalidations at larger granularities with similar results [44], but choose cache-line granularity instructions because they better correspond to existing memory instructions, easing their hardware implementation. Cache-line granularity is also more suitable for other memory managers, such as free-lists and Immix's line and block organization [7]. We leave exploration of larger granularities to future work.

4. METHODOLOGY

This section describes our software and simulator methodology, including the processor and memory architecture model, simulator extensions, JVM, and benchmarks.

4.1 Simulation Methodology

Sniper simulator. We modify Sniper [11], a parallel, high-speed, and cycle-level x86 simulator for multicore systems. We are unaware of any other publicly available cycle-level simulator that executes Java workloads on multicore hardware, which is required to evaluate scrubbing. Sniper uses a higher abstraction level than most cycle-level simulators and exploits parallelism on modern multicore hardware to achieve simulation speeds of up to 2 MIPS. Sniper can transition between a fast functional-only simulation model and a fully detailed simulation mode with timing and microarchitectural state changes. Sniper is validated against Intel Core2 and Nehalem class hardware with average absolute errors of around 20% for performance compared to real hardware, which is in line with other academic architectural simulators. In addition to performance, Sniper models and predicts power consumption using the McPAT framework [17].

Processor architecture. Sniper models a multicore processor with four superscalar out-of-order cores. Table 3 describes the basic architecture characteristics, including the private L1-I, L1-D and L2 caches, and shared last-level cache, which is similar to Intel's Nehalem machine. We model a 32-entry store queue which tracks architecturally committed stores while they are issued to the memory hierarchy; stores do not block commit until this store buffer fills up. Memory writes use a write-fetch write-allocate write-back caching policy. We model write buffers in front of DRAM and simulate a DDR3 DRAM main memory based on specifications from Micron [39].

Component	Parameters
Processor	1 socket, 4 cores
Core	2.66 GHz, 4-way issue, 128-entry ROB
Branch predictor	hybrid local/global predictor
Max. outstanding	48 loads, 32 stores, 10 L1-D misses
Cache line size	64 B, LRU replacement
L1-I	32 KB, 4 way, 4 cycle access time
L1-D	32 KB, 8 way, 4 cycle access time
L2 cache	256 KB per core, 8 way, 8 cycle
L3 cache	shared 8 MB, 16 way, 30 cycle
Coherence protocol	MESI
Memory controller	FR-FCFS scheduling, line-interleaved mapping, open-page policy
DRAM organization	32 GB, 2 channels, 4 ranks/channel, 8 banks/rank, 64 K rows/bank, 8 KB rows
DRAM device	Micron DDR3 [39]

Table 3: Architecture model.

Extensions for Java. We use Jikes RVM [2, 7] and modified Sniper to work with its Just-In-Time (JIT) compilers that generate code during execution. To faithfully simulate multicore hardware running Java workloads, we extended Sniper in a number of ways that are detailed in the following paragraphs.

System call emulation. Because Sniper is a user-level simulator, it may emulate or natively run system calls made by either the application or Jikes RVM. In an initial study, we measured system time with the `strace` and `time` utilities, and found that the benchmarks spend between 1 to 93% of time in system calls on an Intel Nehalem machine. We measured these numbers on the first iteration with replay compilation [9, 16] to reflect system calls during JVM start-up. We found that only two system calls contribute to almost all system time (all others are less than 0.5% of system time), those relating to synchronization: `futex` and `nanosleep`.

Consequently in all the experiments in this paper, we emulate these two system calls in Sniper and run other system calls natively. Sniper emulates futex-based synchronization calls by making threads wait and wake each other up at the correct simulated times. Emulation thus ensures that Sniper accounts for 99.5% of the total execution time. Since Java virtual machines use separate threads for GC, JIT, profiling, and application threads, even single-threaded applications are implicitly multi-threaded and the number of threads almost always exceeds the four cores we model. Because Sniper is a user-level simulator, we add a simple round-robin thread scheduler to Sniper. Sniper selects an available thread for a core once the running thread's time quantum expires (after 1 millisecond), or when the running thread blocks on a synchronization event.

JVM-simulator communication. Simulating cooperative hardware/software mechanisms requires communication between the JVM and hardware simulator. Sniper defines the *magic* instruction *xchg %bx, %bx* for this purpose, which is an x86 instruction that in normal execution has no effect. The simulator intercepts the magic instruction and reads the *%eax* and *%ebx* registers, which specify the type of scrubbing or zeroing instruction and the address.

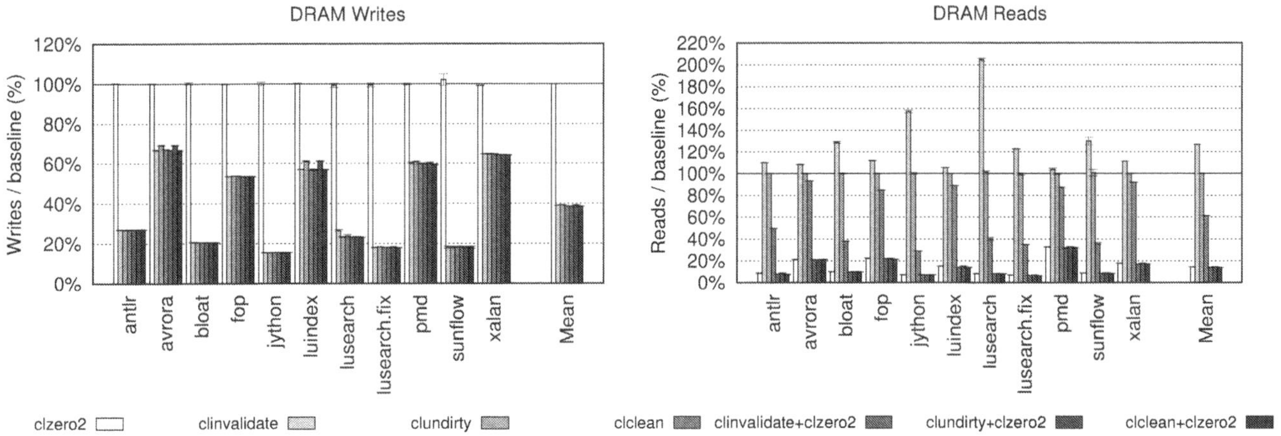

Figure 2: Relative number of DRAM reads and writes for an 8 MB nursery. ***All scrubbing instructions eliminate a large fraction of useless writes and* clclean *also eliminates reads. Zeroing instructions eliminate most DRAM reads. Together they effectively eliminate most useless memory traffic.***

We use Jikes RVM's low-level, low-overhead *syscall* mechanism to invoke Sniper's magic instructions. At the appropriate time, Jikes RVM invokes a scrubbing or zeroing instruction for each of the appropriate cache lines. Sniper models each instruction's effect in hardware, fully accounting for all overheads (including coherence and propagation events to other cache levels).

4.2 Software

Java virtual machine. We modify version 3.1.2 of Jikes RVM [2] to communicate with Sniper when it zeroes and scrubs memory. We specify four garbage collection threads, and for configurable multi-threaded workloads, we specify four application threads. All application and JVM service threads migrate between the four cores (on one socket) using Sniper's scheduler. This configuration works well, as measured by prior work [45].

We use the default *production* Jikes RVM configuration which uses a generational collector with an Immix mature space [7]. We use a practical heap size of 2× the minimum required for each benchmark. This configuration reflects moderate heap pressure. We use the default *boundedNursery*, which initializes the nursery to the bound size, but when the mature space is too limited to accommodate all nursery survivors, it reduces the nursery size accordingly, down to a minimum size of 1 MB. We eliminate the non-determinism of the adaptive compiler by performing replay compilation [9, 16]. The replay JIT compiler applies a fixed optimization plan when it first compiles each method [9, 19]. The plan includes a mix of optimization levels, which is calculated offline from recorded profiling information from numerous executions. We select the plan that gives the best performance, producing a highly optimized base configuration. We report the second invocation of the application, further limiting non-determinism and excluding JIT time to measure application steady-state behavior. We repeat this process three times and report averages and standard deviations in all graphs.

Java benchmarks. We execute 11 benchmarks from the DaCapo suite, taken from versions 2006-10-MR2 and 9.12-bach [8]. We use seven benchmarks from the 9.12-bach DaCapo release: those that work on our version of Jikes RVM and with our simulator. We use two versions of lusearch: the original lusearch and lusearch.fix which eliminates needless allocation (identified by [54]). We use three benchmarks from the 2006-10-MR2 DaCapo suite: antlr, bloat, and fop. Five benchmarks (antlr, bloat, fop, jython, luindex) are single-threaded and six (avrora, lusearch, lusearch.fix, pmd, sunflow, xalan) are multi-threaded.

5. EVALUATION

This section first evaluates the DRAM bandwidth, energy, and performance savings of scrubbing with the 8 MB nursery in detail. We then study the relationship of the nursery size to the last-level cache size, showing that scrubbing is effective at all ratios. The best performing scrubbing instruction alone is *clclean* because it saves both write and read traffic. Combining *clclean* with *clzero2* is the most effective at saving critical off-chip bandwidth and DRAM energy.

5.1 Reduction in DRAM Bandwidth Demand

Figure 2 plots the percentage of DRAM writes and reads saved with *clzero2*, *clinvalidate*, *clundirty*, and *clclean*, individually, and then each scrubbing instruction plus *clzero2*. The results for an 8 MB nursery are normalized to unoptimized runs for each benchmark.

On average, scrubbing alone saves about 60% of DRAM writes as compared with an unoptimized run, as predicted in Section 2.3. In particular, bloat, jython, lusearch, lusearch.fix, and sunflow substantially benefit from scrubbing, saving around 80% of off-chip writes. As expected, *clzero2* has a small effect on DRAM writes, but saves about 86% of DRAM reads.

All three scrubbing instructions (second, third, and fourth bars in Figure 2) are similarly highly effective at reducing DRAM writes. However, differences emerge when we analyze their impact on DRAM reads. The *clinvalidate* instruction increases the number of reads because it evicts all dead lines from cache. Using the common fetch and write-allocate cache policy, a subsequent write (to zero initialize the address upon fresh allocation) must fetch the data again from memory. The *clundirty* instruction does not change the number of reads from memory, since it has no effect on cache replacement.

The best performing scrubbing instruction is *clclean*. It eliminates both useless writes and reads, reducing DRAM reads by about 40% on average. The *clclean* instruction unsets the dirty bit *and*

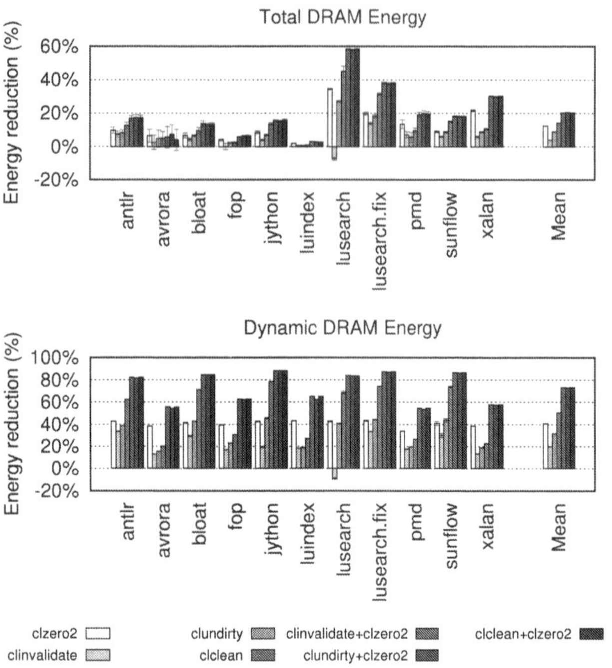

Figure 3: Reduction in DRAM total energy and DRAM dynamic energy for an 8 MB nursery. ***Cooperative cache scrubbing improves total DRAM energy and dramatically improves dynamic DRAM energy.***

moves the line to the LRU position, such that if this set requires a subsequent eviction, the cache will evict the line. The dead and unreachable data is evicted lazily if necessary, and the cache retains more likely useful, live data. Furthermore, *clclean* moves nursery data to the LRU position in a *sequential order*, from the beginning to the end of the nursery address range, which puts addresses from the end of nursery to be evicted next and keeps early nursery addresses, which will be used again soon for allocation. In contrast, *clundirty* evicts nursery data based on last-touch, which is less likely to retain early nursery addresses. The *clclean* instruction thus hits a sweet spot, improving beyond the overly aggressive eviction policy with *clinvalidate* and no change to the eviction policy with *clundirty*.

We next evaluate the impact of each scrubbing instruction when combined with cache-line zeroing and we show that they perform synergistically together. The right three bars of each grouping in Figure 2 show that adding zeroing to scrubbing has little additional effect on writes to DRAM. However, DRAM reads are significantly reduced by adding *clzero2* to scrubbing. Combining zeroing with *clinvalidate* is especially advantageous as it results in a significant decrease in DRAM reads instead of an increase. *Clinvalidate* alone kicks dead data out of cache, and thus requires a fetch on subsequent access. Because the zeroing instruction, however, avoids this fetch by instantiating the data directly in cache, *clinvalidate+clzero2* saves around 86% of DRAM reads. Adding *clzero2* to either *clundirty* or *clclean* similarly saves the DRAM fetch for zeroing nursery data, equalizing the scrubbing instructions that keep nursery data in cache but evict it in different orders. All benchmarks save at least 65% of reads from DRAM. Using scrubbing and zeroing together, we save on average 86% of reads, and overall 75% of DRAM traffic (see Table 4).

5.2 DRAM Energy Reduction

The graphs in Figure 3 plot total and dynamic DRAM energy. The average reduction in dynamic DRAM energy is substantial at 73%. Because the majority of DRAM energy is currently static [39], the average total energy reduction is 20%. Energy reduction is larger than, but mirrors, the performance improvements in Figure 4. Because modern memory systems hide the latency of writes and some reads, reducing memory traffic does not always translate directly into performance. Optimizing with *clclean+clzero2* leads to an overall 20% reduction in total DRAM energy, larger than the average 12% for *clzero2* alone or 14% for *clclean* alone. For lusearch, *clclean* is particularly effective: it saves 45% of total DRAM energy by itself and together with *clzero2*, it saves 58%.

The bottom graph of Figure 3 shows that scrubbing dramatically saves dynamic DRAM energy. Alone, *clzero2* saves 41% of dynamic energy on average. *Clinvalidate* saves 20% on average, while *clundirty* and *clclean* save 32% and 50% of dynamic energy, respectively. Adding *clzero2* to scrubbing improves dynamic energy savings even more: 73% on average. The large savings of both DRAM reads and writes correspond to large reductions in dynamic and total DRAM energy, which will only become a more precious commodity in future systems.

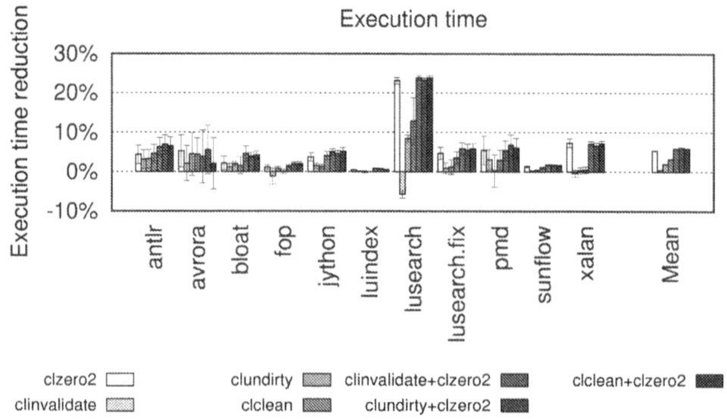

Figure 4: Reduction in execution time for an 8 MB nursery. ***Cooperative cache scrubbing improves performance.***

5.3 Performance

Figure 4 shows the reduction in total execution time for each benchmark when using zeroing, scrubbing, and both optimizations together. Table 4 shows that scrubbing not only reduces memory traffic, it also reduces the average last-level cache (LLC) misses substantially: 86% for the 8 MB nursery. Reductions in memory traffic and decreases in last-level cache misses explain execution time improvements. Because the popular write-back policy coalesces writes and writes generally do not stall the instruction pipeline, performance improvements are modest.

By itself, *clzero2* improves performance by 5%, because of its large reduction in DRAM reads and in last-level cache misses.Even though non-blocking writes should achieve some of the benefits of *clzero2*, we found that the bursts of initializing writes for 32 KB regions overwhelmed the 32 entry store queues on occasion. Avoiding these DRAM-related stalls with *clzero2* removes stalls due to full store queues that occur with normal zeroing store instructions.

Scrubbing with *clinvalidate*, *clundirty*, and *clclean* each alone improves performance on average by 0.5%, 2%, and 3.3%, respectively. *Clclean* reduces execution time by saving reads and writes to memory, as well as reducing last-level cache misses by 39%, proving itself to be the most effective scrubbing instruction. In par-

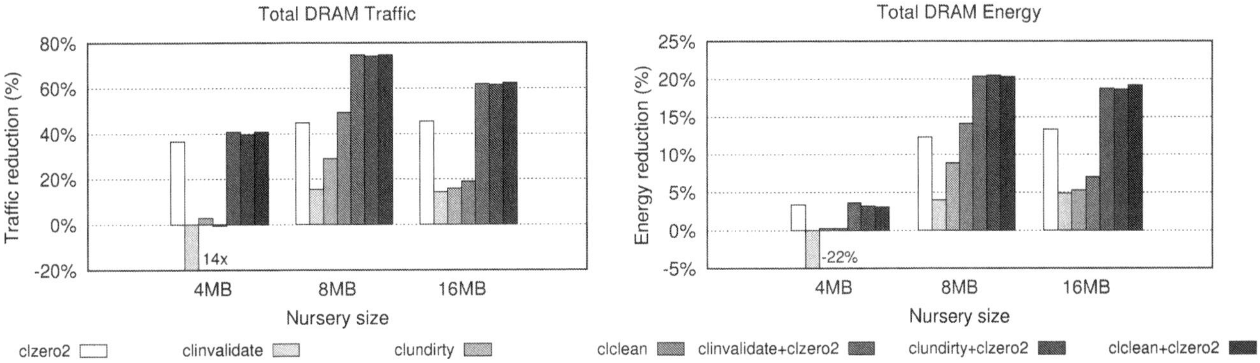

Figure 5: Reduction in DRAM traffic and energy for 4, 8, and 16 MB nurseries, normalized to unoptimized for each nursery size. ***Scrubbing saves DRAM traffic and energy at all nursery sizes, and is particularly effective at nursery sizes equal to or larger than the last-level cache.***

Nursery size	4 MB	8 MB	16 MB
DRAM Reads	-57.54%	-86.10%	-86.35%
DRAM Writes	-12.54%	-61.50%	-35.52%
Total DRAM Traffic	-40.86%	-74.65%	-62.46%
LLC misses	-57.54%	-86.10%	-86.35%
Execution time	-0.84%	-5.92%	-6.93%
Dynamic DRAM Energy	-38.80%	-73.45%	-59.98%
Total DRAM Energy	-3.09%	-20.30%	-19.17%

Table 4: Improvements for all metrics normalized to unoptimized at the same nursery size due to *clclean+clzero2*. *Cooperative cache scrubbing is very effective at reducing DRAM accesses and improving energy efficiency.*

ticular, *clclean* improves the performance of lusearch by 13% because lusearch stresses DRAM bandwidth more than other benchmarks. We recommend *clclean* since it performs best by itself and all scrubbing instructions perform similarly with *clzero2*, saving 6% of execution time by saving substantial DRAM traffic.

5.4 Varying the Nursery Size

The effectiveness of scrubbing is influenced by the ratio of the last-level cache and the nursery size, particularly because we scrub at the last level of cache (which propagates to all levels in an inclusive cache hierarchy). This section presents results for three nursery sizes, and shows that scrubbing is effective on all of them. We expect these results to hold for other similar ratios of nursery and last-level cache sizes. Figure 5 compares both the overall reduction in DRAM traffic and total DRAM energy averaged over all benchmarks on 4 MB, 8 MB, and 16 MB nurseries normalized to no scrubbing for each nursery size. Dynamic DRAM energy savings follow the same trends as traffic, and execution time reductions follow the same trends as total DRAM energy (results omitted due to space limitations). Scrubbing is less effective on very small nursery sizes such as 4 MB, half the size of our 8 MB last-level cache.

The left side of Figure 5 shows that *clinvalidate* saves the least DRAM traffic. In fact, for a 4 MB nursery, which fits in the 8 MB last-level cache, kicking dead cache lines out of the last-level cache after collection increases DRAM traffic by 14× over the unoptimized version due to extra reads from memory. This phenomenon is especially a problem for bloat, jython, lusearch.fix and sunflow, as they incur 22×, 90×, 50×, and 49× increases, respectively, in DRAM reads. (We do not show individual program results due to space limitations.) This increase is large because the unoptimized baseline number of reads is very low. Figure 1 confirms these results by showing that for a 4 MB nursery, almost 100% of dead lines are written to while in cache. With a 16 MB nursery, *clinvalidate* slightly increases DRAM reads (by 5.6%), and lowers DRAM writes (by 36%), leading to an overall 14% reduction in traffic. Results show, however, that when combined with *clzero2*, all scrubbing instructions perform well.

All scrubbing configurations improve DRAM traffic over the unoptimized version (besides *clinvalidate* with the small nursery). With a 4 MB nursery, DRAM traffic is reduced slightly or kept the same for scrubbing, improves by 37% for zeroing, and 40% for both together. With the more realistic 16 MB nursery, scrubbing instructions alone reduce traffic by 14 to 19% from the unoptimized 16 MB amount. While zeroing the 16 MB nursery saves 45% of unoptimized traffic, together scrubbing and zeroing save 62%. Scrubbing and zeroing work together synergistically to save significantly more traffic than either alone, at all nursery sizes.

The right side of Figure 5 shows that all scrubbing configurations improve DRAM energy, except for the degradation for *clinvalidate* with a 4 MB nursery, which reflects the increase in traffic experienced by that configuration. The 8 MB and 16 MB nurseries obtain similar energy improvements with our optimizations, while the smaller nursery sees smaller reductions. With a 4 MB nursery, *clzero* with scrubbing sees an energy reduction of 3 to 3.7%. While *clclean* is most effective at reducing energy with an 8 MB nursery (14%), with the largest nursery it reduces energy by 7%, while speeding up execution time by 2% (not shown). Zeroing alone on a 16 MB nursery reduces energy by 13%, which corresponds to a 6% execution time savings (not shown). Together, scrubbing and zeroing save on average 19% of DRAM energy with a 16 MB nursery, compared to 20% with 8 MB (see Table 4). The larger nursery size with both optimizations achieves the smallest overall execution time across our benchmarks, and a 7% execution time savings over unoptimized. Scrubbing and zeroing together can save significant energy, especially at larger nursery sizes, which are preferred by many JVMs.

Results summary. Table 4 presents savings averaged over the benchmarks for the best configuration, *clclean+clzero2*, for all three nursery sizes, normalized to each nursery size's unoptimized run. The dynamic energy savings have similar trends as DRAM traffic savings. Last-level cache miss savings are the same as DRAM read savings. The results for execution time are smaller than, but follow similar trends as, the total DRAM energy results in Figure 5. While using a small 4 MB nursery saves less traffic and less energy, we still see benefits due to scrubbing. We see the most improvements on larger nursery sizes. While the 16 MB nursery saves less total DRAM traffic than with 8 MB, 62% versus 75%, and less total DRAM energy, 19% versus 20%, the larger nursery saves slightly more last-level cache misses, and leads to a larger performance improvement of 6.9%. Averaging savings across the three nursery sizes, we get improvements of 59% for traffic and 14% and 57% for total and dynamic DRAM energy, respectively. Scrubbing is very effective and robust across nursery sizes, and will likely work well on nurseries larger than the last-level cache in future machines. Furthermore, in multiprogrammed workloads where programs must share the last-level cache, we believe that scrubbing will also improve cache management and decrease competition for bandwidth to main memory, while reducing energy.

6. RELATED WORK

This section surveys work that optimizes cache behavior by using software-hardware cooperation, prefetching, by designing a new architecture, by identifying dead cache lines, and by changing cache set replacement policies.

Cooperative cache management. The ESKIMO system is most closely related to our work [23]. They identify useless write backs in C programs. They propose changes to hardware including a 100 KB map in memory, cache line tags, and instructions for communication between software and hardware. Software communicates allocated and freed data blocks, which may be smaller or larger than the cache line granularity, to hardware to reduce energy and power requirements for DRAM. To optimize cache performance as well as memory performance, they reimplement previous work by Lewis et al. [32] to avoid fetching from memory for writes to addresses in this map. The large hardware map, fine-grained changes to the allocation and free software interfaces, and lack of a memory coherence approach for multicore processors make this work impractical. Whereas ESKIMO targets sequential C programs, our approach works for parallel programs on multicore hardware with small changes to cache coherence mechanisms. On the software side, we exploit contiguous region allocators that identify a large region of memory that is dead at one time, and present an opportunity for en-masse scrubbing of those cache lines. Reducing memory traffic is more important for managed languages, as we consider in this paper, than for explicitly-managed C programs because of the higher allocation rates typically observed in these applications [8]. In summary, our scrubbing instructions are simple, practical to implement, and work well with multicore cache coherence policies.

Prior work extensively analyzed the cost of zero initialization [54], which is required by Java and essentially all managed language specifications. They report that zeroing consumes 2.7-4.5% of execution time on average across several architectures, causes cache pollution, and is responsible for 25% of memory traffic. They propose non-temporal writes of zeroes that go directly to memory, bypassing the cache entirely. This software-only technique and another that spawns a concurrent thread to perform zeroing reduce both the performance overhead due to zeroing instructions and the perturbation in the cache. However, without the hardware support of an in-cache zeroing instruction, their non-temporal zeroing increases traffic to memory and bandwidth usage significantly, sometimes doubling the bandwidth over normal temporal stores [54]. We instead zero cache lines directly without fetching them from memory to save the critical resource of off-chip bandwidth, while minimizing cache displacement.

Prefetching. Prior work proposes a cooperative software-hardware technique to improve cache replacement decisions and prefetching based on program data usage [46, 49, 50]. Static analysis identifies data that both will and will not be reused again and passes this information to hardware as hints on memory instructions. The hardware has one extra bit per cache line to optimize the choice of what to evict from the cache for C and Fortran programs. While this research focuses on software-hardware cooperation, the hints are based on static program information and do not guarantee that the data that should be evicted is dead or will not be used again by the program. Other work has used software-only prefetching to improve garbage collection performance [12, 15].

Co-designed architecture. Prior works propose new memory architectures that are co-designed with the JVM, directly supporting objects and/or garbage collection [38, 51, 53]. While such an architecture can improve memory performance, it requires a radical re-design, whereas our technique works with minimal changes to existing hardware and is language-agnostic.

Write policies. Jouppi investigated cache policies and their effect on performance [26]. The best *write-validate* policy combines no-fetch-on-write and write-allocate for good performance. This prior work motivates zeroing cache lines without reading from memory and limiting write-back traffic to memory, both of which we target in this paper.

Cache replacement and dead cache line prediction. A large body of work focuses on changing the order of replacement for cache lines within a cache set to improve performance, see for example [6, 25, 27, 42, 52]. Hardware approaches also predict which blocks in cache can be evicted based on usage patterns, mainly for more agressive prefetching [1, 18, 28, 29, 30, 34, 36]. This work uses the cache hierarchy more efficiently by replacing cache lines the program will not reference again soon. Any hardware-only approach suffers from mispredictions, and because they lack semantic information about future program accesses, they *must* always write modified data to other levels of the memory hierarchy.

7. CONCLUSION

This paper introduces cache scrubbing, a software/hardware cooperative technique to reduce memory bandwidth demand. We identify useless write backs in modern Java benchmarks running on a modern JVM. We find that 10 to 60% of all write backs to memory, depending on the nursery size, contain dead data in the highly-mutated, short-lived nursery address range. We propose cache scrubbing instructions to remove these useless write backs. Scrubbing requires modest changes to both software and hardware. The Java virtual machine calls scrubbing and zeroing instructions, for regions that are dead or being zeroed, to communicate program semantics to hardware. In order for hardware to scrub and zero lines in cache, we present minor changes to the popular MESI cache coherence protocol, showing how our instructions maintain its invariants.

We explore three simple cache line scrubbing instructions, and evaluate them with an existing zeroing instruction. Our scrubbing instructions may be used by any programming language implementation to reduce memory traffic at the point the runtime identifies cache-line-sized blocks of dead data and this paper shows they are very effective when used with region allocators. We also show that in-cache zeroing is particularly effective for languages that require zero initialization; many current architectures fetch lines that will be completely overwritten with zeroes, wasting a lot of bandwidth and computing resources.

To evaluate these instructions, we built a new simulation methodology and followed existing best practices to simulate multi-threaded Java workloads relatively quickly on multicore hardware. We reveal that while the best scrubbing instruction is *clclean*, which undirties cache lines and moves them to the LRU position, adding *clzero2* to *clclean* overall is the most effective at saving substantial amounts of DRAM traffic, DRAM energy, and execution time across a range of nursery sizes.

In summary, scrubbing effectively diminishes the use of two of the most critical system resources in multicore systems: bandwidth and power. Cooperating between software and hardware will only become more important as future multiprocessors demand increasing levels of efficiency.

Acknowledgements

This work was supported in part by the European Research Council under the European Community's Seventh Framework Programme (FP7/2007-2013) / ERC Grant agreement no. 259295 and by NSF grant SHF-0910818. We would like to thank Karin Strauss for her help on the cache coherence protocol invariants and how scrubbing can maintain them. Also, thank you to Jeff Stuecheli and John Carter for their help on understanding the PowerPC instructions.

8. REFERENCES

[1] J. Abella, A. Gonzalez, X. Vera, and M. O'Boyle. IATAC: A smart predictor to turn-off L2 cache lines. *ACM Transactions on Architecture and Code Optimization (TACO)*, 2(1):55–77, 2005.

[2] B. Alpern, C. R. Attanasio, J. J. Barton, M. G. Burke, P. Cheng, J.-D. Choi, A. Cocchi, S. J. Fink, D. Grove, M. Hind, S. F. Hummel, D. Lieber, V. Litvinov, M. F. Mergen, T. Ngo, J. R. Russell, V. Sarkar, M. J. Serrano, J. C. Shepherd, S. E. Smith, V. C. Sreedhar, H. Srinivasan, and J. Whaley. The Jalapeño virtual machine. *IBM Systems Journal*, 39(1):211–238, 2000.

[3] ARM. ARM946E-S Revision: r1p1 Technical Reference Manual, 2007.

[4] E. D. Berger, B. G. Zorn, and K. S. McKinley. Reconsidering custom memory allocation. In *ACM Object-Oriented Programming, Systems, Languages, and Applications (OOPSLA)*, pages 1–12, Nov. 2002.

[5] S. Blackburn, P. Cheng, and K. S. McKinley. Myths and realities: The performance impact of garbage collection. In *Measurement and Modeling of Computer Systems (SIGMETRICS)*, pages 25–36, 2004.

[6] S. Blackburn and K. S. McKinley. Transient caches and object streams. Technical Report TR-CS-06-03, Australian National University, Department of Computer Science, October 2006.

[7] S. Blackburn and K. S. McKinley. Immix: A mark-region garbage collector with space efficiency, fast collection, and mutator performance. In *ACM Programming Language Design and Implementation (PLDI)*, pages 22–32, 2008.

[8] S. M. Blackburn, R. Garner, C. Hoffman, A. M. Khan, K. S. McKinley, R. Bentzur, A. Diwan, D. Feinberg, F. D., S. Z. Guyer, M. Hirzel, A. Hosking, M. Jump, H. Lee, J. E. B. Moss, A. Phansalkar, D. Stefanović, T. VanDrunen, D. von Dincklage, and B. Wiedermann. The DaCapo benchmarks: Java benchmarking development and analysis. In *ACM Object-Oriented Programming, Systems, Languages, and Applications (OOPSLA)*, pages 169–190, 2006.

[9] S. M. Blackburn, K. S. McKinley, R. Garner, C. Hoffman, A. M. Khan, R. Bentzur, A. Diwan, D. Feinberg, D. Frampton, S. Z. Guyer, M. Hirzel, A. Hosking, M. Jump, H. Lee, J. E. B. Moss, A. Phansalkar, D. Stefanović, T. VanDrunen, D. von Dincklage, and B. Wiedermann. Wake Up and Smell the Coffee: Evaluation Methodology for the 21st Century. *Communications of the ACM*, 51(8):83–89, Aug. 2008.

[10] D. Burger, J. R. Goodman, and A. Kagi. Memory bandwidth limitations of future microprocessors. In *International Symposium on Computer Architecture (ISCA)*, pages 78–89, 1996.

[11] T. E. Carlson, W. Heirman, and L. Eeckhout. Sniper: Exploring the level of abstraction for scalable and accurate parallel multi-core simulation. In *Conference on High Performance Computing Networking, Storage and Analysis (Supercomputing – SC)*, number 52, 2011.

[12] C.-Y. Cher, A. L. Hosking, and T. N. Vijaykumar. Software prefetching for mark-sweep garbage collection: Hardware analysis and software redesign. In *International Conference on Architectural Support for Programming Languages and Operating Systems (ASPLOS)*, pages 199–210, 2004.

[13] C. Click. Azul's experiences with hardware/software co-design. Keynote at ECOOP '09, July 2009.

[14] D. I. Dill, A. J. Drexler, A. J. Hu, and C. H. Yang. Protocol verification as a hardware design aid. In *IEEE International Conference on Computer Design*, pages 522–525, 1992.

[15] R. Garner, S. M. Blackburn, and D. Frampton. Effective prefetch for mark-sweep garbage collection. In *The 2007 International Symposium on Memory Management (ISMM)*, pages 43–54, Oct 2007.

[16] J. Ha, M. Gustafsson, S. Blackburn, and K. S. McKinley. Microarchitectural characterization of production JVMs and Java workloads. In *IBM CAS Workshop*, 2008.

[17] W. Heirman, S. Sarkar, T. E. Carlson, I. Hur, and L. Eeckhout. Power-aware multi-core simulation for early design stage hardware/software co-optimization. In *International Conference on Parallel Architectures and Compilation Techniques (PACT)*, pages 3–12, Sept. 2012.

[18] Z. Hu, S. Kaxiras, and M. Martonosi. Timekeeping in the memory system: Predicting and optimizing memory behavior. In *International Symposium on Computer Architecture (ISCA)*, pages 209–220, 2002.

[19] X. Huang, Z. Wang, S. Blackburn, K. S. McKinley, J. E. B. Moss, and P. Cheng. The garbage collection advantage: Improving mutator locality. In *ACM Object-Oriented Programming, Systems, Languages, and Applications (OOPSLA)*, pages 69–80, 2004.

[20] IBM. Power ISA Version 2.06 Revision B, 2010.

[21] H. Inoue, H. Komatsu, and T. Nakatani. A study of memory management for web-based applications on multicore processors. In *ACM Programming Language Design and Implementation (PLDI)*, pages 386–396, 2009.

[22] Intel. Intel Xeon Phi coprocessor instruction set architecture reference manual, 2012.

[23] C. Isen and L. John. ESKIMO: Energy savings using semantic knowledge of inconsequential memory occupancy for DRAM subsystem. In *ACM/IEEE International Symposium on Microarchitecture*, pages 337–346, 2009.

[24] L. Ivanov and R. Nunna. Modeling and verification of cache coherence protocols. In *IEEE International Symposium on Circuits and Systems*, pages 129–132, 2001.

[25] A. Jaleel, K. B. Theobald, S. C. Steely Jr., and J. Emer. High performance cache replacement using re-reference interval prediction (RRIP). In *International Symposium on Computer Architecture (ISCA)*, pages 60–71, 2010.

[26] N. P. Jouppi. Cache write policies and performance. In *International Symposium on Computer Architecture (ISCA)*, pages 191–201, 1993.

[27] M. Kampe, P. Stenstrom, and M. Dubois. Self-correcting LRU replacement policies. In *Conference on Computing Frontiers*, pages 181–191, 2004.

[28] S. Kaxiras, Z. Hu, and M. Martonosi. Cache decay: Exploiting generational behavior to reduce cache leakage power. In *International Symposium on Computer Architecture (ISCA)*, pages 240–251, 2001.

[29] M. Kharbutli and Y. Solihin. Counter-based cache replacement and bypassing algorithms. *IEEE Transactions on Computers*, 57(4):433–447, 2008.

[30] A.-C. Lai, C. Fide, and B. Falsafi. Dead-block prediction & dead-block correlating prefetchers. In *International Symposium on Computer Architecture (ISCA)*, pages 144–154, 2001.

[31] C. Lefurgy, K. Rajamani, F. L. Rawson III, W. M. Felter, M. Kistler, and T. W. Keller. Energy management for commercial servers. *IEEE Computer*, 36(12):39–48, 2003.

[32] J. A. Lewis, B. Black, and M. H. Lipasti. Avoiding initialization misses to the heap. In *International Symposium on Computer Architecture (ISCA)*, pages 183–194, 2002.

[33] H. Lieberman and C. E. Hewitt. A real time garbage collector based on the lifetimes of objects. *Communications of the ACM (CACM)*, 26(6):419–429, 1983.

[34] W.-F. Lin, S. K. Reinhardt, and D. Burger. Designing a modern memory hierarchy with hardware prefetching. *IEEE Transactions on Computers*, 50(11):1202–1218, 2001.

[35] F. Liu, X. Jiang, and Y. Solihin. Understanding how off-chip memory bandwidth partitioning in chip multiprocessors affects system performance. In *International Symposium on High-Performance Computer Architecture (HPCA)*, pages 57–68, 2010.

[36] H. Liu, M. Ferdman, J. Huh, and D. Burger. Cache bursts: A new approach for eliminating dead blocks and increasing cache efficiency. In *ACM/IEEE International Symposium on Microarchitecture*, pages 222–233, 2008.

[37] K. McMillan. Symbolic model checking. Technical Report CMU-CS-92-131, Carnegie Mellon University, 1992.

[38] M. Meyer. An on-chip garbage collection coprocessor for embedded real-time systems. In *Proceedings of the 11th IEEE International Conference on Embedded and Real-Time Computing Systems and Applications (RTCSA)*, pages 517–524, Washington, DC, USA, 2005.

[39] Micron. TN-41-01: Calculating memory system power for DDR3, 2007.

[40] D. Molka, D. Hackenberg, R. Schone, and M. Muller. Memory performance and cache coherency effects on an Intel Nehalem multiprocessor system. In *Parallel Architectures and Compilation Techniques (PACT)*, pages 261–270, 2009.

[41] M. S. Papamarcos and J. H. Patel. A low-overhead coherence solution for multiprocessors with private cache memories. In *International Symposium on Computer Architecture (ISCA)*, pages 348–354, 1984.

[42] M. K. Qureshi, A. Jaleel, Y. N. Patt, S. C. Steely, and J. Emer. Adaptive insertion policies for high performance caching. In *International Symposium on Computer Architecture (ISCA)*, pages 381–391, 2007.

[43] B. Rogers, A. Krishna, G. Bell, K. Vu, X. Jiang, and Y. Solihin. Scaling the bandwidth wall: Challenges in and avenues for CMP scaling. In *International Symposium on Computer Architecture (ISCA)*, pages 371–382, 2009.

[44] J. B. Sartor. *Exploiting Language Abstraction to Optimize Memory Efficiency*. PhD thesis, The University of Texas at Austin, 2010.

[45] J. B. Sartor and L. Eeckhout. Exploring multi-threaded Java application performance on multicore hardware. In *Proceedings of the ACM international conference on Object oriented programming systems languages and applications (OOPSLA)*, pages 281–296, 2012.

[46] J. B. Sartor, S. Venkiteswaran, K. S. McKinley, and Z. Wang. Cooperative caching with keep-me and evict-me. In *Workshop on Interaction between Compilers and Computer Architectures*, pages 46–57, 2005.

[47] E. Sikha, R. Simpson, C. May, and H. Warren. *The PowerPC Architecture: A Specification for a New Family of RISC Processors*. Morgan Kaufmann Publishers, 1994.

[48] D. Ungar. Generation scavenging: A non-disruptive high performance storage reclamation algorithm. In *Software Engineering Symposium on Practical Software Development Environments (SESPSDE)*, pages 157–167, 1984.

[49] Z. Wang, D. Burger, K. S. McKinley, S. K. Reinhardt, and C. C. Weems. Guided region prefetching: A cooperative hardware/software approach. In *International Symposium on Computer Architecture (ISCA)*, pages 388–398, 2003.

[50] Z. Wang, K. S. McKinley, A. L. Rosenberg, and C. C. Weems. Using the compiler to improve cache replacement decisions. In *Parallel Architectures and Compilation Techniques (PACT)*, pages 199–210, 2002.

[51] M. Wolczko and I. Williams. An alternative architecture for objects: Lessons from the mushroom project. In *ACM OOPSLA Workshop on Memory Management and Garbage Collection*, 1993.

[52] W. A. Wong and J.-L. Baer. Modified LRU policies for improving second-level cache behavior. In *High-Performance Computer Architecture (HPCA)*, pages 49–60, 2000.

[53] G. Wright, M. L. Seidl, and M. Wolczko. An object-aware memory architecture. *Sci. Comput. Program.*, 62(2):145–163, Oct. 2006.

[54] X. Yang, S. M. Blackburn, D. Frampton, J. B. Sartor, and K. S. McKinley. Why nothing matters: The impact of zeroing. In *ACM International Conference on Object Oriented Programming Systems Languages and Applications (OOPSLA)*, pages 307–324, 2011.

[55] Y. Zhao, J. Shi, K. Zheng, H. Wang, H. Lin, and L. Shao. Allocation wall: A limiting factor of Java applications on emerging multi-core platforms. In *ACM Object-Oriented Programming, Systems, Languages, and Applications (OOPSLA)*, pages 361–376, 2009.

KLA: A New Algorithmic Paradigm for Parallel Graph Computations

Harshvardhan Adam Fidel Nancy M. Amato Lawrence Rauchwerger

Parasol Laboratory
Deptartment of Computer Science and Engineering
Texas A&M University
{ananvay, fidel, amato, rwerger}@cse.tamu.edu

ABSTRACT

This paper proposes a new algorithmic paradigm – k-level asynchronous (KLA) – that bridges level-synchronous and asynchronous paradigms for processing graphs. The KLA paradigm enables the level of asynchrony in parallel graph algorithms to be parametrically varied from none (level-synchronous) to full (asynchronous). The motivation is to improve execution times through an appropriate trade-off between the use of fewer, but more expensive global synchronizations, as in level-synchronous algorithms, and more, but less expensive local synchronizations (and perhaps also redundant work), as in asynchronous algorithms. We show how common patterns in graph algorithms can be expressed in the KLA pardigm and provide techniques for determining k, the number of asynchronous steps allowed between global synchronizations. Results of an implementation of KLA in the STAPL Graph Library show excellent scalability on up to 96K cores and improvements of 10x or more over level-synchronous and asynchronous versions for graph algorithms such as breadth-first search, PageRank, k-core decomposition and others on certain classes of real-world graphs.

Categories and Subject Descriptors

D.1.3 [**Programming Techniques**]: Concurrent Programming—*Parallel Programming*; D.2.13 [**Software Engineering**]: Reusable Software—*Reusable Libraries*

Keywords

Parallel Algorithms; Asynchronous Graph Algorithms; Graph Analytics; Big Data; Distributed Computing.

1. INTRODUCTION

Traversals – wherein a computation proceeds from one vertex to another along the edges of a graph – are an important type of graph algorithm, as they form the backbone of several other important graph algorithms (e.g., shortest paths, centrality metrics, connected components). Improving the performance of traversals therefore benefits all algorithms dependent on them. Despite receiving a great deal of attention from many researchers for several decades [26, 13, 5, 21, 27, 8, 17, 15, 19], traversal-based computations remain notoriously difficult to parallelize effectively. Similarly, random walks (such as PageRank) are widely used on web-scale graphs and social networks for link-analysis [7, 23], while algorithms such as k-core decomposition are used to study clustering and evolution of social networks [4]. Such algorithms need effective parallelization as well.

Parallel graph algorithms are currently expressed in level-synchronous or asynchronous paradigms. Level-synchronous paradigms [26, 8] iteratively process vertices of a graph level by level. This model guarantees the current level's computation to have completed before starting the next one through the use of global synchronizations at the end of each level. Level-synchronous algorithms tend to perform well when the number of levels is small, but suffer from poor scalability when the number of levels is large. Bulk synchronous parallel (BSP) algorithms [30] can naturally be expressed in this paradigm. The asynchronous paradigm replaces global synchronizations with point-to-point synchronizations, which can increase the degree of parallelism, but which may also require the completion of redundant work. For example, an asynchronous breadth-first search (BFS) may re-visit vertices multiple times as shorter paths are discovered [24]. Choosing the right paradigm depends on the system, input graph, and algorithm. This implies different implementations and optimizations for algorithms, with no easy way to switch between them.

In this paper, we propose a new paradigm, k-level asynchronous (KLA), that allows parametric control of asynchrony ranging from completely asynchronous execution to partially asynchronous execution to level-synchronous execution. Partial asynchrony is achieved by generalizing the BSP model to allow each superstep to process up to k levels of the algorithm asynchronously.

We implement the KLA paradigm using the STAPL Graph Library (SGL) [14] and evaluate its performance and scalability up to 98,000 cores on a Cray XE6 machine for important classes of graph algorithms including traversals (e.g., BFS, single-source shortest paths, connected components), random walks (e.g., PageRank) and k-core decomposition. Our experimental studies show that KLA improves the performance of these algorithms on some graphs by a factor of 10 or more, at scale.

PACT'14, August 24–27, 2014, Edmonton, AB, Canada.

http://dx.doi.org/10.1145/2628071.2628091 .

In summary, our contribution is threefold:

- **k-level async (KLA) algorithmic paradigm.** We propose a novel paradigm to express parallel graph algorithms that unifies asynchronous and level-synchronous paradigms, while allowing parametric control of asynchrony. We also provide a model to estimate the appropriate level of asynchrony for a given input graph, and a strategy to adaptively determine k.
- **Application of KLA to standard graph computations.** We show how to transform common patterns of asynchronous and level-synchronous graph algorithms to the KLA paradigm.
- **Implementation that achieves scalable performance.** Our implementation of KLA in the STAPL Graph Library shows an improvement of 10x or more over level-synchronous and asynchronous paradigms at large scale (up to 98,000 cores) for graph algorithms such as BFS, PageRank and k-core decomposition.

2. THE KLA PARADIGM

k-level async (KLA) is a novel algorithmic paradigm for parallel processing of graphs. The KLA paradigm bridges traditional level-synchronous and asynchronous paradigms by enabling the level of asynchrony to be parametrically varied from none (level synchronous) to full (asynchronous). The motivation is to improve execution time by using an appropriate combination of expensive global synchronizations, as in level-synchronous algorithms, and less expensive local synchronizations (and possibly redundant work), as in asynchronous algorithms.

This paradigm works in phases, similar to the BSP model. However, each phase is allowed to proceed asynchronously up to k steps by creating asynchronous tasks on active vertices. When $k = 1$, KLA processes the graph one level at a time, i.e., in a level-synchronous fashion. Assuming the level-synchronous variant of the algorithm performs d iterations, if $k \geq d$, then KLA is equivalent to the asynchronous paradigm. However, for $1 < k < d$, the algorithm proceeds in $\lceil \frac{d}{k} \rceil$ phases, referred to as *KLA supersteps* (KLA-SS). Each superstep processes up to k levels asynchronously. The KLA paradigm requires that the algorithmic invariant holds at the point of synchronization. However, in between synchronizations, no guarantee is implied.

Figure 1 provides pseudocode for the KLA paradigm. The paradigm takes two fine-grained vertex-centric functions: a *vertex-operator* and a *neighbor-operator*. The *vertex-operator* describes the computation to be performed on each vertex. It processes the vertex on which it is spawned, and is allowed to visit other vertices by applying the *neighbor-operator* on them. The *vertex-operator* returns *true* if the vertex was actively processed, or *false* if the vertex was not active. A vertex is active if its value is *updated* by the *vertex-operator*, or if it visits neighboring vertices. The paradigm also allows users to optionally provide pre- and post-compute methods, which will be called at the begining and end of each KLA-SS. To express an algorithm in the KLA paradigm, users provide the vertex and the neighbor operators.

In the following sub-section, we describe in more detail how an important graph computation, breadth-first search (and therefore its applications such as single-source shortest paths and connected components) can be expressed in

```
void kla_paradigm(Graph graph, VertexOp wf, NeighborOp uf, int k)
  bool active = true;
  int k_current = 1;

  while( active ) {
    pre_compute(graph, k_current);

    // apply the vertex—operator to each vertex, and reduce to
    // find the no. of active vertices. wf returns true (active), or
    // false (otherwise), and spawns neighbor—operators on neighbors.
    active =
      reduce(map(kla_wf(wf, kla_visit(uf, k)), graph), logical_or());
    global_fence();
    k_current += k; // current level is k more than before.

    post_compute(graph, k_current);
  }
```

Figure 1: Pseudocode for the KLA paradigm.

the KLA paradigm. Other algorithms, such as k-core and PageRank, can also be expressed in the KLA paradigm by using the appropriate vertex and neighbor operators (Figs. 4,5). This is described in Sec. 3.1, which also analyzes implications of applying KLA to algorithms.

2.1 KLA Breadth-First Search

Breadth-first search is a common graph algorithm, widely used as a backbone to implement many other graph algorithms. Multiple algorithms exist to perform BFS in parallel, including the level-synchronous [26, 8, 19] and asynchronous [15, 24] BFS algorithms. Depending on the input graph and the system, choosing the wrong implementation may provide worse performance. We demonstrate how we can significantly improve performance by bridging these two algorithmic approaches using the KLA paradigm and taking advantage of the tunability.

Figure 2 provides an intuition of how the level-synchronous, asynchronous, and KLA versions of BFS differ. From the user's perspective, the driver of the algorithm (Figure 3(a)) does not change, and neither do the BFS vertex and neighbor operators for the algorithm (Figure 3(b,c)). What does change is the `Visit` logic (Figure 2). This determines conditions to allow the computation to proceed on the neighbor vertex being visited. While the visit logic has been simplified in the figure to make it readable, the BFS code closely corresponds to what a user would write.

A KLA BFS results by providing the generic BFS vertex and neighbor operators (Figure 3(b,c)) to the KLA paradigm. The vertex operator can use the functions provided by the paradigm (Visit, VisitAllNeighbors, VisitNeighborIf) to apply the BFS neighbor-operator to neighboring vertices. The vertex operator returns true if it is active for a vertex, and false otherwise. The algorithm terminates when all vertices are inactive, i.e., when all invocations of the vertex operator return false. The requirements for the KLA neighbor-operator are the same as for an asynchronous BFS – it cannot rely on the order in which the vertex is visited and must be resilient to multiple visits. The correctness of the KLA BFS can be proved using simple induction, as shown below.

LEMMA 2.1. *At the end of the i-th KLA BFS KLA-SS, all vertices at distance $\leq i \cdot k$ from the source have been visited and labeled with the correct distances, and no vertices of distance $> i \cdot k$ from the source have been visited.*

```
Visit(NeighOp update, Vertex u, int k_current)
  bool active = update(u)
  if (active)
    bfs_vertex_op(u);
```

(a) Async Visit
spawn tasks

```
Visit(NeighOp update, Vertex u, int k_current)
  bool active = update(u)
  if (active && k_current % k != 0)
    bfs_vertex_op(u);
```

(b) KLA Visit
spawn tasks to depth k

```
Visit(NeighOp update, Vertex u, int k_current)
  update(u);
```

(c) Level-Sync Visit
don't spawn further tasks

Figure 2: Visitation logic for async, KLA and level-sync behavior of BFS.

```
void BFS(Graph graph, Vertex source, int k)
  source.color = GREY;
  kla_paradigm(bfs_vertex_op(), bfs_neighbor_op(), graph, k);
```

(a) BFS algorithm driver

```
bool bfs_vertex_op(Vertex v)
  if (v.color == GREY)       // Active if GREY
    v.color = BLACK;
    VisitAllNeighbors(v, bfs_neighbor_op(_1, v.dist+1));
    return true;             // vertex was Active
  else return false;         // vertex was Inactive
```

(b) vertex-operator

```
bool bfs_neighbor_op(Vertex u, int new_distance)
  if (u.dist > new_distance)
    u.dist = new_distance;   // update distance
    u.color = GREY;          // mark to be processed
    return true;             // vertex was updated
  else return false;
```

(c) neighbor-operator

Figure 3: The fine-grained BFS algorithm.

Proof. The proof is by induction on i, the KLA-SS number. When $i = 0$, only the source has been visited and it is trivially true. Next, we assume that at the end of KLA-SS $(i-1)$, all vertices at distance $\leq (i-1) \cdot k$ from source have been visited and correctly labeled with distances, and vertices at a distance $> (i-1) \cdot k$ are unvisited.

At the beginning of KLA-SS i, only vertices at distance $(i-1) \cdot k + 1$ from source are active. The vertex-operator in Figure 3(b) is applied to all these active vertices and visits their neighbors (Figure 3(b), line 3) if they are at a distance $\leq i \cdot k$ from the source (Figure 2(b), line 3). During the visit, the distance to source is updated only if it decreases; hence, once the correct minimum distance is computed it will not be further updated. Moreover, since the vertex-operator visits all neighbors of active vertices, all edges in the sub-graph induced by the vertices visited during the ith KLA-SS, i.e., at distance $(i-1) \cdot k < d \leq i \cdot k$ from source, will be processed, implying that at some point during the KLA-SS, the correct distance will be computed for all vertices visited in that KLA-SS. □

Corollary 2.2. *KLA BFS will perform* $\lceil \frac{d}{k} \rceil$ *KLA-SSs, where* d *is the number of levels in the graph.*

Corollary 2.3. *If* $k = 1$*, then KLA BFS visits the vertices of the graph in a level-synchronous manner.*

2.2 KLA and the Δ-Stepping SSSP Algorithm

A related approach to KLA is the Δ-stepping single-source shortest path [22] (SSSP) algorithm. It processes multiple *light* edges simultaneously in a single superstep, as long as the smallest tentative distance of an edge's source falls between $i\Delta$ and $(i+1)\Delta$, where i is the current superstep. Then, the *heavy* edges of the vertices that were relaxed for the current superstep are processed, ending the superstep. This greedy approach gives preference to lighter-weight edges, which may improve execution time.

The Δ-stepping algorithm differs from KLA in that it centers around using edge-weights as the metric to prioritize the processing of edges, which has no impact on non-SSSP based algorithms. The KLA paradigm works on the structure of the graph, and not algorithm specifics (edge/vertex weights, etc.). This makes it algorithm agnostic and thus applicable to a broader set of algorithms.

While Δ-stepping is beneficial for solving the single-source shortest path and related problems, it is not applicable to algorithms such as k-core or PageRank. On the other hand, k-core, PageRank and Δ-stepping itself may be expressed using the KLA paradigm. Therefore, KLA is a generalization and extension of the Δ-stepping algorithm to other types of computations and metrics. Section 5.6 compares the traditional Δ-stepping algorithm with its KLA variant.

3. APPLYING KLA TO ALGORITHMS

In this section, we demonstrate how to express graph algorithms in the KLA paradigm. We begin by analyzing the asynchronous behavior for a few important graph algorithms. We then present a classification describing how to apply KLA to additional algorithms.

3.1 Analysis of Example Algorithms in KLA

We analyze three important graph algorithms (BFS, k-core and PageRank) that display different asynchronous characteristics and show how the KLA paradigm may be applied to each. For some algorithms, there is no penalty paid as the asynchrony in the algorithm increases, while in other algorithms, increasing the asynchrony leads to a dramatic increase in redundant work, with the algorithm having to correct previously computed values due to out-of-order arrival of messages. The best performance is obtained by balancing the penalty, if any, due to asynchrony with the cost of global synchronizations. In KLA, this is done by limiting the size of the asynchronous sections by introducing global synchronizations at intervals of depth k.

Breadth-First Search and Graph Traversals. Breadth-first search is an important algorithm due to its widespread direct uses and indirect uses as a part of numerous other algorithms (e.g., betweenness centrality, connected components). We show how to implement KLA BFS in section 2.1. Here, we analyze the implications of applying KLA on BFS.

In a completely asynchronous version of BFS, each vertex starts out with its distance from the source vertex initialized to infinity, and the source vertex's distance initialized to zero. When a vertex receives a message and is updated with a new distance less than its current distance, it propagates this new distance (plus one) to its neighbors. The vertex may receive a shorter distance in the future, which it will also propagate. In this case, the work done by the previous propagation will be redone, resulting in redundant work. However, this scenario cannot be avoided as the vertex is not necessarily aware of the number of messages it is going to receive *a priori*. Because of this, the BFS computation must optimistically propagate every message it receives for a vertex, leading to possible redundant work.

Other graph-traversal algorithms also exhibit similar behavior, along with algorithms dependent on such traversals. This class of algorithms is not aware of the number of incoming messages a vertex will receive *a priori*.

k-core Decomposition. A k-core of a graph G is a maximal connected sub-graph of G in which all vertices have degree at least k. The k-core algorithm is widely used to study clustering and evolution of social networks. It is also used to reduce input graphs to more manageable sizes while maintaining their core-structure. The typical parallel algorithm iteratively deletes vertices with degree less than k until only vertices with degree greater than or equal to k exist.

Figure 4 gives the algorithm for k-core as expressed using KLA. In this algorithm, each vertex starts with a count initialized to its degree. A vertex marks itself deleted if its degree count is less than the specified k value. When a vertex is deleted, it invokes a neighbor-operator over all its adjacent vertices to decrement their degree-counts by one (due to the now deleted edges of the deleted vertex), and activate the adjacent vertex, which can now check its count and repeat the process. This purely asynchronous algorithm relies on determining when to trigger propagation of each vertex based on how many messages it has received. That is, a vertex "knows" the number of messages required for the propagation to take place. Moreover, as there are no constraints on the ordering of the updates (because the degree-count is a one-dimensional scalar being decremented), there is no penalty for increasing asynchrony.

Similarly, the parallel topological sort algorithm also exhibits this behavior. Each vertex starts with a count of its in-degree, and only propagates when the vertex becomes a source, i.e., when its in-degree counter becomes zero.

This class of algorithms is aware of the number of incoming messages needed to activate a vertex *a priori* and is unaffected by the order in which the messages are received.

PageRank. PageRank [7, 23] is an important graph algorithm that is used to rank web-pages on the internet in order of relative importance. As an example of an iterative random walk algorithm, each vertex calculates its rank in iteration i based on the ranks of its neighbors in iteration $i-1$ and then sends out new ranks to its neighbors for the next iteration. The algorithm terminates when either a certain number of iterations have been reached or the ranks have converged.

Even though commonly expressed as a level-synchronous algorithm, PageRank can be converted to a KLA form similar to the k-core algorithm (Figure 5). When a vertex receives the ranks of all its neighbors from iteration $i-1$, it can propagate its rank to its neighbors for the next iteration. For this, each vertex must keep a count of how many ranks

```
bool kcore_vertex_op(Vertex v)
  if (v.degree_count < K && !v.deleted) // Propagate if degree <K
    v.deleted = true;
    VisitAllNeighbors(v, kcore_neighbor_op(_1));
    return true;                // I was Active
  else  return false;           // I was Inactive
```

(a) vertex-operator

```
bool kcore_neighbor_op(Vertex u)
  if (!u.deleted)
    u.degree_count--;          // update my degree
    return true;               // I was updated
  else  return false;
```

(b) neighbor-operator

Figure 4: The k-core algorithm

```
bool pagerank_vertex_op(Vertex v)
  // Propagate if ranks from all neighbors received and <20 iterations
  if (v.num_rcvd_ranks[v.iteration] == v.size() && v.iteration < 20)
    v.rank = 0.15/num_vertices + 0.85*v.sum_rcvd_ranks[v.iteration];
    v.iteration++;
    int n = v.neighbors().size();
    VisitAllNeighbors(v, pr_neigh_op(_1, v.rank/n, v.iteration));
    return true;                      // I was Active
  else  return false;                 // I was Inactive
```

(a) vertex-operator

```
bool pr_neigh_op(Vertex u, double rank, int iteration)
  // update number and rank for given iteration
  u.num_rcvd_ranks[iteration]++;
  u.sum_rcvd_ranks[iteration] += rank;
  return true;                        // I was updated
```

(b) neighbor-operator

Figure 5: The PageRank algorithm.

it has received from the previous iteration. Moreover, in an asynchronous execution, it may also receive ranks for a future iteration before having received all ranks for the $i-1^{th}$ iteration. In such cases, the vertex must buffer this rank in a two-dimensional table, indexed by iteration, for future use. When the vertex propagates and reaches the next iteration, it can use any buffered ranks stored for this new iteration.

As in the case of k-core, each vertex is aware of the number of messages (ranks) it needs to receive to propagate. However, unlike k-core, PageRank also requires ordering information. That is, each vertex must receive all ranks from the previous iteration before processing any ranks from subsequent iterations. Because of the necessary ordering constraint, increasing asynchrony may increase the amount of messages buffered. This is also true for other random walk algorithms that are similar to PageRank, as well as other algorithms like pointer jumping and graph coloring.

3.2 KLA Algorithmic Categories

Based on the characteristics of algorithms discussed in the previous section, we observe that the penalty paid for increasing asynchrony depends on two properties related to the behavior of the algorithm upon a vertex receiving a message from one of its neighbors:

- **Ordering.** Is the algorithm resilient to the ordering of messages from different iterations (i.e., is it algorithmically valid [correct] for messages from iteration $i-1$ to arrive before messages from iteration $i-2$)?

- **Message Count.** Does the algorithm have *a priori* knowledge (on a per-vertex basis) of the number of messages required to activate each vertex?

If the algorithm is resilient to the ordering, it may or may not be aware of the number of messages a vertex needs to receive in order to propagate further. We define propagation to be the necessary condition by which an incoming message along an in-edge triggers a propagation of an update request along all outgoing edges of that vertex. If the algorithm is not resilient to the ordering, it must be aware of the number of messages to propagate per iteration. Note that a fourth category, where the algorithm is not ordering resilient, but the number of messages is not known, does not apply here, as ordering can only be guaranteed if it is certain that there is at least one message that will be received by the vertex per iteration, in which case the number would be known (one).

These properties are useful in determining how to apply KLA to a given algorithm and in understanding the behavior of the algorithm as k is varied. A large set of parallel graph algorithms can be broadly categorized into three categories based on the two properties. All algorithms in a category can be expressed in KLA in a similar manner and will exhibit similar behavior as k is varied. The categories, presented in decreasing order of penalty due to asynchrony (Table 1), are:

- **Type-I**: The number of incoming messages required to propagate a vertex is not known *a priori*. This type of algorithm optimistically propagates a vertex and processes every incoming message, forwarding the results to its outgoing edges, as the vertex is unaware of the total number of messages it may receive. If a different message is received by the vertex at a later time, it is also processed and could generate a new result, which may lead to re-doing some work for subsequent neighboring vertices. Algorithms in this category obtain the most benefit from KLA. Examples of this category include BFS, SSSP, BFS-based (betweenness centrality, connected components, etc.), minimum-spanning tree (GHS and Boruvka), and preflow-push maximum flow.
- **Type-II**: The exact number of incoming messages required to trigger propagation for each vertex is known *a priori*. Such algorithms avoid redoing work, as each vertex serves as a synchronization point and does not propagate until the required number of messages have been received.

  This category may be further subdivided into two types:

  - **Ordered-Type-II**: The output depends on the inter-level ordering of incoming messages. Therefore, messages may need to be buffered if they arrive out-of-order, and then processed once the required number of messages have been received. In such cases, greater asynchrony may lead to a greater occurrence of out-of-order messages, and thus may require greater buffering. Examples include PageRank, random walks, pointer jumping, graph coloring, and particle-swarm optimization.
  - **Unordered-Type-II**: This category includes algorithms where the ordering of incoming messages is not important, and it is sufficient to have received the required number of incoming messages in any order. Examples include k-core and topological sort.

In the next section, we present a model to study the behavior of each category and use it to determine a suitable k for algorithms in that category for a given input graph.

4. DETERMINING k

The performance of KLA algorithms is dependent on the choice of a good value for k. However, it is non-trivial to determine the optimal value of k given an arbitrary input graph, machine and algorithm. Therefore, we present a technique to quickly determine an effective approximate value for k_{opt}. We also present an adaptive strategy that picks an appropriate k based on the current local topology of the graph as the algorithm progresses. This strategy is applicable in the general case. The interpolative method to approximate the value of k_{opt} is useful when executing the algorithm multiple times on the input. Our experimental results show these two techniques work well in practice.

4.1 Adaptive Determination of k

To help users obtain better performance from a single (or a few) run(s) of a KLA algorithm, or when they do not have sufficient information about the input graph, we use a simple adaptive strategy (Adaptive KLA) that dynamically varies k to process the graph. The strategy dynamically chooses the best value for the next iteration based on information from current and previous iterations.

The algorithm starts with $k = 1$ (or some user-defined start value). At the end of each KLA-SS, the value of k is doubled for the next level under the following conditions: 1) high out-degree vertices have not been discovered, 2) the penalty for asynchrony (e.g., wasted work for Type-I or buffering cost for Ordered Type-II) has not exceeded a threshold, and 3) the cost of processing each vertex in the current KLA-SS is equal to or less than the cost of processing each vertex for the previous KLA-SSs. If the thresholds for either out-degree, asynchrony penalty or per-vertex processing cost have been exceeded, the k value is halved. In addition, any high out-degree vertices found in a given KLA-SS are marked for processing in the next KLA-SS to reduce the penalty for processing them prematurely. Finally, if the asynchrony penalty or processing cost exceed a maximum threshold (we empirically found 20% to work well for the machines on which we tested), the value for k is capped, so the algorithm does not suffer from greater asynchronous penalties attempting higher values. The thresholds for asynchrony penalty and processing cost can be chosen depending on the machine, such that for a machine where the cost of communication is much higher than the cost of computation, the threshold can be increased, and vice-versa.

While this technique may not provide the best performance compared to knowing *a priori* the value of k_{opt} (see Sec. 4.2), it is inexpensive in practice. As can be observed from Figure 11, it still provides substantial performance benefits compared to the level-synchronous and asynchronous paradigms by converging to an improved k value, which may then be used for subsequent runs.

4.2 A Model for Approximating k_{opt}

In this section we describe a model for the KLA paradigm that enables us to obtain a good approximation of the value (k_{opt}) for k which results in the lowest execution time for the algorithm based on the input graph and machine. This approach may be used when performing multiple traversals on

Type	Message Count	Message Ordering	Examples
Type-I	Unknown	Not Required	BFS, SSSP, MST, Preflow-Push, CC
Ordered Type-II	Known	Required	PageRank, Pointer Jumping, Graph-Coloring
Unordered Type-II	Known	Not Required	k-core, Topological Sort

Table 1: Characteristics of the three categories of KLA algorithms

a graph to obtain better performance than Adaptive KLA. We use BFS (Type-I) on an undirected, connected graph as an illustration of this model, and show, later in this section, how it applies to Type-II algorithms.

Theoretical Model. Assume a level-synchronous BFS requires d iterations over the graph, processing active vertices in each iteration. As there is an enforced ordering guarantee, there is no wasted work in this paradigm. Therefore, for a graph with n vertices on p processors, the work done in parallel can be V_{max}, the maximum number of vertices to be processed by a processor (ideally, $V_{max} = \frac{n}{p}$). Assuming it takes time α to process each vertex of the graph on average and T_{sync} is the time required by a global-synchronization of p processors in the system, the total time is given by:

$$T^{BFS}_{Level-Sync} = \alpha \cdot V_{max} + d \cdot T_{sync} \quad (1)$$

On the other hand, an asynchronous BFS traversal needs only one global-synchronization for termination detection, but in the process may end up doing redundant work due to loss of ordering guarantees for messages. Assuming a function $\Psi(G)$ gives the amount of redundant work done for graph G (a method for approximating this will be discussed in detail later), the total work per processor now becomes $V_{max} + \Psi^p(G)$, where $\Psi^p(G)$ is the estimated amount of wasted work on a processor. Therefore, the total time for the asynchronous paradigm is given by:

$$T^{BFS}_{Async} = \alpha\,(V_{max} + \Psi^p(G)) + T_{sync} \quad (2)$$

Extending this to the KLA paradigm, the traversal performs $\lceil\frac{d}{k}\rceil$ KLA supersteps. Assuming the wasted work for a given k is given by the penalty-function $\Psi(G, k)$, where $\Psi(G, 1) = 0$ and $\Psi(G, d) = \Psi(G)$, the time now becomes:

$$T^{BFS}_{KLA}(k) = \alpha\,(V_{max} + \Psi^p(G, k)) + \lceil\frac{d}{k}\rceil \cdot T_{sync} \quad (3)$$

The product αV_{max} represents the time taken by the algorithm to complete all useful work in parallel, and can therefore be replaced by T_{Work}:

$$T^{BFS}_{KLA}(k) = T_{Work} + \alpha \cdot \Psi^p(G, k) + \lceil\frac{d}{k}\rceil \cdot T_{sync} \quad (4)$$

When $k = 1$, KLA behaves the same as the level-synchronous paradigm, and for $k = d$, it behaves like the asynchronous paradigm. In the following section, we provide some insight on what causes wasted work.

Modeling the Wasted Work, $\Psi(G, k)$. Wasted work is caused by latency, where a message taking a shorter path arrives after a message through a longer path. This can be caused by two major factors: machine dependent (i.e., network latency) and graph dependent (i.e., distribution of the graph, processing order of adjacent edges of a vertex). As the exact determination of these factors is nondeterministic, we provide a model to approximate the wasted work ($\Psi_{est}(G, k)$) for a given graph in this section.

We classify the edges of an input graph into two categories: E_T, which are the edges in the output BFS tree connecting parents to their children in the BFS, and $E_{NT} = E - E_T$, which are the other edges in the graph. There exist edges in E_{NT} then, that may cause wasted work, because, if these edges are traversed before the corresponding tree edges, the target vertex and its children will need to redo the traversal with shorter paths.

We can further sub-divide E_{NT} into E_{NT_C} and E_{NT_I}. E_{NT_C} are those E_{NT} edges that cross a KLA superstep, i.e., their source vertex is in a different KLA superstep than their target vertex. E_{NT_I} are the subset of remaining E_{NT} edges that have both their source and target inside the same KLA superstep, and therefore are inside an asynchronous execution section. As edges in E_{NT_C} cross a KLA superstep, they cross a global synchronization point. Therefore, they cannot contribute to wasted work, as their traversals will reach the target vertex at the same time as the correct traversal (from the actual BFS parent with the shortest distance-from-source), as guaranteed by the global synchronization. Therefore, we can establish an estimate of the potential wasted work as the cardinality of the set E_{NT_I}:

$$\Psi_{est}(G, k) \precsim E_{NT\_I}(G, k) \quad (5)$$

We know the number of tree edges (E_T) equals $V - 1$. Therefore, $E_{NT} = E - (V - 1)$. Using this, we can approximate the expected number of non-tree edges inside a KLA-SS as:

$$E^{Expected}_{NT\_I}(G, k) = \frac{E - (V - 1)}{d} \times (k - 1) \quad (6)$$

From equations (5) and (6) we get:

$$\Psi_{est}(G, k) \approx \frac{E - (V - 1)}{d} \times (k - 1) \quad (7)$$

This supports our intuition. Small-diameter graphs with large out-degrees have $E >> V$ and $d = O(1)$. Therefore, even a slight increase in k may lead to large amounts of wasted work, which would negate the benefits gained from removing a global synchronization. This implies that such graphs will fair better with smaller k values ($k = 1$). Long-diameter graphs with low out-degrees have $E \approx V$ and $d = O(V)$. This implies that such graphs work best with $k = d$, as the wasted work is negligible. Other graphs such as road networks, geometric meshes, etc. tend to fall in-between, and therefore benefit the most with $1 < k < d$.

Furthermore, small-diameter graphs have a more even distribution of work, as most processors tend to be working in each superstep. Long-diameter graphs exhibit a work-load imbalance due to their low work per superstep. This imbalance can be alleviated by increasing the asynchrony for long-diameter graphs.

Ordered Type-II Algorithms. Type-II algorithms can be modeled in much the same way as Type-I algorithms, apart from the penalty paid for asynchrony. Ordered Type-II algorithms may incur a penalty for buffering messages that arrive out-of-order as the asynchrony is increased. A vertex will have to buffer messages if at least one path that leads to it executes faster than the other paths leading to the same vertex. However, the amount of buffering is bounded to a maximum of k-levels. Therefore, the effect of buffering may be approximated using a linear penalty-function (see Eq. 7): $\Psi_{est.}(G,k) = m \times k + b$, where m and b are input-graph and machine dependent constants. Assume 1) the algorithm requires d iterations over the graph, 2) the time taken by the algorithm to complete all work in parallel is T_{Work}, 3) the cost of buffering is given by β (constant for a given system), and 4) T_{sync} is time required for global-synchronization of p processors in the system. The total execution time for ordered Type-II algorithms is given by:

$$T_{KLA}^{Ord-TII}(k) = T_{Work} + \beta \cdot \Psi_{est}(G,k) + \lceil \frac{d}{k} \rceil \cdot T_{sync} \quad (8)$$

Based on this formula, the constants m and b can be computed by running the algorithm twice with two different k values. This model is useful if the algorithm will be run multiple times iteratively, or for algorithms that iteratively perform the same computation (e.g. PageRank).

Unordered Type-II Algorithms. As there is no penalty for increasing asynchrony in unordered Type-II algorithms, we should ideally observe the best performance with maximum asynchrony. However, for certain graphs with large out-degrees, a completely asynchronous execution may cause network congestion due to a large number of messages in the system. In such cases, the level-synchronous execution should perform best. We observed this effect in social networks and other small-world scale-free graphs. Therefore, unordered Type-II algorithms could be run with $k = 1$ for such high out-degree graphs and asynchronously for other graphs, or using adaptive KLA, which can change k based on out-degree.

Finding k_{opt}: Estimating the Penalty-Function (Ψ_{est}) Determining Ψ exactly is expensive and only gives an upper-bound to the penalty paid for asynchrony. However, it can be closely approximated using a linear model (see Eq. 7). Assuming m gives an estimate of how fast the penalty increases with k, and b is the offset of the line: $\Psi_{est.}(G,k) = m \times k + b$ (both m and b depend on input-graph and machine). Two executions of the algorithm are needed to interpolate Ψ, which will provide the approximate curve of the running-time of the algorithm for varying values of k. The curve's minima can then be used to predict k_{opt}. This approach is mainly useful for application performing multiple traversals, such as in Brandes' betweenness centrality [6]. To find the equation for Ψ_{est}, we run the algorithm with $k = 1$, from which we can obtain the number of iterations (d) and the amortized cost (α) of processing a vertex. Running the algorithm a second time with $k = d$, which was found from the first execution, we can compute the penalty for a completely asynchronous execution of the algorithm ($\Psi_{est}(G,d)$), giving us the slope of the line for Ψ_{est}.

$\Psi_{est}(G,d)$ can be calculated for Type-I algorithms thus: 1) track the global number of visits to the input graph's vertices, 2) subtract from it the actual number of vertices in the graph, 3) divide by the number of processors to get the average wasted work per processor. For ordered Type-II algorithms, the number of visits that need to be buffered can be tracked and averaged across all processors. For unordered Type-II algorithms, the slope is zero.

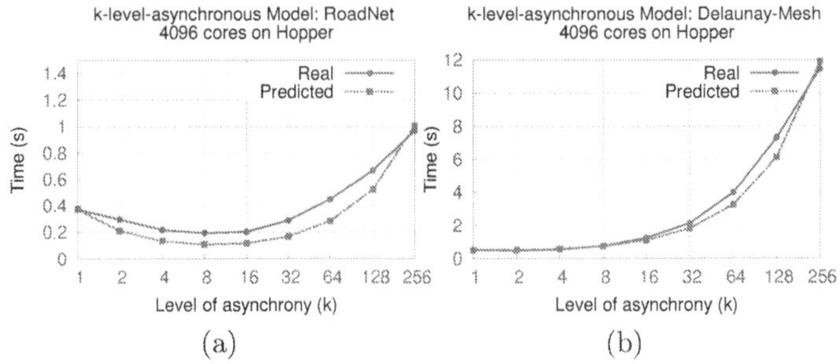

Figure 6: KLA Model: Predicted vs. Actual Execution Times on HOPPER for a Type-I algorithm (BFS).

Using these constants in the appropriate equation (Eq. 4 for Type-I algorithms and Eq. 8 for Type-II algorithms), we can obtain a curve approximating the performance of the algorithm for the given input graph, for different values of k. The k_{opt} is the value for which the curve reaches its minima. We ran KLA on multiple graphs and compared the predicted vs. real k_{opt}, and found the model to approximate the trend well enough to suggest a reasonable k_{opt} value. Figure 6 shows two such results comparing the predicted times given by the KLA model on two different input graphs, to the actual execution times for varying k-values. This model was used to predict k_{opt} for experiments in Sections 5.4 and 5.6.

5. EXPERIMENTS

In this section, we demonstrate the need for a single unifying paradigm with the ability to parametrically control asynchrony. We evaluate the performance of KLA as compared with traditional level synchronous and asynchronous paradigms for a variety of algorithms on various real-world and synthetic graphs.

5.1 Experimental Setup and Input Graphs

Experimental studies were performed on HOPPER – a Cray XE6 machine at the National Energy Research Scientific Computing Center (NERSC) with 153,216 total cores, of which 98,304 cores were available to us. Results reported were averaged over multiple runs to obtain a suitable confidence interval.

KLA was evaluated on representative graphs from different domains, ranging in size from a few million to tens of billions of vertices and edges (Table 2). These include the Graph 500 benchmark input [1], Google and Twitter web-graphs, various road-networks (TX, PA, US, EU and Synthetic) [2, 3], and geometric graphs (Delaunay meshes, geometric meshes and torii) [2, 3]. Input graphs use the default distribution provided by the input files.

5.2 SGL Overview

We implemented the KLA paradigm and some important graph algorithms in the STAPL Graph Library (SGL) [14] to evaluate its performance. SGL consists of a generic parallel graph container (**pGraph**), graph **pViews** [9], and a collection of parallel graph algorithms to allow users to easily process graphs at scale. The **pGraph** container is built using the **pContainer** framework (PCF) [29] provided by the Standard Template Adaptive Parallel Library (STAPL). STAPL [10] is a framework for parallel C++ code develop-

Name	Description	V, E	Source
G500-N	Graph500 Benchmark Input	2^N, 16×2^N	Graph 500 Benchmark
Google	Google Web-Graph	916K, 5.1M	SNAP
Twitter	Twitter Web-Graph	62M, 1.2B	SNAP
RoadNet-TX,PA	Road-networks (TX, PA)	(1.4M, 3.8M), (1M, 3M)	SNAP
RoadNet-US,EU	Road-networks (US, EU)	(24M, 58M), (50M, 54M)	Dimacs Challenge-9
RoadNet-Synthetic	Synthetic Road-network	9.63B, 10.2B	Generated
Delaunay	Delaunay Triangulation Graph	16M, 50M	Dimacs Challenge-10
RGG	Geometric Graph	16M, 132M	Dimacs Challenge-10
Torus	Toroid Mesh	$2.25M \times p$, $9M \times p$	Generated

Table 2: Characteristics of input graphs.

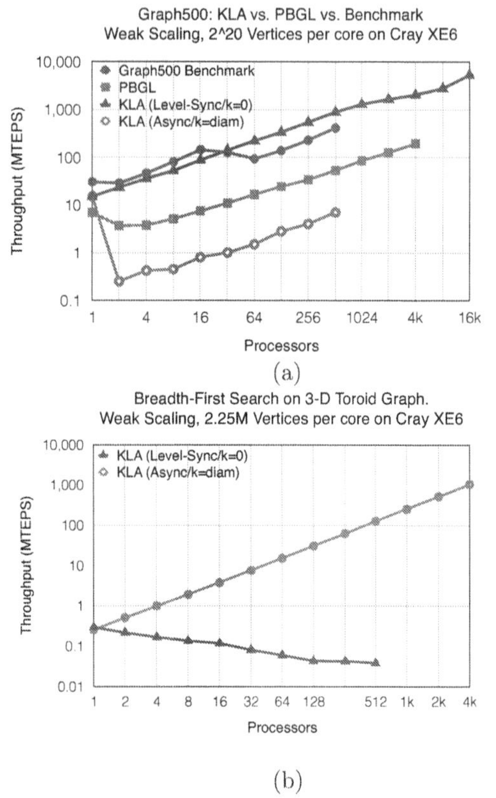

Figure 7: Scalability (Throughput) of BFS on (a) Graph500 benchmark (max. |V|=16B, |E|=256B) and (b) torus (max. |V|=9.2B, |E|=37B).

ment. STAPL's core is a library of components implementing parallel algorithms (`pAlgorithms`) and distributed data structures (`pContainers`).

5.3 Level-Synchronous vs. Asynchronous BFS

To demonstrate the performance differential between level-synchronous and asynchronous paradigms, we compared our implementation of an async BFS to its level-sync variant on a torus graph and the Graph 500 Benchmark graph (shown in Figure 7). These represent two extreme cases for long and short diameter graphs. We use $k = 1$ to emulate level-synchronous behavior and $k = n$ to emulate asynchronous behavior for KLA BFS. In both cases, the algorithm remains the same and only the value of k need vary to suit the input.

The Graph 500 input graph has a short diameter (<16) and vertices with very high out-degrees. For this graph, async BFS performs poorly due to the large number of messages flooding the system and the large amount of wasted work for revisited vertices. The level-sync BFS performs well in this case due to the input graph's low diameter, which implies fewer global synchronization. The torus graph, on the other hand, represents a worst-case scenario for parallel BFS scalability – the algorithm is essentially serialized due to the topology of the torus, which limits the available parallelism. In this scenario, we observed that async BFS performed much better than level-sync BFS, due to the absence of synchronization-points (Figure 7 (b)). These experiments demonstrate that the topology of the graph can significantly affect the performance characteristics of algorithms, and pairing the correct paradigm to the topology can result in a significant performance benefit.

5.4 Evaluation of KLA BFS

In this section we evaluate the performance benefit and scalability of KLA BFS on different types of real-world and synthetic graphs. We observed that for certain graphs, a value of $k > 1$ provides the best performance.

Graph Structure and k_{opt}. To investigate the correlation between the structure of a graph and the choice of k for the KLA algorithm, we ran the KLA BFS on a graph while deforming its shape to vary the diameter from very large (circular chain, $d \approx 128k$) to very small (random graph, $d \approx 8$). We obtained graphs with different diameters by allowing any given vertex to randomly select and connect only to its $\pm m$-closest neighboring vertices, varying m from 2 (circular chain) to n (random network). This is similar to the approach described by Watts and Strogatz [32]. We ran KLA BFS on each deformation for varying values of k, and observed which k was best suited for the given diameter. Figure 8 shows the value of k that gives the best performance for input graphs of varying diameter. This indicates that while a value of $k = 1$ better suits small-diameter graphs, there are also classes of graphs with intermediate diameters for which k_{opt} is between 1 and d. Road network graphs, analyzed in the next section, are one such class of graphs, along with scientific meshes. It is for such graphs that KLA provides improved performance, while maintaining the performance for other inputs and providing a single unifying algorithmic interface.

Road Network Graphs. KLA BFS can be used to accelerate finding routes on a road-map and navigation, as it is well suited to road network graphs due to their relatively long diameters. We obtained road networks for the

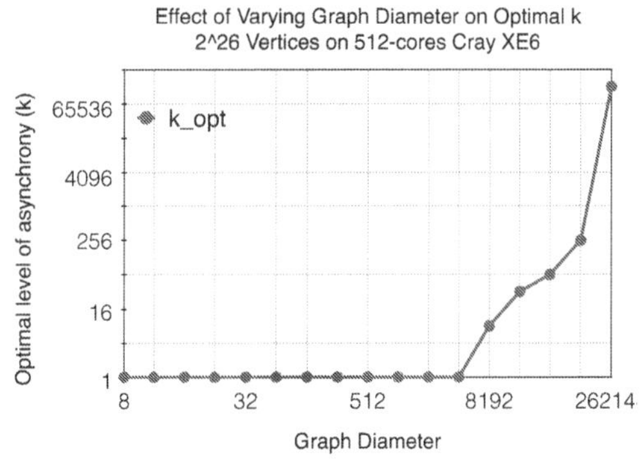

Figure 8: Modeling KLA: Study of effects of graph diameter on the optimal k parameter.

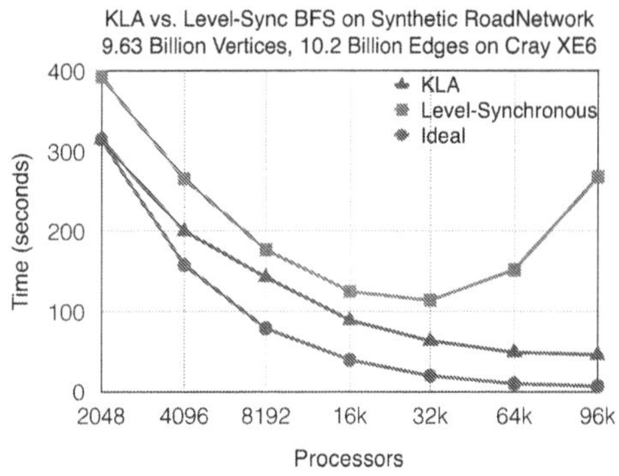

Figure 10: Performance of KLA vs. Level-Sync BFS on synthetic road network, 98,304 cores on HOPPER.

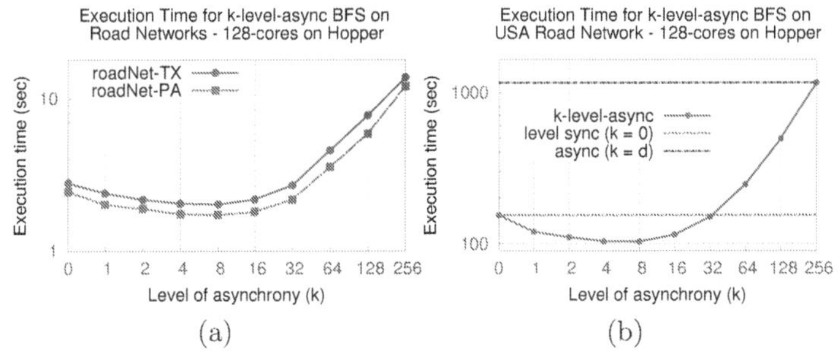

Figure 9: Performance of KLA BFS on road networks for (a) TX, PA and (b) USA on HOPPER.

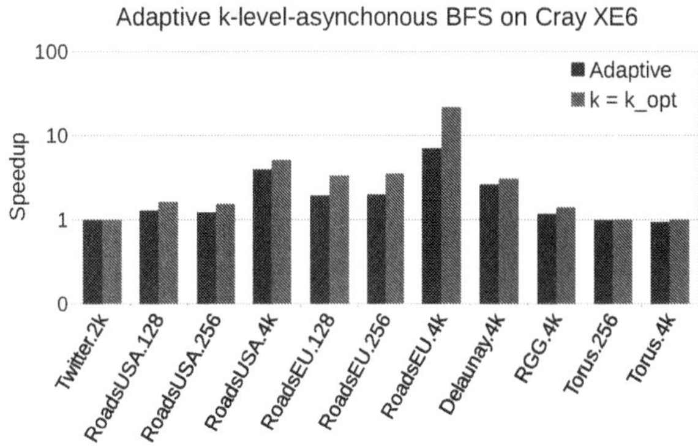

Figure 11: KLA BFS speedup with k_{opt} and Adaptive KLA on various graphs on HOPPER.

state of Texas and Pennsylvania (Figure 9(a)), and the entire U.S.A. (Figure 9(b)). For each of these graphs, the level-synchronous variant, with $k = 1$ proved expensive due to high number of synchronizations. However, owing to the amount of re-done work and the number of messages generated, the purely asynchronous version was also slow. In fact, the best performance was obtained with $1 < k < d$, where the computation was ≈27-33% faster than the fastest traditional paradigm for all three inputs.

Additionally, we generated a synthetic road network by stitching together multiple copies of the European road network, which provided us an input with 9.63 billion vertices and 10.2 billion edges. This input was large enough to allow for a meaningful strong-scaling study to 10^5 cores. Figure 10 compares the scalability of KLA BFS with level-synchronous BFS on this road network. The level-synchronous BFS scales to 32,768 cores, but not beyond. The KLA BFS is able to scale better until 98,304 cores (the maximum available cores). It yields faster running times due to better balancing synchronization costs, which become increasingly expensive for large core counts, with wasted work. This experiment demonstrates that traditional paradigms do not always scale to a large number of cores, where KLA can improve scalability and performance significantly.

5.5 Evaluation of Adaptive KLA BFS

For many applications, the optimal value of k may not be known for a particular input graph. Our Adaptive KLA technique provides improved execution times adaptively based on the graph's topology when users do not have sufficient information about the input graph.

We ran the Adaptive KLA BFS on input graphs from various domains, including road networks (Europe, USA), web graphs (Twitter) and geometric graphs (Delaunay, Random Geometric Graphs (RGG), Torus). We compared the speedup obtained using KLA BFS with k_{opt} to the Adaptive KLA algorithm for each graph. We also ran the level synchronous and asynchronous BFS on these graphs, and used the faster version's running-time as a baseline for calculating the speedup of both KLA BFS and Adaptive KLA BFS. Figure 11 shows the speedup obtained for various graphs over the best traditional paradigm. We observe that KLA with optimal k (k_{opt}) can provide improved performance over traditional paradigms for some input graphs. Due to the small girth of these graphs, not all processors are active in each iteration (this is especially true for higher processor counts) and those processors end up waiting at the global synchronizations in the level-synchronous approach. In contrast, the asynchronous approach may re-visit many vertices, increasing the run-time. KLA allows the traversal to proceed enough so as to recruit more processors in the iteration and yet controls the depth of asynchrony to avoid too many redundant visits, allowing for better scalability and performance. We also observe that Adaptive KLA can improve the performance, although the overhead of adaptivity (as it needs a few iterations to converge) and monitoring the iterations (for wasted work, etc.) keeps it from achieving the same level of performance as KLA with k_{opt}.

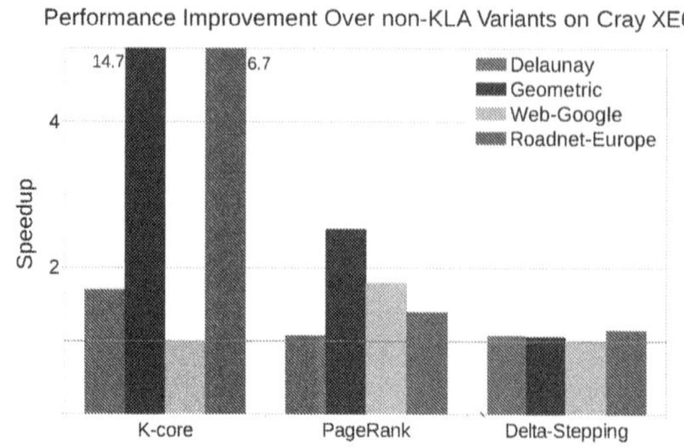

Figure 12: Evaluation of k-core PageRank and SSSP on 16,384 cores on HOPPER.

5.6 Evaluation of Other Types of Algorithms

In this section, we evaluate the performance of three important graph mining and graph analytics algorithms: k-core, PageRank and SSSP. We also compare the Δ-stepping SSSP algorithm with its KLA variant. We run the three algorithms on a variety of input graphs from different domains (road networks, scientific and geometric meshes, and web-graphs) and present their speedup (relative to level-synchronous versions in case of k-core and PageRank, relative to non-KLA Δ-stepping for SSSP) in Figure 12.

k-core. For k-core (Figure 12), we expect the fully asynchronous setting for k to perform fastest. While this is the case for most inputs, graphs with high out-degrees can cause a large number of messages to flood the network, leading to network congestion. In such cases, using the level-sync setting ($k = 0$) provides the best performance, as is observed for the Google web-graph. The benefit provided by KLA for k-core is the ease of algorithm tunability to obtain the best performance for any given input at runtime.

PageRank. PageRank incurs a penalty of buffering for increased asynchrony. However, as the cost of buffering was much lower than the cost for communication and global synchronization on our system, PageRank also saw good performance gains from the KLA paradigm (Figure 12).

Δ-stepping. We also compare an implementation of Δ-stepping SSSP in KLA with non-KLA Δ-stepping SSSP in Figure 12. The results presented show the speedup of the KLA version over the non-KLA version for the best values of Δ and k. We observe from these experiments that, as expected, both variants of Δ-stepping exhibit similar performance for different input graphs, as the KLA paradigm is a generalization of the Δ-stepping algorithm (Section 2.2).

5.7 KLA with Other Graph Frameworks

KLA with Green-Marl. KLA algorithms may also be called recursively in nested sections. We describe such computations using a tuple of k values. Each value in the tuple represents the k for each algorithm being executed in that level of nesting. The arity of the tuple denotes the number of levels of nesting in the algorithm. If the algorithm in the nested section is sequential or non-KLA, the k value for it is ignored ($k = x$). For example, using a shared-memory library for intra-node computation and KLA for inter-node computation, the tuple would be $\langle x, k_1 \rangle$. Figure 13 demonstrates the benefit of using nested-parallel ex-

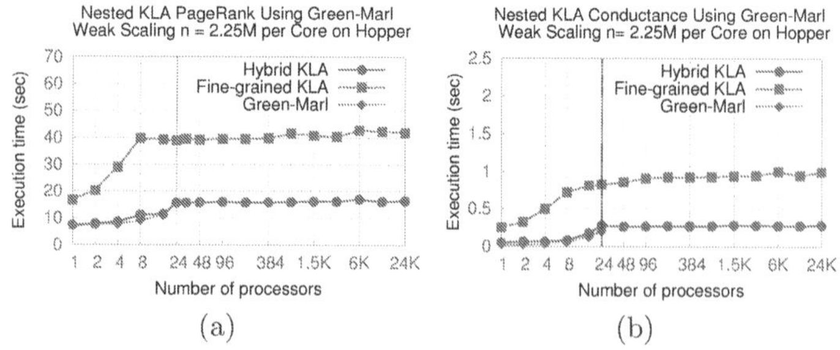

Figure 13: Nested KLA with Green-Marl for (a) PageRank and (b) conductance, up to 24,000 cores.

ecution in the nested KLA paradigm. It takes advantage of an optimized shared-memory library (Green-Marl) for processing partitions of the graph on a shared-memory node and uses KLA version of the algorithm on the upper-level to extend it across distributed nodes in the machine.

In our experiments, we ran two different algorithms – PageRank and cut-conductance – on a mesh graph using the Green-Marl [16] implementation within the node and KLA off-node, and compared them with their single-level KLA implementations in SGL.

KLA in Galois. In addition to the implementation provided for SGL, we illustrate the portability of the KLA technique by applying it within the Galois [15] parallel framework. Galois' execution model relies on shared-memory worklists that determine task scheduling of algorithms. A suite of worklists are provided by the library, including a bulk-synchronous worklist that contains two queues and processes them one after another, and an asynchronous worklist that contains several queues that may be processed in any order, but are prioritized by some metric (e.g. vertex-level).

We modified Galois' bulk synchronous worklist to process vertices in the same KLA-SS asynchronously and to only synchronize after k levels of asynchrony, effectively creating a KLA worklist for Galois. Figure 14 shows the results of executing KLA BFS in Galois for various input graphs. As with KLA in SGL, we see improvements for input graphs with long diameters, whereas short diameter graphs perform best with level-synchronous execution. In certain cases, the KLA worklist is able to achieve more than 90% speedup over the best of the level-synchronous and asynchronous worklists.

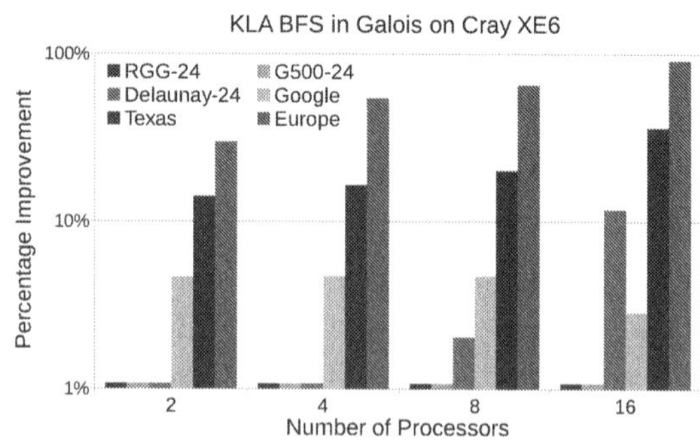

Figure 14: Speedup of KLA BFS in Galois on various graphs relative to the fastest version of Galois (bulk synchronous or asynchronous) on HOPPER.

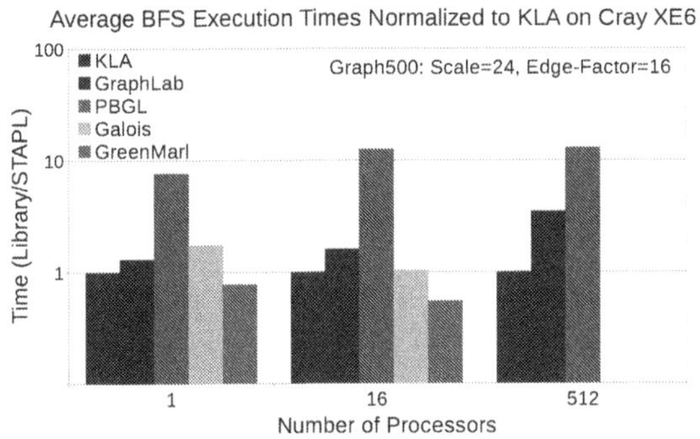

Figure 15: Execution times of Graph500 on various graph libraries normalized to SGL KLA on HOPPER.

6. RELATED WORK

Parallel graph algorithms have long been a subject of research in literature [18, 12]. Our work presents a *general, implementation-independent paradigm* that can provide substantial performance improvements for multiple important graph algorithms. The paradigm itself is applicable to any graph framework supporting asynchronous execution, and while we focus on vertex-centric algorithms, it may also be extended to edge-centric frameworks, as well as expressed in graph-specific languages (graph DSLs). In this work, we mainly focus on implementations using the STAPL Graph Library, however, Section 5.7 shows applicability of KLA to Galois and Green-Marl.

This section reviews some of the relevant parallel graph-processing frameworks. We show a comparison of running times of BFS on the standard Graph 500 benchmark for these libraries with our KLA implementation in Figure 15.

There has been much research in using a level-synchronous approach to express graph algorithms. Most popular graph libraries such as Google's Pregel [21], Parallel Boost Graph Library (PBGL) [13, 11], Multi-Threaded Graph Library (MTGL) [5], along with most stand-alone implementations of parallel graph algorithms (e.g. Graph500 reference implementation [1]), use the level-synchronous paradigm to express and implement parallel algorithms. This paradigm makes it easier to reason about and debug graph algorithms in parallel due to the guarantees it provides, and is straightforward to implement. A detailed comparison of SGL with these libraries was shown in [14]. GRACE [31] and Galois [15] are other shared-memory graph libraries. GRACE allows asynchronous execution while abstracting users from the execution policies. Galois uses optimistic set iterators and operator scheduling to execute algorithms. However, this results in Galois requiring users to handle low-level concurrency issues such as data sharing and deadlock avoidance.

The asynchronous paradigm has also been applied to various graph algorithms [12, 24]. However, they may not be as straightforward to express and reason about as their level-synchronous counterparts. Recently, there have been a few graph processing frameworks that allow asynchronous execution of the algorithms [14, 20, 28, 31]. GraphLab/PowerGraph [20] is one such distributed-memory framework that allows users to choose between synchronous and asynchronous execution at runtime, but it does not support parametric control of asynchrony. It also exposes users to low-level details of parallelism such as memory consistency and concurrency, as they have to choose a consistency model for their application and understand its implications. [22] presents Δ-stepping SSSP, which is discussed in Section 2.2 in detail.

There has even been work on creating domain-specific languages (DSLs) for graph processing. Green-Marl [16] is one such DSL for graph analysis which allows users to express graph-based computations naturally, abstracting parallelism details. The Green-Marl compiler is able to generate code for specific target languages and libraries, which can produce algorithm-specific code with less overhead than the fully generic code in STAPL. It provides an implementation for shared-memory systems using OpenMP. Such a DSL could be extended to generate code for KLA and SGL, allowing users of Green-Marl access to distributed-memory systems, as shown in Section 5.7. Elixir [25] is another DSL which produces Galois code and is designed for concurrent graph processing for shared-memory systems. It also supports loop-unrolling for certain graph algorithms at compile-time, which can reduce global synchronizations in the output code. However, being a compile-time optimization, the algorithm would need to be recompiled for each input with a suitable unroll-factor, which is not a realistic solution.

While it is well known that there exist two ways (asynchronous and level-synchronous) of expressing parallel graph algorithms, the effects of parametrically controlling asynchrony as a general paradigm has not been studied.

7. CONCLUSION

In this paper we have presented a novel approach to designing and implementing parallel graph algorithms — the k-level async (KLA) paradigm — that enables the level of asynchrony of parallel graph algorithms to be parametically varied from none (level-synchronous) to full (asynchronous). We provided guidance on how to express graph algorithms in the KLA paradigm and provided techniques for determining k, the number of asynchronous steps allowed between global synchronizations. Our experimental results show KLA implementation of graph algorithms such as BFS, PageRank and k-core provide good scalability on up to 98,000 cores and improvements of 10x or more over level-synchronous and asynchronous versions of these algorithms.

8. ACKNOWLEDGEMENTS

We would like to thank our anonymous reviewers. This research is supported in part by NSF awards CNS-0551685, CCF-0833199, CCF-0830753, IIS-0916053, IIS-0917266, EFRI-1240483, RI-1217991, by NIH NCI R25 CA090301-11, by DOE awards DE-AC02-06CH11357, B575363, by Samsung, Chevron, IBM, Intel, Oracle/Sun and by Award KUS-C1-016-04, made by King Abdullah University of Science and Technology (KAUST). This material is based upon work supported by the U.S. Department of Energy, National Nuclear Security Administration, under Award Number(s) DE-NA0002376, and used resources of the National Energy Research Scientific Computing Center, which is supported by the Office of Science of the U.S. Department of Energy under Contract No. DE-AC02-05CH11231.

9. REFERENCES

[1] The graph 500 list. http://www.graph500.org, 2013.

[2] Stanford Large Network Dataset Collection. http://snap.stanford.edu/data/index.html, 2013.

[3] 9th DIMACS Implementation Challenge. http://www.dis.uniroma1.it/challenge9/, 2013.

[4] J. I. Alvarez-hamelin, A. Barrat, and A. Vespignani. Large scale networks fingerprinting and visualization using the k-core decomposition. In *Adv. in Neural Inf. Proc. Syst. 18*, pp. 41–50. MIT Press, 2006.

[5] J. W. Berry, B. Hendrickson, S. Kahan, and P. Konecny. Software and algorithms for graph queries on multithreaded architectures. In *Intl. Parallel and Distributed Processing Symp.*, 0:495, 2007.

[6] U. Brandes. A faster algorithm for betweenness centrality. *J. of Math. Sociology*, pp. 163–177, 2001.

[7] S. Brin and L. Page. The anatomy of a large-scale hypertextual web search engine. *Computer Networks and ISDN Systems*, pp. 107–117, 1998.

[8] A. Buluç and K. Madduri. Parallel breadth-first search on distributed memory systems. In *Proc. of Intl. Conf. for High Performance Computing, Networking, Storage and Analysis*, SC '11, pp. 1–12, New York, NY, USA, 2011.

[9] A. Buss, A. Fidel, Harshvardhan, T. Smith, G. Tanase, N. Thomas, X. Xu, M. Bianco, N. M. Amato, and L. Rauchwerger. The STAPL pView. In *Intl. Workshop on Languages and Compilers for Parallel Computing (LCPC), in Lecture Notes in Computer Science (LNCS)*, Houston, TX, USA, 2010.

[10] A. Buss, Harshvardhan, I. Papadopoulos, O. Pearce, T. Smith, G. Tanase, N. Thomas, X. Xu, M. Bianco, N. M. Amato, and L. Rauchwerger. STAPL: Standard Template Adaptive Parallel Library. In *Proc. Annual Haifa Experimental Systems Conference (SYSTOR)*, pp. 1–10, New York, NY, USA, 2010.

[11] N. Edmonds, J. Willcock, and A. Lumsdaine. Expressing graph algorithms using generalized active messages. In *Proc. of Symp. on Principles and Practice of Parallel Programming*, PPoPP '13, pp. 289–290, New York, NY, USA, 2013.

[12] R. G. Gallager, P. A. Humblet, and P. M. Spira. A distributed algorithm for minimum-weight spanning trees. In *Trans. Program. Lang. Syst.*, pp. 66–77, 1983.

[13] D. Gregor and A. Lumsdaine. The Parallel BGL: A generic library for distributed graph computations. In *Parallel Object-Oriented Scientific Computing*, POOSC, 2005.

[14] Harshvardhan, A. Fidel, N. M. Amato, and L. Rauchwerger. The STAPL Parallel Graph Library. In *Languages and Compilers for Parallel Computing*, Lecture Notes in Computer Science, pp. 46–60. Springer Berlin Heidelberg, 2012.

[15] M. A. Hassaan, M. Burtscher, and K. Pingali. Ordered and unordered algorithms for parallel breadth first search. In *Proc. of the Intl. Conf. on Parallel Architectures and Compilation Techniques*, PACT '10, pp. 539–540, New York, NY, USA, 2010.

[16] S. Hong, H. Chafi, E. Sedlar, and K. Olukotun. Green-Marl: A DSL for easy and efficient graph analysis. In *Proc. of the Intl. Conf. on Architectural Support for Prog. Languages and Operating Syst.*, ASPLOS'12, pp. 349–362, New York, NY, USA, 2012.

[17] S. Hong, T. Oguntebi, and K. Olukotun. Efficient parallel graph exploration for multi-core cpu and gpu. In *Proc. of the Intl. Conf. on Parallel Architectures and Compilation Techniques*, PACT '11, pp. 78–88.

[18] J. JàJà. *An Introduction Parallel Algorithms.* Addison–Wesley, Reading, Massachusetts, 1992.

[19] C. E. Leiserson and T. B. Schardl. A work-efficient parallel breadth-first search algorithm (or how to cope with the nondeterminism of reducers). In *Proc. of the Symp. on Parallelism in Algorithms and Architectures*, SPAA '10, pp. 303–314, New York, NY, USA, 2010.

[20] Y. Low, D. Bickson, J. Gonzalez, C. Guestrin, A. Kyrola, and J. M. Hellerstein. Distributed Graphlab: A framework for machine learning and data mining in the cloud. *Proc. of the VLDB Endowment*, pp. 716–727, 2012.

[21] G. Malewicz, M. H. Austern, A. J. Bik, J. C. Dehnert, I. Horn, N. Leiser, and G. Czajkowski. Pregel: A system for large-scale graph processing. In *Proc. of the Intl. Conf. on Management of data*, SIGMOD '10, pp. 135–146, New York, NY, USA, 2010.

[22] U. Meyer and P. Sanders. Delta-stepping : A parallel single source shortest path algorithm. In *ESA '98: Proc. of the European Symp. on Algorithms*, pp. 393–404. Springer-Verlag, 1998.

[23] L. Page, S. Brin, R. Motwani and T. Winograd. The PageRank Citation Ranking: Bringing Order to the Web. 1998.

[24] R. Pearce, M. Gokhale, and N. M. Amato. Multithreaded asynchronous graph traversal for in-memory and semi-external memory. In *Proc. of Intl. Conf. for High Performance Computing, Networking, Storage and Analysis*, SC '10, pp. 1–11, Washington, DC, USA, 2010.

[25] D. Prountzos, R. Manevich, and K. Pingali. Elixir: A system for synthesizing concurrent graph programs. In *Proc. of the Intl. Conf. on Object Oriented Program. Syst. Languages and Applications*, OOPSLA '12, pp. 375–394, New York, NY, USA, 2012.

[26] M. J. Quinn and N. Deo. Parallel graph algorithms. In *ACM Computing Surveys (CSUR)*, pp. 319–348, 1984.

[27] J. H. Reif, editor. *Synthesis of Parallel Algorithms.* Morgan Kaufmann, San Mateo, CA, 1993.

[28] P. Stutz, A. Bernstein, and W. Cohen. Signal/collect: Graph algorithms for the (semantic) web. In *The Semantic Web–ISWC '10*, pp. 764–780. Springer, 2010.

[29] G. Tanase, A. Buss, A. Fidel, Harshvardhan, I. Papadopoulos, O. Pearce, T. Smith, N. Thomas, X. Xu, N. Mourad, J. Vu, M. Bianco, N. M. Amato, and L. Rauchwerger. The STAPL Parallel Container Framework. In *Proc. of Symp. on Principles and Practice of Parallel Programming*, PPoPP, pp. 235–246, San Antonio, TX, USA, 2011.

[30] L. Valiant. Bridging model for parallel computation. *Comm. ACM*, pp. 103–111, 1990.

[31] G. Wang, W. Xie, A. J. Demers, and J. Gehrke. Asynchronous large-scale graph processing made easy. In *CIDR*, 2013.

[32] D. J. Watts and S. H. Strogatz. Collective dynamics of 'small-world' networks. *Nature*, pp. 440–442, 1998.

Tiling and Optimizing Time-Iterated Computations over Periodic Domains

Uday Bondhugula
Department of Computer Science and Automation,
Indian Institute of Science
Bangalore 560012 India
uday@csa.iisc.ernet.in

Vinayaka Bandishti
Department of Computer Science and Automation,
Indian Institute of Science
Bangalore 560012 India
vbandishti@csa.iisc.ernet.in

Albert Cohen
INRIA and École Normale Supérieure
45 rue d'Ulm
Paris 75005, France
Albert.Cohen@inria.fr

Guillain Potron
École Normale Supérieure
and Indian Institute of Science
45 rue d'Ulm
Paris 75005, France
guillain.potron@ens.fr

Nicolas Vasilache
Reservoir Labs
632 Broadway
New York, NY 10012, USA
vasilache@reservoir.com

ABSTRACT

This paper deals with optimizing time-iterated computations on periodic data domains. These computations are prevalent in computational sciences, particularly in partial differential equation solvers. We propose a fully automatic technique suitable for implementation in a compiler or in a domain-specific code generator for such computations. Dependence patterns on periodic data domains prevent existing algorithms from finding tiling opportunities. Our approach augments a state-of-the-art parallelization and locality-enhancing algorithm from the polyhedral framework to allow time-tiling of stencil computations on periodic domains. Experimental results on the swim SPEC CPU2000fp benchmark show a speedup of 5× and 4.2× over the highest SPEC performance achieved by native compilers on Intel Xeon and AMD Opteron multicore SMP systems, respectively. On other representative stencil computations, our scheme provides performance similar to that achieved with no periodicity, and a very high speedup is obtained over the native compiler. We also report a mean speedup of about 1.5× over a domain-specific stencil compiler supporting limited cases of periodic boundary conditions. To the best of our knowledge, it has been infeasible to manually reproduce such optimizations on swim or any other periodic stencil, especially on a data grid of two-dimensions or higher.

Categories and Subject Descriptors

D.3.4 [**Programming Languages**]: Processors—*Compilers, Optimization, Code generation*

PACT'14, August 24–27, 2014, Edmonton, AB, Canada.

http://dx.doi.org/10.1145/2628071.2628106.

Keywords

Tiling; Stencils; Periodic; Automatic parallelization; Polyhedral model

1. INTRODUCTION

Stencil-style computations are widely used in solving partial differential equations over discretized domains. They have been extensively studied by the parallel and high-performance computing community. Stencil computations involve updating points in a data grid of certain dimensionality repeatedly. The computation performed at each point in the grid uses values from its immediate or short distance neighbors. These updates to the grid are repeated a certain number of times or until convergence. Hence, as originally viewed and specified, the computation accesses the entire grid each iteration before accessing it again the next iteration. Such an execution order is memory bandwidth-bound when the data grid does not fit in the last level cache.

Stencil computations can be performed on discretized domains that are either non-periodic or periodic. Non-periodic domains have boundaries that do not change. However, periodic domains are often used to model a portion of a larger space. Periodicity also arises when one models a hollow object. The object is cut and unrolled flat in a lower dimensional space. For example, domains like hollow spheres, cylinders, or tori can be cut and flattened out in 2-d space. Similarly, a ring can be cut and flattened into a 1-d array. When this is done, the points on either boundary have to be treated as neighbors with respect to one another, resulting in wrap-around dependences. These wrap-around dependences create cyclic dependences between tiles in an otherwise valid tiling. Although a lot of effort has been put in optimizing stencil computations, there is very little work on optimizing those with periodicity. This is an important domain of numerical simulation, since periodic boundary conditions are prevalent in partial differential equation solvers. The fact that the SPEC CPU2000fp included the swim (171.swim) as one of its benchmarks is strong evidence of this. The swim benchmark is a weather prediction program that performs finite difference modeling of shallow water equations through periodic boundary conditions on a two dimensional grid [27]. All its running time is spent in the stencil computation. Modeling the earth's atmosphere and surface also involves two-dimensional periodic domains [26].

Tiling for locality and parallelism [17, 37, 41] has been studied intensively for the optimization of stencils with no periodicity. Tiling for locality allows simultaneous reuse in multiple directions—the directions correspond to the loop dimensions being tiled. In particular, the loop that iterates over time in stencils carries temporal reuse while the space loops carry constant reuse as well as spatial reuse along the innermost space dimension. Tiling for parallelism allows reduction in the frequency of synchronization. Tiling for locality and parallelism together makes the computation less dependent on memory bandwidth, and in the context of multicore processors, can make it scale better.

We make a key observation about stencils with periodic boundary conditions: tiling can be enabled by first splitting the iteration domain (or index set) in a very specific way. Then, an extension of existing auto-parallelization and tiling techniques enables the necessary program transformations allowing for dramatic improvement in performance. In particular, our technique improves performance by several factors when compared to code that just tiles and parallelizes the loops that tile and iterate over the data space code.

The rest of this paper is organized as follows. Section 2 introduces the technical background. Section 3 discusses challenges and the feasibility of various approaches. Section 4 and Section 5 describe our solution. Experimental results are presented in Section 6 before concluding in Section 8.

2. BACKGROUND

In this section, we introduce notation and the mathematical background necessary for the sections that follow.

Definition 1 (Hyperplane). A hyperplane is an $n-1$ dimensional affine sub-space of an n dimensional space.

Since we are interested in integer spaces, by a hyperplane we refer to the set of all vectors $x \in \mathbb{Z}^n$ such that $\vec{h}.\vec{x} = k$, for $k \in \mathbb{Z}$. Two vectors $\vec{v_1}$ and $\vec{v_2}$ lie in the same hyperplane if $\vec{h}.\vec{v_1} = \vec{h}.\vec{v_2}$. The set of parallel *hyperplane instances* correspond to different values of k with the row vector $\vec{h}$ normal to the hyperplane.

A hyperplane divides a space into two half-spaces, the positive half-space and the negative half-space. If the coefficients of $\vec{h}$ are integers, the set of integer points are divided into a non-negative half-space ($\vec{h}.x \geq k$) and a negative half-space ($\vec{h}.x \leq k-1$).

Index sets and dependences.

Let $S_1, S_2, \ldots, S_n$ be the statements of a program. The set of all iterations $\vec{i_S}$ of S is called the index set of S and is represented by I_S. Let m_S be the dimensionality of statement S. A program parameter is a symbol that is not modified in the portion of the program being represented. Problem sizes appearing in loop bounds are typical examples of program parameters. Let m_p be the number of program parameters, and $\vec{p}$ be the vector of program parameters. Let E be the set of dependence edges. For an $e \in E$, let D_e be the dependence polyhedron. D_e is a relation between source and target iterations, represented by $\vec{s}$ and $\vec{t}$ respectively, that are in dependence. For example, the vertical dependence instances in Figure 1 and Figure 2 correspond to the dependence polyhedron:

$$D_e = \{\langle\vec{s},\vec{t}\rangle | \vec{s} = (t,i) \wedge \vec{t} = (t',i') \wedge t' = t+1 \wedge i' = i\}$$

2.1 Tiling

Tiling is considered valid if and only if a total order can be constructed for the execution of all tiles, where each tile is being executed atomically. This implies that a tiling is valid if and only if there is no dependence cycle between the tiles. This can be very hard to check statically in general. Hence, compiler optimizers work with sufficient conditions such as that of non-negative dependence components: this was from the pioneering works of Irigoin and Triolet [17] and a large amount of literature on the validity of tiling relates to or derives from it [37, 25, 20, 1, 5]. In particular, the condition involves checking if all components corresponding to (yet unsatisfied) dependences are non-negative for the set of contiguous loop nest dimensions that are being tiled. In a more general polyhedral setting, a tiling hyperplane is an affine function of the form:

$$\phi_S\left(\vec{i_S}\right) = (c_1 \ldots c_{m_S}) \cdot \left(\vec{i_S}\right) + (d_1 \ldots d_{m_p}) \cdot (\vec{p}) + c_0$$

$$c_0, c_1, \ldots, c_{m_S}, d_1, \ldots, d_{m_p} \in \mathbb{Z}, \quad \vec{i_S} \in I_S$$

and a sufficient condition for ϕ_{S_i} to be a statement-wise valid tiling is written as:

$$\phi_{S_p}(\vec{t}) - \phi_{S_q}(\vec{s}) \geq 0, \quad \langle\vec{s},\vec{t}\rangle \in D_e. \tag{1}$$

When the above condition is enforced for all edges e unsatisfied up to that depth, all linearly independent solutions for ϕ in (1) form a band of valid tiling hyperplanes at that depth.

Often, when rectangular tiling is not valid on a given iteration space, it can in many cases be transformed so that rectangular tiling is valid in the new space, i.e., by finding the right set of ϕ's. E.g., a short negative dependence component can be dealt with through loop skewing with respect to an outer loop that satisfies that dependence. However, a well-known scenario in which such a transformation is not possible is when there are long dependences in either direction corresponding to a dimension. As can be seen in Figure 2, periodic stencil computations have such dependences and cannot be tiled along all dimensions readily.

2.2 Stencils

Figure 1 and 2 show the iteration space and dependences for stencil computations without and with periodic boundary conditions, respectively. As can be seen, for non-periodic stencils, all dependences are near-neighbor while for the periodic ones, there are edges wrapping around boundaries.

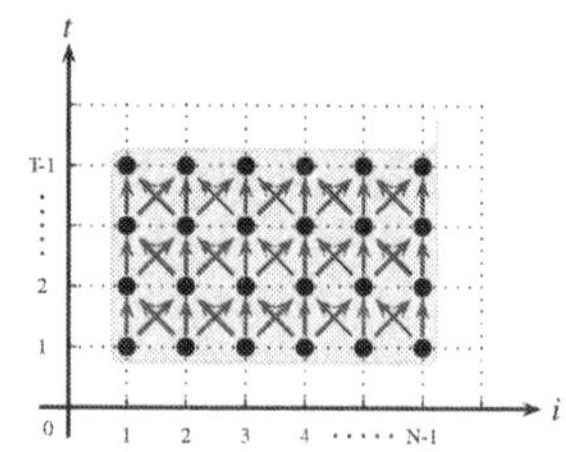

Figure 1: no periodicity

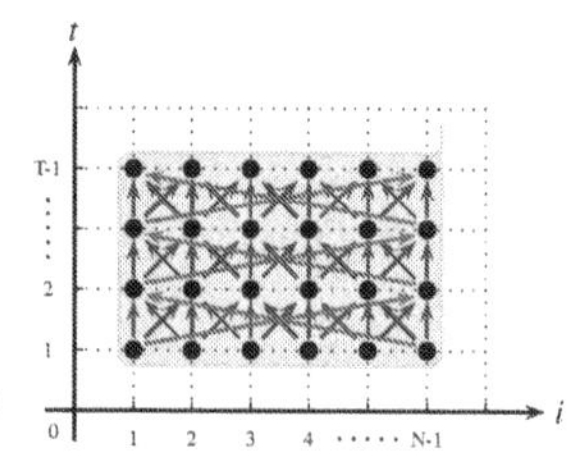

Figure 2: with periodicity

There are multiple ways one could implement the periodic boundary conditions in program code. Figure 3a and 3b show two ways of implementing a simple periodic stencil on a one-dimensional grid. Figure 3b uses a conditional to make the boundary updates access the correct values, while Figure 3a employs copies on to ghost regions to take care of the flow of values across boundaries. When the copy statements are taken into account, the data flow for both codes is equivalent. The conditional can be hoisted out to avoid overhead in the innermost loop. Also, the above code is written with modulo indexing for the time dimension instead of using two copies of the array—the latter is common practice as well. The swim SPEC benchmark in particular uses copies for boundary conditions, and

```
for (t = 0; t < T-1; t++) {
  for (i = 1; i < N+1; i++)
    A[(t+1)%2][i] = (A[t%2][i+1] + 2.0*A[t%2][i] + A[t%2][i-1])/4.0;
  A[(t+1)%2][N+1] = A[(t+1)%2][1];
  A[(t+1)%2][0] = A[(t+1)%2][N];
}
```

(a) periodic (with copies)

```
for (t=0; t <T-1; t++) {
  for (i=0; i<N; i++)
    A[(t+1)%2][i] = ((i+1==N?A[t%2][0]:A[t%2][i+1])
        + 2.0*A[t%2][i] + (i==0?A[t%2][N-1]:A[t%2][i-1]))/4.0;
}
```

(b) periodic (with boundary conditionals)

Figure 3: Stencil: heat-1d equation

uses an old and a new copy for the array instead of indexing the time dimension with a modulo operation.[1]

Time loops and space loops.

The number of times the space grid is updated is determined by the number of iterations in the outermost loop which refer to as the time loop. The loops that update points in the grid are referred to as space loops.

In this context, time tiling refers to tiling the time loop, i.e., the outermost loop. Note that the space loops, being inner parallel loops, can be freely tiled. Time tiling allows temporal reuse to be exploited along the time dimension. This is often the source of a dramatic improvement in single-thread performance, as well as excellent scaling, as time tiled code may be either less memory bandwidth bound or no longer memory bandwidth bound.

For non-periodic stencils, two existing techniques for time tiling are shown in Figure 4. The first one is classical parallelogram-shaped tiling (Figure 4a) that can be obtained by skewing the space dimension(s) with respect to the time loop. Exposing parallelism on such tiles induces a pipelined startup and drain delay, since there is no boundary along which tiles can start in parallel. The second one that we refer to as diamond tiling was recently proposed [3]. It allows concurrent start of all diamonds along the horizontal line: these tiles have no dependences among each other and can start in parallel. It leads to better load balance and maximizes the number of tiles on the wavefront without any pipeline fill-up and drain delays.

3. CHALLENGES AND APPROACHES

This section explores different approaches to the problem of tiling iterated stencil computations with periodic boundary conditions. While these approaches are generally not applicable in a compiler, and sometimes even unsuitable for manual transformation, they provide valuable insights into the challenges involved.

As mentioned earlier, for stencils on periodic domains, the wrap-around dependences at the boundaries create dependence cycles in an otherwise valid tiling. For example, there is no cyclic dependence between tiles in Figure 4a or Figure 4b. However, applying this same tiling to Figure 2 will create a cyclic dependence between tiles at either boundary.

3.1 Merging boundaries

We observe that the cyclic dependence between tiles can be broken if the tiles at either boundary for a dimension can be merged into a single special tile. If the partial tiles at each end match, as is the case in Figure 4b, they could be merged to give a full tile like those in the middle. However, this is not possible in general: depending on the alignment, the height of partial tiles at either boundary may not be the same.

As shown in Figure 5, a proper choice of tile alignment could be found that guarantees matching height for the partial tiles by shifting the tile origin by an amount equal to half the remainder when the dimension length is divided by the tile size. Note that even with such an alignment, if the boundary tiles are not exactly half of a full tile, one would end up with either a smaller full tile or a larger non-convex tile. We will then need to alternate between the two shapes every time tile step. A roadblock to this approach is that it is not practical for compiler automation since it requires the knowledge of fixed tile shape and size, and it does not explicitly say in which cases an invalid tiling can be fixed to make it valid, and which of the tiling schemes is to be chosen. It would also miss other directs way of tiling the space, which would not require such a post-correction. In addition, a stencil in which dependences arise through multiple statements make such a trial and error approach almost infeasible.

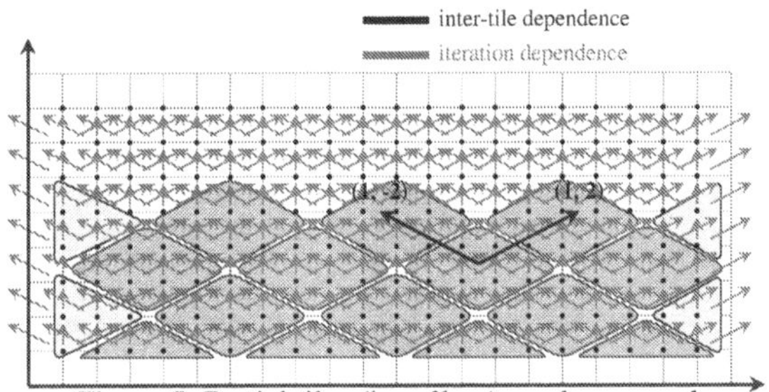

Figure 5: Partial tiles (in yellow) can be merged

3.2 Cut and paste dependent portion

Figure 6 shows an alternative approach where the cyclic dependences are broken through cutting-and-pasting the loop iterations that are transitively affected by periodic boundary conditions. This displacement effectively results in the shortening of the periodic boundary dependences. This is also equivalent to circular loop skewing [38].

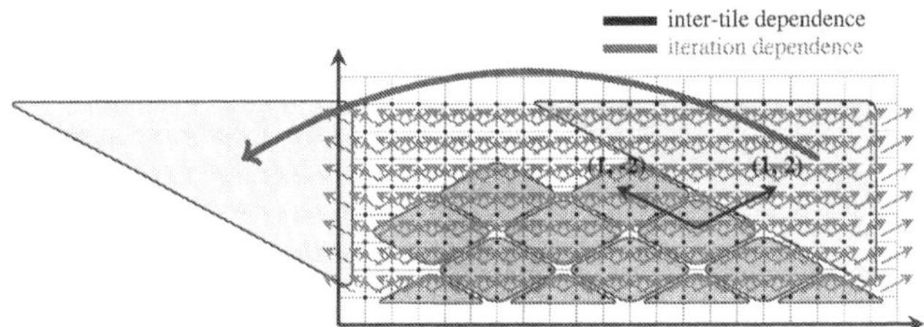

Figure 6: Cut and paste over diamond tiling

This approach requires determining the set of iterations on which another set depends. In other words, it requires computation of a transitive closure of dependences which has remained a very hard problem. Practical approximation schemes for it remain extremely complex and expensive [35]. Libraries like `isl` [35, 36] that do implement transitive closure often recommend avoiding its usage.

[1] Note that using a modulo with respect to two or any power of two does not hurt performance since it directly translates to a bitwise binary operation as opposed to a branch. Alternatively, such modulo indexing can be eliminated through partial unrolling of the loop.

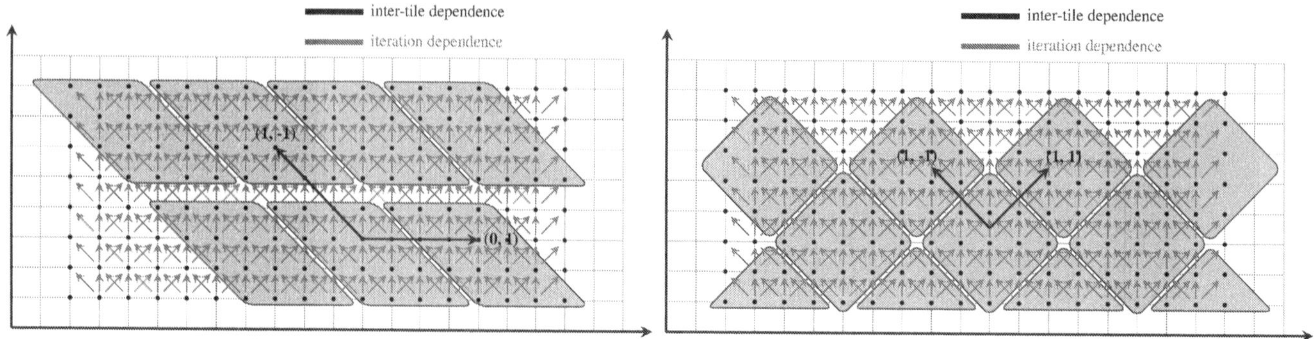

(a) Pipelined parallel tiling (b) Diamond tiling (concurrent start-up)
Figure 4: Two ways of tiling heat-1d (non-periodic)

In particular, to enable time tiling for a code like swim from the spec suite, one needs to compute a transitive closure over tens of dependences across multiple statements. In addition, unlike in the one-dimensional case, the backward slice that a tile depends on is not convex, i.e., it is a union of a large number of convex polyhedra. The number of polyhedra in such a union increases with the dimensionality of space, i.e., the number of space dimensions in the stencil.

3.3 Duplicating computation at boundaries

Redundant computation can be performed at each boundary to eliminate the dependence between boundary tiles resulting from periodic conditions. This is equivalent to replicating computation from the opposite boundary. Doing so would be similar to the approach used in [18] where neighboring tiles were overlapped and redundant computation performed to break a dependence for allowing concurrent start.

Formalizing and implementing this approach would again require one to determine the set of dependent iterations, i.e., to compute the transitive closure. Hence, it would suffer from the same limitations as the "cut and paste approach", and in addition, lead to redundant computation. The amount of redundant computation needed will increase with the size of the tile along the time dimension, and with the dimensionality of the data space.

3.4 Folding

The approach of folding [8, 42] used in the systolic array literature provides an interesting conceptual basis for addressing this problem. The folding approach folds the data domain along the middle of each dimension to bring the boundaries together, placing them one on top of the other. The technique of smashing as described by Osheim et al. [21] uses this idea of folding to describe time tiling for periodic stencil computations. They view smashing as "a data allocation technique rather than a loop/iteration transformation". This statement is partly inaccurate since dependence distances cannot be shortened by allocating, reordering, or laying out data in a particular way. They can only be changed by reordering iterations since the distances correspond to distances in the iteration space. Hence, allocating or storing data does not change the ability to tile unless the iterations themselves were reordered with respect to the order in which they were performed on the original data domain. It is assumed that the authors meant the execution order is also implicitly changed with the new data layout. Figure 7 illustrates the effect of folding on the 1-d heat stencil: the two horizontal halves (in the data space) are stacked on top of each other, converting the long cyclic dependences into short ones.

The folding approach is attractive in that in the folded view of the iteration space, all dependences are short and existing tiling techniques will work without any fixing, replication, or computation of transitive closure. Osheim et al. [21] present the smashing technique as a manual or semi-automatic optimization strategy: there are no heuristics to determine when and how to fold or smash. In addition, visualizing it for higher than two dimensional data grids is not straightforward, and hence, there is a need for a formalism to reason about, express, and compute transformations that achieve the proposed effect. Doing so also automatically solves the code generation problem.

Our approach is strongly influenced by folding, but it handles the periodic boundary constraints through iteration reordering transformations only. We require no changes to the data layout: user-defined data spaces remain unaffected.

4. INDEX SET SPLITTING TO CUT LONG DEPENDENCES

This section describes the first systematic method to enable tiling of stencil computations with periodic boundary conditions. The first step in our approach is to perform a preprocessing that splits the index sets of statements. The second step is to ensure that the transformation space allows the necessary transformations to be found for the new index sets and other performance enhancing transformations can be applied on it. This section deals with the first step while the next one deals with the second.

The method we propose subsumes folding techniques summarized in the previous section. The key reason that a transformation like folding cannot be performed by existing frameworks is that affine transformations typically apply the same affine schedule to the entire index set of a program statement. If the statement's index set is partitioned at compile time into a finite number of partitions, and a possibly different affine transformation may be applied to each one, folding-like transformations fall into the space of valid, *piece-wise affine* transformations. Thus, an *index set splitting* heuristic has to be devised that suits the needs of periodic stencils.

4.1 Short and long dependences

We first explain the classification of dependences as being short or long along a particular dimension. A single dependence represented by an edge e in the dependence graph can correspond to multiple dependence instances, i.e., multiple source and target iteration pairs, $\langle\vec{s},\vec{t}\rangle$ that are in dependence. A dependence instance is *short* along a dimension if its length, i.e., the difference (or distance) between the source and target iteration along that particular dimension can be bounded by a small constant. This constant is typically a small number and it is important that it not be comparable to loop trip counts. We see that a value of five is sufficient in practice. This value is fixed and it is used for any input program and all its dependences. A larger value such as ten could also be used as long as it is not comparable to the trip counts we expect for the problems of interest here. At the same time it should be larger than the stencil width. In practice, choosing this value to classify dependences as short is never a problem. We find that a value like five works well for the entire domain of interest. For example, for a 3-d stencil used, the grid sizes typically of interest while optimizing for execution time are at least a few hundred along each dimension.

A dependence is considered *long* if it is not *short*. Intuitively, a long dependence is one whose length is of the order of iteration space extents and any bound on its length has to involve program parameters that are symbols appearing in loop bounds, typically problem sizes. A dependence whose length varies (depending on the particular source/target instances in dependence) from a small value to a large value is also thus a long dependence. For a dependence edge to be labeled short along a dimension, all of its dependence instances should be short along that dimension; while a single dependence instance being long will label the dependence as being long. In addition, if a dependence is referred to being long in a dimension-independent manner, it implies that there was at least one dimension along which the dependence was long. The above notion of short or long dependences is only meaningful in the context of a schedule for the iterations. When referring to it without mentioning a schedule, these are implicitly assumed to be defined for the identity schedule that corresponds to the original execution order. Applying another schedule will change these dependence distances and their property of being long or short along a dimension. Note that dependence distances for inter-statement dependences are only meaningful under a schedule since the source and target statements could have different dimensionalities. Since a a statement-wise schedule maps all statements to the same set of time dimensions, the distance between the mapped points in the transformed space is meaningful.

In the examples presented so far, the dependence edge that captures the flow of values across the boundaries is a long dependence while all remaining dependences in the grid are short dependences. The length of the arrows in Figure 2 captures this in an obvious way. As an example, for the code in Figure 3b, the long dependence from the left boundary to the right one between $\vec{s} = (t, i)$ and $\vec{t} = (t', i')$ is given by:

$$t' = t + 1 \wedge i = 0 \wedge i' = N - 1 \wedge 0 \le t \le T - 3.$$

The above is long along the inner dimension (i/i') in the positive direction with length $N - 1$ while short along the outer dimension (t/t'). The short blue arrows are short dependences with the distances being standard distance vectors (1,0), (1,1), and (1,-1): these are the well-known constant distance vectors used in compiler literature [2, 4, 38].

4.2 Details of the approach

Key idea.

The approach we describe below attempts to cut all dependences that are long along one dimension roughly at its mid-point, while not affecting how the shorter dependences will be transformed in the resulting space. A hyperplane is used to cut the statement's index set into half spaces. After this cut, a separate affine transformation can be applied to each half space. The goal is to allow transformation frameworks to make all dependences short along at least one more dimension than was previously possible. This is sufficient to enable time tiling for periodic stencils.

We first describe our approach for the case when all dependences are intra-statement. In our context, this is a stencil on a single data grid. An affine hyperplane is defined by two characteristics: its orientation given by its normal vector $\vec{h}$, and its position given by an affine function of the program parameters, $v(\vec{p})$, i.e., $v(\vec{p})$ is of the form $\vec{P} \cdot \vec{p} + r$. Finding a suitable hyperplane cut is the same as finding a suitable orientation and position. The cut itself is given by

$$\vec{h}.\vec{i_S} = v(\vec{p}), \quad \text{i.e.,} \quad \vec{h}.\vec{i_S} = \vec{P} \cdot \vec{p} + r.$$

With such a cut, the index set of S, I_S, is partitioned into two halves given by I_S^+ and I_S^-:

$$I_S^+ = I_S \wedge \{\vec{h}.\vec{i_S} \ge v(\vec{p})\} \qquad I_S^- = I_S \wedge \{\vec{h}.\vec{i_S} \le v(\vec{p}) - 1\}.$$

For example, a possible cut is $2i = N$, cutting the i dimension in the middle; this corresponds to $\vec{h} = (0, 2)$, $\vec{i_S} = (t, i)$, and $v(\vec{p}) = N$ with $\vec{P} = (1)$, $\vec{p} = (N)$, and $r = 0$. Having two linearly independent hyperplanes ($\vec{h}$) would generate four partitions, and so on.

While trying to cut long dependences, we need to make sure the short dependences can continue to remain short, i.e., no short dependence is made long while the long ones are being reduced through a future automatic transformation algorithm. Consider separate affine transformations being applied to each half-space of some cutting hyperplane. If both ends of a short dependence lie on the same side of the hyperplane, the dependence continues to remain short because the same affine transformation is applied on it. If the ends lie on different sides, they both stay at a constant distance from where the dependence crosses the hyperplane. The crossing point thus has to be a fixed point for both affine transformations, and then the dependence will remain short. This provides the intuition that if the long dependences are all cut at their mid-points or at a fixed distance from their mid-points, the source and target iterations of the long dependences can be brought close with the new split index sets while keeping the original short dependences short. Note that it would be valid even if some long dependence instances, potentially belonging to the same dependence edge, are cut at their mid-points while others are cut close to it. We now propose a technique that automatically finds such a cut whenever possible.

The following approach is taken for each dimension along which there are long dependences in *both* directions, positive and negative—since this is what prevents tiling. Let $\vec{s}$ and $\vec{t}$ be the source and target iterations corresponding to a dependence edge e, characterized by dependence polyhedron D_e, that is long along a dimension. In order to cut all dependences within a bounded constant distance from their mid-points, the cutting hyperplane $\vec{h}$ has to satisfy the following:

$$-m \le (v(\vec{p}) - \vec{h} \cdot \vec{s}) - (\vec{h} \cdot \vec{t} - v(\vec{p})) \le m$$

for some $m \in \mathbb{Z}^+$ that we will minimize later. We thus have

$$2v(\vec{p}) - m \le \vec{h} \cdot \vec{s} + \vec{h} \cdot \vec{t} \le 2v(\vec{p}) + m, \quad \langle \vec{s}, \vec{t} \rangle \in D_e. \qquad (2)$$

Note that $\vec{h}$ is unknown while $\vec{s}$, $\vec{t}$ are related through the dependence polyhedron. The above can be linearized with the affine form of the Farkas lemma [28, 11], i.e., if $\vec{f_0}, \vec{f_1}, \ldots, \vec{f_m}$ are the faces of D_e, then there exist $\lambda_i \ge 0$ such that

$$2v(\vec{p}) + m - \vec{h} \cdot \vec{s} - \vec{h} \cdot \vec{t} \equiv \lambda_0 + \lambda_1 \vec{f_1} + \cdots + \lambda_m \vec{f_m} \qquad (3)$$

$$\vec{h} \cdot \vec{s} + \vec{h} \cdot \vec{t} - 2v(\vec{p}) + m \equiv \lambda'_0 + \lambda'_1 \vec{f_1} + \cdots + \lambda'_m \vec{f_m}. \qquad (4)$$

The coefficients of iterators in $\vec{s}$ and $\vec{t}$ from the LHS and RHS can be equated to obtain constraints linear in $\vec{h}$'s coefficients, $\vec{P}$'s coefficients, r, and m. The λ_is, also called Farkas multipliers, can be eliminated locally for each of the long dependences along that dimension, and the constraints aggregated. The constraints are now solved with *the objective to minimize m*. If a solution is found, a hyperplane orientation and position is obtained that cuts within a non-parametric or *constant* distance from the mid-points of all dependence instances in question, and we succeed in finding a split that in turn will allow distinct affine transformations on the split sets that shorten all of these dependences. m is that constant distance since it is free of program parameters ($\vec{p}$). $m = 0$ implies that all mid-points lie on $\vec{h}.\vec{i_S} = v(\vec{p})$. If a solution is not found, there exists no hyperplane that cuts all dependences at a bounded distance from their respective mid-points, and no index set splitting is applied for that dimension. This approach is repeated along all canonical dimensions along which dependences are long in both directions.

Figure 8 shows two other synthetic examples where the cut will lead to better transformations. In general, our technique is robust and resilient to variation in the boundary dependences, width and pattern of the stencils. This is because we minimize the upper bound on the distance of the mid-points of the dependences from the splitting hyperplane, m, as opposed to looking for solutions with $m = 0$. It thus clearly works for the entire domain of interest. Comments on its applicability beyond this domain are made towards the end of the next section.

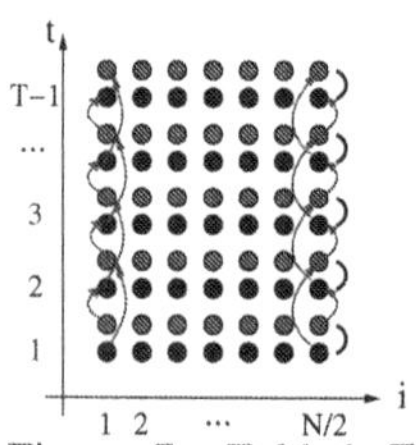

Figure 7: Folded periodic 1-d heat

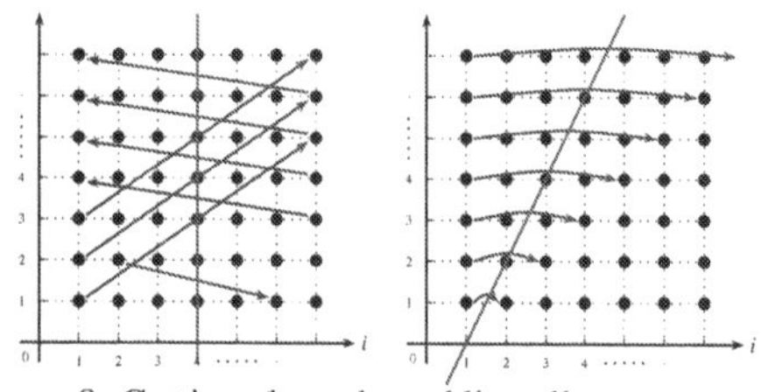

Figure 8: Cutting along the red line allows transformations shortening all dependences

As an example, for the periodic 1-d heat stencil from Figure 2, the split index sets are given by:

$$I_{S^+} = I_S \wedge \{2*i \geq N\} \qquad I_{S^-} = I_S \wedge \{2*i \leq N-1\}.$$

I_S is thus replaced with two statements, with index set I_{S^+} and I_{S^-}. We will show in Section 5 how profitable transformations can be applied automatically with the new statements.

4.3 Multi-statement stencils

In the case of multiple statements, long self-dependences could be hidden since they could be implied transitively through other inter-statement dependences which cannot themselves be classified as long or short. This is the case for stencils written with copies at the boundaries for every time step. If the approach described in the previous section is applied just for the intra-statement dependences in the case of multiple statements, it will not enable tiling even if it succeeds in finding a cut.

This problem can be addressed by computing transitive dependences with respect to a set of dependences. A full transitive closure is not needed: one may only compute transitive dependences for paths leading back to the same statement. Once this is done, the approach described in the previous sub-section is applied to determine the index set splitting. In the case of periodic stencils, such transitivity is over a path of length two. However, if the code is not written with copies but with conditionals (Figure 3b), the need for computing transitive dependences does not arise even with multiple statements. This is the case we encounter for all experimental evaluations.

5. POST-ISS SHORTENING AND TRANSFORMATIONS

In the previous section, we showed that index set splitting *opens the possibility* for dependences being shortened. We now argue that the Pluto framework, that shortens dependences, naturally finds the tiling transformation on the split index sets.

5.1 Pluto scheduling algorithm

We first provide some background on the Pluto scheduling algorithm. Consider a one-dimensional affine transformation for S:

$$\phi_S\left(\vec{i_S}\right) = (c_1 \ldots c_{m_S}) \cdot \left(\vec{i_S}\right) + (d_1 \ldots d_{m_p}) \cdot (\vec{p}) + c_0,$$
$$c_0, c_1, \ldots, c_{m_S}, d_1, \ldots, d_{m_p} \in \mathbb{Z}$$

where $\vec{i_S}$ is an iteration vector of S, m_S is the dimensionality of statement S, m_p is the number of program parameters, i.e., symbols appearing in the program (typically representing problem sizes), and $\vec{p}$ is the vector of those program parameters. Each statement has its own set of c_i and d_i coefficients: c_i correspond to the index set dimensions while d_i correspond to parameters and model parametric shifts. For convenience, the notation we use does not involve a superscript specific to S, i.e., c_i^S, d_i^S.

The Pluto algorithm [5] finds such one-dimensional affine transformations, iterating from the outermost inwards while looking for tilable bands, i.e., for ϕs satisfying

$$\phi_{S_j}(\vec{t}) - \phi_{S_i}(\vec{s}) \geq 0, \quad \langle \vec{s}, \vec{t} \rangle \in D_e. \tag{5}$$

The objective function it uses is that of reducing dependence distances using a parametric upper bounding function that was first proposed as a technique by Feautrier [11].

$$\vec{u} \cdot \vec{p} + w - \left(\phi_{S_j}(\vec{t}) - \phi_{S_i}(\vec{s})\right) \;\geq\; 0, \;\; \langle \vec{s}, \vec{t} \rangle \in D_e \tag{6}$$

$\vec{u}$ and w are then minimized, in order of decreasing priority, using the lexicographic minimum as

$$\text{lexmin}\left(\vec{u}, w, \ldots, c_i^{S_j}, d_i^{S_j}, \ldots\right). \tag{7}$$

5.2 Dependence shortening

Once an index set splitting is performed, the long dependence is still long since a new execution order has still not been specified. The split index sets obtain their schedules from the unsplit index set. For example, the long dependence in Figure 2 (code in Figure 3b that goes from the left boundary to the right one is given by:

$$t' = t + 1 \wedge i = 0 \wedge i' = N - 1 \wedge 0 \leq t \leq T - 3 \tag{8}$$

has the dependence distance along its two dimensions given by the vector $[1, N-1]^T$ and this is long along the second dimension as per the original execution order. We now show that the objective function (6) is well-suited to enable tiling for periodic stencils as well. Note that a solution that corresponds to $\vec{u} = \vec{0}$ is preferred over a solution with $\vec{u} \succ \vec{0}$ since the former would have a better objective function value as per (7). Importantly, $\vec{u} = \vec{0}$ corresponds to a transformation that *shortens all dependence distances* to a constant (due to (6)), the constant itself being given by w that is also minimized as part of (7). Hence, transformations that shorten

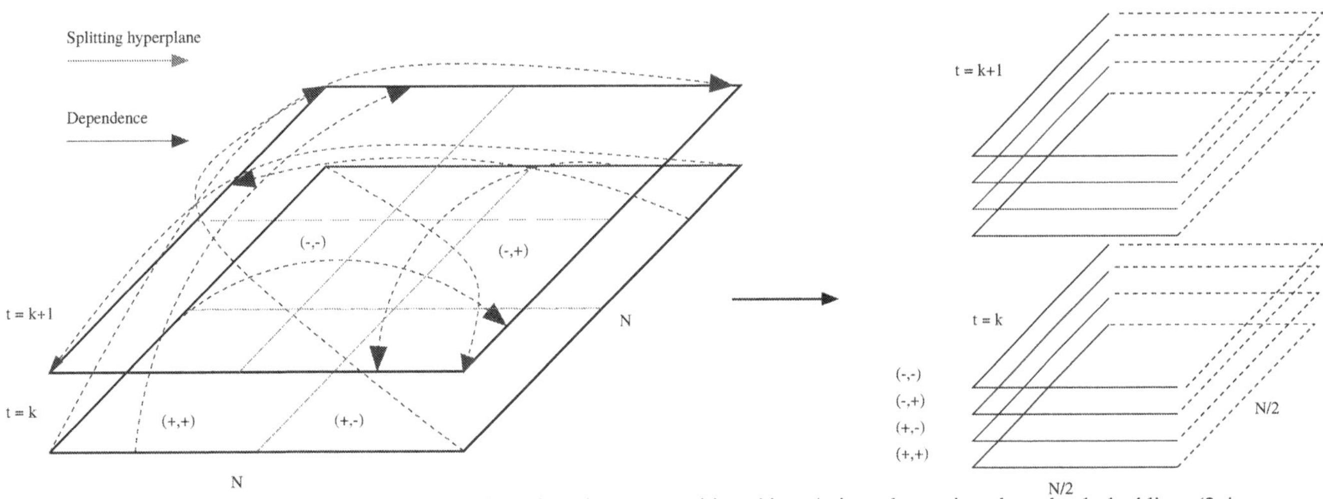

Figure 9: Index set splitting and piece-wise scheduling: iterations are partitioned into 4 pieces by cutting along the dashed lines (2 time steps shown); interleaving the pieces, (shown on the right) results in a space with short dependences only

all dependences to within a fixed constant, which would be w, have a better objective function value than those that do not.

For the dependence in (8), with index set splitting, $\vec{s} = (t,i)$ and $\vec{t} = (t',i')$ are placed into two different index sets, S^+ and S^-. Consider the following transformation on S^+ and S^-:

$$T_{I_S^+}(\vec{i_{S^+}}) = \begin{bmatrix} 1 & 1 \\ 1 & -1 \end{bmatrix} \begin{bmatrix} t \\ i \end{bmatrix} \quad (9)$$

$$T_{I_S^-}(\vec{i_{S^-}}) = \begin{bmatrix} 1 & -1 \\ 1 & 1 \end{bmatrix} \begin{bmatrix} t \\ i \end{bmatrix} + \begin{bmatrix} 1 \\ -1 \end{bmatrix} [N] \quad (10)$$

For S^-, the above can be seen as a composition of $(t,i) \rightarrow (t, N-i)$ with the diamond tiling transformation: $(t,i) \rightarrow (t+i, t-i)$, resulting in transformation $(t-i+N, t+i-N)$: this is the same as (10) written concisely. With the transformation in (9) (10), we get the new dependence distance for dependence (8) as:

$$T_{I_S^-}(\vec{t}) - T_{I_S^+}(\vec{s}) = \begin{bmatrix} (t+1)-(0+N-1)+N \\ (t+1)+(0+N-1)-N \end{bmatrix} - \begin{bmatrix} t+0 \\ t-0 \end{bmatrix} = \begin{bmatrix} 1 \\ 0 \end{bmatrix}$$

Hence, the dependence is made short along both dimensions by T: this is implied by $\vec{u} = \vec{0}$ at both levels. The other long dependence is also shortened similarly by this transformation. Though there are other transformations that also enable such a shortening, this transformation, in addition, also enables concurrent start leading to tiles of shape shown in Figure 4b [3]. However, as long as dependences can be shortened, one can exploit temporal locality along the time dimension and reduce frequency of synchronization with tiling. Thus, the objective is still well-suited for tiling periodic stencils. Another time tiling transformation that will lead to parallelogram tiles of shape in Figure 4a (still with $\vec{u} = 0$ at both levels) is:

$$T(S^+) = (t, t+i) \qquad T(S^-) = (t, t-i+N)$$

As can be viewed geometrically and as a direct fall-out of the index-set splitting proposed in Section 4.2, the transformations that allow shortening of dependences, once index sets have been split, include *reversals* as well as *negative* (backward) *parametric shifts*. In particular, for a 2-d grid in Figure 9, three of four stacked split sets have to be reversed and shifted backwards along one or two dimensions in order to be aligned as depicted. Consequently, negative coefficients are needed in the statement-wise affine transformation functions.

The Pluto algorithm [5] does not allow negative coefficients in its transformations. This is primarily due to the combinatorial difficulty in avoiding the trivial zero solution for ϕ's coefficients as well as in modeling the space of solutions representing linear independent sub-spaces [7]. This trade-off between expressiveness and computational complexity has worked well in practice for many affine loop nests in which reversals are not a prerequisite to enable efficient parallelization. For the important class of computations we consider here, this trade-off is a limitation: the required reversals are not part of the space of valid transformations. Other transformation algorithms like those of Feautrier [11, 12] also avoid negative values in their coefficients. Such algorithms are also designed to extract the maximal amount of fine-grained parallelism, by greedily satisfying dependences as early as possible. This design is incompatible with time tiling. This limitation in Pluto was recently addressed by Bondhugula and Cohen [6], thereby extending it to include transformations that allow reversal and negative parametric shifts in conjunction with other transformations. Since the objective function itself is untouched, index set splitting only enlarges the space of transformations with transformations that were originally in unsplit space still included.

Overall impact.

Note that our technique kicks in only when there are long dependences in both directions along a dimension. We make three observations here: (1) this is sufficient to deal with all stencils on periodic domains, (2) there is obviously no loss of good transformations in cases where the index set splitting does not succeed, and (3) all transformations that were valid on the unsplit index set are also naturally valid on the split index sets. We thus conclude that the approach has no detrimental impact on cases that lie outside the domain for which this technique has been developed. If our technique is applied even when there are long dependences in one direction, the index set splitting may still lead to better parallelization even though tiling was already valid. Evaluating this is out of the scope of this work and is left for future.

5.3 Complementary transformations

Vectorization is key to obtain good single thread performance for stencils [15, 16]. We rely on the native compiler to perform it. To this end, we only make sure that the generated code is preconditioned for good automatic vectorization.

Once dependences are shortened and the code tiled, one need not maintain the execution order implied within a tile, i.e., the split sets can be freely reordered within a tile even if it makes the dependences longer again. This is because the dependence would only be longer inside the tile, preserving the validity of the tiling. Such reordering is helpful for vectorization, prefetching, better cache capacity use within a tile, and register tiling.

Note that the split index sets all use different data for the most part except at the boundaries. Hence, we make the following changes to the schedule:

1. Reverse the reversed split index sets back so that we always have a positive stride. This helps vectorization as well as prefetching.

2. Separate out the split index sets at the tile level so that the entire cache capacity is used for each split index set independently, without interleaving. This ensures we do not artificially mix working sets, and that we keep tile sizes as large as possible. This also reduces cache conflicts and pollution among the split index sets.

Both of the above optimizations significantly improve single thread performance while preserving the benefits of tiling and parallel scaling.

6. EXPERIMENTS

	Intel Xeon E5645	*AMD Opteron 6136*
Microarch	Westmere-EP	Magny-Cours
Clock speed	2.4 GHz	2.4 GHz
Cores / socket	6	8
Total cores	12	16
L1 cache / core	32 KB	128 KB
L2 cache / core	512 KB	512 KB
L3 cache / socket	12 MB	12 MB
Peak GFLOPs	115.2	153.6
Compiler	icc/ifort 12.1.3	icc/ifort 12.1.3
Compiler flags	-O3 -fp-model precise	-O3 -fp-model precise
Linux kernel	2.6.32	2.6.35

Table 1: Details of architectures used for experiments

Benchmark	Problem size
heat-1dp	$1.6\text{x}10^6 \times 1000$
heat-2dp	$16000^2 \times 500$
heat-3dp	$300^3 \times 200$
swim	$1335^2 \times 800$

Table 2: Problem sizes for benchmarks (grid × time steps)

Techniques we described have been implemented into Pluto [22]. Experimental evaluation was performed on two different multi-way SMP multicore setups: an Intel Xeon SMP system and an Opteron SMP one. Table 1 lists their hardware specification. Intel's C, C++, and Fortran compilers version 12.1.3 were used for all experiments, including for compiling codes we automatically generated.

The SPEC CPU2000fp swim benchmark (171.swim) is a weather prediction application that performs finite difference modeling of shallow water equations. It involves periodic boundary conditions on a two dimensional grid. Given that swim is part of the SPEC benchmarks, performance of code generated by a production compiler like *icc* is expected to be highly competitive and a strong reference point. There is no hand-optimized time-tiled code available for swim from prior art. Compiler flags used with *ifort* were "-O3 -ipo". We experimented with other combinations and found these to be the best. Most scores reported on `spec.org` for swim also use these flags for both base and peak tuning configurations. The Pochoir domain-specific compiler could not be used to specify such computation as explained in the next section.

Besides swim, we use three other representative periodic stencil benchmarks, heat-1dp, heat-2dp, and heat-3dp, from the Pochoir suite [33]. Problem sizes used are provided in Table 2. For swim, the reference input that the benchmark is required to be reported with was used—it specifies a 2-d grid of size 1335×1335 with an outer time loop of 800 iterations. For the heat benchmarks, problem sizes used are from the Pochoir suite and are meaningful for the respective computations. Performance for all is compared with Intel's compiler as well as the Pochoir stencil compiler [33] (version 0.5) that is publicly available.

Choice of benchmarks and coverage.

We argue that these benchmarks indeed comprehensively cover the domain of interest. Firstly, all realistic grid dimensionalities are covered. Other variations in input in this domain could come from a different width for the stencil, i.e., a different number of neighbors. However, this only affects the skewing factor needed to perform the tiling. For example, in Figure 4b, the skewing factor is one. The structure of the code and all other transformations and their effects remain the same. In addition, we did not find using different problem sizes or a different computation for the actual point update providing any additional insights. All data sets are significantly larger than the L3 cache.

icc-par or *ifort-par* refers to code auto-parallelized with Intel's C or Fortran compiler respectively, using the '-parallel' flag in addition to the flags specified in Table 1, while *icc-seq* refers to the same without auto-parallelization. *poly-diamond* refers to code we generate that is time tiled using diamond tiling while *poly-pipeline* is tiled with parallelogram shaped tiles. *poly-pipeline* suffers from pipelined startup and drain and thus load imbalance, while diamond tiling allows concurrent startup enabling maximal parallelism; both enable reuse along the time dimension. The tile sizes for *poly-diamond* are set to maximize locality and single thread performance. However, those for *poly-pipeline* are set to guarantee a sufficient number of tiles on the wavefront in the steady-state of the pipeline to keep all processors busy.

Table 3 and Table 4 show the performance of different tiled versions, and compare them with pochoir and the native compiler's auto-parallelization. Table 11 shows scaling for heat-2d periodic on the AMD Opteron. Overall, a very big improvement is seen over *icc-par* as the latter is not expected to time tile such stencils. Lack of time tiling makes the code memory bandwidth-bound yielding no or limited speedup in spite of parallelization. Due to better locality from time tiling, *poly-diamond* code incurs less memory-bandwidth per core, and the improvement with it increases with the number of cores. In some cases, the scaling with *poly-diamond* is not close to ideal since all implementations tend to get memory-bandwidth-bound for a large number of cores. However, the improvement is still very significant. Improvements are higher for lower dimensional stencils than for higher ones as the spatial reuse is lower for the former.

Except in one case, an improvement of 6% to 4× is seen over the Pochoir stencil compiler that is able to tile in the presence of periodicity, though with a different tiling strategy. The mean (geometric) speedup over it on the Intel and Opteron systems is 1.42× and 1.5× respectively. These performance improvements over Pochoir are similar to those observed for non-periodic stencils by Bandishti et al. [3].

Benchmark	1 core				12 cores				Speedup over	
	icc-seq	pochoir	pipeline	diamond	icc-par	pochoir	pipeline	diamond	icc-par	pochoir
heat-1dp	4.50s	2.09s	4.41s	1.66s	0.583s	195ms	2.5s	162.4ms	26.50	1.20
heat-2dp	517.9s	304.1s	459s	305.8s	570s	26.7s	65.5s	25.1s	22.70	1.06
heat-3dp	39.17s	50.27s	41.3s	36.81s	38.19s	11.5s	10.78s	5.07s	7.53	2.26
swim	45.04s	-	34.05s	31.6s	20.4s	-	7.07s	4.07s	5.00	-

Table 3: Running times and speedup with *poly-diamond* on Intel Xeon multicore SMP

Benchmark	1 core				16 cores				Speedup over	
	icc-seq	pochoir	pipeline	diamond	icc-par	pochoir	pipeline	diamond	icc-par	pochoir
heat-1dp	7.16s	3.36s	5.69s	1.88s	9.25s	0.235s	0.789s	0.318s	29.10	0.74
heat-2dp	1424s	504.5s	632.6s	454.8s	1211s	38.47s	65.9s	32.37s	4.12	1.19
heat-3dp	88.5s	93.86s	51.1s	67.55s	38.19s	32.81s	15.95s	8.41s	4.54	3.90
swim	109s	-	59.08s	53.29s	28.00s	-	10.21s	6.61s	4.24	-

Table 4: Running times and speedup with *poly-diamond* on AMD Opteron multicore SMP

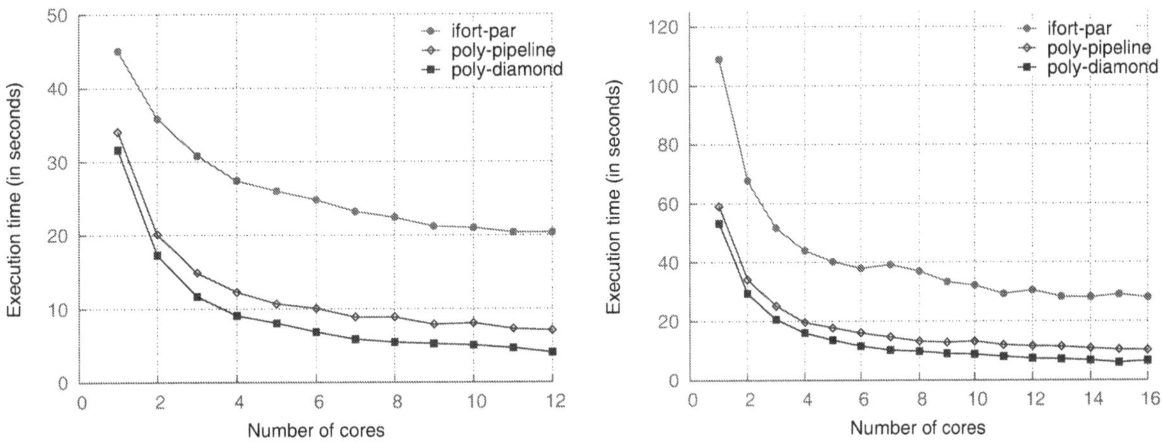

(a) on 2-way SMP Intel Xeon E5645 (12 cores)　　(b) 2-way SMP AMD Opteron (16 cores)

Figure 10: Performance on Swim benchmark from SPEC2000fp

Figures 10a and 10b show improvement on the full swim benchmark. Our approach splits the data domain into four partitions as shown in Figure 9 before applying reversal, shifts, and skewing transformations. Time tiling allows nearly ideal scaling in contrast to *ifort-par* which scales poorly even when the number of cores is low. This behavior has indeed been expected without techniques to exploit reuse along the time dimension. Table 5 supports the claim that improved locality leads to higher performance and better scaling. With inner space loop tiling and parallelization alone, the computation incurs significantly higher number of cache misses and is memory bandwidth-bound. Both *ifort-par* and *poly-diamond* utilize all cores as was reflected from the CPU utilization. *poly-pipeline* suffers from load imbalance due to a pipelined startup and drain phase.

Hardware event	Count (in billions)	
	ifort-par	poly-diamond
L2_RQSTS.LD_HIT	1.23	0.731
L2_RQSTS.LD_MISS	1.74	0.238
L2_RQSTS.LOADS	2.97	0.977
L2_RQSTS.MISS	5.73	0.635
L2 prefetch requests	4.15	0.400
L2 prefetch hits	0.63	0.070
L2 prefetch misses	3.52	0.322

Table 5: Performance counters comparing *ifort-par* with *poly-diamond* for swim on 12 cores on the Intel multicore

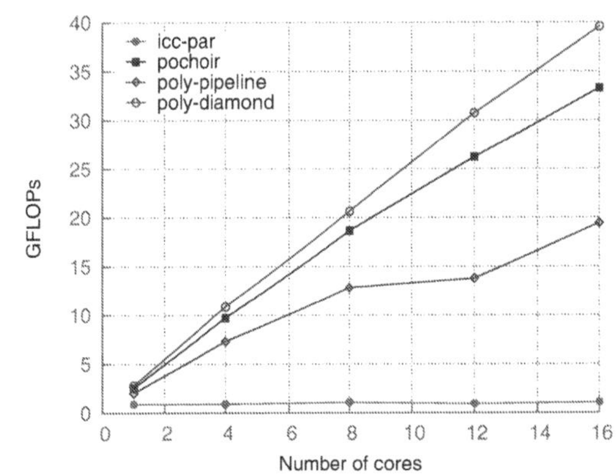

Figure 11: Periodic heat-2d scaling on the Opteron system

The running times of our generated diamond-tiled code for swim on the Intel system and the resulting SPEC rate of 761.67 that we achieve are also better than the highest ever publicly reported on `spec.org`—across all machines (as of 2013). A direct comparison with any of those numbers is however not possible since the machines for which the numbers were reported are different from ours.

Figure 12 shows that time-tiled code for the periodic case provides roughly the same performance as the non-periodic ones. Note that the amount of computation for both periodic and non-periodic,

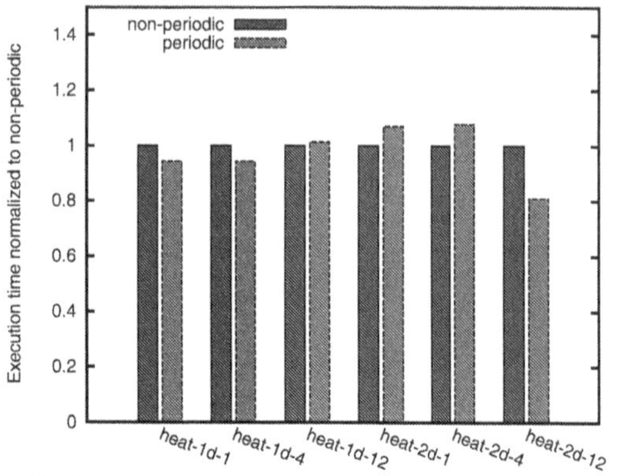

Figure 12: Non-periodic vs periodic stencil performance with time tiling (poly-diamond) on the Intel system (1, 4, 12 cores)

given a particular grid size and number of time iterations, is the same. In one case, surprisingly, the periodic version performs better than the non-periodic. This clearly shows that the non-periodic one could have been optimized better. In general, the periodic stencil code has a more complex structure and is expected to only perform at most as well as the non-periodic one. More optimizations in the polyhedral code generator Cloog could simplify it for better optimization by the native compiler. Overall, these interactions have not yet been studied fully, and this not being the main focus of this paper, are planned for future.

7. RELATED WORK

Recent stencil optimization works that include some domain-specific ones [10, 30, 31, 34, 16] and compiler-based ones [29, 39, 18, 7, 3] do not optimize those with periodic boundary conditions. The Pochoir [33] stencil compiler is the only one, to the best of our knowledge, that supports periodic conditions while applying the optimizations within the scope of this paper. Results indicate that Pochoir is able to perform time tiling via trapezoids regardless of the presence of periodic conditions, but the generated code is not as efficient as with our technique, as discussed in Section 6. We could not find a way to write multiple inter-related stencil computations with Pochoir, and hence the SPEC benchmark swim could not be expressed with it. However, ours being a general-purpose compiler approach driven by data dependences naturally handles such code. Of course, domain-specific optimization efforts have an opportunity to generate better code due to the greater amount of information they have about the problem, and our framework is suitable for integration into domain-specific stencil compilers.

Index-set splitting [14] and iteration space slicing [23] are transformations that partitions iteration domains into smaller sub-domains. This in turn allows different scheduling functions for different pieces of the program and results in more freedom. These seminal works focus on minimizing the dimensionality and latency of admissible schedules. In this work we exploit the degrees of freedom offered by index-set splitting as well as the expressiveness of linear transformations to reduce folding to an index-set splitting problem followed by a dependence shortening transformation problem.

Multiple tiling strategies have been devised to optimize stencil computations for shared and distributed memories. Originally, spatial decomposition through rectangular tiles is applied to the spatial dimensions. Spatial decomposition has the advantage of being simple to achieve but does not exhibit temporal reuse. The 171.swim SPEC CPU2000fp benchmark implements a well-known shallow water simulation model [32, 27]; an earlier version with a smaller data set was already included in the SPEC CPU1995fp suite. It lends itself well to spatial decomposition. However, spatial decomposition alone is not sufficient to reduce the memory-bandwidth consumption of the simulation model. As shown in an earlier work on semi-automatic loop nest optimization, the swim benchmark is amenable to loop fusion across one iteration of the time loop. Such polyhedral-enhanced fusion improves temporal locality and achieved 34% speedup on single-threaded execution [9, 13]. But despite much progress in production and research compilers since 1995, and despite the promises of a boost in the overall SPEC CPU score, time tiling remained inaccessible for the swim benchmark.

Time tiling was proposed to aggregate multiple time iterations and increase temporal reuse compared to tiling only in the data space [39]. Time tiling has roots in Lamport's hyperplane method [19] and is the most widely implemented technique within polyhedral transformation tools and compilers. Due to its reliance on loop skewing to extract parallel wavefronts of tiles, traditional time tiling suffered from two problems: (1) pipelined startup and shutdown phases in which some processors do not have work, and (2) load-imbalance due to insufficient number of tiles along each wavefront. For stencils implementing an explicit residual smoothing scheme such as Jacobi iterations, concurrent startup is possible [18] and results in asymptotically more parallelism than available with the traditional form of skewing-enabled time tiling. A successful tiling scheme which systematically exploits available parallelism is based on diamond tiling [3]. Our contribution builds on these insights, and extends them to stencils with periodic boundary conditions. This results in asymptotically more parallelism and locality on stencils with boundary conditions than was previously available [40].

Choffrut and Culik [8] perform folding on two-dimensional systolic arrays eliminating long wires for connections between elements that are related by reflections and/or rotations. [24] hints at using reflections to find piece-wise linear schedules as opposed to schedules for tiling: however, we found the approach proposed to determine splits itself to be incomplete and preliminary in its description, and very limited in its applicability. Yaacoby et al. [42] presents an algorithm on "uniformizing" dependences in affine recurrence equations in the context of systolic array synthesis through generalized folding. Though the method is unique because of its use of images of dependences and the characterization of affine recurrence equations which can be uniformized, its practical application and subsequent scalability is limited by its reliance on closures of dependence maps, eigenvalues and cycles in the dependence graph. Also, the formalism as described does not capture long dependences across boundaries—this is needed to derive folding for periodic stencils. Overall, our approach is inspired by folding, but, for the problem of tiling and parallelization for the domain of interest here, is more general and made possible by reasoning through index set splitting for dependence shortening. It is also far more robust and resilient to variations in dependence patterns, as argued towards the end of Section 4: it was made possible by minimizing the upper bound on the distance of the splitting hyperplane from the mid-points of long dependences. It thus subsumes reflections. Our approach can also seamlessly deal with any grid dimensionality as opposed to only up to two-dimensional as in the case of [8].

8. CONCLUSIONS

We introduced an automatic method to optimizing time-iterated computations on periodic domains. Our method relies on an original index set splitting scheme. The scheme allowed us to transparently apply tiling transformations with the existing objective function used in Pluto. Experimental results on the swim SPEC

CPU2000fp benchmark showed a speedup of nearly 5× over the highest performance achieved by a highly tuned commercial production compiler. We are not aware of any SPEC numbers for swim that come close to this result, obtained through either manual or automatic means. On other representative stencil computations, our scheme provides performance similar to that achieved with no periodicity. In addition, our technique always matches or outperforms—by up to 4×—a domain-specific stencil capable of handling periodicity in simpler cases. Our method is implemented in an open source research compiler and is available [22].

These results are not only interesting for computational sciences, but also excellent news for programming language and compiler designers. We conclude that it is practically infeasible to manually reproduce the optimizations we performed on swim or any other periodic stencil, especially on a two-dimensional or higher data grid. On the other hand, advanced tools can deal with this complexity, opening dimensions of program optimization that have so far been practically out of the reach of domain experts.

Acknowledgments.

This work was partially funded as part of the ARTEMIS COPCAMS project id. 332913, by the FP7 project CARP id. 287767, and by the INRIA-IISc PolyFlow associate team. We would like to thank P. Sadayappan and Tobias Grosser for their important role during the early stages of this work. We are also thankful to the reviewers of PACT 2014 for their detailed comments.

9. REFERENCES

[1] N. Ahmed, N. Mateev, and K. Pingali. Synthesizing transformations for locality enhancement of imperfectly-nested loops. *International Journal of Parallel Programming*, 29(5), Oct. 2001.

[2] A. V. Aho, R. Sethi, J. D. Ullman, and M. S. Lam. *Compilers: Principles, Techniques, and Tools Second Edition*. Prentice Hall, 2006.

[3] V. Bandishti, I. Pananilath, and U. Bondhugula. Tiling stencil computations to maximize parallelism. In *SC*, pages 40:1–40:11, 2012.

[4] U. K. Banerjee. *Loop Transformations for Restructuring Compilers: The Foundations*. Kluwer Academic Publishers, Norwell, MA, USA, 1993.

[5] U. Bondhugula, M. Baskaran, S. Krishnamoorthy, J. Ramanujam, A. Rountev, and P. Sadayappan. Automatic transformations for communication-minimized parallelization and locality optimization in the polyhedral model. In *ETAPS CC*, 2008.

[6] U. Bondhugula and A. Cohen. Handling negative coefficients in Pluto. Technical Report 1, Indian Institute of Science, Feb. 2014.

[7] U. Bondhugula, A. Hartono, J. Ramanujam, and P. Sadayappan. A practical automatic polyhedral parallelizer and locality optimizer. In *PLDI*, pages 101–113, 2008.

[8] C. Choffrut and K. Culik. Folding of the plane and the design of systolic arrays. *Information Processing Letters*, 17(3):149 - 153, 1983.

[9] A. Cohen, S. Girbal, D. Parello, M. Sigler, O. Temam, and N. Vasilache. Facilitating the search for compositions of program transformations. In *ACM ICS*, pages 151–160, June 2005.

[10] K. Datta, M. Murphy, V. Volkov, S. Williams, J. Carter, L. Oliker, D. A. Patterson, J. Shalf, and K. A. Yelick. Stencil computation optimization and auto-tuning on state-of-the-art multicore architectures. In *Supercomputing*, page 4, 2008.

[11] P. Feautrier. Some efficient solutions to the affine scheduling problem: Part I, one-dimensional time. *IJPP*, 21(5):313–348, 1992.

[12] P. Feautrier. Some efficient solutions to the affine scheduling problem: Part II, multidimensional time. *IJPP*, 21(6):389–420, 1992.

[13] S. Girbal, N. Vasilache, C. Bastoul, A. Cohen, D. Parello, M. Sigler, and O. Temam. Semi-automatic composition of loop transformations. *IJPP*, 34(3):261–317, June 2006.

[14] M. Griebl, P. Feautrier, and C. Lengauer. Index set splitting. *International Journal of Parallel Programming*, 28(6):607–631, 2000.

[15] T. Henretty, K. Stock, L.-N. Pouchet, F. Franchetti, J. Ramanujam, and P. Sadayappan. Data layout transformation for stencil computations on short simd architectures. In *ETAPS International Conference on Compiler Construction (CC'11)*, pages 225–245, Saarbrucken, Germany, Mar. 2011.

[16] T. Henretty, R. Veras, F. Franchetti, L.-N. Pouchet, J. Ramanujam, and P. Sadayappan. A stencil compiler for short-vector simd architectures. In *ACM ICS*, 2013.

[17] F. Irigoin and R. Triolet. Supernode partitioning. In *ACM SIGPLAN Principles of Programming Languages*, pages 319–329, 1988.

[18] S. Krishnamoorthy, M. Baskaran, U. Bondhugula, J. Ramanujam, A. Rountev, and P. Sadayappan. Effective Automatic Parallelization of Stencil Computations. In *ACM SIGPLAN PLDI*, July 2007.

[19] L. Lamport. The hyperplane method for an array computer. In *Proceedings of the Sagamore Computer Conference on Parallel Processing*, pages 113–131, London, UK, 1975. Springer-Verlag.

[20] A. Lim and M. S. Lam. Maximizing parallelism and minimizing synchronization with affine transforms. In *Proceedings of the 24th ACM SIGPLAN-SIGACT symposium on Principles of Programming Languages*, pages 201–214, 1997.

[21] N. Osheim, M. M. Strout, D. Rostron, and S. Rajopadhye. Smashing: Folding space to tile through time. In J. N. Amaral, editor, *LCPC*, pages 80–93. Springer-Verlag, 2008.

[22] PLUTO: A polyhedral automatic parallelizer and locality optimizer for multicores. http://pluto-compiler.sourceforge.net.

[23] W. Pugh and E. Rosser. Iteration space slicing and its application to communication optimization. In *International Conference on Supercomputing*, pages 221–228, 1997.

[24] S. Rajopadhye, L. Mui, and S. Kiaei. Piecewise linear schedules for recurrence equations. In *VLSI Signal Processing V, IEEE Press*, pages 375–384, Oct. 1992.

[25] J. Ramanujam and P. Sadayappan. Tiling multidimensional iteration spaces for multicomputers. *Journal of Parallel and Distributed Computing*, 16(2):108–230, 1992.

[26] D. A. Randall, T. D. Ringler, R. P. Heikes, P. Jones, and J. Baumgardner. Climate modeling with spherical geodesic grids. *Computing in Science and Engg.*, 4(5):32–41, Sept. 2002.

[27] R. Sadourny. The dynamics of finite-difference models of the shallow-water equations. *J. atm. sciences*, 32(4), Apr. 1975.

[28] A. Schrijver. *Theory of Linear and Integer Programming*. John Wiley & Sons, 1986.

[29] Y. Song and Z. Li. New tiling techniques to improve cache temporal locality. In *ACM SIGPLAN PLDI*, pages 215–228, 1999.

[30] R. Strzodka, M. Shaheen, D. Pajak, and H.-P. Seidel. Cache oblivious parallelograms in iterative stencil computations. In *ACM ICS*, pages 49–59, 2010.

[31] R. Strzodka, M. Shaheen, D. Pajak, and H.-P. Seidel. Cache accurate time skewing in iterative stencil computations. In *ICPP*, pages 571–581, 2011.

[32] P. N. Swarztrauber. 171.swim spec cpu2000 benchmark description file. Standard Performance Evaluation Corporation. `http://www.spec.org/cpu2000/CFP2000/171.swim/docs/171.swim.html`, 2000.

[33] Y. Tang, R. A. Chowdhury, B. C. Kuszmaul, C.-K. Luk, and C. E. Leiserson. The pochoir stencil compiler. In *SPAA*, pages 117–128, 2011.

[34] J. Treibig, G. Wellein, and G. Hager. Efficient multicore-aware parallelization strategies for iterative stencil computations. *Journal of Computational Science*, 2(2):130 – 137, 2011.

[35] S. Verdoolaege. isl: An integer set library for the polyhedral model. In K. Fukuda, J. Hoeven, M. Joswig, and N. Takayama, editors, *Mathematical Software - ICMS 2010*, volume 6327, pages 299–302. Springer, 2010.

[36] S. Verdoolaege. Integer Set Library, 2013. An integer set library for program analysis.

[37] M. Wolf. More iteration space tiling. In *Proceedings of Supercomputing '89*, pages 655–664, 1989.

[38] M. Wolfe. *High Performance Compilers for Parallel Computing*. Addison-Wesley Longman Publishing Co., Inc., 1995.

[39] D. Wonnacott. Using time skewing to eliminate idle time due to memory bandwidth and network limitations. In *IPDPS*, pages 171 –180, 2000.

[40] D. Wonnacott and M. Strout. On the scalability of loop tiling techniques. In *International workshop on Polyhedral compilation techniques*, 2013.

[41] J. Xue. *Loop tiling for parallelism*. Kluwer Academic Publishers, Norwell, MA, USA, 2000.

[42] Y. Yaacoby and P. R. Cappello. Converting affine recurrence equations to quasi-uniform recurrence equations. *VLSI Signal Processing*, 11(1-2):113–131, 1995.

ATCache: Reducing DRAM Cache Latency via a Small SRAM Tag Cache

Cheng-Chieh Huang
Institute of Computing Systems Architecture
University of Edinburgh
cheng-chieh.huang at ed.ac.uk

Vijay Nagarajan
Institute of Computing Systems Architecture
University of Edinburgh
vijay.nagarajan at ed.ac.uk

ABSTRACT

3D-stacking technology has enabled the option of embedding a large DRAM onto the processor. Prior works have proposed to use this as a DRAM cache. Because of its large size (a DRAM cache can be in the order of hundreds of megabytes), the total size of the tags associated with it can also be quite large (in the order of tens of megabytes). The large size of the tags has created a problem. Should we maintain the tags in the DRAM and pay the cost of a costly tag access in the critical path? Or should we maintain the tags in the faster SRAM by paying the area cost of a large SRAM for this purpose? Prior works have primarily chosen the former and proposed a variety of techniques for reducing the cost of a DRAM tag access.

In this paper, we first establish (with the help of a study) that maintaining the tags in SRAM, because of its smaller access latency, leads to overall better performance. Motivated by this study, we ask if it is possible to maintain tags in SRAM without incurring high area overhead. Our key idea is simple. We propose to cache the tags in a small SRAM tag cache – we show that there is enough spatial and temporal locality amongst tag accesses to merit this idea. We propose the ATCache which is a small SRAM tag cache. Similar to a conventional cache, the ATCache caches recently accessed tags to exploit temporal locality; it exploits spatial locality by prefetching tags from nearby cache sets. In order to avoid the high miss latency and cache pollution caused by excessive prefetching, we use a simple technique to throttle the number of sets prefetched. Our proposed ATCache (which consumes 0.4% of overall tag size) can satisfy over 60% of DRAM cache tag accesses on average.

Categories and Subject Descriptors

B.3.2 [**Hardware**]: Design Styles—Cache memories

Keywords

DRAM cache; Design; Performance

PACT'14, August 24–27, 2014, Edmonton, AB, Canada.

http://dx.doi.org/10.1145/2628071.2628089.

1. INTRODUCTION

3D-stacking technology has enabled the option of embedding a large DRAM onto the processor. Prior works [18] have proposed to use this as a DRAM cache. Because of its large size (a DRAM cache can be in the order of hundreds of megabytes), the total size of the tags associated with it can also be quite large (in the order of tens of megabytes).

The large size of the tags has created a classic space/time trade-off issue. On the one hand, we would like the latency of a tag access to be small as it would contribute to both hit latency and miss latency. Accordingly, we would like to store these tags in a faster media such as SRAM (*tags-in-SRAM*). However, with hundreds of megabytes of die-stacked DRAM cache, the space overhead of the tags would be huge. For example, it would cost around 12 MB of SRAM space to store all the tags of a 256MB DRAM cache (if we used conventional 64B blocks). Clearly this is too large, considering that some of the current chip multiprocessors have an L3 that is smaller [6].

In order to solve the above problem, Loh and Hill [10] proposed an approach for storing the tags within the DRAM itself (*tags-in-DRAM*). To make this approach practical, they proposed a scheme for embedding the tag and data in the same row buffer, which would enable both tag and data to be accessed in a single *compound access*. Compared to a naive scheme, performing a compound access optimizes the hit latency by obviating the need to reopen a row to access data as shown in Fig. 2 (saving on $tACT$, the time to activate a row). However, it does not optimize the miss latency, since only the tag is accessed on a miss. To reduce the miss penalty, Loh and Hill also proposed a technique for tracking the contents of the DRAM cache in a structure called the *MissMap*. This enables them to avoid a DRAM tag access for misses, with only a few megabytes of SRAM overhead. Subsequently other works [14, 15] proposed miss predictors to achieve the same effect as a MissMap, but with significantly lesser SRAM overhead (in the order of a few kilobytes).

The impracticality of tags-in-SRAM, has led to the above tags-in-DRAM proposals. But how does the performance of recently proposed tags-in-DRAM techniques compare with tags-in-SRAM? We conduct a study to measure the average DRAM access latency for different configurations of DRAM cache, as shown in Fig. 1. Here, tags-in-SRAM refers to a scheme in which tags of all blocks in the DRAM are stored in the SRAM; tags-in-DRAM refers to a scheme that uses Loh and Hill's compound access; MissPred refers to the above, augmented with an oracle miss predictor (100% accuracy

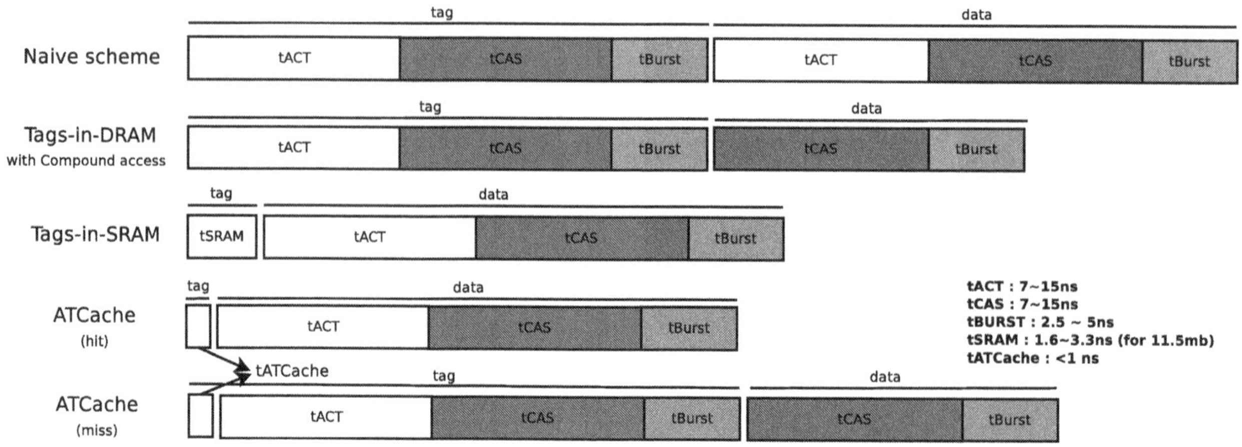

Figure 2: Access latency of different types of DRAM cache.

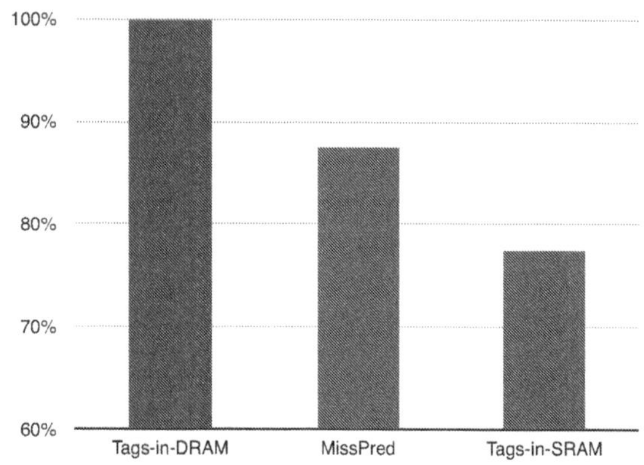

Figure 1: Average latency of the DRAM cache (including main memory access latency). The architectural parameters and workloads are shown in Table 5.

and zero latency). For this study, we use an SRAM access latency of 6 cycles which we modeled using CACTI (32nm, itrs-hp cell); further, we use 7ns for tACT and tCAS and 2.5ns for tBURST for stacked DRAM (other architectural parameters used in this study are shown in Table 5). All results are normalized to the access latency of tags-in-DRAM. As we can see, using the tags-in-SRAM configuration results in a 23.7% reduction in DRAM cache access latency. Furthermore, this latency is 10.2% lesser than MissPred (which is an oracle miss predictor with zero access latency).

Given that there is a significant gap in performance between tags-in-SRAM and tags-in-DRAM, we want to benefit from the tags-in-SRAM approach, but without incurring the cost of a high SRAM overhead. Our key idea is to maintain the tags in the DRAM cache, *but also cache a small amount of tags in SRAM in a dedicated cache.* We call this the *Aggressive Tag Cache (ATCache)*, as we will later show that we can achieve very good performance with a small tag cache. In addition to this, having a small cache is beneficial as this means that the ATCache can be accessed faster than a larger tags-in-SRAM design.

Like a conventional cache, ATCache exploits temporal locality by only caching the tags of recently accessed DRAM cache sets. In a similar vein, it exploits spatial locality by prefetching the tags of adjacent DRAM cache sets. One potential problem is to know how many sets' tags to prefetch, as prefetching too much can lead to cache pollution and also increased miss penalty. To deal with this, we propose a scheme in which we prefetch tags of the adjacent sets only if there is evidence of spatial locality amongst the sets.

We evaluate our approach on the gem5 cycle-accurate simulator [1]. On memory-intensive single-threaded SPEC 2006 benchmarks, our ATCache can achieve 10.3% performance improvement on average compared to a tags-in-DRAM (with compound access) baseline. This compares favorably with the speedup of 6.8% provided by adding a high-accuracy miss predictor (MAP-I) to tags-in-DRAM. Our ATCache can also be integrated with miss predictors. Indeed, on multiprogrammed workloads, our ATCache is 9.3% faster than the tags-in-DRAM baseline, but 10.9% faster when we integrate a miss predictor (MAP-I) to ATCache. Finally, our results are almost as good as a full tags-in-SRAM cache, which provides a performance improvement of 11.9%. Our ATCache only uses 47.375kB space (including the overheads) and around 50kB if we include the MAP-I as part of our design. Therefore, the overall SRAM space consumed is only around 0.5% of a tags-in-SRAM design.

2. BACKGROUND

2.1 DRAM cache

Reducing the latency of tag accesses is fundamental to cache design, as this latency would be added to critical path of the total latency, no matter a hit or miss. Prior works [9, 10, 18] have proposed to use stacked DRAM as a large cache inside the processor chip. By exploiting the high density of stacked DRAM, we are able to have multiple hundreds of megabytes of on-chip DRAM cache. Ideally, we want to architect this large cache with same cache block size as conventional L1 or L2 (which typically use a block size of 32/64 bytes). Consequently, with multiple hundreds of megabytes of DRAM cache, the overhead of storing tags of conventional blocks requires tens of megabytes [3, 9, 10]. In this case, it would be impossible to naively use SRAM (which provides faster access latency at the cost of low density) as storage media.

Table 1: Tag sizes/latencies for different cache sizes.

Cache size	128MB	256MB	512MB	1024MB
Tag size (per block)	24 bits	23 bits	22 bits	21 bits
Total tag size	6MB	11.5MB	22MB	42MB
Latency/hp (cycles)	5	6	7	8
Latency/lstp (cycles)	9	10	12	13

Page-based DRAM cache: A page-based cache (i.e. a much larger cache block size of 2kB to 4kB) has been proposed in several works [8, 9]. With a larger block size, the tag overhead is reduced to hundreds of kilobytes or few megabytes depending on the cache size. With this cache design, there are two major challenges that prior works have addressed. First, a larger cache line size means more data to fetch on a miss. Generally, a DRAM cache miss needs to fetch data from a low-bandwidth off-chip memory. This downside becomes one of the performance bottlenecks of a page-based design. Second, a larger cache line might fetch a significant amount of unused data to the cache. This decreases the effective capacity of the DRAM cache compared to a conventional block size design. To solve the bandwidth problem, Jevdjic et al. [8] proposed a footprint cache which removes the unused blocks from the (page-based) cache line and shows an effective reduction in bandwidth. Their design enables paged-based DRAM cache to outperform block-based caches (tags-in-DRAM, with MissMap) in server workloads [5]. However, in their study, desktop workloads (SPEC 2006) shows about 25% of slow down compared to block-based DRAM cache (with MissMap, 256MB). This is because the spatial footprint in desktop workloads is generally lower than server workloads like web search.

Block-based DRAM cache: Loh and Hill [10, 11] proposed a DRAM cache with conventional block size (64 bytes). In their work, they embedded tags along with their data in the same row buffer (tags-in-DRAM). They architect a 29-way DRAM cache with a 2kB row buffer (29 tags and 29 blocks). One issue with this design is that DRAM cache misses have to pay the high cost of accessing the tags from the DRAM; consequently they also proposed a MissMap, which is a SRAM structure which tracks the contents of DRAM cache in order to skip miss accesses. Since MissMap consumes a reasonably large amount of SRAM (in the order of few megabytes) to maintain the required information, subsequent works [14, 15] proposed miss predictors to predict cache misses with a lower SRAM overhead (in the order of few kilobytes). Subsequently, Qureshi and Loh [14] pointed out that instead of a sequential access of the data and tag, one could use a wider data width (72 bytes) to read tag and data in parallel. In this design, the hit latency of a direct-mapped DRAM cache is close to the latency of accessing only the data. Whereas this approach works great for direct-mapped caches, the downside of this design, however, is its inflexibility in scaling to set associate caches. To support a 4-way cache, for example, every access requires additional 3 tBURSTs for reading 3 more blocks from DRAM cache; assuming a 2.5 ns tBURST for reading a 72-byte block, the additional latency overhead of supporting a 4-way cache is 23 cycles for a 3 GHz processor.

2.2 Tag size and access latency

In this section, we show how we measure the tag sizes of different DRAM cache configurations and also their latencies. Generally, a *tag* for a block refers to several SRAM bits of storage to accommodate not only the tag for that cache block, but also status bits (dirty/valid and cache coherence states) and state associated with the replacement policy. In our system model, the DRAM cache is located a level below the cache coherent shared cache. The minimum requirement of the status register is 2 bits (valid and dirty bits). The number of tag bits depends on processor's addressing capability and the associativity of cache. For a processor with 40-bit address space and 64-byte cache line, a 256MB/16-way cache requires 17 bits for the tag. Let us assume the state associated with the replacement policy requires 4 bits. The overall space requirement for each cache block then is 23 bits, which amounts to around 11.5 MB in total.

We model the latency of tag access using CACTI 6.5 [13]. Specifically, we use 32nm technology and two types of SRAM cell (itrs-hp and itrs-lstp, which represent high performance configuration and low standby power configuration respectively). We report tag latencies for a 3GHz processor cycle. The results are shown in Table 1. As we can see, it shows that even with a low standby power cell, a 11.5MB SRAM tag access (10 processor cycles) can still be faster than minimum tBURST latency (which is about 4 memory cycles which is about 5ns or 15 processor cycles) in DDR3-1600 in DRAM. Substituting the values for tag latencies computed above, it is clear (as shown in Fig. 2) that tags-in-SRAM can provide both better hit (tag + data) and miss (tag) latency than tags-in-DRAM with compound access. In this paper, we will use the above modeled parameters in Table 1 for the tags-in-SRAM approach.

3. OUR METHODOLOGY AND DESIGN

As our study in Fig. 1 shows, a tags-in-SRAM design provides an opportunity to improve both hit and miss latency. The SRAM overhead, however, is a major impediment that limits its practicality. In this paper, we propose a hybrid method in which we maintain full tags in DRAM like Loh and Hill's work [10] but also cache a small number of tags in our proposed cache structure called *ATCache*. To put it simply, similar to a conventional cache which *caches data from memory*, our ATCache *caches the tags of the DRAM cache.*

3.1 Terminology

Before describing our approach, we first define several terminologies that can help explain our design.

SetTag: A SetTag refers to the set of tags of the blocks which belong to the same cache set of a DRAM cache. For example, if the DRAM cache is 16-way associative, then SetTag refers to all the 16 tags in each set. It is worth noting that all 16 tags are necessary to check for a hit or miss in DRAM cache, which is why they are cached together in the ATCache. In other words, a SetTag of an ATCache is analogous to a word of a conventional cache.

SetID: A SetID is an identifier for ATCache to identify if the SetTag for the correct set exists in the ATCache. In other words, a SetID of an ATCache is analogous to a tag of a conventional cache.

Caching ratio: The Caching ratio of an AT cache is the ratio of the size of the ATCache to the total size of the tags required by the DRAM cache. For example, a 256MB/16-way DRAM cache requires 11.5 MB for tags. A caching ratio of 256 corresponds to an ATCache of size 46KB.

Prefetching granularity (PG): In a conventional cache, whenever a word is accessed we also (pre)fetch additional adjacent words belonging to a block to exploit spatial locality. In a similar vein, the prefetching granularity (PG) refers to the number of adjacent SetTags that the ATCache will fetch on a miss. In other words, the PG of an ATCache is analogous to a block size of a conventional cache.

3.2 Locality of tag accesses

The idea of caching is founded on the principles of spatial and temporal locality, which a conventional cache exploits. In this section, we want to examine if spatial and temporal locality exists for tag data accesses also. To this end, we conduct a quick study in which we use a 46kB ATCache (1/256 of total tag size) to store recently accessed tags. Because tags of the same cache set would be accessed together, we store these tags in units of a DRAM cache set (and call it SetTag). In addition to this, to exploit spatial locality we fetch the SetTag of adjacent sets on an ATCache miss; we use the term *prefetching granularity* (PG) to refer to the number of adjacent cache sets that the ATCache will fetch on a miss.

Fig. 3 shows the average miss ratio of the ATCache for different PGs across all single-thread benchmarks that we studied (§ 4) in SPEC 2006. From the figure, the miss ratio of PG/2 is around 63.4%. This means that more than 30% of the tag accesses can be satisfied (hit) by our ATCache for a PG of 2, which is significantly better than a uniformly distributed hit ratio (1/256 $\simeq$ 0.4%). Furthermore, as the PG is increased from 2 through 64, the miss ratio decreases from 63.4% to 20.5%. These all indicate the existence of locality amongst tag accesses.

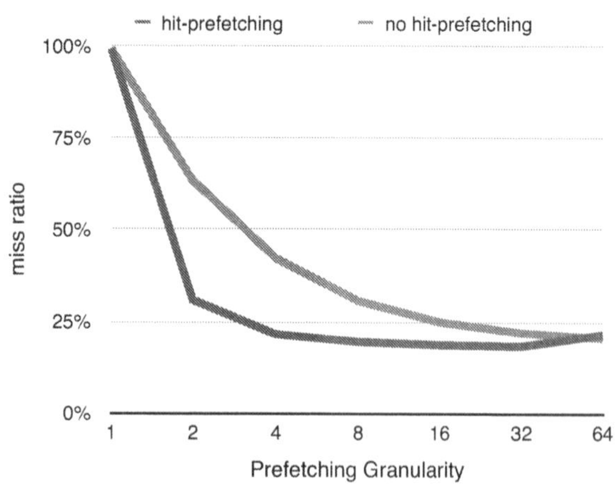

Figure 3: Miss ratio with various PG.

3.3 Hit prefetching

In our prior study, we found that the prefetching granularity (PG) is critical to the performance of ATCache. Prefetching nearby SetTags to the ATCache, generally speaking, is beneficial to miss ratio; however, a large PG can possibly pollute the ATCache which could result in a miss ratio increase, in addition to increasing miss-penalty. We provide a simple solution to achieve a balance between spatial locality, cache pollution, and miss-penalty. We start by fetching the SetTag for a relatively small number of cache sets (say PG/4). Corresponding to the SetTag of each fetched cache set, we maintain a flag that tracks whether or not the SetTag of the current cache set is accessed. Even if one of the prefetched SetTags is actually accessed, we prefetch the SetTags of the next contiguous 4 cache sets – in doing so, we achieve the effect of a larger PG. In case none of the prefetched SetTags are accessed, we do not prefetch any additional SetTags – in doing so, we avoid paying the space and time costs of a larger PG when a larger PG is not beneficial. It is worth noting that the space overhead of this technique is very small. It only requires *one additional bit* in the ATCache's SetID. We conducted a simple experiment to estimate the benefit of hit prefetching; as shown in Fig. 3, we find that with hit prefetching the miss ratio of PG/4 (21.5%) is able to match the miss ratio of PG/32 (22%) without hit prefetching. Since hit prefetching provides a significant benefit, we include it in our baseline system.

3.4 Size, hit ratio and latency

Another important factor to consider in cache design is the interplay between size and the access latency. In most cases, a larger cache size can provide a better hit ratio, but would also mean a higher access latency. In this section, we want to study how the cache capacity affects the ATCache's hit ratio and its latency. Fig. 4 shows the hit ratio for different caching ratios. For this experiment, we use PG/4 with hit prefetching turned on. As we can see, the miss ratio degrades gracefully as the caching ratio is increased. Even with an ATCache size of 11.2KB (caching ratio of 1024), the ATCache can still satisfy over 50% of tag accesses. On the other hand, an ATCache of only 11.2KB will enable it to have a faster access latency of close to 1 cycle in comparison to about 6 cycles for a full tags-in-SRAM design (the latency values are computed using CACTI as discussed earlier in the background section). The reduced tag access latency contributes to better DRAM cache performance as illustrated in Fig. 2.

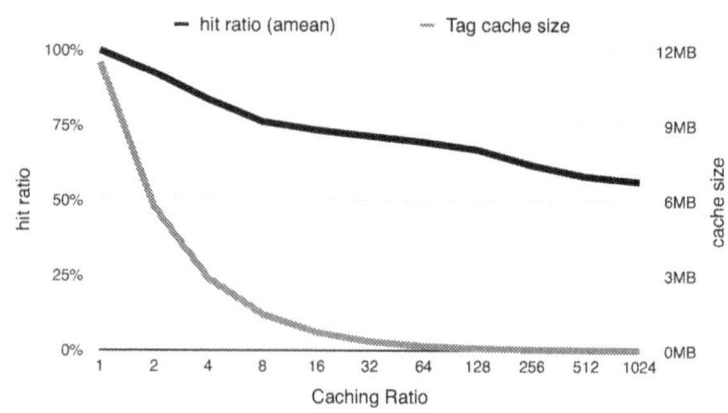

Figure 4: Hit ratio, size for different caching ratios.

3.5 Integration with miss predictor

Prior works have proposed miss predictors [10, 14, 15] which help to improve the performance of a tags-in-DRAM design by reducing the miss penalty. More specifically, they help avoid a DRAM tag access for (what is predicted to be) a DRAM cache miss. Although the latency to access a tag in our design is not as high as the tags-in-DRAM design (since the tags are now stored in the ATCache which is in the SRAM), we can still benefit from a miss predictor. In addition to this, because miss accesses can be handled by the high accuracy predictor, they can skip the ATCache. This means that the ATCache does not need to store the tags corresponding to misses anymore, which in turn increases the effective cache capacity of the ATCache. Therefore, we implement two predictors proposed in prior works – HMP [15] and MAP-I [14]. In our study, we found that both predictors can provides a very high prediction accuracy (Fig.5) with very small space overhead as prior works have observed. In our design we choose to integrate with MAP-I as it provides marginally better predictability.

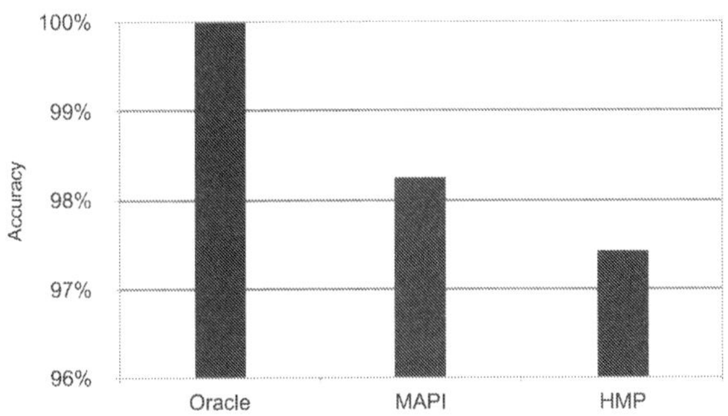

Figure 5: Accuracy of prior proposed predictors.

3.6 Design of ATCache

The design of our ATCache follows the design principles of a conventional cache: the full tags in the DRAM array represents the "main memory" and tags in the ATCache represents the "cached data". The procedure to access the ATCache is illustrated in Table 2 and the access logic is shown in Fig. 6. As we can see, the ATCache requires an additional SetID checking (Step 2A) – which is similar to a tag check for a conventional cache. Now, this represents an additional check compared to a conventional full tags-in-SRAM design. However, it is worth noting that this (step 2A) can be overlapped with step 2B (which is the tag check for DRAM cache). Therefore, the ATCache does not need additional access cycles for an ATCache hit in comparison to a full tags-in-SRAM design.

However, on an ATCache miss, the tags in DRAM have to be accessed and fetched back into the ATCache. So miss processing for ATCache is comparable to a tags-in-DRAM cache, with one small difference. Since step 2A is still required to identify if ATCache contains the correct SetTag, we incur one cycle penalty (step 2A is assumed to take one cycle) to the total access latency when there is an ATCache miss.

3.7 Putting it all together

We illustrate how the ATCache works with a spatial predictor and a miss predictor (MAP-I), with the help of an example (Table 3). This example consists of 5 consecutive DRAM cache accesses and each of them is accessing different cache sets (#sets). In the 1st access, the outcome of MAP-I is a hit which means DRAM cache might contain this data. Then, the system accesses the ATCache but it

Table 2: ATCache access procedure (refer to Fig. 6).

Steps	Description
Step 1	Locate SetID and SetTag in ATCache by a subset of #cache_set (#sub_cache_sets).
Step 2A	Check SetID to determine if ATCache set contains SetTag.
Step 2B	Check SetTag to determine if DRAM cache contains requested data (DRAM cache hit/miss).
Step 3	If step 2A is hit, use step 2B's result to determine hit/miss in DRAM cache. Otherwise, issue compound access to DRAM cache.

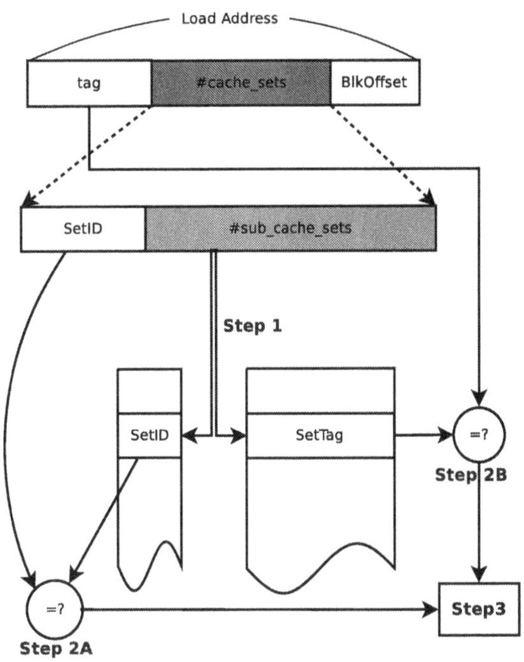

Figure 6: The access logic (also refer to Table 2).

does not contain the corresponding SetTag. Therefore, similar to the tags-in-DRAM approach, an ATCache issues a DRAM compound access for tag and data. The ATCache will also fetch the adjacent cache sets after the compound access. Later, we can see these prefetched adjacent cache sets are accessed in the 3rd access. It is worth noting that a hit prefetching event (§3.3) also is generated in the 3rd access. In the 2nd access, we show a situation in which MAP-I is predicting the access as a miss. In this case, system will skip the access of DRAM cache because of the prediction result and directly fetch data from main memory. In the 4th access, a prefetched set (set 3) is accessed but the sets 4-8 is already brought back by the 3rd access. Therefore, there is no additional access required for our design. Finally, the 5th access is a MAP-I hit and an ATCache miss. Similar to 1st access, the system will issue a compound access and fetch adjacent sets.

3.8 Area overhead

In this paper, we use an ATCache with a caching ratio of 256. In other words, we use a 46kB cache for caching total tags amounting to 11.5MB (256MB/16-way DRAM cache).

Table 3: **Example showing 5 DRAM cache accesses.**

#access	#set	MAP-I	ATCache	description
1	0x1	hit	miss	DRAM compound access and prefetch set 0,2,3 due to prefetching granularity (PG)
2	0x53	miss	X	predicted miss from MAP-I, skip the access
3	0x2	hit	hit	prefetch set 4-8 (hit prefetching)
4	0x3	hit	hit	access data in DRAM cache
5	0x10	hit	miss	DRAM compound access and prefetch set 0x11,0x12,0x13 (same as 1st access)

As shown in Fig. 6, the additional overhead of a ATCache is a bunch of SetIDs. The size for each SetID actually depends on caching ratio and the associativity of the ATCache. Each ATCache block with caching ratio of 256 and associativity of 4 needs $8 + 2$ bits for storing SetID. In addition to SetID, to implement hit prefetching (§3.3, 1 bit per set), the overhead of SetID for each ATCache block slightly increases to 11 bits. In a 256MB/16-way cache, there are 256k cache sets. An ATCache with a caching ratio of 256 would cache only 1k ($256k/256$) sets. Therefore, the overhead of ATCache is around 1.375kB ($11 * 1024/8$ bytes). In total, the ATCache requires about 48kB SRAM space which is less than 0.5% SRAM space compared to tags-in-SRAM's 11.5MB. Table 4 shows the overhead for different cache sizes.

Table 4: Overhead for different cache sizes.

Cache Size	128MB	256MB	512MB	1024MB
Total tag size	6MB	11.5MB	22MB	42MB
ATCache space	24kB	46kB	88kB	168kB
ATCache overhead	704B	1.375kB	2.75kB	5.5kB

4. EXPERIMENTAL METHODOLOGY

4.1 Baseline system

We use the gem5 cycle-accurate simulator [1] in which we consider the L3 to be the DRAM cache; accordingly, we implement the DRAM timing model for the L3. The system parameters that we used are shown in Fig. 5. We show single-threaded results for 11 benchmarks from SPEC 2006 which are considered to be memory-intensive in prior works [14, 15]. In addition to single-threaded benchmarks, we also use the same 11 benchmarks to generate 25 multi-programmed workloads (4-core, as shown in Table 6) and evaluate their performance.

4.2 DRAM cache organizations

In this paper, we evaluate the following DRAM cache designs:

Baseline (Tags-in-DRAM): The DRAM cache design we used as baseline follows Loh an Hill's work [10]. The SetTag and their data are stored in the same row. With compound scheduling, a delay of opening a row (≃ tRCD) can be saved compared to storing them in separate rows. Our baseline

Table 5: System parameters

Processor	3GHz, 4-core, 4-issue OoO, 64 ROB
L1 I/D caches	each 32kB/2way, LRU, 2-cycle, private
L2 cache	4MB/8way, 9-cycle, LRU, shared
Stacked DRAM	256MB, 2-bit SRRIP [7] tRCD-tCAS-tRAS 7-7-25 (ns) tBURST: 2.5ns 16 banks per rank, 1 rank per channel, 4 channel 4kB row buffer, open-page policy
Off-chip DRAM	800MHz (DDR3-1600), x64 interface tRCD-tCAS-tRAS 13.5-13.5-40.5 (ns) tBURST: 5ns 8 banks per rank, 2 ranks per channel, 1 channel 8kB row buffer, open-page policy
On-chip bus	3GHz, 256-bit width
System Bus	1.5GHz, 64-bit width
Miss Predictor	MAP-I [14], 256 entries, 1-cycle latency
ATCache	Caching Ratio:256 (47.375kB incl. overhead) 4-way, 2-cycle latency, hit prefetching
Benchmarks	milc, soplex, omnetpp, gcc, leslie3d, GemsFDTD astar, mcf, bwaves, lbm, libquantum

Table 6: Workload groupings

1-2	soplex-astar-lbm-mcf	lbm-omnetpp-leslie3d-bwaves
3-4	milc-leslie3d-leslie3d-gcc	milc-libquantum-bwaves-gcc
5-6	libquantum-lbm-soplex-libquantum	libquantum-GemsFDTD-soplex-milc
7-8	gcc-milc-libquantum-astar	milc-soplex-bwaves-libquantum
9-10	leslie3d-omnetpp-leslie3d-mcf	lbm-astar-leslie3d-libquantum
11-12	leslie3d-leslie3d-libquantum-milc	mcf-gcc-milc-astar
13-14	omnetpp-libquantum-milc-soplex	gcc-libquantum-libquantum-soplex
15-16	soplex-GemsFDTD-omnetpp-milc	milc-soplex-leslie3d-libquantum
17-18	lbm-libquantum-omnetpp-bwaves	gcc-milc-leslie3d-milc
19-20	omnetpp-omnetpp-libquantum-leslie3d	soplex-mcf-gcc-libquantum
21-22	astar-omnetpp-astar-gcc	mcf-soplex-astar-leslie3d
23-24	bwaves-lbm-libquantum-leslie3d	astar-leslie3d-lbm-mcf
25	bwaves-soplex-bwaves-GemsFDTD	

system uses a 4kB row buffer which is close to a realistic DRAM organization (1kB per device, 4 devices per rank). In our system, a 4kB row buffer can store 4 15-way cache sets (4 x 15 x 64 bytes) and 4 SetTags (4 x 45 bytes). We use an open page policy to manage DRAM banks because we found open page policy gives better performance for our baseline.

NoDRAM (No DRAM cache): In this setting, we remove the DRAM cache from our cache hierarchy. The purpose of this setting is to examine if our system has any performance benefit from the DRAM cache in the first place.

MAP-I: As mentioned in §3.5, we use a MAP-I predictor for predicting misses. We implement a MAP-I predictor with 256 memory access counter (MAC) entries as suggested in prior work [14].

SRAM (Tags-in-SRAM) We use a tags-in-SRAM design which requires 11.5MB (§2.2) SRAM space to store all tags for 256MB DRAM cache. The access latency of the SRAM array is 6 cycles (high performance cell) as we modeled in §2.2. It is worth noting that the high SRAM overhead makes this design impractical.

ATCache: In our proposed design, we use an ATCache with *caching ratio of 256, prefetching granularity (PG) of 4, and associativity of 4*. This means we use $11.5MB/256 =$ 46 kB SRAM tag with 1.375kB overhead. We assume a single cycle latency to identify if the ATCache contains a correct cache set (step 2A in §3.6). A single cycle latency is reasonable considering that the SetID array is only 1.375kB in our design. Since the SRAM array for the ATCache is only

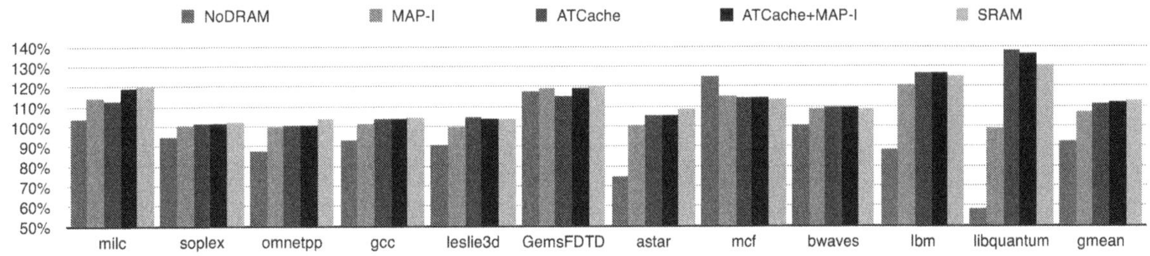

Figure 7: Performance speedup.

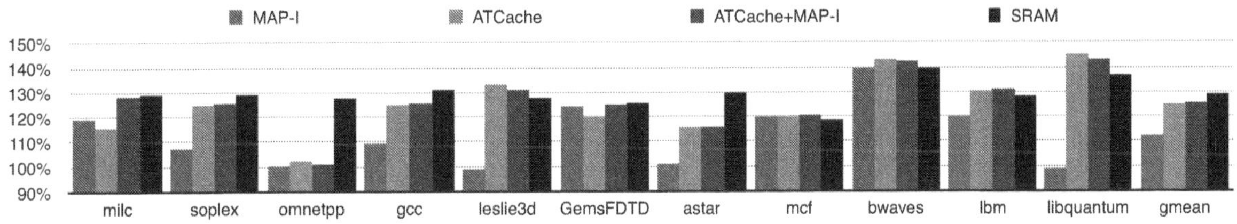

Figure 8: L2 miss latency reduction (higher the better).

46 kB and step 2A and step 2B in §3.6 can be overlapped, we use a 2 cycles for the ATCache hit latency. For a miss in the ATCache, we add a *a 1 cycle lookup latency* (Step 2A) to the total access latency. It is worth noting that similar to miss-predictors in prior works [14], the *ATCache does not cache SetTags for DRAM cache writes.* This is because such writes are not in the critical path of the performance. In summary, in this design we use less than 0.5% of the SRAM space used by tags-in-SRAM.

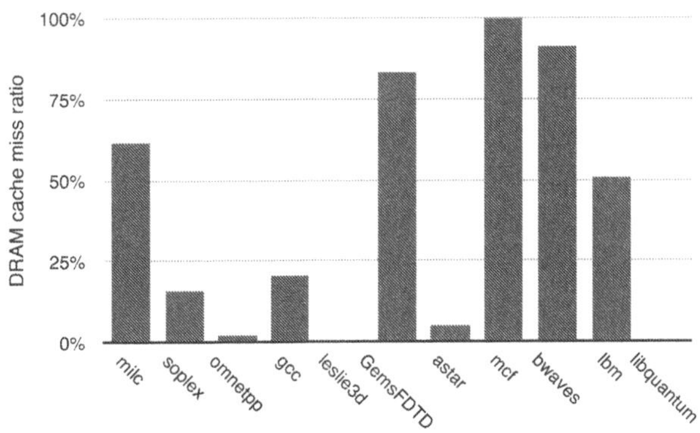

Figure 9: L3 miss ratio.

5. RESULTS

5.1 Performance

The IPC speedups (normalized to the baseline) are shown in Figure 7. From the results, we can see that a system without DRAM cache is 8.6% slower than the tags-in-DRAM baseline; from this we can conclude that the DRAM cache is effective for our system configuration.

We can also observe that a prior proposed miss predictor (MAP-I) improves over the baseline by 6.8%. In contrast, a tags-in-SRAM approach which consumes an impractically large SRAM space (11.5MB) provides a speedup of 12.2%. It is worth noting that this is the gap that the ATCache tries to bridge, while consuming much smaller SRAM space.

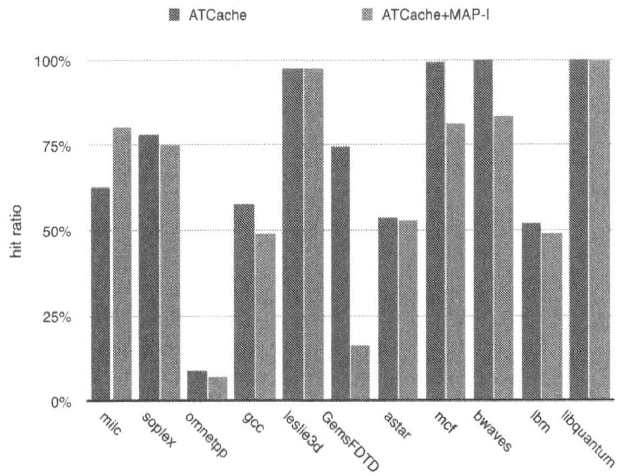

Figure 10: ATCache hit ratio.

We can see that the ATCache achieves 10.3% speedup without MAP-I predictor and 11.9% with the predictor – while consuming only 47.375kB (without MAP-I) and 48kB with MAP-I (256 entries). In other words, we are able to do almost as well as tags-in-SRAM while consuming 0.5% SRAM overhead compared to a tags-in-SRAM design.

In order to understand the speedups in individual benchmarks, we show the miss ratio of each benchmark program in Fig. 9. One interesting aspect to note here is that, by skipping miss accesses, MAP-I can provide a good speedup and even outperforms a tags-in-SRAM design for high miss ratio workloads such as *mcf* and *bwaves*. This is because the latency of accessing MAP-I structure is only one cycle (in comparison to 6 cycles access latency we used for a full tags-in-SRAM cache). However, for benchmarks with a low miss ratio (such as *libquantum*), MAP-I is not as effective and even shows a small slowdown due to its cycle lookup penalty.

On the other hand, with our ATCache we can observe benefit on both high and low miss ratio benchmarks. This is because ATCache reduces both hit latency and miss penalty.

For example, for *libquantum* which has a low miss ratio, we are able to achieve a speedup of 38% over the baseline.

When we integrate MAP-I and ATCache together (ATCache + MAP-I), we can see a speedup boost in moderate miss ratio workloads such as lbm and milc. This is because ATCache's average hit ratio is around 60% (as shown in Fig. 10), but the high accuracy of the MAP-I predictor (with a predictability of close to 98%) can help us further in reducing the DRAM miss penalty. In addition to this, with MAP-I the ATCache can be more effectively used for caching only hit tags. This is exemplified by *milc* benchmark where using an ATCache with MAP-I results in a speedup of 28.9% in comparison with a speedup of 18.9% (MAP-I only) and 11.8% (ATCache only).

However, for low miss ratio benchmarks such as *libquantum*, ATCache+MAP-I shows a small 1% slowdown compared to only ATCache design. This can be attributed to the increased hit access latency (extra cycle) for looking up the MAP-I table.

5.2 L2 miss latency

Fig. 8 shows the L2 miss latency reduction (normalized to the baseline) for all benchmarks. The L2 miss latency here refers to the time it takes for a cache block to be transferred to the L2 from the lower levels upon an L2 miss; in other words, this only includes the L3 (DRAM cache) latency and possibly the main memory latency (in case of a DRAM cache miss). This latency provides us with a more transparent indicator of the benefit of our proposal as it avoids the obfuscating effects of other parameters (such as the effects of the our-of-order processor). As we can see from Fig. 8, with our ATCache we can see up to 45.3% (21.2% on average) reduction in L2 miss latency compared to the baseline. It is worth noting that this is approximately double the reduction provided by MAP-I, which provides a reduction of 11.9% on average. Finally, ATCache+MAP-I is able to provide the maximum reduction over the baseline of 24.5%. From these results, we believe that our technique can effectively improve the performance of the DRAM cache.

5.3 Sensitivity towards caching ratio

In this section, we want to understand the effect of varying the caching ratio. As introduced in §3.1, caching ratio represents the area gain of our technique in comparison to tags-in-SRAM. A caching ratio of 1 refers to a tags-in-SRAM design. Generally, the miss ratio of the ATCache will increase when caching ratio is increased (smaller cache). Fig. 11 shows IPC speedup (average of all benchmarks) for different caching ratios. Here, "IPC (fixed latency)" refers to a configuration where we fixed the access latency of the ATCache to 6 cycles. The speedup in terms of IPC reduces from 12.2% to 9.0% when caching ratio is increased from 1 (tags-in SRAM, 11.5MB) to 256 (≃48kB). Even without accounting for (a) faster access latency that a smaller cache could provide and (b) the miss predictor, we believe this trade-off is still interesting – a reduction in 99.5% space for 3.2% reduction in speedup. "IPC (MAP-I + actual latency)" refers to the realistic configuration in which we consider the effect of a faster SRAM latency due to a much smaller cache (Table 7 shows latencies for different caching ratios) and also the MAP-I predictor. As we can see, the peak speedup in this configuration (ATCache+MAP-I) is for a caching ratio of 64 and the speedup is able to match the speedup of a tags-in-SRAM design (12.2%).

Table 7: Latency in different caching ratios – caching ratio of 1 equals tags-in-SRAM (6 cycles).

Caching Ratio	2	4	8	16	32
latency (cycles)	5	5	4	4	3
Caching Ratio	64	128	256	512	1024
latency (cycles)	3	2	2	1	1

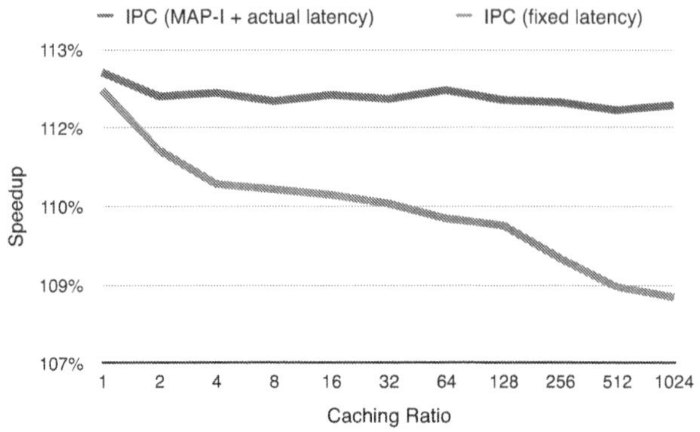

Figure 11: Speedups for different caching ratios. *Caching Ratio: 1* means a *tags-in-SRAM* design.

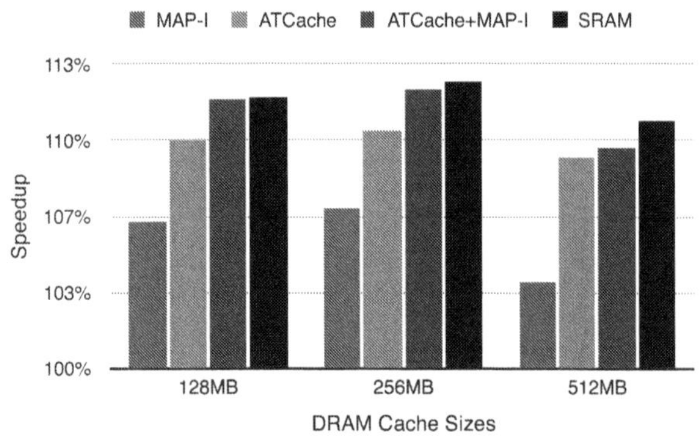

Figure 12: Sensitivity study of DRAM cache sizes.

5.4 Sensitivity towards DRAM cache size

Fig. 12 shows the effect of varying DRAM cache size. We consider 3 different sizes (128MB, 256MB, and 512MB). In this experiment, we use the latencies that we modeled in Table 1 for tags-in-SRAM. For ATCache (we fix caching ratio at 256), we use ATCache latency of 1, 2, and 3 cycles for ATCache size of 24kB (for 128MB DRAM cache), 46kB (for 256MB DRAM cache), and 88kB (for 512MB DRAM cache). From the results, we can see that the ATCache has a 9% to 10% performance improvement over its baseline (tags-in-DRAM) for all sizes. With MAP-I predictor, ATCache+MAP-I is 4% to 5% better than the MAP-I-only.

5.5 Sensitivity towards PG

As our prior studies (§3.2 and §3.3) show, the prefetching granularity (PG) is a key parameter in our design. In this section, we study the effect of varying the PG. In this study, we represent the performance of DRAM cache in terms of its average access latency, normalized to the access latency for PG/1. MAP-I is integrated with the ATCache for this study. As we can see from Fig. 13, increasing the PG from PG/1 to PG/2 , reduces the average latency of DRAM cache by 8.7%. The average latency reaches a minimum for PG/4 (10.1% reduction) and PG/8 (10.5% reduction). When we keep increasing PG, however, the ATCache starts to suffer from cache pollution and increased miss-penalty and shows a degradation in performance. We can clearly observe this with PG/64, whose average latency is 2.5% higher than PG/8. This study also vindicates our decision of choosing PG/4 for our baseline as it is close to the best performing PG.

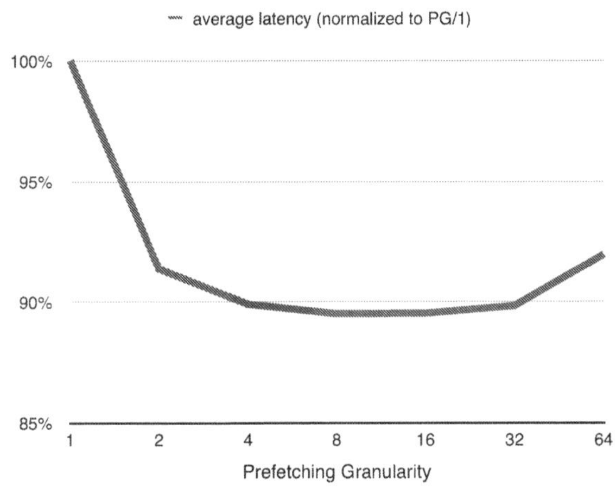

Figure 13: Sensitivity study to PG (with MAP-I).

5.6 Multiprogrammed workloads

IPC: In this section, we study how our design performs under multiprogrammed workloads. We randomly generate 25 workload groups as shown in Table 6, with each group consisting of 4 workloads. The speedup results compared to the baseline system are shown in Figure 14. Each workload group's result is a geometric mean of 4 workloads' speedup. The average is geometric mean of 4 x 25 workloads. As we can see[1], MAP-I provides 5.4% speedup and a full tags-in-SRAM design gives 11.8% speedup over the baseline. On the other hand, ATCache+MAP-I provides up to 12.2% speedup and on average 10.7% speedup over the baseline. Since this is comparable to the speedups we obtained with our uniprocessor workloads, this shows that the ATCache continues to work well under multiprogrammed workloads.

L2 miss latency: To sidestep the effect of different speedup metrics that can be potentially used to summarize the performance of multiprogrammed workloads [12, 4], we compare the L2 miss latency in Fig. 15, as it is arguably a more transparent indicator of the efficacy of ATCache. As we can see from Fig. 15, ATCache with MAP-I predictor shows a 18.4% speedup in L2 miss latency over the baseline; in comparison, tags-in-SRAM shows 21.9% speedup. It is worth noting that a tags-in-SRAM design consumes about 256 times of SRAM space than our design. Again, from these results, we can conclude that our design continues to work effectively in a more memory-intensive scenario.

[1]It is worth noting that a system without DRAM cache is 22.0% slower than our baseline. This is because multiprogrammed workloads have significantly more L2 misses.

6. RELATED WORK

The idea of caching tags has been explored previously. Wang et al. [16] proposed the CAT cache for reducing the area overhead of storing tags in the SRAM cache. CAT cache exploits tag value locality by removing tag value duplication – in doing so, they are able to reduce the area overhead of the tag array with a small performance overhead. However, this work is not applicable in the DRAM cache context since CAT involves accessing the data array first before accessing the tag; this is precisely what works on DRAM cache seek to avoid. Furthermore, whereas the CAT cache exploits tag value locality, the ATCache exploits spatial and temporal locality. It would be interesting to explore if ATCache can be extended to exploit value locality of tags also.

Other works [2, 17] have proposed caching tags to improve cache access latency in the generic setting of a multilevel SRAM cache hierarchy. The key difference between this and our work is the new context (DRAM cache) in which target this idea. By targeting the idea to a novel and concrete context of DRAM caches, we are able to specialize our technique in ways over and beyond the prior works. For example, hit prefetching, through which we gain a significant chunk of our performance, has not been discussed in any of the prior works.

7. CONCLUSION

The advent of the DRAM cache has posed a problem of how to efficiently manage the tags associated with the DRAM cache. One naive option is to store all the tags in SRAM; while this would ensure fast access of the tags, the associated storage cost would render this approach impractical. Consequently prior works have proposed innovative techniques to manage the tags efficiently in DRAM. Nonetheless, we observe, with a help of a study, that it is more performance efficient to manage the tags in SRAM.

Having established this, we propose a simple idea to cache the tags in SRAM so that we can achieve the effect of maintaining all tags in SRAM, without paying the prohibitive cost; we show that there is enough spatial and temporal locality amongst DRAM cache tag accesses to merit caching the tags. Our experimental results show that we achieve similar performance (within 2%) to a very fast tags-in-SRAM design (6 cycles access latency for 11.5MB), while consuming less than 1% of the SRAM space. If we integrate our caching idea with prior proposed miss prediction, we show that we can come within 0.5% of performance achieved with the tags-in-SRAM approach.

8. ACKNOWLEDGMENTS

We thank all the reviewers for their helpful comments. We also thank Bharghava Rajaram for discussions that led to the initial idea. This work is supported by UK India Education and Research Iniative Thematic Partnership Award UKUTP201100256 and the Centre for Numerical Algorithms and Intelligent Software, funded by EPSRC grant EP/G036136/1 and the Scottish Funding Council to the University of Edinburgh.

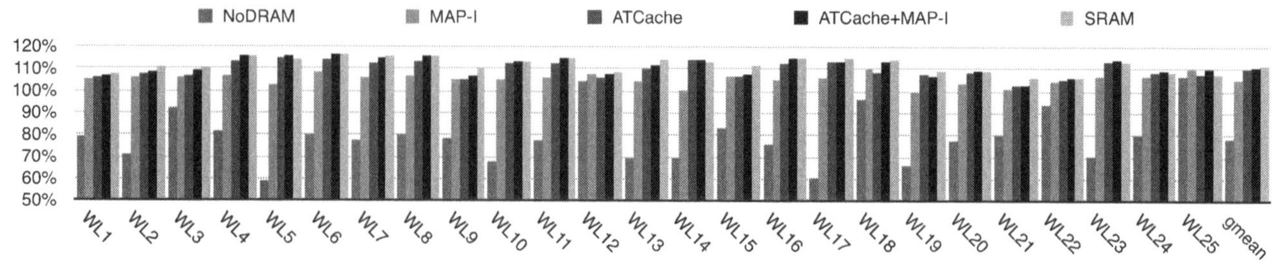

Figure 14: Performance speedup in multiprogrammed workloads.

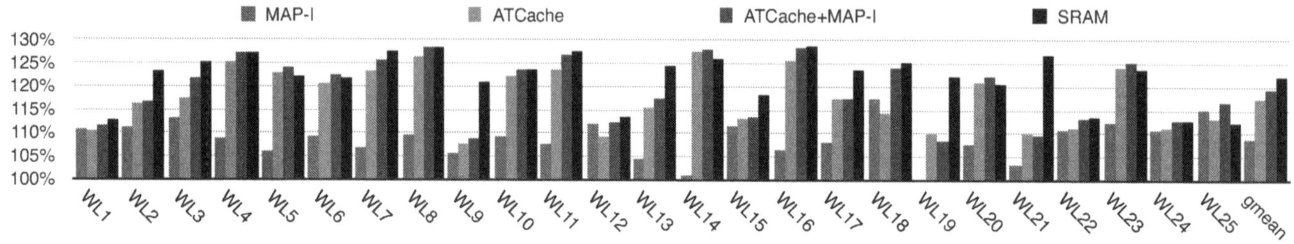

Figure 15: L2 miss latency reduction in multiprogrammed workloads (higher the better).

9. REFERENCES

[1] N. L. Binkert, B. M. Beckmann, G. Black, S. K. Reinhardt, A. G. Saidi, A. Basu, J. Hestness, D. Hower, T. Krishna, S. Sardashti, R. Sen, K. Sewell, M. Shoaib, N. Vaish, M. D. Hill, and D. A. Wood, "The gem5 simulator," *SIGARCH Computer Architecture News*, vol. 39, no. 2, pp. 1–7, 2011.

[2] W. Chou, Y. Nain, H. Wei, and C. Ma, "Caching tag for a large scale cache computer memory system," Sep. 22 1998, uS Patent 5,813,031. [Online]. Available: http://www.google.co.uk/patents/US5813031

[3] X. Dong, Y. Xie, N. Muralimanohar, and N. P. Jouppi, "Simple but effective heterogeneous main memory with on-chip memory controller support," in *SC*, 2010, pp. 1–11.

[4] S. Eyerman and L. Eeckhout, "Restating the case for weighted-ipc metrics to evaluate multiprogram workload performance," *IEEE Computer Architecture Letters*, 2013.

[5] M. Ferdman, A. Adileh, Y. O. Koçberber, S. Volos, M. Alisafaee, D. Jevdjic, C. Kaynak, A. D. Popescu, A. Ailamaki, and B. Falsafi, "Clearing the clouds: a study of emerging scale-out workloads on modern hardware," in *ASPLOS*, 2012, pp. 37–48.

[6] Intel. Haswell processors. [Online]. Available: http://ark.intel.com/products/codename/42174/haswell

[7] A. Jaleel, K. B. Theobald, S. C. S. Jr., and J. S. Emer, "High performance cache replacement using re-reference interval prediction (rrip)," in *ISCA*, 2010, pp. 60–71.

[8] D. Jevdjic, S. Volos, and B. Falsafi, "Die-stacked dram caches for servers: hit ratio, latency, or bandwidth? have it all with footprint cache," in *ISCA*, 2013, pp. 404–415.

[9] X. Jiang, N. Madan, L. Zhao, M. Upton, R. Iyer, S. Makineni, D. Newell, Y. Solihin, and R. Balasubramonian, "Chop: Adaptive filter-based dram caching for cmp server platforms," in *HPCA*, 2010, pp. 1–12.

[10] G. H. Loh and M. D. Hill, "Efficiently enabling conventional block sizes for very large die-stacked dram caches," in *MICRO*, 2011, pp. 454–464.

[11] ——, "Supporting very large dram caches with compound-access scheduling and missmap," *IEEE Micro*, vol. 32, no. 3, pp. 70–78, 2012.

[12] P. Michaud, "Demystifying multicore throughput metrics," *IEEE Computer Architecture Letters*, 2013.

[13] N. Muralimanohar, R. Balasubramonian, and N. P. Jouppi, "Architecting efficient interconnects for large caches with cacti 6.0," *IEEE Micro*, vol. 28, no. 1, pp. 69–79, 2008.

[14] M. K. Qureshi and G. H. Loh, "Fundamental latency trade-off in architecting dram caches: Outperforming impractical sram-tags with a simple and practical design," in *MICRO*, 2012, pp. 235–246.

[15] J. Sim, G. H. Loh, H. Kim, M. O'Connor, and M. Thottethodi, "A mostly-clean dram cache for effective hit speculation and self-balancing dispatch," in *MICRO*, 2012, pp. 247–257.

[16] H. Wang, T. Sun, and Q. Yang, "Cat - caching address tags: A technique for reducing area cost of on-chip caches," in *ISCA*, 1995, pp. 381–390.

[17] T. Wicki, M. Kasinathan, and R. Hetherington, "Cache tag caching," Apr. 3 2001, uS Patent 6,212,602. [Online]. Available: http://www.google.co.uk/patents/US6212602

[18] L. Zhao, R. R. Iyer, R. Illikkal, and D. Newell, "Exploring dram cache architectures for cmp server platforms," in *ICCD*, 2007, pp. 55–62.

SpongeDirectory: Flexible Sparse Directories Utilizing Multi-Level Memristors

Lunkai Zhang[†♮], Dmitri Strukov[◇], Hebatallah Saadeldeen[♮], Dongrui Fan[†], Mingzhe Zhang[‡], Diana Franklin[♮]

[†]State Key Laboratory of Computer Architecture, ICT, Chinese Academy of Sciences

[◇]Electrical and Computer Engineering, UC Santa Barbara

[♮]Department of Computer Science, UC Santa Barbara

[‡]Key Lab of Intelligent Information Processing, ICT, Chinese Academy of Sciences

lunkai.zhang.1984@gmail.com, strukov@ece.ucsb.edu, {fandr, zhangmingzhe}@ict.ac.cn, {heba, franklin}@cs.ucsb.edu

ABSTRACT

Cache-coherent shared memory is critical for programmability in many-core systems. Several directory-based schemes have been proposed, but dynamic, non-uniform sharing make efficient directory storage challenging, with each giving up storage space, performance or energy.

We introduce SpongeDirectory, a sparse directory structure that exploits multi-level memristory technology. SpongeDirectory expands directory storage in-place when needed by increasing the number of bits stored on a single memristor device, trading latency and energy for storage.

We explore several SpongeDirectory configurations, finding that a provisioning rate of 0.5x with memristors optimized for low energy consumption is the most competitive. This optimal SpongeDirectory configuration has performance comparable to a conventional sparse directory, requires 18× less storage space, and consumes 8× less energy.

Categories and Subject Descriptors

B.3.2 [**Memory Structures**]: Design Styles; B.7.1 [**Integrated Circuits**]: Types and Design Styles

Keywords

Sparse Directories; Multi-Level Memristors

1. INTRODUCTION

As the number of processor cores increases, multi-/many-core chips tend to favor directory- over bus-based snooping coherence due to bandwidth needs. Simple directory schemes based on sharer vectors are not scalable, however, because storage increases super-linearly with the number of cores. A scalable, efficient directory scheme is needed for future extreme-scale many-core system. Many directory schemes (e.g., [14][42][44][20][30]) have been proposed to reduce the storage requirements at the cost of energy, latency or complexity. For example, duplicate-tag [14] and tagless [42] directories provide scalable performance and area, but they are not energy efficient. The recently proposed SCD [30] scheme is scalable, but only if it is coupled with a complex ZCache architecture[29].

Requirements for directory coherence storage are quite different among different applications. Some applications have a large number of directory entries, but most directory entries have very few sharers, whereas others have fewer directory entries, with more sharers per entry. Using conventional SRAMs, it is quite complex to provide the flexibility for both situations while keeping overall storage overhead low [11][29].

In this paper, we seek to use emerging memristor technologies to solve this problem. Memristors offer promising characteristics for storage devices—high density, non volatile, low-energy electrical switching, CMOS compatibility [36], and most importantly for this work, the ability to dynamically trade off read and write latency for storage density [3]. This variable-precision storage, projected to be up to seven bits[3] in a single memristor bit, is a perfect match to meet the requirements of different directory storage requirements in different situations. The extra memristors may be used either for more sharers in an entry or for more entries in a set, allowing for flexible needs within and across applications.

This paper makes the following contributions:

- Provide a model projected from empirical data for latency and energy requirements for memristors.
- Introduce an encoding scheme that requires only one memristor bit to store the number of levels being used.
- Design and evaluate a coherence directory with memristors that, with the optimized configuration, saves 18x storage, results in negligible degeneration on overall system performance, and consumes 8× less energy than a conventional directory.

The rest of the paper is organized as follows. We first give a background on memristors and cache coherence directory storage schemes in Section 2. Section 3 presents our Sponge Directory scheme. We then present our methodology and results in Sections 4 and 5. We present a more thorough related work section in Section 6, followed by our conclusions in Section 7.

PACT'14, August 24–27, 2014, Edmonton, AB, Canada.

http://dx.doi.org/10.1145/2628071.2628081.

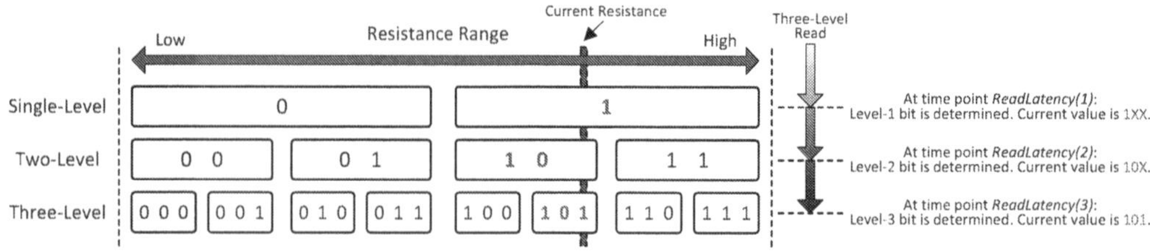

Figure 1: **Multi-level memristor cell, and the step-wise manner of a multi-level memristor read.** The same resistance can be read as different numbers of bits, and the most significant bits are read first.

2. BACKGROUND

The SpongeDirectory is built on two bodies of work – future multi-level memristor technologies and on-chip cache coherence directories. Here, we present the relevant information in those areas.

2.1 Multi-Level Memristor Storage vs Latency

Memristors [39][40] are in the family of resistive memories. Others include Phase Change Memories (PCM) and Spin-Transfer Torque RAM (STTRAM). Memristors, when used as a direct replacement for SRAM, are projected to be significantly more dense than conventional SRAM. Because memristors are analog devices, they can be used for analog computations or, depending on the precision of the storage, storing multiple digital bits in one cell [3]. We propose to exploit this latter characteristic (at the expense of energy and latency).

A memristor cell [39] is a device whose resistance can be changed in a wide range. Holding a voltage above a specific threshold for enough time (i.e., a write pulse) changes the resistance of the memristor cell. An Analog-to-Digital Circuit (ADC) reads the resistance as a digital value. Depending on the ADC setting, the same resistance of a memristor cell could be interpreted as a different number of bits [13][38]. Figure 1 shows that the same resistance can be interpreted as b'1 when the ADC is using one-level accuracy, and as b'10 and b'101, respectively, when the ADC is using two-level and three-level accuracy. Alibart et al. [3] recently showed that a single memristor cell can be used to store up to seven bits of data.

The higher precision of the memristor operations comes at a cost in latency and energy. Here we describe in detail the characteristics of multi-level memristor operations:

2.1.1 Multi-level Memristor Reads

As the number of bits being stored in a single memristor increases, the ADC must distinguish between more values, and the range of resistive values mapping to a single digital value decreases. Therefore, more precise read operations require longer latency.

Another interesting and important characteristic of multi-level memristor read operation is its asymmetry to different bits. Because of this, we will refer to the different bits stored in a single memristor as being stored in different *levels*. Because the most significant bit requires much less precision to be read out than the least significant bit, we refer to the most significant bit as being the shallowest bit, or in the shallowest level, and the least significant bit is the deepest bit, or in the deepest level.

In this paper, we assume a successive approximation ADC [6] which allows us to read out multi-level memristor data in a step-wise manner. If ReadLatency(n) is the time required to read the nth most significant bit, a three-level read operation will be complete at *ReadLatency(3)*. As Figure 1 shows, however, the data in the first level (i.e., the most significant bit or shallowest level) can be read out by *ReadLatency(1)*, and the data in the second level can be used by *ReadLatency(2)*.

The important result is that if we only need to read out the most significant bit of a multi-level memristor, we pay the latency and energy of a less precise memristor.

2.1.2 Multi-level Memristor Writes

In order to write very precise resistance values, multi-level memristors use an iterative write method [3]. That is, a multi-level write is composed of multiple iterations, each iteration consisting of a multi-level read followed by a write pulse.

As we will see in Section 4, a multi-level write can have very high latency (up to hundreds or even thousands of nanoseconds). Fortunately, the operation can be interrupted between iterations to service more critical operations (e.g. a read).

In conclusion, multi-level memristor operations trade operation latency and energy for storage density. Using multiple levels incurs high latencies and energies, but we are able to mitigate these effects with careful data organization and scheduling. The asymmetry in read latency for different levels allows us to access some data at low latency and energy. Finally, while the write latency appears unacceptably high, we can suspend the write while performing more time-critical operations.

2.2 On-chip Coherence Directories

There are several baseline directory architectures used for on-chip coherence, such as sparse directory, duplicate tag directory, and in-cache directory. A duplicate tag directory has been shown not to be energy scalable (since its associativity is linear with number of cores). An in-cache directory requires a special inclusive shared *Last Level Cache* hierarchy. Therefore, among the possible baseline directory architectures, the sparse directory [16] is general purpose and requires the least energy. Recently, a number of proposals (e.g., [12][30][9][4][11]) work on improving the scalability of sparse directories, each with its own trade-off among complexity, storage and performance. Our scalable design provides a new design point in these trade-offs. Specifically, with the help of emerging multi-level memristors, our technique has the lowest storage requirement among all the proposal.s In addition, it as a gentle degradation in performance for rare cases.

Figure 2 provides a logical view of on-chip sparse directory coherence, consisting of a logical uniform directory module and multiple processor cores along with their private caches. To avoid directory and network hot-spotting, the directory module is often divided into multiple directory slices. Each directory slice contains multiple directory entries, typically organized in a set-associative manner, just like caches. Each directory entry usually contains at least the following fields: address tag (address of corresponding memory block), state (three states in a conventional MESI protocol) and sharers (which cores' caches currently contain the memory block).

If a processor core asks for a memory block which does not exist on its private caches, it will issue a coherence request (e.g. GETX in Figure 2) to the sparse directory. The sparse directory then performs corresponding actions (e.g., invalidating all the cached copies of the memory block). The disadvantage of the original sparse directory is its storage requirement, since it must hold all information perfectly. Depending on who is sharing what, there are two sources of storage inefficiency:

- **Storing sharer information in an entry:** In a sharer-vector form, the storage of such information is linear with the number of cores and thus not scalable.
- **Slice-level and set-level non-uniformity:** In theory the number of valid directory entries should never exceed the number of private cache entries. However, due to the set-level and slice-level non-uniformity of sparse directory, the sparse directory often needs to over-provision (usually 2× of the number of private cache entries [8]) the directory entries. The way to solve such a problem usually lies in increasing the actual associativity of the sparse directory (e.g., Cuckoo directory [12]).

In this paper we analyze a conventional 256-core sparse directory (i.e., the *ConvDir* described in Section 4), to shed light on designing low-cost and efficient many-core coherence directory using multi-level memristors. This analysis is analyzes both spatial and temporal behavior.

2.2.1 Directory Design: Timing

In order to exploit the fact that multi-level memristor reads are asymmetric, we need to analyze the timing of traditional conventional sparse directories to determine which items are both commonly accessed and on the critical path, and thus should be in the shallowest levels of the memristors. Figure 3 presents detailed flow graphs of GETX/GETS operations in a sparse directory. Figure 4 shows the number of directory requests with respect to L1 cache and L2 cache requests. Using this information, we make the following set of observations that will guide our design:

- For a typical MESI-based directory coherence system, there are four types directory requests: Exclusive Read (i.e., GETX), Shared Read (i.e.,GETS), Exclusive Write-back (i.e.,PUTX) and Shared Write-back (i.e., PUTS). While GETX and GETS are on the critical path of the execution, PUTX and PUTS are not. *Therefore, we should optimize the latency of GETX and GETS operations.*

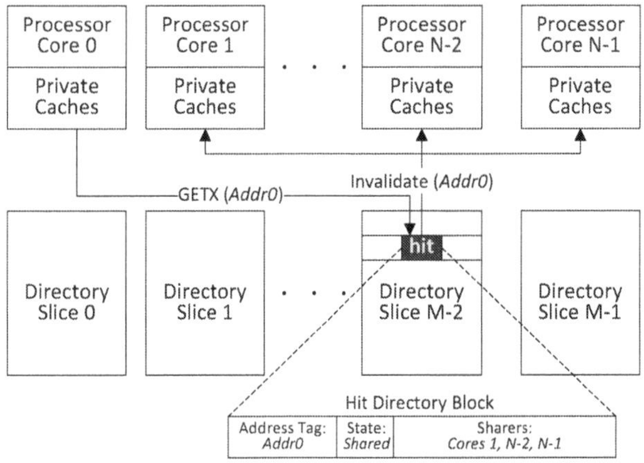

Figure 2: **An example of a sparse directory scheme** used in a multi-/many-core processor to track private cache coherence information. A sparse directory uses set-associative cache-like structures and is is distributed into slices (M slices in this figure).

- From Figure 3, the read operations (in red) are on the critical path of the directory requests, but the write operations (in blue) are not on the critical path. *Therefore, low read latency is more important than write latency.*
- From Figure 3, for all reads, the sparse directory needs to read the tag and state information of all entries in corresponding directory set. On a hit, it usually (cases 1 and 3) needs to read only one sharer from the hit directory's entry. From Figure 4, Case 2 happens relatively rarely. *Therefore, low read latency of tags, states and one sharer is more important than read latency of additional sharers*
- From Figure 4, the number of directory requests are on average over 1144× and 24.9× less than the number of L1 cache requests and L2 cache requests, respectively. According to Amdahl's law, *a moderate degradation of directory performance is unlikely to affect overall system performance.*

2.2.2 Directory Design: Spatial

For each evaluated benchmark, we take a snapshot when the total number of sharers in the directory entries is the largest. Figure 5 is a histogram of how many directory entries have each number of sharers. We can see that benchmarks vary widely in their maximum sharing requirements.

- Some benchmarks (e.g., radix) have a large number of directory entries, but almost all the directory entries are owned by only one sharer. *These benchmarks require more directory entries, but seldom require more sharer storage for each directory entry.*
- Some other benchmarks (e.g., barnes and raytrace) have significantly fewer directory entries, but some of the directory entries have many sharers. *These benchmarks require fewer directory entries, but some of the directories require more storage for sharers.*

Therefore, our proposed directory scheme should be flexible enough to handle both situations - when many directory entries are required and when many sharers are required for some directory entries.

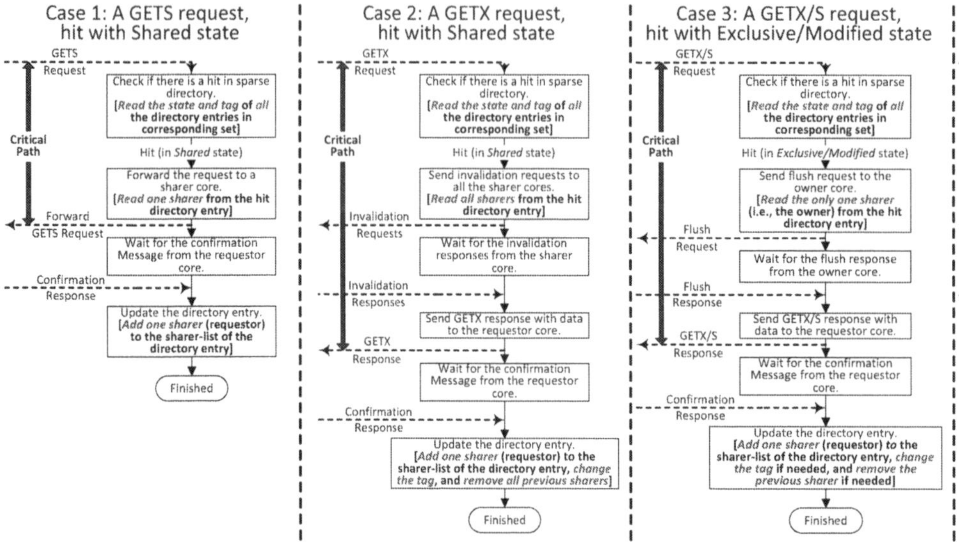

Figure 3: **B**ehaviors of GETX and GETS requests in a conventional sparse directory using MESI protocol showing reads (red) and writes (blue). Goal: reduce latency for common operations on critical path. We see that: (1) Only reads are on the critical path. (2) All reads require state and tag, and most require one sharer. (3) Relatively few operations require reading multiple sharers.

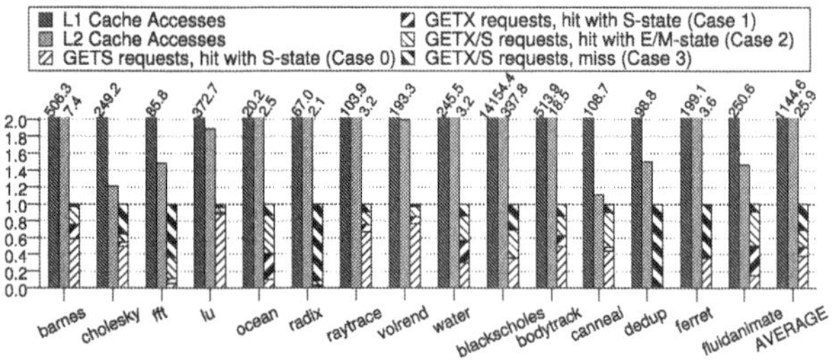

Figure 4: **Number and type of memory accesses normalized to total directory accesses.** Directory accesses are relatively infrequent, therefore latency tolerant.

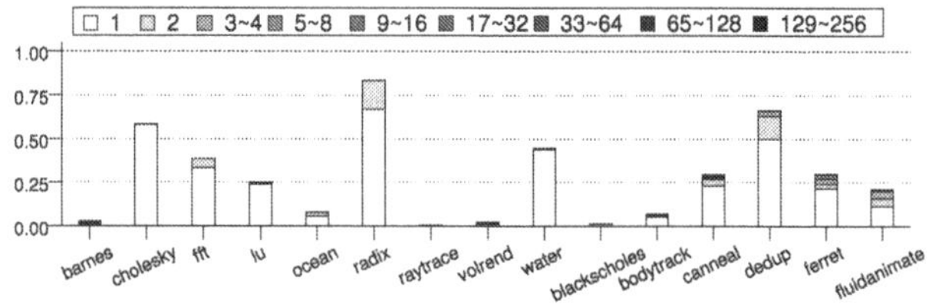

Figure 5: **Number of directory entries with X sharers, normalized to the number of cache blocks** showing variance in need for entries (radix) and sharers (raytrace).

3. SPONGEDIRECTORY

In this section, based on the analysis of both multi-level memristors and sparse directories in Section 2, we propose the detailed architecture of SpongeDirectory. Without the loss of generality, our proposed architecture is for a 256-core system (as described in Section 4).

The storage of each SpongeDirectory slice, like a normal sparse directory slice, is an N-way set-associative memory. Each set has N *blocks* in it. The difference is that the memory is made of multi-level memristor RAMs, therefore each *block* can be configured individually with a number of levels. We call each level of a SpongeDirectory *block* a SpongeDirectory *item*.

3.1 Identifying the Level of a Block

The SpongeDirectory must be able to identify the number of *items* in each *block*. Intuitively, we need to store item count information of all SpongeDirectory *blocks* into a small peripheral RAM. However, this will complicate the design of SpongeDirectory. Here we propose a low-cost but effective mechanism, a *usage bit*, that encodes the number of items stored in a single memristor bit whose value is read only to the deepest filled item.

Each SpongeDirectory *block* has one *usage bit*. If the correspondent *item* is the deepest valid *item* of the block (e.g., the Level 3 *item* in Figure 1), its *usage bit* is 0; otherwise, it is 1. Therefore, A multi-level memristor read can stop once it reads a *usage bit* with value 0.

3.2 SpongeDirectory Entry Formats

A *directory entry* refers to the directory information of a cacheline block. There are two types of *items* — *head items* and *body items*. A *head item* is either invalid or contains the tag, state, and at least one sharer. A new *directory entry* needs only one *head item*, since it only needs its tag, address, and the one sharer that brought it in. As more cores share the cacheline, *body items* are added to store the additional sharers.

We use two different *directory entry* formats for storing sharer information. First, the *sharer pointer* scheme stores information only for sharers, allowing the number of items to grow as the number of sharers grows, but requiring 8 bits per sharer. Second, the *sharer vector* scheme uses only 1 bit per sharer, but requires space for all cores (not just those sharing it). This is efficient for many sharers. Similar to prior work[30], each entry may be configured as either

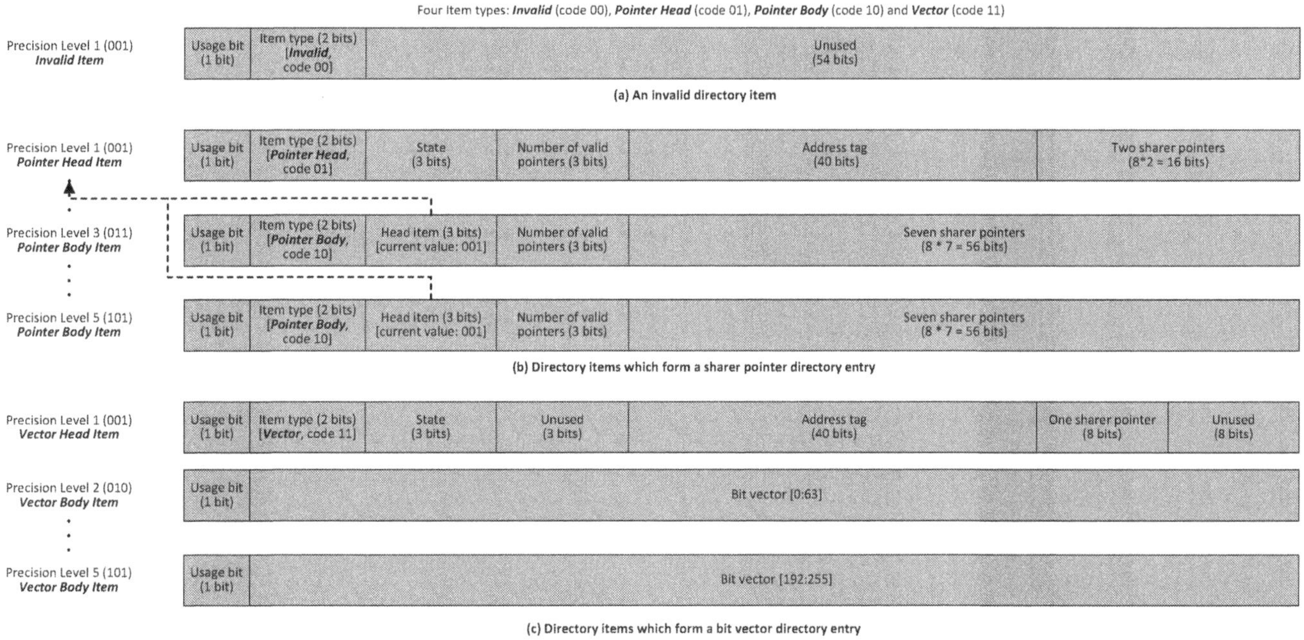

Figure 6: The entry formats of SpongeDirectory

scheme to obtain the advantage of both *sharer pointer* and *sharer vector* schemes.

Figure 6 shows the different formats and how they are utilized with different scenarios.

- *Invalid Items.* Figure 6(a) shows an *invalid item.* This is only used when the block contains no items.
- *Sharer Pointer Head and Body Items.* Figure 6(b) shows an example of a multi-item directory entry using the *sharer pointer* format. The *pointer head item* contains the address tag, state and two sharer pointers. The two *pointer body items* contain all other sharer pointers. Because multiple *directory entries* can be mapped to the same *block*, each body item has a pointer to its head item.
- *Sharer Vector Head and Body Items*: Figure 6(c) shows an example of a *directory entry* using the *sharer vector* format. A *sharer vector directory entry* has a fixed storage requirement for sharer information (in our case, 256 bits, requiring four *items*). With its *head item*, a *sharer vector directory entry* requires all five *items* of a *block*. To ensure fast directory responses, a *sharer vector head item* preserves a sharer pointer.

Figure 7 shows how items would be stored in the same block. We add a few restrictions to reduce read latency:

- A single *block* may contain several *directory entries* in sharer pointer format.
- One *block* can hold up to five *items* (out of a possible seven [3]).
- *Head items* are stored in the shallowest levels for fast completions of cases 1, 3, and 4 in Figure 3.

We also add restrictions to simplify the design:

- All *items* for the same *directory entry* must reside in the same block to simplify accesses.
- A *directory entry* in *sharer vector* format uses the entire *block.*

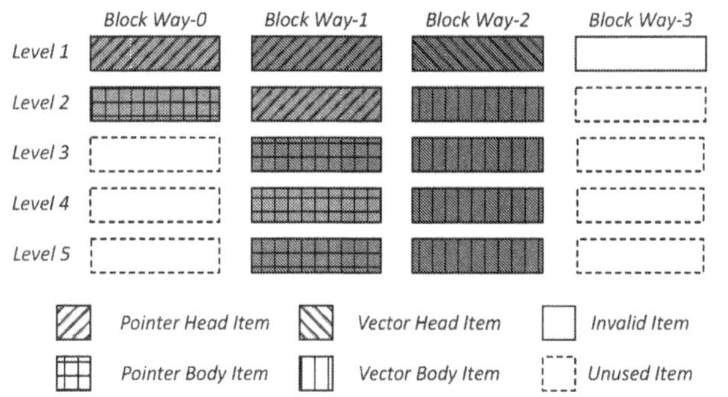

Figure 7: A snapshot of a 4-way SpongeDirectory set. *Items* with the same color belong to the same directory *entry.*

3.3 Minimizing Write Energy

As will be shown in Section 4.2, multi-level memristor writes require significantly more energy than other operations. In addition, it is often the case that just a few bits of an item, and therefore block, need to be changed. In order to save energy consumption, SpongeDirectory only writes the memristor bits of a block that need to change.

- **Inserting or removing *items*** that cross the threshold of the number sharers in an item in *sharer pointer format* requires the entire *block* to be written.
- **Adding a sharer within an *item* in *sharer pointer format*** requires only modification of the target *sharer pointer* and the *pointer count field..*
- **Removing a sharer within an *item* in *sharer pointer format*** may leave a hole, so a sharer pointer may need to be moved. Therefore, the maximum is two *sharer pointers* and the *pointer count field..*
- **Adding a sharer** in *sharer vector format* requires modification of only a single bit.
- **Removing a sharer** in *sharer vector format* modifies only a single bit unless the removed sharer is also in

the *sharer pointer* field of the *head item*. In this case, we also need to modify the *sharer pointer* field.

- **Changing directory entry format** requires the entire block to be written (see below).

3.4 Changing Directory Entry Format

Every *directory entry* is in *sharer pointer* format (with one *head item* and no *body items*) when inserted into the directory, and *sharer pointer items* are added and removed as needed. When the number of sharers surpasses a threshold, SpongeDirectory will upgrade a *sharer pointer directory entry* into *sharer vector* format. All other *directory entries* sharing the same *block* are evicted, sharer pointers are translated to vector locations, and *sharer vector items* are written to the upgraded *directory entry*.

Ideally, as the number of sharers falls below another threshold, a downgrade operation should occur to switch the *sharer vector directory entry* back into *sharer pointer* format. The directory could toggle across the threshold, so we do not downgrade at this time. When a GETX occurs, the resulting directory entry has only one sharer (the requester), so compressing the entry to a single item rather than the entire block is worthwhile, so we only downgrade a *sharer vector directory entry* at this time.

3.5 Buffering Recently Finished Requests

There are still two challenges for SpongeDirectory scheme in some applications: limited write durability and long write latency. As we will show later, if a very small number of blocks are written many times, as in `fluidanimate`, this will hurt the lifetime of that block, as well as suffer delays due to the long write latencies. Therefore, we propose a buffer that holds the most recently finished directory requests to capture subsequent operations to those entries.

4. METHODOLOGY

In this section, we describe the two main aspects to the experiments. First, we describe the different configurations we evaluated. Second, we describe the simulations and models we used to obtain our numerical results.

4.1 Directory Configurations

Our baseline is a conventional sparse directory architecture. In addition, we calculate the storage requirements of the SCD architecture. For the SpongeDirectory configurations, we have several configurations that vary the size, memristor type, organization, and buffering in order to evaluate the effectiveness of our design decisions. Table 2 summarizes the storage requirements of the three basic sizes. All of the variations only change one attribute as compared with *SpongeDirMid*, so we describe only the difference between SpongeDirMid and that configuration.

- **ConvDir** is a conventional sparse directory architecture using a sharer-vector scheme with a 2× provisioning rate.
- **SpongeDirMid** uses energy-optimized memristors with a 0.5× provisioning rate and an 8-entry buffer of the most recently completed requests.
- **SpongeDirSmall** uses a 0.25× provisioning rate.
- **SpongeDirLarge** uses a 1× provisioning rate.
- **SpongeDirMid-NoBuffer** has no buffer of the most recently completed requests.
- **SpongeDirMid-FastMemristor** uses latency optimized memristors.
- **SpongeDirMid-6Levels** uses a narrower format requiring 57 bits per block instead of 65 bits — each *Pointer Head Item* has one sharer pointer instead of two. This will utilize deeper levels more often.
- **SpongeDirMid-SimplePolicy** is SpongeDirMid but does not take advantage of the organization of items within a block. Although head items are stored in the shallowest levels, this reads the entire entry before processing the request.

4.2 Models

For each configuration, we calculate the storage requirements as well as the read latency, write latency, and energy. We developed models for memristors projected from recent experimental data. We used these values as inputs to our simulation infrastructure.

Simulation.

We implement our simulation platform with the multi-threaded GRAPHITE simulator [23], based on Pin [5]. As described in Table 1, we simulate a 256-tile cache coherent many-core system which is distributed in a 16 × 16 mesh network-on-chip. Each tile has split 32KB L1 I/D-caches, a private 512KB L2 cache, and a sparse directory slice.

To take into account the execution time variability of parallel benchmarks [2], we run each simulation multiple times and report the average and standard deviation of each collection of measurements. We evaluate our design using nine SPLASH-2 benchmarks [35] (barnes, cholesky, fft, lu, ocean, radix, raytrace, volrend and water) and six PARSEC benchmarks [7] (blackscholes, bodytrack, canneal, dedup, ferret and fluidanimate). As shown in Figures 4 & 5, these benchmarks exhibit a wide variety of directory behaviors.

To reduce simulation time, Graphite [23] uses relaxed coordination among the threads, and the developers show that the simulation inaccuracy caused by the approach is acceptable. However, this means that the requests of different threads sometimes arrive to a directory slice not in a time order, making it impossible to model the queuing delay of different operations. As a result, we first present the execution time without considering the queuing delay. We then separately present the memristor operation time in the busiest directory slice to show when queuing delay is likely to considerably prolong the execution time.

Storage.

Table 2 shows the storage requirements of the directory schemes, which is affected by two parameters: (1)storage of each *directory block*; (2)*provisioning rate* of the sparse directory scheme, defined as the total number of *directory blocks* divided by the total number of cache blocks in all private caches.

For the first parameter, due to their multiple storage formats, both SCD and SpongeDirectory require smaller *directory blocks* than a conventional sparse directory.

The *provisioning rate* of a conventional sparse directory is 2×. Because SCD mimics a much larger associativity with its Zcache-like infrastructure, it only needs a provisioning rate of 1×. Each *SpongeDirectory block* can be configured to hold multiple *directory entries*, further

Table 1: Simulation Parameters

Frequency	1GHz
Processor	in-order, x86-64 ISA, IPC equals to 1 except on memory accesses, 64-byte cacheline size
L1 Caches	private split 32KB I/D-caches per processor, 4-way, parallel access, 2-cycle latency, 0.82pJ tag lookup, 88.71pJ data access.
L2 Caches	private, 512KB per processor, 8-way, sequential access, 11-cycle latency, 4.62pJ tag access, 74.70pJ data access.
Coherence Protocol	MESI protocol, split request-response, with forward, sequential consistency.
Directories	Critical directory access latency = data path latency (5 cycles) + critical RAM operation latency + network/memory latency. ConvDir: RAM read/write latency: 1 cycle (1ns); buffering 8 most recent requests. SpongeDirectories: by default, buffering 8 most recent requests, using energy-optimized memristors, head item shallower policy and 5-level memristors, a sharer pointer format directory entry having at most three *items*.
Network	16 × 16 MESH network, 4 cycles per hop. 1 process/hierarchy per tile.
Memories	350 cycle latency.

Table 2: Compared directory architectures. SpongeDirectory formats in Figure 6.

	Directory type	RAM type	Block organization	Prov. rate	Directory RAM storage per tile (caches have 624.375 KB RAM per tile)
SpongeDirSmall	SpongeDirectory	memristor	4-way, 512 sets	0.25×	65 bits per block (5 levels/bit) ->~16KB (2.56% cache)
SpongeDirMid (default)	SpongeDirectory	memristor	4-way, 1024 sets	0.5×	65 bits per block (5 levels/bit) ->~32KB (5.13% cache)
SpongeDirLarge	SpongeDirectory	memristor	4-way, 2048 sets	1.0×	65 bits per block (5 levels/bit) ->~64KB (10.25% cache)
SpongeDirMid -6Levels	SpongeDirectory	memristor	4-way, 1024 sets	0.5×	57 bits per block (6 levels/bit) ->~28KB (4.48% cache)
ConvDir	Conventional Sparse Directory	SRAM	4-way, 4096 sets	2.0×	307 bits / block: 3-bit state, 40-bit tag, 8-bit sharer pointer, 256-bit vector -> 614 KB per tile (98.3% of cache).
SCD	SCD [30]	SRAM	Zcache [29], 4 ways, 2048 sets	1.0×	71 bits per block: 3-bit state, 40-bit tag, 2-bit type, 26-bit sharer info field -> 71 KB per tile (11.37% of cache).

Table 3: Energy and Latencies of the modeled directory storage.

Architecture	Size	Storage type	1-level read latency		1-level read energy		Area	
			latency-optimized	energy-optimized	latency-optimized	energy-optimized	latency-optimized	energy-optimized
SpongeDirSmall	16KB	memristor	1.651ns	4.763ns	41.464pJ	3.172pJ	11000.6um^2	3563.8um^2
SpongeDirMid	32KB	memristor	1.698ns	5.463ns	41.775pJ	4.008pJ	11464.8um^2	6363.0um^2
SpongeDirLarge	64KB	memristor	1.809ns	6.739ns	42.397pJ	4.167pJ	12411.4um^2	8011.9um^2
SpongeDirMid -6Levels	28KB	memristor	1.670ns	5.439ns	36.582pJ	3.341pJ	10404.7um^2	5671.0um^2
ConvDir	614KB	SRAM-based 4-way cache	< 1.000ns		tag: 11.58pJ data: 74.70pJ		968655um^2	

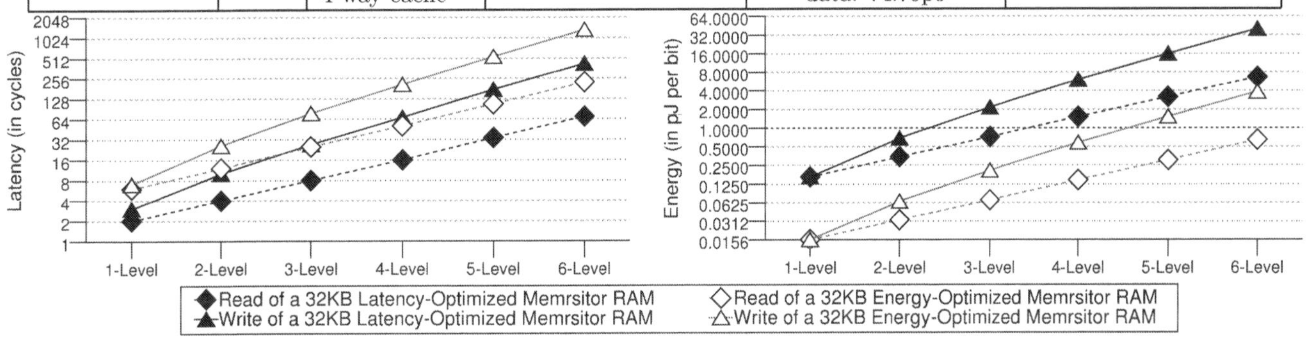

Figure 8: The latency and energy consumption of 32KB multi-level memristor RAMs used in *SpongeDirMid*.

$$ReadLatency(n) = \lceil ReadLatency(1) * ExpoBase^{n-1} \rceil \quad (1)$$

$$WriteLatency(n) = \lceil (ReadLatency(n) + WritePulseLat) * n \rceil \quad (2)$$

$$ReadEnergy(n) \approx ReadEnergy(1) * ExpoBase^{n-1} \quad (3)$$

$$WriteEnergy(n) \approx ReadEnergy(n) * n \quad (4)$$

reducing its provisioning rate. We evaluated three sizes of *SpongeDirectories* — 0.25×, 0.5×, and 1×.

In conclusion, *SpongeDirectory* has smallest because it utilizes both a compact *directory block* format as well as a low *provisioning rate*. This results in *SpongeDirMid* (our default SpongeDirectory configuration) requiring 1/18th of the storage of a conventional sparse directory and less than half of SCD.

Memristor and SRAM-Cache Modeling.

For the detailed modeling of memristors, we use nvsim [10] to obtain the read latency and energy of single-level memristor RAMs under at 22nm process. Cacti 6.5 is used to obtain energy characteristics of SRAM structures. Prior work [37] demonstrated that in designing the memristor-based RAM, there is a trade off between latency, energy and area. We explore two design points: *Latency-Optimized* and *Energy-Optimized.*

As Table 3 shows, memristors in the *Latency-Optimized* configuration are almost twice as fast as the *Energy-Optimized* configuration, but they consume almost 10x the energy and require more area. In addition, we see that for the *Energy-Optimized* configuration, all SpongeDirectory configurations consume substantially less energy than a conventional directory when accessing the lowest level.

Previous work on multi-level PCM reading technology [21] shows that the read latency increases *exponentially* with the number of bits stored in the PCM cell. For a multi-level memristor, we model the same read latency trend—Equation 1 shows how the latency is computed in a multi-level read. *ReadLatency(n)* refers to the latency of an n-level read. *ExpoBase* refers to the exponential base of the modeled multi-level memristor technique.

As mentioned in Section 2.1.2, a multi-level write is composed of multiple iterations, with each iteration consisting of a multi-level read followed by a write pulse. Alibart et al. [3] show that, for a multi-level write, the number of iterations grows linearly with the number of write levels. Equation 2 reflects this curve. *ReadLatency(n)* refers to the latency of an n-level read, and *WritePulseLatency* refers to the latency of a write pulse.

A write pulse consumes trivial energy compared to a read pulse [32], so we make an approximation that the energy consumption of a memristor operation equals the energy consumption of its read sub-operations. Since the power consumption of the read operation is constant (because the read voltage is constant), we obtain Equations 3 & 4 for energy consumption of multi-level read/write operations.

For *ExpoBase*, we use the empirical number 2.1, which is derived from Alibart et al.'s work [3]. Memristor write pulses can be less than one nanosecond [32], therefore we assign $WritePulseLatency = 1ns$ in Equation 2. Figure 8 shows the latency and energy consumption of multi-level operations on 32KB memristor RAMs (with Latency-Optimized or Energy-Optimized configurations).

5. RESULTS

In this section, we present the evaluation of SpongeDirectory in terms of eviction rate, critical directory access latency, overall performance, directory energy consumption and lifetime. For clarity, in each graph, we remove any variations whose results are nearly identical to *SpongeDirMid.*

5.1 Eviction Rate

Eviction rate is the most straight-forward metric for evaluating the effectiveness of a sparse directory scheme. Given a particular configuration of the directory, evictions occur when there is no place in the desired set to place a new entry.

We can see from Figure 9 that, even with a provisioning rate of only 0.25×–1×, SpongeDirectory has a low eviction rate (on average all less than 1%). Evictions occur in SpongeDirectory for three reasons: format upgrades, non-uniform accesses, and lack of capacity.

When SpongeDirectory upgrades directory entries from the sharer pointer format to the sharer vector format, all other entries in the same block are evicted. These evictions could be reinstated at the cost of extra complexity for upgrades. However, given the fact that this occurs rarely in our experiments, there is little justification to introduce this complication.

Directory entries are sometimes non-uniformly distributed [12], leading to evictions in the hotspot directory sets. The SpongeDirectory gains much more associativity by increasing the number of levels it uses (at the cost of latency and energy consumption). For example, *SpongeDirSmall* can exhibit a lower eviction rate than *ConvDir* (`canneal` and `ferret`). As we will see in Section 5.3, this advantage sometimes helps SpongeDirectory achieve higher performance than a much larger conventional directory.

While extra levels provides more tolerance in a particular set than the conventional directory, the overall capacity of *SpongeDirSmall* is less than the conventional directory. 0.25× * 5 levels = 1.25×, which is still substantially smaller than conventional directory's 2×. Thus, the conventional directory can hold many more entries, as long as they are not concentrated in certain sets. This is illustrated in `radix`, where *SpongeDirSmall* experiences an eviction rate of 7.98% because of insufficient capacity in the hotspot *SpongeDirectory* slice.

5.2 Critical Read Operation Latency

As discussed in Section 2.2, the performance of a directory scheme is dependent on critical reads. In Figure 11, we present the latency of critical read accesses of different directory architectures. Compared to a conventional sparse directory, SpongeDirectories require many more cycles (on average 7.56 cycles for *SpongeDirSmall,* 4.44 cycles for *SpongeDirMid* and 4.39 cycles for *SpongeDirLarge,* compared with 0.58 cycles for *ConvDir*) to perform critical read accesses.

This long latency is due to two factors of the memristor technology. First, as an emerging technology, memristor devices still have much longer access latency compared with mature SRAM devices (Table 3). Second, multi-level memristor operations require more latency. Even with

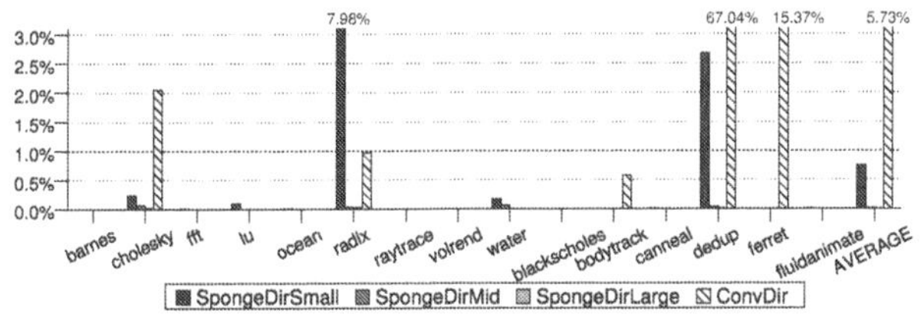

Figure 9: **Directory Eviction Rate**

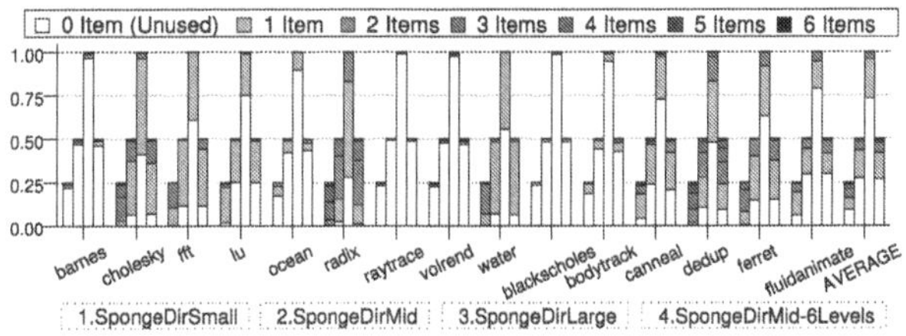

Figure 10: **SpongeDirectory Blocks with Different Items, Normalized to Number of Cache Blocks**

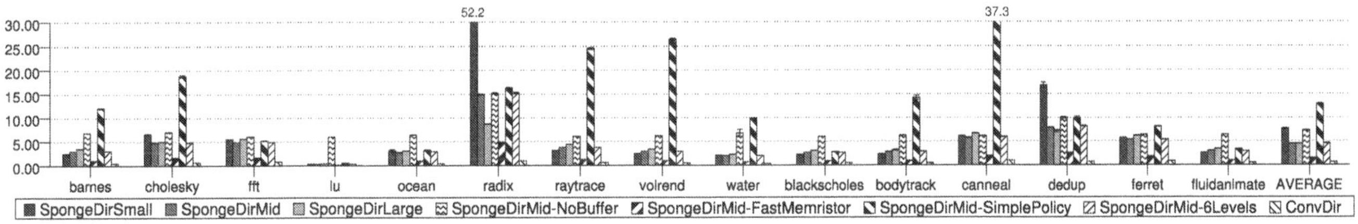

Figure 11: **Average Latency of Critical Read Operations (cycles)**

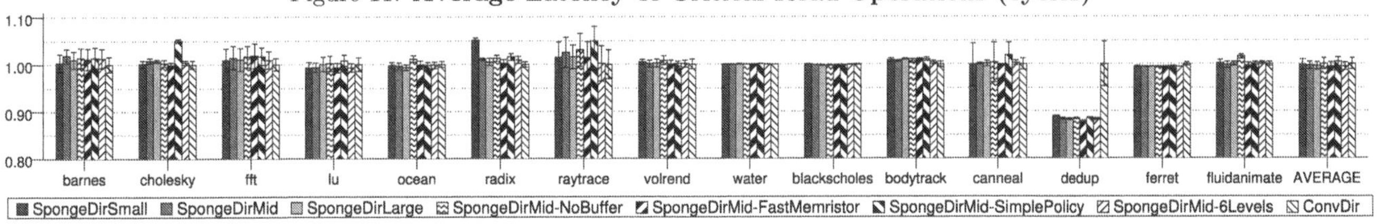

Figure 12: **Normalized Execution Time** (without considering directory request queuing)

careful design to reduce accesses to deeper levels, the lower the provisioning rate, the more often these deeper levels are used.

As shown in Figure 11, design choices such as provisioning rate, buffering, which memristors we use, and the organization policies, affect the critical read latency. Figure 10 shows the most direct reason for rising latency - increased accesses to deeper levels.

Provisioning Rate affects evictions and how often deep levels are acessed. Two benchmarks, `radix` and `dedup`, exhibit long critical latency (52.2 and 16.3 cycles respectively) for *SpongeDirSmall* due to increased accesses to deep levels.

Request Buffering helps reduce the critical latency because part of the requests are bypassed from accessing memristors. On average, the critical read latency of *SpongeDirMid-NoBuffer* is 2.71 cycles longer than *SpongeDirMid*.

Memristor Design can choose to optimize for either latency or energy. Optimizing for latency (*SpongeDirMid-FastMemristor*) is 2× faster (on average 1.47 cycles versus 4.44 cycles) than optimizing for energy (*SpongeDirMid*).

Item Organization Policies were chosen to increase the number of accesses to lower levels. Not utilizing this optimization (*SpongeDirMid-SimplePolicy*) can result in much longer critical read latency—for `cholesky`, 18.79 cycles compared with 4.81 cycles.

Narrower format also increases the access to deeper levels, as shown by *SpongeDirMid-6Levels*. While it did not greatly affect the critical read latency, it has a larger effect on the time when the memristor is busy (see Section 5.3).

5.3 Overall Performance

The overall performance of different schemes is determined by two factors — critical latency in the RAM discussed in Section 5.2 and the queuing time to wait for previous directory operations to finish. As discussed in Section 4, Graphite cannot model the second phenomena. Therefore, we first show the overall execution time not taking into account directory queuing time. We then show the percentage time the busiest slice was being used and discuss the effect of queuing time on overall performance.

Execution Time without Queueing Time.

Figure 12 provides a comparison of overall performance due to read latency between the SpongeDirectory and conventional sparse directory. This represents two competing effects - higher evictions in the conventional sparse directory versus higher read latencies in the SpongeDirectory.

Overall, SpongeDirectory is competitive despite its lower provisioning, more compact format (resulting in 18x fewer bits) and longer memristor access latency.

Closer inspection of the eviction rates and levels used within SpongeDirectory explain the variance in the results. Benchmark `dedup` has a much lower eviction rate in the SpongeDirectory than the conventional directory, and, although higher levels are quite often used, all SpongeDirectory configurations experience a 10% performance gain.

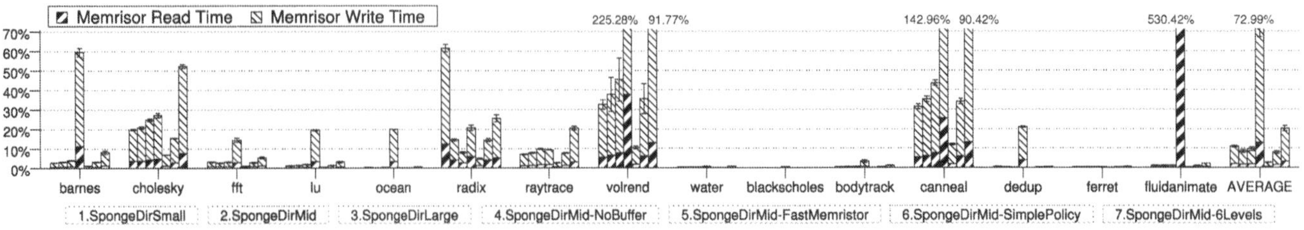

Figure 13: **Percentage time busiest SpongeDirectory slice is serving requests**

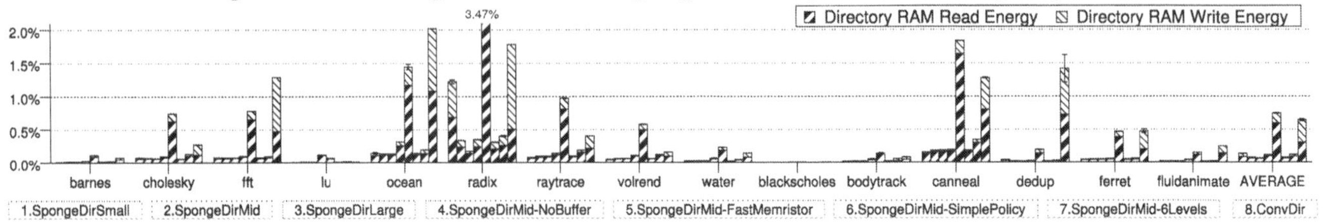

Figure 14: **Percentage of on-chip memory dynamic energy**

We observe two cases of obvious slowdown of SpongeDirectories, and we look for the detailed reasons:

- `cholesky` on *SpongeDirMid-SimplePolicy*: `cholesky` needs much longer critical read latency in the *SpongeDirMid-SimplePolicy* than all other directory architectures. This indicates that careful item organization of the SpongeDirectory is indeed necessary.

- `radix` on *SpongeDirSmall*: `radix` suffers from both a high eviction rate and long critical read latency due to accesses in deep levels. Therefore, we need more capacity than the 0.25× provisioning rate of *SpongeDirSmall* to avoid such pathologically bad behavior.

Considering Queueing Time.

With the help of suspendable multi-level memristor writes, long-latency non-critical memristor accesses typically do not slow down critical directory operations. However, this is based on the assumption that there is enough time when the RAM is not performing critical reads to fit in non-critical, long-latency writes. If the memristor RAM is very busy, the critical requests might be blocked because the limited directory processing buffers are all taken by awaiting non-critical requests.

Figure 13 shows the percentage of memristor access time in the busiest SpongeDirectory slice. For *SpongeDirMid*, the average value is 8.37% (up to 35.1% when running `canneal`), which is acceptable. However, several other *SpongeDirectory* design choices sometimes cause unacceptably long memristor operation time :

- **No request buffering** leads to memristor operation time in the busiest slice which is longer than total exection time for `fluidanimate`, `volrend`, and `canneal`. This would result in a slowdown of at least 1.5x-5.3x.

- **Using six levels instead of five levels** leads to memristor operation time in the busiest slice which is almost same with total exection time for `canneal` and `volrend`, likely slowing down those two applications.

- **Small provisioning rate** (*SpongeDirSmall*) leads to high occupancy in the busiest slice of `radix` - 61.45% of overall execution time.

When we consider the overall execution time and time the busiest slice was being utilized, the reasons for our default parameters are clear. Although *SpongeDirMid-FastMemristor* individual operations are considerably faster than with *SpongeDirMid*, this advantage is not reflected in terms of overall execution, nor an unacceptably large percentage time the the busiest directory slice was being used. Therefore, we do not need to use latency-optimized memristors to maintain competitive performance. In addition, it is clear that buffering is critical. *SpingeDirMid* provides the best trade-off between a low eviction rate, small storage, and good performance. Finally, a wider format that uses only 5 levels is worth the small extra area.

5.4 Dynamic Directory Energy Consumption

Figure 14 shows the breakdown of dynamic energy consumption of different directory schemes. We see that, on average, all of the SpongeDirectories configurations with energy-optimized memristors consume less energy than a conventional directory. *SpongeDirMid* consumes about half the energy of a conventional directory. Even *SpongeDirMid-FastMemristor*, which consumes by far the most energy, consumes only slightly more energy than a conventional directory.

If we compare the these configurations, we see that:

- It is clear that the performance benefit from latency-optimized memristors is far outweighted by the energy benefit of energy-optimized menristors.

- Request buffering further reduces the energy consumption. When executing `ocean`, *SpongeDirMid* consumes half the energy of *SpongeDirMid-NoBuffer*.

- A small provisioning rate can substantially increase the energy consumption. For example, when executing `radix`, *SpongeDirSmall* consumes nearly three times more energy than *SpongeDirMid* due to increased accesses to deeper levels.

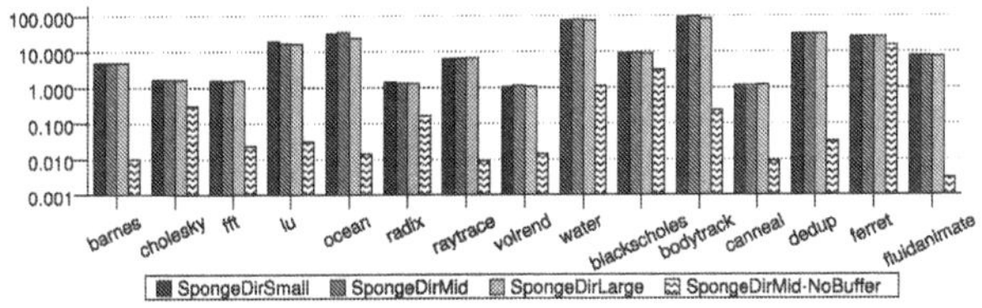

Figure 15: **Worst Case Lifetime (in Years)**

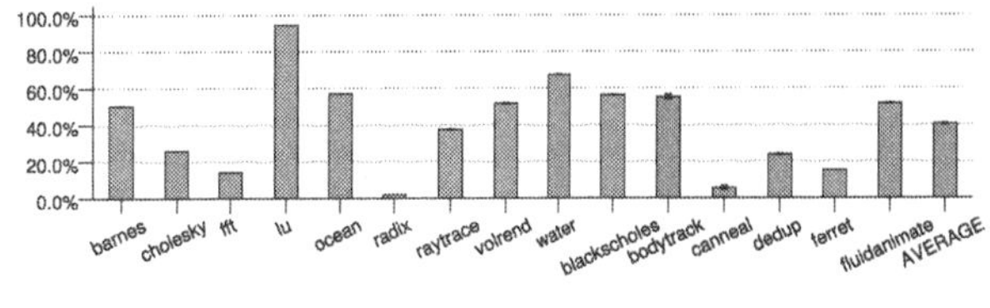

Figure 16: **Percentage of Bypassed Memristor Accesses of SpongeDirMid due to Buffering**

5.5 Memristor Lifetime

Based on statistics provided by Yang et al.'s work [40], we assume the endurance of each SpongeDirectory block is 10^{12} writes and report the lifetime of the most hotspot SpongeDirectory block in Figure 15. We can make two major conclusions. First, the provisioning rate does not have a large effect on worst-case lifetime. The worst-case lifetime of *SpongeDirMid* over all benchmarks is over 1 year. Since the hotspot SpongeDirectory block is unlikely to be the same block over long runs, we anticipate the overall lifetime of *SpongeDirMid* to be at least several years.

Second, request buffering is required for a feasable memristor implementation. Without buffering (*SpongeDirMid-NoBuffer*), in most cases the worst lifetime is below 1 year (down to 0.003 year in `fluidanimate`). This is because buffering is very effective at reducing the access rate of applications with high accesses to specific blocks when it is critical, as shown in Figure 16. This shows the percentage of bypassed memristor accesses with directory request buffering. For some benchmarks, a large percentage of directory requests are bypassed (up to 94.29% for `lu`); whereas for some other benchmarks, few directory requests are bypassed (down to 2.08% for `radix`). Note that, even though `radix` has a small bypass rate, request buffering still increases the worst case lifetime by 7.6 times. This is because the buffered requests are exactly the ones visiting hotspot *blocks*.

5.6 Summary

In summary, experimental results show that *SpongeDirMid* is a reasonable design choice. This design choice uses the following configurations for reasons:

- 0.5× **provisioning rate** provides a balance between good performance (compared to smaller) and storage space (compared to larger).
- **Buffering of eight most recently finished requests** dramatically increases the lifetime of the memristors and reduces the amount of time the memristors are busy (allowing for critical reads to interrupt long-latency write operations).
- **Using energy-optimized memristors** substantially reduces the total energy and area requirements with negligible reductions in overall performance.
- **Using a head shallower item organization policy** reduces overall execution time in some cases (e.g., `cholesky`).
- **Using a wider, shallower 5-level memristor scheme instead of a narrower, 6-level scheme** decreases the overall memristor operation time, allowing for more critical reads to interrupt long-latency write operations in some cases (e.g., `canneal`).

6. RELATED WORK

6.1 Multi-level Non-Volatile Memory

Recently, several projects have focused on architectural support for multi-level non-volatile memories (multi-level NVMs) from different angles. Qureshi et al. [25] improved the access latency of multi-level PCM by using a hardware-software hybrid scheme, which converts a multi-level PCM page into two single-level PCM pages when used often. Several projects [18][19] [24][34] focus on improving the MLC NVM write performance/energy/endurance by improving the NVM infrastructure and memory controller. Jiang et al. [17] also worked on improving the performance of a multi-level STT-RAM. Saadeldeen et al. [27] use memristors for branch prediction. Sampson et al. [28] propose to improve the performance, lifetime or density of multi-level PCM with an approximate storage technique.

However, to our knowledge, no previous work has used multi-level NVM to solve the coherence directory scaling problem.

6.2 Coherence Directory

Many projects have attempted to reduce the storage of on-chip directories as well as tolerate the variability in sharers and entries. The SpongeDirectory provides extra storage at the expense of higher latency and energy, whereas these schemes reduce storage needs or use those bits more efficiently. Most of these schemes could be combined with SpongeDirectory to provide even more area savings.

Building hierarchical directories [33][15][1][20][22] is another way to reduce directory storage while still preserving exact sharer information. Martin et al. proposed a hierarchical solution for the in-cache directory [22] which embeds coherence information into a hierarchy of inclusive caches. They show that such a approach is efficient in terms of area, network traffic and energy. However, such hierarchical designs create complexity challenges. Another scheme, *Waypoint* [20], uses small directory caches on chip, overflowing extra directory entries to a special part of cacheable user-space memory. It requires over substantially higher directory lookup latency when there is an on-chip directory miss.

The Cuckoo Directory [12] was partly motivated by the observation that set-level non-uniform accesses to directory entries could induce an excessive number of invalidations. This uses a complex hashing technique which achieves almost the same invalidation rate as a fully associative sparse directory with only moderate (about 1.5×) over-provisioning. However, this scheme does not seek to reduce the sharer storage within a directory entry, thus it is not scalable in storage for many-core systems.

The SpongeDirectory is inspired by *Scalable Coherence Directory (SCD)* [30] which introduced a pointer-vector hybrid scheme to encode sharer information. SCD "borrows" blocks from underutilized sets, whereas the SpongeDirectory uses technology to provide extra space within the same set. SCD relies on high directory associativity, like Cuckoo Directory (Zcache [29]). Such schemes are complimentary to SpongeDirectory and could be used to provide further space savings.

Compression has been used by storing some information at the page level[9][26], using dual-grained tracking[4], and using many granularities[41][11]. Others have used varying compression schemes [31, 43, 42, 44].

7. CONCLUSIONS

In order to scale up coherence directories for future extra-scale many-core system, we propose SpongeDirectory, a sparse directory scheme utilizing multi-level memristor RAMs. Each SpongeDirectory block is able to dynamically change its number of levels (thus total storage), according to current dynamic requirement.

Evaluations on a 256-core extreme-scale processor show that a SpongeDirectory optimized for low energy consumption has the performance of a conventional sparse directory with over 18× the storage space while using 8× less energy.

Finally, SpongeDirectory uses technology to accommodate variation in directory demands. This could be combined with other schemes to reduce overall storage requirements such as using organization (i.e. SCD) or compression.

8. ACKNOWLEDGEMENTS

We would like to thank Lei Liu and our anonymous reviewers for their thoughtful comments. This work is supported in part by NSF grant CCF-1017578, the National Grand Fundamental Research 973 Program of China under Grant No. 2011CB302501, the Foundation for Innovative Research Groups of the National Natural Science Foundation of China under Grant No. 60736012, and the National Natural Science Foundation of China under Grant No. 61332009 and 61202059, and a gift from Google.

9. REFERENCES

[1] M. E. Acacio, J. Gonzalez, J. M. Garcia, and J. Duato, "A two-level directory architecture for highly scalable cc-numa multiprocessors," *Parallel and Distributed Systems, IEEE Transactions on*, vol. 16, no. 1, pp. 67–79, 2005.

[2] A. Alameldeen and D. Wood, "Variability in architectural simulations of multi-threaded workloads," in *9th IEEE International Symposium on High-Performance Computer Architecture*, 2003, pp. 7–18.

[3] F. Alibart, L. Gao, B. Hoskins, and D. B. Strukov, "High-precision tuning of state for memristive devices by adaptable variation-tolerant algorithm," *CoRR*, vol. abs/1110.1393, 2011.

[4] M. Alisafaee, "Spatiotemporal coherence tracking," in *45th Annual IEEE/ACM International Symposium on Microarchitecture*, 2012, pp. 341–350.

[5] M. Bach, M. Charney, R. Cohn, E. Demikhovsky, T. Devor, K. Hazelwood, A. Jaleel, C.-K. Luk, G. Lyons, H. Patil *et al.*, "Analyzing parallel programs with pin," *IEEE Computer*, vol. 43, no. 3, pp. 34–41, 2010.

[6] R. J. Baker, *CMOS: circuit design, layout, and simulation.* Wiley-IEEE Press, 2011, vol. 18.

[7] C. Bienia, S. Kumar, J. P. Singh, and K. Li, "The PARSEC benchmark suite: Characterization and architectural implications," in *17th International Conference on Parallel Architectures and Compilation Techniques*, 2008, pp. 72–81.

[8] P. Conway, N. Kalyanasundharam, G. Donley, K. Lepak, and B. Hughes, "Cache hierarchy and memory subsystem of the AMD Opteron processor," *IEEE Micro*, vol. 30, pp. 16–29, Mar.–Apr. 2010.

[9] B. A. Cuesta, A. Ros, M. E. Gómez, A. Robles, and J. F. Duato, "Increasing the effectiveness of directory caches by deactivating coherence for private memory blocks," in *38th International Symposium on Computer Architecture*, 2011, pp. 93–104.

[10] X. Dong, C. Xu, Y. Xie, and N. P. Jouppi, "NVSim: A circuit-level performance, energy, and area model for emerging nonvolatile memory," *IEEE Trans. on CAD of Integrated Circuits and Systems*, vol. 31, no. 7, pp. 994–1007, 2012.

[11] L. Fang, P. Liu, Q. Hu, M. C. Huang, and G. Jiang, "Building expressive, area-efficient coherence directories," in *Proceedings of the 22nd international conference on Parallel architectures and compilation techniques*, 2013, pp. 299–308.

[12] M. Ferdman, P. Lotfi-Kamran, K. Balet, and B. Falsafi, "Cuckoo directory: A scalable directory for many-core systems," in *17th IEEE International Symposium on High-Performance Computer Architecture*, 2011, pp. 169–180.

[13] L. Gao, F. Merrikh-Bayat, X. Guo, D. B. Strukov, and K.-T. Cheng, "Digital-to-analog and analog-to-digital conversion with metal oxide memristors for ultra-low power computing," in *IEEE/ACM International Symposium on Nanoscale Architectures*, 2013, pp. 19–22.

[14] G. Grohoski, "Niagara-2: A highly threaded server-on-a-chip," in *Hot Chips 20*, 2008.

[15] S.-L. Guo, H.-X. Wang, Y.-B. Xue, C.-M. Li, and D.-S. Wang, "Hierarchical cache directory for CMP," *Journal of Computer Science and Technology*, vol. 25, pp. 246–256, Mar. 2010.

[16] A. Gupta, W.-D. Weber, and T. Mowry, "Reducing memory and traffic requirements for scalable directory-based cache coherence schemes," in *19th International Conference on Parallel Processing*, 1990, pp. 312–321.

[17] L. Jiang, B. Zhao, Y. Zhang, and J. Yang, "Constructing large and fast multi-level cell stt-mram based cache for embedded processors," in *Design Automation Conference (DAC), 2012 49th ACM/EDAC/IEEE*, 2012, pp. 907–912.

[18] L. Jiang, B. Zhao, Y. Zhang, J. Yang, and B. R. Childers, "Improving write operations in mlc phase change memory," in *High Performance Computer Architecture (HPCA), 2012 IEEE 18th International Symposium on.* IEEE, 2012, pp. 1–10.

[19] M. Joshi, W. Zhang, and T. Li, "Mercury: A fast and energy-efficient multi-level cell based phase change memory system," in *High Performance Computer Architecture (HPCA), 2011 IEEE 17th International Symposium on.* IEEE, 2011, pp. 345–356.

[20] J. H. Kelm, M. R. Johnson, S. S. Lumettta, and S. J. Patel, "WAYPOINT: Scaling coherence to thousand-core architectures," in *19th International Conference on Parallel Architectures and Compilation Techniques*, 2010, pp. 99–110.

[21] J. Li, C.-I. Wu, S. C. Lewis, J. Morrish, T.-Y. Wang, R. Jordan, T. Maffitt, M. Breitwisch, A. Schrott, R. Cheek *et al.*, "A novel reconfigurable sensing scheme for variable level storage in phase change memory," in *Memory Workshop (IMW), 2011 3rd IEEE International*, 2011, pp. 1–4.

[22] M. M. K. Martin, M. D. Hill, and D. J. Sorin, "Why on-chip cache coherence is here to stay," *Commun. ACM*, vol. 55, pp. 78–89, Jul. 2012.

[23] J. E. Miller, H. Kasture, G. Kurian, C. Gruenwald, N. Beckmann, C. Celio, J. Eastep, and A. Agarwal, "Graphite: A distributed parallel simulator for multicores," in *16th IEEE International Symposium on High-Performance Computer Architecture*, 2010, pp. 1–12.

[24] D. Niu, Q. Zou, C. Xu, and Y. Xie, "Low power multi-level-cell resistive memory design with incomplete data mapping," in *Computer Design (ICCD), 2013 IEEE 31st International Conference on.* IEEE, 2013, pp. 131–137.

[25] M. K. Qureshi, M. M. Franceschini, L. A. Lastras-Montaño, and J. P. Karidis, "Morphable memory system: A robust architecture for exploiting multi-level phase change memories," in *37th International Symposium on Computer Architecture*, 2010, pp. 153–162.

[26] A. Ros and S. Kaxiras, "Complexity-effective multicore coherence," in *21st International Conference on Parallel Architectures and Compilation Techniques*, 2012, pp. 241–252.

[27] H. Saadeldeen, D. Franklin, G. Long, C. Hill, A. Browne, D. Strukov, T. Sherwood, and F. T. Chong, "Memristors for neural branch prediction: a case study in strict latency and write endurance challenges," in *Proceedings of the ACM International Conference on Computing Frontiers*, 2013, p. 26.

[28] A. Sampson, J. Nelson, K. Strauss, and L. Ceze, "Approximate storage in solid-state memories," in *Proceedings of the 46th Annual IEEE/ACM International Symposium on Microarchitecture*, 2013, pp. 25–36.

[29] D. Sanchez and C. Kozyrakis, "The ZCache: Decoupling ways and associativity," in *43rd Annual IEEE/ACM International Symposium on Microarchitecture*, 2010, pp. 187–198.

[30] ——, "SCD: A scalable coherence directory with flexible sharer set encoding," in *18th IEEE International Symposium on High-Performance Computer Architecture*, 2012, pp. 1–12.

[31] R. Simoni, "Cache coherence directories for scalable multiprocessors," Stanford University, Technical Report CSL-TR-92-550, Oct. 1992.

[32] A. C. Torrezan, J. P. Strachan, G. Medeiros-Ribeiro, and R. S. Williams, "Sub-nanosecond switching of a tantalum oxide memristor," *Nanotechnology*, vol. 22, no. 48, 2011.

[33] D. A. Wallach, "PHD: a hierarchical cache coherent protocol," Master's thesis, Massachusetts Institute of Technology, 1992.

[34] J. Wang, X. Dong, G. Sun, D. Niu, and Y. Xie, "Energy-efficient multi-level cell phase-change memory system with data encoding," in *Computer Design (ICCD), 2011 IEEE 29th International Conference on*, 2011, pp. 175–182.

[35] S. C. Woo, M. Ohara, E. Torrie, J. P. Singh, and A. Gupta, "The SPLASH-2 programs: Characterization and methodological considerations," in *22nd International Symposium on Computer Architecture*, 1995, pp. 24–36.

[36] Q. Xia, W. Robinett, M. W. Cumbie, N. Banerjee, T. J. Cardinali, J. J. Yang, W. Wu, X. Li, W. M. Tong, D. B. Strukov, and Others, "Memristor-CMOS Hybrid Integrated Circuits for Reconfigurable Logic," *Nano letters*, vol. 9, no. 10, pp. 3640–3645, 2009.

[37] C. Xu, X. Dong, N. P. Jouppi, and Y. Xie, "Design implications of memristor-based rram cross-point structures." in *DATE*, 2011, pp. 734–739.

[38] C. Xu, D. Niu, N. Muralimanohar, N. P. Jouppi, and Y. Xie, "Understanding the trade-offs in multi-level cell reram memory design," in *Design Automation Conference (DAC), 2013 50th ACM/EDAC/IEEE.* IEEE, 2013, pp. 1–6.

[39] J. J. Yang, M. D. Pickett, X. Li, O. A. A., D. R. Stewart, and R. S. Williams, "Memristive switching mechanism for metal//oxide//metal nanodevices," *Nature Nanotechnology*, vol. 3, pp. 429–433, 2008.

[40] J. J. Yang, D. B. Strukov, and D. R. Stewart, "Memristive devices for computing," *Nature Nanotechnology*, vol. 8, pp. 13–24, 2013.

[41] J. Zebchuk, B. Falsafi, and A. Moshovos, "Multi-grain coherence directory," in *Proceedings of the 46th Annual IEEE/ACM International Symposium on Microarchitecture (MICRO 2013)*, no. EPFL-CONF-195669, 2013.

[42] J. Zebchuk, V. Srinivasan, M. K. Qureshi, and A. Moshovos, "A tagless coherence directory," in *42nd Annual IEEE/ACM International Symposium on Microarchitecture*, 2009, pp. 423–434.

[43] H. Zhao, S. Arrvindh, S. Dwarkadas, and V. Srinivasan, "SPATL: Honey, i shrunk the coherence directory," in *20th International Conference on Parallel Architectures and Compilation Techniques*, 2011, pp. 33–44.

[44] H. Zhao, A. Shriraman, and S. Dwarkadas, "SPACE: Sharing pattern-based directory coherence for multicore scalability," in *19th International Conference on Parallel Architectures and Compilation Techniques*, 2010, pp. 135–146.

EFetch: Optimizing Instruction Fetch for Event-Driven Web Applications

Gaurav Chadha Scott Mahlke Satish Narayanasamy
University of Michigan, Ann Arbor
{gauravc, mahlke, nsatish}@umich.edu

ABSTRACT

Web 2.0 applications written in JavaScript are increasingly popular as they are easy to use, easy to update and maintain, and portable across a wide variety of computing platforms. Web applications receive frequent input from a rich array of sensors, network, and user input modalities. To handle the resulting asynchrony due to these inputs, web applications are developed using an event-driven programming model. These event-driven web applications have dramatically different characteristics, which provides an opportunity to create a customized processor core to improve the responsiveness of web applications.

In this paper, we take one step towards creating a core customized to event-driven applications. We observe that instruction cache misses of web applications are substantially higher than conventional server and desktop workloads due to large working sets caused by distant re-use. To mitigate this bottleneck, we propose an instruction prefetcher (EFetch) that is tuned to exploit the characteristics of web applications. We find that an *event signature*, which captures the current event and function calling context, is a good predictor of the control flow inside a function of an event-driven program. It allows us to accurately predict a function's callees and their function bodies and prefetch them in a timely manner. For a set of real-world web applications, we show that the proposed prefetcher outperforms commonly implemented next-2-line prefetcher by 17%. Also, it consumes 5.2 times less area than a recently proposed prefetcher, while outperforming it.

Categories and Subject Descriptors

B.3.2 [**Memory Structures**]: Design Styles—cache memories

Keywords

Event-driven web applications; JavaScript; Instruction Prefetching

PACT'14, August 24–27, 2014, Edmonton, AB, Canada.

ACM 978-1-4503-2809-8/14/08 ...$15.00.
http://dx.doi.org/10.1145/2628071.2628103.

1. INTRODUCTION

Web 2.0 has revolutionized the way we use personal computers today. Modern websites are extremely dynamic, feeding personalized contents to the users according to their preferences. Web 2.0 has also enabled a new class of client-side web applications such as web emails, interactive maps, and social networks. A web application is essentially a program that runs within a web browser. Web applications are increasingly popular today due to the ease with which users can run these applications within their web browsers without having to download and install them on their personal computers. Web applications also allow developers to instantly update and maintain them. Furthermore, as they can run within almost any web browser, they are highly portable across diverse systems ranging from servers and desktops to tablets and smart phones.

A large fraction of the Web 2.0 content are being programmed using JavaScript today, as it is commonly supported in most popular web browsers in use. Web applications written in scripting languages receive input from diverse sources such as user clicks, accelerometers, microphones, and other sensors. These rich array of input sources provide large asynchronicity to the input stream of web applications. As a result, *event-driven* programming models naturally arise among popular web development platforms. An event-driven model makes it easy to integrate input from a rich array of sensors and user input modalities.

Event-driven web applications typically execute thousands of events in a second. Runtime characteristics of the event-driven web applications developed using scripts are dramatically different from the conventional server or desktop applications, which have been the primary focus for most processor optimizations studied till today.

As Moore's Law continues to hold true, we may be able to continue to increase the number of processor cores in a chip. However, due to the end of Dennard scaling, it is also likely that we may not be able to power-up and operate all the processor cores at the same time. Heterogeneous processors are a likely solution to mitigate this "dark silicon" problem [9]. Given that web applications constitute a dominant use for consumer devices, we envision that one or more of the cores in a heterogeneous multi-core processor could be "Web Cores" that are customized for executing web applications.

In this paper, we take the first step towards designing a WebCore by identifying an important performance bottleneck in event-driven web applications, namely, instruction fetch, and propose an instruction prefetcher, **E**vent **Fetch** or EFetch, to mitigate it. We studied several Web 2.0 applications and discovered that L1 instruction cache misses to be a critical performance bottleneck. Instruction fetch is a more severe problem for web applications than it is for certain server applications that have been used in the past instruction fetch optimization studies [10, 11]. While the L1 instruction cache misses per kilo-instructions (mpki) is on the order of 1-3 for conventional applications, it is nearly 25 on average for popular web applications, e.g., Facebook, Gmail, Amazon, CNN, Google maps.

Event-driven web applications experience poor instruction cache performance for several reasons. First, the size of JavaScript code associated with most web sites is very large, ranging from 200 KB to several megabytes [19]. Second, not only is their instruction footprint larger than conventional programs, but they also do not exhibit much temporal locality for instruction addresses. The reason is that, diverse set of events are invoked in response to external inputs, resulting in too many hot functions. Also, each of those events is designed such that it executes for a fairly short period of time (thousands of instructions on average, millions in the worst case) to ensure responsiveness. In a conventional application, iteration counts of hot loops could be in hundreds of thousands, which causes them to exhibit much more temporal locality. But, loops in web applications rarely ever iterate for a long time. Finally, only about a tenth of a function body gets accessed when a function is invoked. This combined with rich control flow within a function, results in poor spatial locality.

L1 instruction cache misses significantly degrade performance. On average, across the web applications studied, performance can be increased by 53% if all L1-I cache misses are eliminated. Unlike data cache misses, out-of-order execution cannot hide the latency of an instruction cache miss that stalls the pipeline. While there is a rich literature on designing instruction prefetchers to address this problem [12, 18, 27, 22], past prefetcher designs have significant limitations when applied to event-driven programs. They either rely on spatial locality [12, 22], address access patterns [27], predictability of branches [8], or require fairly large hardware structures [10].

In this paper, we define *event signatures* to design a custom prefetcher for web applications. An event signature is a hash of current event-identifier and function call context signature (a hash of call addresses of functions at the top of call stack). The web browser is responsible for constructing an identifier for an event and initializing a special hardware *event register* before beginning to process an event's handler. We observe that the event signature is a good predictor of the control flow inside a function, which in turn allows us to predict a function's callees and their function bodies.

In addition to the event register, our WebCore architecture has a hardware *callee predictor table* that keeps track of the set of callees invoked from a function under an event signature context. On encountering a previously seen event signature, WebCore issues prefetch requests to its callees. A prefetcher is effective only if it can prefetch the cache blocks ahead of their use. In our design, we prefetch the next function to be called, going down the program call graph in a depth-first manner, staying one function ahead of the program execution. A *predictor stack* keeps track of the predicted call graph and validates as the trailing program makes progress. In the case of a mispredicted call, a recovery is initiated to start the prefetch from the correct functional call context.

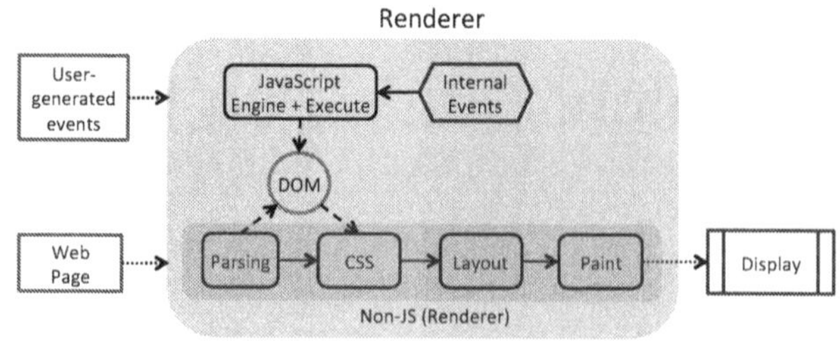

Figure 1: Software components of a renderer process in a browser.

We study a representative website from each class of web applications: e-commerce (`amazon`), interactive maps (`google maps`), search (`bing`), social networking (`facebook`), news (`cnn`), utilities (`google docs`), and data-intensive applications (`pixlr`). We show that WebCore's prefetcher (EFetch) outperforms commercially implemented next-2-line prefetcher by 17%. It also outperforms a recently proposed prefetcher, PIF [10], while consuming 5.2 times less area.

2. BACKGROUND AND MOTIVATION

In this section, we briefly describe a web browser system and the event-driven programming model used to write Web 2.0 applications.

2.1 Web Browser Software Architecture

A web browser consists of several processes. For each user session ("tab"), the browser spawns off a renderer process, which performs the critical tasks of a browser. A main process in the web browser receives events from the external system and delivers them to the appropriate renderer process.

The software components of a renderer process are shown in Figure 1. They are responsible for tasks such as parsing `HTML` content, layout, and paint. When it encounters events that need to be processed by executing a JavaScript (JS) program, it invokes the JavaScript engine. The JavaScript engine starts executing the source code in the interpreted mode first, and then dynamically compiles hot functions into native code.

Web applications are written in JavaScript using an event-driven programming model. Figure 3 shows an example execution of a web application. A looper thread in the renderer process constantly polls an event-queue. It dequeues one event at a time and invokes the necessary JavaScript handler function to process the event. The events may be generated internally or in response to an external input. A critical rule that web developers adhere to is that durations of events are short. This is necessary to ensure that a web application is responsive to the user. If an event has to wait for any long-latency operation (e.g., downloading a web page), instead of stalling, the event handler would register an event callback to be invoked when the long-latency operation has completed, and then return.

2.2 Motivation for WebCore

Characteristics of event-driven programs are significantly different from the conventional programs. We studied several microarchitectural characteristics of web applications

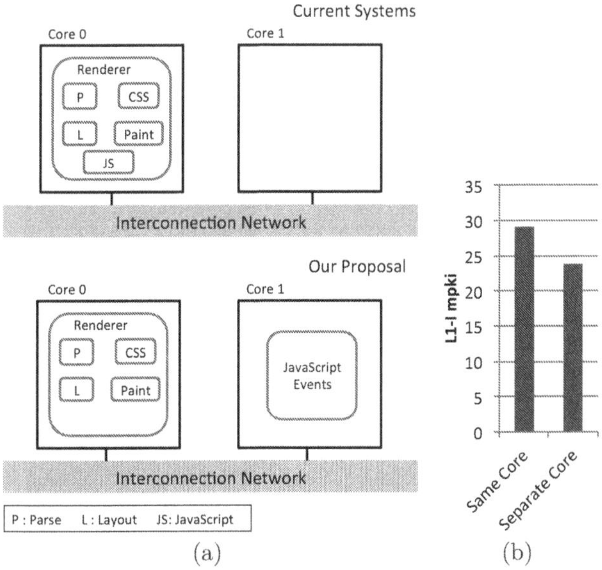

Figure 2: (a) Isolating JavaScript Events, (b) L1-I mpki when executing JS events along with the entire Renderer (Same Core) or Isolated (Separate Core)

and discovered that instruction cache misses and branch mispredictions are significantly higher than most conventional programs studied in the past.

Web applications suffer from an instruction fetch bottleneck due to the event-driven nature of these programs. These applications execute a wide range of functions in response to different events initiated by the user and the external system. Furthermore, each function in JavaScript executes for only a few hundreds of instructions to ensure responsiveness. As a result, event-driven JavaScript programs exhibit little temporal locality. They also tend to expose relatively less spatial locality due to rich control flow within the body of a function, which is written to handle a variety of control states within the web application. Finally, the instruction footprint of web applications on average is about 200 KB but could be as high as 2 MB (e.g., `google maps`).

As the processor industry moves towards heterogeneous multi-core processors, we envision that one or more cores could be customized to exploit the characteristics of web applications. In such a scenario, the JS component of the web browser would execute on a dedicated processor core ("Web Core") different from the one used for executing the other parts of the renderer process as shown in Figure 2(a).

Figure 2(b) shows the L1 instruction cache (I-cache) mpki when we execute the JS events along with all the renderer process. On average, L1 I-cache mpki could be as high as 29. I-cache mpki reduces to about 24 when we execute the native code produced by the JS engine on a separate core. Though, by executing the JS events on a separate core, L1 data cache suffers from coherence misses. However, the impact of this is very small, mitigated, in part, by the additional L1 cache capacity on the separate core. There is a loss of 2.1% in performance compared to running the JS events with the renderer process. In our study, we seek to optimize the I-cache performance of a "Web Core" that is dedicated to execute the instructions corresponding to the JS events.

Figure 4 shows the I-cache mpki for the several web applications we studied. For reference, it also shows the average mpki we observed for conventional PARSEC [6] and SPECint 2006 [2] workloads. I-cache mpki for web applications could be as high as 26 (`bing`), where for SPECint 2006 it is about 2.

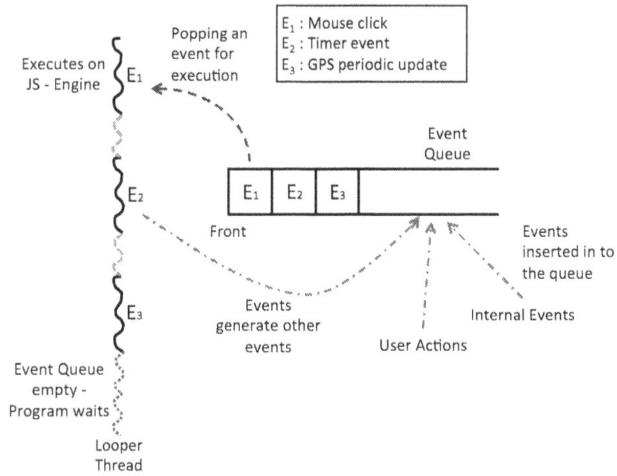

Figure 3: Event-Driven Programming Model

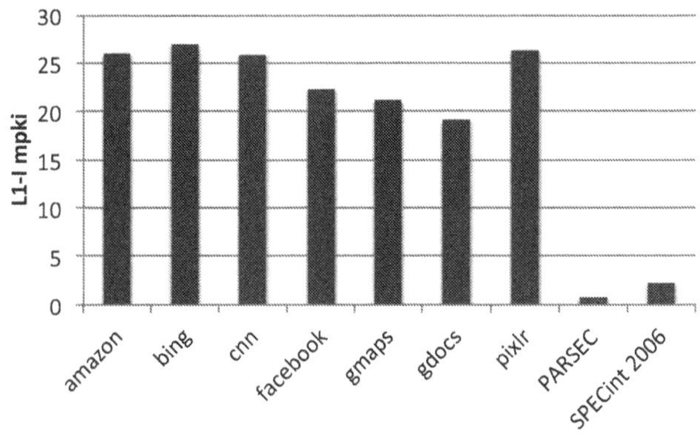

Figure 4: Comparison of L1-I cache mpki

Figure 5 shows the cumulative I-cache L1 miss rates observed due to different cache blocks accessed. As the figure shows, we need over 10,000 cache blocks to cover 80% of misses for web applications. However, a few hundred cache blocks can cover almost all the I-cache misses for the conventional PARSEC programs, or a couple thousand for SPECint 2006 programs. These results indicate the need for an instruction prefetcher that is customized to exploit the characteristics of the event-driven JavaScript web applications.

3. DESIGN

In this section we first discuss the key insights, an overview, and the architecture design of *EFetch*, an instruction cache prefetcher for event-driven Web applications.

3.1 Observations and Insights

Our design for prefetching the instruction stream ahead of its use, banks on our observation that the event signature is highly correlated with the stream of instructions executed in event-driven applications. In other words, event signature is a good predictor of the control flow inside a function, which in turn allows us to predict a function's callees and their function bodies. In fact, we can accurately predict the order

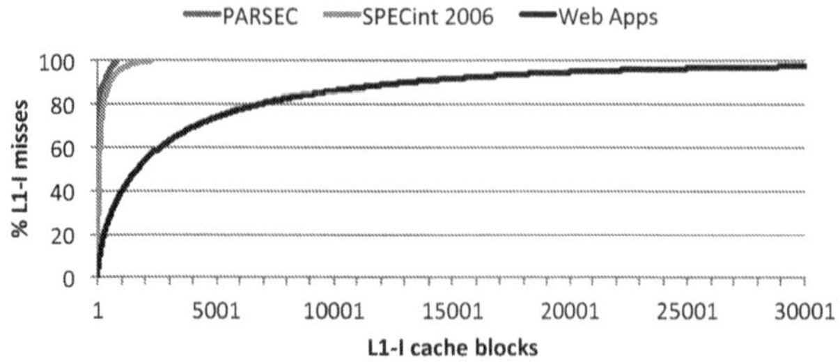

Figure 5: Cumulative Distribution of L1-I cache misses across cache blocks

in which the callees of a function are invoked. By keeping track of the cache block addresses accessed with the event signature those cache blocks can be prefetched when the same event signature is seen again.

But, a prefetcher is good only if it can prefetch the cache blocks ahead of their use. For this reason, in our design we also keep track of the functions called (callees) corresponding to an event signature. This way, we can prefetch the next function to be called, going down the program call graph (Figure 7) in a depth-first manner, staying ahead of the program execution.

However, we should not keep prefetching deep down the call graph without the program advancing, because of the following reasons:

- The accuracy of predicting the next function to be executed reduces as we go further ahead of the program execution. This could lead to erroneous prefetches, polluting the cache.
- It is likely that by the time the function whose cache blocks were prefetched very early, gets called, those cache blocks might have gotten evicted. This not only results in poorer coverage, but also wastes energy.

3.2 Prefetching Policy

In EFetch, we use the event signature as a key, formed by a simple XOR of the event-ID with *context depth* most recent function call addresses (*context depth* = 3 in our final design). Our design depends on the predictability of the functions called and the function bodies executed under this key. So, we keep track of the functions invoked (callees) under different keys. Additionally, the function body addresses accessed within the callees are also recorded with these keys.

During program execution, on a function call, an event signature is formed from the event-ID and the call context. If this event signature has been seen before, the first callee recorded earlier is predicted to be the next function called and its predicted function body is prefetched. For example, in Figure 7, when f_1 gets called, g_1 is prefetched (step 0 in Figure 8). Since it is important for the prefetcher to stay ahead of program execution, the next predicted function is prefetched. In trying to hide memory latency, the prefetcher can, potentially, go further down the call graph and prefetch more functions ahead of time. However, we lose accuracy in predicting the next function the deeper we go down a call graph. Also, in our workloads, due to high hit rate of instructions in the L2 cache, we only need to hide the L1-I cache miss latency. Thus, we prefetch only the next predicted function (except in the case of leaf functions).

When the program catches up (step 1), the prefetcher goes down the callgraph, prefetching the next function (h_1). On returning from a callee, the next callee is prefetched.

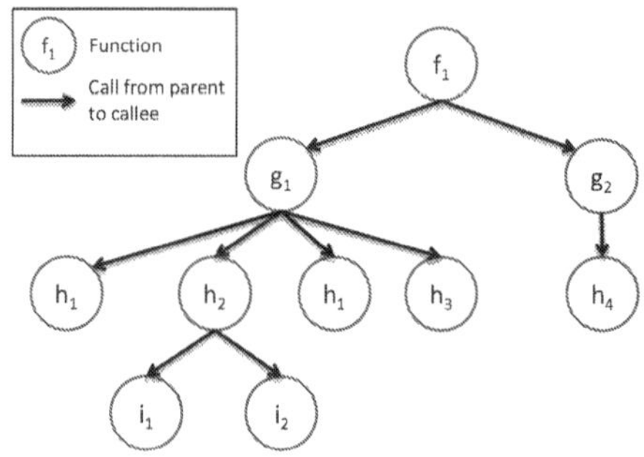

Figure 7: A pre-order traversal of this call graph shows the order in which the functions are called.

Step	Call Stack	Functions Prefetched
0	f_1	g_1
1	$f_1 g_1$	h_1, h_2
2	$f_1 g_1 h_1$	-
3	$f_1 g_1$	-
4	$f_1 g_1 h_2$	i_1, i_2
	...	

Step	Call Stack	Functions Prefetched	
5	$f_1 g_1$	h_3	← h_2 returns
6	$f_1 g_1 h_1$	-	
7	$f_1 g_1$	-	
8	$f_1 g_1 h_3$	-	
9	$f_1 g_1$	-	
10	f_1	g_2	
	...		

Figure 8: Functions prefetched on different points of program execution

If the prefetched callee is a leaf function, we can predict the next callee (its sibling) with high accuracy. So, in case of a leaf function, we prefetch its next sibling (h_2 in step 1). If the sibling is also a leaf function, that gets prefetched too and so on. The prefetcher stops if the sibling is a non-leaf function, even if there are more siblings in the callee list which are leaf functions. This is because, it is unclear how deep the call graph might go when executing the non-leaf function, and prefetching upcoming leaf siblings might be too early.

If a callee gets mispredicted (on a non-leaf function call, the function called does not match the last prefetched function), the prefetcher stops and synchronizes itself with the actual function call stack. Thereafter, prefetches continue just like before.

3.3 Predicting Callees and Prefetching Future Accesses

EFetch design architecture has been illustrated in Figure 6. The event-ID is stored in the event-ID register. It is formed by the browser using the type of event and the JavaScript function address. *EA* is a unit that forms addresses from their compact stored representation consisting of a base address and a bit vector.

The current function call stack of the program is maintained in the *Call Stack*, each entry of which is a function call address. On a function call, the function call address is pushed onto the *Call Stack* and the event signature is computed. The event signature and the function call address is then used to index in to the *Callee Predictor* to obtain the list of callees and their function bodies to be prefetched.

The *Callee Predictor* records the function bodies and callees corresponding to different event signatures. To save space, this information is maintained in two tables (Figure 6), one

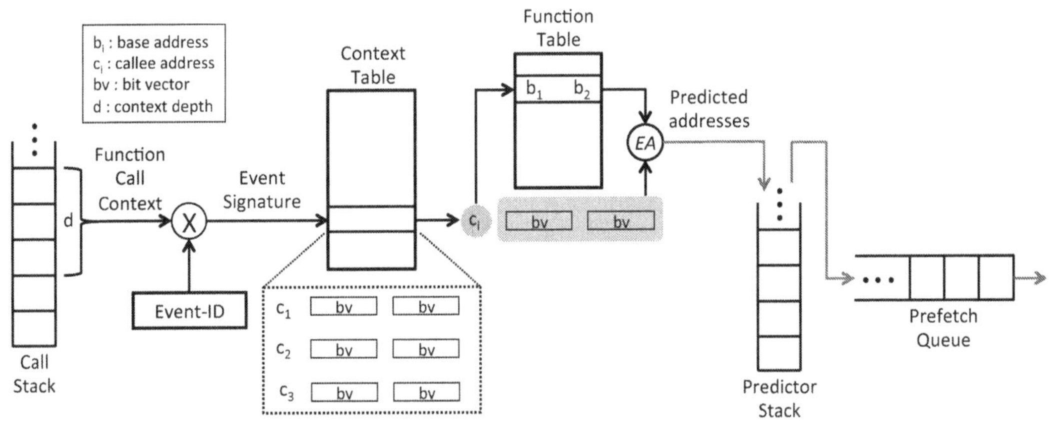

Figure 6: Prefetcher Design Overview.

indexed by the *context key* - *Context Table*, the other indexed by the function call address - *Function Table*. The list of callees is stored in the *Context Table*, and their function bodies to be prefetched is obtained from the *Function Table* (Section 3.4).

If an entry is found in the Callee Predictor, the list of callees is read out, and pushed on to the *Predictor Stack* such that the first predicted callee is on the top of the stack. The *Predictor Stack* is used to maintain the state of the prefetcher and synchronize it with the *Call Stack*. Each entry of this structure stores a function address and four status bits (Section 3.4).

The function body addresses of the function at the top of the *Predictor Stack* (if it has not been prefetched yet) are pushed in to the *Prefetch Queue*. Addresses present in this queue are then prefetched.

If the prediction of callees was correct, it is guaranteed that the top of the *Predictor Stack* matches the next function the program invokes. Thus, when the program invokes the next function, the function at the top of the *Predictor Stack* is validated, and prefetching under the new event signature is initiated. When the program returns from a function, the entry at the top of the *Predictor Stack* is popped.

If the prefetcher mispredicts the next function to be executed, detected by a mismatch in the function called and function present at the top of the *IPStack*, prefetching is halted. The *Predictor Stack* is cleared from the top till the parent of the current function. This is because, except till the parent of the current function, the prefetcher does not know how the call graph looks. This way, on a misprediction, the prefetcher aligns itself with the real *Call Stack*.

3.4 Design of Hardware Structures

Event-ID register : This register stores the event-ID uniquely identifying an event. This ID is formed by the browser using these two pieces of information - the type of event (mouse click, mouse scroll, timed event, etc.) and the JavaScript function called to handle the event. Using a special instruction (added in our design) this event-ID is stored in the event-ID register.

Call stack : This structure maintains the current function call stack of the program. Each entry in this stack is a function call address. On every function call, the call address of the function is pushed on to this stack. Conversely, on every return, the entry at the top of the stack is popped out. It has 32 entries. If the structure overflows, the oldest entries are discarded.

Prefetch Queue : Prefetch requests are made from this structure. It maintains a queue of L1-I cache block addresses to be prefetched. We observe that the L1-I cache blocks accessed in a function are contiguous with a few discontinuities. Therefore, we record pairs of a base address with an associated bit vector representing the nearby blocks, similar to the scheme used in [10].

Callee Predictor : This structure is used to record the function bodies and callees with respect to event signatures. This is a combination of two tables (Figure 6), one indexed by the event signature - *Context Table*, the other indexed by the function address - *Function Table*. Each entry in the *Function Table* is a list of two base addresses (offsets from the function address at cache line granularity), pointing at different points in the function body. Each entry in the *Context Table* is an ordered list of three unique callees (ordered by their first call) and two bit vectors for each callee. These are callees of the function at the top of the call stack for this event signature (Figure 6). The callees and the bit vectors are read from the *Context Table*. The callee address is used to index in to the *Function Table*. The base addresses read out from the *Function Table* combined with the bit vectors form the function body addresses to be prefetched. Both tables have 4k entries each.

Predictor Stack : It maintains the state of the prefetcher and is used to synchronize it with the Call Stack. This is a 32-entry stack, each entry of which stores a function call address and four status bits. Following is a description of what each bit implies if it is set :

- Prefetch bit : Instruction cache blocks of this function have been pushed on to the prefetch queue.
- Leaf bit : This is a leaf function.
- Parent Executing bit : This is a function whose prefetch requests have been pushed on to the Prefetch Queue; it has completed execution, but its parent has not.
- Mispredict bit : There has been a misprediction and this is the last correctly predicted function.

3.5 Prefetching Algorithm and Example

In our design we predict the instructions to be fetched by predicting the next function to be called. Here, the **top of the stack** means the first entry in the *Predictor Stack* that does not have its Parent Executing bit set.

On a function call (Figure 9(a)), given the current function call context and the event-ID, the event signature is formed. If the top of the *Predictor Stack* matches the function called, it implies the prediction was correct. The event signature is used to index in to the Callee Predictor. If there is no entry, nothing is done. If there is an entry, the prefetcher reads the list of callees and pushes them in reverse order in to the *Predictor Stack*. This is so that the callees can be popped off the stack in the order in which they are predicted to be called.

If there is a mismatch, we try to match the function called with any entry in the *Predictor Stack* going up from the top. If it matches any entry, it means this function has been called again in the same invocation of its parent, and that we have prefetched it before. So nothing more is to be done.

If the current function does not match any entry, it means the prefetcher mispredicted the current function call. In this case, prefetching is halted and the *Predictor Stack* is cleared until the parent of the current function. This is because, except till the parent of the current function, the prefetcher does not know how the call graph looks. Prefetching restarts once either the parent returns, or if by using the current function as part of the event signature, the prefetcher can make predictions.

On all occasions, if the top of the *Predictor Stack* has not been prefetched, prefetch requests for its function body addresses are made. Its Prefetch bit is then set marking that it has been prefetched. The prefetcher now waits for the program to catch up. We do not want to prefetch too far ahead of the program execution, unless it is a leaf function, in which case its sibling is prefetched as well.

Similarly, on a function return (Figure 9(b)), if the top of the *Predictor Stack* matches the function returned, its Parent Executing bit is set and its callees, if any, are popped. If there is a mismatch however, we try to match the function returned with any entry in the *Predictor Stack* going up from the top. If we find a match, it means the function has completed a previous call, and nothing more is to be done.

If the Mispredict bit of the top of the *Predictor Stack* is set, it implies that a callee was mispredicted and the *Predictor Stack* had already been cleared up till this entry before. Otherwise, if the top of the *Predictor Stack* has not been prefetched, follow the last step of the algorithm as in the case of a function call.

In our design, a prefetch request is made only if the cache block is not present in the L1-I cache.

Figure 8 shows which function is prefetched relative to program execution. Following the algorithms described in Figures 9(a) and 9(b), Figure 10(a) shows a step-by-step walk-through of the states of the Predictor Stack as an example program executes. At the start of the call graph (Figure 7), the Predictor Stack has f_1 at the top of the stack and it has already been prefetched (Prefetch bit set).

In Step 1, when g_1 is called, it matches the top of the stack, implying the prediction was correct. Its callees are pushed on to the stack. h_1 is prefetched. Since it's a leaf function, the next callee, h_2 is also prefetched. This is not a leaf function, so prefetching stops, waiting for the program to catch up. Similarly, when h_2 is called in step 4, both of its callees being leaves are prefetched, without waiting for the call to the first callee i_1.

When h_1 is called again in step 6, it does not match the top of the stack. However, it does match an earlier entry since it was its second call by its parent - g_1. This is, therefore, not a misprediction. This function has already been prefetched.

The above is a case where the prefetcher always predicted correctly. Figure 10(b) shows a case where everything proceeds as before until h_3 is called, at which point a misprediction is detected, since the next predicted callee is h_6.

When h_3 is called in step 8 the top of the stack does not match the function called or any entries with their Parent Executing bit set. A misprediction is detected - the Predictor Stack is cleared until g_1; it's Mispredict bit is set, and the newly called function (h_3) is pushed on to the Predictor Stack, with it's Prefetch bit set. This way the *Predictor Stack* is synchronized with the *Call Stack*.

When h_3 returns, the top of the stack (g_1) has a Mispredict bit set, so nothing more is done.

// On a function (*f*) call

1. **if** top (*Predictor Stack*) == *f*
   a. Callees of *f*, if any, are pushed on to the *Predictor Stack* in reverse order
2. **else if** *f* matches any entry in the *Predictor Stack* going up from top (*Predictor Stack*)
   // *f* was called and prefetched before.
   // Nothing more to be done
3. **else**
   // the function call was mispredicted
   a. The *Predictor Stack* is cleared until the parent of *f*
   b. The *Mispredict* bit of top (*Predictor Stack*) is set
   c. *f* is pushed onto the *Predictor Stack*
   d. The *Prefetch* bit of *f* is set
4. **if** f_x (= top (*Predictor Stack*)) has not been prefetched (its *Prefetch* bit is not set)
   a. Prefetch f_x
   b. Set its Prefetch bit
   c. if f_x is a leaf function (its *Leaf* bit is set)
      i. f_x = sibling of f_x not been prefetched, go to step 4a

(a) Algorithm followed on a function call

// On a function (*f*) return

1. **if** top (*Predictor Stack*) == *f*
   a. Its *Parent Executing* bit is set
   // *f* has returned but its parent has not. Its parent is the
   // new top (*Predictor Stack*)
   b. Its callees, if any, are popped from the *Predictor Stack*
2. **else if** *f* matches any entry in the *Predictor Stack* going up from top (*Predictor Stack*)
   // *f* has completed a previous call
   // Nothing more to be done
3. **if** *Mispredict* bit of top (*Predictor Stack*) is set
   // a callee was mispredicted
   // Nothing more is done
4. **if** f_x (= top (*Predictor Stack*)) has not been prefetched (its *Prefetch* bit is not set)
   a. Prefetch f_x
   b. Set its Prefetch bit
   c. if f_x is a leaf function (its *Leaf* bit is set)
      i. f_x = sibling of f_x not been prefetched, go to step 4a

(b) Algorithm followed on a function return

Figure 9: Prefetching Design Algorithms

4. METHODOLOGY

In this work we have attempted to evaluate the behavior of event-driven JavaScript (JS) web workloads. This

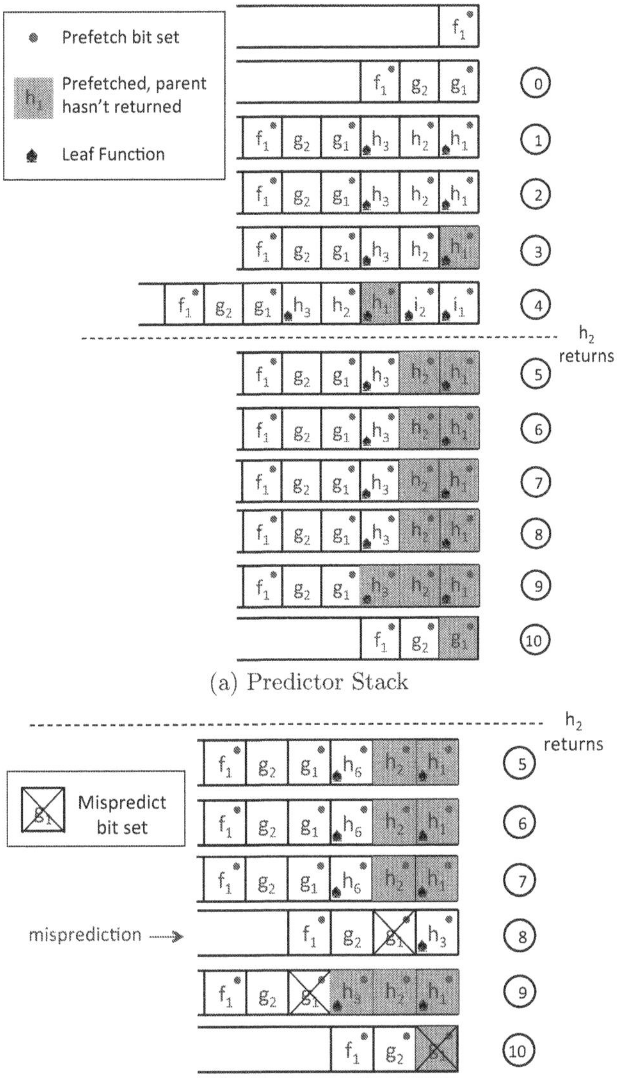

(a) Predictor Stack

(b) Predictor Stack on a misprediction

Figure 10: Prefetching example

nature of JavaScript execution is not captured by existing JavaScript benchmark suites like Octane [1] and Sunspider [3]. Real-world JavaScript web workloads, as executed in the rendering of popular web pages, bear little resemblance to the benchmark suites, as shown in [19]. An important difference is the lack of event-driven execution in existing benchmark suites. For the above reasons, for this work, we have created workloads from real web sites, studied their characteristics and evaluated our design using them.

4.1 Web Applications

Figure 11 lists the 7 real web applications that we have used in this study. These websites were chosen since they are both important and popularly visited, and they cut across a diverse range of tasks users typically perform on the web browser. Our applications cover e-commerce (amazon.com), search (bing.com), news (cnn.com), social networking (facebook.com), mapping (maps.google.com), online document editing (docs.google.com) and online image editing (pixlr.com).

Web Site	Actions performed	#events executed	# JS-Execute instructions
amazon (amazon.com)	Search for a pair of headphones, click on one result, go to a related item	7,787	432,875,253
bing (bing.com)	Search for the term "Roger Federer", go to new results	4,858	258,961,747
cnn (cnn.com)	Click on the headline, go to world news	13,409	1,230,395,548
fb (facebook.com)	Visit own homepage, go to communities, go to pictures	9,305	2,165,554,555
gmaps (maps.google.com)	Search for driving directions between two addresses, get public transit directions, get biking directions	7,298	2,722,470,912
gdocs (docs.google.com)	Open a spreadsheet, insert data, add 5 values	1,714	808,941,337
pixlr (pixlr.com/editor)	Add various filters to an image uploaded from the computer	465	26,424,174

Figure 11: Web Sites visited and actions taken, and a measure of the size of the benchmarks

Core	4-wide, 1.66 GHz OoO, 96-entry ROB, 16-entry LSQ
L1-(I,D)-Cache	32 KB, 2-way, 64 B lines, 2 cycle hit latency, LRU
L2 Cache	2 MB, 16-way, 64 B lines, 21 cycle hit latency, LRU
Main Memory	4 GB DRAM, 101 cycle access latency, 12.8 GB/s bandwidth
Branch Predictor	Pentium M branch predictor 15 cycle mis-predict penalty 2k-entry Global Predictor, 256-entry iBTB 2k-entry BTB, 256-entry Loop Branch Predictor
Interconnect	Bus
Energy modeling	V_{dd} = 1.2 V, 45 nm

Figure 12: Details of the architecture simulated

The actions taken on visiting each site (a browsing session), are meant to represent a typical behavior of a user on a short, but complete visit to the site. We kept the browsing sessions short, partly because it becomes logistically difficult to capture and study long-term uses of web applications, but also because some of these websites would typically be used in this manner. For example, searching for specific information or reading news headlines.

4.2 Workload Setup

We instrumented the open source web browser Chromium, running on Ubuntu 12.04. It uses the V8 JavaScript engine, also used in Google Chrome. Our instrumentation setup works as follows:

- We first, instrumented the C++ code used to implement the V8 JavaScript engine in Chromium. This helped us separate out the JavaScript part from the rest of the browser in the execution stream.
- Next we visit a website and perform the actions described in Figure 11. In order to create a workload that is repeatable, we captured the instruction trace of the browser [1], using the trace-recording component

[1]specifically, the Renderer component of the web browser

of SniperSim [7]. This generates binary trace files containing information about the instructions executed, the direction of branches and the memory addresses accessed.

- Finally, we fed these instruction traces, into the SniperSim simulator, and evaluated our design.

The architecture simulated is based on a mobile system - Exynos 5250. The architectural configuration is detailed in Figure 12.

In our experiments we have simulated the code executed by the web browser for JavaScript execution. This also includes native code executed as part of library calls.

5. RESULTS

In this section we first validate the premises our design is based on, going on to evaluate it, comparing it with previously proposed instruction prefetcher designs.

5.1 Prefetch Accuracy and Coverage

The basic premises that our design is based on are that event signatures are highly correlated with the control flow inside functions and that they are repetitive.

The first premise implies that both the body of the function and its callees are also highly correlated with the event signature. The second premise ensures that event signatures can be used to predict the callees and the function bodies. We, therefore, keep track of the list of callees of a function and their function bodies associated with the event signature.

We use the following two metrics to validate the design choices made in our prefetching scheme.

- Prefetch **accuracy** is defined as the percentage of prefetch hits (blocks that were prefetched and later were a hit in the cache) over all prefetch requests issued.
- **Coverage** is the percentage of misses that became prefetch hits as a results of prefetching - (#prefetch hits)*100/(#prefetch hits + #misses).

Each data point in all plots discussed in this section shows an average over all benchmarks.

5.1.1 Callee Set Prediction Accuracy

Any advantage to be gained from our design banks on the predictability of the list of callees using the event signature, since having made this prediction correctly, the prefetcher can prefetch the bodies of the functions predicted.

The list of callees is ordered by the first call to that callee. Maintaining an ordered list is important, since we are trying to predict the very next function to be called, staying one function ahead of program execution.

In Figure 14, we evaluate the predictability of the most recently seen callee set for that event signature. Here, a prediction is called accurate, if both the callees and their order is predicted correctly. As is evident from the figure, predicting that the last seen callee set for that event signature is going to be the next callee set is highly accurate.

5.1.2 Predicting Function Body

Having predicted the next function (callee) to be executed, it is important for the prefetcher to be able to predict the correct part of the function body to prefetch. Due to varying control flow within a function, different parts of the function body may get executed on different calls.

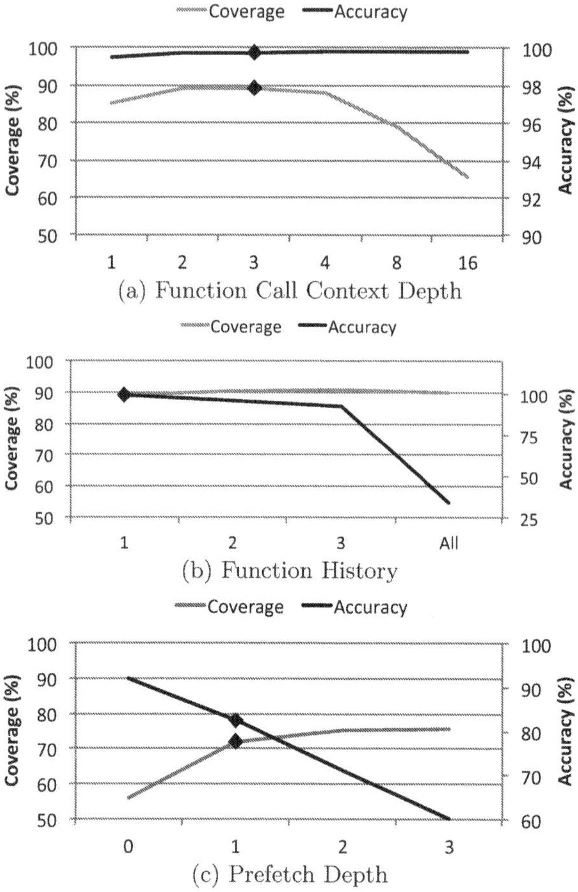

Figure 13: Variation in *Coverage* and *Accuracy* with varying *Function Call Context Depth*, *Function History* and *Prefetch Depth*. The diamond marks the final design choice

Given that, event signature is a good predictor for callees, it is expected that it will be a good predictor for function bodies. However, this prediction is not perfect, consequently different parts of the function body might execute with the same event signature. This opens up another dimension to this problem - how much of the executed function body history to keep track of with the event signature. In Figure 13(b), we explore precisely this point. Here, a function history of n, means that we keep track of and prefetch the function body addresses executed the last n times this function was called with the same event signature. This figure shows a study of an ideal case, where a predicted I-cache block is brought in to the cache only when it is needed. There is no notion of timeliness - a block is considered prefetched as soon as it is predicted. This figure shows that the function body seen the last time is a good predictor of the function body going to be executed next. Using more history, does not significantly help cover more misses (coverage does not improve), but loses accuracy since it is prefetching more cache blocks that are not accessed.

5.1.3 Function Call Context Depth

Using function call context (and event-ID) to predict the callees of a function and their function bodies being the cor-

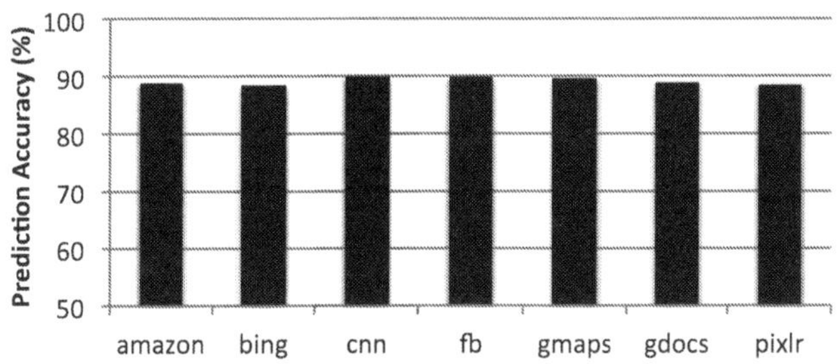

Figure 14: Callee Set Prediction Accuracy

nerstone of our design, how much of the call stack (number of functions) to use to form the event signature is a vital question. It is logical to believe that using more functions to form the event signature will result in better accuracy in predicting callees and function bodies, since we have more precise context information. However, there can be two problems with using a deeper context history

- It might take long for the prefetcher to learn the different contexts. Whenever we do not have the context in our table, we can not prefetch anything, thereby losing coverage.
- Using a deeper context history, results in the prefetcher using potentially stale information for a shallower context.

In our studies we found out that the first potential problem does not have a significant effect on our scheme. The prefetcher sees and is thus able to learn the frequently used long contexts fairly early. The second potential problem, does have significant effects. A shallower context can appear in multiple deeper contexts. Therefore, if we use a deep context, we are likely to see older history (stale information) for the shallower context. As we have seen from the discussion in Section 5.1.2, using recent history results in better predictions. Using too deep a context is also counterintuitive, since in that case we would be trying to correlate functions that may not necessarily have any bearing on the control flow of a child function. For e.g. library function calls like printf(). Its usage is common across a wide range of user functions, and it is internal call stack might have little correlation to the main() function.

Figure 13(a) validates the above hypotheses. Coverage reduces with increasing context depth without any noticeable change in accuracy.

5.1.4 Predicting Ahead of Program Execution

As discussed earlier, it is important for the prefetcher to stay ahead of program execution.

However, there are two issues with trying to prefetch too early - first, the cache block might get evicted by the time the program needs it; second, prediction accuracy of the prefetcher drops the further it goes ahead of the program, thereby issuing erroneous prefetches, causing pollution in the cache. Figure 13(c) confirms precisely the above arguments.

In our workloads, the L2 miss rate for instructions is 2.8%, thus for most L1-I misses we only need to prefetch early enough to hide L2 access latency. A prefetch depth of 1 is thus sufficient.

5.1.5 Final Design Choice

In our final design we use a context depth of 3 and a prefetch depth of 1. We only keep track of the last seen callee set and function body. A diamond marks our final design parameters in the earlier plots.

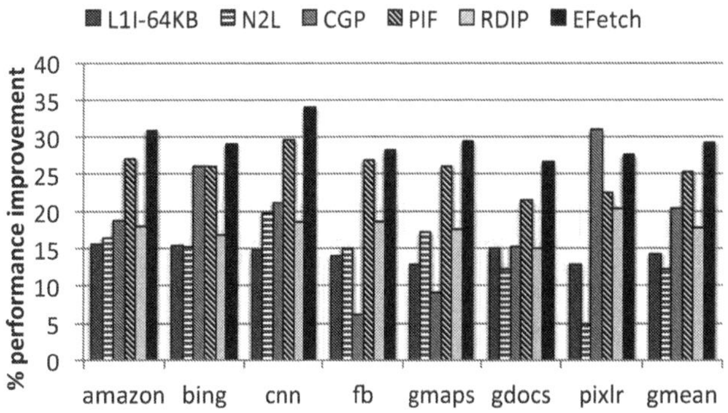

Figure 16: Performance achieved compared to No Prefetching (NP) as the baseline

5.2 Performance

In this section we will compare and contrast our design with other relevant designs.

- *NP* is a design with no instruction prefetcher. This is our baseline.
- *N2L* prefetches the next 2 cache lines.
- *CGP* is our implementation of Call Graph Prefetching [5].
- *PIF* is our implementation of the Proactive Instruction Fetch [10].
- *RDIP* is our implementation of Return-Address-Stack directed instruction prefetching [13].
- *EFetch* is our design.

In Figure 15, we show the number of prefetch hits, misses and erroneous prefetches as a percentage of the sum of prefetch hits and load misses. EFetch issues far fewer erroneous prefetches than PIF. Erroneous prefetches are those prefetches that never get hit before they are evicted. They hurt performance by polluting the cache kicking out potentially useful blocks, wasting L1-L2 bandwidth and consequently wasting energy. Unlike EFetch, PIF, which maintains a temporal stream of cache block accesses, has no way of knowing when the event signature has changed, and thus, keeps prefetching off the end of the temporal stream. This scheme ensures high coverage, but also suffers from low accuracy. EFetch also issues some erroneous prefetches since it assumes the last seen callee set and their function bodies will be the same as this time for a particular event signature, which is not always true. However, it recovers quickly - on the very next function call or return. N2L does not perform well. This is to be expected due to the small function sizes, large number of function calls and complex control flow inside functions.

EFetch performs better than RDIP, by achieving better coverage, even though it loses out slightly in accuracy. RDIP achieves better accuracy since its signatures are able to point at discrete call sites within functions. However, for web workloads, this leads to a very large number of signatures that need to be kept track of, overflowing their table size, causing loss in coverage. Also, RDIP only keeps track of L1-I

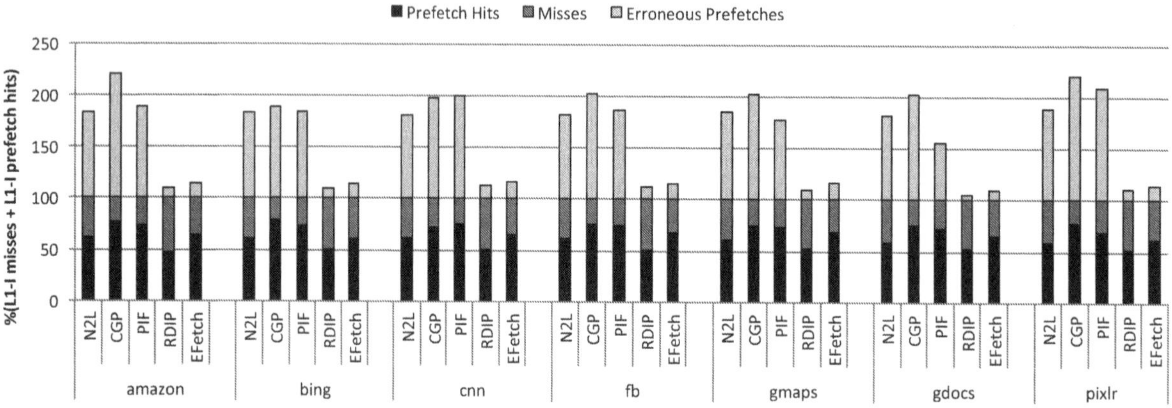

Figure 15: Each bar is divided in to three segments: *Prefetch Hits* are misses removed by prefetching. *Misses* are the remaining L1-I cache misses. *Erroneous Prefetches* are prefetches made which were never used (until their eviction from L1-I cache).

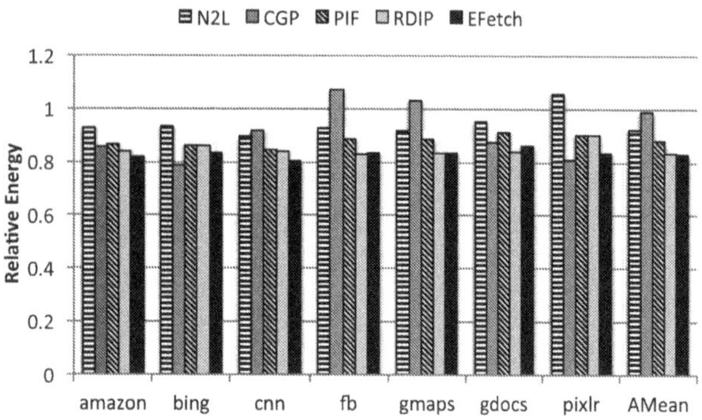

Figure 17: Energy expended compared to No Prefetching (NP) as the baseline

cache misses. The exact misses can change between dynamic instances of signatures, due to cache capacity and conflict misses. EFetch keeps track of all L1-I cache accesses. For web workloads, it is still able to keep hardware costs down due to small function sizes and better compaction of cache addresses.

Figure 16 shows the performance improvement of the different designs. EFetch performs as well or better than the other designs on all benchmarks. L1I-64KB has an L1 instruction cache of 64KB, roughly equal to the sum of the L1-I cache size in our baseline (NP) and the hardware storage overhead of EFetch. On average, EFetch outperforms L1I-64KB by 15%, N2L by 17%, CGP by 8.9%, PIF by 3.9% and RDIP by 11.5%.

5.3 Storage Overheads

We use 4K entry tables - context table, function table. Each entry in the context table stores 3 callee addresses and 2 bit vectors, along with a tag. Callee addresses are stored in the form of offsets in to the function table, using 12 bits each. The tag is 14 bits long. Therefore, a context table entry is 56 bits long.

Each entry in the function table stores 2 base addresses in the form of offsets from the function address, plus a tag. An offset needs 4 bits, tag is 14 bits in size, so each entry is 22 bits.

Both tables have 4k entries each, so a total storage of 4k*(56 + 22) bits = 39 kB is required. Comparing this with PIF, which needs 136 kB for the history buffer and 68 kB for the index table for a storage overhead of 204 kB, we get similar or better performance for 5.2 times less hardware storage cost.

Design	Structure	Size (KB)	Access Energy (pJ)	Static Power (mW)
CGP [5]	Call Graph History Cache	32	44.8	28.6
PIF [10]	History Buffer Index Table	136 68	39.3 25	119.9 62.2
RDIP [13]	Miss Table	63	32.6	49
EFetch	Callee Predictor Table	39	21.5	33.9

Table 1: Energy and power estimates used for hardware structures

5.4 Energy

We evaluated the energy expended by the different instruction prefetcher designs using McPat 0.8 [14]. CACTI 5.3 [26] was used to determine the per-access energy and static power of the additional hardware structures as shown in Table 1.[2] Figure 17 shows that EFetch uses less energy than all other designs, owing to its better trade-off between prefetcher accuracy and coverage. We noticed from our evaluation that the energy consumed by hardware structures added for instruction prefetching is very minimal, ranging from 0.01% of the total energy consumed for EFetch to 1.06% for PIF. Thus, to minimize energy consumed, it is not the additional hardware structures that need to be optimized, but the erroneous prefetches.

6. RELATED WORK

Instruction fetch stalls cause a significant performance degradation, leading to a rich-body of work trying to solve this problem. The earliest solutions to this problem included next-line prefetching, taking advantage of sequen-

[2] We have validated these numbers with the authors of RDIP

tial instruction fetch [4]. This initial idea was expanded upon and next-N-line and instruction stream prefetchers were proposed [12, 18, 27, 22] using varying kinds of events to control the aggressiveness and lookahead of the prefetcher. Next–line prefetchers are simple and work well for sequential code. However, they have poor accuracy and are not able to prefetch ahead in time for code with frequent branches and function calls.

To be able to more effectively prefetch instructions ahead of time in branch and call heavy code, several branch predictor based prefetchers [8, 20, 21, 24] have been proposed. Run-ahead execution [16], wrong-path instruction prefetching [17] and using an idle thread [15] or speculative threads [25, 28] can be used to generate future instruction accesses. Ferdman et. al. [10] showed that by using the instruction fetch sequence instead of the commit sequence, these approaches suffer from interference caused by wrong-path execution. Also these don't have sufficient lookahead when the branch predictor traverses loops.

The discontinuity prefetcher [23] handles fetch discontinuities. It's able to alleviate some of the issues with other branch-predictor based prefetchers by operating at an instruction block granularity. But it's lookahead is limited to one fetch discontinuity to avoid over-prediction. The branch history guided prefetcher (BHGP) [24] keeps track of branch instructions and imminent instruction cache misses, which are prefetched upon the next occurrence of the branch. However, they cannot differentiate between different invocations of the same branch (which will have a bearing on the branch outcome and instruction cache misses seen) leading to lower coverage or accuracy. Our work, differs from the above in that it targets event-driven web applications, where each event can be completely independent of the others, thereby executing completely different code from one event to the next. Also, we use event-ID and the function call stack to predict the callees of function and their function bodies, and thus is neither affected by wrong-path execution nor is unable to differentiate between different invocations of the same function.

PIF [10] addresses the limitations of branch-predictor directed prefetching by recording temporal instruction committed streams and fetch misses. By using the committed stream of instructions, it remains unaffected by the predictability of individual branches and wrong-path instructions. To similarly be able to avoid disruptions caused by wrong-path instructions, our scheme updates the state of the prefetch structures as call and return instructions commit. Instead of using temporal streams of instructions, we utilize the event-ID and call graph information to predict the instruction cache blocks.

PIF needs to keep track of a large window of instructions committed to be able to predict the temporal stream accurately. The size of the hardware structures exceeds 200 kB, while our design needs less than 40 kB.

A recently proposed instruction prefetcher, RDIP [13], exploits the information stored in the return address stack (RAS) and uses the return addresses of functions called, to predict and thereby prefetch the next segment of function executed. This scheme was evaluated on traditional server workloads. RDIP relies on function call context being a good predictor of the next function called. Unlike RDIP, EFetch targets event-driven web applications. To do so, it utilizes the event-ID along with the function call context (event signature) to predict the next function executed. In addition to differences discussed in Section 5.2, EFetch prefetches only the part of the function body executed the last time with the same event signature, avoiding erroneous prefetches. RDIP, on the other hand, accumulates L1-I cache misses incurred over all previous instances when the signature was seen.

Annavaram, Patel and Davidson used the current function to guide instruction prefetching for database applications in [5]. EFetch, on the other hand is designed for event-driven web applications. By making use of the event-ID and multiple functions in the call context, EFetch is able to differentiate between invocations to the same function, and there is merit in this scheme, since it is a good predictor of varying control flow inside the function. Also, EFetch fetches only that part of the function body, that it predicts will get executed. This is of significant importance for event-driven web workloads which are composed of a large number of very small functions, with some frequently executed very large functions. Importantly, on a single invocation of these large functions, only a small part of them is executed and it is composed of discontiguous I-cache blocks. An approach like the one in [5], would hurt performance by, on the one hand, fetching I-cache blocks beyond the boundary of small functions, and on the other hand, fetching contiguous cache blocks of the few very large functions, even though many of these I-cache blocks will go unused.

7. CONCLUSION

Event-driven web applications are becoming a dominant set of programs used in client-side computing. Unfortunately, processor architecture optimizations studied in the past are not designed to take advantage of the unique characteristics of event-driven web applications.

In this paper we identified L1 instruction cache misses to be an important performance bottleneck in the web applications. This issue is significantly more severe than it is for conventional server applications. We proposed a new prefetcher that used event signatures (formed from function calling context and event-ID) to accurately prefetch instruction cache blocks. We demonstrated that the proposed prefetcher outperforms past designs, and also has modest storage requirements.

8. ACKNOWLEDGEMENTS

We would like to thank the anonymous reviewers for their valuable comments and feedback. This research was supported by National Science Foundation grants CAREER-1149773 and SHF-1217917 and funding from Intel Corporation.

9. REFERENCES

[1] Octane benchmark suite. https://developers.google.com/octane/.

[2] SPEC CPU 2006. http://www.spec.org/cpu2006/.

[3] Sunspider benchmark suite. https://www.webkit.org/perf/sunspider/sunspider.html.

[4] D. Anderson, F. Sparacio, and R. M. Tomasulo. The ibm system/360 model 91: Machine philosophy and instruction-handling. *IBM Journal of Research and Development*, 11(1):8–24, 1967.

[5] M. Annavaram, J. M. Patel, and E. S. Davidson. Call graph prefetching for database applications. *ACM Transactions on Computer Systems (TOCS)*, 21(4):412–444, 2003.

[6] C. Bienia, S. Kumar, J. P. Singh, and K. Li. The parsec benchmark suite: Characterization and architectural implications. In *Proceedings of the 17th International Conference on Parallel Architectures and Compilation Techniques*, PACT '08, pages 72–81, New York, NY, USA, 2008. ACM.

[7] T. E. Carlson, W. Heirman, and L. Eeckhout. Sniper: Exploring the level of abstraction for scalable and accurate parallel multi-core simulations. In *International Conference for High Performance Computing, Networking, Storage and Analysis (SC)*, Nov. 2011.

[8] I.-C. K. Chen, C.-C. Lee, and T. N. Mudge. Instruction prefetching using branch prediction information. In *Computer Design: VLSI in Computers and Processors, 1997. ICCD'97. Proceedings., 1997 IEEE International Conference on*, pages 593–601. IEEE, 1997.

[9] H. Esmaeilzadeh, E. Blem, R. S. Amant, K. Sankaralingam, and D. Burger. Dark silicon and the end of multicore scaling. In *Computer Architecture (ISCA), 2011 38th Annual International Symposium on*, pages 365–376. IEEE, 2011.

[10] M. Ferdman, C. Kaynak, and B. Falsafi. Proactive instruction fetch. In *Proceedings of the 44th Annual IEEE/ACM International Symposium on Microarchitecture*, MICRO-44 '11, pages 152–162, New York, NY, USA, 2011. ACM.

[11] M. Ferdman, T. F. Wenisch, A. Ailamaki, B. Falsafi, and A. Moshovos. Temporal instruction fetch streaming. In *Microarchitecture, 2008. MICRO-41. 2008 41st IEEE/ACM International Symposium on*, pages 1–10. IEEE, 2008.

[12] N. P. Jouppi. Improving direct-mapped cache performance by the addition of a small fully-associative cache and prefetch buffers. In *Computer Architecture, 1990. Proceedings., 17th Annual International Symposium on*, pages 364–373. IEEE, 1990.

[13] A. Kolli, A. Saidi, and T. F. Wenisch. Rdip: Return-address-stack directed instruction prefetching. In *Proceedings of the 46th Annual IEEE/ACM International Symposium on Microarchitecture*, pages 260–271. ACM, 2013.

[14] S. Li, J. H. Ahn, R. D. Strong, J. B. Brockman, D. M. Tullsen, and N. P. Jouppi. Mcpat: an integrated power, area, and timing modeling framework for multicore and manycore architectures. In *Microarchitecture, 2009. MICRO-42. 42nd Annual IEEE/ACM International Symposium on*, pages 469–480. IEEE, 2009.

[15] C.-K. Luk. Tolerating memory latency through software-controlled pre-execution in simultaneous multithreading processors. In *Computer Architecture, 2001. Proceedings. 28th Annual International Symposium on*, pages 40–51. IEEE, 2001.

[16] O. Mutlu, J. Stark, C. Wilkerson, and Y. N. Patt. Runahead execution: An alternative to very large instruction windows for out-of-order processors. In *High-Performance Computer Architecture, 2003. HPCA-9 2003. Proceedings. The Ninth International Symposium on*, pages 129–140. IEEE, 2003.

[17] J. Pierce and T. Mudge. Wrong-path instruction prefetching. In *Microarchitecture, 1996. MICRO-29. Proceedings of the 29th Annual IEEE/ACM International Symposium on*, pages 165–175. IEEE, 1996.

[18] A. Ramirez, O. J. Santana, J. L. Larriba-Pey, and M. Valero. Fetching instruction streams. In *Proceedings of the 35th annual ACM/IEEE international symposium on Microarchitecture*, pages 371–382. IEEE Computer Society Press, 2002.

[19] P. Ratanaworabhan, B. Livshits, and B. G. Zorn. Jsmeter: Comparing the behavior of javascript benchmarks with real web applications. In *Proceedings of the 2010 USENIX conference on Web application development*, pages 3–3. USENIX Association, 2010.

[20] G. Reinman, B. Calder, and T. Austin. Fetch directed instruction prefetching. In *Microarchitecture, 1999. MICRO-32. Proceedings. 32nd Annual International Symposium on*, pages 16–27. IEEE, 1999.

[21] G. Reinman, B. Calder, and T. Austin. Optimizations enabled by a decoupled front-end architecture. *Computers, IEEE Transactions on*, 50(4):338–355, 2001.

[22] A. J. Smith. Sequential program prefetching in memory hierarchies. *Computer*, 11(12):7–21, 1978.

[23] L. Spracklen, Y. Chou, and S. G. Abraham. Effective instruction prefetching in chip multiprocessors for modern commercial applications. In *High-Performance Computer Architecture, 2005. HPCA-11. 11th International Symposium on*, pages 225–236. IEEE, 2005.

[24] V. Srinivasan, E. S. Davidson, G. S. Tyson, M. J. Charney, and T. R. Puzak. Branch history guided instruction prefetching. In *High-Performance Computer Architecture, 2001. HPCA. The Seventh International Symposium on*, pages 291–300. IEEE, 2001.

[25] K. Sundaramoorthy, Z. Purser, and E. Rotenberg. Slipstream processors: improving both performance and fault tolerance. *ACM SIGPLAN Notices*, 35(11):257–268, 2000.

[26] S. Thoziyoor, N. Muralimanohar, J. Ahn, and N. Jouppi. Cacti 5.3. *HP Laboratories, Palo Alto, CA*, 2008.

[27] C. Zhang and S. A. McKee. Hardware-only stream prefetching and dynamic access ordering. In *Proceedings of the 14th international conference on Supercomputing*, pages 167–175. ACM, 2000.

[28] C. Zilles and G. Sohi. Execution-based prediction using speculative slices. In *Computer Architecture, 2001. Proceedings. 28th Annual International Symposium on*, pages 2–13. IEEE, 2001.

XStream: Cross-core Spatial Streaming based MLC Prefetchers for Parallel Applications in CMPs

Biswabandan Panda, Shankar Balachandran
Department of Computer Science & Engineering
Indian Institute of Technology Madras
Chennai, India
{biswa,shankar}@cse.iitm.ac.in

ABSTRACT

Hardware prefetchers are commonly used to hide and tolerate off-chip memory latency. Prefetching techniques in the literature are designed for multiple independent sequential applications running on a multicore system. In contrast to multiple independent applications, a single parallel application running on a multicore system exhibits different behavior. In case of a parallel application, cores share and communicate data and code among themselves, and there is commonality in the demand miss streams across multiple cores. This gives an opportunity to predict the demand miss streams and communicate the predicted streams from one core to another, which we refer as cross-core stream communication.

We propose cross-core spatial streaming (XStream), a practical and storage-efficient cross-core prefetching technique. XStream detects and predicts the cross-core spatial streams at the private mid level caches (MLCs) and sends the predicted streams in advance to MLC prefetchers of the predicted cores. We compare the effectiveness of XStream with the ideal cross-core spatial streamer. Experimental results demonstrate that, on an average (geomean), compared to the state-of-the-art spatial memory streaming, storage efficient XStream reduces the execution time by 11.3% (as high as 24%) and 9% (as high as 29.09%) for 4-core and 8-core systems respectively.

Categories and Subject Descriptors

C.1.4 [**Parallel Architectures**]:

Keywords

Prefetching; multi-core

1. INTRODUCTION

Hardware Prefetching plays an important role in reducing the execution time of programs. In commercial chip-multiprocessors (CMPs), different types of hardware prefetchers are employed at the mid level caches (MLCs). For example, Intel's Nehelam uses a spatial prefetcher and a stream prefetcher at the private MLCs [2]. Stream based prefetchers fetch data in the form of streams wherein a stream is a *sequence of cache-line-aligned memory addresses*. A demand miss stream corresponds to demand miss addresses only. Temporal (Spatial) streams are streams that recur temporally (spatially). **Streams that spread and recur across multiple cores are known as cross-core streams**.

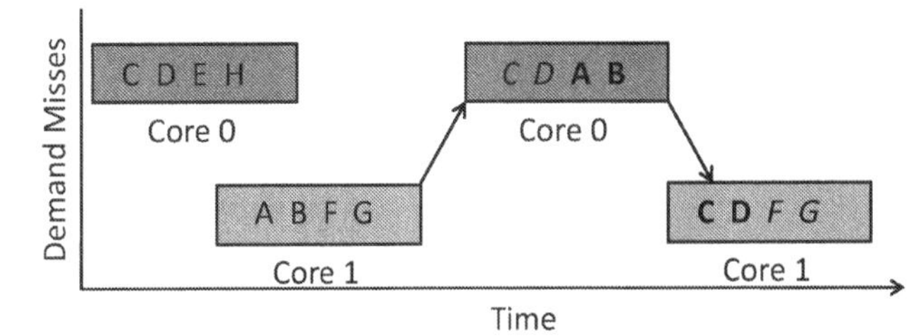

Figure 1: Example of cross-core streaming. A, B, C, and D are part of cross-core streams, and E, F, G, and H are part of intra-core streams.

Figure 1 shows an example of cross-core streams for a 2-threaded application. The X axis denotes the logical time order and the Y axis shows the demand miss addresses (aligned to cache line address) from two cores (core 0 and core 1). It can be seen that, the demand misses observed in one core recur in other cores. For example, demand misses to A and B are first observed in core 1 and later recur in core 0. Similarly, misses to C and D are first observed in core 0 and later recur in core 1. These miss streams are cross-core miss streams. Streams local to a core may result in hits if the stream prefetcher prefetches in-time. In this example, C and D get hits at core 0 and F and G get hits at core 1. But a cross-core spatial stream oblivious prefetcher can not eliminate the misses to cross-core streams A and B (shown in bold) in core 0 and similarly to C and D (shown in bold) in core 1.

Past works related to hardware cross-core stream prefetching, such as temporal memory streaming (TMS) [19] and store-ordered streaming (SORDS) [20] have been explored to minimize the coherent read misses. TMS [19] and SORDS [20] exploit migratory and producer-consumer sharing patterns respectively. These techniques are proposed for distributed shared memory (DSM) systems and when applied to CMPs,

PACT'14, August 24–27, 2014, Edmonton, AB, Canada.

ACM 978-1-4503-2809-8/14/08 ...$15.00.
http://dx.doi.org/10.1145/2628071.2628073.

require impractical storage (more than 20 MB on a 4-core CMP) to train the streams. Also these techniques store the predicted streams at the DRAM, which results in increased DRAM traffic. In contrast to TMS and SORDS, Somogyi et al.'s spatial memory streaming (SMS) prefetcher [14] is a practical technique that exploits the spatial streams that recur. In general, temporal streaming based techniques get better coverage and accuracy than spatial streaming but at the cost of the complexity of managing the off-chip storage. On the other hand, spatial streaming based techniques are simple, storage efficient and can eliminate the cold-start misses. *In this work, our focus is on on-chip spatial streaming technique and how to make it aware of the cross-core spatial streams.* For the cross-core spatial stream awareness, we propose cross-core spatial streaming (XStream). XStream predicts and communicates the spatial streams from one MLC prefetcher to the other predicted MLC prefetchers. XStream is based on two observations. First, in case of parallel applications, large fraction of memory space participates in cross-core sharing and communication. Second, there is ample time gap between occurrence of a stream in one core and recurrence of the same in others. *Prefetching techniques oblivious to cross-core streams may potentially reduce the execution time of parallel applications. However by exploiting the cross-core streams, significant reduction in the execution time can be achieved.*

To illustrate the importance of cross-core spatial streams in prefetching, Figure 2 shows the reduction in the execution time that can be achieved with the ideal cross-core MLC prefetchers normalized to the SMS prefetcher. The ideal cross-core prefetcher is an oracle that is aware of all the cross-core spatial streams. It uses local streams along with the cross-core spatial streams for its in-time prefetching. For this experiment, we assume that the ideal cross-core prefetcher has infinite storage to detect and communicate the cross-core streams in-time. Figure 2 shows that for 4 (8) threaded PARSEC [6] applications running on a 4 (8) core CMP, on an average (geomean), more than 23% (19%) reduction in the execution time can be achieved by making the SMS aware of cross-core streams. Given the scope of reduction, we propose XStream. The contributions of this paper are as follows:

- We identify commonality in spatial streams that spread and recur across multiple cores and propose cross-core spatial streaming (XStream), a storage efficient prefetching technique where an MLC prefetcher communicates its spatial streams to the other predicted MLC prefetchers. (Sections 3 and 4)
- We also introduce the notion of cross-core timeliness for the in-time communication of cross-core spatial streams across multiple MLC prefetchers. Cross-core timeliness plays an important role in improving the effectiveness of XStream. (Section 4.4)
- We show the effectiveness of XStream using all the applications from the PARSEC [6] benchmark suite. Compared to the cross-core stream oblivious SMS [14], XStream achieves an average (geomean) speedup of 11.3% and 9% for 4-core and 8-core systems respectively. On a 4-core CMP, XStream gets close to the ideal reduction of 23.3% with the ideal cross-core spatial streamer. (Section 6)

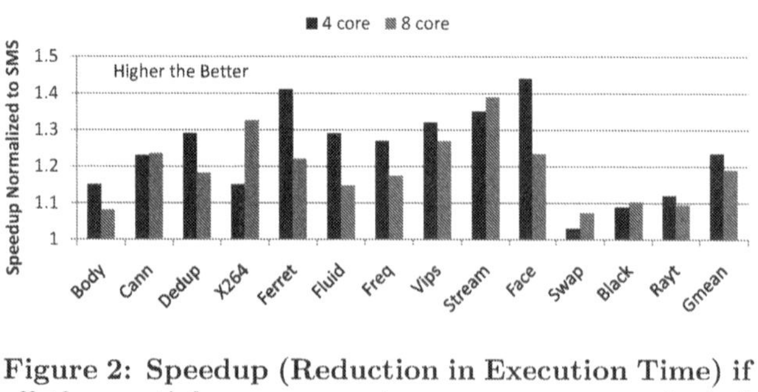

Figure 2: Speedup (Reduction in Execution Time) if all the spatial cross-core streams are communicated in-time.

2. BACKGROUND

In this section, we describe the baseline system design and the sharing patterns observed in the case of shared memory parallel applications. We also describe the design of state-of-the-art SMS prefetcher.

2.1 Baseline CMP Design

We consider a baseline CMP system that consists of multiple cores and multiple DRAM channels. Each core has a private L1 and L2 cache. Last level cache (LLC, which is L3) is shared among all the cores. Each core has prefetchers at the private MLC, which sends prefetch requests to the LLC. In case of a miss at the shared LLC, prefetch request is forwarded to the DRAM. The baseline system uses two hardware prefetchers at the MLC. One for instruction miss streams and the other for data miss streams. In the baseline system, *demand miss streams trigger prefetches, instead of demand access streams as the use of access streams put additional pressure on miss status holding registers (MSHRs) and access streams from multiple cores interfere heavily at the LLC and at the DRAM controllers.* In PARSEC, instruction streams are more predictable compared to data streams. So the system uses a simple stream prefetcher for instructions with 32 stream entries with prefetch degree of 4 and prefetch distance of 64. For data miss streams, the system uses the SMS [14] prefetcher. Both the prefetchers generate prefetch requests which are buffered in a prefetch queue. Prefetch queue (PFQ) is a first-in first-out buffer (FIFO) from which the oldest prefetch request is sent to the MSHRs. The MLC fill buffers are fused with the MSHRs. The baseline system inserts the prefetch responses with non-exclusive cache coherence states.

2.2 Cross-core Sharing Patterns

In shared memory parallel applications, threads share data and code. Based on the demand requests (reads or writes), and the threads that are making these requests, the sharing patterns for each spatial region can be classified into three categories [4]: (1) `Read-only`: In a given interval, a spatial region exhibits read-only sharing if it is written or read by one thread and then read by one or more threads later.
(2) `Migratory`: A spatial region exhibits migratory sharing if the threads get exclusive access to a spatial region back to back.
(3) `Producer-consumer`: A spatial region exhibits producer-consumer sharing if it is written by one thread and then read

Idea	Hardware Overhead for a 4-core CMP	Hardware overhead : Total MLC size (256 KB*4)	Supports Cross-core Streaming?
TMS [19]	24 MB	24 : 1	Yes
SORDS [20]	22 MB	22 : 1	Yes
STMS [18]	12 MB	12 : 1	Yes
STEMS [13]	6.4 MB	6.4 : 1	No
SMS [14]	256 KB	0.25 : 1	No
XStream	303.5 KB	0.28 : 1	Yes

Table 1: Overview of streaming techniques for a 4-core CMP.

by threads other than the writer before the writer writes again.

2.3 Spatial Memory Streaming (SMS)

Table 1 compares various streaming techniques in terms of their hardware overhead and support for cross-core streaming. Table 1 shows that, except SMS and XStream, all the other streaming techniques demand impractical storage[1]. *For a private MLC of 256 KB, it is not practical to use additional on-chip hardware of more than 6 MB for hardware prefetching and all the techniques mentioned in the Table 1, except SMS and XStream, require off-chip hardware support.* Compared to SMS, our XStream supports cross-core streaming with additional on-chip hardware of 47.5 KB.

SMS is a hardware prefetching technique that exploits spatial locality present in demand access streams. SMS logically partitions the system memory space into fixed size spatial regions wherein each spatial region consists of multiple cache lines, represented by bits in a bit vector. The training process for a spatial region kicks off on the occurrence of the very first demand access to any address in that spatial region. *The training is completed when any cache line within that region is evicted or invalidated.* SMS uses three hardware tables: (1) filter table (FT), (2) accumulation table (AT) and (3) pattern history table (PHT). FT and AT are implemented as content addressable memories (CAMs). Both FT and AT are part of a single table called active generation table (AGT). On a demand access, filter table filters out the spatial region tag and the spatial signature, which is PC + *offset* (PC/*offset*). PC is the program counter associated with the access and *offset* is the distance of a cache line from the base address of the spatial region tag, in terms of #cache lines. The base address of a spatial region tag is the higher order bits of the address.

On subsequent demand accesses to the cache line addresses within a spatial region tag, accumulation table records the accessed cache line addresses (in the form of bits in the bit vector). Once a spatial region is trained (upon eviction/invalidation of a cache line), active generation table sends the bit vector to the pattern history table. Pattern history table (which is indexed by the spatial signature) stores the predicted bit vector and the spatial signature (PC/*offset*), and uses it to trigger future prefetch requests. At the end of every training phase, the bit vector in the pattern history table is updated to the *set intersection* of the existing bit vector with the bit vector sent by the active generation table. In future, a demand access to a trained spatial signature triggers prefetch requests for the bits (corresponding cache line addresses), which are set in the bit vector. Figure 3 shows the detailed design of SMS prefetcher where a region consists of 4 cache lines represented by 4 bits in the bit vector. On the very first access to an address A+1, filter table stores the spatial region tag (as A) and PC/*offset* (as PC/1). Accumulation table stores and updates the bit vector for the demand accesses as shown in ① and ② of Figure 3. ③ of Figure 3 shows the completion of the training process and transfer of the spatial signature (PC/1) along with its trained bit vector (0 0 1 1) from active generation table to pattern history table. *Even-though SMS is an efficient prefetching technique, it falls short for parallel applications because of its cross-core stream obliviousness. In this work we address this.*

[1]We do not use simple stream and stride prefetcher as both of them are not effective for PARSEC benchmark suite.

3. MOTIVATION FOR XSTREAM

Motivation 1: Figure 4 shows the fraction of spatial signatures that recur across multiple cores. On an average, for 4-threaded PARSEC [6] applications, on a 4-core CMP, **80% of the spatial signatures recur in 2 or more cores, which we call cross-core spatial signatures (XCore signatures)**. The rest 20% are intra-core spatial signatures. We observe that a minimum of 160 spatial signatures (in `swaptions`), and a maximum of 4068 spatial signatures (in `facesim`), recur at-least 4 times and in more than one core. Also, there is a time gap (on an average, more than 32K clock cycles with minimum of 3 clock cycles, and maximum of 1 million clock cycles) between a particular spatial signature being accessed by one core and later recurring at a different core. This provides opportunity to exploit this behavior. Figure 5 shows the fraction of MLC data misses (which belong to the recurred spatial signatures) satisfied at the LLC, DRAM, and at the remote cores' L1 and L2. From Figure 5, it is clear that 90% of the MLC data misses are satisfied either at the L3 or at the DRAM. **Though 80% of the spatial signatures are cross-core, less than 10% of the data that belongs to these cross-core signatures are present in any of the private MLCs when the spatial signatures recur.**

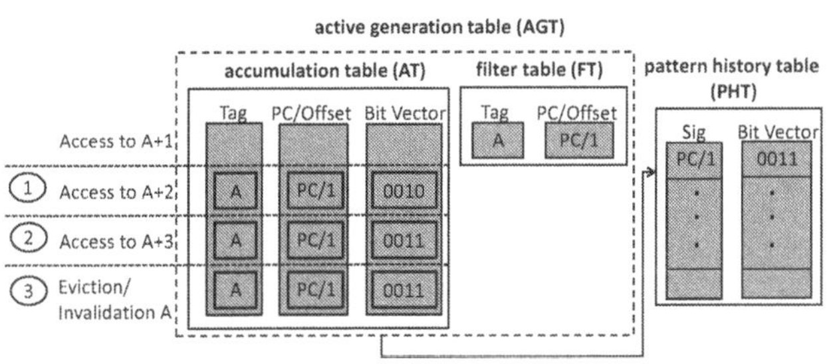

Figure 3: Hardware structure of SMS prefetcher. Sig stands for spatial signature (PC/*offset*).

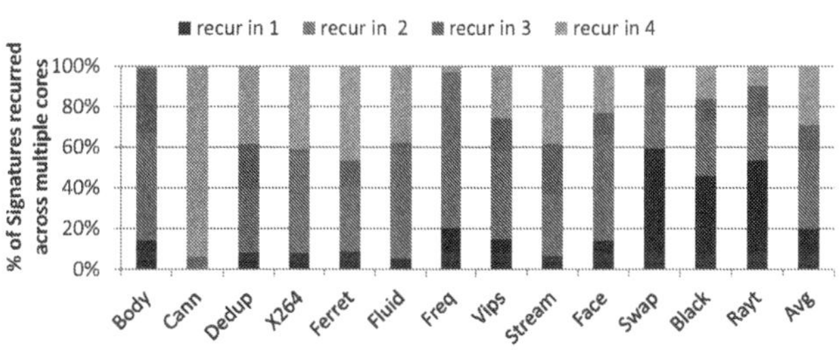

Figure 4: Recurrence of spatial signatures across multiple cores on a 4-core CMP.

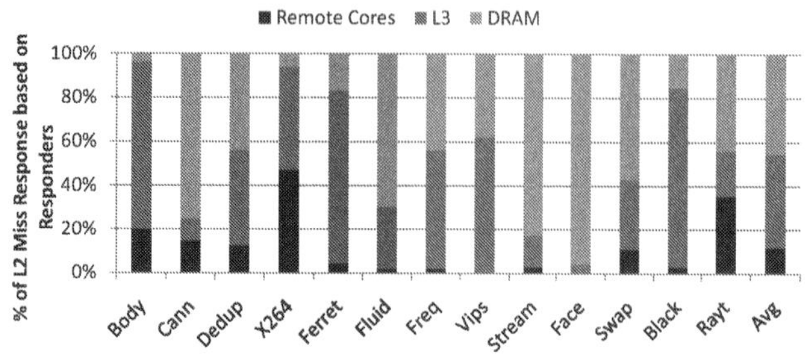

Figure 5: Distribution of MLC demand responses based on the responders on a 4-core CMP.

Motivation 2: Past works related to cross-core streaming target specific kinds of sharing patterns such as migratory [19] and producer-consumer [20], and reduce the read coherent misses. With the current industry trend, more number of cores on a chip share the LLC and the fraction of coherent read misses will be small. **Hence it is important to minimize all types of MLC data misses and not just the coherence misses and it is necessary to handle all kinds of sharing patterns.**

With these motivations, we propose cross-core spatial streaming (XStream), a simple and storage efficient hardware prefetching technique that is aware of cross-core spatial streams.

4. CROSS-CORE SPATIAL STREAMING

In this section, we describe and explain the working of the proposed XStream technique. XStream works in two phases and both the phases work in tandem.

Phase 1: The first phase detects cross-core spatial streams along with the IDs of cores involved in it. In this phase, the MLC prefetchers send their spatial signatures along with their corresponding bit vectors to a shared hardware table named cross-core spatial stream detector (XStream Detector). For every spatial signature, XStream Detector stores these bit vectors along with their core IDs in a temporal order and identifies the commonality in them. In case of a commonality between the bit vectors, it identifies the master prefetcher (*prefetcher of the core in which a spatial signature is trained first before it recurs in other cores*) and the worker prefetcher (*prefetcher of the core that follows the spatial signature of the master core*) associated with a spatial signature.

Phase 2: During the second phase, the future demand misses[2] to the trained signature at the master prefetcher trigger the communication of the spatial streams (in terms of a bit vector) to the predicted worker prefetcher in-time. The worker prefetcher updates its bit vector based on the bit vector communicated by the master prefetcher. Future demand misses at the worker core trigger prefetch requests based on the updated bit vector. *Note that the master prefetcher does not prefetch for the worker prefetcher. The worker prefetcher is solely responsible for sending the prefetch requests for its own private MLC.* Next we describe the XStream Detector.

[2]As mentioned in Section 2.1, we use demand miss triggered prefetching.

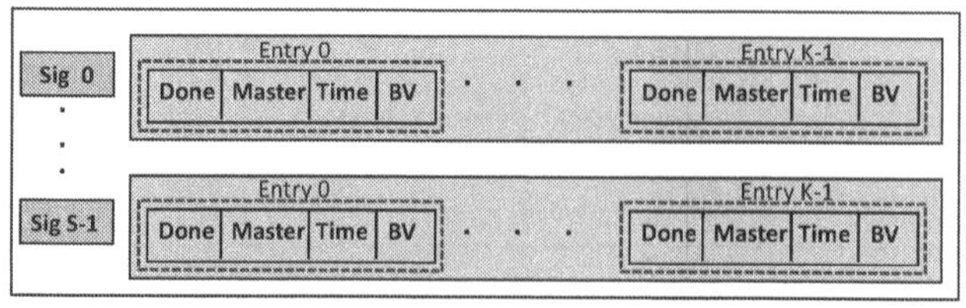

Figure 6: Hardware structure of the XStream Detector. BV stands for bit vector.

4.1 XStream Detector

To detect cross-core spatial streams, we use XStream Detector, a hardware table, which is shared by all the MLC prefetchers. We place XStream Detector beside the shared LLC with access latency similar to that of L3 cache. Figure 6 shows the structure of the XStream Detector We connect XStream Detector to all the private MLC prefetchers. XStream Detector keeps track of the trained spatial signatures sent by MLC prefetchers. When a spatial signature is trained and sent by the AGT to the PHT in SMS, it is also communicated to the XStream Detector. XStream Detector maintains S number of signatures wherein each signature stores K entries. Each entry consists of a `bit vector`, `Master` field, that stores the core ID of the MLC prefetcher that has sent the trained signature, `Time` field, that indicates the clock cycle at which a signature is inserted into the XStream Detector and `Done` field, that indicates whether a bit vector has already participated in the XStream detection process or not. If `Done` field is set, the bit vector is no more eligible to participate in the XStream detection process. For a given spatial signature, the entries associated with it follow the temporal order (entry 0 is the oldest entry and entry k-1 is the youngest entry). To minimize the noise in the process of detecting cross-core spatial streams, AGT communicates a `bit vector` to the XStream Detector only if the #1s in that `bit vector` satisfies a threshold called numones_{thresh}.

XStream Detector also uses a threshold called $\text{cross-core}_{thresh}$. For two bit vectors, say BV_0 and BV_1, $\text{cross-core}_{thresh}$ counts the #1s in the set intersection operation between BV_0 and BV_1. $\text{cross-core}_{thresh}$ quantifies the commonality between two bit vectors. We also modify the PHTs with additional fields. Figure 7 shows the enhanced PHT with three additional fields (Worker, Time and Init fields, shown in bold) along with the baseline PHT. The `worker` field, added in each entry stores the core ID that follows the spatial signature. `Time` field indicates the difference in clock cycles between the occurrence of a stream in the master core and the recurrence of the same in the worker core. The third additional field, namely `Init` field, which indicates whether the master prefetcher has initiated the process of communicating the bit vector to the worker prefetcher. If set, the

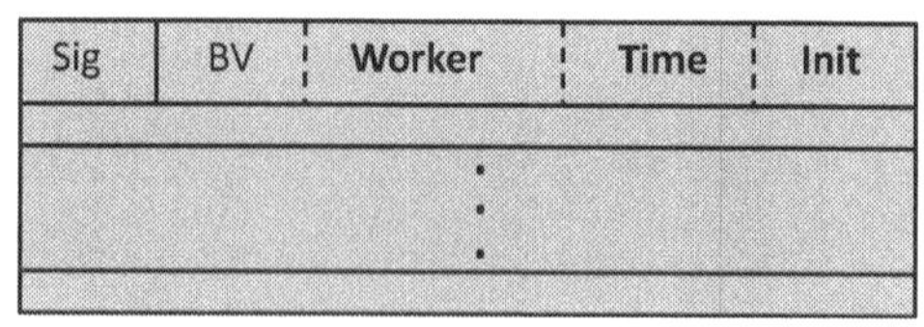

Figure 7: Hardware structure of enhanced PHT. BV stands for bit vector.

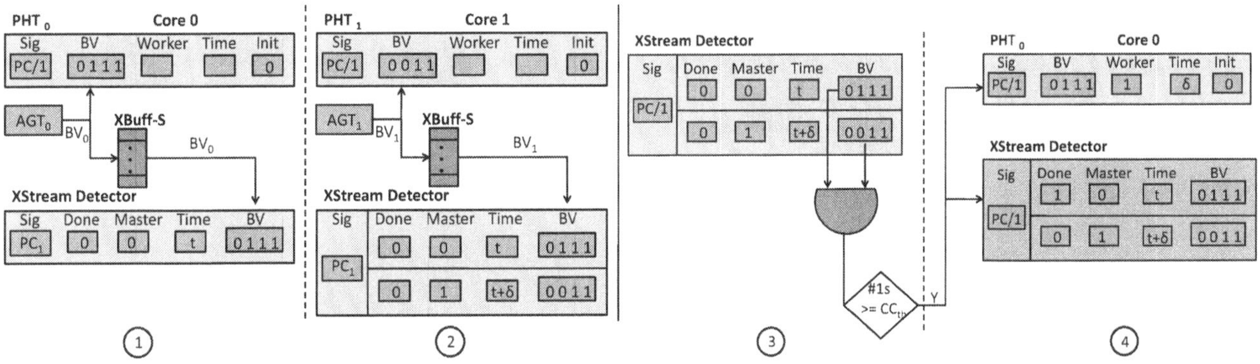

Figure 8: Steps involved in the XStream detection. X_Y denotes X of core Y. CC_{th} is cross-core$_{thresh}$. Each entry of XBuff-P stores the BV along with the predicted worker core ID. Similarly each entry of XBuff-S stores the BV along with the master core ID.

`Init` field indicates that the master prefetcher has initiated the process. We now describe the XStream detection phase.

4.2 XStream Detection

Figure 8 shows the steps involved in the XStream detection phase and the contents of the hardware structures at the end of each step. With the help of XStream detector, XStream detects the cross-core spatial streams along with the master and worker prefetchers involved with it. We describe the details of detection phase and communication phase for a dual core CMP (with core 0 and core 1) in the following steps.

Step ①: In ① of Figure 8 (a), for a spatial signature PC/1, AGT of core ID 0 (AGT_0) sends the `bit vector` to PHT_0 and to the shared XStream Detector through the shared X buffer (XBuff-S). As multiple AGTs can send their `bit vectors` at the same time, XStream Detector uses a small buffer named XBuff-S, which buffers the `bit vectors` sent by the AGTs. XBuff-S stores the `bit vector` along with the sender core ID. XStream Detector stores the `bit vector`, sender core ID (`Master`) (as 0) and the `Time` (t) at which the spatial signature enters XStream Detector.

Step ②: As shown in ② of Figure 8 (a) , in the future, say at time t + δ, AGT of core ID 1 (AGT_1) sends its `bit vector` for the signature PC/1 to PHT_1 and to the shared XStream Detector. It can be observed that, the BVs sent by core ID 0 and core ID 1 are indexed by a common spatial signature PC/1. For every signature, when a `bit vector` enters XStream Detector, the XStream Detector tries to find commonality between `bit vectors` and in the process it searches for eligible `bit vectors` (`Done` field zero) with the `Master` field different from the current sender core ID (`Master`).

Step ③: In ③ of Figure 8 (b), for PC/1, XStream Detector searches for the first eligible `bit vector` from its current entry to entry 0 (for every spatial signature, entry 0 stores oldest entry). In this case, XStream Detector gets a hit for the `bit vector` sent by the core ID 0 in ①. Then to find commonality between the `bit vectors` of different cores (in this example, core ID 0 and core ID 1), it performs the *set-intersection* (bitwise AND) of BV_0 and BV_1 and counts the #1s in it.

Step ④: If the #1s crosses a threshold called cross-core$_{thresh}$, in ④ of Figure 8 (b), XStream Detector treats the prefetcher of core ID 0 as the master prefetcher and the prefetcher of core ID 1 as the worker prefetcher of PC/1. XStream Detector communicates the time difference between insertions of `bit vectors` from two different cores (core ID 0 and core ID 1) to the master core ID (core ID 0). In this case, the difference is δ time units. Along with the time difference, it sends the worker core ID (core ID 1) also. As shown in ④ of Figure 8 (b), PHT of master core (core ID 0) updates its `Worker` field with 1 and `Time` field with δ. At the same time XStream Detector sets the `Done` bit for the entry maintained by core ID 0.

4.3 XCore Communication

In this section, we describe the next phase of XStream, which is called as the XCore communication phase. The communication phase kicks in when the AGT of a master prefetcher sends its `bit vector` to a trained cross-core spatial signature (spatial signature with a valid `Worker` and `Time` field in the PHT). In case of a valid `Worker` field, the master prefetcher sends its `bit vector` to the predicted worker prefetcher (through XBuff-P) based on the `Time` field[3]. A spatial signature is eligible for XCore communication if its `Worker` field is different from the core ID it belongs to. For example, a spatial signature of core ID 0 is eligible for XCore communication if its `Worker` field contains any valid core ID except 0. Figure 9 illustrates the steps involved in this phase.

Steps ①-③: In ① of Figure 9, AGT of core ID 0 communicates the `bit vector` along with the core ID to the shared XBuff-S. In ② of Figure 9, XBuff-S transfers the `bit vector` along with the core ID to the XStream Detector. ① and ② of Figure 9 correspond to ① of Figure 8 (a). In ① of Figure 9, when PHT_0 receives the trained `bit vector`, it counts the #1s in BV_0. If the #1s crosses numones$_{thresh}$ and the corresponding `Worker` field is different from its own core ID then it sets the `Init` bit. In this example, the bit is set for PC/1 in PHT_0. Once the `Init` bit is set, the master prefetcher can communicate the `bit vector` to the worker prefetcher. In ③ of Figure 9, PHT_0 communicates BV_0 to the private cross-core buffer (XBuff-P) of core ID 0 after δ

[3]It helps the master prefetcher gauge how much time it has, to communicate the `bit vector` to the worker prefetcher before the worker core may start demanding the cache lines.

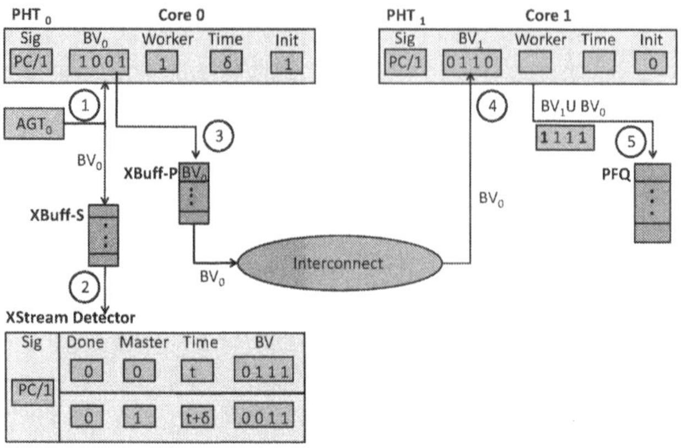

Figure 9: Steps involved in the XCore communication.

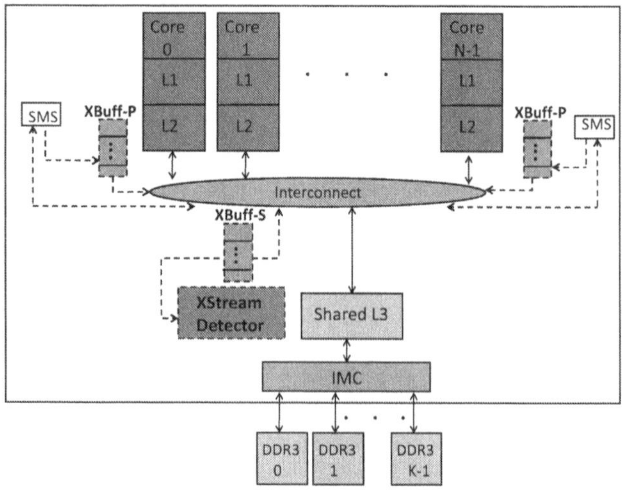

Figure 10: Enhanced CMP with XStream. Dashed blocks and dashed lines are from XStream.

units of time, where δ is predicted time initiated during the detection phase. At a given moment, multiple PHTs can send their `bit vectors` and their predicted `Worker` fields for the cross-core communication. To buffer them, we use XBuff-P. Kindly note, we subtract the average communication latency (65 clock cycles, with minimum of 25 clock cycles, and maximum of 83 clock cycles) between PHT$_0$ and PHT$_1$ from the δ, at the time of XStream detection. This helps XStream to communicate the streams in-time.

Steps ④-⑤: Based on the interconnect scheduling, PHT$_1$ gets BV$_0$ as shown in ④ of Figure 9. PHT$_1$ updates its `bit vector` BV$_1$ to the *set union*[4] (bitwise OR) of BV$_0$ and BV$_1$. In the future, when a demand miss to the trained entry in PHT$_1$ occurs, it triggers the prefetch requests based on the updated bit vector (set union of BV$_1$ and BV$_0$) as shown in ⑤ of Figure 9. In this way, the spatial locality, both within and across the cores, are exploited at the worker prefetcher.

4.4 XCore Timeliness

The effectiveness of XStream depends on two factors: 1) how timely a `bit vector` is communicated from the master prefetcher to the worker prefetcher (XCore timeliness) and 2) the accuracy of the XStream detector.

XStream maintains timeliness using the clock domain that drives the LLC, to clock all the per core PHTs, the interconnect as well as the XStream Detector. XStream maintains a set of local registers (local to each PHT), which stores the current clock cycle. It also maintains a shared global register in the XStream Detector. During the XStream detection phase, when an entry is inserted into the XStream Detector, the Time field is set to the current clock cycle based on the global register. In future, when a bit vector from a different core satisfies crosscore$_{thresh}$ as shown in ④ of Figure 8, the XStream Detector sends the time difference (in terms of the difference in clock cycles) between the insertions of the bit vectors by two different cores to the master prefetcher. In future, when AGT of the master prefetcher sends its bit vector to PHT, it checks for the numones$_{thresh}$. If it satisfies numones$_{thresh}$, it checks the `Worker` field and the `Time` field. Based on the current clock cycle, PHT of the master core schedules the communication of the bit vector after Time clock cycles from the current clock cycle and sends it to XBuff-P. For example if the present clock cycle is x, the master core schedules the communication at $x + \delta$, where δ is the content of the `Time` field. All the registers are reset at fixed intervals. To reduce the hardware overhead, we store the `Time` field in an encoded format.

Our experiments show that the on an average, the estimates of δ are accurate 67% of the time. A slight difference $(+/-\ 3)$ between the actual and the predicted encoded δ values leads to an accuracy of 83.2%. Incorrect delta estimates can affect the timeliness and the overall accuracy and a fine grain feedback mechanism (feedback on delta estimates per spatial signature) can be used to further improve the accuracy of delta estimates. It is important to note that the clock domain that is used at the LLC is typically different from the clock domain that drives the processor cores (similar to intel's haswell [1]). Also, this domain is unaffected by power modes of the cores and the C-states at which the cores may be in. This choice of clock domain source for XStream ensures that all the steps in Sections 4.2 and 4.3 are executed with respect to the same reference clock, thus ensuring correct operation no matter what states the cores are in. In our experimental setup, the clock domain for LLC is clocked at the same rate as that of the cores.

4.5 Special Cases

In this section, we highlight some of the special cases that can happen in a CMP with more than 2 cores.

Case 1: In the enhanced PHT, we store the core ID of only one worker core but within a small window of time, a spatial signature can have more than one worker core. XStream resolves this issue implicitly. For example, in a 4-core CMP, for a given spatial signature, with core i as the master core if core j, k and l follow core i then PHTs of core i, core j and core k store core j, k and l in their respective `Worker` fields. In this way, XStream does not incur extra hardware to store more than one worker core.

Case 2: Section 4.4 describes the mechanism by which the master prefetcher sends its `bit vector` to the worker prefetcher. But there are scenarios where a spatial signature recurs multiple times at the master core before it recurs at the worker core. In this case, XStream communicates the latest `bit vector` from the master prefetcher to the worker prefetcher.

[4]Set union operation between two bit vectors preserve both the local and cross-core bits.

System Address Space	32 bits
Hashed Spatial Signature (PC/*offset*)	16 bits
Size of the Spatial Region	2 KB
Width of the Bit Vector	32 bits
Private Cross Core Buffer(XBuff-P)	8 entries
Shared Cross Core Buffer(XBuff-S)	8 entries
$numones_{thresh}$, $cross\text{-}core_{thresh}$	8
Local and Global Clock Registers	16 bits

Table 2: Parameters specific to XStream.

Figure 10 shows the new hardware added to the baseline CMP system to make it cross-core streams aware. The additional hardware and the interconnect transactions are shown as dashed blocks and dashed lines.

5. HARDWARE IMPLEMENTATION

5.1 Storage, Energy, and Power Requirements

Table 2 shows the details of the various parameters used in XStream. For all the parameters mentioned in Table 2, we sweep through values in powers of two and we find that the combination of values mentioned in Table 2 achieves the maximum coverage. We use 4K entry PHT, which is organized as an associative cache with tag and data arrays. XStream Detector, the heart of XStream keeps track of 4096 signatures. Both PHT and XStream Detector are indexed using the spatial signature (PC/*offset*). We vary the number of spatial signatures (in powers of two) and compared the coverage achieved by XStream and we find that the table with 4096 signatures gives the best coverage. Table 3 shows the storage, energy, and power requirements of XStream on a 4-core CMP. We use CACTI 6.0 [10] with 45nm technology to obtain the access energy, static power, access time, and the area overhead. As XStream does not augment additional bits in the AGT, the storage requirement of AGT is same as that of the baseline SMS. In PHT, XStream augments a few additional fields. The major chunk of storage overhead comes from the XStream Detector. The ideal cross-core streamer requires 64 MB of additional storage for in-time cross-core communication. The storage requirements of each table are as follows:

- Per core AGT: 16 way, 64 entries (4 sets * 16 entries).
  Tag Store: 64 * (32[5] - 11[6] - log_2 (4)) bits = **0.14 KB**
  Data Store: 64 * (32 + 21[7] + 16) bits = **0.53 KB**
- Per core PHT: 8 way, 4096 entries (512 sets * 8 entries).
  Tag Store: 4096 * (16 - log_2 (512)) bits = **3.5 KB**
  Data Store: 4096 * (32 + 4 + 2 + 1) bits = **19.5 KB**
- Shared XStream Detector: 4096 entries
  Data Store: 4096 * (32 + 16 + 16 + 2 + 1) bits = **33.5 KB**

Data store of the PHT uses `bit vector` (32 bits), `Time` (4 bits), `Worker` (2 (3) bits for 4 (8) cores), and `Init` (1 bit) fields. The size of PHT in the baseline SMS is (4096 * 32) bits = 16 KB. So XStream incurs additional 3.5 KB per core (14 KB for a 4-core CMP) for PHT. *The total hardware overhead of XStream for a 4-core CMP is* 14 KB + 33.5 KB = 47.5 KB, *which is a little more than* $\frac{1}{6}$*th of a single MLC (256 KB).* XStream Detector table is implemented as an SRAM (not as SRAM cache) with 4096 signatures and each signature consists of 8 entries. Each entry consists of `bit vector` (32 bits), `Signature` (16 bits), `Time` (16 bits[8]), `Master` (2 (3) bits for 4 (8) cores) and `Done` (1 bit) fields. XStream Detector is also power efficient with power consumption of less than 60mW. In terms of area, the overhead because of XStream Detector is a little more than $\frac{1}{14}$th of a single MLC (2.74 mm^2). XStream also uses encoders (16 : 4) for encoding the 16 bit clock cycle into 4 bit `Time` field and combinational circuits to count the #1s (`popcount`) present in `bit vectors`. The encoding logic takes less than a cycle to encode and the `popcount` circuit takes less than 4 clock cycles[9] to count the #1s in a bit vector. XStream also uses 32 bit registers (one per core at the private SMS and one at the shared XStream Detector) to store the `popcounts`.

[5]32 bits because of address space and not because of the bit vector.

[6]log_2 (2 KB), where 2 KB is the size of the spatial region.

[7]spatial region tag.

	PHT (Per Core)	XStream Detector (Shared)
Size	19.5 KB	33.5 KB
Access Energy	0.024nJ	0.008nJ
Static Power	24.77mW	59.04mW
Access Time	0.61ns	0.24ns
Area (Data Array)	0.13 mm^2	0.19mm^2
Area (Tag Array)	0.07 mm^2	-

Table 3: Storage, Energy, and Power requirements.

Processor	4-core and 8-core CMP, 3.7 GHz Out of Order
Fetch/Decode/Commit width	8
ROB/LQ/SQ/Issue Queue	192/96/64/64 entries
L1 D/I Cache	32 KB,4 way
L2 Unified Cache	256 KB,8 way
L3 Shared Unified Cache	2(4) MB for 4(8) cores, 16 way
MSHRs	16, 32, 64(128) MSHRs at L1, L2, L3 with 4(8) cores, Targets per MSHR = 4
Cache Line Size	64B in L1, L2 and L3
Replacement Policy	LRU at L1 and L2, EAF [12] at the shared L3
Prefetchers at L2	Data - SMS [14], Inst - Stream Prefetcher, with Prefetch Degree = 4 and Prefetch Distance = 16
Coherence Protocol	MOESI
On-chip Interconnect	Crossbar Topology, Transfer/Arbitration Latency - 4/5 clock cycles, Channel Width - 64B Peak Bandwidth/link - 29.9 GB/s
DRAM Controller	On-chip, Open Row, 64 read & write queues, FR-FCFS scheduler, drain-when-full
DRAM Bus	split-transaction, 800 MHz, BL=8
DRAM	DDR3 1600 MHz (11-11-11) 1(2) channels for 4(8) core CMPs, 2 Ranks/channel and 8 Banks/Rank Peak Bandwidth = 12.8 GB/s

Table 4: Parameters of the simulated system.

[8]This unencoded field is different from the encoded 4 bit `Time` field of PHT.

[9]We verify it using Synopsys design compiler for 45nm technology.

Application	Programming Model	Communication Pattern	Prefetcher Sensitivity	XCore Ratio	MLC MPKI	LLC MPKI	MLC PPKI	Pf Accuracy (in %)
bodytrack	Data	Read Only	Low	High	0.73	0.46	0.15	36
canneal	Irregular	Read Only	Low	High	17.85	9.09	0.8	15
dedup	Pipeline	Migratory, P & C	High	High	1.80	0.90	1.40	59
x264	Pipeline	Read Only	High	High	0.76	0.73	0.22	67
ferret	Pipeline	Migratory, P & C	Low	High	6.52	0.85	4.00	70
fluidanimate	Data	Read Only	High	Medium	1.82	1.78	0.23	47
freqmine	Data	Read Only	High	Medium	4.76	0.04	0.40	50
vips	Data	Read Only	Medium	High	1.73	1.16	0.09	48
streamcluster	Data	Read Only	High	High	11.32	5.55	14.07	46
facesim	Data	Read Only	High	High	1.68	14.69	9.02	95
swaptions	Data	Read Only	Low	Low	0.02	0.09	1.53	86
blackscholes	Data	Read Only	Low	Low	0.22	0.10	0.18	89
raytrace	Data	Read Only	Medium	Low	0.18	0.36	0.14	51

Table 5: Characteristics of PARSEC benchmarks. P & C stands for producer & consumer, MPKI stands for misses per kilo instructions. PPKI stands for prefetch issued per kilo instructions. We define Pf Accuracy in Section 6.5.

5.2 On-chip Interconnect Support

To support XStream, we introduce three new interconnect transactions, which we name as XStream transactions. The first transaction named `X-request`, is a transaction between MLC prefetchers and the shared XStream Detector. The transaction consists of the `bit vector` along with the core ID of the sender core. The second transaction named `X-response` is a response transaction between XStream Detector and the master prefetcher. The transaction consists of the `Worker` and the `Time` fields. The third transaction named `X-comm` is between the MLC prefetchers, which carries the `bit vector` from the master prefetcher to the worker prefetcher.

5.3 Timeliness

To support in-time transfer of `bit vectors`, we use multiple local registers at the MLCs and a global register at the XStream Detector. Both local and global registers are 16 bits wide. We reset these registers after every 64K clock cycles. We use encoding logic, which converts a 16 bit clock cycle into a 4 bit `Time` field of PHT. `Time`= $\lfloor \frac{clockcycle}{4096} \rfloor$, where the `Time` field varies from 0 to 15. When XStream Detector sends the `Worker`, it also sends the encoded `Time`. All the PHT entries store these 4 bit `Time` fields. The `Time` field of a spatial signature is decremented every 4K clock cycles. Once a `Time` field becomes zero, PHT of the master core sends the `bit vector` along with the `Worker` core ID to its private XBuff-P. We fine tune the width of the local and global registers based on the average interconnect latency and average residence time of cache lines at the MLC to capture the XCore timeliness.

6. EXPERIMENTAL EVALUATION

6.1 Methodology

We use gem5 Full System (FS) [7] simulator to simulate 4-core and 8-core CMP. We run PARSEC [6] benchmarks on 4-core and 8-core simulated systems and take a detailed look at the cross-core spatial streams. For our evaluation, we consider the parallel region of each program as our region-of-interest (ROI) with `sim-large` as the input size. Due to the slow FS simulation speed of gem5, we run all the applications for 2 billion instructions within ROIs. We use the execution time of an application to measure the performance. To minimize the variability in execution time, we pin the software threads to the hardware threads (cores) and we run all the simulations five times and take the average of the execution time as the final execution time.

Table 4 shows the parameters of our simulated system. We compare XStream with the baseline SMS prefetcher (which is oblivious to the cross-core streaming) and with the ideal cross-core spatial streamer that has the knowledge of all the cross-core streams.

We also compare XStream with shared SMS (SSMS), wherein the demand miss streams from all the cores are trained by a common AGT (of 128 entries) and the predicted streams are stored at a common PHT (of 8192 entries). Both the AGT and PHT steal a fraction of LLC space to predict and store the streams. SSMS is similar to SHIFT [8]. SHIFT is proposed for the lean core servers in which the instruction streams are common across all the cores. SHIFT does not store the instruction streams of each core locally, SHIFT stores the instruction streams of only one core at the LLC and all the other cores use it for prefetching. SHIFT can also be extended for data streams provided a significant fraction of the data streams are common across all the cores. But in the case of shared memory parallel applications, the degree (#cores involved in XCore communication) of XCore communication varies throughout the parallel phase of an application. The major difference between SHIFT and SSMS is that SHIFT uses the stream of a particular core and all other cores use it for prefetching, but SSMS uses a single AGT and PHT to train and store the streams coming from all the cores. Table 5 shows the programming models, sharing patterns and various metrics related to MLC, LLC, and MLC prefetchers. Kindly note that these values are for a 4-core CMP with SMS as the MLC hardware prefetcher. In Table 5, prefetcher sensitivity refers to the degree of reduction in execution time with SMS over a system without prefetching. The sensitivity of an application is considered to be `High` if the reduction is more than 10%, `Medium` if the reduction is in between 2% to 10%, and `Low` if the reduction is less than 2%. XCore ratio refers to the ratio of XCore signatures to the sum of XCore signatures and intra-core signatures. This ratio is only for the spatial signatures that recur at-least 4 times. XCore ratio is considered to be `High` if the ratio is greater than 0.85, `Medium` if the ratio is in between 0.60 and 0.85, and `Low` if it is less than 0.6.

6.2 Execution Time

We evaluate XStream on both 4-core and 8-core systems. Figure 11 compares the execution time of SSMS, XStream, and the ideal cross-core prefetcher normalized to SMS on a 4-core CMP. On an average (geomean), compared to SMS, XStream reduces the execution time by 11.3%. Applications such as `dedup`, `vips`, `streamcluster`, `ferret`, and `facesim` are the major benefactors with reductions of 13%, 20%, 22%, 24%, and 28% respectively. Cores associated with these applications communicate heavily as compared to rest of the PARSEC applications.

SSMS does a poor job compared to SMS because of the cross-core noise that comes from non-recurring non-cooperative streams. We use 256 and 8192 entries (provides the best coverage) for the shared AGT and PHT respectively in SSMS. `swaptions` and `blackscholes` have negligible cross-core spatial streams and their performance with SSMS is similar to their performance with SMS. The ideal cross-core spatial streamer reduces the execution time by 23.13%. Figure 12 compares the reduction in execution time with XStream and with the ideal cross-core prefetcher normalized to SMS on an 8-core system. *We do not compare XStream with SSMS because SSMS causes increase in the execution time for all the benchmarks except* `swaptions` and `blackscholes`. For 8-core CMP, on an average (geomean), XStream reduces the execution time by 9.4%. `streamcluster`, `x264`, `ferret`, and `vips` are the major benefactors with reduction of 29.09%, 15%, 14% and 15.2% respectively.

6.3 Analysis

Table 5 shows that the applications such as `dedup`, `x264`, `facesim` and `streamcluster` are highly sensitive to prefetching and their XCore ratio is also high. XStream delivers its best for these applications except for `x264`. For `x264`, XStream increases the LLC pollution (eviction of demand lines because of prefetching, that are later used) by 6%.

`facesim` uses an iterative Newton-Raphson method over a matrix, which is used by multiple cores. Hence, it has high cross-core spatial correlation. `dedup` and `ferret` use pipeline programming model where each stage of the pipeline is occupied by one or more threads and each stage communicates heavily to its successor stage. Applications such as `canneal` also shows high XCore ratio but XStream fails to deliver performance because of irregular and non-deterministic behavior of spatial signatures that recur.

Applications such as `swaptions` and `blackscholes` do not communicate heavily. `blackscholes` uses data parallel model and it partitions its data structures in such a way that each thread works in its own partition, which limits the XCore communication. So XStream reduces the execution time of `swaptions` and `blackscholes` only by 2% and 3%.

From all the applications mentioned in Table 5, `ferret` has an interesting trend. `ferret` is an application which belongs to the `Low` prefetch sensitive class but with XStream, the execution time reduces significantly. Figure 11 shows, there is a gap between XStream and the ideal cross-core prefetcher. One of the factors that limits XStream as compared to the ideal cross-core prefetcher is the number of harmful prefetches issued by XStream. To bridge the gap between the ideal cross-core prefetcher and XStream, we propose feedback-driven XStream in Section 6.9. On a 4-core system, applications such as `dedup`, `ferret`, `x264` and `facesim` suffer from this trend. *For these applications, more than 88% of the harmful prefetches are issued from 37 spatial signatures. Out of these 37 spatial signatures, only 9 of them issue useful prefetches.*

On an 8-core system, `streamcluster` has an interesting behavior as it communicates consistently with other threads but after a fixed window of 128K clock cycles, the communication becomes intensive. This happens in case of `fluidanimate` also.

Impact of XCore Timeliness: XCore timeliness plays an important role in improving the effectiveness of XStream. To quantify the effect of timeliness, we compare XStream with and without XCore communication. In case of XStream without in-time communication, the AGT of the master core sends the `bit vector` to the PHT of the master core and communicates the same to the worker core also. Compared to XStream with in-time communication, on an average (geomean), XStream without in-time communication increases the execution time by 6.5% (7.18%) on 4-core (8-core) system. On a 4-core system, applications such as `dedup` and `facesim` show an increase of 35% and 29.2% in their respective execution times as compared to XStream with in-time communication. The XCore timeliness plays a bigger role for the 8-core system. Applications such as `facesim`, `dedup`, `fluidanimate` and `x264` are sensitive to the in-time communication of the streams.

6.4 MLC and LLC Miss rates

Figure 13 compares the reduction in MLC and LLC miss rates for 4-core system with SMS and XStream. On an average, XStream reduces the MLC miss rate (average across all the private MLCs) from 37% (with SMS) to 20%. Similarly at the LLC, on an average, XStream reduces the miss rate from 44% (with SMS) to 39%. *Please note, miss rate here indicates only the demand miss rate and it does not account for additional prefetch requests and their misses at the LLC.* Figure 15 shows the reduction in MLC and LLC miss rates for an 8-core system. On an average, XStream reduces the

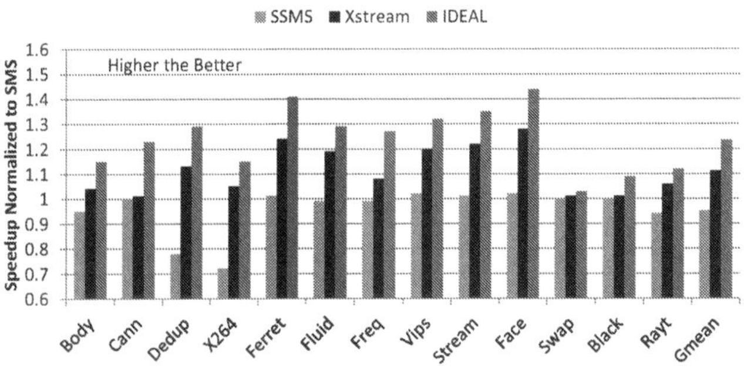

Figure 11: Speedup (Reduction in Execution time) on a 4-core CMP.

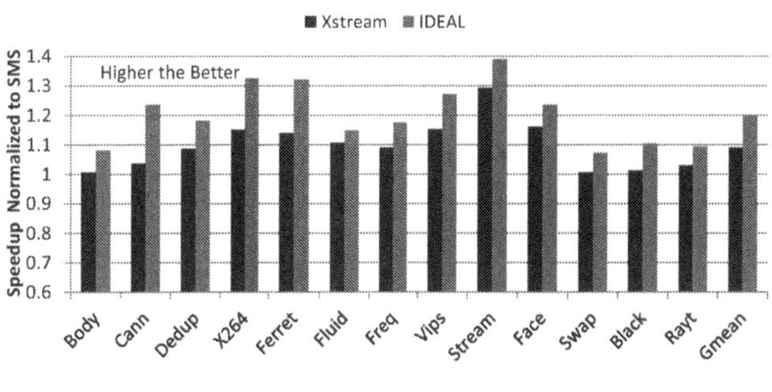

Figure 12: Speedup (Reduction in Execution time) on an 8-core CMP.

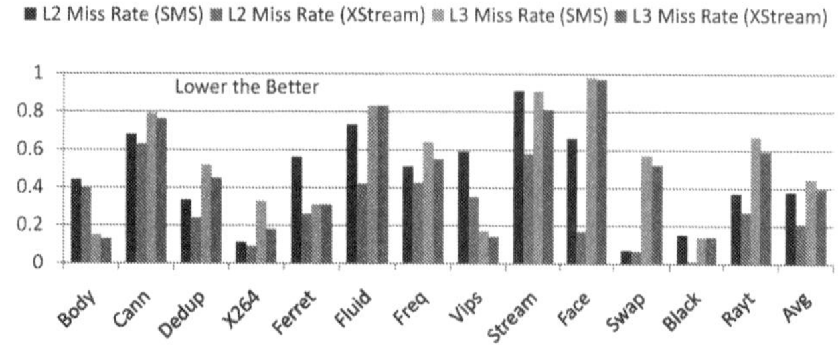

Figure 13: Miss rate on a 4-core CMP.

MLC miss rate from 60% (with SMS) to 46% and LLC miss rate from 42% (with SMS) to 34%. The reduction in miss rates help XStream in reducing the execution time.

6.5 Accuracy, Coverage, and Pf Traffic

Prefetch accuracy (in %) of XStream is defined as

$$\text{Prefetch Accuracy} = \frac{\#\text{Used Lines}}{\#\text{Pf Issued}} * 100 \quad (1)$$

wherein `Used Lines` is the demand hits to the prefetched cache lines and `Pf Issued` is the prefetch requests sent to the LLC because of XStream only (we do not add the prefetch requests issued because of the local streams). To find the accuracy, we augment each cache line with an additional bit that is set if the line is brought in to the cache because of cross-core streaming (not because of the intra-core spatial streaming). To achieve this, we change the PHT by augmenting an additional bit for every bit in the `bit vector`. This additional bit is set whenever a bit is set in the `bit vector` because of the XCore communication.
Prefetch coverage (in %) of XStream is defined as

$$\text{Prefetch Coverage} = \frac{\#\text{Used Lines}}{\#\text{Demand Misses} + \#\text{Used Lines}} * 100 \quad (2)$$

where `Demand Misses` stands for data misses at the MLC. Additional Pf traffic is the additional prefetch requests issued by the XStream as compared to SMS. *Kindly note that this traffic does not include the communication between PHTs and communication between a PHT and the XStream Detector.* Figure 14 shows that, on an average (not geomean), for 4-core CMP, XStream delivers an accuracy of 63.7% and a coverage of 39.61% with additional prefetch traffic of 19.07%. Applications such as `swaptions` and `blackscholes` have high accuracy with low coverage. The reason behind this behavior is the #prefetches issued by XStream, which is very low (additional 10% compared to SMS). Figure 16 shows the accuracy, coverage, and additional traffic because of XStream on an 8-core CMP. We also quantify the additional interconnect bandwidth consumed because of XStream detection and communication. On an average, for 4-core and 8-core CMP, XStream consume additional interconnect bandwidth of 18% and 15.53% respectively. *This additional bandwidth is because of the communication of streams from PHTs to the shared XStream Detector and from master prefetcher to worker prefetcher.* Applications such as `vips`, `dedup`, and `facesim` consumes an additional bandwidth of more than 40% as compared to the baseline SMS. Table 6 summarizes the overall results of XStream for 4-core and 8-core systems.

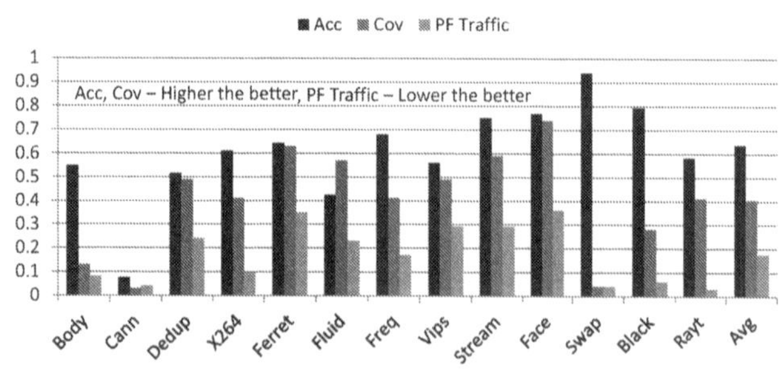

Figure 14: Accuracy, Coverage, and additional Pf Traffic in % of XStream on a 4-core CMP.

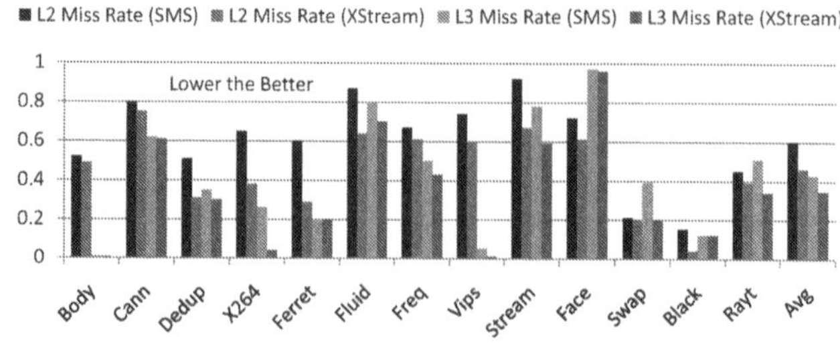

Figure 15: Miss rate on an 8-core CMP.

6.6 Comparison with TMS and SORDS

We do not compare XStream with TMS [19] and SORDS [20] because as compared to the baseline SMS, both of them perform poorly with the practical on-chip hardware budget of 256 KB per core. Both [19] and [20] perform better than SMS when we increase the hardware budget to 2 MB per core (with hardware budget of less than 2 MB per core, TMS is unable to beat SMS).

6.7 Scalability

When we move from a 4-core to a 8-core system, the average reduction in the execution time drops from 11.3% to 9.4%. The scalability of XStream depends on the factors which deal with the application behavior such as 1) degree of XCore communication and 2) application scaling.

degree of XCore communication: If more number of threads participate in crosscore streams, we can anticipate an increase in Xcore communication. For applications such as `x264` and `streamcluster`, this is the case. On moving to a 8-core system from a 4-core system, the degree of Xcore communication increases for these applications resulting in reduction of execution time.

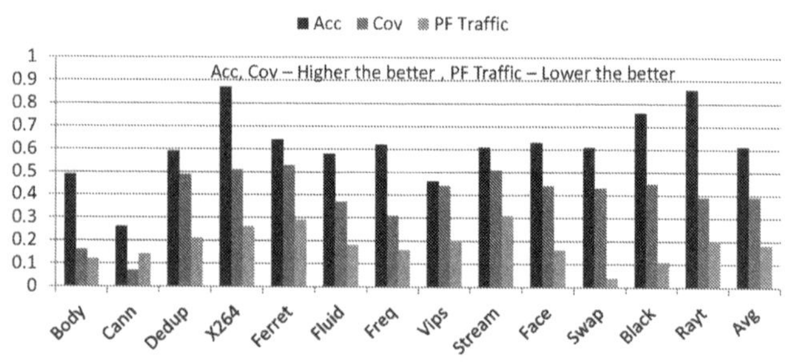

Figure 16: Accuracy, Coverage, and additional Pf Traffic in % of XStream on an 8-core CMP.

	Reduction in Execution Time	Additional Pf Traffic	Additional Interconnect Bandwidth
4-core	11.3%(max of 24%)	19.07%	18%
8-core	9% (max of 29.09%)	17.69%	15.53%

Table 6: Summary of results for XStream.

application scaling: XStream scales poorly if the ratio of the number of software threads spawned to the number of cores is high. For instance, dedup and ferret spawn $2 + 3n$ threads and $2 + 4n$ threads respectively in an n core system. The other factor that can limit the true scaling of an application is the number of synchronization primitives (such as locks) used and how frequently synchronization is required. The number of locks acquired by a particular thread per number committed kilo instruction (LPKI) is a clear indicator of application scaling. For instance fluidanimate(1.36), freqmine(0.03) and vips(0.01) have orders of magnitude higher LPKI than others. Naturally, these applications do not scale well with core count and see a drop in the savings of execution time.

organization of XStream framework: Another important factor related to scaling is to understand how scalable the hardware organization of XStream is for 4-core and 8-core systems, the shared XStream detector with an on-chip interconnect such as crossbar does a good job but for many-core systems (16-core and above), shared XStream detector with a crossbar may become a scalability bottleneck. On an average, on each link, XStream uses 57% of the spared interconnect bandwidth in XStream detection and communication but with the increase in the core count, the bandwidth utilization goes down because of more number of cores compete for XStream detector. As part of our future work, we would like to explore a distributed XStream, wherein chunks of XStream will be distributed with the LLC banks and also over a scalable interconnect such as ring.

6.8 Sensitivity Studies and Tradeoffs

We analyze the sensitivity of XStream to the #signatures present in XStream Detector and to the size of MLC and L1 on a 4-core CMP. Our baseline evaluation has 4096 signatures at the XStream Detector with 256 KB of MLC and 32KB of L1 D-cache. With 2048 signatures, the coverage of XStream decreases by 18% for applications such as `canneal`, `fluidanimate`, and `facesim`. These applications have more than 4000 distinct XCore signatures. For MLC size of 64 and 128 KB, XStream reduces the execution time by 13.27% and 15.24% respectively. In case of MLC size of 512 KB, XStream reduces the execution time by 10.91%. If one is allowed to change only L2's size to increase performance, the size of L2 has to be increased to at-least 1MB/core (512KB/core is enough for applications such as `bodytrack` and `blackscholes`) to match the performance of XStream. Our experiments also show that the increase in size of L1 from 32KB to 64KB/128KB provides only a marginal improvement of less than 1.5% over the baseline.

6.9 Feedback Driven XStream

The performance of XStream can be further improved with prefetch throttling techniques such as feedback directed prefetching (FDP) [15]. FDP throttles the prefetcher by changing the prefetch degree and prefetch distance based on prefetch metrics such as accuracy, coverage, and cache pollution. As SMS does not use parameters such as prefetch degree and prefetch distance, simple integration of FDP with XStream is not possible. So we use the prefetch accuracy to enable/disable cross-core prefetching. For every prefetch request generated because of the cross-core bits, we add an additional bit with the prefetch requests and the responses. We also add an additional bit for each cache line brought into the cache because of cross-core streaming. After every 64K clock cycles, we enable XStream if the prefetch accuracy is more than 0.45 else we disable it. On an average (geomean), feedback driven XStream reduces the execution time by 14.25% over SMS. Due to space constraints, we do not present the performance results in detail. Feedback driven XStream reduces the Pf traffic by 7.45% over XStream. XStream when integrated with pollution filtering mechanism [21] reduces the execution time by 12.38% and 10.17% on 4-core and 8-core system respectively.

6.10 Effect On Multiprogrammed Workloads

We assess the effectiveness of the proposed XStream by evaluating it in a multiprogrammed scenario also. In multiprogrammed setup, multiple independent applications run independently with minimal or no XCore communication. The XCore communication comes from the operating system code and not from the independent applications. We test the robustness of XStream by simulating 32 4-core and 16 8-core workload mixes from SPEC 2006 benchmark suite [3] and in terms of weighted speedup, XStream performs similar to SMS.

7. RELATED WORK

TMS: Wenisch et al.'s TMS prefetcher [19] exploits temporal correlation among coherent miss streams at the L1 D-cache that spread across the cores. TMS minimizes the coherent read misses in DSMs. The idea targets commercial workloads and scientific applications and it works well for applications with migratory sharing pattern. The major disadvantage of this approach is the large hardware overhead (24 MB on an 4 core CMP) and frequent use of cache directories. Wenisch et al.'s STMS [18] implements TMS by storing the streams at the DRAM Though 48 MB is a small fraction of memory for large scale servers, it is not the case for CMPs. Modern day CMPs use multiple levels of cache with the last level cache (LLC) being shared by all cores. which results in additional DRAM traffic and consumption of additional L2-L3 bandwidth. In an 8-core CMP, on an average, compared to SMS, STMS increases the DRAM traffic by 51%. Wenisch's Ph.D. thesis [17] proposed an extension of TMS to CMPs and showed the effectiveness of TMS on a 4-core CMP. Similar to TMS in DSMs, TMS in CMPs incurs hardware overhead of 9 MB per core.

SORDS: Wenisch et al.'s SORDS prefetcher [20] exploits the producer-consumer sharing pattern. The main observation of SORDS is the correlation between the producer and consumer cores. Based on this observation, SORDS stores the streams generated by the producer that is initiated by a write request. On a future demand miss at the consumer core, SORDS forwards the streams produced by the producer core. Similar to TMS, SORDS incurs additional storage of 22 MB on a 4-core CMP.

STeMS: Somogyi et al.'s spatio temporal memory streaming (STeMS) [13] prefetcher is based on the temporal correlation among streams within a spatial region. STeMS correlates the temporal streams that are local to a particular core and it is oblivious to the cross-core streams. STeMS incurs storage overhead of 6.52 MB on a 4-core CMP. Also, TMS and SORDS consult the cache coherence directory to decide which core's main memory holds the temporal streams.

Cross-core Stride Prefetcher: Panda et al. proposed a cross-core stride prefetcher [11] , which exploits spatial strides (based on the demand misses at L1) present within and across the cores. The idea is similar to Bhattacharjee et al.'s ICC [5], which is an inter-core cooperative prefetching framework proposed for TLBs. The authors evaluated their framework for a 2 level cache hierarchy. Though cross-core strides dominate the demand misses at the L1, MLC misses do not contribute to cross-core strides. In case of PARSEC, on an average, cross-core strides are of more than 128 cache lines. In applications such as `blackscholes` and `facesim`, on an average, 42% of strides cross the virtual page boundaries and cross-core strides contribute negligibly in applications such as `streamcluster` and `ferret`. Apart from cross-core streaming techniques, there are data forwarding techniques which forward data from one core to another. Data forwarding method, proposed by Koufaty et al. [9] uses compiler hints to forward data across the cores. The effectiveness of these techniques depend on the cache size because on an average, on a 4-core CMP, with MLC of 256 KB, 82% of the time, data forwarded by one core gets evicted before the same gets consumed by the other core. Other techniques such as Data Marshaling [16] eliminates cross-core write misses with the help of marshal instructions in staged execution models.

8. CONCLUDING REMARKS

This paper proposed cross-core spatial streaming (XStream), a prefetching technique for the MLCs that exploits cross-core spatial streams. With negligible hardware overhead, XStream results in 11.3% and 9% reduction in execution time for 4-core and 8-core CMPs, respectively. As part of future work, we would like to extend XStream for multi-chip configurations, where each chip will have 4-cores to 8-cores and an XStream framework of one chip can communicate spatial streams to XStream frameworks of other chips.

9. ACKNOWLEDGMENTS

The authors thank the anonymous reviewers and the Shepherd of this paper Ravishankar Iyer for their valuable suggestions. Special thanks to Anju Moosad, T V Kalyan, Tripti Warrier, Akanksha Jain, Vivek Seshadri, Madhu Mutyam and Mainak Chaudhuri for their insightful feedback on the intial versions of this paper. Biswabandan is supported by the TCS Ph.D. fellowship. This work is also supported by the IBM India SUR grant. The authors gratefully acknowledge the support of TCS and IBM.

10. REFERENCES

[1] `http://www.hotchips.org/wp-content/uploads/hc_archives/hc25/HC25.80-Processors2-epub/HC25.27.820-Haswell-Hammarlund-Intel.pdf`.

[2] Intel 64 and ia32 architecture software developer's manuals. `http://www.intel.com/products/processor/manuals/`.

[3] Spec benchmark suite. `http://www.spec.org/cpu2006/`.

[4] N. Barrow Williams, C. Fensch, and S. Moore. A communication characterisation of splash-2 and parsec. In *IISWC*, 2009.

[5] A. Bhattacharjee and M. Martonosi. Inter-core cooperative tlb for chip multiprocessors. In *ASPLOS*, 2010.

[6] C. Bienia, S. Kumar, J. P. Singh, and K. Li. The parsec benchmark suite: characterization and architectural implications. In *PACT*, 2008.

[7] N. Binkert, B. Beckmann, G. Black, S. K. Reinhardt, A. Saidi, A. Basu, J. Hestness, D. R. Hower, T. Krishna, S. Sardashti, R. Sen, K. Sewell, M. Shoaib, N. Vaish, M. D. Hill, and D. A. Wood. The gem5 simulator. *SIGARCH Comput. Archit. News*, 39(2), Aug. 2011.

[8] C. Kaynak, B. Grot, and B. Falsafi. Shift: Shared history instruction fetch for lean-core server processors. In *MICRO*, 2013.

[9] D. Koufaty, X. Chen, D. K. Poulsen, and J. Torrellas. Data forwarding in scalable shared-memory multiprocessors. *IEEE Trans. Parallel Distrib. Syst.*, 7(12), 1996.

[10] R. B. N. Muralimanohar and N. P. Jouppi. Cacti 6.0: A tool to understand large caches. technical report, university of utah and hewlett packard laboratories. 2007.

[11] B. Panda and S. Balachandran. Hardware prefetchers for emerging parallel applications. In *PACT*, 2012.

[12] V. Seshadri, O. Mutlu, M. A. Kozuch, and T. C. Mowry. The evicted-address filter: A unified mechanism to address both cache pollution and thrashing. In *PACT*, 2012.

[13] S. Somogyi, T. F. Wenisch, A. Ailamaki, and B. Falsafi. Spatio-temporal memory streaming. In *ISCA*, 2009.

[14] S. Somogyi, T. F. Wenisch, A. Ailamaki, B. Falsafi, and A. Moshovos. Spatial memory streaming. In *ISCA*, 2006.

[15] S. Srinath, O. Mutlu, H. Kim, and Y. N. Patt. Feedback directed prefetching: Improving the performance and bandwidth-efficiency of hardware prefetchers. In *HPCA*, 2007.

[16] M. A. Suleman, O. Mutlu, J. A. Joao, Khubaib, and Y. N. Patt. Data marshaling for multi-core architectures. In *ISCA*, 2010.

[17] T. F. Wenisch. Temporal memory streaming. phd thesis, carnegie mellon university. 2007.

[18] T. F. Wenisch, M. Ferdman, A. Ailamaki, B. Falsafi, and A. Moshovos. Practical off-chip meta-data for temporal memory streaming. In *HPCA*, 2009.

[19] T. F. Wenisch, S. Somogyi, N. Hardavellas, J. Kim, A. Ailamaki, and B. Falsafi. Temporal streaming of shared memory. In *ISCA*, 2005.

[20] T. F. Wenisch, S. Somogyi, N. Hardavellas, J. Kim, C. Gniady, A. Ailamaki, and B. Falsafi. Store-ordered streaming of shared memory. In *PACT*, 2005.

[21] X. Zhuang and H. Lee. A hardware-based cache pollution filtering mechanism for aggressive prefetches. In *ICPP*, 2003.

What is the Cost of Weak Determinism?

Cedomir Segulja and Tarek S. Abdelrahman
The Edward S. Rogers Sr. Department of Electrical and Computer Engineering
University of Toronto
seguljac@eecg.toronto.edu, tsa@eecg.toronto.edu

ABSTRACT

We analyze the fundamental performance impact of enforcing a fixed order of synchronization operations to achieve weak deterministic execution. Our analysis is in three parts, performed on a real system using the SPLASH-2 and PARSEC benchmarks. First, we quantify the impact of various sources of nondeterminism on execution of data-race-free programs. We find that thread synchronization is the prevalent source of nondeterminism, sometimes affecting program output. Second, we divorce the implementation overhead of a system imposing a specific synchronization order from the impact of enforcing this order. We show that this fundamental cost of determinism is small (slowdown of 4% on average and 32% in the worst case) and we identify application characteristics responsible for this cost. Finally, we evaluate this cost under perturbed execution conditions. We find that demanding determinism when threads face such conditions can cause almost 2x slowdown.

Categories and Subject Descriptors

D.1.3 [**Programming Techniques**]: Concurrent Programming—*Parallel Programming*; D.2.8 [**Software Engineering**]: Metrics—*Performance Measures*; D.3.4 [**Programming Languages**]: Processors—*Run-time Environments*

Keywords

determinism; deterministic execution; multithreading

1. INTRODUCTION

One of the main reasons why parallel programs are demanding to write, debug, and test is the *nondeterminism* of program output and/or the way this output is produced [19, 31]. Recently, there has been a stream of systems that suppress nondeterminism by forcing threads to access shared resources, i.e., communicate, in a deterministic manner. They propose different thread synchronization orders, or *schedules*, and also incur different overheads (Table 1).

PACT'14, August 24–27, 2014, Edmonton, AB, Canada.

http://dx.doi.org/10.1145/2628071.2628099.

System	Schedule	Weak vs. Strong	Max. Overhead
Grace [7]	serial	strong	3.6x
Dthreads [25]	round-robin	strong	4x
Conversion [29]	round-robin	strong	5x
Parrot [13]	round-robin	weak	3.8x
Kendo [33]	dynamic	weak	1.6x
RCDC [16]	dynamic	strong	1.7x
RFDet [26]	dynamic	strong	2.6x
DMP [14]	hybrid	strong	1.7x
CoreDet [4]	hybrid	strong	10x
Calvin [22]	hybrid	strong	1.7x

Table 1: State-of-the-art deterministic systems. The overheads, reported in [5] and in the respective papers, show that the authors themselves find that determinism comes at a cost.

Some of the above systems provide determinism only for data-race-free programs, which is commonly referred to as *weak determinism* [33]. Others secure determinism even in the presence of data races and this stronger guarantee is therefore named *strong determinism* [33]. In addition to this difference, these systems come in both hardware [14, 16, 22] and software [7, 33, 4, 25, 13, 29, 26] flavors, and enforce determinism using a variety of techniques, including speculation [7, 14], buffering [14, 25, 16, 22, 26] and version control [29]. This makes it difficult to understand if one system is better than another due to the schedule being enforced or due to differences in implementations. In other words, it is unclear whether the performance degradation under deterministic systems stems from forcing the execution to be deterministic, or from the enforcement mechanisms being used. Thus, we pose the question: implementation overhead set aside, *what is the fundamental cost of determinism?*

In this paper, we seek to answer this question in the context of data-race-free programs, that is, for weak determinism. Guaranteeing deterministic thread communication for this class of programs reduces to ensuring that synchronization operations are executed deterministically. In the rest of this paper, we use the term "determinism" to simply refer to weak determinism, unless noted otherwise.

We run a data-race-free version of SPLASH-2 [40] and PARSEC [8] benchmark suites on a dual chip 16-core Xeon E5-2660 machine and empirically study the cost of making synchronization deterministic under a given schedule. We use a schedule-record-replay framework to divorce the implementation overhead of generating a schedule from the fundamental impact of enforcing the schedule. The framework also allows us to evaluate the performance of deterministic execution across different execution environments by perturbing the execution in a controlled manner.

Our study has three parts. In the first, we quantify to what extent does nondeterminism occur in program execution. In the process, we identify previously unreported sources of nondeterminism, like lazy binding, initialization of C++ static variables and compiler vectorization. Our analysis confirms the common belief that thread synchronization is the most significant contributor to nondeterminism in data-race-free programs.

In the second part of our study, we evaluate the performance impact of enforcing a schedule on program execution. By employing our schedule-record-replay framework, we find a lower bound on the execution time that can be achieved with any deterministic execution that enforces the same schedule. The analysis reveals that the cost of deterministic execution is smaller than previously thought: only 4% on average and never greater than 32% increase in the run time compared to a nondeterministic execution. We further pinpoint program characteristics that are relevant for identifying whether or not a program will incur significant performance degradation when executed with a schedule.

In the last part of our study, and again using the same framework, we evaluate the cost of enforcing a schedule across multiple execution environments (e.g., with the presence of context switches, background processes and execution on asymmetric architectures). We find that insisting on the same schedule when threads face uneven conditions like unbalanced system loads or an asymmetric architecture can slow down execution by as much as 2x.

While the technique we use to measure the cost of determinism applies only to data-race-free programs, we believe that the insights that our work provides are also of interest to systems that supply determinism for arbitrary parallel programs (i.e., strong determinism). First, for both weak and strong determinism, the order in which threads execute synchronization operations (e.g., lock acquire/release, condition variable signal/wait) must be resolved deterministically. Second, although strongly deterministic systems must additionally deal with data races, recent advances in this area have demonstrated that strong determinism requires no extra program serialization in addition to the serialization caused by deterministically ordering synchronization operations [29, 26].

Contributions. To the best of our knowledge, our study of data-race-free benchmarks is the first to:

- Quantify the impact of various sources of nondeterminism on program execution on a real machine.
- Determine the fundamental performance cost of enforcing weak determinism and correlate it to application characteristics.
- Evaluate the fundamental cost of requiring the same deterministic execution across a range of environments.

The rest of this paper is organized as follows. Section 2 defines determinism, discusses sources of nondeterminism, and summarizes the existing approaches of enforcing deterministic thread synchronization. Section 3 describes our schedule-record-replay framework. Section 4 details the platform, benchmarks, and the metrics we use in our study. Section 5 presents and analyzes our empirical results. Section 6 presents related work, and Section 7 concludes.

2. BACKGROUND

2.1 What is Determinism?

Determinism is a program property that requires observing the same output whenever the program runs with the same input. However, depending on what one assumes *program output* and *program input* to mean, many flavours of determinism arise. These flavours apply to both data-race-free and arbitrary parallel programs, i.e., they are orthogonal to the notion of weakly vs. strongly deterministic implementations. Here we highlight common definitions of determinism and state the one we adopt in this paper.

2.1.1 Program Output

One often considers only the end program result to be the output (*external determinism* [19]). However, while debugging, the intermediate values or even instruction operands might be considered as the program output. Determinism is then defined more rigorously as the repeatability of the sequence of instructions each thread executes, along with the values of operands used by each instruction (*internal determinism* [19]). Between these two extremes, other formulations are possible; an excellent discussion of plausible definitions of determinism is given by Lu and Scott [27]. In particular, the executions are *SyncOrder* deterministic if they, in addition to agreeing in the final result, contain the same synchronization operations, executed by the same threads in the same order.

For both data-race-free and arbitrary parallel programs, SyncOrder determinism allows for some differences between executions (changes in the addresses of variables via ASLR as described in Section 2.2.2, or benign data changes due to data races), as long as they have no effect on synchronization order and program result. However, it still limits the number of possible thread interleavings and hence greatly increases test coverage [13].

All existing deterministic systems provide determinism of at least SyncOrder semantics, and they deterministically resolve the order of synchronization operations. Hence, when assessing the lower bound on the cost of determinism, we adopt SyncOrder determinism and require threads to synchronize in a deterministic manner.

2.1.2 Program Input

A natural definition of the input includes supplied program arguments and file/network input. However, certain software and hardware parameters may also influence the program output (e.g., process memory layout or the size of hardware structures). Practical approaches to determinism can be classified in three groups according to how they cope with these parameters. One class considers these parameters to be program input as well, by silently assuming they do not vary across executions. Another class forces these parameters to be constant (e.g., *system-level determinism* [2, 6] by providing a custom OS). Finally, some approaches actually do guarantee determinism when certain system parameters vary (e.g., *unbounded determinism* [22] by providing determinism across micro-architectural variations).

We believe that it is more useful to provide determinism across a wide range of system setting. Thus, we consider system parameters to be a source of nondeterminism rather than a program input.

2.2 What Causes Nondeterminism?

Here we describe causes for executions of the same program not to be identical in the *strict sense of internal determinism.* Most of these sources are already known, however, we do identify some sources not previously reported and that we discovered while running our benchmarks.

While each of the sources we discuss instigates nondeterminism on its own, it is important to note that these sources do interact and hence are not completely orthogonal.

2.2.1 Thread Communication

One well-known source that leads to nondeterminism is thread communication, i.e., accesses to shared resources by different threads. Small variations in the execution environment, such as the state of hardware caches, TLBs or the presence of other applications, may make accesses to shared resources by different threads occur in different orders across multiple program runs. This, in turn, can cause threads to execute different instruction sequences and possibly affect program output.

Prior work has identified accesses to shared program variables [19, 31] and shared library resources (e.g., variables and I/O objects) [33, 4] as potentially occurring in different orders, leading to nondeterminism. However, we have also discovered accesses to other shared resources, not introduced by programmers and library writers, as giving rise to nondeterminism. These accesses are manifested through subtle compiler/run-time interactions. For example, the run-time symbol resolution (also known as lazy binding) [17], speeds up program load time, but it also causes the first thread to reach a given shared library call to do the extra work of symbol resolution. Since the "first" thread can be different across program runs, so can the number of instructions executed by each thread, making executions not internally deterministic. C++ local static variables initialized with a non-compile-time constant also cause the first thread to reach the corresponding function to do the extra work, again making executions nondeterministic.

2.2.2 Process Address Space Layout Variations

Address space layout randomization (ASLR), changes in Linux environment variables, modification of shared libraries, preloading additional libraries (e.g., to debug segmentation faults using `libSegFault.so`), cause changes in the addresses of program instruction and data across multiple runs, making them not identical by the strict definition of internal determinism.

Additional variability may arise when the address variations are coupled with code that inspects addresses. For example, compiler auto-vectorization, which takes advantage of the vector units available in modern processors (e.g., SSE/AVX on x86 and AltiVec/VMX on PowerPC), is implemented via loop peeling and/or loop versioning to dynamically at run-time guarantee aligned accesses [9]. These transformations result in code in which the total number of executed instructions depends on the input data alignment, and hence, could change due to the address space layout variability. Similarly, certain library (or compiler built-in) functions (e.g., `memcpy` and `memset`), follow different code paths based on input alignment in order to use the widest data type transfers supported by the hardware. Finally, the application code itself can be dependent on memory addresses.

2.2.3 System and Library Dependences

Certain library and system calls are nondeterministic. Some are such by construction (e.g., `rand` or `gettimeofday`), others through their semantics. For example, Linux's `read` system call is allowed to return smaller number of bytes than requested [14]. Different runs of the same program that must read a certain number of bytes may execute a different number of `read` calls.

2.3 How to Achieve Determinism?

The bulk of work on determinism seeks to ensure that threads communicate in a deterministic manner [14, 33, 7, 4, 22, 16, 25, 13, 29, 26]. For data-race-free programs, this problem reduces to guaranteeing that synchronization operations are executed deterministically. While data races add complexity to a deterministic system, it has been recently shown that racey access can be made deterministic without adding any program serialization in addition to the one caused by deterministically ordering synchronization operations [29, 26].

Thread synchronization order is described formally using the notion of a *schedule.* A schedule is a directed acyclic graph consisting of nodes that represent executed synchronization operations of a multi-threaded program. The edges of a schedule denote the causal partial relationship between synchronization operations, i.e., the Lamport's happened-before relation [24].

The schedules generated and enforced by the state-of-the-art deterministic systems (Table 1) are best described by the notion of a *turn.* At any given time during execution, it is only one thread's turn and only while a thread has the turn can it execute synchronization operations. Depending on when a thread passes its turn, the following schedules emerge.

In the *serial schedule* [7] a thread holds on to its turn until the end of its execution, effectively imitating an execution in which threads are executed synchronously in program order (i.e., as function calls). In the *round-robin schedule* [25, 13] a thread passes its turn after each executed synchronization operation. In the *dynamic schedule* [33, 16, 26] the turn is passed on each tick of a per-thread deterministic *logical clock.* The original proposal by Olszewski et al. [33] uses store instructions to maintain logical clocks, i.e., a thread passes its turn upon executing one memory store. The *hybrid schedule* [14, 4, 22] uses the logical clock to break down the execution of each thread into *quanta* and enforces the serial schedule during each quantum – a thread passes its turn only when it reaches the end of one quantum. A thread's quantum ends when it executes N ticks, where N is an input parameter of this schedule. Additionally, a thread also could end its quantum after executing a synchronization operation – this variation is known as the "reduced serial mode" [4].

While primarily introduced to handle programs with data races, we note that the hybrid schedule can be seen as a generalization of the serial schedule (when $N = \infty$), the round-robin schedule (when $N = \infty$ and a quantum also ends upon executing a synchronization operation) and the dynamic schedule (when $N = 1$). We utilize this aspect when building a framework for finding the cost of enforcing these schedules.

It is important to note that the notion of a turn is conceptual, and many executions satisfy the same schedule. For example, the implementation of the serial schedule executes threads speculatively to regain parallelism while respecting the serial schedule [7]. The systems using the dynamic schedule avoid the overhead of turn passing and force a thread to wait when executing a synchronization operation until its logical clock becomes the lowest across all threads [33]. Nonetheless, the existing systems suffer overheads not fundamental to deterministic synchronization (e.g., rollbacks in case of speculation, or forcing a total order of synchronization operations). While we use the concept of a turn, we ensure that threads wait only when necessary to conform to the partial order of synchronization dictated by a given schedule.

3. OUR FRAMEWORK

We use a schedule-record-replay framework (Figure 1) to evaluate the cost of making synchronization operations in data-race-free programs deterministic under a given schedule. When evaluating the performance of a program under a specific schedule, we execute it *twice*: the first time to generate the schedule, and the second time to enforce the schedule. The key concern is to impose the schedule as efficiently as possible, in order to obtain the best execution time achievable with that schedule.

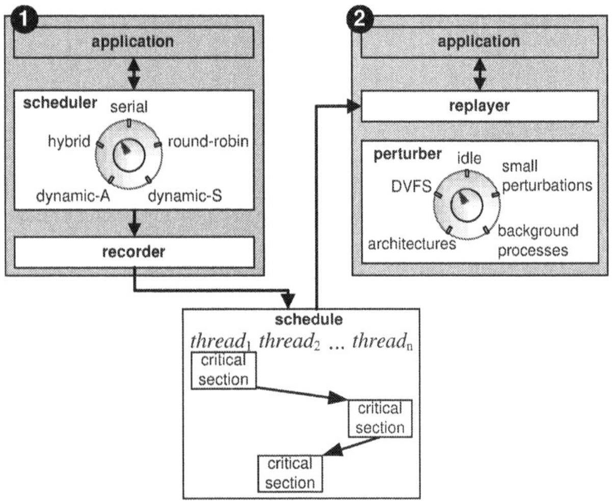

Figure 1: The schedule-record-replay framework.

During the first run, we run the program with the *scheduler* that generates and enforces fixed synchronization order. The scheduler has a "knob" that allows us to select the schedule to be evaluated. During this run, the *recorder* captures the order of synchronization operation under the schedule and dumps it to a file. In the second run, the *replayer* imposes the saved recorded schedule, guaranteeing the same deterministic execution as in the first run, but without the scheduler's overhead.

The replayer should force threads to wait only when absolutely necessary for the schedule to be respected and it should do so with little overhead. If we can achieve that, then the run time of the second run is a close-to-best time that can be attained with any system enforcing the same schedule.

The framework also has a *perturber* component, as shown in Figure 1. The perturber, similar to the scheduler, has a knob that allows us to choose the execution environment in which the performance of a given schedule is measured. We discuss each component of this framework in turn.

3.1 Scheduler

The scheduler intercepts Pthreads synchronization operations and orders them by implementing the schedules described in Section 2.3. Using the insight that the hybrid schedule can be seen as a generalization of all the other schedules, our scheduler implements the hybrid schedule with parameterizable quantum duration, and by varying the quantum duration we get the serial, round-robin, and the dynamic schedule.

We use the hardware performance counters and Linux's `perf_event` API to implement logical clocks. For the dynamic schedule, we implemented two versions of logical clocks: one that uses only the number of store instructions [33], and one that uses the number of *all* instructions [16, 26]. We refer to the resulting schedules as *dynamic-S* and *dynamic-A*, respectively. For the hybrid schedule, we use the number of all instructions to implement logical clocks, set the phase duration to 100,000 instructions, and do not use the reduced serial phase. These settings have been found previously to on average give the best performance with the CoreDet [4] implementation of the hybrid schedule [25].

The determinism of logical clocks, necessary to ensure a deterministic schedule, can be compromised when there are other sources of nondeterminism besides thread synchronization (e.g., lazy binding, auto-vectorization with ASLR, and nondeterminism in library calls). Thus, to ensure correctness of the dynamic and hybrid schedule, we pause logical clocks during the execution of nondeterministic library functions and disable lazy binding and auto-vectorization. This is done only during the record run, and not during the replay run.

The use of logical clocks that tick on each instruction can compromise the determinism of schedules. This is because performance counters report slightly different number of instructions even for identical instruction sequences, as reported in [39]. However, our framework is unaffected by this issue. We use the scheduler only during the recording run, and then enforce the recorded order with the replayer, making the replayed execution deterministic. This is one advantage of our schedule-record-replay framework that decouples schedule generation from schedule enforcement. Indeed, we verify this deterministic execution using a series of microbenchmarks and a data-race-free version of RACEY [21].

3.2 Recorder

The recorder captures the scheduled order of synchronization operations. Due to space considerations, we focus our description on critical sections, but our framework supports the other commonly used synchronization primitives (barriers and condition variables) as well.

When a critical section is executed, the relevant information (the identifiers of the thread executing the critical section and of the lock that protects the critical section) are atomically appended to an array shared by all threads. Although this creates an over-constrained, total order of synchronization operations, the schedule (i.e., the partial order sufficient to guarantee repeatability) is easily reconstructed based on the thread and lock identifiers: a synchronization operation A must occur before a synchronization B if and only if A precedes B in the shared array and A and B have the same lock or thread identifier. The potential application slowdown during the recording run is not an issue, since the recorder is used solely to capture a schedule, while it is the task of the replayer to efficiently execute this schedule.

3.3 Replayer

During replay, the schedule is represented with multiple arrays, *one per thread*. Each byte of a thread's array corresponds to one critical section that the thread will execute and its value is the id of the *next* thread to enter a critical section protected by the same lock. This encoding supports programs with up to 256 threads. A thread traverses its array during the execution, consuming one byte for each executed critical section. Thus, laying out the elements of a thread's array in the order in which the thread will enter critical sections (which is known from the recording run) enables good cache behavior.

We use the replay lock and unlock operations, shown in Figure 2, that replace corresponding Pthreads routines and are inspired by ticket locks [28]. We hijack the Pthreads mutex structure (**pthread_mutex_t**), and use it to store the identifier of the next thread to acquire the lock: a thread can enter a critical section only if the value currently stored in the mutex structure equals the thread identifier. The initial value of the mutex structure is set during the mutex initialization routine (**pthread_mutex_init**) and then updated with the identifier of the next thread to acquire the lock (retrieved from the aforementioned threads's array) upon exiting a critical section.

```
int pthread_mutex_lock(pthread_mutex_t *mutex){
  // the mutex structure holds the identifier of the next thread to
  // acquire the lock.
  volatile char *nextThreadID = (char*) mutex;
  char thisThreadID = get_threadID();
  // wait until the previous thread releases the lock.
  while (*nextThreadID != thisThreadID);
  return 0;
}

int pthread_mutex_unlock(pthread_mutex_t *mutex){
  char *nextThreadID = (char*) mutex;
  // allow the next thread to acquire the lock by updating the mutex
  // structure.
  *nextThreadID = get_nextThreadID();
  return 0;
}
```

Figure 2: Replay lock and unlock operations.

3.3.1 Optimizations

The replayer's lock routine requires identifying a running thread (the **get_threadID** macro). Library routines such as **gettid** or **pthread_self**, or the use of the thread-local storage, would provide the thread identifier, albeit at the price of a function call. This overhead can be avoided by carefully allocating the stack of each thread. Placing stacks in a consecutive memory region aligned to a ($stackSize \times nThreads$) boundary allows to obtain a unique number in $[0, nThreads - 1]$ for each thread by just manipulating the stack pointer (only 3 register-to-register x86 instructions), and we use this number as the thread identifier.

Inspired by Linux's **current** macro [12], we place the pointer to the current element of a thread's array at the bottom of the thread stack. This allows a fast implementation of the **get_nextThreadID** macro: after the address of this pointer is calculated by manipulating the stack pointer, the identifier of the next thread to acquire the mutex is accessed by simply incrementing and dereferencing this pointer.

Hence, with the exception of a few assembly instructions that manipulate the stack pointer and make memory accesses only to thread-private data and are of high spatial locality, and aside from the store during the unlock operation, a replayed run includes only the fundamental operation necessary to enforce a schedule: waiting during a lock acquire for the immediately preceding thread to leave the critical section. We verify that this implementation of the replayer indeed incurs negligible overhead in Section 5.2.1.

3.4 Perturber

One benefit of determinism is that once the program is deployed in the field, it continues to behave as tested, i.e., "*deployed determinism has the potential to make testing more valuable, as execution in the field will better resemble inhouse testing*" [15]. This however, makes efficient deterministic execution especially challenging, since programs are run under various conditions (e.g., OS-caused perturbations such as context switches and page faults, dynamic CPU frequency scaling) and on various systems (e.g., symmetric vs. asymmetric architectures). The perturber imitates various execution environments programs face in the field.

3.4.1 Small Perturbations

The perturber simulates small execution perturbations such as context switches, thread migrations and page faults via Linux signals and wait periods. To simulate a perturbation in a thread, a signal is sent to this target thread which mimics the magnitude of the perturbation by just waiting a certain time period. We determined the smallest possible perturbation delay in the target thread execution using a micro-benchmark as about a 5μs. This allows us to imitate the first-order effects of context switches and thread migrations (which are typically on the order microseconds [3]) and page faults (milliseconds [20]). Hence, we randomly insert two types of delays (10μs and 1ms delays) so that they occur with the following frequency: one 10μs delay for each 1ms of execution time and one 1ms delay for each 100ms of execution time. The perturber implements two scenarios: balanced perturbations (same delays in each thread) and unbalanced perturbations (the frequency of delays varies over threads, ranging from the above frequency to 1/8 of it).

3.4.2 Background Processes

To account for the presence of other processes, the perturber spawns a number of background threads which repeatedly execute a work-sleep pattern in which they first spin in an empty loop (keeping the processor busy) and then sleep (allowing for other threads to run). By varying the duration of the work vs. sleep phases we control the impact that the background threads have on the core utilization and other running threads. Again the perturber implements two scenarios: a low-intensity balanced one in which there is a one background thread running on each core and each thread spends just 5% of its cycles working, and an intense unbalanced one where there is only one background thread but it spends 50% of it cycles working.

3.4.3 *Dynamic Voltage and Frequency Scaling (DVFS)*

The perturber uses Linux's `cpufreq` system to explore the performance of deterministic execution under different DVFS policies. First, by utilizing Linux's `ondemand` governor, the perturber implements a scenario in which power-performance balance is required, and the OS dynamically adjusts the CPU frequency. Second, by using the `userspace` governor, the perturber sets the frequency of some processor cores to the lowest value (1.2 GHz) while periodically switching the frequencies of the other cores between 1.2 and 2.2 GHz. This simulates the per-core DVFS approach [23].

3.4.4 *Non-Uniform Memory Access*

To explore the effects that a non-uniform memory access (NUMA) architecture has on deterministic execution, the perturber spreads the threads across the two nodes of our NUMA machine in a round robin manner. Otherwise, the threads are contained in a single NUMA node, experiencing uniform memory accesses.

3.4.5 *Asymmetric Architectures*

We employ the aforementioned `userspace` governor to create asymmetry. The perturber implements a scenario where half of the threads are running on the cores that are more powerful than the others (2.2 GHz vs. 1.2 GHz) and a scenario where only one thread is running on a powerful core.

4. EXPERIMENTAL METHODOLOGY

4.1 Benchmarks

We use the SPLASH-2 [40] and PARSEC [8] benchmarks released with the PARSEC 3.0 suite. From this suite of 27 benchmarks, we exclude two benchmarks from all of our experiments: `freqmine`, which does not have a Pthreads version (and our framework currently only works with Pthreads), and `canneal`, which employs a lock-free synchronization strategy, and conversion to a version that uses Pthreads synchronization primitives would result in code bearing little similarity to the original `canneal` code.

We tested all the other benchmarks for data races using ThreadSanitizer [36], and found races in 16 out of 25 benchmarks. Our examination of the code revealed that races were used when it is perceived that proper synchronization is unnecessary or that it would decrease performance. Additionally, some of the races were undoubtedly program bugs: even with the assumption of sequentially consistent memory model in the presence of data races (which none of the modern programming languages, compilers, and architectures provide) these data races lead to undesired program behaviour.

We fixed all the reported data races by adding synchronization and compared the performance of the original benchmarks to the data-race-free ones. An increase in the execution time was noticed only in three cases: `barnes`(11%), `radiosity`(5%) and `raytrace_parsec`(8%). This confirms that there is little to be gained by introducing "benign" racy accesses, as previously hypothesized by Boehm [11]. For the rest of this study, we use the data-race-free version of benchmarks as a baseline.

Unless stated otherwise, all the benchmarks were compiled with GCC 4.6 using default compilation settings of PARSEC 3.0 with added the `-march=native` flag to obtain binaries optimized for our machine. The input used is `simlarge`: decent parallel speedup was obtained for this input while the running time of a single experiment was short enough in order to run all the experiments in a reasonable amount of time.

4.2 Platform

The machine we use has two Xeon E5-2660 chips. A single chip consists of 8 cores and operates at a frequency between 1.2 GHz and 3.0 GHz. Each core supports two-way hyper-threading which yields a total of 32 hardware threads. There is 16 GB of main memory per chip, and cores have faster access to 16 GB of their chip and slower access to 16 GB of the other chip, i.e., this is a NUMA system. The operating system is Ubuntu 12.04, kernel version 3.2.

When quantifying sources of nondeterminism, we run the benchmarks to utilize all 32 hardware threads and use the "default" OS settings: ASLR is enabled, the OS controls thread scheduling, and the processor frequency varies based on the workload. On the other hand, when evaluating the cost of making synchronization deterministic, we execute both nondeterministic and deterministic runs in a more controlled environment. This way, any difference we observe across runs can be confidently attributed to differences between the schedules and not to other factors.

For the controlled environment, we disable hyper-threading and ASLR, fix the frequency to 2.2 GHz, and explicitly pin application threads to cores (one thread per core). We then configure the benchmarks to run on 8 cores since this allows us to evaluate the effect of a NUMA system on deterministic execution (Section 3.4.4). Two exceptions are `dedup` and `ferret` that for an 8-core configuration spawn much more than 8 threads and our one-thread-per-core approach is not possible. Thus, we run `dedup` and `ferret` in a 4- and 3-core configuration, respectively. The number of threads in the `x264` benchmark is proportional to the number of input frames and much larger than 8; hence, we exclude this benchmark when evaluating the cost of determinism.

4.3 Metrics

4.3.1 *Execution Variability*

To quantify the extent to which executions are not identical in the strict sense of internal determinism, we utilize the hardware performance counters to detect changes in the executed instruction streams. We record the total number of *repeatable* hardware events for each thread over 10 program runs. These events are repeatable in the sense that their number is always the same for the runs with identical instruction traces. Hence, changes in the recorded number of events undoubtedly indicate the presence of nondeterminism.

The events we monitor are store instructions, conditional branches, and not taken branches. These were the only repeatable events correctly accounted for by the performance counters on our platform. We define the *variability of a thread* as the range (across multiple executions) of the number of events in that thread, normalized by the average number of events in all the threads. For example, in a program that on average triggers 50 events, a thread's variability of 10% indicates that the difference in the number of events occurred in that thread between multiple runs was as much as 5 events. The *execution variability* is simply the sum of per-thread variabilities:

$$variability = \sum_{t \in threads} variability_t = \sum_{t \in threads} \frac{\max\limits_{r \in runs} e_{t,r} - \min\limits_{r \in runs} e_{t,r}}{\sum\limits_{\substack{r \in runs \\ t \in threads}} e_{t,r} \;/\; \#runs}$$

where $variability_t$ and $e_{t,r}$ denote variability of the thread t and the number of events that occurred in that thread during program run r, respectively.

It is possible for executions with different instruction traces to have the same number of events, and hence, our approach can fail to detect nondeterminism. The fine-grain nature of events we monitor makes this unlikely, but we do recognize that our results are a lower bound on variability. While we could, for example, collect a complete per-thread execution trace, this would significantly perturb execution.

4.3.2 *Deterministic Slowdown*

We quantify the performance impact of imposing a certain schedule by comparing the execution time of a replay run enforcing the schedule with that of a nondeterministic run. We repeat both the replay and nondeterministic run at least 10 times and as many times as needed to get the standard error of the average execution time of each run below 0.5%. We then report the *ratio* of the average execution time of the deterministic replay run to the nondeterministic run. We refer to this value as the *deterministic slowdown*. Using bootstrap [18], we established that each reported deterministic slowdown is accurate to ±1.5%, with 95% confidence.

For fairness, we use the same controlled environment for both the deterministic and nondeterministic runs, as described in Section 4.2. Further, since the replayer uses spin-based synchronization, we use scalable spinning synchronization [28] in the nondeterministic run as well. This improves the nondeterministic execution time across all the benchmarks (by as much as 2x for `streamcluster`). Finally, when quantifying the impact of a schedule under varying system conditions, we ensure that the same conditions are applied during both the replay and nondeterministic run.

5. EXPERIMENTAL EVALUATION

5.1 Quantifying Nondeterminism

Table 2 shows the average number of the events triggered in each benchmark across multiple runs, and the resulting execution variability (in the "all" column). Additionally, the benchmarks for which changes in the output occurred at least once have the corresponding variability cell grayed. This clearly demonstrates that the nondeterminism in multi-threaded programs execution is real, significant, and that it sometimes even leads to a different program output.

We further break the variability down to the sources discussed in Section 2.2. The "sync.", "lazy." and "C++" columns show the variability due to thread communication stemming from respectively: (*i*) program synchronization, (*ii*) lazy binding, and (*iii*) initialization of C++ local static variables. The "vec." column displays the variability due to the ASLR and the compiler auto-vectorization. Lastly, the "lib." column presents the variability occurred during library calls, caused by a combination of (*i*) thread communication that occurs during the execution of library calls, (*ii*) the ASLR, and (*iii*) nondeterministic timing functions.

	Benchmark	Average Number of Events (billions)	Execution Variability (%)					
			all	thread communication			vec.	lib.
				sync.	lazy.	C++		
splash	barnes	10.13	3.43	3.11	$3.85\cdot10^{-5}$	0	0	$1.01\cdot10^{-6}$
	cholesky	0.16	2.95	5.93	$3.56\cdot10^{-4}$	0	$1.98\cdot10^{-4}$	$5.41\cdot10^{-4}$
	fft	3.45	$2.31\cdot10^{-4}$	$2.27\cdot10^{-5}$	$2.44\cdot10^{-5}$	0	0	$3.03\cdot10^{-5}$
	fmm	4.83	9.49	8.20	$3.54\cdot10^{-5}$	0	$2.07\cdot10^{-8}$	$1.05\cdot10^{-5}$
	lu_cb	4.86	1.95	4.54	$2.94\cdot10^{-5}$	0	$4.94\cdot10^{-7}$	$1.47\cdot10^{-5}$
	lu_ncb	4.83	2.36	1.31	$1.21\cdot10^{-5}$	0	$4.76\cdot10^{-7}$	$2.01\cdot10^{-5}$
	ocean_cp	1.67	2.28	2.61	$1.41\cdot10^{-4}$	0	$3.17\cdot10^{-4}$	$2.46\cdot10^{-6}$
	ocean_ncp	1.55	0.06	0.09	$2.66\cdot10^{-4}$	0	$1.12\cdot10^{-4}$	$3.17\cdot10^{-6}$
	radiosity	23.05	11.28	15.75	$2.44\cdot10^{-6}$	0	0	$1.60\cdot10^{-7}$
	radix	2.62	$5.97\cdot10^{-3}$	0.01	$6.67\cdot10^{-5}$	0	0	$4.29\cdot10^{-5}$
	raytrace	7.78	4.37	3.44	$7.50\cdot10^{-6}$	0	0	$9.54\cdot10^{-5}$
	volrend	2.89	32.53	40.25	0	0	0	$2.35\cdot10^{-6}$
	water_nsquared	22.03	10.29	11.18	$1.06\cdot10^{-5}$	0	0	$1.18\cdot10^{-7}$
	water_spatial	5.68	8.71	12.36	$4.79\cdot10^{-5}$	0	0	$1.86\cdot10^{-5}$
parsec	blackscholes	0.92	$3.53\cdot10^{-4}$	0	$2.19\cdot10^{-4}$	0	0	$1.73\cdot10^{-6}$
	bodytrack	2.90	8.46	3.61	$1.94\cdot10^{-5}$	0	$3.34\cdot10^{-6}$	$1.72\cdot10^{-3}$
	dedup	11.58	22.90	9.56	$1.69\cdot10^{-5}$	0	0	$6.60\cdot10^{-3}$
	facesim	6.07	0.04	$7.84\cdot10^{-4}$	$1.68\cdot10^{-5}$	0	$3.32\cdot10^{-5}$	0.05
	ferret	7.06	31.93	33.81	$7.96\cdot10^{-6}$	0	$1.42\cdot10^{-8}$	$4.54\cdot10^{-3}$
	fluidanimate	3.85	0.06	0	$7.58\cdot10^{-5}$	0	0	0.07
	raytrace	4.78	3.45	4.00	$4.70\cdot10^{-5}$	$5.46\cdot10^{-5}$	0	$4.01\cdot10^{-6}$
	streamcluster	1.06	$2.98\cdot10^{-4}$	0	$8.24\cdot10^{-5}$	0	0	$1.50\cdot10^{-6}$
	swaptions	6.41	$9.23\cdot10^{-5}$	0	$8.82\cdot10^{-5}$	0	0	$1.02\cdot10^{-5}$
	vips	6.77	3.41	3.80	$4.43\cdot10^{-8}$	0	0	$8.04\cdot10^{-3}$
	x264	1.83	$1.41\cdot10^{-3}$	$1.39\cdot10^{-3}$	$3.20\cdot10^{-5}$	0	0	$4.09\cdot10^{-5}$

Table 2: Variability in SPLASH-2 and PARSEC benchmarks.

The variability for each column was obtained by examining 10 runs in which only the target source of nondeterminism was contributing to execution variability. This was done by either removing other sources of nondeterminism; i.e., by enforcing a fixed synchronization order using the record-replay framework, by disabling lazy binding and auto-vectorization, and by transforming local static variables into global ones, or by isolating the nondeterminism inside library calls (e.g., printfs, scanfs, file I/O, and memory allocation) by pausing the performance counters during their execution.

It is important to note that the presented variability breakdown is not exact: the total variability is not equal to the sum of individual variabilities. This is because the individual variabilities do interact with each other and they are also collected on different sets of runs. Nonetheless, the breakdown reflects the extent to which the executions experienced variability due to each particular source of nondeterminism.

We make the following observations:

- Not surprisingly, program synchronization is the most significant contributor to nondeterminism, and it sometimes affects program output.

- Other sources of nondeterminism result in much less variability but do materialize. This has important implications for existing deterministic systems that rely on determinism of logical clocks. These systems typically handle nondeterminism during library calls, but assume none of the additional nondeterminism we discovered in this study. Consequently, the combination of auto-vectorization and the ASLR can compromise guarantees of strongly deterministic systems. For weakly deterministic systems, lazy binding and static initialization, in addition to vectorization, can undermine their deterministic guarantees.

5.2 The Cost of Determinism

5.2.1 *Replayer's Efficiency*

Ideally, the replayer should impact execution only by forcing a thread to wait before executing a synchronization operation until the preceding scheduled synchronizations have finished. Yet, our replayer has three sources of overhead. First, although the replayer's macros (`get_threadID` and `get_nextThreadID`) are highly optimized, they are of nonzero latency. Second, having each thread traverse its (potentially large) array that represents synchronization operations could possibly disturb the memory subsystem and slow down other memory accesses. Finally, a write to a lock during replayer's unlock operation can potentially cause unnecessary communication between processors executing the threads not directly involved in the transfer of the lock. The last issue can be avoided by having a per-thread dedicated variable in each lock, as done with array-based queue locks [28]. However, modifying the replayer in this way brought no performance improvement. Thus, we conclude that this issue does not have a visible performance impact on our benchmarks.

The impact of the first two overhead sources should ideally be evaluated by comparing our replayer to an ideal replayer with no overhead, but this is not possible. Thus, we compare a nondeterministic run to a nondeterministic run in which the synchronization operations have been modified to execute the `get_threadID` and `get_nextThreadID` macros, but not to enforce any particular schedule. Since no schedule is enforced, the array elements that are being accessed during the modified nondeterministic run may not correspond to the synchronization operations being executed. Nonetheless, the underlying effect is still present: executing synchronization operations includes the additional latency and causes each thread to sequentially traverse a dedicated memory region.

The result of this comparison is shown in Figure 3, which displays the execution time of the nondeterministic run including replayer's overhead normalized w.r.t. the execution time of the unmodified nondeterministic run (the error bars show 95% confidence interval). As seen, the execution times are nearly identical. Thus, we consider the execution time obtained by our framework during the replay run to provide a lower bound on the execution time that can be achieved with any deterministic execution enforcing the same schedule.

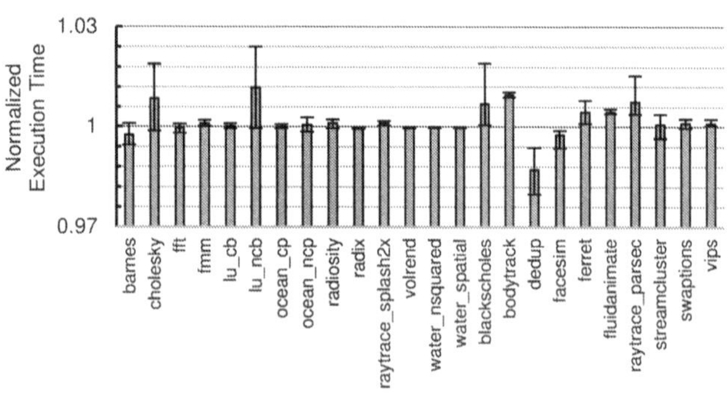

Figure 3: The efficiency of the replayer.

5.2.2 *Deterministic Slowdown*

The "Deterministic Slowdown" column of Table 3 shows the deterministic slowdown for each schedule. We make the following observations:

- The performance of a significant number of benchmarks (10 out of 24) is unaffected by the schedule being enforced and is the same in both the nondeterministic and deterministic case.
- Enforcing the serial schedule comes with a significant cost of up to 7.71x slowdown. Moreover, this schedule degrades the performance of certain benchmarks to that extent that their deterministic execution is slower than the single-threaded execution, i.e., the deterministic slowdown is higher than the parallel speedup in these cases.
- The round-robin schedule on average incurs modest slowdown of 1.60x, although it can also result in a significant performance degradation of more than 5x.
- The dynamic schedules induce a small slowdown, both on average and in the worst case. The dynamic-A schedule, which uses the number of all instructions to implement logical clocks, performs exceptionally well: *the slowdown never raises above 1.32x, and it is only 1.04x on average.*
- The hybrid schedule, similar to the dynamic schedules, generates only a small average slowdown of 1.18x. However, it can result in up to 2.69x slowdown.

This demonstrates that, at least for our set of benchmarks and our platform, and implementation overhead set aside, *the fundamental cost of weak determinism is small.*

5.2.3 *Analysis*

The slowdown during a deterministic run can occur due to the change in the time threads spend waiting while performing synchronization (*wait time*), and/or the time threads spend working (*work time*). The increase in the wait time is caused by a schedule forcing threads to wait longer than in the nondeterministic case, while the change in the work time may occur due to a schedule forcing a different control path, leading to an execution with different amount of work, or to an execution with the same amount of work but changed efficiency (e.g., improved/deteriorated data locality).

Figure 4 display the work time under schedules normalized w.r.t. the work time of the nondeterministic run, showing that these are very close, with the exception of **dedup**. Profiling reveals that the amount of work is identical in both the deterministic and nondeterministic run of **dedup**, but the execution efficiency changes. The compress stage of the **dedup** pipeline, where threads allocate and access a large number of memory buffers, experiences significantly less page faults under the nondeterministic and the round-robin runs compared to the other schedules. A schedule in this case determines the order in which threads allocate memory and this evidently influences Linux's page allocation policy. Aside from this peculiarity, the work time does not increase under deterministic runs. Thus, we focus on the increase in the wait time.

Intuition suggests that the lock frequency should relate to the wait time during deterministic runs, since more/less

	Benchmark	Deterministic Slowdown					Parallel Speedup	Analysis					
		serial	round-robin	dynamic-S	dynamic-A	hybrid		lock freq.	lock span	round-aware lock span	clock imbalance (store inst.)	clock imbalance (all inst.)	type of parallelism
splash	barnes	1.11	0.97	0.95	0.95	0.99	6.87	$2.75 \cdot 10^{2}$	0.14	0.00	0.03	0.01	static partitioning w/ irreg sync
	cholesky	3.41	2.40	1.08	1.05	1.09	3.98	$5.70 \cdot 10^{1}$	0.90	0.36	0.08	0.04	dynamic load balancing
	fft	4.36	1.02	1.02	1.02	1.02	7.21	1.16	0.50	0.00	0.00	0.00	static partitioning
	fmm	6.34	1.33	1.16	1.13	1.19	6.68	$2.67 \cdot 10^{2}$	0.77	0.10	0.01	0.02	static partitioning w/ irreg sync
	lu_cb	1.00	1.00	1.00	1.00	1.00	7.32	$1.44 \cdot 10^{-3}$	0.00	0.00	0.03	0.01	static partitioning
	lu_ncb	1.01	1.00	1.01	1.01	1.01	4.04	$5.74 \cdot 10^{-4}$	0.00	0.00	0.03	0.05	static partitioning
	ocean_cp	1.00	1.00	1.00	1.00	1.00	4.71	$4.59 \cdot 10^{-2}$	0.00	0.00	0.01	0.01	static partitioning
	ocean_ncp	1.00	1.00	1.00	1.00	1.00	7.83	$2.67 \cdot 10^{-2}$	0.00	0.00	0.00	0.01	static partitioning
	radiosity	7.58	3.03	1.09	1.07	2.69	7.00	$8.45 \cdot 10^{2}$	1.00	0.36	0.03	0.01	dynamic load balancing
	radix	1.00	1.00	1.00	1.00	1.00	7.70	$2.63 \cdot 10^{-3}$	0.00	0.00	0.00	0.02	static partitioning
	raytrace	7.71	2.93	1.08	1.03	1.88	7.71	$3.67 \cdot 10^{1}$	1.00	0.31	0.02	0.01	dynamic load balancing
	volrend	6.12	1.91	1.08	1.02	1.67	6.37	$5.97 \cdot 10^{1}$	0.75	0.68	0.09	0.03	dynamic load balancing
	water_nsquared	1.00	1.00	1.00	1.00	1.00	6.85	3.14	0.00	0.00	0.08	0.04	static partitioning
	water_spatial	1.00	1.00	1.00	1.00	1.00	6.44	$8.20 \cdot 10^{-3}$	0.00	0.00	0.16	0.01	static partitioning
parsec	blackscholes	1.01	1.00	1.00	1.00	1.00	7.98	0.00	0.00	0.00	0.00	0.00	static partitioning
	bodytrack	5.86	1.04	1.05	1.05	1.05	5.85	2.52	0.87	0.01	0.01	0.01	dynamic load balancing
	dedup	5.03	1.76	1.63	1.32	1.33	4.01	$1.43 \cdot 10^{1}$	0.95	0.67	1.08	0.29	pipeline parallelism
	facesim	6.21	1.00	1.00	1.00	1.00	6.20	6.09	0.92	0.35 (0.00)	0.02	0.00	dynamic load balancing
	ferret	6.20	3.20	1.59	1.24	1.26	2.92	$6.80 \cdot 10^{-2}$	1.00	0.66	0.87	0.14	pipeline parallelism
	fluidanimate	1.81	1.00	0.99	0.97	0.97	6.00	$1.10 \cdot 10^{3}$	0.56	0.00	0.10	0.01	static partitioning w/ irreg sync
	raytrace	7.27	1.52	1.07	1.01	1.02	7.17	$1.58 \cdot 10^{1}$	1.00	0.66	0.01	0.00	dynamic load balancing
	streamcluster	1.00	1.00	1.00	1.00	1.00	6.14	$9.19 \cdot 10^{-3}$	0.00	0.00	0.08	0.07	static partitioning
	swaptions	1.00	1.00	1.00	1.00	1.00	7.93	0.00	0.00	0.00	0.00	0.00	static partitioning
	vips	7.62	5.28	1.32	1.06	1.05	7.62	5.87	1.00	0.96	0.50	0.14	background I/O threads
	average slowdown	**3.61**	**1.60**	**1.09**	**1.04**	**1.18**							
	maximum slowdown	**7.71**	**5.28**	**1.63**	**1.32**	**2.69**							

Table 3: Deterministic slowdowns, parallel speedup of the nondeterministic run w.r.t. the single-threaded run, the number of lock acquires per million cycles and the program characteristics that impact the performance under schedules.

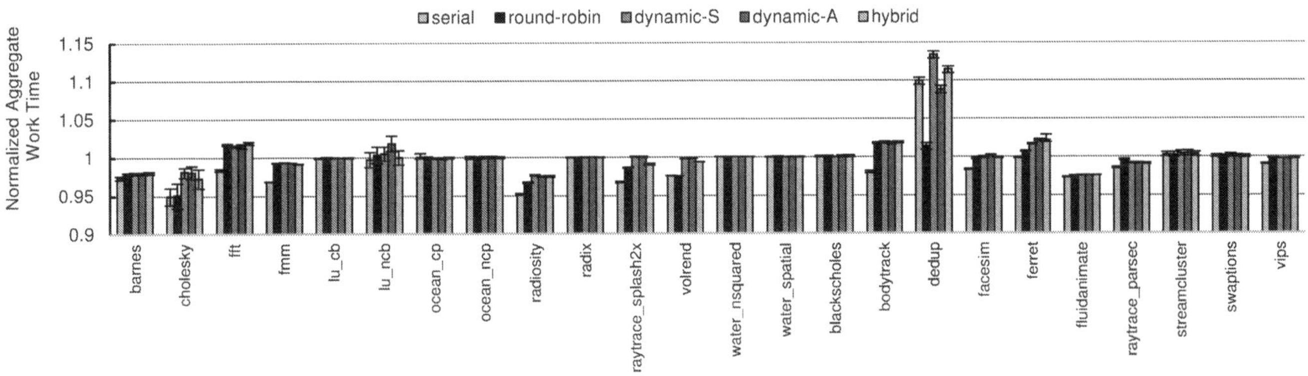

Figure 4: The total time threads spent working under schedules, normalized w.r.t. the work time in the nondeterministic run.

synchronization gives more/less opportunity for a schedule to force threads to wait. However, Table 3 shows this is not always the case: synchronization-intense `barnes` experiences only a small slowdown of 1.11x and only under the serial schedule, while the synchronization-light `ferret` suffers a performance degradation under all schedules. Thus, we analyze two application characteristics that can better relate to deterministic performance: the *lock span* and *clock imbalance*.

Lock span. The *lock span* is obtained during nondeterministic execution as the time between earliest and latest lock acquires, relative to the total run-time (Figure 5). More precisely, the lock span is calculated by measuring the time elapsed from the earliest to latest acquire of each lock, finding the maximum over all the locks and normalizing this time by the total execution time. We hypothesize that a low lock span translates to a low deterministic slowdown. In the worst case, the earliest and the latest acquire of a lock in the nondeterministic run get reordered during a deterministic run. In this case, the increase in the wait time will be roughly equal to the time difference between these two uses of the lock in the nondeterministic run. Hence, applications with small time differences between any two lock acquires should experience little to no increase in wait time.

Two extensions are required in order to properly account for benchmarks that suffer load imbalance or use barriers. First, for the imbalanced benchmarks, a potential increase in the wait time of a "shorter' thread translates to increase in the program execution time only when this thread is forced to wait for long enough to become the "longest" thread. Thus, when calculating the locks span, we decrease the time elapsed between the earliest and latest use of a lock by the maximum observed difference between the run times of threads. Second, when barriers are used to divide program into phases, the use of a lock in different program phases can never be reordered by a schedule, so it can not contribute to the execution time increase. Hence, we calculate the lock span as the sum of per-phase lock spans.

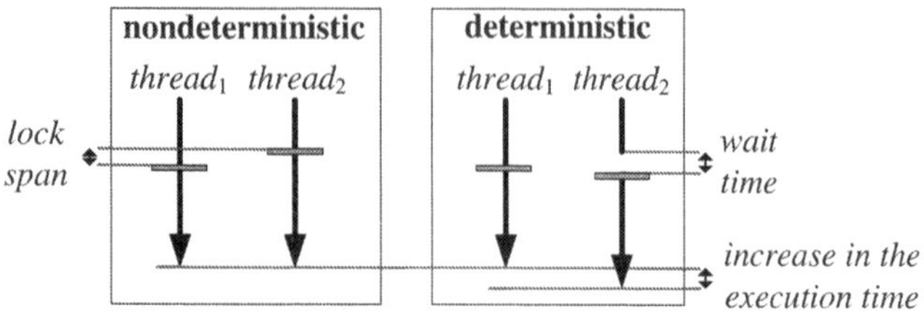

(a) Low lock span.

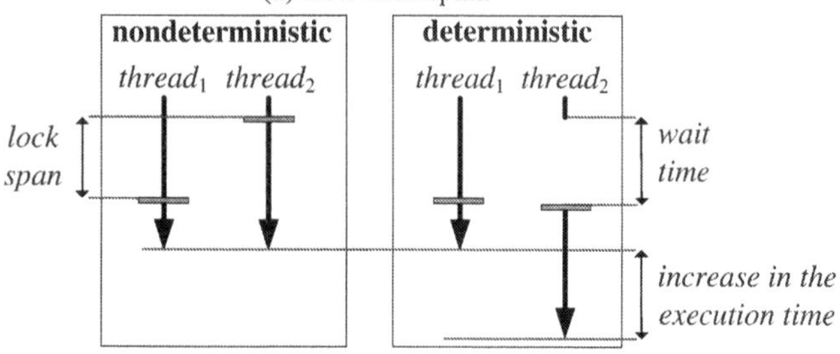

(b) High lock span.

Figure 5: The lock span is measured during a nondeterministic run as the time between earliest and latest lock acquires (denoted with thick grey lines). When a deterministic run imposes a different order of lock acquires, a low/high lock span translates to low/high increase in the execution time.

The lock span values are shown in Table 3. The 10 benchmarks that have lock span lower than 0.001 show no slowdown under deterministic runs. The `barnes` benchmark, which has a low lock span of 0.14, experiences only 1.11x slowdown in the worst case. *A low lock span translates to good performance under any schedule.* Looking at the remaining benchmarks, it is evident that *a high lock span translates to significant slowdown under the serial schedule but not necessarily under the other schedules.*

The inability of the lock span to fully characterize the performance under the round-robin, dynamic and hybrid schedules stems from the fact that the earliest and latest acquire of a lock do not always get reordered, as assumed in the definition of the lock span. We define the *round-aware lock span* in the same way as the lock span with the difference that it only considers two acquires of a lock as a potential source of slowdown if these acquires indeed can be reordered under the round-robin schedule. When calculating the round-aware lock span, each lock acquire is given an index that denotes its order among other acquires done by the same thread; the time between two acquires is considered only if the "earlier" lock has a larger index than the "later" lock.

As Table 3 shows, *a low round-aware lock span translates to good performance under the round-robin schedule, while a high round-aware lock span suggests a significant performance degradation under the same schedule.* One exception is `facesim`: it uses condition variables to effectively create a barrier, leading to incorrect detection of program phases used during the lock span calculation. After manually replacing condition variables in question with barriers, we recorded the expectedly low value of 0.001.

Clock imbalance. The *clock imbalance* is obtained by collecting a ratio of the end logical time to physical time for each thread and calculating the relative standard deviation of these ratios. We hypothesize that applications with high clock imbalance are likely to incur visible deterministic slowdown under the dynamic schedule. When the logical clocks closely follow the physical time, the deterministic run under the dynamic schedule mimics a nondeterministic one, and no slowdown occurs. Logical clocks that run at varying physical time rates across threads, provide the dynamic schedule with a poor estimate of the physical time. Hence, threads may be forced to wait longer than in the nondeterministic run.

Table 3 shows the clock imbalance when the logical clock is incremented only on a store instructions and when it is incremented on every instruction. Three benchmarks (`dedup`, `ferret` and `vips`) that have a high clock imbalance when only stores instructions are used have the largest slowdowns under the dynamic-S schedule. The clock imbalance becomes lower when using all instructions, and so do the slowdowns under the dynamic-A schedule. *Applications with a high clock imbalance are likely to incur visible slowdown with the dynamic schedule.*

The benchmarks in question employ the pipeline model of parallelism where different threads perform different pipeline stages or use background I/O threads, which explains why logical clocks do not run at the same rate in these cases.

The hybrid schedule uses logical clocks but it also depends on the duration of a quantum. Thus, the performance of the hybrid schedule is a function of both the clock imbalance and the quantum duration parameter. We leave the detailed analysis of the hybrid schedule performance for future work.

Conclusions. Our analysis shows that deterministic slowdowns are mainly caused by an increase in wait time. Lock span and clock imbalance indicate to what degree this increase occurs. These application characteristics can be used as heuristics to predict whether or not an application will incur significant slowdown under a given schedule.

5.3 The Cost of Determinism in the Field

Table 4 shows the deterministic slowdown for each of the perturber settings described in Section 3.4 with the dynamic-A schedule. Additionally, we have grayed the cells for which there is more than 10% change in the slowdown *compared to the slowdown* from Table 3.

The data shows that the cost of determinism stays the same for most of the benchmarks and across most of the execution environments we test. However, the performance cost does increase for certain benchmarks when threads face significantly skewed conditions (unbalanced system load and asymmetric architectures). In the worst case, deterministic execution causes a slowdown of almost 2x. This suggests that guaranteeing a fixed synchronization order across significantly different execution environments is probably too slow for production use. Looking at the application characteristics, we found that the increase typically happens for programs that implement dynamic load balancing, where the nondeterministic execution is able to adjust the per-thread work to the changing execution conditions, while the deterministic execution is not.

	Benchmark	Small Perturb.		Bkgd. Proc.		DVFS		NUMA	Asym. Arch.	
		bal.	ubal.	bal.	ubal.	auto	manual		8/8	1/15
splash	barnes	0.95	0.96	0.96	0.97	0.92	0.96	0.91	0.94	0.92
	cholesky	1.05	1.05	1.06	1.25	1.06	1.02	1.08	1.03	1.06
	fft	1.01	1.02	1.07	1.02	1.01	1.01	1.01	1.00	1.01
	fmm	1.13	1.13	1.19	1.24	1.13	1.13	1.14	1.15	1.13
	lu_cb	1.00	1.00	0.99	1.03	1.00	1.00	1.00	1.00	1.00
	lu_ncb	1.01	1.01	1.01	1.03	0.97	1.01	1.03	0.99	1.01
	ocean_cp	1.00	1.00	1.00	1.01	1.00	1.00	1.00	1.00	1.00
	ocean_ncp	1.00	1.00	1.00	1.00	1.00	1.00	1.00	1.00	1.01
	radiosity	1.07	1.08	1.19	1.94	1.13	1.07	1.11	1.46	1.16
	radix	1.00	1.00	1.00	1.00	1.00	1.00	1.00	1.00	1.00
	raytrace	1.03	1.03	1.14	1.92	1.08	1.02	1.03	1.44	1.14
	volrend	1.03	1.03	1.08	1.19	1.06	1.02	1.03	1.38	1.09
	water_nsquared	1.00	1.00	1.00	1.00	1.00	1.00	1.00	1.02	1.00
	water_spatial	1.00	1.01	1.00	1.08	1.00	1.00	1.00	1.00	1.00
parsec	blackscholes	1.00	1.00	1.01	1.00	1.00	1.00	1.00	1.00	1.00
	bodytrack	1.04	1.06	1.05	1.51	1.04	1.05	1.03	1.33	1.07
	dedup	1.33	1.33	1.35	1.31	1.29	1.33	1.32	1.64	1.54
	facesim	1.00	1.01	1.00	1.00	0.99	1.00	1.00	1.00	1.00
	ferret	1.24	1.25	1.19	1.29	1.21	1.25	1.15	1.37	1.58
	fluidanimate	0.97	0.97	0.97	0.98	0.97	0.97	0.97	0.98	0.97
	raytrace	1.00	1.01	1.07	1.77	1.05	1.01	1.02	1.39	1.09
	streamcluster	1.00	1.00	1.01	1.00	1.00	1.00	1.00	1.00	1.00
	swaptions	1.00	1.00	1.00	1.00	1.00	1.00	1.00	1.00	1.00
	vips	1.06	1.07	1.09	1.09	1.15	1.06	1.06	1.43	1.33
	average slowdown	**1.04**	**1.04**	**1.06**	**1.19**	**1.04**	**1.04**	**1.04**	**1.15**	**1.09**
	maximum slowdown	**1.33**	**1.33**	**1.35**	**1.94**	**1.29**	**1.33**	**1.32**	**1.64**	**1.58**

Table 4: The slowdowns under various execution settings.

5.4 Comparison with a Deterministic System

To investigate the extent to which the implementation overheads increase the cost of determinism, we compare our results with the performance under Parrot [13]. Parrot is a weakly deterministic system that employs the round-robin schedule. We compare the execution times obtained when running the benchmarks with Parrot to the results obtained for the round-robin schedule using our framework. We run Parrot with its default settings. We do not apply code annotations to improve Parrot's performance (as done in [13]), since these lead to a different schedule, and more importantly, introduce nondeterminism.

Figure 6 shows the execution time under Parrot, normalized w.r.t. the execution time of the round-robin schedule obtained by our framework (we could not get `vips` to run with Parrot). The implementation overhead significantly exacerbates the cost of determinism, especially for `fluidanimate`. This benchmark executes many critical sections; however, these are protected with many different locks in order to avoid contention. While Parrot generates the same round-robin schedule as our scheduler, it enforces it by allowing only one thread at a time to enter a critical section (as all other deterministic systems do, with an exception of Grace [7] that uses speculation). This unnecessarily imposes a total order of synchronization operations and leads to poor performance.

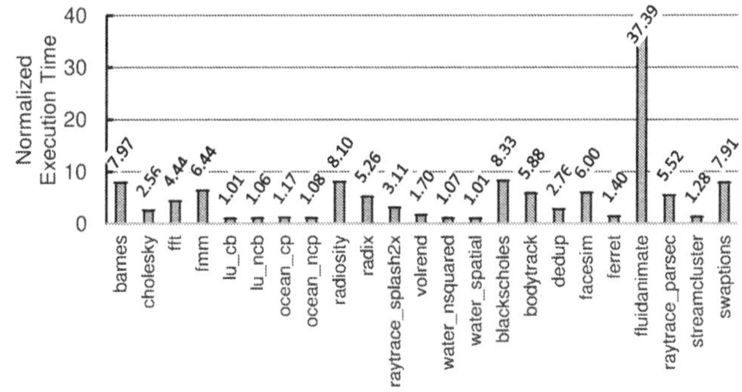

Figure 6: Comparison with Parrot.

6. RELATED WORK

Quantifying Sources of Nondeterminism. Various sources of nondeterminism have been previously identified (unordered thread communication [19, 31], address space layout [30, 38], system dependences [35, 34]). However, our study is the first to measure the extent to which they make executions internally or externally nondeterministic and to identify nondeterminism due to lazy binding, initialization of C++ static variables and compiler auto-vectorization in the presence of ASLR. Devietti et al. [14] measure how frequently, across multiple runs, a particular dynamic instance of a load reads data created from a different dynamic instance of a store. This quantifies variability in thread communication (which may or may not induce program nondeterminism) and not the *extent* to which unordered thread communication introduces nondeterminism. Alameldeen and Wood [1] and Mytkowicz et al. [30] quantify the variability in the execution time of multi-threaded workloads, while our study focuses on the variability in the execution trace and program output.

The Cost of Determinism. Liu et al. [25] and Olszewski et al. [33] measure execution times under the round-robin and dynamic schedules, respectively, when the additional features (e.g., memory protection) or overheads (e.g., interrupts used to maintain logical clocks) of their deterministic systems are disabled or isolated. Their analysis blends the cost of both enforcing *and* generating the schedules (e.g., includes the overhead of passing and waiting for the turn). In contrast, we use a record-replay approach to measure the cost of enforcing only the necessary scheduling constraints.

Nguyen et al. [32] recently reported significant deterministic slowdowns of a few PARSEC and PBBS [10] benchmarks under CoreDet [4]. Hypothesizing that other deterministic systems would perform similarly, they argued that there is a substantial cost to determinism for applications that perform orders of magnitude more synchronization than the PARSEC benchmarks. We evaluate the fundamental cost of determinism on a large set of benchmarks, including ones having several orders of magnitude more synchronization than the PARSEC benchmarks studied in [32] (e.g., `fluidanimate` and `radiosity`). Our results show that, under the right schedule and when implementation overhead is set aside, there is little fundamental cost to determinism.

Determinism in the Field. Alameldeen and Wood [1] demonstrate that by analyzing a certain technique in a narrow environment, one can reach wrong conclusions, especially for multi-threaded workloads. Hower et al. [22] design an architecture for deterministic execution and show how to guarantee determinism across its different implementations. While they do evaluate the overhead of the additional support for determinism-across-implementations on a *single* implementation, they do not evaluate the performance impact of requiring the same deterministic execution across *different* implementations, which is what we study. The use of DVFS in order to simulate asymmetry on otherwise symmetric machine was previously done by Shelepov et al. [37].

Record-Replay. Record-replay systems (see [35] for a good summary) are generally designed for debugging and are typically concerned with low overhead recording. We employ a record-replay technique in order to decouple the overhead of generating a schedule from the fundamental performance impact of enforcing it, and we focus on a low overhead replay.

7. CONCLUSION

In this paper, we use a schedule-record-replay system to divorce implementation overhead from the fundamental cost of enforcing a fixed synchronization order in data-race-free parallel programs. We find that this fundamental cost is significantly lower than previously thought; for the dynamic schedule, it is no more than 32% slowdown in parallel execution and 4% on average. However, in the presence of skewed execution conditions, this cost can slow down execution by a factor of almost 2x. We propose and assess two new program characteristics, lock span and clock imbalance, that indicate how suited a given schedule is for a given program. Finally, we show that deterministic guarantees of systems that rely on the determinism of logical clocks can be compromised because of other sources of nondeterminism that make these clocks nondeterministic.

Our study focuses on data race free programs, i.e., on weak determinism. However, we believe that our results are of interest to both weakly and strongly deterministic systems. While handling data races increases the complexity and performance penalty of strongly deterministic systems, researchers have been successful in reducing the overhead of deterministically resolving data races to the point where the only program serialization is caused by synchronization operations. Evaluating the tightness of the lower bound empirically determined here for data-race-free programs in the context of strong determinism is an interesting direction for future work.

The findings of this study open several opportunities for work on determinism. First, they suggest that there remains room for lowering implementation overheads in existing proposals for deterministic systems. Second, they suggest that insisting on a fixed schedule for programs in production is probably too costly. Thus, it may be necessary to relax the definition of determinism, e.g., by allowing an execution to follow any of the multiple permitted schedules for a single program input. Finally, our findings give insights into program characteristics that impact the cost of enforcing determinism, which may guide the design of future deterministic systems.

8. ACKNOWLEDGMENTS

We thank the anonymous reviewers for their many helpful comments. We also thank the members of our research group for their feedback on the manuscript.

9. REFERENCES

[1] A. Alameldeen and D. Wood. Variability in Architectural Simulations of Multi-Threaded Workloads. In *Proc. of HPCA*, pages 7–18, 2003.

[2] A. Aviram, S.-C. Weng, S. Hu, and B. Ford. Efficient System-Enforced Deterministic Parallelism. In *Proc. of OSDI*, pages 1–16, 2010.

[3] A. Bastoni, B. Brandenburg, and J. Anderson. Cache-Related Preemption and Migration Delays: Empirical Approx. and Impact on Schedulability. In *Proc. of OSPERT*, pages 33–44, 2010.

[4] T. Bergan, O. Anderson, J. Devietti, L. Ceze, and D. Grossman. CoreDet: A Compiler and Runtime System for Deterministic Multithreaded Execution. In *Proc. of ASPLOS*, pages 53–64, 2010.

[5] T. Bergan, J. Devietti, N. Hunt, and L. Ceze. The Deterministic Execution Hammer: How Well Does it Actually Pound Nails? In *Proc. of WODET*, 2011.

[6] T. Bergan, N. Hunt, L. Ceze, and S. D. Gribble. Deterministic Process Groups in dOS. In *Proc. of OSDI*, pages 1–16, 2010.

[7] E. D. Berger, T. Yang, T. Liu, and G. Novark. Grace: Safe Multithreaded Programming for C/C++. In *Proc. of OOPSLA*, pages 81–96, 2009.

[8] C. Bienia. *Benchmarking Modern Multiprocessors.* PhD thesis, Princeton University, 2011.

[9] A. J. C. Bik, M. Girkar, P. M. Grey, and X. Tian. Automatic Intra-register Vectorization for the Intel Architecture. *Int. J. Parallel Program.*, 30(2):65–98, 2002.

[10] G. E. Blelloch, J. T. Fineman, P. B. Gibbons, and J. Shun. Internally Deterministic Parallel Algorithms Can Be Fast. In *Proc. of PPOPP*, pages 181–192, 2012.

[11] H.-J. Boehm. Position Paper: Nondeterminism is Unavoidable, but Data Races are Pure Evil. In *Proc. of RACES*, pages 9–14, 2012.

[12] D. Bovet and M. Cesati. *Understanding The Linux Kernel.* 2005.

[13] H. Cui, J. Simsa, Y.-H. Lin, H. Li, B. Blum, X. Xu, J. Yang, G. A. Gibson, and R. E. Bryant. Parrot: A Practical Runtime for Deterministic, Stable, and Reliable Threads. In *Proc. of SOSP*, pages 388–405, 2013.

[14] J. Devietti, B. Lucia, L. Ceze, and M. Oskin. DMP: Deterministic Shared Memory Multiprocessing. In *Proc. of ASPLOS*, pages 85–96, 2009.

[15] J. Devietti, B. Lucia, L. Ceze, and M. Oskin. DMP: Deterministic Shared-Memory Multiprocessing. *IEEE Micro*, 30(1):40–49, 2010.

[16] J. Devietti, J. Nelson, T. Bergan, L. Ceze, and D. Grossman. RCDC: A Relaxed Consistency Deterministic Computer. In *Proc. of ASPLOS*, pages 67–78, 2011.

[17] U. Drepper. How to Write Shared Libraries. `http://www.akkadia.org/drepper/dsohowto.pdf`, 2011.

[18] B. Efron and R. Tibshirani. *An Introduction to the Bootstrap.* 1993.

[19] P. Emrath and D. Padua. Automatic Detection of Nondeterminacy in Parallel Programs. In *Proc. of PADD*, pages 89–99, 1988.

[20] J. Hennessy and D. Patterson. *Computer Architecture, Fifth Edition: A Quantitative Approach.* 2011.

[21] M. Hill and M. Xu. Racey: A Stress Test for Deterministic Execution. `http://www.cs.wisc.edu/~markhill/racey.html`.

[22] D. Hower, P. Dudnik, M. Hill, and D. Wood. Calvin: Deterministic or Not? Free Will to Choose. In *Proc. of HPCA*, pages 333 –334, 2011.

[23] W. Kim, M. S. Gupta, G.-Y. Wei, and D. Brooks. System Level Analysis of Fast, Per-Core DVFS Using On-Chip Switching Regulators. In *Proc. of HPCA*, pages 123–134, 2008.

[24] L. Lamport. Time, Clocks, and the Ordering of Events in a Distributed System. *Comm. ACM*, 21(7):558–565, 1978.

[25] T. Liu, C. Curtsinger, and E. D. Berger. DTHREADS: Efficient Deterministic Multithreading. In *Proc. of SOSP*, pages 327–336. ACM, 2011.

[26] K. Lu, X. Zhou, T. Bergan, and X. Wang. Efficient Deterministic Multithreading Without Global Barriers. In *Proc. of PPOPP*, pages 287–300, 2014.

[27] L. Lu and M. Scott. Toward a Formal Semantic Framework for Deterministic Parallel Programming. In *Proc. of DISC*, pages 460–474, 2011.

[28] J. Mellor-Crummey and M. Scott. Algorithms for Scalable Synchronization on Shared-Memory Multiprocessors. *ACM Trans. Comput. Syst.*, 9(1):21–65, Feb. 1991.

[29] T. Merrifield and J. Eriksson. Conversion: Multi-version Concurrency Control for Main Memory Segments. In *Proc. of EuroSys*, pages 127–139, 2013.

[30] T. Mytkowicz, A. Diwan, M. Hauswirth, and P. F. Sweeney. Producing Wrong Data Without Doing Anything Obviously Wrong! In *Proc. of ASPLOS*, pages 265–276, 2009.

[31] R. Netzer and B. Miller. What are Race Conditions? *ACM Lett. Program. Lang. Syst.*, 1(1):74–88, Mar. 1992.

[32] D. Nguyen, A. Lenharth, and K. Pingali. Deterministic Galois: On-demand, Portable and Parameterless. In *Proc. of ASPLOS*, pages 499–512, 2014.

[33] M. Olszewski, J. Ansel, and S. Amarasinghe. Kendo: Efficient Deterministic Multithreading in Software. In *Proc. of ASPLOS*, pages 97–108, 2009.

[34] H. Patil, C. Pereira, M. Stallcup, G. Lueck, and J. Cownie. PinPlay: A Framework for Deterministic Replay and Reproducible Analysis of Parallel Programs. In *Proc. of CGO*, pages 2–11, 2010.

[35] G. Pokam, C. Pereira, K. Danne, L. Yang, S. King, and J. Torrellas. Hardware and Software Approaches for Deterministic Multi-Processor Replay of Concurrent Programs. *Intel Technology Journal*, 13(4):20–41, 2009.

[36] K. Serebryany and T. Iskhodzhanov. ThreadSanitizer: Data Race Detection in Practice. In *Proc. of WBIA*, pages 62–71, 2009.

[37] D. Shelepov, J. C. Saez Alcaide, S. Jeffery, A. Fedorova, N. Perez, Z. F. Huang, S. Blagodurov, and V. Kumar. HASS: A Scheduler for Heterogeneous Multicore Systems. *SIGOPS Oper. Syst. Rev.*, 43(2):66–75, 2009.

[38] V. Weaver and S. McKee. Can Hardware Performance Counters be Trusted? In *Proc. of IISWC*, pages 141–150, 2008.

[39] V. Weaver, D. Terpstra, and S. Moore. Non-Determinism and Overcount on Modern Hardware Performance Counter Implementations. *Proc. of ISPASS*, pages 215–224, 2013.

[40] S. Woo, M. Ohara, E. Torrie, J. Singh, and A. Gupta. The SPLASH-2 Programs: Characterization and Methodological Considerations. In *Proc. of ISCA*, pages 24–36, 1995.

ILP and TLP in Shared Memory Applications: A Limit Study

Ehsan Fatehi and Paul V. Gratz
Electrical and Computer Engineering
Texas A&M University
email: {efatehi|pgratz}@tamu.edu

ABSTRACT

With the breakdown of Dennard scaling, future processor designs will be at the mercy of power limits as Chip Multi-Processor (CMP) designs scale out to many-cores. It is critical, therefore, that future CMPs be optimally designed in terms of performance efficiency with respect to power. A characterization analysis of future workloads is imperative to ensure maximum returns of performance per Watt consumed. Hence, a detailed analysis of emerging workloads is necessary to understand their characteristics with respect to hardware in terms of power and performance tradeoffs. In this paper, we conduct a limit study simultaneously analyzing the two dominant forms of parallelism exploited by modern computer architectures: Instruction Level Parallelism (ILP) and Thread Level Parallelism (TLP). This study gives insights into the upper bounds of performance that future architectures can achieve. Furthermore it identifies the bottlenecks of emerging workloads. To the best of our knowledge, our work is the first study that combines the two forms of parallelism into one study with modern applications. We evaluate the PARSEC multithreaded benchmark suite using a specialized trace-driven simulator. We make several contributions describing the high-level behavior of next-generation applications. For example, we show these applications contain up to a factor of 929X more ILP than what is currently being extracted from real machines. We then show the effects of breaking the application into increasing numbers of threads (exploiting TLP), instruction window size, realistic branch prediction, realistic memory latency, and thread dependencies on exploitable ILP. Our examination shows that theses benchmarks differed vastly from one another. As a result, we expect no single, homogeneous, micro-architecture will work optimally for all, arguing for reconfigurable, heterogeneous designs.

Categories and Subject Descriptors

C.2 [**Processor Architectures**]: Multiple Data Stream Architectures (Multiprocessors); F.1.2 [**Computation By Abstract Devices**]: Modes of Computation—*Parallelism and concurrency*

Keywords

Instruction-Level Parallelism (ILP); Thread-Level Parallelism (TLP); PThreads; Limits

PACT'14, August 24–27, 2014, Edmonton, AB, Canada.

ACM 978-1-4503-2809-8/14/08 ...$15.00.
http://dx.doi.org/10.1145/2628071.2628093 .

1. INTRODUCTION

Moore's law [19], which states that the amount of transistors on integrated circuits doubles in a given period, has been the underlying driver of computer advancement for nearly half a century. For many decades, there has been an increase in performance and decrease in power consumption per-transistor as device technology scaled. This phenomenon is known as Dennard scaling [7]. In the last decade, however, the power and performance increase dictated by Moore's Law with Dennard scaling have had diminishing returns. As a result, relying on Moore's law to gain performance has become more difficult due to power constraints. Recently, this trend drove computer architects to chip-multi-processor (CMP) designs with ever increasing core counts to better leverage these extra transistors. As core counts continue to increase, however, power and performance are unable to proportionally match the previous pace of improvement [9]. Future designs must compensate for inefficient transistor scaling with respect to energy and performance. A characterization analysis of future workloads is imperative in order to ensure that future designs achieve maximum returns in performance with respect to power consumption.

The current industry approach to CMP architecture design is to replicate a single core multiple times. These homogeneous CMPs are expected to sufficiently run current and near-future applications. This is an ineffective approach to multi-core design, however, as it is only motivated by reducing costs and design effort. Bhadauria et al.showed that current processors are not sufficient for emerging multi-threaded applications [3]. They concluded that current architectures should increase the number of functional units on each core, reduce core size (using in-order execution rather than Out-of-Order execution), and increase core count in order to improve performance and reduce power.

Typical processor architectures exploit two forms of parallelism in order to achieve scaling performance with increasing transistor density: Instruction Level Parallelism (ILP) and Thread Level Parallelism (TLP). ILP is exploited by architectures that fetch and execute multiple instructions per cycle from a single instruction stream or thread. Maximizing ILP often requires highly complex microarchitectural techniques such as out-of-order (OoO) execution with large instruction windows. These OoO engines consist of hardware managed pools of instructions searched to find ready-to-execute instructions. As a result, ILP exploitation often comes at a high cost in terms of power. Alternately, TLP is exploited by splitting a problem up into multiple threads that can be run simultaneously on more than one processor. Utilizing TLP in typical applications requires that the programmer specify how the problem is partitioned among those threads and defines the exact communication needed between the threads. Scaling performance with processor count requires that TLP applications have a highly balanced load, otherwise overheads will quickly lead to diminishing returns with increasing processor count.

While the processor designs of the 1990's and early 2000's predominantly relied upon ILP exploitation to scale performance, the breakdown of Dennard scaling has driven computer architects towards CMP designs. CMPs integrate many cores onto one die, exploiting TLP to improve performance. TLP exploitation does not preclude ILP exploitation, so having multiple cores on a single die opens up many different design combinations. It is unlikely that a single universal CMP design would be optimal for all applications. A key design challenge lies in determining how to partition chip resources in CMPs between ILP and TLP exploitation. At a high level, chip resources can be spent two ways: increasing the size of each core (for greater ILP exploitation), or by creating additional cores (for greater TLP exploitation). Understanding when to add cores or change core size is pivotal in optimal multi-core design. The first step is to understand the trade-offs in ILP and TLP in modern applications. To the best of our knowledge there has been no such thorough study in recent years that analyzes such trade-offs in ILP and TLP in modern applications. This gap in knowledge is, in part due to the multi-core era being in its infancy compared to other advancements in computer architecture. While there have been many ILP studies done in the past [21, 27, 16, 11, 20, 2, 6], none of them attempt to understand the relationship between ILP and TLP. Further, none have attempted to answer the question, does TLP exploitation reduce ILP and to what degree.

The main focus of this work is the analysis of next-generation workloads along the axes of ILP and TLP exploitation. The intent is to aid in making more informed CMP architectural design decisions. Generally, increasing core size (by increasing cache size, instruction window size, the number of functional units, etc.) results in an increase in ILP extraction; while increasing core count results in an increase in TLP extraction. However, for applications with imbalanced loads, a heterogeneous CMP design composed of a few high ILP cores, and many of low ILP cores (for TLP extraction) might achieve higher overall efficiency. An example of this architecture is shown in Figure 1. Our limit study is aimed at narrowing the design choices available by giving guidelines on how future micro-architectures should be designed. We begin by conducting a ground-up workload characterization analysis.

In this paper, we perform an ILP and TLP limit study on emerging multi-threaded workloads. We designed a trace-driven simulator that constructs an instruction-level Data Flow Graph (DFG) from each thread in multi-threaded applications that includes inter-thread dependencies. Using this simulator we evaluate ILP and TLP using the PARSEC shared memory multiprocessor benchmark suite [4]. These experiments determine how TLP extraction affects the ILP availability, how ILP is affected by window size, and the affects of ILP on thread dependencies. We also study the critical path (CP) of each benchmark with the goal of studying both the thread-level load balance and the instruction-level parallelism of the CP segments, thus indicating how wide a core must be to achieve a given calculated performance.

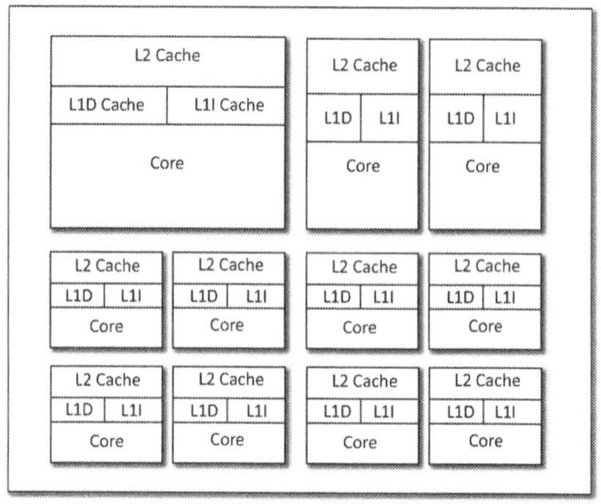

Figure 1: Example of a multi-core hetergeneous architecture.

Our experiments explore the demands of these applications with respect to hardware architectures, such as exploring the effects of realistic branch prediction and memory latency. Analysis of these multi-threaded applications provide insight on trade-offs in multi-core designs. This work answers the following seven questions:

1. *What is the upper bound on ILP?* We provide quantitative data on how much ILP headroom is available in modern applications in relation to how much is currently extracted. We find that current architectures are far removed from the ILP limits found using our methodology. For example, current machine ILP can differ by as much as 929x versus a processor with infinite resources.

2. *What is the threading inefficiency of each benchmark?* We quantitatively explore workload imbalance in these applications. Understanding the load imbalance will help identify bottlenecks in the microarchitectural design. With increasing TLP the load imbalance increases, but we find the rate of the inefficiency depends greatly on the complexity of the particular benchmark.

3. *What is the impact on ILP as we scale cores?* We quantify the actual trade-off in TLP and ILP for these applications. This will help determine whether it is better to increase core size or to add more cores. We find, generally, increasing TLP extraction does indeed affect ILP. The relation between the two is however, highly dependent on the benchmark.

4. *What is the impact on ILP when imposing instruction window size restrictions?* We examine how ILP increases with window size for these applications. We find that there is large amount of ILP that is not being exploited within a 128 to 512 instruction distance. Often more than 10x the amount found in real machines. The majority of ILP, however, is much further than 5000 instructions away making it unlikely a traditional instruction window will be able to capture the majority of ILP available.

5. *What is the effect of thread dependencies on ILP?* We attempt to quantify the impact that high level thread dependencies have on performance reduction. We find that all but one benchmark's performance was significantly impacted by thread dependencies. As core count increases, the performance reduction caused by thread dependencies increases. Although, the performance reduction occurs at different rates dependent on the application.

6. *What is the impact on ILP when imposing realistic memory system latency and branch prediction accuracy restrictions?* We examine how ILP is affected when imposing realistic memory latency and branch prediction for these applications. We find that there is on average a 31% reduction in ILP when adding realistic memory latency model depending on the benchmark, and on average 67% reduction when adding realistic branch prediction. Overall, branch prediction is the stronger bottleneck than memory latency under these constraints. These results provide motivation to put more effort into improving branch prediction, despite the field being very mature.

7. *What are the critical path's thread composition characteristics?* We attempt to provide an understanding the critical path characteristics with the perspective of gaining performance and reducing power. We find the composition of the critical path to be interesting and potentially exploitable.

With respect to the experiments listed above we found that no benchmark reacted in a similar manner for all seven questions. This suggests that an optimal multi-core design (with respect to power and performance) is highly dependent on the application running on it, arguing for a dynamic and heterogeneous design. Although there have been many limit studies in the past, we revisit the topic using next-generation parallel applications adding many more experiments to give a more in-depth understanding of parallel applications. The rest of this paper is organized as follows: Section 2, discusses our motivation for conducting a limit study. Section 3 presents methodology in how we measured ILP, and TLP limits. Section 4 presents our results. Section 5 shows related work and finally we conclude in Section 6.

2. MOTIVATION

There have been many ILP limit studies to date[21, 27, 16, 11, 20, 2, 6]. These studies, however, often contradict each other, by making inconsistent assumptions with respect to ideal hardware capabilities, compiler capabilities and lacking consistency in the types of benchmarks used. In addition, these studies are almost exclusively more than 20 years old. Since then, the applications used in general purpose computing have evolved significantly to now work on much larger data sets with new and more complex algorithms. As such the applications in the prior studies are now largely outdated. Furthermore, we are aware of no study that has focused on the interaction between ILP and TLP. The purpose of our study is to understand the degree in which TLP extraction affects ILP availability. Understanding these tradeoffs is important because exploiting TLP and ILP require different approaches to processor design. Exploiting TLP requires multiple-cores, while exploiting ILP requires larger cores. As it becomes more difficult to exploit the additional transistors gained by Moore's law, it is imperative to put these transistors to the best possible use with respect to performance and power efficiency. Analyzing the upper bound limits allows insight to the remaining parallelism. Understanding the trade-offs between ILP and TLP will help give insight on the optimal core counts and core makeup for a specific application with respect to power and performance.

3. EXPERIMENTAL DESCRIPTION

This section first discusses how our ILP and TLP limit study is conducted. We then go over the benefits of a trace-driven approach to study the limits of ILP in multi-threaded applications. Finally we cover our methodology for calculating the upper bound limits of benchmarks.

3.1 Limit Study

To measure the upper bound ILP limits found in shared-memory multi-threaded applications, we begin by assuming an ideal processor core model. This ideal model consists of infinite physical registers, perfect branch prediction, perfect memory-address aliasing (addresses are known, thus unrelated loads can move in front of stores). This model also includes unlimited hardware resources (unlimited instruction window, functional units, and single cycle memory latency). Furthermore, to explore the limits of TLP we remove all inter-thread synchronization constructs from the code (e.g. Locks, Barriers, etc.), while preserving true inter-thread data dependencies to ensure correctness. ILP and performance limits were then modeled via analysis of the application's true data dependencies (either through the register file or memory). From this starting point we then begin adding constraints, such as restricting window size and enforcing synchronization constructs. We then examine how the application's performance and ILP are affected by these constraints versus an ideal machine. Constraints are changed one by one or in combination of a few. This helps identify bottlenecks in the benchmarks under test. What sets our study apart from other studies is our ability to directly observe the tradeoffs in ILP and TLP in this class of parallel applications. As we increase/decrease the amount of TLP (by increasing/decreasing the number of threads) we are able to observe how this impacts ILP.

3.2 Trace-Driven Approach

Previous TLP studies were analytically performed with simple assumptions of application scaling [9, 12]. Analyzing benchmark traces that are generated from an execution-driven simulator (which simulates real machine behavior) can provide much more accurate bounds on performance. Our trace-driven approach allows us to capture the actual dynamic instruction stream of multi-threaded benchmarks. These dynamic instruction streams have perfect branch prediction, memory-addresses are disambiguated, along with perfect memory (zero latency). A trace driven approach provides accuracy that an analytical approach cannot replicate. An analytical approach usually involves simplification to model real behavior. We chose to use execution traces rather than static code analysis since static code lacks memory disambiguation and control flow information.

Prior to feeding these traces into our trace-driven simulator, the traces are pre-processed once to work out all dependencies among instructions both intra-thread (through the register file and memory) and inter-thread (through memory). These traces are then fed into our trace-driven simulator, which then constructs a dynamic Data Flow Graph (DFG) for each thread, stitching together those threads with

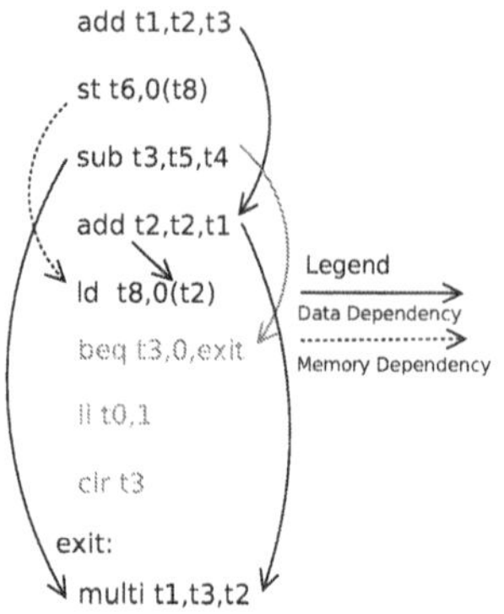

(a) Assembly fragment with dependencies highlighted. Wrong-path and control flow instructions grayed.

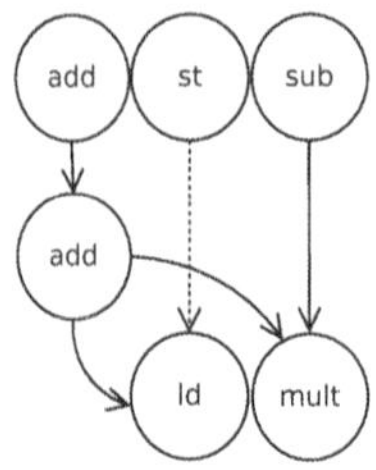

(b) Data-flow graph (DFG) for code in part (a).

Figure 2: Data-flow graph (DFG) for assembly fragment.

the dependencies between threads through memory. Figure 2 illustrates the process for a single thread. Figure 2a shows a simple assembly pseudo-code fragment with register data dependencies highlighted with solid lines, and memory data dependencies shown with dashed lines. In this example, the effective address of the store (*st*) and load (*ld*) alias to the same memory location forming a true data dependence through memory. Note that the branch instruction as well as the instructions on the branch not taken path are grayed out in the figure to represent the wrong path instructions. In our limit study we assume perfect branch prediction, therefore these instructions are not used in the DFG construction.

Figure 2b shows the corresponding DFG, that would typically be created with our simulator. The nodes represent instructions, and the edges represent producer-consumer data dependencies among the instructions. For the purpose of this limit study, all instructions are assumed to take one cycle. The maximum height of the DFG represents the number of cycles that this code fragment would take to execute in an ideal machine. In the example, the height of the DFG is three, thus with infinite resources and one cycle per instruction the code would take three cycles to execute.

3.2.1 Calculating Single-Threaded Average ILP

Using the DFG it becomes easy to extract ILP of the program. Here we define ILP_{ST_AVG} of a given single thread (ST) to be the average (AVG) number of instructions that can be executed in each cycle under the given machine constraints. Equation(1), is used to calculate ILP_{ST_AVG}.

$$ILP_{ST\_AVG} = \frac{I_{all}}{H} \tag{1}$$

In this equation, I_{all} is the total number of instructions in the DFG, and H is the height of the DFG, representing cycle count of the ideal machine. For the DFG shown in Figure 2b, the ILP_{ST_AVG} is $\frac{6}{3} = 2$.

3.2.2 Calculating Multi-Threaded Average ILP

Extending this model to multiple threads in shared memory applications requires additional modeling of the dependencies between threads. Dependencies between threads are examined in two ways. First, to ensure correctness, the DFG generator models the true dependencies through memory caused by stores in one thread feeding to loads of the same address in another thread. Second, we also can model the dependencies in between threads caused by synchronization constructs inserted by the programmer in the code (e.g. locks, barriers, etc.). Figure 3a illustrates this process by showing a simplified parallel code fragment containing thread synchronization via a barrier. For this example, we assume two threads execute the "*worker_thread*" function simultaneously, each performing writes to parts of the shared array $x[]$. Later these threads read the array $x[]$, after being synchronized by the *pthreads_barrier_wait*() to ensure correctness. Figure 3b shows the DFG for these two threads with the thread synchronizing barrier in place. In this example, the height Thread 1's DFG (H_1) is six because it inherits Thread 2's height at the barrier (since it has the greater H of the two at this synchronization point). Here, H_2 is five. As per Equation(1), the ILP_{ST_AVG} of Thread 1 is 1.33 (The total number of instructions in Thread 1, I_1 is 8) and for Thread 2 is 2 (I_2=10). These results are averaged across threads to calculate the average ILP of multi-threaded (MT) application DFGs following Equation (2).

$$ILP_{MT\_AVG} = \frac{\sum_1^N (I_{alln}/H_n)}{N} \tag{2}$$

Here H_n, is the height of thread n's DFG, for threads 1 to N where N is the total number of threads in the benchmark. I_n is the total number of instructions in a given thread. For the DFG shown in Figure 3b, the ILP_{MT_AVG} is $\frac{1.33+2}{2}$ = 1.665.

3.2.3 Calculating Multi-Threaded Critical Path ILP

ILP_{MT_AVG} calculates the program's ILP under the assumption that the application scales ideally with thread count. Unfortunately applications do not typically scale perfectly, hence we introduce a new ILP metric in this section which gives attempts to provide a more useful estimation of the effective ILP for multi-threaded applications. Figure 3 illustrates the issue. In Figure 3b, although H_1 (the H of Thread 1) sets the lower-bound limit on execution time for this example, we note that Thread 1 alone does not determine the overall height (H_{max}) of this multi-threaded program. Here, speeding up execution in Thread 1 would not lead to a significant performance increase. Because, although Thread 1 has a higher H after the barrier, it inherits the H of four from Thread 2 at the barrier. Thus both Thread 1 and Thread 2 have an impact on the overall H_{max} of the program. Instructions from Thread 2 prior to the barrier and instructions from Thread 1 after the barrier form the *critical path* (CP) of the application. We define the program's CP (indicated by the darkened circles in Figure 3a) as the dependency chain of *thread segments* through the program that determines the H_{max}, *ie.* the execution time of the program in the limit. Much insight can be extracted from per-thread ILP as well as the critical path ILP. In this example, the number of instructions on the CP is 11, and the CP takes six cycles to execute, therefore we define the ILP_{MT_CP}=1.83 instructions/cycle for this code. To calculate ILP_{MT_CP}, equation(3) is used.

$$ILP_{MT\_CP} = \frac{\sum_1^k I_{kn}}{H_{max}} \tag{3}$$

In this equation, I_{kn} is the segment of instructions that are under the height (H_{max}) defining segments of each thread in the DFG.

Further insight can be gained on the limits of ILP and TLP scaling when thread synchronization semantics are removed. This approach allows an exploration of limits of

```
void worker_thread{
.....
...
while(loop)
.....
....
x[j] = y[j]*n;
pthread_barrier_wait (&barrier);
z[j]=x[i];
}
```

(a) Multi-Threaded pseudo-code fragment.

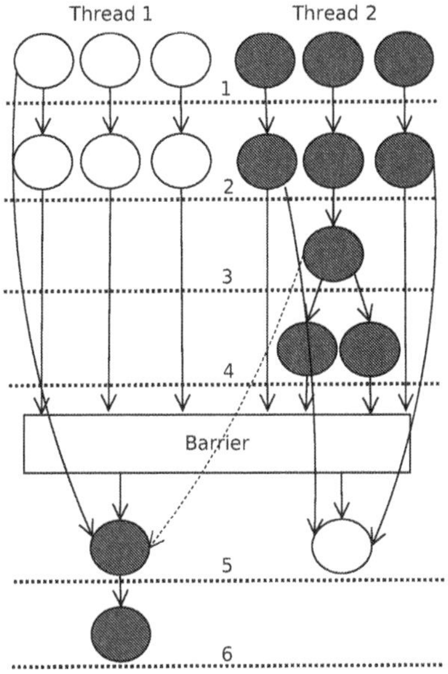

(b) DFG for code in part (a) assuming two concurrent threads. Both in-memory dependencies and thread synchronization constructs honored.

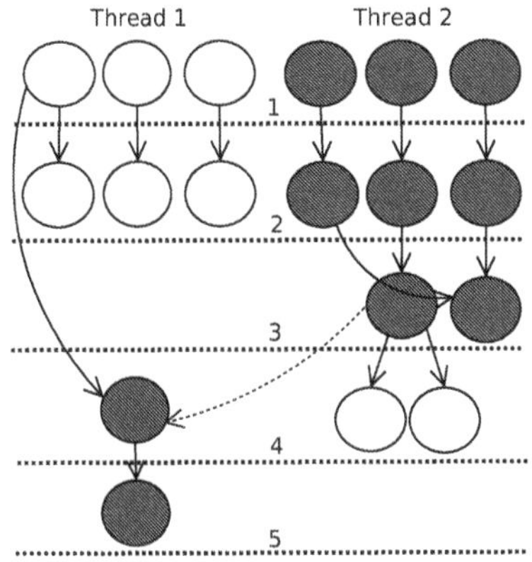

(c) DFG for code in part (a) with thread synchronization constructs removed.

Figure 3: Multi-Threaded code fragment and associated DFG, with and without thread synchronization constructs honored. Darkened nodes represent instructions along the critical path.

cross-synchronization boundary speculation. Figure 3c shows the DFG for the code fragment when all thread synchronization semantics are removed. In this case, correctness is ensured by continuing to enforce direct producer/consumer relationships between threads through memory. As the figure shows the overall H_{max} is reduced to five because two, now non-critical, instructions in Thread 2 are removed from the program's CP. The new CP has I_{CP}=10 and an ILP_{CP}=2 due to the increased efficiency of the resultant code path. We denote this measure of the ILP of the critical path without synchronization semantics as $ILP_{MT\_CP\_NS}$. Note that here we are again measuring the dependency chain of *thread segments*, not solely the dependency chain of instructions themselves. Thus, there are two instructions at $H = 3$ in Thread 2 that are counted as critical, despite the fact that one of them is not directly on the critical path connected to Thread 1.

Defining a CP metric, is a difficult and somewhat fraught question, with several possible derivations. Ultimately, we chose the current CP metric because we felt it provided more insight than the alternative approaches. In particular, the current metric captures the average dynamic ILP width of the CP segment in question, thus indicating how wide a core must be to achieve the performance shown. Alternate approaches would not show the true ILP width of the CP and thus provides less useful information about the desired width of the machine needed to execute it.

3.2.4 Threading Inefficiency

While ILP_{MT_CP} provides information about the width of the machine needed to achieve a given performance on multi-threaded applications, it does not give a full picture of the relative balance between threads. Here we introduce a new term, called *threading inefficiency* (TI). TI is a measure of the relative imbalance between the CP (in terms of instruction count) versus the average thread. TI is calculated according to Equation (4).

$$TI = \frac{I_{CP}}{\frac{I_{all}}{N}} \tag{4}$$

In this formula, I_{CP} is the total number of instructions in the CP and I_{all} is the total number of instructions in all threads.

Analyzing the TI, particularly as thread count increases, provides insight into the overheads of scaling out to many cores. The CP is the longest path in the execution of a program, therefore the maximum speed up of a program is limited by its CP. When TI is greater than 1, the CP is greater than the average thread length, it indicates the workload is uneven. For example, a TI of 10 means the CP is 10 times larger than the average thread length, which we would interpret as the application being highly imbalanced.

4. EVALUATION

In this section we first discuss some details of the methodology of our study and then present our results.

4.1 Methodology

To conduct the work presented here, we generated dynamic instruction stream traces using the gem5 Simulator [5] and the PARSEC Benchmark Suite [4] compiled for the Alpha ISA [10]. All the PARSEC benchmarks that our simulation infrastructure supports are presented. To save space in the graphs, the benchmark names are abbreviated to their first two letters. The abbreviations are as follows: **BL** - Blackscholes, **BO** - Bodytrack, **CA** - Canneal, **DE** - Dedup, **FE** - Ferret, **FL** - Fluidanimate, **VI** - Vips, and **X2** - X264.

Once traces were generated, we pre-process them by identifying data, instruction, and thread dependencies, similar

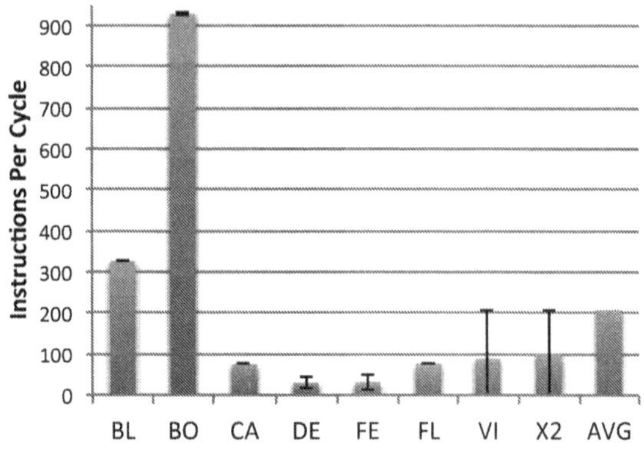

(a) ILP_{MT_AVG} for N=2

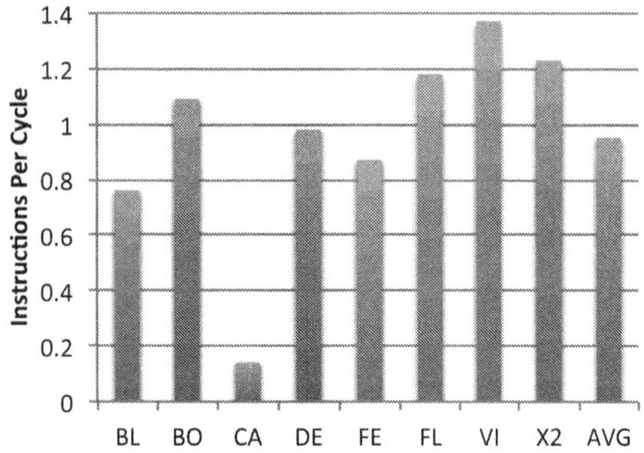

(b) ILP on a real machine (2.3 GHz AMD processors)

Figure 4: ILP Limits

to the example given above Figure 3. An individual trace set was generated for each of the examined numbers of threads (N_{min}). These traces are then fed into our off-line analysis tools which create a dynamic DFG. For this paper our tools dynamically generate different DFGs dependent upon window size and the presence or absence of thread synchronization semantics, as shown in Figure 3.

One issue with a trace-driven approach, were traces are generated once and then analyzed off-line, is lock acquisition order may change under different execution constraints, particularly in benchmarks which utilize fine grained locking. In the set of PARSEC benchmarks which we are able to execute in this infrastructure, this only applies to Canneal. In our prior work we found this effect to cause a relatively minor impact in the measured performance, generally <10%.

Due to time constraints, small input sizes are used for all figures. Only instructions in the Region of Interest (ROI) were examined. In order to ensure that the integrity of this idealized limit study was not effected by input size we selected a few benchmarks to run using small, medium and large input sizes. After studying the results closely we found that the behavioral trends extracted from small input were mirrored in the medium and large inputs as well. We also ran the native input on real machines, and found the trends remained the same.

4.2 ILP and TLP Limit Study Results

Our limit study explores seven important questions as described in Section 1. We answer these questions by evaluating PARSEC benchmarks in our limit study. We believe answering and analyzing the following questions will help provide insight into what future architectures should look like for next-generation workloads.

4.2.1 *What is the Upper Bound on ILP?*

Determining the upper bound on ILP available in multi-threaded benchmarks helps quantify its availability for exploitation. If there is a plethora of ILP being left on the table, then this will be clear motivation to develop better techniques to exploit ILP. To answer this question we simulated our traces with unlimited resources and no thread synchronization semantics however data and register dependencies are still preserved. Although these benchmarks do have single threaded versions, we found that they behaved significantly different from the multi-threaded versions. There are many algorithmic transformations that are tied to the sequential versus the parallel versions of the code. We therefore felt the serial versions were not similar enough to provide useful results. To have a consistent baseline, we start at the minimum number of parallel threads possible for each benchmark, N_{min}=2, meaning there will be at minimum 2 threads spawned for each benchmark. [1] We calculate the upper bound ILP (ILP_{MT_AVG}) using the equation(2).

Figure 4a shows the resulting ILP_{MT_AVG} for each benchmark. Here the whiskers show the standard deviation (SD) of ILP among threads. The ILP_{MT_AVG} varies from 29-929 Instructions/Cycle with an average across the benchmarks of 200. As shown by the whiskers, **FE**, **DE** , **VI** and **X2** show a noticeable variance in the ILP difference among threads, while the other benchmarks show little variance.

The **first observation** we derive from this data is that there is significant variance in ILP between benchmarks. For **DE** and **BO** (lowest and highest respectively), the ILP varied by a factor of 32x. **DE** finds and removes redundancies from data streams with a technique called deduplication. The application has heavy communication among threads. Despite having several parallel stages, each stage is highly dependent on the previous stage thus restricting ILP. **BO** processes images/videos and keeps track of a human body. Its has high ILP because the frame input is fixed and all processing is dependent on that frame. The input does not alter, and therefore, can be parallelized very effectively (the highest of all benchmarks).

For comparison, we ran these benchmarks on real machines, with N_{min}=2, using the native input set. We then measured the ILP_{MT_AVG}; results are shown on Figure 4b. This yielded our **second observation**, not only do some of these benchmarks fare poorly (**CA**) in real machines in terms of ILP, they are orders of magnitudes less than what could theoretically be achieved. There is no doubt, a great deal of ILP is left on the table in these applications. This argues that greater effort should be spent in finding ways to exploit ILP in next-generation hardware. These results are motivation to push for more research in aggressive speculation to maximize ILP gains.

[1]Note that, when configured as N_{min}=2, the PARSEC benchmarks will spawn a variable number of threads greater than or equal to that number. In particular, **BL**, **BO**, **CA**, and **FL** each spawn 2 threads, while **DE**, **FE**, **VI**, and **X2** spawn 12, 10, 4 and 6 threads respectively.

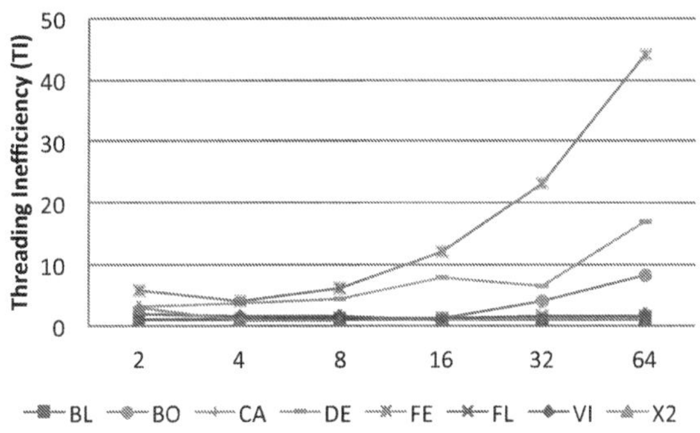

Figure 5: Threading inefficiency (TI) of PARSEC benchmarks for N_{min} = 2 through 64.

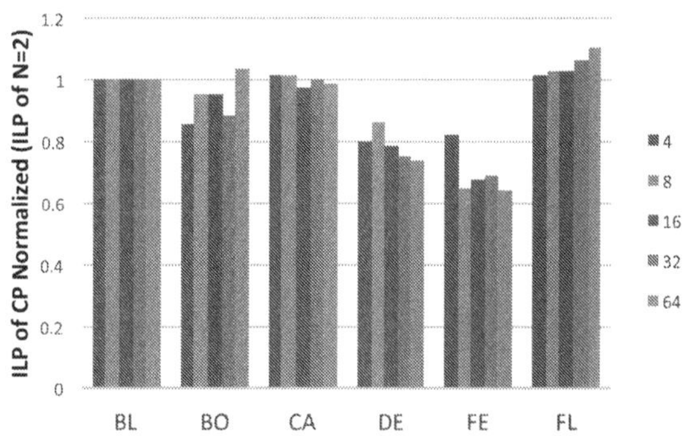

Figure 6: Normalized ILP of the CP without synchronization semantics ($ILP_{MT\_CP\_NS}$) for N_{min}=4 through 64. Normalized against CP ILP for N_{min}=2.

4.2.2 *What is the threading inefficiency of each benchmark?*

Figure 5 shows the TI, as defined by Equation 4, for all benchmarks from N_{min}= 2-64. For the case of **X2** and **VI** , we were unable to generate values of N_{min} greater than 2 due to infrastructure problems, so they will be left out of the analysis in this and the following questions. This experiment uses the same configuration as discussed in Section 4.2.1. From Figure 5 we notice two distinct groups of behaviors. In the first group, containing **CA**, **BL**, and **FL** , TI increases slowly with thread count and TI never exceeds 2x. **BL** shows the best TI, approximately 1 for all N_{min}. **BL** represents an embarrassingly parallel program, as it remains well balanced as threads increase. In **BL**, the problem space is evenly partitioned among the cores and there is very little interaction among the threads until the program completes [4].

The second group consists of **FE** , **DE** , and **BO** . In these benchmarks TI increases dramatically with thread count. The underlying parallel algorithms in this group involve a great deal of inter-thread dependencies at a high level. This increase still occurs despite removing all thread synchronization overhead (inter-thread data dependencies are always respected to ensure correctness). Bienia et. al. found these benchmarks to be the only ones using the Pthread condition synchronization function in our study [4]. Pthread condition variables are used by a thread to suspend or wake up other threads for the purpose of synchronizing data. These results indicate that, despite ignoring the condition thread synchronization semantics, overheads of coordinating parallelization remain high for these applications. The parallel threads generated by this group also spawned various types of worker threads that had different types of jobs to do. These threads relied on prior stages of thread pools to reach a certain checkpoint before executing. This leads to our **third observation**, there is a dramatic increase in TI for benchmarks that require threads to heavily depend on each other (a good rule of thumb is when a parallel program uses a significant number of Pthread condition instructions). In other words the more complex the parallel algorithm is, the more difficult it is to scale. While this observation may be thought of as "intuitive", what we add is the quantification of scaling overhead. Furthermore, we find that depending on the complexity of the benchmark, the penalty of scaling can be amplified. It should be emphasized that the degree of inefficiency varies among benchmark. **FE** had the worst TI (44), and **BL** had the best (1). Knowing the TI of each benchmark is not enough to to optimize your returns on hardware, rather it is a combination of resources available with respect to CP, ILP, and cycle time. Threading inefficiency is a useful metric, which we will use to help interpret data we present in the questions below.

4.2.3 *What is the impact on ILP as core count scales?*

In this experiment we study the effects of the CP's ILP (ILP_{MT_CP}), as we increase TLP (by adding more threads). Here we ran benchmarks setting N_{min} to 2 through 64, simulating ideal cores. We again ignored all thread synchronization semantics, thus following the discussion for extracting $ILP_{MT\_CP\_NS}$ described at the end of Section 3.2.3, and illustrated in Figure 3c. Figure 6 shows the ILP of the CP for the varying N_{min}. Showing the ILP of the CP gives a much more accurate understanding of the tradeoffs between ILP and TLP caused by inefficiencies in multi-threaded load balancing. The CP takes into account all threads of a program. It is typical for a benchmark to spawn additional threads as it continues to execute. For some benchmarks such as **FE**, setting N_{min}=64 will yield a CP which touches on as many as 258 threads (many of these threads are short-lived). It is important to understand that an increase in ILP does not necessarily indicate it is better for the overall program in terms of performance and speedup. One must take into account the CP's instruction count and the application's TI to understand the presented CP ILP values.

From Figure 6 we see **CA**, **FL** and **BL** are the only benchmarks that only show a small loss in ILP as N_{min} increases. Furthermore, in **FL**, the ILP actually increases forN_{min}=32 and 64. It is worth noting that these are the simplest of all benchmarks, in terms of parallelism model (they are data-parallel). For these benchmarks it would make sense to keep core sizes the same as cores are added to compensate for the increase in TLP. **DE** and **FE** see ILP reductions of 27% and 45% respectively as you scale out to 64 cores. For these applications, a good tradeoff that conserves power as N_{min} increases is to reduce the size of the cores. **BO** is the most interesting as the CP ILP is best at 2 and 64, it shows less ILP for intermediate N_{min}. Thus the optimal ILP for **BO** is found at 64 cores. For this benchmark, it makes sense to maximize the size of all cores for N_{min}=64 cores, however, note that this benchmark has among the worst TI (Figure 5). This brings us to our **fourth observation**, as you increase the number of cores, the optimal core size to optimize performance with respect to power varies greatly with application (it should match ILP trends). Creating extra overhead due to scaling often gives additional ILP, but that does not speak to whether it is beneficial or not, in order to properly process this, the TI must be taken into account (shown in Figure 5).

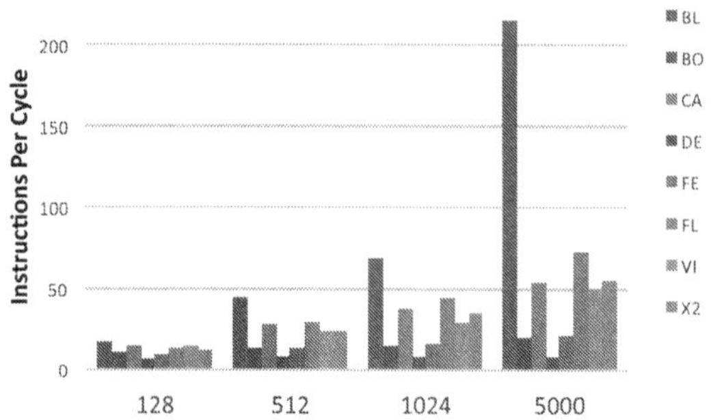

(a) $ILP_{MT\_CP\_NS}$ for N=2

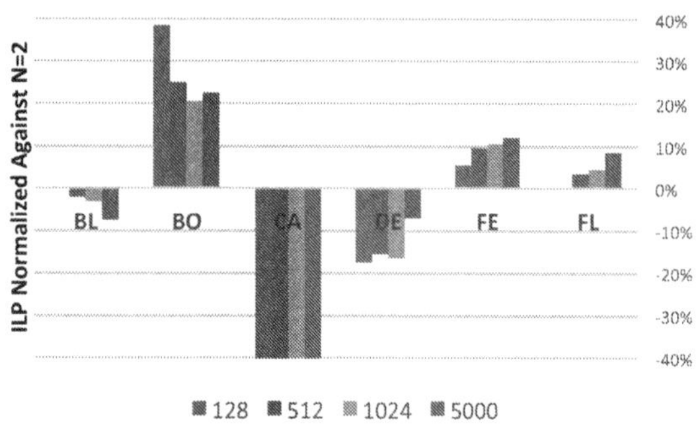

(b) $ILP_{MT\_CP\_NS}$ for N=64, normalized against N=2

Figure 7: Instruction window constraint impact on $ILP_{MT\_CP\_NS}$.

4.2.4 What is the impact of instruction window size restrictions?

In this experiment, we vary the simulated instruction window size. This experiment explores the search distance required to achieve significant ILP gains. The results should also help inform design decisions with respect to die area and power. Figure 7a shows the $ILP_{MT\_CP\_NS}$ with window size constraints placed on each benchmark, for N_{min}=2. From the results, it is clear that window size heavily impacts ILP. As the figure shows, an instruction window size of 128 restricts max ILP to roughly 7-18 depending on the benchmark. Compared to the results for an infinite window (Figure 4a) this reflects a loss in ILP available of 4-59x. When using a 5000 window size the applications gain more than half the ILP that we see in an infinite window for **CA**, **BL** and **FL**.

Looking at instruction window sizes of 128 and 512 (a 4x increase in size), we see slightly above 2x the returns in ILP for **BL**, **CA** and **FL**. As noted previously these are the simplest benchmarks in terms of parallelism model (all 3 are using data-parallel algorithms [4]). Diminishing returns set in for ILP as window sizes increase from 512 to 1024 and finally to 5000. For the rest of the benchmarks the bulk of the ILP is found beyond instruction windows of size 5000. These benchmarks are much more complex, and as a result this additional ILP is likely from different phases

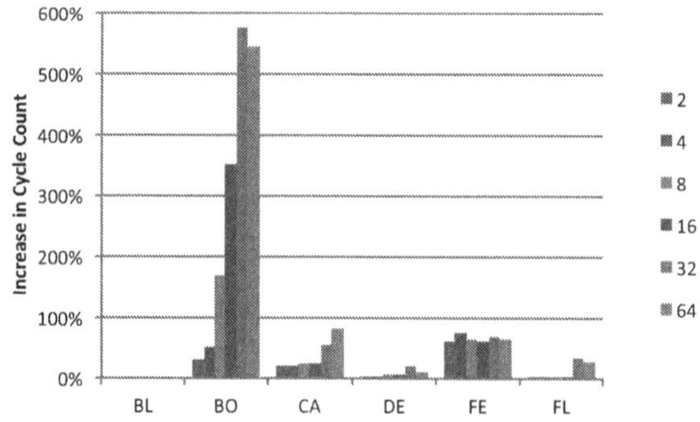

(a) Impact of thread synchronization semantics on H.

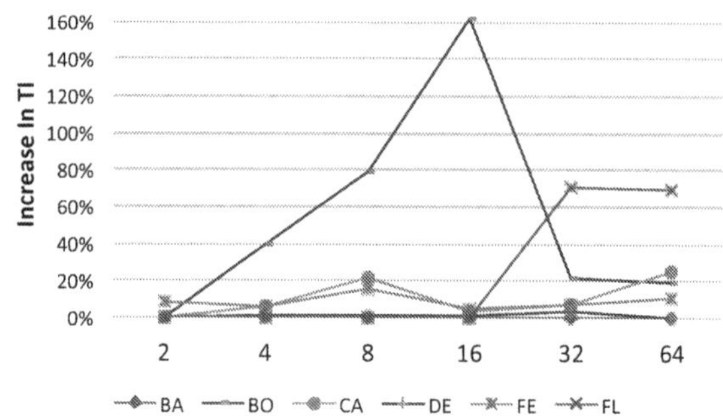

(b) Impact of thread synchronization semantics on TI.

Figure 8: Impact of thread synchronization semantics.

of the parallel algorithm. They also have different parallel stages, which have significant instruction parallelism relative to each other. Our **fifth observation** is that we see that ILP is being heavily restricted by window size.

In half the benchmarks, most of the ILP can be mined from within a distance of 5000 instructions (**BL, CA, FL**), while in the other half (**X2, VI, FE, DE, BO**), the ILP is found much further than a distance of 5000 instructions away, making it more difficult to capture using a traditional instruction window. Improving performance in the first group might involve increasing the instruction window, while the second group would require much more aggressive speculation techniques. We speculate near ILP (<5000 windows) is likely to include what is traditionally considered to be Data-level Parallelism (loop bodies etc.) while far ILP is more likely to come from different program phases and related phenomena ILP as mentioned prior.

In Figure 7b we show the change in $ILP_{MT\_CP\_NS}$ comparing N_{min} of 2 and 64. We find the ILP of the CP changes as you increase N_{min}. In some benchmarks the increase in TLP takes away from the ILP when imposing window constraints. For **BL**, it makes little difference, while for **FE**, **FL** and **BO** we notice an increase in ILP as we increase TLP. However for **CA** and **DE** we notice ILP is reduced. Therefore depending on the benchmark, increasing TLP does not necessarily decrease the amount of ILP when using window size constraints. When we do observe an increase in ILP it is worth noting that this at a cost of an increase in threading inefficiency.

4.2.5 *How do thread synchronization semantics effect ILP?*

Thread synchronization semantics (i.e. locks, barriers and condition variables) are inserted by programmers to synchronize data access between threads, with the goal of removing races and ensuring correctness. Often theses semantics are implemented very conservatively, sacrificing program performance to reduce programming time and complexity. For example, a programmer may insert a lock to synchronize all accesses to an array even when different threads are not actually working on the same elements of that array, and hence there is no actual data dependence between threads accessing the array. Furthermore, there are often independent instructions beyond a synchronization semantic that could be executed in parallel while waiting on the synchronization semantic. In this section, we explore the potential benefit of speculation beyond synchronization semantics on the ILP of the CP. Thus, here we move from measuring $ILP_{MT\_CP\_NS}$ to ILP_{MT_CP} as illustrated in Figure 3b.

Intuitively, we expect that removing the thread synchronization semantics imposed by the programmer will reduce H, the DFG height (ie. the estimated cycle count). Here we quantify the actual impact on performance by focusing on the changes in H of each benchmark. When simulating without synchronization primitives, we still honor the true data dependencies between threads, therefore applications behave as if an idealized, fine-grain synchronization was used. For this experiment, we compared H for each benchmark at each N_{min} with thread synchronization semantics enabled against a parallel run with thread synchronization semantics ignored (as was done in all experiments to this point in the paper). A large increase in H with thread synchronization semantics enabled would provide motivation for revisiting TLP exploitation techniques as well as motivation for creating new techniques to speculate past thread synchronization semantics as discussed in Section 5.3.

Figure 8a shows the increase in H with thread synchronization semantics enabled versus with thread synchronization semantics disabled. Figure 8b shows increase in TI due to thread synchronization semantics. **BL**, being an embarrassingly parallel program, shows no effect from thread synchronization semantics. **CA** is an interesting case, as it contains the finest-grain synchronization of all the applications, using load locks and store conditional instructions directly to create atomic locks. It also uses high level barriers to synchronize all the threads. **CA** at 64 threads, shows an 80% slow down when enabling thread synchronization semantics. In this case it is the use of these barriers that inhibits performance. **FE** has the biggest increase in cycle time at $N_{min} = 4$ (slowing down nearly as much at 80%), which is interesting since it is a pipelined parallel algorithm (multiple stages in the program applications, where some stages are parallel), spawning many more than the minimum N threads for each case. **FL** does not see any performance impact from thread synchronization semantics until N_{min}=32-64. **DE** , another pipeline parallel benchmark, has very minimal slowdown when enabling thread synchronization semantics, along with **BL** it stands to benefit the least. **BO** is particularly interesting as it has an significant impact on cycle time due to thread synchronization semantics. This leads to our **sixth observation**, there is sufficient motivation to develop new and aggressive thread dependency speculation techniques, particularly for $N_{min} \geq 32$. Its worth noting, although intuitive, almost every benchmark experiences a significant increase in threading inefficiency due to synchronization semantics.

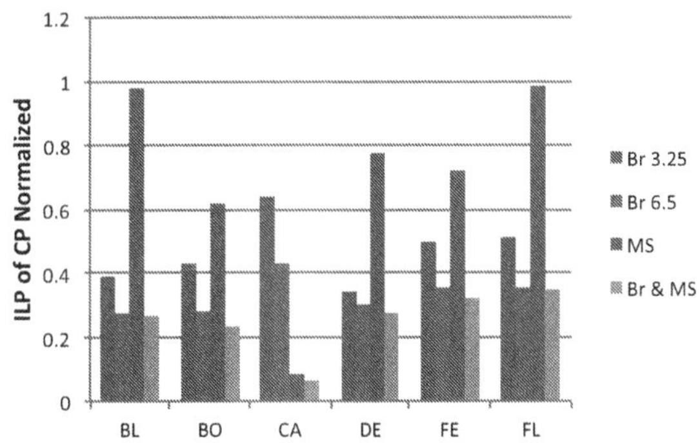

Figure 9: ILP_{MT_CP} with Branch, Memory Latency, and both, normalized against Nmin=64, thread semantics enabled and a 128 instruction window.

4.2.6 *What is the impact on ILP of realistic memory system latency and branch prediction accuracy?*

To explore the impact of realistic constraints on memory system latency and branch prediction accuracy we perform four experiments. In the first two experiments we add realistic branch prediction (Br) modeling different prediction accuracies. In the third experiment we add realistic memory latency using a cache simulator (MS). Finally, for the last experiment we add both MS and Br simultaneously. For these experiments we set N_{min}=64, with thread dependencies enabled, using a 128 instruction window. For branch prediction simulations we implement a realistic model of 6.5 branch misses per thousand instructions (MPKI), which represents current typical branch predictor performance [14]. For our realistic memory system we implemented simple cache hierarchy, modeling private L1 and L2 caches and a shared L3 last-level cache. The sizes of each cache are 256KB, 512KB, and 2MBs respectively. The three levels of the cache have an access delay of 1, 10, 30 respectively, a L3 cache miss results in a 150 cycle delay. Here we chose 2MB of L3 cache since we are using the small input set of PARSEC the memory footprint is likely smaller than native input sets. However, the trends should remain the same for larger input sets when using a larger last level cache. Figure 9 shows our results for these experiments. The results show that there is an average 31% reduction in ILP_{MT_CP} when adding memory system model delay, and an average 67% reduction when adding a realistic branch misprediction rate of 6.5 MPKI (*Br* 6.5). **BL** and **FL** have very little ILP_{MT_CP} degradation when implementing a realistic memory system. Interestingly, **CA** has the worst cache ILP_{MT_CP} performance, being reduced by 92%. The results for **CA**, are consistent with Bienia et .al's [4] work, where **CA** is known to be severely restricted by cache size. Generally, with the exception of **CA**, we find that branch misprediction has a nearly uniform, and drastic impact on the ILP available. To further explore this impact, we improved the MPKI by a factor of 2, (from 6.5 to 3.25) shown as *Br* 3.25 in the figure. Improving MPKI by a factor of 2 results in an ILP improvement of 14%-51% depending on the application. Our **seventh observation**, is branch prediction is the stronger bottleneck of the two under these constraints. These results provide motivation to continue

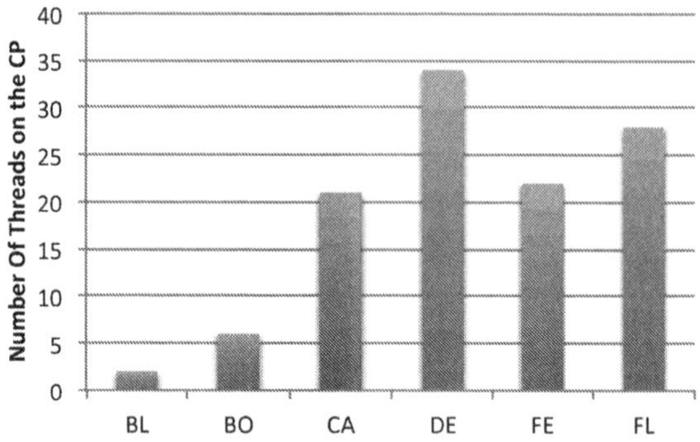

(a) Number of threads on the CP.

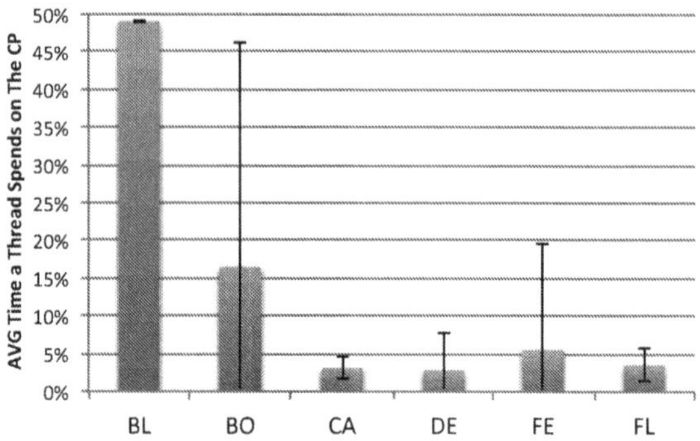

(b) Average time spent on CP. Whiskers show one standard deviation.

Figure 10: Characteristics of the critical path (CP).

expending resources to improve branch prediction, despite it being a mature field of research [13, 14, 24]. In our last experiment, we add both Br (6.5 MPKI) and MS constraints simultaneously. The results in Figure 9 show the combination tends to follow the most constrained of either Br or MS depending on the benchmark.

4.2.7 *What are the defining characteristics of the critical path?*

Finally, we examine the characteristics of the critical path (CP) for each benchmark. In this experiment, we utilize a configuration that most realistically resembles a forward looking chip-multiprocessor, 64 cores, with a 128 instruction window using a realistic memory latency and branch prediction (6.5 MPKI), as well as thread synchronization semantics enabled. We recorded what threads were on the critical path, as well as how much of the CP was made up of each thread. We then filtered the results and removed any thread on the CP that made up less than 1/(Total Threads on the CP) when $N_{min} = 64$ (some threads spawn more than others as explained in Section 4.2.1). Since the CP is the longest path from start to end of execution, it makes sense to speed up the CP by using the highest performing cores available. By characterizing the CP, we can determine the practicality and or difficulty of CP thread migration for the sake of acceleration. Figure 10 shows this data along two axes.

Figure 10a shows the number of threads that make up the CP of each benchmark. The bars in Figure 10b show the average time a thread spends on the CP, while the whiskers on each bar show one SD of thread time on the CP. Using these two graphs, we are able to highlight a few observations. **BL** has two threads on the CP, each containing 50% of the CP. **FE** had 34 threads on the CP that we considered critical; interestingly, it spawned a total of 258 threads. Out of the 34 critical threads in **FE** one thread dominated the CP by occupying 62% of the time. In **BO**, there were 6 threads on the CP, with one thread dominating, occupying 77% of the time. Thus we feel it would be beneficial to have one or two bigger cores, to execute the dominant threads on the CP for both benchmarks. The other benchmarks had many threads making up their CP. For these applications, it is likely still advantageous to have a few larger cores to execute the CP and migrate threads to those cores on the CP when they become critical, this is particularly true for applications with poor TI. This follows into our **eight observation**, there exists a potential for performance gain by creating larger cores and migrating threads to that core when they are on the CP. This approach, however, will require research to explore techniques that can identify thread criticality in real time [8, 26].

4.2.8 *Summary Of Observations*

In this section, we explore the limits and trade-offs between ILP and TLP in modern, shared-memory multi-threaded applications. Here, we summarize our observations from the experiments conducted. Current architecture designs are far from achieving even a fraction of the ILP that is available in these applications. Clearly, there remains a huge headroom for improvement with respect to ILP exploitation. This suggests for more creative techniques to maximize ILP while maintaining power requirements. Although traditionally ILP extraction has been viewed as extremely power intensive, recent commercial processor designs indicate that this may be possible. In particular, comparing Intel's Haswell versus Ivy Bridge processors, through a concerted effort to reduce power, Intel has managed to reduce power consumption by 50% while slightly increasing ILP extraction for two processors *in the same 22nm process technology* [1]. Even within a distance of 128 instructions, there remains a substantial amount of ILP that is not being mined by current architectures. Within a 5000 instruction window the simplest data-parallel programs can extract nearly half the upper bound of ILP calculated in this paper. In more complex benchmarks, such as those that use parallel-pipeline algorithms, a majority of the ILP is much further away and likely impossible to capture using a traditional instruction window. Therefore there is a good motivation to *increase window size*, as well as to find innovative ways to capture ILP that is much further away using a much more *aggressive speculation techniques*. In order to explore the impact of realistic design constraints on ILP we added simple branch prediction and memory system models, and found that branch prediction is more important of the two with respect to ILP under these constraints. Despite branch prediction cost overhead and the maturity of this field, *it may be worthwhile to expend resources to improve branch predictors, potentially even over increasing cache size* [13, 14, 24].

We find that increasing TLP does effect ILP, but the trade-offs are not consistent among all benchmarks. The trade-offs depends on the benchmark, a good rule of thumb for parallel algorithms: the simpler the parallel algorithm the less likely TLP will negatively effect ILP. Therefore as core counts increase, core size *should be dependent upon the application.* From a practical viewpoint, this argues for heterogeneous architectures (only powering up core size appropriate for the given application) or dynamic architectures.

We find that thread synchronization semantics can greatly impact program performance, although the amount depends on the application. There is as much as a 6x slowdown due to these semantics. The overhead of thread synchronization semantics on performance become quite noticeable as programs scale to larger numbers of cores. Therefore, there should be more *effort in trying to speculate beyond synchronization semantics.*

As cores continue to scale the more likely there will be an increase in load imbalance. This increased load imbalance puts pressure on certain threads causing them to become more critical than others. This argues for heterogeneous designs which map threads to high performance cores when those threads become critical. Since we find the critical path often migrates from thread to thread many times during the application's runtime, we find that there is a critical need to *identify critical threads during runtime*, to enable performance critical thread migration. Generally in our results we find that no two benchmarks reacted the same across all our tests, thus the *optimal design for each benchmark is different*, when factoring in limited resources and power constraints. This also argues for heterogeneous designs which dynamically powers up the appropriate sized cores for efficient execution of each benchmark.

5. RELATED WORK

In the following section, we discuss related work that pertains to our limit study. We start by examining past limit studies, and end on a survey of related toolsets that are similar in terms of measuring ILP and TLP.

5.1 Past ILP Limit Studies

Historically, many researchers have published ILP limit studies [21, 27, 16, 11, 20, 2, 6], however since the majority of these studies date back several decades, there have been numerous technology advances in the computer architecture field since their publication. Most importantly, none of them have covered the trade-offs and limits between ILP and TLP. In the following subsection, we highlight some significant limit studies.

Wall et al. [27] published one of the first studies of ILP limits with respect to register renaming, branch prediction, loop unrolling, and window size. The paper concluded that with ideal techniques that are currently available to exploit ILP, parallelism rarely exceeds 5-7. A study by Butler et al. [6] conducted around the same time showed parallelism to be around 17 for the SPEC Suite. Their paper showed that with optimal hardware design, machines can achieve realistic parallelism of 2-5. A limit study by Austin et al. [2] involved creating single-threaded DFGs similar to our methodology using SPEC benchmarks. They showed ILP ranges from 13 to 23. Austin et al. concluded a very large instruction window is needed to capture the majority of the parallelism. Lam et al. [16] demonstrated that control flow is a bottleneck in exploiting ILP, our branch prediction experiments reinforce this finding. The authors concluded that, to increase ILP, restrictions on control flow must be eased. Three novel techniques were introduced that helped alleviate control flow, increasing ILP to its full potential: speculative execution, control dependence analysis, and executing various paths in program execution simultaneously. The studies conducted by Wall, Butler, Austin and Lam et al. are the foundation of our limit study, as we seek to replicate their research in a multi-threaded era, where applications now include inter-thread dependencies. The findings in these papers are inconsistent with each other. The ILP limits found in Austin et al.'s were most similar to our finding and coincidentally had a very similar methodology to us. Their and our work both show parallelism to be several orders of magnitude greater than what was found in the other papers. We speculate that the reason why we found the upper bound to be orders of magnitude higher than most work previous is because modern programs are much larger, more complex and operate on much more data allowing for more data-parallel ILP extraction.

Postiff et al. [21] examined ILP in SPEC95 benchmarks. Their approach to find additional ILP was unique compared to previous methods published prior; which involved removing disruptions in the instruction stream caused by the stack pointer. They showed that there is plenty of ILP in an application; however, it is spread out quite expansively. They also concluded that compilers must be involved in mining ILP. This work differs from ours, as Postiff et al.'s work involved modifications to the traces, removing compiler-added code. In contrast we removed only operating system code from our traces. Gonzalez et al. [11] argued that there was a lack of effort to increase ILP by trying to solve the data dependency problem, showing it is a major bottleneck. The solution proposed was to create data speculation techniques to predict values of data dependencies. The study showed that additional ILP could be exploited by removing pseudo data dependencies and substituting their values with values generated with a prediction algorithm. The paper demonstrated that significant improvements can be achieved by predicting arithmetic data values when using an infinite window. In their work, they noted that speculation techniques would greatly benefit large/infinite instruction windows. Our work agrees with both Gonzales et al. and Postiff et al. [11, 21] findings that ILP is spread out across an application. We show that the majority of ILP can be captured using window sizes greater than 5000 in a few of the benchmarks.

Pai et al. [20] is one of the newer limit studies. The researchers aimed at exploring DLP, since at that time, Single instruction, multiple data (SIMD) had become quite popular. The authors looked into how much DLP is available in a program; as they pointed out, previous studies had not distinguished between TLP and DLP. They found that there is a high degree of available DLP in applications. In our work, we do not directly distinguish between DLP and ILP; we speculate that the majority of ILP captured in our experiments using a window <5000 are a result of DLP.

The most recent study was done by McFarlin et al. [18] in 2013, and is a loosely based limit study that attempts to calculate the upper bounds the OoO Engine performance. Their research focused on the OoO scheduler, and was split into two parts. The first part involves reworking scheduling order of instructions with respect to functional units and operands. Secondly, they looked at scheduling improvements based on hardware speculation support. Based on their study they came up with recommendations on what is needed to have an optimal OoO Engine, such as the need to optimize instructions scheduling statically. They also found that the critical path is highly dependent on load and branch instructions, and addressing these issues can greatly increase performance. In our work, we do not study the impact an OoO Engine with respect to ILP, as we assume in all our experiments that functional units are an unlimited resource.

We note that many of the past limit studies covered above are somewhat outdated; benchmarks have evolved, and they have been designed to take advantage of TLP. These previous studies workloads used much smaller data sets and different/comparatively less complex algorithms. Further, no previous study examined the relation between TLP and ILP, thread synchronization effects and thread load balancing in multi-threaded applications with respect to the critical path. There is a dearth of studies regarding trade-offs and limits on current benchmarks when it comes to ILP and TLP. These studies need to be updated to reflect behavior of future applications. This is our motivation for pursuing the work in this paper.

5.2 Past TLP Limit Studies

One of the most influential modern studies on the tradeoffs of TLP and ILP was written by Hill et al. [12], where Ahmdal's Law was applied to various multicore topologies. Hill et al. developed theoretical mathematical models to determine what type of topology would work best in running multi-threaded applications. Various combinations of dynamic, asymmetric, and symmetric topologies were examined. The work was done at a high level and was designed to stimulate thought rather than provide concrete evidence on the best topologies to utilize when considering multithreaded applications. In this paper, we aimed to provide some answers to the questions proposed in Hill et al.'s paper. Esmaeilzadeh et al. [9] modeled multicore scaling limits factoring in single, multi-core, and device scaling for the purpose of measuring speed for parallel applications in the next five generations of technology. Esmaeilzadeh et al. used simplified models and did not fully elaborate on TLP and ILP trade-offs, which is the main focus of this paper. Our work differs from theirs as they derived their results and conclusions based on a number of simplified assumptions (the authors modeled characteristics of benchmarks derived from other papers). Our work is distinctive in that we try to reflect real workloads as close as possible using real benchmark traces as the basis of our limit study. In other words instead of modeling their characteristics, we used empirical data to reach our conclusions.

5.3 TLP Speculation Techniques

In Section 4.2.5 we showed there is significant performance to be gained by removing thread synchronization semantics in the majority of benchmarks analyzed. These results give motivation to revisit old techniques to speculate beyond synchronization primitives as well as motivation to create new techniques. In this section we go over a few techniques in the past that are designed to speculate beyond synchronization primitives gain performance.

Thread Level Speculation (TLS) was introduced in the mid 90s by Steffan et al. [25]. TLS is a technique that generates automatic parallelization of single threaded programs starting at the compiler level. Speculative threads are generated based on the compiler "guessing" whether blocks of codes are independent. These threads are executed at runtime speculatively. Martinez et al. [17], extended TLS to work with parallel applications. The authors argued that many thread synchronization primitives were placed in nonoptimal positions in code. Thus, forcing independent code to be dependent due to the constrictions of thread synchronization primitives. Martinez et al.'s work introduced the ability to speculate beyond barriers, locks and flags.

Another TLP speculation technique is Speculative Lock Elision (SPE), developed by Rajwar et al. [22]. SPE detects whether a critical section is truly critical at runtime. If a critical section is determined to have false inter-thread dependencies the locks are removed and the critical section is executed. Thus, this allows threads not to wait to acquire a lock, therefore reducing execution time of the parallel application.

This paper adds to previous work done by showing the upper bound of performance when removing all thread synchronization primitives. The results shown in Section 4.2.5 provide motivation to revisit these previous techniques as well as create new ones.

5.4 Trace-Driven Tool Sets

To the best of our knowledge, we have built the first simulator that is able to analyze thread and instruction dependencies for benchmarks of current and emerging workloads. There exist a few simulators, however, that share the some of the same characteristics. MaxPar [15] is a simulator developed in 1985 that analyzes data and instruction dependencies in parallel systems. The overall goal of the simulator was to measure the inherent parallelism in parallel applications. Since then, there have been many changes such as underlying ISA, compilers, etc. Our simulator is similar to MaxPar, except to accommodate the benchmarks of today and it can handle inter-thread dependencies. Tasksim [23] is a hybrid simulator that combines both traces and realtime execution of multi-threaded applications. This hybrid system has the ability to generate a single trace and use that trace to run N threads, thus saving time generating traces for given number of cores. The drawback to this simulator is that it does not support many popular parallel languages. They support three languages, with the most notable being OpenMP 3.0. Our simulator is different in that for each set of N threads, you must re-run the traces. Our simulator bypasses high level languages (HLL) and runs at the assembly level; as a result our simulator places no restrictions on HLL or threading model.

6. CONCLUSIONS

In this paper, we conducted a limit study on next-generation multi-threaded benchmarks. We found that there remains a significant amount of ILP in these benchmarks which has yet to be mined. Compared to real machines as much as 929x more ILP is available. We found the upper bound on ILP averaged around 200 instructions/cycle for all benchmarks, far exceeding current high-performance processor cores. Much of this ILP, however, is much further than 5000 instructions away. The plethora of ILP found should be motivation for the computer architecture community to revisit old techniques as well attempt to create new techniques to extract this ILP. As TLP increases, there is often a trade off in ILP, and it can decrease as much as 45%, depending on the complexity of the parallel algorithm. We also found that thread dependencies had a detrimental effect on cycle time, increasing it as much 9x. Adding realistic branch prediction, and realistic memory latency resulted in ILP degradation of 67% and 31% on average respectively. From this study it is clear that there are large performance improvements to be had when it comes to next-generation parallel workloads. In particular, the results of this study argue that research into more aggressive thread synchronization speculation techniques can have a significant performance impact. They also argue that research into run-time critical path identification will be critical to the success of asymmetric multi-core designs. From the all the experiments that we conducted, there were no two benchmarks that reacted the same way to all our tests, leading us to believe that the optimal design for each benchmark is different, with respect to performance and power.

7. ACKNOWLEDGMENTS

This research is supported in part by the National Science Foundation under grant CCF-1320074. We recognize Collin Cusce, David Kadjo, and Zhe Wang for their assistance developing this work. We also thank the anonymous reviewers who's feedback greatly influenced the final form of this paper, and particularly Prof. Wonsun Ahn for his advice and shepherding of this work.

8. REFERENCES

[1] S. Anthony. Intel: Haswell will draw 50% less power than Ivy Bridge. http://www.extremetech.com/computing/156739-intel-haswell-will-draw-50-less-power-than-ivy-bridge.

[2] T. M. Austin and G. S. Sohi. Dynamic dependency analysis of ordinary programs. In *the 19th Annual International Symposium on Computer Architecture (ISCA)*, pages 342–351, 1992.

[3] M. Bhadauria, V. M. Weaver, and S. A. McKee. Understanding parsec performance on contemporary cmps. In *the 2009 IEEE International Symposium on Workload Characterization (IISWC)*, pages 98–107, 2009.

[4] C. Bienia, S. Kumar, J. P. Singh, and K. Li. The PARSEC Benchmark Suite: Characterization and Architectural Implications. In *The 17th International Conference on Parallel Architectures and Compilation Techniques*, 2008.

[5] N. Binkert, B. Beckmann, G. Black, S. K. Reinhardt, A. Saidi, A. Basu, J. Hestness, D. R. Hower, T. Krishna, S. Sardashti, R. Sen, K. Sewell, M. Shoaib, N. Vaish, M. D. Hill, and D. A. Wood. The gem5 simulator. *ACM Computer Architecture News*, 39(2):1–7, May 2011.

[6] M. Butler, T.-Y. Yeh, Y. Patt, M. Alsup, H. Scales, and M. Shebanow. Single instruction stream parallelism is greater than two. In *the 18th Annual International Symposium on Computer Architecture (ISCA)*, pages 276–286, 1991.

[7] R. H. Dennard, F. H. Gaensslen, V. L. Rideout, E. Bassous, and A. R. LeBlanc. Design of ion-implanted mosfet's with very small physical dimensions. *IEEE Journal of Solid-State Circuits*, 9(5):256–268, 1974.

[8] K. Du Bois, S. Eyerman, J. B. Sartor, and L. Eeckhout. Criticality stacks: Identifying critical threads in parallel programs using synchronization behavior. In *the 40th Annual International Symposium on Computer Architecture (ISCA)*, pages 511–522, 2013.

[9] H. Esmaeilzadeh, E. Blem, R. St. Amant, K. Sankaralingam, and D. Burger. Dark silicon and the end of multicore scaling. In *the 38th annual international symposium on Computer architecture (ISCA)*, pages 365–376, 2011.

[10] M. Gebhart, J. Hestness, E. Fatehi, P. Gratz, and S. W. Keckler. Running PARSEC 2.1 on M5. Technical report, The Univ. of Texas at Austin, Dept. of Comp. Sci., 2009.

[11] J. González and A. González. Limits of instruction level parallelism with data speculation. In *Proc. of the VECPAR Conf*, pages 585–598. Citeseer, 1998.

[12] M. D. Hill and M. R. Marty. Amdahl's law in the multicore era. *Computer*, 41(7):33–38, July 2008.

[13] D. Jimenez. Piecewise linear branch prediction. In *the 32nd International Symposium on Computer Architecture (ISCA)*, pages 382–393, June 2005.

[14] D. A. Jimenez. An optimized scaled neural branch predictor. In *the 2011 IEEE 29th International Conference on Computer Design (ICCD)*, pages 113–118, 2011.

[15] D. kai Chen. Maxpar: An execution driven simulator for studying parallel systems. Technical report, University of Illinois at Urbana-Champaign, 1989.

[16] M. S. Lam and R. P. Wilson. Limits of control flow on parallelism. In *the 19th Annual International Symposium on Computer Architecture (ISCA)*, pages 46–57, 1992.

[17] J. F. Martínez and J. Torrellas. Speculative synchronization: Applying thread-level speculation to explicitly parallel applications. *SIGOPS Oper. Syst. Rev.*, 36(5):18–29, Oct. 2002.

[18] D. S. McFarlin, C. Tucker, and C. Zilles. Discerning the dominant out-of-order performance advantage: Is it speculation or dynamism? In *the Eighteenth International Conference on Architectural Support for Programming Languages and Operating Systems (ASPLOS)*, pages 241–252, 2013.

[19] G. Moore. Cramming more components onto integrated circuits. *Electronics Magazine*, April 1965.

[20] S. Pai, R. Govindarajan, and M. Thazhuthaveetil. Limits of data-level parallelism. *14th Annual IEEE International Conference on High Performance Computing*, Dec. 2007.

[21] M. A. Postiff, D. A. Greene, G. S. Tyson, and T. N. Mudge. The limits of instruction level parallelism in spec95 applications. *SIGARCH Comput. Archit. News*, 27(1):31–34, Mar. 1999.

[22] R. Rajwar and J. R. Goodman. Speculative lock elision: Enabling highly concurrent multithreaded execution. In *the 34th Annual ACM/IEEE International Symposium on Microarchitecture (Micro)*, pages 294–305, 2001.

[23] A. Rico, A. Duran, F. Cabarcas, Y. Etsion, A. Ramirez, and M. Valero. Trace-driven simulation of multithreaded applications. In *the 2011 IEEE International Symposium on Performance Analysis of Systems and Software (ISPASS)*, pages 87 –96, april 2011.

[24] A. Seznec. A new case for the tage branch predictor. In *the 44th Annual IEEE/ACM International Symposium on Microarchitecture (Micro)*, pages 117–127, 2011.

[25] J. Steffan and T. Mowry. The potential for using thread-level data speculation to facilitate automatic parallelization. In *the 4th International Symposium on High-Performance Computer Architecture (HPCA)*, 1998.

[26] M. A. Suleman, O. Mutlu, M. K. Qureshi, and Y. N. Patt. Accelerating critical section execution with asymmetric multi-core architectures. *SIGPLAN Not.*, 44(3):253–264, Mar. 2009.

[27] D. W. Wall. Limits of instruction-level parallelism. In *the fourth international conference on Architectural support for programming languages and operating systems (ASPLOS)*, pages 176–188, 1991.

Versatile and Scalable Parallel Histogram Construction

Wookeun Jung
Department of Computer Science and Engineering
Seoul National University,
Seoul 151-744, Korea
wookeun@aces.snu.ac.kr

Jongsoo Park
Parallel Computing Lab, Intel Corporation
2200 Mission College Blvd.,
Santa Clara, California 95054, USA
jongsoo.park@intel.com

Jaejin Lee
Department of Computer Science and Engineering
Seoul National University,
Seoul 151-744, Korea
jaejin@snu.ac.kr

ABSTRACT

Histograms are used in various fields to quickly profile the distribution of a large amount of data. However, it is challenging to efficiently utilize abundant parallel resources in modern processors for histogram construction. To make matters worse, the most efficient implementation varies depending on input parameters (e.g., input distribution, number of bins, and data type) or architecture parameters (e.g., cache capacity and SIMD width).

This paper presents versatile histogram methods that achieve competitive performance across a wide range of input types and target architectures. Our open source implementations are highly optimized for various cases and are scalable for more threads and wider SIMD units. We also show that histogram construction can be significantly accelerated by Intel® Xeon Phi™ coprocessors for common input data sets because of their compute power from many cores and instructions for efficient vectorization, such as gather-scatter.

For histograms with 256 fixed-width bins, a dual-socket 8-core Intel® Xeon® E5-2690 achieves 13 billion bin updates per second (GUPS), while a 60-core Intel® Xeon Phi™ 5110P coprocessor achieves 18 GUPS for a skewed input. For histograms with 256 variable-width bins, the Xeon processor achieves 4.7 GUPS, while the Xeon Phi coprocessor achieves 9.7 GUPS for a skewed input. For text histogram, or word count, the Xeon processor achieves 342.4 million words per seconds (MWPS). This is 4.12×, 3.46× faster than PHOENIX and TBB. The Xeon phi processor achieves 401.4 MWPS, which is 1.17× faster than the Xeon processor. Since histogram construction captures essential characteristics of more general reduction-heavy operations, our approach can be extended to other settings.

Categories and Subject Descriptors

D.1.3 [**Programming techniques**]: Concurrent programming—*Parallel programming*; C.1.2 [**Processor architecture**]: Multiple Data Stream Architectures (Multiprocessors)—*Single-instruction-stream, multiple-data-stream processors*

Keywords

Histogram; Algorithms; Performance; SIMD; Multi-core

PACT'14, August 24–27, 2014, Edmonton, AB, Canada.

http://dx.doi.org/10.1145/2628071.2628108 .

1 Introduction

While the most well known usage of histograms is image processing algorithms [8], histogramming is also a key building block in various emerging data-intensive applications. Common database primitives such as join and query planning often use histograms to estimate the distribution of data in their pre-processing steps [18, 25, 34]. Histogramming is also a key step in fundamental data processing algorithms such as radix sort [31] and distributed sorting [19]. Typically, these data-intensive applications construct histograms in their pre-processing steps so that they can adapt to input distributions appropriately.

Histogramming is becoming more important because of two trends: (1) increasing amount of data and (2) increasing parallelism in computing systems.

Histograms for Profiling Big Data: The amount of data that needs to be analyzed now sometimes exceeds tera bytes and is expected to be continuously increasing, if not accelerating [5]. This sheer amount of data often necessitates quickly profiling the data distribution through histograms. For tera bytes of data, just scanning them may take several minutes, even when the data are spread across hundreds of machines and read in parallel [5]. Therefore, quickly sampling to profile the data is valuable both to interactive users and to software routines, such as query planners. This pre-processing often involves constructing histograms since they are a versatile statistical tool [24].

Histograms for Load Balancing in Highly Parallel Systems: The parallelism of modern computing systems is continuously increasing, where histograms often play a critical role in achieving a desired utilization through load balancing. NVIDIA GPUs are successfully adopted to high-performance computing, where each card provides hundreds of hardware threads. Intel has also recently announced Xeon Phi™ coprocessors with ≥240 hardware threads. Not only does the parallelism within each compute node increases (scale up), but also the number of nodes used for data-intensive computation increases rapidly up to thousands in order to overcome limited memory capacity and disk bandwidth per node (scale out) [21]. Unless carefully load balanced, these parallel computing resources can be vastly underutilized. Histograms are often constructed in a pre-processing step to find a load balanced data partition, for example, in distributed bucket sorting [19].

When histogramming is incorporated as a pre-processing, its efficiency is crucial in achieving a desired overall performance. For example, if the load-balanced partitioning itself is not parallelized in a scalable way, it can quickly become a bottleneck. Nevertheless, efficient histogram construction is a challenging problem that has been a subject of many studies [6, 20]. The difficulty mainly stems from the following two characteristics.

First, *an efficient histogram construction method widely varies depending on histogram parameters and architecture characteristics.* For example, the way bins are partitioned substantially changes suitable approaches. This work considers three common types of histograms that are supported or implemented by widely used tools for data analysis such as R [15], IPP [33], TBB [28], and MapReduce [13, 35].

- *Histograms with fixed-width bins* is the most common type of histogram. Histograms in this type consist of bins with the same width. For example, typical image histograms have 256 bins with width 1 for each when each of RGB color components is represented by 8-bit integers.

- *Histograms with variable-width bins* is a general type of histogram that can express histograms with any distribution of bin ranges. Histograms in this type are useful to represent skewed distributions more accurately by increasing the binning resolution for densely populated ranges. Logarithmically scaled bins are an example, which are efficient for analyzing the data in a Zipf distribution [11]. The execution time of constructing histograms with variable-width bins is often dominated by computing bin indices when a non-trivial number of bins exist. In this case, binary search, or something similar, is required (§3).

- *Histograms with unbounded number of bins* is a type of histograms where the number of bins are undetermined beforehand. A typical example is text histograms, or word counting, where each bin corresponds to an arbitrary-length word. We use associative data structures such as hash table to represent the unbounded bins. Other important examples also exist such as histograms of the human genome data and histograms of numbers with arbitrary precision. In addition, by performing operations other than summation during histogram bin updates, we can implement the reduction phase of MapReduce programs with associative and commutative reduction operations.

Other histogram parameters and architectural characteristics also affect the choice of histogram construction method. For example, skewed inputs speedup methods with thread-private histograms because of fewer cache misses, while they slow down methods with shared histograms because of more conflicts (§2).

Second, *histogram construction is challenging to parallelize in a scalable way because bin values to be updated are data-dependent leading to potential conflicts.* There are primarily two approaches to parallelize histogramming at the thread level: (1) maintaining shared histogram bins through atomic operations and (2) maintaining per-thread private histogram bins and reducing them later. The latter is faster when private histograms together fit in the on-chip cache avoiding core-to-core cache line transfers and atomic operations. Conversely, when the working set overflows the on-chip cache, the private histogram method becomes slower due to increased off-chip DRAM accesses. Likewise, for histograms with associative data structures, using shared data structures needs concurrency control, while using private data structures needs non-trivial reduction techniques (§4.2). The unpredictable conflicts from data-dependent updates are even more problematic to fully utilize wide SIMD units available in modern processors. To address this difficulty, architectural features such as scatter-add [6] and gather-linked-and-scatter-conditional [20] have been proposed, but they are yet to be implemented in production hardware.

Therefore, we need (1) a *versatile* histogram construction method for a wide range of histogram parameters and target architectures, and (2) a *scalable* histogram construction method that effectively utilizes multiple cores and wide SIMD units in modern processors. To this end, we make the following contributions:

- We present a collection of *scalable* parallelization schemes for each type of histogram and target architecture (§2). For histograms with fixed-width bins, we implement a shared histogram method and a per-thread private histogram method, each optimized for different settings (§2). For histograms with variable-width bins, we implement a binary-search method (§3) and a novel partitioning-based method with adaptive pivot selection. Since the partitioning-based method has a higher scalability with respect to the SIMD width, it outperforms the binary-search method in Xeon Phi™ coprocessors when the number of bins is reasonably small and/or the input is skewed.

- We showcase the usefullness of many-core processors in constructing histograms that is seemingly dominated by memory operations. Although many-core processors such as NVIDIA GPUs and Intel® Xeon Phi™ have impressive compute power, it can be realized only when those cores and wide SIMD units are effectively utilized. Therefore, their applicability is not often shown outside compute intensive scientific operations. We show that hardware gather-scatter and unpack load-pack store instructions in Xeon Phi™ coprocessors [3] are key features that accelerate data-intensive operations. For example, they help achieve 6–15× vectorization speedups in our partition-based method and hash function computations.

- We demonstrate the competitive performances of our histogram methods in two architectures, (1) dual-socket 8-core Intel® Xeon® processor with Sandy Bridge (SNB hereafter) and (2) 60-core Intel® Xeon Phi™ coprocessor with Knights Corner (KNC hereafter) (§5). For histograms with fixed-width bins, SNB achieves near the memory-bandwidth-bound performance, 12-13 billion bin updates per second (GUPS) for inputs in the uniform random and Zipf distributions. KNC achieves better performance (17–18 GUPS) thanks to its increased memory bandwidth and hardware gather-scatter support. For histograms with 256 variable-width bins,

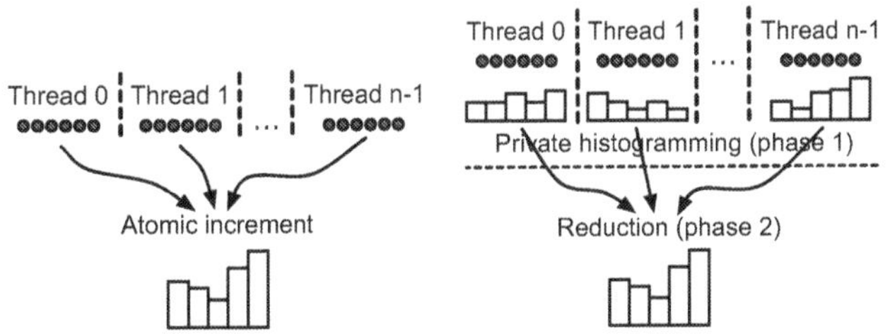

(a) Shared histogram method (b) Private histogram method

Figure 1: Parallel histogram algorithms for fixed-width bins.

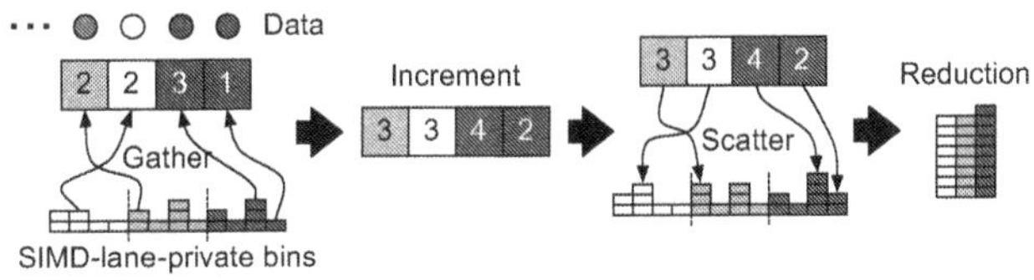

Figure 2: SIMDified bin update with gather-scatter instructions.

SNB achieves 4.7 GUPS using the fastest known tree search method [17] extended to AVX. On KNC, our novel adaptive partition algorithm shows better performance than binary search algorithm, achieving 5.3–9.7 GUPS. For text histograms using a Wikipedia input, SNB shows 345 million words per second (MWPS) (3.4 and 4.1× faster than TBB and PHOENIX, respectively), and KNC shows 401.4 MWPS using SIMD instructions.

- We implement an open-source histogram library that incorporates the optimizations mentioned above (available at [2]).

2 Histograms with Fixed-width Bins

This section and the following two describe our algorithms optimized for each bin partitioning type, input distribution, and target architecture. Histogramming can be split into two steps: *bin search* and *bin update*.

Depending on how bins are partitioned, the relative execution time of each step varies. When the width of bins is fixed, bin search step is a simple arithmetic operation. Therefore, a major fraction of the total execution time is accounted for the bin update step that mainly consists of memory operations with potential data conflicts. Conversely, when bins have variable widths or are unbounded, histogramming time is dominated by the bin search step.

For histograms with fixed width bins (in short, fixed-width histograms), the bin search step is as simple as computing `(int)((x-B)/W)`, where `W` and `B` denote the bin width and the bin base, respectively.

This is followed by the bin update step, which increments the corresponding bin value. Since the simple bin search step consists of a small number of instructions, the memory latency of the bin update step can easily become the bottleneck. Consequently, the primary optimization target for fixed-width histograms is the memory latency involved in the bin update step. This is particularly true in multi-threaded settings because of the overhead associated with synchronizing bin updates to avoid potential conflicts.

2.1 Thread-Level Parallelization

We consider two methods for thread-level parallelization, depending on how the bin values are shared among threads. These methods – shared and private – are illustrated in Fig. 1.

The *shared histogram method* in Fig. 1(a) maintains a single shared histogram, whose updates are synchronized via atomic increment instructions. The *private histogram method* in Fig. 1(b) maintains a private histogram per thread, which is reduced to a global histogram later. The reduction phase can also be parallelized.

The private histogram method has advantages of avoiding (1) the overhead of atomic operation itself (roughly 3× slower than a normal memory instruction according to our experiments), (2) the serialization of the atomic operations when multiple threads are updating the same bin simultaneously, and (3) coherence misses incurred by remotely fetching cache lines that have been updated by other cores recently. The last two issues are particularly problematic to the shared histogram method when there are a few bins or the input data is skewed.

The shared histogram method on the other hand has advantages of avoiding (1) off-chip DRAM accesses when the duplicated private histograms together overflow the last level cache (LLC) and (2) the overhead of reduction when the number of bins is relatively large compared to the number of inputs.

The target architecture also affects the choice between private and shared methods. For example, the private histogram method is more suitable to KNC with private LLCs.

2.2 SIMD Parallelization

The bin search step can be vectorized via SIMD load, subtract, and division instructions. The reduction step in the private histogram method is similarly vectorized. However, vectorizing the bin update step requires atomic SIMD instructions, such as scatter-add [6] or gather-linked-and-scatter-conditional [20] because of potential conflicts across SIMD lanes. Unfortunately, these hardware supports are yet to be implemented in the currently available processors.

When the number of bins is sufficiently small, we can maintain per-SIMD-lane private histogram at the expense of higher memory pressure. In KNC, with this per-SIMD-lane privatization, we take advantage of hardware gather-scatter instructions to vectorize the bin update step.

For example, Fig. 2 illustrates the vectorized bin update step with 3 bins and 4-wide SIMD. Since the vector width is four, there are four slots for each bin. Depending on the input values, distinguished by the colors in Fig. 2, we read the corresponding bin values using a gather instruction, increment the bin values, and write the updated bin values using a scatter instruction. Note that the per-SIMD-lane privatization prevents a collision between the 3rd and 4th data elements. Without the privatization, the 3rd bin value would have been incremented twice. After processing the whole input data in this manner, we need to reduce the four simd-lane-private slots into one bin to get the result. When reducing, we simply sum up the private bins using scalar instructions.

Gather-scatter instructions in KNC are particularly useful for skewed inputs because the instructions are faster

N	Number of input elements
M	Number of bins
K	SIMD width, a power of two (4, 8, and 16)
P	Number of threads

Table 1: Abbreviations of important factors.

when fewer cache lines are accessed, resulting in larger SIMD speedups [22]. In SNB, since gather-scatter instructions are not supported, we do not vectorize the bin update step.

3 Histograms with Variable-width Bins

The bin search step with variable-width bins is considerably more involved than that with fixed-width bins. Assuming bin boundaries are sorted, the bin search step is equivalent to the problem of inserting an element into a sorted list; we find the index that corresponds to a given data value by comparing it with bin boundary values. Thus, this step no longer takes a constant time as in the case of fixed-width histograms hence the bin search step is typically the most time consuming. This renders the method for thread-level parallelization (i.e., shared vs. private) a lesser concern because it is easy to parallelize the bin search step without write data sharing.

We consider two approaches of the bin search step for variable-width bins: *binary search* and *partitioning*. The partitioning method resembles quick sort except that we pick pivots differently and that we stop when the input is partially sorted. This partitioning method has execution time asymptotically similar to that of the binary search method, but it scales better with wider SIMD. Therefore, the partitioning method generally outperforms the binary search method in KNC.

3.1 Binary Search

To be scalable with respect to the number of bins, we use binary search for searching bin indices. Its running time is $O(NlogM)$, where N and M denote the number of inputs and bins, respectively (Table 1).

SIMD Parallelization. Binary search can be vectorized and blocked for caches using the algorithm described in Kim *et al.* [17]. We extend their work using SSE instructions to AVX and KNC instructions. The main idea behind vectorizing binary search is increasing the radix of binary search from 2 to K, where K is the SIMD width. Instead of comparing the input value with the median, we execute an SIMD comparison instruction with a K-element vector with M/Kth, $2M/K$th, ..., and $(K-1)M/K$th elements. Consequently, the process becomes K-ary search.

The result of comparison indicates which chunk the data would be in, and we recursively continue the comparison for the chunk. Since the radix of the search tree is K instead of 2, the reduction of the tree height and the corresponding SIMD speedup are both log_2K.

3.2 Partitioning

The partitioning method is based on the partition operation in quicksort. At each step, we pick a pivot value from the bin boundaries for partitioning. At the beginning the median of boundaries is picked as a pivot. Using the pivot, we partition the data into two chunks by reading each element,

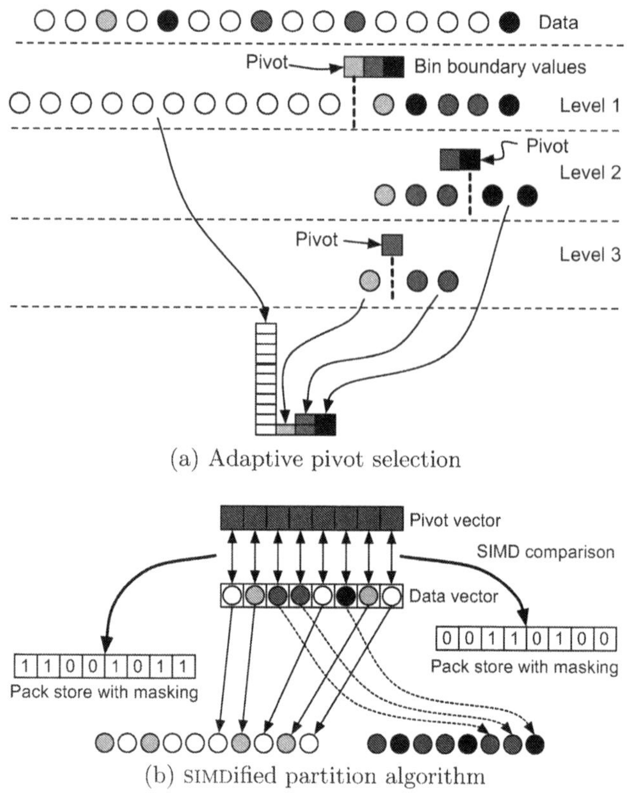

(a) Adaptive pivot selection

(b) SIMDified partition algorithm

Figure 3: Partitioning algorithms for variable-width bins.

comparing it with the pivot, and writing it to one of the chunks according to the comparison. We continue partitioning these two chunks recursively until inputs are partitioned into M chunks. Note that M is the number of histogram bins. Then, histogram bin values are computed by simply counting the number of elements in each chunk.

Although the asymptotic complexity of the partitioning method is the same as the binary search method (if $M \ll N$, which is typically the case), its SIMD speedup, K, is larger than that of the binary search method, log_2K. § 5 shows that this leads to better performance of the partitioning method in KNC that has wide SIMD instructions. This is also facilitated by the following optimization techniques.

Adaptive Partitioning. For the skewed data, we can improve the performance of partition algorithm by selecting the pivot values adapting on the input distribution. The main idea is to prune out a large chunk of data earlier so that we eliminate later operations on that chunk. Fig 3(a) shows how adaptive pivot selection improves performance. In this example, the input data is skewed to the first bin. Thus, we pick the first boundary as a pivot level 1 instead of the median. After partitioning, we do not need to partition the chunk at the left-hand side because all its elements belong to the first bin of histogram. In other words, we prune out the data elements skewed to the first bin at level 1. We apply the normal partitioning algorithm to the other chunk at level 1. Since this chunk is much smaller than the chunk at the left-hand side, the overhead of continuing partitioning it is also small.

The detailed algorithm is as follows. First, we check if the data is skewed. We sample some data elements and build a small histogram using a simple method like binary search. If the input data is skewed to the ith bin, we perform pruning. When $i = 1$ or $i = M$, we partition the data into two chunks. This case is similar to the case in Fig 3(a). Otherwise, we pick the ith and $(i+1)$th boundary values as pivots and partition the data into three chunks: $C1$, $C2$, and $C3$. $C1$ has elements smaller than the ith boundary value, the elements in $C2$ belong to the ith bin, and $C3$ has elements bigger than or equal to the $(i+1)$th boundary value. For $C2$, we count the number of its elements and update the ith bin. We apply the normal partition algorithm to $C1$ and $C3$.

Note that, with high probability, random samples match the overall data pattern. Suppose that $X\%$ of the input falls into ith bin. The number of samples that fall into the bin follows the binomial distribution, which can be approximated as the normal distribution with an enough number of samples. A rule of thumb for the number of samples, n, is that both $n \times X/100$ and $n \times (1 - X/100)$ are greater than 10[9]. Then, with high probability, close to $X\%$ of the samples fall into the bin.

SIMD Parallelization. The partition method can be accelerated by vectorizing the comparison. Fig 3(b) describes how the partition method can be SIMDified. Instead of comparing each element with the pivot, we compare a vector register populated with input data elements to another vector register filled with repeated pivot values. Based on the comparison result, we write each data element to different chunks using an *pack store with masking* instruction (KNC supports this type of instructions [3]). Since SNB does not support such instructions and has narrower SIMD, the binary search method is faster than the partitioning method in SNB.

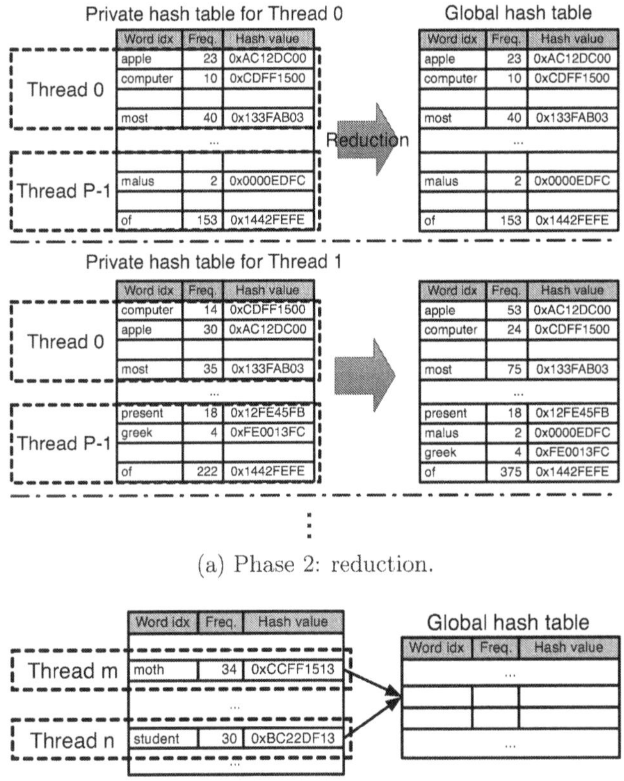

(a) Phase 2: reduction.

(b) Collisions in Phase 2.

Figure 4: Parallel text histogram construction using thread-private hash tables.

4 Histograms with Text Data

For the text histogram, or word counting, we need an associative data structure to represent an unbounded number of bins. We use hash tables each of whose entry records a word and its frequency. The bin search step consists of hashing and probing, and the bin update step increments the frequency in case of hit. This section presents our serial, thread-level parallel, and SIMD implementations of the hash table.

We assume that the whole input text is stored in an one-dimensional byte array, and we preprocess the raw text data to get indices and lengths of words in the input text. The index of a word is the index of the byte array element that contains the first character of the word. As a result, each word is represented by a pair of the index and the length of the word. The input to our algorithm is a list of these pairs. Consequently, this representation of input data can be applied to an arbitrary data type.

4.1 Serial Hash Table Implementation

Our SNB implementation uses a hash function based on the CRC instruction in the SSE instruction set [1, 16]. To the best of our knowledge, this is the fastest hash function for x86 processors with a reasonably high degree of uniformity in distribution [16]. Using the CRC instruction achieves a throughput of 4 characters (one 32-bit word) per instruction.

KNC, however, does not support the SSE instruction set, thus we need to rely on normal ALU instructions. We use `xxHash` that hashes a group of 4 characters at a time with 11 instructions. When implemented in SNB, `xxHash` shows a throughput 1.3 times lower than that of the CRC-based hash function (4.9 GB/s vs. 6.3 GB/s for Xeon E5-2690). Nevertheless, `xxHash` can be SIMDfied for KNC as described in § 4.3.

Based on the formula proposed in the red dragon book [7], the quality measures of hash functions in CRC-based hashing and `xxHash` are 1.02 and 1.01, respectively. An ideal function gives 1, and a hash function with a quality measure below 1.05 is acceptable in practice [16].

Each hash table entry stores the hash value, occurrence frequency, and index of the associated word. For each word, we first compute its hash value. Using the hash value, we obtain the index to a hash table entry. If the entry is empty, the word has not been processed yet, hence we insert a new entry to the table. Otherwise, we check if it is a hit. We compare the hash values first before comparing the word itself and the word stored in the entry to avoid expensive string comparison. For a hit, we increment the frequency field. Otherwise, a collision occurs. We move on to the next entry and repeat the previous steps. Hash collisions are resolved with an open addressing technique with linear probing. This improves cache utilization significantly.

4.2 Thread-Level Parallelization

A straightforward way of parallelizing text histogram construction would be using a concurrent hash table, such as `unordered_map` in Intel TBB [28]. However, such shared hash tables incur a lot of transactional overhead induced by atomic read, insert, update, and delete operations. Since we do not use the data stored in the hash table in the middle of histogram construction and we are only interested in the final result stored in the hash table, text histogram construction can exploit a *thread-private hash table.*

Each thread maintains its own private hash table during histogram construction, and each thread takes care of some portion of the input. After processing all the input data, we reduce private hash tables to a single hash table. Using thread-private hash tables, we achieve better scalability. We avoid expensive atomic operations and coherent cache misses that are introduced by a shared hash table.

Our parallel text histogram construction consists of two phases: private histogram construction and reduction. Assume that there are P threads. In the private histogram construction phase, each thread takes a chunk of input data and builds its own private hash table. No synchronization is required between threads.

In the reduction phase (Phase 2 in Fig. 4(a)), the thread-private hash tables are reduced to a single global hash table that contains the desired histogram. Note that we cannot perform entry-wise addition of multiple private hash tables in the reduction phase. For example, the first entry of Thread 0's table in Fig. 4(b) corresponds to a word "apple", whereas that of Thread 1's table corresponds to "computer" (it is the word for the second entry in Thread 0's table). This happens when the words "computer" and "apple" incur hash collisions and threads 0 and 1 encounter the two words in a different order.

To exploit thread-level parallelism in the reduction phase, we divide each private table into P chunks. Each thread takes a chunk of table entries and reduces them into the global table. The reduction procedure is similar to that of building a private hash table with the following differences:

1. No need to recalculate hash values because they are already stored in the source.
2. For a hit in the global table, we add the frequency of the source entry to that of the global entry.
3. Needs some atomic instructions to insert a new entry into the global table. Fig. 4(c) illustrates this issue. Two different threads m and n are trying to insert different words into the same entry in the global table. This happens when the global table does not have both words yet. To ensure atomicity, we use the compare-and-swap instruction.

Note that atomic instructions, such as compare-and-swap, are not needed to update frequency field for a hit. The case when two different threads update the same entry never occurs because there are no duplicated entries for a single word in the private hash table. Thus, each thread always works on a different word.

4.3 SIMD Parallelization

Vectorization of the hash table manipulation involves the following non-trivial challenges: First, the length of words varies unlike numerical data. We consider two vectorization techniques for such variable-length data. One is vectorization within a word (i.e., horizontal vectorization), while the other is vectorization across words (i.e., vertical vectorization). The horizontal vectorization wastes a significant fraction of vector lanes when many words are shorter than the

```
hashval = init
for i from 0 to length - 1 {
  part = text[wordIdx + i]
  hashval = Hash(hashval, part)
}
```

(a) A hash function using scalar instructions.

```
hashval_vec = init_vec
for i from 0 to max(length_vec) - 1 {
  valid_mask = compare(length_vec, i, LEQ)
  part_vec = gather(valid_mask ,text, wordIdx_vec + i)
  hashval_vec = SIMDHash(valid_mask, v_hashval, part_vec)
}
```

(b) A vectorized hash function.

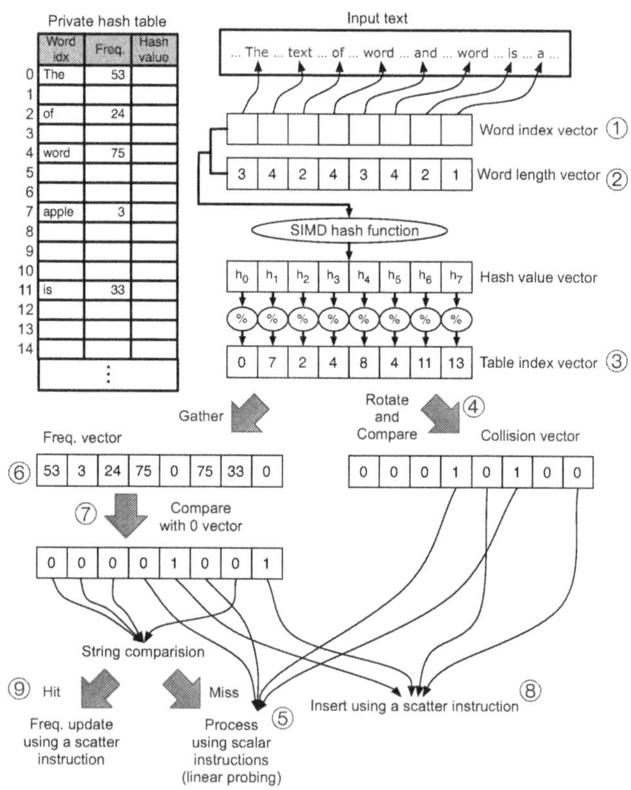

(c) Vectorized hash table manipulation.

Figure 5: SIMD optimization of text histogram construction.

vector width. It involves cross-SIMD operations that have long latencies, such as permutation. Thus, vertical vectorization typically performs better but with its own challenge of dealing with differences in the length of words. In Xeon Phi, most vector operations support masking that is very helpful to address this challenge.

Second, memory access patterns are irregular. Words are placed in scattered locations, and the ability to efficiently access non-consecutive memory locations is essential. The gather and scatter instructions supported by Xeon Phi also play a critical role in addressing this challenge. Therefore, we limit our SIMD parallelization to the vertical vectorization technique on KNC only.

SIMD hash functions. Fig. 5(a) shows the pseudo code for a scalar hash function. This is our baseline. The hash function consists of two operations: loading a portion of the word (line 3) and computing the hash value (line 4). These two operations are repeatedly executed until we process the entire word. Thus, number of iterations equals the length of the word (line 2).

The vectorized hash function is conceptually similar to the scalar one and shown in Fig. 5(b). Each SIMD lane holds a portion of different words. The hash value is computed using the same equation as that of the scalar implementation, but operating on 16 words per function call. Note that the portions of different words are stored in scattered memory locations. To load these different portions, we use a gather instruction (line 4). Its second argument specifies the base address, and the third argument is used as a offset vector. With the gather instruction, we compose $part_{vec}$ with the values stored at $text + wordIdx_{vec}[0] + i$, ..., $text + wordIdx_{vec}[15] + i$. We iterate until the loop index exceeds the length of the longest word (line 2). To avoid unnecessary computation and gather instructions for shorter words, we mask out the corresponding SIMD lanes. The mask is obtained by comparing the lengths of the words and the loop index (line 3). If the loop index is bigger than the length of a word, the corresponding SIMD lane is masked out. This SIMDification technique speeds up our hash function 6.3–10.7 times.

SIMDified hash table manipulation. The algorithm for hash table manipulation can also be vectorized using gather and scatter instructions. Fig. 5(c) illustrates the vectorized version of the algorithm described § 4.1. This vectorization algorithm focuses on vectorizing the insertion operation to the hash table and the case of a hit.

The word index vector (①) and length vector (②) are inputs to the SIMD hash function. We access the table entries using the table index vector (③) obtained after calling the SIMD hash function.

Our SIMDification is subject to SIMD lane collisions: i.e., two SIMD lanes may try to access the same hash table entry simultaneously. To avoid this, we check if there exists a collision between SIMD lanes by comparing all pairs of SIMD lane values (④). We do not vectorize the case of a collision because collisions occur very rarely. We observe that less than 0.5% of hash table accesses result in collisions. We process them using scalar instructions (⑤).

After obtaining the frequency vector (⑥) using a gather instruction with the table index vector, we check if the corresponding hash table entries are empty (⑦). If the entry is empty and there is no collision, we insert a new entry using a scatter instruction (⑧). To check for a hash table hit, we perform string comparison. If a hit, we update the frequency using a scatter instruction (⑨). Otherwise we process the case using scalar instructions (⑤). This SIMDification technique speeds up our thread-private hash table manipulation 1.1–1.2 times.

	Intel SNB	Intel KNC
Sockets×Cores×SMT	2×8×2	1×60×4
Clock (GHz)	2.9	1.05
L1/L2/L3 Cache (KB)	32 / 256 / 20,480	32 / 512 / -
SIMD Width (Bits)	128 (SSE), 256 (AVX)	512
Single Precision GFLOP/s	742	2,016
STREAM Bandwidth (GB/s)	76	150

Table 2: Target architecture specification.

Best Performance (GUPS)		Fixed-width		Variable-width	
Input	# of Bins	SNB	KNC	SNB	KNC
Uniform	256	13	17	4.7	5.3
	32K	6.3	0.98	1.7	0.52
Skewed (Zipf α=2)	256	13	18	4.6	9.7
	32K	12	11	2.7	0.83

Table 3: Performance summary for numerical histograms.

5 Experimental Results

Two processor architectures that this paper evaluates are summarized in Table 2, and more details are as follows:

Intel Xeon E5-2690 (Sandy Bridge EP). This architecture features a super-scalar, out-of-order micro-architecture supporting 2-way hyper-threading. It has 256 bit-wide (i.e., 8-wide single-precision) SIMD units that execute the AVX instruction set. This architecture has 6 functional units [1]. Three of them are used for computation (ports 0,1, and 5), and the others are used for memory operations (ports 2 and 3 for load, and ports 2-4 for store). While three arithmetic instructions can be executed in parallel ideally, AVX vector instructions have limited port bindings and typically up to 2 AVX instructions can be executed in a cycle.

Intel Xeon Phi 5110P coprocessor (Knights Corner). This architecture features many in-order cores, each with 4-way simultaneous multithreading support to hide memory and multi-cycle instruction latency. To maximize area and energy efficiency, these cores are less aggressive: i.e., they have lower single-thread instruction throughput than the SNB core and run at a lower frequency. However, each core has 512-bit vector registers, and its SIMD unit executes 16-wide single-precision SIMD instructions. KNC has a dual-issue pipeline that allows prefetches and scalar instructions to be co-issued with vector operations in the same cycle [3, 14].

5.1 Numerical Histograms

We use 128M single precision floating point numbers (i.e., 512 MB data) as the input. We run histogram construction 10 times and report the average execution time. We use Intel® compiler 13.0.1 and OpenMP for parallelization.

Table 3 lists the best histogramming performance (in billion bin updates per second, GUPS) for each input type and

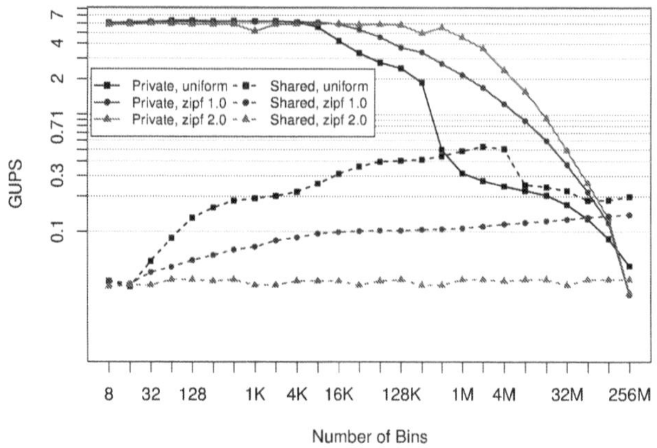

Figure 6: Comparison of private and shared bins in SNB for fixed-width bins.

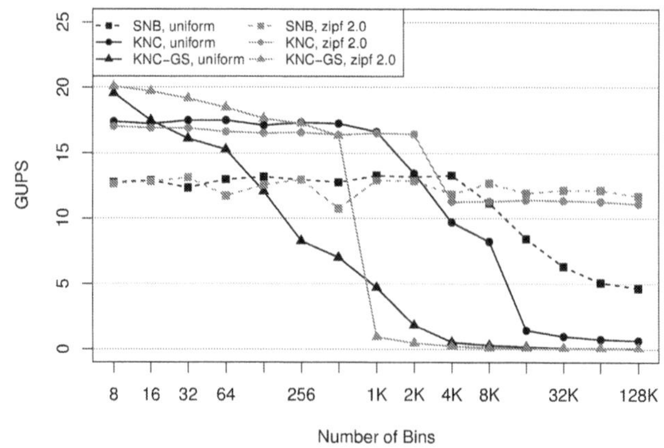

Figure 7: Performance for private bins in SNB and KNC with fixed-width bins.

target architecture. As expected, fixed-width histogramming is faster, but the gap is not so large because the latter provides opportunity to utilize the increasing ratio of compute to memory bandwidth in modern processors (e.g., exploiting wide SIMD). For more bins, the performance drops due to increasing cache misses (both with fixed-width and variable-width bins) and increasing compute complexity (with variable-width bins). When the input data are skewed (here, a Zipf distribution with parameter α=2), the performance improves due to increasing temporal locality of accessing bins (fixed-width and variable-width bins) and the partitioning with adaptive pivot selection method used for variable-width bins in KNC.

For 256 fixed-width bins, KNC outperforms SNB, and the gap widens with skewed inputs. For 32K bins and uniform random inputs, KNC becomes slower than SNB, when the private bins do not fit on-chip caches in KNC, while they do in SNB. The trend is similar with variable-width bins. The following sections provide more detailed analyses of experimental results.

5.1.1 Numerical histograms with Fixed-width Bins

This section presents experimental data for histograms with fixed-width bins. We show the impact of two different data distributions: uniform random and Zipf.

Comparison between private and shared bins. Fig. 6 compares the performance of private bins with that of shared bins on SNB when 16 threads are used. The y-axis is in the logarithmic scale. The black lines of Fig. 6 shows the performances for the data in a uniform randomly distribution. When the number of bins is small, the private bin method is considerably faster than the shared bin method. When increasing the number of bins, the performance of private bins does not change until 4K bins (16 KB per thread and 32 KB per core) when the total size of bins reaches the L1 cache capacity (32 KB). For 512K bins, their total size exceeds the shared L3, resulting in an abrupt drop. At this point, the performance of shared bins becomes better than that of private bins. The performance of private bins continuously decreases due to the reduction overhead caused by many private bins. The performance of shared bins is proportional to the number of bins up to 4M bins because the contention to the same bin between different threads is being reduced. Similar to the case of private bins, we find an abrupt drop at 4M bins because of the L3 cache capacity misses.

To see the effect of skewness on the performance, we use data in Zipf distributions [11]. The degree of skewness in a Zipf distribution is denoted by α. The bigger it is, the more the distribution is skewed. The frequency of a value in a Zipf distribution varies as a power of α (i.e., the frequency follows a power law), and the distribution is skewed towards small values. In this figure, we use Zipf distributions with α values 1 and 2. For $\leq$4K bins, the input distribution does not affect the performance of private bins because L1 caches can hold the working set. Otherwise, the private bin method performs better with skewed inputs than with the uniform distribution; because of the skewness, fewer cache misses occur.

In contrast, the shared bin method performs worse with skewed inputs because of coherence misses. Another reason is that more contention to the same bins between different threads results in more memory access serialization.

Scalability of private and shared bins. When private bins are used, thread-level scalability is closely related with the LLC capacity. When the total size of private bins is smaller than the LLC and $\leq$4 threads are used, the performance scales almost linearly. However, using >4 threads increases LLC misses and degrades the performance for both of SNB and KNC.

When shared bins are used (only for SNB), we also need to consider the likelihood of contention between threads to the same bin (through atomic instructions) and coherence misses. For 4K bins, the degree of bin sharing between private caches in different threads is large, hence performing worse than the sequential version. For a larger number of bins, the degree of sharing is smaller, and, in contrast to the private bin case, using more threads does not incur more LLC (i.e., L3) misses. Therefore, for larger number of bins, the method with shared bins provides modest speedups ($\sim$2×) with 8 cores and performs better than the private bin method.

Performance. Fig. 7 shows the performance of our histogram algorithms for fixed-width bins. Algorithms used for SNB, KNC, and KNC-GS are described in §2. Both SNB

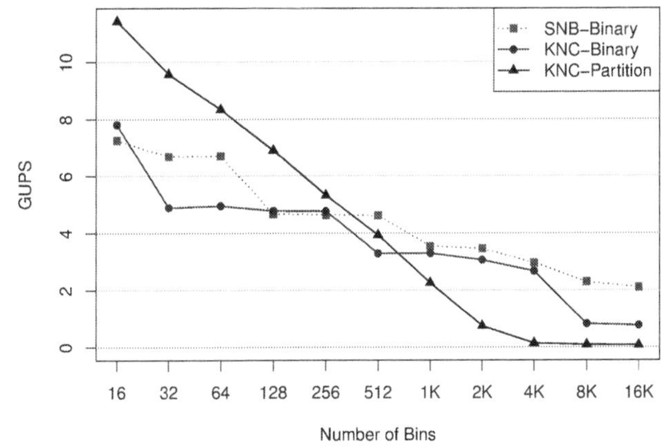

Figure 8: Performance in SNB and KNC for variable-width bins and uniform randomly distributed inputs.

and KNC use private bins here. KNC-GS is the case when KNC uses gather-scatter instructions. Both KNC and KNC-GS use four threads per core (total 240 threads), and SNB uses two threads per core (total 32). We vary the number of bins.

Black lines in Fig. 7 shows the performance for data in uniform distribution. For common cases where ≤2K bins are used, KNC performs better than SNB. For larger number of bins, SNB exploits the cache capacity per thread bigger than KNC. The performance of KNC starts dropping at 2K bins (8 KB) because four threads per core fully utilize the capacity of the L1 cache (32 KB).

For all cases but 8 and 16 bins with data in uniform distribution, KNC is faster than KNC-GS. Since a single scatter instruction updates 16 data simultaneously in KNC-GS [22], it uses 16 copies of the same original bin to avoid data conflicts, and later reduces them. These 16 copies reside in the same cache line. This implies that a single gather-scatter instruction accesses 16 different cache lines in the worst case. However, when the number of bins is smaller under the uniform random distribution, the gather-scatter is more likely to access the same cache line. This is the reason why KNC-GS is faster than KNC at 8 and 16 bins. When the input is skewed, KNC-GS can perform better in a wider range of number of bins as will be shown shortly.

To see the effect of skewness on the performance of each algorithms, we use Zipf distribution with $\alpha = 2$ in this experiment. For the data in the Zipf distribution, the result of KNC-GS is worth noticing. The performance of KNC-GS for the Zipf distribution is better than KNC and SNB for ≤512 bins. Note that the performance of KNC-GS for the uniform distribution is better than KNC and SNB only up to 16 bins. Similar to the case of the uniform distribution, gather-scatter instructions are likely to access fewer cache lines with fewer bins. When the distribution is skewed, gather-scatter instructions are likely to access even fewer cache lines. This accounts for the reason why KNC-GS is better than KNC and SNB up to 512 bins with the Zipf distribution, instead of 16 bins as with the uniform distribution. We believe that histogramming ≤512 bins for skewed inputs captures an important common case.

5.1.2 *Numerical histograms with Variable-width Bins*

This section discusses the result for a histogram with variable-width bins. Since the thread-level scalability of our algorithms is almost linear, we skip the discussion of the thread-level scalability.

Data in the uniform random distribution. Fig. 8 shows the performance of our algorithms for a histogram with variable-width bins and the data in the uniform random distribution. The binary search and partitioning algorithms described in §3.1 and §3.2 are used in this experiment. Note that the partitioning algorithm is not implemented for SNB because SNB does not support instructions to efficiently vectorize it, namely unpack load and pack store.

For ≤256 bins, KNC-Partition performs the best. The performance of the binary search algorithm discontinuously drops at every point where the number of bins is a power of the SIMD width (say K). This is because the binary search algorithm uses the same complete SIMD K-ary search tree even though the number of bins are different. For example, the algorithm shows the same performance at 128 and 512 bins because both cases need complete 8-ary binary search trees with the same height of 3. However, for >256 bins, KNC-Partition is slower than SNB-Binary or KNC-Binary because its execution time partly scales linearly as more bins are used, instead of scaling logarithmically. As explained in §3.2, the time complexity of the partitioning method is $O(NlogM + \frac{N}{B}M)$, where the second term corresponds to counting the number of elements in each chunk at the end of processing each block with size B. In order to avoid cache misses, B is limited to the on-chip cache capacity, resulting in the execution time proportional to the number of bins when many bins are used.

Note that the performance of SNB-Binary is competitive with that reported in Kim et. al [17], which is known to be the fastest tree search method. For 64K bins, they report 0.28 GUPS using SSE instructions, while 1.2 GUPS is achieved with the version of our implementation that uses the same SSE instructions. If normalized to the same clock frequency and the number of cores, their performances are similar.

For 256 bins, SNB-Binary is 2.2× faster than the binary search method implemented using scalar instructions in SNB (i.e., SIMD speedup in SNB is 2.2×). The same speedup in KNC is larger (4.0×) due to wider SIMD. The SIMD speedup of KNC-Partition is 15×, which exhibits the scalability of the partitioning method with respect to SIMD width.

For >256 bins, SNB-Binary is faster than KNC-Binary, which is caused by different cache organizations. First, the cache capacity per thread is smaller in KNC, when both KNC and SNB fully use their hardware threads: L1 capacity per thread is 8 KB in KNC and 16 KB in SNB. Second, SNB has a shared L3, which efficiently stores the read-only tree shared among threads.

Data in Zipf distributions. Fig. 9 shows the performance of our algorithm with variable-width bins and inputs in Zipf distributions. In addition to the binary search and basic partitioning methods, we use the partitioning method that performs the adaptive pivot selection described in §3.2 once at the top partitioning level. We can observe that the input distribution does not noticeably affect the performance of binary search, by comparing Fig. 8 and 9.

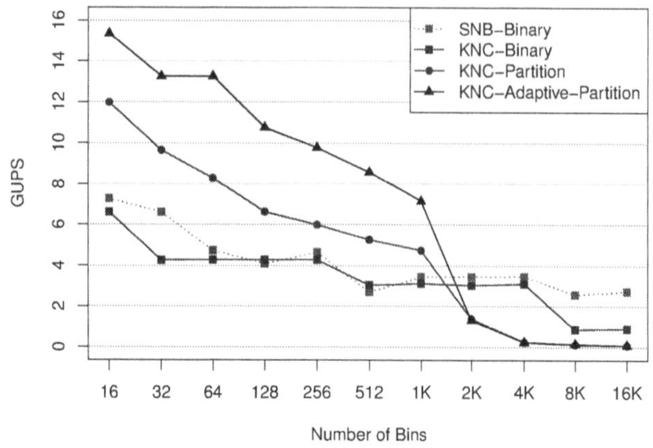

Figure 9: Performance in SNB and KNC for variable-width bins and inputs in Zipf distributions.

	Wikipedia	Genome
Size (MB)	116	192
Word occurrence (10^6)	16.7	16.7
Distinct word occurrence (10^6)	3.4	10.4
Average length of word	4.9	9
Distribution	Zipf	Near Uniform random

Table 4: Input data used for the text histogram.

KNC-Partition with Zipf distributions in Fig. 9 is significantly faster than KNC-Partition with the uniform distribution in Fig. 8 for ≤1K bins and slightly faster for >1K bins. The skewness of the input data affects the partitioning step, and it is more likely to happen that all the elements in the SIMD vector being partitioned are less than the pivot, resulting in a single partition. This in turn reduces the number of memory writes and improves performance.

For ≤1K bins, KNC-Adaptive-Partition performs the best, which shows the effectiveness of our adaptive pivot selection. For >1K bins, the linear performance scaling with respect to the number of bins overwhelms the performance.

5.2 Text Histograms

This section describes the performance of our text histogram implementation with the input data described in Table 4. **Wikipedia** is a text corpus obtained from the Wikipedia website [4], which is commonly used to evaluate word count applications [13, 35]. We select 2^{24} words excluding meta language tags, and the length of words follows Zipf distribution. **Genome** is a collection of fixed-length strings extracted from human DNA sequences (the same number of words extracted as that of **Wikipedia**). **Genome** is much less skewed (close to the uniform distribution) and has more distinct words than **Wikipedia**.

Fig. 10 shows the execution time break down of various text histogram construction techniques. SNB in Fig. 10 corresponds to the thread-level parallelization technique described in §4.2 on SNB. It uses two threads per core (total 32 threads). KNC-SCALAR corresponds to the same thread-level parallelization technique on KNC with 4 threads per core, total 240 threads. KNC-VECTORIZED is the vectorized version presented in §4.3 on KNC.

For **Wikipedia**, throughputs are 342.4 MWPS (million words per second), 209.7 MWPS, and 401.4 MWPS with SNB, KNC-SCALAR, and KNC-VECTORIZED, respectively. For **Genome**, throughputs are 104.9 MWPS, 93.7 MWPS, 142.2 MWPS with SNB, KNC-SCALAR, and KNC-VECTORIZED, respectively. KNC-VECTORIZED is faster than SNB by 1.17× for **Wikipedia** and 1.36× for **Genome**.

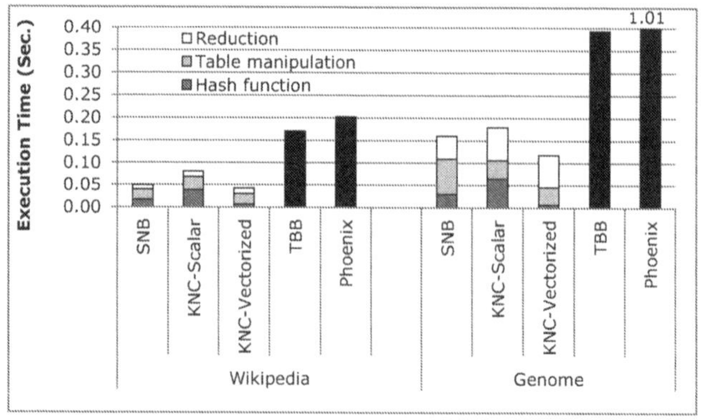

Figure 10: Execution time break down of the text histogram construction.

Lower throughputs are achieved for **Genome** because (1) it has a longer average word length that leads to longer hash function time, and (2) it has more distinct words and is less skewed resulting in longer table manipulation and reduction time.

The hash function time of SNB is 2.1–2.2× faster than that of KNC-SCALAR because (1) a CRC-based hash function is used in SNB, which is 1.3× faster than **xxHash** in SNB, and (2) SNB is faster than KNC when executing scalar instructions. Nevertheless, KNC-VECTORIZED achieves 6.3× and 10.7× SIMD speedups for each input set, resulting in 2.8× and 5.0× faster hash function times than SNB. The SIMD speedup for **Wikipedia** is lower than that of **Genome** because the varying length of words incurs inefficiencies in SIMDification. The result implies the possibility of accelerating other hash-based applications using Xeon Phi.

Compared to hash function computation, hash table manipulation is a memory intensive task, resulting in ≤ 1.2× SIMD speedups. Optimizations with gather/scatter instructions are also limited because hash table manipulation accesses scattered memory locations. In contrast, the hash function access contiguous memory locations.

6 Related Work

When shared data are updated in an unpredictable pattern, a straightforward parallelization scheme is using atomic operations, such as compare-and-swap and fetch-and-add [30]. If the computation associated with updates is associative, we can use the privatization and reduction approach [27] to avoid the cost of atomic operations. In histogramming, we show that the approach with atomic operations can be faster when the target architecture provides a shared LLC and private bins overflow the LLC. We envision that the transactional memory feature [29] (available in the Haswell architecture) will provide yet another option, particularly useful when the number of bins is large so that the probability of conflict is low.

Since parallelizing histogram is challenging particularly at the SIMD level, hardware supports have been proposed [6, 20]. In the gather-linked-and-scatter-conditional proposal [20], scatter-conditional succeeds only for the SIMD lanes that have not been modified after the previous gather-linked (i.e., a vector version of load-linked and store-conditional). The updates for the unsuccessful parts can be retried through the mask bits resulted from the scatter-conditional.

The following sections compare our approach with related work on CPUs and GPUs. We measure the performance of the related work on CPUs on the Intel SNB machine used in §5.

6.1 Comparison with related work on CPUs

Fixed-width numerical histograms. We first compare our approach with Intel® Integrated Performance Primitives (IPP), a widely used library for multi-media processing that is highly optimized for x86 architectures [33]. To exploit thread-level parallelism with IPP, OpenMP parallel section is used with private bins for numerical histograms. Since methods with private bins scale well when bins fit in the LLC, we compare single-threaded performance with small enough number of bins.

For 256 fixed-width bins, our approach achieves comparable performance (ours 1.2 vs. IPP 1.1 GUPS). Since IPP supports only 8 or 16-bit integers (`ippiHistogramEven` function), we use 16-bit integers as inputs for both. Even though IPP does not support more than 65536 bins yet, our implementation will outperform IPP when there are many bins (with shared bins) or when KNCs are used (with gather-scatter instructions) because ours is optimized for multiple input types and target architectures.

Variable-width numerical histograms. For 256 and 32K variable-width bins, 11× speedup is realized: we achieve 0.22 and 0.086 GUPS respectively, while IPP achieves 0.02 and 0.008 GUPS.

In addition, we compare our implementation with R, a widely used tool for statistical computation [15]. We measure the performance of the `hist` function in R by specifying `breaks` vector that represents the bin boundary. We compare the result with our variable-width method because the `hist` function does not support the fixed-width method explicitly. We also compare the result with the single core performance of our implementation because multi-threaded extension of the `hist` function is not supported in R. For 256 and 32K bins, our implementation is 200× and 40× faster than R, respectively.

Text histograms. We compare our approach with Intel Thread Building Block [28], and Phoenix, a MapReduce framework for SMP [35]. We run them on SNB (shown in Fig. 10).

In TBB, we use `concurrent_unordered_map` because it is faster than `concurrent_hash_map`, and we do not need concurrent removes for word count. We do not measure the pre-processing time of converting character buffers to C++ `strings`, and only measure the histogram construction time. TBB is 3.46× and 2.45× slower than our SNB implementation for `Wikipedia` and `Genome`, respectively. The larger speedup for `Wikipedia` is from fewer bins and skewed data that result in more contention when a shared data structure is used. A similar behavior is observed with fixed-width numerical histograms, where the private method becomes faster relative to the shared method with fewer bins or skewed data.

For PHOENIX, we use the word count example provided in the PHOENIX suite. For fair comparison, we measure the time for *reduce* phase only, excluding *map*, merge, and sort phases. PHOENIX is 4.12× and 6.29× slower than our SNB implementation.

6.2 Comparison with related work on GPUs

Numerical histograms. We also compare our result on KNC with previous work using GPU, `TRISH` [10] and `Cuda-histogram` [26]. For the 128 fixed-width bins with 32-bit input data, `TRISH` shows about 19 GUPS on GTX 480 while our implementation shows 17 GUPS. `TRISH` does not support more than 256 bins. `Cuda-histogram` does not report numbers for the 32-bit input data. They only reported numbers for 8-bit input data for less than 256 bins. On the other hand, for more than 256 bins, our implementation (17 GUPS) outperforms `Cuda-histogram` (12-16 GUPS) on Tesla M2070.

Overall, GPU-based implementations do not show competitive performance consistently for a wide range of input types, and also are restrictive with respect to the input type and the number of bins. They use private bins that are later reduced. For fast memory accesses, GPU shared memory has to be used, and, due to its limited capacity, the maximum number of private bins each thread can have is 85.

Therefore, in 256-bin implementations, a group of threads share bins and update them via atomic instructions, resulting in slowdown. In contrast, our histogram implementation supports various bin and input element types (although single-precision floating point numbers are mostly evaluated in this paper, our library also supports other types).

There are other work on histogram construction on GPU but with slower performance than `TRISH` and `Cuda-histogram`. NVIDIA Performance Primitives (NPP) provide a parallel histogram implementation, but it only supports byte inputs and a limited number of fixed-width bins [23]. Gregg and Hazelwood [12] report the performance of NPP histogram implementation as 2.6 GUPS for unit-width bins with [0, 64) and [0, 256) ranges in Tesla C2050. Shams and Kennedy [32] overcome the limitation of the NPP histogram implementation such as a limited number of bins by scanning the input multiple times. Each time it updates a subset of bins. With 8800 GTX, they report 2.8 GUPS for 256 bins, but the performance drops quickly as more bins are used: e.g., 0.64 GUPS for 3K bins.

Text histograms. We compare our approach with MARS, a MapReduce framework on GPUs [13]. We use a word count implementation provided in MARS. It does not have a *reduce* phase. Instead, *group* phase processes the result of the *map* phase and gives the number of each word. Thus, we measure the execution time of the *group* phase only on NVIDIA GTX 480 for fair comparison.

It is 107× and 127× slower than our KNC-VECTORIZED implementation for `Wikipedia` and `Genome`, respectively. Note that MARS sorts the result of its *map* phase in the *group* phase. This results in a significant overhead.

7 Conclusions and Future Work

This paper presents *versatile* and *scalable* histogram methods that achieve competitive performances across a wide range of input types and target architectures via scalability with respect to the number of cores and SIMD width. We expect that a large fraction of techniques presented in this paper can be applied to more general reduction-heavy computations whose parallelization strategy is likely to be similar. We also show that, when the increasing compute density of modern processors are efficiently utilized, the performance gap between fixed-width and variable-width histogramming can become as small as ~2× for 256 bins, encouraging variable-width histogramming that can represent the input distribution more precisely. We show that many-core Intel® Xeon Phi™ coprocessors can achieve >2× throughput than dual socket Xeon® processors for variable-width histograms, where instructions that facilitate efficient vectorization, such as gather-scatter and unpack load-pack store, play key roles. The gather-scatter instructions also greatly help speedup the hash function time in text histogram construction, and the same SIMD hash function implementation can be applied to other data-intensive applications that use hash functions.

Based on the techniques presented in this paper, we implemented a publicly available histogram library [2]. We will improve the library so that it will be able to adapt at run time to a variety of different input types and target architectures. This library will significantly alleviate the burden of programmers in writing efficient histogramming code. We showed that our method for text histogram construction outperforms word counting implemented in Phoenix (a MapReduce framework for SMP), and we expect that our method can be applied to the reduce phase of other MapReduce applications.

8 Acknowledgements

This work was supported by the National Research Foundation of Korea (NRF) grant funded by the Korea government (MSIP) (No. 2013R1A3A2003664). ICT at Seoul National University provided research facilities for this study.

References

[1] Intel® 64 and IA-32 Architectures Optimization Reference Manual. http://www.intel.com/content/dam/doc/manual/64-ia-32-architectures-optimization-manual.pdf.

[2] Adaptive Historgram Template Library. https://github.com/pcjung/AHTL.

[3] Intel® Xeon Phi™ Coprocessor Instruction Set Architecture Reference Manual. http://software.intel.com/sites/default/files/forum/278102/327364001en.pdf.

[4] Wikipedia:Database download. http://en.wikipedia.org/wiki/Wikipedia:Database_download.

[5] S. Agarwal, A. Panda, B. Mozafari, A. P. Iyer, S. Madden, and I. Stoica. Blink and It's Done: Interactive Queries on Very Large Data. In *International Conference on Very Large Data Bases (VLDB)*, 2012.

[6] J. H. Ahn, M. Erez, and W. J. Dally. Scatter-Add in Data Parallel Architectures. In *International Symposium on High-Performance Computer Architecture (HPCA)*, 2005.

[7] A. V. Aho, M. S. Lam, R. Sethi, and J. D. Ullman. *Compilers: principles, techniques, & tools*, volume 1009. Pearson/Addison Wesley, 2007.

[8] G. A. Baxes. *Digital Image Processing: Principles and Applications*. Wiley, 1994.

[9] L. D. Brown, T. T. Cai, and A. DasGupta. Interval estimation for a binomial proportion. *Statistical Science*, 16(2):101–133, 05 2001.

[10] S. Brown and J. Snoeyink. Modestly faster histogram computations on GPUs. In *Innovative Parallel Computing (InPar), 2012*, 2012.

[11] J. Gray, P. Sundaresan, S. Englert, K. Baclawski, and P. J. Weinberger. Quickly Generating Billion-Record Synthetic Databases. In *International Conference on Management of Data (SIGMOD)*, 1994.

[12] C. Gregg and K. Hazelwood. Where is the Data? Why You Cannot Debate CPU vs. GPU Performance Without the Answer. In *International Performance Analysis of Systems and Software (ISPASS)*, 2011.

[13] B. He, W. Fang, Q. Luo, N. K. Govindaraju, and T. Wang. Mars: a mapreduce framework on graphics processors. In *Proceedings of the 17th international conference on Parallel architectures and compilation techniques*, pages 260–269. ACM, 2008.

[14] A. Heinecke, K. Vaidyanathan, M. Smelyanskiy, A. Kobotov, R. Dubtsov, G. Henry, A. G. Shet, G. Chrysos, and P. Dubey. Design and Implementation of the Linpack Benchmark for Single and Multi-Node Systems Based on Intel® Xeon Phi™ Coprocessor. In *IEEE International Parallel and Distributed Processing Systems (IPDPS)*, 2013.

[15] R. Ihaka and R. Gentleman. R: A language for data analysis and graphics. *Journal of computational and graphical statistics*, 5(3), 1996.

[16] P. Kankowski. Hash functions: An empirical comparison. http://www.strchr.com/hash_functions.

[17] C. Kim, J. Chhugani, N. Satish, E. Sedlar, A. D. Nguyen, T. Kaldewey, V. W. Lee, S. A. Brandt, and P. Dubey. FAST: Fast Architecture Sensitive Tree Search on Modern CPUs and GPUs. In *International Conference on Management of Data (SIGMOD)*, 2010.

[18] C. Kim, T. Kaldewey, V. W. Lee, E. Sedlar, A. D. Nguyen, N. Satish, J. Chhugani, A. D. Blas, and P. Dubey. Sort vs. Hash Revisited: Fast Join Implementation on Modern Multi-Core CPUs. In *International Conference on Very Large Data Bases (VLDB)*, 2009.

[19] C. Kim, J. Park, N. Satish, H. Lee, P. Dubey, and J. Chhugani. CloudRAMSort: Fast and Efficient Large-Scale Distributed RAM Sort on Shared-Nothing Cluster. In *International Conference on Management of Data (SIGMOD)*, 2012.

[20] S. Kumar, D. Kim, M. Smelyanskiy, Y.-K. Chen, J. Chhugani, C. J. Hughes, C. Kim, V. W. Lee, and A. D. Nguyen. Atomic Vector Operations on Chip Multiprocessors. In *International Symposium on Computer Architecture (ISCA)*, pages 441–452, 2008.

[21] P. Lofti-Kamran, B. Grot, M. Ferdman, S. Volos, O. Kocberber, J. Picorel, A. Adileh, D. Jevdjic, S. Idgunji, E. Ozer, and B. Falsafi. Scale-Out Processors. In *International Symposium on Computer Architecture (ISCA)*, 2012.

[22] J. Park, P. T. P. Tang, M. Smelyanskiy, D. Kim, and T. Benson. Efficient Backprojection-based Synthetic Aperture Radar Computation with Many-core Processors. In *International Conference for High Performance Computing, Networking, Storage and Analysis (SC)*, 2012.

[23] V. Pdlozhnyuk. Histogram calculation in CUDA. http://docs.nvidia.com/cuda/samples/3_Imaging/histogram/doc/histogram.pdf.

[24] K. Pearson. Contributions to the Mathematical Theory of Evolution. II. Skew Variation in Homogeneous Material. *Philosophical Transactions of the Royal Society of London*, 186, 1895.

[25] V. Poosala, P. J. Haas, Y. E. Ioannidis, and E. J. Shekita. Improved Histograms for Selectivity Estimation of Range Predicates. In *International Conference on Management of Data (SIGMOD)*, 1996.

[26] T. Rantalaiho. Generalized Histograms for CUDA-capable GPUs. https://github.com/trantalaiho/Cuda-Histogram.

[27] L. Rauchwerger and D. A. Padua. The LRPD Test: Speculative Run-Time Parallelization of Loops with Privatization and Reduction Parallelization. *IEEE Transactions on Parallel and Distributed Systems*, 10(2), 1999.

[28] J. Reinders. *Intel Threading Building Blocks: Outfitting C++ for Multi-core Processor Parallelism.*

[29] J. Reinders. Transactional Synchronization in Haswell. http://software.intel.com/en-us/blogs/2012/02/07/transactional-synchronization-in-haswell.

[30] J. W. Romein. An Efficient Work-Distribution Strategy for Gridding Radio-Telescope Data on GPUs. In *International Conference on Supercomputing (ICS)*, 2012.

[31] N. Satish, C. Kim, J. Chhugani, A. D. Nguyen, V. W. Lee, D. Kim, and P. Dubey. Fast Sort on CPUs and GPUs: A Case for Bandwidth Oblivious SIMD Sort. In *International Conference on Management of Data (SIGMOD)*, 2010.

[32] R. Shams and R. A. Kennedy. Efficient Histogram Algorithms for NVIDIA CUDA Compatible Devices. In *International Conference on Signal Processing and Communication Systems*, 2007.

[33] S. Taylor. *Optimizing Applications for Multi-Core Processors, Using the Intel Integrated Performance Primitives.* 2007.

[34] W. Wang, H. Jiang, H. Lu, and J. X. Yu. Bloom Histogram: Path Selectivity Estimation for XML Data with Updates. In *International Conference on Very Large Data Bases (VLDB)*, 2004.

[35] R. M. Yoo, A. Romano, and C. Kozyrakis. Phoenix rebirth: Scalable mapreduce on a large-scale shared-memory system. In *Workload Characterization, 2009. IISWC 2009. IEEE International Symposium on*, pages 198–207. IEEE, 2009.

Bitwise Data Parallelism in Regular Expression Matching

Robert D. Cameron, Thomas C. Shermer, Arrvindh Shriraman,
Kenneth S. Herdy, Dan Lin, Benjamin R. Hull, Meng Lin
School of Computing Science
Simon Fraser University
Surrey, British Columbia
{cameron,shermer,ashriram,ksherdy,lindanl,bhull,linmengl}@sfu.ca

ABSTRACT

A new parallel algorithm for regular expression matching is developed and applied to the classical grep (global regular expression print) problem. Building on the bitwise data parallelism previously applied to the manual implementation of token scanning in the Parabix XML parser, the new algorithm represents a general solution to the problem of regular expression matching using parallel bit streams. On widely-deployed commodity hardware using 128-bit SSE2 SIMD technology, our algorithm implementations can substantially outperform traditional grep implementations based on NFAs, DFAs or backtracking. 5X or better performance advantage against the best of available competitors is not atypical. The algorithms are also designed to scale with the availability of additional parallel resources such as the wider SIMD facilities (256-bit) of Intel AVX2 or future 512-bit extensions. Our AVX2 implementation showed dramatic reduction in instruction count and significant improvement in speed. Our GPU implementations show further acceleration.

Categories and Subject Descriptors

D.1.3 [**Programming Techniques**]: Concurrent Programming—*parallel programming*; D.3.3 [**Programming Languages**]: Processors—*compilers*; F.2.2 [**Analysis of Algorithms and Problem Complexity**]: Nonnumerical Algorithms and Problems—*pattern matching*

Keywords

regular expression matching; parallel bit streams

1. INTRODUCTION

The use of regular expressions to search texts for patterns has a long history and remains an important technique. Thompson [21] is credited with the first construction to convert regular expressions to nondeterministic finite automata (NFA). Following Thompson's approach, a regular expression of length m is converted to an NFA with $O(m)$ states. Using the NFA it is possible to search a text of length n in $O(mn)$ time. Frequently, a more efficient choice is to convert an NFA into a deterministic finite automata (DFA). A DFA maintains a single active state throughout the matching process and hence, using a DFA it is possible to search a text of length n in $O(n)$ time[1].

A significant proportion of the research in fast regular expression matching can be regarded as the "quest for efficient automata" [15]. In [2], Baeza-Yates and Gonnet presented a new approach to string search based on bit-level parallelism. This technique takes advantage of the intrinsic parallelism of bitwise operations within a computer word. Thus, given a w-bit word, the number of operations that a string search algorithms performs can be reduced by a factor w. Building on this observation, the Shift-Or algorithm simulates an NFA using bitwise operations and achieves $O(\frac{nm}{w})$ time in the worst-case [13]. A disadvantage of the Shift-Or approach is an inability to skip input characters. Simple string matching algorithms, such as the Boyer-Moore family of algorithms [3, 7], skip input characters to achieve sublinear times in the average case. The Backward Nondeterministic Dawg Matching (BNDM) pattern matching algorithm [24] combines the advantages of the Shift-Or approach with the ability to skip characters. The nrgrep tool is based on the BNDM algorithm. It is generally considered the fastest grep tool for matching complex patterns, and achieves similar performance to the fastest existing string matching tools for simple patterns [13].

Recently, there has been considerable interest in the use of parallel hardware such as multicore processors (CPUs), graphics processing units (GPUs), field-programmable gate arrays (FPGAs), or specialized architectures such as the Cell Broadband Engine (Cell BE) to accelerate regular expression matching. Generally, speedups are achieved by using parallel hardware features to improve the throughput of multiple instances of a matching problem at a time, i.e., by matching against sets of patterns or multiple input streams. In contrast, our approach uses parallelism to accelerate the throughput of a single problem instance, i.e., a single regular expression matched against a single input stream.

In related work targeting multicore hardware, Scarpazza and Braudaway [20] demonstrated that text processing algorithms that exhibit irregular memory access patterns can

[1]It is well known that the conversion of an NFA to an equivalent DFA may result in *state explosion*, i.e., the number of resultant DFA states may increase exponentially.

PACT'14, August 24–27, 2014, Edmonton, AB, Canada.

ACM 978-1-4503-2809-8/14/08 ...$15.00.
http://dx.doi.org/10.1145/2628071.2628079.

be efficiently executed. Pasetto et al [16] presented a flexible tool that performs small-ruleset regular expression matching at a rate of 2.88 Gbps per chip on Intel Xeon E5472 hardware. Naghmouchi et al [18, 12] demonstrated that the Aho-Corasick (AC) string matching algorithm [1] is well-suited for parallel implementation on multicore CPUs, GPUs and the Cell BE. Salapura et al [17] advocated the use of vector-style processing for regular expressions in business analytics applications and leveraged the SIMD hardware available on multicore processors to achieve a speedup of greater than 1.8 over a range of data sizes. On the Cell Broadband Engine, Scarpazza and Russell [19] described a pattern matching implementation that delivered a throughput of 40 Gbps for a small dictionary of approximately 100 patterns and a throughput of 3.3-3.4 Gbps for a larger dictionary containing thousands of patterns. Iorio and van Lunteren [8] presented a string matching implementation for automata that achieved 4 Gbps on the Cell BE. On GPUs, Tumeo et al [22] presented a chunk-based implementation of the AC algorithm for accelerating string matching on GPUs. Lin et al., proposed the Parallel Failureless Aho-Corasick (PFAC) algorithm to accelerate pattern matching on GPU hardware and achieved 143 Gbps raw data throughput, although system throughput was limited to 15 Gbps [9]. Most recently, Mytkowicz et al [11] have developed a method for combining SIMD parallelism and data parallelism on multicore hardware. Of each of these related works, this approach stands out since it also focuses on the acceleration of matching against a single input stream.

Whereas the existing approaches to parallelization have been based on adapting traditional sequential algorithms to emergent parallel architectures, we introduce both a new algorithmic approach and its implementation on SIMD and GPU architectures. This approach relies on a bitwise data parallel view of text streams as well as a surprising use of addition to match runs of characters in a single step. The closest previous work is that underlying bit-parallel XML parsing using 128-bit SSE2 SIMD technology together with a parallel scanning primitive also based on addition [4]. However, in contrast to the deterministic, longest-match scanning associated with the ScanThru primitive of that work, we introduce here a new primitive MatchStar that can be used in full generality for nondeterministic regular expression matching. We also introduce a long-stream addition technique involving a further application of MatchStar that enables us to scale the technique to n-bit addition in $\lceil \log_{64} n \rceil$ steps. We ultimately apply this technique, for example, to perform synchronized 4096-bit addition on GPU wavefronts of 64 threads.

There is also a strong keyword match between the bit-parallel data streams used in our approach and the bit-parallelism used for NFA state transitions in the classical algorithms of Wu and Manber [23], Baez-Yates and Gonnet [2] and Navarro and Raffinot [14]. However those algorithms use bit-parallelism in a fundamentally different way: representing all possible current NFA states as a bit vector and performing parallel transitions to a new set of states using table lookups and bitwise logic. Whereas our approach can match multiple characters per step, bit-parallel NFA algorithms proceed through the input one byte at a time. Nevertheless, with the BNDM extensions, the nrgrep [13] program remains among the strongest competitors in regular expression matching performance, so we include it in our comparative evaluation.

The remainder of this paper is organized as follows. Section 2 briefly describes regular expression notation and the grep problem. Section 3 presents our basic algorithm and MatchStar primitive using a model of arbitrary-length bit-parallel data streams. Section 4 discusses the block-by-block implementation of our techniques including the long stream addition techniques for 256-bit addition with AVX2 and 4096-bit additions with GPU SIMT. Section 5 describes our overall SSE2 implementation and carries out a performance study in comparison with existing grep implementations. Given the dramatic variation in grep performance across different implementation techniques, expressions and data sets, Section 6 considers a comparison between the bit-stream and NFA approaches from a theoretical perspective. Section 7 then examines and demonstrates the scalability of our bitwise data-parallel approach in moving from 128-bit to 256-bit SIMD on Intel Haswell architecture. To further investigate scalability, Section 8 addresses the implementation of our matcher using groups of 64 threads working together SIMT-style on a GPU system. Section 9 concludes the paper with a discussion of results and areas for future work.

2. REGULAR EXPRESSIONS AND GREP

We follow common POSIX notation for regular expressions. A regular expression specifies a set of strings through a pattern notation. Individual characters normally stand for themselves, unless they are one of the special characters `*+?[{\(|^$.` that serve as metacharacters of the notation system. Thus the regular expression `cat` is a pattern for the set consisting of the single 3-character string "`cat`". The special characters must be escaped with a backslash to prevent interpretation as metacharacter, thus `\$` represents the dollar-sign and `\\\\` represent the string consisting of two backslash characters. Character class bracket expressions are pattern elements that allow any character in a given class to be used in a particular context. For example, `[@#%]` is a regular expression that stands for any of the three given symbols. Contiguous ranges of characters may be specified using hyphens; for example `[0-9]` for digits and `[A-Za-z0-9_]` for any alphanumeric character or underscore. If the caret character immediately follows the opening bracket, the class is negated, thus `[^0-9]` stands for any character except a digit. The period metacharacter `.` stands for the class of all characters.

Consecutive pattern elements stand for strings formed by concatenation, thus `[cd][ao][tg]` stands for the set of 8 three-letter strings "`cat`" through "`dog`". The alternation operator `|` allows a pattern to be defined to have two alternative forms, thus `cat|dog` matches either "`cat`" or "`dog`". Concatenation takes precedence over alternation, but parenthesis may be used to change this, thus `(ab|cd)[0-9]` stands for any digit following one of the two prefixes "`ab`" or "`cd`".

Repetition operators may be appended to a pattern to specify a variable number of occurrences of that pattern. The Kleene star operator `*` specifies zero-or-more occurrences matching the previous pattern, while Kleene plus `+` specifies one-or-more occurrences. Thus `[a-z][a-z]*` and `[a-z]+` both specify the same set: strings of at least one lower-case letter. The postfix operator `?` specifies an optional component, i.e., zero-or-one occurrence of strings matching the element. Specific bounds may be given within braces: `(ab){3}` specifies the string "ababab", `[0-9A-Fa-f]{2,4}` specifies strings of two, three or four hexadecimal digits, and `[A-Z]{4,}` specifies strings of at least 4 consecutive capital letters.

The grep program searches a file for lines containing matches to a regular expression using any of the above notations. In addition, the pattern elements `^` and `$` may be used to match respectively the beginning or the end of a line. In line-based tools such as grep, `.` matches any character except newlines; matches cannot extend over lines. Normally, grep prints all matching lines to its output. However, grep programs typically allow a command line flag such as `-c` to specify that only a count of matching lines be produced; we use this option in our experimental evaluation to focus our comparisons on the performance of the underlying matching algorithms.

3. BIT-PARALLEL DATA STREAMS

Whereas the traditional approaches to regular expression matching using NFAs, DFAs or backtracking all rely on a byte-at-a-time processing model, the approach we introduce in this paper is based on quite a different concept: a data-parallel approach to simultaneous processing of data stream elements. Indeed, our most abstract model is that of unbounded data parallelism: processing all elements of the input data stream simultaneously. In essence, data streams are viewed as (very large) integers. The fundamental operations are bitwise logic, stream shifting and long-stream addition.

Depending on the available parallel processing resources, an actual implementation may divide an input stream into blocks and process the blocks sequentially. Within each block all elements of the input stream are processed together, relying on the availability of bitwise logic and addition scaled to the block size. On commodity Intel and AMD processors with 128-bit SIMD capabilities (SSE2), we typically process input streams 128 bytes at a time. In this case, we rely on the Parabix tool chain [10] to handle the details of compilation to block-by-block processing. On the latest processors supporting the 256-bit AVX2 SIMD operations, we also use the Parabix tool chain, but substitute a parallelized long-stream addition technique to avoid the sequential chaining of 4 64-bit additions. Our GPU implementation uses scripts to modify the output of the Parabix tools, effectively dividing the input into blocks of 4K bytes. We also have adapted our long-stream addition technique to perform 4096-bit additions using 64 threads working in lock-step SIMT fashion.

A key concept in this streaming approach is the derivation of bit streams that are parallel to the input data stream, i.e., in one-to-one correspondence with the data element positions of the input streams. Typically, the input stream is a byte stream comprising the 8-bit character code units of a particular encoding such as extended ASCII, ISO-8859-1 or UTF-8. However, the method may also easily be used with wider code units such as the 16-bit code units of UTF-16. In the case of a byte stream, the first step is to transpose the byte stream into eight parallel bit streams, such that bit stream i comprises the ith bit of each byte. These streams form a set of basis bit streams from which many other parallel bit streams can be calculated, such as character class bit streams such that each bit j of the stream specifies whether character j of the input stream is in the class or not. Figure 1 shows an example of an input byte stream in ASCII, the eight basis bit streams of the transposed representation, and the character class bit streams `[a]`, `[z9]`, and `[0-9]` that may be computed from the basis bit streams using bitwise logic. Zero bits are marked with periods (`.`) so that the one bits stand out. Transposition and character class construction are straightforward using the Parabix tool chain [10].

input data	`a453z--b3z--az--a12949z--ca22z7--`
B_7	`.................................`
B_6	`1...1..1.1..11..1.....1..11..1...`
B_5	`111111111111111111111111111111111`
B_4	`.1111...11...1...111111....1111..`
B_3	`....111..111.111...1.1111....1.11`
B_2	`.11..11...11..11....1..11.....111`
B_1	`...11..111...1....1...1..1.1111..`
B_0	`1.11.11.1.111.1111.1.1.1111...111`
`[a]`	`1...........1...1.........1......`
`[z9]`	`....1....1...1.....1.11......1...`
`[0-9]`	`.111....1........11111.....11.1..`

Figure 1: Basis and Character Class Streams

input data	`a453z--b3z--az--a12949z--ca22z7--`
M_1	`.1...........1...1.........1.....`
M_2	`.1111........1...111111....111...`
M_3	`.....1........1.....1.11......1..`

Figure 2: Marker Streams in Matching `a[0-9]*[z9]`

Marker Streams. Now consider how bit-parallel data streams can be used in regular expression matching. Consider the problem of searching the input stream of Figure 1 to finding occurrence of strings matching the regular expression `a[0-9]*[z9]`. Note that this is an ambiguous regular expression, which could match texts such as `a12949z` in multiple ways. The matching process involves the concept of *marker streams*, that is streams that mark the positions of current matches during the overall process. In this case there are three marker streams computed during the match process, namely, M_1 representing match positions after an initial `a` character has been found, M_2 representing positions reachable from positions marked by M_1 by further matching zero or more digits (`[0-9]*`) and finally M_3 the stream marking positions after a final `z` or `9` has been found. Without describing the details of how these streams are computed for the time being, Figure 2 shows what each of these streams should be for our example matching problem. Our convention that a marker stream contains a 1 bit at the next character position to be matched, that is, immediately past the last position that was matched. Note that all three matches from the third occurrence of `a` are correctly marked in M_3.

MatchStar. MatchStar takes a marker bitstream and a character class bitstream as input. It returns all positions that can be reached by advancing the marker bitstream zero or more times through the character class bitstream.

input data	`a453z--b3z--az--a12949z--ca22z7--`
M_1	`.1...........1...1.........1.....`
$C =$ `[0-9]`	`.111....1........11111.....11.1..`
$T_0 = M_1 \wedge C$	`.1...............1.........1.....`
$T_1 = T_0 + C$	`....1...1.............1......11..`
$T_2 = T_1 \oplus C$	`.1111............111111....111...`
$M_2 = T_2 \vee M_1$	`.1111........1...111111....111...`

Figure 3: $M_2 = \textbf{MatchStar}(M_1, C)$

Figure 3 illustrates the MatchStar method. In this figure, it is important to note that our bitstreams are shown in natural left-to-right order reflecting the conventional presentation of our character data input. However, this reverses the normal order of presentation when considering bitstreams as numeric values. The key point here is that when we perform bitstream addition, we will show bit movement from left-to-right. For example, `111.` + `1...` = `...1`.

The first row of the figure is the input data, the second and third rows are the input bitstreams: the initial marker position bitstream and the character class bitstream for digits derived from input data.

In the first operation (T_0), marker positions that cannot be advanced are temporarily removed from consideration by masking off marker positions that aren't character class positions using bitwise logic. Next, the temporary marker bitstream is added to the character class bitstream. The addition produces 1s in three types of positions. There will be a 1 immediately following a block of character class positions that spanned one or more marker positions, at any character class positions that weren't affected by the addition (and are not part of the desired output), and at any marker position that wasn't the first in its block of character class positions. Any character class positions that have a 0 in T_1 were affected by the addition and are part of the desired output. These positions are obtained and the undesired 1 bits are removed by XORing with the character class stream. T_2 is now only missing marker positions that were removed in the first step as well as marker positions that were 1s in T_1. The output marker stream is obtained by ORing T_2 with the initial marker stream.

In general, given a marker stream M and a character class stream C, the operation of MatchStar is defined by the following equation.

$$\text{MatchStar}(M, C) = (((M \wedge C) + C) \oplus C) \vee M$$

Given a set of initial marker positions, the result stream marks all possible positions that can be reached by 0 or more occurrences of characters in class C from each position in M.

MatchStar differs from ScanThru of the Parabix tool chain in that it finds all matches, not just the longest match. This is necessary for general matching involving possibly ambiguous regular expressions.

Compilation. Using the marker stream and MatchStar concept, we now outline our compilation algorithm. This is implemented in a Java program. First the regular expression is parsed and represented as an abstract syntax tree. Second, the various character classes used in the regular expression are extracted. The character class compiler of the Parabix framework is invoked to generate the bit stream equations required for each character class. Then the syntax tree is walked to generate code for each type of regular expression structure as follows.

- An initial marker stream M_0 is set to be all ones, indicating that every position in the input file is a potential match if we have not yet examined any pattern elements.
- If we have a regular expression formed as an alternation of subexpressions, we compile each of these in turn, providing the current input marker stream as input to each of them. The final marker streams of the compiled forms of each subexpression are then just combined using a bitwise-or to produce the overall final marker stream of the alternation. That is, a match occurs at any position that can be reached by matching any one of the alternatives.
- If we have a marker stream formed as a concatenation of subexpressions, then we compile each of these in turn, providing the output marker stream of each compilation as the input marker stream for the compilation of the next pattern element.
- If a regular expression is a character class expression or a single character, then we form the bitwise-and of the current marker stream and the character class stream to filter out current marker positions that do not have a match to the class. The result is then shifted forward one position to identify the successful matches.
- If a regular expression is an optional expression of the form `R?` for some subexpression `R`, then the output marker stream is simply formed as the bitwise-or of the input marker stream (zero occurrences of `R` matched) and the output stream produced by compiling `R` in the context of the current input marker stream (one occurrence matched).
- If a regular expression is a repetition of a character class of the form `C*`, then the compiled form uses the MatchStar operation to produce the output marker stream from the input stream and the compiled stream for character class `C`.
- If a regular expression is a repetition of a non character class of the form `R*`, then a Pablo while loop is created conditioned on a control marker stream still having bits marking match positions to be considered. The body of the while consists of the compiled form of the expression `R`, taking as input the marker stream at the beginning of the iteration and producing as output all positions that can be reached from the input positions in a single step. These output positions are candidates for further iteration, but positions that have already been considered are removed. This guarantees termination of the loop; iteration continues only if a new marker position is reached that has not been previously considered as an output. The final output is the bitwise-or of matches determined in each loop iteration.
- If a regular expression is a bounded repetition of the form `R{m,n}`, then it is compiled according to the

equivalent form consisting of m concatenations of R followed by $n - m$ concatenations of R?.

- If a regular expression is a bounded repetition of the form R{m,}, then it is compiled according to the equivalent form consisting of m concatenations of R followed by R*.

The output of the regular expression compiler is then fed as input to the Pablo compiler of the Parabix tool chain. The result is then compiled with a C++ compiler linked with the Parabix run-time libraries.

4. BLOCK-AT-A-TIME PROCESSING

The unbounded stream model of the previous section must of course be translated an implementation that proceeds block-at-a-time for realistic application. In this, we primarily rely on the Pablo compiler of the Parabix toolchain [10]. Given input statements expressed as arbitrary-length bitstream equations, Pablo produces block-at-a-time C++ code that initializes and maintains all the necessary carry bits for each of the additions and shifts involved in the bitstream calculations.

In the present work, our principal contribution to the Parabix tool chain is to incorporate the technique of long-stream addition described below. Otherwise, we were able to use Pablo directly in compiling our SSE2 and AVX2 implementations. Our GPU implementation required some scripting to modify the output of the Pablo compiler for our purpose.

Long-Stream Addition. The maximum word size for addition on commodity processors is typically 64 bits. In order to implement long-stream addition for block sizes of 256 or larger, a method for propagating carries through the individual stages of 64-bit addition is required. However, the normal technique of sequential addition using add-with-carry instructions, for example, is far from ideal.

We use the following general model using SIMD methods for constant-time long-stream addition up to 4096 bits. Related GPU solutions have been independently developed[6], however our model is intended to be a more broadly applicable abstraction. We assume the availability of the following SIMD/SIMT operations operating on vectors of f 64-bit fields.

- `simd<64>::add(X, Y)`: vertical SIMD addition of corresponding 64-bit fields in two vectors to produce a result vector of f 64-bit fields.
- `simd<64>::eq(X, -1)`: comparison of the 64-bit fields of `x` each with the constant value -1 (all bits 1), producing an f-bit mask value,
- `hsimd<64>::mask(X)`: gathering the high bit of each 64-bit field into a single compressed f-bit mask value, and
- normal bitwise logic operations on f-bit masks, and
- `simd<64>::spread(X)`: distributing the bits of an f bit mask, one bit each to the f 64-bit fields of a vector.

Here, the `hsimd<64>::mask(X)` and `simd<64>::spread(X)` model the minimum communication requirements between the parallel processing units (SIMD lanes or SIMT processors). In essence, we just need the ability to quickly send and receive 1 bit of information per parallel unit. The `hsimd<64>::mask(X)` operation gathers 1 bit from each of the processors to a central resource. After calculations on the gather bits are performed, we then just need an operation to invert the communication, i.e., sending 1 bit each from the central processor to each of the parallel units. There are a variety of ways in which these facilities may be implemented depending on the underlying architecture; details of our AVX2 and GPU implementations are presented later.

Given these operations, our method for long stream addition of two $f \times 64$ bit values X and Y is the following.

1. Form the vector of 64-bit sums of x and y.

   $$\mathtt{R} = \mathtt{simd\langle 64\rangle::add(X,\ Y)}$$

2. Extract the f-bit masks of X, Y and R.

   $$\mathtt{x} = \mathtt{hsimd\langle 64\rangle::mask(X)}$$

   $$\mathtt{y} = \mathtt{hsimd\langle 64\rangle::mask(Y)}$$

   $$\mathtt{r} = \mathtt{hsimd\langle 64\rangle::mask(R)}$$

3. Compute an f-bit mask of carries generated for each of the 64-bit additions of X and Y.

   $$\mathtt{c} = (\mathtt{x} \wedge \mathtt{y}) \vee ((\mathtt{x} \vee \mathtt{y}) \wedge \neg \mathtt{r})$$

4. Compute an f-bit mask of all fields of R that will overflow with an incoming carry bit. This is called the *bubble mask.*

   $$\mathtt{b} = \mathtt{simd\langle 64\rangle::eq(R,\ -1)}$$

5. Determine an f-bit mask identifying the fields of R that need to be incremented to produce the final sum. Here we find a new application of MatchStar.

   $$\mathtt{i} = \mathtt{MatchStar(c*2,\ b)}$$

   This is the key step. The mask `c` of outgoing carries must be shifted one position (`c*2`) so that each outgoing carry bit becomes associated with the next digit. At the incoming position, the carry will increment the 64-bit digit. However, if this digit is all ones (as signaled by the corresponding bit of bubble mask `b`, then the addition will generate another carry. In fact, if there is a sequence of digits that are all ones, then the carry must bubble through each of them. This is just MatchStar.

6. Compute the final result Z.

   $$\mathtt{Z} = \mathtt{simd\langle 64\rangle::add(R,\ simd\langle 64\rangle::spread(i))}$$

Figure 4 illustrates the process. In the figure, we illustrate the process with 8-bit fields rather than 64-bit fields and show all field values in hexadecimal notation. Note that two of the individual 8-bit additions produce carries, while two others produce FF values that generate bubble bits. The net result is that four of the original 8-bit sums must be incremented to produce the long stream result.

A slight extension to the process produces a long-stream full adder that can be used in chained addition. In this

X	19	31	BA	4C	3D	45	21	F1
Y	22	12	45	B3	E2	16	17	36
R	3B	43	FF	FF	1F	5B	38	27
x	0	0	1	0	0	0	0	1
y	0	0	0	1	1	0	0	0
r	0	0	1	1	0	0	0	0
c	0	0	0	0	1	0	0	1
c*2	0	0	0	1	0	0	1	0
b	0	0	1	1	0	0	0	0
i	0	1	1	1	0	0	1	0
Z	3B	44	0	0	1F	5B	39	27

Figure 4: Long Stream Addition

case, the adder must take an additional carry-in bit `p` and produce a carry-out bit `q`. This may be accomplished by incorporating `p` in calculating the increment mask in the low bit position, and then extracting the carry-out `q` from the high bit position.

i = `MatchStar(c*2+p, b)`

q = `i >> f`

As described subsequently, we use a two-level long-stream addition technique in both our AVX2 and GPU implementations. In principle, one can extend the technique to additional levels. Using 64-bit adders throughout, $\lceil \log_{64} n \rceil$ steps are needed for n-bit addition. A three-level scheme could coordinate 64 groups each performing 4096-bit long additions in a two-level structure. However, whether there are reasonable architectures that can support fine-grained SIMT style at this level is an open question.

Using the methods outlined, it is quite conceivable that instruction set extensions to support long-stream addition could be added for future SIMD and GPU processors. Given the fundamental nature of addition as a primitive and its particular application to regular expression matching as shown herein, it seems reasonable to expect such instructions to become available. Alternatively, it may be worthwhile to simply ensure that the `hmask` and `spread` operations are efficiently supported.

5. SSE2 IMPLEMENTATION

Implementation Notes. Our regular expression compiler directly uses the Parabix tool chain to compile regular expression into SSE2-based implementations. Our compiler essentially scripts three other compilers to perform this work: the Parabix character class compiler to determine basic bit stream equations for each of the character classes encountered in a regular expression, the Pablo bitstream equation compiler which converts equations to block-at-a-time C++ code for 128-bit SIMD, and gcc 4.8.2 to generate the binaries. The Pablo output is combined with a `grep_template.cpp` file that arranges to read input files, break them into segments, and print or count matches as they are encountered.

Comparative Implementations. We evaluate our bitwise data parallel implementation versus several alternatives. We report data for two of these: gre2p and nrgrep version 1.12.

The gre2p program is a grep version implemented using the recently developed RE2 regular expression library, using a systematic DFA-based approach (as well as some NFA fallback techniques) [5]. The NFA class is represented by nrgrep, one of the strongest competitors in regular expression matching performance. We also considered GNU grep 2.10, agrep 3.41 as an alternative NFA-based implementation and pcregrep 8.12 as a backtracking implementation, but do not report data for them. GNU grep is a popular open-source implementation that is claimed to be primarily DFA-based with heuristics for important special cases. The agrep implementation does not support some of the common regular expression syntax features and is limited to patterns of at most 32 characters. As a backtracking implementation, pcregrep supports more regular expression features, but is not competitive in performance in any example we tested.

We performed our SSE2 performance study using an Intel Core i5-4570 (Haswell) processor (3.2 GHz, 4 physical cores, 32+32 kB (per core) L1 cache, 256 kB (per core) L2 cache, 6 MB L3 cache) running the 64-bit version of Ubuntu 12.04 (Linux).

Our performance evaluation focuses on the running time of the regular expression matching process itself, excluding the preprocessing time for regular expression compilation. However, the overhead of the Parabix transform to bit stream form is included in our reported results.

Test Expressions. Each grep implementation was evaluated against the six regular expressions shown in Table 1. @ matches the at-sign character. This expression demonstrates the overhead involved in matching the simplest possible regular expression, a single character. Date, Email, and URI provide examples of commonly used regular expression. This set of expressions were modified from the *Benchmark of Regex Libraries*. Hex matches delimited byte strings in hexadecimal notation, and enforces the constraint that the number of hex digits is even. This expression illustrates the performance of a repetition operator implemented using a while loop in our system. StarHeight is an artificial expression designed to further stress while loop implementation with 4 levels of Kleene closure. All tests were run on a version of a *Linux 3Dfx howto* file of 39,421,555 bytes.

Results. Figure 5 compares each of the grep implementations, with relative performance reported in CPU cycles per byte.

The performance in matching the @ regular expression establishes the base line cost for regular expression processing. All programs report 15,788 matching lines of the 1,086,077 lines in the file. The Parabix SSE2 implementation is clearly the fastest in this case with a cost of 0.95 CPU cycles per byte. The bulk of this represents the overhead of the Parabix transform, the bitwise logic to calculate the single `[@]` character class stream is relatively trivial. It is interesting to note that this example does not represent a baseline cost for either nrgrep or gre2p, each of these benefit from character skipping optimizations in their implementations.

Our results for the matching the Date expression to find the 668 lines containing dates show an increase from 0.95 to 1.22 cycles per byte, corresponding to the additional logic for the regular expression matching steps according to our algorithm. For this relatively simple expression, however, nrgrep outperforms our implementation by taking significant

<table>
<tr><th>Name</th><th>Expression</th></tr>
<tr><td>@</td><td><code>@</code></td></tr>
<tr><td>Date</td><td><code>([0-9][0-9]?)/([0-9][0-9]?)/([0-9][0-9]([0-9][0-9])?)</code></td></tr>
<tr><td>Email</td><td><code>([^ @]+)@([^ @]+)</code></td></tr>
<tr><td>URI</td><td><code>(([a-zA-Z][a-zA-Z0-9]*)://|mailto:)([^ /]+)(/[^]*)?|([^ @]+)@([^ @]+)</code></td></tr>
<tr><td>Hex</td><td><code>[ ](0x)?([a-fA-F0-9][a-fA-F0-9])+[.:,?!]</code></td></tr>
<tr><td>StarHeight</td><td><code>[A-Z]((([a-zA-Z]*a[a-zA-Z]*[ ])*[a-zA-Z]*e[a-zA-Z]*[ ])*[a-zA-Z]*s[a-zA-Z]*[ ])*[.?!]</code></td></tr>
</table>

Table 1: Regular Expressions

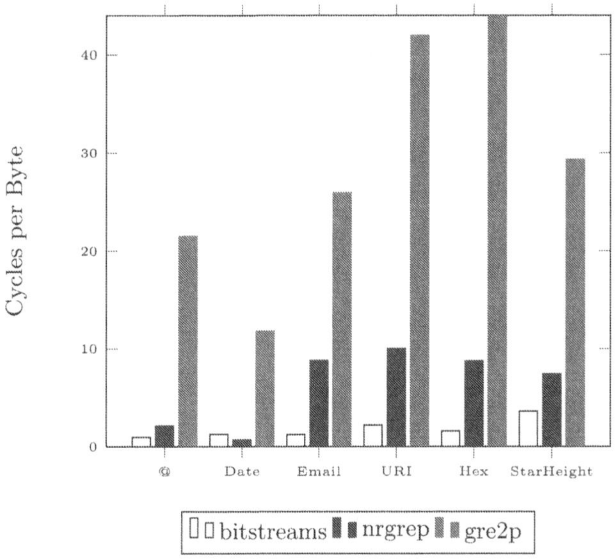

Figure 5: Cycles per Byte

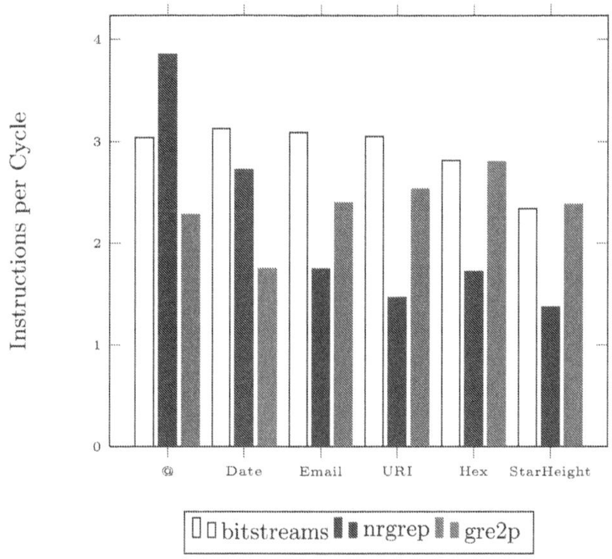

Figure 6: Instructions per Cycle

advantage of character skipping. Each time that nrgrep encounters a character that cannot appear in a date it jumps six character positions rather than searching every character in the input text. gre2p also shows a significant benefit from the character skipping optimization.

The results for the Email expression illustrate the relative advantage of the bitstreams method when the expression to be matched does not permit character skipping in the NFA- or DFA-based implementations. In this example, our implementation outperforms nrgrep by a factor of 7X, and gre2p by 23X. There are 15,057 lines matching the Email regex.

The URI expression illustrates the performance of the grep programs with additional regular expression complexity. All three implementations require more time than for the Email expression, with similar but slightly lower performance ratios maintained. In this example, the performance advantage of the bitstreams implementation drops to about 4.5X over nrgrep and 19X over gre2p. 32557 lines are matched by the URI regex.

The results for Hex expression illustrate the bitstreams performance in the case of a Kleene-+ operator compiled to a while loop. Performance is nevertheless quite good; our implementation uses just 1.6 cycles per byte to find the 130,243 matching lines. The gre2p program performs quite poorly here, off the chart at 114 cycles per byte. This is lower than the bitstreams implementation by about 70X. In this example, nrgrep maintains its relative performance to the bitstreams implementation, about 5.5X slower.

A more complex triply-nested repetition structure is required by the bitstreams implementation of the StarHeight expression. In this case, there is a noticeable drop off in the performance advantage of the bitstreams implementation over the nrgrep and gre2p. Nevertheless a 2X advantage over nrgrep is still observed.

Figure 6 shows the efficiency of processor resource usage achieved by the three programs on each of the test expression in terms of instructions per cycle (IPC). For the first four expressions, in particular, the bitstreams implementation uses the processor resources quite efficiently, avoiding penalties due to cache misses and branch mispredictions. However, with the while loop structures in processing the Hex and StarHeight expressions, branch mispredictions increase considerably and there is a noticeable drop-off in IPC. The gre2p program suffers from significant penalties for the smaller expressions, but otherwise achieves a good IPC rate. On the other hand, nrgrep IPC drops off with expression complexity, suffering from significant penalties due to mispredictions in the character-skipping logic and cache misses in table lookups.

Overall, the bitstreams SSE2 implementation significantly outperformed both nrgrep and gre2p. In addition, the performance of bitstreams generally scales well with regular expression complexity, although nested Kleene closures are an issue.

6. RUNNING-TIME COMPARISON WITH BASE NFA IMPLEMENTATIONS

Our experimental results indicate that regular expression matching using bitstreams can outperform current implementations of NFA- (and DFA-) based matching. It is worth exploring why this is so, and under what conditions one might expect bitstreams to perform better than NFA- or DFA-based matchers, and vice-versa.

The bitstream method starts with a preprocessing step: the compilation of the regular expression using the algorithm presented above as well as the compilers of the Parabix toolchain. Compilation is an offline process whose time is not counted in our performance measures, as each of these are research tools that have neither been optimized nor integrated. This leads to a bias in our results, as our timings for nrgrep and gre2p include the time taken for preprocessing. We minimize the bias by performing our tests with reasonably large inputs, so that the text-scanning costs dominate the preprocessing costs. We assume that the length m of regular expressions is typically less than 100 bytes and that data files are typically over 10 MB. Provided that a well-engineered implementation of our regular expression compilation algorithm together with the compilers of the Parabix tool chain requires no more than $10000m$ cycles, the overhead of compilation will not substantially increase the running time. As our regular expression algorithm is $O(m)$, and the other steps of the Parabix tool chain require $O(m \log m)$ time, we expect that such performance is well within reason. It is important to note that our algorithms construct neither NFAs nor DFAs and so are no subject to the exponential-time behaviour of NFA-to-DFA transformation.

For simplicity, we will first assume that the input regular expressions are restricted to having Kleene closures only of single characters or alternations of single characters. This is a broad class of regular expressions, covering the majority of common uses of grep.

Let Σ be our input alphabet and $\sigma = |\Sigma|$. As we are comparing techniques in practice, we assume that Σ is a standard input alphabet, such as ASCII ($\sigma = 128$), UTF-8 ($\sigma = 256$), UTF-16 ($\sigma = 65536$), or UTF-32 ($\sigma = 1114112$). This assumption allows us to equate the number of bits in the encoding of a character (a parameter for the bitstream method) with $\log \sigma$.

The bitstream method compiles a regular expression of size m into bitstream code that is $O(m \log \sigma)$ statements long (with one operation per statement; it is essentially three-address code). This is translated to machine code and placed inside a loop[2] that executes once per w characters, where w is the width of the processor's word. Also inside this loop is the transposition step that converts character-encoded files into their bitstream representation; this transposition takes $O(\log \sigma \log \log \sigma)$ work per loop iteration.

In total, this is $O(m \log \sigma + \log w + \log \sigma \log \log \sigma)$ work per iteration. In current practice, we have $\log w$ around 8 (for 256-bit architectures), and $\log \sigma$ at least 7. Thus, $m \log \sigma$ will dominate $\log w$ with current and foreseeable technology–we do not expect to see $\log w$ skyrocket. So we can absorb the $\log w$ term and state the work as $O(m \log \sigma + \log \sigma \log \log \sigma)$ per iteration. We multiply this by $O(\frac{n}{w})$ iterations to give $O(\frac{n(m+\log \log \sigma) \log \sigma}{w})$ work.

We further note that all of the work in the loop is done by superscalar instructions, with the exception of the additions, which require carry propagation. There will be at most C of these additions in the loop, where C is the number of concatenation and Kleene star operations in the regular expression; $C < m$.

Almost all intermediate bitstreams in the loop body can be kept in registers, requiring no storage in memory. Good register allocation–and limited live ranges for bitstream variables–keeps register spillage to a minimum. For those bitstreams that do require storage in memory, long buffers are allocated, allowing the successive iterations of the loop to access successive memory locations. That is, for the few streams requiring it, memory is accessed in a sequential fashion. As this is the best case for hardware prefetching, we expect few cache misses with bitstream method.

We compare this with base NFA methods; by "base" here we mean NFA methods that do not skip input characters. The performance of input-skipping methods can be approximated by first analyzing the performance of the base method and then multiplying this by the expected fraction of examined (non-skipped) input.

In the base NFA method, a state set of approximately m states is kept as a bit set in $\frac{m}{w}$ machine words (or $\frac{m}{8}$ bytes). For each character c of the input, a precomputed transition table, indexed by the c and the current state set, is accessed. Since there are $2^{\Theta(m)}$ state sets, the transition table will have $\sigma 2^{\Theta(m)}$ entries. Each entry is a new state set, which requires $\frac{m}{8}$ bytes. Thus, the transition table is of size $\sigma m 2^{\Theta(m)}$, which is quite large: it can become expensive to precompute, and it consumes a lot of memory. For even fairly small m a table of this size will probably not fit in cache memory. Thus, we would expect many cache misses with this base method.

To improve the table size, several authors have separated the transition table into several tables, each indexed by a subset of the bits in the bit set representing the current state. Suppose one uses k bits of the state set to index each table. Ignoring ceilings, this requires $\frac{m}{k}$ tables, each with $\sigma 2^k$ entries of $\frac{m}{8}$ bytes apiece. Each table therefore takes up $m 2^{k-3} \sigma$ bytes, and so the collection of them takes up $\frac{m^2 2^{k-3} \sigma}{k}$ bytes. At each character, the NFA algorithm does one lookup in each table, combining the results with $\frac{m}{k} - 1$ boolean OR operations.

The original NFA method of Thompson uses $k = 1$, which gives a m tables of $\frac{m\sigma}{4}$ bytes each, along with m lookups and $m - 1$ boolean OR operations to combine the lookups, per character.

Navarro and Raffinot use $k = \frac{m}{2}$, giving 2 tables of $2^{\frac{m}{2}-3} m\sigma$ bytes each, two lookups per character, and 1 boolean OR operation per character to combine the lookups.

In Table 2, we summarize the theoretical analysis of these NFA methods, listing the number of table lookups per input character and the size of the tables for various values of m, the number of states. We assume the ASCII character set ($\sigma = 128$); any of the UTF character sets would yield larger tables.

Of particular importance to the speed of NFA methods is whether the table lookups result in cache hits or not. If the tables are small enough, then they will fit into cache and

[2]Technically, it is inside two loops: an inner one that executes once per w characters in a large buffer, and an outer one that successively fetches buffers until the input is exhausted.

k		1	4	8	$\frac{m}{2}$	m
lookups		m	$\frac{m}{4}$	$\frac{m}{8}$	2	1
	m					
	5	0.8	1.6	12.5	1.3	2.5
memory	10	3.1	6.2	50.0	10.0	160.0
(KiB)	15	7.0	14.1	112.5	120.0	7680.0
	20	12.5	25.0	200.0	640.0	327680.0
	25	19.5	39.1	312.5	6400.0	13107200.0

Table 2: lookups per character and memory consumed by tables in NFA methods (in kibibytes)

lookups will all be cache hits, taking minimal time. In this case, the time per input character will be a small constant times the number of lookups.

If the tables are not small enough to fit into cache, some proportion of the lookups will generate cache misses. This will stall the processor and these stalls will come to dominate the computation time. In this case, the time per input character will be some large constant (a cache miss can take about two orders of magnitude longer than a cache hit) times the number of lookups.

Using 256KiB as an estimate of the size of a current standard data cache, we can consider those entries of Table 2 above 256 to be relatively slow. We can summarize these theoretical predictions by saying that the NFA methods with small k scale well with an increase in NFA states, but with large k the method is limited to a small number of states.

We can now directly (but roughly) compare the NFA methods with bitstream methods. Consider small-k (say, $k <= 4$) NFA methods. For the reasonable range of m, the tables fit into cache. The running time is predicted to be a small constant times the $\frac{m}{k} >= \frac{m}{4}$ lookups. The small constant, which we will under approximate with 4 cycles, is for the table addressing computation, combining the lookups with boolean OR, and final state detection and handling. Thus, the running time per input character may be lower-bounded by $4 * \frac{m}{4}$, or simply m, cycles.

Our method, on the other hand, takes time $O(\frac{m \log \sigma + \log \log \sigma \log \sigma}{w})$ per input character, where the constant inside the big-Oh is approximately 2 for the first part of the numerator and 6 for the second part. Furthermore, we expect no cache misses due to the regular stride of our memory accesses. For UTF-8 (or ASCII), this time becomes at most $2\frac{8m}{w} + 6\frac{24}{w} = \frac{16m+144}{w}$ cycles per character.

For processors with a 128-bit word, this is $\frac{16m+144}{128} = \frac{m}{8} + \frac{9}{8}$ cycles per character. Comparing this with the at least m cycles per character of the base NFA methods, we expect these NFA methods to be competitive with our method only when the size of the regular expression is 1. As the size of the regular expression increases, we expect our method to approach a factor-of-8 improvement over the base NFA methods.

In theory, our improvement factor should scale closely with the word size; so that for processors with a 256-bit word, we expect an 16x improvement, and for processors with a 512-bit word, we expect a 32x improvement. In practice, we expect some reduction in these improvement ratios for various reasons, including the need for while-loops to implement nested Kleene closures as well as processor limitations in memory bandwidth, for example.

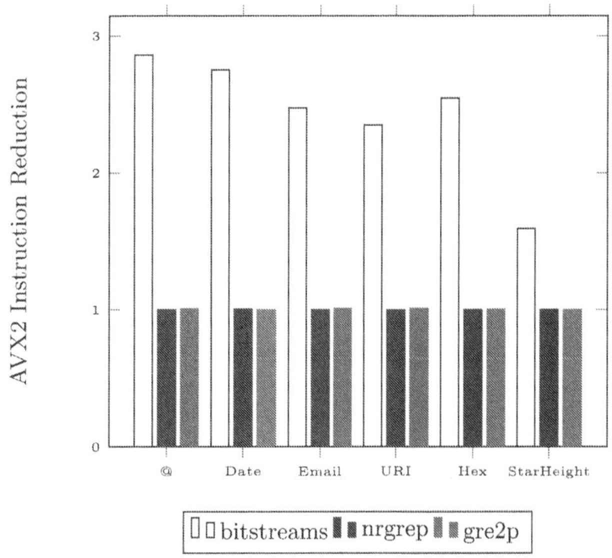

Figure 7: AVX2/SSE2 Instruction Reduction

7. SIMD SCALABILITY

Although commodity processors have provided 128-bit SIMD operations for more than a decade, the extension to 256-bit integer SIMD operations has just recently taken place with the availability of AVX2 instructions in Intel Haswell architecture chips as of mid 2013. This provides an excellent opportunity to assess the scalability of the bitwise data-parallel approach to regular expression matching.

For the most part, adapting the Parabix tool chain to the new AVX2 instructions was straightforward. This mostly involved regenerating library functions using the new AVX2 intrinsics. There were minor issues in the core transposition algorithm because the doublebyte-to-byte pack instructions are confined to independent operations within two 128-bit lanes.

AVX2 256-Bit Addition. Bitstream addition at the 256-bit block size was implemented using the long-stream addition technique. The AVX2 instruction set directly supports the `hsimd<64>::mask(X)` operation using the `_mm256_movemask_pd` intrinsic, extracting the required 4-bit mask directly from the 256-bit vector. The `hsimd<64>::spread(X)` is slightly more complex, requiring a short sequence of instructions to convert the computed 4-bit increment mask back into a vector of 4 64-bit values.

We also compiled new versions of the `egrep` and `nrgrep` programs using the `-march=core-avx2` flag in case the compiler is able to vectorize some of the code.

Figure 7 shows the reduction in instruction count achieved for each of the applications. Working at a block size of 256 bytes at a time rather than 128 bytes at a time, the bitstreams implementation scaled very well with reductions in instruction count over a factor of two in every case except for StarHeight. Although a factor of two would seem an outside limit, we attribute the change to greater instruction efficiency. AVX2 instructions use a non destructive three-operand form instead of the destructive two-operand form of SSE2. In the two-operand form, binary instructions must

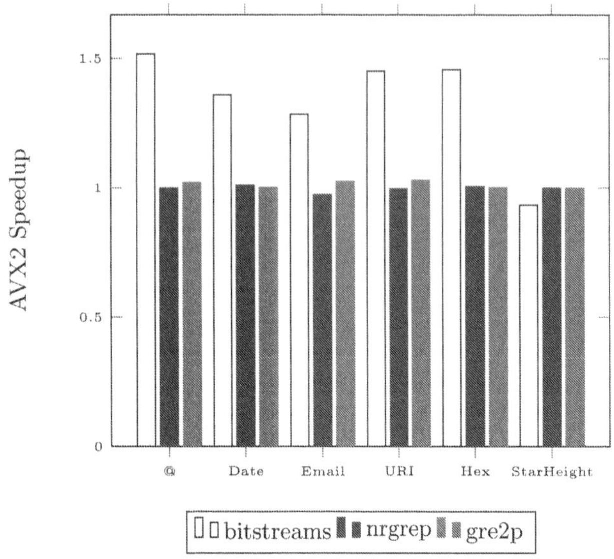

Figure 8: AVX2/SSE2 Speedup

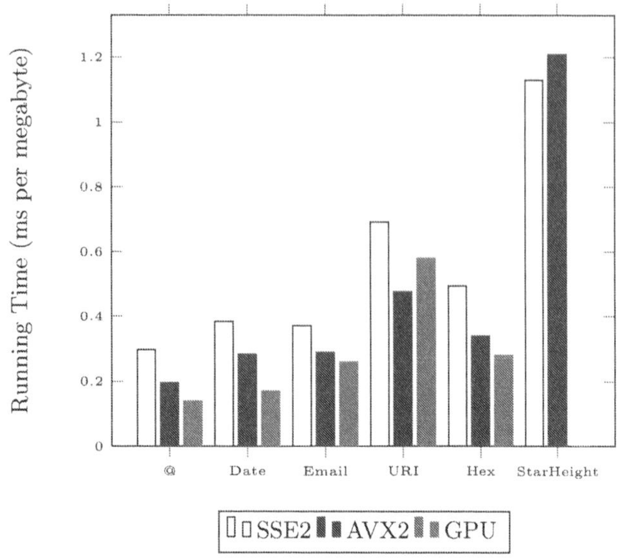

Figure 9: Running Time

Expression	Bitstream/AVX2 grep Speedup		
	vs. nrgrep	vs. gre2p	vs. GNU grep -e
At	3.5X	34X	1.6X
Date	0.76X	13X	48X
Email	9.5X	28X	12X
URI	6.6X	27X	518X
Hex	8.1X	105X	267X
StarHeight	1.9X	7.6X	97X

Table 3: Bitsream Speedup vs. Comparators

always use one of the source registers as a destination register. As a result the SSE2 object code generates many data movement operations that are unnecessary with the AVX2 set.

As expected, there was no observable reduction in instruction count with the recompiled grep and nrgrep applications.

As shown in Figure 8 the reduction in instruction count was reflected in a significant speedup in the bitstreams implementation in all cases except StarHeight. However, the speedup was considerably less than expected. The bitstreams code on AVX2 has suffered from a considerable reduction in instructions per cycle compared to the SSE2 implementation, likely indicating that our grep implementation has become memory-bound. However, the performance of StarHeight deserves particular comment, with an actual slowdown observed. When moving to 256 positions at a time, the controlling while loops may require more iterations than working 128 positions at a time, because the iteration must continue as long as there are any pending markers in the block. Nevertheless, the overall results on our AVX2 machine were quite encouraging, demonstrating very good scalability of the bitwise data-parallel approach. Significantly, the @ regular expression is matched at 0.63 cycles/byte using our AVX2 implementation indicating a considerable reduction in the overhead cost of the Parabix transform.

Table 3 shows the final performance results showing the speedup factors achieved by the bitstreams/AVX2 implementation vs nrgrep and gre2p. We have also added comparison with GNU grep (version 2.16), as it is well known and sometimes used as a basis for comparisons.

8. GPU IMPLEMENTATION

To further assess the scalability of our regular expression matching using bit-parallel data streams, we implemented a GPU version in OpenCL. We arranged for 64 work groups each having 64 threads. The size of work group and number of work groups is chosen to provide the best occupancy as calculated by the AMD App Profiler. Input files are divided in data parallel fashion among the 64 work groups. Each work group carries out the regular expression matching operations 4096 bytes at a time using SIMT processing. Although the GPU does not directly support the mask and spread operations required by our long-stream addition model, we are able to simulate them using shared memory. Each thread maintains its own carry and bubble values in shared memory and performs synchronized updates with the other threads using a six-step parallel-prefix style process. Others have implemented long-stream addition on the GPU using similar techniques, as noted previously.

We performed our test on an AMD Radeon HD A10-6800K APU machine. On the AMD Fusion systems, the input buffer is allocated in pinned memory to take advantage of the zero-copy memory regions where data can be read directly into this region by the CPU and also accessed by the GPU for further processing. Therefore, the expensive data transferring time that is needed by traditional discrete GPUs is hidden and we compare only the kernel execution time with our SSE2 and AVX implementations as shown in Figure 9. The GPU version gives up to 55% performance improvement over SSE version and up to 40% performance improvement over AVX version. However, because of implementation complexities of the triply-nested while loop for the StarHeight expression, it has been omitted.

Although we intended to process 64 work groups with 4096 bytes each at a time rather than 128 bytes at a time on SSE or 256 bytes at a time on AVX, the performance improvement is less than 60%. The first reason is hardware limitations. Our kernel occupancy is limited by register usage and not all the work groups can be scheduled at the same time. The second reason is that the long-stream addition implemented on GPU is more expensive than the implementations on SSE or AVX. Another important reason is the control flow. When a possible match is found in one thread, the rest of the threads in the same work group have to execute the same instructions for further processing rather than jump to the next block with a simple IF test. Therefore, the performance of different regular expressions is dependent on the number of long-stream addition operations and the total number of matches of a given input. Perhaps surprisingly, the overhead of the Parabix transformation was not a dominant factor, coming in at 0.08 ms/MB.

9. DISCUSSION

Contributions. A new class of regular expression matching algorithm has been introduced based on the concept of bit-parallel data streams together with the MatchStar operation. The algorithm is fully general for nondeterministic regular expression matching; however it does not address the nonregular extensions found in Perl-compatible backtracking implementations. Taking advantage of the SIMD features available on commodity processors, its implementation in grep offers consistently good performance in contrast to available alternatives. For moderately complex expressions, 10X or better performance advantages over DFA-based gre2p and 5X performance advantage over nrgrep were frequently seen. While lacking some special optimizations found in other engines to deal with repeated substrings or to perform skipping actions based on fixed substrings, it nevertheless performs competitively in all cases.

A model for parallelized long-stream addition has also been presented in the paper, allowing our techniques to scale beyond the blocks of 128 bytes we use with the SSE2 implementation. This model allowed straightforward extension to the 256-byte block size used in our AVX2 implementation and should continue to scale well up for SIMD vectors up to 4096 bytes in length based on 64-bit additions. The model also supports GPU implementation with some additional effort.

Related Work. Much of the previous work in parallelizing of regular processing has dealt with the problem of using parallel resources to handle multiple instances of a matching problem in parallel. It is thus complementary to our approach which focuses on parallelization to accelerate the matching of a single instance. From this perspective, the recent work of Mytkowicz et al [11] stands out as an important comparator in that it also focusses on acceleration of matching for a single input stream. Mytkowicz use the SIMD byte-shuffle capabilities found, for example, in the SSSE3 instruction sets to perform small-table parallel lookups for multiple potentially active states of a FSM. Data parallelism is achieved by initially considering all possible states at the beginning of each data segment, but then relying on convergence and range-coalescing optimizations to quickly reduce the number of active states in play. Examining a large collection of regular expressions used in practice, these techniques were found to be effective, allowing matching to proceed with just one or two shuffles per input symbol.

However, the Mytkowicz approach is still fundamentally considering input elements one byte at a time and would be hard pressed to compete with our reported results of 1-4 CPU cycles per input byte. It is also dependent on the availability of the SIMD byte-shuffle operation, which is unavailable in SIMD instructions sets such as SSE2 and ARM Neon, for example. Our SIMD implementation relies only on the availability of SIMD pack operations to efficiently implement the Parabix transform; SIMD pack is widely available in current SIMD instruction sets. It is also a special case of the more general shuffle operations and hence available on any processor that supports byte shuffle. The Parabix approach also has the further advantage that performance scales with increasing SIMD instruction width, as illustrated by our AVX2 performance results in comparison to SSE2.

It is perhaps surprising that the classic nrgrep application is still competitive in performance for expressions that allow the BNDM algorithm to perform significant character skipping. Although the length of possible skipping reduces with the complexity of the input expression considered, many applications of grep searching tend to use simple expressions in practice. Nevertheless, the Parabix approach offers consistently high performance often faster than nrgrep by a factor of 5X or more.

Ongoing and Future Work. Based on the techniques presented here a fully integrated grep version with a dynamic code generator implemented with LLVM is being developed by another team working with the Parabix technology (Dale Denis, Nick Sumner and Rob Cameron). An initial version is available at `http://parabix.costar.sfu.ca/icGREP`. With icgrep-0.8, total compile-time overhead to translate our test expressions into executable x86 code ranges from 0.002 seconds to 0.008 seconds for our test cases. Although this represents a tolerable overhead of 0.64 cycles/byte for our 40 MB test file, we expect that a substantial reduction of this overhead is feasible.

Further work on the compilation algorithms includes the extending the algorithms to use MatchStar in Kleene-* repetitions beyond those of single characters (bytes). Each such extension would replace while-loop iteration with addition and bitwise logic. For example, the repetitions of variable-length UTF-8 byte sequences can be compiled without while loops by taking advantage of synchronizing properties of UTF-8.

Future work also includes the development of multicore versions of the underlying algorithms to further accelerate performance and to handle regular expression matching problems involving larger rule sets than are typically encountered in the grep problem. Such implementations could have useful application in tokenization and network intrusion detection for example. Additional GPU implementation work could take advantage of specialized instructions available on particular platforms but not generally avaiable through OpenCL. For both multicore and GPU implementations, data-parallel division of input streams could benefit from techniques such as the principled speculation of Zhao et al [25], for example.

Other area of interest include extending the capabilities of the underlying method with addition features for substring capture, zero-width assertions and possibly backreference matching. Adding Unicode support beyond basic Unicode character handling to include full Unicode character class support and normalization forms is also worth investigating.

10. ACKNOWLEDGMENTS

This research was supported by grants from the Natural Sciences and Engineering Research Council of Canada and MITACS, Inc.

11. REFERENCES

[1] A. V. Aho and M. J. Corasick. Efficient string matching: an aid to bibliographic search. *Communications of the ACM*, 18(6):333–340, June 1975.

[2] R. Baeza-Yates and G. H. Gonnet. A new approach to text searching. *Communications of the ACM*, 35(10):74–82, 1992.

[3] R. S. Boyer and J. S. Moore. A fast string searching algorithm. *Communications of the ACM*, 20(10):762–772, 1977.

[4] R. D. Cameron, E. Amiri, K. S. Herdy, D. Lin, T. C. Shermer, and F. P. Popowich. Parallel scanning with bitstream addition: An XML case study. In *Euro-Par 2011 Parallel Processing*, pages 2–13. Springer, 2011.

[5] R. Cox. Regular expression matching in the wild, 2010.

[6] R. Crovella. Long stream addition with CUDA. Stack Overflow question 12957116, 2012.

[7] R. N. Horspool. Practical fast searching in strings. *Software: Practice and Experience*, 10(6):501–506, 1980.

[8] F. Iorio and J. V. Lunteren. Fast pattern matching on the cell broadband engine. In *2008 Workshop on Cell Systems and Applications (WCSA), affiliated with the*, 2008.

[9] C. Lin, C. Liu, L. Chien, and S. Chang. Accelerating pattern matching using a novel parallel algorithm on GPUs. *IEEE Transactions on Computers*, 62(10), 2013.

[10] D. Lin, N. Medforth, K. S. Herdy, A. Shriraman, and R. Cameron. Parabix: Boosting the efficiency of text processing on commodity processors. In *18th International Symposium on High Performance Computer Architecture (HPCA)*, pages 1–12. IEEE, 2012.

[11] T. Mytkowicz, M. Musuvathi, and W. Schulte. Data-parallel finite-state machines. In *19th International Conference on Architectural Support for Programming Languages and Operating Systems (ASPLOS)*, pages 529–542, 2014.

[12] J. Naghmouchi, D. P. Scarpazza, and M. Berekovic. Small-ruleset regular expression matching on GPGPUs: quantitative performance analysis and optimization. In *Proceedings of the 24th ACM International Conference on Supercomputing*, ICS '10, pages 337–348, New York, NY, USA, 2010. ACM.

[13] G. Navarro. Nr-grep: A fast and flexible pattern matching tool. *Software Practice and Experience (SPE*, 31:2001, 2000.

[14] G. Navarro and M. Raffinot. A bit-parallel approach to suffix automata: Fast extended string matching. In *Combinatorial Pattern Matching*, pages 14–33. Springer, 1998.

[15] G. Navarro and M. Raffinot. Fast and flexible string matching by combining bit-parallelism and suffix automata. *ACM Journal of Experimental Algorithmics (JEA)*, 5:2000, 1998.

[16] D. Pasetto, F. Petrini, and V. Agarwal. Tools for very fast regular expression matching. *Computer*, 43(3):50–58, 2010.

[17] V. Salapura, T. Karkhanis, P. Nagpurkar, and J. Moreira. Accelerating business analytics applications. In *18th International Symposium on High Performance Computer Architecture (HPCA)*, pages 1–10. IEEE, 2012.

[18] D. P. Scarpazza. Top-performance tokenization and small-ruleset regular expression matching. *International Journal of Parallel Programming*, 39(1):3–32, 2011.

[19] D. P. Scarpazza and G. F. Russell. High-performance regular expression scanning on the Cell/BE processor. In *Proceedings of the 23rd International Conference on Supercomputing*, pages 14–25. ACM, 2009.

[20] D. P. Scarpazza, O. Villa, and F. Petrinni. Fast string searches & multicore processors mapping fundamental algorithms on parallel hardware, 2008.

[21] K. Thompson. Programming techniques: Regular expression search algorithm. *Communications of the ACM*, 11(6):419–422, 1968.

[22] A. Tumeo, O. Villa, and D. Sciuto. Efficient pattern matching on GPUs for intrusion detection systems. In *Proceedings of the 7th ACM International Conference on Computing Frontiers*, pages 87–88. ACM, 2010.

[23] S. Wu and U. Manber. Agrep - a fast approximate pattern-matching tool. *Usenix Winter 1992*, pages 153–162, 1992.

[24] S. Wu and U. Manber. Fast text searching: allowing errors. *Communications of the ACM*, 35(10):83–91, 1992.

[25] Z. Zhao, B. Wu, and X. Shen. Challenging the "embarrassingly sequential": parallelizing finite state machine-based computations through principled speculation. In *19th International Conference on Architectural Support for Programming Languages and Operating Systems (ASPLOS)*, pages 543–558, 2014.

Adaptive Heterogeneous Scheduling for Integrated GPUs

Rashid Kaleem*
Dept. of Computer Science
University of Texas at Austin
rashid@cs.utexas.edu

Rajkishore Barik
Intel Labs
Santa Clara, CA
rajkishore.barik@intel.com

Tatiana Shpeisman
Intel Labs
Santa Clara, CA
tatiana.shpeisman@intel.com

Brian T. Lewis
Intel Labs
Santa Clara, CA
brian.t.lewis@intel.com

Chunling Hu
Intel Labs
Santa Clara, CA
chunling.hu@intel.com

Keshav Pingali
Dept. of Computer Science
University of Texas at Austin
pingali@cs.utexas.edu

ABSTRACT

Many processors today integrate a CPU and GPU on the same die, which allows them to share resources like physical memory and lowers the cost of CPU-GPU communication. As a consequence, programmers can effectively utilize both the CPU and GPU to execute a single application. This paper presents novel adaptive scheduling techniques for integrated CPU-GPU processors. We present two online profiling-based scheduling algorithms: *naïve* and *asymmetric*. Our asymmetric scheduling algorithm uses low-overhead online profiling to automatically partition the work of data-parallel kernels between the CPU and GPU without input from application developers. It does profiling on the CPU and GPU in a way that doesn't penalize GPU-centric workloads that run significantly faster on the GPU. It adapts to application characteristics by addressing: 1) load imbalance via irregularity caused by, e.g., data-dependent control flow, 2) different amounts of work on each kernel call, and 3) multiple kernels with different characteristics. Unlike many existing approaches primarily targeting NVIDIA discrete GPUs, our scheduling algorithm does not require offline processing.

We evaluate our asymmetric scheduling algorithm on a desktop system with an Intel 4th Generation Core Processor using a set of sixteen regular and irregular workloads from diverse application areas. On average, our asymmetric scheduling algorithm performs within 3.2% of the maximum throughput with a CPU-and-GPU oracle that always chooses the best work partitioning between the CPU and GPU. These results underscore the feasibility of online profile-based heterogeneous scheduling on integrated CPU-GPU processors.

*The work presented in this paper has been supported by NSF grants CCF 1337281, CCF 1218568, ACI 1216701, and CNS 1064956.

PACT'14, August 24–27, 2014, Edmonton, AB, Canada.
Copyright 2014 ACM 978-1-4503-2809-8/14/08 ...$15.00.
http://dx.doi.org/10.1145/2628071.2628088 .

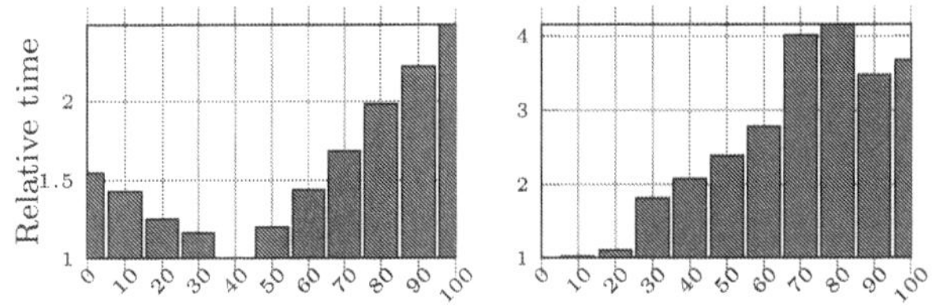

Figure 1: Relative execution time of **BH**-BarnesHut (left) and **FD**-Facedetect (right) as ratio of work offloaded to the GPU is varied from 0% to 100% in increments of 10% (*lower is better*). **BH** is optimal at 40% and **FD** is optimal at 0%.

Categories and Subject Descriptors

D.4.1 [**Operating Systems**]: Process Management—*Scheduling*; D.1.3 [**Software**]: Programming—*Parallel programming*

Keywords

Heterogeneous computing; integrated GPUs; scheduling; load balancing; Irregular applications;

1. INTRODUCTION

In many modern processors such as Intel's IvyBridge and Haswell processors, and AMD's Trinity and Richland processors, the GPU is resident on the same die as the CPU and has the same address space. Such processors present new challenges to application developers, as achieving maximum performance often requires simultaneous use of both CPU and GPU. Moreover, the optimal division of work between the CPU and GPU is very application dependent. As an example, consider Fig. 1, which shows the performance of Barnes-Hut (**BH**) and Face detection (**FD**) on an Intel Haswell machine as the proportion of work assigned to the GPU is varied from 0% to 100% (the applications and the machine are described in more detail in Sec. 7). The y-axis in both graphs shows execution time normalized to the best running time for each application. For **BH**, the best running time is obtained when 40% of the work is done on the GPU. **FD** in contrast does not benefit at all from GPU execution and performs best when run on multicore CPU.

Ideally, the scheduler should partition work between CPU and GPU automatically and efficiently without any input from the application developer. The division of work between the CPU and a GPU has been the subject of a number of prior studies [4,12,18,22,24,32]. Their techniques fall into three broad categories:

- *Off-line training* [18,22,24]: Train the runtime scheduling algorithm on input data set and then use the previously obtained information on the real run. The success of this approach depends crucially on how accurately the training reflects what happens during the real run. Moreover, the training must be repeated for each new platform.
- Use a *performance model* [4,19]: Accurate performance models are notoriously difficult to construct, particularly for irregular workloads since runtime behavior is very dependent on characteristics of the input data.
- Extend standard *work-stealing* with restrictions on stealing [12,32]: Since the GPU cannot initiate communication with the CPU, only extensions where work is pushed to GPUs can address load imbalance. Such approaches incur overheads on the CPU execution since the CPU has to act on behalf of the GPU workers.

Most of the prior work has been performed in the context of discrete GPUs, where data must be communicated between CPU memory and GPU memory over slow interconnect such as the PCIe bus. This high-latency communication limits the CPU to offload relatively coarse-grain tasks to the GPU. Integrated GPUs dramatically reduce the cost of data communication between CPU and GPU, so finer grain work sharing between the CPU and GPU than has been explored by prior work becomes possible.

In this paper, we present novel scheduling techniques for integrated CPU-GPU processors that leverage online profiling. Our techniques profile a fraction of the work-items on each device and decide how to distribute the workload between the CPU and GPU based on the measured device execution rates. Because our algorithm is fully online, it does not require any prior training and carries no additional overhead when applied to applications with new data sets or new platforms.

While seemingly simple, scheduling based on online profiling must avoid several pitfalls to produce good results. *First*, it should perform the profiling with near zero overhead, effectively utilizing all available resources, as otherwise, the profiling cost might significantly reduce the benefit of subsequent heterogeneous execution. *Second*, it should accurately measure the execution ratio of different devices, which might be non-trivial in the presence of load imbalance that often occurs in irregular applications. *Finally*, it should be able to effectively handle diverse realistic workloads including those with multiple kernels and multiple invocations of the same kernel, accounting for the fact that optimal execution might require different CPU/GPU partitioning of the different kernel invocations or different kernels.

Our approach addresses these challenges and demonstrates that, if implemented correctly, profile-based scheduling has very little overhead and produces an efficient execution strategy which competes with an offline *Oracle* model. We do note that these benefits are for integrated GPU systems where the offload cost is very small.

Specifically, our contributions are as follows:

1. We present a simple *naïve* profiling based scheduling algorithm that partitions work between CPU and GPU cores of an integrated GPU system without requiring any application-specific information from the application writer. We analyze the overhead associated with such a scheme.
2. We improve our naïve profiling scheme and devise a novel *asymmetric scheduling* algorithm that eliminates some of the overheads associated with naïve profiling. We show that asymmetric profiling introduces zero overhead in the profiling phase.
3. Furthermore, we extend our asymmetric scheduling algorithm with several adaptive schemes to address load imbalance due to irregularities within a *parallel_for* loop and also across multiple *parallel_for* invocations.
4. We present an experimental evaluation of our algorithms on an Intel 4th Generation Core Processor using an extensive set of *sixteen* benchmarks which comprise of a mix of regular and irregular code. On average, our asymmetric scheduling algorithm performs within 5.8% of the maximum throughput obtained by an exhaustive search algorithm. Furthermore, our asymmetric algorithm with adaptivity can further improve the efficiency and achieves within 3.2% of the exhaustive search algorithm.

The layout of the paper is as follows. Sec. 2 outlines the problem statement for heterogeneous execution and discusses it's complexity. Sec. 3 summarizes our programming model and runtime. Sec. 4 describes our naïve profiling algorithm and analyzes it's overhead. Sec. 5 describes our asymmetric profiling scheduling algorithm. We describe the details of our implementation in Sec. 6. This is followed by the evaluation of the proposed schemes as well as a brief description of the benchmarks and hardware in Sec. 7 followed by discussion of the results. We discuss related work in Sec. 8 and conclude in Sec. 9.

2. PROBLEM STATEMENT

The heterogeneous programming framework we use provides a *parallel_for* loop construct for the data-parallel execution of independent loop iterations. Our applications have one or more data-parallel *parallel_for* loops. We would like to determine the optimal partitioning of loop iterations between the CPU and the GPU that minimizes the execution time of the *parallel_for*.

Why is this hard? Several factors make automatic heterogeneous scheduling challenging for CPU+GPU processors:

- The CPU and GPU have different device characteristics. CPU cores are typically out-of-order, have sophisticated branch predictors, and use deep cache hierarchies to reduce memory access latency. GPU cores are typically in-order, spend their transistors on a large number of ALUs, and hide memory latency by switching between hardware threads. This dissimilarity leads to significant differences in execution performance. Certain applications may execute significantly faster on one device than the other. As a result, executing even a small amount of work on the slower device may hurt performance.
- Certain *parallel_for* iterations may take more time than others. Without apriori information about the loop's behavior, it is hard to optimally divide work between the CPU and GPU automatically.
- Iterations may show execution irregularity due to, e.g., data-dependent control flow operations. Without knowl-

edge of the input data, it is hard to determine the optimal partitioning.

- There can be more than one *parallel_for* in an application and each may be invoked more than once, as in the second *parallel_for* in Fig. 2. Since one parallel loop can have the side effect of warming the cache for a second loop, understanding the interactions among the different parallel loops is important to optimally partition work. Similarly, interactions between the multiple invocations of the same parallel loop can also be important for optimal work scheduling.

As a result, devising an automatic heterogeneous scheduling algorithm to handle all these situations is a daunting task. In the remainder of this paper, we do not address interactions among two or more parallel loops, but plan to address it in future work. Furthermore, we do not specially treat *parallel_for* loops that do not have enough parallelism to keep all GPU resources busy. In the future, we plan to execute these loops entirely on the CPU.

3. BACKGROUND

This section briefly describes our heterogeneous programming model and then discusses various existing approaches to heterogeneous execution.

3.1 C++ programming model

We use the Concord [5] C++ framework to evaluate the benefits of our different scheduling algorithms. However, our scheduling techniques should apply to other programming frameworks with similar data-parallel APIs such as OpenMP, OpenACC, and C++ AMP. Concord is a heterogeneous C++ programming framework for processors with integrated GPUs, and is designed to allow general-purpose, object-oriented, data-parallel programs to take advantage of GPU execution. It provides two parallel constructs for offloading computations to the GPU: a *parallel_for* loop and a *parallel_reduce* loop. These APIs are similar to popular data-parallel multi-core C++ programming models such as TBB [1], OpenMP, Cilk [23], and Galois [28]). Both these constructs take as arguments the number of data-parallel iterations and the closure object which encompasses the parallel code. Concord does not guarantee that different loop iterations will be executed in parallel, and does not guarantee floating point determinism in reductions. Also, programmers should make no assumption about the order in which different iterations are done. For the rest of the paper, we only focus on the *parallel_for* construct – similar techniques apply to *parallel_reduce*.

Fig. 2 shows an example Concord C++ program demonstrating the use of two *parallel_for* constructs. The first *parallel_for* increments every element of an N-element array a using the data-parallel kernel in *Foo::operator* once (single invocation kernel), while the later loop decrements the elements of a using the *Bar::operator* kernel multiple times (multiple invocation kernel). The classes *Foo* and *Bar* contain the environment (e.g., a) for the parallel code specified in the *operator* functions.

3.2 Heterogeneous execution model

Supporting data parallelism in a heterogeneous system requires two things. *First*, executable versions of a kernel must be compiled for each system device. Like systems such as *Dandelion* [31] and *Lime* [16], *Concord* [5] addresses this

```
// Functor class implementing one loop body
class Foo {
  int *a;
  void operator(int i) { a[i] += f(i); }
};
// Functor class implementing another loop body
class Bar {
  int *a;
  void operator(int i) { a[i] -= g(i);}
};
...
Foo *f1 = new Foo();
// Single invocation of a data-parallel loop
parallel_for(N, *f1);
...
Bar *f2 = new Bar();
// Multiple invocations of a data-parallel loop
for (int i=M; i<P; i++)
   parallel_for(i, *f2);
```

Figure 2: Example demonstrating Concord *parallel_for*

by translating a high-level language kernel to separate native executables for the CPU and GPU. *Second*, a *scheduling* mechanism is required to determine where each *parallel_for* iteration will be executed. There are different approaches to scheduling *parallel_for* iterations across multiple devices of a heterogeneous system that aim to minimize execution time. We summarize them below.

3.2.1 Offline profiling

The application is first run using a training data set and profiled. The profiling data is used to select the scheduling policy for subsequent application runs against real data. *Qilin* [24] performs an offline analysis to measure the kernel's execution rate on each device (CPU and GPU). These rates are used to decide the distribution of work for each device. Qilin uses a linear performance model to chose the scheduling policy based on the size of the input data set. In general, there are two main drawbacks of offline-profiling. *First*, the scheduling policy chosen depends on the training data, i.e., if the training data differs significantly from the actual data used in subsequent runs, the scheduling policy is likely to be suboptimal. *Second*, new execution rates and work distributions must be determined for each new target platform.

3.2.2 Online approaches

In online approaches, the decision of where to execute *parallel_for* iterations is made at runtime. The programmer does not have to train the system on representative inputs for each target platform. We discuss some common online approaches below.

- **Work-stealing** [9] is a popular way to address load imbalance in multi-core execution. However, a GPU differs from the CPU in one important aspect when addressing load imbalance. Current GPUs cannot initiate communication with the CPU or execute atomic operations visible to the CPU which means a GPU cannot request work from non-local work pools. The GPU cannot use persistent threads to steal work from a common pool because of the relaxed CPU-GPU memory consistency, which only guarantees that GPU memory updates will be visible after the GPU code terminates. Furthermore, the GPU is statically scheduled: once items are scheduled to be processed on the GPU, the order in which they are processed is undefined and hence we can make no assumptions about

which items can be stolen from the GPU's local pool by other threads.
One simple approach to addressing load imbalance that avoids these limitations is to have a dedicated *GPU proxy thread* running on the CPU to perform work-stealing on behalf of the GPU. The GPU proxy thread can steal a number of loop iterations to execute on the GPU, then wait for the GPU to complete their execution or until all iterations have been processed by either the CPU or the GPU. The time to execute a number of loop iterations on the GPU is a key performance bottleneck. If we choose many iterations in order to reduce the overhead of launching work on the GPU, the GPU might stall loop termination while the CPU threads are out of work. On the other hand, if we choose too few iterations, this will increase the number of GPU offload requests as well as underutilize the GPU hardware, as we show later in Sec. 4.2.

- **Profiling-based** is an online profiling based approach. The application kernel is dynamically profiled and used to determine the distribution of workload between the CPU and the GPU. The key to this approach is that the profiling phase should not introduce any overhead that can not be compensated by the benefits obtained by doing it. We present two online-profiling based techniques in the next two sections and analyze their overheads.

4. NAÏVE PROFILING

In this section, we propose a heterogeneous scheduling algorithm based on a simple online profiling scheme and analyze the associated overheads.

It is well-known that regular applications with little or no load imbalance are well-suited for GPUs whereas multi-core CPUs equipped with accurate branch predictors are capable of performing well across regular or irregular, balanced or imbalanced workloads. As a result, we first determine the characteristics of a workload using an online profiling run in order to determine the rate of execution on each device. This profiling information is used to decide the percentage of remaining iterations to assign to each device.

Fig. 3 shows our naïve profiling scheduling algorithm. It executes in two phases – *profiling phase* and *execution phase*. When a kernel is executed for the first time over N items, the runtime forks a proxy thread that offloads Nf_p iterations to the GPU, where f_p is a ratio between 0 and 1[1], and measures the rate G_r at which the GPU processes the kernel. Concurrently, the runtime thread itself processes another Nf_p iterations on the multicore CPU and computes the CPU rate C_r. Both threads merge on a barrier after completing the profiling phase where they compare the two rates G_r and C_r. Based on these rates, the runtime distributes the remaining iterations to the CPU and GPU in the execution phase. New rates are computed and cached for future invocations of the same kernel. For already-seen kernels, the runtime uses the old values of C_r and G_r to distribute iterations.

The naïve profiling based scheduling algorithm may introduce overheads in both the phases: (1) in the *profiling phase*, one of the devices completes execution before the other one; (2) if the iterations used in the profiling phase are not representative of the entire iteration space (applications with imbalance and irregularity fall into this category), then the *execution phase* may introduce some more overheads. We address both these overheads with an asymmetric scheduling algorithm (Sec. 5). Below, we first provide theoretical analysis of our naïve profiling algorithm and then discuss how f_p is determined.

[1]We discuss choosing f_p in Sec. 4.2.

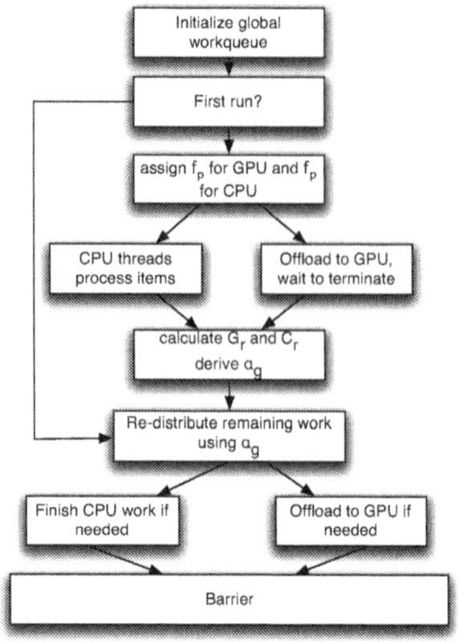

Figure 3: Naïve profiling

4.1 Analysis

Let α_g denote the ideal ratio for distribution to the GPU, and the remaining $1 - \alpha_g$ to the CPU. If we denote the rate with which CPU executes work items as C_r and GPU as G_r, we would like to find the ratio α_g of work items to be offloaded to the GPU such that:

$$\frac{N\alpha_g}{G_r} = \frac{N(1-\alpha_g)}{C_r} \tag{1}$$

Where N is the total number of work items to be processed due to a call to the *parallel_for*. Using this formula, we can derive the value of α_g as:

$$\alpha_g = \frac{G_r}{G_r + C_r}$$

Intuitively, α_g specifies how fast the GPU is compared to the CPU. So if the two devices are processing items at the same rate ($C_r = G_r$), we would have $\alpha_g = 0.5$.

The ideal time to execute the N work-items can be expressed as:

$$T_{ideal} = \frac{N}{C_r + G_r} \tag{2}$$

Real execution time will consist of the T_{prof}, time to profile Nf_p work on CPU and GPU, and T_{exec}, time to execute the remaining items according to the measured distribution ratio β_g.

$$T_{real} = T_{prof} + T_{exec} \tag{3}$$

The distribution ratio β_g computed by the profiling may differ from the ideal distribution ratio α_g that allows both devices to terminate at the same time. This could happen, for example, if the workload is highly irregular or if the profiling stage is too short. How much the execution time T_{exec}

differs from the ideal time to execute $(1-2f_p)N$ remaining items depends on the difference between α_g and β_g, as stated in the theorem below. Ideally, we would like profiling to derive β_g as close to α_g as possible.

THEOREM 1. *The overhead of executing P iterations using distribution ratio β_g instead of the ideal ratio α_g is proportional to the difference between β_g and α_g.*

PROOF. *The overhead is the difference of execution times with β_g and α_g.*

$$T_{overhead} = max[\frac{N\beta_g}{G_r} - \frac{N\alpha_g}{G_r}, \frac{N(1-\beta_g)}{C_r} - \frac{N(1-\alpha_g)}{C_r}]$$

$$= max[N(\frac{\beta_g - \alpha_g}{G_r}), N(\frac{\alpha_g - \beta_g}{C_r})] \quad (4)$$

The above difference is clearly proportional to $\beta_g - \alpha_g$. □

Another source of overhead with the naïve profiling algorithm is a suboptimal distribution of work during the profiling phase. The profiling time is the maximum of time to execute Nf_p items on each of CPU and GPU.

$$T_{prof} = max[\frac{Nf_p}{G_r}, \frac{Nf_p}{C_r}] \quad (5)$$

The profiling phase can impose significant overhead if the difference between G_r and C_r is very large. For example, assume that the GPU is 10x faster than the CPU ($G_r = 10C_r$). In this case,

$$T_{prof} = max[\frac{Nf_p}{10C_r}, \frac{Nf_p}{C_r}] = \frac{Nf_p}{C_r}$$

If we assume $f_p = 5\%$, the time taken by the profiling phase becomes $\frac{0.05N}{C_r}$. As the GPU is 10x times faster than the CPU, it completes its profiling run in one tenth of the time. If the GPU would continue working during the rest of the profiling run it could complete nine times as much work, that is, another 45% of the total work. Even if the profiling is accurate, and the remaining work is divided between the CPU and GPU using the ideal distribution ratio $\alpha_g = 0.9$, the time the GPU has spent idle during the profiling stage will have significant negative effect on total execution time.

4.2 Determining profiling size

Determining the right number of iterations or work-items to use for profiling is important. Picking *too many* items for the profiling phase can increase the profiling overhead since one device may have to wait for the other device to complete execution. On the other hand, picking *too few* work items for the GPU can underestimate GPU performance since it is underutilized. Ideally, the profiling size should be large enough to utilize all the available GPU parallelism. To illustrate this point, we demonstrate the impact of different profiling sizes on two kernels: one regular kernel and the other irregular.

Regular kernel: Fig. 4 shows the impact of choosing different profiling sizes on the performance of a simple synthetic kernel running on the integrated GPU (details of our experimental platform are provided in Sec. 7). This kernel computes the sum of integers from 1 to 2048 per work-item. There are no memory accesses and no thread divergences in the kernel. We report the GPU execution rate, G_r, as we

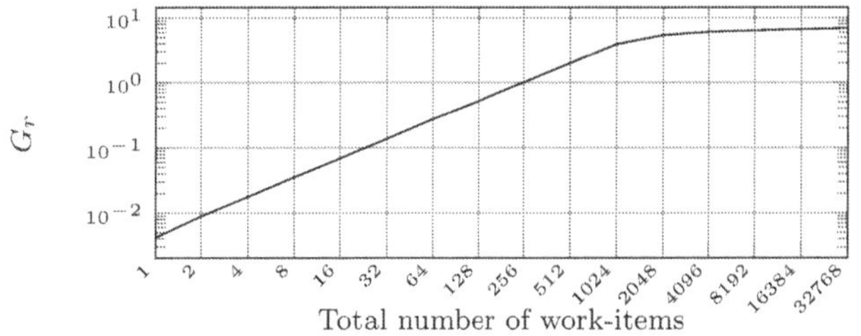

Figure 4: Plot showing the change in G_r with increasing number of work-items for a regular kernel. (Note the logarithmic scales.)

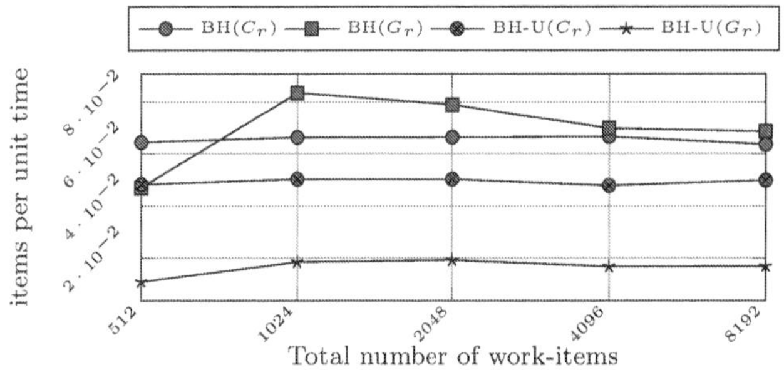

Figure 5: Plot showing average C_r and G_r for different values of Nf_p for BarnesHut (**BH**) and BarnesHut-unoptimized (**BH-U**).

increase the number of work-items offloaded to the GPU. As we increase the number of items, we see an increase in G_r as the GPU takes the same amount of time to process more items. The rate stabilizes at 2048 items, which implies that the GPU hardware was underutilized when processing less than 2048 items. Ideally, we would like to have at least 2048 items to profile accurately and not underutilize this specific GPU.

Irregular kernel: Irregular kernel code may complicate the choice of a good profiling chunk size. Fig. 5 shows the average execution rates for both **BH-U** and **BH**[2] when we process items in chunk sizes ranging from 512 to 8192. We show the execution rates separately for the CPU (C_r) and GPU(G_r). The CPU performance is relatively stable for both **BH** and **BH-U** (the difference in time per item for the two versions is due to the improved locality with **BH**), and not affected by increasing chunk size. However, for **BH-U** on the GPU, G_r increases sharply from 512 to 1024 and is relatively stable for larger values. A similar but less subtle trend is visible for **BH** on the GPU as well.

The impact of picking a small chunk size for GPU profiling is visible in Fig. 5. If we pick a chunk size of 512 for **BH-U**, we get the GPU rate $\frac{1}{92}$, and the CPU rate $\frac{1}{21}$, which leads to an offload ratio α_g of 0.17. However, if we pick 1024 as the chunk size, we get a different rate for the GPU $\frac{1}{54}$ and for the CPU $\frac{1}{19}$ leading to an GPU offload ratio of 0.27, which is close to the static optimal 0.30.

To summarize, we want to use the smallest number of items that fully utilize the GPU. The integrated GPU we use in our experimental evaluation has 20 execution units (EU), 7 threads per EU, each thread being 16-way SIMD

[2]**BH** is an optimized version of Barnes-Hut algorithm (**BH-U**), where the bodies are sorted in a breadth-first-search order from the root.

for a total of 2240 work-items that can execute at one time. This information can be obtained automatically by querying the GPU device using the OpenCL API[3]. So, we use 2048 as the profiling size for our evaluation which agrees with our empirical observation above for both regular and irregular kernels.

5. ASYMMETRIC PROFILING

In this section, we describe our asymmetric profiling algorithm that addresses the overheads of the naïve profiling algorithm and additionally, provides adaptive strategies that handle load imbalance due to irregularity and multiple invocations per kernel.

The first overhead in naïve profiling was caused by waiting on a barrier when one of the devices finishes execution before the other. We address this overhead in asymmetric profiling as follows: we initially have a shared pool of work consisting of the entire parallel iteration space, and we pick a portion f_p of items to be offloaded to the GPU using the proxy GPU thread. The CPU workers continue to pick items from the shared global pool and locally collect profiling information. When the GPU proxy thread finishes profiling, it performs the following steps in order; it (1) computes the distribution ratio by reading each worker's local profiling statistics (during this time, the CPU workers continue to work on the shared pool), (2) empties the shared pool, (3) adds the CPU portion of the work to one of the CPU worker's work-stealing queue, and (4) finally offloads GPU portion of the work to GPU. Fig. 6 illustrates the algorithm. It is important to note that while the GPU is executing, CPU workers continue to work from the shared pool, thereby eliminating the overhead seen in naïve profiling.

One of the design choices for asymmetric scheduling is to start with a shared pool in the profiling phase instead of work-stealing. This is justified since at the beginning we have no knowledge of how to partition work among CPU workers and the proxy GPU worker. For example, for applications with irregularities, it may be costly to partition the work up front into the work-stealing queues.

If both the devices are kept busy in the profiling phase by having sufficient number of parallel iterations, it can be seen that the profiling phase will introduce zero overhead in the asymmetric profiling algorithm (theoretical analysis is provided below in Sec. 5.1). Similar to the naïve profiling, the vanilla version of asymmetric profiling may still introduce overhead in the execution phase if the iterations used in profiling phase are not representative of the entire iteration space. We address this in Sec. 5.2.

5.1 Analysis

We now analyze the overhead of asymmetric profiling compared to the ideal execution scenario. We concentrate on the analysis of the profiling phase, as the behavior of the execution phase in the base algorithm is identical to that of naïve profiling. Assuming the runtime offloads f_p fraction of the original items to the GPU and allows CPU threads to execute as long as the GPU is busy, the time taken by the GPU to complete Nf_p items is $t_p = \frac{Nf_p}{G_r}$. At the same time, CPU completes an additional t_pC_r items assuming there is enough

[3]CL_DEVICE_MAX_COMPUTE_UNITS, CL_DEVICE_MAX_WORK_GROUP_SIZE, and CL_DEVICE_NATIVE_VECTOR_WIDTH_INT.

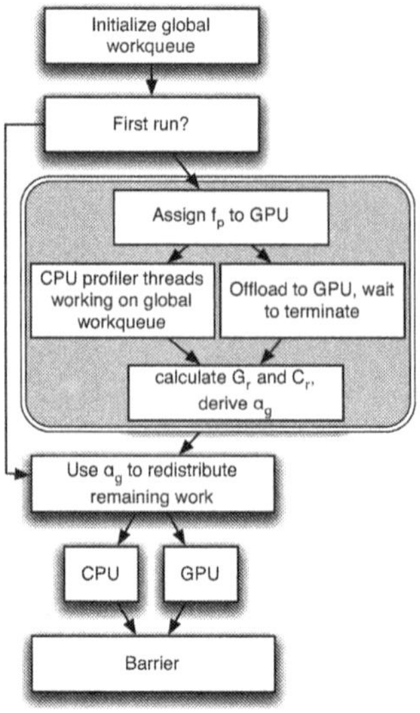

Figure 6: Asymmetric profiling

work to keep it busy. In this case, the overhead of the profiling is zero, as both GPU and CPU work all the time. On the other hand, if the amount of work offloaded to GPU is so large that there is not enough work items for CPU, there is a non-zero overhead. This observation is formally stated by the following theorem.

THEOREM 2. *Overhead of the profiling phase in the asymmetric profiling algorithm is zero if* $f_p < \alpha_g$.

PROOF. *The number of items executed by CPU is maximum of the amount of work it can perform in* t_p *time and the remaining work:*

$$N_c = max(t_pC_r, (1 - f_p)N)$$

The first argument to max is greater than the second, when $t_pC_r > (1 - f_p)N$, *which simplifies to* $f_p > \alpha_g$. *In this case, the total amount of work executed by CPU and GPU is* $N_p = Nf_p + \frac{Nf_pC_r}{G_r}$. *In the ideal case, this work can be executed by CPU and GPU working together in* $\frac{N_p}{C_r+G_r}$ *time. This time is equal to the profiling phase time* $\frac{Nf_p}{G_r}$ *as can be shown by simple algebraic transformations. The overhead of the profiling phase is, thus, zero.* □

In practice, f_p is likely to be greater than α_g only when CPU is significantly faster than GPU. For example, if we offload 5% of work to GPU for profiling, CPU should be at least 19x faster than GPU to trigger non-zero overhead. To handle such cases our work can be combined with static profiling techniques such as [18] to determine if the workload has a strong CPU bias and use CPU-biased asymmetric profiling instead of the GPU-biased one.

5.2 Addressing load imbalance

In order to address bias due to the initial profiling, the profiling can be repeated until a certain termination condition is reached, after which the benefits of re-profiling diminish. This ensures that we profile more than once to understand the application-level imbalance better. We consider two termination conditions: *convergence* and *size*.

Convergence-based strategy repeats profiling until β_g converges. For example, we could re-profile until computed ratios differ by no more than 0.05. The assumption with convergence strategy is that once the distribution ratio stops changing, it is close to the ideal ratio α_g. Convergence strategy works well when distribution ratio indeed stabilizes after temporary converging. On the otherhand, *size*-based strategy repeats the profiling until a certain portion of the work items has been completed. For example, we could re-profile till the number of remaining items is more than 50%. Size-based strategy works well when *i)* running CPU threads in profiling mode does not impose a lot of overhead, and *ii)* the irregularity of the workload gets amortized over fixed portion of the items.

When re-profiling, it is important to keep both CPU and GPU busy. As has been shown by Theorem 2, asymmetric profiling incurs no overhead only when there is sufficient amount of work to keep CPU busy while GPU performs its fixed portion of work. The profiling strategy, thus, should keep the total fraction of items offloaded to GPU below the ideal distribution ratio α_g, or, more practically, below its approximation, β_g, from a prior profiling run.

It is important to note that there can be scenarios where neither size-based or convergence-based strategies can determine the optimal partitioning – for example, triangular loop inside a *parallel_for* loop. We believe such scenarios are rare in practice – none of the sixteen benchmarks we studied exhibit this kind of behavior.

5.3 Multiple invocations per kernel

In programs where the kernel is executed multiple times, the programmer can assume the first invocation as a profile run to obtain the rate of execution on both devices. After the first run, whenever we execute some items on one or both devices, we observe the execution rates and update our offload ratio β_g according to the selected update strategies described below.

5.3.1 Update functions:

Given an execution of some items on the devices, we use (C_r, G_r, C_n, G_n), where C_r and G_r are rates and C_n, G_n are number of items processed by the CPU and GPU respectively. Two variants we propose are :

1. **Greedy**: Simply use the G_r, C_r to compute β_g. This is always used the first time a rate is computed since we assume no initial distribution of work-items.
2. **Sample weighted**: Compute $w = \frac{C_n+G_n}{C_n+G_n+T_n}$, where T_n is the number of items used to compute the rate so far, and $\beta_g^{new} = \frac{G_r}{G_r+C_r}$. And set the new ratio to be $\beta_g = w\beta_g^{new} + (1-w)\beta_g$. Update $T_n += C_n + G_n$.

We also evaluate a device-weighted variant, which weights the rate computed by each device by the number of items processed by the device for that profiling run. We do not observe a significant improvement in the performance of device-weighted updates. We use the *sample-weighted* updates for our experimental results.

6. IMPLEMENTATION

In this section, we briefly discuss the implementation details that is used in the evaluation in Sec. 7. We start with details on the compiler infrastructure, followed by a summary of the heterogeneous runtime describing when and where the scheduling decision takes place.

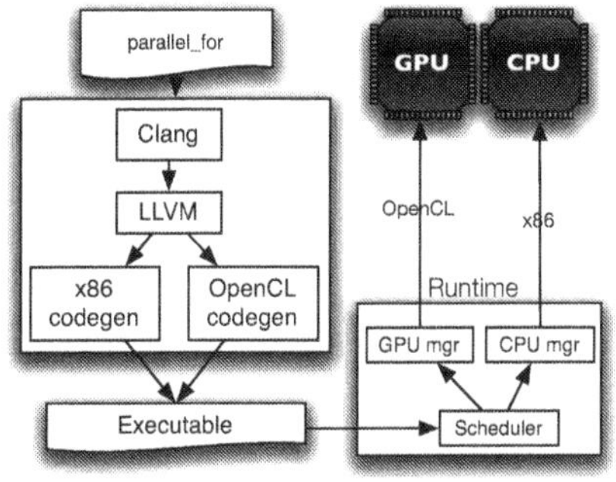

Figure 7: Compiler and runtime

Compiler: Our evaluation uses data-parallel C++ applications where the parallel regions are expressed using Concord *parallel_for* constructs as described in Sec. 3.

Fig. 7 depicts our overall compilation and runtime framework. We use the CLANG and LLVM infrastructure to compile our C++ programs. The static compiler identifies kernels and generates both native CPU and GPU OpenCL code for them. It then emits a host-side executable containing all code including the OpenCL code.

Runtime: During program execution, the runtime loads the embedded OpenCL code and just-in-time compiles it to GPU *ISA* using the vendor-specific OpenCL compiler. It also decides how to distribute the work between the CPU and GPU. It implements work-stealing on the CPU, with one of the CPU worker threads (the GPU proxy thread) offloading to the GPU as guided by online profiling. The observed distribution ratio, β_g, for our scheduling algorithms (described in Sec. 4 and Sec. 5) is computed in the GPU proxy thread which then redistributes the parallel iterations among the CPU and GPU cores.

7. EVALUATION

We now present an evaluation of our techniques. We begin with an overview of the hardware and software environment. We next describe the benchmarks used in the evaluation and their static and runtime characteristics. Finally, we present performance results and follow it up with a summary.

7.1 Environment

We evaluated our scheduling techniques on a desktop computer with a 3.4GHz Intel 4th Generation Core i7-4770 Processor with four CPU cores and with hyper-threading enabled. The integrated GPU is an Intel HD Graphics 4600 with 20 execution units (EUs), each with 7 hardware threads where each thread is 16-wide SIMD, and running at a turbo-mode clock speed from $350MHz$ to $1.2GHz$. The system has 8GB system memory and is running 64-bit Windows 7.

7.2 Benchmarks

We consider a diverse set of applications (sixteen in total) to evaluate our proposed runtime system. These applications span a spectrum of application domains and exhibit different behaviors: single kernel vs. multiple kernels, single invocation vs. multiple invocations, and regular vs. irregular. Most of these were ported from existing sources: TBB [1], Rodinia [13], and Parsec [8]. We also developed some applications from scratch. The details of our benchmarks are shown in Table 1.

Name	Abbrv.	Input	# kernels	kernel-name	invocations	Oracle-time(s)	num iter per kernel	Dynamic. Instr.
BarnesHut	BH [6]	1M bodies, 1 step	1	Barneshut	1	6.852	1000000	1.96×10^{11}
BarnesHut(unoptimized)	BH-U [6]	1M bodies, 1 step	1	Barneshut	1	9.194	1000000	1.98×10^{11}
LavaMD	LMD [13]	-boxed1d 10	1	kernel	1	0.582	1000	2.02×10^{10}
Matrix Multiply	MM	2048 by 2048 float matrix	1	testc	1	1.506	4194304	7.08×10^{10}
Ray Tracer	RT	sphere=256,material=3,light=5	1	kernel	1	2.426	10240000	3.25×10^{11}
Breadth first search	BFS	W-USA ($\|V\|$=6.2M, $\|E\|$=1.5M)	1	relax	1748	14.05	6262104	5.68×10^{11}
Black Scholes	BS [8]	64K	1	mainwork	2000	0.32	65536	6.17×10^{10}
Connected Component	CC	W-USA ($\|V\|$=6.2M, $\|E\|$=1.5M)	1	merge	2147	22.37	6262104	1.54×10^{12}
Face Detect	FD [2]	3000 by2171 Solvay-1927	1	HaarDetect	132	1.884	22-1370340	6.09×10^{10}
Heartwall	HW [13]	test.avi	1	kernel	5	0.924	51	4.62×10^{10}
N-Body	NB	4096 bodies	1	Slowpar	101	4.506	20475	3.91×10^{11}
Seismic	SM [1]	1950 by 1326, 100 frames	1	UpdateStress	100	2.048	25791520	1.43×10^{11}
Shortest Path	SP	W-USA ($\|V\|$=6.2M, $\|E\|$=1.5M)	1	relax	2577	30.66	6262104	9.17×10^{11}
BTree	BT [13]	big-command	2	kernel_cpu	1	0.586	1000000	1.66×10^{11}
				kernel_cpu_2	1		1000000	
Computational fluid dynamics	CFD [13]	missile - 0.3M	4	compute-time	6000	24.072	232704	1.49×10^{12}
				compute-flux	6000		232704	
				compute-step	2000		232704	
				init	1		232704	
Particle Filter	PF [13]	(128, 128, 10), 80K particles	7	find-index	9	4.646	8000	3.50×10^{11}
				calculate-u	9		8000	
				divide-weights	9		8000	
				update-weights	9		8000	
				particle-filter-like	9		8000	
				initial-arrays	1		8000	
				initial-weights	1		8000	

Table 1: Key statistics for the kernels of benchmarks used in the evaluation. *Oracle-time* is the time taken by the best offline distribution, and is also used as the normalizing factor in Fig. 9 and Fig. 10.

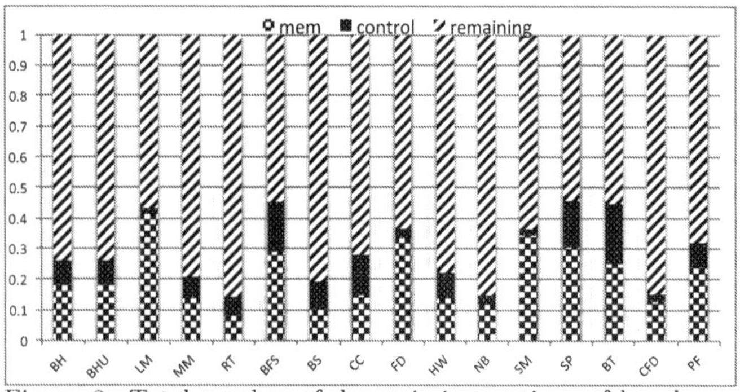

Figure 8: Total number of dynamic instructions of benchmarks divided into three categories: *memory*, *control*, and *remaining*, obtained via a serial CPU execution. The number of dynamic instructions is given in Table 1(column 9).

The compile-time and run-time characteristics of our benchmarks are tabulated in Table 1. The order of the benchmarks we use are as follows: (1) single kernel and single invocation (**BH**, **BH-U**, **LMD**, **MM**, **RT**); (2) single kernel and multiple invocations (**BFS**, **BS**, **CC**, **FD**, **HW**, **NB**, **SM**, **SP**); (3) multiple kernels and multiple invocations (**BT**, **CFD**, **PF**). The table shows the number of times a kernel is invoked in column 6. The *Oracle-time* in column 7 reports the absolute execution time for an *Oracle* approach described in Sec. 7.3 – this serves as the baseline for the runtime evaluation in Fig. 9 and Fig. 10, which are normalized to this time. Column 8 reports the number of parallel iterations per kernel invocation. Column 9 reports the number of instructions executed at runtime per benchmark.

To better understand the irregularities in our benchmarks, we also analyze the dynamic instruction traces for a single-threaded CPU execution via *Intel VTune Amplifier* to determine the run-time behavior of our applications[4]. Fig. 8 shows the division of the instructions into three categories: *memory* operations (load and store instructions), *control* instructions, and *remaining*, which can be a crude estimate for the *compute* instructions. The absolute number of dynamic instructions is given in column 9 of Table 1. Applications such as **BH**, **BH-U**, **BFS**, **CC**, **SP**, **BT**, and **PF** show considerable amount of control flow irregularities where as **FD**, and **SM** show significant amount of memory related operations. Since these applications are not hand-tuned for GPUs, the memory related operations may not necessarily be coalesced and give an indication of non-coalesced memory accesses on the GPU. Also note that benchmarks with large amount of control flow irregularities may not perform well on the GPU.

7.3 Comparison schemes

We compare the following scheduling strategies to distribute the parallel iterations between the CPU and GPU:

1. **CPU**: Multi-core CPU execution based on TBB. The *parallel_for* invocation is simply forwarded to the TBB runtime to complete the execution.
2. **GPU**: GPU-only execution, where all items are offloaded to the GPU via OpenCL.
3. **Oracle**: The best performance obtained by exhaustive search of different amount of parallel_for iterations assigned to the CPU and GPU. The GPU works on some percentage of the parallel iterations while the CPU works on the remaining ones. The percentage is varied from 0% to 100% on the GPU in increments of 10%

[4]Note that this measurement provides an upper-bound of the irregularities present in a benchmark.

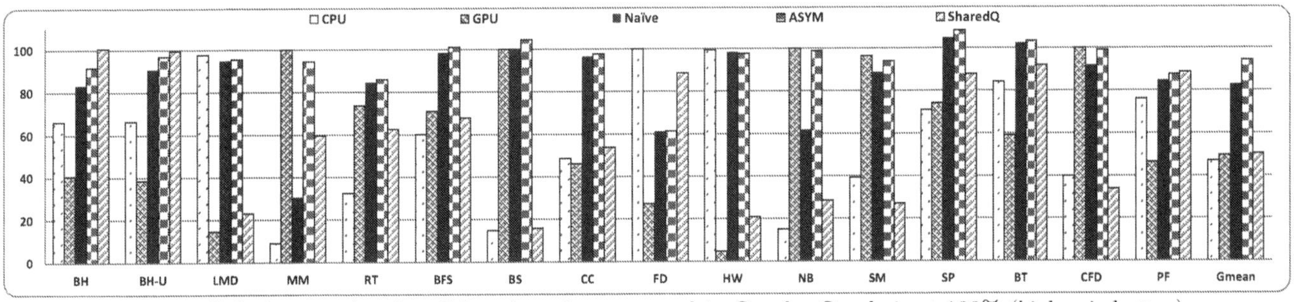

Figure 9: Relative speedup for all benchmarks compared to Oracle. Oracle is at 100% (higher is better).

and the best performance obtained is selected. The best percentage for single kernel benchmarks is given in Table 2(row 1) and the absolute runtime for those percentages is given in Table 1(column 7). We select the runtime obtained by such a technique as the baseline for all comparisons.

4. **Naïve**: The naïve profiling scheme described in Sec. 4 where we use the same profiling size for both the CPU and the GPU.
5. **ASYM**: The asymmetric profiling scheme described in Sec. 5. We use the *sample weighted* variant for multiple invocation kernels.
6. **SharedQ**: We also compare against a shared queue implementation where a GPU proxy-thread atomically grabs a fixed chunk of work (profile size) and offloads it to the GPU while CPU threads also atomically obtain work-items from the same global queue. Since there will be contention on the shared queue, this approach may suffer as the number of workers increase[5].

We also evaluate two variants of our asymmetric profiling algorithm to address load imbalance, as described in Sec. 5.2:

- **ASYM+CONV**: A convergence-based update strategy, where half of remaining items are used for reprofiling until convergence is achieved. Convergence is reached when the β_g computed on two successive profiling steps do not differ by more than 0.05.
- **ASYM+SIZE**: A size-based update strategy, where we repeatedly profile with f_p items on the GPU until at least half of the total items are left.

7.4 Results

Heterogeneous execution: First we highlight the significance of heterogeneous execution compared to single device execution. We compare the single-device execution (either on the CPU or the GPU) against the offline optimal model (Oracle). Fig. 9 shows that there is an obvious advantage to heterogeneous execution: (1) using only the multicore CPU, we can achieve 47.07% of Oracle on average; (2) using only the GPU, we can achieve 49.67% of Oracle on average. Clearly, heterogeneous execution results in 2× improvement in runtime compared to the best of executing on the CPU-alone or the GPU-alone. These results emphasize the improvement of heterogeneous execution over single device execution.

Naïve profiling: Naïve profiling as described in Sec. 4 performs online profiling on a fraction of the parallel iterations to determine the offload ratio, β_g. Although the profiling information obtained is able to outperform single-device execution as illustrated in Fig. 9, it only performs at 82.7% of the Oracle on average. There are two sources of inefficiency in naïve profiling: (1) The *overhead of profiling* can dominate the execution time for workloads that are highly biased towards a particular device. For instance **NB** and **MM** are both highly biased towards the GPU. With a fixed profiling size on both devices, the scheduler has to wait at the barrier for both devices to report the rates to determine the distribution. If the GPU profiling finishes early, the scheduler waits for the CPU to complete the profiling step resulting in a large overhead. (2) The *inaccuracy of profiling information*, although not evident, is another source of inefficiency. For instance, **FD** only obtains 61.2% of the Oracle, because the profiling information obtained is not representative of the entire iteration space. The inaccuracy can also be observed in optimal distribution percentages (as shown in Table 2) for benchmarks with single *parallel_for* kernels.

	BH	BH-U	LMD	MM	RT	BFS	BS	CC	FD	HW	NB	SM	SP
Oracle	40	40	0	100	70	70	100	70	0	0	100	70	50
Naïve	52.4	44.3	0	89.6	84.4	72.8	94.9	73.9	31.1	0	77.3	77	71
ASYM	47.9	41.7	0	92.5	84.3	72.8	96.2	73.8	32.9	0	89.6	92.1	70.6
ASYM+SIZE	39.6	40.2	0	92.2	69.7	61.1	96.0	68.8	18.4	0	88.3	92.2	59.2
ASYM+CONV	41.2	40.6	0	92.4	70.6	73.1	96	73.8	33.2	0	89	92.7	70.7

Table 2: GPU work percentages computed by different schemes for single-kernel applications.

Asymmetric profiling: As described in Sec. 5, asymmetric profiling does not suffer from the overhead of waiting on a barrier to compare the rates for both devices. Most applications benefit from using asymmetric profiling compared to naïve profiling. That is, it performs on average at 94.2% efficiency compared to the Oracle. The biggest improvement is observed in applications that show a high GPU bias such as **NB** and **MM**. This is because the distribution ratio β_g can be decided quickly, and hence the overhead of profiling is reduced significantly (close to zero[6]). We note, however, that **BH** and **FD** do not benefit from the vanilla version of asymmetric profiling. This is, as explained before, due to the inaccuracy of the profiling information as evident from the distribution computed by asymmetric profiling differing from the optimal distribution obtained by the Oracle (as shown in Table 2). Note that benchmarks such as **BS**, **BT**, **BFS**, and **SP** improve performance better than Oracle using asymmetric profiling – this is because the Oracle is obtained in increments of 10%.

ASYM+CONV: In order to address the load imbalance and the inaccuracy of profiling information, we rely on re-

[5]Note that our SharedQ implementation does not use the optimization strategies described in Sec. 5.3.

[6]This overhead in our implementation consists of : for N workers, we read a local counter from each worker and perform N additions and 3 divisions, which is negligible compared to the total execution time of an application.

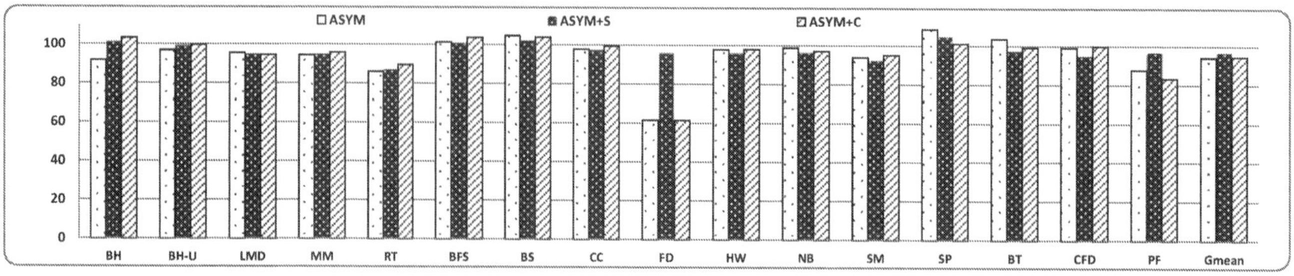

Figure 10: Comparison of different adaptive schemes. Vertical axis shows relative speedup vs. Oracle (higher is better).

peated profiling to achieve more accurate information. The convergence based approach repeatedly profiles until the offload ratio, β_g, determined by consecutive profiling phases differs by less than 0.05. This does introduce an overhead of repeated profiling, but the benefit of more accurate profiling information should offset this overhead. **ASYM+CONV** can achieve on average 94.6% of Oracle as shown in Fig. 10. The biggest improvement is observed in the applications that have some irregularity, for instance **BH**. The convergence based approach determines a more accurate distribution ratio, as evident from the percentages reported in Table 2 (47% for **ASYM** versus 41% for **ASYM+CONV**) is more closer to the optimal value 40%. Similarly, for **RT**, the ratio reported becomes 69% versus the optimal 70%.

However, we observe that this approach still does not improve **FD**, and furthermore the efficiency of **PF** goes down. Both of them are false positives as they converge fairly quickly in **ASYM+CONV** approach. The source of inefficiency for **FD** stems from the algorithm: the cascade of classifiers is grouped to discard failing face images early. The profiling phase obtained from the initial rounds converges in two iterations on these cascade of classifiers, which is not representative of later stages that search further for faces in parts of the image not discarded by earlier stages. For **PF**, an inaccurate rate due to convergence makes the performance drop from 87% for **ASYM** to 83% for **ASYM+CONV**. Clearly, in order to improve the efficiency of **FD** and **PF**, the profiling information has to be resilient to local optima. Also note that, **FD** shows a large amount of memory related irregularities and **PF** shows a large amount of control flow and memory irregularities (as shown in Fig. 8).

ASYM+SIZE: Instead of relying on convergence, we use half of the work-items to determine the profiling ratio and use this ratio to distribute the remaining items. This approach proves the best performing overall since it does not rely on an initial portion of the work-items to determine the rate and does not converge on a local maxima. There is an overhead to repeated profiling which reduces the efficiency for some applications, but not significantly. However, the biggest winner is **PF**, which performs at 96% of Oracle, followed by **FD**, which performs at 95% of Oracle. Overall, the size-based approach performs at 96.8% (geo-mean) efficiency of the Oracle, thereby clearly demonstrating that it is the best strategy across all benchmarks.

7.5 Summary

In conclusion, we show that:

- *Heterogeneous* execution improves the execution time of our applications by 2× compared to a single device execution (either the multicore CPU or the GPU).
- A simple profiling technique, such as Naïve profiling, can provide reasonably good performance, on average 82% of the Oracle.
- *Asymmetric* profiling is necessary to reduce the overhead of online profiling and improves the efficiency of heterogeneous execution to 94.2% compared to the Oracle.
- Some applications such as **FD**, **RT** and **BH** require repeated profiling to obtain optimal distribution of work. Our adaptive scheme **ASYM+SIZE** obtains the best distribution with minimal profiling overhead and achieves 96.8% efficiency compared to the Oracle.

8. RELATED WORK

Making GPUs more accessible to programmers has been an increasingly active research area [5, 14, 16, 31]. Below we discuss prior work that particularly focus on scheduling and load balancing in heterogeneous architectures.

8.1 Heterogeneous execution

There have been increasing efforts [4, 24, 27, 35] to make heterogeneous execution of applications more efficient. A load balancing scheme for discrete devices, *HDSS*, is presented in [7], and is similar to our convergence based approach. [25] describes a model-driven 2D-FFT scheduling for matrix computations across two devices. [29] describes a dynamic scheduling strategy for heterogeneous execution for generalized reductions and structured grids based on a cost model.

Qilin [24] is an API and runtime to support execution of applications across the CPU and the GPU. Programmers use the API to manage data movement and provide implementation of kernels for both devices. The system performs offline profiling to determine parameters for a linear performance model which is used to determine distributions for real runs. The *StarPU* [4] system is a data management and runtime framework similar to *Qilin* [24]. It supports user defined scheduling policies along with a set of pre-defined policies for dynamic workload scheduling. *SKMD* [22] supports execution of single kernel on multiple devices. It relies on static analysis of kernels to determine workload distribution. More recently, [35] presents a heterogeneous library for executing dense linear algebra. [27] presents a compiler and runtime to address portable performance across heterogeneous systems. They utilize evolutionary algorithms to search optimal algorithms from *PetaBricks* [3] specifications. Pandit et al. [26] balance CPU and GPU workload by restricting

CPU to executing work in coarse-grain chunks with all CPU threads synchronizing at the end of each chunk. While this approach works well for their regular PolyBench workloads, our work targets both regular and irregular applications.

Ravi et al. [30] use work-sharing to distribute work between the CPU and a discrete GPU. Their non-uniform chunk size-based work distribution resembles our baseline SharedQ approach that is 53.5% slower than our **ASYM** approach. Grewe et al. [17] use machine learning to divide work between the CPU and GPU when there is contention from other programs. In contrast, we use online profiling and do not require offline training or other prior knowledge of the applications and platform. Scogland et al. [34] present several scheduling techniques for systems with discrete devices. Their most sophisticated approach resembles our naïve profiling that we found yields only 82% of Oracle performance compared to 96.8% for **ASYM+CONV**.

Our work is different from the above work in several aspects. Data transfer is not a factor in our scenario – thus making the offloading cost to minimal. Besides the wide-variety of regular workloads studied in previous works, we handle irregular workloads as well. It is hard to get optimal partitioning for them through offline and machine model based approaches. We do not require knowledge of the underlying architectures, no offline processing, and we do not require separate program execution needed by [29] to decide the parameters in their cost model for each application.

8.2 Load balancing among multiple GPU cores

Cederman et al. [11] and Chatterjee et al. [12] address load balancing of workloads across different execution units on a GPU. In particular, they use work-stealing between tasks running on the different streaming multiprocessors (SM) of a discrete GPU. The host CPU populates the initial work-stealing queues. Each SM maintains its own work-stealing queue and steals [9] work from other SMs. This is possible due to the availability of an atomic *CAS* operation on the GPU between its SMs. However, since no current hardware supports those operations between the CPU and GPU, this approach does not extend to the general case, in particular to integrated GPUs like ours. [15] describe a fine-grained load balancing scheme by running persistent kernels which communicate with the host via task-queues. Abstracting multiple GPUs as a single virtual device [21] has also shown to be a useful way to support multiple GPUs. A performance prediction based on modeling of multiple GPUs is presented in [33].

9. CONCLUSIONS AND FUTURE WORK

Heterogeneous execution on integrated GPUs and SoCs will be a key feature of future architectures [20]. Dynamic load balancing will be essential to realize the full potential of these architectures. We presented a set of scheduling algorithms that use load balancing to minimize application execution time on integrated GPUs. To improve accuracy, these algorithms make use of low-cost online profiling. After presenting a naïve profiling algorithm, we describe asymmetric profiling scheme that mitigates some overheads in the naïve scheme. We also explored two extensions to asymmetric profiling that address load imbalance: size-based and convergence-based. We observed that these two techniques help to address irregularities in application behavior and can achieve within 3.2% of the maximum throughput obtained by an exhaustive search algorithm using a diverse set of sixteen benchmarks running on Intel's 4th Generation Core Processor. In the future, we want to extend our work to consider computer systems with multiple CPUs, discrete GPUs, and discrete accelerators [10] such as the Intel Xeon Phi coprocessor. While discrete GPUs and accelerators have greater communication costs and longer latencies, they have higher power budgets and higher computational potential. A key issue to consider will be the data-transfer overhead between different devices. Finally, we would like to extend our scheduling algorithms to handle unpredictable system loads.

10. REFERENCES

[1] Intel thread building blocks.

[2] Opensource computer vision library.

[3] J. Ansel, C. Chan, Y. L. Wong, M. Olszewski, Q. Zhao, A. Edelman, and S. Amarasinghe. Petabricks: a language and compiler for algorithmic choice. In *Proceedings of the 2009 ACM SIGPLAN conference on Programming language design and implementation*, PLDI '09, pages 38–49, NY, USA, 2009. ACM.

[4] C. Augonnet, S. Thibault, R. Namyst, and P.-A. Wacrenier. Starpu: a unified platform for task scheduling on heterogeneous multicore architectures. *Concurrency and Computation: Practice and Experience*, 23(2):187–198, 2011.

[5] R. Barik, R. Kaleem, D. Majeti, B. Lewis, T. Shpeisman, C. Hu, Y. Ni, and A.-R. Adl-Tabatabai. Efficient mapping of irregular C++ applications to integrated GPUs. In *IEEE/ACM International Symposium on Code Generation and Optimization (CGO)*, 2014.

[6] J. Barnes and P. Hut. A hierarchical $O(N \log N)$ force calculation algorithm. *Nature*, 324:446–449, 1986.

[7] M. E. Belviranli, L. N. Bhuyan, and R. Gupta. A dynamic self-scheduling scheme for heterogeneous multiprocessor architectures. *ACM Trans. Archit. Code Optim.*, 9(4):57:1–57:20, Jan. 2013.

[8] C. Bienia, S. Kumar, J. P. Singh, and K. Li. The PARSEC benchmark suite: characterization and architectural implications. In *Proceedings of the 17th international conference on Parallel architectures and compilation techniques*, PACT '08, pages 72–81, NY, USA, 2008. ACM.

[9] R. D. Blumofe and C. E. Leiserson. Scheduling multithreaded computations by work stealing. *J. ACM*, 46(5):720–748, Sept. 1999.

[10] C. Cascaval, S. Chatterjee, H. Franke, K. Gildea, and P. Pattnaik. A taxonomy of accelerator architectures and their programming models. *IBM Journal of Research and Development*, 54(5):5:1–5:10, 2010.

[11] D. Cederman and P. Tsigas. On dynamic load balancing on graphics processors. In *Proceedings of the 23rd ACM SIGGRAPH/EUROGRAPHICS Symposium on Graphics Hardware*, GH '08, pages 57–64, Aire-la-Ville, Switzerland, 2008.

[12] S. Chatterjee, M. Grossman, A. Sbirlea, and V. Sarkar. Dynamic task parallelism with a GPU work-stealing runtime system. In *Languages and Compilers for Parallel Computing*, volume 7146 of

Lecture Notes in Computer Science, pages 203–217. Springer Berlin Heidelberg, 2011.

[13] S. Che, M. Boyer, J. Meng, D. Tarjan, J. W. Sheaffer, S.-H. Lee, and K. Skadron. Rodinia: A benchmark suite for heterogeneous computing. In *Proceedings of the 2009 IEEE International Symposium on Workload Characterization (IISWC)*, IISWC '09, pages 44–54, Washington, DC, USA, 2009. IEEE Computer Society.

[14] S. Che, J. W. Sheaffer, and K. Skadron. Dymaxion: optimizing memory access patterns for heterogeneous systems. In *Proceedings of 2011 International Conference for High Performance Computing, Networking, Storage and Analysis*, SC '11, pages 13:1–13:11, NY, USA, 2011. ACM.

[15] L. Chen, O. Villa, S. Krishnamoorthy, and G. Gao. Dynamic load balancing on single- and multi-GPU systems. In *IEEE International Symposium on Parallel Distributed Processing (IPDPS)*, pages 1–12, 2010.

[16] C. Dubach, P. Cheng, R. Rabbah, D. F. Bacon, and S. J. Fink. Compiling a high-level language for GPUs: (via language support for architectures and compilers). In *Proceedings of the 33rd ACM SIGPLAN Conference on Programming Language Design and Implementation*, PLDI '12, pages 1–12, NY, USA, 2012. ACM.

[17] D. Grewe, Z. Wang, and M. O'Boyle. OpenCL task partitioning in the presence of GPU Contention. In S. Rajopadhye and M. Mills Strout, editors, *Languages and Compilers for Parallel Computing*, Lecture Notes in Computer Science. Springer Berlin Heidelberg, 2013.

[18] D. Grewe, Z. Wang, and M. O'Boyle. Portable mapping of data parallel programs to OpenCL for heterogeneous systems. In *IEEE/ACM International Symposium on Code Generation and Optimization (CGO)*, pages 1–10, 2013.

[19] S. Hong and H. Kim. An integrated GPU power and performance model. *SIGARCH Comput. Archit. News*, 38(3):280–289, June 2010.

[20] S. Keckler, W. Dally, B. Khailany, M. Garland, and D. Glasco. GPUs and the future of parallel computing. *Micro, IEEE*, 31(5):7–17, 2011.

[21] J. Kim, H. Kim, J. H. Lee, and J. Lee. Achieving a single compute device image in OpenCL for multiple GPUs. In *Proceedings of the 16th ACM symposium on Principles and practice of parallel programming*, PPoPP '11, pages 277–288, NY, USA, 2011. ACM.

[22] J. Lee, M. Samadi, Y. Park, and S. Mahlke. Transparent CPU-GPU collaboration for data-parallel kernels on heterogeneous systems. In *Proceedings of the 22nd international conference on Parallel architectures and compilation techniques*, PACT, 2013.

[23] C. E. Leiserson. The cilk++ concurrency platform. In *Proceedings of the 46th Annual Design Automation Conference*, DAC '09, pages 522–527, NY, USA, 2009. ACM.

[24] C.-K. Luk, S. Hong, and H. Kim. Qilin: exploiting parallelism on heterogeneous multiprocessors with adaptive mapping. In *Proceedings of the 42nd Annual IEEE/ACM International Symposium on Microarchitecture*, MICRO 42, pages 45–55, NY, USA, 2009. ACM.

[25] Y. Ogata, T. Endo, N. Maruyama, and S. Matsuoka. An efficient, model-based CPU-GPU heterogeneous FFT library. In *IEEE International Symposium on Parallel and Distributed Processing. IPDPS.*, pages 1–10, 2008.

[26] P. Pandit and R. Govindarajan. Fluidic kernels: Cooperative execution of opencl programs on multiple heterogeneous devices. In *Proceedings of Annual IEEE/ACM International Symposium on Code Generation and Optimization*, CGO '14, pages 273:273–273:283, NY, USA, 2014. ACM.

[27] P. M. Phothilimthana, J. Ansel, J. Ragan-Kelley, and S. Amarasinghe. Portable performance on heterogeneous architectures. In *Proceedings of the eighteenth international conference on Architectural support for programming languages and operating systems*, ASPLOS '13, pages 431–444, NY, USA, 2013. ACM.

[28] K. Pingali, D. Nguyen, M. Kulkarni, M. Burtscher, M. A. Hassaan, R. Kaleem, T.-H. Lee, A. Lenharth, R. Manevich, M. Méndez-Lojo, D. Prountzos, and X. Sui. The tao of parallelism in algorithms. In *Proceedings of the 32nd ACM SIGPLAN conference on Programming language design and implementation*, PLDI '11, pages 12–25, NY, USA, 2011. ACM.

[29] V. Ravi and G. Agrawal. A dynamic scheduling framework for emerging heterogeneous systems. In *High Performance Computing (HiPC), 2011 18th International Conference on*, pages 1–10, Dec 2011.

[30] V. T. Ravi, W. Ma, D. Chiu, and G. Agrawal. Compiler and runtime support for enabling generalized reduction computations on heterogeneous parallel configurations. In *Proceedings of the 24th ACM International Conference on Supercomputing*, ICS '10, pages 137–146, NY, USA, 2010. ACM.

[31] C. J. Rossbach, Y. Yu, J. Currey, J.-P. Martin, and D. Fetterly. Dandelion: a compiler and runtime for heterogeneous systems. In *Proceedings of the Twenty-Fourth ACM Symposium on Operating Systems Principles*, SOSP '13, pages 49–68, NY, USA, 2013. ACM.

[32] A. Sbîrlea, Y. Zou, Z. Budimlíc, J. Cong, and V. Sarkar. Mapping a data-flow programming model onto heterogeneous platforms. In *Proceedings of the 13th ACM SIGPLAN/SIGBED International Conference on Languages, Compilers, Tools and Theory for Embedded Systems*, LCTES '12, pages 61–70, NY, USA, 2012. ACM.

[33] D. Schaa and D. Kaeli. Exploring the multiple-GPU design space. In *IEEE International Symposium on Parallel Distributed Processing. IPDPS.*, pages 1–12, 2009.

[34] T. Scogland, B. Rountree, W. chun Feng, and B. De Supinski. Heterogeneous task scheduling for accelerated OpenMP. In *IEEE 26th International Parallel Distributed Processing Symposium (IPDPS)*, pages 144–155, May 2012.

[35] F. Song and J. Dongarra. A scalable framework for heterogeneous GPU-based clusters. In *Proceedinbgs of the 24th ACM symposium on Parallelism in algorithms and architectures*, SPAA '12, pages 91–100, NY, USA, 2012. ACM.

Warp-Aware Trace Scheduling for GPUs

James A. Jablin
Brown University
Dept. of Computer Science
jjablin@cs.brown.edu

Thomas B. Jablin
University of Illinois at Urbana-Champaign
Dept. of Electrical and Computer Engineering
jablin@illinois.edu

Onur Mutlu
Carnegie Mellon University
Dept. of Electrical and Computer Engineering
onur@cmu.edu

Maurice Herlihy
Brown University
Dept. of Computer Science
herlihy@cs.brown.edu

ABSTRACT

GPU performance depends not only on thread/warp level parallelism (TLP) but also on instruction-level parallelism (ILP). It is not enough to schedule instructions within basic blocks, it is also necessary to exploit opportunities for ILP optimization beyond branch boundaries. Unfortunately, modern GPUs cannot dynamically carry out such optimizations because they lack hardware branch prediction and cannot speculatively execute instructions beyond a branch.

We propose to circumvent these limitations by adapting Trace Scheduling, a technique originally developed for microcode optimization. Trace Scheduling divides code into traces (or paths), and optimizes each trace in a context-independent way. Adapting Trace Scheduling to GPU code requires revisiting and revising each step of microcode Trace Scheduling to attend to branch and warp behavior, identifying instructions on the critical path, avoiding warp divergence, and reducing divergence time.

Here, we propose "Warp-Aware Trace Scheduling" for GPUs. As evaluated on the Rodinia Benchmark Suite using dynamic profiling, our fully-automatic optimization achieves a geometric mean speedup of 1.10× on a real system by increasing instructions executed per cycle (IPC) by a harmonic mean of 1.12× and reducing instruction serialization and total instructions executed.

Categories and Subject Descriptors

D.3.4 [**Programming Languages**]: Processors - Code Generation, Compilers, Optimization

General Terms

Languages, Performance

PACT'14, August 24–27, 2014, Edmonton, AB, Canada.

ACM 978-1-4503-2809-8/14/08 ...$15.00.
http://dx.doi.org/10.1145/2628071.2628101.

Keywords

GPU; compiler optimization; instruction-level parallelism; global instruction scheduling; trace scheduling

1. INTRODUCTION

GPU architectures use a Single-Instruction, Multiple-Thread (SIMT) model marshaling thousands of threads across hundreds of cores, each thread having its own register state but all threads sharing one program counter. Threads are managed in groups called *warps* in CUDA, or alternatively wavefronts in OpenCL. Warp size varies, but for CUDA, warps contain 32 threads. GPUs schedule an entire warp of threads at once and warp threads cannot be scheduled separately. GPUs interleave warp execution to increase resource utilization and instruction throughput.

Each new generation of GPUs provides increasing levels of resources such as more registers, shared memory, functional units, and arithmetic cores. Most efforts to manage GPU resource utilization [17, 20, 25, 31, 32] have focused on thread or warp-level parallelism (TLP). Our contribution in this paper is to focus attention on the complementary use of instruction-level parallelism (ILP) to improve resource utilization. While this subject is well-understood for CPU architectures, it has received little attention for GPUs.

Modern GPU architectures [30] have neglected ILP for two major reasons. First, they typically lack branch prediction and hardware support for speculation. Second, the conventional GPU application has abundant TLP. However, as GPUs become more general purpose, it will become increasingly necessary to improve GPU performance by exploiting ILP within a single thread. By contrast many CPUs, recognizing the relative scarcity of ILP within basic blocks, implement hardware branch prediction, enabling faster execution by successfully guessing branch outcomes and fetching and executing instructions.

Trace Scheduling [9], first developed for microcode optimization, attempts to decrease execution time by exposing ILP across branch boundaries through static global instruction scheduling. Generally, Trace Scheduling organizes sequences of *basic blocks,* a series of instructions free of control flow besides the last instruction, into regions called *traces.* Optimization efforts then focus on scheduling instructions within traces. Trace Scheduling proceeds in three steps. *Trace selection* partitions basic blocks into traces. *Trace formation* extends traces to expose additional opportunities for the final step, *local scheduling*. *Local scheduling* schedules instructions within each trace to reduce execution time.

Trace scheduling, as used previously for microcode, is not immediately applicable to GPUs. The principal challenge is avoiding warp divergence, which occurs when a warp's threads take different execution paths. GPUs serialize the different executions, executing first one path, then the other, at substantial cost to performance. It is well-established [6, 10–12, 18, 19, 23, 24] that avoiding divergence is performance critical.

This paper describes *Warp-Aware Trace Scheduling*, a new technique for GPU global instruction scheduling. Our optimization consists of three major steps, customized for the GPU execution model. The first step selects traces that start at basic blocks that are likely to be divergence-free. These traces define the earliest non-divergent entry for scheduling instructions for speculative execution. The second step harnesses the GPU's native compiler infrastructure for predication. In the final step, the instruction scheduler schedules long-latency memory operations (and their dependent instructions) as early as possible in a trace.

Because GPUs have little or no exception handling, any such speculation must be conservative; a failed speculation may reduce performance, but will not require rolling back speculative computations. For this reason, we only speculate on global memory `load`'s and arithmetic instructions. When appropriate, the scheduler moves instructions from divergent to non-divergent basic blocks, reducing divergence time.

We make the following contributions:

1. Comprehensive rethinking and redesign of CPU-oriented trace scheduling techniques to accommodate GPU requirements such as avoiding divergence when possible, and reducing divergence time otherwise.
2. Development and evaluation of Warp-Aware Trace Scheduling, a fully-automatic ILP optimization for reducing execution time.

Across the entire Rodinia Benchmark Suite [5], run on a real system (NVIDIA GTX 670), Warp-Aware Trace Scheduling achieves a geometric mean speedup of 1.10× by improving instructions executed per cycle (IPC) by a harmonic mean of 1.12× and reducing instruction serialization and total instructions executed. Our results suggest that Warp-Aware Trace Scheduling can be a promising way of improving single-thread performance on GPUs, thereby enabling the architecture to execute a wider variety of programs. More aggressive speculation, made possible by adding new *speculative* `load` and *exception* `check` instructions (see Section 4.3 for further details), and complementary optimization will likely further increase performance.

The organization for the rest of the paper follows. Section 2 describes PTX and our profiling infrastructure. Section 3 motivates the importance of optimizing GPU ILP. Section 4 first provides a brief overview of Trace Scheduling, and then in subsequent subsections details our approach to adapting Trace Scheduling to the GPU. Afterward, Section 5 describes our experimental methodology, and Section 6 reports Warp-Aware Trace Scheduling's results on the Rodinia Benchmark Suite. Section 7 interprets and discusses our results, and Section 8 describes related work. Section 9 posits future research opportunities to complement and improve Warp-Aware Trace Scheduling, and Section 10 concludes.

2. BACKGROUND

To evaluate Warp-Aware Trace Scheduling, we develop a PTX-to-PTX optimizer for fully automating profiling, analyzing, and optimizing PTX [29], NVIDIA's pseudo-assembly language. Subsequently, the graphics driver compiles PTX into executable binary code. Our PTX toolchain records dynamic program profiles, information to guide Warp-Aware Trace Scheduling. While this section describes PTX, our technology and ideas easily extend to HSA-based systems. HSAIL [13], a low-level intermediate language, functions similarly to PTX but supports a variety of processor architectures from HSA Foundation members AMD, ARM, Imagination, MediaTek, Qualcomm, Samsung, and Texas Instruments.

For profiling purposes, we implement our own instrumentation system rather than use the CUDA Profiling Tools Interface (CUPTI) [28]. While CUPTI is capable of collecting an extensive array of metrics, it can not collect each thread's behavior at every branch. Hence the need for our own instrumentation.

Our tool takes as input a GPU program, and as output, it produces an instrumented version of the program. Code destined for GPU execution is called the GPU *kernel*. In the instrumented version of the kernel, code is inserted before every conditional branch to collect each threads' branch behavior. The inserted code uses each thread's ID to update a unique counter for each branch direction. Consequently, there is one counter per branch per thread. Library calls to our tool are inserted before kernel invocations to allocate and initialize GPU memory for branch counters and after kernel invocations to compile the counters' results. Each branch's statistics are reduced to a single percentage, the probability of taking the branch. The probability is the number of times the branch was taken divided by the total number of times the branch was visited times 100.

PTX contains the following controlflow instructions: `@`, `call`, `ret`, `exit`, and `bra`. We avoid interprocedural analysis because after optimization for the Rodinia benchmarks, full inlining occurs and no `call` instructions exist. Regardless, our current implementation of Warp-Aware Trace Scheduling is intraprocedural. Since our profiler only instruments top-level functions, the instructions `ret` and `exit` behave identically, ending execution. All PTX instructions may conditionally execute based on a guard predicate, `@{!}p`. The `!` symbol is optional and performs logical negation. The `bra` instruction defines conditional and unconditional branching. In PTX, indirect branches are supported but unimplemented. However, indirect function calls are implemented. Conditional branches are formed by applying a guard predicate to an unconditional branch. For the purposes of this paper, a branch refers to a two-way conditional branch. The rest of the paper reflects this definition. Our optimizer effectively profiles the Rodinia benchmarks and reflects PTX ISA version 3.2 [29].

For efficient GPU global instruction scheduling, it is necessary to be aware of the GPU execution model and warp divergence (see Section 1). Warp-Aware Trace Scheduling minimizes execution time by exposing ILP while avoiding divergence and reducing divergence time. Generally, GPU execution proceeds as warps execute one common instruction at a time. However, when threads of a warp fail to identically evaluate a branch, lockstep warp execution halts. The warp's threads *diverge*; the warp splits and its threads take different execution paths. Execution proceeds in this fashion until all the warp's threads *converge* again, and all the warp's threads continue in lockstep.

In addition to its tracing capabilities, our tool also performs analysis and optimization, representing GPU programs as a controlflow graph (CFG) and dataflow graph (DFG). A CFG node represents a basic block (BB), a single-entry single-exit code region. CFG edges are directed and represent potential paths of control flow. In a DFG, nodes represent instructions, and edges represent variable definitions (outgoing edges), and variable uses (incoming edges) through registers. The DFG does not contain edges for data flow through memory. Instrumenting, analyzing, and predicting occur automatically, only employing information available in the GPU program's source code.

3. MOTIVATION

Warp-Aware Trace Scheduling improves GPU resource utilization by increasing ILP [30] to decrease overall execution time. GPU utilization is measured by thread-level parallelism (TLP), the number of resident warps, and additionally, instruction-level parallelism (ILP). Table 1 summarizes the GPUs' historical technical specifications *per thread block* and *per streaming multiprocessor (SM)*. New GPU architectures contain more local hardware resources (Special Function Units, Instruction Issue, and Arithmetic Cores) exceeding the nominal growth in number of threads per SM. Beyond NVIDIA GPUs, this progression is also depicted in other companies' GPU hardware [1,15].

While adjusting *occupancy*, the ratio of the number of resident warps to the maximum number of resident warps, to expose TLP is routine, no suitably obvious and automatic solution exists for increasing ILP. If these trends persist, ILP will have expanding performance implications. We propose to automatically and efficiently extract ILP using Warp-Aware Trace Scheduling.

ILP describes the potential overlap between executing instructions. On the GPU, SMs schedule instructions from ready warps of a block. At every instruction issue, an SM's warp scheduler selects a ready warp, if any, and issues the warp's next instruction to the warp's threads. The duration between instruction issue and completion is called *latency*. Achieving full utilization requires "hiding" all latency; at every clock cycle, all warp schedulers should have an instruction ready to issue.

4. GLOBAL INSTRUCTION SCHEDULING

Warp-Aware Trace Scheduling is a GPU-specific type of global instruction scheduling. Global instruction scheduling exposes ILP by grouping code, commonly basic blocks, into regions and scheduling instructions within each region, independently of other regions, to reduce execution time. Generally, global scheduling performs the following steps:

Step	Section	Description
1. Trace Selection	4.1	assign basic blocks to regions
2. Trace Formation	4.2	facilitate local scheduling, potentially adding nodes and edges
3. Local Scheduling	4.3	schedule instructions within each region

<table>
<tr><th rowspan="2">Specification</th><th colspan="8">Compute Capability</th></tr>
<tr><th>1.0</th><th>1.1</th><th>1.2</th><th>1.3</th><th>2.0</th><th>2.1</th><th>3.0</th><th>3.5</th></tr>
<tr><td>per Block</td><td colspan="8"></td></tr>
<tr><td>Max Number of Threads</td><td colspan="4">512</td><td colspan="4">1024</td></tr>
<tr><td>per SM</td><td colspan="8"></td></tr>
<tr><td>Max Resident Blocks</td><td colspan="6">8</td><td colspan="2">16</td></tr>
<tr><td>Max Resident Warps</td><td colspan="2">24</td><td colspan="2">32</td><td colspan="2">48</td><td colspan="2">64</td></tr>
<tr><td>Max Shared Memory</td><td colspan="4">16KB</td><td colspan="4">48KB</td></tr>
<tr><td>Number of 32-bit Registers</td><td colspan="2">8K</td><td colspan="2">16K</td><td colspan="2">32K</td><td colspan="2">64K</td></tr>
<tr><td>Special Function Units</td><td colspan="4">2</td><td>4</td><td>8</td><td colspan="2">32</td></tr>
<tr><td>Instruction Issue (per Clock Cycle)</td><td colspan="4">0.25</td><td>1</td><td>2</td><td colspan="2">8</td></tr>
<tr><td>Arithmetic Cores</td><td colspan="4">8</td><td colspan="2">32</td><td colspan="2">192</td></tr>
</table>

Table 1: Historical streaming multiprocessor (SM) and thread block characteristics based on CUDA Compute Capability

Faraboschi *et al.* [8] provide a comprehensive survey of global instruction scheduling.

The following sections address our modifications to Trace Scheduling's basic steps to create Warp-Aware Trace Scheduling for GPUs. Global scheduling algorithms may use different definitions of region. Our scheduling algorithm defines region as a trace, pioneered by Fisher [9], and more extensively described by Ellis [7]. A trace is a set of basic blocks where each basic block is a predecessor of the next basic block, and the set is cycle free. The rest of the paper refers to regions as traces.

4.1 Trace Selection

Trace selection, the first step in global scheduling, groups sequences of frequently executed basic blocks into traces. Generally, given a weighted controlflow graph (CFG), trace selection chooses a *seed* node, a start node for the trace, and *grows* a trace, adding an adjacent node to the trace. All nodes are only visited once and the process repeats until all nodes are visited. The goal is to recognize paths of frequently executed basic blocks, identifying the program's critical path.

In contrast to prior work, trace selection for GPUs must adapt to the GPU-specific challenge of avoiding warp divergence. The challenge is creating traces defining the earliest non-divergent entry for scheduling instructions for speculative execution. Algorithms 1 and 2 present our GPU Trace Selection and Best Successor Of algorithms. Compared with prior work [8], our algorithms differ in two important respects: seed selection and trace growth to promote efficient local scheduling and divergence avoidance for GPUs.

Prior work selects traces by traversing CFG nodes or edges weighted by profile-generated execution frequency of basic blocks or branch paths respectively. Then, in prior work, trace selection *grows* traces *forward*, traversing the seed's child nodes, and *backward*, traversing the seed's parent nodes.

If divergence exists among frequently executed basic blocks, prior approaches to seeding and growing traces could make it worse, scheduling instructions from non-divergent

Algorithm 1 GPU Trace Selection Algorithm

```
function TRACE SELECTION(Set nodes)
/* nodes sorted by CFG tree-height and divergence. */
    while there are unvisited nodes do
        seed = next unvisited node   /* Select a seed */
        Mark seed visited
        current = seed
        loop                         /* Grow trace forward */
            s = BEST SUCCESSOR OF(current)
            if s == 0 exit loop
            Add s to the trace
            Mark s visited
        end loop
    end while
end function
```

Algorithm 2 GPU Best Successor Of Algorithm

```
1  function BEST SUCCESSOR OF(Node src)
2      Edge e = the highest probability edge
3          among all src's outgoing edges
4      if PROBABILITY(e) ≤ MIN_PROB return 0
5      n = e's target
6      if n is visited return 0
7      return n
8  end function
9
10 function PROBABILITY(Edge e)
11     return e's weight
12 end function
```

basic blocks to divergent basic blocks. Instead, our algorithm begins by generating a list of seeds, nodes likely to be non-divergent. From these seeds the algorithm only grows forward, never backward. Therefore all trace roots are likely non-divergent. This assists local scheduling to avert divergence and reduce divergence time (see Section 4.3). Finally, we substitute dynamic profiling of program branch behavior instead of execution frequency because branch behavior provides additional insight differentiating basic block's warp behavior.

As mentioned previously (see Section 2), we developed a PTX optimizer for automatically profiling, analyzing, and optimizing PTX [29], CUDA's virtual instruction set architecture (ISA). Our PTX toolchain records dynamic program profiles to guide Warp-Aware Trace Scheduling.

Our GPU TRACE SELECTION algorithm starts with a set of seed nodes, gathered using a breadth-first traversal on the CFG and sorted by the following properties:

- Control-equivalent to program entry node
- Loop head
- Contains PTX synchronization or communication instructions (*e.g.* `bar` and `membar`)[†]
- Control-equivalent to a basic block containing PTX synchronization or communication instructions

Ties are broken by most likely predicted successor. The result is a list sorted by breadth-first tree-height of likely non-divergent nodes. For reference, the definitions for dominance, post-dominance, and control-equivalence [2] are included below:

Definition (Dominance). A node $\boldsymbol{A}$ dominates a node $\boldsymbol{B}$ if and only if all paths from the start node to $\boldsymbol{B}$ go through $\boldsymbol{A}$.

Definition (Post-Dominance). A node $\boldsymbol{A}$ post-dominates a node $\boldsymbol{B}$ if and only if all paths from $\boldsymbol{B}$ to the exit node go through $\boldsymbol{A}$.

Definition (Control-Equivalence). A node $\boldsymbol{A}$ is control-equivalent to a node $\boldsymbol{B}$ if $\boldsymbol{A}$ dominates $\boldsymbol{B}$ and $\boldsymbol{B}$ post-dominates $\boldsymbol{A}$.

After choosing a seed, GPU TRACE SELECTION only grows traces forward. Warp-Aware Trace Scheduling's objective is to schedule instructions as early as possible and in non-divergent basic blocks. Traces with non-divergent roots represent this intent. We do not allow traces to grow backward because of the need to avoid divergence.

In prior work, Smith [33] also only grew traces forward, but in his algorithm the next unscheduled basic block is selected as the new seed, contrary to the general approach of identifying the next node by highest execution count. Our TRACE SELECTION algorithm prioritizes non-divergent basic blocks, necessarily skipping basic blocks.

During trace growth, the GPU BEST SUCCESSOR OF algorithm (Algorithm 2) determines the most likely successor based on branch prediction. The MIN_PROB variable (line 4) is a cutoff criterion to stop trace growth when a likely successor cannot be determined since the branch prediction does not distinguish divergent and non-divergent branches, an additional reason for our deliberate approach to seed choice. Our results (see Section 6) evaluate the applicability of branch prediction without regard for warp behavior. Searching for a MIN_PROB value maximizing performance, MIN_PROB was experimentally determined to be 65.

The example CFG in Figure 1 contains three traces ($A \rightarrow B \rightarrow C$, $D \rightarrow E \rightarrow F$, and $G \rightarrow I$), four `if`-statements (A,B,C; D,E,F; J,K,L; and G,H,I), and one loop (D,E,F). The example contains one branch, J, affected by the MIN_PROB criterion. Nodes A, C, D, J, F, and G include conditional branches. Nodes B, E, K, and H end with unconditional branches. Nodes A, C, G, and I form a control-equivalent set. D is control-equivalent to F and J is control-equivalent to L. Note too, Trace #1 stops at C because D is a loop head and Trace #2 stops at F because traces cannot traverse a backedge (see definition of trace, Section 4). Node J does not start a trace because its branch fails the MIN_PROB criterion. While the example demonstrates the MIN_PROB criterion's effects on a branch off the critical path, a branch like J could just as likely lie on the critical path.

A reversal in a single branch's behavior can drastically affect trace selection. Suppose C's edge probabilities were reversed, $C \rightarrow D$ is predicted 5 and $C \rightarrow J$ is predicted 95. Three traces would be selected, $A \rightarrow B \rightarrow C \rightarrow J$, $D \rightarrow E \rightarrow F$, and $G \rightarrow I$. Longer traces tend to increase local scheduling opportunities.

4.2 Trace Formation

Compared to prior work, Warp-Aware Trace Scheduling forms traces most similar to Fisher's original proposal for

[†]instructions that assume uniform, non divergent warp behavior

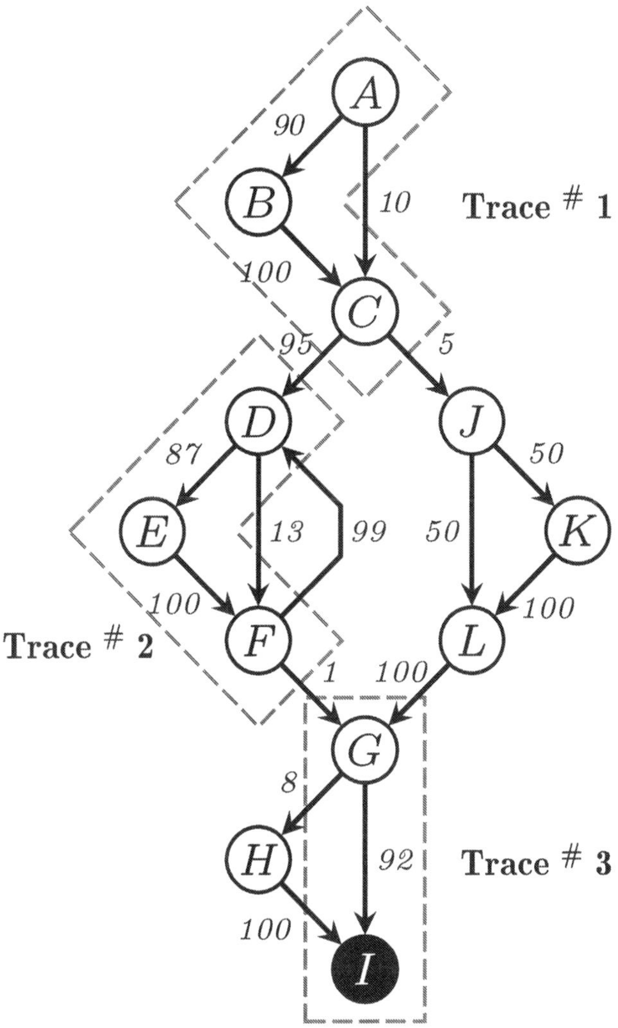

Figure 1: An example controlflow graph (CFG) with three traces: Trace #1 ($A \rightarrow B \rightarrow C$), Trace #2 ($D \rightarrow E \rightarrow F$), and Trace #3 ($G \rightarrow I$). Nominally, all single nodes, not already in a trace represent a trace (*e.g.* H).

CPUs [9]. However, unlike prior work, GPU trace formation respects program source code block structure, leaving it intact. All explicit attempts to form longer traces are conspicuously absent. However, contrary to Fisher, GPU traces are implicitly enlarged. After Warp-Aware Trace Scheduling, during the code's subsequent passage through the GPU compiler toolchain, predication is automatically performed. For PTX synchronization instructions, GPU trace formation adds extra edges to the trace to create scheduling constraints to preserve correct program behavior.

Many prior works, for example Superblock [14] and Hyperblock [22] scheduling, advanced structure-transforming innovations to decrease implementation effort of bookkeeping, expand traces, and enable optimization. Superblock scheduling forms longer traces by removing side entrances via tail duplication, and Hyperblock scheduling explicitly applies predication.

PTX code sequence *before*...				
⋮			...	
25		setp.*.*	%p0,	...;
⋮			...	
28	@%p0	bra	BB0;	
29			...	
⋮			...	
39			...	
40		BB0:		
⋮			...	
... and *after* `if`-conversion				
⋮			...	
25		setp.*.*	%p0,	...;
29	@!%p0		...	
⋮	@!%p0		...	
39	@!%p0		...	
⋮			...	

Table 2: Example PTX code sequence showing the application of `if`-conversion using predication

After Warp-Aware Trace Scheduling, `ptxas` (or the CUDA device driver) compiles PTX to SASS [26]. SASS supports predication which `ptxas` employs for optimization, like `if`-conversion. To complement NVIDIA's toolchain, Warp-Aware Trace Scheduling ignores opportunities to form longer traces, relying on `ptxas` and later predicate-modifying optimizations (see Section 9 for how to potentially weaken dependence on NVIDIA's GPU toolchain to explicitly lengthen GPU traces).

GPU trace formation expects PTX code sequences, matching the pattern in the top half of Table 2, will be optimized to straightline code. The instruction on line 25 sets the branch's condition and on line 28, the branch to label (basic block) `BB0` is executed if predicate register `%p0` is `true`, skipping lines 29 through 39. The code sequence in the bottom half of Table 2 represents the above sequence after applying `if`-conversion, using predication. After `if`-conversion, line 28 is removed and code between lines 29 and 39 will conditionally execute based on `!%p0`. The `!` symbol performs logical negation.

For PTX synchronization instructions, GPU trace formation adds extra edges to the trace to create scheduling constraints to preserve correct program behavior.

4.3 Local Instruction Scheduling

Local scheduling, historically referred to as local compaction, moves instructions within but not between traces to improve ILP. Consider two instructions, $\boldsymbol{A}$ and $\boldsymbol{B}$, and $\boldsymbol{B}$ is a conditional branch. Moving $\boldsymbol{A}$ above $\boldsymbol{B}$ is called *upward code motion* and the opposite transformation, moving $\boldsymbol{A}$ *below* $\boldsymbol{B}$, is called *downward code motion*. Dependences define execution-order constraints between instructions. During upward code motion, an instruction breaks its control dependence on the preceding branch. If the instruction's new basic block has multiple successors, this motion is

	Restricted [4]	General [4]	Boosting [34]	**Deviant (ours)**
Scheduling Restrictions	*Legal* and *Safe*	*Legal*	none	excludes texture, shared, and constant memory operations and all `store` instructions
Hardware Support	none	non-trapping instructions	shadow register file, shadow store buffer, and support for re-executing instructions	none
Exception Handling for Speculative Instructions	prohibited	ignored	supported	absent

Table 3: Characterizing global scheduling models from prior work and our new GPU model (found on the far right). Most GPUs contain limited exception handling capabilities (shown in more detail in Table 4); The GPU provides no mechanism to detect exceptions.

Exception	**Support**
Arithmetic	
Integer Floating-Point	No mechanism to detect occurrence[‡]
Memory	
Texture Constant Shared Global	CUDA runtime error "unknown error" at conclusion of kernel execution, available on host device (CPU)

Table 4: GPU exception handling by instruction type (for NVIDIA GPUs)

speculative because it is uncertain whether the instruction's result will be needed. The following restrictions govern code motion:

Legal – Preserve sequential correctness
Safe – Prevent any exception caused by speculative execution from terminating execution

Prior work enforced exception handling to varying degrees with hardware and software support. Table 3 describes the general scheduling models' policies and enforcement strategies to obey the aforementioned restrictions. The rightmost column in Table 3 summarizes our new GPU scheduling model. In general, the GPU is *unsafe* (see CUDA C Programming Guide [27], Section F.2). On the GPU, arithmetic exceptions, like integer and floating-point division by zero, underflow, and overflow, are not signaled, no mechanism exists to detect the exception, and execution continues normally. Additionally, as Table 3 and Table 4 indicate, all GPU memory operations are *unsafe*, speculatively executing a memory operation can cause an error and may be reported only after kernel execution concludes. Warp-Aware Trace Scheduling conforms to the CUDA Programming Model's exception handling policy. We say the GPU global scheduling model is **deviant** because GPU execution continues even if errors occur, failing to conform to (*deviating* from) prior scheduling models.

Because GPUs have such weak exception handling mechanisms, our scheduler only speculates on global `load`'s and arithmetic instructions and prohibits speculation of all `store` instructions and texture, shared, and constant memory operations. Looking forward, we recommend adding new instructions, a *speculative* `load` and an *exception* `check`, providing a *safe* and practical solution to govern data speculation, similar to instructions (`PREFETCH`*h*) used by current Intel 64 architectures [16]. A *speculative* `load` always succeeds, never causes a page fault, and sets a *valid* flag. *exception* `check` tests the *valid* flag.

Warp-Aware Trace Scheduling's local trace scheduler performs *no scheduling on instructions within basic blocks.* It *only* performs *scheduling on instructions between basic blocks.* During PTX-to-SASS translation, `ptxas` performs register allocation and scheduling within basic blocks. When scheduling instructions between basic blocks, Warp-Aware Trace Scheduling's local trace scheduler only applies *upward code motion*, removing instructions from the top of one basic block and appending them to the bottom of their new basic block. The local trace scheduler never moves an instruction down, not even an instruction in its native basic block. Remember the details of GPU trace selection in Section 4.1. By construction, trace roots are the earliest, likely non-divergent basic block to schedule into. The scheduler greedily schedules instructions to minimize execution time on the critical path, so it is possible that at scheduling's conclusion some basic block schedules have been lengthened. The main objective is to increase ILP and additionally, separate dependent global memory `load`'s and `store`'s, scheduling `load`'s as early as possible, because generally, `load`'s and `store`'s respectively begin and end chains of dependent instructions.

4.3.1 Bookkeeping

To maintain program correctness (*legality*) during scheduling, it may be necessary to insert copies of moved instructions, a process called *bookkeeping*, also known as *compensation*. The instruction copies are referred to as compensation code. Due to GPU-specific warp behavior, Warp-Aware Trace Scheduling's bookkeeping is tightly controlled

[‡]CUDA C Programming Guide [27], Section G.2. Floating-Point Standard

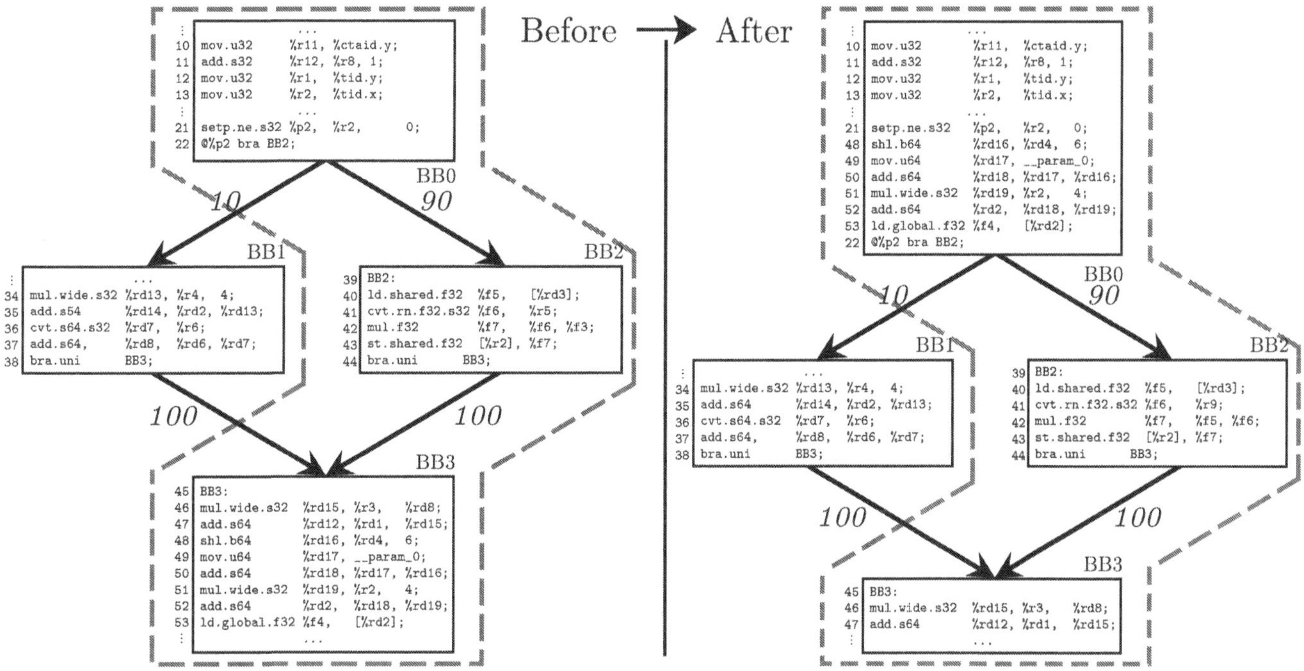

Figure 2: Example local scheduling of an `if-else`-statement. The `if` is predicted likely *not taken*. Consequently, during local scheduling, instructions from BB3 (lines 48 − 53) are *moved upward* into BB1. After local scheduling note line 53, a global memory `load`, will be speculatively executed.

to avoid inserting instruction copies into divergent basic blocks, thereby reducing divergence time.

Typically, compensation is required to correct misspeculation. However, Warp-Aware Trace Scheduling only speculates global `load`'s, never `store`'s, and maintains original basic block boundaries and order of conditional branches. Consequently, Warp-Aware Trace Scheduling is *recovery-free* (*i.e.* it requires no support for misspeculation to preserve program correctness).

Starting from the trace root's successors, the local trace scheduler, respecting data dependences, attempts upward code motion to schedule instructions on the trace from root to leaf, preferring to schedule in the trace's root to potentially achieve earliest possible execution. If an instruction cannot be scheduled in the root and another convergent basic block cannot be found, the scheduler begins to schedule the next instruction. Loops are scheduled independently. The scheduler operates without a model of instruction latencies. Consequently, our approach greedily schedules based on branch prediction, and as previously mentioned can produce unbalanced basic blocks, preferring to schedule instructions to minimize critical path execution. The result is a scheduler that attempts to minimize overall execution time and divergence time, without inducing additional warp divergence or increasing divergence time.

Figure 2 demonstrates warp-aware local scheduling on an `if-else`-statement. The example contains one trace: BB0 → BB2 → BB3. The figure's left side depicts the original code sequence, <u>before</u> local scheduling, and the right side depicts the optimized code sequence, <u>after</u> local scheduling. No instructions are moved from BB2 because these instructions (lines 41–43) depend on the shared `load` instruction on line 40. The scheduler only speculates on global `load`'s. Most of BB3's instructions (lines 48–53) are *moved upward* into basic block BB1. However, instructions on line 46 and 47 remain because line 47 depends on line 46, which in turn depends on line 37 (register `%rd8`). While it is possible to move the instructions on lines 46 and 47 to BB1, local scheduling is not optimized to avoid increasing execution time. The scheduler considers CFG structure and branch profiling to identify divergence and avoid it as well as increasing divergence time. In this instance, considering BB0 → BB1's edge weight (*10*), the scheduler determines that BB1 is a divergent basic block and prevents scheduling extra instructions into it. If the scheduler determined BB1 non-divergent, the scheduler would schedule instructions on lines 46 and 47 to both BB1 and BB2.

5. EXPERIMENTAL METHODOLOGY

We evaluated Warp-Aware Trace Scheduling using the Rodinia Benchmark Suite [5]. The benchmarks were compiled using CUDA 5.5 with full optimization (O3), targeted for a compute capability 3.0 device (sm_30) using the NVIDIA driver version 319.37, the driver version accompanying CUDA 5.5. Programs were profiled, analyzed, and optimized using the optimizer we developed and previously discussed (see Section 4.1). All results are from execution on an NVIDIA GTX 670 (a compute capability 3.0 device), not simulation.

Results for each benchmark were measured as an average of at least 10 runs and reflect kernel, not whole program, performance. Different input sets were used for training and testing. Besides performance, the results before and after our optimization are identical. While current GPUs contain weak exception handling capabilities, Warp-Aware Trace Scheduling maintains sequential correctness (*i.e.* legal-

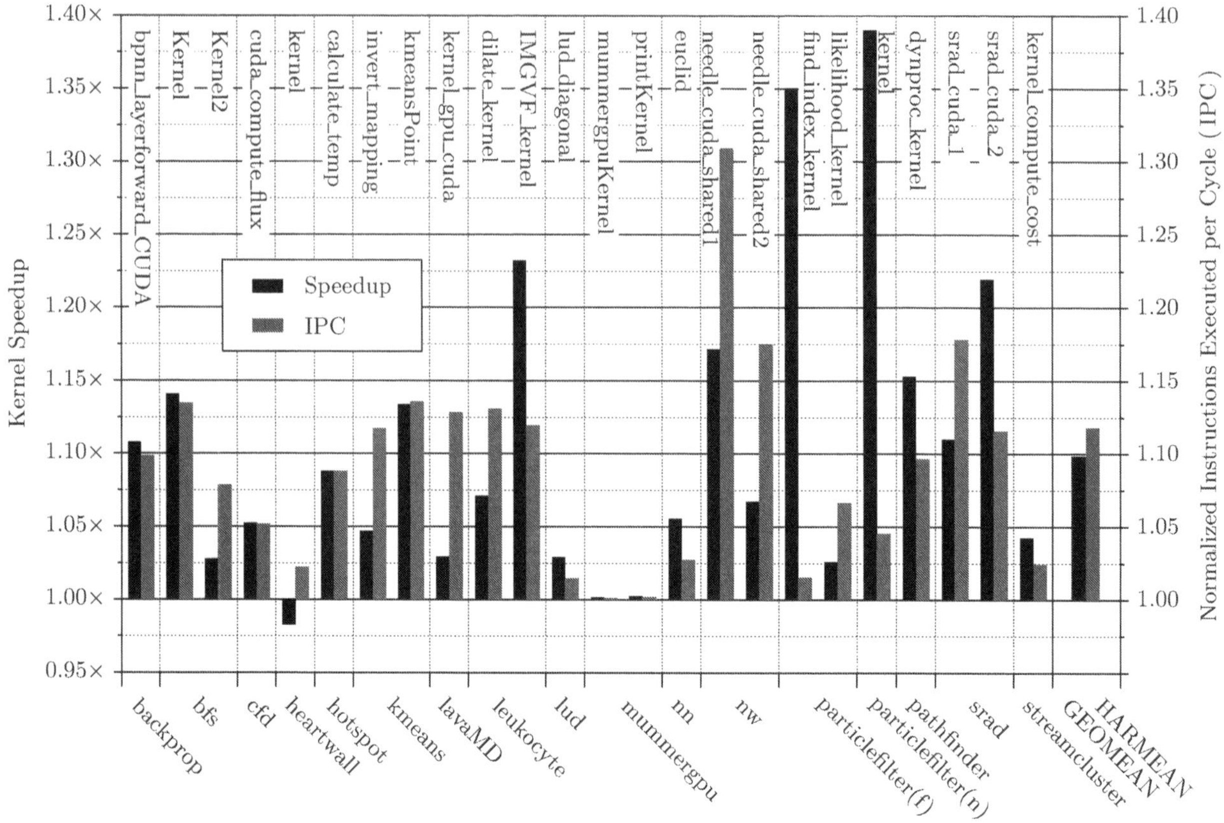

Figure 3: Kernel speedup and normalized instructions executed per cycle (IPC) with Warp-Aware Trace Scheduling on the Rodinia benchmarks. Geometric mean speedup and harmonic mean IPC are found on the right.

ity, see Section 4.3). Our technique only speculates global `loads`, never `stores` (see Section 4.3).

6. RESULTS

Figure 3 demonstrates the performance benefit of Warp-Aware Trace Scheduling applied to the Rodinia Benchmark Suite on a real system. On Figure 3's dual y-axis, kernel speedup is on the left and normalized instructions executed per cycle (IPC)[§] is on the right. IPC results were recorded using NVIDIA's profiler and represent relative IPC after Warp-Aware Trace Scheduling over the baseline (original) IPC. The bottom x-axis shows benchmark names and on the top x-axis, the corresponding names of the benchmark's kernels.

Shown on the far right of Figure 3, across the Rodinia benchmarks, the geometric mean speedup is 1.10×. In terms of speedup, notable standouts include **particlefilter(n)**'s *kernel*, 1.34×; **particlefilter(f)**'s *find_index_kernel*, 1.35×; **leukocyte**'s *IMGVF_kernel*, 1.23×; and **srad**'s *srad_cuda_2*, 1.22×. **heartwall** produces the only negative speedup performance mark at 0.98×.

Comparing speedup to IPC, the results are markedly correlated. Intuitively, identifying and improving IPC on critical program paths can reduce overall execution time. On the far right, across the Rodinia benchmarks, the IPC's harmonic mean is 1.12×.

[§]the number of executed instructions divided by the number of SMs divided by elapsed clocks

6.1 Performance Analysis

If Warp-Aware Trace Scheduling automatically identifies no opportunities, it leaves the kernel unchanged. Specifically, Warp-Aware Trace Scheduling dismisses kernels if:

- there are too few (or no) branches to speculate
- trace selection fails; unpredictable critical path
- the program contains insufficient ILP

Intuitively, if no branches exist in a program, there are no basic block boundaries to schedule across, and global scheduling will have marginal performance benefit. In our evaluation, the branches in Rodinia's kernels are mostly predictable, containing a majority of branches with lopsided ratios (*e.g.* 90 − 10). Based on our trace selection's MIN_PROB criterion (see Section 4.1), too many 50 − 50 branches, or other suitably balanced branches, can thwart identification of program critical path and trace generation. Finally, if the program contains insufficient ILP to expose, again, global instruction scheduling will be ineffective.

We inspected SASS to affirm our technique's results and identify and understand related **ptxas** optimizations. Scrutinizing the differences in SASS before and after applying our optimization we concluded our optimization had successfully identified program's critical path and divergent basic blocks and hoisted instructions above branches. Since SASS is not executable binary microcode but rather just another (virtual) low-level assembly language, more thorough analysis was done using NVIDIA's profiler, collecting statistics from hardware counters. Analyzing complementary hardware counters reported by NVIDIA's profiler suggests modest increases to cache misses and instruction replay overhead in order to expose additional ILP and increase IPC is a desirable tradeoff to achieve higher overall performance.

Warp-Aware Trace Scheduling is applied before `ptxas` optimization and register allocation. On average the total number of used registers increased by 4. In particular, kernels in **lud**, **nw**, and **srad** showed the greatest increases in number of used registers by 17, 16, and 14, respectively but these increases did not affect occupancy (see Section 3).

6.2 IPC Analysis

Note that increasing IPC (instruction throughput) does not always result in a corresponding improvement in execution time. For instance, notice the difference between IPC and speedup for **nw**'s *needle_cuda_shared1* (see Figure 3). Increasing IPC may also increase the percentage of replayed instructions, a negative performance metric. The percentage of replayed instructions is calculated as:

$$\left(\frac{\text{instructions issued} - \text{instructions executed}}{\text{instructions issued}}\right) \times 100,$$

the difference between the number of instructions issued by the number of instructions executed, and:

$$\text{instructions issued} \geq \text{instructions executed}.$$

Replay is a hardware optimization to hide instruction latency. When a variable, long-latency instruction, such as a `ld/st` instruction stalls the pipeline, the stalling warp is removed from the pipeline and the pipeline starts executing ready instructions from a previously waiting warp. Later, the original stalling instructions will be reissued and hopefully, execute faster. A replay could occur due to a local cache miss, memory bank conflict, and non-uniform memory access.

To further investigate and identify the source of performance improvements, for each benchmark we used NVIDIA's profiler to gather global memory replay overhead, shared memory replay overhead, and instruction replay overhead. For benchmarks that showed positive performance improvements, no correlation between either replay overhead and IPC, or replay overhead and speedup was found. These results reinforce our hypothesis that IPC can substitute for TLP (*e.g.* occupancy), to improve GPU resource utilization and attain higher performance, even at the expense of increases to negative performance metrics.

6.3 Summary

Warp-Aware Trace Scheduling, like prior global scheduling techniques, primarily focuses on reducing execution time by increasing ILP (IPC) on the critical path. However, its unique features to avoid divergence and reduce divergence time contribute to improved performance. Targeting and reducing divergence time achieves reductions in negative performance metrics, such as instruction serialization and total instructions executed. The next section describes Figure 3's results, focusing on increasing ILP, avoiding divergence, and reducing divergence time for faster program execution.

7. DISCUSSION

This section studiously interprets some benchmarks' performance results reported in the previous section. First, Table 5 reflects on benchmarks' kernels not amenable to Warp-Aware Trace Scheduling. To begin, Warp-Aware Trace Scheduling disregards kernels that contain limited or no branches, no control flow. **backprop**'s *bpnn_adjust_weights_cuda* only contains one branch. Dynamic profiling indicates it is taken and immediately encounters an `exit` instruction. Consequently, global scheduling would be ineffective.

In **leukocyte**'s *GICOV_kernel*, few branches exist and each basic block's arithmetic intensity, the ratio of arithmetic instructions to off-chip memory instructions, is high. Consequently, increasing ILP will have only marginal performance benefit because sufficient ILP exists within each basic block. **lud**'s *lud_internal* contains no branches. **lud**'s second kernel, *lud_perimeter*, contains few lopsided (*e.g.* 90 − 10) branches and many even (*e.g.* 50 − 50) branches. Attempting to select expansive traces in *lud_perimeter* fails.

In **particlefilter(f)**, *normalize_weights_kernel* has a sufficient number of branches and its critical path is clearly defined. However, its critical path skips an extreme amount of the program; most often, the kernel exits without performing much computation.

For **particlefilter(f)**'s other kernel, *sum_kernel*, intense computation is only found within its single loop. Warp-Aware Trace Scheduling restricts upward code motion to within traces, never between traces. It is likely *sum_kernel* would benefit from loop unrolling, a complementary optimization to trace scheduling (for further details, see Section 9).

Returning to Figure 3, these kernels generally contain predictable branches, enable selection and formation of long traces, and contain sufficient ILP to effectively employ global scheduling.

Among Rodinia, **cfd**'s *cuda_compute_flux* is unique in its use of the `unroll` pragma. This pragma tells the compiler to replace a loop with a repeated sequence of the loop's instructions, with fewer branch instructions between. For *cuda_compute_flux* after unrolling, no loops, no backedges, remain, allowing Warp-Aware Trace Scheduling to select a single long trace from the kernel.

Only **heartwall**'s *kernel* produces negative speedup. Note the fractional increase in IPC. Here, while Warp-Aware Trace Scheduling was effective uncovering ILP, slowdown was produced because our heuristics to avoid divergence failed, scheduling extra instructions to divergent basic blocks. Considering the ILP exposed and our conservative approach to speculation, reversing *kernel*'s negative performance may still not achieve distinct performance benefits. For **heartwall**, the overriding performance problem is not limited ILP but rather low global memory bandwidth due to inefficient memory access patterns.

A marked contrast exists between IPC and speedup for **lavaMD**'s *kernel_gpu_cuda*. For *kernel_gpu_cuda*, Warp-Aware Trace Scheduling fails to appreciably improve execution time because loops are scheduled independently and *kernel_gpu_cuda*'s global memory instructions are isolated in two tight loops.

Both **mummergpu**'s kernels are problematic for global scheduling. *printKernel*'s execution time is dominated by one large loop containing numerous divergent branches with

Benchmark	Kernel	Number of branches	Critical Path (MIN_PROB)	Arithmetic Intensity
backprop	bpnn_adjust_weights_cuda	1	✗	✗
cfd	cuda_initialize_variables	∅	✓	✓
	cuda_time_step	∅	✓	✓
	cuda_compute_step_factor	∅	✓	✓
gaussian	Fan1	1	✓	✓
	Fan2	✓	✗	✗
leukocyte	GICOV_kernel	✗	✓	✓
lud	lud_perimeter	✓	✗	✓
	lud_internal	∅	✓	✓
particlefilter(f)	normalize_weights_kernel	✓	✓	✗
	sum_kernel	✗	✓	✗

Table 5: Rodinia benchmarks' kernels for which Warp-Aware Trace Scheduling identified insufficient ILP opportunities to justify application of global scheduling techniques

few global `load`'s to speculate. With safer data speculation support, like the solution proposed in Section 4.1, more aggressive speculation could enable higher performance. *mummergpuKernel*'s problems only differ in that it contains nested loops. A loop optimization, or the combination of global scheduling and loop optimization, may produce better results.

Warp-Aware Trace Scheduling achieves impressive performance results for **particlefilter(n)**'s *kernel* and **particlefilter(f)**'s *find_index_kernel*. But the increase in IPC, an indicator of the degree of ILP, is minimal. In these kernels, Warp-Aware Trace Scheduling's results are attributable to reduced divergence time and scheduling instructions from divergent basic blocks to non-divergent basic blocks. Comparing the original and optimized kernels using NVIDIA's profiler shows a marked reduction in instruction serialization and total instructions executed.

8. RELATED WORK

Trace Scheduling, initially proposed by Fisher [9], now dominates current approaches to global instruction scheduling. Works related to Fisher's Trace Scheduling mostly vary regarding trace shape and schedule construction. For further information, Faraboschi *et al.* [8] survey global instruction scheduling and region shapes.

Specifically, much related work pertains to enhancing ILP on VLIW/EPIC (IA-64) architectures. These architectures employ dynamic hardware branch prediction as well as hardware parallelism detection and extraction techniques. GPUs are simple in-order SIMT (Single-Instruction Multiple-Thread) architectures without hardware branch prediction and analogous hardware parallelism detection and extraction. Without enhancement, Trace Scheduling could not successfully navigate between the GPU architecture's pitfalls and challenges. Warp-Aware Trace Scheduling emits performance by adapting global scheduling to the GPU execution model and avoiding divergence.

Regarding static GPU controlflow analyses to enable optimization, Coutinho *et al.* [6] propose a static branch divergence analysis. Their analysis could complement but not substitute for dynamic profiling because Warp-Aware Trace Scheduling requires accurate determination of program critical path, not just differentiation of divergent and non-divergent instructions.

Various software-only GPU-specific optimizations generally target divergence. Branch fusion, proposed by Coutinho *et al.* [6], merges common code from divergent program paths using their aforementioned static branch divergence analysis. Han *et al.* [12] describe two optimizations: iteration delaying and branch distribution. Iteration delaying improves performance by targeting a divergent branch within a loop, executing iterations following the branch and delaying execution of iterations that do not follow the branch until later. Hopefully, the delayed iterations execute with more threads, achieving higher resource utilization. Branch distribution functions similarly to branch fusion.

9. FUTURE WORK

We plan to investigate the following strategies to expose additional ILP for higher performance: trace expansion, local scheduling, and misspeculation support. Warp-Aware Trace Scheduling could benefit from trace-enlarging techniques, like Superblock scheduling's tail duplication [14] and Hyperblock scheduling's predication [22]. If loops dominate runtime, potential loop optimizations include loop unrolling and Software Pipelining [21].

Regarding local scheduling, our current approach could be augmented with accurate modeling of instruction latencies. Further, alternative list scheduling heuristics could produce more efficient schedules. Our local scheduler only applies *upward* code motion, but precedent suggests *downward* code motion could provide additional performance benefits.

Finally, with precise exceptions and efficient misspeculation support, more aggressive speculation is possible. Section 4.3 describes adding new *speculative* `load` and *exception* `check` instructions. Currently, only a fraction of potential, long latency, memory instructions are speculated and no `store` instructions since current GPUs provide no hardware support for handling exceptions.

Using ILP rather than TLP to support effective latency hiding could lead to additional optimizations, trading kernel characteristics, like occupancy, for higher performance. For instance, register pressure can have negative performance impact. Substituting ILP for TLP could reduce register pressure without exceeding the warp scheduler's ability to hide long-latency memory instructions.

Potentially, with divergence analysis like the analysis proposed by Coutinho *et al.* [6], dependence on trace selection's MIN_PROB criterion could be reduced or eliminated. Local scheduling could also benefit from more accurate identification of divergence.

Discussed in more detail in Section 4.1, traces are identified using dynamic profiling. Alternatively, trace selection could use static branch prediction heuristics [3]. However, no study exists demonstrating static GPU branch prediction to be suitable, sufficient in branch coverage and accuracy, for enabling optimization. Additionally, our current profiling approach could be enhanced to allow application of Warp-Aware Trace Scheduling during just-in-time (JIT) compilation. Currently, our profiling approach's overhead makes this impractical.

10. CONCLUSION

This paper presented a detailed implementation and evaluation of Warp-Aware Trace Scheduling, the first fully-automatic speculative global scheduling optimization for GPUs. We revisited and revising Trace Scheduling's three major steps for the GPU architecture. First, during trace selection, the kernel is partitioned into traces with likely *non-divergent* roots. Next, in trace formation, our implementation adds edges to synchronization instructions to constrain scheduling and preserve correct program behavior. Finally, instructions within traces are scheduled to improve ILP and hide global memory latency, if possible, breaking control dependences and speculating on instruction execution. Furthermore, our local scheduling effectively avoids divergence and reduces divergence time.

Our evaluation of Warp-Aware Trace Scheduling on a real GPU system demonstrates significant performance improvements in execution time and IPC for 17 benchmarks and 24 kernels. Overall, Warp-Aware Trace Scheduling automatically achieves a geometric mean 1.10× speedup using dynamic profiling, improving IPC by 1.12× (harmonic mean), and reducing instruction serialization and total instructions executed. These current results reinforce our implementation approach and basic concepts for our global instruction scheduling technique. Executing our plans for future work, composing additional optimizations with Warp-Aware Trace Scheduling, we anticipate more higher performance improvements.

11. ACKNOWLEDGMENTS

James A. Jablin is supported by the Department of Energy Office of Science Graduate Fellowship Program (DOE SCGF), made possible in part by the American Recovery and Reinvestment Act of 2009, administered by ORISE-ORAU under contract no. DE-AC05-06OR23100.

We acknowledge the support of Intel Science and Technology Center for Cloud Computing.

12. REFERENCES

[1] Advanced Micro Devices, Inc. *AMD Graphics Cores Next (GCN) Architecture*, 2012.

[2] A. V. Aho, M. S. Lam, R. Sethi, and J. D. Ullman. *Compilers: Principles, Techniques, and Tools (2nd Edition)*. Addison-Wesley Longman Publishing Co., Inc., Boston, MA, USA, 2006.

[3] T. Ball and J. R. Larus. Branch Prediction for Free. In *Proceedings of the ACM SIGPLAN 1993 conference on Programming language design and implementation*, PLDI '93, pages 300–313, New York, NY, USA, 1993. ACM.

[4] P. P. Chang, S. A. Mahlke, W. Y. Chen, N. J. Warter, and W.-m. W. Hwu. IMPACT: An Architectural Framework for Multiple-Instruction-Issue Processors. In *Proceedings of the 18th annual international symposium on Computer architecture*, ISCA '91, pages 266–275, New York, NY, USA, 1991. ACM.

[5] S. Che, M. Boyer, J. Meng, D. Tarjan, J. W. Sheaffer, S.-H. Lee, and K. Skadron. Rodinia: A Benchmark Suite for Heterogeneous Computing. In *IEEE International Symposium on Workload Characterization, 2009. IISWC 2009.*, pages 44–54, October 2009.

[6] B. Coutinho, D. Sampaio, F. M. Q. Pereira, and W. Meira Jr. Divergence Analysis and Optimizations. In *Proceedings of the 2011 International Conference on Parallel Architectures and Compilation Techniques*, PACT '11, pages 320–329, Washington, DC, USA, 2011. IEEE Computer Society.

[7] J. R. Ellis. *Bulldog: A Compiler for VLIW Architectures (Parallel Computing, Reduced-Instruction-Set, Trace Scheduling, Scientific)*. PhD thesis, New Haven, CT, USA, 1985.

[8] P. Faraboschi, J. Fisher, and C. Young. Instruction Scheduling for Instruction Level Parallel Processors. *Proceedings of the IEEE*, 89(11):1638–1659, 2001.

[9] J. A. Fisher. Trace Scheduling: A Technique for Global Microcode Compaction. *IEEE Trans. Comput.*, 30(7):478–490, July 1981.

[10] W. W. L. Fung and T. M. Aamodt. Thread Block Compaction for Efficient SIMT Control Flow. In *Proceedings of the 2011 IEEE 17th International Symposium on High Performance Computer Architecture*, HPCA '11, pages 25–36, Washington, DC, USA, 2011. IEEE Computer Society.

[11] W. W. L. Fung, I. Sham, G. Yuan, and T. M. Aamodt. Dynamic Warp Formation and Scheduling for Efficient GPU Control Flow. In *Proceedings of the 40th Annual IEEE/ACM International Symposium on Microarchitecture*, MICRO 40, pages 407–420, Washington, DC, USA, 2007. IEEE Computer Society.

[12] T. D. Han and T. S. Abdelrahman. Reducing Branch Divergence in GPU Programs. In *Proceedings of the Fourth Workshop on General Purpose Processing on Graphics Processing Units*, GPGPU-4, pages 3:1–3:8, New York, NY, USA, 2011. ACM.

[13] HSA Foundation. *HSA Programmer's Reference Manual: HSAIL Virtual ISA and Programming Model, Compiler Writer's Guide, and Object Format (BRIG)*, May 2013.

[14] W.-M. W. Hwu, S. A. Mahlke, W. Y. Chen, P. P. Chang, N. J. Warter, R. A. Bringmann, R. G. Ouellette, R. E. Hank, T. Kiyohara, G. E. Haab, J. G. Holm, and D. M. Lavery. The Superblock: An Effective Technique for VLIW and Superscalar

Compilation. *J. Supercomput.*, 7(1-2):229–248, May 1993.

[15] Intel Corporation. *Performance Interactions of OpenCL Code and Intel® - Quick Sync Video on Intel HD Graphics 4000*, 2012.

[16] Intel Corporation. *Intel 64 and IA-32 Architectures Software Developer's Manual*, September 2013.

[17] A. Jog, O. Kayıran, N. Chidambaram Nachiappan, A. K. Mishra, M. T. Kandemir, O. Mutlu, R. Iyer, and C. R. Das. OWL: Cooperative Thread Array Aware Scheduling Techniques for Improving GPGPU Performance. In *Proceedings of the Eighteenth International Conference on Architectural Support for Programming Languages and Operating Systems*, ASPLOS '13, pages 395–406, New York, NY, USA, 2013. ACM.

[18] A. Jog, O. Kayıran, A. K. Mishra, M. T. Kandemir, O. Mutlu, R. Iyer, and C. R. Das. Orchestrated Scheduling and Prefetching for GPGPUs. In *Proceedings of the 40th Annual International Symposium on Computer Architecture*, ISCA '13, pages 332–343, New York, NY, USA, 2013. ACM.

[19] O. Kayıran, A. Jog, M. T. Kandemir, and C. R. Das. Neither More nor Less: Optimizing Thread-level Parallelism for GPGPUs. In *Proceedings of the 22Nd International Conference on Parallel Architectures and Compilation Techniques*, PACT '13, pages 157–166, Piscataway, NJ, USA, 2013. IEEE Press.

[20] D. B. Kirk and W.-m. W. Hwu. *Programming Massively Parallel Processors: A Hands-on Approach.* Morgan Kaufmann Publishers Inc., San Francisco, CA, USA, 1st edition, 2010.

[21] M. Lam. Software Pipelining: An Effective Scheduling Technique for VLIW Machines. In *Proceedings of the ACM SIGPLAN 1988 conference on Programming Language design and Implementation*, PLDI '88, pages 318–328, New York, NY, USA, 1988. ACM.

[22] S. A. Mahlke, D. C. Lin, W. Y. Chen, R. E. Hank, and R. A. Bringmann. Effective Compiler Support for Predicated Execution Using the Hyperblock. In *Proceedings of the 25th annual international symposium on Microarchitecture*, MICRO 25, pages 45–54, Los Alamitos, CA, USA, 1992. IEEE Computer Society Press.

[23] J. Meng, D. Tarjan, and K. Skadron. Dynamic Warp Subdivision for Integrated Branch and Memory Divergence Tolerance. In *Proceedings of the 37th Annual International Symposium on Computer Architecture*, ISCA '10, pages 235–246, New York, NY, USA, 2010. ACM.

[24] V. Narasiman, M. Shebanow, C. J. Lee, R. Miftakhutdinov, O. Mutlu, and Y. N. Patt. Improving GPU Performance via Large Warps and Two-level Warp Scheduling. In *Proceedings of the 44th Annual IEEE/ACM International Symposium on Microarchitecture*, MICRO-44, pages 308–317, New York, NY, USA, 2011. ACM.

[25] J. Nickolls, I. Buck, M. Garland, and K. Skadron. Scalable Parallel Programming with CUDA. *Queue*, 6(2):40–53, Mar. 2008.

[26] NVIDIA Corporation. *CUDA Binary Utilities*, July 2013.

[27] NVIDIA Corporation. *CUDA C Programming Guide*, July 2013.

[28] NVIDIA Corporation. *CUPTI*, July 2013.

[29] NVIDIA Corporation. *Parallel Thread Execution ISA v3.2*, July 2013.

[30] NVIDIA Corporation. *Tuning CUDA Applications For Kepler*, July 2013.

[31] J. Ragan-Kelley, C. Barnes, A. Adams, S. Paris, F. Durand, and S. Amarasinghe. Halide: A Language and Compiler for Optimizing Parallelism, Locality, and Recomputation in Image Processing Pipelines. In *Proceedings of the 34th ACM SIGPLAN Conference on Programming Language Design and Implementation*, PLDI '13, pages 519–530, New York, NY, USA, 2013. ACM.

[32] S. Ryoo, C. I. Rodrigues, S. S. Baghsorkhi, S. S. Stone, D. B. Kirk, and W.-m. W. Hwu. Optimization Principles and Application Performance Evaluation of a Multithreaded GPU Using CUDA. In *Proceedings of the 13th ACM SIGPLAN Symposium on Principles and Practice of Parallel Programming*, PPoPP '08, pages 73–82, New York, NY, USA, 2008. ACM.

[33] M. D. Smith. Support for Speculative Execution in High-Performance Processors. Technical report, Stanford, CA, USA, 1992.

[34] M. D. Smith, M. S. Lam, and M. A. Horowitz. Boosting Beyond Static Scheduling in a Superscalar Processor. In *Proceedings of the 17th annual international symposium on Computer Architecture*, ISCA '90, pages 344–354, New York, NY, USA, 1990. ACM.

CAWS: Criticality-Aware Warp Scheduling for GPGPU Workloads

Shin-Ying Lee and Carole-Jean Wu
Computer Science and Engineering
School of Computing, Informatics, and Decision Systems Engineering
Arizona State University
Tempe, AZ 85281
{lee.shin-ying,carole-jean.wu}@asu.edu

ABSTRACT

The ability to perform fast context-switching and massive multi-threading is the forte of modern GPU architectures, which have emerged as an efficient alternative to traditional chip-multiprocessors for parallel workloads. One of the main benefits of such architecture is its latency-hiding capability. However, the efficacy of GPU's latency-hiding varies significantly across GPGPU applications.

To investigate this, this paper first proposes a new algorithm that profiles execution behavior of GPGPU applications. We characterize latencies caused by various pipeline hazards, memory accesses, synchronization primitives, and the warp scheduler. Our results show that the current round-robin warp scheduler works well in overlapping various latency stalls with the execution of other available warps for only a few GPGPU applications. For other applications, there is an excessive latency stall that cannot be hidden by the scheduler effectively. With the latency characterization insight, we observe a significant execution time disparity for warps within the same thread block, which causes sub-optimal performance, called the warp criticality problem.

To tackle the warp criticality problem, we design a family of criticality-aware warp scheduling (CAWS) policies by scheduling the critical warp(s) more frequently than other warps. Our results on the breadth-first-search, B+tree search, two point angular correlation function, and K-means clustering show that, with oracle knowledge of warp criticality, our best-performing scheduling policy can improve GPGPU applications' performance by 17% on average. With our designed criticality predictor, the various scheduling policies can improve performance by 10-21% on breadth-first-search. To our knowledge, this is the first paper to characterize warp criticality and explore different criticality-aware warp scheduling policies for GPGPU workloads.

Categories and Subject Descriptors

C.1 [**Processor Architectures**]: Parallel Architectures;
C.4 [**Performance of Systems**]: Design Studies

PACT'14, August 24–27, 2014, Edmonton, AB, Canada.

ACM 978-1-4503-2809-8/14/08 ...$15.00.
http://dx.doi.org/10.1145/2628071.2628107.

Keywords

GPGPU; warp/wavefront scheduling; GPU performance characterization

1. INTRODUCTION

The ability to perform fast context-switching and massive multi-threading has been the forte of modern Graphics Processing Unit (GPU) architectures, which have emerged as an efficient alternative to traditional chip multiprocessors (CMPs) for parallel workloads. Therefore it is becoming more and more common today to execute general-purpose GPU (GPGPU) workloads on the highly-parallel architecture. GPUs are based on the *Single Instruction Multiple Thread* (SIMT) computing paradigm where multiple threads are grouped together to form a *warp* or *wavefront*. Threads in a warp are mapped to a *Single Instruction Multiple Data* (SIMD) execution unit such that all threads execute the same instruction, but with different data. For example, NVIDIA Kepler GPU supports up to 64 concurrent warps within a streaming multiprocessor (SM).

The benefit of fast context-switching and the large number of warps is *latency-hiding*: whenever the execution of a warp is stalled, it can be swapped out and another warp can be swapped in for immediate execution to maximize resource utilization without any penalty. These stalls could be caused by pipeline hazards, such as control or structural hazards, or memory accesses.

To investigate GPU's latency hiding ability, we develop an algorithm that attributes latencies caused by data dependency, control and structural hazards, as well as latencies from instruction and data cache accesses. Our results show that the current round-robin warp scheduler in the baseline GPU architecture works well in overlapping various types of latency stalls experienced by a warp with executions of other available warps in the warp pool for some GPGPU applications. In these applications, all warps are created *equal*, with homogeneous distribution of latency breakdown and execution time.

However, for certain applications, e.g., *breadth-first-search* (*bfs*), *not* all warps are created equal. We observe a significant execution time disparity for warps belonging to the same thread group (*thread block*). Since a thread block cannot be scheduled to execute until all warps in the previous thread block have finished executing, this results in sub-optimal computing resource utilization, as the warps which finished executing earlier have to wait for the longest-running warp to finish before another thread block can be swapped in for execution. We call this the *warp criticality* problem, which is similar to its multi-threaded CPU application counterpart [2] and is due to the internal synchronization of the application. For some thread blocks in *bfs*, we observe warp execution time disparity to be over 50% compared to the ideal scenario, where all warps in the thread block finish execution at the same time. This indicates that there is ample room for execution time improvement if we can reduce the warp execution time disparity.

The critical warp behavior is exacerbated by additional *scheduling delay* that is imposed upon the critical warp (the slowest-running warp) and, as a result, overall application performance is degraded.

To address the warp criticality problem, we delve deeper into *bfs*'s application code to identify the source of warp criticality and explore a set of warp scheduling algorithms to improve the execution time of the longer running warps in a thread block. Many prior works have looked at various warp scheduling algorithms to improve GPU performance, e.g., prefetch-aware scheduling [12], memory-aware scheduling [9, 10, 12, 11, 16, 18]. However, to the best of our knowledge, this work is the first to characterize warp criticality and explore different criticality-aware warp scheduling (CAWS) algorithms for modern GPU architectures.

The concept behind CAWS is simple: by scheduling the critical warps more frequently than other warps, we can effectively reduce the execution time of the critical warp, and hence reduce the total execution time of an application, since the next thread block can now be scheduled to execute and finish earlier. The ultimate goal of the criticality-aware scheduling policies is to *equalize* the execution time of all warps.

With the oracle knowledge of criticality for all warps in a thread block, our CAWS policies improve the performance of GPGPU workloads by 17% on average. In addition to the oracle knowledge, with application program hints, our average-based CAWS policy achieves performance improvement on *bfs* of 21%. Overall, our CAWS policies can improve performance by 10-21% with the warp criticality prediction.

Contributions: The key contributions of this paper are:

1. We characterize the stall cycles for GPU warps due to pipeline hazards and memory subsystem latencies, which gives insights into the latency-hiding ability of the massively parallel GPU architecture.
2. We identify and characterize the critical warp behavior of GPGPU applications on a modern GPU architecture, which has not been addressed in prior work.
3. We show that the critical warp behavior can be alleviated by scheduling warps according to their criticalities.
4. We design, implement, and evaluate a family of criticality-aware warp scheduling algorithms to address the critical warp issue. These new scheduling algorithms increase computing resource utilization and improve execution performance for GPGPU applications by 17%.

The rest of the paper is organized as follows. Section 2 describes our simulation infrastructure and the methodology we use to evaluate warp-criticality. Section 3 characterizes the latency-hiding ability of the modern GPU architectures and outlines the execution latency breakdown. We present and formalize the warp-criticality problem of *bfs* in Section 4 and explore a range of criticality-aware scheduling algorithms in Section 5. Section 6 presents our result analysis for the scheduling policies explored in this paper.

Architecture	*NVIDIA Fermi GTX480*
Num. of SMs	*15*
Max. # of Warps per SM	*48*
Max. # of Blocks per SM	*8*
# of Schedulers per SM	*2*
# of Registers per SM	*32768*
Shared Memory	*48KB*
L1 Data Cache	*16KB per SM (32-sets/4-ways)*
L1 Inst Cache	*2KB per SM (4-sets/4-ways)*
L2 Cache	*768KB (64-sets/16-ways/6-banks)*
Min. L2 Access Latency	*120 cycles*
Min. DRAM access Latency	*220 cycles*
Warp Size (SIMD Width)	*32 threads*

Table 1: GPGPU-sim configurations.

Section 7 presents related work in this area. Section 8 discusses various challenges we faced in designing the CAWS algorithms and known-issues in other GPGPU applications, and Section 9 concludes the paper.

2. METHODOLOGY

2.1 Simulation Infrastructure

In order to investigate the warp criticality problem, we use GPGPU-sim (version 3.2.0) [1] to profile the behavior of GPGPU applications. GPGPU-sim is a cycle-level performance simulator that models a general-purpose GPU architecture supporting NVIDIA CUDA and its PTX ISA. We run GPGPU-sim with the default configuration representing NVIDIA Fermi GTX480 architecture. Figure 1 shows the relevant microarchitecture components modeled in our simulation environment and Table 1 describes the simulation configuration and parameters. In addition to the baseline round-robin warp scheduler modeled in GPGPU-sim, we implement a range of criticality-aware warp schedulers which can be employed to reduce the execution time of the critical warps. Details of the criticality-aware warp schedulers are described in Section 5.1.

2.2 Workload

We choose 18 GPGPU applications from the Rodinia [4] and Parboil [19] benchmark suites to characterize the latency-hiding feature in modern GPUs. Table 2 lists the details of these 18 benchmarks along with the description, the input data set used for our characterization study, and the computation/memory-intensive characters.

3. CHARACTERIZING THE LATENCY HIDING ABILITY OF GPU WARP SCHEDULER

3.1 Background

At every cycle, GPU's warp scheduler selects an available warp from the warp pool for execution (Figure 1). If there is a ready instruction in the selected warp's instruction buffer without any pipeline hazards, this warp instruction is ready for execution; otherwise it is stalled due to one of the following factors: instruction fetch scheduling policy, instruction cache miss, data cache miss, data hazard, control hazard, structural hazard, or delay caused by the warp scheduling

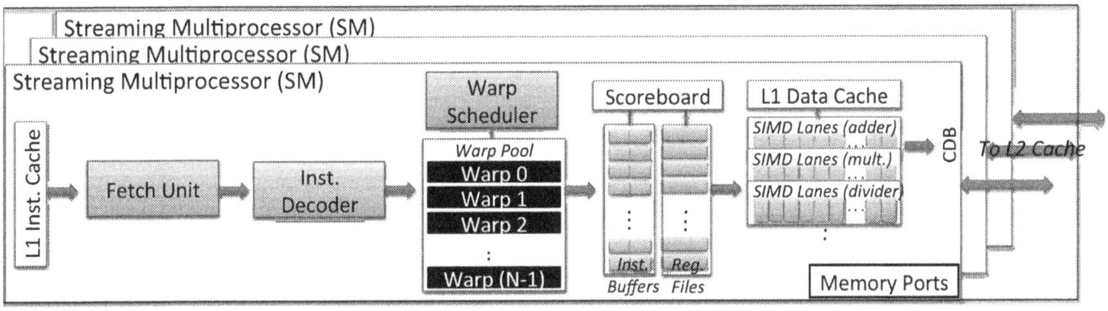

Figure 1: GPU pipeline modeled.

Benchmark	Description	Data Set	Category [5, 11]
b+tree	graph algorithm	1 million nodes	memory intensive
backprop	pattern recognition	65536 nodes	memory intensive
bfs	graph algorithm	65536 nodes	memory intensive
gaussian	matrix operations	1024x1024 matrix	computation intensive
heartwall	medical image processing	656x744 grey scale AVI	computation intensive
hotspot	physics simulation	512x512 nodes	computation intensive
kmeans	data mining algorithm	494020 nodes	memory intensive
lavaMD	physics simulation	10 nodes	computation intensive
leukocyte	medical image processing	640x480 grey scale AVI	computation intensive
lud	matrix operations	2048x2048 matrix	computation intensive
myocyte	biological simulation	100 nodes	computation intensive
needle	data mining algorithm (bioinformatics)	1024x1024 nodes	memory intensive
particle	medical image processing	128x128x10 nodes	computation intensive
pathfinder	graph algorithm	100000 nodes	computation intensive
srad_1	image processing	502x458 nodes	computation intensive
srad_2	image processing	2048x2048 nodes	memory intensive
streamcluster(small)	data mining algorithm	32x4096 nodes	memory intensive
streamcluster(mid)	data mining algorithm	64x8192 nodes	memory intensive
tpacf	geometry and physics computation	487x100 nodes	memory intensive

Table 2: GPGPU Benchmarks.

policy. In order to evaluate the effectiveness of the GPU warp scheduler's latency hiding ability, we first need to identify the sources of warp execution time delays. In the following, we explain each of the potential factors that can delay a warp's instruction from getting executed:

Warp scheduler. At every cycle, the warp scheduler depicted in Figure 1 selects a warp for execution based on the warp scheduling policy. In the baseline GPU architecture, we use a fair round-robin scheduler to select warps in the warp pool. For instance, if there are 48 active warps in the pool, the warp scheduler will iterate over the 48 warps cycle-by-cycle issuing one instruction per warp. A warp is selected for instruction issue and execution every 48 cycles and will have up to 47 cycles delay from the round robin scheduling policy to hide any latency stall cycles from itself.

Instruction buffer and instruction cache miss. In order to store instructions fetched from the instruction cache, each warp has a two-entry instruction buffer. When a warp selected for execution has no instruction(s) in its instruction buffer, additional latency penalty is paid because of the empty instruction buffer caused by instruction cache misses.

Structural hazard. If there is an available instruction in the selected warp's instruction buffer, the instruction will be placed in the scoreboard while also accessing the source operands in the register file. This is when structural hazards caused by contentions in the register file banks and at the various functional units are examined. If the decoded instruction cannot proceed for execution due to the unavailability of the register file bank or due to the unavailability of the required functional unit, the warp needs to be stalled.

Control hazard. Unlike CMPs that are often equipped with advanced branch predictor units, GPUs do not currently implement branch prediction logics and rely on the massive multi-threading feature to overlap the latency caused by control hazards. However, it is possible for a warp to experience additional control hazard stalls. For example, if a branch or function call instruction falls onto the *taken* path for a particular warp, and there is no other active warp in the pool at this time instance to help hide the branch address resolution latency, the particular warp then has to spend additional cycle(s) until its target address is calculated.

Data hazard. In addition to the stalls coming from structural and control hazards, data dependency can introduce additional penalty to an active warp. Currently, there is no data forwarding logics implemented in GPUs. Therefore, warps have to wait until data dependency is resolved before it can proceed execution. We highlight here that if an instruction is dependent on an older load instruction experiencing a cache miss, this particular dependent instruction will spend a significant amount of stall cycles until the data hazard is cleared.

MSHR and data cache miss. Memory load and store

Algorithm 1: Baseline Fair Round-Robin Scheduling.

```
1 while NoReadyWarp AND NotVisitedAllWarps do
2     warp = findNextWarp();
3     probe(warp);
4     if readyWarp then
5         issue(warp);
```

Algorithm 2: Warp Latency Breakdown (the *probe* function in Algorithm 1).

```
  Input: w: warp
1 w.Scheduling += CurrTime - w.PrevTime;
  w.PrevTime = CurrTime;
2 if Sync then
3     w.Sync++;
4 else if EmptyInstFetchBuffer then
5     w.Fetch++;
6 else if prevBranchTaken then
7     w.CtrlHazard++;
8 else if DataDependency then
9     if onOlderDataCacheMiss then
10        if
          w.CurrPendingAddr ≠ w.PrevPendingAddr
          then
11            w.DataHazard++; w.PrevPendingAddr =
              w.CurrPendingAddr;
12        else
13            w.DataCacheMiss++;
14    else
15        w.DataHazard++;
16 else if FU_unavailable then
17     w.StructuralHazard++;
18 else
19     w.Exec++;
```

instructions can experience additional latency stalls if the miss status holding registers (MSHRs) for the data cache are highly contended or if a data cache miss is encountered. Depending on the availability of the MSHRs and where the requested data reside, the amount of latency can vary.

Synchronization primitives. In addition to pipeline hazards, cache miss, and scheduling latencies, implicit and explicit synchronization primitives in GPU programs can stall warp execution as well. This delay mainly comes from how the communication between the parallel threads is structured.

3.2 Latency Attribution Algorithm

To illustrate how the different stall factors can contribute to a warp's execution time, we develop an algorithm to count and reason about where stall cycles come from for warps. Because latencies caused by the various stall factors can be significantly overlapped in GPUs, it is a challenging task to accurately and faithfully attribute stall cycles to the corresponding cause.

At every cycle, the baseline warp scheduler looks for a ready warp by iterating over the active warps in the instruction issue stage at the GPU pipeline (Algorithm 1). For each of the visited warps, whether they are ready or not, we record the execution status of the warp by instrumenting the baseline warp scheduler's implementation with a monitoring function, called *probe()*, in Line 3 of Algorithm 1. If the visited warp is not ready, the monitoring function will investigate the sources of stalls and update the corresponding latency counting logics; otherwise, the visited warp is ready for execution.

Next, we delve deeper into the monitoring function and present our latency attribution algorithm. First, we want to calculate the time during which a warp does not execute any new instruction because of the scheduling policy. This is determined to be the difference between the time when a warp is checked and the time when this particular warp was last checked. The time difference signifies how long the selected warp needs to wait until it can potentially issue the next instruction, i.e., the scheduling delay.

After the scheduling latency is determined, the monitoring function next examines whether the selected warp is ready or not. If ready, the *w.Exec* counter is incremented (Line 19 of Algorithm 2). Otherwise, the monitoring function investigates the stall factors sequentially – synchronization primitives, no available instructions in the instruction buffer or instruction cache misses, control hazard, data hazard, data cache misses, and structural hazard. Because a warp can be stalled due to multiple stall factors at the same time (the latency hiding feature by the massive multi-threading GPUs), we want to be cautious about not double-counting latencies overlapped by several stall factors. For example, if a warp is stalled because of data dependency on an older, load instruction that misses in the data cache, we attribute only the first stall cycle to the data hazard factor and any additional, subsequent stall cycle(s) to the data cache miss factor. This is because the underlying reason for the warp stall is the data cache miss encountered by the previous memory miss. If there is no following dependent instruction on a previous load cache miss (while the cache miss is being serviced), our algorithm does not attribute any stall cycle for this data cache miss. Therefore, it is important to note that the latency shown under data cache miss category represents only the latency penalties that stalled pipeline execution.

We also want to highlight that since GPUs rely on the fast switching between the massive number of available warps to improve pipeline resource utilization, even if a warp encounters no delay from pipeline hazards, memory accesses, or synchronization overhead, it still suffers from delays caused by the scheduling policy. For example, if a fair round-robin scheduling policy is applied for a GPU application that has 48 warps running on an SM core, each warp will spend 47 cycles waiting until its next ready instruction can be executed. These 47 scheduling cycles will be used to overlap with other latencies caused by e.g., structural hazards, for a particular warp. These stall cycles are shown in the scheduling latency instead of structural hazards, since the additional latencies are hidden by the warp scheduler which overlaps the scheduling latency with the execution of other ready warps.

3.3 Characterization Results

Figure 2 presents the latency characterization results for the Rodinia and Parboil applications. The x-axis presents the latency breakdown of the GPGPU applications sorted by the degree of the scheduler's latency-hiding ability while

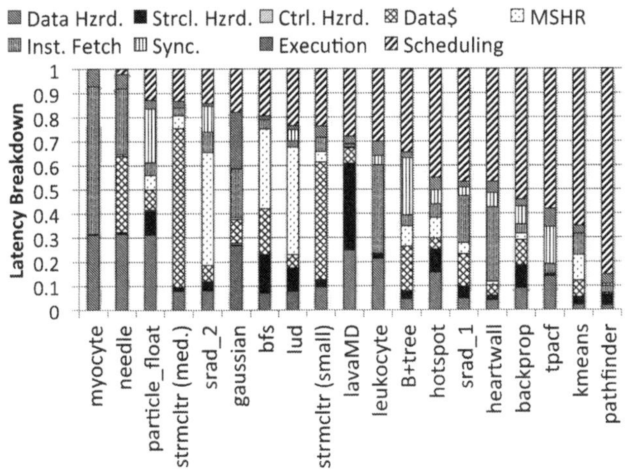

Figure 2: Latency breakdown for the Rodinia and Parboil applications.

Algorithm 3: The *bfs* algorithm

```
while not yet visited all nodes do
    kernel_1() { /* running on GPU */
    if node[tid].mask == true then
        node[tid].mask = false;
        i = 0;
        while i < node[tid].no_of_connected_nodes do
            id = node[tid].child[i]
            if node[id].visited == false then
                node[id].update = true;
    }
    /* an implicit barrier here */
    kernel_2() { /* running on GPU */
    if node[tid].update == true then
        node[tid].update = false;
        node[tid].mask = true;
        node[tid].visited = true;
    }
    /* an implicit barrier here */
```

---

the y-axis shows the latency stalls attributed by the various factors discussed in Section 3.1. The latency stall results are across all warps in each of the applications. The sections of the bars illustrate the stall cycles contributed by each stalling factor. Applications toward the right are the ones that benefit from the baseline round-robin (RR) scheduling policy whereas the applications toward the left are the ones whose latency stall cycles cannot be hidden by the scheduler.

First, we investigate the effectiveness of latency hiding ability of the baseline RR scheduling policy by focusing on the *Scheduling* bars. The RR scheduling policy is able to hide the majority of the warp stall cycles in applications, such as *backprop*, *tpacf*, *kmeans*, and *pathfinder*. These applications are considered as *well-behaving* GPGPU applications. On the other hand, the latency-hiding ability of the RR scheduling policy is poor for applications such as *myocyte* and *needle*. This is because there lacks warp-level parallelism in these two applications. In other words, there are not sufficient active warps in the warp pool.

The next two factors dominating stall cycles are from *Inst. Fetch* and *Data$* – stalls caused by waiting for ready instructions in the instruction buffer and by waiting for data to be served from the cache memory. Applications, such as *myocyte*, *needle*, and *tpacf*, suffer from instruction fetch stalls significantly. For *myocyte* and *needle*, this is again due to the lack of warp-level parallelism. When there are enough active warps in the pool, warps will "prefetch" instructions for each other. However, since the number of active warps in these two applications is small, instruction fetch often results in a cache miss. Furthermore, the scheduler cannot overlap the instruction fetch latency with other concurrent warps. As a result, the applications spend a significant amount of time waiting for available instructions for execution.

On the other hand, the reason that *tpacf* suffers from long instruction fetch stall cycles is because it has a high static instruction working set that does not fit to the instruction cache entirely. Despite having a high degree of warp-level parallelism, *tpacf* still encounters high instruction fetch latencies. Moreover, having a high degree of warp-level parallelism makes the instruction cache contention problem even more critical. Fast warps evict cache lines from the instruction cache that will be re-referenced by slow warps later. As a result, slow warps take a large amount of time to resolve instruction cache misses.

Applications such as *streamcluster(small)* and *streamcluster(medium)* suffer from long-latency data cache misses. As explained in Section 3.1, this *Data$* miss latency reflects the amount of cycles dependent instructions need to wait for, but not the amount of cycles memory accesses in the application take. The significant amount of stall cycles caused by data cache misses indicate that *streamcluster* heavily accesses the memory hierarchy and suffer significantly from its low degree of memory-level parallelism.

We next look at the amount of latency stalls contributed by the three classic types of pipeline hazards, i.e., data, structural, and control hazards. Data hazard stalls are caused by the particular instruction ordering within an application. We observe that applications, e.g., *myocyte*, *needle*, and *particle_float*, suffer from data hazard stalls more than other GPGPU applications. Structural hazard stalls are caused by the competition for pipeline resources, in this case, the functional units in the pipeline. Applications, such as *lavaMD*, spend a significant amount of time waiting for the structural hazard to be resolved. This is because the warps in *lavaMD* heavily compete for the load/store unit in the pipeline. Over all GPGPU applications, we do not see much stall penalty caused by control hazards. Compared with CPU applications, the Rodinia GPGPU applications contain less branch instructions [13]. Furthermore, since the branch resolution latency is relatively small, it can often be easily hidden by the scheduler.

In addition to structural hazard caused by the unavailability of functional units, contention in the miss status holding registers (MSHRs) can cause additional penalty. *lud*, in particular, experiences a significant amount of delay by the unavailability of MSHRs. This is because warps in *lud*, a memory-bandwidth intensive program [4, 11], often request data from the memory in a bursty manner. As a result, the performance of *lud* is significantly degraded by MSHR contention. Such contention happens to *srad_2* and *bfs* as well. Our studies show that by increasing the number of MSHR

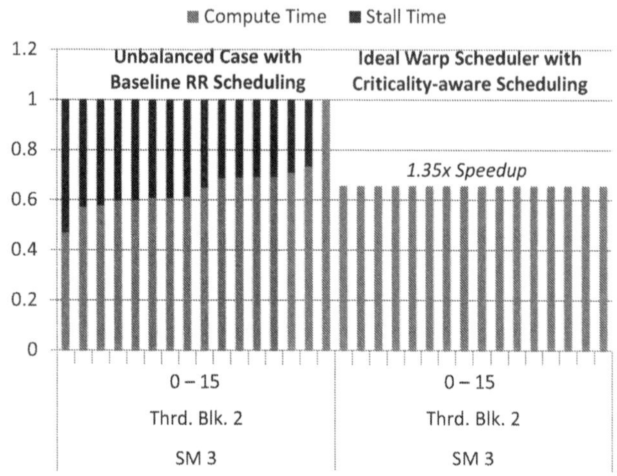

Figure 3: Speedup for ideal criticality-aware warp scheduler.

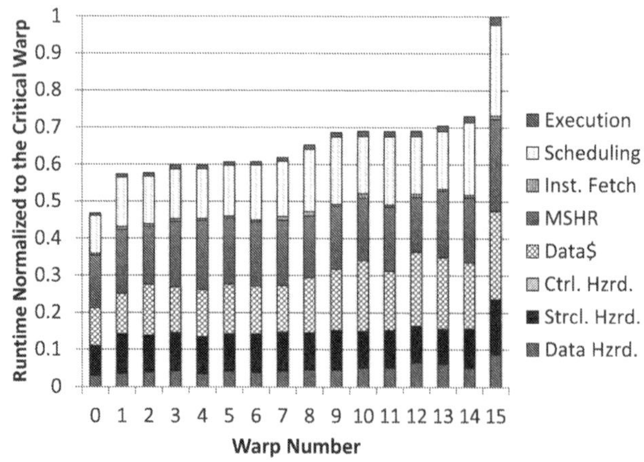

Figure 4: Latency breakdown for the *bfs* algorithm (sorted by execution time).

entries from 32 to 64, MSHR stall cycle is halved for *bfs*.

Finally, the *Sync.* component in Figure 2 indicates the amount of time warps wait on barriers (e.g., the *syncthread()* API calls) in the kernel. *b+tree*, *particle_float*, and *tpacf* are three applications whose warps spend a large amount of time synchronizing on barriers. This significant synchronization time is caused by workload imbalance between the warps.

4. MOTIVATION: WARP CRITICALITY PROBLEM IN THE *BFS* APPLICATION

4.1 The Breadth-First Search Application

We use the breadth-first search (*bfs*) application from the Rodinia and Parboil benchmark suites as a motivating example to highlight the warp criticality problem. *bfs* performs breadth-first graph traversal to search for a specific item in a tree.

The CUDA version of *bfs* contains two kernels that are called repeatedly in a loop. Both kernels have a thread block size of 512 threads that are grouped into 16 warps. These warps are then mapped to the available SMs on the GPU. The first kernel expands the search frontier from the current node to the next node level that contains multiple child nodes. The second kernel performs the actual visit and then sets up the conditions for the next iteration of the first kernel. All threads are synchronized at the end of each kernel. Algorithm 3 illustrates the breadth-first-search algorithm. At the end of two kernels, all warps are synchronized implicitly, without an explicit use of barriers, before all warps can proceed.

4.2 The Warp Criticality Problem

Figure 3 shows the amount of idle time the non-critical warps spend waiting for the critical warp to arrive at the end of the first kernel in `bfs`. The bars plot the compute and idle time normalized to the critical warp, *Warp* 15 (sorted by execution time), in Thread Block 2, SM 3. These show large warp stall times, with a worst-case stall time of 53% for Warp 0. In contrast, the right set of bars depict an oracle criticality prediction, in which the warp scheduler preferentially selects and executes warps based on their degrees of criticality, resulting in a speedup of 35%.

We further investigate the latency breakdown for all warps in this thread block that is executed in lockstep. Figure 4 compares the latency breakdown of each warp in the thread block. We observe that the critical warp (*Warp 15*) in this particular thread block (Thread Block 2, SM3) suffers from longer *Scheduling*, *MSHR*, *Data$*, and *Strcl. Hzrd.* latency delays than other warps. As we will later see in the paper, our proposed criticality-aware scheduling policies can reduce these latencies for the critical warp and result in faster thread block execution time.

4.3 Identification of the Source of Criticality in *bfs*

To root-cause the sources of warp criticality in *bfs*, we investigate several important contributing factors that can potentially slow down warps in a thread block. We explore the impact of instructions per cycle, the impact of the number of instruction and data cache misses in different levels of the GPU cache hierarchy, code size, etc. Figure 5 compares the degree of correlation between the warp criticality and the different factors. The bars represent the magnitude of the different factors explored in this work normalized to that of the critical warp. Comparing the trend of the different bars, it is apparent that CPI and data cache misses do not correlate well with warp execution time, whereas the number of iterations and the number of dynamic instructions in a warp do, implying that these are potential indicators for warp criticality.

In the *bfs* algorithm, based on the input data set, each node has a different number of child nodes as illustrated in Algorithm 3. A warp has to traverse through all connected nodes in the graph. Because the number of child nodes varies in each node level, the amount of work distributed to the warps in the same thread block varies as well. This causes an imbalanced workload distribution among the warps. The warp which needs to traverse through more child nodes (the iteration count in Line 6 of Algorithm 3) finishs more slowly and becomes the critical warp in the thread block. In fact, the warp execution time is directly proportional to the number of iterations of the algorithm. Therefore, we believe that the number of iterations specified in *bfs* could be a good indicator for predicting the degree of warp criticality for this

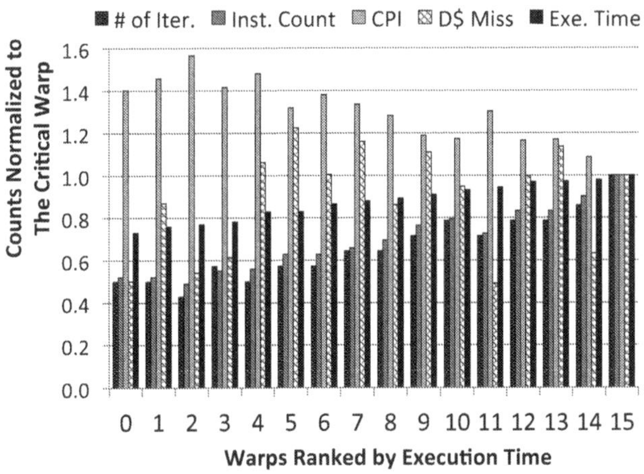

Figure 5: The comparison of execution time and different factors (normalized to the critical warp).

application.

Since the major contributing factor causing the warp execution speed disparity in *bfs* is the dynamic code size, and the knowledge of the code structure becomes available when the compiler analyzes and transforms the high-level C/C++ code to the PTX intermediate representation, we can insert this hint to predict the warps criticality in each thread block by including the feature into the LLVM compiler [14].

5. CRITICALITY-AWARE WARP SCHEDULING POLICIES

To reduce warp execution time disparity, we explore a family of criticality-aware warp scheduling (CAWS) policies and seek to bridge the execution time gap between the warps. We first explain how each scheduling policy works and present the performance results of the scheduling policies when oracle knowledge of warp criticality is available. Then we investigate the kind of information that can be useful to the design of a warp criticality predictor and help us identify warp criticality at runtime. Finally, we compare the performance results for the baseline round-robin and the family of CAWS policies designed in this paper.

5.1 Exploration of Scheduling Policies

Round-robin (RR) scheduling. As the name suggests, the round-robin (RR) policy schedules warps in an iterative manner. All warps in the warp pool are treated *equally* regardless of their degree of criticality and are given the same amount of time resource in the baseline GPU.

Thread block based CAWS (CAWS-blk) scheduling. This scheduling policy aims to improve the execution time of a thread block (limited by the execution time of the longest running, critical warp in the thread block) by giving more time resource to the most critical warp in the thread block. By giving higher priority to the most critical warp at the thread block granularity, CAWS-blk allows thread blocks to finish faster, such that hardware resources become available to other thread blocks earlier. Consequently, the resource contention is alleviated.

Streaming-multiprocessor based CAWS (CAWS-SM) scheduling. Instead of improving the execution time of the critical warp local to a particular thread block, we design a global, the CAWS-SM policy that aims to improve the execution time of the critical warp(s) within the same SM but across different thread blocks. The idea behind this policy is to equalize the execution time of all warps on an SM. CAWS-SM selects the top N critical warps from the warp pool to accelerate, where N equals to the number of thread blocks on an SM in the design. The SM-based policy is particularly helpful when some of the thread blocks mapped to the same SM do not contain any critical warp and other thread blocks contain one or more critical warps.

Average based CAWS (CAWS-avg) scheduling. Instead of giving more time resource to the top critical warp in a particular thread block (e.g., CAWS-blk) or within a particular SM (e.g., CAWS-SM), we design a CAWS-avg scheduling policy that identifies a number of critical warps (ranging from none to m) within either a thread block or a SM which require more time resource, where m is determined by the average execution time of all warps scaled by a factor. CAWS-avg evaluates warp criticality by the average execution time of all warps. When the disparity of execution time for warps in an SM is insignificant, giving the slowest warp a higher priority may cause criticality inversion, which occasionally happens in CAWS-SM and CAWS-blk. The advantage of CAWS-avg is to avoid the occurrence of criticality inversion.

5.2 Implementation of Scheduling Policies

5.2.1 *Priority Counter*

We design a per-warp priority counter that indicates the degree of warp criticality. The counter value determines when a warp is going to be selected by the scheduler for execution. For example, given there are 48 active warps in the pool in the baseline RR scheduling policy, all warps would initially have counter values from 0 to 47. The warp with a zero counter value is to be scheduled and its counter is reset based on its priority. In this case, the counter for the selected warp is always reset to be 47 since all warps are treated equally and have the same priority in the baseline policy. In addition to the selected warp, counters for other warp are decremented by one.

5.2.2 *Counter Value*

Since the value of the priority counter determines how often a warp is scheduled for execution (a smaller value indicates a warp is more important and needs to be scheduled more often), we have to carefully select the counter value for the critical warp(s). For example, to give critical warp(s) 20% more time resource, the scheduler will have to schedule the critical warp(s) 20% more frequently compared to other warps in the pool. This means that, in a pool of 48 warps, the counter value of the critical warps should be reset to 0.8 * 48 and so on.

5.2.3 *Counter Configuration for the Scheduling Policies*

In *bfs*, we recognize that the execution disparity between the fastest and the slowest warps is approximately 20% on average. To compare the effectiveness of the CAWS policies explored in this paper, we experiment with a counter configuration that guarantees 20% more time resource to the high-priority, critical warp(s) identified in each policy by resetting the value of the priority counters to 40 for critical warps and to 48 for the remaining warps

For the CAWS-avg policy in particular, we divide all warps in the pool into three priority levels. Warps with execution

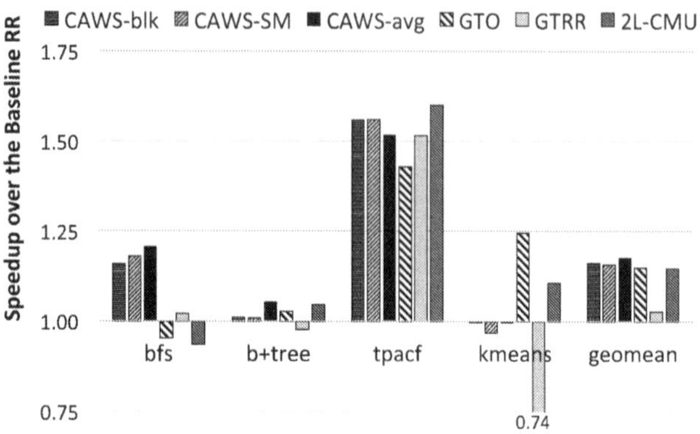

Figure 6: Speedup comparison for the different warp scheduling policies (normalized to the round-robin scheduler).

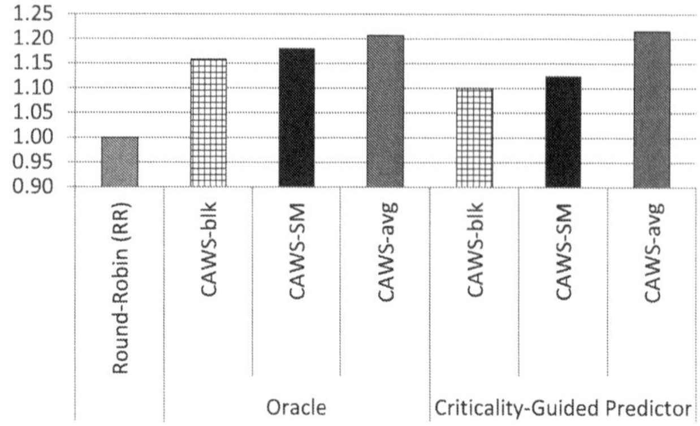

Figure 7: Speedup comparison for the different CAWS policies on *bfs* (normalized to the round-robin scheduler).

time more than 20% of the average are determined to be critical warps and are given 20% more time resource. As discussed in the previous section, this implies that the counter value for these warps are reset to 40 for a pool of 48 warps. Warps with execution time less than 20% of the average are determined to be fast warps and are given 20% less time resource by setting the counter value accordingly. Finally, the remaining warps in the pool will adopt the default counter value as the baseline RR policy.

6. RESULT ANALYSIS

In this section, we choose four benchmarks from the Rodinia and Parboil benchmark suites to represent four distinct GPGPU workload behavior. We use the benchmarks to highlight the specific characteristics of the workloads and to evaluate the effectiveness of our proposed CAWS schemes in detail.

1. **Rodinia/Parboil Breadth-First-Search (bfs) kernel#1** A workload imbalance GPGPU application depicted in Section 4. Warps have disparate execution path resulting from different number of iterations. Warps with heavier workloads experience more instructions and take longer time to finish.
2. **Rodinia B+tree Search (b+tree)** An application that has multiple small parallel regions (a region between two consecutive barrier instructions). Warps in *b+tree* reach barrier instructions frequently and spend a large amount of time on waiting for synchronization with warps from the same thread block.
3. **Parboil Two Point Angular Correlation Function (tpacf)** A GPGPU application whose static instruction count is larger than the capacity of instruction cache. Faster warps force the instruction cache to evict cache lines that will soon be reused by other warps. Its instruction fetch and instruction cache access pattern causes slow warps to wait for the next instruction, which degrades the overall system throughput.
4. **Rodinia K-means Clustering (kmeans) kernel#1** A memory intensive GPGPU application where warps require large memory space to store private data and have a high degree of intra-warp data access [18]. This memory access behavior creates memory contention at the data cache, resulting in frequent cache misses.

6.1 Criticality Encoding

We encode warp criticality information based on the warp execution time with the baseline round-robin policy to guide the CAWS schedulers. Furthermore, in order to keep the simulation region consistent and to create a fair comparison metric, in this paper, we only use the first round of kernel execution to present and analyze the performance of different warp scheduling policies.

6.2 Overall Performance

We first apply the oracle criticality knowledge on top of CAWS to observe the performance improvement. Figure 6 shows the speedup comparison for different state-of-the-art GPU warp scheduling schemes with CAWS using the oracle criticality encoding. Compared with the baseline round-robin policy, CAWS schedulers can achieve an average of 22% speedup by equalizing warp execution time, which outperform the state-of-the-art warp schedulers, such as GTO [18], GTRR [18], and 2L-CMU [16].

Imbalance GPGPU Workload. For *bfs*, CAWS tends to accelerate warps with heavy workloads or having longer execution path. The critical warps receive more time slots to process their tasks. As a result, the execution time within a thread block or SM becomes more balanced, minimizing the warp idle time. By adopting GTO and 2L-CMU schedulers, instead of making improvement, the performance degrades. This is because GTO and 2L-CMU greedily dispatch time slots to one warp and/or a group of warps. Without considering warps' criticality, the critical warps do not always reside in the high priority groups and will experience performance degradation. Consequently, GTO and 2L-CMU worsen *bfs*'s warp execution time disparity and criticality problem.

Fine-grained Parallel Region Workload. *b+tree* comprises multiple parallel regions which have only 5-10 instructions. Warps in *b+tree* do not exhibit a clear execution time disparity because the application frequently perfoms synchronization instructions. For this type of GPGPU applications, employing CAWS to accelerate the critical warps does not receive speedup as much as applications in the Imbalance GPGPU Workload category. Nevertheless, our average-based (CAWS-avg) policy still improves performance by 5% on *b+tree*, which outperforms all other warp schedul-

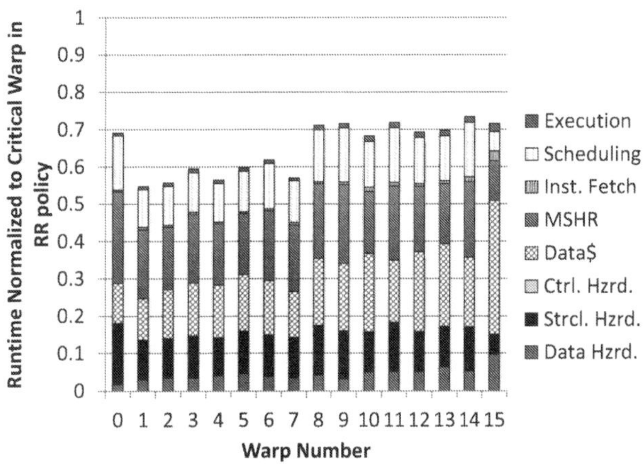

Figure 8: Latency breakdown for the *bfs* algorithm under the oracle, CAWS scheduling policy.

ing policies.

Large Instruction Working Set Workload. The criticality problem of *tpacf* stems from insufficient instruction cache capacity. Slow warps spend more time waiting for the next instruction to be fetched from the instruction cache. Employing CAWS, warps reach and execute a particular instruction roughly at the same time. Therefore CAWS reduces the instruction cache miss rate and shortens the average wait time resulting from instruction fetch latency. Overall, *tpacf* gains approximately 1.5x speedup by applying the various CAWS schemes.

Large Data Working Set Workload. The fourth class of applications represented by *kmeans* does not benefit much from CAWS. This is because the execution time difference and the criticality problem for *kmeans* is due to memory contention in the data cache. Our experiment results show that the critical warps in *kmeans* mainly suffer from the high L2 cache miss count. In this case, giving higher priority to the slow warps and prioritizing critical warps does not alleviate its memory contention nature. Moreover, it may introduce criticality inversion. While critical warps receive more time slots to run, it implies that the fast warps' private data gets evicted from data cache more frequently. Eventually, the fast warps turn into critical warps due to longer memory access latencies. For GTRR, because it applies a round-robin manner to greedily schedule a new warp, the data locality is hardly kept. Therefore, GTRR degrades *kmeans*'s performance significantly. On the other hand, GTO and 2L-CMU scheduler tend to maintain data locality which relieves memory contention at the data cache and thereby significantly improves the performance for *kmeans*.

In summary, the GPGPU applications with an imbalanced warp workloads benefit the most from the CAWS schemes proposed here. While we use four applications to represent and evaluate the diverse, heterogeneous characteristics of the GPGPU workloads here, our results on other GPGPU applications show similar behavior for each category. Taking a step further, we next show how the criticality information can be predicted and expressed to the scheduler in practice for *bfs*, the application that benefits the most from CAWS.

To realize a practical implementation for the family of CAWS policies, we design the iteration-based criticality predictor tailored for *bfs*. As discussed in Section 4.3, the loop iteration count serves as a good indicator for the amount of workload assigned to each warp.

Figure 7 compares the performance of various CAWS policies with the baseline round-robin policy when the oracle knowledge of the critical warp(s) is available versus when using the criticality-guided predictor.

When oracle knowledge of warp criticality is available, the average-based (CAWS-avg) scheduling policy improves *bfs*'s execution time the most, by 21%. The thread-block-based (CAWS-blk) and streaming-multiprocessor-based (CAWS-SM) scheduling policies also improve the performance of *bfs* by 16% and 18%, respectively. Overall, the iteration-based CAWS prediction policies *all* improve the execution time for *bfs*. The performance speedup under the CAWS policies, i.e., the CAWS-blk and the CAWS-SM policies, is less when compared to using the oracle warp criticality knowledge. This is not surprising since the loop iteration counts may not correlate perfectly with warp criticality. Table 3 compares the speedup with respect to the predictor accuracy. Given the prediction accuracy of 87.5% and 79.2% for the CAWS-blk and the CAWS-SM policies, *bfs* still sees 10-12% performance speedup over the baseline RR policy. The CAWS-avg policy still performs the best, even with the iteration-based criticality predictor, and improves the performance of *bfs* by 21%.

Policy	Speedup	Accuracy
CAWS-blk	1.10	87.50%
CAWS-SM	1.12	79.17%
CAWS-avg	1.21	95.4%

Table 3: Prediction accuracy of the criticality-guided predictor.

The varying degree of performance improvement by the these scheduling policies comes from (1) the distribution pattern of warp execution time and (2) the priority counter implementation. For example, if there exists one obvious critical warp among all warps within a thread block or within a SM, all three scheduling policies would perform equally well. However, if the execution time difference between the most critical warp (the longest-running warp) and the next critical warp (the second longest-running warp) is not significant, the occurrence of criticality inversion is likely. In other words, by giving more resources to the critical warp in the three criticality-aware scheduling policies, it is likely for the second critical warp to become the most critical warp instead.

Furthermore, the priority counter implementation may worsen the criticality inversion problem. For example, if the counter value is not configured carefully, the most critical warp may receive more resources than needed. As a result, it increases the likelihood of criticality inversion. Table 4 compares the frequency of criticality inversion in each of the three scheduling policies with respect to the execution time improvement and shows that the increasing frequency of criticality inversion hinders the amount of performance gain in the scheduling policy. When there is no criticality inversion, e.g., in the CAWS-avg policy, we can achieve the most performance benefit with the CAWS policy.

Next, to illustrate how the CAWS policies can effectively reduce the execution time of the critical warp(s), we compare the execution time of all warps in the particular thread

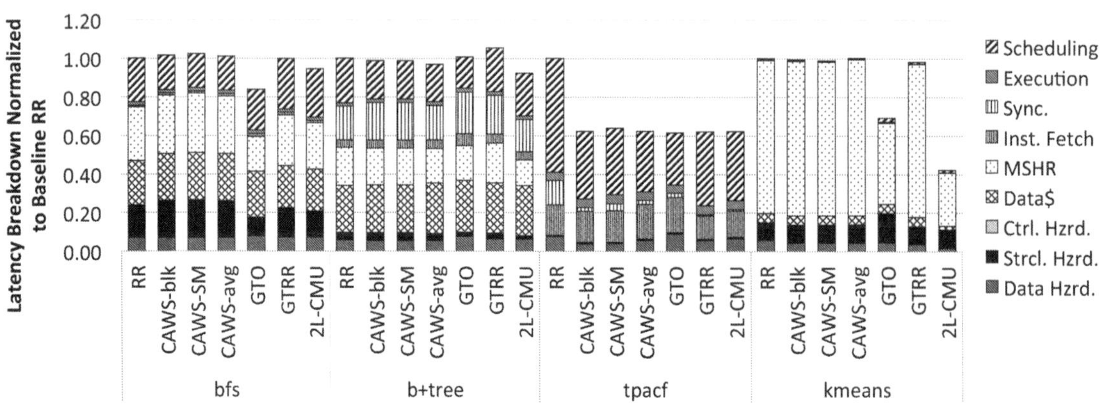

Figure 9: Latency breakdown of different warp scheduling policies at first round of kernel execution (normalized to the round-robin scheduler).

Policy	Speedup	Criticality Inversion
CAWS-blk	1.16	8.89%
CAWS-SM	1.18	2.22%
CAWS-avg	1.21	0%

Table 4: The speedup and frequency of criticality inversion within a thread block.

block (Thrd Blk 2, SM3) used previously in Section 4 and Figure 4. Figure 8 shows the execution time and the latency breakdown for all the warps in the thread block under the oracle, CAWS-avg scheduling policy. The execution time of the critical warp (*Warp 15*) is reduced by 28.4% when compared to using the baseline RR scheduling policy. This execution time improvement comes primarily from the reduction in the scheduling delay (*Scheduling*), the contention in the MSHR entries (*MSHR*), and the contention in the functional units (*Strcl. Hzrd*). These latency components are exactly the ones that the CAWS policy intends to improve. When comparing to the warp latency breakdown under the baseline RR scheduling policy in Figure 4, the *Data$* latency component is increased under the oracle, CAWS-avg policy. This is because the *Data$* stall cycles of the critical warp are better hidden by the RR scheduling policy. Overall, by applying the oracle, CAWS-avg policy, the execution time of this particular thread block is improved by 27%.

6.3 Latency Characterization and CAWS

We revisit the latency breakdown approach (Algorithm 2) to analyze the behavior of different GPU warp scheduling policies. Figure 9 shows the average latency of each warp in the first round kernel execution. Note that because the latency breakdown counts the average of all warps, it is not directly proportional to the overall execution time, especially for a workload-imbalanced application such as *bfs*.

As shown in Figure 9, a significant amount of *bfs*'s execution time is spent at the MSHR and data cache. This is because *bfs* has a large dataset, which does not completely fit into the data cache. Moreover, in the data cache, the data re-reference rate is very low. Hence it requires high memory bandwidth to accommodate the data requests. This insight reflects on the latency characterization. *bfs* substantially suffers from *Strcl. Hzrd.*, *MSHR*, and *Data$*. These latencies are coming from warps generating a burst of memory requests and competing for memory resources including the load/store units. Applying CAWS or GTRR does not reduce memory traffic in the memory system and thereby the latencies of these factors do not change a lot. GTO and 2L-CMU schedulers exploit a small number of active warps to lessen the amount of outstanding memory requests, consequently reducing the memory latency.

b+tree suffers from memory system and synchronization time. The reason *b+tree*'s *MSHR* and *Data$* latency cannot be overlapped by *scheduling* is its fine-grained parallel regions. Fast warps arrive at the barrier quickly and become idle. These fine-grained parallel regions result in insufficient warp-level parallelism. The latency breakdown shows that applying CAWS does not further improve the latency hiding ability of the scheduler.

For *tpacf*, observing from the latency breakdown, the baseline RR scheduler hides *tpacf*'s execution latency well. Indeed, the main factor limiting *tpacf*'s performance is instruction fetch latency. As mentioned in Section 3.3, the instruction fetch latency can be hidden well unless an application lacks warp-level parallelism. Under all scheduling policies, i.e., CAWS, GTRR, GTO, and 2L-CMU, the scheduling latency is significantly reduced. This is due to less instruction cache miss count with these advanced warp scheduling algorithms. Furthermore, benefiting from the significantly reduced instruction fetch latency, the *sync.* time also decreases. This implies that the criticality problem is alleviated. Furthermore, Figure 9 also shows that the time for warps to reach a barrier instruction becomes negligible under the advanced scheduling policies.

The latency breakdown of *kmeans* under the RR scheduler demonstrates that this application suffer from memory access latency primarily. A significant portion of the execution delay is at the *MSHR* and *Data$*. In addition to RR, adopting CAWS or GTRR policies does not alleviate its memory contention nature. Therefore the latency characterization does not show a significant change. On the other hand, unsurprisingly, using GTO or 2L-CMU scheduler, the *MSHR* and *Data$* latencies are reduced. This is because GTO and 2L-CMU scheduling policies keep data locality in the data cache better and, as a result, reduce the latencies related to data memory references.

7. RELATED WORK

Prior work have looked at various warp scheduling policies to improve GPU performance. In this section, we discuss the scheduling policies that are most related to this work.

Many prior work [9, 10, 12, 11, 16, 18] focused on improving the memory aspect of the GPU warp scheduling algorithm. Gebhart et al. [9] and Narasiman et al. [16] proposed to split warps into different subgroups and keep only one group of warps active at a time. The warp scheduler is only able to issue instructions from the active group of warps. These algorithms prevent all warps from stalling at the same time by ensuring the warps in the pool do not encounter long latency memory operations or compete for the register file banks at the same time. These scheduling policies allow the GPU warp scheduler to tolerate memory latency better while reducing the idle time of GPU cores. In contrast, this paper aims to reduce the delay caused by scheduling policies as well as the delay caused by the structural hazards in particular. These additional latency penalties worsen the execution time of the critical warp(s) and can degrade the overall performance of GPGPU applications.

Rogers et al. [18] proposed a family of static and dynamic greedy scheduling approaches, GTRR, GTO, and CCWS, to improve intra-warp data locality. These greedy scheduling algorithms aim to improve the hit rate at D-cache. However, the greedy approaches are only apt for improving memory intensive applications. For imbalance GPGPU workloads, such as *bfs*, employing the greedy scheduling policies, e.g. GTO and GTRR, does not help improve performance. On the other hand, the proposed CAWS policies designed for imbalance GPGPU workloads are shown to improve performance for such workloads while not hurting the performance of memory intensive applications.

In addition to improving the memory behavior of GPGPU applications, prior studies proposed to use scheduling policies to reduce the likelihood of branch and memory divergence occurrence on GPUs. When branch or memory divergence happens, the utilization of GPU resources becomes sub-optimal. Therefore, algorithms, e.g., [7, 8, 15, 16, 20], are designed to dynamically select and combine cross-warp threads that are executing the same instruction to the same warp, such that cross-warp threads can now execute on the same SIMD unit, and thereby improve the utilization of the SIMD lanes. Instead of applying such compaction-based algorithms, Rhu and Erez [17] proposed to overlap the execution of a divergent warp to further improve the latency hiding ability of the scheduler. All of these scheduling algorithms attempt to improve GPU performance by increasing the utilization of functional units but are not designed to address the warp criticality problem studied in this paper.

Besides the various warp scheduling policies discussed here for modern GPUs, scheduling is a rich research field in CPUs. While we cannot cover all scheduling policies, we focus on a few that are most related to our work here. Bhattacharjee and Martonosi [2] observed the thread criticality problem for parallel threads executing on CMPs. Since the performance of a parallel application is constrained by the critical (the slowest running) thread, the execution time of the parallel application is significantly affected by the execution time of the critical thread. To alleviate the execution time disparity between the different parallel threads, Bhattacharjee and Martonosi designed the thread criticality predictor (TCP) that is largely based on per-thread cache behavior and showed that TCP can be used to guide task stealing as well as to improve energy efficiency of the CMP. Many other mechanisms, e.g., [3, 6], were inspired by the thread criticality concept for parallel applications running on CMPs and proposed techniques to reduce the execution time of the critical thread(s) and thereby improve overall parallel application performance.

While the warp criticality problem presented in this paper is similar to the thread criticality problem that is observed in parallel applications executing on CMPs, due to the distinct difference between GPU and CPU architectures, the effects introduced by the critical warp(s) and thread(s) vary as well. Because of the fast context-switching and massive multi-threading in modern GPUs, our characterization results have shown that a significant amount of warp stall cycles can be well hidden in GPUs (but this is not the case in CMPs).

To the best of our knowledge, this work is the first that performs warp latency characterization in detail and presents the warp criticality problem in GPGPU applications. Taking a step further, we design and evaluate a range of criticality-aware scheduling policies with both oracle and an iteration-based warp criticality predictor for improving the performance of the breadth-first-search algorithm on modern GPUs.

8. DISCUSSION

The performance of the criticality-aware scheduling policys depends significantly on the performance of the criticality predictor, and it is challenging to design the criticality predictor for modern GPUs executing GPGPU applications. First, as shown in Section 6.1, the performance improvement seen in *bfs* depends on how frequently criticality inversion occurs, which is governed by the implementation of the per-warp priority counters. If the priority counter is not configured appropriately, it is easy to overestimate the amount of resources that should be given to the critical warp and, consequently, other non-critical warps will be slowed down.

Second, the performance improvement of *bfs* is also affected by the prediction accuracy. Because of the diverse GPGPU application behavior, the factors causing the warp execution time disparity vary from application to application. Hence, it is a non-trivial task to design a warp criticality predictor which works well for all GPGPU applications.

Lastly, we also find that the parallel regions in between two consecutive synchronization points in GPGPU applications are much more fine-grained than CPU applications. This implies that the time for the criticality predictor to learn and to accelerate the execution of the critical warp(s) is tight. We find this especially true for applications, e.g., *backprop*, *hotspot*, *particle_float*, etc., in the fine-grained parallel region application represented by *b+tree*.

9. CONCLUSION

This paper presents a detailed characterization and evaluation for the latency-hiding capability of modern GPU architectures, highlighting the different factors that comprise the execution latency in the GPU pipeline, across a wide range of GPGPU applications. We find that the fast context-switching and massive multi-threading architecture can effectively hide much of the latency by swapping in and out warps. However, for certain GPGPU applications, such as *breadth-first-search*, the performance of the overall application is limited by certain critical warps. To address such a performance issue, we identify the sources of criticality and design a family of simple and lightweight scheduling policies that aim to *equalize* the execution of all warps to achieve maximum hardware resource utilization and minimize the overall application execution time. Our results show that, given oracle knowledge of warp criticality, the overall performance can be improved by as much as 17% on average. We design practical warp criticality predictors that can improve performance by 10-21% on *bfs*. To the best of our knowledge, this paper is the first to identify the warp criticality problem in modern GPU architectures and to design CAWS policies for managing massively parallel threads. We hope that, with the significant performance improvement for *bfs* and potentially other GPGPU workloads, this work inspires better criticality counter designs tailored to the warp criticality problem in modern GPUs.

10. ACKNOWLEDGEMENTS

We would like to thank Wenhao Jia, Margaret Martonosi, and the anonymous reviewers for their feedback. This work is supported by Arizona State University.

11. REFERENCES

[1] A. Bakhoda, G. Yuan, W. W. L. Fung, H. Wong, and T. M. Aamodt. Analyzing cuda workloads using a detailed gpu simulator. In *Proc. of the 2009 International Symposium on Analysis of Systems and Software (ISPASS-2009)*, Apr 2009.

[2] A. Bhattacharjee and M. Martonosi. Thread criticality predictors for dynamic performance, power, and resource management in chip multiprocessors. In *Proc. of the 36th International Symposium on Computer Architecture (ISCA-36)*, Jun 2009.

[3] K. D. Bois, S. Eyerman, J. B. Sartor, and L. Eeckhout. Criticality stacks: Identifying critical threads in parallel programs using synchronization behavior. In *Proc. of the 40th International Symposium on Computer Architecture (ISCA-40)*, Jun 2013.

[4] S. Che, M. Boyer, J. Meng, D. Tarjan, J. W. Sheaffer, S.-H. Lee, and K. Skadron. Rodinia: A benchmark suite for heterogeneous computing. In *Proc. of the 2009 International Symposium on Workload Characterization (IISWC-2009)*, Oct 2009.

[5] S. Che, J. W. Sheaffer, M. Boyer, L. G. Szafaryn, L. Wang, and K. Skadron. A characterization of the rodinia benchmark suite with comparison to contemporary cmp workloads. In *Proc. of the 2010 International Symposium on Workload Characterization (IISWC-2010)*, Dec 2010.

[6] E. Ebrahimi, R. Miftakhutdinov, C. Fallin, C. J. Lee, J. A. Joao, O. Mutlu, and Y. N. Patt. Parallel application memory scheduling. In *Proceedings of the 44th International Symposium on Microarchitecture (MICRO-44)*, Dec 2011.

[7] W. L. W. Fung and T. M. Aamodt. Thread block compaction for efficient simt control flow. In *Proc. of the 17th International Symposium on High Performance Computer Architecture (HPCA-17)*, Feb 2011.

[8] W. L. W. Fung, I. Sham, G. Yuan, and T. M. Aamodt. Dynamic warp formation and scheduling for efficient gpu control flow. In *Proc. of the 37th International Symposium on Computer Architecture (ISCA-37)*, Jun 2010.

[9] M. Gebhart, R. D. Johnson, D. Tarjan, S. W. Keckler, W. J. Dally, E. Lindoholm, and K. Skadron. Energy-efficient mechanisms for managing thread conteext in throughput processors. In *Proc. of the 38th International Symposium on Computer Architecture (ISCA-38)*, Jun 2011.

[10] W. Jia, K. A. Shaw, and M. Martonosi. MRPB: Memory request prioritization for massively parallel processors. In *Proc. of the 20th International Symposium on High Performance Computer Architecture (HPCA-20)*, Feb 2014.

[11] A. Jog, O. Kayiran, N. Chidambaram, A. K. Mishra, M. T. Kandemir, O. Mutlu, R. Iyer, and C. R. Das. Owl: Cooperative thread array aware scheduling techniques for improving gpgpu performance. In *Proc. of the 18th International Conference on Architectural Support for Programming Languages and Operating Systems (ASPLOS-13)*, Mar 2013.

[12] A. Jog, O. Kayiran, A. K. Mishra, M. T. Kandemir, O. Mutlu, R. Iyer, and C. R. Das. Orchestrated scheduling and prefetching for gpgpus. In *Proc. of the 40th International Symposium on Computer Architecture (ISCA-40)*, Jun 2013.

[13] A. Kerr, G. Diamos, and S. Yalamanchili. A characterization and analysis of ptx kernels. In *Proc. of the 2009 International Symposium on Workload Characterization (IISWC-2009)*, Oct 2009.

[14] C. Lattner and V. Adve. Llvm: A compilation framework for lifelong program analysis & transformation. In *Proc. of the 2004 International Symposium on Code Generation and Optimization (GCO-2004)*, Mar 2004.

[15] J. Meng, D. Tarjan, and K. Skadron. Dynamic warp subdivision for integrated branch and memory divergence tolerance. In *Proc. of the 37th International Symposium on Computer Architecture (ISCA-37)*, Jun 2010.

[16] V. Narasiman, M. Shebanow, C. J. Lee, R. Miftakhutdinov, O. Mutlu, and Y. N. Patt. Improving gpu performance via large warps and two-level warp scheduling. In *Proc. of the 44th International Symposium on Microarchitecture (MICRO-44)*, Dec 2011.

[17] M. Rhu and M. Erez. The dual-path execution model for efficient gpu control flow. In *Proc. of the 19th International Symposium on High Performance Computer Architecture (HPCA-19)*, Feb 2013.

[18] T. G. Rogers, M. O'Connor, and T. M. AAmodt. Cache-conscious wavefront scheduling. In *Proc. of the 45th International Symposium on Microarchitecture (MICRO-45)*, Dec 2012.

[19] J. A. Stratton, C. Rodrigues, I.-J. Sung, N. Obeid, L.-W. Chang, N. Anssari, G. D. Liu, and W.-M. W. Hwu. The Parboil technique report, Mar 2012.

[20] A. S. Vaidya, A. Shayesteh, D. H. Woo, R. Saharoy, and M. Azimi. Simd divergence optimization through intra-warp compaction. In *Proc. of the 40th International Symposium on Computer Architecture (ISCA-40)*, Jun 2013.

Invyswell: A Hybrid Transactional Memory for Haswell's Restricted Transactional Memory

Irina Calciu
Brown University
Providence, RI, USA
irina@cs.brown.edu

Justin Gottschlich
Intel Labs
Santa Clara, CA, USA
justin.e.gottschlich@intel.com

Tatiana Shpeisman
Intel Labs
Santa Clara, CA, USA
tatiana.shpeisman@intel.com

Gilles Pokam
Intel Labs
Santa Clara, CA, USA
gilles.a.pokam@intel.com

Maurice Herlihy
Brown University
Providence, RI, USA
mph@cs.brown.edu

ABSTRACT

The Intel Haswell processor includes restricted transactional memory (RTM), which is the first commodity-based hardware transactional memory (HTM) to become publicly available. However, like other real HTMs, such as IBM's Blue Gene/Q, Haswell's RTM is best-effort, meaning it provides no transactional forward progress guarantees. Because of this, a software fallback system must be used in conjunction with Haswell's RTM to ensure transactional programs execute to completion. To complicate matters, Haswell does not provide escape actions. Without escape actions, non-transactional instructions cannot be executed within the context of a hardware transaction, thereby restricting the ways in which a software fallback can interact with the HTM. As such, the challenge of creating a scalable hybrid TM (HyTM) that uses Haswell's RTM and a software TM (STM) fallback is exacerbated.

In this paper, we present Invyswell, a novel HyTM that exploits the benefits and manages the limitations of Haswell's RTM. After describing Invyswell's design, we show that it outperforms NOrec, a state-of-the-art STM, by 35%, Hybrid NOrec, NOrec's hybrid implementation, by 18%, and Haswell's hardware-only lock elision by 25% across all STAMP benchmarks.

Categories and Subject Descriptors

D.1.3 [**Programming Techniques**]: Concurrent Programming

General Terms

Algorithms; Design

Keywords

Hybrid Transactional Memory; Transactional Memory; Intel Haswell Restricted Transactional Memory

PACT'14, August 24–27, 2014, Edmonton, AB, Canada.

ACM 978-1-4503-2809-8/14/08 ...$15.00.
http://dx.doi.org/10.1145/2628071.2628086 .

1. INTRODUCTION

Traditionally, locks have been the predominant mechanism used to synchronize shared memory in multithreaded programs [16]. Yet, developing software that correctly and efficiently uses locks is notoriously challenging, even for the most seasoned programmers. Transactional memory (TM) has been proposed as an alternative to locks, where much of the mechanical complexity of synchronization is managed by the underlying system, not the programmer [15, 30].

Experience with software transactional memory (STM), where transactions are implemented entirely in software, has demonstrated the simplicity of transactional programming, but has raised challenging performance issues. Modern STMs tend to be scalable at high thread counts [9], meaning that beyond a certain point (and up to a limit), adding more threads typically increases throughput for many benchmarks, yielding performance that is often competitive with fine-grained locking. Unfortunately, these STMs tend to perform poorly at low or medium thread counts, because of non-amortized transactional overhead, resulting in performance that is not competitive with fine-grained locking.

To improve the performance of transactions, hardware vendors such as Intel and IBM have included support for hardware transactional memory (HTM). One such example is Intel's Haswell processor [18], which includes restricted transactional memory (RTM), a cache-based HTM design that uses the microarchitecture's existing cache coherence protocol to manage transactional conflicts. Yet, it is unclear how RTM can be most effectively used by software. One cannot simply substitute hardware transactions for software transactions, because RTM, like other HTMs, such as IBM's Blue Gene/Q [31] and System z [19], is *best-effort*, providing no progress guarantees. [1] Whether a transaction succeeds depends on whether its data set fits in the processor's cache, whether the transaction finishes without interruption, and a myriad of other architectural and platform-specific limitations best hidden from the programmer.

It has been recognized that effectively integrating best-effort HTM with the software that uses it requires an intermediate software fallback when hardware transactions fail. Such a system is called hybrid transactional memory (HyTM) [6,

[1] Although System z supports constrained transactions, which are guaranteed to commit, we believe this does not present a generalized mechanism for HTM forward progress as constrained transactions are size-restricted.

4, 7, 22], where hardware and software transactions execute under the umbrella of a single TM system. In this paper, we present a novel HyTM, called *Invyswell*, that uses hardware transactions from Haswell's RTM in conjunction with software transactions from a heavily modified design of InvalSTM [11], an STM designed to provide scalability and performance for large transactions with notable contention.

Invyswell enables the concurrent execution of both hardware and software transactions with the aim of being performant for all transaction sizes and degrees of contentions. Haswell's RTM performs best for small transactions with low contention, as it imposes no instrumentation overhead, but is limited to a "requester-wins" contention policy. InvalSTM performs best for large transactions with high contention, because it can make highly informed contention management decisions through its commit-time invalidation process. Yet, challenges remain in finding an efficient solution for the "transactional twilight zone" - midsize transactions that are small enough to successfully execute in hardware but have a non-trivial degree of contention. Furthermore, even after designing a TM that addresses the unique challenges of each of these categories, that system must ensure that each individual component does not negatively impact the overall performance by mismanaging transactions for which it was not intended. Invyswell addresses this by using a sophisticated design that employs several hardware and software modes of execution. This gives the system the flexibility to trade execution overhead for precision in conflict detection.

Haswell's RTM does not support *escape actions*, non-transactional instructions executed within transactions [24]. This limitation complicated our design, especially with respect to opacity [12], a correctness conditions that guarantees consistency of eventually-aborted transactions. Another challenge we encountered was designing Invyswell's *contention manager* (CM), a decision-making process aimed at improving throughput, due to the different isolation properties for hardware and software transactions. The lack of escape actions further complicated this issue, as well, as it restricts the way a hardware transaction can abort a software transaction before the hardware transaction itself commits.

We evaluate Invyswell's performance using the STAMP benchmark suite. Invyswell's performance compares favorably to that of pure software, pure hardware, and hybrid solutions. Invyswell is 35% faster than NOrecSTM [5], a state-of-the-art software transactional memory, and 18% faster than NOrecHy [4], a state-of-the-art hybrid transactional memory, as shown in Figure 1. It also outperforms Haswell's native *hardware lock elision* (HLE) [17, 25], a hardware mechanism that attempts to elide locks by executing critical sections as transactions and supports transactional re-execution with single global lock fallback implemented purely in hardware. Although on the average Invyswell is only 25% faster than HLE, the performance difference is significant for some benchmarks with large transactions, where Invyswell outperforms HLE by 2× to 5.4×.

This paper makes the following contributions:

1. We present a hybrid transactional memory for Haswell RTM, called Invyswell, which features a novel design based on InvalSTM and an adaptive system supporting five transaction types.
2. We propose a novel method for precise conflict detection between hardware and software transactions using Bloom filters, which works well even for HTMs *without* support of escape actions.

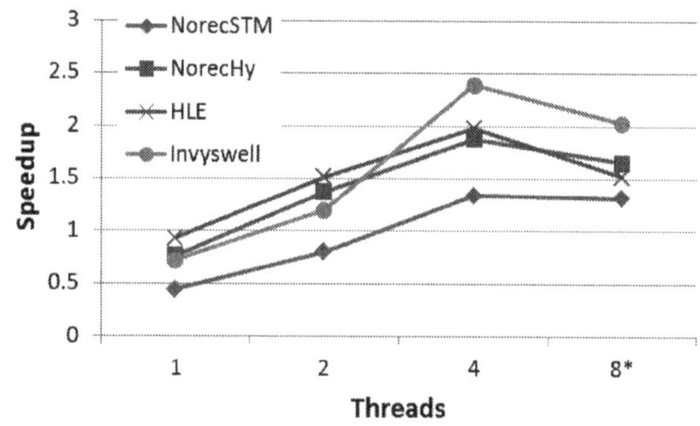

Figure 1: STAMP Performance Differential by Geometric Mean. *Hyperthreading is enabled for 8 threads. (Note: NOrec and Hybrid NOrec are abbreviated as NorecSTM and NorecHy, respectively, in the legend)

3. We demonstrate that achieving the best performance requires HyTM even in presence of HLE. Our evaluation on the STAMP benchmark suite shows that Invyswell outperforms HLE by up to 3.5× (25% on average) and state-of-the-art software and hybrid solutions by more than 18%.
4. We describe challenges and design tradeoffs for a Haswell HyTM, paving the way for even better systems in the future.

2. RELATED WORK

TM systems [13] fall into three rough categories: *software* (STM), *hardware* (HTM), and *hybrid* (HyTM). Most of the research literature concerns STM systems [1, 8, 11, 14, 23, 26, 29]. There are too many such systems to discuss them individually, but in this paper, we compare our HyTM to NOrec [5], a state-of-the-art STM that uses value-based validation, deferred update and lazy conflict detection.

Recently, Intel [18] and IBM [31, 19] announced new processors with hardware support for transactions, and it seems likely that others will follow. Like Herlihy and Moss's original TM proposal [15], these systems rely on modified cache coherence protocols to achieve atomicity and isolation. Haswell also supports *hardware lock elision* [25], a scheme where annotated lock-based critical sections are executed speculatively, but are retried pessimistically if speculation fails.

HyTM schemes promise to provide the best of both worlds: the efficiency of HTM with the scalability of STM. The first papers to articulate this point are from Damron et al. [6] and Kumar et al. [21]. Later work in this area includes PhTM [22], intended for Sun's Rock architecture and Riegel et al.'s work [27] intended for AMD's proposed Advanced Synchronization Facility (ASF). More recently, Wang et al. [31] proposed a HyTM for IBM Blue Gene/Q's best-effort HTM, based on a Single-Global-Lock fallback. In this paper, we compare Invyswell to Hybrid NOrec [4], a state-of-the-art hybrid transactional memory.

3. OVERVIEW OF INVALSTM

One of the key differences between InvalSTM and other STMs is that it performs commit-time invalidation [11]. This approach requires that a transaction identify and resolve

```
SpecSW
tx_begin:
fetch_and_add(&sw_cnt, 1);
do { local_cs = commit_sequence;
} while (local_cs & 1);
tx_read:
if addr in write hash table
   return val;
add addr to read bf;
val = *addr;
validate();
return val;
tx_write:
if (status == INVALID) restart;
add addr to write bf;
add addr,val to local hash table;
tx_end:
if (readonly)
  fetch_and_sub(&sw_cnt, 1);
  return;
acquire commit_lock;
validate();
if !CM_can_commit() restart();
fetch_and_sub(&sw_cnt, 1);
commit();
tx_post_commit:
invalidate();
release commit_lock;

LiteHW
tx_end:
if (!commit_lock && !sw_cnt) _xend();
else _xabort();
```

(a) SpecSW and LiteHW Events.

```
BFHW
tx_read: add addr to read bf
tx_write: add addr to write bf
tx_end:
if (!commit_lock)
    ++hw_post_commit;
    _xend();
else
  if (!conflict with SW txn)
      ++hw_post_commit;
      _xend();
else _xabort();
tx_post_commit:
if (!readonly) invalidate();
fetch_and_sub(&hw_post_commit, 1);

IrrevocSW
tx_begin: acquire commit_lock
tx_read: add addr to read bf
tx_write: add addr to write bf
tx_end: Do nothing
tx_post_commit:
if (!readonly) invalidate();
release commit_lock

SglSW
tx_begin:
acquire commit_lock
++commit_sequence
tx_end:
++commit_sequence
Release commit_lock
```

(b) BFHW, IrrevocSW, and SglSW Events.

Figure 2: Transactional Events for Invyswell's Five Different Transaction Types.

conflicts with all other in-flight (i.e., concurrently executing) transactions during its commit phase. InvalSTM achieves this by storing read and write sets in transaction-specific Bloom filters so it can perform conflict detection using constant-time set intersection. With commit-time invalidation, InvalSTM has complete knowledge of all conflicts between a committing transaction and other in-flight transactions, allowing it to make informed decisions on how to best mitigate contention. *All* InvalSTM transactions perform validation to achieve opacity in $O(N)$ total computational complexity, where N is the number of read elements, which is notably faster than the $O(N^2)$ overhead incurred by incremental validation and can drastically reduce the opacity cost for large transactions. Additionally, read-only transactions commit without incurring any commit-time serialization overhead.

For these reasons, InvalSTM naturally complements Haswell's RTM. Haswell's RTM can be used for small transactions and low thread counts, while InvalSTM can be used for large transactions and high thread counts. Moreover, Haswell's RTM can leverage InvalSTM's use of Bloom filters for conflict detection by augmenting Haswell's hardware transactions with Bloom filters to enable many hardware transactions to execute concurrently with many software transactions. These Bloom filters are a good fit for Haswell's cache-based HTM design because they can be structured for constant-sized cache line alignment, thereby minimizing the negative impact of introducing hardware-to-software conflict detection into an already restricted HTM space. Finally, because InvalSTM's read-only transactions do not introduce any serialization in their execution, the performance overhead for transactions is transparent to Haswell RTM's faster executing hardware transactions. This enables Haswell's RTM to perform without interference when read-only software transactions are executing within InvalSTM, regardless of their size.

4. INVYSWELL'S DESIGN

In this section, we describe Invyswell, a HyTM that supports the concurrent execution of multiple hardware and multiple software transactions while guaranteeing forward progress. Invyswell uses Haswell's RTM [18] and a modified version of InvalSTM [11]. In InvalSTM, when a transaction is ready to commit, it marks conflicting in-flight transactions as invalid. InvalSTM uses Bloom filters for fast conflict detection between software transactions. Invyswell also uses Bloom filters at times, but not always, for conflict detection between hardware and software transactions.

Because Haswell's RTM does not support escape actions, the communication between in-flight hardware and software transactions is essentially impossible without introducing conflicts between them. For example, if a software transaction writes to memory shared by a hardware transaction, the latter will abort. Yet, communication between hardware and software transactions might be useful to improve the precision of conflict detection between them, thereby increasing throughput in cases when conflicts do not occur.

To manage this space, Invyswell generally performs conflict detection between a hardware and a software transaction *after* the hardware transaction has committed. This enables increased throughput in cases where no conflicts exist while minimizing the chance of aborting a hardware transaction because of communication with in-flight software transactions.

Furthermore, Invyswell exploits the observation that hardware transactions do not need to check for conflicts with software transactions until just before committing, a mechanism called *lazy subscription*, which was introduced by Dalessandro et al. in their NOrec HyTM system [4]. By using lazy subscription, Invyswell reduces the "window of vulnerability" in which a write to a software transaction's conflict detection metadata (e.g., its read set, its execution lock, etc.) will abort a non-conflicting, in-flight hardware transaction.

Invyswell supports five transactions types, motivated by the need for progress guarantees and adaptability to different types of workloads. Two types are in hardware, lightweight (LiteHW) and bloom filter-based (BFHW), and three types are in software, speculative (SpecSW), irrevocable (IrrevocSW), and single global lock (SglSW). The pseudocode for these transaction is shown in Figure 2. Invyswell's state transitions between them are shown in Figure 3.

4.1 SpecSW: An HTM-Friendly InvalSTM

Invyswell's first type of transaction is the speculative software transaction (SpecSW), which is similar to an InvalSTM transaction, and is shown in Figure 4. It tracks its read and write locations in transaction-specific Bloom filters and stores its write set's values in a hash table for deferred update during its commit phase. Note that a memory barrier is necessary after inserting a memory location in a read bloom

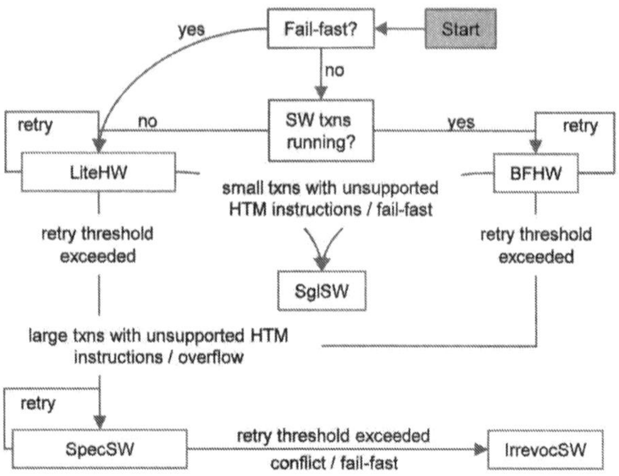

Figure 3: Invyswell's State Machine Describing the Transitions Between the Different Transaction Types.

filter and before reading the value from memory. At commit-time, a SpecSW performs invalidation, where it compares its write Bloom filter against all other in-flight SpecSWs' read Bloom filters. If a conflict is found, it consults the contention manager (CM) on how to proceed. The CM then either aborts the committing transaction or permits it to commit. If permitted to commit, the SpecSW transaction updates all write locations and then marks all conflicting in-flight transactions as invalid. During a SpecSW's execution, it checks to see if it has been marked as invalid prior to each read and write and prior to committing. If it has, it aborts and it retries again as a SpecSW or another type as illustrated in Figure 3.

A key difference between Invyswell and InvalSTM is that SpecSWs perform invalidation *after* committing changes to memory, unlike InvalSTM, which performs invalidation *before*. The reason for doing this is the following. In InvalSTM, new transactions acquire an in-flight lock to insert their transaction ID into an in-flight linked list. If Invyswell did the same, hardware transactions would have to read this lock before committing, to ensure correctness in their conflict detection. However, reading such a lock could subsequently cause many unnecessary hardware transaction aborts because whenever a new SpecSW was added to the list the in-flight lock would be acquired, automatically aborting all hardware transactions that previously read it.

To avoid this behavior, Invyswell performs invalidation after committing SpecSW's changes to memory and uses a slotted array for the in-flight SpecSWs, rather than a linked list. The combination of these changes results in Invyswell's elimination of the InvalSTM in-flight lock, thereby reducing the likelihood of unnecessary hardware transaction aborts. Instead, if a new transaction starts while the committing transaction is updating memory, it will be detected by the invalidation phase of the committing transaction, which will follow the memory update phase. Alternatively, if the new transaction starts after the memory was already updated, it could be missed by the invalidation phase. However, this new transaction is guaranteed to only read consistent states because the committing transaction has finished updating the memory, making the bloom filter check unnecessary for this transaction.

Initially, this modification results in the loss of opacity for SpecSWs, however, we restore opacity for SpecSWs by adding inexpensive validation to each read as described in Section 4.7. This change makes SpecSWs compatible with hardware transactions that can invalidate in-flight SpecSWs and it permits Invyswell to eliminate the need for an in-flight lock and the per-transaction locks that are required by InvalSTM.

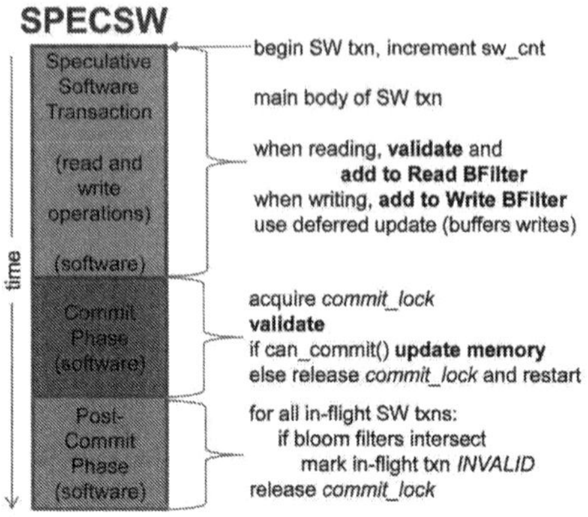

Figure 4: Speculative Software Transaction (SpecSW).

4.2 BFHW: Hardware-Software Conflict Detection

Invyswell's second type of transaction is the Bloom filter hardware transaction (BFHW). BFHWs execute in hardware and, like SpecSWs, record the memory locations they read and write in transaction-specific software Bloom filters.

At commit time, if a BFHW sees the software `commit_lock` is free, it increments the `hw_post_commit` counter, which subsequently prevents SpecSWs from committing or reading new values while its value is non-zero, and then commits its speculative writes to memory and performs post-commit invalidation on all in-flight SpecSWs, where all conflicting transactions are marked as invalid. The BFHW then decrements the `hw_post_commit` counter to indicate its post-commit phase has completed, allowing software transactions to again commit, as shown in Figure 5.

The `hw_post_commit` counter is necessary because there is a window of vulnerability after a BFHW has committed, but before it has finished executing the invalidation phase, when SpecSWs can read inconsistent values written by the BFHW. Without the `hw_post_commit` counter these SpecSWs will be marked as *invalid* by the BFHW during its invalidation phase, but they could still execute momentarily returning inconsistent reads, causing SpecSWs to lose their opacity.

Alternatively, if the `commit_lock` is taken when a BFHW enters its commit phase, this means a SpecSW is committing. In this scenario, the simplest option is for the BFHW to abort, because there may be a conflict with the committing SpecSW. However, because BFHWs track their read and write accesses, Invyswell can instead perform conflict detection between the committing BFHW and the committing SpecSW via Bloom filter set intersection. If an overlap is found, the BFHW is aborted. Otherwise, no conflict exists between the BFHW and the SpecSW, and, because their respective read and write sets are immutable during their commit phases, the BFHW is permitted to commit.

When a SpecSW commits, it releases the `commit_lock` before clearing its read and write sets. This ensures that if the SpecSW commits before a committing BFHW performs conflict detection against the committing SpecSW, that the BFHW is automatically aborted because the write performed by the SpecSW to the `commit_lock` would trigger a hardware conflict with the BFHW from its prior read.

Note that if a BFHW transaction aborts, its `hw_post_commit` counter increment never becomes visible, because it is part of its speculative write set. Moreover, the new counter value becomes visible only when the hardware transaction commits. If a SpecSW reads this counter after it has been written to by a BFHW, but before the BFHW has committed, the BFHW will be automatically aborted by Haswell RTM's strong isolation property, thereby avoiding a race.

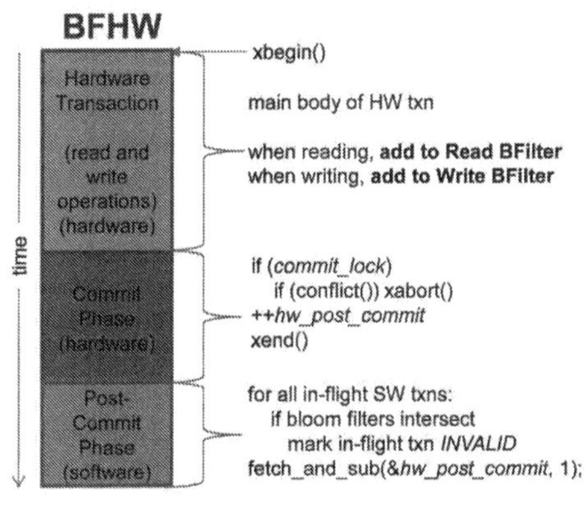

Figure 5: Bloom Filter Hardware Transaction (BFHW).

4.3 LiteHW: Optimizing for Small Transactions

Although BFHWs enable the concurrent execution of hardware and software transactions, they come with added overhead because each load and store requires an associated Bloom filter insert operation. Invyswell addresses this limitation with its third type of transaction, the LiteHW.

LiteHWs are lightweight hardware transactions, which execute without read or write annotations. They can only commit if there are no in-flight software transactions when they begin their commit phase. Unfortunately, because LiteHWs do not maintain read or write set metadata, if a software transaction is in-flight when a LiteHW enters its commit phase, Invyswell must assume a conflict exists between the LiteHW and the software transaction and, therefore, must abort the LiteHW. LiteHWs determine if there is an in-flight software transaction by reading the `commit_lock` and the software transaction counter, `sw_cnt`, prior to committing. Because LiteHWs do not perform conflict detection against software transactions, they require no post-commit phase.

4.4 IrrevocSW: Progress Guarantees

InvalSTM guarantees forward progress by using transaction-specific priorities that are incremented each time a transaction is aborted. Using this mechanism, a continuously aborted transaction will eventually yield the highest priority and is guaranteed to commit. Invyswell's BFHWs, however, deviate from this model and instead commit memory changes first and perform invalidation second, at which point all conflicting software transactions are aborted. Because of this change, there is a danger that BFHWs could repeatedly abort high-priority SpecSWs, resulting in their starvation.

To address this problem, Invyswell introduces a fourth transaction type, the IrrevocSW, a direct update irrevocable transaction type that cannot be aborted. To ensure irrevocability, IrrevocSWs acquire the `commit_lock` as soon as they begin their execution and hold it until they have committed. To enable conflict detection with other transactions, an IrrevocSW transactions records its read and write locations in Bloom filters. An IrrevocSW needs no commit phase, because its writes are in-place. Its post-commit phase invalidates conflicting in-flight SpecSWs. While an IrrevocSW is executing, SpecSWs are required to perform validation and are disallowed from committing. Furthermore, LiteHW transactions must abort if their commit phase overlaps with any part of an IrrevocSW's execution. However, BFHWs can execute concurrently with an IrrevocSW. Yet, to ensure correctness, a BFHW needs to check for conflicts with the IrrevocSW transaction prior to committing its changes to memory and it must abort itself if a conflict is found.

4.5 SglSW: Progress Guarantees with Reduced Overhead

Small transactions that execute instructions not supported by Haswell's RTM need to be executed in software. However, both SpecSWs and IrrevocSWs add transactional metadata that may be too expensive for transactions that only access a few memory elements. To address this need, Invyswell employs a final transaction type that uses a single global lock without any associated transactional metadata.

This transaction type, SglSW, uses direct update and is irrevocable. SglSW is fast, but it does not allow the concurrent execution of other software transactions. Because SglSW does not track its reads or writes, it cannot perform conflict detection. Instead, it uses a sequence lock to force all in-flight SpecSWs to abort and acquires the `commit_lock` when it begins its execution to prevent IrrevocSWs from starting. BFHW and LiteHW transactions abort if an SglSW is executing when they try to commit. However, SglSWs allows for some overlap in execution with BFHWs and LiteHWs, as long as the executing SglSW commits before the hardware transactions do, thereby ensuring that the hardware's strong isolation property aborts any BFHWs and LiteHWs that conflict with the SglSW.

4.6 Transitioning Between Transaction Types

Transactions are scheduled opportunistically, first as fast, high-risk hardware transactions, then as slower, low-risk software transactions as shown in Figure 3. Each transaction is first tried in hardware, as LiteHW or BFHW, depending on whether other software transactions are present. If the hardware abort status suggests that a transaction is unlikely to succeed in hardware, then it is retried as a SpecSW. If it fails again, it is either retried as a SpecSW or it is escalated to irrevocable status, preventing it from aborting and ensuring progress. The transitions between the different types are decided automatically at runtime based on a heuristic that is application-independent. [2]

[2] Due to limitations in Intel's first generation HTM (e.g., imprecision on a transaction's abort status and limitations of only four concurrent hardware threads, eight with hyperthreading) Invyswell's state transitions deviate slightly from that shown in Figure 3. In particular, we use a modified design that transitions to SglSW when SpecSWs fail.

4.7 SpecSW Validation

InvalSTM performs invalidation before committing a transaction's writes to memory. It uses a per-transaction `invalid` flag which is set to true when a committing transaction invalidates a conflicting in-flight transaction. For reasons described in Section 4.1, Invyswell departs from this design and performs invalidation after committing a SpecSW's writes to memory. Unfortunately, this change makes InvalSTM's approach to ensure opacity – using the transaction's `invalid` flag – insufficient for SpecSWs. Instead, on every new read that is not present in a SpecSW's write set, Invyswell inserts the new read location into the SpecSW's Bloom filter and only then is the SpecSW permitted to read the value. This ensures that a potential conflict will not be missed by another transaction's invalidation phase. Next, the SpecSW performs the validation process shown in Figure 6. This validation process is necessary because of the interactions SpecSWs can have with different transactions and the inconsistent reads they might cause, as we explain next.

SglSW.

First, a SpecSW read could be inconsistent due to a concurrently executing SglSW. Because SglSWs do not store reads and writes using Bloom filters, conflict detection cannot be performed between them and a SpecSW. Thus, the SpecSW must abort if the `commit_sequence` has changed (Line 1 in Figure 6) after it was read at `tx_begin` (Figure 2).

IrrevocSw.

Second, a concurrently executing IrrevocSW or a committing SpecSW could cause an inconsistent read. Thus, the SpecSW read must check if the read location is in the Bloom filter of the transaction holding the `commit_lock` (Line 2 in Figure 6). If so, it must abort. If `commit_lock` changes during the read validation, the conflict may go unnoticed by the validation code. However, if the lock has changed, it means the transaction that released it must have finished the invalidation phase. Therefore, it is sufficient to check if the SpecSW has been invalidated in the meantime (Line 4 in Figure 6).

BFHW.

Finally, a SpecSW must wait for all committed BFHWs to finish invalidation (`hw_post_commit` to reach zero) before using a new read value (Line 3 in Figure 6). If the SpecSW is not marked as invalid, the read is safe (Line 4 in Figure 6).

```
1. if commit_sequence changed: restart();
2. if conflict with committing SW txn: restart();
3. while (hw_post_commit!=0);
4. if (status==INVALID): restart();
```

Figure 6: Overview of Invyswell's SpecSW Validation Process.

4.8 Contention Manager (CM)

SpecSWs consult the CM during the commit phase to acquire permission to commit. As in InvalSTM, the CM considers all in-flight transactions that would be aborted if the committing transaction was allowed to commit. Any CM policy can be used. Invyswell uses iBalanced [10], which makes decisions based on priority, read and write set sizes, and other factors.

Invyswell has trade-offs that the original InvalSTM design does not have. For example, InvalSTM's ability to make decisions based on complete knowledge of in-flight transactions is lost. Essentially, there is no CM for Invyswell's hardware transactions because Haswell's RTM does not support escape actions, and thus a hardware transaction has to abort all conflicting software transactions after the hardware transaction has committed. The side-effect of this approach is that, conceptually, hardware transactions are likely to scale to high thread counts only when there is little to no contention, even if mitigation of that contention could be possible with an intelligent CM. On the other hand, software transactions retain a complete knowledge of the CM decision-making process, enabling them to scale for high thread counts amidst high contention when the contention can be managed to provide wide transactional throughput.

5. CORRECTNESS

Figures 2 and 3 show the five types of Invyswell transactions and the transitions between them, respectively. In this section, we give an informal explanation why these five transaction types can run concurrently with one another without violating atomicity, as shown in Figure 7. However, atomicity by itself does not guarantee that aborted transactions are opaque; that is, that they only observe consistent states, a topic we discuss in Section 5.1.

Types	BFHW	LiteHW	SpecSW	IrrevocSW	SglSW
BFHW	yes	yes	yes	yes	yes
LiteHW	yes	yes	yes	yes	yes
SpecSW	yes	yes	yes	yes	no
IrrevocSW	yes	yes	yes	no	no
SglSW	yes	yes	no	no	no

Figure 7: Invyswell's Concurrent Execution Matrix.

LiteHW and BFHW vs. LiteHW and BFHW.

Haswell's hardware transactions are *strongly isolated*, meaning that their changes to memory become visible to other threads only on commit, whether those threads are executing a transaction or not. The hardware automatically detects conflicts between these types of transactions, and any conflict will abort at least one transaction. There is no need for additional mechanisms to synchronize concurrently executing LiteHWs and BFHWs with respect to each other.

LiteHW vs. Software Transactions.

LiteHWs can execute concurrently with Invyswell's software transactions, but they cannot commit while such software transactions are executing. A LiteHW that overlaps execution with a software transaction (SpecSW, IrrevocSW, or SglSW) can commit only after the software transaction has committed, otherwise the resulting execution may be not serializable. A LiteHW that tries to commit while a software transaction is executing will abort. Such behavior is detected by the `sw_cnt` counter and the commit lock (see Figure 2).

BFHW vs. SpecSW or IrrevocSW.

Unlike LiteHWs, BFHWs use software Bloom filters to keep track of the memory locations they access. By performing explicit conflict detection with these Bloom filters, BFHWs can commit in the presence of software transactions. If a committing SpecSW conflicts with an in-flight BFHW, then the BFHW will automatically be aborted by the hardware when the SpecSW writes its speculative data to memory. If a committing BFHW conflicts with an in-flight SpecSW, the SpecSW will be aborted during the BFHW's post-commit invalidation phase. Moreover, BFHWs' use of lazy subscription means it is sufficient to compare the Bloom filters of BFHWs and SpecSWs at the end of the hardware transaction.

Postponing conflict detection to the end of the BFHW's execution narrows the window in which it will be aborted by false conflicts. Moreover, SpecSWs' Bloom filters do not change while it is committing, so a BFHW can read them without being aborted due to metadata interference (i.e., non-transactional interference). Note that SpecSWs that are doomed to abort after a BFHW invalidates them could read inconsistent memory before they notice they were aborted, generating faulty behavior. For this reason, atomicity by itself is not the only TM correctness property that Invyswell guarantees, an issue we discuss in Section 5.1.

SpecSW vs. SpecSW.

Conflict detection between multiple SpecSWs uses invalidation. A committing SpecSW checks for conflicts with other in-flight SpecSWs and, if conflicts are found, the committing SpecSW either aborts itself or invalidates the SpecSWs it conflicts with. No SpecSW can commit during another SpecSW's invalidation process because the committing SpecSW holds the commit lock.

IrrevocSW vs. Software Transactions.

An IrrevocSW acquires the commit lock as soon as it becomes active, ensuring that no other software transaction can become irrevocable (i.e., other IrrevocSWs and SglSWs cannot start) or commit. When an IrrevocSW commits, it invalidates in-flight conflicting SpecSWs.

SglSW vs. Everything.

When an SglSW begins, it acquires the commit lock and aborts all other concurrently executing transactions. While it holds that lock, SglSWs and IrrevocSWs are prevented from starting, and LiteHWs and BFHWs cannot commit. The SglSW also updates the `commit_sequence` lock at the transaction's start and end, aborting all concurrently executing SpecSWs and BFHWs.

5.1 Opacity and Sandboxing

Opacity is a correctness property that ensures that aborted transactions do not observe inconsistent states [12]. The principal challenge to achieving opacity for Invyswell occurs when a hardware transaction and a software transaction conflict. Haswell's hardware transactions are strongly isolated, but InvalSTM's software transactions are not, so care must be taken when managing their interaction.

Invyswell's initial modification to InvalSTM's design permits doomed SpecSWs, i.e. SpecSWs that are guaranteed to abort, to observe inconsistent states because committing SpecSWs perform invalidation *after* writing their changes to memory. To prevent these transactions from observing inconsistent states, Invyswell performs validation at commit-time and before each new read as described in Section 4.7.

Unlike SpecSWs, Invyswell's IrrevocSWs and SglSWs cannot observe inconsistent states because these transactions are never aborted and are, therefore, never doomed. Finally, Haswell's shared memory writes executed by a hardware transaction become visible only when the transaction commits, and writes by aborted transactions never become visible. Moreover, Haswell's transactions are (mostly) sandboxed, meaning that faulty behavior caused by inconsistent reads will cause the transaction to abort. Unfortunately, however, there is one leak in the Haswell sandbox, described in detail in the next section.

5.2 Hardware Sandboxing Limitations

For the most part, hardware sandboxing ensures that no consistency violation within a hardware transaction can affect other transactions. There is, however, one vexing "loophole", an unlikely sequence of events in which (1) mutually inconsistent reads cause a spurious memory write, (2) which overwrite an address later used as the target of an indirect jump in that same transaction, (3) thereby causing a jump to a location that happens to contain either an `_xend` (commit transaction) instruction, or immediate data that looks like one. Executing this instruction without the final commit lock check could prematurely commit an inconsistent set of changes.

This hazard, however unlikely, presents a challenge for any HyTM system implemented in an unmanaged language. Broadly speaking, without escape actions, hardware transactions cannot guarantee transactional consistency if they execute concurrently with either in-place update software transactions or with the commit phase of a deferred update software transaction.

To address this hazard, Invyswell's hardware transactions check the `commit_lock` before doing an indirect jump using function pointers. Simple optimizations can reduce the cost of such a policy. For example, there is no need to check the lock if the transaction has an empty write set, because it could not have corrupted the jump address. If a transaction makes multiple indirect jumps, it suffices to check the lock before the first jump, because once read, the `commit_lock` remains in the transaction's read set, and the transaction will be aborted if the lock is changed externally.

In the results presented in Section 7, we performed these optimizations by hand. For some benchmarks, we found that early checking slightly improved performance, probably because transactions with indirect jumps are often longer, hence less likely to succeed in hardware, and more likely to benefit from a quicker fallback to software.

In the long term, there is a trend toward compiler support to help with this issue. The danger posed by indirect jumps in transactions is similar to the danger posed by common security threats such as buffer overflow in general-purpose programs. The security literature has many examples of compiler techniques to protect jump addresses, such as moving vtables and return addresses in a separate memory space [2] marked as read-only. The latest GCC supports security functionality to check vtable integrity.

Static validity checking for function pointers is difficult, in general, but feasible for common special cases, such as initializers. GCC uses devirtualization and inlining for the most likely target for indirect pointers for optimization levels -O2 or higher. When inlining is possible, GCC can make indirect jumps direct. A transactional compiler could be more aggressive about eliminating or protecting indirect jumps.

6. OPTIMIZATIONS

In this section, we describe the modifications that we made to Invyswell's original design to improve its performance. We found these optimizations to be effective for the first-generation Intel Haswell RTM processor, however, some optimizations are designed specifically for performance of low thread counts (as indicated by the * below) and may degrade performance as thread counts increase. As a result, when Intel's RTM scales to higher thread counts, these "low thread count" changes should be eliminated.

Hardware Transactions.

Hardware transactions are retried with exponential back-off. Before starting a hardware transaction, the `commit_lock` and the software transaction counter, `sw_cnt`, are read non-transactionally to increase the likelihood of finding these data cached, and to optimize for the case when only hardware transactions are active.

Validation.

Consider two SpecSWs, T_A and T_B. Assume that T_A has entered its commit phase and T_B is about to validate a read. Furthermore, assume that T_B has higher priority than T_A and that they conflict with one another. When T_B performs its validation, it could notice that T_A has acquired the commit lock and abort because of the conflict it identifies. At the same time, T_A could consult the CM and abort because T_B has a higher priority, resulting in both transactions aborting because of each other. A similar situation could also occur between a committing SpecSW and a committing BFHW.

To avoid such scenarios, we introduce two global flags, `hw_check` and `sw_check`, in addition to the `commit_lock`, to indicate the different phases of a SpecSW's commit phase. At the highest level, these flags are used to ensure that SpecSWs and BFHWs are only aborted by a SpecSW that is guaranteed to commit. These flags change the SpecSW and BFHW commit process in the following way.

At commit, a SpecSW, called T_C, acquires the `commit_lock` and then consults the CM to receive permission to commit. If permitted to commit, T_C sets the `hw_check = true` to signal to BFHWs that it is committing its writes to memory. With this approach, BFHWs only read the `hw_check` flag at commit-time, instead of the `commit_lock`, which ensures that a BFHW can only be aborted by a SpecSW that will eventually commit, rather than reading the `commit_lock`, where a BFHW could be aborted by a SpecSW that has only started its commit phase but may eventually be aborted by the CM.

Next, T_C waits for the `hw_post_commit` counter to reach zero and, once it has, it checks if it was invalidated by a concurrently committing BFHW. If still valid, T_C sets the `sw_check = true`, which informs other SpecSWs about to read new memory to perform conflict detection against T_C's Bloom filters. At this point, T_C and many concurrently reading SpecSWs may perform simultaneous conflict detection on each other. If conflicts are found, the reading SpecSWs are aborted. If no conflicts are found between reading SpecSWs and T_C, the reading SpecSWs subsequently check their `valid` flag to ensure they were not invalidated by T_C, which may have performed conflict detection before the reading SpecSWs had, and subsequently cleared its Bloom filters before the reading SpecSWs could identify conflicts with them. Any reading SpecSWs that are still valid are permitted to continue their execution. Without the `sw_check` flag, the scenario of conflicting transactions T_A and T_B might occur. With it, a reading SpecSW's validation can only fail if it conflicts with a concurrently executing SpecSW that is guaranteed to commit.

**Bloom Filters.*

In principle BFHWs and IrrevocSWs enable more concurrency than LiteHWs or SglSWs, yet, in practice the overhead associated with BFHWs' and IrrevocSWs' Bloom filters can negate their concurrency benefits. This is especially true at low thread counts where there is not enough concurrency to justify such overhead. Because of this, we use SglSWs, rather than IrrevocSWs, as the fallback from SpecSWs for our experiments (see Figure 3), as SglSWs do not employ Bloom filters. However, once RTM becomes available with higher core counts, we plan to reinstate IrrevocSWs as the fallback for SpecSWs because they enable SpecSWs to execute alongside them, while SglSWs do not.

To reduce the overhead of BFHWs, we optimize away their read set Bloom filters. This optimization is possible because BFHWs only invalidate SpecSWs – SpecSWs never invalidate BFHWs – thereby only requiring write-write and write-read conflict detection for BFHWs invalidation phase. [3] However, this change prohibits BFHWs and SpecSWs from committing concurrently, which the original Invyswell design permitted. For low thread counts, however, we have found this change to only positively impact performance. Yet, for higher thread counts, this change will likely degrade performance and, therefore, it would be advisable to revert back to Invyswell's original Bloom filter design.

**Fail-Fast.*

When there is contention, many SpecSWs will repeatedly abort before reaching their retry threshold and falling back to SglSWs. The amount of wasted work that this process can incur could be substantial if contention is consistent, or even bursty, throughout the entire benchmark.

To address this, we add a counter to count the number of high-priority software transactions aborted during the invalidation phase. Whenever a thread notices that this number is over a threshold, it increments a racy shared counter. Once this counter reaches a pre-defined threshold, our optimized system switches to Fail-Fast mode, which only uses LiteHWs and SglSWs. We have found this optimization to be efficient because it identifies the cases when STMs are wasting work with too many retries, which eventually fail to irrevocable mode. In these cases, we have found it is better to use irrevocable software transactions immediately.

Read-Only.

We employed optimizations for both read-only SpecSWs and BFHWs. Read-only SpecSWs can commit when they reach commit phase without acquiring the commit lock, even if they were invalidated. First, the validation process in the read annotations ensures that the transaction's read set was consistent at the time of the last read. Second, read-only SpecSWs, as well as read-only BFHWs do not need to perform invalidation, as they can be serialized before conflicting in-flight software transactions.

[3]BFHWs can be aborted by other hardware transactions, but that is handled automatically by the hardware.

7. EXPERIMENTAL RESULTS

Our experimental results were gathered on an Intel Haswell four-core processor (Core i7-4770) with RTM and HLE support, running at 3.40GHz. Each core has a 32KB L1 cache, and a total of 8GB RAM shared across all cores. We enabled hyperthreading to collect data for up to eight threads. Because of L1 cache sharing due to hyperthreading, we noticed that at eight threads some hardware transactions that previously executed without failure began to abort due to overflow, thereby degrading performance. We used the GCC 4.8 compiler with -O3 optimizations for all benchmarks.

We used the STAMP benchmark suite [3] to measure the speedup that Invyswell provides relative to sequential execution. We compare this speedup against NOrec, which we call NorecSTM, Hybrid NOrec, which we abbreviate as NorecHy, and Haswell's HLE. For each of these systems, we executed each STAMP benchmark five times and present the median result as shown in Figure 8. Variance was generally low, except for Bayes.

Invyswell Details.

We instrumented the STAMP code using its macros to use a thread-local transaction type indicator for choosing which code path to execute. This instrumentation incurs a run-time performance penalty. A compiler could generate different code paths for these transaction types, but it would not need to generate a code path for each type. In particular, LiteHW and SglSW have similar read/write annotations, as do BFHW and IrrevocSW. Moreover, the overhead incurred for manual instrumentation is higher than the overhead incurred by compiler instrumentation.

Hardware transactions are retried N times, where $N = 10$ for our experiments, unless the abort status indicates that the transaction is unlikely to succeed in hardware, in which case the transaction is immediately retried in software. SpecSWs are retried M times, where $M = 4$, and used SglSW as a fallback if the number of retries is exceeded. Invyswell was configured to use 1024 bits and the spooky-hash function [20] for its Bloom filters. Outside of normal Bloom filter trade-offs of precision versus size, there is an additional trade-off with Bloom filters for Invyswell's hardware transactions between their precision and the aborts they cause by overflow. [4] We found 1024 bits to be a good balance across all benchmarks. For example, the Yada benchmark emits many Bloom filter false positives and makes this tradeoff apparent. Increasing the Bloom filters' size improves SpecSW performance but degrades BFHW, as it causes more aborts.

Hybrid NOrec and Invyswell.

Hybrid NOrec has many variants, many of which require nonspeculative loads. [27] requires both nonspeculative loads and nonspeculative stores. These variants cannot be implemented using TSX, and are not considered in this paper. The version of NOrec evaluated in this paper uses the two location variant and the sw_exists filter described in [4]. [5]

Hybrid NOrec has two types of transactions, hardware and software. Both types can execute at the same time. To ensure hardware transactions do not see inconsistent memory states, they eagerly subscribe to the software transactions' commit lock as soon as they begin their execution. When a software transaction begins its commit phase, hardware transactions are automatically aborted. When a hardware transaction commits, it increments a shared counter, which notifies software transactions that they must perform value-based validation to ensure consistency. To perform validation, each software transaction maintains its own list of read memory locations. To reduce list insert computational overhead, each software transaction inserts new read element directly to the list's tail, even if the item is already in the list, resulting in $O(1)$ insert time complexity. A disadvantage of this approach is that the read list can become large if a software transaction reads many locations, thereby increasing the time it takes to perform validation, where the entire list must be walked. Each software transaction performs validation in $O(N)$ time, where N is the size of the read set, for every new read added to the transaction's read set after a software or hardware transaction has committed.

In contrast to Hybrid NOrec, Invyswell has two hardware transaction types, three software transaction types, and performs conflict detection using Bloom filters, not lists, which house the memory accessed by both hardware transactions (BFHW) and software transactions (SpecSW and IrrevocSW). With Bloom filters, Invyswell's conflict detection is performed in $O(1)$ time, yet, because Invyswell uses invalidation, it has additional overhead that Hybrid NOrec does not have, where invalidation is performed after committing a transaction's speculative writes to memory.

Invyswell's LiteHWs are similar to Hybrid NOrec's hardware transactions, but Invyswell's BFHWs have no Hybrid NOrec counterpart. Although BFHWs incur overhead not found in Hybrid NOrec's hardware transactions – the storing of read and write set data in Bloom filters – this overhead is amortized on large transactions because of the finer grained conflict detection that it enables. The improved precision of conflict detection enables wider transactional throughput between hardware and software transactions if they don't conflict (e.g., Figure 8f's benchmark).

If Invyswell did not include BFHWs, nearly all of Labyrinth's transactions would execute as software transactions, because Invyswell's LiteHWs often get aborted by the long-running software transactions. However, with BFHW, hardware and speculative software transactions (SpecSWs) can execute concurrently and both types of transactions can commit, as there are not many conflicts. NOrec hardware transactions do not exhibit Bloom filter overhead but, instead, incur overhead on its software transactions, which must do value based validation, re-validating the entire read set after each transactional commit. As 50% of the transactions in Labyrinth cannot succeed in hardware, the performance of both HyTMs is similar to that of NOrec STM.

Another important difference between Invyswell and Hybrid NOrec is how fast software transactions execute for different transaction sizes. Invyswell's SpecSW transactions, which are similar to InvalSTM's transactions, are fast for large transactions, while NOrec's software transactions are

[4]The larger the Bloom filter, the better its precision, but the more likely a hardware transaction using such a Bloom filter will abort due to cache overflow, because the Bloom filter must be part of the hardware transaction's speculative state stored, in this case, in Haswell's L1D cache.

[5]Our implementation of Hybrid NOrec included all the optimizations used in [4]. In addition, we tried a variant of this algorithm that had hardware transactions lazily subscribe to the software commit lock, which also used the indirect jump annotations that we used for Invyswell. This version performed similarly to Hybrid NOrec's normal eager subscription, so we omitted the results for clarity.

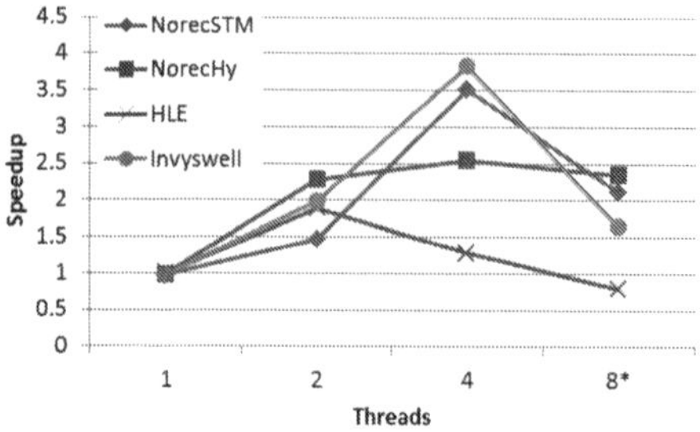

(a) Bayes.

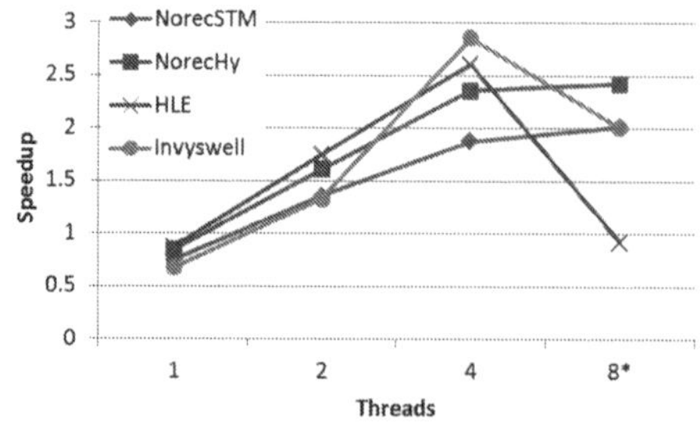

(b) Genome.

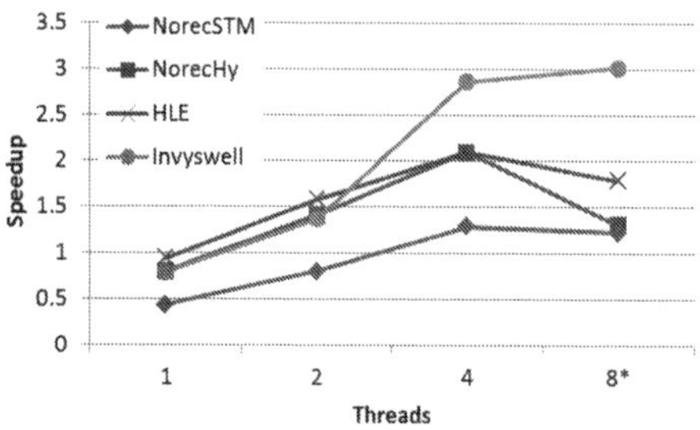

(c) Intruder.

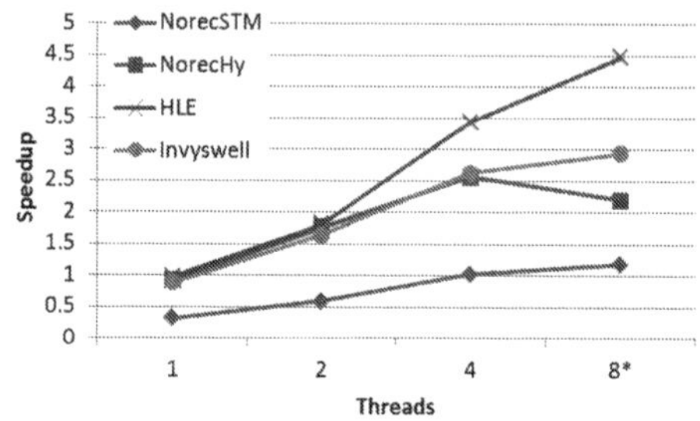

(d) kmeans low.

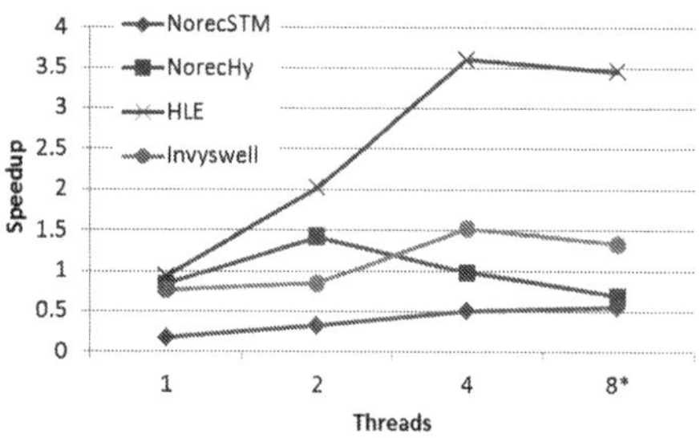

(e) kmeans high.

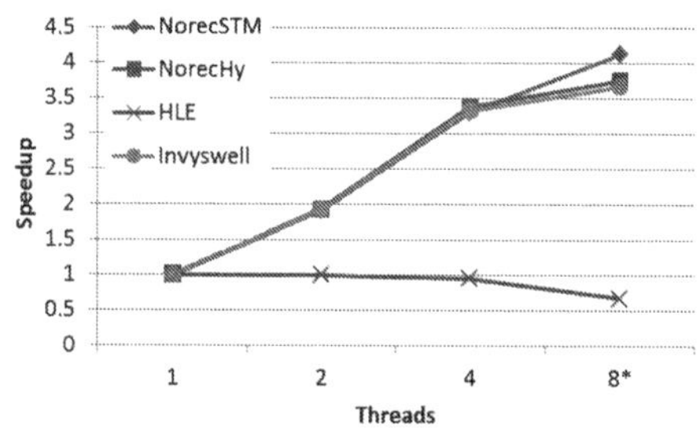

(f) Labyrinth.

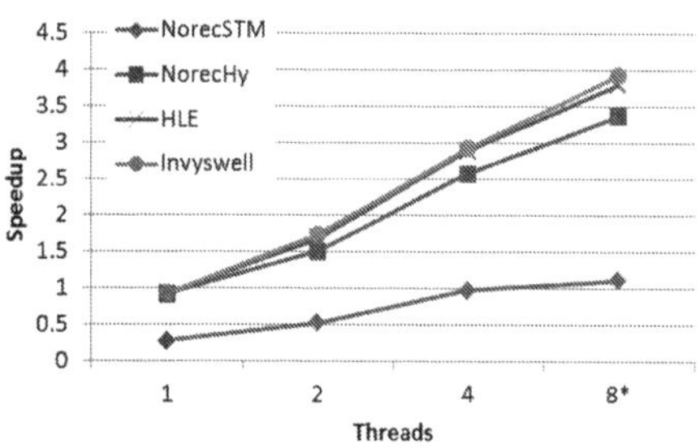

(g) ssca2.

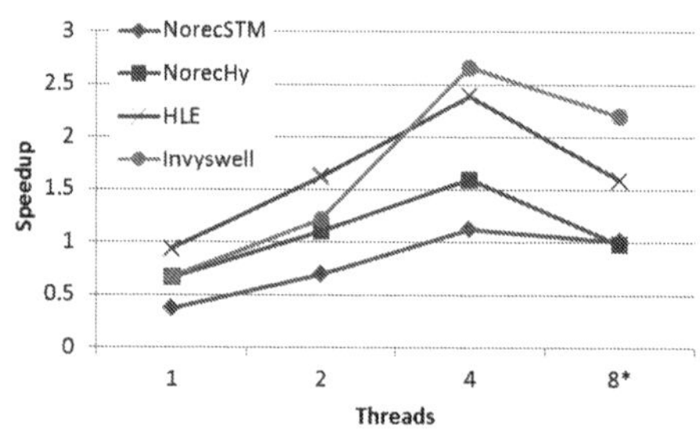

(h) Vacation low.

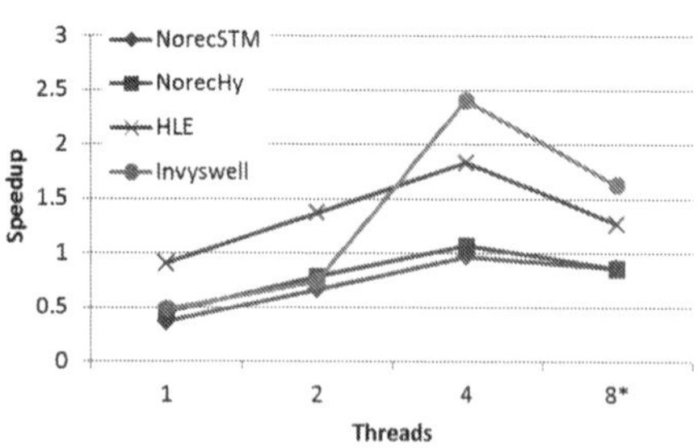

(i) Vacation high.

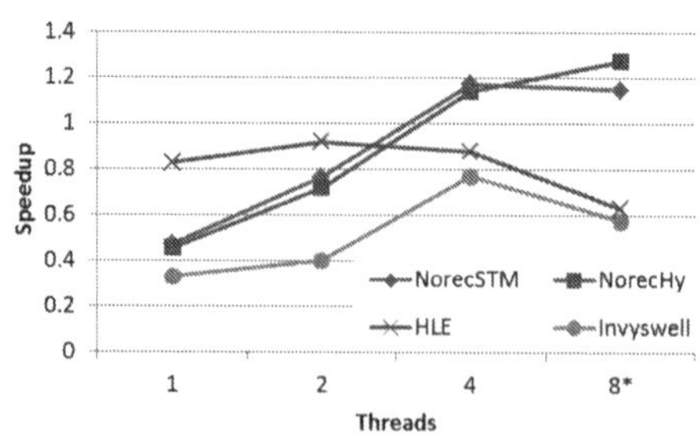

(j) Yada.

Figure 8: Speedup on STAMP Benchmarks (Note: 8 threads using hyperthreading).

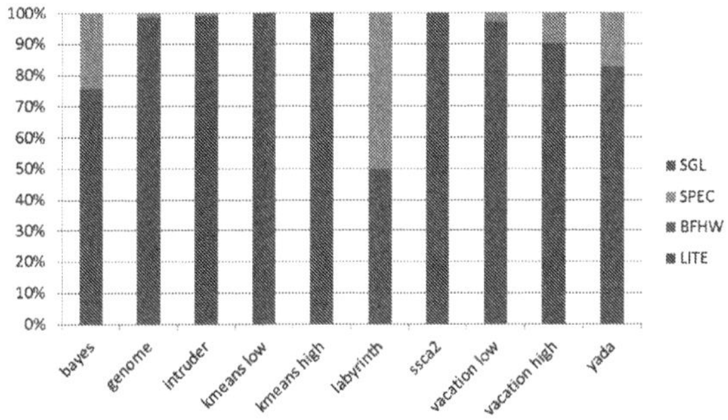

(a) Invyswell Transaction Types: 1-threaded execution.

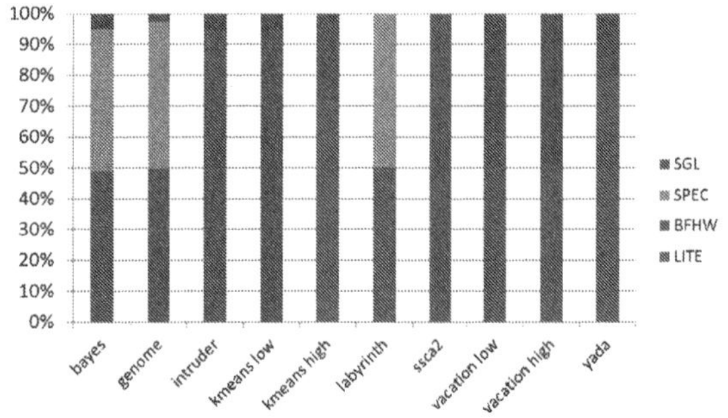

(b) Invyswell Transaction Types: 8-threaded execution.

Figure 9: Percentage of Transaction Types for Invyswell for 1-Threaded and 8-Threaded Executions.

fast for small transactions without many reads to re-validate. Yet, because Haswell's RTM can successfully execute most smaller size transactions (those without unsupported instructions), we believe SpecSWs are the natural choice as a fallback mechanism for hardware transactions.

Nevertheless, there is an interesting effect that occurs in the presence of hyperthreading, where hardware transactions overflow at smaller sizes than they would without hyperthreading because of cache sharing between two hyperthreads on the same core. For example, in Genome (Figure 8b), at eight threads about 50% of hardware transactions spill to software, for both HyTMs, because of overflow. Because of this, Hybrid NOrec performs better than Invyswell for Genome at eight threads. However, we believe this is an artifact of hyperthreading, as Invyswell is notably faster than Hybrid NOrec for Genome at four threads, where significantly fewer hardware transactions spill to software. With this in mind, we expect Invywell to perform better as HTMs scale in core count, as only large transactions will overflow the cache, resulting in the use of Invysell's SpecSWs only in the cases in which they were intended.

NOrec and HyTMs.

STMs typically scale at higher thread counts, but often perform poorly at low thread counts, especially for small and mid-sized transactions. NOrec, referred to as NorecSTM in our figures, like any STM, incurs instrumentation overhead that limits performance for small (Ssca2, Kmeans) and mid-sized (Intruder, Vacation, Genome) transactions. For such benchmarks, Invyswell can outperform NOrec by a factor of 3.5× (8g). Hybrid NOrec also outperforms NOrec on these benchmarks, indicating that a hybrid is necessary over an STM. However, Invyswell can be twice as fast as Hybrid NOrec (8c) because of its more lightweight SglSWs, in which Hybrid NOrec has no software equivalent.

As expected, NOrec performs best for benchmarks with longer transactions, and bigger read and write sets, such as Bayes, Labyrinth and Yada (Figures 8a, 8f, and 8j, respectively). Hybrid NOrec closely approaches the NOrec's speedup, as most of the benefit in these cases comes from the software transactions. In Figure 8a, NOrec is 2.1× faster than sequential execution, while Invyswell is 1.6× faster. For completeness, we included results for Bayes, but its high variance suggests that these results should be interpreted with caution [28].

Labyrinth (Figure 8f) has long transactions, where the first portion of the transaction manipulates non-shared memory. For this benchmark, 50% of the transactions cannot complete in hardware, so HLE's performance degrades to that of a lock. In contrast, NOrec yields high throughput because it enables concurrency between its transactions. Because Haswell does not support non-transactional loads and stores, all local operations performed inside a transaction are also transactional, putting pressure on the cache. Therefore, both Hybrid NOrec and Invyswell are negatively affected, resulting in performance similar to NOrec.

Hardware Lock Elision (HLE).

HLE is implemented entirely in hardware and has no instrumentation overhead, but uses a non-scalable single global lock fallback when transactions fail. For large benchmarks, such as Bayes or Labyrinth, even at small thread counts, Invyswell outperforms HLE by a notable margin. This is because many transactions overflow the cache and fall back to software, being serialized by the lock used in HLE. For medium sized benchmarks, Invyswell also outperforms HLE. However, for small transactions, HLE benefits most from the lack of overhead, so it is faster than Invyswell on benchmarks such as Kmeans Low and Kmeans High. Ssca2 is also a benchmark with small transactions, but Invyswell and HLE perform similarly.

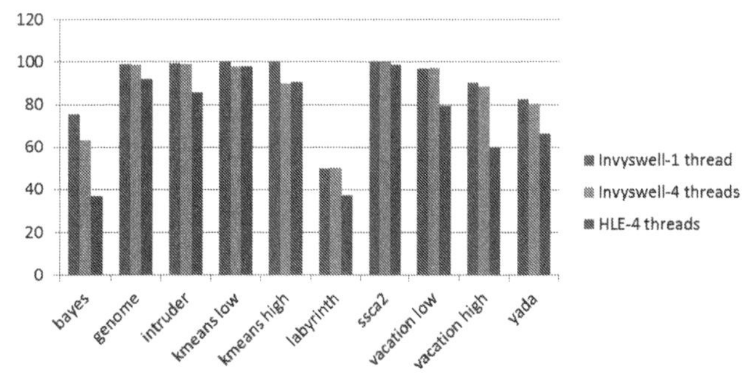

Figure 10: Percentage of Committed Hardware Transactions.

Figure 10 shows the percentage of committed hardware transactions for one thread and four threads for both Invyswell and HLE. The one-threaded execution indicates, in general, the percentage of transactions that fail in hardware because of unsupported instructions or overflow. This provides a baseline of the maximum number of hardware transaction commits that are possible for each benchmark. We also found that the number of HLE hardware transactions that begin is higher than the total number of committed transactions. This suggests that HLE also retries failed transactions before falling back to its global lock.

Invyswell's percentage of committed hardware transactions at four threads is similar to its percentage at one thread, and it is higher than HLE's percentage at four threads. This makes the argument that Invyswell generally makes more efficient use of hardware resources than the hardware (i.e., HLE) itself. Figures 9a and 9b show the breakdown of Invyswell's transaction types for one thread and eight threads executions. The eight-threaded execution suffers from the effects of hyperthreading, so the number of hardware transactions successfully committed is lower than for the one thread execution.

Overall, Invyswell outperforms HLE. For Yada, however, HLE is faster than Invyswell despite using fewer hardware transactions. This benchmark has large transactions and high contention, causing a lot of conflicts between transactions. In this case, Invyswell suffers from many false positives in its Bloom filter set intersection. We noticed an increase in performance for SpecSWs as we increase the size of the Bloom filters. However, as we previously explained, larger Bloom filters negatively impact BFHWs. Therefore, the size of the Bloom filters represents a tradeoff to balance the performance of SpecSWs and BFHWs.

Discussion.

In general, Invyswell outperforms prior methods across all STAMP benchmarks. Not only does Invyswell outperform HLE for all but the smallest transactions, it is inherently more flexible, because the programmer has explicit control over CM and failover policies. Although Invyswell is adapted from the earlier InvalSTM design, the existence of hardware transactions that bypass the CM means that the two systems are divergent, in terms of design and behavior.

Hardware transactions can fail for a variety of reasons, including resource exhaustion, timing anomalies, or illegal instructions. For future work, there is a need for better adaptive CM to identify when a particular approach is not working well, and when to switch to a more effective alternative.

8. CONCLUSIONS

We described Invyswell, a HyTM that combines Haswell's RTM transactions with software transactions from a heavily modified version of InvalSTM. We evaluated Invyswell on a 3.4 GHz 4-core Haswell processor capable of supporting up to eight hardware threads and compared it to to Haswell's native hardware lock elision (HLE), a state-of-the-art STM (NOrec), and a state-of-the-art HyTM (Hybrid NOrec).

Our main goals with Invyswell were to *(i)* improve performance for small- to medium-sized transactions, configurations where the instrumentation costs of STMs typically cause them to perform poorly and *(ii)* to extend InvalSTM's design to support the concurrent execution of both hardware and software transactions. We found that very small transactions are handled well by a simple combination of hardware transactions with fallback to a single global lock. The most interesting challenges were *(i)* modifying InvalSTM to provide some degree of precision in its conflict detection between concurrently executing hardware and software transactions and *(ii)* improving mid-size transaction performance, transactions that are small enough to benefit from hardware transactions, but too large to work well with a single global lock.

We evaluated a variety of transactional mechanisms, both hardware and software, on a range of STAMP benchmarks. As one might expect for such heterogeneous benchmarks, no single mechanism was best for every benchmark, but overall, Invyswell outperformed prior methods by more than 18%.

Haswell supports *hardware lock elision* (HLE), which allows an annotated critical section to be first executed speculatively as a hardware transaction, and then, if that transaction fails, to be re-executed non-speculatively using the original lock. HLE already provides some of the functionality of HyTM, so it is natural to ask whether Haswell needs HyTM at all. We find that HyTM is indeed needed: on average, Invyswell is about 25% faster than HLE across all benchmarks. Moreover, for benchmarks with large transactions, such as Bayes and Labyrinth, HLE does not scale and it is 2×-5.4× slower than Invyswell. The principal reason HLE does not eliminate the need for HyTM is that HyTM allows for better contention management. HLE follows a hard-wired policy of falling back to a lock after failure, but HyTM can make more intelligent and flexible decisions about resolving conflicts, taking advantage of software-based transactions, and making more effective transitions between speculative and various non-speculative synchronization mechanisms.

We tested alternative software mechanisms that trade overhead for precision. Conflict detection can be coarse and fast (SglSW) or more precise and slower (IrrevocSW and SpecSW). In the thread-count range supported by our platform, coarse-and-fast usually slightly outperforms precise-and-slower. We conjecture that precise conflict detection will become more attractive in future hardware platforms with more cores, where Invyswell is likely to perform well.

Any HyTM faces the challenge of providing opacity, which ensures that all transactions only observe consistent states. This is more difficult than it may seem, because the composition of two opaque mechanisms (for example, Haswell's RTM and InvalSTM) is not necessarily opaque. RTM's lack of escape actions complicated our task. Escape actions could make it substantially easier to ensure opacity, and to provide more effective conflict management. For example, a hardware transaction could invalidate software transactions during its commit phase, rather than after it, allowing, in some cases, for it to abort itself to improve overall throughput, as was the case in InvalSTM's original design.

Our experience suggests that hybrid mechanisms can improve the performance of small to mid-size transactions that can execute in hardware, compared to software-only or hardware lock-elision mechanisms. We conjecture that this difference will become even more pronounced when Haswell platforms with more cores become available.

Acknowledgements

We thank Andi Kleen, Michael Spear, and the anonymous reviewers for useful feedback. We have tried our best to address all of their excellent comments.

9. REFERENCES

[1] A.-R. Adl-Tabatabai, C. Kozyrakis, and B. Saha. Transactional programming in a multi-core environment. In K. A. Yelick and J. M. Mellor-Crummey, editors, *PPoPP*, page 272. ACM, 2007.

[2] P. Broadwell, M. Harren, and N. Sastry. Scrash: A system for generating secure crash information. In *Proceedings of the 12th Conference on USENIX Security Symposium - Volume 12*, SSYM'03, pages 19–19, Berkeley, CA, USA, 2003. USENIX Association.

[3] C. Cao Minh, J. Chung, C. Kozyrakis, and K. Olukotun. Stamp: Stanford transactional applications for multi-processing. In *IISWC '08: Proceedings of The IEEE International Symposium on Workload Characterization*, September 2008.

[4] L. Dalessandro, F. Carouge, S. White, Y. Lev, M. Moir, M. L. Scott, and M. F. Spear. Hybrid norec: a case study in the effectiveness of best effort hardware transactional memory. In *Proceedings of the sixteenth international conference on Architectural support for programming languages and operating systems*, ASPLOS XVI, pages 39–52, New York, NY, USA, 2011. ACM.

[5] L. Dalessandro, M. F. Spear, and M. L. Scott. Norec: streamlining stm by abolishing ownership records. In *Proceedings of the 15th ACM SIGPLAN Symposium on Principles and Practice of Parallel Programming*, PPoPP '10, pages 67–78, New York, NY, USA, 2010. ACM.

[6] P. Damron, A. Fedorova, Y. Lev, V. Luchangco, M. Moir, and D. Nussbaum. Hybrid transactional memory. In *Proceedings of the 12th international conference on Architectural support for programming languages and operating systems*, ASPLOS XII, pages 336–346, New York, NY, USA, 2006. ACM.

[7] D. Dice, Y. Lev, M. Moir, and D. Nussbaum. Early experience with a commercial hardware transactional memory implementation. In *Proceedings of the 14th international conference on Architectural support for programming languages and operating systems*, ASPLOS XIV, pages 157–168, New York, NY, USA, 2009. ACM.

[8] D. Dice, O. Shalev, and N. Shavit. Transactional locking II. In *Proc. of the 20th International Symposium on Distributed Computing (DISC 2006)*, pages 194–208, 2006.

[9] A. Dragojević, P. Felber, V. Gramoli, and R. Guerraoui. Why stm can be more than a research toy. *Commun. ACM*, 54(4):70–77, Apr. 2011.

[10] J. E. Gottschlich, M. P. Herlihy, G. A. Pokam, and J. G. Siek. Visualizing transactional memory. In *Proceedings of the 21st international conference on Parallel architectures and compilation techniques*, PACT '12, pages 159–170, New York, NY, USA, 2012. ACM.

[11] J. E. Gottschlich, M. Vachharajani, and J. G. Siek. An efficient software transactional memory using commit-time invalidation. In *Proceedings of the International Symposium on Code Generation and Optimization (CGO)*, April 2010.

[12] R. Guerraoui and M. Kapalka. On the correctness of transactional memory. In *Proceedings of the ACM SIGPLAN Symposium on Principles and practice of parallel programming*, pages 175–184, New York, NY, USA, 2008. ACM.

[13] T. Harris, J. R. Larus, and R. Rajwar. *Transactional Memory, Second Edition*. Morgan and Claypool, 2010.

[14] M. Herlihy, V. Luchangco, M. Moir, and W. N. Scherer, III. Software transactional memory for dynamic-sized data structures. In *Proceedings of the twenty-second annual symposium on Principles of distributed computing*, PODC '03, pages 92–101, New York, NY, USA, 2003. ACM.

[15] M. Herlihy and J. E. B. Moss. Transactional memory: Architectural support for lock-free data structures. In *Proceedings of the International Symposium on Computer Architecture*. May 1993.

[16] M. Herlihy and N. Shavit. *The Art of Multiprocessor Programming*. Elsevier, Inc., 2008.

[17] Intel Corporation. Hardware lock elision in Haswell. Retrieved from `http://software.intel.com/sites/products/documentation/doclib/stdxe/2013/composerxe/compiler/cpp-win/GUID-A462FBC8-37F2-490F-A68B-2FFA8010DEBC.htm`.

[18] Intel Corporation. Transactional Synchronization in Haswell. Retrieved from `http://software.intel.com/en-us/blogs/2012/02/07/transactional-synchronization-in-haswell/`, 8 September 2012.

[19] C. Jacobi, T. Slegel, and D. Greiner. Transactional memory architecture and implementation for ibm system z. In *Proceedings of the 2012 45th Annual IEEE/ACM International Symposium on Microarchitecture*, MICRO '12, pages 25–36, Washington, DC, USA, 2012. IEEE Computer Society.

[20] Jenkins, B. SpookyHash: a 128-bit non-cryptographic hash (2010). Retrieved from `http://burtleburtle.net/bob/hash/spooky.html`, 25 June 2014.

[21] S. Kumar, M. Chu, C. J. Hughes, P. Kundu, and A. Nguyen. Hybrid transactional memory. In *Proceedings of the eleventh ACM SIGPLAN symposium on Principles and practice of parallel programming*, PPoPP '06, pages 209–220, New York, NY, USA, 2006. ACM.

[22] Y. Lev, M. Moir, and D. Nussbaum. PhTM: Phased transactional memory. In *TRANSACT '07: 2nd Workshop on Transactional Computing*, aug 2007.

[23] V. J. Marathe and M. Moir. Toward high performance nonblocking software transactional memory. In *PPoPP '08: Proceedings of the 13th ACM SIGPLAN Symposium on Principles and practice of parallel programming*, pages 227–236, New York, NY, USA, 2008. ACM.

[24] M. J. Moravan, J. Bobba, K. E. Moore, L. Yen, M. D. Hill, B. Liblit, M. M. Swift, and D. A. Wood. Supporting nested transactional memory in logtm. In *Proceedings of the 12th international conference on Architectural support for programming languages and operating systems*, ASPLOS XII, pages 359–370, New York, NY, USA, 2006. ACM.

[25] R. Rajwar and J. R. Goodman. Speculative lock elision: enabling highly concurrent multithreaded execution. In *MICRO*, pages 294–305. ACM/IEEE, 2001.

[26] T. Riegel, C. Fetzer, and P. Felber. Time-based transactional memory with scalable time bases. In *Proceedings of the nineteenth annual ACM symposium on Parallel algorithms and architectures*, SPAA '07, pages 221–228, New York, NY, USA, 2007. ACM.

[27] T. Riegel, P. Marlier, M. Nowack, P. Felber, and C. Fetzer. Optimizing hybrid transactional memory: the importance of nonspeculative operations. In *Proceedings of the 23rd ACM symposium on Parallelism in algorithms and architectures*, SPAA '11, pages 53–64, New York, NY, USA, 2011. ACM.

[28] W. Ruan, Y. Liu, and M. Spear. Stamp need not be considered harmful. In *Ninth ACM SIGPLAN Workshop on Transactional Computing*. Mar 2014.

[29] B. Saha, A.-R. Adl-Tabatabai, R. L. Hudson, C. C. Minh, and B. Hertzberg. McRT-STM: a high performance software transactional memory system for a multi-core runtime. In *PPOPP*. ACM SIGPLAN 2006, Mar. 2006.

[30] N. Shavit and D. Touitou. Software transactional memory. In *Proceedings of the Principles of Distributed Computing*. Aug 1995.

[31] A. Wang, M. Gaudet, P. Wu, J. N. Amaral, M. Ohmacht, C. Barton, R. Silvera, and M. Michael. Evaluation of blue gene/q hardware support for transactional memories. In *Proceedings of the 21st international conference on Parallel architectures and compilation techniques*, PACT '12, pages 127–136, New York, NY, USA, 2012. ACM.

Consolidated Conflict Detection for Hardware Transactional Memory

Lihang Zhao
Information Sciences Institute
University of Southern California
Marina del Rey, CA 90292
lihangzh@isi.edu

Jeffrey Draper
Information Sciences Institute
University of Southern California
Marina del Rey, CA 90292
draper@isi.edu

ABSTRACT

Hardware Transactional Memory (HTM) promises to ease multithreaded parallel programming with uncompromised performance. Microprocessors supporting HTM implement a conflict detection mechanism to detect data access conflicts between transactions. Understanding the on-chip network bandwidth utilization of such mechanisms is important as the energy and latency cost of routing packets across the chip is growing alarmingly. We investigate the communication characteristics of a typical conflict detection mechanism. A variety of traffic overheads are identified, which accounts for a combined 56% of the total transactional traffic in a wide spectrum of applications. To combat this problem, we propose C2D (Consolidated Conflict Detection), a novel micro-architectural technique to consolidate conflict detection to a logically central (but physically distributed) agent to reduce the bandwidth utilization of conflict detection. Full system evaluation shows that the proposed technique, if applied to conventional eager conflict detection, can reduce 35% of the traffic and hence 27% of the network energy. The consolidated eager conflict detection generates less traffic than a lazy conflict detection scheme thereby closing the gap between bandwidth utilization of eager and lazy conflict detection.

1. INTRODUCTION

Over the past decade, the shared memory chip multiprocessor (CMP) has emerged as a *sine qua non* to exploit the increasing transistor density for sustainable performance improvement. Traditionally, locks are used to synchronize concurrent accesses to the shared memory. However, programming with locks is challenging: coarse-grain locks limit performance while fine-grain locks increase complexity. Transactional Memory (TM) promises to simplify parallel programming by providing atomic and isolated execution of code blocks (i.e., transactions). A TM system can be implemented in the software stack or with hardware support. Our work focuses on the hardware approach (HTM), as its tight integration with evolving parallel architecture continues to produce ample research opportunities.

PACT'14, August 24–27, 2014, Edmonton, AB, Canada.

http://dx.doi.org/10.1145/2628071.2628076 .

A conflict occurs when multiple transactions access a data block and at least one access is a store. Undetected conflicts could lead to incorrect transaction execution. Thus, HTM systems implement a conflict detection mechanism. Two architectural features are important for such a mechanism. First, the system must track the memory locations being accessed transactionally (i.e., transaction footprint). Second, the system tests any transaction's requests against other transactions' footprints to identify conflicts. In practice, HTM systems (both academic proposals [2, 26, 21] and commodity designs [18, 38]) typically distribute the bookkeeping of the transaction footprint to individual cores using either extra state bits in the L1 cache or hardware signatures [37]. In general, conflicts can be detected and resolved either eagerly when transactions access the memory or lazily when transactions commit. In the eager approach, when there is a data request, the sharer cores are interrogated via coherence messages to detect conflicts between the local transaction and the requestor. Detected conflicts are resolved with the Ack/Nack (negative acknowledgment) mechanism of the underlying coherence protocol.

Understanding the bandwidth utilization of the conflict detection mechanism is important, as the interplay between the on-chip network and the HTM system can significantly affect the performance/joule of the microprocessor [39]. In our study, we identify the traffic overheads in eager conflict detection, which aggravates the already problematic coherence traffic. The first major overhead comes from the interrogation process in which numerous cores are contacted to detect conflicts against the requestor. When the request fails due to conflicts, these cores continue as if the request has not been issued. Thus, the sole reason they are notified of the request is because conflicts can only be detected distributively by individual cores. Ideally, a core should be aware of a conflicting request only when its transaction execution must be throttled to avoid the conflict. The interrogation process initiates inter-transaction communication more frequently than necessary. Another traffic overhead is the data transfer to requestors whose requests fail due to conflicts. The data is discarded by the requestors thereby rendering the data transfer futile and wasted. Despite the waste, the home node sends data to requestors speculatively in order to hide the latency of detecting conflicts distributively. Without the speculation, the cache access latency increases from 3-hop to 4-hop. According to our experiments with a representative eager HTM running a set of scientific and commercial applications, the interrogation and wasted data transfer accounts for 20% (up to 37%) and 36% (up to 50%) of the to-

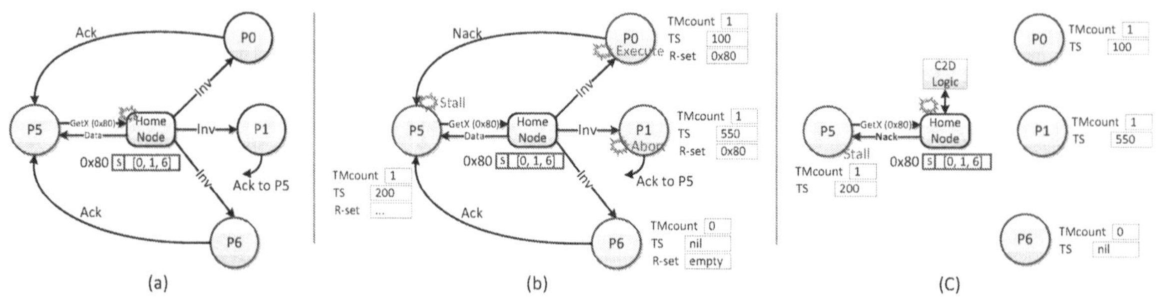

Figure 1: Examples comparing (a) data race detection, (b) distributive conflict detection and (c) consolidated conflict detection. Explosive marks indicate the operation of race condition detection in (a) or conflict detection in (b) and (c).

tal transactional traffic respectively. It is worth noting that the traffic overhead also plagues lazy HTMs that enforce pessimistic concurrency control on the write set of committing transactions. The traffic overhead is expected to grow as CMPs become increasingly distributed and, applications with coarse-grain transactions are emerging.

Limiting the energy consumption of on-chip networks is imperative as networks account for a substantial portion of the system energy budget even with elaborate low-power circuit techniques [17, 16]. Unfortunately, the distributive conflict detection exacerbates energy due to its excessive traffic overhead, which not only indicates higher dynamic energy but also nullifies the power-gating effort to reduce the static energy as routers have less opportunity to be gated-off [9].

To this end, we propose *Consolidated Conflict Detection* (C2D), a micro-architectural technique to minimize the bandwidth utilization of conflict detection. Conceptually, transactions send their requests to a logically central agent for conflict detection. The agent bookkeeps sufficient transactional metadata to detect and resolve conflicts, thereby removing the need to interrogate remote cores. Moreover, by mapping the agent to the home node, the home node no longer needs to speculate on the fate of the requests. That is, the home node does not send data to requestors if the requests fail due to a conflict. So, the wasted data transfer is eliminated without penalizing the cache latency. The consolidation of conflict detection does not create a scalability bottleneck because the logically central agent is physically distributed to the home nodes. Thus, conflicts on different partitions of the shared memory are processed by different home nodes in parallel. The implementation complexity is at most moderate. No change is required to the underlying coherence protocol except a few more bits in the coherence messages. Our evaluation shows that the proposed technique can reduce 35% (up to 66%) of the network traffic in an eager conflict detection scheme thereby reducing the network energy by 27% (up to 43%). Performance is improved by 2.7% on an average. Moreover, a consolidated eager conflict detection approach generates 20% less traffic than a lazy HTM, closing the gap between the bandwidth utilization of the eager and lazy conflict detection. The contributions of this work are three-fold.

- We identify numerous inefficiencies in the bandwidth utilization of the eager conflict detection mechanism, which could become a fundamental limiting factor when deploying HTM on large CMPs.
- Rather, we propose a novel technique to minimize the communication in conflict detection. To the best of our knowledge, this work is the first to address the traffic overhead of HTM conflict detection.
- We evaluate the proposed technique in extensive full system simulations to demonstrate its effectiveness in reducing network traffic of eager conflict detection.

The rest of this paper is organized as follows. Section 2 discusses the background and challenges in conflict detection to motivate this work. We present the basic idea in Section 3 and discuss the implementation details in Section 4. Experimental results are presented in Section 5. Section 6 reviews related work, and Section 7 summarizes this work.

2. BACKGROUND AND MOTIVATION

This section first contrasts conflict detection with the detection of race conditions in the cache coherence scheme. Then, we show that the inherent difference between these two tightly coupled schemes leads to excessive coherence traffic. Furthermore, the traffic overhead of a conventional conflict detection mechanism is quantified.

2.1 Detecting Data Races in Cache Coherence

The key functionality of a cache coherence protocol is to detect data races (i.e., data access conflicts) between processor cores. This discussion assumes a directory-based write-invalidate protocol as it provides a viable solution for scaling the cache coherence. The directory is a logically central structure to track which cores hold a private copy of a data block. This core ownership information enables a race condition to be detected at the home node. Once a race condition is detected, the home node sends invalidation messages to the sharer cores demanding them to relinquish the requested data block. The sharer cores must be contacted because the requestor always wins the race. Figure 1(a) illustrates the race condition detection. A key insight is that the detection of data races is centralized. The home node bookkeeps the necessary information and handles the races.

2.2 Conflict Detection in HTM

The detection of a conflict in HTM is analogous to the detection of a race condition as both prevent conflicting accesses to shared memory. Thus conflict detection typically piggybacks onto the coherence protocol. However, the home node cannot identify the active transactions that have accessed a data block because the directory tracks core ownership instead of transaction ownership [1]. So, unlike data races, conflicts are generally not detected at the home node.

[1]It is assumed that conflict detection between transactional and non-transactional accesses is provided.

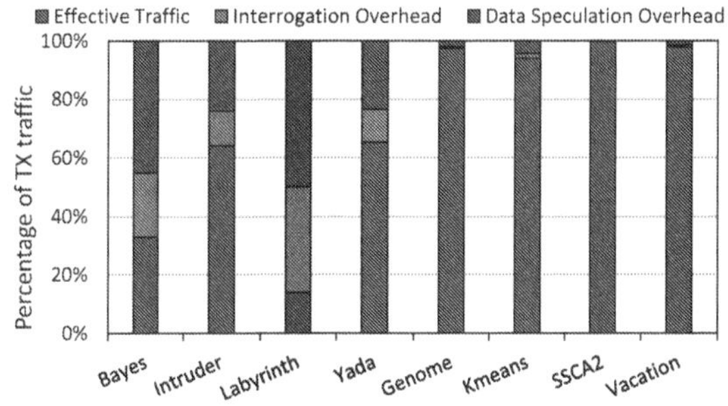

Figure 2: Breakdown of transactional traffic.

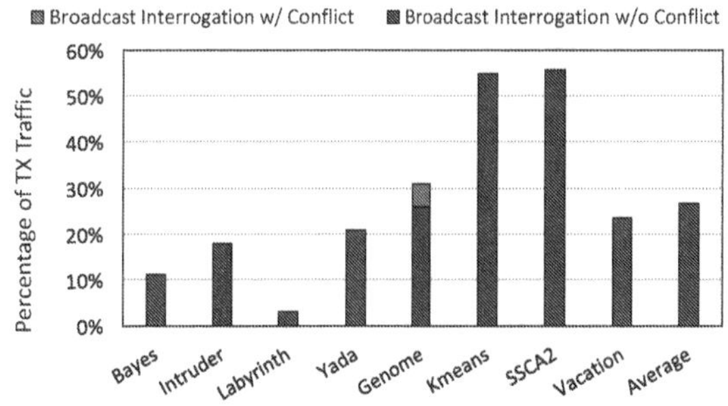

Figure 3: Broadcast traffic as a percentage of the total transactional traffic.

Typical HTM systems distribute the conflict detection capability to individual cores. Each core tracks the read and write address set of local transactions among other metadata. When the home node receives a request, it interrogates (via coherence invalidation) the cores in the sharer vector to detect conflicts. The interrogated cores detect conflicts between any local transaction and the requestor. If a conflict is detected, the core could either send a Nack (negative-Acknowledgement) message to the requestor and continue its execution or send an Ack (Acknowledgement) and aborts any local transaction. Different cores receiving the same interrogation could make different decisions to resolve the conflict. As long as one core nacks the request, the requestor stalls its transaction and retries the request. Although the requestor-always-win approach in cache coherence could be used to resolve transaction conflicts, previous studies [6, 18] show that more sophisticated conflict resolution policies are necessary for such concerns as forward progress and performance. So, eager HTM designs [26, 21, 36] typically implement more effective policies that arbitrate between transactions based on certain prioritization heuristics. Without loss of generality, the baseline HTM in this paper adopts the time-based policy [28] that prioritizes older transactions (smaller timestamp).

Figure 1(b) depicts an example of the conflict detection. P0 and P1 signal conflicts between the local transaction and the requestor as the store address is found in the local transaction's read set. P0 and P1 resolves the conflicts using the timestamps respectively. P6 skips conflict detection as it is not in an active transaction. Note the conflicts are detected distributively.

2.3 The Communication Overhead of Conflict Detection

A conflict between two parties, namely the requestor and the set of sharer transaction(s), can be resolved by stalling or aborting one party while allowing the other party to proceed. If the requestor can proceed with its request, the communication cost of interrogation is inevitable as the sharer transactions must be notified to abort themselves. Nonetheless, if the sharer transactions can proceed, they can be ignorant of the request. These transactions are interrogated by the home node anyway because the home node is unable to detect conflicts. In this case, the cost of interrogation is not well justified and thus should be minimized. Here, we define the *interrogation overhead* in conflict detection as the coherence requests (responses) to (from) various cores to detect conflicts that stop the requestors. In Figure 1(b), the Inv, Ack and Nack messages are all interrogation overhead. This overhead can be removed if the home node can detect conflicts.

Moreover, a *data speculation overhead* is the wasted data traffic to speculatively transfer data to requestors whose requests fail due to conflicts. In Figure 1(b), the data packet from the home node to P5 constitutes the data speculation overhead as P5's GetX request fails. The root cause of the data speculation overhead is that the home node itself cannot detect conflicts encountered by the requests it serves. Thus, it sends data speculatively assuming the requests will survive the conflict detection. The speculation hides the latency for interrogating remote cores for conflict detection at the cost of superfluous traffic.

The home node relies on the directory to identify sharer processors to be interrogated for conflict detection. When a data block is evicted from the shared cache, the corresponding directory entry (as part of the cacheline tag) is also evicted. In unbounded HTMs [2, 26, 4], when a transaction requests the evicted block, conflicts are possible because the block could still belong to the memory footprint of another active transaction. However, the home node cannot identify the processors that have accessed the block. So, it conservatively broadcasts the interrogation to all cores but the requestor for conflict detection. The bandwidth utilization is significant. This approach is too conservative especially for applications with infrequent contentions as most of the cores receiving the broadcast interrogation do not conflict with the requestor nor even execute a transaction. We define the *broadcast overhead* as the broadcast interrogations to processor cores (and responses from them) that do not conflict with the requestor. Note that conflicts can still be detected correctly if the broadcast overhead is removed.

We quantify the traffic overhead in an eager conflict detection on a 16-core CMP (see Section 5 for experiment detail). As it is observed in Figure 2, the interrogation overhead and data speculation overhead account for an average 20% and 36%, respectively, of the total transactional traffic. The aggregated overhead traffic even exceeds the effective traffic in two applications. Figure 3 shows the cost of broadcasting interrogations as a percentage of the total transactional traffic. An average 27% (up to 56%) of the transactional traffic is the broadcast overhead. Only a very small fraction of the broadcast interrogations encounter a conflict. So, the broadcast is indeed too conservative. While the first two overheads mainly plague workloads with moderate to high contention, the broadcast overhead is more substantial in low contention workloads. Thus, the communication overhead in conflict detection can affect a wide range of applications regardless of the frequency of conflicts.

3. C2D: CONSOLIDATED CONFLICT DETECTION

The key thesis of this proposal is the re-assigning of conflict detection from individual conflicting cores to the home node so that the on-chip bandwidth utilization of conflict detection mechanisms can be minimized. The home node is an ideal point for the consolidated conflict detection as all the coherence requests get serialized at the home node. With necessary metadata of concurrent transactions, the home node is capable of correctly and promptly detecting conflicts, requiring no interrogation to remote cores. If a request should be nacked, the home node directly nacks the requestor and skips the data transfer to the requestor. Hence, other cores are completely isolated from the request. Communication to the sharer transactions is initiated only when they should abort or stall to make way for the requestor. A simple example of the C2D scheme is illustrated in Figure 1(c). Unlike the conventional scheme in Figure 1(b), conflicts are detected at the home node using the C2D logic. The home node resolves the conflict by nacking P5's request as its transaction is younger. Note neither interrogation nor speculative data transfer is initiated. Also, P1's transaction is not aborted by the nacked request thereby preserving more concurrency.

The nucleus of the C2D design is a cost-effective mechanism to bookkeep transactional metadata at the home node, which enables the home node to handle conflicts. A minimal set of transactional metadata essential for conflict detection and resolution includes:

1. Transaction ownership of data blocks.
2. The ordering to serialize conflicting transactions.

Provided the above metadata is readily available at the home node, the C2D logic can (1) identify conflicting transactions and (2) resolve the conflicts. In subsequent discussion, the bookkeeping mechanisms are described. Then, we discuss the C2D logic that processes conflicts.

3.1 Morphable Ownership Tracker

The transaction ownership of a data block is the set of sharer transactions whose read or write set contains the block address. The home node tracks the transaction ownership so as to identify conflicting transactions. This feature is provided by the Morphable Ownership Tracker (MOS-Tracker). Its organization is shown in Figure 4. Conceptually, the MOS-Tracker has P entries to bookkeep P sets of addresses being accessed transactionally by each of the P

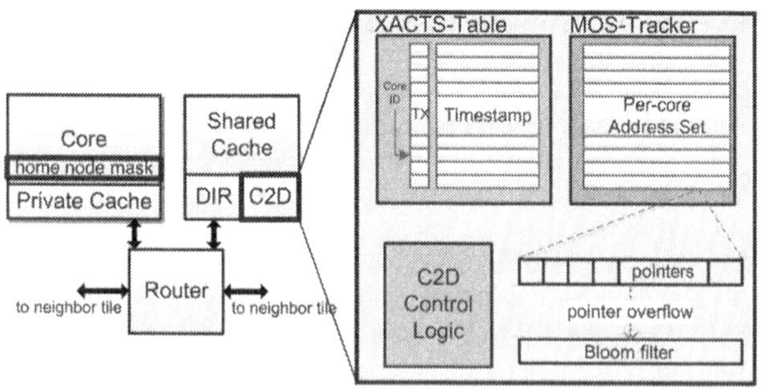

Figure 4: Architectural overview of a CMP tile. Bold rectangles indicate C2D-specific components.

processors. Each entry is equivalent to a combined read and write set. If a processor is not executing a transaction, its MOS-tracker entry is an empty set. It is important to note that the set is a subset of a transaction's memory footprint as it tracks transactional accesses to the addresses that are mapped to only the home node. As the home node handles conflicts only on those addresses, it is unnecessary to track the transaction ownership for other addresses. Performing a set-membership test of an address against the MOS-Tracker entries generates the *transactional sharer vector*, which is a bit vector identifying the processors executing an sharer transaction. The transactional sharer vector and the coherence state together indicate the data sharing activity of concurrent transactions (described in Table 1).

The MOS-Tracker supports three operations.

Insert. An address is inserted into an entry when the home node receives a coherence message from a transaction to unblock the directory. All the transactional accesses that encounter a L1 miss can be tracked this way. For other accesses served from the L1, the requestors explicitly notify the home node with the requests. The *hit notification* goes through the load store queue. The traffic overhead of hit notifications is marginal for two reasons. First, the shared data being accessed within transactions often exhibits a migratory sharing behavior [13, 32]. So it is common that the first access to the data in a transaction misses in the L1 and goes to the home node. Second, repeated hit notification is prevented by marking the already-notified cachelines with extra L1 state bits. Quantified results of the notification traffic are presented in Section 5.

Test. A set membership test of an incoming address against all the P entries in the MOS-Tracker generates the P-bit transactional sharer vector. If the directory has a valid sharer vector for the requested block, the test operation can skip the entries corresponding to cores not present in the sharer vector as the transactional sharer vector is a subset of the sharer vector. Only when the sharer vector is invalid will a MOS-Tracker test walk through all the sets. In subsequent section, we present a design that allows the test of individual entries to proceed in parallel.

Reset. The MOS-Tracker clears an entry corresponding to a core when the home node is notified by the core of the end of the transaction. This notification is discussed in the next section.

Motivated by the observation that a large fraction of transactions have a small set of read and write addresses while a few transactions have a large set of read and write addresses, we design the MOS-Tracker as a morphable structure that tracks a small set of addresses precisely while tracking an unbounded set of addresses conservatively. When the number of accesses to track is small, the MOS-Tracker uses the limited pointer scheme to bookkeep the addresses precisely. As transactions progress, the number of transactional accesses could overflow the pointer slots. Under such circumstances, the MOS-Tracker morphs into a set of Bloom filters [3] to track the addresses conservatively but without false negatives. As in a conventional transaction signature, false positives in the MOS-Tracker can cause conservative serialization of transactions but do not jeopardize correctness and forward progress. Recall the morphable design can completely avoid false positives when the address set is small. A cost-effective implementation of the MOS-Tracker is presented in next section.

Table 1: Data sharing activities and conflict requests at different combinations of coherence state and transactional sharer vector

Coherence State	Tx Sharer Vector Size	Data Sharing Activity	Conflict Request
NP	0	Data is not present in the on-chip cache. No active transaction has accessed it.	None
NP	1	Data is not present in the on-chip cache. An active transaction has accessed (read or write) it.	GetS, GetX
NP	>1	Data is not present in the on-chip cache. 1+ active transactions have read it.	GetX
S	0	Data is shared. No active transaction has accessed it.	None
S	≥ 0	Data is shared. 1+ active transactions have read the block.	GetX
M	0	Data is modified and not in any private cache. No active transaction has accessed it.	None
M	1	Data is modified and not in any private cache. A transaction has accessed (read or write) it.	GetS, GetX
MT	0	Data is modified and in private cache. No active transaction has accessed it.	None
MT	1	Data is modified and in private cache. A transaction has written to it.	GetS, GetX

3.2 Transaction Status Table

The home node is augmented with a Transaction Status Table (XACTS-Table) to record the status of concurrent transactions. It tracks each transaction's rank in the global transaction ordering, which is used for conflict resolution. The conflict resolution policy is largely orthogonal to C2D: any policy is applicable to C2D as long as it provides a unanimous transaction ordering throughout the system. Without loss of generality, C2D adopts the time-based policy [28]. A timestamp is generated at the beginning of each transaction, and is tagged to every coherence message from the transaction. Transactions with smaller timestamp win the conflict resolution. The structure of the XACTS-Table is depicted in Figure 4. The table is indexed using core id. Each entry has a `TS` field to record the timestamp and a `TX` bit to indicate the validity of the timestamp.

Maintaining the XACTS-Table requires every transaction to explicitly notify the home nodes with its beginning and end. However, the requirement can be relaxed based on the observation that transactions cannot conflict on a data block if they have not requested the data from the home node. So the home nodes need not update a transaction's status in the XACTS-Table until they receive a request (or a hit notification) from the transaction. As a result, a transaction does not explicitly notify its home node when it begins. The home node updates the transaction's timestamp when a request (or a hit notification) from the transaction is received. When a transaction ends, it notifies only the home nodes to which the transaction has sent requests. To identify the home nodes being contacted by a running transaction, each core is augmented with a simple bit vector called the *home node mask*. When the core sends a transactional request or hit notification to a home node, the corresponding bit is set. When the transaction ends, the home node mask identifies the home nodes that should receive a notification of the transaction end.

3.3 The C2D Logic

Now, we discuss the C2D logic that detects and resolves conflicts using the transactional metadata from the MOS-Tracker and XACTS-Table. It operates in parallel with the shared cache access thereby not penalizing the cache latency.

When a home node receives a coherence data request, the C2D logic retrieves the transactional sharer vector of the requested block from the MOS-Tracker. The requestor is masked out from the vector. If the vector is empty, the request is conflict free because no other transaction is accessing the data. So, the home node proceeds to serve the request as in a normal coherence protocol. Otherwise, if the vector is not empty, the home node examines the combination of the vector, coherence state and request type to detect any violation of the "single-writer-multi-reader" invariant that signals a conflict between the requestor and the sharers. Table 1 describes the state combinations that lead to conflicts. Note that the C2D logic conservatively signals a conflict when there is a GETS request to a block that is in the NP state and has been accessed in an active transaction. Nonetheless, the home node no longer has to assume all the cores are conflicting with the requestor when the requested block is in the NP state.

Once conflicts are detected, the C2D logic resolves the conflict by serializing the conflicting transactions. The transaction timestamp in the XACTS-Table is used to determine the serializing ordering: transactions with larger timestamps (younger) are serialized after those with smaller timestamps (older). Unlike the distributive scheme that enforces the ordering between the requestor and individual sharer transactions separately, the C2D logic treats the sharer transactions as a group. Specifically, if a requestor should be serialized after at least one sharer transaction, then all the sharer transactions can proceed safely. The home node sends a Nack to the requestor causing it to stall. More concurrency is preserved as the consolidated conflict resolution avoids the myopic aborting of some sharer transactions by requests that are nacked by other sharers. If all the sharer transactions should be serialized after the requestor, the home node sends to the sharers an invalidation message with a special flag (`AbortFlag`) asserted. Upon receiving the invalidation, the sharer transactions either abort or trap into a contention manager. An Ack message is sent from each sharer to the requestor. Figure 5 summarizes the conflict detection and resolution procedure implemented in the C2D logic. Note that the operations can be readily pipelined for higher throughput.

4. IMPLEMENTATION DETAILS

4.1 Implementing MOS-Tracker

The MOS-Tracker bookkeeps one address set per core either in a limited pointer format when the set size is small or in a Bloom filter format when the set size exceeds the pointer capacity. The implementation should address two main challenges. First, the common case latency of MOS-Tracker operations should be bounded by the L2 access latency (usually between 10 to 20 cycles) so that the conflict detection does not penalize the L2 access. Second, the morphing between two formats should be transparent. Otherwise, requests could be blocked by the C2D logic due to the unavailability of transaction ownership information. These challenges must be addressed with area- and energy-efficient hardware.

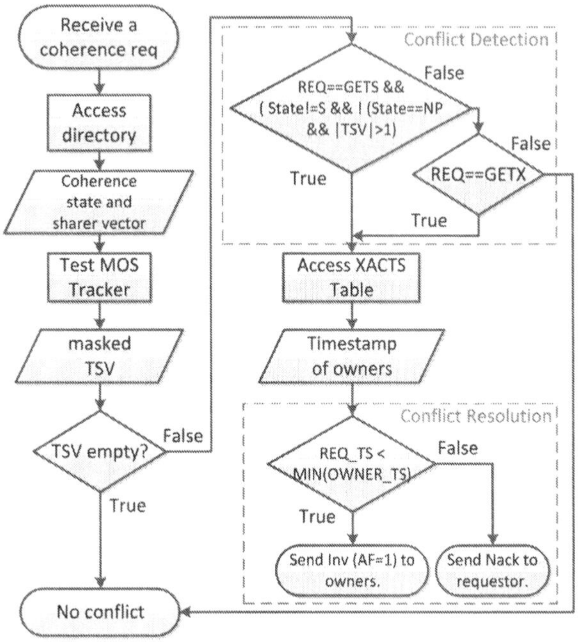

Figure 5: Procedure of the C2D logic to detect and resolve conflicts. AF: AbortFlag. TSV: Transactional Sharer Vector.

The proposed MOS-Tracker implementation is presented in Figure 6. The basic storage structure is a simple single-ported SRAM array. In the pointer mode, each row contains pointer slots addressable with the column address. The first slot always points to the next free pointer slot in the row. One logical MOS-Tracker entry can span one or more rows. Here, we consider a straightforward 1-to-1 mapping between rows and entries. The test operation walks through rows in search for the target address. The output is the P-bit transactional sharer vector. A wide read port and parallel comparison accelerates the test. The sharer vector and test output from the filter-mode SRAMs can assist to skip the rows that need not be tested. So, the test typically finishes within the L2 access latency.

In the filter mode, the SRAM combines the per-core Bloom filters as all the filters use the same hash function. The hashed address reads out a P-bit vector, where each bit corresponds to a bucket in a per-core Bloom filter. The test operation requires a single read access. Inserting an address into core i's filter requires two accesses. One access reads out the P-bit vector and the other access writes back the modified P-bit vector with the ith bit set to one. Resetting core i's filter clears the ith bit in each P-bit word. [30] describes a cost-effective circuit design of a small SRAM with flush clear function.

A minimalist MOS-Tracker consists of two SRAM arrays: one in filter mode and the other initially configured to pointer mode. The final transactional sharer vector is generated by AND-ing the P-bit vector from each SRAM. More filter-mode SRAMs can help reduce false positives. k filter-mode SRAM arrays with k hash functions constitute a set of parallel Bloom signatures [29] for the P cores, where k is a design parameter. One pointer-mode SRAM is usually sufficient to track the accesses of fine-grain transactions. Allocating

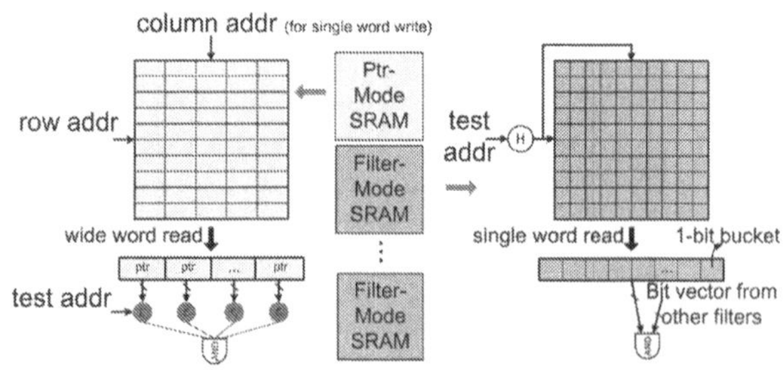

Figure 6: A hardware implementation of the MOS-Tracker. H stands for hashing

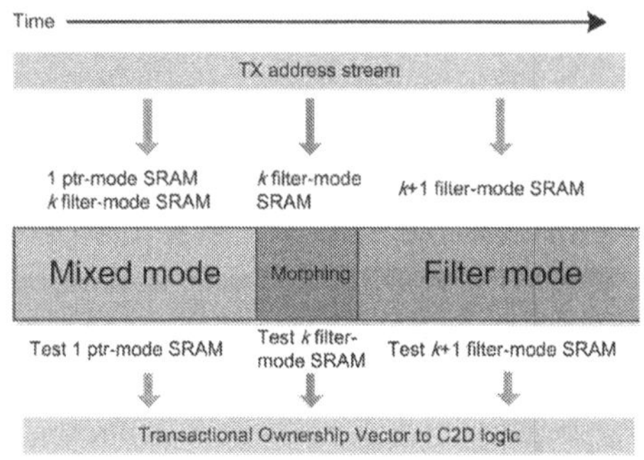

Figure 7: Execution phases of the MOS-Tracker.

additional SRAM arrays for pointer storage results in diminishing return and elongated test latency.

The pointer-mode SRAM morphs to filter mode when pointers overflow a row. Morphing can be performed by a software handler in two steps. First, the address pointers are flushed to a temporary storage. Then, these addresses are re-inserted into the empty Bloom filter. The morphing SRAM remains offline until the handler returns. The MOS-Tracker can still track transaction ownership as the filter-mode SRAMs have virtually continuous availability. So, morphing is transparent to the C2D logic. The morphed SRAM can return to pointer mode when no core is in a transaction. If frequent morphing is expected or detected, the SRAM can be pinned to filter mode by a programmer or a runtime mechanism. Figure 7 depicts the MOS-Tracker's execution phases.

The minimalist design with two SRAM arrays delivers good overall performance according to our experiments. Each SRAM in the design has 4096 bits organized as a 16x16 array. The word width is 16 bits. The pointer-mode SRAM stores 8 address pointers (32-bit each) in a row. If both SRAMs are in the filter mode, the per-core filter is equivalent to a parallel Bloom signature with 2 hash functions and 256 bits per hash function. When combining the MOS-Tracker in all the 16 home nodes, the aggregated address tracking capability is either 128 addresses/core or 8K-bit signature/core. The total number of bits required is 128K. The hardware cost is compensated by the removal of conventional signatures.

4.2 Analysis of False Positive in C2D

It is well known that false positives in Bloom-filter based signatures indicate conflicts when no actual conflict exists. Thus, false positives are usually detrimental to performance by causing unnecessary stalls or aborts. In the distributive

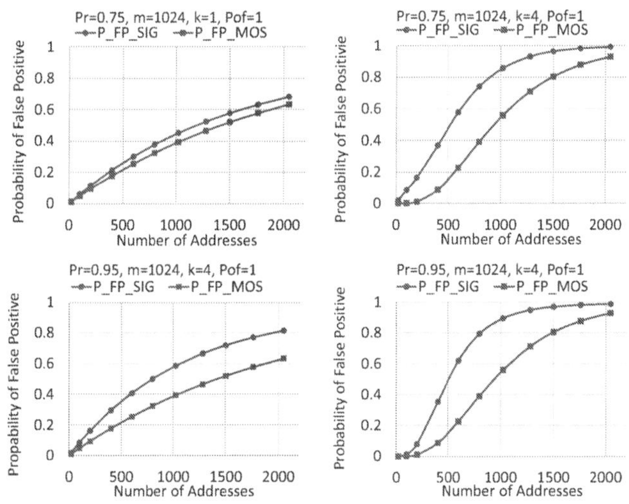

Figure 8: Probability of a false positive as a function of the number of addresses being inserted.

conflict detection, false positives occur in either the read or write signature. In the consolidated scheme, false positives occur in the MOS-Tracker. We use an analytical model to compare the frequency of false positives in the two conflict detection schemes assuming a similar hardware budget. Specifically, our model considers: *i)* two parallel Bloom signatures [29] tracking the read and write set of a transaction and *ii)* one MOS-Tracker entry tracking the address set of a transaction. Each parallel Bloom signature uses k bit-selection hash functions and k SRAMs, each with m/k bits. n_r addresses are inserted into the read signature and n_w addresses are inserted into the write signature. Let us assume the probability of an address being a read address (P_r) is $n_r/(n_r+n_w)$. By extending the formal model proposed by Sanchez et al. [29], the probability of a false positive in the signatures is:

$$P_{FP_{sig}} \cong \left(\frac{n_r}{n_r+n_w}\right)\left(1-e^{-\frac{n_r k}{m}}\right)^k + \left(\frac{n_w}{n_r+n_w}\right)\left(1-e^{-\frac{n_w k}{m}}\right)^k \quad (1)$$

The MOS-Tracker uses the same k hash functions and k SRAMs. Each SRAM has $2m$ bits so that the total bit count is equivalent to that of the two signatures. However, as the MOS-Tracker bookkeeps p address sets (one per transaction), $2m/kp$ bits are dedicated to track a transaction's address set. Assume a transaction's memory footprint is uniformly distributed among the p home nodes, the probability of a false positive in the MOS-Tracker is:

$$P_{FP_{MOS}} \cong P_{of}\left(1-e^{-\frac{\frac{n_r+n_w}{p}k}{\frac{2m}{p}}}\right)^k = P_{of}\left(1-e^{-\frac{\frac{n_r+n_w}{2}k}{m}}\right)^k \quad (2)$$

P_{of} is the probability of pointer overflow. The P_{FP} is plotted in Figure 8. P_{of} is fixed at one to obtain the upper bound. As shown, if a fixed number of bits are invested to implement either the read and write signature or the MOS-Tracker, the latter has less frequent false positives as the combined tracking of read and write set in one bit field can improve the signature utilization [11].

Table 2: Benchmark input parameters

Benchmark	Input Parameters	Abort Rate
Bayes	32 var, 1024 records, 2 edge/var	97.1%
Intruder	2k flow, 10 attack, 4 pkt/flow	77.6%
Labyrinth	32*32*3 maze, 64 paths	98.6%
Yada	1264 elements, min-angle 20	47.9%
Genome	32/512 nucleotides, 16384 segments	1.3%
Kmeans	65k pts, 32d, 16 clusters, thld 0.1e-4	7.4%
SSCA2	16k nodes, 9 len, 9 para edge	0.3%
Vacation	1M record, 4K req, 60% coverage	38%

Table 3: Baseline System

Core	16 SPARC V9 cores, 2GHz, in-order, CPI=1
L1 Cache	32KB, split I/D, 4-way associative, write-back, 1 cycle latency
L2 Cache	8MB, 8-way associative, 16 banks interleaved, 20 cycles latency
Coherence	MESI protocol, static cache bank directory
Memory	4 GB, 4 memory controllers, 200 cycles latency
Network	4x4 2D mesh, DOR, 4 flits/VC, 2 VCs/vnet, 5 vnet, 2GHz 4-stage router, 128-bit link
HTM	2x2Kbit signature/core, 2 multi-bit-selection hashings, 256-entry log buffer, 25-cycle backoff

5. EVALUATION

5.1 Methodology

We evaluate the efficacy of the proposed C2D technique using cycle-accurate full system simulation [22]. The Ruby memory timing module [23] models a detailed memory subsystem. We use Garnet [1] and Orion2 [19] to model the timing and power of a packet-switched on-chip network respectively. For our analysis, we collect execution statistics from at least twenty runs of each workload in the STAMP benchmark [24], which is extensively used by the TM community. Table 2 lists the input parameters of the benchmark.

The simulation uses a tiled CMP as the baseline architecture. Each tile has an in-order SPARC core, L1 data and instruction cache and an address-interleaved L2 bank. The L2 is inclusive. Cache coherence is maintained by a directory-based MESI protocol. The directory is distributed among the tiles by augmenting the L2 tags with directory information. The tiles are connected by a 2D mesh router network. The canonical 4-stage router uses virtual channel flow control and dimension-ordered routing. The link width is 128 bits. A coherence control message (64 bits) is transmitted in 1 flit, and a coherence data message (576 bits) requires 5 flits. We estimate the router and link energy for 40nm technology and 0.9V on-chip voltage.

The baseline HTM system follows the log-based approach [26] for eager version management. A hardware log buffer is used to accelerate abort recovery. Cores track the transaction read and write set with two 2Kbit parallel Bloom signatures [29]. Each signature uses two bit-selection hash functions. Conflicts are detected eagerly and distributively by piggybacking onto the coherence protocol. The protocol is extended with sticky states [26] to allow transactions to overflow the L1. Conflicts are resolved in hardware using the time-based policy. A backoff mechanism delays transaction restarts by a fixed time to mitigate conflicts. Detailed system parameters are shown in Table 3.

For the evaluation of C2D, we apply the C2D technique to the baseline eager conflict detection (**Eager-Base**) approach to implement the consolidated eager conflict detection (**Eager-C2D**). The coherence controller is augmented with a XACTS-Table, a MOS-Tracker and the C2D logic.

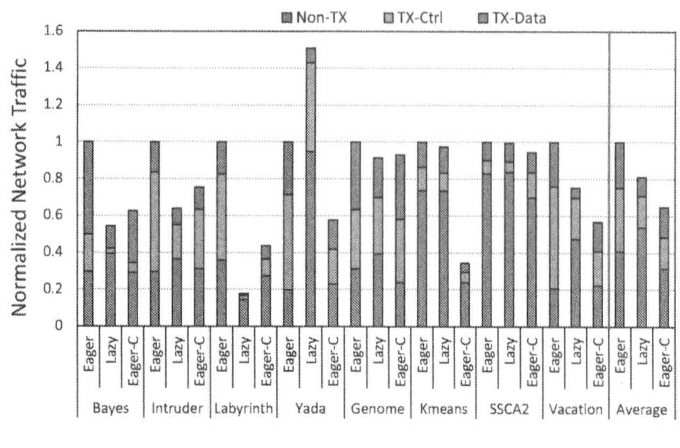

Figure 9: Normalized on-chip network traffic.

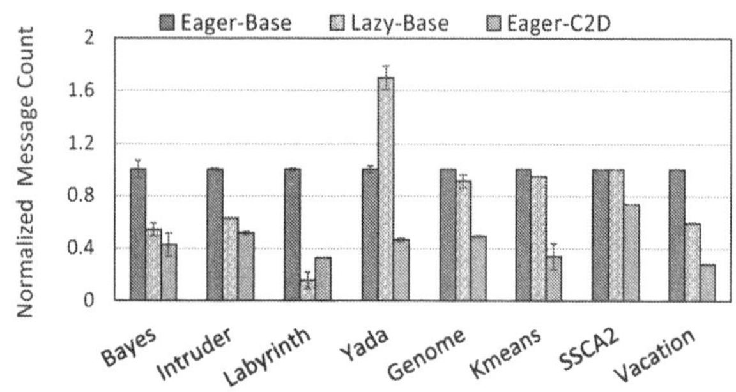

Figure 10: Normalized Coherence Message Count.

Each MOS-Tracker has two 4Kbit SRAMs with the same hash functions as the baseline. These mechanisms operate in parallel with L2 access, thereby not penalizing the 20-cycle L2 response latency. We also present results from a lazy HTM system (**Lazy-Base**), as lazy systems are considered more gracious in bandwidth utilization due to the laziness in conflict detection. The lazy HTM is as described in [6].

5.2 Impact on Network Traffic

Figure 9 shows the impact of various conflict detection schemes on the network traffic, which is measured as router traversals by flits. All the results are normalized to Eager-Base. As it is observed, the C2D technique reduces 39% (up to 57% in Labyrinth) of the network traffic when applied to the eager conflict detection scheme. Specifically, C2D reduces 60% of the transactional control traffic in the baseline eager system because the consolidation eliminates the need to interrogate remote transactions in order to detect conflicts. In particular, Labyrinth exhibits an 81% reduction in transactional control traffic. In Labyrinth, each thread is executing coarse-grain transactions that read a global maze grid, calculate a path between two points, and add the path to the grid. So, a writer transaction conflicts with all the concurrent sharer transactions. In the conventional scheme, all the sharer transactions must be interrogated to detect the conflicts. Enabled by C2D, the home node can detect the conflicts thereby significantly reducing the control messages devoted to interrogation. Meanwhile, C2D reduces 34% of the transactional data traffic as it obviates the data transfer from the home node to requestors whose requests are nacked.

Table 4: Notification traffic in Eager-C2D

Benchmark	TX End	L1 Hit
Bayes	0.06%	0.22%
Intruder	4.98%	6.70%
Labyrinth	0.04%	0.20%
Yada	0.24%	1.09%
Genome	2.07%	2.91%
Kmeans	1.14%	1.66%
SSCA2	3.41%	2.03%
Vacation	0.91%	2.48%

As the broadcast overhead exists in unbounded HTM designs only, we also performed experiments configuring the C2D to reduce all but the broadcast overhead to examine its impact on best-effort HTMs. The resulting average traffic reduction is 25% instead of 39%. The traffic reduction in the four high-contention workloads is 38% instead of 40%. So, both unbounded and best-effort HTMs can benefit similarly from C2D.

Lazy HTM systems typically exhibit more gracious bandwidth utilization than eager systems due to the laziness in conflict detection. However, lazy conflict detection does have undesirable characteristics such as complicated overflow handling and longer aborting recovery. The results in Figure 9 confirm that the Lazy-Base generates 19% less traffic than the Eager-Base. Nonetheless, the Eager-C2D generates 24% less traffic than the lazy system. Thus, the C2D technique could preserve the benefits of detecting conflicts eagerly without paying the extra bandwidth cost. Lazy systems can also benefit from the C2D as they also detect conflicts eagerly to isolate memory updates of committing transactions. We leave such a study to our future work.

Figure 10 shows the normalized coherence message count in each application. The Eager-C2D reduces 55% of the coherence messages compared with the Eager-Base and 45% of the messages compared with the Lazy-Base. The reduction in coherence message count is directly translated to coherence traffic savings. So, unlike the TMNOC scheme which reduces network traffic by reducing the average hop count [39], C2D achieves traffic savings by reducing the coherence messages being injected into the network.

As discussed in Section 3, processor cores need to notify the home node with two events: *1)* the transaction end and *2)* transactional L1 hit. The notification traffic is already accounted for in the transactional control traffic of Eager-C2D in Figure 9. Here, we show the two types of notification traffic as a percentage of total network traffic in Table 4. On average, the transaction end notification accounts for 1.61% of the traffic, and the L1 hit notifications account for 2.16% of the traffic. The added traffic is dwarfed by the traffic savings of the C2D scheme.

5.3 Reduction in Network Energy

One of the fundamental goals of the C2D technique is to reduce the network energy consumption for conflict detection. Figure 11 presents the normalized energy consumption of the on-chip network (including routers and links). On an average, Eager-C2D achieves an energy saving of 27.1% compared with the distributed conflict detection in the Eager-Base. Lazy-Base has a smaller network energy footprint than Eager-C2D in four workloads. However, the lazy scheme consumes significantly more energy than both eager schemes in Yada and SSCA2. Overall, Eager-C2D consumes 19% less network energy than Lazy-Base. The savings are mainly from the diminishing dynamic energy as

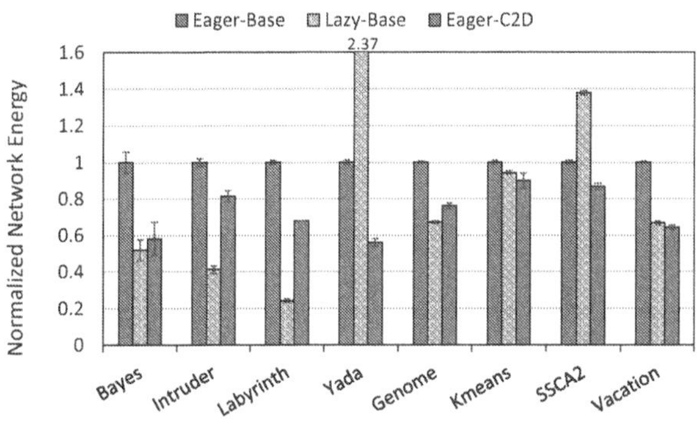

Figure 11: Normalized network energy.

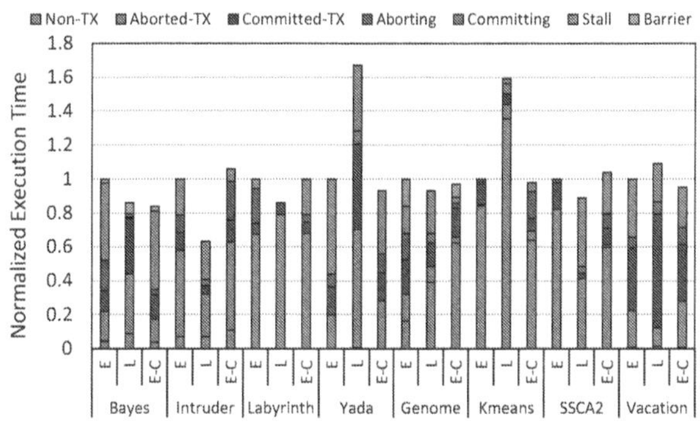

Figure 12: Normalized execution time.

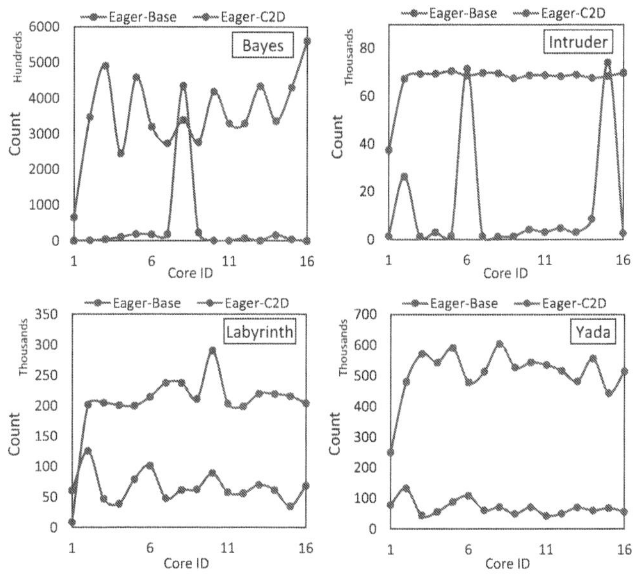

Figure 13: Conflict detections performed at each tile.

C2D reduces the flits being transmitted over the network. Further investigation is needed to see if even more energy savings could be achieved, given that fewer flits could result in substantial idle periods in the routers making power gating feasible for static energy savings.

5.4 Impact on Performance

Figure 12 shows the normalized execution time. On average, the C2D scheme reduces execution time by 2.7%. Six workloads exhibit performance improvement of up to 16.3%. Two workloads (Intruder and SSCA2) are slowed down by around 5%. As discussed, the C2D can avoid transaction aborting caused by unsuccessful requests. However, if the transaction needs to abort eventually, delaying the aborting cause the transaction to either take longer to recover (Intruder) or stall peer transactions longer (SSCA2). The results of these two workloads echo the findings in [10] that early termination of ultimately conflicting transactions could sometimes improve performance. Nonetheless, the majority of the workloads in our evaluation do benefit from the increased concurrency. As a matter of fact, the performance potential of C2D is not fully revealed as the network bandwidth is not a bottleneck in the evaluated workloads. The reduction in network traffic will lead to more significant performance improvements in use cases with intensive core-to-core communication (e.g., highly multithreaded applications and workload consolidation).

The relative performance between Lazy-Base and the two eager systems varies from one workload to another. This variation also leads to the fluctuation of Lazy-Base's network energy consumption (see Figure 11). On average, Lazy-Base is 1.12x slower than Eager-C2D. However, many other dimensions (e.g., version management) beside conflict detection contribute to the performance difference between lazy and eager HTMs [15, 6]. The design tradeoffs within the numerous dimensions are explored in a plethora of research proposals. Our technique focuses on the bandwidth utilization and, is shown to close the bandwidth utilization gap between eager and lazy systems with negligible impact (even a slight improvement) on overall performance.

5.5 Reduction on Conflict Detection

Performing conflict detection is an energy-intensive operation. Moreover, it can stall the instruction retiring [18]. The ongoing execution is further disrupted if subsequent conflict resolution needs to trap into a contention manager. Thus, frequent conflict detection at each tile is undesired. Figure 13 shows the number of conflict detections performed at each tile. We only present results from applications with a medium to high number of contentions. The results from the other applications show a similar trend as that in Yada. As it is observed, C2D can reduce the number of conflict detections to be performed at most tiles. Also, the total number of conflict detections is reduced significantly. Thus, the consolidation of the activity of conflict detection reduces the frequency of the processor cores being distracted to perform conflict detection.

Another important observation from Figure 13 is that the consolidation of conflict detection does not create a performance or traffic bottleneck because no tile performs significantly more conflict detection than in the distributed scheme. In the C2D scheme, the per-home-node conflict detection count is essentially determined by the memory layout of transactional data. Apparently, home nodes of the conflict hot spots will handle more conflicts. For instance, in Bayes and Intruder, 90% of the conflicts that cause transaction aborting occur on three memory blocks [40]. Thus, these two applications have a few home nodes that perform more frequent conflict detection. In comparison, the conflict hot spots in Labyrinth and Yada are more evenly distributed in the memory space, and so are the per-home-node conflict detections.

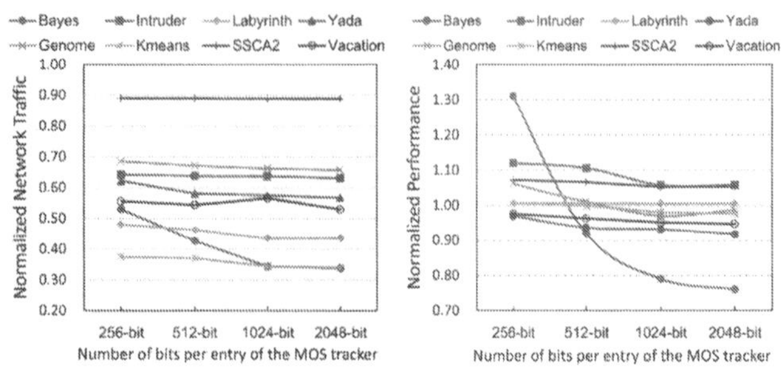

Figure 14: Sensitivity to MOS-Tracker entry size.

5.6 Sensitivity Study

The MOS-Tracker entry size is the bit field size dedicated to tracking the address set of one transaction. The entry size could affect the effectiveness of the C2D scheme as it determines the probability of false positives. In the pointer mode, a larger entry can track more address pointers for a transaction. Thus, the entry is less likely to morph into the imprecise filter mode. In the filter mode, a larger bit field results in fewer conflicts when storing different hash values, thereby lowering the probability of false positives. We conducted a sensitivity analysis of the network traffic as well as performance to varying MOS-Tracker entry size. In this study, the SRAMs are pinned to the filter mode to simulate the worst case scenario (i.e., always imprecise). The results are shown in Figure 12. The values are normalized to Eager-Base.

Regardless of the entry size, Eager-C2D consistently generates less network traffic than the Eager-Base. A majority of the applications see a slight reduction in network traffic when the bit field size increases. The reduction is within 5% except for Bayes which has 19% less traffic when the entry size increases from 256 bits to 2048 bits. The execution time shows a similar sensitivity to the entry size: the performance change is within 7% in all applications but Bayes. The reason why Bayes is sensitive to the MOS-Tracker entry size is that it mainly uses coarse-grain transactions with nearly 150 accesses (up to 3750 accesses) to distinctive cache lines. In fact, transactions in Bayes are much coarser than the transactions in the remaining workloads in the STAMP benchmark. Thus, a small MOS-Tracker entry cannot track the sizable set of addresses with a sufficiently low probability of false positives. As the entry size increases beyond 1024 bits, the traffic and performance are stabilized indicating that a 1024-bit MOS-Tracker entry at each home node is adequate to track the address set of coarse-grain transactions in Bayes. Overall, both the traffic and performance of the evaluated applications are relatively insensitive to the entry size of the MOS-Tracker; however, upcoming applications with coarse-grain transactions will benefit from a larger entry size.

5.7 Hardware Cost Estimation

We generate the 16x16x16bit single-ported SRAM using a commercial memory compiler targeting 65nm TSMC bulk CMOS technology. The SRAM operates at 2GHz and supports power gating. The area of the SRAM array is 14346.9 um^2 and the access time is less than half a cycle. We estimate the area overhead based on the 16-core Rock processor which provides HTM support and is manufactured using 65nm bulk CMOS technology [35]. If The Rock processor augments each of the 16 nodes with two of the 4K-bit SRAMs, it adds a meager 1.16% to the overall area.

6. RELATED WORK

Conflict detection in typical HTM systems. The idealized Unbounded Transactional Memory [2] stores all the transaction information in a single complex data structure. As the logs are shared by all the processors, conflicts can be detected without contacting remote processors. Subroutines are invoked to access the data structure so as to detect conflicts and commit transactions. In comparison, C2D centralizes a minimal set of metadata at the physically distributed home nodes for conflict detection. The metadata management is in hardware.

Chafi et al. [8] propose a scalable lazy HTM design based on the Transactional Coherence and Consistency (TCC) model. Due to continuous transaction execution in the TCC model, the core ownership in the directory is equivalent to transaction ownership. Thus, conflicts can be readily detected at the home node without incurring extra traffic. Our technique offers a similar advantage to eager systems using a conventional coherence and consistency model.

Bobba et al. [5] describe a novel approach that uses tokens to count sharer transactions per memory block. The home node detects a conflict by checking the token count in the directory. The home node does not track the exact identify of the sharer transactions. So, it interrogates remote processors when a conflict is detected. In contrast, the C2D technique tracks the sharer transactions and their relative rank in conflict resolution, thereby avoiding the interrogation when the conflict causes the requestor to stall.

A more common approach is to distribute the transactional bookkeeping as well as the conflict detection logic to individual processors. A family of HTM designs that support in-place update [2, 26, 20, 21] uses the distributive approach and piggybacks onto the coherence protocol to notify processors with potentially conflicting requests. EazyHTM [34] and Pi-TM [27] follows the same approach to detect conflicts eagerly; however, conflict resolution is deferred to the commit phase to preserve more concurrency. Due to the distributive nature of conflict detection, the conflict detection traffic overhead discussed in Section 2 manifests in these designs and, hence, can be mitigated using the proposed C2D technique.

Shriraman et al. [31] describe a hybrid scheme for conflict detection and management. The proposed FlexTM uses per-processor hardware (e.g., signatures, conflict summary table) for transactional bookkeeping. Conflicts are identified and recorded as individual processors receive forwarded L1 requests. FlexTM promotes full flexibility by exposing the hardware mechanisms to the software stack. If integrated into FlexTM, the C2D technique can reduce the bandwidth utilization of the Eager conflict detection mode as the home node directory responds properly to requestors about the conflicts without the need for further contacting the sharer processors in many cases.

Extensive research in HTM has paved the way for commercial implementations. The IBM Blue Gene/Q [36] implements transactional bookkeeping into the ways of L2 cache as the core design cannot be modified. Conflicts are detected at the L2 cache level. However, augmenting L2 blocks for transactional bookkeeping constitutes a considerable cost as well as intricacies in L2 designs. A more recent HTM implementation from IBM [18]adopts a distributve approach for conflict detection. The transactional bookkeeping is done at the L1s, and the system interrogates the L1s for conflict detection. The C2D technique can reduce the network traffic in such a system.

Techniques to reduce HTM traffic. Titos et al. [33] notice that a large fraction of the transactional traffic is wasted due to high contention. Zhao et al. [39] identify the pathological traffic waste due to failed requests and, hence propose a technique to opportunistically filter out requests that are predicted to fail. Unfiltered requests still incur the traffic overheads discussed and addressed in this work. Fung et al. [12] note the significant interconnect traffic to detect conflicts between thousands of transactions in the context of GPGPU. To reduce the traffic, the authors propose a hierarchical scheme that detect intra-warp and inter-warp conflicts in two phases.

Signatures for Transactional Memory. Ceze et al. [7] pioneered the use of hardware signature as a compact representation of a thread's access information. Since then, hardware signatures have been frequently adopted in TM designs [37, 25]. Sanchez et al. [29] explore the design of signatures with a formal analysis model. The authors advocate the use of parallel Bloom signatures that improve area-efficiency with single-ported SRAM. In our technique, the home node uses the parallel Bloom signature to track a transaction's footprint. We extend their model to analyze false positives in the MOS tracker. Choi et al. [11] propose to use a single signature to track all the accesses of a transaction. Their unified signature approach can enlarge the signature coverage without additional area overhead. The MOS tracker also uses a single signature to track a transaction's footprint. However, the home node can distinguish between read and write addresses using the coherence metastate in the directory.

7. CONCLUSION

The on-chip network bandwidth utilization of the conflict detection mechanism is of importance to the performance/joule of HTM-capable microprocessors. In this paper, we found that the traffic overhead of conflict detection accounts for a significant portion of the total network traffic. The root cause of this inefficiency is the distribution of conflict detection capability to individual cores across the entire chip. To reduce the bandwidth utilization of conflict detection, we propose a novel technique to consolidate the conflict detection into the logically central (but physically distributed) home nodes so that a home node can handle conflicts correctly and promptly without initiating further on-chip communication. While full system simulations show that C2D has a negligible impact on performance (1.03x speedup), it dramatically reduces network traffic and can be implemented with a meager area overhead. The consolidation technique, if adopted in the eager conflict detection mechanism, reduces the network traffic by 35%, thereby saving 27% of the network energy.

8. REFERENCES

[1] N. Agarwal, T. Krishna, L.-S. Peh, and N. K. Jha, "Garnet: A Detailed On-chip Network Model inside a Full-System Simulator," in *Procs. of Int'l Symp. on Performance Analysis of Systems and Software*, 2009.

[2] C. S. Ananian, K. Asanovic, B. C. Kuszmaul, C. E. Leiserson, and S. Lie, "Unbounded Transactional Memory," in *Procs. of the 11th Int'l. Symposium on High-Performance Computer Architecture*, 2005.

[3] B. H. Bloom, "Space/time Trade-offs in Hash Coding with Allowable Errors," *Communication ACM*, vol. 13, no. 7, Jul. 1970.

[4] C. Blundell, J. Devietti, E. C. Lewis, and M. M. K. Martin, "Making the Fast Case Common and the Uncommon Case Simple in Unbounded Transactional Memory," in *Procs. of 34th Int'l. Symposium on Computer Architecture*, 2007.

[5] J. Bobba, N. Goyal, M. D. Hill, M. M. Swift, and D. A. Wood, "TokenTM: Efficient Execution of Large Transactions with Hardware Transactional Memory," in *Procs. of the 35th Annual Int'l. Symposium on Computer Architecture*, 2008.

[6] J. Bobba, K. E. Moore, H. Volos, L. Yen, M. D. Hill, M. M. Swift, and D. A. Wood, "Performance Pathologies in Hardware Transactional Memory," in *Procs. of the Int'l. Symposium on Computer Architecture*, 2007.

[7] L. Ceze, J. Tuck, J. Torrellas, and C. Cascaval, "Bulk Disambiguation of Speculative Threads in Multiprocessors," in *Procs. of the 33rd Annual Int'l. Symposium on Computer Architecture*, 2006.

[8] H. Chafi, J. Casper, B. D. Carlstrom, A. McDonald, C. C. Minh, W. Baek, C. Kozyrakis, and K. Olukotun, "A Scalable, Non-Blocking Approach to Transactional Memory," in *Procs. of 13th Int'l. Symposium on High Performance Computer Architecture*, 2007.

[9] L. Chen and T. M. Pinkston, "NoRD: Node-Router Decoupling for Effective Power-Gating of On-Chip Routers," in *Procs. of the 2012 45th Annual IEEE/ACM Int'l. Symposium on Microarchitecture*, 2012.

[10] W. Choi and J. Draper, "Locality-aware Adaptive Grain Signatures for Transactional Memories," in *Parallel Distributed Processing (IPDPS), 2010 IEEE Int'l. Symposium on*, 2010.

[11] W. Choi and J. Draper, "Improving Utilization of Hardware Signatures in Transactional Memory," *Parallel and Distributed Systems, IEEE Transactions on*, vol. 24, no. 11, Nov 2013.

[12] W. W. L. Fung and T. M. Aamodt, "Energy Efficient GPU Transactional Memory via Space-time Optimizations," in *Procs. of the 46th Annual IEEE/ACM Int'l. Symposium on Microarchitecture*, 2013.

[13] A. Gupta and W.-D. Weber, "Cache Invalidation Patterns in Shared-Memory Multiprocessors," *Computers, IEEE Transactions on*, vol. 41, no. 7, Jul 1992.

[14] L. Hammond, B. D. Carlstrom, V. Wong, M. Chen, C. Kozyrakis, and K. Olukotun, "Transactional Coherence and Consistency: Simplifying Parallel Hardware and Software," *IEEE Micro*, vol. 24, no. 6, pp. 92–103, 2004.

[15] T. Harris, A. Cristal, O. Unsal, E. Ayguade, F. Gagliardi, B. Smith, and M. Valero, "Transactional Memory: An Overview," *Micro, IEEE*, vol. 27, no. 3, pp. 8–29, May 2007.

[16] Y. Hoskote, S. Vangal, A. Singh, N. Borkar, and S. Borkar, "A 5-GHz Mesh Interconnect for a TeraFlops Processor," *Micro, IEEE*, vol. 27, no. 5, pp. 51–61, Sept 2007.

[17] J. Howard, S. Dighe, S. Vangal, G. Ruhl, N. Borkar, S. Jain, V. Erraguntla, M. Konow, M. Riepen, M. Gries, G. Droege, T. Lund-Larsen, S. Steibl, S. Borkar, V. De, and R. Van Der Wijngaart, "A 48-core IA-32 Processor in 45 nm CMOS using On-die Message-passing and DVFS for Performance and Power Scaling," *Solid-State Circuits, IEEE Journal of*, vol. 46, no. 1, pp. 173–183, Jan 2011.

[18] C. Jacobi, T. Slegel, and D. Greiner, "Transactional Memory Architecture and Implementation for IBM System z," in *Procs. of the 2012 45th Annual IEEE/ACM Int'l. Symposium on Microarchitecture*, 2012.

[19] A. B. Kahng, B. Li, L.-S. Peh, and K. Samadi, "Orion 2.0: A Fast and Accurate NOC Power and Area Model for Early-stage Design Space Exploration," in *Procs. of the Conference on Design, Automation and Test in Europe*, 2009.

[20] M. Lupon, G. Magklis, and A. Gonzalez, "FASTM: A Log-based Hardware Transactional Memory with Fast Abort Recovery," in *Procs. of the 18th Int'l. Conference on Parallel Architectures and Compilation Techniques*.

[21] M. Lupon, G. Magklis, and A. Gonzalez, "A Dynamically Adaptable Hardware Transactional Memory," in *Procs. of 43th Int'l. Symposium on Microarchitecture*, 2010.

[22] P. S. Magnusson, M. Christensson, J. Eskilson, D. Forsgren, G. Hallberg, J. Hogberg, F. Larsson, A. Moestedt, and B. Werner, "SIMICS: A Full System Simulation Platform," *Computer*, vol. 35, 2002.

[23] M. M. K. Martin, D. J. Sorin, B. M. Beckmann, M. R. Marty, M. Xu, A. R. Alameldeen, K. E. Moore, M. D. Hill, and D. A. Wood, "Multifacet's General Execution-driven Multiprocessor Simulator (GEMS) Toolset," *SIGARCH Comput. Archit. News*, vol. 33, November 2005.

[24] C. C. Minh, J. Chung, C. Kozyrakis, and K. Olukotun, "STAMP: Stanford Transactional Applications for Multi-Processing," in *Procs. of Int'l. Symposium on Workload Characterization*, 2008.

[25] C. C. Minh, M. Trautmann, J. Chung, A. McDonald, N. Bronson, J. Casper, C. Kozyrakis, and K. Olukotun, "An Effective Hybrid Transactional Memory System with Strong Isolation Guarantees," in *Procs. of the 34th Annual Int'l. Symposium on Computer Architecture*, 2007.

[26] K. E. Moore, J. Bobba, M. J. Moravan, M. D. Hill, and D. A. Wood, "LogTM: Log-based Transactional Memory," in *Procs. of 12th Int'l. Symposium on High Performance Computer Architecture*, 2006.

[27] A. Negi, R. Titos-Gil, M. E. Acacio, J. M. Garcia, and P. Stenström, "Pi-TM: Pessimistic Invalidation for Scalable Lazy Hardware Transactional Memory," in *Procs. of the 18th Int'l. Symposium on High Performance Computer Architecture*, 2012.

[28] R. Rajwar and J. R. Goodman, "Transactional Lock-free Execution of Lock-based Programs," *SIGARCH Comput. Archit. News*, vol. 30, no. 5.

[29] D. Sanchez, L. Yen, M. D. Hill, and K. Sankaralingam, "Implementing Signatures for Transactional Memory," in *Procs. of the 40th Annual IEEE/ACM Int'l. Symposium on Microarchitecture*, 2007.

[30] K. Sawada, T. Sakurai, K. Nogami, T. Shirotori, T. Takayanagi, T. Iizuka, T. Maeda, J. Matsunaga, H. Fuji, K. Maeguchi, K. Kobayashi, T. Ando, Y. Hayakashi, A. Miyoshi, and K. Sato, "A 32 Kbyte Integrated Cache Memory," *Solid-State Circuits, IEEE Journal of*, vol. 24, no. 4, pp. 881–888, Aug 1989.

[31] A. Shriraman, S. Dwarkadas, and M. L. Scott, "Flexible Decoupled Transactional Memory Support," in *Procs. of the 35th Annual Int'l. Symposium on Computer Architecture*, 2008.

[32] P. Stenström, M. Brorsson, and L. Sandberg, "An Adaptive Cache Coherence Protocol Optimized for Migratory Sharing," in *Procs. of the 20th Annual Int'l. Symposium on Computer Architecture*, 1993.

[33] J. Titos, M. Acacio, and J. Garcia, "Characterization of Conflicts in Log-based Transactional Memory (LogTM)," in *Parallel, Distributed and Network-Based Processing, 2008. PDP 2008. 16th Euromicro Conference on*, 2008.

[34] S. Tomić, C. Perfumo, C. Kulkarni, A. Armejach, A. Cristal, O. Unsal, T. Harris, and M. Valero, "EazyHTM: Eager-Lazy Hardware Transactional Memory," in *Procs. of the 42Nd Annual IEEE/ACM Int'l. Symposium on Microarchitecture*, 2009.

[35] M. Tremblay and S. Chaudhry, "A Third-generation 65nm 16-core 32-thread plus 32-scout-thread CMT SPARC Processor," in *Solid-State Circuits Conference, 2008. ISSCC 2008. Digest of Technical Papers. IEEE Int'l.*, 2008.

[36] A. Wang, M. Gaudet, P. Wu, J. N. Amaral, M. Ohmacht, C. Barton, R. Silvera, and M. Michael, "Evaluation of Blue Gene/Q Hardware Support for Transactional Memories," in *Procs. of the 21st Int'l. Conference on Parallel Architectures and Compilation Techniques*, 2012.

[37] L. Yen, J. Bobba, M. R. Marty, K. E. Moore, H. Volos, M. D. Hill, M. M. Swift, and D. A. Wood, "LogTM-SE: Decoupling Hardware Transactional Memory from Caches," in *Procs. of 13th Int'l. Symposium on High Performance Computer Architecture*, 2007.

[38] R. M. Yoo, C. J. Hughes, K. Lai, and R. Rajwar, "Performance Evaluation of Intel® Transactional Synchronization Extensions for High-Performance Computing," in *Procs. of Int'l. Conference for High Performance Computing, Networking, Storage and Analysis*, 2013.

[39] L. Zhao, W. Choi, L. Chen, and J. Draper, "In-network Traffic Regulation for Transactional Memory," in *Procs. of Int'l. Symp. on High Performance Computer Architecture*, 2013.

[40] L. Zhao, W. Choi, and J. Draper, "SEL-TM: Selective Eager-Lazy Management for Increased Concurrency in Transactional Memory," in *Procs. of IPDPS*, 2012.

DeSTM: Harnessing Determinism in STMs for Application Development

Kaushik Ravichandran
Georgia Institute of Technology
Atlanta, Georgia, USA
kaushikr@gatch.edu

Ada Gavrilovska
Georgia Institute of Technology
Atlanta, Georgia, USA
ada@cc.gatech.edu

Santosh Pande
Georgia Institute of Technology
Atlanta, Georgia, USA
santosh@cc.gatech.edu

ABSTRACT

Non-determinism has long been recognized as one of the key challenges which restrict parallel programmer productivity by complicating several phases of application development. While Software Transactional Memory (STM) systems have greatly improved the productivity of programmers developing parallel applications in a host of areas they still exhibit non-deterministic behavior leading to decreased productivity. While determinism in parallel applications which use traditional synchronization primitives (such as locks) has been relatively well studied, its interplay with STMs has not. In this paper we present DeSTM, a deterministic STM, which allows programmers to leverage determinism through the implementation, debugging and testing phases of application development.

In this work we first adapt techniques which introduce determinism in applications which use traditional synchronization (such as locks) to work in conjunction with certain STMs. As one would expect, this does lead to performance degradation over a non-deterministic execution. Next we present, DeSTM, which uses novel techniques exploiting the properties of these STMs to dramatically improve the performance of deterministic executions. Further, DeSTM allows programmers to randomly change the deterministic schedule in a controlled fashion giving programmers access to a wide variety of execution schedules during application development.

We demonstrate our approach on the STAMP benchmark suite. We first study the overheads that determinism introduces in STM applications and then demonstrate how DeSTM is able to improve performance of deterministic execution significantly, by over 50% in some applications and on average by about 35%. DeSTM also actually helped us detect, what we believe is a bug, in one of the benchmarks. Further, our approach is programmer friendly requiring no changes to application code.

PACT'14, August 24–27, 2014, Edmonton, AB, Canada.

http://dx.doi.org/10.1145/2628071.2628094.

Categories and Subject Descriptors

D.1.3 [**Programming Techniques**]: Concurrent Programming—*Parallel programming*

Keywords

STM; Software Transactional Memory; Determinism

1. INTRODUCTION

Software Transactional Memory (STM) [30, 16] systems are becoming increasingly popular as an effective and programmer friendly solution to writing concurrent code. STMs present programmers with an atomic construct which can be used to wrap accesses to shared data. In these atomic sections (also known as *transactions*) reads and writes logically occur at a single instance of time. STMs operate by speculatively running these atomic sections in parallel and monitoring their runtime execution for memory conflicts. A conflict causes the STM to perform an abort, rollback and retry on one of the transactions, leading to a correct parallel execution and the illusion of atomicity. Memory accesses are logged behind the scenes to perform rollbacks.

STMs side-step many of the issues that occur in lock based code such as deadlock, livelock, lock placement, data consistency, atomicity and priority inversion. In addition, the atomic interface that STMs use greatly enhances the conceptual understanding of multi-threaded code. Transactions also have the property of being composable which makes them easier to reason about. Another advantage STMs bring to the table is their speculative behavior. This results in increased parallelism since threads do not need to wait to access a resource, allowing different threads to modify distinct parts of a data structure in parallel resulting in performance improvements. STMs have been found suitable for parallelizing many applications, providing performance gains with minimal programmer effort [6].

However, one of the key challenges which restrict parallel programmer productivity is the non-determinism of parallel code. While STMs have reduced the complexity of development of parallel code when compared with lock based code they are still non-deterministic in nature leading to decreased programmer productivity. Non-determinism describes the phenomenon where code behaves differently during different executions despite there being no non-determinism in the inputs.

Serial code is inherently deterministic in nature and is the programming model that most programmers are accustomed to. Deterministic behavior is also much easier to reason

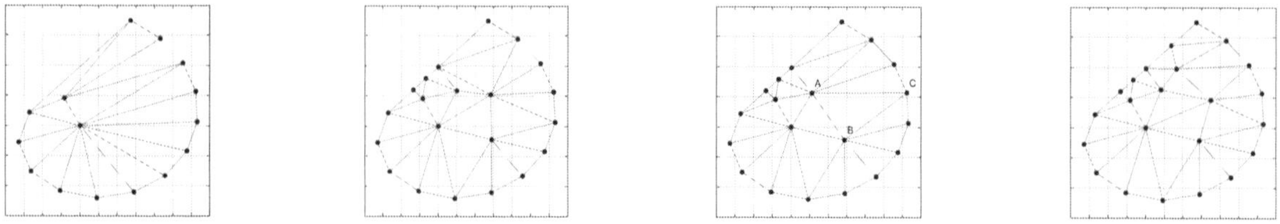

(a) Input Mesh (b) Serial Output (c) Parallel Output 1 (d) Parallel Output 2

Figure 1: Input and Output Meshes for the *yada* Benchmark

about. In parallel applications, however, non-determinism arises due to the parallel application itself and/or due to the parallel machine and its runtime. The difficulties that non-determinism introduces has long been recognized [32]. STMs further amplify these issues by being speculative in nature.

There has been growing interest in applying determinism to parallel applications with several systems discussing a wide variety of techniques [26, 2, 21, 23]. Prior work, has however primarily focused on introducing determinism into parallel applications which use traditional synchronization primitives such as locks. With one of the major goals of STMs being increased programmer productivity, they serve as a prime candidate for the inclusion of determinism thereby further strengthening their appeal.

While there is a growing consensus that determinism is important, there is still disagreement as to what extent of determinism is desired (and worth paying for). There are in fact a wide range of types of determinism ranging from applications which are just data-race free to those which use synchronous parallelism (parallelism proceeding in lock step). A middle ground which balances between these extremes, that is often settled on, is known as *Internal Determinism* [4] and is what we adopt as well. *Internal Determinism* requires key aspects of intermediate steps of the application to be deterministic.

Another type of determinism is *External Determinism.* Applications which exhibit this type of determinism are only required to produce the same output when run on the same input (execution may vary internally, even at key points, as long as the output is the same) and are said to be *determinate.*

Internal Determinism, the type we adopt, has many advantages. In addition to leading to external determinism [27], it also provides many benefits such as ease of development, ease of reasoning about code, ease of debugging and ease of testing [4]. Internal Determinism requires that key intermediate steps during execution be deterministic. In an STM execution these are transactional commits and aborts and hence we provide determinism at this granularity.

We were able to classify the STAMP benchmark suite [6] into *Externally Deterministic* and *Externally Non-deterministic* applications, as shown in Table 1. In *bayes* the learn score changes between runs. In *kmeans* the clustering varies between runs. In *labyrinth* the paths generated varies and in *yada* the resulting triangulation varies between runs. Note that each of the varying results is correct and acceptable.

Irrespective of whether STM applications exhibit *external* determinism, all STM applications inevitably exhibit *internal* non-determinism. Similar to the non-deterministic

Externally Non-deterministic	Externally Deterministic
bayes	genome
kmeans	intruder
labyrinth	ssca2
yada	vacation

Table 1: Classification of STAMP Benchmarks

order of critical section execution in parallel applications which use traditional synchronization primitives (such as locks), the order of executing transactions is highly non-deterministic. It is these differences in ordering that lead to non-deterministic behavior [1]. One could in fact also argue, that the STM notion of *aborts* introduces yet another source of non-determinism into an already crowded landscape. Aborts ensure correct STM operation by rolling back offending transactions when atomicity constraints have been violated. Hence, while the execution of an instruction in a critical section using locks guarantees visibility of its effects (in some cases at the end of the critical section), no such guarantee can be made for an instruction in an STM transaction due to the notion of aborts. In fact, its behavior in subsequent attempts may be completely different due to intervening commits. Its effects will be made visible only after a successful commit (after all aborts), introducing complications during implementation and debugging [37, 14]. Introducing determinism eases the burden on the programmer significantly.

Let's take a look at how non-determinism manifests itself in a real world application. Consider the *yada* benchmark from the STAMP STM suite. The *yada* benchmark implements Ruppert's algorithm for Delaunay mesh refinement [29], a technique for generating unstructured meshes of triangles which satisfy certain guarantees such as bounds on angles. It is not *externally deterministic* since it does not produce the same output every time it is run (however, each output is correct and acceptable). It is often used in interpolation, rendering, terrain databases, geographic information systems and also to find solutions for partial differential equations by the finite element method. Figure 1 shows the input mesh (Figure 1a), the output mesh during serial execution (Figure 1b) and two sample output meshes during parallel executions (Figure 1c and Figure 1d). Non-determinism complicates application development phases:

Implementation Programmers typically follow an iterative process where they write a piece of code, make sure it works correctly and then loop back continuing the implementation process. This approach implicitly assumes determinism in

[1]If the order in which the operations execute changes the result then this leads to *external non-determinism* in addition to *internal non-determinism*

intermediate execution stages. While this is a given when writing serial code, it does not hold for parallel code. Figure 1b shows the serial output. This serial output as well as the internal steps used to obtain it never change, irrespective of how many times it is run [2]. Non-determinism throws a wrench in the iterative implementation process.

Debugging Consider two sample output meshes obtained during parallel execution (Figure 1c and Figure 1d). Consider the triangle marked ABC in Figure 1c. If the application encounters a bug while generating triangle ABC, a typical debugging cycle includes running the application a few times and gathering relevant information about that particular triangle. With non-deterministic execution subsequent executions might not even contain that triangle (as can be seen in Figure 1d and even Figure 1b)! This severely effects debugging.

Testing Testing is often performed by comparing output with a *golden* (correct) output. As one can see from the output meshes in Figure 1 there is no correct output that can be used for comparison in this situation. This hampers testing of code.

Introducing determinism into STMs helps programmers. In this work we first adapt techniques which introduce determinism in applications which use traditional synchronization to work in conjunction with certain STMs (see Section 3.1 for applicability). As one would expect, introducing determinism does lead to performance degradation over a non-deterministic execution. Next we present, DeSTM, which uses novel techniques exploiting the properties of these STMs to dramatically improve the performance of deterministic executions. Determinism typically imposes a fixed execution schedule. However, DeSTM also allows programmers to randomly change the deterministic schedule in a controlled fashion giving programmers access to a wide variety of execution schedules during development. We use TL2 [10], a popular STM framework to demonstrate our approach.

We evaluate our approach using the STAMP benchmark suite. We first study the overheads that determinism introduces in STM applications and then demonstrate how DeSTM is able to improve performance of deterministic execution significantly, by over 50% in some applications and on average by about 35%. DeSTM also actually helped us detect, what we believe is a bug, in the *vacation* benchmark (this bug pattern helped us identify a similar issue in another benchmark where it manifests itself at lower compiler optimization levels). Further, our approach is programmer friendly and does not require any changes to application code.

The remainder of this paper is organized as follows. In Section 2 we discuss the classical double barrier approach to determinism. In Section 3 we discuss some of the general ideas behind determinism in STMs. In Section 4 we discuss how to adapt the classical double barrier technique to STMs. In Section 5 we present DeSTM. In Section 6 we present a comprehensive evaluation (as well as a discussion on the issue in the *vacation* benchmark). We present related work in Section 7 and discuss future work and conclude in Section 8.

[2]Certain algorithms like random algorithms exhibit varying behavior on each run. However, these are also typically still controlled by a seed or other external factors which should be quantified as *inputs*.

2. DETERMINISM IN MULTI-THREADED CODE

Double Barrier Technique.

The classical approach to introducing determinism into a multi-threaded application which uses traditional synchronization primitives (such as locks) involves using a turn based algorithm coupled with double barriers [21]. This gives each thread a turn in which it can make modifications to shared state as shown in Figure 2. Turns are typically implemented using a token passing algorithm. Ownership of the token indicates that the thread may make modifications after which it passes the token to the next thread. The execution is divided into two phases: the *Parallel Phase* and the *Serial Phase* with each Parallel Phase being called a *round.*

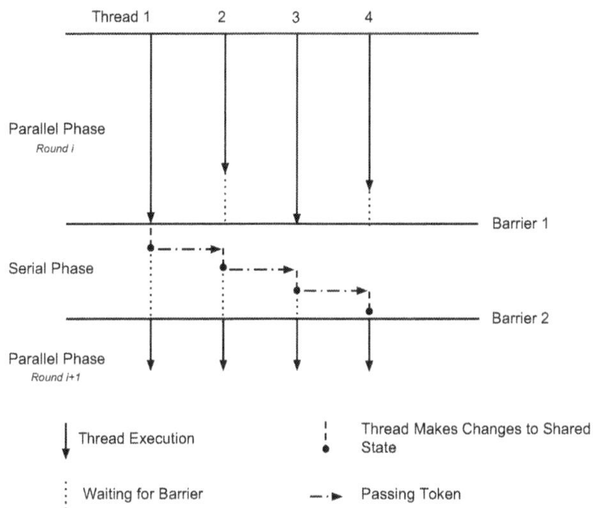

Figure 2: The Double Barrier Technique

Parallel Phase.

In this phase changes made by individual threads are contained or isolated in some manner (one technique is to convert threads into isolated processes [21]). This ensures that any modifications by threads to shared state are not visible to other threads in the parallel phase. Note, threads execute freely without any synchronization in this phase.

Threads continue running until they reach Barrier 1 (the first barrier). The placement of Barrier 1 varies between implementations (systems such as Dthreads [21] use synchronization boundaries such as barriers and locks). Once threads reach Barrier 1 they switch over to the Serial Phase.

Serial Phase.

In this phase the token passing algorithm gives each thread a turn to make its changes to shared state after which it passes the token to the next thread in a round robin fashion and proceeds to wait at Barrier 2 (the second barrier). Turns ensures that all changes to shared state are made in a deterministic order and the barriers ensure that changes do not effect execution of the Parallel Phase. Once all threads reach Barrier 2 they then begin the next *round* of the Parallel Phase.

Section 4 discusses how to adapt this to STMs.

3. DETERMINISM IN STMS

3.1 Applicability and Limitations

There are a wide variety of STM designs and implementations. In this work we focus on introducing determinism into a popular subset of STMs which use global clocks to provide opacity and commit time locking (Section 4.3 in [16] provides an excellent description of this class of STMs). Commit time locking systems use lazy versioning and make changes to shared state only during commit. Lazy versioning systems buffer updates until commit time and are also referred to as deferred update or write-back systems. A number of STMs employ this design including TL2, DeuceSTM (CTL configuration) [19], SMV [28] and TinySTM (CTL configuration) [34]. Our approach can not be applied to other types of STMs which do not use global clocks such as InvalSTM [15] (uses invalidation). Further, our approach to determinism is applicable to STM applications which use well-formed code (that read/write to shared state within transactions). We built our approaches on top of TL2, a popular STM framework.

3.2 STM Recap

Before moving on we quickly recap how this class of STM infrastructures work (for a more detailed description see Section 4.3 in [16]). At the start of a transaction, the STM samples the *global clock* and stores it in a per-transaction variable (typically called the *read version*). Within a transaction, reads are logged and occur from shared memory itself (if not previously written to by the same transaction) and writes to shared memory are logged (in a buffer). After the execution of the transaction, the STM attempts to commit any changes, with its *Commit Protocol*. The commit protocol checks if any other threads have modified any locations read to or written by this transaction (by comparing the current version number of the memory locations with the *read version*). If the locations have been modified, it is a *conflict* and the STM aborts the transaction and retries. Such a situation will arise if any of these memory locations have been modified after the transaction has started. If all the memory locations are unmodified, the transaction locks all of them and commits by writing the changes from its buffer into shared memory, updating the memory locations' version numbers and by incrementing the *global clock*. After a successful commit of a transaction the thread continues its execution past the atomic construct.

3.3 Internal Determinism

As discussed in Section 1 *internal determinism* requires key aspects of intermediate steps of the application to be deterministic. For STM applications the key steps are transactional commits and aborts. We provide determinism at this level.

The *trace* An execution of an STM application generates a certain commit/abort order. A commit can be represented by the string T<thread_number>-C and an abort can be represented by the string T<thread_number>-A. A sorted sequence of these strings by time is referred to as the *trace*. For example, T1-C:T2-C:T1-C:T2-A describes 2 threads with 3 commits and 1 abort between them. For STM applications which use our deterministic framework this trace is unique. The programmer can also choose to output this trace to aid development.

3.4 Invariants

During STM application development, the number of commits and aborts along with other statistics are typically output at the end of an execution. These numbers vary significantly from run to run in a typical execution. However, by introducing determinism into the execution, by virtue of having a unique *trace*, the number of commits and aborts that occur *must* be constant across different runs, hence becoming invariant. This extra piece of information serves as an additional tool to help programmers identify potential issues since varying counts in a deterministic execution point to a bug.

In fact, once we introduced determinism into applications from the STAMP suite we observed that for the *vacation* benchmark, the commit and abort counts varied across runs. This quickly lead us to find, what we believe is a bug, in the actual benchmark code (see Section 6.5 for a discussion).

3.5 Non-determinism due to Memory Conflicts

There can be unusual sources of non-determinism in STMs which need to be removed. For example, consider the mechanism used to detect conflicts. While different implementations use different mechanisms to implement conflict detection, TL2 maintains versioned write locks for memory locations which indicate whether a location is locked as well as a version number to detect conflicts (as discussed in Section 3.2). Memory locations are mapped to a limited number of versioned write locks through a hash function, ensuring that the number of locks needed is modest. Detecting conflicts using this technique can sometimes lead to false conflicts. That is, if the addresses of A and B map to the same versioned write lock (through the hash function), two concurrent transactions one of which operates on A and the other on B will conflict despite not actually conflicting with each other, a false conflict. A false conflict, however, also introduces non-determinism. Let's see why.

While the hash function itself is deterministic the memory locations that serve as input to the hash function are not. Address Space Layout Randomization (ASLR) is a security technique which randomly arranges the positions of key data areas in the application (including the stack and heap) in the process's virtual address space on each run. This causes the virtual memory addresses used in each run to be different.

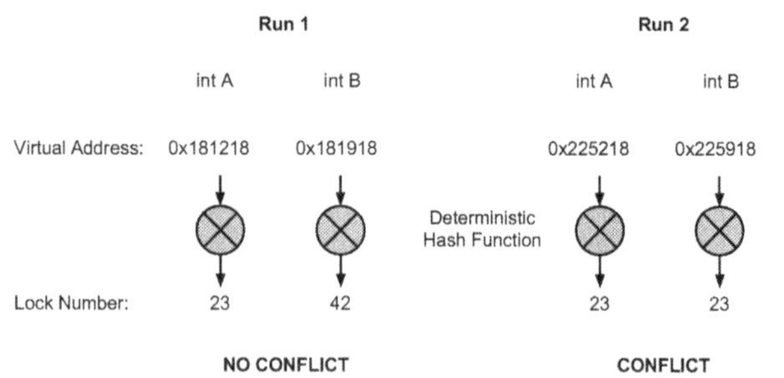

Figure 3: The Effects of ASLR on STM Conflict Detection

Figure 3 depicts the scenario where concurrent accesses to two integers A and B results in a false conflict in one case and does not result in a conflict in another. This causes one of the transactions in Run 2 to abort while these particular accesses will not cause either transaction in Run 1 to abort. This leads to different traces and non-deterministic execution.

In our prototype implementation we solved this problem by turning ASLR off [3] [4]. Indeed, ASLR improves security by protecting against certain buffer overflow attacks which our approach would be vulnerable to. A permanent solution to this problem would involve developing an ASLR aware hash for STMs (potentially using differences from the start addresses of memory segments) and is outside the scope of this paper.

Depending on the underlying STM implementation other sources of non-determinism such as non-deterministic wait loops, non-deterministic counter and version number updates also need to be disabled.

4. DOUBLE BARRIER TECHNIQUE FOR STMS

We now discuss how to adapt the classical double barrier technique (Section 2) to these STM systems. To use the double barrier technique we first need to provide isolation to different threads while they are running in the Parallel Phase. While previous techniques have often developed specialized mechanisms (for example by converting threads into isolated processes [21]), the STMs we consider (Section 3.1), naturally provide complete isolation through their atomic constructs. All modifications made to shared data are automatically isolated from other running transactions, while still providing parallelism making them especially suitable for deterministic executions.

The start of the commit protocol of a transaction provides a convenient location to place Barrier 1, switch over to the Serial Phase and begin token passing. This forces a thread to wait for the token in order to begin its commit protocol. Once it owns the token it executes its commit protocol completely and then passes the token to the next thread in a round robin fashion. The next thread then gets a chance to execute its commit protocol. This causes threads to take turns modifying the shared state in a deterministic fashion. Recall, that modifications to shared state are made only during the commit protocol. A successful commit entails locking all modified memory locations, writing the changes from the local buffer, updating their version numbers and incrementing the *global clock*. Note, that at the end of the commit protocol a transaction does not necessarily commit its changes to memory but can also abort if it finds changes to memory it has used which violate its atomicity constraints. However, notice that whether a commit or an abort occurs is in fact deterministic. This is because a thread begins its commit protocol only when it is the token owner, implying that threads before it have completed their respective commit protocols resulting in a deterministic memory state. Barrier 2 is placed at the end of the commit protocol. This ensures that threads can not continue executing before all transactions finish updating their changes to shared state.

Figure 4 depicts this technique. This approach leads to *both* an internally and externally deterministic execution. As one would expect this does slow down execution time when compared to a non-deterministic execution (see Section 6 for an evaluation). In TL2, we implemented these barriers using pthread barriers.

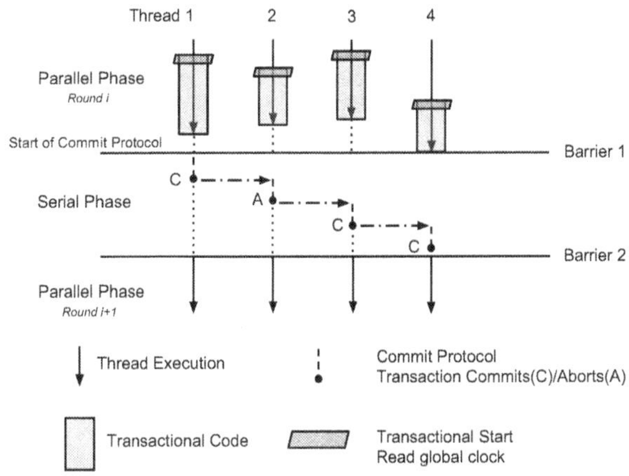

Figure 4: The Double Barrier Technique

5. DESTM

We now present DeSTM, which improves performance of deterministic execution significantly by exploiting properties of these STMs.

Notice in Figure 4 that Thread 1 has to wait for all threads to arrive before it can begin its commit protocol. This requirement was put in place to ensure that changes to shared state are not made while other threads are executing in the Parallel Phase. However, by using this STM model (Section 3.2) it is in fact safe to commit changes while other threads are still executing. Let's see why.

Consider the situation in Figure 4 where Thread 1 writes to memory location z in its transaction. These writes are logged by the STM into a buffer. Let us also assume that Thread 2 is writing to the same memory location z in its transaction. Under the double barrier technique, changes made by Thread 1 will be committed to shared memory during its commit protocol. When Thread 2 executes its commit protocol it will observe these changes (by observing the version number on the location's lock) and abort.

However, these STMs also in fact perform the same operation (checking version number on a location's lock) at every memory read and write during execution of the transaction itself (in addition to the checks in the commit protocol). This allows it to detect atomicity violations early and abort instead of waiting until the commit protocol to detect the violation and abort. Hence, if we allow Thread 1 to commit changes before all threads reach Barrier 1 it is actually safe. At most, this will only cause Thread 2 to abort its transaction early in the Parallel Phase itself instead of during its commit protocol in the Serial Phase. Both possibilities still always cause an abort leading to an *internally* and *externally* deterministic execution.

Note, to maintain determinism we still need to pass a token between different threads to maintain ordering. This allows us to relax the requirement of having threads wait at Barrier 1 to begin their commit protocol but rather allow them to begin as soon as they are token owners.

This might suggest that we can get rid of both the barriers entirely and allow a thread to commit when it has the token. However, this is not the case. Let us examine this situation

[3]Several techniques can be used to turn off ASLR. For example via the ADDR_NO_RANDOMIZE personality flag or via the *setarch* linux command

[4]GDB also turns off ASLR to aid debugging

in more detail and see what happens when we try to remove each of the barriers.

5.1 Removing Barrier 1

Hypothetically removing Barrier 1, let us assume that the only constraint to start the commit protocol is the ownership of the token. Consider two Threads (1 and 2) running in the Parallel Phase (both in the same round, *Round i*), the first one executing transaction X and the second executing transaction Y. Thread 1 owns the token which it will pass it to the next thread, Thread 2, when it completes its commit protocol. Figure 5 depicts two possible outcomes in this scenario.

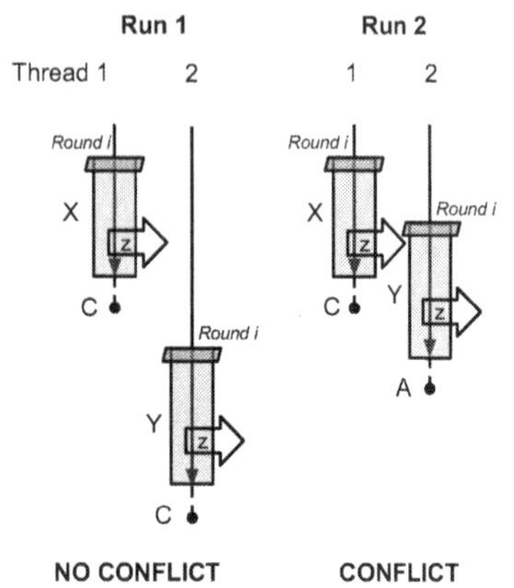

Thread 1 is the token owner and passes it to Thread 2 once done

Figure 5: Effect of Removing Barrier 1

Let's say one of the variables that both these transactions read and write is, say z. In *Run 1* Thread 1 finds that it owns the token and hence commences its commit protocol on transaction X and commits successfully. After it commits, Thread 2 begins the execution of its transaction Y. In this case, despite the fact that it is reading and writing to the same variable z, since transaction Y starts (reads the current *global clock*) after transaction X commits there is no conflict (since it is reading from the latest value) allowing Thread 2 to commit transaction Y successfully.

Consider an alternative ordering, in *Run 2*. In this situation, Thread 2 begins the execution of its transaction Y *prior* to Thread 1's commit of transaction X. Now, since z is being modified in between the execution of transaction Y, transaction Y will abort (either early during a read/write or during the commit protocol). In effect, this lack of ordering constraints introduces non-deterministic behavior. To solve this problem we can add a constraint:

Constraint 1.

A transaction may begin its commit protocol when it owns the token ***and only*** *after every other transaction has started in that round (i.e. after each has read the current global clock).*

Constraint 1 solves the race condition of whether other transactions have started in a round, leading to a deterministic execution while still being significantly relaxed over having a complete barrier, Barrier 1.

In our implementation built on TL2, Constraint 1 is implemented by using a synchronized start counter on a per round basis. After a transaction successfully starts, it increments this counter. When a transaction wants to commit it first ensures that all threads have started by waiting until the count is equal to the number of running threads (taking into consideration new threads starting and threads ending).

5.2 Removing Barrier 2

Barrier 2 makes every thread wait after the execution of its commit protocol for every other thread to complete its commit protocol. Considering that the STM is protecting reads and writes, would removing Barrier 2 continue to provide determinism? After all, threads would still need to wait for the token to begin their commit protocol for the next round. However, removing Barrier 2 entirely does not lead to a deterministic execution. Let's see why.

Hypothetically removing Barrier 2, consider two threads running in the Parallel Phase, with Thread 1 executing Transaction X in *Round* i and Thread 2 executing Transaction Y in *Round* $i-1$. This can happen after Thread 1 has completed its execution of the previous round and has moved on to the current round while Thread 2 is still working on a transaction in the previous round. Note, that in this situation Thread 2 is still the token owner as it has not yet completed execution of Transaction Y in *Round* $i-1$. Figure 6 depicts two possible outcomes in this scenario.

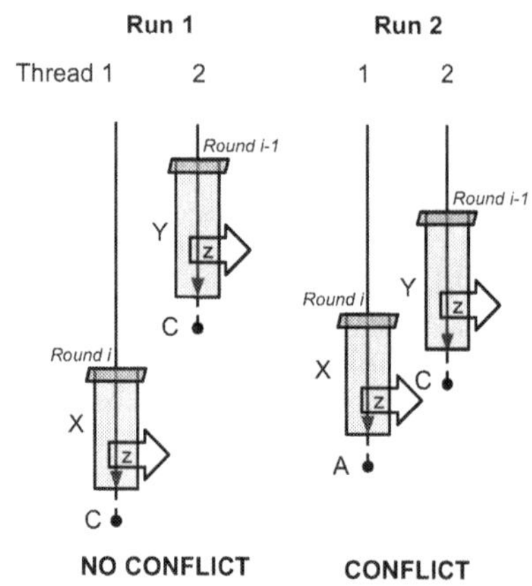

Thread 2 is the token owner in the previous round and passes to Thread 1 once done

Figure 6: Effect of Removing Barrier 2

Similar to the previous example, let's say one of the variables that both these transactions read and write is z. Thread 2 finishes the execution of Transaction Y in *Round* $i-1$ and passes the token to Thread 1. In *Run 1*, Thread 1 happens to start (reads the current *global clock*) its transaction after Thread 2 has committed its transaction in the previous round. In this situation there is no conflict. However, in *Run 2*, Thread 1 happens to start the transaction *prior* to Thread 2 commiting transaction Y. Hence, when Thread 1 attempts to commit transaction X it will see that the value of z has been modified since it started leading to an abort (either early during a read/write or during the commit protocol). The possibility of these two outcomes leads to non-determinism. To solve this problem we can add a constraint:

Constraint 2.

A transaction may start ***only*** *after every other transaction in the previous round has completed its commit protocol.*

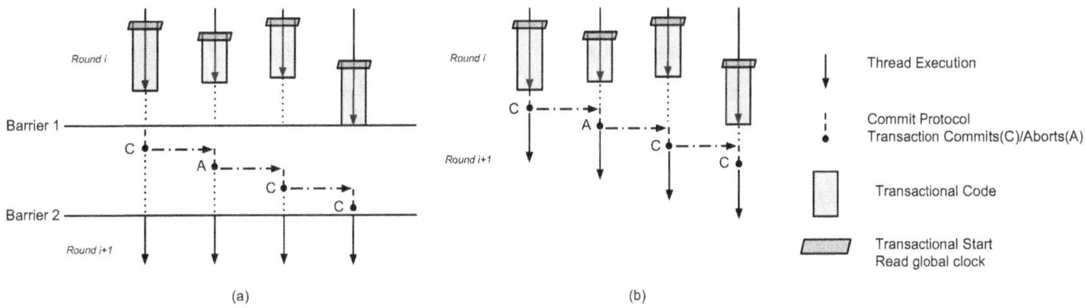

Figure 7: Comparison Between the Two Techniques

Constraint 2 solves the race condition between transactions in the previous round and the current round, leading to a deterministic execution while still being significantly relaxed over having a complete barrier, Barrier 2.

In our implementation built on TL2, Constraint 2 is implemented by using a synchronized commit protocol counter on a per round basis which threads wait on to start a transaction. Once set by the last thread in the previous round (taking into consideration new threads starting and threads ending), threads pass through this check.

Constraint 1 and 2 coupled with the token passing algorithm are sufficient to guarantee a deterministic execution. Constraint 1 and Constraint 2 replace Barrier 1 and Barrier 2. These constraints are very relaxed when compared to the requirements that full barriers impose. Barrier 1 requires all threads to complete execution of a transaction before any of them can start the commit protocol, whereas Constraint 1 is considerably more flexible. Barrier 2 requires each thread to wait at the end of its commit protocol for all other threads to complete their commit protocols before it can continue. Constraint 2, is again, considerably more flexible than this.

Figure 7 compares the two execution models. Figure 7(a) shows the execution of 4 threads executing transactions using the double barrier technique adapted to STMs and Figure 7(b) shows the same execution under DeSTM. We can clearly see that removing the two barriers and replacing them with more flexible constraints leads to significantly improved execution time in *Round i*.

5.3 Randomizing the Execution Schedule

Token passing follows a round robin approach, being passed from Thread i to Thread $(i+1)$ (wrapping around). Figure 8 presents the pseudocode. The *next_token_owner* array contains the next thread that each thread should pass the token to (For example, *next_token_owner*[2] = 3 implies Thread 2 will pass the token to Thread 3). Note, for this discussion thread indices are 0 based.

Under such a scheme the token always passes in a round robin fashion (Figure 9(a)). Each round uses the same pattern. This leads to a single deterministic execution schedule.

To expose other deterministic schedules to the programmer, DeSTM provides a flag which can be used to randomize the *next_token_owner* array for every round. However, a simple approach of just randomizing the array does not work. Consider the randomized *next_token_owner* array shown in Figure 9(b). Despite the array being randomized the passing pattern produced by this randomization has *multiple cycles*, between Thread 0 and 3 as well between Thread 1 and 2.

```
// Stores the current token owner.
int token_owner;

// Stores next thread each thread passes token to.
// For example: next_token_owner[2] = 3;
// Implies that thread 2 will pass the token to thread 3.
int next_token_owner[NUM_THREADS];

// Initialize with a round robin pattern.
initialize() {
  for (i = 0; i < NUM_THREADS; ++i) {
    next_token_owner[i] = (i + 1) % NUM_THREADS;
  }
}

// Look up the next_token_owner array and pass the token.
pass_token() {
  lock token_owner;
  token_owner = next_token_owner[thread_id];
  unlock token_owner;
}
```

Figure 8: Token Passing Mechanism

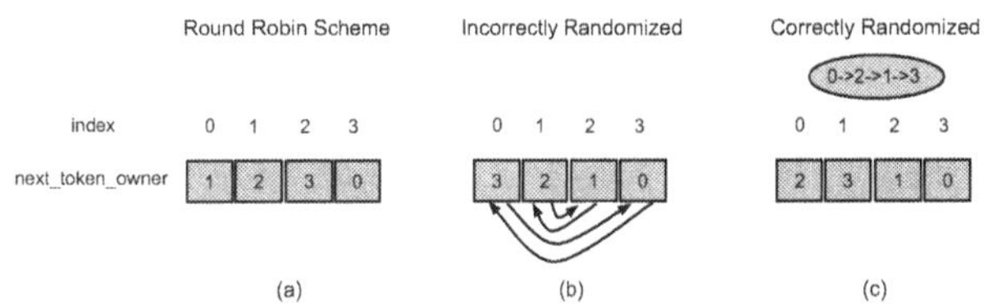

Figure 9: Randomizing the *next_token_owner* Array

To generate a correctly randomized *next_token_owner* array, DeSTM first generates a random *Passing String* (shown in the green oval in Figure 9(c)). This can be generated by a simple random permutation of a string containing all thread identifiers. The *next_token_owner* is then generated from this string. This ensures that the *next_token_owner* array is correct, containing only a single cycle with every identifier. Generating a new *Passing String* every round allows DeSTM to generate a new execution schedule each round [5].

The randomization is controlled by a single random *SEED*. The programmer can modify the random order provided by varying the *SEED*. This randomization technique allows the runtime to expose numerous execution schedules for use during implementation, debugging and testing.

6. EVALUATION

In this section we present a comprehensive evaluation of the double barrier approach and DeSTM. Our prototype im-

[5] Due to a limitation in our current implementation every passing string we generate must begin with the first thread identifier (Thread 0), however the rest of the passing string is random.

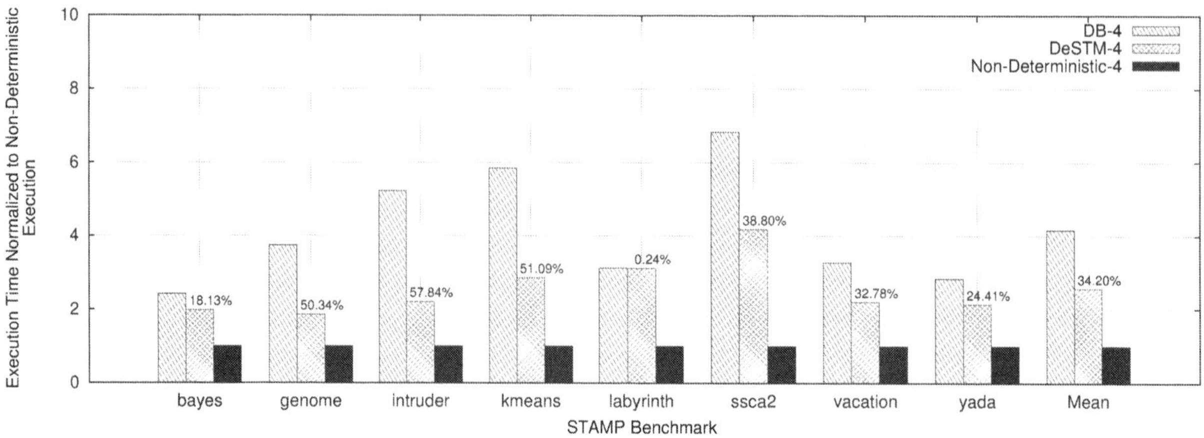

Figure 10: Performance Comparison Between DB Approach, DeSTM and Non-Deterministic Executions

plementation of DeSTM is built on top of TL2 (0.9.6). We use the STAMP benchmark suite (0.9.10).

All experiments were performed on a dual socket machine with two Intel Xeon CPU E5540 processors at 2.53GHz with 4 cores each for a total of 8 cores. The machine was running Ubuntu 12.04.3 LTS (Kernel Version: 2.6.35-32-generic). All experiments were compiled with gcc 4.6.3 with the O3 optimization level. All experiments are the average over 10 runs. All benchmarks were run with recommended inputs [6]. We will be making our binaries available [7].

6.1 Determinism

We first experimentally verified that the execution traces (see Section 3.3) were unique across a large number of runs for all STAMP benchmarks. We ran 200 runs of each STAMP benchmark using the large recommended input and 20000 runs of each benchmark using the small recommended input with both the Double Barrier approach and DeSTM. All runs executed deterministically producing the same output *and* trace (external *and* internal determinism) [8].

6.2 Performance

Next we compare the performance of these techniques:

- **Non-Deterministic** This the baseline non-deterministic implementation consisting of the STAMP benchmark suite running on top of TL2 with no modifications. It does not link with any of our libraries.
- **Double Barrier (DB)** In this approach we adapt the classical double barrier technique to work with TL2 as described in Section 4.
- **DeSTM** This version provides deterministic executions using the techniques described in Section 5.

Figure 10 reports the results we obtained. The results report the execution time of *DeSTM* and the *DB* approach normalized to the execution time of the non-deterministic execution. Each benchmark was run with 4 threads (degree of parallelism) for each technique (including the Non-Deterministic execution). The labels on the DeSTM bars indicate the percentage performance improvement of DeSTM over the DB approach.

Discussion.

We see that when determinism is applied to STMs by adapting the classical Double Barrier (DB) approach overheads are relatively large (sometimes more than 6x). On an average the execution time of the DB approach is little more than 4x that of the non-deterministic execution with the same number of threads.

DeSTM is able to significantly improve on execution time of the classical DB approach by more than 50% for some benchmarks (*genome*, *intruder* and *kmeans* benchmarks) and on an average by almost 35%. On average the execution time of DeSTM is only a little more than 2 times that of the non-deterministic execution.

The performance gains that DeSTM exhibits varies between benchmarks. Recall, that DeSTM relaxes the requirements of the two barriers replacing them by simpler constraints which leads to less time idling and more parallelism, translating to performance benefits. We see that in all the benchmarks DeSTM outperforms the DB approach. The *labyrinth* benchmark exhibits only a small performance gain under DeSTM (0.24%). This is due to its extremely unbalanced workload in which some transactions are extremely short while some are extremely large. This high imbalance overpowers any benefits that can be gained by DeSTM. However, in all the other benchmarks DeSTM exhibits significant improvements over the DB approach.

Also, note that in no situation does DeSTM perform worse than DB. The constraints that DeSTM imposes are always more relaxed than having barriers hence always leading to better performance.

Overall, the overheads exhibited by deterministic executions using DeSTM are modest. With non-determinism being one of the key challenges to parallel application development we argue that these overheads are certainly acceptable during application development.

6.3 Scalability

In this section we report results for execution time with a varying number of threads. Figure 11 reports the results we obtained. The execution times are normalized to the execution time of a single threaded execution with TL2 (which

[6]As specified in benchmark README files
[7]http://www.cc.gatech.edu/~kravicha/destm/destm.html
[8]One benchmark, *vacation*, had what we believe is a bug, which first needed to be fixed. See Section 6.5 for details.

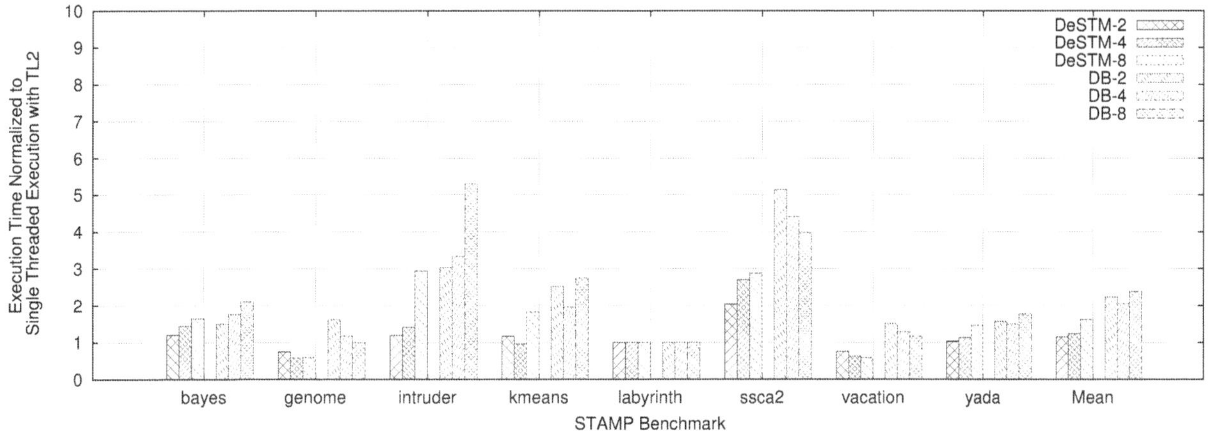

Figure 11: Scalability of the DB and DeSTM Executions

does not link with any of the code which induces determinism).

Discussion.

Increasing the number of threads in a deterministic execution typically causes more synchronization overheads. This is because, there are now a larger number of threads to wait for either during barrier synchronization (DB approach) or while waiting for the constraints to get satisfied (DeSTM). Imbalances in execution time between transactions hence get magnified leading to higher synchronization overheads. On the other hand, increasing the number of threads also serves to decrease the amount of work each thread needs to do. The results in Figure 11 represent the effective outcome of this trade-off and is highly application dependent. We observe that some benchmarks demonstrate improved performance with increasing number of threads (*genome*, *vacation* and up until 4 threads *kmeans*) while others do not. The *labyrinth* benchmark shows constant execution time regardless of the number of threads. This is because in addition to exhibiting highly unbalanced behavior (as explained in Section 6.2), the benchmark exhibits very high contention patterns, allowing only one or two transactions to commit per round regardless of number of threads used.

The scalability trends between the DB approach and DeSTM are similar. A very interesting observation is that *even the slowest DeSTM execution* on a given benchmark is *faster than the fastest execution using the DB approach* demonstrating that DeSTM is able to reduce overheads in deterministic executions quite significantly.

6.4 Overheads

While the two previous sections compared the performance of deterministic executions to non-deterministic executions, in this section we provide a breakdown of the overheads in a deterministic execution. The experiments were run with 4 threads. The results we obtained are reported in Figure 12.

Discussion.

As discussed in Section 5, DeSTM improves the performance of deterministic execution by removing the requirements of the barriers and replacing them with more flexible constraints. Figure 12 shows the different components of the overhead in deterministic executions and illustrates how DeSTM is able to effectively reduce time waiting at the barriers. Notice how the percentage of overhead caused by waiting due to the barriers is much larger than that of the waiting due to the constraints. This significant reduction in time spent at barriers allows DeSTM to effectively reduce execution time of deterministic executions.

Note again, how the highly unbalanced transaction profile in *labyrinth* causes almost all the overhead in the DB approach to occur while waiting for Barrier 1 (the other two components are present but are not visible due to scale).

We also measured the overheads due to randomizing the execution schedule (see Section 5.3) but it was less than 1% in each of the benchmarks and hence we omitted these overheads in this discussion.

6.5 Invariant Based Bug Identification

As discussed in Section 3.3, the introduction of determinism into an STM application causes every execution to have a unique trace, by virtue of which the number of commits and aborts also remain constant in every run. During STM application development, these numbers are typically output at the end of an execution. While, these values change significantly between runs in a typical execution, with determinism they do not and this fact can potentially serve as a valuable debugging tool. When these counts (or in general the execution trace) vary between deterministic runs, it points to the existence of a bug in the code. Bug free code *will* have a unique trace. The differences between the execution traces serve as an extremely helpful starting point to locate and fix the bug.

While we were running the STAMP benchmarks with DeSTM, we observed that for the *vacation* benchmark [6] these counts (and also the execution traces) varied between runs, suggesting a bug. Further investigation quickly lead us to find, what we believe is a bug, in the benchmark code.

Figure 13 shows the original code. The $maxPrices$ and $maxIds$ arrays (local variables) are used to find the maximum prices of items and their corresponding identifiers. A typical if check is used to identify the maximum price on $line11$. STMs typically provide a $LOCAL\_WRITE$ API which should be used when writing to local variables so that these writes are rolled back correctly when a transaction aborts. However, in this case the API calls were inadvertently missed causing the values in the array to restore in-

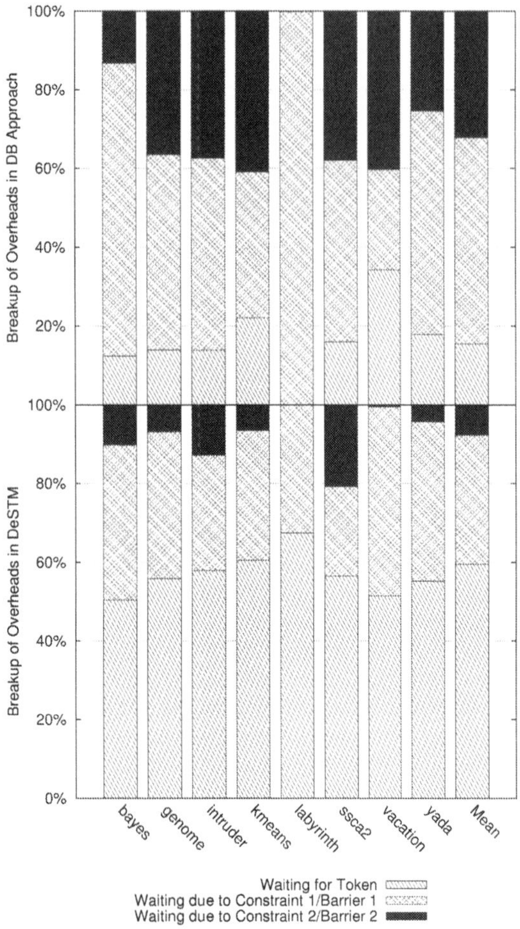

Figure 12: Breakdown of Overheads in Deterministic Executions

correctly (subsequent retries after an abort use old values) [9]. This in turn caused the addition of the Customer on *line*18 to sometimes not occur (causing insertions for certain customers to be missed). This in turn led to different traces with different commit and abort patterns.

Once the variability in the traces was identified (DeSTM outputs lots of debugging information in traces) we were able to pin point the original transaction which caused the variant behavior and the initialization issue which caused it. While there are several approaches to fix the issue, we

[9]Sometimes regardless of whether the the *LOCAL_WRITE* API is used, the values of local variables will restore correctly. Such a situation arises when the local variable in question is stored in a register. STMs implement abort/retries with the *longjmp/setjmp* functions (or its variants) which restore registers correctly after a rollback (*longjmp*). Whether a local variable is stored in a register or not is compiler dependent and hence this behavior cannot be relied upon to restore values. Portable methods include declaring the variables inside the transactional scope or using the *LOCAL_WRITE* API while writing to the variable. In the above example code, *isFound* is stored in a register and hence gets restored correctly while the two arrays *maxPrices* and *maxIds* do not, leading to an inconsistent state after a rollback.

```
1  void client_run(void* argPtr) {
2    ...
3    // Part of a larger switch statement inside a loop.
4    // The following two arrays are declared as locals on
       the stack.
5    long maxPrices[NUM_RESERVATION_TYPE] = { -1, -1, -1 };
6    long maxIds[NUM_RESERVATION_TYPE] = { -1, -1, -1 };
7    ...
8    TM_BEGIN();
9    ...
10     // This is inside a loop.
11     if (price > maxPrices[t]) {
12       maxPrices[t] = price;
13       maxIds[t] = id;
14       isFound = TRUE;
15     }
16   ...
17   if (isFound) {
18     Add Customer;  // Adds customer information.
19   }
20   Perform operations with Customer;
21   ...
22   TM_END();
23   ...
24 }
```

Figure 13: Original *vacation* Code

```
void client_run(void* argPtr) {
  ...
  ...
  TM_BEGIN();
  // Initialize these inside.
  long maxPrices[NUM_RESERVATION_TYPE] = { -1, -1, -1 };
  long maxIds[NUM_RESERVATION_TYPE] = { -1, -1, -1 };
  ...
  TM_END();
}
```

Figure 14: Fixed *vacation* Code

resorted to simply moving the initialization code for the two arrays *maxPrices* and *maxIds* inside the transactional scope. This ensures that when the transaction restarts after an abort the arrays are reset correctly. Figure 14 shows the changes made to the code.

Based on this bug pattern we looked for potential issues in other benchmarks. A similar issue also seems to be present in the *bayes* benchmark at the O0 optimization level, however unlike the *vacation* benchmark, at higher optimization levels the offending variable is optimized away by the compiler, hiding the bug. Nonetheless, it is not safe to depend on the compiler to optimize away the variable. *genome*, also seems to exhibit a similar issue but unlike *bayes* or *vacation* it does not affect correctness.

7. RELATED WORK

There has been a burgeoning interest in determinism for parallel applications. While determinism and the challenges it imposes has a rich history dating back to atleast the 1960s [18, 12, 27, 32] there has been a surge of interest recently in approaches which seek to remove non-determinism from parallel applications from several angles including hardware [8, 17, 9], operating systems [1], programming languages/models [5, 4] and several runtime approaches [26, 36, 2, 3, 21, 22]. With the growing importance of parallel programming in today's multi-core architectures the need for leveraging determinism to ease development is clear.

Olszewski et al. presented Kendo [26] one of the first systems to provide determinism for race-free programs by serializing synchronizations in a deterministic order. Similar to their approach our system provides deterministic guarantees until the first race in the code. One of the strengths of such techniques is that it allows programmers to systematically eliminate all races in an iterative process [26]. CoreDet [2] and Dthreads [21] present techniques to introduce determinism into arbitrary multi-threaded code which rely on the POSIX threading APIs and discuss the classical double barrier technique. Others [23, 22] have built on this work and discuss how to improve performance by relaxing synchronization requirements. However, all of these works have aimed to provide determinism to parallel applications which use traditional synchronization techniques such as locks. As such they are not applicable to code which uses software transactional memory due to differences in the nature of abstractions and due to the predominantly low-level synchronization primitives used in STM implementations. STMs have been found to be an extremely useful tool in reducing the complexity of parallel programming. Integrating determinism in STMs is crucial in further easing the development of parallel programs and is a theme we explore in this work.

Bocchino et al. [5] present DPJ (Deterministic Parallel Java) and argue that parallel programming should be deterministic by default and present a type and effect system for Java. Blelloch et al. [4] present a programming model for "nested-parallel" programs through commutative and linearizable operations. StreamIt [33] is able to provide determinism by virtue of the streaming model that it adopts. Cilk [11] is able to provide determinism for a certain subset of legal programs and its Nondeterminator race detector tool [7] can be used to identify data races. DeSTM on the other hand introduces determinism into applications that are being developed using the transactional programming model.

With transactional memory increasing in popularity there has been increased interest in aiding the development process. Gottschlich et al. discuss techniques used to debug transactional applications [14] and present a visualization tool in [13]. Debuggers [37] and novel performance bottleneck analysis tools [38] for transactional memories help programmers during the development cycle. While, nondeterminism has been long recognized as one of the key challenges to parallel application development, its interplay with STMs has been relatively unexplored. Determinism in STMs was discussed in the preliminary work of Smiljkovic et al. [31] which proposes using the classical double barrier approach (similar to our DB approach but with extra barriers at transaction start). On the other hand, in this work we present DeSTM which exploits properties of certain STMs, removes strict synchronization requirements imposed by barriers and improves performance of deterministic executions significantly while also allowing programmers to specify multiple deterministic execution schedules.

Record and Replay (RnR) [20, 24, 25, 35] techniques can be used to replay previously recorded executions, another important tool used to assist the debugging process. RnR techniques for STMs have also been developed [14].

8. CONCLUSION

In this paper we presented DeSTM, an infrastructure which allows programmers to leverage determinism through the implementation, debugging and testing phases of STM application development. We motivated the need for determinism and discussed why it is especially powerful to couple it with STMs which strive to improve parallel programmer productivity. We discussed the classical double barrier approach and presented DeSTM which further exploits the properties of certain STMs to significantly improve the performance of deterministic executions. Non-determinism is one of the remaining key challenges that programmers face during development, and we believe that DeSTM enhances the ease of programming using STMs.

Future Work.

We are looking at methods to extend this technique to automatically identify bugs in transactional applications and to further improve performance. Another avenue of work which a reviewer brought up, is investigating how these techniques extend to STMs which do not use global clocks or version numbers for memory locations to track conflicts.

9. ACKNOWLEDGMENTS

The authors would like to thank the anonymous reviewers for their comments and suggestions. The authors also gratefully acknowledge the support of NSF grants CNS-1320752 and CCF-1018544.

10. REFERENCES

[1] A. Aviram, S.-C. Weng, S. Hu, and B. Ford. Efficient system-enforced deterministic parallelism. In *Proceedings of the 9th USENIX Conference on Operating Systems Design and Implementation*, OSDI'10, pages 1–16, Berkeley, CA, USA, 2010. USENIX Association.

[2] T. Bergan, O. Anderson, J. Devietti, L. Ceze, and D. Grossman. Coredet: A compiler and runtime system for deterministic multithreaded execution. In *Proceedings of the Fifteenth Edition of ASPLOS on Architectural Support for Programming Languages and Operating Systems*, ASPLOS XV, New York, NY, USA, 2010. ACM.

[3] E. D. Berger, T. Yang, T. Liu, and G. Novark. Grace: Safe multithreaded programming for c/c++. In *Proceedings of the 24th ACM SIGPLAN Conference on Object Oriented Programming Systems Languages and Applications*, OOPSLA '09, pages 81–96, New York, NY, USA, 2009. ACM.

[4] G. E. Blelloch, J. T. Fineman, P. B. Gibbons, and J. Shun. Internally deterministic parallel algorithms can be fast. In *Proceedings of the 17th ACM SIGPLAN Symposium on Principles and Practice of Parallel Programming*, PPoPP '12, New York, NY, USA, 2012. ACM.

[5] R. L. Bocchino, Jr., V. S. Adve, D. Dig, S. V. Adve, S. Heumann, R. Komuravelli, J. Overbey, P. Simmons, H. Sung, and M. Vakilian. A type and effect system for deterministic parallel java. In *Proceedings of the 24th ACM SIGPLAN Conference on Object Oriented Programming Systems Languages and Applications*, OOPSLA '09, pages 97–116, New York, NY, USA, 2009. ACM.

[6] C. Cao Minh, J. Chung, C. Kozyrakis, and K. Olukotun. STAMP: Stanford transactional applications for multi-processing. In *IISWC '08: Proceedings of The IEEE International Symposium on Workload Characterization*, September 2008.

[7] G.-I. Cheng, M. Feng, C. E. Leiserson, K. H. Randall, and A. F. Stark. Detecting data races in cilk programs that use locks. In *Proceedings of the Tenth Annual ACM Symposium on Parallel Algorithms and Architectures*, SPAA '98, pages 298–309, New York, NY, USA, 1998. ACM.

[8] J. Devietti, B. Lucia, L. Ceze, and M. Oskin. Dmp: Deterministic shared memory multiprocessing. In *Proceedings of the 14th International Conference on Architectural Support for Programming Languages and Operating Systems*, ASPLOS XIV, pages 85–96, New York, NY, USA, 2009. ACM.

[9] J. Devietti, J. Nelson, T. Bergan, L. Ceze, and D. Grossman. Rcdc: A relaxed consistency deterministic computer. In *Proceedings of the Sixteenth International Conference on Architectural Support for Programming Languages and Operating Systems*, ASPLOS XVI, pages 67–78, New York, NY, USA, 2011. ACM.

[10] D. Dice, O. Shalev, and N. Shavit. Transactional locking ii. In *Proceedings of the 20th International Conference on Distributed Computing*, DISC'06, pages 194–208, Berlin, Heidelberg, 2006. Springer-Verlag.

[11] M. Frigo, C. E. Leiserson, and K. H. Randall. The implementation of the cilk-5 multithreaded language. In *Proceedings of the ACM SIGPLAN 1998 Conference on Programming Language Design and Implementation*, PLDI '98, pages 212–223, New York, NY, USA, 1998. ACM.

[12] P. B. Gibbons. A more practical pram model. In *Proceedings of the First Annual ACM Symposium on Parallel Algorithms and Architectures*, SPAA '89, pages 158–168, New York, NY, USA, 1989. ACM.

[13] J. E. Gottschlich, M. P. Herlihy, G. A. Pokam, and J. G. Siek. Visualizing transactional memory. In *Proceedings of the 21st International Conference on Parallel Architectures and Compilation Techniques*, PACT '12, pages 159–170, New York, NY, USA, 2012. ACM.

[14] J. E. Gottschlich, R. Knauerhase, and G. Pokam. But how do we really debug transactional memory programs? In *Presented as part of the 5th USENIX Workshop on Hot Topics in Parallelism*, Berkeley, CA, 2013. USENIX.

[15] J. E. Gottschlich, M. Vachharajani, and J. G. Siek. An efficient software transactional memory using commit-time invalidation. In *Proceedings of the 8th Annual IEEE/ACM International Symposium on Code Generation and Optimization*, CGO '10, pages 101–110, New York, NY, USA, 2010. ACM.

[16] T. Harris, J. Larus, and R. Rajwar. *Transactional Memory, 2nd Edition*. Morgan and Claypool Publishers, 2nd edition, 2010.

[17] D. R. Hower, P. Dudnik, M. D. Hill, and D. A. Wood. Calvin: Deterministic or not? free will to choose. In *Proceedings of the 2011 IEEE 17th International Symposium on High Performance Computer Architecture*, HPCA '11, pages 333–334, Washington, DC, USA, 2011. IEEE Computer Society.

[18] R. M. Karp and R. E. Miller. Parallel program schemata. *J. Comput. Syst. Sci.*, 3(2):147–195, May 1969.

[19] G. Korl, N. Shavit, and P. Felber. Noninvasive concurrency with java stm.

[20] T. J. LeBlanc and J. M. Mellor-Crummey. Monitoring and debugging of distributed real-time systems. chapter Debugging Parallel Programs with Instant Replay, pages 301–311. IEEE Computer Society Press, Los Alamitos, CA, USA, 1995.

[21] T. Liu, C. Curtsinger, and E. D. Berger. Dthreads: Efficient deterministic multithreading. In *Proceedings of the Twenty-Third ACM Symposium on Operating Systems Principles*, SOSP '11, pages 327–336, New York, NY, USA, 2011. ACM.

[22] K. Lu, X. Zhou, T. Bergan, and X. Wang. Efficient deterministic multithreading without global barriers. In *Proceedings of the 19th ACM SIGPLAN Symposium on Principles and Practice of Parallel Programming*, PPoPP '14, pages 287–300, New York, NY, USA, 2014. ACM.

[23] T. Merrifield and J. Eriksson. Conversion: Multi-version concurrency control for main memory segments. In *Proceedings of the 8th ACM European Conference on Computer Systems*, EuroSys '13, pages 127–139, New York, NY, USA, 2013. ACM.

[24] P. Montesinos, L. Ceze, and J. Torrellas. Delorean: Recording and deterministically replaying shared-memory multiprocessor execution ef?ciently. In *Proceedings of the 35th Annual International Symposium on Computer Architecture*, ISCA '08, pages 289–300, Washington, DC, USA, 2008. IEEE Computer Society.

[25] S. Narayanasamy, C. Pereira, and B. Calder. Recording shared memory dependencies using strata. In *Proceedings of the 12th International Conference on Architectural Support for Programming Languages and Operating Systems*, ASPLOS XII, pages 229–240, New York, NY, USA, 2006. ACM.

[26] M. Olszewski, J. Ansel, and S. Amarasinghe. Kendo: Efficient deterministic multithreading in software. In *Proceedings of the 14th International Conference on Architectural Support for Programming Languages and Operating Systems*, ASPLOS XIV, pages 97–108, New York, NY, USA, 2009. ACM.

[27] S. S. Patil. Record of the project mac conference on concurrent systems and parallel computation. chapter Closure Properties of Interconnections of Determinate Systems, pages 107–116. ACM, New York, NY, USA, 1970.

[28] D. Perelman, A. Byshevsky, O. Litmanovich, and I. Keidar. Smv: Selective multi-versioning stm. In *Proceedings of the 25th International Conference on Distributed Computing*, DISC'11, pages 125–140, Berlin, Heidelberg, 2011. Springer-Verlag.

[29] J. Ruppert. A delaunay refinement algorithm for quality 2-dimensional mesh generation. In *Selected Papers from the Fourth Annual ACM SIAM Symposium on Discrete Algorithms*, SODA '93, pages 548–585, Orlando, FL, USA, 1995. Academic Press, Inc.

[30] N. Shavit and D. Touitou. Software transactional memory. In *Proceedings of the Fourteenth Annual ACM Symposium on Principles of Distributed Computing*, PODC '95, pages 204–213, New York, NY, USA, 1995. ACM.

[31] V. Smiljkovic, C. Fetzer, O. Unsal, A. Cristal, and M. Valero. Deterministic execution of tm-based applications, 2013. Abstract: http://www.eurotm.org/action-meetings/wtm2013/program/abstracts, Related Report: http://www.gsd.inesc-id.pt/~mcouceiro/eurotm/stsm/smiljkovic.pdf, Related presentation: http://www.gsd.inesc-id.pt/~mcouceiro/eurotm/wtm2013/smiljkovic.pdf.

[32] G. L. Steele, Jr. Making asynchronous parallelism safe for the world. In *Proceedings of the 17th ACM SIGPLAN-SIGACT Symposium on Principles of Programming Languages*, POPL '90, pages 218–231, New York, NY, USA, 1990. ACM.

[33] W. Thies, M. Karczmarek, and S. P. Amarasinghe. Streamit: A language for streaming applications. In *Proceedings of the 11th International Conference on Compiler Construction*, CC '02, pages 179–196, London, UK, UK, 2002. Springer-Verlag.

[34] TinySTM. http://www.tmware.org/tinystm.

[35] M. Xu, R. Bodik, and M. D. Hill. A "flight data recorder" for enabling full-system multiprocessor deterministic replay. In *Proceedings of the 30th Annual International Symposium on Computer Architecture*, ISCA '03, pages 122–135, New York, NY, USA, 2003. ACM.

[36] J. Yu and S. Narayanasamy. A case for an interleaving constrained shared-memory multi-processor. In *Proceedings of the 36th Annual International Symposium on Computer Architecture*, ISCA '09, pages 325–336, New York, NY, USA, 2009. ACM.

[37] F. Zyulkyarov, T. Harris, O. S. Unsal, A. Cristal, and M. Valero. Debugging programs that use atomic blocks and transactional memory. In *Proceedings of the 15th ACM SIGPLAN Symposium on Principles and Practice of Parallel Programming*, PPoPP '10, pages 57–66, New York, NY, USA, 2010. ACM.

[38] F. Zyulkyarov, S. Stipic, T. Harris, O. S. Unsal, A. Cristal, I. Hur, and M. Valero. Discovering and understanding performance bottlenecks in transactional applications. In *Proceedings of the 19th International Conference on Parallel Architectures and Compilation Techniques*, PACT '10, pages 285–294, New York, NY, USA, 2010. ACM.

PATS: Pattern Aware Scheduling and Power Gating for GPGPUs

Qiumin Xu and Murali Annavaram
Ming Hsieh Department of Electrical Engineering, University of Southern California
Los Angeles, CA
{qiumin, annavara} @usc.edu

ABSTRACT

General purpose computing using graphics processing units (GPGPUs) is an attractive option to achieve power efficient throughput computing. But the power efficiency of GPGPUs can be significantly curtailed in the presence of divergence. This paper evaluates two important facets of this problem. First, we study the branch divergence behavior of various GPGPU workloads. We show that only a few branch divergence patterns are dominant in most workloads. In fact only five branch divergence patterns account for 60% of all the divergent instructions in our workloads. In the second part of this work we exploit this branch divergence pattern bias to propose a new divergence pattern aware warp scheduler, called PATS. PATS prioritizes scheduling warps with the same divergence pattern so as to create long idleness windows for any given execution lane. The long idleness windows are then exploited for efficiently power gating the unused lanes while amortizing the gating overhead. We describe the architectural implementation details of PATS and evaluate the power and performance impact of PATS. Our proposed design significantly improves power gating efficiency of GPGPUs with minimal performance overhead.

Categories and Subject Descriptors

C.1.4 [**Computer Systems Organization**]: Processor Architectures—*Parallel Architectures*

Keywords

branch divergence; GPGPU; pattern; power gating; warp scheduling

1. INTRODUCTION

General purpose graphics processing unit (GPGPU) is the execution platform of choice for many massively parallel applications. The large number of parallel execution resources in a GPU are exposed in a hardware independent manner to the application layer through programming/runtime environments such as CUDA [2] or OpenCL [23]. Thus significant effort is invested in porting parallel applications to run on GPUs. Within each application computationally intensive kernels are identified and these kernels are parallelized into thousands of concurrent threads (also called work items). Depending on the execution resource constraints in GPUs, such as the size of register files, several threads are first packed into a concurrent thread array (CTA). Each CTA itself is then sub-divided into groups of threads (typically 32 threads), and each of these thread groups is called a warp in the Nvidia terminology or wavefront in the AMD terminology. GPUs use single instruction multiple thread (SIMT) execution model, where a single instruction is executed concurrently on several execution lanes (called SIMT lanes) using multiple data items. All threads within a warp need to only fetch and decode a single instruction thereby amortizing the cost of generating control information. Furthermore, threads within a warp do not have data dependence and do not need to synchronize. Hence, the simplified control coupled with massive parallel hardware makes GPUs a power efficient choice for throughput-oriented computing.

It has been shown in several recent works [11, 12, 22, 25, 29] that when general purpose applications are ported to run on GPUs, these applications fail to fully utilize all the available hardware resources due to branch and memory divergence. Whenever a branch instruction is executed within a warp, some threads may take the branch while other threads traverse the not-taken path. To independently control the execution behavior of each thread within a warp, an active mask vector is used. Each thread's execution is controlled by whether the corresponding active mask bit is set or reset. If the bit is set the corresponding thread will execute and update the architectural state. If the bit is unset then that thread's computation does not update any of the architectural state. The SIMT execution model requires that all threads with taken and not-taken path to be executed sequentially.

In the presence of branch divergence the power efficiency of GPUs can be compromised significantly. Recognizing the importance of sustaining power efficiency in the presence of divergence, a wide range of solutions [3, 4, 30, 31] have been proposed. Most of these solutions propose to power gate unused resources. In addition to power gating unused resources, many other orthogonal approaches to improve power efficiency have also been studied [13, 14, 18, 26, 27]. Some examples of these solutions range from reducing regis-

PACT'14, August 24–27, 2014, Edmonton, AB, Canada.

http://dx.doi.org/10.1145/2628071.2628105 .

ter file accesses through caching register content [13], 2-level warp schedulers to improve memory access behavior [27].

The focus of this research is two fold. First, we study the branch divergence behavior of various general purpose workloads running on GPUs. The surprising result we observed is that in a 32 thread warp, out of possibly 2^{32} branch divergence patterns, each benchmark exhibits very few divergence patterns. In other words, many warps branch exactly the same as other warps in the program. Our results indicate that on average 60% of the warps in a variety of workloads have fewer than five branch divergence patterns.

The second part of this paper then uses this critical knowledge to improve power gating efficiency in the presence of branch divergence. As shown in prior work [18], GPU execution units account for 20.1% of dynamic power consumption. In [4], the authors report that static leakage power accounts for 50% of total power consumption in integer units and 90% total power consumption in floating point units. Thus at least 10% of the total GPU power consumption is attributed to leakage power. The authors in [30] applied power gating at a coarser granularity of an entire SM, when it is not in use. Recent work [4] applied power gating at a finer granularity of gating either all the integer units or all the floating point units. Floating point units can be shut off, when there are only integer instructions in the pipeline, and vice-versa. In this work, we exploit the branch divergence pattern similarity to shutdown unused SIMT lanes. Based on the observation that the same divergence pattern occurs repeatedly across multiple warps within a CTA and even across CTAs, we propose to co-schedule warps with similar divergence patterns. When a set of SIMT lanes are unused in one warp, we co-schedule warps with similar SIMT lane idleness behavior to create longer idle periods in each SIMT lane. This long idleness is essential to reduce the overheads of power gating.

To summarize, the following are the contributions of this work:

Explore the divergence patterns: We studied several divergent benchmarks from the Rodinia [8], Parboil [1], and ISPASS [5] benchmark suites and show that there are only a few branch divergence patterns in each benchmark. State-of-the-art two-level round robin scheduler [13] schedules warps agnostic to the active mask patterns and thus warps with different divergence patterns are interleaved. This interleaving results in short SIMT lane idleness and a naive SIMT lane level power gating scheme would cause frequent wake-ups resulting in large power gating overheads.

Pattern-aware two-level warp scheduler: To address the inefficiency of two-level warp scheduler, we propose pattern aware two-level scheduler (PATS). PATS prioritizes issuing cluster of warps which have similar active mask patterns. PATS thus stretches the idle period length of SIMT lanes improving power gating efficiency.

Deterministic lookahead to prevent gating penalty: Finally, we present a runtime approach that dynamically tracks the active masks of soon-to-be executed warps waiting in the operand collector buffer. By looking ahead into the execution window, we can proactively wakeup an idle execution unit or stop power gating any execution resource that may be needed in the near future further improving power gating efficiency.

The rest of the paper is organized as follows: Section 2 presents divergence pattern analysis of GPU workloads. Section 3 highlights the challenges of per lane power gating and motivates the need for a divergence pattern aware scheduling technique. Sections 4 discusses the proposed PATS techniques and the required microarchitectural support. Section 5 presents the simulation methodology and results. We discuss related work in section 6 and conclude in section 7.

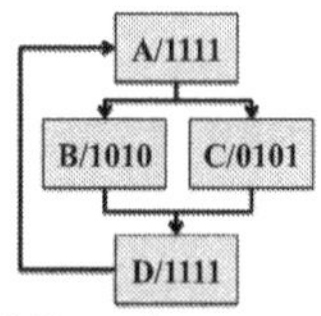

(a) Example program

PC	Iter	Aggregate Active Mask	Instruction Count	Warp Count
B	1	3 1 1 1	100	3
B	2	3 3 1 0	100	3
C	1	0 2 2 2	20	3
C	2	0 0 1 2	20	3

(b) Divergence statistics table

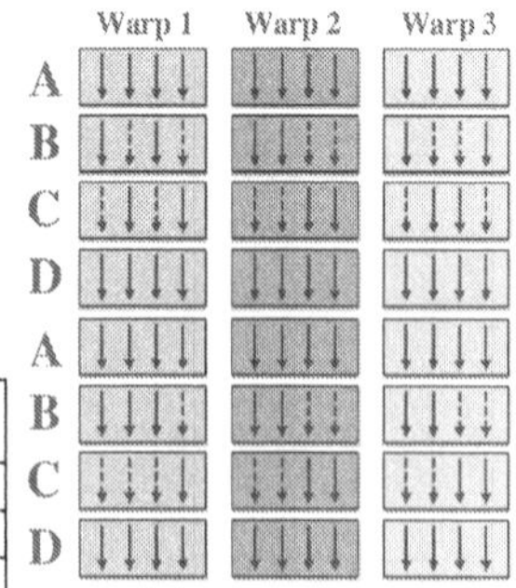

(c) Multiple warps diverge differently at same PC in different iterations.

Figure 2: Illustration of divergence pattern behavior

2. DIVERGENCE PATTERNS

To study the branch divergence patterns we ran 19 benchmarks from several benchmark suites, including Rodinia [8], Parboil [1], and ISPASS [5]. The benchmarks are listed in Table 1. These benchmarks were used in the most recent GPU power gating work [4] and exhibit diverse range of behaviors: five of these benchmarks are purely integer benchmarks, four of them are floating point dominant and four of them are non-divergent benchmarks.

We simulated the benchmarks using GPGPU-Sim v3.2.1 [5]. The default NVIDIA GTX480-like configuration is used. The baseline is a fermi-like architecture containing 15 streaming multiprocessors (SMs). Each SM has two shader processor (SP) units, one load/store unit and one special function unit (SFU) to handle complex computations such as sine and cosine. There are 16 double-clocked CUDA cores in each of the SP units, and thus each SP unit can execute one warp containing 32 threads each cycle. Each CUDA core has a separate integer and floating point pipeline. The register file size is 128 KB per SM, and the maximum warps per SM is 48. The default scheduler, unless stated otherwise, is greedy then oldest first scheduler. We use GPUWattch [18] and McPAT [20] for power estimations.

Before we present the branch divergence pattern analysis, we provide a quick overview of how active masks are used to control divergent execution within a GPU. Figure 2(a) illustrates that basic block A is executed by all the threads within a warp; we assume for illustration simplicity that there are four threads per warp. Hence, the active mask is set to "1111" when A is executed. The last instruction in A is a branch and the branch can take two paths B or C. The first thread and third thread execute B, while others branch to C. Thus the active mask in B is "1010" while the active mask in C is "0101". We refer to the divergent active mask as a *divergence pattern*. This divergence can be handled either by software predication or using hardware stack [12]. The first instruction in B and C is referred to as an *immediate divergent point*.

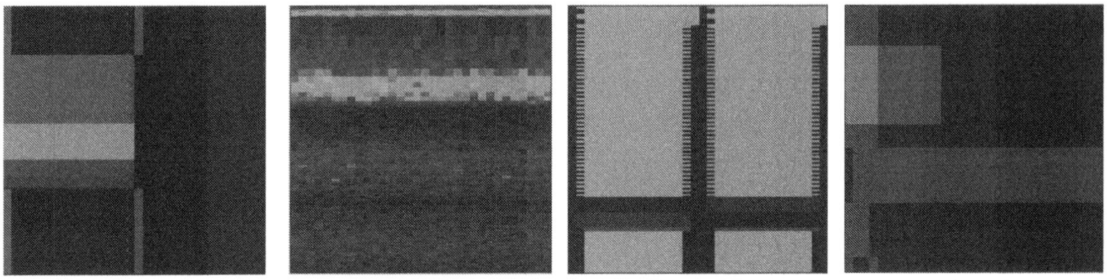

(a) backprop (b) bfs (c) hotspot (d) LPS

(e) lbm (f) nw (g) pathfinder (h) srad

Figure 1: Divergence patterns for divergent benchmarks

GPU applications use the notion of a kernel to execute the parallel component of the workload. Usually the kernel code is repeatedly executed by many warps. Furthermore, each warp may iteratively execute the same set of divergent points but with potentially different active masks at each iteration. Such an execution could potentially result in a huge number of divergent patterns. Figure 2(c) shows an illustration where three different warps (warp1, warp2, warp3) running the same control flow code shown in Figure 2(a) for two iterations. In both iterations the basic block A and D are executed by all threads in all warps. But basic blocks B and C could be executed by different combinations of threads in each warp as illustrated in the figure. For instance, basic block B is executed with three different active masks "1010", "1100", "1001" by the three warps in the first iteration, and "1110", "1100", "1100" are the active masks of the three warps in the second iteration. In this example a total of five patterns are seen during the execution of the basic block B. Hence, when there are 48 warps, each with a 32-bit active mask, that execute thousands of iterations of the same control flow sequences, there could be thousands of different branch divergence patterns.

In order to capture the variance in the number of active masks, we use a *divergence statistics table*. Figure 2(b) shows this table for the warp execution behavior seen in basic blocks B and C in the illustration in Figure 2(c). For every diverging basic block, there is one entry per each iteration that block is executed. The column titled *Aggregate Active Mask* sums up the active masks of all warps across the CTAs currently executing in the SM that branch to the specific basic block in one iteration. For instance, in our illustration, the first iteration of B was executed by three warps with active masks "1010", "1100", and "1001". Thus the aggregate active mask field stores "3111", which is simply the sum of all active masks for the given iteration of a basic block. This field implies SIMT lane one was used three times during one iteration of the basic block, while all other lanes were used once. The *instruction count* field in the table is simply the dynamic count of instructions executed in the given iteration of that basic block. The last column, *warp count*, counts the number of warps with at least one active mask bit that executed the basic block during one iteration in the corresponding row.

After defining the basic terminology above, we now present a graphic representation of the divergence statistics table. The divergence pattern data for a subset of 8 benchmarks is shown in Figure 1. Due to space limitation we restrict showing the results to these 8 representative benchmarks in this section.

In each of this figure the X-axis of the graph ranges from 1 to 32, indicating the warp width. For each iteration of every diverging basic block there is one point on the Y-axis. The Y-axis is a sorted list of the starting program counter addresses (PC) of each diverging block concatenated with the iteration number. For instance, consider a program with just three diverging basic blocks, and the starting PCs of these basic blocks are PC1, PC2 and PC3. Let us say the execution sequence of these diverging blocks is PC1, PC2, PC3, PC1, PC1. In this execution sequence, the diverging basic block starting at PC1 is executed three times; PC2 and PC3 were executed once. As mentioned before we simulated a Fermi-like configuration where at most 48 warps from one kernel can execute concurrently in a single SM. Thus at most 48 warps could have executed each of the diverging basic blocks. Referring to divergence statistics table in Figure 2(b), the maximum value for any given SIMT lane in the aggregate active mask field will be 48 during any one iteration of the three basic blocks, PC1, PC2 or PC3. The aggregate active mask vector of PC1's first iteration is then plotted as a single horizontal line in Figure 1. We then plot the second and third instance of PC1's aggregate active mask which are plotted as the second and third horizontal lines. Once PC1 is processed, we then plot PC2's aggregate

Name	R	Pattern	Count	%DynDiv	% Total	Name	R	Pattern	Count	%DynDiv	% Total
backprop	1	10000000000000000100000000000000	720896	51.6%	6.2%	cutup	1	11111111111111110000000000000000	45254	97.1%	1.7%
(12.0%)	2	11111111111111110000000000000000	675863	48.4%	5.8%	**(1.7%)**	2	00000000000000001111111111111111	1331	2.9%	0.05%
bfs	1	00000000000000000000000000000100	19392	1.15%	0.96%	nw	1	11111111111111110000000000000000	8265664	46.3%	46.3%
	2	00000000000100000000000000000000	19147	1.13%	0.95%		2	11111111111111100000000000000000	638976	3.6%	3.6%
(73.8%)	3	00000000000000010000000000000000	19009	1.12%	0.94%	**(100%)**	3	11111111111111000000000000000000	638976	3.6%	3.6%
	4	00000000000000000000000000010000	18726	1.11%	0.93%		4	11111111111110000000000000000000	638976	3.6%	3.6%
	5	00000000000000000000000100000000	18646	1.10%	0.92%		5	11111111111100000000000000000000	638976	3.6%	3.6%
hotspot	1	00111111111111000011111111111100	788310	48.5%	22.4%	pathfinder	1	11111111111111110000000000000000	925	3.6%	0.36%
	2	01111111111111100111111111111110	529994	36.7%	32.6%		2	00000000000000000000000000000111	600	2.3%	0.24%
(46.2%)	3	00000000000000000111111111111110	81692	5.0%	2.3%	**(10.1%)**	3	11100000000000000000000000000000	600	2.3%	0.24%
	4	01111111111111100000000000000000	78076	4.8%	2.2%		4	00000000000000000000000000000011	500	1.9%	0.20%
	5	00111111111111110011111111111111	50836	3.1%	1.4%		5	00011111111111111111111111111111	425	1.6%	0.17%
LPS	1	11110000000000000000000000000000	292700	32.6%	10.5%	srad	1	11111111111111101111111111111110	3538944	31.7%	4.7%
	2	01111111111111111111111111111111	205636	22.9%	7.4%		2	00000000000000010000000000000001	2621440	23.5%	3.5%
(32.2%)	3	11100000000000000000000000000000	185636	20.7%	6.7%	**(15.0%)**	3	00000000000000000000000000000001	884736	7.9%	1.2%
	4	11111111111100000000000000000000	72200	8.0%	2.6%		4	00000000000000010000000000000000	851968	7.6 %	1.1%
	5	10101010101000000000000000000000	34500	3.8%	1.2%		5	00000000000000001111111111111110	458752	4.1%	0.6%
b+tree	1	11111111111111111111111111110000	1088043	54.6%	5.87%	lbm	1	11111111111111111111111000000000	5518624	32.0%	15.4%
	2	10000000000000000000000000000000	206918	10.4%	1.12%		2	01111111111111111111111111111111	4319520	25.1%	12.0%
(10.8%)	3	00000000000000010000000000000000	32530	1.63%	0.18%	**(48.0%)**	3	11111111111111111111111100000000	3471008	20.1%	9.7%
	4	00000001000000000000000000000000	26830	1.35%	0.14%		4	00000000000000000000000100000000	488992	2.8%	1.4%
	5	00000000100000000000000000000000	26662	1.34%	0.14%		5	10000000000000000000000000000000	419424	2.4%	1.2%
gaussian	1	11111111111111110000000000000000	11452316	97.0%	96.6%	heartwall	1	01111111111111111111111111111111	10150173	1.75%	0.72%
	2	11110000000000000000000000000000	102305	0.87%	0.86%		2	11111111111111111111111111111110	10136403	1.74%	0.72%
(99.6%)	3	11101110111011100000000000000000	56186	0.48%	0.47%	**(41.5%)**	3	00111111111111111111111111111111	10107945	1.74%	0.72%
	4	10001000100010000000000000000000	54678	0.46%	0.46%		4	11111111111111111111111111111100	10100907	1.74 %	0.72%
	5	11001100110011000000000000000000	54678	0.46%	0.46%		5	00011111111111111111111111111111	9916848	1.71%	0.71%
MUM	1	00000000000000000000000000000010	11196	1.04%	0.78%	WP	1	11111110111111101111111011111110	592802	23.6%	8.2%
	2	00000000000000000001000000000000	10164	0.94%	0.71%		2	11111111111111110000000000000000	339682	13.5%	4.7%
(75.4%)	3	00000000000000000000000000000100	9334	0.87%	0.65%	**(34.8%)**	3	11111110111111100000000000000000	42289	1.69%	0.59%
	4	00000000000000000000000100000000	9290	0.86%	0.65%		4	00000001000000000000000000000000	27022	1.08 %	0.37%
	5	00000000010000000000000000000000	9218	0.86%	0.65%		5	00000000000000000000000010000000	18801	0.75%	0.26%
*kmeans, lavaMD, LIB, mri-q, sgemm have 0% diverged instructions											

Table 1: 5 most common divergence patterns for 19 benchmarks.

```
for(int t = 0; t < rows - 1; t += pyramid_height){
    for (int i = 0; i < t; i++){
        computed = false;
        if(tx >= i+1 && tx <= BLOCK_SIZE-i -2){
            computed = true;
            do_computation();}}}
```

Figure 3: Divergence control flow of pathfinder

```
for(int i=nodes[tid].start; i<(nodes[tid].edges +
    nodes[tid].start); i++){
    int id = edges[i];
    if(!visited[id]){
        do_something();}}}
```

Figure 4: Divergence control flow of bfs

active mask for each iteration followed by PC3's aggregate active mask.

Each row of the graph shows the value of the aggregate active mask vector in color scale. Red maps to 48, which is the maximum number of warps concurrently executing in a shader core in Fermi. Green maps to 24. Dark blue maps to zero, means that none of the 48 warps has an active thread in that SIMT lane for the given PC in a given iteration. To differentiate the importance of each basic block we use the total instruction count as defined earlier as the weight of each line that is plotted. If PC1 has 100 instructions, and PC2 has 20 instructions, the line for active mask for PC1 will be 5 times thicker than a line for PC2.

As shown in Figure 1, many benchmarks exhibit visually interesting divergence patterns. Except for bfs, other benchmarks have divergence patterns that are neatly blocked and zeros (dark blue) are clustered together. This pattern implies that the same branch divergence behavior is encountered across multiple iterations of the divergent block. But even more critically the divergence similarity is also quite persistent across different divergent basic blocks.

To understand the reason for this strong divergence similarity across multiple iterations of the same basic block and across different basic blocks in many benchmarks, we analyzed the source code of each benchmark and identified the potential divergence points and the conditions used within branch instructions at the divergence point. The most common reason for this divergence similarity occurs when a branch condition is dependent on a thread-specific static value. The example code in Figure 3 for the pathfinder benchmark shows the branch condition in the inner most loop of the pathfinder [8] benchmark. The *if* branch is taken or not depends on the value of the x component of thread id (variable *tx*). For each iteration of the outermost loop the innermost loop iterates as many times as the outmost loop's index (variable *t*).This condition is true for all the warps executing the kernel. Once inside the inner loop a warp diverges simply based on the thread-id, as shown in the "if" condition within the inner loop.

Each horizontal line in Figure 1 for pathfinder has an aggregate active mask pattern of shrinking ones, as less threads in a warp satisfy the "if" condition after each outer loop iteration. But the weight of each line (thickness) is the same since the total instruction count executed on each iteration is identical. The range of the qualified thread ids decreases with pyramid height on both sides in each of the innermost loop iteration, and thus the graph in Figure 3 has triangle patterns. The benchmark nw also has a similar branching behavior where the innermost loop branch is dependent on the thread-id and the innermost loop iteration count is set by the outermost loop. Hence, whenever the branch condition is dependent on a statically determined value, such as thread-id, the branch divergence patterns will remain stable across all warps. Similar observation was made in [25].

On the other hand, as shown in Figure 4, the bfs benchmark kernel#1 has a branch condition that is dependent on the value of the graph node visited by that thread in that iteration. Therefore, as shown in Figure 1b, the divergence pattern of bfs benchmark is unpredictable within each warp as well across different iterations.

We show the five most common divergence patterns for each benchmark in Table 1. The column titled *Count* shows the total number of instructions (dynamic count) executed under each pattern. The column titled $\%DynDiv$ shows the instructions (dynamic count) that executed under that divergence pattern as a fraction of all the instructions that diverged. The column titled $\%Total$ shows the dynamic count of instructions that executed under that divergence pattern as a fraction of all the instructions, both diverged and non-diverged, executed in that application. The percentage value under the name of each application shows the fraction of total diverged instruction over all the instructions executed. For backprop there are only two divergence patterns throughout the entire application, while for bfs there is no dominant divergence pattern since each pattern accounts for roughly 1% of the total diverged instructions. In our evaluations we noticed that bfs has 2000 divergence patterns and most of these divergence patterns have many leading zeros and just a few ones. Since there is no else condition in the bfs branch code, shown in Figure 4 there are no complementary divergence patterns with leading ones. Even though pathfinder has well defined structure to its divergence patterns, as explained earlier, the height of the pyramid determines the number of divergence patterns that can be seen. If the pyramid is short there will be few divergence patterns, and vice-versa. In our execution the pyramid is quite tall and hence there are many patterns, each accounting for only a fraction of the total divergence patterns. Many benchmarks exhibit five or more divergence patterns, but the top two divergence patterns account for more than 50% of the diverged instructions. On average, the five most common patterns account for 60.3% of total diverged instructions.

3. CHALLENGES IN PER LANE POWER GATING IN GPUS

There are many potential usages to exploit the predictable branch divergence behavior shown in the previous section. One such usage is power gating. We propose to explore the possibility of power gating unused SIMT lanes by exploiting the repeated branch divergence patterns. With technology scaling, static power is becoming prominent [7]. In [4] the authors state that static power accounts for more than 50% of the total power consumption in a GPU. Power gating is a well know technique for reducing static power consumption, but it has to be used with caution. Otherwise, the power gating overheads can lead to negative performance impact as well as increase the power consumption. As is shown in [15], the overheads include break-even time and wakeup delay. The energy overhead to sleep as well as the overhead to wakeup have to be compensated before power gating can provide any power savings. Thus the longer a unit is power gated, it continues to save static energy and eventually the static energy savings cross over the power overheads of using the sleep transistor. The number of cycles in power gated state when this cross over occurs is called the break-even time. When the gated unit is needed for computation there is a cost to wake up the unit since the unit has to be powered on to reach full V_{dd}, which is called the wakeup delay. A typical value for break-even time is about 9-19 cycles [15], and a typical value for wakeup delay is about 3-9 cycles, for logic blocks that are similar in size to the execution units in GPUs. In the remaining paper, by default we use a break-even time of 14 cycles and wakeup delay of 3 cycles. We also include our energy saving and performance results for 9-19 cycles of break-even time and 3-15 cycles of wake-up delay in the sensitivity analysis section of the paper.

Applying power gating per SIMT lane poses new challenges. First, in order to effectively apply power gating at the granularity of a SIMT lane, it is necessary to keep the SIMT lane idle for long enough periods. However, the typical idleness window of a SIMT lane is significantly shorter than the required break-even time. In fact, our results show that, for the hotspot benchmark, 72% of idle periods for any single integer unit is less than five cycles. The primary reason for the short idle periods is the scheduling decisions made by the default two-level scheduler [24], which schedules all ready warps in a round robin fashion. Therefore warps with different divergence patterns are interleaved with each other. In particular if a warp with a divergent behavior is co-scheduled with a warp that fully utilizes all the SIMT lanes, then the idle period of each SIMT lane is constantly interrupted by the warp that needs to use all the SIMT lanes.

In [4] the authors proposed to power gate all the integer or floating point pipelines within each SM as a whole. Thus they needed to pay the wakeup penalty only when they issue an instruction that requires the gated unit type (INT or FP). But with SIMT lane power gating of either an integer or floating point unit, even if a scheduled warp requires just one gated SIMT lane resource then the *entire warp* must pay the penalty of wakeup. Thus the probability of paying the wakeup penalty increases significantly with per lane power gating.

Blackout is a technique proposed in [4] to reduce the negative effects of power gating. The authors proposed to force a unit to stay in sleep mode for at least the break-even time. When this technique is applied for the entire cluster of INT or FP units the scheduler simply forces all the warps that require that cluster to wait for the blackout period to complete. Given that there are plenty of warps with either INT or FP instructions the scheduler can still find sufficient number of warps of a given type to schedule even if the other instruction type resource is in the blackout state. Thus blackout in effect clusters the warps that need the same resource together. But this technique when applied to a SIMT lane power gating may cause significant performance penalties. When blackout is applied at the SIMT lane granularity, the warp scheduler has to essentially find other warps that also don't use that SIMT lane. Unfortunately, there are warps with a fully utilized active mask that are interspersed with divergent warps in the ready queue. Our results show that on average there is a 3.4% performance overhead when blackout is applied on per lane power gating, as the warp scheduler is unable to issue a warp that needs a lane in the blackout state. In the worst case scenario, it causes 14% performance overhead in the MUM benchmark.

Thus to tackle the challenges listed here there is a critical need to develop a new power gating approach for per lane power gating to work well. In the next section, we describe our three proposed techniques: Pattern Aware Two-level Scheduler (PATS), Deterministic Look Ahead Ready (LAR), Pattern and Instruction Type Aware scheduler (PATS++). We show that these techniques target the challenges effectively with minimal overhead.

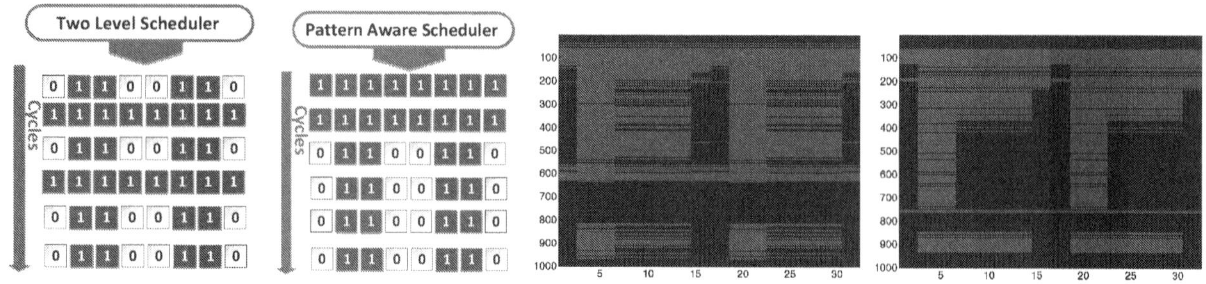

(a) Interleavely scheduled warps (b) warps of same pattern is prioritized (c) Two level scheduler (d) Pattern aware scheduler

Figure 5: Effect of warp scheduler on idle cycles

4. PATTERN AWARE TWO-LEVEL SCHEDULER (PATS)

We propose PATS to prioritize scheduling warps with similar divergence patterns. The prioritized scheduling technique could prolong the length of idle cycles for any given SIMT lane. Figure 5 illustrates the key idea of pattern aware scheduler. For the purpose of illustration, we assume there are eight threads per warp (rather than the 32 threads used in our results) and hence there are eight SIMT lanes to support the execution of each warp. In Figure 5a and Figure 5b, a warp is scheduled for execution on eight SIMT lanes. Again for demonstration purposes, let us assume that the break-even time is three cycles, and zero idle detect time and zero wakeup delay. In Figure 5a, the default scheduler is not cognizant of the divergence patterns. Hence, different patterns interleave with each other in the scheduler. Although many lanes are intermittently active, none of the lanes has long enough idle window to offset the break-even time of three cycles. Figure 5b shows the behavior with PATS. PATS uses the same set of warps as before, but prioritizes issuing warps with the same divergence patterns. Thus warps with the same divergence are scheduled as a cluster creating long idleness windows of 4 cycles for idle SIMT lane thereby increasing the opportunity to power gate.

Figure 5c and Figure 5d show the lane idleness behavior from an actual execution trace of the 32 integer units collected from the hotspot benchmark. The X-axis represents 32 lanes from left to right and the Y-axis represents the time progression from top to bottom. In Figure 5c, the default two level round robin scheduler in GPGPUSim v3.2.1 is used. As explained earlier, we assume that each SM has two shader processors (SPs) each with 16 double clocked SIMT lanes and each SIMT lane has a separate INT and FP pipeline. Two warps can be issued to the two SPs in any clock. Any full warp is assigned to one SP, by simply scheduling the odd and even SIMT lanes one after the other in two half clocks. Thus the divergence pattern for a warp is converted from a 32-bit value to a 16-bit value by OR-ing odd bits with even bits. We then concatenate the active masks of two instructions that were issued in the same cycle as a 32 bit value in this illustration. An active mask bit value of zero is represented as blue and the red color represents an active mask bit value of 1. Although the default two level scheduler is able to find some stretches of idleness, the SIMT lane idleness is interrupted by fully active warps. In fact, in this Figure 5c the longest stretch of idleness is 200 cycles for one SIMT lane and most SIMT lanes have fewer than 20 idle cycles. The PATS approach, shown in Figure 5d, has extended periods of idleness for many SIMT lanes. For instance, the longest blue blocks in the middle SIMT lanes have 497 continuous idle cycles.

4.1 Design Issues of Pattern Aware Two-level Scheduler (PATS)

In this section, we describe the micro-architectural modifications needed in a GPU pipeline to implement PATS. PATS can be built on top of any existing warp scheduler, such as greedy then oldest scheduler [27] or two-level round robin scheduler [24]. To concretely present the implementation we built PATS on top of the two-level scheduler. We extend the default two-level scheduler with three enhancements: (1) Pattern table, (2) Per pattern warp subset and (3) Warp charger.

Pattern table: We augment the warp scheduler with a 7-entry pattern table. Each entry is a 16-bit vector that holds the most common divergence patterns. Note that, as mentioned earlier, each warp is scheduled in two half cycles on 16 double clocked CUDA cores in our implementation. If one was to use 32 CUDA cores without double clocking, then the entry size will be 32 bits. In addition, each entry has a 6-bit warp count field that counts the number of warps with the same divergence pattern, and 1-bit valid field. Note that at most 48 warps can be resident in each SM, and hence, the warp count field is six bits. All entries are initialized as invalid at the beginning. The pattern table is updated only at the beginning and at the end of each divergence. In current GPU designs each time a warp encounters a divergence or reconvergence point, the SIMT stack is updated. As described in prior work [12], at the divergence point the divergent active masks are pushed on top of the existing SIMT stack entries and at the re-convergence point the SIMT stack entry at the top is popped. We propose the following addition to the SIMT stack update process. Every time an entry is pushed on top of the SIMT stack the active mask vector that is being pushed on the SIMT stack is read out and it is matched against the top five active mask entries of the pattern table. If there is a hit in the pattern table, then the 6-bit warp count is incremented. Every time the SIMT stack entry is popped the active mask that is being removed is also matched with the top five pattern table entries. On a hit the warp count field is decremented. If the warp count field reaches zero that implies there are no active warps cur-

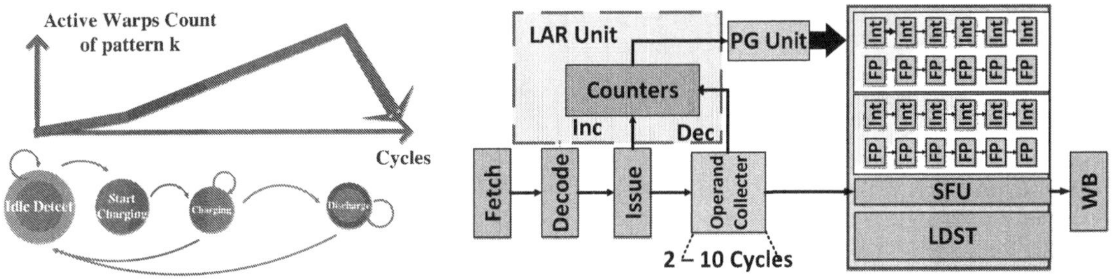

(a) Warp charger state machine (b) GPU SIMD pipeline with LAR
Figure 6: Illustrations of WarpCharger and the deterministic look ahead ready (LAR) approach

rently executing with the same active mask. Hence, the entry whose warp count reaches zero is invalidated.

If there is no hit in the pattern table, then the active mask that is being pushed on top of the SIMT stack is allocated an entry in the pattern table. First, the insertion process tries to find an invalid entry in one of the top five pattern table entries. If no invalid entry is available, it implies that there are already five divergence patterns in the machine with at least one warp with that pattern still active. Rather than perform a complex replacement algorithm, we use the last two entries in the pattern table to find an approximate match. Entries 6 and 7 in the pattern table are special entries with at least four leading zeros (entry 6) or four trailing zeros (entry 7). The basic intuition is that if a pattern can not be exactly matched with the top five patterns then we try to see if the pattern has leading or trailing zeros. This is based on our empirical observation that many patterns in fact have either trailing or leading zeros. Rather than match perfectly, we try to match the current active mask approximately when the pattern table has five valid entries already. If the current active mask has no trailing or leading zeros we simply treat it as a random pattern, and we do not store that entry in the pattern table.

We also designed a simple optimization to reduce the number of patterns that are considered for insertion into the pattern table. This optimization is based on the observation that if the divergent code is short and is executing only a few instructions before diverging again or reaching a reconvergence point, then there is no reason to insert this short lived divergence pattern into the pattern table. Hence, every time a new divergence point is reached we simply subtract the current PC from the re-convergence PC (RPC). If there is a separation of at least 100 bytes between PC and RPC, which roughly translates into 12 instructions, then we consider that divergent active mask pattern for insertion into the pattern table. Otherwise, we simply ignore that pattern. This optimization effectively reduces the number of searches and insertions in the pattern table for short lived patterns. Note that RPC and PC are both already available in existing SIMT stack hardware and hence this distance can be easily computed. Furthermore, note that this optimization is not perfect since the distance between RPC and PC is not the true metric for measuring the size of a divergent path. We needed to measure the distance between PC and jump PC within an $if - then - else$ condition to truly measure the size of the if and $else$ paths. Nonetheless this rough optimization works well by reusing existing data fields in the SIMT stack.

Per pattern type active warps subset: Since our goal is to schedule warps with same divergence patterns together, we first need to identify warps with similar divergence patterns. Each active mask entry that is pushed on the top of the stack is assigned a pattern id. In our implementation we simply use the pattern table index number where the pattern was matched as the pattern id. We augment the SIMT stack with a 3-bit pattern id which essentially stores the pattern table index where the pattern is currently matched for each warp. For instance, if the active mask vector matched entry 4 then that active mask is tagged as pattern number 4. Note that this process of searching for patterns and assigning patter id is not in the critical path. The active mask is pushed on to the SIMT stack and the matching process is conducted off the critical path. Once the active mask is associated with a pattern type (which is the pattern table index in our case), there is no need to repeat the pattern assignment until the next divergence point. This pattern id is then used by the scheduler to decide which warps to issue. This decision is made in conjunction with a warp charger logic which we will describe next.

Warp charger: The last hardware enhancement proposed in our work is the warp charger. Warp charger has the responsibility to gather a large number of warps with the same divergence pattern so that the scheduler can issue them in a clustered fashion. As illustrated in Figure 6a, the warp charger starts by simply picking the first valid entry in the pattern table and decides to charge that divergence pattern and enters into a charge state. In the charge state it informs the scheduler the pattern id number it has decided to charge. Then the scheduler gives lowest priority to that pattern id when it is scheduling warps. Thus it holds off issuing warps with that pattern id thereby allowing other warps to issue. The scheduler stores the pattern id of the pattern that is being charged in a 3-bit register. Then every time a warp enters the active queue in a two-level scheduler, it checks the pattern id of the entering warp with the pattern id it has marked for charging. If there is a match it increments a charge counter. Once the counter reaches a threshold, which is set at eight in our current implementation, then the warp charger enters the discharge state.

In the discharge state the warp charger informs the scheduler that pattern id that it wants to discharge. The scheduler then issues only warps with the discharge pattern id. Note that the warp charge counter is incremented only when a warp enters the active queue. Hence, during the discharge process all warps that are being discharged will be already available in the active queue of the two-level scheduler. If the scheduler can't find enough warps with the discharge pattern id in any given cycle, it stalls issuing warps rather than issue a different divergence pattern. This approach may appear too aggressive in providing power gating at the expense of performance. But note that the discharger only informs the scheduler when it sees a minimum of eight warps in the active queue with the same divergence pattern. Since each warp may execute many instructions cumulatively the length of idle cycles for any given SIMT lane in the current divergence pattern can be significantly enhanced. Hence, in practice warp discharger increases the effectiveness of power gating by allowing the power gating hardware to safely shutdown all SIMT lanes that are going to be unused during the discharge process. The discharge process stops when the warp count of that divergence pattern reaches zero. Then the warp charger selects the first valid pattern id from the pattern table to charge and informs the scheduler to give lowest priority to the selected divergence pattern.

Note that the warp charger works well to deal even with benchmarks with highly random warp divergence patterns. For benchmarks, such as bfs, that have many random warp divergence patterns the warp charger may pick one pattern for charging. In charge state the scheduler only gives lower priority to the selected divergence pattern. But if there are no other warps to issue the scheduler will ignore the warp charge request and continue to issue the charging patterns. Thus the warp charger provides an excellent opportunity to improve power gating efficiency without negatively impacting performance.

4.2 Gating penalty avoidance using deterministic lookahead

In this section we describe an approach avoid unnecessary sleep and wakeup penalty for power gating a SIMT lane. We propose a new technique called deterministic look ahead ready (LAR) approach. Our key idea is inspired by determinist clock gating [19], which points out that for many stages in the pipeline, the circuit block's usage is deterministic for several cycles into the future. Hence, clock gating can be disabled and enabled with near-zero penalty by exploiting this determinism. Our key observation is that as soon as a warp is issued to the operand collector stage, this warp will come into the execution unit in the immediate near future. Note that the operand collector stage is simply a pipeline stage used in GPUs to read the register input operands after a warp is already scheduled for execution. Since register reads can take multiple cycles in GPUs the operand collector stage buffers the input operands and waits for all input operand reads to complete before executing the instruction. The typical time a warp stays in the operand collector is 2-10 cycles. Thus given this knowledge it is prudent to not activate any power gating for a SIMT lane that is going to be used by any warp that entered the operand collector stage. Thus our power gating hardware will not initiate power gating any SIMT lane as long as there is at least one warp in the operand collector stage that requires the SIMT lane being considered for power gating.

Figure 6b shows a SIMT pipeline and the implementation of LAR. A per lane counter is used to track the pending warps in the operand collector. Whenever a warp is issued to the operand collector buffer, the appropriate counter in the active lane will be increment by one. When the warp leaves the operand collector, that counter will be decremented by one. Power gating logic is disabled whenever the counter value of that lane is non-zero.

4.3 Pattern and Instruction Aware Scheduler (PATS++)

PATS as described in the previous section simply uses pattern similarity to prioritize warp scheduling for each SIMT lane. Hence, the assumption is that we apply power gating for the entire SIMT lane. Recall that in our baseline architecture each CUDA core has a separate INT and FP pipeline. We use the baseline with a separate INT and FP pipelines since modern hardware designs have separate INT and FP pipelines due to vastly different representation of INT and FP numbers. We enhance PATS to take advantage of the availability of separate INT and FP units. In this section we design PATS++ which is essentially PATS that also takes into account instruction type (INT or FP) when making a warp scheduling decision. Thus PATS++ combines pattern similarity information with instruction type information. The 3-bit pattern id information is enhanced with a 2-bit instruction type field (INT/FP/SFU/LDST). The scheduler then prioritizes a warp with the same pattern for scheduling but when there are multiple warps with the same pattern available it also prioritizes issuing the warp that has the same instruction type as the previously issued warp.

Each time a warp enters the active warp queue, PATS++ checks whether it is an INT or FP instruction and increments a 6-bit counter for either INT or FP type. Initially the warp scheduler selects INT type as a priority. But if the INT counter goes down to zero it simply switches to prioritize FP type and toggles back to INT when the FP counter goes to zero.

4.4 Hardware Overheads

We assume that the per lane power gating technique is implemented as shown in [15]. The approach uses idle detect logic and ready instruction detect logic. The idle detect logic can be implemented as a counter that will be incremented every time an idle cycle is detected and cleared whenever a ready instruction is detected. Whenever the counter hits the idle detect threshold, the power gating logic will trigger the power gating signal for that specific SIMT lane.

Scheduler: PATS requires each warp entry in the scheduler to store an additional 3-bit pattern id.

Pattern table: As mentioned before, a 7-entry pattern table is required in the branching unit. Each entry has a 16-bit active mask pattern, a three bit pattern id, a valid bit, and 6 bit warp counter. In total, we need 23 bits per entry and a total of 161 bits of storage for the pattern table. For comparison logic, 16 XOR gates are used to compare SIMT stack entry that is being pushed or popped sequentially with each entry in the pattern table. One could also increase the comparison speed with additional XOR gates, but in our implementation we only compare the SIMT stack entry with each pattern table entry sequentially.

Warp charger: The warp charger stores a 3-bit pattern id that is currently selected for charging. The charger accumulates a count of all ready warps with a matching pattern id. The counter is 3 bits since we accumulate up to eight warps before starting the discharge process. In addition, there is one bit to indicate the charge or discharge state.

PATS++: PATS++ requires two-bit instruction type field attached to each warp entry, in addition to the 3-bit pattern id. It also requires two 6-bit counters to count the number of INT ready and FP ready warps.

Whenever the idle detect counter for a given SIMT lane hits the idle detect threshold, the power gating logic will trigger the power gating signal for that specific SIMT lane. In our approach even when counter value exceeds the threshold we first check the LAR to override the idle detection counter. The per lane power gating controller does not interact with the warp scheduler or warp discharger directly. The warp scheduler works only in conjunction with the warp discharger to provide longer idle windows, which simply translate into improved power gating efficiency. This decoupling between the scheduler and power gating controller simplifies our proposed design.

We also explored the option of letting the warp discharger proactively inform the power gating controller when it is ready to discharge. In this approach the warp discharger can tell the power gating controller which lanes are going to be idle during the discharge phase. But the approach requires coordination between the two sides. Furthermore even when warp discharge begins due to inherent delays within the pipeline, such as bank conflicts when reading a register, there is no way to predict exactly when the discharged warps enter the execution stage. Hence, the added benefits of this coordination were not sufficiently large to justify this complexity.

5. EVALUATION

5.1 Methodology

We evaluated our proposed techniques for energy saving and performance using GPGPU-Sim v3.2.1 [5]. As mentioned earlier, the default NVIDIA GTX480-like configuration provided with GPGPU-sim is used. We use GPUWattch [18] and McPAT [20] for power estimations. We evaluated our results using 19 benchmarks from Rodinia [8], Parboil [1], and ISPASS [5] benchmarks.

Static Energy Impact: Figure 7a and Figure 7b show the static energy savings by taking into account the power gating overhead. There are four bars in each chart. The first bar (labeled *PerLane*) shows the static energy savings when the default power gating approach [15] is applied to each of the INT and FP units within each SIMT lane. We use a break-even time of 14 cycles and wakeup delay of 3 cycles. On average this default approach saves 33.0% of the static energy for INT units and 45.4% for FP units. Note that some divergent benchmarks like backprop and MUM, the energy savings are virtually non-existent due to significantly increased transitions between wakeup and sleep states. For the same reason, cutcp even has negative energy savings.These negative savings are due to frequent interruptions to a gated SIMT lane due to short idle cycles.

The second bar labeled *Gates* shows power savings of gates approach as described in [4]. In this approach an entire cluster of INT or FP units is power gated and they also use blackout approach, which was briefly described earlier in Section 3. Gates is most beneficial for benchmarks with a good instruction mix, like cutcp, LIB and mri-q. Those benchmarks have lots of integer instruction as well as floating point instructions. On the other hand, as is shown in Figure 7b, b+tree, bfs, lavaMD, MUM, nw, pathfinder don't

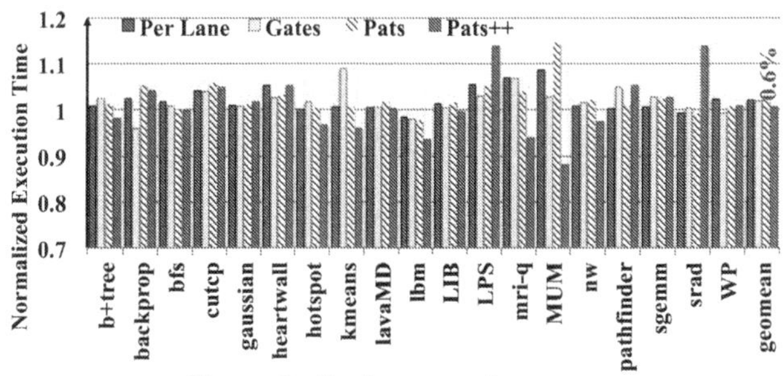

Figure 8: Performance Impact

have any FP instructions. In this case, gates is unable to find other instruction types to prevent issuing INT instructions. As a result, static energy savings for INT units are limited with gates.

The third bar (labeled *PATS*) shows the savings when we apply PATS. PATS provides 12% and 6% more energy savings on divergent benchmarks for INT and FP units compared to gates. PATS improves energy savings on many divergent benchmarks with dominant patterns, like backprop, lbm and srad. Even for benchmarks without strongly dominant divergence patterns, like bfs and MUM, PATS can still achieve energy savings. Note that in gates the authors used blackout that forces a unit to stay gated even if the idle window is small. PATS does not use blackout; thus for cutup and mri-q, which have many short idle cycles, the unit cycled frequently resulting in negative savings with PATS. It is clear that PATS would not work well on non-divergent benchmarks, and therefore kmeans and lavaMD , which are non-divergent workloads, do not benefit from PATS. The 90% energy saving of kmeans is mainly attributed to many instances of long idle cycles for SIMT lanes.

The last bar labeled $PATS++$ shows the power savings with our enhanced PATS that gives priority to instruction type in addition to the pattern id. Clearly, PATS++ provides the best power savings compared to any of the previously proposed techniques. Only LPS and pathfinder have a slight degradation with PATS++ compared to PATS. Figure7b shows the energy savings of floating point units. b+tree, bfs, lavaMD, MUM, nw show almost 100% savings, because those are integer only benchmarks. We excludes those for calculating average energy savings in the FP charts. For other benchmarks, we can see similar trends as INT. PATS and PATS++ both can outperform prior techniques. On average, PATS++ improves energy savings by 14% for both INT and FP units.

Overall, PATS++ saves 52.1% of the INT unit static energy and 66.4% of FP unit static energy. Execution unit leakage accounts for roughly 10% of the total GPU energy consumption. Therefore, PATS++ would gain 5%~6% overall GPU energy savings. Note, there's no dominant component in GPU that consumes most of the energy. Execution units, register files, and DRAM each account for 20% energy consumption. To improve GPU energy efficiency, we have to improve each component. This paper focus on saving execution unit power. With technology scaling down, as static energy consumption increases the contribution of PATS++ can be even more significant.

Performance Impact: Figure 8a shows the performance impacts of all the techniques mentioned above. The Y-axis is the execution time normalized to the default scheduler

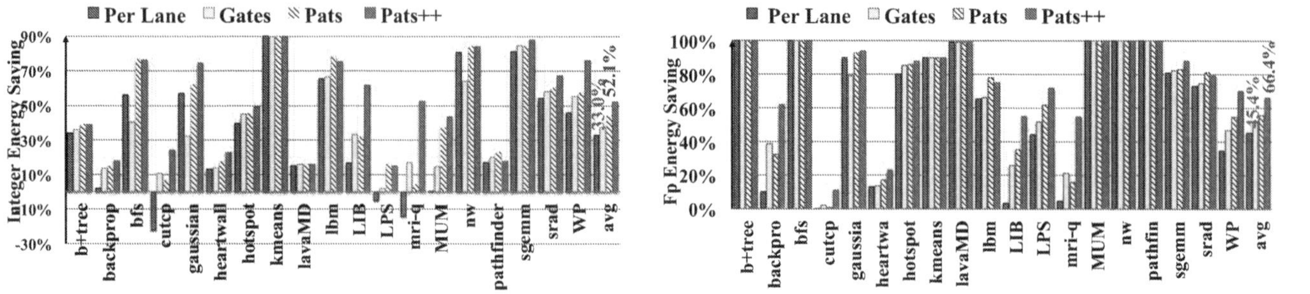

(a) Integer unit (b) Float point unit

Figure 7: Static energy savings of proposed techniques.

without power gating. Per lane has an average of 2% performance overhead. In the worst case, it can incur about 8% of performance loss for MUM. The performance loss is primarily due to power gating of SIMT lanes, which are just gated but then immediately required for execution by a fully active warp. Gates suffers about 1% performance loss and benchmarks with limited instruction mix cause the worst case performance degradation. PATS alone degrades performance by 2% but PATS++ reduces the overhead to 0.6%. The way gates, PATS and PATS++ change the scheduling order of warps may occasionally lead to increase in the performance for some benchmarks as a side effect. Most of these improvements were due to memory access re-ordering that lead to slightly improved cache hit rates.

Sensitivity to Power Gating Parameters: Figure 9b and Figure 9a show the performance and energy savings sensitivity to power gating parameters for both default per lane and PATS++. We increase the break-even time and wake-up delay in this study. Overall when the break-even time increased to 19 cycles, PATS++ still provides 50% of static energy saving in integer units and 65% of floating point units. Wakeup delay increase has the most significant impact on both performance and energy savings. But PATS++ has significantly slower degradation than the default technique of per lane power gating.

Implementation Complexity: Header/footer transistor for gating must be sized based on the amount of switching current. Thus per-lane gating transistor is smaller than the per-cluster gating transistor. The total gating transistor area, whether one uses per lane or per cluster, is roughly the same. The primary cost is the control logic overhead. We use NCSU PDK 45nm library to estimate the area and power overhead for various registers, counters and logic blocks used in PATS and PATS++. We also extract the power and area of an SM from GPUWattch [18]. An SM occupies $48.1mm^2$ and consumes 1.92 W of dynamic power and 1.61 W of leakage power. The total area overhead of PATS++ is $6269.1um^2$, resulting in 0.01% area overhead. The dynamic power is 0.015 W and the leakage power is 6.6e-5 W, accounting for 0.78% of the dynamic power and 0.004% leakage power overhead.

6. RELATED WORK

Handling SIMD divergence: Handling SIMD divergence has been focus of many prior works in GPU. Fung et al, first proposed dynamic warp formation [12] to dynamically regroup threads with different home lanes executing

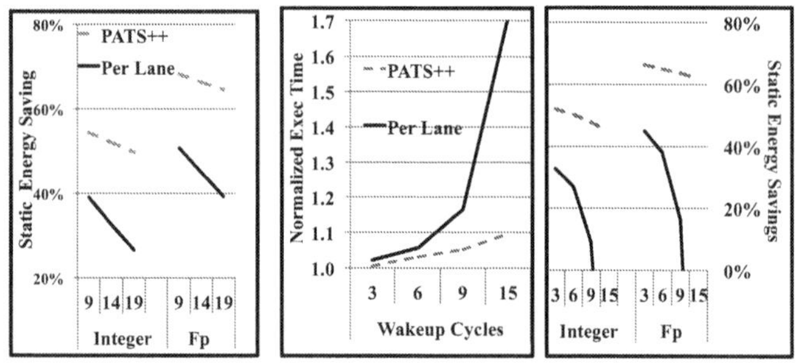

(a) Break-even time (b) Wake-up delay (bet=14)

Figure 9: Sensitivity of power gating parameters

the same instruction into a new warp. Thread block compaction [11] was then proposed to exploit the observation that divergence within a thread block occurs with high temporal locality. Recent research [25] shows that many idle lanes are aligned because branch conditions are dependent on programmable values such as thread ids, therefore requiring shuffling lanes to create better warp compaction. Intra-warp compaction [29], also targeted eliminating the aligned idleness of SIMT lanes to improve compaction opportunities. In our work, on the other hand, we exploit the aligned SIMT lane idleness to improve power gating efficiency.

Predictive power management techniques: Power management usually requires predicting when to engage the power management technique. Various techniques have been proposed to improve prediction accuracy. Idle detect is one simple but effective prediction method proposed in power gating [15], based on the observation that if a unit is idle in the previous time window, it probably would stay in idle state. In [16], a global phase history table is used to track different execution phases in microprocessor for dynamic power management. In deterministic clock gating [19], the author utilized deterministic information available a few cycles ahead to realize zero overhead clock gating. In our research, we utilize these prior approaches to power gate SIMT lanes but we then enhance and adapt them within the GPU execution context.

Power gating: Power gating techniques has been widely applied in processors [15, 21], caches [10], and NOCs [9]. Prior work on GPU power gating focused on gating a coarser granularity of SM cores [30] or an entire SP cluster based on instruction types [4]. In our work, we propose lane-level power gating and we compare with [4] to show that PATS++

can exploit lane level idleness for improving power efficiency further.

GPU power saving: Various researchers have looked at orthogonal approaches to improving GPU power efficiency. Several works [3, 13, 32] proposed to save register file power. Leng [18] saves dynamic power of the execution units and register file by clock gating and DVFS. However, our research mainly targets reducing static power by using lane-level power gating.

GPU schedulers: GPU scheduling has been extensively studied. Two-level scheduler [13] improves energy efficiency by keeping only a small subset of active warps in the active queue. Narasiman [24] has proposed another two-level scheduler that divides large warps into smaller fetch groups. Jog [17] proposed warp scheduler which enables efficient prefetching policies. Rogers [27] proposed a cache locality based warp scheduler to improve performance. PATS can be built on top any scheduler although our implementation used two-level scheduer.

Power aware schedulers: Power aware schedulers for CPUs and multicore systems [6, 28] have been studied extensively. Previous works focused on dynamic runtime power management and DVFS. Our research utilized the GPU-specific control flow divergence patterns to reduce execution unit static power.

7. CONCLUSION

GPUs provide a power efficient execution platform for many massively parallel throughput oriented applications. But when general purpose applications are ported to run on GPUs these applications suffer from inefficient resource utilization due to branch and memory divergence. This paper focuses on two aspects of this problem. First, we study the branch divergence behavior of various general purpose workloads running on GPUs and show that branch divergence patterns exhibit strong bias and only a few patterns dominate the execution in many workloads. We then exploit this knowledge to effectively power gate SIMT lanes within a GPGPU. We propose pattern aware two-level warp scheduler (PATS) that increases the idleness time of a SIMT lane. We design and evaluate PATS and an enhanced PATS++ approaches to show that the proposed approaches outperform prior GPGPU power gating techniques.

8. ACKNOWLEDGMENTS

We thank anonymous reviewers for their valuable comments on this work. We thank Mohammad Abdel-Majeed and Daniel Wong for sharing the gates power gating infrastructure for comparison purposes and Hyeran Jeon for helping with the simulation infrastructure. This work was supported by DARPA-PERFECT-HR0011-12-2-0020 and NSF-CAREER-0954211.

9. REFERENCES

[1] Parboil benchmark suite. http://impact.crhc.illinois.edu/parboil.php.

[2] Nvidia cuda compute unified device architecture - programming guide, 2008. http://developer.download.nvidia.com.

[3] M. Abdel-Majeed and M. Annavaram. Warped register file: A power efficient register file for gpgpus. In *Proceedings of the International Symposium on High Performance Computer Architecture (HPCA)*, 2013.

[4] M. Abdel-Majeed, D. Wong, and M. Annavaram. Gating aware scheduling and power gating for gpgpus. In *Proceedings of the 46th Annual IEEE/ACM International Symposium on Microarchitecture (MICRO)*, 2013.

[5] A. Bakhoda, G. Yuan, W. Fung, H. Wong, and T. Aamodt. Analyzing cuda workloads using a detailed gpu simulator. In *IEEE International Symposium on Performance Analysis of Systems and Software (ISPASS)*, 2009.

[6] D. Bautista, J. Sahuquillo, H. Hassan, S. Petit, and J. Duato. A simple power-aware scheduling for multicore systems when running real-time applications. In *IEEE International Symposium on Parallel and Distributed Processing (IPDPS)*, 2008.

[7] S. Borkar. Design challenges of technology scaling. In *Proceedings of the 32th Annual IEEE/ACM International Symposium on Microarchitecture (MICRO)*, 1999.

[8] S. Che, M. Boyer, J. Meng, D. Tarjan, J. W. Sheaffer, S.-H. Lee, and K. Skadron. Rodinia: A benchmark suite for heterogeneous computing. In *Proceedings of the IEEE International Symposium on Workload Characterization (IISWC)*, 2009.

[9] L. Chen and T. Pinkston. Nord: Node-router decoupling for effective power-gating of on-chip routers. In *45th Annual IEEE/ACM International Symposium on Microarchitecture (MICRO)*, 2012.

[10] K. Flautner, N. S. Kim, S. Martin, D. Blaauw, and T. Mudge. Drowsy caches: simple techniques for reducing leakage power. In *Proceedings of the 29th Annual International Symposium on Computer Architecture (ISCA)*, 2002.

[11] W. W. L. Fung and T. M. Aamodt. Thread block compaction for efficient simt control flow. In *Proceedings of the International Symposium on High Performance Computer Architecture (HPCA)*, 2011.

[12] W. W. L. Fung, I. Sham, and G. Y. andTor M. Aamodt. Dynamic warp formation and scheduling for efficient gpu control flow. In *Proceedings of the 40th Annual IEEE/ACM International Symposium on Microarchitecture (MICRO)*, 2007.

[13] M. Gebhart, D. Johnson, D. Tarjan, S. Keckler, W. Dally, E. Lindholm, and K. Skadron. Energy-efficient mechanisms for managing thread context in throughput processors. In *Proceedings of the 38th Annual International Symposium on Computer Architecture (ISCA)*, 2011.

[14] S. Z. Gilani, N. S. Kim, and M. J. Schulte. Power-efficient computing for compute-intensive gpgpu applications. In *Proceedings of the International Symposium on High Performance Computer Architecture (HPCA)*, 2013.

[15] Z. Hu, A. Buyuktosunoglu, V. Srinivasan, V. Zyuban, H. Jacobson, and P. Bose. Microarchitectural techniques for power gating of execution units. In *Proceedings of the International Symposium on Low Power Electronics and Design, (ISLPED)*, 2004.

[16] C. Isci, G. Contreras, and M. Martonosi. Live, runtime phase monitoring and prediction on real systems with

application to dynamic power management. In *Proceedings of the 39th Annual IEEE/ACM International Symposium on Microarchitecture (MICRO)*, 2006.

[17] A. Jog, O. Kayiran, A. Mishra, M. Kandemir, O. Mutlu, R. Iyer, and C. Das. Orchestrated scheduling and prefetching for gpgpus. In *Proceedings of the 40th Annual International Symposium on Computer Architecture (ISCA)*, 2013.

[18] J. Leng, T. Hetherington, A. ElTantawy, S. Gilani, N. S. Kim, T. M. Aamodt, and V. J. Reddi1. Gpuwattch: Enabling energy optimizations in gpgpus. In *Proceedings of the 40th Annual International Symposium on Computer Architecture (ISCA)*, 2013.

[19] H. Li, S. Bhunia, Y. Chen, T. N. Vijaykumar, and K. Roy. Deterministic clock gating for microprocessor power reduction. In *Proceedings of the International Symposium on High Performance Computer Architecture (HPCA)*, 2003.

[20] S. Li, J. H. Ahn, R. D. Strong, J. B. Brockman, D. M. Tullsen, and N. P. Jouppi. Mcpat: an integrated power, area, and timing modeling framework for multicore and manycore architectures. In *Proceedings of the 42nd Annual IEEE/ACM International Symposium on Microarchitecture (MICRO)*, 2009.

[21] A. Lungu, P. Bose, A. Buyuktosunoglu, and D. J. Sorin. Dynamic power gating with quality guarantees. In *Proceedings of the 14th ACM/IEEE international symposium on Low power electronics and design (ISLPED)*, 2009.

[22] J. Meng, D. Tarjan, and K. Skadron. Dynamic warp subdivision for integrated branch and memory divergence tolerance. In *Proceedings of the 37th Annual International Symposium on Computer Architecture (ISCA)*, 2010.

[23] A. Munshi. The opencl specification. In *Khronos OpenCL Working Group*, 2008.

[24] V. Narasiman, M. Shebanow, C. J. Lee, R. Miftakhutdinov, O. Mutlu, and Y. N. Patt. Improving gpu performance via large warps and two-level warp scheduling. In *Proceedings of the 44th Annual IEEE/ACM International Symposium on Microarchitecture (MICRO)*, 2011.

[25] M. Rhu and M. Erez. Maximizing simd resource utilization in gpgpus with simd lane permutation. In *Proceedings of the 40th Annual International Symposium on Computer Architecture*, 2013.

[26] M. Rhu, M. Sullivan, J. Leng, and M. Erez. A locality-aware memory hierarchy for energy-efficient gpu architectures. In *Proceedings of the 46th Annual IEEE/ACM International Symposium on Microarchitecture (MICRO)*, 2013.

[27] T. G. Rogers, M. O'Connor, and T. M. Aamodt. Cache-conscious wavefront scheduling. In *Proceedings of the 45th Annual IEEE/ACM International Symposium on Microarchitecture (MICRO)*, 2012.

[28] C. Scordino and G. Lipari. Using resource reservation techniques for power-aware scheduling. In *Proceedings of the 4th ACM international conference on Embedded software (EMSOFT)*, 2004.

[29] A. S. Vaidya, A. Shayesteh, D. H. Woo, R. Saharoy, and M. Azimi. Simd divergence optimization through intra-warp compaction. In *Proceedings of the 40th Annual International Symposium on Computer Architecture (ISCA)*, 2013.

[30] P.-H. Wang, C.-L. Yang, Y.-M. Chen, and Y.-J. Cheng. Power gating strategies on gpus. *ACM Transactions on Architecture and Code Optimization (TACO)*, 2011.

[31] Y. Wang, S. Roy, and N. Ranganathan. Run time power gating in caches of gpus for leakage energy savings. In *Design, Automation and Test in Europe Conference and Exhibition (DATE)*, 2012.

[32] W. Yu, R. Huang, S. Xu, S.-E. Wang, E. Kan, and G. Suh. Sram-dram hybrid memory with applications to efficient register files in fine-grained multi-threading. In *Proceedings of the 38th Annual International Symposium on Computer Architecture (ISCA)*, 2011.

Heterogeneous Microarchitectures Trump Voltage Scaling for Low-Power Cores

Andrew Lukefahr, Shruti Padmanabha, Reetuparna Das, Ronald Dreslinski Jr.
Thomas F. Wenisch, and Scott Mahlke
Advanced Computer Architecture Laboratory
Ann Arbor, MI, USA
{lukefahr, shrupad, reetudas, rdreslin, twenisch, mahlke}@umich.edu

ABSTRACT

Heterogeneous architectures offer many potential avenues for improving energy efficiency in today's low-power cores. Two common approaches are dynamic voltage/frequency scaling (DVFS) and heterogeneous microarchitectures (HMs). Traditionally both approaches have incurred large switching overheads, which limit their applicability to coarse-grain program phases. However, recent research has demonstrated low-overhead mechanisms that enable switching at granularities as low as 1K instructions. The question remains, in this fine-grained switching regime, which form of heterogeneity offers better energy efficiency for a given level of performance?

The effectiveness of these techniques depend critically on both efficient architectural implementation and accurate scheduling to maximize energy efficiency for a given level of performance. Therefore, we develop *PaTH*, an offline analysis tool, to compute (near-)optimal schedules, allowing us to determine Pareto-optimal energy savings for a given architecture. We leverage *PaTH* to study the potential energy efficiency of fine-grained DVFS and HMs, as well as a hybrid approach. We show that HMs achieve higher energy savings than DVFS for a given level of performance. While at a coarse granularity the combination of DVFS and HMs still proves beneficial, for fine-grained scheduling their combination makes little sense as HMs alone provide the bulk of the energy efficiency.

Categories and Subject Descriptors

C.1.4 [**Architectures**]: Heterogeneous systems

Keywords

Heterogeneous Multicores; DVFS; Fine-Grained Architectures; Energy Efficiency

PACT'14, August 24–27, 2014, Edmonton, AB, Canada.

http://dx.doi.org/10.1145/2628071.2628078 .

1. INTRODUCTION

Transistor scaling has historically allowed architects to build complex processor designs with ever-decreasing energy consumption. However, with the end of Dennard scaling [7], architects must seek new alternatives to improve energy efficiency [14]. A variety of proposed techniques trade off a small decrease in performance for a large reduction in energy consumption through utilizing a range of energy efficient execution modes. The most common technique, Dynamic Voltage/Frequency Scaling (DVFS) creates energy efficient modes by lowering the voltage and frequency. The second technique, Heterogeneous Microarchitectures (HMs), reduces energy by migrating execution to a more efficient, but lower performing, core microarchitecture. Traditionaly both DVFS and HMs incurred large overheads to transition between modes, limiting their applicability to coarse-grained program phases [21, 22]. However, recent efforts [19, 26, 27, 30] have drastically reduced these transition penalties, enabling switching between modes at much finer granularities.

A scheduler divides the application into numerous intervals and migrates execution to the most appropriate mode for each interval. Sub-optimal scheduling decisions reduce the realized energy savings, masking the efficiency potential of the underlying architecture. A naive approach to bound the efficiency potential of each heterogeneous architecture is to exhaustively explore *all* possible schedules. Unfortunately the complexity of this approach increases exponentially with the number of intervals and the number of modes. Emerging architectures capable of fine-grained switching further confound such analysis by drastically increasing the number of intervals in which a scheduling decision must be made. To manage this massive state space, we have developed Pareto-optimal Tradeoffs for Heterogeneity, or *PaTH*, an offline analysis tool that determines (near-)optimal scheduling decisions and calculates the Pareto-optimal tradeoff space between performance and energy savings for a specific architecture and workload.

We then use *PaTH* to explore the design space of heterogeneous low-power core architectures to determine which architectures offer the best energy savings for a given performance level. *PaTH* enables us to study the effects of intelligent scheduling as well as heterogeneity in low-power cores. Prior works, such as [2, 13], which relied on static analysis, required both HMs and DVFS to provide sufficient energy-efficient performance levels. Counter-intuitively, we find that fine-grained scheduling allows HMs to achieve higher energy efficincy for similar performance levels alone, effectively rendering fine-grained DVFS unnecessary. Overall, this paper offers the following contributions:

- We evaluate the effect of scheduling on different forms of heterogeneity on low-power cores. We study the potential tradeoffs of traditional DVFS and HMs, as well as emerging fine-grained DVFS and HMs for single-threaded applications. Overall, our results show that HMs are able to provide higher energy savings than DVFS for a given level of performance. Additionally, we find that fine-grained scheduling with HMs alone negates the need for fine-grained DVFS.
- We further analyze individual benchmarks and show significant variation in their use of DVFS and HMs to achieve Pareto-optimal performance/energy tradeoffs. We analyze common behavioral patterns across applications and their affinity to various forms of heterogeneity.
- This analysis is possible through *PaTH*, an offline analysis tool that can evaluate Pareto-optimal tradeoffs between performance and energy for a given architecture. By relying on approximations that bound the Pareto-optimal tradeoffs within an accuracy of $\pm 2.5\%$, *PaTH* efficiently searches the entire state space of possible schedules with a tractable analysis turnaround time.

2. BACKGROUND

The most prevalent heterogeneity techniques for trading performance for energy efficiency are DVFS and HMs. Today both suffer from large transition overheads. However, researchers have proposed approaches to minimize the transition latencies for both techniques.

2.1 Dynamic Voltage and Frequency Scaling

In CMOS technologies, significant power savings are possible by lowering the voltage. However, this necessitates lowering the frequency to meet timing constraints, leading to a performance loss. In prior technology generations, the frequency and voltage scaled roughly equally. Therefore, a reduction in voltage would yield a roughly equivalent reduction in frequency (and performance) but allow a much higher overall power reduction, justifying the loss in performance. However, typically low-power cores rely on low-leakage technologies, which sacrifice voltage scaling for decreased static power consumption. This, in combination with shrinking technology nodes, means voltage reductions are requiring larger corresponding reductions in frequency (and performance), marginalizing much of the benefits of voltage scaling.

2.1.1 Coarse-Grained Approaches

Traditional DVFS designs rely on off-chip voltage regulators, built using very large filtering components and connected over long wires, requiring tens of microseconds to change the voltage [19]. To amortize the overhead of voltage transitions, the granularity of switching was limited to Operating System (OS) scheduling intervals.

For these architectures, a variety of techniques have been proposed to decide when to switch DVFS levels, either at compile time [39] or dynamically using a JIT [37], or the OS [40, 35, 15]. Additionally, there have been studies that attempt to find the theoretical best performance/energy tradeoffs for a DVFS system using a given number of voltage/frequency levels [38, 16].

2.1.2 Fine-Grained Approaches

On-chip regulators bring the voltage regulator on the same chip as the core, reducing the wire length and the need for large capacitors, allowing more rapid transitions between voltage levels. These regulators can transition across the full voltage range in less than 20ns, but currently suffer from $\sim 20\%$ power conversion efficiency losses [18, 23]. Eyerman and Eeckhout study the benefits of on-chip regulators to save energy for an individual off-chip cache miss [10].

A competing technique, *dual-rail supplies*, uses two separate off-chip regulators and allows an individual core to connect to either of the two supply rails [27, 8]. Again, this technique provides sub-20ns transitions, but at the cost of an additional $\sim 10\%$ area overhead to route the extra power rail [8]. Furthermore, this technique limits the possible voltage choices to the number of rails. Li et al. propose a controller that uses dual-rail supplies to scale down the voltage and frequency on individual L2 cache misses [25].

2.2 Heterogeneous Microarchitectures

An alternative heterogeneity technique is to use single-ISA heterogeneous multicore systems, which reduce energy consumption by switching to a more efficient core when power-hungry structures in a high performance core are underutilized [21]. Researchers have conducted extensive studies of the types of cores required for multiple workloads [22], operating system codes [28], and ILP and MLP intensive codes [31].

2.2.1 Coarse-Grained Approaches

ARM Ltd. designed big.LITTLE [12], a heterogeneous multicore system, consisting of both a high performance out-of-order core (Cortex-A15) and low power in-order core (Cortex-A7). While the A7 sacrifices $\sim\frac{1}{2}$ the performance of the A15 running Dhrystone, it consumes $\sim 6x$ less power. This combination of performance and power allow the A7 to operate $\sim 3x$ more energy efficiently than the A15. As both cores have separate L2 caches, the transition between cores and rebuilding of the cache state can require as long as 20K cycles, forcing coarse-grained switching.

The challenge of when to switch between HMs is similar to changing voltages with DVFS. Van Craeynest et al. [36] propose a model that measures CPI, MLP, and ILP to predict the performance on the inactive processor. Other techniques discover an application's core bias by monitoring stall sources [20] or building architectural signatures [33] to allow the OS to migrate the application to the most appropriate core.

2.2.2 Fine-Grained Approaches.

The first approach to achieve fine-grained HMs is to enable adaptive cores by resizing hardware structures to be more efficient [1], allowing the core to lower its power consumption with minimal impact on performance. Proposed architectures attempt to optimize individual structures, such as the IQ, ROB, LSQ, and cache sizes [3, 1, 4, 9, 24].

An alternative approach is to share structures between multiple cores, most commonly caches and pipelines. Cache sharing solutions rely on multiplexing the L1 caches between multiple cores to eliminate much of the state transfer overheads when switching [29, 32]. Other researchers have proposed multiplexing pipeline stages between cores to achieve heterogeneity [30]. The hybrid approach combines two separate pipelines that share caches and a unified frontend. However, this hybrid approach has higher design complexity, and it increases the power consumption of the more energy efficient core by a reported $\sim 9\%$ [26].

2.3 Tradeoff Analysis

As both heterogeneity techniques tradeoff performance for energy savings, at a coarse granularity researchers have attempted to decide which technique is preferable. Grochowski et al. conclude that both DVFS and HMs are necessary for the best energy/performance tradeoffs [13]. Azizi et al. analyze the performance/energy tradeoffs for both DVFS and HMs and conclude that HMs can deliver large performance jumps, while DVFS delivers very good incremental performance changes [2], However, their study assumes a static mapping of applications to cores, neglecting the potential benefits of scheduling.

3. PARETO-OPTIMAL TRADEOFFS FOR HETEROGENEITY

One of the main challenges to performing a study of heterogeneity tradeoffs is to find an algorithm which optimally selects the best combination of HMs and/or DVFS in each region of execution, while minimizing the energy consumption subject to a performance constraint. For HMs, we consider high performance out-of-order core (**Big**) and energy efficient in-order core (**Little**). For DVFS, we consider six different voltage/frequency levels. A single core at a specific frequency is henceforth referred to as a **mode**. The Pareto-optimal mode for each region can vary depending on the performance constraint. Therefore, to maximize energy savings, we need to determine the Pareto-optimal mode for each region of the application *for all possible performance constraints.*

We approach this challenge by executing the application under all possible modes and dividing the application into independent blocks, called **quanta**, while collecting energy and performance characteristics for each. We form schedules by selecting a unique mode for each quantum. We then attempt to examine all possible schedules to determine the subset of schedules that forms an optimum performance/energy tradeoff. As this will prove intractable, we rely on an approximation technique that allows us to compute the performance/energy tradeoffs within a bounded level of error. We further include an optimization technique that allows us to prune large trees of provably non-optimal schedules without having to compute their energy and delay.

3.1 Quanta Independence

We claim that quanta can be evaluated independently of each other provided the switching overheads are sufficiently negligible. We analyze independence in the two scenarios, where consecutive quanta use the same mode (non-switching) or different modes (switching). In Section 5.3, we further evaluate the effects of switching overheads.

Independence: Given two sequential quanta, i and $i+1$, x_i and x_{i+1} represent the core/voltage modes for quanta i and $i+1$, respectively. The choice of x_{i+1} is *independent* of x_i if $Energy(x_{i+1}|x_i)$ and $Delay(x_{i+1}|x_i)$ are constant for all x_i, i.e. given any mode, x_i, for quantum i, the resulting energy and delay for mode x_{i+1} in quantum $i+1$ does not change.

For fine-grained architectures, a quantum is assumed to consist of 1K committed instructions. We argue this length represents the lower bound at which the overheads of switching modes are negligible, allowing quanta to be evaluated independently in fine-grained architectures. For coarse-grained architectures, we assume a quantum length of 10M instructions.

In the non-switching case ($x_i = x_{i+1}$), there is no mode change so there is no departure from the behavior of the original program run, i.e. no overheads for switching modes. Any inter-quanta interactions, e.g., overlapped cache miss or updated branch prediction, are accounted for in the existing execution trace.

For the switching case ($x_i \neq x_{i+1}$), the claim of independence relies on being able to switch modes with minimal overheads. HMs are typically designed to share caches and pipeline stages in an attempt to minimize switching overheads [26]. DVFS approaches rely on either moving the power supply on-chip or building multiple off-chip power supplies [19, 25].

As switching can potentially occur as frequently as every 1K instructions, the effects of pipeline interactions need to also be considered. For example, if an out-of-order core executes two consecutive quanta, a load miss in the second quantum may be partially overlapped by another miss in the previous quantum. However, if a switch occurs, this overlap may not occur, and the load miss in the second quantum will incur the full miss latency. These interactions were studied in greater detail in our prior work which concluded that for fine-grained architectures, the effects of these interactions were negligible provided the quantum length does not shrink below 1K instructions [26].

The claim of independence is easy to illustrate for traditional coarse-grained architectures, which were designed to rely on large quanta sizes to ensure negligible switching overheads. These architectures have transition latencies in the tens of thousands of cycles resulting in negligible impact when contrasted with the millions of cycles required for the quanta's computation.

3.2 Exhaustive Schedules

While executing the instructions in a quantum, a core incurs some delay and consumes some energy. These values differ between core/voltage modes due to their different implementations. Example performance and energy characteristics for three quanta of a fictional big.LITTLE system are shown in Table 1. For the sake of simplicity, no voltage scaling is shown. A schedule is formed by making a unique mode choice for each quantum.

Schedule: $X = \{x_1, ..., x_n\}$, an ordered mapping to a single mode, x_i for each possible quantum, i.

The easiest approach to finding the lowest energy consumption for a given level of performance is to exhaustively compute all possible schedules, calculate their resulting energy and delay characteristics, and find the lowest energy schedule for each delay. Table 2 is an exhaustive list of all possible schedules of the example in Table 1. For this example, we assume negligible switching overhead. The delay for schedule {B,L,B} is calculated by summing the delay

	Quantum 1		Quantum 2		Quantum 3	
Core	Delay	Energy	Delay	Energy	Delay	Energy
Big	10 ms	50 mJ	20 ms	60 mJ	30 ms	60 mJ
Little	20 ms	20 mJ	40 ms	50 mJ	35 ms	40 mJ

Table 1: Example Characteristics. Delay and energy characteristics for a fictional big.LITTLE system over three quanta of 10M instructions each.

Number	Schedule	Delay (ms)	Energy (mJ)
1	{B,B,B}	60	170
2	{B,B,L}	65	150
3	{B,L,B}	80	160
4	{B,L,L}	85	140
5	{L,B,B}	70	140
6	{L,B,L}	75	120
7	{L,L,B}	90	130
8	{L,L,L}	95	110

Table 2: Exhaustive Schedule Characteristics. Delay and energy characteristics for *all possible schedules* of the fictional Big (B) and Little (L) cores over the quanta of Table 1.

for choosing the Big core for quantum 1 ($10ms$), the Little core for quantum 2 ($40ms$), and the Big core for quantum 3 ($30ms$), yielding a total of $80ms$. The energy is computed similarly.

3.3 Pareto Frontier

Using exhaustive schedules we can compute the best schedule, and corresponding energy consumption, for a given performance level. Given an exhaustive list of schedules and their corresponding energy and delay characteristics, we can combine all Pareto optimal schedules to form the Pareto frontier of the energy/delay tradeoff.

Pareto Optimal Schedule: A schedule $X = \{x_1, ..., x_n\}$ is a *Pareto Optimal Schedule* if and only if there exists no schedule, $Y = \{y_1, ..., y_n\}$, over the same quanta, such that $X \neq Y$, $Energy(Y) < Energy(X)$, *and* $Delay(Y) < Delay(X)$.

Figure 1 illustrates the characteristics of the schedules of Table 2. The point (90 ms,130 mJ), formed by the schedule {L,L,B}, is made non-Pareto optimal by the point (75ms, 120mJ), formed by {L,B,L}. Together the Pareto optimal points form the Pareto frontier, which represents the best possible tradeoffs between energy and delay.

3.4 Pareto Optimal Regions

Pareto frontiers can effectively express the best energy-performance tradeoffs but they require exhaustively exploring all possible schedules. The computational complexity required to compute all schedules is n^q, where n is the number of possible core modes and q is the number of quanta. As further described in Section 4, we consider 12 possible core modes and 1M quanta. The number of possible schedules quickly becomes too large to exhaustively search the exact Pareto frontier.

One of *PaTH*'s main contributions is an algorithm to produce the Pareto Optimal tradeoffs within a bounded level of error while still exploring the entire design space in a tractable amount of time. Our approach is divided into four

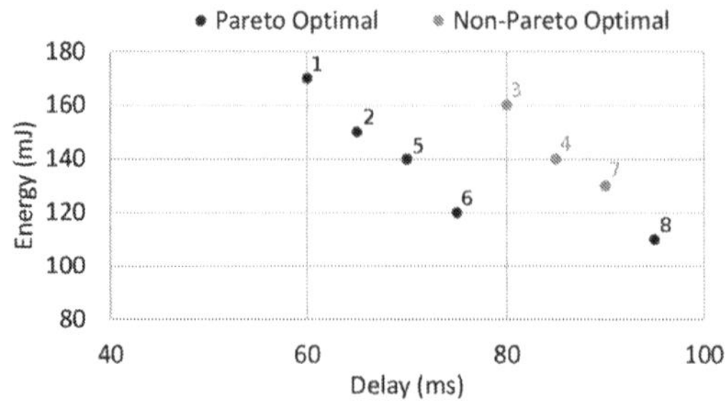

Figure 1: Pareto Frontier of Schedule Characteristics. The resulting energy and delay characteristics for all possible schedules of Table 2. Some schedules *both consume more energy and require more delay* than others, (i.e. are up and to the right), making them *non-Pareto optimal schedules.* The remaining Pareto optimal schedules form the Pareto frontier.

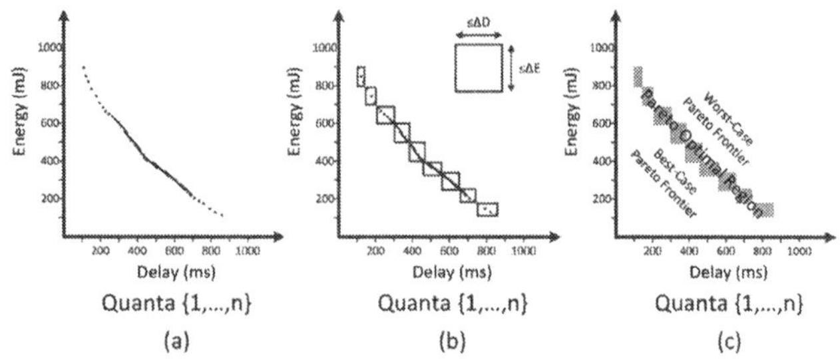

Figure 2: Approximating the Pareto Frontier. When the segment's Pareto frontier is complete (a), it needs to be approximated to allow merging with another segment's frontier (a). This is accomplished by grouping all schedules that differ by $\leq \Delta E$ and $\leq \Delta D$ (b). These schedules are then approximated by both a best-case schedule, with the least energy and delay possible for all encompassed schedules and worst-case schedule, with the highest energy and delay possible (c). Together these approximate schedules form the best-case and worst-case frontiers. The exact Pareto frontier must lie between them in the Pareto optimal region.

steps: (1) group the execution into analyzable *segments*, where each segment consists of many quanta, (2) exhaustively compute the Pareto frontier within a segment, (3) approximate all segments by introducing a bounded amount of error, and (4) convolve segments together to form the overall Pareto frontier.

By using a divide-and-conquer approach, we can compute the Pareto frontier in parallel by computing Pareto frontiers for sequential segments of the application simultaneously and convolving them to form the overall frontier. Convolution, however, requires summing the energy and delay of each schedule on the first segment's Pareto frontier (for quanta $\{1, ..., n\}$) with each schedule on the second segment's Pareto frontier (for quanta $\{n+1, ..., m\}$). The quadratic time complexity of this operation again yields an intractable problem. Therefore, before combining each partial frontier, we first use *approximation* to reduce the number of schedules that must be convolved in order to make the computation manageable.

To approximate each segment's Pareto frontier while maintaining a bounded error, we replace many schedules that

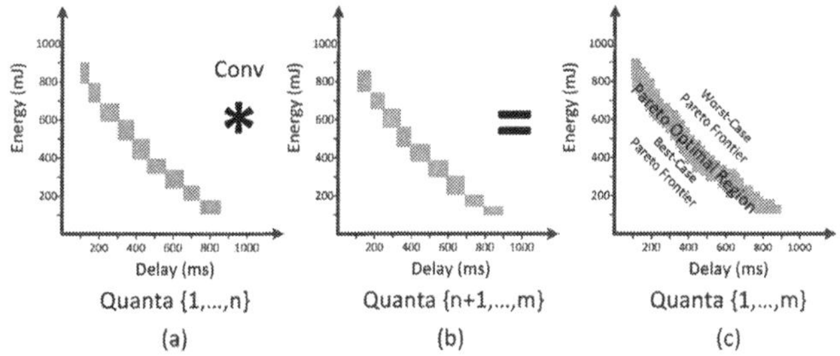

Figure 3: Merging Two Pareto Frontiers Segments. To combine quanta {1,..,n} with {n+1,..,m}, the approximated frontier from Figure 2 (a) must be convolved with the succeeding segment (b). This results in a combination of all possible best and worst-case schedules of the first segment with all possible best and worst-case schedules of the second segment, resulting in a Pareto optimal region for quanta {1,..,m} (c). The schedules that result from the convolution will bound the true Pareto frontier in the Pareto optimal region. For our analysis, we bound the total error introduced by approximation and merging to ±2.5% of the true Pareto frontier.

have similar energy *and* delay with two approximated schedules, as illustrated in Figure 2. We first select the highest energy schedule, and select nearby schedules until we meet the bound on either the energy *or* the delay error. We then replace all encompassed schedules with two approximated schedules, a best-case and worst-case. The best-case schedule consists of the least energy and least delay of any encompassed schedule. Note that least energy typically comes from a different schedule than the least delay. This schedule is Pareto optimal to all encompassed schedules. The worst case schedule is similar, but with the worst energy and delay, implying all encompassed schedules are Pareto optimal to the worst-case schedule. Together, these two schedules bound the actual Pareto frontier between them in the **Pareto optimal region**.

As illustrated in Figure 3, when combining two segments, we convolve all the best and worst-case schedules for the first segment with all best and worst-case schedules of the second segment. Hence, the combined Pareto frontier comprises two curves, representing the upper and lower bounds of the Pareto optimal region within which the true frontier must lie. By limiting the error introduced during the approximation phase such that the difference between the worst case frontier and the best case frontier is sufficiently small, we achieve a bounded estimate of the true Pareto frontier to an accuracy of ±2.5%. Our approach is a departure from traditional approaches which either optimize locally within a segment but do not combine them, [19, 39], or rely on approximations to combine segments but do not provide an overall error guarantee, [38].

3.5 Early Schedule Pruning

Rather than exhaustively computing all possible schedules within a segment to form the Pareto frontier, we can utilize early schedule pruning to reduce the number of schedules that must be generated. This optimization takes advantage of independence to detect non-optimal sub-schedules before all subsequent schedules are enumerated, removing unnecessary computation without introducing any error.

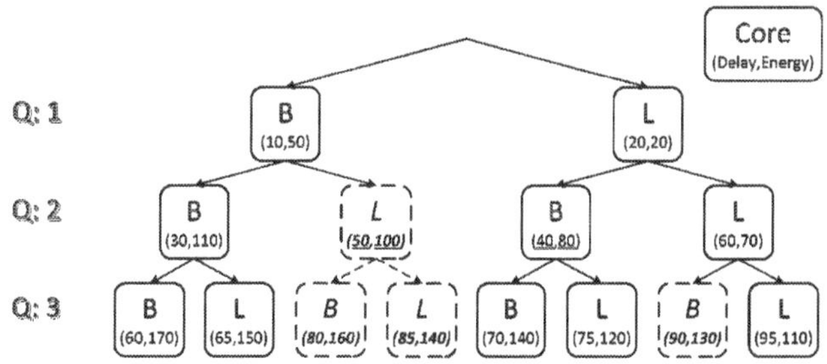

Figure 4: Early Scheduling Pruning Optimization. Once a sub-schedule becomes non-Pareto optimal (illustrated with a dashed border), all subsequent schedules will remain non-Pareto optimal and need not be considered. For example, the schedule {B,L} is made non-Pareto optimal by schedule {L,B}. Therefore all schedules based on {B,L} will never be Pareto optimal and need not be computed.

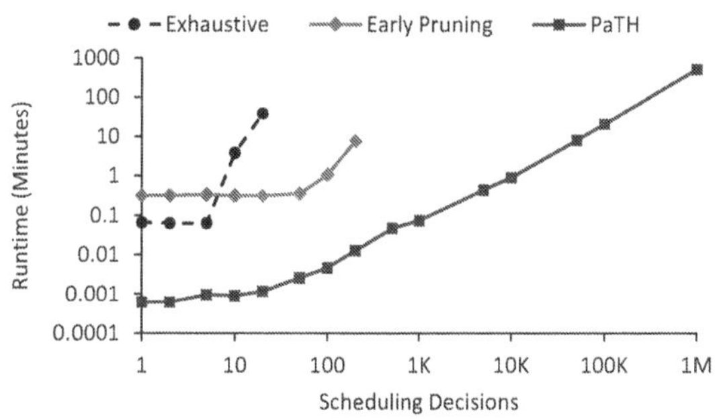

Figure 5: Runtime Overheads. Exhaustive computes all possible schedules, Early Pruning prunes non-optimal sub-schedules early. *PaTH* uses bounded approximations, and can analyze much larger scheduling windows. Scheduling decisions represent 1K and 10M instructions for fine-grained and coarse-grained approaches, respectively.

Non-Optimal Sub-schedule: Any schedule, $Z = \{x_1, ..., x_n, z_{n+1}\}$, that includes a *non-optimal sub-schedule*, $X = \{x_1, ..., x_n\}$, is also *non-optimal* as there must exist a sub-schedule, $Y = \{y_1, ..., y_n\}$, such that there exists a schedule, $Z^* = \{y_1, ..., y_n, z_{n+1}\}$, that yields $Energy(Z^*) < Energy(Z)$ and $Delay(Z^*) < Delay(Z)$.

Let us again consider the quanta from Table 1. Figure 4 illustrates the formation of schedules as a tree. The first level contains two sub-schedules, {B} and {L}, for a Big or Little core. The second level contains four sub-schedules, and the third has eight complete schedules. However, note that if we compute the energy and delay for all sub-schedules on the second level, we observe that the schedule {B,L} is made non-Pareto optimal by the schedule {L,B}. Any schedule that begins with {B,L} will always be non-Pareto optimal by a equivalent schedule that begins with {L,B}. Therefore schedules derived from the {B,L} sub-schedule need not be computed as they will never be on the Pareto frontier.

3.6 Runtime Overheads

Figure 5 illustrates the runtime overheads associated with forming the Pareto optimal tradeoffs for *gcc* with various approaches. The runtime measurements for *PaTH* were collected on an Intel 2.2GHz 8-core machine with hyper-

Architectural Feature	Parameters
Big Core	3-Issue Out-Of-Order
	2048 Entry BTB
	Tournament Predictor
	15 stage pipeline
	48 ROB entries
	82 entry register file
Little Core	2-Issue In-Order
	512 Entry BTB
	2-Bit Predictor
	8 stage pipeline
	32 entry register file

Table 3: Experimental coarse-grained core parameters

Architectural Feature	Parameters
Frontend	3-Issue
	2048 Entry BTB
	Tournament Predictor
Big Backend	3-Issue Out-Of-Order
	15 stage pipeline
	48 ROB entries
	82 entry register file
Little Backend	2-Issue In-Order
	8 stage pipeline
	32 entry register file

Table 4: Experimental fine-grained core parameters

threading. The Exhaustive approach computes all solutions to form the exact frontier while Early Pruning computes an identical frontier, but can eliminate non-optimal sub-schedules to reduce computation overhead. *PaTH* relies on bounded approximations and parallelization to scale to a much higher number of decisions.

The large overhead at the beginning of both Exhaustive and Early Pruning is due to memory pre-allocation. While Exhaustive only computes the Pareto frontier once, Early Pruning must compute the Pareto frontier for each quantum, causing higher overheads initially before the cumulative benefits of early pruning become effective. However, neither approach can tractably analyze more than 1K decisions. *PaTH*'s bounded approximations and parallelism allow it to analyze 1M decisions, or 1B instructions for fine-grained approaches, in a little over 8 hours.

3.7 Multi-Threaded Extension

While we have relied on *PaTH* to evaluate single-threaded applications, the tool can also optimize multi-threaded applications. When each core is optimized individually knowledge of thread interactions is lost, potentially wasting energy savings. *PaTH* can also optimize both *within* a core as well as *across* cores. If given c cores and q quantums, rather than selecting one mode for the quantum it must select c modes, one for each core. However, this increases the computational complexity from n^q to $(cn)^q$. This increase in computational complexity requires additional optimization steps in *PaTH*, which are left for future work.

4. METHODOLOGY

As the goal of this work is to determine the relative benefits of competing forms of heterogeneity, we model the power and performance for fine-grained DVFS and HMs, as well as their combination. Additionally, we model more traditional coarse-grained equavalent systems for comparison.

Memory	Size	Access Cycles	Latency
L1 Instruction Cache	32 KB	1 cycle	-
L1 Data Cache	32 KB	2 cycles	-
L2 Cache	1 MB	-	7.5ns
Main Memory	1024MB	-	40ns

Table 5: Experimental memory system

	28nm LP-FDSOI
Voltage (V)	Frequency (MHz)
1.1	2000
1.0	1800
0.9	1500
0.8	1200
0.7	900
0.6	600

Table 6: Realistic DVFS Levels. Achievable frequencies for a given voltage domain for *28nm Low Power - Fully Depleted Silicon on Insulator*. Data taken from [11].

4.1 Architecture Modeling

For fine-grained HMs, we mimic the architecture proposed by our prior work which relies on a single core with two separate backends, the Big (out-of-order) and Little (in-order) [26]. These multiplex access to shared L1 caches, fetch engine, and branch predictor. We require that only one backend is active at a time. Additionally, the Little backend now must access structures that were designed for a higher performance Big backend. The power implications of this architecture are further discussed in Section 4.2.

We choose to model both ideal fine-grained DVFS as well as *dual-rail* DVFS. Ideal DVFS (or just DVFS), is capable of utilizing the full voltage/frequency range of the core at a fine granularity, but *neglects the on-chip regulator conversion losses* [19]. The Dual-Rail (DR) model allows the core to rapidly transition between separate off-chip voltage supplies. As additional voltage rails incur area and/or metal layer overheads, we assume a *limit of two voltage/frequency modes* [8].

At a coarse granularity, we use separate caches and frontends to create a system similar to ARM's big.LITTLE. This system is capable of utilizing both microarchitectures and the full frequency range. However, it is limited to only being able to switch as often as every 10M instructions.

To model performance, we use the gem5 simulator [5]. We use full system simulations for 1B instructions (after fast forwarding for 2B instructions) using the ARM ISA running on Ubuntu 11.04. We evaluate the potential core modes using the SpecInt 2006 benchmarks compiled using gcc with the -O2 optimization flag. The microarchitectural parameters for the coarse-grained and fine-grained core models are given in Tables 3 and 4 respectively. The memory system latencies are shown in Table 5. We assume the frequency of both the L1 instruction and data caches scale with the core, resulting in constant access cycles, while the L2 cache and Main Memory are maintained at a constant frequency, resulting in constant access latency.

Model	Core	Perf. (MIPS)	Avg. Power (mW)	Efficiency (MInsts/J)
Coarse	Big	1986	2056	965
	Little	1191	369	3227
Fine	Big	1986	2081	954
	Little	1230	393	3129

Table 7: Modeling Baselines. The performance, power, and energy efficiency characteristics of our modeled architectures.

4.2 Power Modeling

Rather than relying on a simple scaling equation, our approach relies on realistic voltage/frequency modes for a modern technology. As such, we use published voltage and frequency levels for an ARM A9 processor using a cutting-edge process technology, 28nm Fully Depleted Silicon On Insulator (FDSOI) [11]. Table 6 gives the specific voltage and frequency levels used in this study. *The voltage levels that occurred most frequently in the schedules generated by PaTH, 1.1V and 1.0V, form the supplies for the DR systems.*

We model core power consumption using McPAT [34]. To determine the optimum performance/energy tradeoffs more accurately, we compute the energy consumption for each quantum individually. Similarly to [6], we extend McPAT to save CACTI models and re-use them for each quantum, and augment it to allow non-standard voltages. Finally, we update McPAT's internal scaling models to more accurately reflect current manufacturing technologies by using ITRS projections from 2012 to add the 28nm FD-SOI technology node [17].

For *coarse-grained* approaches, we assume a perfect transition and that inactive cores *are power-gated* when not in use. For fine-grained ideal DVFS, we assume a perfect on-chip regulator [19]. Based on [25], when raising voltages we assume execution continues at the original frequency until the voltage stabilizes, whereupon execution switches to the higher frequency. When lowering voltages, execution switches to the lower frequency before gradually lowering the voltage to match. Similarly to [26], we assume that, due to the rapid switching between microarchitectures, *fine-grained* HMs *are not power-gated*, and can only save energy through clock-gating. This implies both backends will be dissipating static energy even though only one is active.

Additionally, when using multiple backends, the shared structures must be provisioned to support the highest performance backend, effectively over-provisioning for the more energy efficient backend, reducing it's overall energy efficiency. The over-provisioning results in a Little backend whose power consumption is higher than a custom designed energy-efficient core. The fine-grained HMs must rely on operating in energy efficient mode more frequently to overcome the reduced energy efficient mode savings.

4.3 Architecture Baselines

The performance, average power, and energy efficiency for the baseline architectures for the SPECINT2006 benchmarks are given in Table 7. Note that, due to an over-provisioned frontend, the fine-grained Little achieves a slightly higher performance than it's coarse-grained counterpart. Secondly, note that both fine-grained architectures have both a higher average power and lower efficiency than their coarse-grained counterparts due to overheads of sharing architectural components and increased leakage energy of the inactive backend. As a brief comparison, Table 8 illustrates the relative differences between microarchitectures for both our coarse-grained system and ARM's when running Dhrystone [12].

System	Evaluation	ΔPerformance	ΔEnergy
Industry	ARM A7/A15	1.9x	3.5x
Modeled	Gem5+Mcpat	2.09x	3.01x

Table 8: Model Comparison. A comparison of the energy and performance differences between our modeled coarse-grained HMs and an industrial equivalent [12].

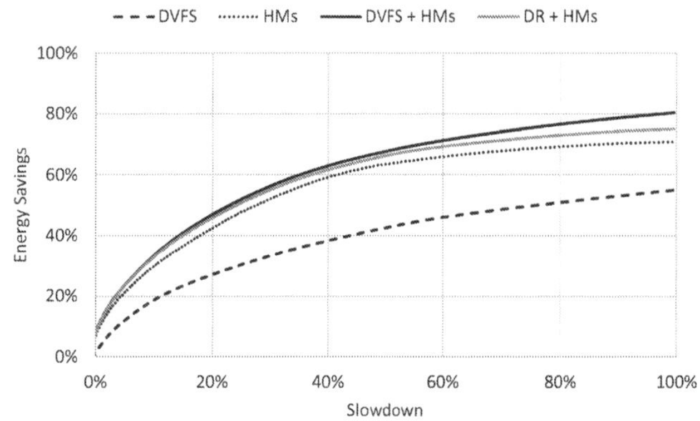

Figure 6: Pareto Frontier for Fine-Grained Switching. Note that HMs achieve more energy savings than DVFS. Additionally DVFS + HMs and DR + HMs achieve only modest improvements to HMs.

5. TRADEOFFS IN HETEROGENEITY

Using *PaTH*, we can now study the performance/energy tradeoffs between different forms of heterogeneity. Section 6 provides more in-depth analysis on how program characteristics affect the tradeoff.

We study four different fine-grained **heterogeneous configurations**: only ideal voltage heterogeneity (DVFS), only microarchitectural heterogeneity (HMs), a combination of the two (DVFS + HMs), and a combination of HMs and a dual-rail voltage system (DR + HMs). The DR design utilizes only two voltage/frequency modes. The details of these configurations are further discussed in Section 4.

5.1 Fine-Grained Comparison

Figure 6 illustrates the Pareto frontier of energy savings and slowdown for each fine-grained heterogeneous configuration. The slowdown and energy savings are normalized to the performance and energy of the highest performance microarchitecture (Big) at the highest frequency(2GHz), where a 100% slowdown indicates a doubling of the runtime. To interpret the tradeoff, observe the energy savings for each heterogeneous configuration at a specific slowdown. Higher lines indicate better configurations, as they achieve higher energy savings for a given slowdown.

Figure 6 illustrates that HMs are able to achieve higher energy savings for a given level of slowdown than DVFS regardless of the slowdown level. Analysis of the microar-

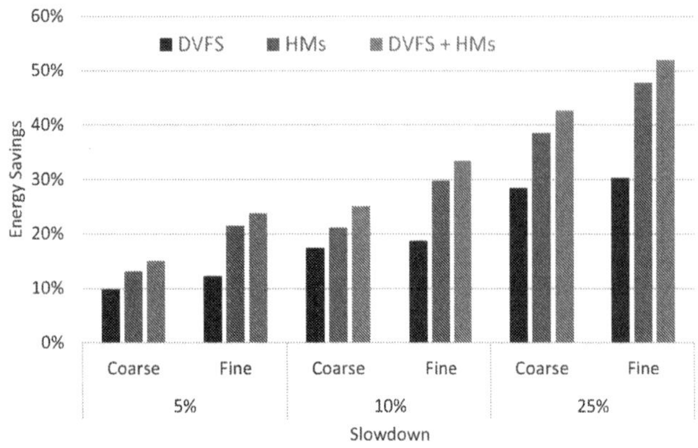

Figure 7: Impact of Switching Granularity. At smaller slowdowns, the benefits of fine-grain switching are more apparent. Also, HMs achieve better tradeoffs than both coarse-grained DVFS + HMs and fine-grained DVFS.

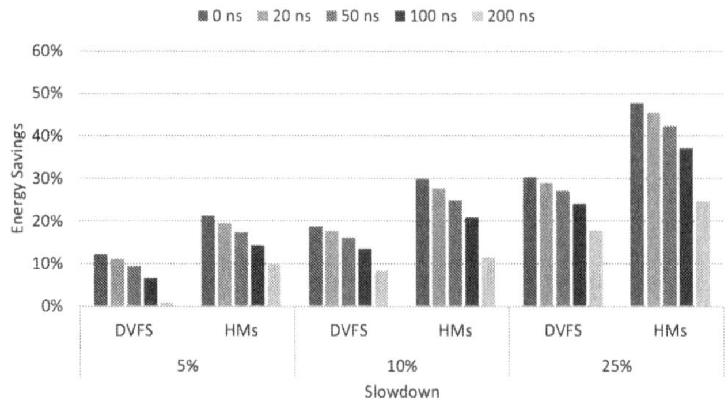

Figure 8: Impact of Switching Overheads Note that even experiencing a 100ns delay, HMs are still able to achieve better tradeoffs than idealistic DVFS.

chitectures helps confirm this observation. DVFS can only operate a complex architecture slower, which only yields its maximum effectiveness when stalled on memory-bound phases. However, HMs can switch to a simpler architecture (with a shorter pipeline) while maintaining the same frequency. Therefore HMs are able to improve efficiency under more phases with poor performance, such as low ILP or high branch misprediction levels, as well as memory-bound phases. Figure 6 indicates that the combination of DVFS + HMs offers an additional 3-4% energy savings over only HMs until about 60% slowdowns. *Thus HMs, rather than DVFS, provide more opportunities to switch to a more energy efficient mode without suffering significant performance loss.* Please see Section 6 for more in-depth analysis based on program behavior.

5.2 Switching Granularity

Figure 7 compares the tradeoffs for each heterogeneous configuration with different switching granularities, both fine-grained (1K instruction quanta) and coarse-grained (10M instruction quanta). Here we observe that at coarse switching granularities, DVFS saves 10%, 17% and 28% of the energy while HMs delivers 13%, 21%, and 38%. Finally, with DVFS + HMs, energy savings of 15%, 25% and 43% are possible.

Focusing on the benefits of fine-grained switching, we observe that DVFS provides an additional 2% energy savings for a given level of performance over coarse-grained DVFS. However HMs are able to save 7-10% more energy than coarse-grained HMs. The minimal improvement of fine-grained DVFS is caused by the nature of the phases it targets. L2 misses, where DVFS garners it's primary benefits, tend to occur in bursts, allowing them to be captured by both coarse and fine-grained approaches. However, fine-grained HMs are able to capture short phases of multiple branch mispredicts or low-ILP that cannot be captured by coarse-grained HMs or DVFS. These additional capabilities allow *HMs to benefit more from fine-grained switching than DVFS.*

Focusing on a 5% slowdown, we observe that coarse-grained DVFS + HMs allow 15% energy savings, a 3x energy savings return for the performance loss. Fine-grained HMs alone are able to achieve a 21% energy savings. Finally, using a fine-grained DVFS + HMs system, the core is able to save 25% of the energy consumption with a 5% slowdown, a 5X energy savings return for the performance loss. *Fine-grained architectures are able to save 10% more energy than the best coarse-grained approach.*

5.3 Switching Overheads

Thus far in our analysis we have neglected the overheads of switching. However, switching as frequently as every 1K instructions could have an impact on the tradeoff. To model the overheads of switching, we augment *PaTH* to track the number of switches for each schedule and then factor in various levels of fixed overhead per switch. As discussed in Section 4.2, we assume that fine-grained DVFS systems switch between different levels without any execution stalls, but suffer the power consumption for the highest voltage during the transition. For transitions between fine-grained HMs, we assume the execution halts for a fixed number of cycles, and during that delay both microarchitectures are consuming their average power.

Figure 8 illustrates the results of factoring in delays of various lengths. The achieved energy savings are shown with 0 (ideal), 20, 50, 100, and 200 ns delays. As the exact transition latency is design dependent, we have included a wide range of latencies. Kim et al. developed an on-chip voltage regulator capable of scaling over the full voltage range in 20ns [18]. Lukefahr et al. report a fine-grained HM that incurs less than 1% overhead for switching at granularities of 1K instructions, indicating a less than 20ns switching delay.

As shown in Figure 8, at a 5% slowdown, HMs suffer a 2%, 4%, 7%, and 12% drop in energy savings for 20, 50, 100, and 200 ns latencies. Similarly DVFS suffers a 1%, 3%, 6%, and 11% drop. The observation is that even with a 100ns latency cost per switch, HMs are still able to achieve higher energy savings than ideal DVFS.

5.4 Leakage Overheads

For fine-grained HMs we assume the inactive backend is clock-gated but not power-gated. Therefore, another major variable in the performance/energy tradeoff for these architectures is the leakage energy incurred by the inactive backend. When in Little mode, the leakage energy of Big adds extra energy overheads to Little. Figure 9 illustrates the impact on energy savings when we increase the assumed leak-

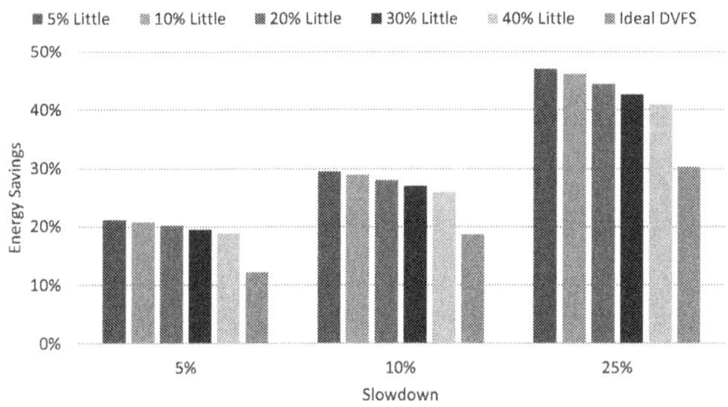

Figure 9: Impact of Leakage Energy Overheads for Fine-Grained HMs. Each bar illustrates the energy savings as Big's leakage energy adds overheads to the total power in Little mode. Here, even with a 40% power overhead from Big's leakage, fine-grained HMs still achieve better performance/energy tradeoffs than ideal DVFS.

age power overheads of Big relative to Little's total power. Note the Little backend adds insignificant leakage while the Big backend is active. Different Pareto-optimal schedules result as leakage is increased, causing *PaTH* to shift some quanta to a higher performance mode. At a 5% slowdown level, a majority of the application is still run on the Big backend to meet performance requirements, resulting in a minor impact of leakage energy as the Little backend is not as heavily utilized, However, as the allowed slowdown increases, the Little backend is increasingly utilized and the overall energy savings reflect the additional leakage incurred when using the Little backend. Even with an additional 40% leakage power overhead, fine-grained HM's are still able to achieve better energy savings for a given level of performance than ideal DVFS. By analyzing the results from [11], for a low leakage 28nm FDSOI process, we expect the overhead of the Big's leakage to add an additional 10-20% power overhead when in Little mode.

5.5 Discussion

Prior works, most notably [2], relied on static application-to-core allocation to derive their performance/energy pareto frontiers. They arrive at two core designs, then used voltage scaling to provide incremental performance improvements at the cost of additional energy. However, our results indicate that HMs provide a superior tradeoff space than DVFS. In fact, our results suggest that building fine-grained DVFS is unnecessary when fine-grained HMs are available. Additionally, we show that these results are not affected by sensitivity to either switching overheads or leakage energy.

We believe there are two main differences that help to explain the discrepancy between prior works. First, we have more restrictive DVFS scaling due to the limitations imposed by the use of low-leakage transistors for low-power cores. Second, prior studies neglect to include the benefits of intelligent scheduling. By using scheduling to intelligently switch between different HMs, we can achieve many of the same performance levels available through DVFS with a higher energy savings.

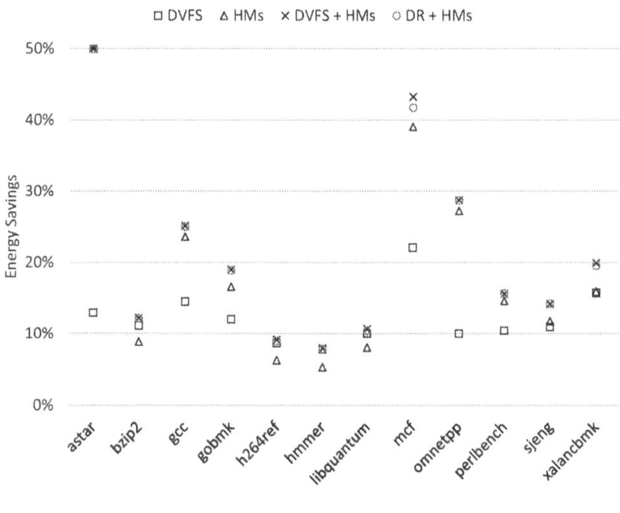

Figure 10: Per Benchmark Energy Savings for a 5% Slowdown

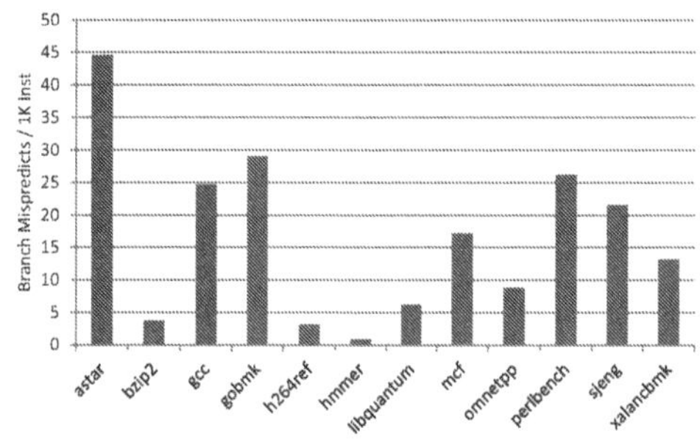

Figure 11: Branch mispredictions per thousand instructions

6. PROGRAMMATIC BEHAVIOR

Heterogeneity provides energy savings by mapping low performance application phases to more energy efficient modes (lower voltage or simpler microarchitecture). The goal of this section is to study the programmatic behavior of individual benchmarks and examine their predisposition to the different forms of heterogeneity through illustrative case studies. Figure 10 illustrates the wide range of potential energy savings for the different techniques across all the benchmarks studied. This range indicates that some benchmarks are better able to utilize DVFS, others HMs, and still others see little benefit from either fine-grained approach.

6.1 Expectations

To begin our study, we show a few metrics that we believe are most useful in explaining why some benchmarks prefer one form of heterogeneity over another. These metrics include branch mispredicts (Figure 11), L2 cache accesses (Figure 12), and instructions per cycle (Figure 13). These measurements were taken using the highest frequency level for the Big microarchitecture.

The first metric, branch mispredicts, is chosen to illustrate a scenario which puts Little at an advantage. The Little core, with its shorter pipeline length, can recover from branch mispredictions faster. Additionally, during periods of high mispredictions, lowering the frequency of a Big core neither increases branch prediction accuracy nor reduces

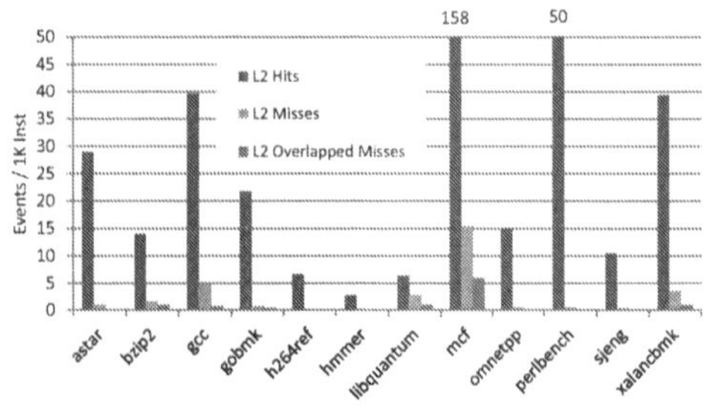

Figure 12: Categorized L2 accesses per thousand instructions

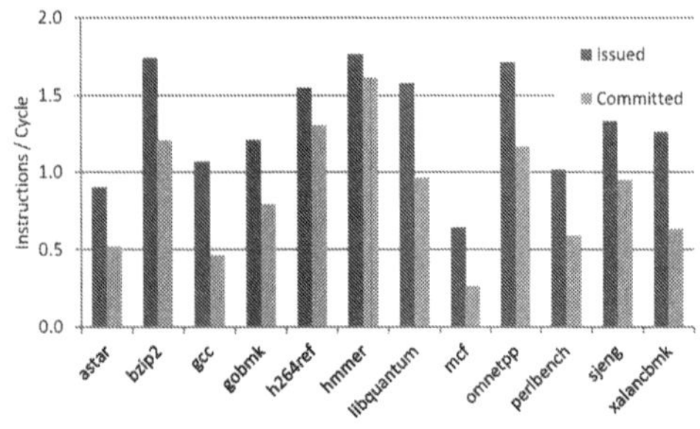

Figure 13: Issued and committed instructions per cycle in a thousand instruction window

misprediction penalties. Therefore, we consider benchmarks with highly unpredictable control flow to be more amenable to HMs.

The next metric is L2 cache accesses, which include three separate quantities, L2 hits, L2 misses, and L2 overlapable misses. As a high performance Big core cannot avoid stalling on L2 misses, these offer an ideal opportunity to switch to a Little core. However, if the L2 misses are independent, they can be issued in parallel by a Big core operating at a lower voltage. This is not possible with the Little core, which cannot exploit this parallelism. Therefore, if the application is generating a large number of independent L2 misses, DVFS is a better option. Alternatively, if it has large number of dependent L2 misses HMs are a better option.

Finally, the third metric is instructions per cycle. We observe that for several computation-bound benchmarks, neither form of heterogeneity is significantly utilized. The performance of these benchmarks is limited primarily by the frequency and issue width. Therefore they prefer the highest frequency on the core with the highest issue width. As DVFS reduces frequency, and HMs reduce issue width, both approaches deliver less than average energy returns.

Given Figures 11-13, we expect that *bzip2*, *hmmer*, *h264ref* should be computation-bound. More control-bound applications, such as *astar*, *gobmk*, and *perlbench*, which have higher branch misprediction rates and lower numbers of L2 misses, should prefer HMs. *mcf*, *libquantum*, *xalancbmk*, which have higher L2 miss rates and numerous parallel loads, should prefer DVFS. The remaining benchmarks have intermediate levels of both branch mispredictions and L2 misses, and we expect them to be able to utilize some combination of both types of heterogeneity.

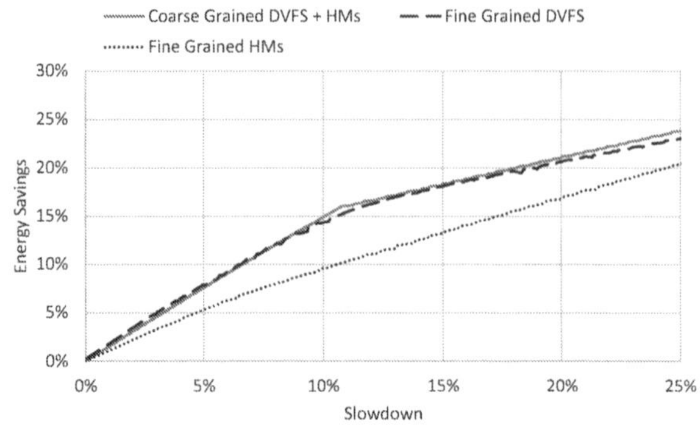

Figure 14: Pareto Frontier for *hmmer*. Note DVFS achieves better tradeoffs than HMs. Also the coarse-grained and fine-grained tradeoffs are nearly identical.

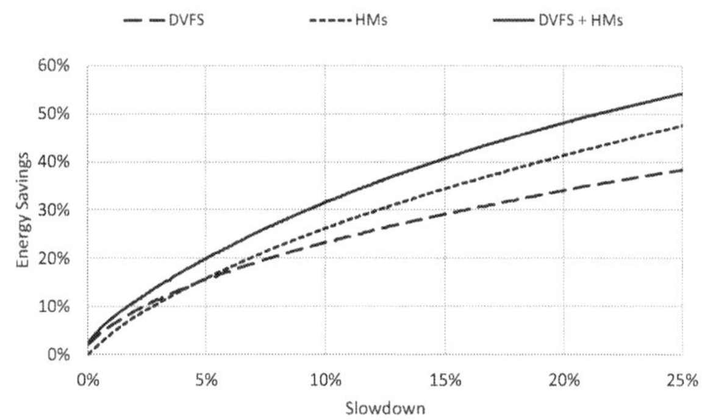

Figure 15: Pareto Frontier for *xalancbmk*. Note the much higher energy savings achieved using DVFS than HMs for small levels of slowdown.

6.2 Benchmark Classifications

The first, and perhaps least interesting, class of benchmarks are the computation-bound. In Figure 14, we have chosen *hmmer* as the representative of this class. Due to the stable long-term phases of this benchmark, fine-grained approaches gain almost nothing over a coarse-grained approach. Also, these benchmarks prefer DVFS simply because the performance difference between modes is smaller. *hmmer* effectively utilizes a 10% slower DVFS level to incur a 10% slowdown. However, its energy saving returns are only slightly better than the performance loss required to achieve it.

The first memory-bound application we study is *xalancbmk*. This benchmark has a moderate amount of L2 misses, but a large fraction of them can be overlapped. Figure 15 illustrates that the Pareto frontier for fine-grained DVFS is above (i.e. saves more energy than) fine-grained HMs, until around a 5% performance loss. For this benchmark DVFS, which can exploit parallel L2 misses, gives a better return than HMs. The return is because Little, while more energy efficient, must stall on every L2 miss. Beyond 5%, there is not a sufficient number of parallel loads to continue to make DVFS more efficient.

The second memory-bound benchmark we highlight is *mcf*. Figure 12 shows high levels of memory parallelism that indicate this benchmark should prefer to use DVFS. However, Figure 16 illustrates that it actually prefers HMs. This counter-intuitive result can be explained by noting that *mcf*

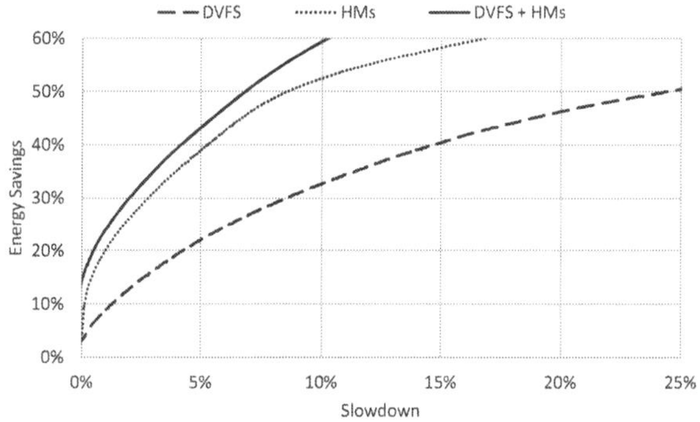

Figure 16: Pareto Frontier for *mcf***.** Unlike expected, HMs are preferred to DVFS.

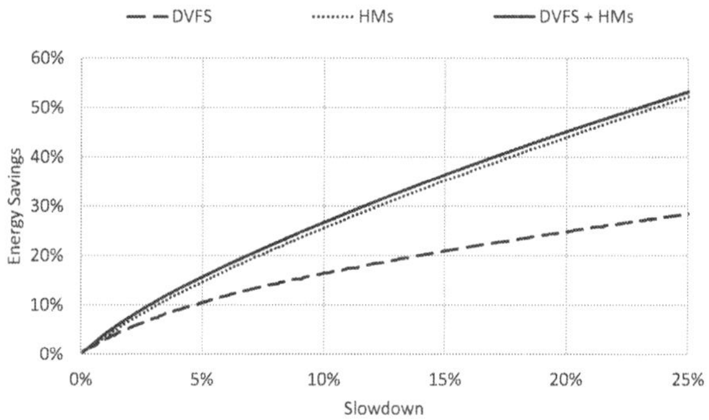

Figure 17: Pareto Frontier for *perlbench***.** Note the utilization of HMs due to L2 pointer-chasing.

exhibits phased behaviors. While the initial phase contains a large number of parallel loads, after the phase change the number of parallel loads reduces considerably. Therefore, while the average parallel load count is still relatively high, a majority of this parallelism comes in the first phase of the execution. Therefore, *mcf* prefers to run a combination of DVFS and HMs to optimize individual execution phases.

The final application class consists of control-bound applications. For this example we choose to scrutinize *perlbench*, which has one of the highest branch misprediction rates. This benchmark also has a large number of L2 hits which tends to form dependence chains. Figure 17 illustrates that a combination of frequent branch mispredictions and serial memory accesses causes this benchmark to prefer HMs. In fact, *perlbench* maps so well to HMs that the addition of DVFS adds almost no benefit.

6.3 Coarse vs. Fine Grain

Now we return our attention to how switching granularity affects individual benchmarks. Benchmarks like *hmmer*, shown in Figure 14, which have stable long-term phases, allow coarse-grained approaches to fare as well as fine-grained. However, benchmarks with unstable phase behavior benefit from using a fine-grained system.

Figure 18 illustrates the benefits of fine-grained HMs for *omnetpp*. While coarse-grained HMs achieve a nearly linear tradeoff, fine-grained HMs are able to achieve 3x more savings than coarse-grained HMs at a 10% slowdown target. Figure 19 illustrates that if measured at a fine granularity, *omnetpp* shows two finely interleaved main performance

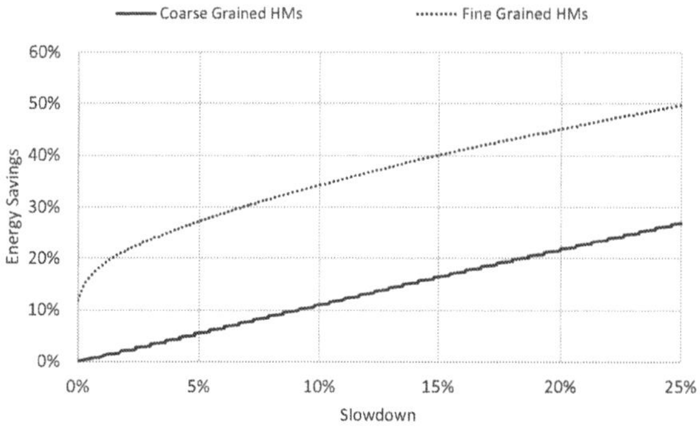

Figure 18: Pareto Frontier for *omnetpp***.** Fine grained HMs achieve better tradeoffs than coarse-grained HMs.

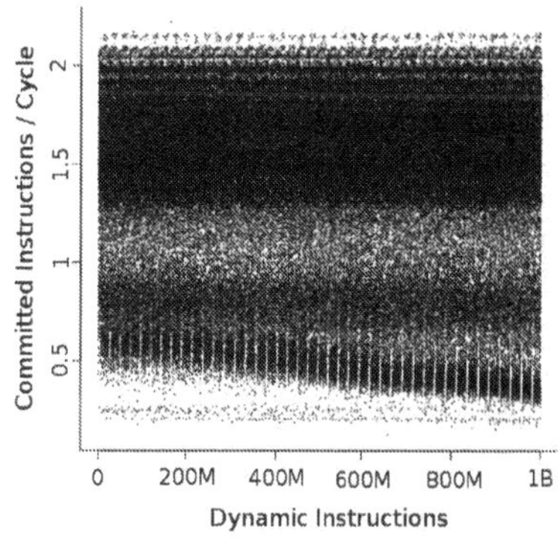

Figure 19: Committed Instruction / Cycle for *omnetpp***.** Each point represents 1K dynamic instructions. Note the high performance band, which benefits from out-of-order, and the low performance band , which does not.

bands, one higher and one lower. Fine-grained switching is required to exploit them. The Big mode is required for the higher band, but the lower band can be run on the Little mode with nearly the same performance, reducing the energy consumed without impacting performance. As the low performance bands are not caused by parallel L2 misses, DVFS cannot target these phases as effectively as HMs.

6.4 Combined Heterogeneity

In some benchmarks, DVFS performs well for some phases of the application and HMs for others. Often initially DVFS achieves a better tradeoff, but there are a limited number of phases that can exploit DVFS, so HMs begin to dominate for higher slowdowns. This leads to a scenario where both are used simultaneously. A variety of benchmarks utilize both DVFS and HMs synergistically to achieve increased energy savings, e.g, *xalancbmk* and *mcf* of Figures 15 and 16.

7. CONCLUSION

This paper explored the implications of scheduling using different forms of heterogeneity to maximize energy efficiency for a given level of performance. We developed *PaTH*, an offline analysis tool that is capable of determining the Pareto-optimal performance/energy tradeoffs for a heterogeneous architecture. *PaTH* is capable of efficiently searching the enormous state space of possible schedules with tractable analysis turnaround time, by relying on bounded approximations to find the Pareto-optimal performance/energy tradeoffs within an accuracy of ±2.5%. We then use *PaTH* to show the performance and energy tradeoffs for DVFS and HMs, as well as their combination.

Overall, our results show that HMs are able to provide higher energy efficiency than DVFS for a given level of performance. While at a coarse granularity the combination of DVFS and HMs still proves beneficial, for fine-grained scheduling their combination makes little sense as HMs alone provide the bulk of the energy efficiency. Additionally, we analyzed the effects of switching granularity and overheads on the choice of heterogeneity. Finally, we demonstrated that different benchmarks prefer different types and amounts of heterogeneity.

8. ACKNOWLEDGEMENTS

This work is supported in part by ARM Ltd and by the National Science Foundation under grant SHF-1217917. The authors would like to thank the fellow members of the CCCP research group, our shepherd (Osman Unsal), and the anonymous reviewers for their time, suggestions, and valuable feedback.

9. REFERENCES

[1] D. Albonesi, R. Balasubramonian, S. Dropsbo, S. Dwarkadas, E. Friedman, M. Huang, V. Kursun, G. Magklis, M. Scott, G. Semeraro, P. Bose, A. Buyuktosunoglu, P. Cook, and S. Schuster, "Dynamically tuning processor resources with adaptive processing," *IEEE Computer*, vol. 36, no. 12, pp. 49 -58, Dec. 2003.

[2] O. Azizi, A. Mahesri, B. C. Lee, S. J. Patel, and M. Horowitz, "Energy-performance tradeoffs in processor architecture and circuit design: a marginal cost analysis," in *Proceedings of the 37th annual international symposium on Computer architecture*, 2010, pp. 26–36.

[3] R. Bahar and S. Manne, "Power and energy reduction via pipeline balancing," *Proc. of the 28th Annual International Symposium on Computer Architecture*, vol. 29, no. 2, pp. 218–229, 2001.

[4] R. Balasubramonian, D. Albonesi, A. Buyuktosunoglu, and S. Dwarkadas, "Memory hierarchy reconfiguration for energy and performance in general-purpose processor architectures," in *Proc. of the 27th Annual International Symposium on Computer Architecture*, 2000, pp. 245–257.

[5] N. Binkert, B. Beckmann, G. Black, S. K. Reinhardt, A. Saidi, A. Basu, J. Hestness, D. R. Hower, T. Krishna, S. Sardashti, R. Sen, K. Sewell, M. Shoaib, N. Vaish, M. D. Hill, and D. A. Wood, "The gem5 simulator," *SIGARCH Comput. Archit. News*, vol. 39, no. 2, pp. 1–7, Aug. 2011.

[6] T. Carlson, W. Heirman, and L. Eeckhout, "Sniper: Exploring the level of abstraction for scalable and accurate parallel multi-core simulation," in *High Performance Computing, Networking, Storage and Analysis (SC), 2011 International Conference for*, 2011, pp. 1–12.

[7] R. Dennard, F. Gaensslen, H.-N. Yu, V. LEO RIDEOVT, E. Bassous, and A. R. Leblanc, "Design of ion-implanted mosfet's with very small physical dimensions," *Solid-State Circuits Society Newsletter, IEEE*, vol. 12, no. 1, pp. 38–50, 2007.

[8] R. Dreslinski, "Near threshold computing: From single core to many-core energy efficient architectures," Ph.D. dissertation, University of Michigan, 2011.

[9] C. Dubach, T. M. Jones, E. V. Bonilla, and M. F. P. O'Boyle, "A predictive model for dynamic microarchitectural adaptivity control," in *Proceedings of the 2010 43rd Annual IEEE/ACM International Symposium on Microarchitecture*, ser. MICRO '43, 2010, pp. 485–496.

[10] S. Eyerman and L. Eeckhout, "Fine-grained dvfs using on-chip regulators," *ACM Trans. Archit. Code Optim.*, vol. 8, no. 1, pp. 1:1–1:24, Feb. 2011.

[11] P. Flatresse, G. Cesana, and X. Cauchy, "Planar fully depleted silicon technology to design competitive soc at 28nm and beyond," Feb. 2012, http://www.soiconsortium.org/link-812.php.

[12] P. Greenhalgh, "Big.little processing with arm cortex-a15 & cortex-a7," Sep. 2011.

[13] E. Grochowski, R. Ronen, J. Shen, and P. Wang, "Best of both latency and throughput," in *Computer Design: VLSI in Computers and Processors, 2004. ICCD 2004. Proceedings. IEEE International Conference on*, 2004, pp. 236–243.

[14] M. Horowitz, E. Alon, D. Patil, S. Naffziger, R. Kumar, and K. Bernstein, "Scaling, power, and the future of cmos," in *Electron Devices Meeting, 2005. IEDM Technical Digest. IEEE International*, 2005, pp. 7 pp.–15.

[15] C. Isci, A. Buyuktosunoglu, C. Cher, P. Bose, and M. Martonosi, "An analysis of efficient multi-core global power management policies: Maximizing performance for a given power budget," in *Proc. of the 39th Annual International Symposium on Microarchitecture*, Dec. 2006, pp. 347–358.

[16] T. Ishihara and H. Yasuura, "Voltage scheduling problem for dynamically variable voltage processors," in *Proceedings of the 1998 international symposium on Low power electronics and design*, ser. ISLPED '98, 1998, pp. 197–202.

[17] ITRS, "International technology roadmap for semiconductors 2012," 2012, http://www.itrs.net/.

[18] W. Kim, D. Brooks, and G.-Y. Wei, "A fully-integrated 3-level dc-dc converter for nanosecond-scale dvfs," *IEEE Journal of Solid-State Circuits*, vol. 47, no. 1, pp. 206 -219, Jan. 2012.

[19] W. Kim, M. S. Gupta, G.-Y. Wei, and D. Brooks, "System level analysis of fast, per-core dvfs using on-chip switching regulators," in *Proc. of the 14th International Symposium on High-Performance Computer Architecture*, 2008, pp. 123–134.

[20] D. Koufaty, D. Reddy, and S. Hahn, "Bias scheduling in heterogeneous multi-core architectures," in *Proc. of the 5th European Conference on Computer Systems*, 2010, pp. 125–138.

[21] R. Kumar, K. I. Farkas, N. P. Jouppi, P. Ranganathan, and D. M. Tullsen, "Single-ISA Heterogeneous Multi-Core Architectures: The Potential for Processor Power Reduction," in *Proc. of the 36th Annual International Symposium on Microarchitecture*, Dec. 2003, pp. 81–92.

[22] R. Kumar, D. M. Tullsen, and N. P. Jouppi, "Core architecture optimization for heterogeneous chip multiprocessors," in *Proc. of the 15th International Conference on Parallel Architectures and Compilation Techniques*, 2006, pp. 23–32.

[23] H.-P. Le, J. Crossley, S. R. Sanders, and E. Alon, "A sub-ns response fully integrated battery-connected switched-capacitor voltage regulator delivering 0.19 w/mm 2 at 73% efficiency," in *Solid-State Circuits Conference Digest of Technical Papers (ISSCC), 2013 IEEE International.* IEEE, 2013, pp. 372–373.

[24] J. Lee, V. Sathisha, M. Schulte, K. Compton, and N. S. Kim, "Improving throughput of power-constrained GPUs using dynamic voltage/frequency and core scaling," in *Proc. of the 20th International Conference on Parallel Architectures and Compilation Techniques*, 2011, pp. 111–120.

[25] H. Li, C.-Y. Cher, T. N. Vijaykumar, and K. Roy, "Vsv: L2-miss-driven variable supply-voltage scaling for low power," in *Proceedings of the 36th annual IEEE/ACM International Symposium on Microarchitecture*, ser. MICRO 36, 2003, pp. 19–28.

[26] A. Lukefahr, S. Padmanabha, R. Das, F. M. Sleiman, R. Dreslinski, T. F. Wenisch, and S. Mahlke, "Composite cores: Pushing heterogeneity into a core," in *Proc. of the 45th Annual International Symposium on Microarchitecture*, 2012, pp. 317–328.

[27] T. N. Miller, X. Pan, R. Thomas, N. Sedaghati, and R. Teodorescu, "Booster: Reactive core acceleration for mitigating the effects of process variation and application imbalance in low-voltage chips," in *Proc. of the 18th International Symposium on High-Performance Computer Architecture*, vol. 0, 2012, pp. 1–12.

[28] J. Mogul, J. Mudigonda, N. Binkert, P. Ranganathan, and V. Talwar, "Using asymmetric single-isa cmps to save energy on operating systems," *IEEE Micro*, vol. 28, no. 3, pp. 26–41, May 2008.

[29] H. Najaf-abadi, N. Choudhary, and E. Rotenberg, "Core-selectability in chip multiprocessors," in *Parallel Architectures and Compilation Techniques, 2009. PACT '09. 18th International Conference on*, 2009, pp. 113–122.

[30] H. Najaf-abadi and E. Rotenberg, "Architectural contesting," in *High Performance Computer Architecture, 2009. HPCA 2009. IEEE 15th International Symposium on*, 2009, pp. 189–200.

[31] G. Patsilaras, N. K. Choudhary, and J. Tuck, "Efficiently exploiting memory level parallelism on asymmetric coupled cores in the dark silicon era," *ACM Trans. Archit. Code Optim.*, vol. 8, no. 4, pp. 28:1–28:21, Jan. 2012.

[32] K. K. Rangan, G.-Y. Wei, and D. Brooks, "Thread motion: fine-grained power management for multi-core systems," in *Proc. of the 36th Annual International Symposium on Computer Architecture*, 2009, pp. 302–313.

[33] D. Shelepov, J. C. Saez Alcaide, S. Jeffery, A. Fedorova, N. Perez, Z. F. Huang, S. Blagodurov, and V. Kumar, "Hass: A scheduler for heterogeneous multicore systems," *SIGOPS Oper. Syst. Rev.*, vol. 43, no. 2, pp. 66–75, Apr. 2009.

[34] L. Sheng, H. A. Jung, R. Strong, J.B.Brockman, D. Tullsen, and N. Jouppi, "Mcpat: An integrated power, area, and timing modeling framework for multicore and manycore architectures," in *Proc. of the 42nd Annual International Symposium on Microarchitecture*, 2009, pp. 469–480.

[35] J. Suh and M. Dubois, "Dynamic mips rate stabilization in out-of-order processors," in *Proc. of the 36th Annual International Symposium on Computer Architecture*, 2009, pp. 46–56.

[36] K. Van Craeynest, A. Jaleel, L. Eeckhout, P. Narvaez, and J. Emer, "Scheduling heterogeneous multi-cores through performance impact estimation (pie)," in *Proceedings of the 39th International Symposium on Computer Architecture*, ser. ISCA '12, 2012, pp. 213–224.

[37] Q. Wu, M. Martonosi, D. W. Clark, V. J. Reddi, D. Connors, Y. Wu, J. Lee, and D. Brooks, "A dynamic compilation framework for controlling microprocessor energy and performance," in *Proceedings of the 38th annual IEEE/ACM International Symposium on Microarchitecture*, ser. MICRO 38, 2005, pp. 271–282.

[38] F. Xie, M. Martonosi, and S. Malik, "Bounds on power savings using runtime dynamic voltage scaling: an exact algorithm and a linear-time heuristic approximation," in *Low Power Electronics and Design, 2005. ISLPED '05. Proceedings of the 2005 International Symposium on*, 2005, pp. 287–292.

[39] ——, "Compile-time dynamic voltage scaling settings: opportunities and limits," in *Proceedings of the ACM SIGPLAN 2003 conference on Programming language design and implementation*, ser. PLDI '03, 2003, pp. 49–62.

[40] ——, "Efficient behavior-driven runtime dynamic voltage scaling policies," in *Proceedings of the 3rd IEEE/ACM/IFIP international conference on Hardware/software codesign and system synthesis*, ser. CODES+ISSS '05, 2005, pp. 105–110.

RCS: Runtime Resource and Core Scaling for Power-Constrained Multi-core Processors

Hamid Reza Ghasemi and Nam Sung Kim
University of Wisconsin-Madison, U.S.A.
{ghasemi, nskim3}@wisc.edu

Abstract

Providing a sufficient voltage/frequency (V/F) scaling range is critical for effective power management. However, it has been fraught with decreasing nominal operating voltage and increasing manufacturing process variability that makes it harder to scale the minimum operating voltage (VMIN). In this paper, we first present a resource and core scaling (RCS) technique that jointly scales (i) the resources of a processor and (ii) the number of operating cores to maximize the performance of power-constrained multi-core processors. More specifically, we *uniformly* scale the resources that are both associated with each core (*e.g.*, L1 caches and execution units (EUs)) and shared by all the cores (*e.g.*, last-level cache (LLC)) as a means to compensate for lack of a V/F scaling range. Under the maximum power constraint, disabling some resources allows us to increase the number of operating cores, and vice versa. We demonstrate that the best RCS configuration for a given application can improve the geometric-mean performance by 21%. Second, we propose a runtime system that predicts the best RCS configuration for a given application and adapts the processor configuration accordingly at runtime. The runtime system only needs to examine a small fraction of runtime to predict the best RCS configuration with accuracy well over 90%, whereas the runtime overhead of prediction and adaptation is small. Finally, we propose to *selectively* scale the resources in RCS (dubbed sRCS) depending on application's characteristics and demonstrate that sRCS can offer 6% higher geometric-mean performance than RCS that uniformly scales the resources.

Categories and Subject Descriptors

C.1.2 [**Multiple Data Stream Architecture (Multiprocessors)**]: Parallel processors

Keywords

Power-constrained multi-core processor; voltage/frequency scaling; resource and core scaling; machine learning

1. Introduction

V/F scaling has been the most powerful knob to trade performance with power consumption of a processor. Incorporated with scaling the number of operating cores, scaling V/F can maximize performance of multi-core processors under the maximum power constraint (or simply power constraint in this paper) [1,2,3]. With technology scaling, however, the range of V/F scaling for processors has been continuously decreased because it becomes very costly to scale VMIN of on-chip memory structures [4,5]. Consequently, future processors may not be able to support V/F scaling unless a significantly higher chip area and/or power cost is paid to implement low-VMIN on-chip memory structures.

In this study, we envision a multi-core processor in which the number of operating cores can be fewer than that of integrated cores due to the maximum power constraint. To maximize the performance of such a power-constrained multi-core processor, we first present an RCS technique that jointly scales the amount of resources (both associated with each core and shared by all the cores) and the number of operating cores. RCS allows us to exploit a diverse degree of thread- and instruction-level parallelism (TLP and ILP) exhibited in various parallel applications. For an application with high TLP but low ILP, using more cores with less resources can lead to higher performance than fewer cores with more resources, and vice versa. We demonstrate that choosing the best RCS configuration for a given application can improve the geometric-mean performance by 21%. Furthermore, we propose to selectively scale the resources in RCS (dubbed sRCS) considering the runtime characteristics of a given application. We demonstrate that sRCS can offer 6% higher geometric-mean performance than RCS and it is as effective as RCS incorporated with V/F scaling in a limited range.

Second we propose a runtime system that predicts the best RCS configuration and adapts the processor accordingly for a given application at runtime. Our runtime system periodically examines various counter values that indicate the performance of a processor and the utilization of key resources such as EUs, L1/L2 caches, and off-chip DRAM bandwidth. We observe that predicting the best RCS configuration based on these counter values becomes a complex multi-dimensional classification problem. Thus, we take a machine learning (ML) approach that can be very effective for diverse classification problems. Although various ML approaches have been explored for dynamic multi-core resource management (*e.g.*, memory scheduling [6]), our novel contribution is to investigate key counters and predictor architecture that can maximize accuracy of predicting the best RCS configuration. On average, the best configuration predictor exhibits 93% accuracy after monitoring counter values for only a small fraction of runtime. As it examines a more fraction of runtime, the accuracy approaches to 100%. Upon the correct prediction of the best configuration, our runtime system can achieve 93% of maximum performance improvement that can be achieved by the oracular RCS (*i.e.*, applying the best RCS configuration from the start of executions). This improvement with the runtime system includes the overhead of changing RCS configurations and running a given application with sub-optimal RCS configurations for the predictor to determine the best RCS configuration at runtime.

The remainder of this paper is organized as follows. Section 2 describes the related work. Section 3 provides our experimental methodology. Section 4 demonstrates the potential performance improvement using RCS. Section 5 analyzes the impact of RCS

PACT'14, August 24–27, 2014, Edmonton, AB, Canada.

http://dx.doi.org/10.1145/2628071.2628095

on core power consumption. Section 6 proposes a runtime RCS system and analyzes its efficacy. Section 7 evaluates the effectiveness of sRCS and compares it against RCS with limited V/F scaling. Section 8 concludes this study.

2. Related Work

In processors, the resources are often over-provisioned to provide high performance for diverse applications while not all applications fully utilize all the processor resources. To address such inefficiency in traditional *uniprocessors*, several prior studies investigated the benefits of adaptive resource scaling to reduce power consumption [7,8,9,10]. Iyer *et al.* observed that the utilization of architectural components considerably changes over long runtime periods, and explored an adaptive resource scaling technique to minimize average power consumption [7]. Albonesi *et al.* explored various hardware/software techniques to adapt resources of a uniprocessor for higher power efficiency [8]. Lee *et al.* examined a wide range of uniprocessor design space to analyze performance/power efficiency trends and limits of adaptively reconfiguring the resources of uniprocessors [9]. Kontorinis *et al.* proposed a table-driven adaptive resource scaling technique with a runtime algorithm, reducing a considerable amount of peak power consumption with little performance loss [10]. Finally, it is noteworthy that a resource scaling technique was implemented in ARM Cortex-A15 [11]. In contrast to ours, these efforts focus on uniprocessors and do not capture the effect of spreading threads over more or fewer cores and scaling the shared resources like last-level cache (LLC) on performance.

Homayoun *et al.* proposed a configurable heterogeneous processor architecture exploiting 3D stacking technology [12]. The resources are shared between vertically stacked cores at a fine granularity. As a result, each core can borrow/lend the resources from/to other cores as needed by the thread running on a core. Watanabe *et al.* proposed a flexible in-order uniprocessor architecture to cope with a shrinking range of V/F scaling [5]. The number of instruction engines (IEs) and EUs are scaled up/down independently to maximize the performance of *single-thread* applications. However, they do not explore any runtime system for dynamically provisioning cores resources and the number of operating cores at runtime. Kim *et al.* proposed *TFlex* in which flexible medium sized in-order cores can be dynamically scaled up/down to provide a spectrum of one large single core to many small cores [13]. Although they provide a trade-off between ILP and TLP, they do such a trade-off in the context of explicit data graph execution (EDGE) architecture that employs distributed microarchitectural protocols. Furthermore, they do not offer a runtime system to predict the best configuration at runtime. Khubaib *et al.* proposed a microarchitecture that can transform an OoO core into an in-order core by totally disabling the resources required for OoO execution; it switches between a single- to a multi-core processor whenever the number of active threads is more than one (*e.g.*, 2 threads) [14]. However, they do not propose a mechanism that can determine the best number of active cores at runtime. Therefore, they do not re-configure cores for highly threaded applications. In contrast, we dynamically scale up/down the amount of most key resources and the number of operating cores at runtime. Ipek *et al.* proposed a core fusion architecture in which medium OoO core can be fused to form a large OoO core [15]. However, they require a compiler and/or programmer to insert two special instructions (i.e., FUSE/SPLIT) for reconfiguration. In contrast, ours does not need to change applications for reconfiguration at runtime. Petrica *et al.* exploited resource scaling as a means to compensate for a lack of the V/F scaling range in multi-core processors [4] as we do in this study and proposed an adaptive approach to fill the gap between fine-grained adaptive microarchitecture and a core-level power-gating technique [4]. In contrast to ours, they do not jointly scale the number of operating cores as well as shared resources such as LLC.

Suleman *et al.* proposed a feedback-driven approach to maximize performance by dynamically varying the number of threads at runtime [16]. Although we share a similar mechanism to dynamically change the number of operating cores at runtime, they fixed the number of cores in their study. Moore and Childers also proposed a dynamic approach that can choose the optimal number of threads based on offline- and online- methods [17]. Finally, some prior studies investigated adaptive approaches based on ML, control theory, etc. for dynamic resource, core, and/or voltage/frequency scaling techniques for power and/or thermal management or performance improvement under the power constraint [18,19,20,21,22], all of which differ from ours capturing the effect of spreading threads over more or fewer cores and scaling the shared resources on performance.

Finally, scaling only frequency (i.e., F scaling) can be an alternative to V/F scaling when the V/F scaling range is limited. While F scaling is orthogonal to resource scaling, it cannot effectively manage over-provisioned resources as resource scaling can.

3. Simulation Methodology

For evaluation, we use a full-system cycle-level simulator, GEMS [23] and a power modeling framework, McPAT [24]. We configure GEMS similar to an Intel® Xeon processor; take the corresponding configuration from the McPAT package; and use the 32nm technology for power estimation; see Table 1 for the detailed parameters when all the resources are enabled. The processor has 12 cores, but it can operate only 8 cores with full resources enabled due to the power constraint.

We use 11 benchmarks: JBB, OLTP, APACHE, and ZEUS from commercial workloads [25]; WUPWISE, MGRID, APPLU, and EQUAKE from SPEC-OMP [26], and SWAPTIONS, BODYTRACK, and BLACKSHOLES from PARSEC [27] (denoted by JBB, OLTP, APCH, ZEUS, WPWS, MGRD, APLU,

Table 1: Key parameters of a 12-core processor with the full core resources.

# of cores	12	NoC topology	crossbar switch
Core fetch/issue/retire	4/4/4	Core	OoO
IL1/DL1	Private 32KB/32KB	ALU/multiplier/FPU	4/2/4
ITLB/DTLB	32/32 entries	LSQ	32/32 entries
BTB	2K	Register file (integer/floating-point)	128/128
Branch predictor	YAGS: 20-15-15	Load replay penalty	10 cycles
Branch mis-prediction penalty	11 cycle	ROB/IQ	64/32 entries
L2/MSHR	Shared 8MB/16 entries	Technology	32nm
Cache coherency protocol	Directory-based MESI	V/F	0.9V /3.2GHz

EQK, SWSP, BDTK, and BKSL). Depending on the degree of contentions related to synchronizations, each thread often executes a varying number of instructions [16]. Thus, for fair and consistent comparisons across configurations and intervals, we ensure that each configuration executes the same number of *transactions* instead of instructions; a transaction typically corresponds to an iteration of a global loop in each executed thread. We run each benchmark for 40 intervals comprised of 2- to 4-billion instructions; each interval is equivalent to tens to hundreds of *ms* in real machine's time. Note that the software threads are scheduled by the OS and executed with fewer cores in a time-multiplexed manner. Since these parallel benchmarks have far more software threads than 12 cores, the negative performance impact of load imbalance is small (and reflected in the simulation) [28,29].

4. RCS under Power Constraint

To exploit ILP in applications, a processor core is designed to execute multiple in-flight instructions in an OoO fashion. The more resources (*e.g.*, larger L1/L2 caches and more EUs) a core has, the higher performance is for applications with high ILP. Similarly, the more cores a processor has, the more threads it can concurrently execute for applications with high TLP, leading to higher overall performance. However, due to the power constraint, we cannot increase both the amount of resources per core and the number of operating cores at the same time. Consequently, we often have to trade the amount of resources per core with the number of integrated cores at design time. Moreover, we uniformly scale chosen resources of each core, coupled with the number of operating cores such that the processor does not exceed the power constraint for the worst-case power consumption. Hence, the number of feasible RCS configurations is limited to a small number (*i.e.*, three in this study), making it more tractable for implementing a runtime system.

As the prior studies observed, many execution phases of applications often underutilize given core resources due to various reasons (*e.g.*, limited ILP and small memory footprint) [7,8,10,30]. In such a case, disabling some core resources such as L1 caches and/or EUs may not notably impact *single-thread* performance, while it can considerably reduce the maximum power consumption of each core. This in turn allows us to operate more cores (and thus increase the performance of applications with high TLP) under the power constraint. In contrast, if the applications exhibit high ILP but low TLP, disabling some cores but enabling more resources per operating core can lead to higher performance.

Figure 1 illustrates a hypothetical example of RCS for a quad-core processor. Assume that the maximum power consumption of the processor is limited to 90W; we only consider the power consumption of cores after excluding the power consumption by shared components such as memory controllers and network-on-chip (NoC) interconnect, etc. in this example. When all the resources of each core are enabled, the maximum power consumption of each core operating at 0.9V/3.2GHz is 30W. Therefore, only three cores can operate due to the power constraint. However, when the amount of resources of some architectural components such as L1 caches, instruction queue (IQ), load-store queue (LSQ), and EUs is reduced by half, the maximum power consumption of each core can be reduced from 30W to 22.5W at the same V/F. This in turn allows us to operate all four cores.

Figure 2 shows the normalized execution time (ET) of three different RCS configurations that simultaneously vary the amount of core resources and the number of operating cores such that all three configurations consume approximately the same maximum power at 0.9V/3.2GHz. The ET of each configuration is normalized to that of the 8-core configuration. The key parameters of three RCS configurations are listed in Table 2; we will discuss how the maximum power consumption of each architectural component scales as the amount of core resources scales in Section 5.

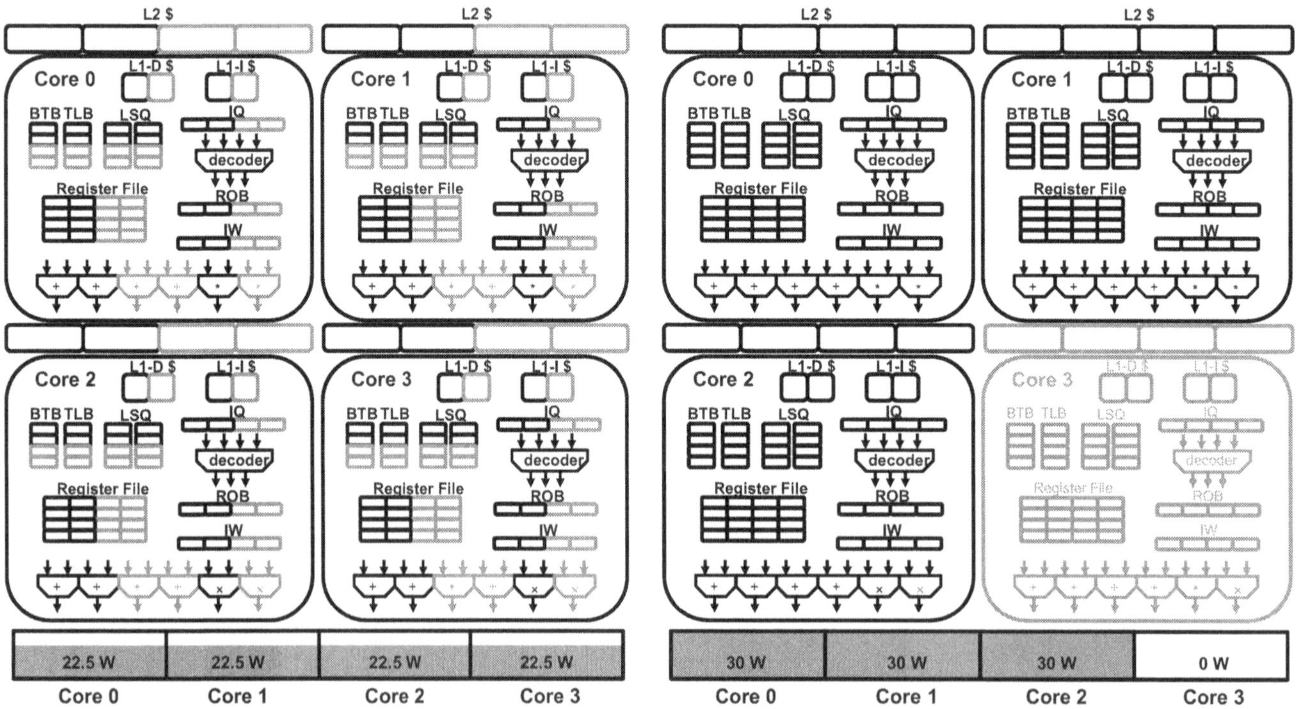

Figure 1: A hypothetical example of RCS under the maximum power constraint (90W) for a quad-core processor: (a) all four cores are active with a half of resources disabled (22.5W per core) (b) only three cores are active with the full resources enabled (30W per core). The disabled resources are represented with the gray color.

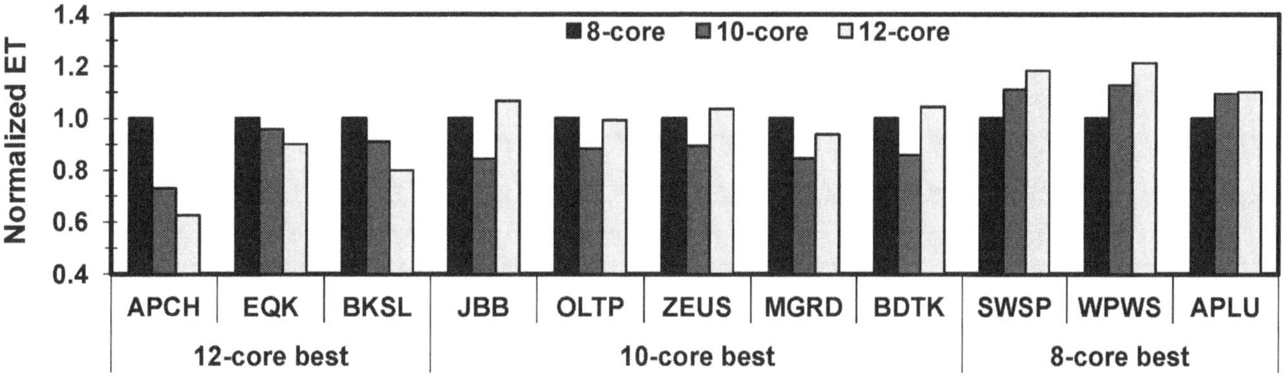

Figure 2: ET comparison of 8-, 10-, and 12-core configurations that consume approximately the same maximum power. The ET of each application is normalized to that of the 8-core configuration.

Table 2: Key parameters of three RCS configurations consuming approximately the same maximum power.

Processor configuration	8-core	10-core	12-core
L2(MB)	8	6	4
IL1(KB)/DL1(KB)	32/32	32/32	16/16
TLB	32	32	16
ALU/complex ALU/FPU	4/2/4	2/1/2	1/1/1
LSQ	32/32	32/32	16/16
ROB/IQ	64/32	64/32	32/16
YAG branch predictor	20/15/15	20/15/15	10/8/8

We determine these RCS configurations after performing many experiments to analyze the impact of core resource scaling on performance and maximum power consumption of the processor. We then *prioritize* the architectural components for resource scaling based on (i) the changes of power efficiency (i.e., performance divided by power) after scaling the resources and (ii) the complexity of implementing resource scaling. We choose to apply the resource scaling only for the architectural components that exhibit relatively large power reduction with small performance degradation; Table 7 in Section 7 presents the changes of power efficiency for major architectural components after reducing the amount of resources by half to motivate our sRCS technique. For instance, we do not reduce the size of physical register-file (PRF) in all three RCS configurations, because reducing the size of PRF decreases considerably more performance than power consumption. Similarly, we reduce the size of the TLB, LSQ, re-order buffer (ROB), IQ, and branch predictor only for the 12-core configuration, as shown in Table 2, because they can exhibit notable performance degradation compared to power reduction. Finally, we can vary the fetch width of cores as a category of resource scaling technique, but we do not exploring it in this study.

Figure 2 clearly demonstrates that the best RCS configuration, which offers the highest performance, varies from benchmark to benchmark. For example, the 8-core configuration provides the highest performance for APPLU, WUPWISE, and SWAPTIONS, while the 12-core configuration gives the highest performance for APACHE, EQUAKE, and BLACKSHOLES; the 12-core configuration offers 31% higher geometric-mean performance than the 8-core configuration for these benchmarks. In other words, the amount of resources per core is more critical for APPLU, WUPWISE, and SWAPTIONS, which exhibit high ILP but low TLP and/or have large memory footprints, to achieve the highest performance under the power constraint. On the other hand, the number of operating cores is more critical for APACHE, EQUAKE, and BLACKSHOLES, which generally exhibit high TLP but low ILP and/or small memory footprints, to achieve the highest performance. The performance of the 10-core configuration is the highest for JBB, OLTP, ZEUS, MGRD, and BDTK, indicating that the amount of resources per core and the number of operating core should be balanced to achieve the highest performance. Overall, choosing the best RCS configurations for the benchmarks that benefit from the 10- and 12-core configurations can provide 21% higher geometric-mean performance than the 8-core configuration.

5. Impact of RCS on Power Consumption

In Section 4, we demonstrated that the best RCS configuration leading to the highest performance varies from benchmark to benchmark due to various requirements of each application in terms of the amount of resources per core and the number of operating cores. In modern processors, key architectural components such as on-chip caches, buffers, and queues (*i.e.*, on-chip memory structures) are designed in a modular fashion so that their size or width can be easily adapted for derivative architectures targeting various market segments (*i.e.*, mobile, desktop, and server). These on-chip memory structures are typically comprised of multiple arrays and each array is equipped with a local power-gating device that can be turned it on/off independently [31]. The number of operating EUs can be varied by fine-grained power-gating, which has been explored by the industry due to the growing need for supporting aggressive power management techniques [32]. In general, we share the same (i) hardware mechanism to scale the resource of each architectural component and (ii) associated overhead with [7,8,10]. In addition, the number of operating cores is scaled up/down by turning on/off per-core power-gating devices, which are supported by most commercial multi-core processors [33,34].

Table 3 tabulates both the absolute and percentage power consumption of key architectural components of all three RCS configurations. The maximum power consumption or thermal design power (TDP) of the 8-, 10-, and 12-core configurations is approximately the same (~185W). Note that the TDP of an Intel® dual-core Xeon processor manufactured with 65nm technology is 150W [35]; the TDP of an Intel's 6-core processor manufactured with 32nm technology and operating at a similar frequency is 130W [36]. The power consumption of each core in 8-, 10-, and 12-core configurations is 23.1W, 18.5W, and 15.4W, respectively. The core power consumption number of each configuration includes each core's share of the power consumption of architectural components shared by all the cores, such as memory controllers, NoC, etc. The columns denoted by "L2 + Dir," "IL1+ITLB+BTB," "DL1+DTLB+LSQ," "INT," "FP," and "Oth-

Table 3: Breakdown of maximum power consumption of cores for different processor configurations.

Processor Configuration		L2 + Dir	IL1 + ITLB + BTB	DL1 + DTLB + LSQ	IQ + ROB	INT	FPU	Others	Core Total
8-core	Power	4.91W	0.43W	0.86W	0.87W	2.88W	2.12W	11.00W	23.07W
	% in Core Tot.	21.3%	1.8%	3.7%	3.8%	12.5%	9.2%	47.7%	100%
10-core	Power	3.22W	0.43W	0.86W	0.87W	1.44W	1.06W	10.59W	18.46W
	% in Core Tot.	17.4%	2.3%	4.7%	4.7%	7.8%	5.7%	57.4%	100%
12-core	Power	2.01W	0.31W	0.69W	0.69W	0.98W	0.53W	10.23W	15.44W
	% in Core Tot.	13.0%	2.0%	4.5%	4.5%	6.4%	3.4%	66.2%	100%

ers" show the maximum power consumption and percentage values in maximum power consumption of L2 cache and coherent protocol directory; IL1 cache, ITLB, BTB, and branch predictor; DL1 cache, DTLB, and LSQ; integer ALUs, multipliers, and dividers; floating-point adder, multipliers, and dividers; and all other components. In the following section, we discuss how the maximum power consumption of each architectural component is calculated.

Set-associative memory components: The first group of memory components is set-associative memory structures such as L2 (and its coherent protocol directory), IL1/DL1, and BTB. For these memory components, dynamic memory resizing techniques have been widely used in commercial processors to reduce leakage power consumption at runtime [37]. It is possible to shut down a subset of arrays that constitute either ways or sets depending on a cache design. Although disabling some arrays can reduce the leakage power consumption of the memory components, the dynamic power consumption remains the same. This is because it does not reduce the switching capacitance of accessed arrays; only a subset of arrays in large memory components is accessed regardless of the number of arrays. For example, to shut down 2MB of an 8MB 8-way cache we can disable ¼ of arrays constituting all the available ways or sets without impacting the number of parallel accesses to the cache. Scaling the size of L2 to 6MB and 4MB (and the associated coherent protocol directories) reduces the maximum power consumption of the 10- and 12-core configurations by 16.97W ((4.91W − 3.22W) × 10) and 35.85W ((4.91W − 2.01W) × 12), respectively, while scaling the size of IL1/DL1 to 16KB reduces the maximum power consumption of the 12-core configuration by 1.68W ((0.94W − 0.80W) × 12).

Fully-associative memory components: The second group of memory components is fully-associative memory structures such as ROB, DTLB, ITLB, IQ, and LSQ. These components usually are designed using content-addressable memory (CAM) and some combinational circuits such as comparators and multiplexers. Similar to set-associative memory structures, it is possible to shut down a subset of total entries and the associated comparators to reduce their leakage power consumption without impacting the critical path delay [38]. However, this does not reduce the capacitance of tag matching buses that are connected to all the comparators including the disabled ones. Note that a large fully-associative memory component can be designed with multiple CAM arrays that are connected in a hierarchical way. In such a case, disabling a subset of CAM arrays can also reduce dynamic power consumption, but we assume that disabling some entries in the fully-associative memory components only reduces leakage power consumption for a conservative estimation in this study. For instance, disabling a half of the total entries in ITLB, DTLB, BTB, LSQ, and ROB can reduce the maximum power consumption of the 12-core configuration by 3.25W ((1.12W − 0.85W) × 12). In summary, scaling the size of memory components for the 10- and 12-core configurations can reduce the maximum power consumption of the processor by 16.97W and 40.38W, respectively; as indicated in Table 2, only L2 cache size is reduced in the 10-core configuration. This is in turn exploited to increase the number of operating cores (with less on-chip memory resources).

EUs: The impact of scaling the number of ALUs, complex ALUs (multipliers and dividers), and FPUs on power consumption is very straightforward. Disabling a subset of such units using fine-grain power- and clock-gating techniques can reduce both dynamic and leakage power consumption. However, this does not reduce the power consumption of the shared operand and result buses that are connected to the inputs and outputs of these units. Scaling the number of EUs can reduce the maximum power consumption of the processor by 24.97W ((4.99W − 2.50W) × 10) and 41.80W ((4.99W − 1.51W) × 12) for the 10- and 12-core configurations, respectively. This power reduction is substantial enough to operate one or more cores under the power constraint. Note that the instruction issue mechanism must be aware of disabled EUs and it should not issue instructions to the disabled EUs.

Others: In this study, we do not apply the resource scaling techniques for the remaining architectural components although we can for some of them (i.e., the number of memory controllers; the width of fetch, decode, and issue stages; the size of PRF; etc.) to limit the scope of the study.

Putting it together: McPAT can provide the breakdown of maximum dynamic and leakage power consumption of each component in a processor. We begin with the estimation of the maximum power consumption of a 12-core processor with the full resources per core to accurately consider the power consumption of all the shared resources (*e.g.*, on-chip interconnect, memory controllers, etc.) and extract dynamic and leakage power consumption of each component including its subcomponents (*e.g.*, arrays, decoders, etc. in L1/L2). Then, we subtract the dynamic and/or leakage power consumption of disabled subcomponents based on the methodology discussed in this section. Scaling the chosen resources of each core reduces the maximum power consumption of each core by 4.6W and 7.6W for the 10- and 12-core configurations, as summarized in Table 3. Such power reduction can provide enough power headroom to operate two and four more cores for the 10- and 12-core configurations than for the 8-core configuration since each core consumes approximately 18.5W and 15.5W, respectively.

6. Runtime System

In this section, we propose a runtime system that can determine (i) the best RCS configuration for a given application and (ii) adapt the processor accordingly. Then, we evaluate its effectiveness and discuss its runtime overhead.

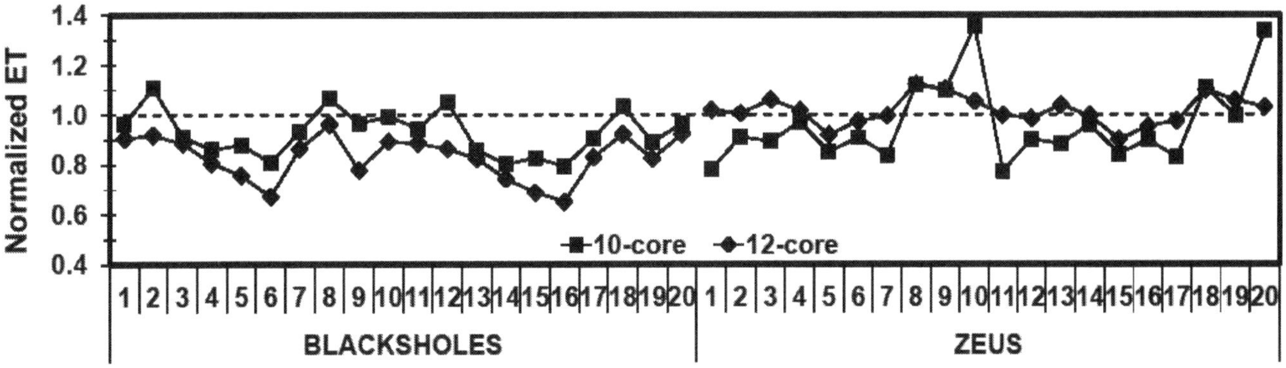

Figure 4: ET vs. runtime interval of the 8-, 10-, and 12-core configurations. The ET of each application is normalized to that of the 8-core configuration at each runtime interval.

Table 4: Performance improvement with dynamic over static configurations.

JBB	ZEUS	OLTP	MGRD	WPWS	BDTK
0.8%	4%	0.5%	1.6%	0.1%	31%

6.1 Performance Comparison at Each Interval

Figure 4 plots the ETs of 8-, 10-, and 12-core configurations that run BLACKSHOLES and ZEUS, at each runtime interval. The ETs of the 10- and 12-core configurations are normalized to that of the 8-core configuration at each interval. Each interval in a benchmark is comprised of the same number of transactions to perform the same amount of work, typically corresponding to 60- to 150-million instructions (*i.e*, tens to hundreds of *ms*) depending on a benchmark and its interval.

While a particular RCS configuration always outperforms two other RCS configurations across all the intervals for APACHE, SWAPTIONS, EQUAKE, and BLACKSHOLES, the RCS configuration leading to the highest performance changes over intervals for ZEUS, OLTP, JBB, MGRID, APPLU, WUPWISE, and BODYTRACK. For instance, the 12-core configuration always shows higher performance than the 8- and 10-core configurations across all the runtime intervals for BLACKSHOLES. On the other hand, either the 8- or 10-core configuration can provide the highest performance at some runtime intervals for ZEUS.

Assume that we can oracularly choose the best RCS configuration that can lead to the highest performance at each interval (*i.e.*, the best *dynamic* RCS) and compare its overall performance

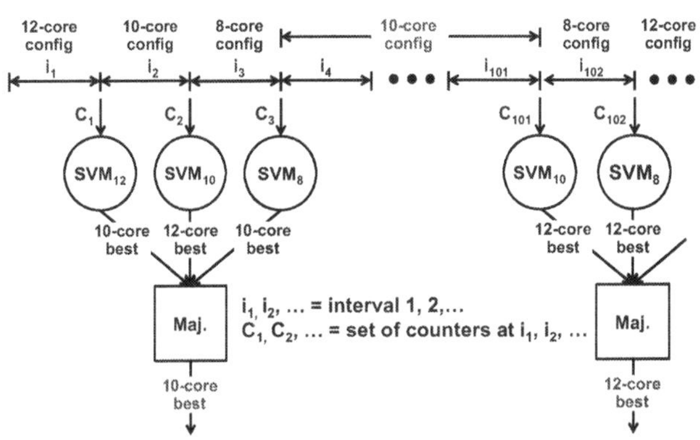

Figure 3: Proposed predictor architecture, comprised of 3 sub-predictors based on SVMs, to determine the best RCS configuration for *n* = 1.

with the best performance that can be achieved by applying only one of the RCS configurations across all the intervals for each application (*i.e.*, the best *static* RCS). Among the applications that benefit from the dynamic RCS, as tabulated in Table 4, the dynamic RCS can provide notably higher performance only for BODYTRACK and ZEUS than the best static RCS, while offering only negligibly higher performance for JBB, OLTP, MGRID, and WUPWISE.

6.2 Best Configuration Predictor

Considering small performance improvements using the dynamic RCS over the best static RCS, we focus on developing a predictor that can determine the best (static) RCS configuration at runtime in this section.

Need for using an ML approach: A simple performance sampling technique can be sufficient, if we can repeat the execution of the same interval for all three configurations, which is nontrivial and costly considering the duration of intervals; we cannot just compare performance of configuration *A* at interval *i* with that of *B* at interval *i*+1 to determine which configuration is better, because the performance reference points are different at interval *i* and *i*+1. Consequently, determining the best configuration at runtime needs to consider numerous performance counters, leading to a complex multi-dimensional classification problem in which an ML approach can be very effective.

Predictor architecture: To determine the best RCS configuration, we choose to use support vector machine (SVM) because of its superiority to other ML algorithms such as artificial neural network (ANN) for many classification problems. SVM is a supervised learning model and widely used for classification and regression analysis. An SVM takes a set of inputs (*i.e.*, performance counter values) and predicts which of two possible classes forms the output (*i.e.*, the best RCS configuration) as a non-probabilistic binary linear classifier. For example, an SVM predicts whether or not a particular RCS configuration (e.g., 12-core configuration) is the best for given counter values. Hence, a simple predictor can be comprised of *M* SVMs where *M* is the number of feasible RCS configurations (= 3 in our study).

Figure 3 shows our proposed predictor architecture comprised of 3 sub-predictors (SVM_8, SVM_{10}, and SVM_{12}), each of which consists of 3 SVMs, and how it determines the best RCS configuration. Each predictor only receives inputs from the associated RCS configuration. For instance, SVM_{10} only receives inputs generated by the 10-core configuration and predicts whether or not the best RCS configuration is the 8-, 10, or 12-core configuration; see "Predictor inputs" to justify why we split the predictor into three sub-predictors.

Table 5: Summary of inputs to SVMs.

Category	Counters
System performance	IPC and ET
Memory resources	access/miss rate of (L2, L1D, L1I) and bandwidth utilization of off-chip DRAM channel
Core resources	utilization/stall of (ROB, IQ, ALU, FPU, LSQ) and branch prediction accuracy

The predictor explores all three feasible RCS configurations over $3 \times n$ consecutive intervals, starting with the 12-core configuration; see Section 6.3 for the justification of starting with the 12-core configuration. At the end of each n consecutive intervals, the sub-predictor, which is associated with the current RCS configuration, predicts the best RCS configuration based on the collected counter values during the intervals. At the end of the third n consecutive intervals, the predictor first decides the best RCS configuration based on the majority rule; in Figure 3 where $n = 1$, SVM_8 and SVM_{12} predict that the 10-core configuration is the best while SVM_{10} predicts that the 12-core configuration is the best. Thus, the predictor decides that the 10-core configuration is the best.

When all three sub-predictors disagree, the predictor chooses the best configuration based on the sub-predictor with the highest confidence (*i.e.*, the longest distance to the SVM's hyper-plane). Second, the runtime system takes necessary actions to apply the decided configuration to the processor; see Section 6.3 for the necessary actions and their overhead to change the processor configuration. Finally, it maintains the decided RCS configuration for a pre-determined period of time (e.g., 100 intervals) as illustrated in Figure 3 and/or until it detects a substantial change of given application's execution phase (e.g., [39]).

Predictor inputs: Table 5 categorizes the counters, taken by the best-configuration predictor, into three groups. The first "System Performance" group includes each core's IPC and ET to evaluate the performance benefit of the current configuration. The second "Memory Resource" group consists of access and miss rates of each core's on-chip caches and bandwidth utilization of each off-chip DRAM channel. These counters indicate whether or not a given application is memory-intensive (*i.e.*, the on-chip cache sizes and/or off-chip DRAM bandwidth is sufficient for a given application); for some applications, increasing the number of threads does not improve performance due to limited off-chip DRAM bandwidth [16]. The third "Core Resource" group encompasses utilization and stall rates of ROB, IQ, FPU, and ALU as well as a rate of branch miss-prediction. These counters demonstrate how much the core configuration is matched with the resource requirement of a given application. We consider the utilization counters for SVM_8 since all core resources are fully activated but they may not be fully utilized. On the other hand, we take the stall counters for SVM_{12} because only a small amount of core sources are activated and thus they may cause more stalls due to limited core resources. For SVM_{10} we take both utilization and stall counters because the 10-core configuration is between those two cases. Since we need to consider different counters depending on what is the current RCS configuration, we split the predictor into 3 sub-predictors, each of which is customized for each RCS configuration, leading to higher accuracy according to our preliminary evaluations (that are not shown in this paper due to limited space).

Predictor training: We take an off-line training method in this study due to long cycle-level simulation time for evaluations involving an on-line training approach. For an off-line training method, we collect 40 sets of chosen counter values from 40 execution intervals of a benchmark running on a particular RCS configuration; the number of sets per configuration per benchmark is limited by our simulation time constraint but it can be far more with real hardware. We also obtain 2×40 sets by moving-averaging counter values over 2 and 4 intervals, respectively. For three feasible RCS configurations per benchmark, we have total 3×120 (=360) sets and they will be associated with and trained to predict the best RCS configuration of the benchmark. Then $L \times 120$ sets collected from L benchmarks running on a particular RCS configuration are applied to sub-predictor associated with the RCS configuration for the training. For example, we apply 10×120 sets from 10 benchmark executed on the 8-core configuration to SVM_8 that is comprised of 3 outputs (*i.e.*, "8-core-best," "10-core-best," and "12-core-best"). Among the 10×120 sets, the 3×120 sets from APACHE, EQUAKE, and BLACKSHOLES and 3×120 sets from APPLU, WUPWISE, and SWAPTIONS will be trained to predict "12-core-best" and "8-core-best," respectively, during the training phase of SVM_8. The remaining sets from the rest of the benchmark will be trained to predict "10-core-best." This process is repeated for SVM_{10} and SVM_{12}. Finally, to evaluate the prediction accuracy for a given benchmark, we exclude all the input sets from the benchmark being evaluated during the off-line training phase.

Predictor accuracy: Figure 5 shows the accuracy of the proposed predictor. The geometric-mean prediction accuracy is 84%, 93%, 99%, and ~100% for n = 1, 2, 3, and 4, respectively. To calculate the prediction accuracy for a benchmark, we try all possible combinations of randomly picking 1, 2, 3, and 4 consecutive intervals out of 40 available intervals from each RCS configuration. Most benchmarks show close to 100% prediction accuracy when n is greater than 2. However, some benchmarks such as

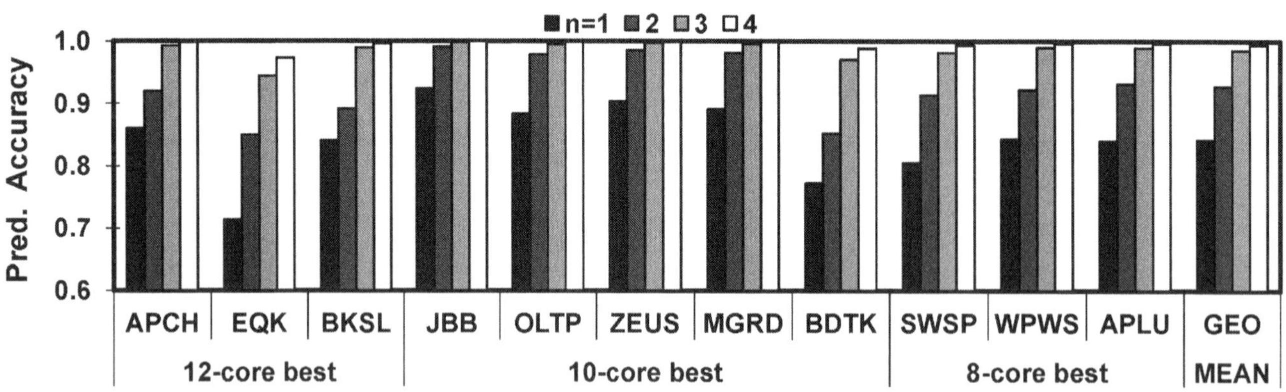

Figure 5: Prediction accuracy for n = 1, 2, 3, and 4 intervals.

Table 6: Performance improvement of oracular and runtime RCS with n = 2. The performance of the 10- and 12-core configurations is normalized to that of 8-core configuration.

	12-core best			10-core best					8-core best		
	APCH	EQK	BKSL	JBB	OLTP	ZEUS	MGRD	BDTK	SWSP	WPWS	APLU
Oracle	60.0%	11.1%	25.0%	18.5%	13.2%	11.9%	18.3%	16.6%	0.0%	0.0%	0.0%
Runtime	54.4%	10.1%	22.6%	15.7%	11.8%	10.4%	16.7%	14.3%	-1.4%	-1.7%	-1.1%
Runtime/Oracle	90.1%	91.2%	90.3%	84.9%	88.9%	87.0%	91.5%	86.1%	98.6%	98.7%	99.3%

BODYTRACK and EQUAKE exhibit relatively poor prediction accuracy because of a very wide range of performance variance across intervals. Note that, EQUAKE shows very small performance difference between configurations. Therefore, inaccurate prediction does not impact performance notably. In summary, we can predict the best RCS configuration with well over 90% accuracy by observing only 15% of total intervals, 2 intervals per configuration (= 6 intervals) out of 40 intervals in this experiment.

This proposed predictor can provide very high prediction accuracy to determine the best RCS configuration that can lead to the highest overall performance over a large number of intervals even for applications in which the best RCS configuration changes over intervals (e.g., ZEUS, OLTP, JBB, MGRID, APPLU, WUPWISE); we can consider that these applications show phase behavior in a time scale of seconds [39]. Considering the simulation time, we limit the number of intervals to 40, which corresponds to a few seconds for most applications. However, some applications show the phase behavior over time scale larger than a few seconds [39]. For such applications, we can periodically apply the prediction technique and adjust the configuration according to capture a large time-scale phase behavior. To this end, Isci *et al.* proposed a runtime technique to monitor and predict the runtime phases of applications to increase power efficiency using DVFS [39]. Sherwood *et al.* propose Simpoint to find a portion of program that is representative of the entire program's execution [40]. Later, Lau *et al.* propose an on-line technique to predict different phases of applications and resource requirement at runtime [41]. Similar techniques can be adopted to determine whether or not we need to update the best RCS configuration.

SVM versus ANN: In this study, we also evaluate a predictor based on multi-layer, feed-forward ANN trained by a scaled conjugate gradient back propagation algorithm. Such an ANN structure can be also used to predict the best configuration in a similar way to our SVM-based predictor. For our evaluation, we first replace the classification algorithm based on SVM with ANN while maintaining the predictor architecture (cf. Figure 3) and inputs to the predictor (cf. Table 5). Second, we vary the number of layers and nodes (*i.e.*, perceptrons) along with other parameters such as initial weights of the ANN-based predictor. Third, we train and experiment these ANN-based predictors several times since the training process is non-deterministic. Finally, we choose the best predictor for the comparison with the SVM-based predictor.

Our experiments show that the SVM-based predictor can offer more robust predictions than the ANN-based predictor. For n = 1, 2, 3, and 4, the geometric-mean prediction accuracy of the ANN-based predictor is 75%, 79%, 82%, and 84% while that of the SVN-based predictor is 84%, 93%, 99%, and ~100%, respectively. For higher prediction accuracy, the ANN-based predictor needs to consider more intervals (*e.g.*, 5 or 6) than the SVM-based predictor. This leads to longer execution with a sub-optimal configuration. Note that ANN may not be suitable for our proposed technique in contrast to the study by Bitirgen *et al.* [18], because we need to apply a large number of inputs to the predictor to track various changes in states and utilizations of processor resources. On the other hand, considering many inputs makes ANN more vulnerable to noise in input data sets than SVM.

6.3 Necessary Support and Runtime Overhead

To decide the best RCS configuration, the predictor begins to collect counter values for n (= 2 in this study) consecutive intervals for each configuration in the order of 12-, 10-, and 8-core configurations. In other words, we change the RCS configuration at most three times. This gradually turns on more core resources for fewer operating cores. Therefore, scaling down the core resources (*i.e.*, reducing the size of on-chip memory components and flushing core pipelines) occurs at most once (*i.e.*, from the 8-core configuration back to either 10- or 12-core configuration) during a substantial period of runtime. Then we maintain the best RCS configuration determined by the predictor until we observe a considerable phase change from a given application, which may occur every a few seconds [39]. Thus, we expect that the overall overhead of runtime RCS should be very small; see Table 6 for runtime overhead. The key hardware mechanisms to support runtime RCS are already available in the power control unit (PCU), a microprocessor, which monitors performance and power consumption of each core; dynamically adjusts V/F state; manages the sequences of turning on/off cores and a part or all of on-chip caches, etc., in a multi-core processor [37].

Changing the number of operating cores: Since applications typically have more software threads than 12 cores [28,29], these many threads are executed with fewer cores in a time-multiplexed manner. Before changing the number of operating cores at runtime, the runtime RCS system notifies the change to the thread scheduler so that it can dispatch an appropriate number of software threads to the cores; we assume the same OS thread-scheduler as [16] for changing the number of active threads at runtime and it takes only few μs for switching of threads between cores [42] while one interval in our evaluation is equivalent to tens of *ms*.

Reducing on-chip shared cache size: When the cache size should be reduced due to a change of the configuration, the cache controller writes back all the dirty cache lines to the main memory and then decreases the L2 cache size. This starts by walking through all the cache lines in the cache section that is going to be shut down. To evict any cache line in "M" state, the cache controller sends the data to the main memory and updates the directory to "I." To evict any cache line in "E" state, the cache controller just updates the directory to "I." To evict any cache line in "S" the cache controller sends an invalidation request for the cache line to the NoC and waits to get invalidation acknowledgements from all the sharers. Then, the controller sends the data to the main memory and updates the directory to "I." After completing this process, the cache controller reduces the cache size. The performance impact of changing the size of a large shared cache even every 1*ms* is reported to be less than 0.5% on average [43].

Flushing core pipelines and order of downsizing: When the amount of core resources should be scaled down, first the cores stop fetching new instructions and wait until outstanding

Table 7: Impact of resource scaling of each component on power efficiency of the 10-core configuration.

	Half L2s	Half L1s	Half TLBs	Half ALUs	Half FPUs	Half PRF	Half LSQ	Half IQ
ZEUS	0.32%	-2.59%	0.02%	6.53%	4.86%	-5.02%	0.01%	-5.77%
JBB	-5.77%	-2.74%	0.02%	6.13%	4.86%	-6.71%	0.01%	-8.48%
OLTP	-1.44%	-3.40%	0.02%	6.50%	4.86%	-4.48%	0.01%	-6.23%
APACHE	-8.96%	-2.07%	0.02%	3.87%	4.86%	-8.16%	0.01%	-9.46%
EQUAKE	10.70%	-18.53%	0.02%	3.32%	4.33%	-4.11%	0.01%	-3.10%
BODYTRACK	-5.39%	-13.39%	0.02%	-5.62%	4.75%	-3.56%	0.01%	-7.29%

misses are serviced. Second, we allow all the previously fetched instructions in the IQs/ROBs to be executed and retired and begin to flush L1 caches in parallel across cores to be disabled. The ROB has 64 entries, so it takes at least 16 cycles for a 4-wide core to retire all the instructions when there is no outstanding cache miss. Finally, while the L2 cache is flushed and downsized, the processor can shut down a portion of the resources of the cores using a fine-grained power-gating technique and lets the instructions be fetched in the new RCS configuration. We assume/model that we halt the core(s) and flush/initialize the pipeline(s) and caches for the components impacted by power-gating on/off during the reconfiguration; the sleep/wake-up latency of fine-grained power-gating just considering the stabilization of power distribution network (PDN) of EUs is in the order of a couple of cycles for ALUs [32] and tens of cycles for FPUs; in our modeling, we assume 10 and 100 cycles for shutting down ALUs and FPUs, respectively.

Predictor computational overhead: The current predictor implementation is based on *libsvm* containing redundant routines for development and debugging. We measure the computational overhead of the predictor by running the binary in our simulator configured with the parameters shown in Table 1. We observe that it takes 0.47ms, 1.53ms, and 1.58ms for SVM_8, SVM_{10}, and SVM_{12} to predict the best configuration using a single core (out of 8, 10, 12 available cores). This overhead can be substantially shortened and eliminated by developing optimized SVM code and run it on the PCU.

Overall overhead of runtime RCS: Our runtime RCS significantly differs from typical fine-grained dynamic power-gating techniques that turn on/off components based on activity changes of architectural components during a relatively short period of runtime. Note that the sleep/wake-up latency of power-gating just considering the stabilization of PDN is less than tens of *ns* [44]; most performance penalty is incurred only when the size of on-chip caches is reduced. Furthermore, the overhead of either completing or invalidating in-flight instructions is negligible (as discussed earlier), because we need at most one configuration change that requires a shutdown of resources in a long period.

Modeling and evaluating the overhead of runtime RCS, we observe that runtime RCS applied for 40 intervals can deliver 92% of the maximum performance improvement achieved by an oracular RCS (*i.e.*, using the best RCS configuration from the start of executions) on average; Table 6 compares the performance improvement of the oracular and runtime RCS, and the performance of 10- and 12-core configurations is normalized to that of 8-core configuration. 9% lower performance than the oracular RCS is resulted by three factors: (i) execution of some intervals with the sub-optimal configurations; (ii) the performance penalty of increasing/decreasing on-chip caches, flushing core pipeline, and turning on/off cores; and (iii) execution of predictor code. Finally, we limit the number of intervals to 40 due to excessive simulation time, but we expect the runtime RCS to provide higher performance with more intervals, amortizing the cost of (i) and (ii).

7. sRCS

Previously, we explored RCS that *uniformly* scales some chosen resources that are both associated with each core and shared by all the cores. In this section, we explore RCS that *selectively* scale the resources of each core (sRCS) to better exploit the unique characteristics of memory- and compute-oriented applications.

Motivation: Table 7 shows the impact of scaling the resources of each component on power efficiency (*i.e.*, performance/Watt) of the 10-core configuration. We scale each architectural component's resource at a time and measure the relative change of performance and maximum power consumption. Reducing the size of IL1, DL1, PRF, and IQ by half notably degrades the power efficiency of all the examined applications. On the contrary, reducing the number of FPUs by half improves the power efficiency of all the examined applications. Scaling the L2 size and the number of integer ALUs exhibits varying impacts on power efficiency depending on applications; see the shaded columns in Table 7. For instance, the power efficiency of EQUAKE considerably improves with half L2 cache size while that of APACHE, JBB and BODYTRACK notably degrades. Similarly, all applications except for BODYTRACK show improvement in power efficiency when the number of ALUs is reduced by half. For JBB, we can hypothesize that increasing the L2 size while decreasing the number of ALUs can further improve performance under the power constraint.

Performance improvement: For sRCS, we provide four sub-configurations including the original 10-core configuration considered earlier. The number of operating cores is ten for all four sub-configurations, but one sub-configuration (*i.e.*, 10-core memory-oriented configuration) has the full 8MB L2 cache size like the 8-core configuration with fewer ALUs and FPUs like the 12-core configuration. The two other sub-configurations (*i.e.*, 10-core alu- and fpu-oriented configurations) have 4MB L2 cache size like the 12-core configuration but with more ALUs or FPUs like the 8-core configuration. Table 8 summarizes these four sub-configurations and highlights their key differences among the sub-configurations from the original 10-core configuration (*i.e.*, 10-

Table 8: Key parameters of cores for four 10-core sub-configurations consuming approximately the same maximum power.

Processor configuration	Memory oriented	Balanced (original)	ALU oriented	FPU oriented
L2(MB)	8	6	4	4
IL1(KB)/DL1(KB)	32/32			
TLB	32			
ALU/Complex ALU/FPU	2/1/1	2/1/2	4/2/1	1/1/4
LSQ	32/32			
ROB/IQ	64/32			
YAG branch predictor	20/15/15			

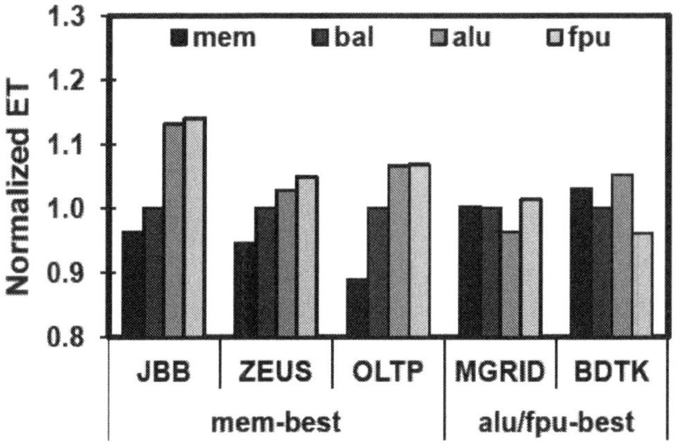

Figure 6: ET comparison of four 10-core sub-configurations with SRS. The ETs are normalized to the 10-core balanced configuration.

core balanced configuration) are shown in the two shaded rows. All four sub-configurations consume approximately the same maximum power (~185W). Note that we cannot provide sRCS for the 8- and 12-core configurations in this study. This is because we only have three configurations; (i) the 8-core configuration uses all the resources of each component while (ii) the 12-core configuration uses a bare minimum amount of resources for ALUs and FPUs in each core. Therefore, there is no way to increase (or decrease) the amount of resources of these two configurations. However, with more cores, we expect that more configurations can support sRCS, but we leave it as future work.

Figure 6 compares the ETs of four 10-core sub-configurations. The ETs are normalized to the 10-core balanced configuration. The three commercial workloads, JBB, OLTP, and ZEUS that benefit from the 10-core original configuration show further improvement with the 10-core memory-oriented configuration since they exhibit very low ALU and FPU utilization with high cache misses. In contrast, MGRID and BODYTRACK show further improvement with the 10-core alu- and fpu-oriented configurations, respectively. On average, sRCS can provide 6% performance improvement additional to 11% performance improvement for the applications that exhibit the highest performance with the 10-core baseline original configuration.

Finally, let us consider all the applications that exhibit the highest performance with the 8- and 12-core configurations (APACHE, EQUAKE, BLACKSHOLES, SWAPTIONS, WUPWISE, and APPLU). For these applications, we compare the high-

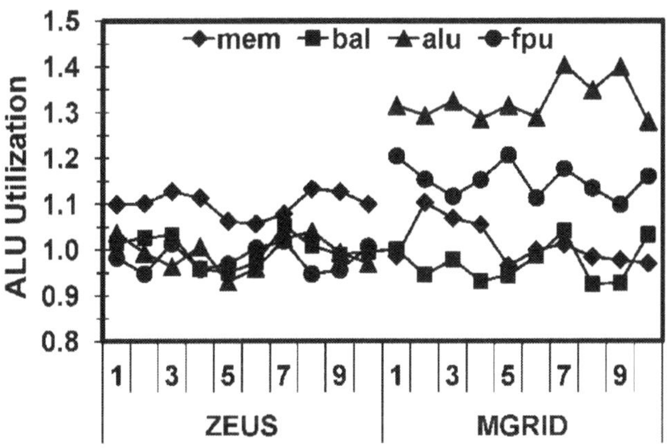

Figure 7: ALU utilization vs. runtime interval of four 10-core sub-configurations with sRCS. The ALU utilizations are normalized to the 10-core balanced configuration.

Table 9: Key parameters and operating points of three 10-core sub-configurations + limited V/F scaling consuming approximately the same maximum power.

Processor configuration	Low-V	Balanced (original)	High-V
V/F	2.7GH/z0.85V	3.2GHz/0.9V	3.6GHz/0.95V
L2(MB)	8	6	4
ALU/complex ALU/FPU	4/2/4	2/1/2	1/1/1

est performance with either the 8- or 12-core configuration to that with the best 10-core sub-configuration. We observe that the performance of the best 10-core sub-configuration is never higher than that of the 8- or 12-core configurations for these applications.

Best sub-configuration predictor: Determining the best 10-core sub-configuration can be performed in two steps. First, the predictor proposed in Section 6.2 determines the best configuration out of the original 8-, 10-, and 12-core configurations. Second, if the chosen best RCS configuration can support sRCS (*i.e.*, the 10-core configuration in this study), we determine the best sub-configurations. Figure 7 shows the ALU utilization comparison of four 10-core sub-configurations at each runtime interval for ZEUS and MGRID. First, all the five applications, which exhibit the highest performance with the 10-core balanced configuration, consistently favor one particular 10-core sub-configuration (*e.g.*, the memory- and alu-oriented configurations for ZEUS and MGRID, respectively). Second, the minimum ALU utilization of the best sub-configuration is almost always higher than the other sub-configurations across all the intervals that we examine; we only show 10 intervals for each application in Figure 7 and the analysis for the time period substantially longer than 40 intervals is left as future work. In such a case, we can use the ALU utilization to determine the best sub-configuration. This gives almost 100% prediction accuracy for sampling only one interval for each sub-configuration for all the five applications.

Comparison with RCS + limited V/F scaling range: Assuming a limited V/F scaling range can be still available, we compare RCS + limited V/F scaling with sRCS. Table 9 tabulates the key configuration parameters and operating points of three 10-core sub-configurations. We can afford larger L2 cache and more EUs at 0.85V at the cost of lower operating frequency (*i.e.*, low-V 10-core configuration) while we can operate all the cores at higher frequency (3.6GHz instead of 3.2GHz) at the expense of smaller L2 cache and fewer EUs at 0.95V (*i.e.*, "high-V" 10-core configuration). Similar to sRCS, we examine only the 10-core configuration because the 8- and 12-core configurations cannot support low- and high-V configurations, respectively; although the 8- and 12-core configurations can support high- and low-V configurations, respective, in this study, we limit our study to the 10-core configuration to contrast this result to sRCS.

Figure 8 compares the normalized ET of the low-V and high-V 10-core configurations with the best 10-core configuration using sRCS. We only evaluate the applications exhibiting the highest performance with the (balanced) 10-core configuration to contrast this result to sRCS. The low-V 10-core configuration provides 6%-19% higher performance than the balanced 10-core configuration while the high-V 10-core configuration offers 2.4% higher performance for OLTP; JBB shows the highest performance with the balanced 10-core configuration. In comparison, ZEUS, JBB and OLTP with the best 10-core sRCS configuration show 4%-10% higher performance while MGRD and BDTK exhibit 8% and 15% lower performance than the best of the two 10-core configurations using limited V/F scaling.

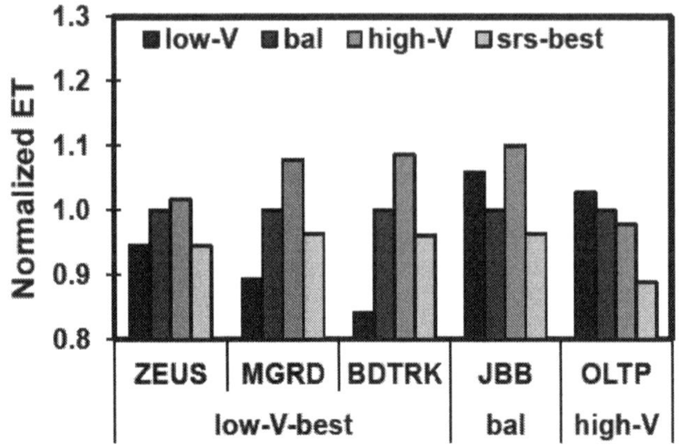

Figure 8: ET comparison of 10-core configurations with a limited V/F scaling and the best sRCS. The ETs are normalized to the 10-core balanced configuration.

8. Conclusion

With technology scaling, supporting a sufficient V/F scaling range for effective power management techniques becomes too expensive in terms of either chip area and/or power consumption. Facing such a challenge, we exploit resource scaling as a mean to compensate for lack of a V/F scaling range and propose an RCS technique to improve performance of power-constrained multi-core processors in this paper. Our experimental results demonstrate that our RCS can improve the geometric-mean performance by 21% over the baseline 8-core configuration. Second, we propose a runtime system that predicts the best RCS configuration for a given application and adapts the processor accordingly at runtime. The predictor based on an ML algorithm only needs to examine 15% of runtime intervals to achieve accuracy well over 90% and our runtime RCS can offer 92% of the maximum performance that can be achieved by the oracular RCS. Third, we propose sRCS, which can give more optimized configurations than RCS for individual applications. We demonstrate that sRCS can provide 6% higher geometric-mean performance than RCS.

Acknowledgement

The authors would like to thank Ken Vu and Srini Ramani at IBM for their continuous suggestion and support. This work was supported in part by generous grants from IBM, NSF (CCF-0953603 and CCF-1016262), and DARPA (HR0011-12-2-0019). Nam Sung Kim has a financial interest in AMD and Samsung Electronics.

Reference

[1] C. Isci, A. Buyuktosunoglu, C.-Y. Cher, P. Bose, and M. Martonosi, "An Analysis of Efficient Multi-core Global Power Management Policies: Maximizing Performance for a Given Power Budget," in *IEEE/ACM MICRO*, 2006, pp. 347-358.

[2] J. Lee, V. Sathisha, M. Schulte, K. Compton, and N. Kim, "Improving Throughput of Power-constrained GPUs Using Dynamic Voltage/Frequency and Core Scaling," in *ACM PACT*, 2011, pp. 111-120.

[3] J. Li and J.F. Martinez, "Dynamic Power-Performance Adaptation of Parallel Computation on Chip Multiprocessors," in *IEEE/ACM HPCA*, 2006, pp. 77- 87.

[4] P. Petrica, A.M. Izraelevitz, D. Albonesi, and C. Shoemaker, "Flicker: A Dynamically Adaptive Architecture for Power Limited Multicore Systems," in *IEEE/ACM Int. Symp. Computer Architecture (ISCA)*, 2013.

[5] Y, Watanabe, J. Davis, and D. Wood, "WiDGET: Wisconsin Decoupled Grid Execution tiles," in *IEEE/ACM Int. Symp. on Computer Architecture (ISCA)*, 2010.

[6] J. Martinez and E. Ipek, "Dynamic Multicore Resource Management: A Machine Learning Approach," *IEEE Micro*, vol. 29, no. 5, pp. 8-17, Sep/Oc 2009.

[7] A. Iyer and D. Marculescu, "Microarchitecture-level Power Management," *IEEE T. Very Large Scale Integration System (TVLSI)*, vol. 10, no. 3, pp. 230-239, Jun 2003.

[8] D. Albonesi *et al.*, "Dynamically Tuning Processor Resources with Adaptive Processing," *IEEE Computer*, vol. 36, no. 12, pp. 49-58, Dec 2003.

[9] B. Lee and D. Brooks, "Efficiency Trends and Limits from Comprehensive Microarchitectural Adaptivity," in *ACM ASPLOS*, 2008.

[10] V. Kontorinis, A. Shayan, D. Tullsen, and R. Kumar, "Reducing Peak Power with a Table-driven Adaptive Processor Core," in *IEEE/ACM Int. Symp. on Microarchitecture (MICRO)*, 2009, pp. 189-200.

[11] T. Lanier. Exploring the Design of the Design of the Cortex-A15 Processor. [Online]. http://www.arm.com/files/pdf/at-exploring_the_design_of_the_cortex-a15.pdf

[12] H. Homayoun, V. Kontorinis, A. Shayan, T.-W. Lin, and D. Tullsen, "Dynamically Heterogeneous Cores through 3D Resource Pooling," in *IEEE/ACM Int. Symp. on High-Peformance Computer Architecture (HPCA)*, 2012, pp. 1-12.

[13] C. Kim *et al.*, "Composable Lightweight Processors," in *IEEE/ACM Int. Symp. on Microarchitecture (MICRO)*, 2007, pp. 381-394.

[14] K. Khubaib, M.A. Suleman, M. Hashemi, C. Wilkerson, and Y.N. Patt, "MorphCore: An Energy-Efficient Microarchitecture for High Performance ILP and High Throughput TLP," in *IEEE/ACM Int. Symp. on Microarchitecture (MICRO)*, 2012, pp. 305-316.

[15] E. Ipek, M Kirman, N. Kirman, and J.F. Martinez, "Core Fusion: Accommodating Software Diversity in Chip Multiprocessors," in *IEEE/ACM Int. Symp. on Computer Architecture (ISCA)*, 2007, pp. 186-197.

[16] M.A. Suleman, M.K. Qureshi, and Y.N. Patt, "Feedback-driven Threading: Power-efficient and High-performance execution of Multi-threaded Workloads on CMPs," in *ACM Int. Conf. on Architectural Support for Programming Languages and Operating Systems (ASPLOS)*, 2008, pp. 277-286.

[17] R.W. Moore and B.R. Childers, "Using Utility Prediction Models to Dynamically Choose Program Thread Counts," in *IEEE Int. Symp. Performance Analysis of Systems and Software (ISPASS)*, 2012, pp. 135-144.

[18] R. Bitirgen, E. Ipek, and J.F. d Martinez, "Coordinated Management of Multiple Interacting Resources in Chip Multiprocessors: A Machine Learning Approach," in *IEEE/ACM Int. Symp. on Microarchitecture (MICRO)*, 2008, pp. 318-329.

[19] K. Meng, R. Joseph, R.P. Dick, and L. Shang, "Multi-optimization Power Management for Chip Multiprocessors,"

in *ACM Int. Conf. on Parallel Architectures and Compilation Techniques (PACT)*, 2008, pp. 177-186.

[20] K. Ma, X. Li, M. Chen, and X. Wang, "Scalable Power Control for Many-core Architectures Running Multi-threaded Applications," in *IEEE?ACM Int. Symp. on Computer Architecture (ISCA)*, 2011, pp. 449--460.

[21] R. Cochran, C. Hankendi, A.K. Coskun, and S. Reda, "Pack & Cap: Adaptive DVFS and Thread Packing under Power Caps," in *IEEE/ACM Int. Symp. on Microarchitecture (MICRO)*, 2011, pp. 175-185.

[22] X. Wang, K. Ma, and Y. Wang, "Adaptive Power Control with Online Model Estimation for Chip Multiprocessors," *IEEE T. on Parallel and Distributed Systems (TPDS)*, vol. 22, no. 10, pp. 1681-1696, Oct 2011.

[23] M.M.K. Martin *et al.*, "Multifacet's General Execution-Driven Multiprocessor Simulator (GEMS) toolset," *SIGARCH Comput. Archit. News*, vol. 33, no. 4, pp. 92-99, Nov 2005.

[24] Sheng Li *et al.*, "McPAT: An Integrated Power, Area, and Timing Modeling Framework for Multicore and Manycore Architectures," in *IEEE/ACM Int. Symp. on Microarchitecture (MICRO)*, 2009, pp. 469-480.

[25] A.R. Alameldeen *et al.*, "Evaluating Non-Deterministic Multi-Threaded Commercial Workloads, " in *IEEE Computer Architecture Evaluation Using Commercial Workloads Workshop (CAECW)*, 2002, pp. 30-38.

[26] Standard Performance Evaluation Corporation. SPEC OMP V3.2. [Online]. http://www.spec.org/omp/

[27] C. Bienia and K. Li, "PARSEC 2.0: A New Benchmark Suite for Chip-multiprocessors," in *Workshop on Modeling, Benchmarking and Simulation (MoBS)*, 2009.

[28] N. Barrow-Williams, C. Fensch, and S. Moore, "A Communication Characterisation of SPLASH-2 and PARSEC," in *IEEE Int. Symp. on Workload Characterization (IISWC)*, 2009, pp. 86-97.

[29] N.R. Fredrickson, A. Afsahi, and Y. Qian, "Performance Characteristics of OpenMP Constructs, and Application Benchmarks on a Large Symmetric Multiprocessor," in *ACM Int. Conf. on Supercomputing (ICS)*, 2003, pp. 140-149.

[30] B. Lee and D. Brooks, "Efficiency Trends and Limits from Comprehensive Microarchitectural Adaptivity," in *ACM Int. Conf. on Architectural Support for Programming Languages and Operating Systems (ASPLOS)*, 2008, pp. 36-47.

[31] M. Khellah *et al.*, "A 4.2Ghz, 130Mb/cm2, Dual-Vcc SRAM in 65nm CMOS Featuring Active Power Management with Autonomous Compensation of PVT Variation & Aging Impacts," in *IEEE Int. Symp. on Solid Circuit Conf. (ISSCC)*, 2006, pp. 2572-2581.

[32] J.W. Tschanz *et al.*, "Dynamic Sleep Transistor and Body Bias for Active Leakage Power Control of Microprocessors," *IEEE J. of Solid-State Circuits (JSSC)*, vol. 38, no. 11, pp. 1838-1845, Nov 2003.

[33] D Foley *et al.*, "AMD'S Llano Fusion APU," in *IEEE HOTCHIPS*, 2011.

[34] S. Damaraju *et al.*, "A 22nm IA multi-CPU and GPU System-on-Chip," in *IEEE ISSCC*, 2012, pp. 56-57.

[35] [Online]. http://ark.intel.com/products/27287/Intel-Xeon-Processor-7140M-16M-Cache-3_40-GHz-800-MHz-FSB

[36] (2011) Intel Core i7-3960X Processor. [Online]. http://ark.intel.com/products/63696

[37] A. Naveh, "Power and Thermal Management in the Intel Core Duo Processor," *Intel Technology J.*, vol. 10, no. 2, pp. 109-122, 2006.

[38] I. Park, C. L. Ooi, and T. N. Vijaykumar, "Reducing Design Complexity of the Load/Store Queue," in *IEEE/ACM Int. Symp. on Microarchitecture (MICRO)*, 2003, p. 411.

[39] C. Isci, A. Buyuktosunoglu, and M. Martonosi, "Long-term Workload Phases: Duration Predictions and Applications to DVFS," *IEEE Micro*, vol. 25, no. 5, pp. 39-51, Sep-Oct 2005.

[40] E. Perelman, G. Hamerly, M. Van Biesbrouck, T. Sherwood, and B. Calder, "Using SimPoint for Accurate and Efficient Simulation," in *ACM SIGMETRICS*, 2003, pp. 318-319.

[41] J. Lau, S. Schoenmackers, and B. Calder, "Transition Phase Classification and Prediction," in *IEEE/ACM Int. Symp. on High-Peformance Computer Architecture (HPCA)*, 2005, pp. 278-289.

[42] R. Strong, J. Mudigonda, J.C. Mogul, N. Binkert, and D. Tullsen, "Fast Switching of Threads between Cores," *ACM Oper. Syst. Rev.*, vol. 43, no. 2, pp. 35-45, Apr 2009.

[43] H.R. Ghasemi, S.C. Draper, and N.S. Kim, "Low-voltage On-chip Cache Architecture Using Heterogeneous Cell Sizes for High-performance Processors," in *IEEE/ACM Int. Symp. on High-Peformance Computer Architecture (HPCA)*, 2011, pp. 38-49.

[44] D.-C. Juan, Y.-T. Chen, M.C. Lee, and S.-C. Chang, "An Efficient Wake-up Strategy Considering Spurious Glitches Phenomenon for Power Gating Designs," *IEEE T. Very Large Scale Integration System (TVLSI)*, vol. 18, no. 2, pp. 246 - 255, Feb 2010.

Realm: An Event-Based Low-Level Runtime for Distributed Memory Architectures

Sean Treichler
Stanford University
Stanford, CA
sjt@cs.stanford.edu

Michael Bauer
Stanford University
Stanford, CA
mebauer@cs.stanford.edu

Alex Aiken
Stanford University
Stanford, CA
aiken@cs.stanford.edu

ABSTRACT

We present Realm, an event-based runtime system for heterogeneous, distributed memory machines. Realm is fully asynchronous: all runtime actions are non-blocking. Realm supports spawning computations, moving data, and *reservations*, a novel synchronization primitive. Asynchrony is exposed via a light-weight event system capable of operating without central management.

We describe an implementation of Realm that relies on a novel *generational event* data structure for efficiently handling large numbers of events in a distributed address space. Microbenchmark experiments show our implementation of Realm approaches the underlying hardware performance limits. We measure the performance of three real-world applications on the Keeneland supercomputer. Our results demonstrate that Realm confers considerable latency hiding to clients, attaining significant speedups over traditional bulk-synchronous and independently optimized MPI codes.

Categories and Subject Descriptors

D.1.3 [**Programming Techniques**]: Concurrent Programming; D.2.12 [**Software Engineering**]: Interoperability

Keywords

Realm; Legion; distributed memory; deferred execution; events; reservations; heterogeneous architectures; runtime

1. INTRODUCTION

All parallel programs can be thought of as graphs with nodes representing operations to be performed and edges representing ordering constraints, such as control or data dependences. To simplify the task of mapping parallel programs to distributed memory machines, runtime systems take several distinct approaches to expressing and manipulating these graphs.

In *implicit representation* systems, the runtime is unaware of the dependences between operations and the burden of orchestrating and optimizing the program for each target architecture falls primarily on the programmer; MPI [36] and X10 [17] are examples of systems in which the programmer encodes the partial order on the execution of operations using primitives for launching parallel work and performing synchronization. In *explicit representation* systems, the runtime has direct access to the graph of operations and takes responsibility for all synchronization and scheduling. Explicit representation systems can yield both higher performance (because an automated system can exploit opportunities for overlapping operations that are too difficult for a programmer to express) and more portable performance (because choices for a particular machine are not baked in to the program). Recent examples of explicit representation systems include Sequoia [22], Tarragon [18], and Deterministic Parallel Java (DPJ) [10].

Most explicit systems for distributed memory machines are *static*, meaning the dependence graph of operations is available at compile time. In contrast, *dynamic* explicit systems must manage the graph as it is generated on-line by the client, and any runtime system overheads will limit performance. The additional cost of communication in distributed memory machines makes dynamically handling graph construction and execution challenging, traditionally relegating the scope of dynamic explicit systems to shared memory machines. However, dynamic explicit systems are essential when dealing with applications with data-dependent parallelism or reacting to large variations in hardware performance. As applications become more irregular and the performance of distributed machines exhibits more variation due to heterogeneity and power saving techniques[35], dynamic explicit systems will become important for achieving high performance.

In this paper we present Realm, a dynamic, explicit representation runtime system for heterogeneous, distributed memory machines. Realm uses a light-weight *event* system to dynamically represent the program graph. Client applications use Realm events to encode control dependences between computation, data movement, and synchronization operations. Using *generational events*, a novel implementation technique, Realm compresses the representation of many events into a single generational event and eliminates the need for Realm (or the programmer) to manage the lifetime of every event. This allows events to be passed by value and stored in arbitrary data structures without reference-counting overhead or explicit deallocation performed by program code. The reduction in storage costs and overhead allows Realm to provide the benefits of a dynamically-generated

PACT'14, August 24–27, 2014, Edmonton, AB, Canada.

ACM 978-1-4503-2809-8/14/08 ...$15.00.
http://dx.doi.org/10.1145/2628071.2628084 .

explicit representation even for programs that are distributed across many nodes.

We begin in Section 2 with more discussion of related work in parallel runtime systems. Section 3 covers how lightweight Realm events enable a *deferred execution model*, how deferred execution differs from standard asynchronous models, and motivates the need for the other novel features of Realm including *reservations* and *physical regions*. Section 4 gives an overview of the Realm interface. Each subsequent section highlights one of our primary contributions:

- Section 5 describes the use of Realm events and how events are implemented with generational events. The low cost of managing events in Realm is central to the overall design, as Realm clients allocate events at rates in the tens of thousands per second per node.
- Section 6 introduces *reservations* for performing synchronization in a deferred execution model, thereby enabling relaxed execution orderings not expressible in many explicit systems. We show how reservations are typically used by Realm clients and present an efficient implementation.
- Section 7 covers Realm's *physical region system* and how it supports data movement in a deferred execution model. We also cover Realm's novel support for bulk reductions.
- Section 8 evaluates Realm on a collection of microbenchmarks that stress-test our implementations of events, reservations, and data movement operations. We show that the performance of Realm's primitives approach the limits of the underlying hardware.
- Section 9 details the performance of three real-world applications written in both an implicit representation model and in Realm's explicit deferred execution model. In one case we also compare against an independently written and optimized MPI code. We find that applications using Realm range from 22-135% faster than equivalent implicit versions.

2. BACKGROUND AND RELATED WORK

In this section we discuss both related work and the distinctions between implicit/explicit and static/dynamic runtime systems in more detail. The presentation of Realm begins in Section 3. A categorization of a number of (but by no means all) classic and recent parallel runtimes is given in Table 1.

The most widely used high-performance parallel runtime is MPI [36], which is an implicit representation system. MPI implements a bulk-synchronous model in which programs are divided into phases of computation, communication, and synchronization [24]. A common bulk-synchronous idiom is a loop that alternates phases:

```
while (...) {
   compute(...); // local computation
   barrier;
   communicate(...);
   barrier;
}
```

By design, computation and communication cannot happen at the same time in a bulk synchronous execution, idling significant machine resources. Thus, MPI has evolved to include asynchronous operations for overlapping communication and computation. Consider the following MPI-like code:

```
receive(x, ...);
Y;   // see discussion
sync;
f(x);
```

Here x is a local buffer that is the target of a `receive` operation copying data from remote memory. The `receive` executes asynchronously—the main thread continues execution with Y while the `receive` is also executing—but the only way to safely use the contents of x is to perform a `sync` operation that blocks until the `receive` completes.

It is the responsibility of the programmer to find useful computation Y to overlap with the `receive`. There are several constraints on the choice of Y. The execution time of Y must not be too short (or the latency of the `receive` will not be hidden) and it must not be too long (or the continuation f(x) will be unnecessarily delayed). Since Y can't use x, Y must be an unrelated computation, which can result in non-modular code that is difficult to maintain.

Thus, the programmer is responsible not only for adding sufficient synchronization but also for static scheduling (e.g., overlapping Y with the `receive`). Other implicit runtimes have the same issue, as only the programmer has the knowledge of what can be parallelized. The PGAS languages (UPC [12], Titanium [40] and Co-Array Fortran [33]) are, for the purposes of this discussion, very similar to MPI. Other programming models that differ significantly from the bulk synchronous model still require user-placed and potentially blocking synchronization to join asynchronous computations (e.g., Cilk's *spawn/synch* [9], X10's [17] and Habanero Java's [14] *asynch/finish* and Chapel's rich collection of synchronization constructs [15]). The actor model provided by Charm++ [29] is a form of implicit representation, as the runtime has no knowledge of what messages will be sent by a message handler until it is actually executed. Charm++ also provides futures that allow asynchronous computations to be called; a thread using a future executes an implicit synchronization operation if the value is not yet available.

Static explicit systems vary widely in how they represent the graph of dependent operations. Some, including classic dataflow systems such as Id [4], provide languages that are very close to the underlying static graphs. There are also recent examples, particularly for coarse-grain static dataflow

Implicit Representation Systems	
MPI [36] GASNet [41] Co-Array Fortran [33] UPC [12] Titanium [40] Chapel [15] X10 [17] HJ [14] Cilk [9] Charm++ [29]	
Explicit Representation Systems	
Static	*Dynamic*
TAM [19] Id [4] Sequoia [22, 26] DPJ [10] Tarragon [18] CnC [31, 11] Lucid [27] CGD [37]	StarPU [5] TAM [19] Realm

Table 1: Categorization of parallel runtimes.

[27, 37]. Tarragon [18] is a good example of the wide range of possible semantics for static systems, having a more actor-like instead of purely dataflow semantics for its graphs. Another example is Concurrent Collections (CnC) [11], which incorporates both control and data dependence edges in the graph. In other static explicit systems the static graph is is constructed as a compiler's intermediate representation; examples are Sequoia [22] and Deterministic Parallel Java (DPJ) [10].

A significant advantage of static dependence graphs is that they can be scheduled at compile time, resulting in very low runtime overheads, which in turn enables exploitation of finer-grain parallelism. Furthermore, because the dependence graph is explicit, the user is relieved of specifying the overlap of operations, allowing the implementation more scope for optimizations and different strategies for different platforms. There are two disadvantages to static explicit systems. The first is that dynamic decision making, while not impossible, must be encoded as a choice among a static set of possibilities, leading to cumbersome implementations that would be simple in a dynamic setting. The other issue is that partial orders specified by graphs cannot express some useful weaker dependence patterns, and in fact some explicit systems have added constructs that capture weaker ordering constraints at the cost of more complex semantics and implementations [3].

In contrast, there are few previous dynamic explicit systems for distributed memory machines. TAM is a low-level runtime for dataflow languages that targets conventional hardware. TAM is a hybrid static/dynamic system and is listed in Table 1 in both categories. At a fine grain (roughly, within a function body) TAM is quite static, which is necessary to exploit very fine grain parallelism. At coarser granularity TAM is dynamic, with the graph of dependences between *frames* evolving at runtime. TAM, which was designed for much smaller machines than today's heterogeneous supercomputers, leaves the runtime management of the dynamic parts of the graph to the client. TAM also has no facilities for relaxed execution orderings nor for bulk reductions. Parallex [23, 28] is a more recent system with similarities to TAM, in that it is thread-based and latency-hiding is achieved through cooperative multithreading.

StarPU [5] is closer to Realm, providing a similar interface to build a dynamically generated control-dependence graph. Like Realm, it provides separate data movement primitives that appear as operations in the graph. StarPU has no primitive equivalent to Realm's reservations for expressing synchronization in a deferred execution environment, and does not support bulk reductions, two of the novel features of Realm. Furthermore, StarPU's *tags*, which play the role of Realm's events, are managed by the client, not by StarPU, which means they cannot be optimized for time or space consumption. It is important to note that the goals of StarPU and Realm are also different: Realm is intended to be a low-level runtime for higher-level languages and runtimes that will run efficiently on very large heterogeneous machines; StarPU is designed with a pragmatic C-level interface to be used directly by programmers.

Ompss also provides a dynamically constructed, explicit graph of operations[20]. Ompss' graphs are heavier weight than Realm's, including data as well as control dependences. This prevents Ompss from replicating the important performance optimizations performed by Realm for distributed memory machines. Realm also differs in providing reservations as well as physical regions and associated operations, such as bulk reductions.

Many distributed systems use a publish/subscribe abstraction for supporting communication that has similarities to Realm's events and event waiters[2, 13]. Work has also been done on using object-oriented languages to build event-based distributed systems[21, 25, 16]. Events in these systems are much heavier weight and often carry large data payloads. Many systems focus on resiliency instead of performance[34].

3. DEFERRED EXECUTION

On distributed memory architectures communication costs can easily dominate performance. Thus, all distributed memory runtime systems must provide mechanisms for hiding long latency communication. Dynamic explicit runtimes have a unique additional problem: the operations to construct the dynamic graph are themselves potentially long latency. However, by providing a well-designed client interface, Realm is able to use the same mechanism to hide both forms of latency.

In Realm, all operations execute asynchronously. When invoked, every Realm operation returns immediately with an *event* that *triggers* when the operation completes. Furthermore, every Realm operation takes an event as a precondition, and the operation is guaranteed not to begin until the precondition event has triggered. Consider an application that needs to run operations A and B on different nodes, where A produces data a that must be copied to the input b of B, and also operations C and D, where D depends on C. The Realm client would issue the following calls:

```
Event e1 = p1.spawn(A,... ,NO_EVENT);
Event e2 = a.copy_to(b,e1);
Event e3 = p2.spawn(B,... ,e2);
Event e4 = p1.spawn(C,... ,NO_EVENT);
Event e5 = p1.spawn(D,... ,e4);
```

Here `p.spawn(X,...)` means operation `X` is to be run on processor `p`. The use of events `e1`, `e2`, and `e4` as preconditions tells Realm how to construct the dynamic dependence graph:

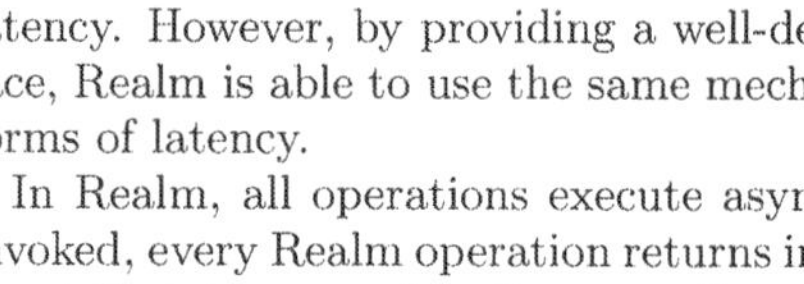

This example illustrates two important points. First, events in Realm represent control dependences only—events carry no data and copies are themselves operations in the graph. The simplicity of events enables the representation and optimizations discussed in Section 5.

Second, from the client's point of view these five statements execute without delay—all the operations are launched asynchronously and the client is never required to block on any Realm operation. In general, the use of events as dependences between operations allows clients to launch arbitrarily deep acyclic graphs of dependent operations without the need to block on intermediate results. To the best of our knowledge, this execution model has no name in the literature; we refer to it as *deferred execution*.

For contrast, consider how this example would be executed by an implicit runtime. First A would be spawned asynchronously. Next, the asynchronous copy from a to b would block pending the availability of a. Up to this point, the two models are the same: A is running and the copy is waiting on the completion of A. However, in standard asynchronous execution the client makes no further progress because it has the responsibility of waiting until it is safe to issue the copy. In deferred execution, this responsibility is delegated to the runtime, and the client can immediately continue with the spawn of B, even if the data in a is not yet ready. Deferred execution allows the client to continue to build the explicit graph, enabling the runtime to discover and construct the graph for the independent chain of operations C and D while A is executing. Furthermore, once processor $p1$ is available after executing A, the two chains of operations can execute in parallel. A similar effect can be achieved in implicit systems by hoisting C and D above B, but this solution places the burden for scheduling on the programmer (recall Section 2).

A key to enabling deferred execution in Realm is making events inexpensive. With the client able to issue operations far ahead of the actual execution, a large number of events are needed to track the dependences between operations. As we show in Section 9, Realm clients can generate tens of thousands of unique events per second per node during execution. In Section 5, we describe the implementation of generational events that are crucial to making events cheap and deferred execution practical.

Realm's novel operations are integrated into the deferred execution model as well. For example, a reservation request immediately returns an event that triggers when the reservation is granted. In this way, reservations are a deferred execution version of locks that do not block and allow another operation's execution to be dependent on the reservation's acquisition. Similarly, Realm's data movement operations are deferred. Realm's support for novel bulk reductions allows clients to construct sophisticated asynchronous reduction trees that match the shape of the machine's memory hierarchy. We illustrate a real-world application that leverages this feature in Section 9.

4. REALM INTERFACE

Realm is a low-level runtime, providing a small set of primitives for performing computations on heterogeneous, distributed memory machines. The focus is on providing the necessary mechanisms, while leaving the policy decisions (e.g. which processor to run a task on, what copies to perform) under the complete control of the client. While that client may be a programmer coding directly to the Realm interface, the expected usage model for Realm is as a target for higher-level languages and runtimes.

The Realm interface is shown in Figure 1. Except for the static singleton machine object, object instances are lightweight *handles* that uniquely name the underlying object. Every handle is valid everywhere in the system, allowing handles to be freely copied, passed as arguments, and stored in the heap. For performance, Realm does not track where handles propagate. In the case of events, this creates an interesting problem of knowing when it is safe to reclaim resources associated with events (see Section 5).

In the rest of this section we explain Realm processor and machine objects. In subsequent sections we present Realm's events, reservations, and physical regions.

```
class Event {
  const unsigned id, gen;
  static const Event NO_EVENT;

  bool has_triggered() const;
  void wait() const;
  static Event merge_events(const set<Event> &to_merge);
};

class UserEvent : public Event {
  static UserEvent create_user_event();
  void trigger(Event wait_on = NO_EVENT) const;
};
class Processor {
  const unsigned id;
  typedef unsigned TaskFuncID;
  typedef void (*TaskFuncPtr)(void *args,size_t arglen,Processor p);
  typedef map<TaskFuncID, TaskFuncPtr> TaskIDTable;

  enum Kind { CPU_PROC,GPU_PROC /* ... */ };
  Kind kind() const;

  Event spawn(TaskFuncID func_id,const void *args,size_t arglen,
            Event wait_on) const;
};
class Reservation {
  const unsigned id;
  Event acquire(Event wait_on = NO_EVENT) const;
  void release(Event wait_on = NO_EVENT) const;

  static Reservation create_reservation(size_t payload_size = 0);
  void *payload_ptr();
  void destroy_lock();
};
class Memory {
  const unsigned id;
  size_t size() const;
};

class PhysicalRegion {
  const unsigned id;
  static const PhysicalRegion NO_REGION;

  static PhysicalRegion create_region(size_t num_elmts, size_t elmt_size);
  void destroy_region() const;

  ptr_t alloc();
  void free(ptr_t p);

  RegionInstance create_instance(Memory memory) const;
  RegionInstance create_instance(Memory memory,
                          ReductionOpID redopid) const;
  void destroy_instance(RegionInstance instance,
                     Event wait_on = NO_EVENT) const;
};

class RegionInstance {
  const unsigned id;

  void *element_data_ptr(ptr_t p);
  Event copy_to(RegionInstance target, Event wait_on = NO_EVENT);
  Event reduce_to(RegionInstance target, ReductionOpID redopid,
            Event wait_on = NO_EVENT);
};
class Machine {
  Machine(int *argc, char ***argv,
       const Processor::TaskIDTable &task_table);

  void run(Processor::TaskFuncID task_id,
        const void *args, size_t arglen);

  static Machine* get_machine(void);
  const set<Memory>& get_all_memories(void) const;
  const set<Processor>& get_all_processors(void) const;

  int get_proc_mem_affinity(vector<ProcMemAffinity> &result, ...);
  int get_mem_mem_affinity(vector<MemMemAffinity> &result, ...);
};
```

Figure 1: Runtime Interface.

4.1 Processors

Lines 14-25 of Figure 1 show the interface for `Processor` objects. Processors name every computational unit within the machine. Processors have a kind, currently either CPU or GPU (line 20). Exposing heterogeneous processor types through a common interface allows the client to alter the task mapping without having multiple code paths for launching tasks and keeps the Realm interface open to extension for new processor kinds (e.g. FPGAs).

The `spawn` method (line 23) launches a new *task* on a processor, adding a new node to Realm's dynamic control dependence graph. The spawn operation is invoked on a processor handle, enabling a task on one processor to launch another task on any other processor in the system. Spawn takes an optional event that must trigger before the task begins execution and returns a (fresh) event that triggers when the task completes. For example, Figure 2 shows a portion of a Realm event graph generated from a real client application [6]. Tasks are rectangles in Figure 2. The right-hand side of the graph shows the actual application-level tasks, while the left-hand side shows *mapping* tasks launched by the higher-level runtime to dynamically compute the placement of the application tasks and data. In Figure 2, the application-level tasks are launched on the GPU from the mapping tasks running on a CPU. Dashed lines indicate that one task is launched by another task.

4.2 Machine

Realm provides a singleton `Machine` object (lines 65-78 of Figure 1) that handles initialization and run-time introspection of the hardware. The `Machine` object is created at program start, providing a task table mapping task IDs to function pointers, and then invokes the `run` method (line 69). Any task can call the `get_machine` method (line 72) and use it to obtain lists of all `Memory` (line 73) and `Processor` (line 74) handles. Using the affinity methods (lines 76-77), the client can also determine which memories are accessible by each processor and with what performance, as well as which pairs of memories can support copy operations.

4.3 Implementation

Our implementation of Realm for heterogeneous clusters of both CPUs and GPUs is built on Pthreads, CUDA for GPUs[1], and the GASNet cluster API[41] for portability across interconnect fabrics. The cluster is modeled as having two kinds of processors (a `CPU` processor for each CPU core and a `GPU` processor for each GPU, matching the scheduling granularity of Pthreads and CUDA respectively) and four kinds of memory (distributed GASNet memory accessible by all nodes via RDMA operations, system memory on each node, GPU device memory, and zero-copy memory, which is a segment of system memory that has been mapped into both the CPU and GPU's address spaces). Internally, Realm maintains a queue for each processor of tasks that are ready to execute (i.e., those for which the precondition event has triggered); when the processor becomes idle Realm executes the next task in the queue.

Realm features requiring communication rely on GASNet's *active messages*, which consist of a command and payload sent by one node to another. Upon arrival at a destination node, a handler routine is invoked to process the message[39].

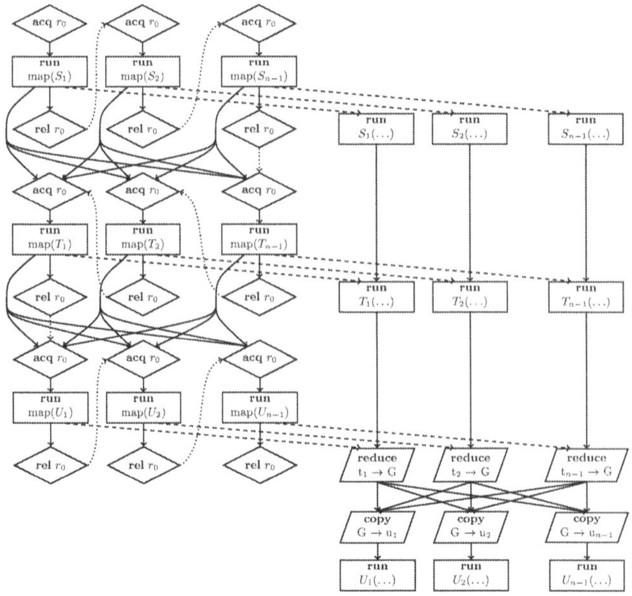

Figure 2: A Realm Event Graph

5. EVENTS

Events describe dependences between operations in Realm. In Figure 2, events are solid black arrows between operations, indicating one operation must be performed before another. Events express control dependences only—events order operations but do not imply anything about data dependences and do not involve data movement.

Lines 1-13 of Figure 1 show the event interface. An instance of the `Event` type names a unique event in the system. `NO_EVENT` (line 3) is a special instance that by definition has always triggered. The event interface supports testing whether an event has triggered (line 5) and waiting on an event to trigger (line 6), but the preferred use of events is passing them as preconditions to other operations. If an operation has more than one precondition, those events are merged into an aggregate event with the `merge_events` call (line 7). The aggregate event does not trigger until all of the constituent events have triggered. In most cases, events are created as the result of other Realm calls, and the implementation is responsible for triggering these events. However, clients can also create a `UserEvent` (line 10) that is triggered explicitly by the client.

5.1 Event Implementation

Events are created on demand and are *owned* by the creating node. The `Event` type is a light-weight *handle*. The space of event handles is divided statically across the nodes by including the owner node's ID in the upper bits of the event handle. This allows each node to assign handles to new events without conflicting with another node's assignments and without inter-node communication. The inclusion of the node ID in event handles also permits any node to determine an event's owning node without communication.

When a new event e is created, the owning node o allocates a data structure to track e's state (*triggered* or *untriggered*) and e's local list of *waiters*: dependent operations (e.g., copy operations and task launches) on node o. The first reference to e by a remote node n allocates the same data structure on n. An *event subscription* active message is then sent to

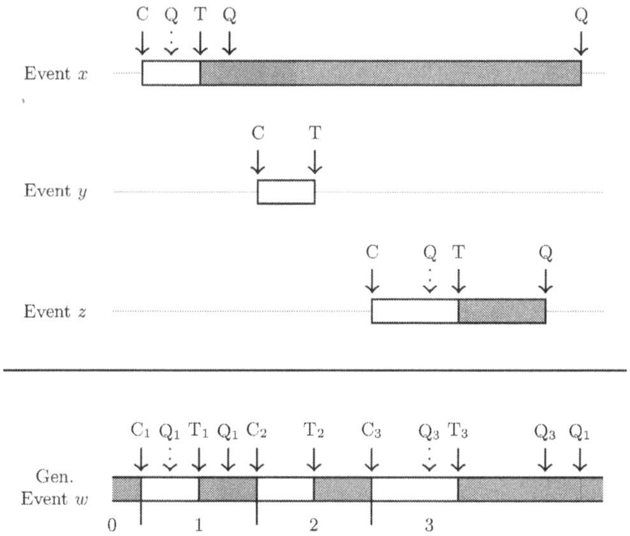

Figure 3: Generational Event Timelines

node o indicating node n should be informed when e triggers. Any additional dependent operations on node n are added to n's local list of e's waiters without further communication. When e triggers, the owner node o notifies all local waiters and sends an *event trigger* message to each subscribed node. If the owner node o receives a subscription message after e triggers, o immediately responds with a trigger message.

The triggering of an event may occur on any node. When it occurs on a node t other than the owner o, a trigger message is sent from t to o, which forwards that message to all other subscribed nodes. The triggering node t notifies its local waiters immediately; no message is sent from o back to t. While a remote event trigger results in the latency of a triggering operation being at least two active message flight times, it bounds the number of active messages required per event trigger to $2N-2$ where N is the number of nodes monitoring the event (which is generally a small fraction of the total number of machine nodes). An alternative is to share the subscriber list so that the triggering node can notify all interested nodes directly. However, such an algorithm is both more complicated (due to race conditions) and requires $O(N^2)$ active messages. Any algorithm super-linear in the number of nodes in the system will not scale well, and as we show in Section 8.1, the latency of a single event trigger active message is very small.

5.2 Generational Events

There are several constraints on the lifetime of the data structure used to represent an event e. Creation and triggering of e can each happen only once, but any number of operations may depend on e. Furthermore, some operations depending on e may not even be requested until long after e has triggered. Therefore, the data structure used to represent e cannot be freed until all these operations depending on e have been registered. Some systems ask the programmer to explicitly create and destroy events[5], but this is problematic when most events are created by Realm rather than the programmer. Other systems address this issue by reference counting event events[30], but reference counting adds client and runtime overhead even on a single node, and incurs even greater cost in a distributed memory implementation.

Instead of freeing event data structures, our implementation aggressively recycles them. Compared to reference counting, our implementation requires fewer total event data structures and has no client or runtime overhead. The key observation is that one *generational event* data structure can represent one untriggered event and a large number (e.g., $2^{32}-1$) of already-triggered events. We extend each event handle to include a generation number and the identifier for its generational event. Each generational event records how many generations have already triggered. A generational event can be reused for a new generation as soon as the current generation triggers. (Any new operation dependent on a previous generation can immediately be executed.) To create a new event, a node finds a generational event in the triggered state (or creates one if all existing generational events owned by the node are in the untriggered state), increases the generation by one, and sets the generational event's state to untriggered. As before, this can be done with no inter-node communication.

An example of how multiple events can be represented by a single generational event is shown in Figure 3. Timelines for events x, y, and z indicate where creation (C), triggering (T) and queries (Q) occur. Queries that succeed (i.e. the event has triggered) are shown with solid arrows, while those that fail are dotted. The lifetime of an event extends from its creation until the last operation (trigger or query) performed on it. Although the lifetime of event x overlaps with those of y and z, the untriggered intervals are non-overlapping, and all three can be mapped on to generational event w, with event x being assigned generation 1, y being assigned 2, and z being assigned 3. A query on the generational event succeeds if the generational event is either in the triggered state or has a current generation larger than the one associated with the query.

Nodes maintain generational event data structures for both events they own as well as remote events that they have observed. Remote generational event data structures record the most recent generation known to have triggered as well as the generation of the most recent subscription message sent (if any). Remote generational events enable an interesting optimization. If a remote generational event receives a query on a later generation than its current generation, it can infer that all generations up to the requested generation have triggered, because the new generation(s) of the event were able to be created by the event's owner. All local waiters for earlier generations can be notified even before receiving the event trigger message for the current generation.

In Section 8 we show that the latency of event triggering is very low, even in the case of dense, distributed graphs of dependent operations. In Section 9 we show that our generational event implementation results in a large reduction in space requirements to record events for real applications.

6. Reservations

Recall that the tasks on the right of Figure 2 are the actual application-level tasks and that the mapping tasks on the left dynamically compute where the application-level tasks should run. The higher-level runtime's mapping tasks may be run in any order, but each requires exclusive access to a shared data structure. In most systems, locks are used for atomic data access. However, standard locking primitives do not integrate well with deferred execution, as the requestor must wait (or constantly poll) for the lock to be granted. *Reservations* are a new synchronization mechanism that serve the purpose of locks in Realm's dynamically generated control dependence graph of deferred operations.

Reservations (lines 26-34 of Figure 1) are requested using the `acquire` method. Rather than waiting when the reservation is held (or returning a "retry" response), the request returns immediately with an event that will trigger when the reservation is eventually granted. Reservations are released with the `release` method. As with other Realm operations, the `acquire` and `release` methods accept an event parameter as a precondition (lines 28-29). A chain of event dependences should always exist between paired acquire and release invocations.

Another important difference between reservations and locks is that the processor requesting the reservation need not be the one that uses it. A common Realm idiom is to acquire a reservation on behalf of a task being launched. For example, in Figure 2, acquire requests (`acq` diamonds) are made for the reservation protecting the higher-level runtime's meta-data. The event returned by these requests then becomes the precondition for launching the mapping tasks, which actually use the meta-data. The reservation releases (`rel` diamonds) are made before the mapping tasks even run, but are conditioned on the completion of the mapping tasks. Dotted arrows between acquire and release nodes indicate one possible execution order of reservation grants and requests. Note that completion events for mapping calls are made preconditions for later reservation requests. This prevents acquire requests from later mapping tasks from being processed before other preconditions have been satisfied, which could lead to deadlock. Preconditions on reservation acquires also allow the acquisition of multiple reservations to follow a specific order, analogous to the standard technique for avoiding deadlock when requesting multiple locks simultaneously.

Often reservations are used to guard small allocations of data. To improve support for this idiom in a distributed environment, we allow a small (less than 4KB) *payload* of data to be associated with a reservation. The payload is guaranteed to be coherent while the reservation is held. The payload size is specified when the reservation is created (line 31) and a pointer to the local copy of the payload is obtained from the `payload_ptr` method (line 32).

Events and reservations give Realm expressiveness equivalent to the interfaces of implicit representation systems for ordering and serialization. Realm also makes these operations deferred and composable, neither of which is possible in other runtime interfaces.

6.1 Reservation Implementation

Like events, reservations are created on demand, using a space of handles statically divided across the nodes. Reservation creation requires no communication and the handle is sufficient to determine the creating node. However, whereas event ownership is static, reservation ownership may migrate; the creating node is the initial owner, but ownership can be transferred to other nodes. Since any node may at some point own a reservation r, all nodes use the same data structure with the following fields to track the state of r:

- *owner node* - the most recently known owner of r. If the current node is the owner, this information is correct. If not, this information may be stale, but the recorded node will have more recent information about the true owner and will forward the request.
- *reservation status* - records whether r is currently held; valid only on the current owner.
- *local waiters* - a list of pending local acquire requests. This data is always valid on all nodes.
- *remote waiters* - a set of other nodes known to have pending acquire requests; valid only on the current owner.
- *local payload pointer and size* - a copy of r's payload

Each time an acquire request is made, a new event is created to track when the grant occurs. The current node then examines its copy of the reservation data structure to determine if it is the owner. If the current node is the owner and the reservation isn't held, the acquire request is granted immediately and the event is triggered. If the reservation is held, the event is added to the list of local waiters. Note that the event associated with the acquire request is the only data that must be stored. If the current node isn't the owner, a *reservation acquire* active message is sent to the most recently known owner. If the receiver of an acquire request message is no longer the owner, it forwards the message on to the node it has recorded as the owner. If the current owner's status shows the reservation is currently held, the requesting node's ID is added to the remote waiters set. If the reservation is not held, the ownership of the reservation is given to the requesting node via a *reservation transfer* active message, which includes the set of remaining remote waiters and an up-to-date copy of the reservation's payload.

Similarly, a release request (once its preconditions have been satisfied) is first checked against the local node's reservation state. If the local node is not the owner, a *release* active message is sent to the most recently known owner, which is forwarded if necessary. Once the release request is on the reservation's current owning node, the local waiter list is examined. If the list is non-empty, the reservation remains in the acquired state and the first acquire grant event is pulled off the local waiter list and triggered. If the local waiter list is empty, the acquire state is changed to not-acquired, and the set of remote waiters is examined. If there are remote waiters, one is chosen and the corresponding node becomes the new owner via a reservation transfer.

The unfairness inherent in favoring local waiters over remote waiters is intentional. When contention on a reservation is high (the only time fairness is relevant), the latency of transferring a reservation between nodes can be the limiter on throughput. Minimizing the number of reservation transfers maximizes reservation throughput (see Section 8.2).

7. PHYSICAL REGIONS

Traditionally, most interfaces for data movement in distributed memory architectures only support copies of untyped buffers (e.g. MPI send operations). However, it is often useful to associate operations on data, such as reductions, in conjunction with data movement. Performing bulk data movement and reductions simultaneously can significantly reduce their cost compared to performing the operations separately. To support bulk reductions, where each element of a collection is the result of a reduction, Realm needs to know the type (or at least the size) of the elements in the collections involved. Realm relies on a system of typed *physical regions* to manage the layout and movement of data in a deferred execution model.

A physical region defines an addressing scheme for a collection of elements of a common type. To a first approximation, physical regions of elements of type T are arrays of T with additional metadata to support efficient copies, reductions, and allocation/deallocation of elements within the region. Realm supports creating multiple *instances* of a physical region in different memories for replication or data migration. Because all instances of a physical region r use the same addressing scheme, Realm has sufficient information to perform deferred copies between instances of r.

Lines 35-64 of Figure 1 show a subset of the interface for physical regions (we omit portions of the interface due to space constraints). Each physical memory is named by a `Memory` object (line 35). Physical region objects are constructed by defining the maximum number and size of elements (line 44). Physical region instances are created in a specific `Memory` (line 50). To maintain performance transparency, there is no virtualization of memory—each `Memory` is sized based on a physical capacity and a new instance can be allocated only if sufficient space remains. Instances must be explicitly destroyed, which can be contingent on an event (lines 53-54).

Elements can be dynamically allocated or freed within a physical region (lines 47-48). Elements are accessed by Realm pointers of type `ptr_t`. By definition, a Realm pointer into physical region r is valid for every instance of r regardless of its memory location (line 60). This allows Realm pointers to be stored in data structures and reused later, even if instances have been moved around. In common cases, pointer indexing reduces to inexpensive array address calculations which are compiled to individual loads and stores.

Realm supports copy operations between instances of the same physical region (line 61). Copy operations in Figure 2 are rhomboids marked `copy`. Like all other Realm operations, copy requests accept an event precondition and return an event that triggers upon completion of the copy. Realm does not guarantee the coherence of data between different instances; coherence must be explicitly managed by the client via copy operations.

7.1 Reduction Instances

If a task only performs reductions on an instance, a special reduction-only instance may be created (lines 51-52). In Figure 2, each task `Ti` is mapped to use reduction-only instance t_i to accumulate reductions in the GPU zero-copy memory. Using the `reduce_to` method (lines 62-63), these reduction buffers are eventually applied to a normal instance residing in GASNet memory. We detail this pattern in a real-world application in Section 9. Bulk reduction operations are rhomboids marked `reduce` in Figure 2.

Reduction-only instances differ in two important ways from normal instances. First, the per-element storage in reduction-only instances is sized to hold the "right-hand side" of the reduction operation (e.g., the v in $struct.field \mathrel{+}= v$). Second, individual reductions are accumulated (atomically) into the local reduction instance, which can then be sent as a batched reduction to a remote target instance. When multiple reductions are made to the same element, they are *folded* locally, further reducing communication. The fold operation is not always identical to the reduction operation. For example, if the reduction is exponentiation, the corresponding fold is multiplication:

$$(r[i] \mathrel{**}= a) \mathrel{**}= b \quad \Leftrightarrow \quad r[i] \mathrel{**}= (a * b)$$

The client registers reduction and fold operations at system startup (omitted from Figure 1 due to space constraints). Reduction instances can also be folded into other reduction instances to build hierarchical bulk reductions matching the memory hierarchy.

Realm supports two classes of reduction-only instances. A *reduction fold instance* is similar to a normal physical region in that it is implemented as an array indexed by the same element indices. The difference is that each instance element is a value of the reduction's right-hand-side type, which is often smaller than the region's element type (the left-hand-side type). A reduction operation simply folds the supplied right-hand-side value into the corresponding array location. When the reduction fold instance p is reduced to a normal instance r, first p is copied to r's location, where Realm automatically applies p to r by invoking the reduction function once per location via a cache-friendly linear sweep over the memory.

The second kind of reduction instance is a *reduction list instance*, where the instance is implemented as a list of reductions. A reduction list instance logs every reduction operation (the pointer location and right-hand-side value). When the reduction list instance p is reduced to a normal physical region r, p is transferred and replayed at r's location. In cases where the list of reductions is smaller than the number of elements in r the reduction in data transferred can yield better performance (see Section 8.3).

8. MICROBENCHMARKS

We evaluate our Realm implementation using microbenchmarks that test whether performance approaches the capacity of the underlying hardware. All experiments were run on the Keeneland supercomputer[38]. Each Keeneland KIDS node is composed of two Xeon 5660 CPUs, three Tesla M2090 GPUs, and 24 GB of DRAM. Nodes are connected by an Infiniband QDR interconnect.

Nodes	1	2	4	8	16
Mean Trigger Time (μs)	0.329	3.259	3.799	3.862	4.013

Figure 4: Event Latency Results.

8.1 Event Latency and Trigger Rates

We use two microbenchmarks to evaluate event performance. The first tests event triggering latency, both within and between nodes. Processors are organized in a ring and each processor creates a user event dependent on the previous processor's event. The first event in the chain of dependent events is triggered and the time until the triggering of the chain's last event is measured; dividing the total time by the number of events in the chain yields the mean trigger time. In the single-node case, all events are local to that node, so no active messages are required. For all other cases, the ring uses a single processor per node so that every trigger requires the transmission (and reception) of an event trigger active message.

Table 4 shows the mean trigger times. The cost of manipulating the data structures and running dependent operations

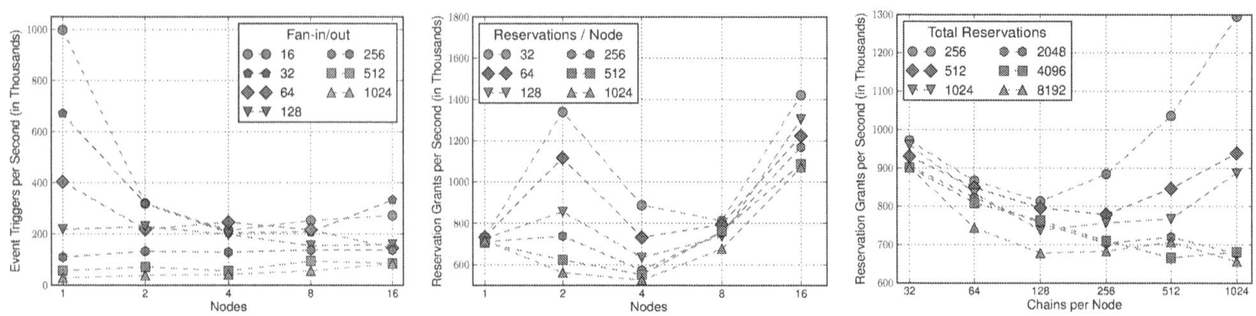

(a) Event Trigger Rates (b) Reservations for Fixed 1024 Chains (c) Reservations for Fixed 8 Nodes

Figure 5: Microbenchmark Results.

is shown by the single-node case, which had an average latency of only 329 nanoseconds. The addition of nearly 3 microseconds when going from one node to two is attributable to the latency of a GASNet active message; others have measured similar latencies[7]. The gradual increase in latency with increasing node count is likely related to the point-to-point nature of Infiniband communication, which requires GASNet to poll a separate connection for every other node.

Our second microbenchmark measures the maximum rate at which events can be triggered by our implementation. Instead of a single chain, a parameterized number (the *fan-in/out factor*) of parallel chains are created. The event at step $i+1$ of a chain depends on the ith event of every other chain. The events within each step of the chains are distributed across the nodes. Recall from Section 5 that the aggregation of event subscriptions limits the number of event trigger active messages to one per node (per event trigger) even when the fan-in/out factor exceeds the node count.

Figure 5a shows the event trigger rates for a variety of node counts and fan-in/out factors. For small fan-in/out factors, the total rate falls off initially going to two nodes as active messages become necessary, but increases slightly again at larger node counts. Higher fan-in/out factors require more messages and have lower throughput that also increases with node count. Although the number of events waiting on each node decreases with increasing node count, the minimal scaling indicates the bottleneck is in the processing of the active message each node must receive rather than the local redistribution of the triggering notification.

The compute-bound nature of the benchmark shows that active messages do not tax the network and leave bandwidth for application data movement. The event trigger rates in this microbenchmark are one to two orders of magnitude larger than the trigger rates required by the real applications described in Section 9.

8.2 Reservation Acquire Rates

The reservation microbenchmark measures the rate at which reservation acquire requests can be granted. A parameterized number of reservations are created per node and their handles are made available to every node. Each node then creates a parameterized number of *chains* of acquire/release request pairs, where each request attempts to acquire a random reservation and is made dependent on the previous acquisition in the chain. Thus the total number of chains across all nodes gives the total number of acquire requests that can exist in the system at any given time. All chains are started at the same time and the time to process all chains is divided into the total number of acquire requests to yield an average reservation grant rate.

Figure 5b shows the reservation grant rate for a variety of node counts and reservations per node. The number of chains per node is varied so that the total number of chains in the system is 1024 in all cases. For the single-node cases, the insensitivity to the number of reservations indicates that the bottleneck is in the computational ability of the node to process the requests. For larger numbers of nodes, especially for the larger numbers of reservations per node (where contention for any given reservation is low), the speedup with increasing node count suggests the limiting factor is the rate at which reservation-related active messages can be sent (nearly every request will require a transfer of ownership). In nearly all cases, the performance actually increases with decreasing number of reservations. Although contention increases, favoring local reservation requestors makes contention an advantage, reducing the number of reservation-related active messages that must be sent per reservation grant.

The benefit of reservation unfairness is more clearly shown in Figure 5c. Here the node count is fixed at 8 and reservation grant rates are shown for a variety of total reservation counts and number of chains per node. At 32 chains per node (256 chains total) contention is low and the grant rate is high. As the number of chains per node increases there is more contention for reservations and the grant rate drops. For smaller reservation counts, further increases in the number of chains results in improved grant rates. On each line the increase occurs when the chains per node exceeds the total number of reservations, which is where the expected number of requests per reservation per node exceeds one. As soon as there are multiple requestors for the same reservation on a node, the unfairness of reservations reduces the number of reservation ownership transfers, yielding better performance.

8.3 Reduction Throughput

To evaluate reduction instances we use a histogram microbenchmark where all nodes perform an addition reduction to a physical region in the globally visible GASNet memory. Using the reduction interface (Section 7) reductions are performed in five ways:

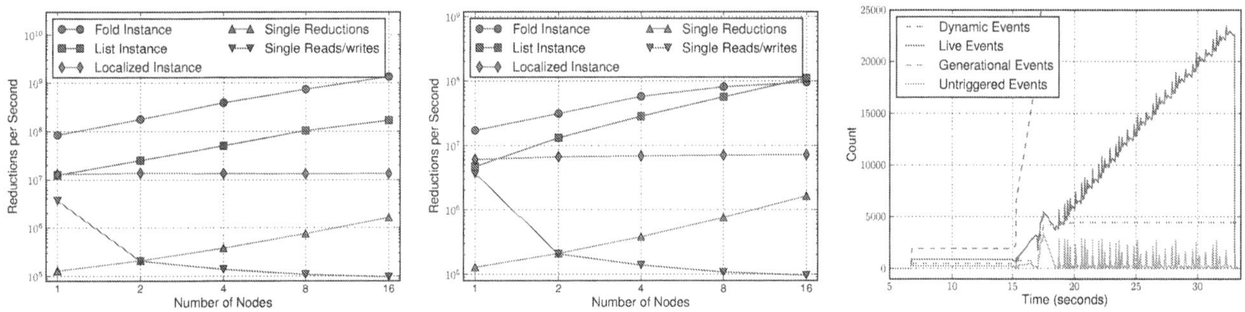

(a) Dense Reduction Benchmark (b) Sparse Reduction Benchmark (c) Event Lifetimes - Fluid Application

Figure 6: Performance of Reductions and Events.

- Single Reads/Writes - Each node acquires a reservation on the global physical region and for each reduction reads a value from the region, performs the addition, and writes the result back. The reservation is released after all reductions are performed.
- Single Reductions - Each reduction is individually sent as an active message to the node whose system memory holds the target of the reduction.
- Localized Instance - Each node takes a reservation on the global physical region, copies it to a new instance in its own system memory, performs all reductions to the local region, copies the region back, and releases the reservation.
- Fold Instance - Each node creates a local fold reduction instance. All reductions are folded into the instance, which is then copied and applied to the global region.
- List Instance - Each node creates a local list reduction instance. Reductions are added to the list reduction instance, which is then copied and applied to the global region.

We ran two experiments, one with dense reductions and one with sparse reductions. In both cases a large random source of data is divided into chunks, which are given to separate reduction tasks. Eight reduction tasks are created for each node, one per processor. The dense case uses a histogram with 256K buckets and each reduction task performs 4M reductions (Figure 6a). The sparse case uses a histogram with 4M buckets, but only 64K reductions are performed by each task (Figure 6b).

In the dense experiment, the reduction fold instances perform best and scale well with the number of nodes, achieving over a billion reductions per second in the 16 node case. List instances also scale well, but perform about an order of magnitude worse than fold instances in the dense case. The use of a separate active message for each reduction operation is another two orders of magnitude worse—data must be transferred in larger blocks to be efficient. The localized instance approach works well for a single node, but its serial nature doesn't benefit from increasing node counts. Finally, the only time the latency of performing individual RDMA reads and writes isn't disastrous is on a single node, where the reads and writes are all local.

The sparse case is similar, except the reduction fold case suffers from the overhead of transferring a value for every bucket even though most buckets are unmodified. The reduction list case continues to scale well, surpassing the reduction fold performance at larger node counts and showing that list instances are better suited for scaling sparse reduction computations.

9. APPLICATION EVALUATION

To quantify the performance of our Realm implementation real-world applications we target an existing high-level runtime system[6] to the Realm interface. We use the same three applications as [6] and profile several aspects of performance. We first look at the use of Realm events by the applications in Section 9.1. Section 9.2 covers the use of reservations. Finally, in Section 9.3 we estimate the performance benefits conferred by Realm relative to implicit representation systems.

All three applications we investigate are multi-phase and require parallel computation, data exchange, and synchronization between phases. *Circuit* is an electrical circuit simulation. The circuit is represented as an irregular graph where the edges are wires and nodes are where wires meet. The graph is dynamically partitioned into pieces that are distributed around the machine and the simulation is run for many time steps, each of which involves three distinct phases with a variety of access patterns. Figure 7 (reproduced from [6]) shows the placement of physical regions for storing node and wire data in different machine memories for one time step. Wire and private nodes for each piece can remain in device memory for each GPU. Physical regions for shared and ghost node data are placed in zero-copy memory to facilitate direct data movement to/from GASNet memory. Reduction instances in zero-copy memory buffer reductions from the `Distribute Charge` task running on the GPU before they are folded back to GASNet memory using a bulk reduction. The Realm event graph in Figure 2 directly corresponds to the operations shown in Figure 7.

Fluid is a distributed memory port of the PARSEC fluidanimate benchmark[8], which models fluid flow as particles moving through a volume divided into cells. Each time step involves multiple phases, each updating different properties of the particles based on neighboring particles. The space of cells is partitioned and neighboring cells in different partitions must exchange data between phases. These exchanges are done point-to-point by chaining copies and tasks using events rather than employing a global bulk-synchronous approach to exchange neighboring particle information.

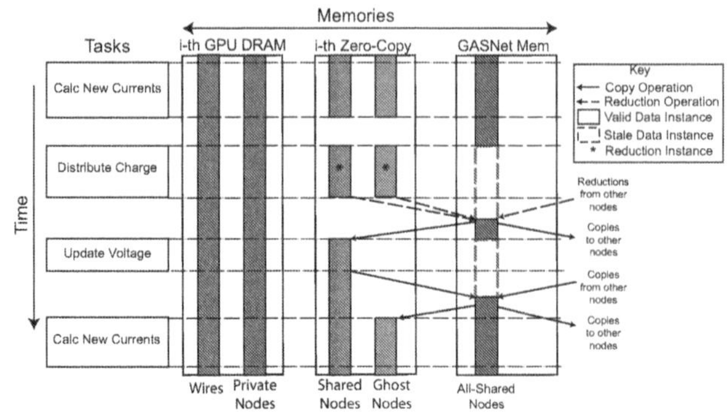

Figure 7: Data Placement and Movement for Circuit.

AMR is an adaptive mesh refinement benchmark based on the third heat equation example from the Berkeley Labs BoxLib project[32]. AMR simulates the two dimensional heat diffusion equation using three different levels of refinement. Each level is partitioned and distributed across the machine. Time steps require both intra- and inter-level communication and synchronization. Dependences between tasks from the same and different levels are again expressed through events.

9.1 Event Lifetimes

To illustrate the need for generational events data structures, we instrumented Realm to capture information about the lifetime of events. The usage of events by all three applications was similar, so we present representative results from just one. Figure 6c shows a timeline of the execution of the Fluid application on 16 nodes using 128 cores. The dynamic events line measures the total number of event creations. A large number of events are created—over 260,000 in less than 20 seconds of execution—and allocating separate storage for every event would clearly be difficult for long-running applications.

An event is *live* until its last operation (e.g., query, trigger) is performed. After an event's last operation a reference counting implementation would recover the event's associated storage. The live events line in Figure 6c is therefore the number of needed events in a reference counting scheme. In this example, reference counting reduces the storage needed for dynamic events by over 10X, but with the additional overhead associated with reference counting. This line also gives a lower bound for the number of events when the application performs explicit creation and destruction of events.

As discussed in Section 5.2, our implementation requires storage that grows with the maximum number of untriggered events, a number that is 10X smaller than even the maximal live event count. The actual storage requirements of our Realm implementation are shown by the generational events line, which shows the total number of generational events in the system. The maximum number of generational events needed is slightly larger than the peak number of untriggered events because nodes must create a new event locally if they have no available (i.e. triggered) generational events, even if there are available generational events on remote nodes. Overall, our implementation uses 5X less storage than a reference counting implementation and avoids any related overhead. These savings would likely be even more dramatic for longer runs of the application, as the number of live events is steadily growing as the application runs, while the peak number of generational events needed appears to occur during the start-up of the application. Overall this demonstrates the ability of generational events to represent large numbers of live events with minimal storage overhead.

9.2 Reservation Performance

The Circuit and AMR applications both made use of reservations, creating 3336 and 1393 reservations respectively. Of all created reservations in both applications, 14% were migrated at least once between nodes. The grant rates for both applications are orders of magnitude smaller than the maximum reservation grant rates achieved by our reservation microbenchmarks in Section 8.2. Thus, for these benchmarks reservations were needed to express non-blocking synchronization and were far from being a performance limiter.

9.3 Comparison with Implicit Representations

We now attempt to estimate the performance gains attributable to the latency hiding provided by deferred execution. To compare with a standard implicit implementation, we modified each Realm application to wait for events in the application code immediately before the dependent operation rather than supplying them as preconditions. While this methodology has the disadvantage that our approximation of an implicit runtime may not be as fast as a purpose-built one, it has the great advantage of controlling for the myriad possible performance effects in comparing two completely different implementations: any performance differences will be due exactly to the more relaxed execution ordering enabled by deferred execution.

Figure 8a shows three curves for the AMR application: the original Realm version, the implicit version, and an independently written and optimized MPI implementation [32]. Observe that the implicit version is competitive with the independent MPI code, which is some evidence that using the implicit version as a reference point is reasonable. Both the Realm and implicit versions start out ahead of MPI due to better mapping decisions provided by the higher-level runtime[6]. The Realm implementation of AMR uses a simple all-to-all pattern for its communication. The additional latency inherent in this pattern is hidden well by the deferred execution model, but is a bottleneck for the implicit version, resulting in up to 102% slowdown at 16 nodes. The MPI version continues to scale by using much more complicated asynchronous communication patterns, but the need for blocking synchronization primitives still results in exposed communication latency, causing a 66% slowdown relative to Realm on 16 nodes.

It is worth emphasizing that in principle the MPI code can be just as fast as (or faster than) Realm—there is nothing in Realm that a programmer cannot emulate with sufficient effort using the primitives available in any implicit runtime system. However, as discussed in Section 2, this programming work is substantial, difficult to maintain, and often machine specific; it is our experience that few programmers undertake it.

Figures 8b and 8c show performance results for the Circuit and Fluid applications respectively; for these applications we do not have independently optimized distributed memory implementations and so we compare only the Realm and implicit implementations. Each plot contains performance curves for both implementations on two different problem

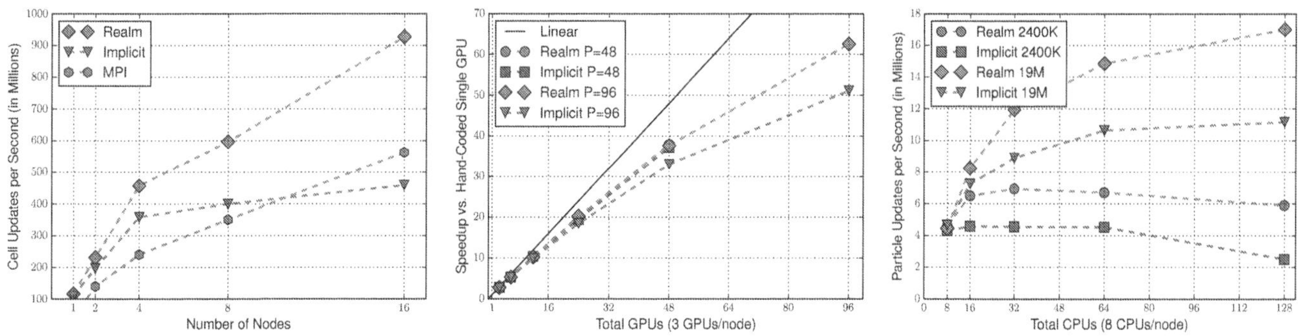

(a) AMR Application: 16384 Cells (b) Circuit Application (c) Fluid Application

Figure 8: Comparisons with a Generic Implicit System.

sizes. Circuit is compute-bound and the implicit implementation performs reasonably well. By 16 nodes, however, the overhead grows to 19% and 22% on the small and large inputs respectively. Fluid has a more evenly balanced computation-to-communication ratio and suffers more by switching to the implicit model. At 16 nodes, performance is 135% and 52% worse than the deferred execution implementations on the small and large problem sizes respectively. Ultimately the input problem size for the fluid application is too small to strong scale beyond 16 nodes as the computation-to-communication ratio approaches unity.

10. DISCUSSION AND CONCLUSION

Modern supercomputers bear little resemblance to their predecessors. Current machines are composed of heterogeneous processors and dynamic networks. As these machines continue to scale, the latencies associated with communication, data movement, and computation will both grow and become increasingly volatile[35]. Under these circumstances, implicit representation systems that place the burden of hiding latencies on the programmer, such as MPI, will no longer be practical.

Dealing with the growing and variable latencies of future hardware will require dynamic explicit representation programming systems. Dynamic explicit programming systems are aware of program operations and their control dependences. Consequently they can dynamically react to latencies at runtime and discover schedules that are impractical for human programmers to specify. The crucial component for a dynamic explicit system is a deferred execution model. Deferred execution allows explicit representation systems such as Realm to discover as much parallelism as possible, enabling them to automatically hide long latency operations by overlapping them with additional work. Furthermore, deferred execution allows dynamic explicit systems to hide the latency of constructing the graph of operations and performing scheduling at runtime. As distributed architectures become increasingly prevalent, we believe that explicit representation systems with deferred execution models, such as Realm, will be essential for achieving high performance and fully leveraging the underlying hardware.

To the best of our knowledge Realm constitutes the first low-level runtime system that implements a fully deferred execution model with primitives for deferring computation, data movement, and synchronization. Events are the mechanism for composing operations allowing Realm clients to execute without blocking. Generational event data structures make handling the large number of events created during real application executions tractable. Reservations provide a novel primitive for performing synchronization in a deferred execution model. Support for composing data movement with computations like reductions is achieved through physical regions with different layouts such as reduction instances. All of these components are essential for an expressive programming system capable of high performance.

Going forward, we expect Realm to provide a useful foundation for the construction of higher-level programming systems such as Legion[6]. The simple primitives of the Realm API are expressive, but also capable of abstracting many different hardware architectures. Combined with the automatic latency hiding of a Realm implementation, the Realm API provides a natural layer of abstraction for the development of portable higher-level systems targeting both current and future architectures.

We have presented Realm, a dynamic explicit low-level runtime system based on a deferred execution model. We have described the interesting aspects of our Realm implementation, specifically the use of generational event data structures, our implementation of reservations, and the use of reduction physical instances. Using microbenchmarks we demonstrated that our Realm implementation approaches the fundamental performance limits of the underlying hardware. We also showed that our Realm implementation improved the performance of three real-world applications up to 135% over implicit representation programming systems.

Acknowledgments

This research was supported by the Army High Performance Research Center under grant W911NF-07-2-0027-1, Los Alamos National Laboratories Subcontract No. 173315-1 through the U.S. Department of Energy contract DE-AC52-06NA25396, an NVIDIA Fellowship, and the Keeneland Computing Facility under NSF contract OCI-0910735.

11. REFERENCES

[1] "CUDA programming guide 5.5," 2014.

[2] M. Aguilera *et al.*, "Matching events in a content-based subscription system," in *Proc. PODC*, 1999, pp. 53–61.

[3] Arvind, R. Nikhil, and K. Pingali, "I-structures: Data structures for parallel computing," *ACM Trans. Program. Lang. Syst.*, 1989.

[4] R. Arvind, Nikhil and K. Pingali, "Id Nouveau reference manual, part II: Semantics," MIT, Tech. Rep., 1987.

[5] C. Augonnet *et al.*, "StarPU: A Unified Platform for Task Scheduling on Heterogeneous Multicore Architectures," *Concurrency and Computation: Practice and Experience*, vol. 23, pp. 187–198, Feb. 2011.

[6] M. Bauer *et al.*, "Legion: Expressing locality and independence with logical regions," in *Supercomputing (SC)*, 2012.

[7] C. Bell *et al.*, "Optimizing bandwidth limited problems using one-sided communication and overlap," in *Proc. IPDPS*, 2006.

[8] C. Bienia, "Benchmarking modern multiprocessors," Ph.D. dissertation, Princeton University, January 2011.

[9] R. Blumofe *et al.*, "Cilk: An efficient multithreaded runtime system," in *Proc. PPoPP*, 1995, pp. 207–216.

[10] R. Bocchino *et al.*, "A type and effect system for deterministic parallel Java," in *Proc. OOPSLA*, 2009, pp. 97–116.

[11] Z. Budimlić *et al.*, "Concurrent collections," *Scientific Programming*, vol. 18, no. 3, pp. 203–217, 2010.

[12] W. Carlson *et al.*, "Introduction to UPC and language specification," UC Berkeley Technical Report, 1999.

[13] A. Carzaniga, D. Rosenblum, and A. Wolf, "Design and evaluation of a wide-area event notification service," *ACM Trans. Comput. Syst.*, pp. 332–383, 2001.

[14] V. Cavé, J. Zhao, J. Shirako, and V. Sarkar, "Habanero-Java: The new adventures of old X10," in *Proc. of Principles and Practice of Programming in Java*. ACM, 2011, pp. 51–61.

[15] B. Chamberlain, D. Callahan, and H. Zima, "Parallel Programmability and the Chapel Language," *Int'l Journ. of High Performance Computing Applications*, 2007.

[16] D. Chang, "CORAL: A concurrent object-oriented system for constructing and executing sequential, parallel and distributed applications," in *Proc. OOPSLA/ECOOP*, 1991.

[17] P. Charles *et al.*, "X10: An Object-Oriented Approach to Non-uniform Cluster Computing," in *Proc. OOPSLA*, 2005, pp. 519–538.

[18] P. Cicotti and S. Baden, "Asynchronous programming with Tarragon," in *Proc. High Performance Distributed Computing*, 2006, pp. 19–23.

[19] D. Culler *et al.*, "TAM: A compiler controlled threaded abstract machine," *Jour. of Parallel and Distributed Computing*, pp. 347–370, 1993.

[20] A. Duran *et al.*, "Ompss: A proposal for programming heterogeneous multi-core architectures," *Parallel Processing Letters*, vol. 21, no. 02, pp. 173–193, 2011.

[21] P. Eugster, R. Guerraoui, and C. Damm, "On objects and events," in *Proc. OOPSLA*, 2001, pp. 254–269.

[22] K. Fatahalian *et al.*, "Sequoia: Programming the Memory Hierarchy," in *Supercomputing*, November 2006.

[23] G. Gao, T. Sterling, R. Stevens, M. Hereld, and W. Zhu, "Parallex: A study of a new parallel computation model," in *International Symposium on Parallel and Distributed Processing*, 2007, pp. 1–6.

[24] A. Gerbessiotis and L. Valiant, "Direct bulk-synchronous parallel algorithms," *Journal of Parallel and Distributed Computing*, vol. 22, no. 2, pp. 251–267, 1994.

[25] T. Harrison *et al.*, "The design and performance of a real-time CORBA event service," in *Proc. OOPSLA*, 1997, pp. 184–200.

[26] M. Houston *et al.*, "A portable runtime interface for multi-level memory hierarchies," in *Proc. PPoPP*, 2008, pp. 143–152.

[27] R. Jagannathan, "Coarse-grain dataflow programming of conventional parallel computers," in *Adv. Topics in Dataflow Computing*, 1995.

[28] H. Kaiser, M. Brodowicz, and T. Sterling, "Parallex: An advanced parallel execution model for scaling-impaired applications," in *Proceedings of the International Workshop on Parallel Processing*, 2009, pp. 394–401.

[29] L. Kale and S. Krishnan, "CHARM++: A portable concurrent object oriented system based on C++," in *Proc. OOPSLA*, Sep. 1993, pp. 91–108.

[30] "The OpenCL Specification, Version 1.0," The Khronos OpenCL Working Group, December 2008.

[31] K. Knobe, "Ease of use with concurrent collections (cnc)," *Hot Topics in Parallelism*, 2009.

[32] A. N. M. Lijewski and J. Bell, "Boxlib," 2011.

[33] R. Numrich and J. Reid, "Co-array Fortran for parallel programming," *SIGPLAN Fortran Forum*, pp. 1–31, 1998.

[34] K. Ostrowski, K. Birman, D. Dolev, and C. Sakoda, "Implementing reliable event streams in large systems via distributed data flows and recursive delegation," in *Proc. DEBS*, 2009, pp. 15:1–15:14.

[35] E. Rotem *et al.*, "Power-management architecture of the intel microarchitecture code-named sandy bridge," *Micro, IEEE*, pp. 20–27, 2012.

[36] M. Snir *et al.*, *MPI-The Complete Reference*, 1998.

[37] A. Soviani and J. Singh, "Optimizing communication scheduling using dataflow semantics," in *Proc. ICPP*, 2009, pp. 301–308.

[38] J. Vetter *et al.*, "Keeneland: Bringing heterogeneous GPU computing to the computational science community," *Computing in Science Engineering*, pp. 90–95, 2011.

[39] T. von Eicken *et al.*, "Active messages: A mechanism for integrated communication and computation," in *ISCA*, 1992, pp. 256–266.

[40] K. Yelick *et al.*, "Titanium: A high-performance Java dialect," in *Workshop on Java for High-Performance Network Computing*, 1998.

[41] ——, "Productivity and performance using partitioned global address space languages," in *Proc. PASCO*, 2007, pp. 24–32.

kMAF: Automatic Kernel-Level Management of Thread and Data Affinity

Matthias Diener
Informatics Institute, UFRGS
Porto Alegre, Brazil
mdiener@inf.ufrgs.br

Eduardo H. M. Cruz
Informatics Institute, UFRGS
Porto Alegre, Brazil
ehmcruz@inf.ufrgs.br

Philippe O. A. Navaux
Informatics Institute, UFRGS
Porto Alegre, Brazil
navaux@inf.ufrgs.br

Anselm Busse
Communication and Operating Systems Group, TU Berlin
Berlin, Germany
anselm.busse@tu-berlin.de

Hans-Ulrich Heiß
Communication and Operating Systems Group, TU Berlin
Berlin, Germany
hans-ulrich.heiss@tu-berlin.de

ABSTRACT

One of the main challenges for parallel architectures is the increasing complexity of the memory hierarchy, which consists of several levels of private and shared caches, as well as interconnections between separate memories in NUMA machines. To make full use of this hierarchy, it is necessary to improve the locality of memory accesses by reducing accesses to remote caches and memories, and using local ones instead. Two techniques can be used to increase the memory access locality: executing threads and processes that access shared data close to each other in the memory hierarchy (thread affinity), and placing the memory pages they access on the NUMA node they are executing on (data affinity). Most related work in this area focuses on either thread or data affinity, but not both, which limits the improvements. Other mechanisms require expensive operations, such as memory access traces or binary analysis, require changes to hardware or work only on specific parallel APIs.

In this paper, we introduce kMAF, a mechanism that automatically manages thread and data affinity on the kernel level. The memory access behavior of the running application is determined during its execution by analyzing its page faults. This information is used by kMAF to migrate threads and memory pages, such that the overall memory access locality is optimized. Extensive evaluation with 27 benchmarks from 4 benchmark suites shows substantial performance improvements, with results close to an oracle mechanism. Execution time was reduced by up to 35.7% (13.8% on average), while energy efficiency was improved by up to 34.6% (9.3% on average).

PACT'14, August 24–27, 2014, Edmonton, AB, Canada.

ACM 978-1-4503-2809-8/14/08 ...$15.00.
http://dx.doi.org/10.1145/2628071.2628085.

Categories and Subject Descriptors

B.3.2 [**MEMORY STRUCTURES**]: Design Styles—*Cache memories, Virtual memory*; D.4.1 [**OPERATING SYSTEMS**]: Process Management—*scheduling*

Keywords

Thread affinity, Data affinity, NUMA, Cache hierarchies

1. INTRODUCTION

The memory hierarchy of modern parallel architectures presents challenges for thread scheduling and memory management of the operating system. When scheduling threads, their performance depends on which core each thread is executed, since the memory access performance varies depending on the core and the memory hierarchy [15]. These differences in the memory access latency between cores are due to shared cache levels, different bandwidths and latencies in the interconnections [38]. Regarding memory management, the memory hierarchy introduced non-uniform memory access (NUMA) due to multiple memory controllers in the system. Because of the NUMA characteristics, the performance of memory accesses also depends on which NUMA node each memory page is allocated, affecting overall performance and energy consumption [1]. For these reasons, it is important to consider the memory accesses of an application for thread scheduling and memory management [6].

Improving the locality by establishing an affinity of threads to cores and data to NUMA nodes has several benefits [35]. When threads that share data are executing on cores that share a cache, less cache misses are expected due to a reduction of cache line replications [10]. Moreover, when the cores executing threads that share data are nearby in the memory hierarchy, the latency to access the shared data is reduced. A lower overhead from cache coherence protocols can also be expected when shared data is not replicated [29]. Regarding data affinity, when the data accessed by the core is located on the local NUMA node, the access latency is lower compared to an access to a remote NUMA node [33].

Several previous proposals aim to optimize the affinity of threads and data considering the memory access behavior. Most approaches focus on either thread affinity [2, 13, 14] or data affinity [1, 12, 28, 34], but perform them only separately. Some mechanisms rely on execution traces [14, 28], which cause a high overhead [3] and can not be used if the behavior of the application changes between executions. Mechanisms that focus on specific parallel programming paradigms [22, 30] are not a generic solution for data and thread affinities. Other approaches use indirect information about the memory access behavior [2], which can result in less accurate affinities.

In this paper, we propose a *kernel memory affinity framework (kMAF)*, which manages both thread and data affinity according to the memory access behavior of parallel applications. kMAF detects which data each thread accesses during the execution of the application by using the virtual memory implementation of the operating system. This information is used together with information about the hardware topology to calculate optimized affinities and migrate threads and memory pages.

kMAF presents several advantages compared to the current state-of-the-art. As the affinity management is performed on the kernel level, kMAF requires no changes to the application or its runtime libraries, and is therefore compatible with a large variety of parallelization models. Furthermore, it is hardware-independent and only requires that the architecture supports virtual memory with paging. As kMAF works completely during the execution of the parallel application, it needs no time-consuming analysis phase or any previous information about the behavior of the application.

We implemented kMAF in version 3.8 of the Linux kernel and evaluate it on a 4-node NUMA system using four sets of parallel benchmarks: The OpenMP implementation of the NAS Parallel Benchmarks (NPB) [21], PARSEC [4], which uses the Pthreads and OpenMP APIs, the MPI-based HPC Challenge Benchmark (HPCC) [26] and the hybrid MPI+OpenMP implementation of NPB [37]. Results show significant performance and energy efficiency improvements compared to the original thread and data affinity management of the Linux kernel.

The rest of the paper is organized as follows: In the next section, we introduce metrics to characterize the memory access behavior of parallel applications and evaluate their suitability for thread and data affinity. Section 3 introduces kMAF, our proposed mechanism. The evaluation methodology is shown in Section 4. Section 5 presents and analyzes experimental results. Related work is discussed in Section 6. Finally, Section 7 summarizes our conclusions.

2. BACKGROUND: AFFINITY IN SHARED MEMORY ARCHITECTURES

In this section, we begin with a brief outline of the benefits of managing the thread and data affinity of parallel applications. We then introduce a set of metrics that can be used to determine the potential for affinity management of a parallel application and use these metrics to analyze several sets of parallel benchmarks.

2.1 Benefits of Affinity Management

The management of thread and data affinity aims to improve the accesses to shared and private data in parallel applications.

Managing the thread affinity improves the efficiency of the interconnections, reducing inter-chip traffic that has a higher latency and lower bandwidth than intra-chip interconnections. It also reduces the number of cache misses of parallel applications. In read-only situations, executing threads on the same shared cache reduces data replication, thereby increasing the cache space available to the application [10]. In read-write or write-write situations, an optimized affinity also reduces cache line invalidations.

Managing data affinity improves the locality on NUMA machines by reducing the number of accesses to remote memory banks. As thread affinity, it improves the efficiency of the interconnections. This increases the memory bandwidth available in the system and reduces the average memory access latency.

It is important to note that thread affinity is a prerequisite for data affinity. Data affinity alone is not able to improve locality when more than one thread accesses the same pages, since the threads may be executing on cores of different NUMA nodes. In this situation, only the threads that are executing on the same node where the data is located would benefit from the locality. With the thread affinity, threads that share a lot of data would be executed on the same node, improving the effectiveness of the data affinity.

2.2 Quantifying Application Memory Access Behavior

To determine the importance of thread and data affinity for a parallel application, we introduce metrics to describe the memory accesses behavior of a parallel application.

2.2.1 *Metrics for Thread Affinity*

Throughout this paper, we refer to memory accesses to the same address by two different threads as *sharing*. As thread affinity management focuses mostly on caches, we look at sharing at the cache line granularity, which is 64 Bytes on most architectures. The first metric we introduce is based on the intuition that to benefit from thread affinity, it is necessary to have groups of threads that share the same data among each other, and not with other threads. Conversely, if all threads share the same amount of data in the same way among them, no improvements from thread affinity can be expected.

To formalize this intuition, consider a matrix M, in which each element $M[i][j]$ contains the amount of sharing between threads i and j. We can determine the potential for thread affinity of the application by analyzing the differences between the amount of sharing between the threads. For that purpose, we calculate the *heterogeneity* of the sharing behavior with Equation 1, where T is the number of threads. The higher the heterogeneity, the higher the potential for thread affinity, since there are higher differences between the amounts of sharing. If heterogeneity is low, the amount of sharing between the threads is similar, thus any thread affinity applied would result in similar performance for accesses to shared data.

$$Heterogeneity = \frac{\sum_{i=1}^{T}\sum_{j=1}^{T}\left(\frac{\sum_{k=1}^{T} M[i][k]}{T} - M[i][j]\right)^2}{T^2} \qquad (1)$$

Apart from the heterogeneity, another important metric is the *amount* of sharing between the threads, which we calculate with Equation 2. When there is little sharing, thread affinity has less potential for improvements, even when the heterogeneity is high. Therefore, both the amount and heterogeneity of the sharing must be taken into account when analyzing the potential for thread affinity of a parallel application.

$$SharingAmount = \frac{\sum_{i=1}^{T} \sum_{j=1}^{T} M[i][j]}{T^2} \quad (2)$$

2.2.2 *Metrics for Data Affinity*

The potential for data affinity of a page is proportional to the amount of memory accesses from a single NUMA node. That is, if a page presents most of its accesses from the same node, it has more potential for data affinity than a page that is accessed from several nodes. We call the highest number of memory accesses to a page from a single NUMA node compared to the number of accesses from all nodes the *exclusivity* of the page. The higher the exclusivity of a page, the higher its potential for data affinity. The exclusivity for a page is calculated with Equation 3, where NA is a vector containing the number of memory accesses, each element $NA[i]$ is the number of memory accesses from node i, and N is the number of NUMA nodes.

$$PageExclusivity = \frac{max(NA)}{\sum_{i=1}^{N} NA[i]} \quad (3)$$

The exclusivity is minimal when a page has exactly the same amount of accesses from all nodes. In this case, the exclusivity is given by $1/N$. The exclusivity achieves its maximum when all accesses to the corresponding page originate from the same NUMA node. In this case, the exclusivity is 1.

It is also important to take the amount of memory accesses to a page into account. The higher the amount of accesses, the higher the potential for data affinity. Combining these two metrics, the pages that have a lot of memory accesses and high exclusivity are the ones with the highest potential for data affinity. It is important to note that the thread affinity influences both data affinity metrics, since they consider the NUMA node that generated the memory accesses, not the threads themselves. This underlines our previous statement that data affinity depends on thread affinity.

The exclusivity describes a single page. To calculate the average exclusivity for the whole application, we scale the exclusivity of each page with the number of memory accesses to it, and divide it by the total number of memory accesses. This operation is shown in Equation 4, where $PageExclusivity_i$ is the exclusivity of page i, $Accesses_i$ is the number of memory accesses to page i, and P is the number of pages. As for the page exclusivity, the minimum and maximum of the average exclusivity is $1/N$ and 1, respectively, where N is the number of NUMA nodes in the system.

$$AvgExclusivity = \frac{\sum_{i=1}^{P} PageExclusivity_i \cdot Accesses_i}{\sum_{i=1}^{P} Accesses_i} \quad (4)$$

Another requirement for data affinity is that the memory usage of the application must be significantly higher than the cache size of the system. If the memory that an application uses fits into the processor caches, only minor improvements from a data affinity policy can be expected, as the caches can filter most of the memory accesses.

2.3 Benchmark Examples

In this section, we analyze several benchmarks to determine their suitability for affinity management by using the metrics introduced in the previous section.

2.3.1 *Methodology*

We analyze the potential for thread and data affinities with applications from 4 benchmark suites, whose details are summarized in Table 1. We run the OpenMP version of the NAS Parallel Benchmarks (NPB) [21], in which all applications except DC were executed using input size *C*. For DC, input size *B* was chosen as it is the largest input size of this benchmark. The second benchmark suite is PARSEC [4], which contains applications that are based on the OpenMP and Pthreads APIs. It was executed using the *native* input size. The HPC Challenge benchmark (HPCC) [26] is a single application based on MPI that consists of 16 phases with different computational and memory access characteristics. The fourth benchmark suite is the Multi-zone version of the NAS Parallel Benchmarks [37], which are hybrid applications implemented using MPI and OpenMP.

To analyze these applications, we created a simulator for the Pin dynamic binary analysis tool [25] that monitors all memory accesses of the parallel application. We use this simulator to calculate the heterogeneity, amount of accesses to shared data and the exclusivity. For the thread affinity metrics, we consider memory accesses by 2 threads in the same cache line as sharing. For the data affinity, we will present results for page sizes of 4 KByte and 2 MByte. The benchmarks were executed with 64 threads on a simulated 4-node NUMA architecture. We assign the threads to the NUMA nodes in such away that the exclusivity is maximized.

2.3.2 *Results*

The average exclusivity of all pages is presented in Figure 1 for 4 KByte and 2 MByte page sizes. To visualize the exclusivity of individual pages, we round the exclusivity of each page to the nearest 10% and group pages with the same rounded exclusivity together. Figure 2 depicts this visualization for 4 KByte pages. Figure 3 shows the values for heterogeneity and amount of sharing.

Table 1: Overview of the benchmarks used in the evaluation, showing parallelization API, benchmark names, input size and average memory usage per application.

Benchmark suite	Parallel API	Benchmark names	Input size	Memory usage
NAS-OMP v3.3.1	OpenMP	BT, CG, DC, EP, FT, IS, LU, MG, SP, UA	*C* DC:*B*	6.1 GByte
PARSEC v2.1	Pthreads, OpenMP	Blackscholes, Bodytrack, Facesim, Ferret, Freqmine, Raytrace, Swaptions, Fluidanimate, Vips, X264, Canneal, Dedup, Streamcluster	*native*	4.8 GByte
HPCC v1.4.3	MPI	HPCC (1 application with 16 phases)	4000^2 matrix	19.3 GByte
NAS-MZ v3.3.1	MPI, OpenMP	BT-MZ, LU-MZ, SP-MZ	*C*	5.8 GByte

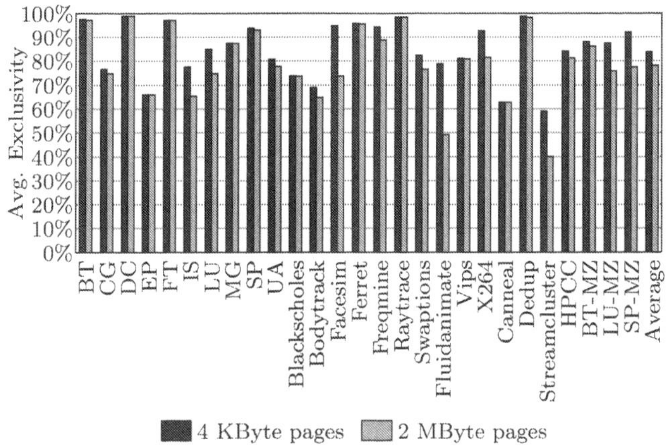

Figure 1: Average exclusivity for different page sizes.

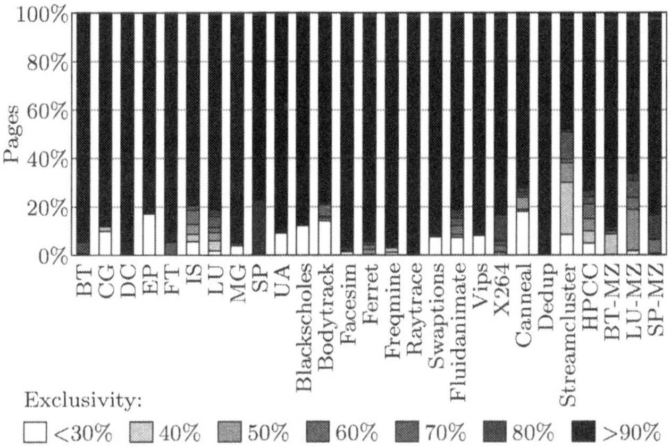

Figure 2: Page exclusivity for 4 KByte pages. The rounded exclusivity is shown in gray scale.

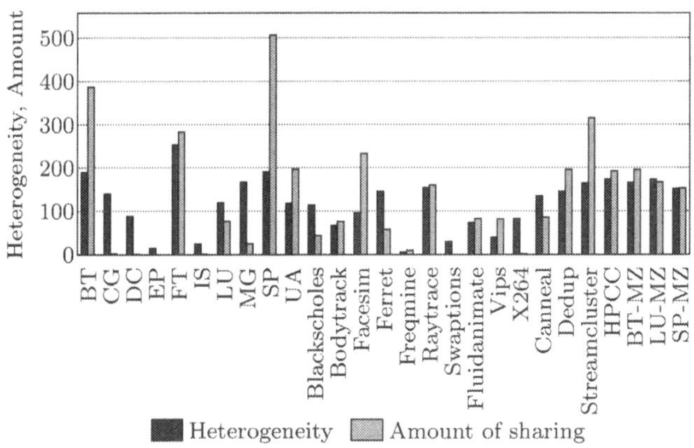

Figure 3: Sharing patterns.

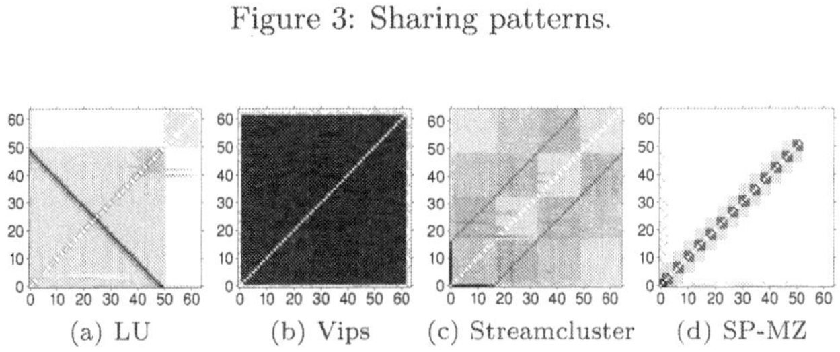

Figure 4: Example affinity matrices. Axes represent thread IDs. Cells show the amount of sharing for each pair of threads or processes. Darker cells indicate more sharing.

In most applications, the exclusivity is high, showing the importance of data affinity. Even in Streamcluster, which presents the lowest value, approximately 60% of its pages have a high exclusivity. On the other hand, the metrics for thread affinity (heterogeneity and amount of sharing), are not high for all applications, such as in Freqmine and EP. In these applications, although there is not much sharing between the threads, data affinity is important because each thread still needs to access its private data.

Some applications, such as SP and Dedup, have high values for exclusivity, heterogeneity and amount of sharing, and therefore can benefit from both thread and data affinity. CG and DC have a high heterogeneity but only share little data. EP and Swaptions have a very low total memory usage (less than 65 MByte), such that few improvements from data affinity are expected, since most of the memory they use fits into the caches. It is important to note that even when increasing the page size from 4 KByte to 2 MByte, the exclusivity only decreases slightly, from 83.6% to 78.3% on average for all benchmarks.

Figure 4 shows the sharing patterns of four benchmarks. Darker cells indicate more sharing between threads or processes. In several benchmarks, such as BT, MG and SP, most sharing happens between neighboring threads, such as threads 0 and 1. LU shows data sharing between more distant threads, with almost no sharing between threads 52–63. In Vips, the amount of sharing between all threads is almost the same. It therefore has a low heterogeneity, as indicated by Figure 3. Streamcluster shows a pipeline sharing pattern, where groups of threads of the same pipeline stage access the same data. HPCC has a complex pattern with sharing between neighboring and more distant threads. Additionally, nearly every of the 16 phases has a different sharing pattern.

2.3.3 Summary of Benchmark Behavior

Summarizing our analysis of the benchmarks, we can affirm that a large majority of them are suitable for data affinity. Less benchmarks are suitable for thread affinity. However, for the reasons mentioned previously, it is necessary to manage the thread affinity to fully benefit from the data affinity. Another important result is that when increasing the page size from 4 KByte to 2 MByte, the exclusivity of the memory accesses of most applications decreases only very slightly. This indicates that data affinity is important even when considering large pages.

3. KMAF: AUTOMATIC AFFINITY MANAGEMENT IN THE KERNEL

Our proposal, the *Kernel Memory Affinity Framework (kMAF)*, uses the virtual memory implementation of the operating system to characterize the memory access behavior of parallel applications during their execution and uses this information to optimize the affinity of the running application. kMAF requires no changes to the hardware, and is compatible with all architectures that use virtual memory with paging.

An overview of kMAF is shown in Figure 5. It consists of the following four parts, denoted A–D in the figure:

A. Determine the memory access behavior. Information about the parallel applications' memory access behavior is collected at the OS level through its page faults.

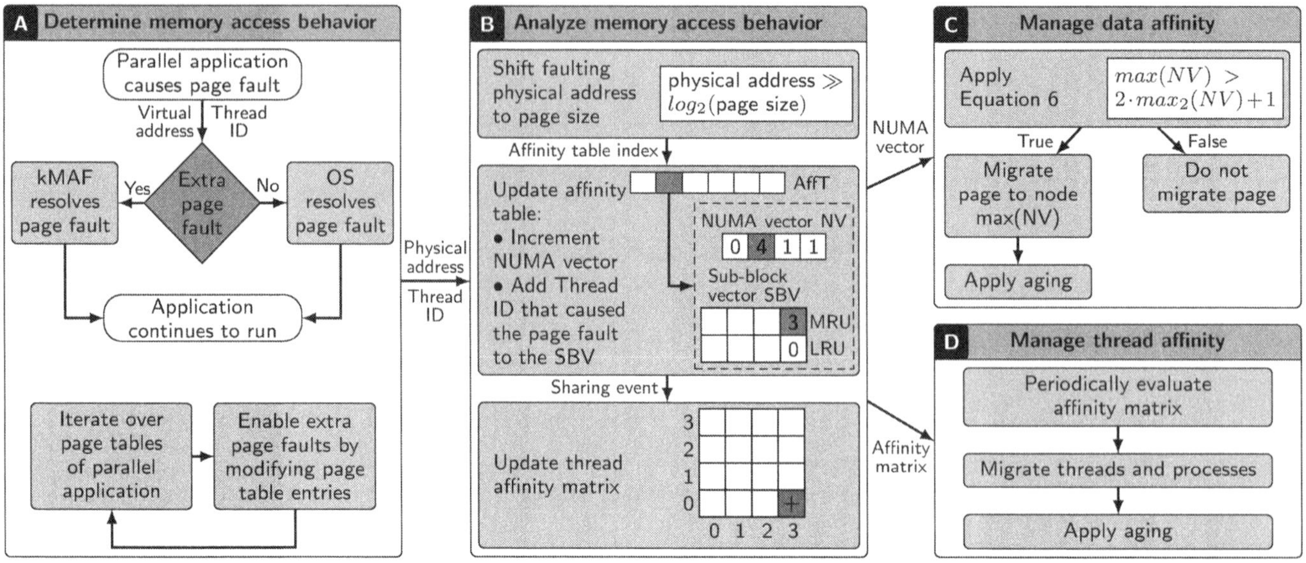

Figure 5: Overview of kMAF. In the example, a parallel application consisting of four threads is executing. The system contains 4 NUMA nodes. Each page is split into 4 sub-blocks, with 2 positions for threads (MRU and LRU). Thread 3, executing on NUMA node 1, causes a page fault. kMAF increments the NUMA vector in position 1, and adds thread 3 to the sub-block vector in the MRU position. Since the sub-block had been accessed previously by thread 0, it is moved to the LRU position, and a sharing event is stored in the affinity matrix by incrementing it in cell (0,3). The NUMA vector is evaluated by Equation 6, and the page gets migrated to node 1, since the condition is fulfilled.

B. Analyze the memory access behavior. The information about memory accesses is stored in a per-page list, together with the NUMA nodes that accessed the page and the threads that accessed sub-blocks of the page.

C. Manage data affinity. The per-node number of accesses to memory pages is analyzed to check if they should be migrated to a different NUMA node.

D. Manage thread affinity. kMAF periodically applies a mapping algorithm to determine if threads need to be migrated.

3.1 Determine Memory Access Behavior

Gathering information about memory accesses at the operating system level presents a challenge, as the accesses are usually performed directly by the hardware. Previous research [11, 13] has shown that memory access information can be gathered by analyzing the page faults of parallel applications. We adapt the idea of these mechanisms for kMAF to determine the memory access behavior. It is based on two fundamental concepts, which are described in this section.

3.1.1 Sampling Memory Accesses via Page Faults

Whenever an application accesses a memory address and its corresponding page is not set as present in the page table, the OS is notified about the faulting virtual address, as well as the thread ID that caused the fault. By tracking page faults that happen in the same memory area, it is possible to detect which threads are accessing shared data. Threads belonging to the same process use the same page table and therefore share the same virtual and physical address space. If threads belong to different processes, they do not share a page table. Shared memory regions between threads from different processes have the same physical memory address, but not necessarily the same virtual address. In order to support the detection of sharing in these multi-process applications, kMAF uses the physical address for detection. Since the full address is available during the page fault, it is possible to use different memory area sizes, such as the cache line or page size, for detection. This also makes the detection independent from the page size of the hardware.

3.1.2 Increasing Accuracy via Extra Page Faults

It is important to note that only one page fault per page happens during normal operation, which would limit the accuracy of the detection mechanism. This limitation can be overcome by enabling multiple page faults per page. These extra page faults are injected by kMAF by periodically iterating over the page tables of the parallel application and clearing the page present bit of pages that can be shared between threads. As these extra page faults do not represent missing information in the page table, they can be resolved quickly by kMAF itself without the normal kernel routines, thus minimizing their overhead.

In processes that contain only one thread, kMAF only enables extra page faults in pages that are shared with other processes. In multi-threaded processes, extra page faults are enabled for all data segments, since the operating system does not keep track of which threads access each page.

3.2 Analyze Memory Access Behavior

We store information about the memory access pattern in an *Affinity Table (AffT)*. Each table entry contains information about one physical page frame. To locate the entry of a page in the affinity table, we bit shift the physical address to the right, removing the offset bits inside a page, as shown in Equation 5.

$$AffTIndex = PhysAddr \gg log_2(PageSize) \quad (5)$$

In each affinity table entry, kMAF stores the number of accesses from each NUMA node to each page in the *NUMA vector (NV)*. The number of counters in the NUMA vector is equal to the number of NUMA nodes in the system. The number of bits used to store each counter can be configured. A high number of bits provides more accuracy, but requires more memory to store the counter.

To manage thread affinity, we store the IDs of the threads that access each page in the *sub-block vector (SBV)*. As we need a finer granularity than the page size to determine thread affinity, each page is divided into several sub-blocks of equal size. To support this feature, each entry of the affinity table contains several fields that store the threads that access each sub-block of the page. For each sub-block, the number of IDs of threads that access it can be configured. Tracking more threads can lead to a higher accuracy, but requires more memory and could lead to false positives. False positives may occur because threads that have not accessed the sub-block for a long time should not be considered a sharer of the sub-block.

The thread ID that generated the page fault is stored in the MRU position in the SBV entry that corresponds to the sub-block of the memory address. In case the sub-block has been accessed before by other threads, these other threads are moved towards the LRU position. Furthermore, we record a sharing event by incrementing the affinity matrix in the cells that correspond to all pairs of threads in the SBV entry.

3.3 Manage Data Affinity

To manage the data affinity, on every page fault kMAF evaluates the NUMA vector of the page that caused the fault to determine the exclusivity of the page. We calculate the exclusivity by looking at the number of accesses from the NUMA nodes. If the highest number of accesses from a node is more than double the second highest number, the page will be migrated to the node with the highest number of accesses, if it is not already located on that node. Equation 6 formalizes this behavior, where $max(NV)$ is the highest value of the NUMA vector, and $max_2(NV)$ is the second highest value of the NUMA vector.

$$Migrate = \begin{cases} true & \text{if } max(NV) > 2 \cdot max_2(NV) + 1 \\ false & \text{otherwise} \end{cases} \quad (6)$$

The idea behind this equation is to prevent early migration of pages, during application initialization, but enable quick migration as soon as a pattern is established. We delay any page migration until we set the thread affinity for the first time, to avoid unnecessary page migrations due to page sharing between the threads, and to benefit from a higher exclusivity of the pages when threads that access the same page execute on the same NUMA node. We also perform aging in the NUMA vector to be able to better react to changes in the memory access behavior. Every time a page is migrated, we divide all counters of the NUMA vector by 2 to reduce the impact of old values on the data affinity.

3.4 Manage Thread Affinity

To optimize the mapping of processes and threads to processing units (PUs), kMAF periodically evaluates the thread affinity matrix. To be able to react quickly to changes in the memory access behavior, we selected a quick graph partitioning algorithm that generates the mapping and execute it with a period of 100 ms. Furthermore, we apply an aging mechanism to the affinity matrix to reduce the influence of old values in the matrix.

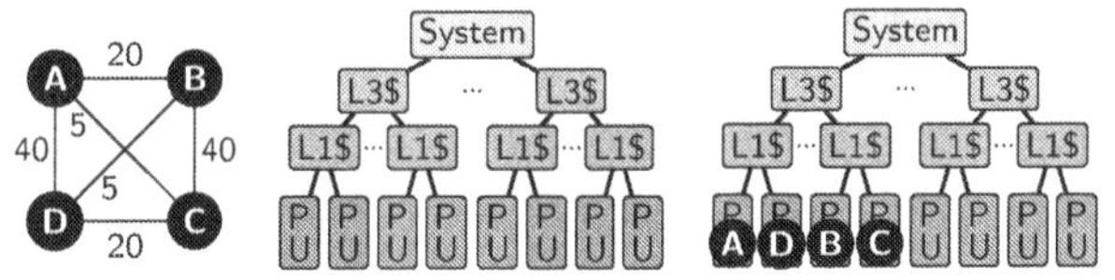

(a) Input: Affinity graph. (b) Input: Hierarchy graph of the machine. (c) Output: Mapping of threads to PUs.

Figure 6: Inputs and output of the mapping algorithm.

3.4.1 Calculating the Thread Mapping

The information provided by the sharing detection is used to calculate an optimized mapping from processes and threads to PUs during the execution of the parallel application. The mapping problem is NP-hard [5], therefore it is necessary to use efficient heuristic algorithms to calculate the mapping. Online mapping requires algorithms with a short execution time, since it directly impacts the overhead on the executing application.

The mapping problem is modeled with two undirected graphs, an affinity graph and a hierarchy graph. In the affinity graph, vertices represent threads and edges represent the amount of affinity between them. Figure 6a shows an example affinity graph for four threads A–D. In the hierarchy graph, vertices represent levels of the memory hierarchy and PUs, while edges represent the interconnections between them. In the hierarchy graph, we do not consider levels whose arity is 1. For instance, if there is only one L3 cache for each NUMA node, there is no need to include the NUMA node level in the hierarchy graph when calculating the thread affinity. Figure 6b depicts a simplified hierarchy graph for the hardware architecture that will be used in the evaluation. The affinity graph is obtained from the affinity matrix during runtime, while the hierarchy graph is generated from the hardware information provided by the kernel.

To calculate the mapping, we use the dual recursive bipartitioning algorithm of the Scotch mapping library [31], version 6.0. We selected this algorithm because it has a short execution time while providing good results [32], and is therefore suitable for online mapping. The algorithm receives the affinity and hierarchy graphs as input, and outputs the PU for each thread such that the total cost of memory accesses is minimized, as shown in Figure 6c. This information is used to migrate the threads to their assigned PUs.

3.4.2 Aging Mechanism

After calculating the mapping, we apply an aging technique in the affinity matrix, multiplying its values by a factor of 0.75, to reduce the influence of old values in the matrix and make it easier to detect changes in the memory access behavior during execution. We also evaluated other factors between 0.6 and 0.95, but the results are not very sensitive to this value. We chose the value 0.75 because the operation can be performed efficiently with a subtraction and a bit shift operation: $M_{new}[i][j] = M_{old}[i][j] - (M_{old}[i][j] \gg 2)$, where i and j are the indices of the affinity matrices M_{old} and M_{new}.

3.5 Overhead of kMAF

kMAF introduces storage and runtime overheads, which will be discussed in this section.

3.5.1 Storage Overhead

The storage overhead is the amount of memory required to store the affinity table and thread affinity matrix.

Affinity Table. Equation 7 describes the size of each entry in the affinity table, $AffTentry_{size}$. In the equation, $NVcounter_{size}$ is the number of Bytes used to store each counter of the NUMA vector, N is the number of NUMA nodes, $Sub\text{-}block_{size}$ is the granularity chosen to detect thread affinity, $ThreadID_{size}$ is the number of bytes required to store a thread ID in the sub-block vector, and $\#Sharers$ is the number of tracked threads per sub-block. Equation 8 calculates the size of the affinity table, where $\#AffTentry$ is the number of entries of the affinity table.

$$AffTentry_{size} = NVcounter_{size} \cdot N + \frac{Page_{size}}{Sub\text{-}block_{size}} \cdot ThreadID_{size} \cdot \#Sharers \quad (7)$$

$$MemUsageAffT = \#AffTentry \cdot AffTentry_{size} \quad (8)$$

To calculate the storage overhead, we use the following configuration: $NVcounter_{size}$: 2 Bytes, $Sub\text{-}block_{size}$: 1 KByte, $ThreadID_{size}$: 2 Bytes and $\#Sharers$: 2. The system has a $Page_{size}$ of 4 KByte and 4 nodes. The same configuration will be used in the experiments. In this scenario, each entry of the affinity table requires 20 Bytes and the affinity table overhead is 0.49% of the total memory in the system.

Thread Affinity Matrix. The memory usage of the thread affinity matrix is given by Equation 9, where T is the number of threads of the parallel application and $TAffMentry_{size}$ is the size of each element of the matrix in bytes. For an element size of 4 Bytes and an application with 64 threads, the memory usage of the thread affinity matrix is 16 KByte.

$$MemUsageTAffM = T^2 \cdot TAffMentry_{size} \quad (9)$$

3.5.2 Runtime Overhead

The runtime overhead consists of the time required to introduce extra page faults, resolve these faults, and calculate thread and data affinity, plus the migrations. The complexity to introduce extra page faults increases linearly with the number of processes of the parallel application, as we need to iterate over each page table. Resolving the extra page faults from kMAF has a constant time complexity. The complexity of calculating the thread affinity depends on the algorithm adopted. The algorithm we adopted has a complexity of $O(T^3)$, where T is the number of threads of the parallel application [18]. For data affinity, the time complexity is $O(N)$, where N is the number of NUMA nodes. The overhead of the migrations depends on the actual implementation in the kernel. In Section 5.4, we will evaluate the runtime overhead on a running application.

3.6 Summary of kMAF

An example of the operation of kMAF is shown in the caption of Figure 5. kMAF is independent from the parallelization model, as the memory access behavior is determined directly from the memory accesses themselves. For the same reason, it also supports hybrid applications that use several models. kMAF works during the execution of the parallel application, and requires no modification to the application, its runtime system or expensive operations such as tracing. Methods that rely on tracing are not able to handle applications in which the access behavior changes between or during executions. Furthermore, changing the input data or the number of threads can also lead to different behaviors.

kMAF is also highly OS and hardware independent. It can be applied to all platforms that use virtual memory with paging, which covers the majority of the current computer architectures. No architecture specific information, such as a special hardware counter, is necessary. As the detection is completely dynamic, kMAF can be combined with other techniques that alter the behavior of a parallel application, such as modifying the number of processes and threads during execution [23] and migrating MPI processes between cluster nodes [9].

4. METHODOLOGY

We evaluated kMAF on a 4-node NUMA machine, where each node consists of an 8-core Intel Xeon X7550 processor that supports Simultaneous Multithreading (SMT). Each core has private L1/L2 caches, while the L3 cache is shared between all the cores in the processor. The machine parameters are summarized in Table 2.

We experimented with the same 27 benchmarks and input sizes that were described in Section 2.3.1. As the machine can run 64 threads concurrently, most benchmarks were executed with this number of threads or processes. In benchmarks where this is not possible, such as X264 and Streamcluster, we executed with a number as close as possible to 64. For the hybrid NAS-MZ benchmarks, several configurations of processes and threads were evaluated: 1 process with 64 threads, 2 processes with 32 threads each and 4 processes with 16 threads each. As the results were very similar, we show only the values for the 4 processes with 16 threads configuration. All benchmarks were compiled with gcc, version 4.6.3. For the benchmarks that use MPI, we used the Open MPI framework [16], version 1.5.1, which uses KNEM [17] for communication in shared memory.

Five different mapping mechanisms were compared:

Operating System (OS). The OS is the baseline for the experiments. We use an unmodified Linux kernel, version 3.8. We evaluated the standard first-touch policy and the AutoNUMA approach [11]. However, results were very close to each other (less than 2% difference), so we only show the results using the first-touch policy.

Oracle. For the oracle mechanism, we collected memory access traces as described in Section 2.3.1, and used information from the traces to perform an optimized thread and data mapping for the applications.

Table 2: Configuration of the evaluation system and kMAF.

	Parameter	Value
System	Processors	4x Intel Xeon X7550, 8 cores, 2-SMT
System	Caches	32 KByte L1, 256 KByte L2, 18 MByte L3
System	Memory	128 GByte DDR3-1333, 4 KByte page size
kMAF	NUMA vector	4x 1 Byte per page
kMAF	Sub-block vector	4x 2 entries per page (1 KByte size)
kMAF	Thread ID size	16 Bits each

Compact. The compact mapping, similar to existing implementations in some OpenMP frameworks [20], performs a round-robin scheduling of threads to cores that takes into account the memory hierarchy.

Random. For the random mapping, we generated random mappings of threads to cores and memory pages to NUMA nodes, one for each execution.

kMAF. We implemented kMAF in version 3.8 of the Linux kernel and use it with the configuration shown in Table 2.

All experiments were executed 20 times. For each experiment, we show the average values, as well as the confidence interval for a confidence level of 95% in a Student's t-distribution. All results are normalized to the baseline, the OS. We measured execution time, L3 cache misses and traffic on the QuickPath Interconnect (QPI) with the help of the Intel performance counter monitor (PCM) [19].

5. RESULTS

This section presents and discusses the results of kMAF compared to other affinity mechanisms, following the methodology shown in Section 4. We present four sets of results: performance, energy consumption, performance using only thread or data affinity, and the runtime overhead of kMAF.

5.1 Performance

The results of execution time, L3 cache misses and QPI traffic can be found in Figures 7, 8 and 9, respectively. The reduction of the cache misses, with an average of 11.1% in kMAF, are due to the more efficient thread affinity, since it reduces the cache line replication. Data affinity alone does not have a significant influence on cache misses. The reduction of the QPI traffic, with an average of 19.0%, happened due to the optimized thread and data affinity, as the data is located more often in the local memory banks. Both these metrics were responsible for the reduction of the execution time, with an average of 13.8% for kMAF.

To illustrate how thread affinity also affects data affinity, consider Streamcluster. In Streamcluster, the exclusivity is low but the heterogeneity and amount of sharing is high. However, the reduction of QPI traffic is higher than the reduction of cache misses. The reason is that the better fitting thread affinity results in a placement of threads that share data on the same NUMA node, thus reducing QPI traffic. Cache misses were not reduced to the same degree. Therefore, although the indicators of Streamcluster show a higher potential for thread affinity, we are able to observe this by looking at QPI traffic, not at cache misses.

For applications that are more influenced by data affinity than thread affinity, the performance is similar regardless of the thread affinity applied. For instance, Vips has a high exclusivity and low heterogeneity and amount of sharing, which makes its reduction of QPI traffic larger than the reduction of cache misses. However, these indicators do not always correlate. One example is DC, whose indicators are similar to the ones of Vips, but the results show a higher reduction of cache misses than QPI traffic.

Most applications are more sensitive to the data affinity than the thread affinity, which can be observed in the results by the fact that the QPI traffic presented a higher reduction than cache misses. This happens because, even if an application does not share much data among its threads, each thread will still need to access its own private data, which can only be improved through data affinity. It is important to note that this does not mean that data affinity is more important than thread affinity, because, as previously stated, the effectiveness of data affinity depends on thread affinity.

For each benchmark, several affinity policies were tested. On average, execution time was reduced by 13.8%, 15.3%, 3.2% and 1.2% compared to the OS by kMAF, Oracle, Compact and Random, respectively. We can observe that kMAF presented performance improvements close to the Oracle, which demonstrates that kMAF handled both thread and data affinities correctly. By analyzing the Compact and Random affinities, we note that simple affinity strategies are not sufficient to handle a variety of applications, since they have very different characteristics. Also, this shows that our performance improvements are due to a better affinity, and not due to unnecessary migrations introduced by the operating system.

5.2 Energy Consumption

Apart from performance, energy improvements represent an important goal of affinity management. Optimizing affinity can reduce the energy consumption through a more efficient use of the computing resources, such as the caches and interconnections. Furthermore, reducing execution time by itself also saves static energy. We measure the system energy consumption during the execution of each application with the help of the Báseboard Management Controller (BMC), which exposes the energy consumption of the system through IPMI. We compare kMAF to the same affinity mechanisms that were used in the performance experiments.

Figure 10 contains the energy consumption results normalized to the results of the baseline (OS). As expected, the applications that benefit more from affinity management show higher energy savings. As in the performance results, SP had the highest reduction of energy consumption, of 34.6%. On average, energy consumption was reduced by 9.3% by kMAF and by 11.1% by the Oracle. As before, Compact and Random only reduced energy consumption slightly compared to the baseline (4.1% and 2.9%, respectively).

5.3 Managing Thread and Data Affinity Separately

In Section 2.1, we mentioned that setting thread affinity is a requirement for data affinity. To evaluate the influence of thread and data affinity, we executed kMAF only with the thread affinity and data affinity part, and let the OS handle the respective other affinity. We use the OS thread and data affinity as the baseline, as before.

Figure 11 shows the execution time for the three configurations, normalized to the baseline. For most benchmarks, the improvements from the thread affinity only are higher than for the data affinity only. On average, data affinity reduced execution time by 2.0%, thread affinity by 6.4%. It is important to note that the improvements from managing thread and data affinity jointly, as shown in Section 5.1, are higher than the sum of improvements when managing the affinities separately. This shows that integrated mechanisms are necessary for optimal results.

5.4 Runtime Overhead

Since kMAF operates during the execution of the parallel application, it causes an overhead, as discussed in Section 3.5.2. The overhead can be attributed to the following

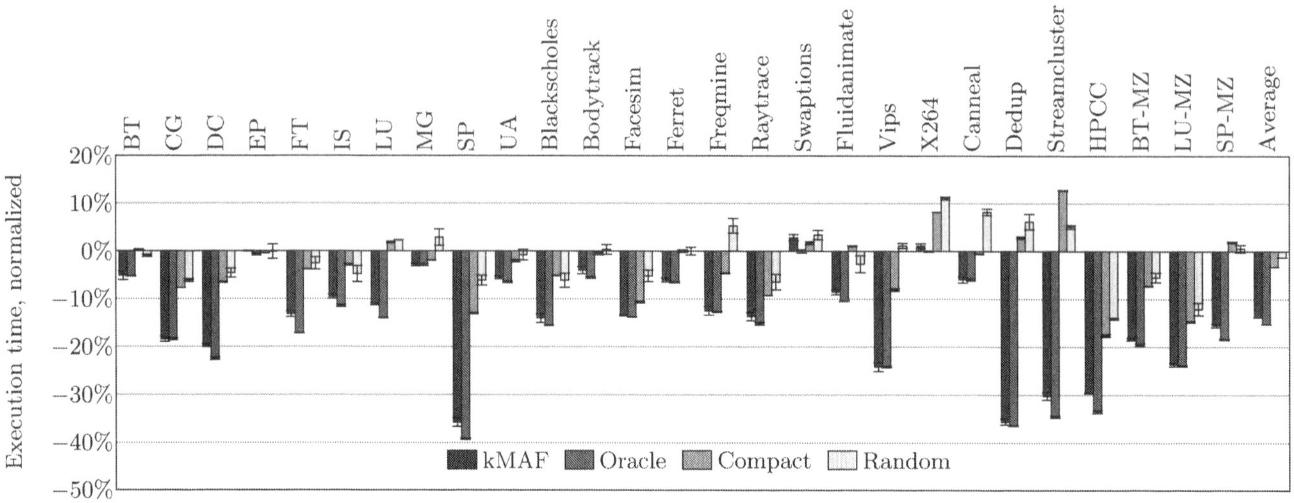

Figure 7: Execution time, normalized to the OS.

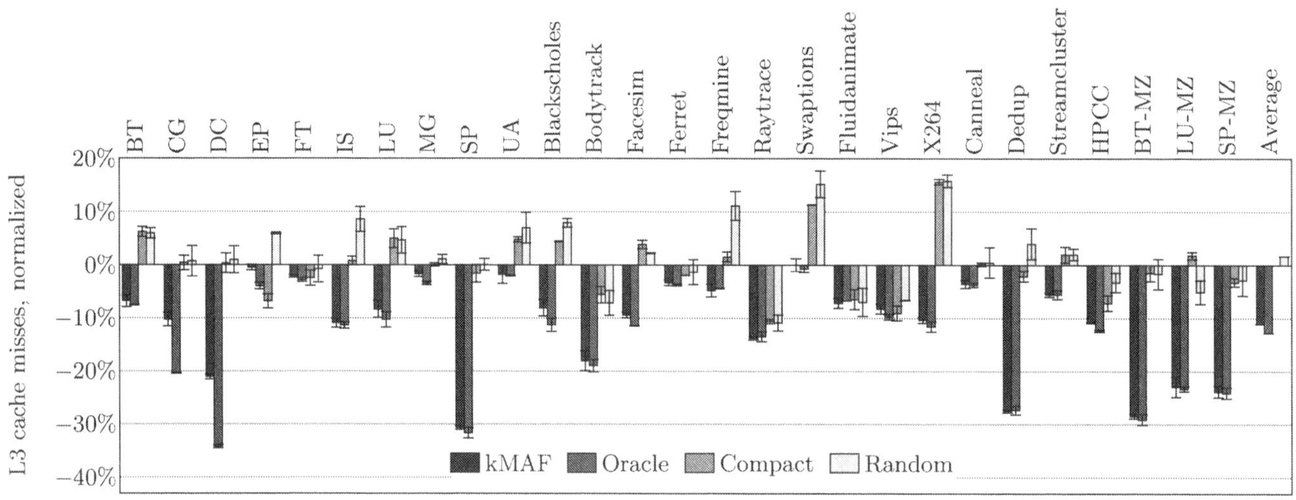

Figure 8: L3 cache misses, normalized to the OS.

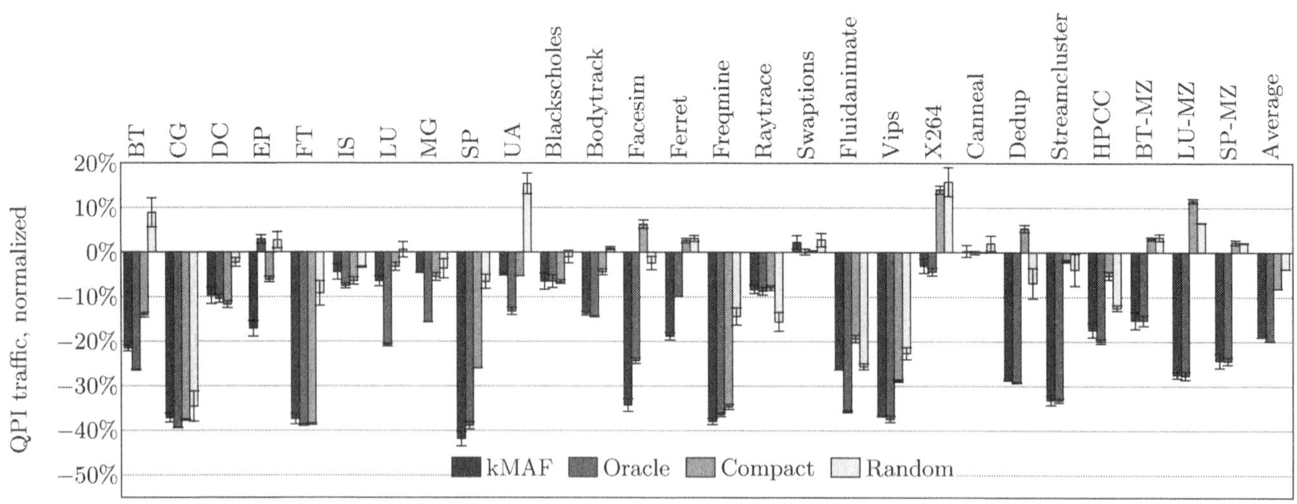

Figure 9: QPI traffic, normalized to the OS.

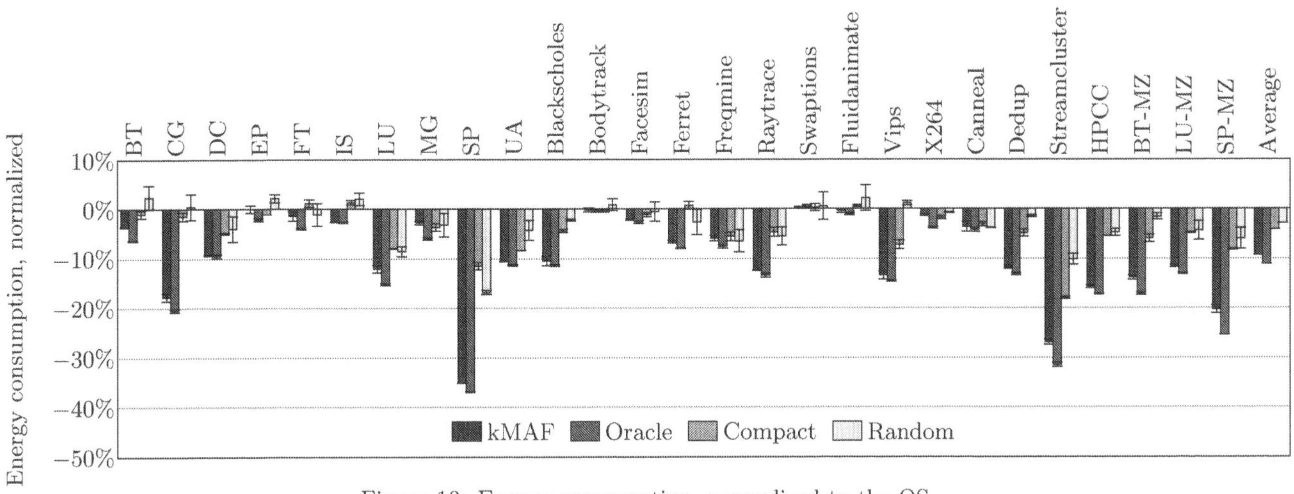

Figure 10: Energy consumption, normalized to the OS.

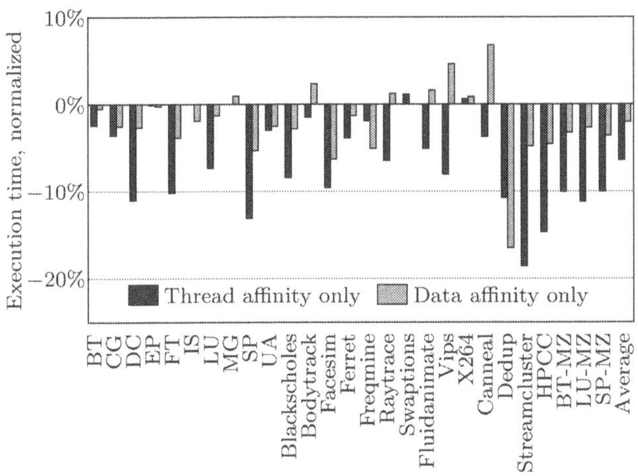

Figure 11: Application execution time when running kMAF with only thread or data affinity, normalized to the OS.

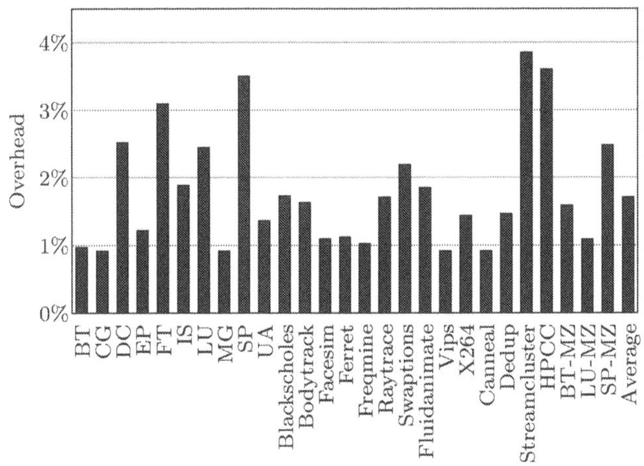

Figure 12: Total runtime overhead of kMAF as the percentage of the execution time of each application.

reasons: Extra page faults cause additional interrupts to the operating system, accesses to the affinity table and matrix, migration of pages between NUMA nodes, calculation of the thread mapping and the migration of threads. To approximate the overhead for the application, we measured the time spent in the kernel routines for each source of overhead, such as the time spent in the page fault handler for the extra page faults. Figure 12 shows the overhead for each application, as the percentage of each application's execution time. For all benchmarks, the overhead is less than 4%, with an average of 1.8%.

6. RELATED WORK

Several related mechanisms that focus on thread and process affinity considering the memory accesses have been proposed. In parallel applications that use explicit functions to share data, such as MPI communication functions, most previous proposals make use of information gathered from MPI primitives to generate a communication pattern. Frameworks such as the MPI Parallel Environment (MPE) [8] and eztrace [36] can be used to trace MPI messages between processes. Process affinity of MPI based applications is also evaluated in [7], but with the assumption that the affinities are previously known. In [30], the affinity can be either provided by the programmer, or be automatically detected by monitoring the MPI messages, as in [9]. A similar technique is used in [22]. These mechanisms utilize MPI primitives and are therefore not a generic solution for process and thread affinities. For multithreaded applications based on shared-memory frameworks, such as OpenMP and Pthreads, most traditional mapping mechanisms use memory access traces [3, 14] to characterize and map the application's threads. Tracing has a high overhead and can not be used if the application's behavior changes between executions.

Traditional data affinity policies, such as *first-touch*, *next-touch* [24] and *interleave* [12], have been used by operating systems to allocate memory on NUMA machines. In the case of first-touch, which is the default placement policy of Linux, a memory page is allocated in the NUMA node of the thread that causes its first page fault, and the page is never migrated. In the next-touch policy, pages are migrated to the node that performs the next access to them, leading to many migrations in pages that are accessed from different nodes. Recent versions of the Linux kernel can optionally balance the memory pages between NUMA nodes (AutoNUMA [11]). Both the interleaving policy and the NUMA balancing did not have a measurable influence on the results for the benchmarks we executed (less than 2% difference compared to first-touch).

Different approaches have been proposed to overcome these issues. For instance, Awasthi et al. [1] use information from the memory controller, such as the queuing delays and row-buffer hit rates, to guide data affinity policies. However, this mechanism does not consider thread affinity. Similarly, Marathe et al. [28] present a page placement scheme for NUMA platforms. Their framework captures information from hardware counters to feed an affinity decision logic. However, their work requires the identification of the stable execution phase of the parallel application through traces.

Tikir and Hollingsworth [34] use UltraSPARC III hardware monitors to guide data affinity, but do not set thread affinity. They propose adding an address translation counter to the TLB, and gather statistics from cache misses and TLB misses. Their proposal is limited to architectures with software-managed TLBs, while ours works in any architecture that supports virtual memory. Similarly, Marathe and Mueller [27] use the Power Management Unit (PMU) of the Itanium-2 architecture to perform data mapping. Their profiling mechanism imposes a high overhead, as it requires traps to the operating system on every high latency memory load operation or TLB miss. Hence, they enable the profiling mechanism just during the beginning of each application, losing the opportunity to handle changes during the execution of the application. Carrefour [12] uses instruction based sampling (IBS), available on AMD architectures, to collect statistics about page accesses during runtime, and uses them to improve data affinity. Data affinity alone is not able to improve locality when more than one thread accesses the same pages, since the threads may be executed in cores of different NUMA nodes.

Azimi et al. [2] set the affinity of threads based on information from the hardware counters of Power5 processors that sample the memory addresses of accesses resolved by remote caches. Accesses solved by local caches are not considered, generating an incomplete thread affinity pattern. Our previous work, SPCD [13], uses the page faults of a parallel application to set thread affinity. Only thread affinity was performed in these mechanisms, which does not improve the locality of memory accesses in NUMA architectures.

7. CONCLUSIONS

Parallel architectures with complex memory access characteristics represent the state-of-the-art. To fully benefit from these architectures, it is important to analyze the memory access characteristics of parallel applications and use this information to optimize the locality of memory accesses. This can be done in two complementing ways: by running threads that access shared data close to each other in the memory hierarchy (thread affinity) and to place memory pages on the NUMA node that accesses them the most (data affinity).

In this paper, we presented metrics and a methodology to analyze the memory access behavior of parallel applications to determine their potential for thread and data affinity. We introduced kMAF, which is a framework that automatically manages affinity on the operating system level. It requires no hardware changes and is compatible with all architectures that use virtual memory with paging. Furthermore, it requires no previous information about the applications' behavior, and no changes to the applications themselves or their runtime libraries.

Experiments with a wide range of parallel applications with different memory access characteristics showed that kMAF was able to improve performance substantially, up to 35.7% (13.8% on average). Energy consumption was also reduced, by up to 34.6% (9.3% on average). Results were close to an oracle mechanism, and substantially better than simpler mechanisms that do not take application behavior into account. We also show that combining thread and data affinity can lead to higher improvements than performing them separately.

For the future, we intend to expand kMAF to the system as a whole, without focusing on a single running application.

Acknowledgment

The authors thank Laércio L. Pilla, Francis B. Moreira, Emmanuell D. Carreño and the anonymous reviewers for their comments. This work was partially supported by CNPq, FAPERGS and CAPES.

8. REFERENCES

[1] M. Awasthi, D. W. Nellans, K. Sudan, R. Balasubramonian, and A. Davis, "Handling the Problems and Opportunities Posed by Multiple On-Chip Memory Controllers," in *Parallel Architectures and Compilation Techniques (PACT)*, 2010.

[2] R. Azimi, D. K. Tam, L. Soares, and M. Stumm, "Enhancing Operating System Support for Multicore Processors by Using Hardware Performance Monitoring," *ACM SIGOPS Operating Systems Review*, vol. 43, no. 2, Apr. 2009.

[3] N. Barrow-Williams, C. Fensch, and S. Moore, "A Communication Characterisation of Splash-2 and Parsec," in *IEEE International Symposium on Workload Characterization (IISWC)*, 2009.

[4] C. Bienia and K. Li, "Parsec 2.0: A new benchmark suite for chip-multiprocessors," in *Annual Workshop on Modeling, Benchmarking and Simulation*, 2009.

[5] S. Bokhari, "On the Mapping Problem," *IEEE Transactions on Computers*, vol. C-30, no. 3, 1981.

[6] S. Borkar and A. A. Chien, "The Future of Microprocessors," *Communications of the ACM*, vol. 54, no. 5, 2011.

[7] B. Brandfass, T. Alrutz, and T. Gerhold, "Rank reordering for MPI communication optimization," *Computers & Fluids*, Jan. 2012.

[8] A. Chan, W. Gropp, and E. Lusk, "User's Guide for MPE Extensions for MPI Programs," 1998.

[9] H. Chen, W. Chen, J. Huang, B. Robert, and H. Kuhn, "MPIPP: An Automatic Profile-guided Parallel Process Placement Toolset for SMP Clusters and Multiclusters," in *International Conference on Supercomputing*, 2006.

[10] Z. Chishti, M. D. Powell, and T. N. Vijaykumar, "Optimizing Replication, Communication, and Capacity Allocation in CMPs," *ACM SIGARCH Computer Architecture News*, vol. 33, no. 2, May 2005.

[11] J. Corbet, "Toward better NUMA scheduling." [Online]. Available: http://lwn.net/Articles/486858/
[12] M. Dashti, A. Fedorova, J. Funston, F. Gaud, R. Lachaize, B. Lepers, V. Quema, and M. Roth, "Traffic Management: A Holistic Approach to Memory Placement on NUMA Systems," in *Architectural Support for Programming Languages and Operating Systems (ASPLOS)*, 2013.
[13] M. Diener, E. H. M. Cruz, and P. O. A. Navaux, "Communication-Based Mapping Using Shared Pages," in *IEEE International Parallel & Distributed Processing Symposium (IPDPS)*, 2013.
[14] M. Diener, F. L. Madruga, E. R. Rodrigues, M. A. Z. Alves, and P. O. A. Navaux, "Evaluating Thread Placement Based on Memory Access Patterns for Multi-core Processors," in *IEEE International Conference on High Performance Computing and Communications (HPCC)*, 2010.
[15] J. Feliu, J. Sahuquillo, S. Petit, and J. Duato, "Understanding Cache Hierarchy Contention in CMPs to Improve Job Scheduling," in *International Parallel and Distributed Processing Symposium (IPDPS)*, 2012.
[16] E. Gabriel, G. E. Fagg, G. Bosilca, T. Angskun, J. J. Dongarra, J. M. Squyres, V. Sahay, P. Kambadur, B. Barrett, and A. Lumsdaine, "Open MPI: Goals, concept, and design of a next generation MPI implementation," in *Recent Advances in Parallel Virtual Machine and Message Passing Interface*, 2004.
[17] B. Goglin and S. Moreaud, "KNEM: A generic and scalable kernel-assisted intra-node MPI communication framework," *Journal of Parallel and Distributed Computing*, vol. 73, no. 2, Feb. 2013.
[18] T. Hoefler and M. Snir, "Generic topology mapping strategies for large-scale parallel architectures," in *International Conference on Supercomputing (ICS)*, 2011.
[19] Intel, "Intel Performance Counter Monitor - A better way to measure CPU utilization," 2012. [Online]. Available: http://www.intel.com/software/pcm
[20] ——, "Using KMP_AFFINITY to create OpenMP thread mapping to OS proc IDs," 2012. [Online]. Available: http://software.intel.com/en-us/articles/using-kmp-affinity-to-create-openmp-thread-mapping-to-os-proc-ids
[21] H. Jin, M. Frumkin, and J. Yan, "The OpenMP implementation of NAS Parallel Benchmarks and Its Performance," 1999.
[22] C. Karlsson, T. Davies, and Z. Chen, "Optimizing Process-to-Core Mappings for Application Level Multi-dimensional MPI Communications," in *IEEE International Conference on Cluster Computing (CLUSTER)*, 2012.
[23] D. Li, B. R. de Supinski, M. Schulz, K. Cameron, and D. S. Nikolopoulos, "Hybrid MPI/OpenMP Power-Aware Computing," in *IEEE International Parallel & Distributed Processing Symposium (IPDPS)*, 2010.
[24] H. Löf and S. Holmgren, "affinity-on-next-touch: Increasing the Performance of an Industrial PDE Solver on a cc-NUMA System," in *International Conference on Supercomputing*, 2005.
[25] C. Luk, R. Cohn, R. Muth, and H. Patil, "Pin: Building Customized Program Analysis Tools with Dynamic Instrumentation," in *ACM SIGPLAN Conference on Programming Language Design and Implementation (PLDI)*, 2005.
[26] P. Luszczek, J. J. Dongarra, D. Koester, R. Rabenseifer, B. Lucas, J. Kepner, J. Mccalpin, D. Bailey, D. Takahashi, J. Jack, and R. Rabenseifner, "Introduction to the HPC Challenge Benchmark Suite," 2005.
[27] J. Marathe and F. Mueller, "Hardware Profile-guided Automatic Page Placement for ccNUMA Systems," in *ACM SIGPLAN Symposium on Principles and Practice of Parallel Programming (PPoPP)*, 2006.
[28] J. Marathe, V. Thakkar, and F. Mueller, "Feedback-Directed Page Placement for ccNUMA via Hardware-generated Memory Traces," *Journal of Parallel and Distributed Computing*, vol. 70, no. 12, 2010.
[29] M. M. K. Martin, M. D. Hill, and D. J. Sorin, "Why On-Chip Cache Coherence is Here to Stay," *Communications of the ACM*, vol. 55, no. 7, Jul. 2012.
[30] G. Mercier and E. Jeannot, "Improving MPI Applications Performance on Multicore Clusters with Rank Reordering," in *European MPI Users' Group conference on Recent advances in the message passing interface (EuroMPI)*, 2011.
[31] F. Pellegrini, "Static Mapping by Dual Recursive Bipartitioning of Process and Architecture Graphs," in *Scalable High-Performance Computing Conference (SHPCC)*, 1994.
[32] M. J. Rashti, J. Green, P. Balaji, A. Afsahi, and W. Gropp, "Multi-core and Network Aware MPI Topology Functions," in *Recent Advances in the Message Passing Interface*, 2011.
[33] C. P. Ribeiro, J.-F. Mehaut, A. Carissimi, M. Castro, and L. G. Fernandes, "Memory Affinity for Hierarchical Shared Memory Multiprocessors," in *International Symposium on Computer Architecture and High Performance Computing (SBAC-PAD)*, 2009.
[34] M. M. Tikir and J. K. Hollingsworth, "Hardware monitors for dynamic page migration," *Journal of Parallel and Distributed Computing*, vol. 68, no. 9, Sep. 2008.
[35] J. Torrellas, "Architectures for extreme-scale computing," *IEEE Computer*, vol. 42, no. 11, 2009.
[36] F. Trahay, F. Rue, M. Faverge, Y. Ishikawa, R. Namyst, and J. Dongarra, "EZTrace: a generic framework for performance analysis," in *International Symposium on Cluster, Cloud and Grid Computing (CCGrid)*, May 2011.
[37] R. F. Van der Wijngaart and H. Jin, "NAS Parallel Benchmarks, Multi-Zone Versions," 2003.
[38] W. Wang, T. Dey, J. Mars, L. Tang, J. W. Davidson, and M. L. Soffa, "Performance Analysis of Thread Mappings with a Holistic View of the Hardware Resources," in *IEEE International Symposium on Performance Analysis of Systems & Software (ISPASS)*, 2012.

Shuffling: A Framework for Lock Contention Aware Thread Scheduling for Multicore Multiprocessor Systems

Kishore Kumar Pusukuri Rajiv Gupta Laxmi N. Bhuyan
Department of Computer Science and Engineering
University of California, Riverside
Riverside, USA 92521
{kishore, gupta, bhuyan}@cs.ucr.edu

ABSTRACT

On a cache-coherent multicore multiprocessor system, the performance of a multithreaded application with high lock contention is very sensitive to the distribution of application threads across multiple processors (or Sockets). This is because the distribution of threads impacts the frequency of lock transfers between Sockets, which in turn impacts the frequency of last-level cache (LLC) misses that lie on the critical path of execution. Since the latency of a LLC miss is high, an increase of LLC misses on the critical path increases both lock acquisition latency and critical section processing time. However, thread schedulers for operating systems, such as Solaris and Linux, are oblivious of the lock contention among multiple threads belonging to an application and therefore fail to deliver high performance for multithreaded applications.

To alleviate the above problem, in this paper, we propose a scheduling framework called *Shuffling*, which migrates threads of a multithreaded program across Sockets so that threads seeking locks are more likely to find the locks on the same Socket. Shuffling reduces the time threads spend on acquiring locks and speeds up the execution of shared data accesses in the critical section, ultimately reducing the execution time of the application. We have implemented Shuffling on a 64-core Supermicro server running Oracle Solaris 11™ and evaluated it using a wide variety of 20 multithreaded programs with high lock contention. Our experiments show that Shuffling achieves up to 54% reduction in execution time and an average reduction of 13%. Moreover it does not require any changes to the application source code or the OS kernel.

Categories and Subject Descriptors

D.4.1 [**Process Management**]: Scheduling

Keywords

Multicore; scheduling; thread migration; lock contention; last-level cache misses

PACT'14, August 24–27, 2014, Edmonton, AB, Canada.
Copyright 2014 ACM 978-1-4503-2809-8/14/08 ...$15.00.
http://dx.doi.org/10.1145/2628071.2628074.

1 Introduction

The cache-coherent multicore multiprocessing architecture was designed to overcome the scalability limits of the symmetric multiprocessing architecture. Today, multicore multiprocessor (or multi-socket) systems with a large number of cores are ubiquitous [4, 5, 6]. For applications with high degree of parallelism it is often necessary to create large number of threads and distribute them across the multiple multicore Sockets to utilize all the available cores [32]. However, shared-memory multithreaded applications often exhibit high *lock times* (i.e., > 5%) due to frequent synchronization of threads [20, 28]. The lock time is defined as the percentage of elapsed time a process has spent waiting for lock operations in user space [26]. Figure 1(a) presents the lock times of 20 multithreaded programs including SPEC jbb2005 [41], PBZIP2 [30], and programs from PARSEC [2], SPEC OMP2001 [41], and SPLASH2 [49] suites. As we can see, the lock times for these programs are quite high.

On a multicore multisocket system, the performance of a multithreaded application with *high lock contention* is highly sensitive to the distribution of threads across Sockets (or multicore processors). In this paper, we demonstrate that the time spent on acquiring locks, as experienced by competing threads, can increase greatly depending upon the Sockets on which they are scheduled. When a lock is acquired by a thread, the time spent on acquiring it is longer if lock currently resides in a cache line of a remote Socket as opposed to the Socket on which the acquiring thread is running. In addition, once the thread acquires the lock, access to shared data protected by the lock is also likely to trigger LLC misses. This causes the thread to spend longer time in the critical section. When the competing threads of a multithreaded application are distributed across multiple Sockets, the above situation arises often and it increases lock transfers between Sockets. Frequent lock transfers between Sockets significantly increases long latency LLC misses that fall on the *critical path* of execution. Moreover, the larger the number of threads, the higher is the lock contention problem which causes LLC misses associated with inter-Socket transfer of locks and the shared data they protect. As shown in Figure 1(b), most of the programs exhibit high LLC miss rates (i.e., > 3 MPKI). LLC miss rate is defined as the last level cache misses per thousand instructions (MPKI). Since the latency of LLC miss is high, the increase in LLC misses on the critical path increases both lock acquisition latency and critical section processing time, thereby leading to significant performance degradation.

PARSEC: bodytrack (BT), fluidanimate (FA), facesim (FS), streamcluster (SC); SPEC OMP2001: applu (AL), ammp (AM), apsi (AS), equake (EQ), fma3d (FM), gafort (GA), galgel (GL), mgrid (MG), swim (SM), wupwise (WW); SPLASH2: ocean (OC), raytrace (RT), radix (RX), volrend (VL); PBZIP2 (PB); SPEC jbb2005 (JB).

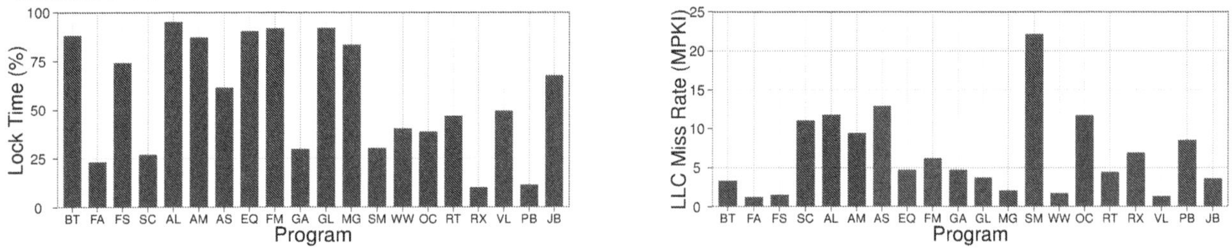

(a) Lock times. (b) LLC Miss Rate.

Figure 1: We studied 33 programs including SPEC jbb2005, PBZIP2, and program from PARSEC, SPEC OMP2001, and SPLASH2 suites. We thoroughly evaluate programs with high lock times (i.e., > 5%). Among the 33 programs, the above 20 programs have high lock times. Therefore, we considered these 20 programs throughout this paper. Lock times and LLC miss rates of these 20 programs are shown here. The programs are run with 64 threads on 64 cores spread across 4 Sockets. The description of the machine is shown in Figure 2.

Our Solution -- Shuffling. To address the above problem, we propose a scheduling framework called *Shuffling*, which aims to reduce the variance in the lock arrival times of the threads scheduled on the same Socket. The lock arrival times are the times at which threads arrive at the critical section just before they successfully acquire the lock. *By scheduling threads whose arrival times are clustered in a small time interval so that they can all get the lock without losing the lock to a thread on another Socket.* Thus Shuffling ensures that once a thread releases the lock, it is highly likely that another thread on the same Socket will successfully acquire the lock, and LLC misses will be avoided. Consequently, Shuffling reduces the lock acquisition time and speeds up the execution of shared data accesses in the critical section, ultimately reducing the execution time of the application.

We implemented Shuffling on a 64-core, 4-Socket machine running Oracle Solaris 11 and evaluated it using a large set of multithreaded programs. The results show that for 20 programs with high lock times Shuffling achieves up to 54% (average 13%) reduction in execution time. For the remaining 13 programs with very low lock times, the change in performance was insignificant (within 0.5%). Moreover, Shuffling outperforms the state-of-the-art cache contention management technique [3, 52]. Finally, Shuffling is an attractive approach because its *overhead is negligible* and it *does not require any changes to the application source code or the OS kernel.*

The key contributions of our work are as follows:

- We identify the important reasons for why modern OSs fail to achieve high performance for multithreaded applications with high lock contention running on multicore multiprocessor systems.
- We develop a scheduling framework called *Shuffling* which orchestrates migration of threads between Sockets with the goal of simultaneously maintaining load balance and reducing lock transfers between Sockets to reduce LLC misses on the critical path.

The rest of the paper is organized as follows. In Section 2 we show why distribution of threads impacts lock transfers between Sockets. In Section 3 we provide design and implementation of Shuffling. In Section 4, we evaluate Shuffling with a wide variety of multithreaded programs. Related work and conclusions are given in Sections 5 and 6.

Supermicro 64-core server:
4 × 16-Core 64-bit AMD Opteron^{TM} 6272 (2.1 GHz);
L1/L2: 48 KB / 1000 KB; Private to a core;
L3: 16 MB shared by 16 cores; RAM: 64 GB;
Memory latency (local : remote) = (128 nsec : 201 nsec);
Operating System: Oracle Solaris 11^{TM}.

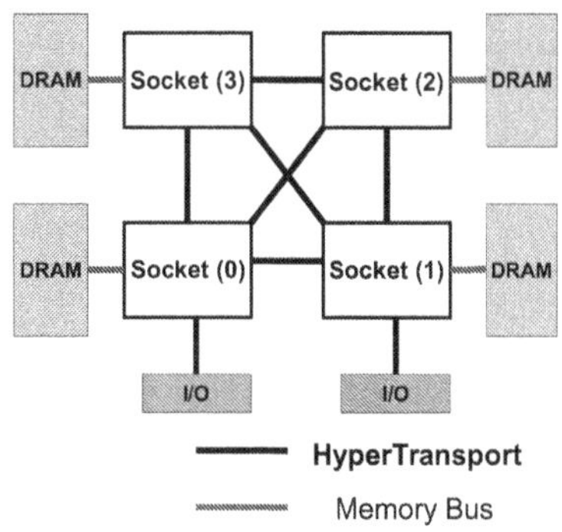

Figure 2: Our 64-core machine has four 16-core Sockets (or Processors). We interchangeably use Socket and Processor.

2 Lock Contention and LLC Misses

Although thread schedulers of modern operating systems, such as Solaris and Linux, are effective in scheduling multiple single threaded programs, they fail to effectively schedule threads of a multithreaded program on a cache-coherent multiprocessor system. Since they do not distinguish between threads representing single threaded applications from threads of a single multithreaded application, the decisions made by these schedulers are oblivious to the lock contention among the threads of a multithreaded program. Lock contention results when multiple threads compete to acquire the same lock. For example, consider a typical synchronization where several threads compete for a lock to enter a critical section in the Bodytrack (BT) [2] computer vision application on the 64 core 4-Socket machine described in Figure 2.

BT is an Intel RMS workload which tracks a 3D pose of a marker-less human body with multiple cameras through an image sequence. BT has a persistent thread pool and the main thread executes the program and sends a task to the thread pool whenever it reaches a parallel kernel. The program has three parallel kernels :1) Edge Detection;

```
// entry of worker thread function
...
// get a lock
ticket = loopTickets.getTicket();
while(ticket < GradientArgs.src->Height() - 2) {
 for(i = ticket; i < GradientArgs.src->Height() -
     2 && i < ticket + WORKUNIT_SIZE_GRADIENT;
     i++) {
       GradientMagThresholdPthread(i + 1, ...);
 }
  ticket = loopTickets.getTicket();
}
...
```

Figure 3: Code snippet around a parallel kernel of BT.

2) Calculate Particle Weights; and 3) Particle Resampling. The parallel kernels use locks to distribute the work among threads to dynamically balance the load. To understand the effect of the distribution of threads across Sockets on the performance, on our multicore system, we studied code around the first parallel kernel Edge Detection. BT employs a gradient based edge detection mask to find edges. The result is compared against a threshold to eliminate spurious edges. Edge detection is implemented in function Gradient-MagThreshold and the code snippet around the function is shown in Figure 3 [2].

Each worker thread of BT tries to *acquire a lock* so it can enter the critical section. In the critical section the thread runs GradientMagThreshold function in a loop. As expected, lock contention increases with the number of threads. The worker threads perform both read and write operations on the *shared data*. This code involves a series of *successful (Acquire Lock; Execute Critical Section; Release Lock)* operation sequences that are performed by the participating threads. The execution time of an operation sequence increases if LLC misses occur when acquiring the lock and performing read and write operations on the shared data.

2.1 The Cost of LLC Misses

If $T(Acq_i; Exec_i; Rel_i)$ denotes the time for the ith successful operation sequence, and there are a total of n threads competing for the lock, then the total time is given by $\sum_{i=1}^{n} T(Acq_i; Exec_i; Rel_i)$. On a cache-coherent multiprocessor machine, the time for each successful (Acquire; Exec; Release) can vary significantly. Let us consider two consecutive operations $(Acq_i; Exec_i; Rel_i)$ and $(Acq_{i+1}; Exec_{i+1}; Rel_{i+1})$ such that they are performed by two threads located at Sockets $Socket_i$ and $Socket_{i+1}$ respectively. The time for the second operation pair, i.e. $T(Acq_{i+1}; Exec_{i+1}; Rel_{i+1})$ can vary as follows:

- $T(Acq_{i+1}; Exec_{i+1}; Rel_{i+1})$ is *low* (T_{low}) when the threads that perform operations $(Acq_i; Exec_i; Rel_i)$ & $(Acq_{i+1}; Exec_{i+1}; Rel_{i+1})$ are located on the same Socket, i.e. $Socket_i = Socket_{i+1}$ because then LLC hits occur when the lock, and the shared data it protects, are accessed;

- $T(Acq_{i+1}; Exec_{i+1}; Rel_{i+1})$ is *high* (T_{high}) when the threads that perform operations $(Acq_i; Exec_i; Rel_i)$ & $(Acq_{i+1}; Exec_{i+1}; Rel_{i+1})$ are located on different Sockets, i.e. $Socket_i \neq Socket_{i+1}$ because LLC misses occur when the lock, and the shared data it protects, are accessed.

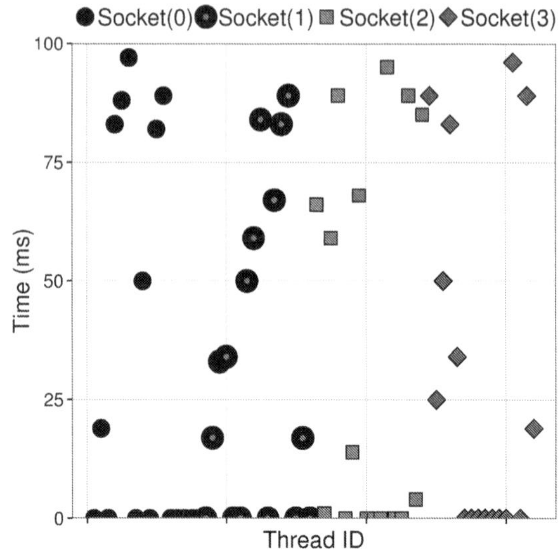

Figure 4: Lock arrival Times of the 64 threads of BT with **Solaris** across all the four Sockets. DTrace [8] scripts were used to collect the lock arrival times of 64 threads of BT before acquiring the lock in a 100 milliseconds interval. Threads with the same symbol arrived on the same Socket.

The above variation is due to the high cost of lock transfer between Sockets on a cache coherent multisocket system. Our machine uses the MOESI cache coherency protocol [42]. In this protocol a cache line can be in one of five states: *Modified, Owned, Exclusive, Shared, and Invalid*. Therefore, following the execution of $(Acq_i; Exec_i; Rel_i)$, the cache line containing the lock is in *Modified* state. If the $Socket_{i+1}$ is different from $Socket_i$, then the cache line must be transferred from $Socket_i$ to $Socket_{i+1}$ when $(Acq_{i+1}; Exec_{i+1}; Rel_{i+1})$ is executed.

2.2 High Frequency of LLC Misses and its Cause

Next, we show how often the above event sequences entail overhead of T_{low} vs. T_{high}. For a given number of threads, the total number of *successful* (*Acquire*; *Exec*; *Release*) operations performed is the same. However, how often these operations require T_{low} and T_{high} overhead varies based on the distribution of threads across the four Sockets. When running BT with 64 threads on 64 cores across 4 Sockets with the default Solaris scheduler, around 68% of the time lock transfers between two Sockets take place. In other words, T_{high} cost must be paid for over $2/3^{rd}$ of the time with the default Solaris scheduler. Therefore, with Solaris, high overhead LLC misses happen frequently which degrades performance as these LLC misses are on the critical path. LLC miss has high latency, for example, it is 201 nanoseconds for our machine. These high latency LLC misses on the critical path significantly increase both *lock acquisition latencies* and *critical section processing times*.

The frequent lock transfers between Sockets in multiprocessor system increases execution time of the critical path and significantly degrades performance of multithreaded applications. This problem becomes very prominent for applications with high lock contention. As Figure 1 shows, BT experiences high lock contention. Its LLC miss rate is also high – 3.3 MPKI (Misses Per Thousand Instructions).

Next let us examine the reason for frequently encountered LLC misses. Figure 4 shows the times (say *lock arrival times*) at which threads arrive at the critical section just before they successfully acquire the lock and execute the event sequence (*Acquire*; *Execute*; *Release*). The x-axis plots thread ids and the y-axis plots the corresponding lock arrival times. We use DTrace [8] scripts to collect the *lock arrival times* of the 64 threads in a 100 milliseconds (ms) snapshot. As we can see in Figure 4, the lock arrival times of threads on each Socket are spread across a wide time interval for the default Solaris scheduler. For example, as we can see in Figure 4, on Socket(0), a thread arrived at the critical section at around 20 ms timestamp, but no other thread arrives at the critical section on Socket(0) till the 50 ms timestamp. Therefore, even though the lock is available before the 50 ms timestamp, none of the threads have arrived at the critical section on Socket(0) to acquire it until the 50 ms timestamp. Therefore, the likelihood that the lock will be acquired before the 50 ms timestamp by a thread on a different Socket is very high. This will trigger lock transfer, along with the shared data protected by the lock, between Sockets. Thus LLC misses will occur due to lock acquisition as well accesses to shared data in the critical section. Since these LLC misses are on the critical path, significant degradation in performance results.

3 The Shuffling Framework

To address the above problem, we propose a scheduling framework called *Shuffling*, which aims to reduce the variance in the arrival times of the threads scheduled on the same Socket. *By scheduling threads whose arrival times are clustered in a small time interval so that they can all get the lock without losing the lock to a thread on another Socket.* Therefore, Shuffling ensures that once a thread releases the lock it is highly likely that another thread on the same Socket will successfully acquire the lock and LLC misses will be avoided. Consequently, Shuffling reduces the lock acquisition time and speeds up the execution of shared data accesses in the critical section, ultimately reducing the execution time of the application.

Let us assume that the expected arrival times at critical section for all the threads are known. We can distribute the threads across the Sockets as follows. We sort the threads according to their expected arrival times and divide them into equal sized groups, one group per Socket to maintain load balance across the Sockets. Moreover, each group can be formed by taking consecutive threads from the sorted list to minimize the variance in arrival times for threads in each group. Finally, by migrating the threads, we distribute the threads across the Sockets according to the above schedule.

We observe that, instead of moving locks and shared data they protect between the Sockets, Shuffling moves the threads between the Sockets. *Migrating threads between Sockets is preferable to moving locks, and shared data they protect, between Sockets.* This is because when multiple threads are contending for locks and shared data, they are not doing useful work and hence the thread migration cost is not expected to impact the execution time. On the other hand, Shuffling reduces LLC misses on the critical path of execution. Moreover, it preserves the number of threads on each Socket, i.e. *load balance* across the Sockets is maintained. We also observe, that it reduces inter-Socket thread migrations compared to default Solaris. Thus shuffling improves application performance.

Algorithm 1: The Shuffling Framework.

Input: N: Number of threads; C: Number of Sockets.

```
repeat
    i. Monitor Threads -- sample lock times of N threads.
    if lock times exceed threshold then
        ii. Form Thread Groups -- sort threads according to lock times and divide them into C groups.
        iii. Perform Shuffling -- shuffle threads to establish newly computed thread groups.
    end
until application terminates;
```

The key problem that we face is -- how to determine the expected arrival times of threads. One way to achieve this is to analyze the application code and instrument it to collect this information. This task is complicated by the fact that an application typically contains many critical sections and it would require analyzing the application before it can be run to take advantage of Shuffling. However, *we would like to develop a Shuffling algorithm that does not modify application code and can be applied on-the-fly to any application that is run on the system.* Therefore we base our shuffling algorithm on thread *lock times* that can be collected by using simple OS level monitoring utilities. As we show later in this section, sorting and grouping of threads according to their *lock times* is effective in reducing the variance in the arrival times of the threads scheduled on each Socket.

3.1 The Shuffling Algorithm

The overview of Shuffling is provided in Algorithm 1. Shuffling is implemented by a daemon thread which executes throughout an application's lifetime repeatedly performing the following three steps: monitor threads; form thread groups; and perform thread shuffling. The first step monitors the behavior of threads in terms of the percentage of elapsed time they spend on waiting for locks. If this time exceeds a preset threshold (we use 5% of elapsed time as the threshold), shuffling is triggered by executing the next two steps. The second step forms groups of similarly behaving threads using the lock times collected during the monitoring step. Finally the third step performs thread shuffling to ensure that threads belonging to the same thread group are all moved to the same CPU. Next we describe these steps in greater detail.

(i) Monitor Threads. We monitor the fraction of execution time that each thread spends waiting for locks in user space -- this is referred to as the *lock time*. *Threads that experience similar lock times will be placed in the same group* as they are likely to represent threads that contend with each other for locks and keep the lock located on the same Socket. The daemon thread maintains per thread data structure that holds the lock time values collected for the thread as well as the id of the Socket on which the thread is running. The design of the monitoring component involves two main decisions: a) selecting an appropriate sampling interval for lock times and b) selecting an appropriate shuffling interval i.e., time interval after which we form new thread groups and carry out shuffling. We explain the selection of these intervals in Section 3.2.

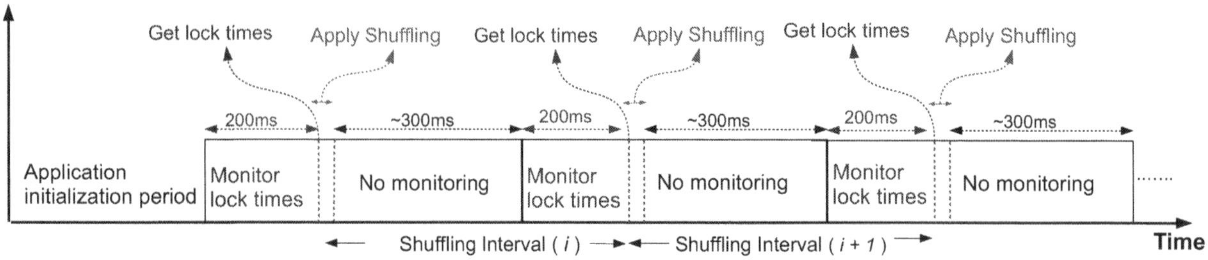

Figure 5: Frequency of Monitoring and Shuffling.

(ii) Form Thread Groups. At regular intervals (i.e., *shuffling interval*), the daemon thread examines the profile (i.e., lock time) data collected for the threads, and if the lock times exceed the minimum preset threshold, it constructs thread groups such that one group per Socket is formed. We would like the lock time behavior of threads within each group to be similar. Therefore we sort the threads according to their lock times and then divide them into as many groups of consecutive threads as the Sockets being used to run the application. For example, when all Sockets are being used, the first group is assigned to Socket(0), the second to Socket(1), the third to Socket(2), and the fourth to Socket(3). Since the size of each thread group is the same, load balance across the Sockets is maintained.

(iii) Perform Shuffling. This step simply affects the thread groups computed for each of the Sockets in the preceding step. That is, at regular intervals (i.e., shuffling interval), Shuffling simultaneously migrates as many threads as needed across Sockets to realize the new thread groups computed in the previous step [1]. In this step we expect only a subset of threads to be migrated as many threads may already be bound to a set of cores on the Sockets where we would like them to be. It is also possible that in some programs, over many shuffling intervals, the behavior of threads does not change significantly. If this is the case, the thread groups formed will not change, and hence no threads will be migrated. Thus, effectively the shuffling step is skipped altogether and monitoring is resumed. In other words, when thread migrations are not expected to yield any benefit, they will not be performed.

3.2 Frequency of Monitoring and Shuffling

In developing a practical implementation of the Shuffling framework we must make several *policy* decisions. First, we must select an appropriate *sampling interval* for collecting lock time data of the threads before thread groups can be formed for shuffling. Second, we must select an appropriate *shuffling interval*, i.e. duration between one application of shuffling and the next.

3.2.1 Sampling Interval.

We monitor the lock times of threads through the proc file system. Although small sampling interval allows fine-grain details of the lock time data to be collected, it increases the monitoring overhead. Therefore selecting an appropriate sampling interval is very important. To select an appropriate sampling interval, we measured the system overhead of

[1]For balancing load across cores, Shuffling delegates the job of migrating threads *within cores* of a Socket to the default Solaris thread scheduler.

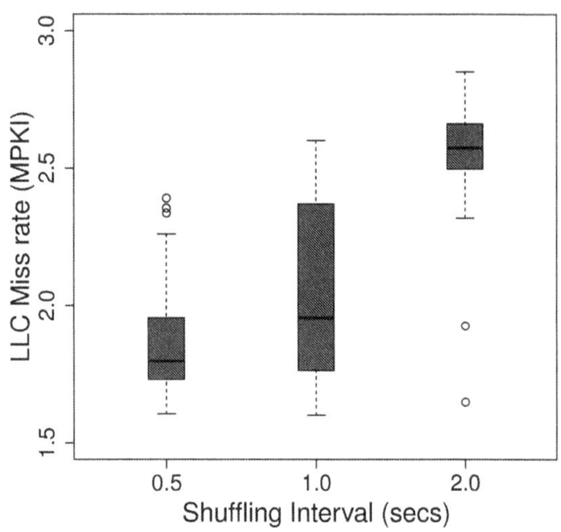

Figure 6: LLC Miss Rates vs Shuffling Interval: shuffling with 500 milliseconds interval provides sustained reduction in LLC miss rate.

Shuffling with different lock time sampling intervals when programs are running with 64 threads on our machine. When we use time intervals less than 200 milliseconds (ms) (e.g., 50 ms, 100 ms), the system overhead is significantly higher. This is due to the high rate of cross-calls, which lead to high system time [26]. Therefore, the Shuffling framework uses 200 ms time interval for collecting lock times. The overhead of monitoring lock times with 200 ms is *less* than 1% of system time, which is negligible.

3.2.2 Shuffling Interval.

Shuffling interval significantly impacts the performance improvements as it affects lock transfer rate between Sockets, and thus affects LLC misses in the critical path. Therefore, for finding an appropriate shuffling interval, we measured the LLC miss-rate with different shuffling intervals as shown in Figure 6 by running BT with 64 threads on 64 cores with the Shuffling framework. As we can see in Figure 6, shuffling with 500 ms interval provides sustained reduction in LLC miss rate and gives best performance for BT. Although we can shuffle with an interval less than 500 ms by using small lock time sampling intervals, as explained above, it increases system overhead and limits performance benefits. Therefore, we have chosen 500 ms as a shuffling interval in this work.

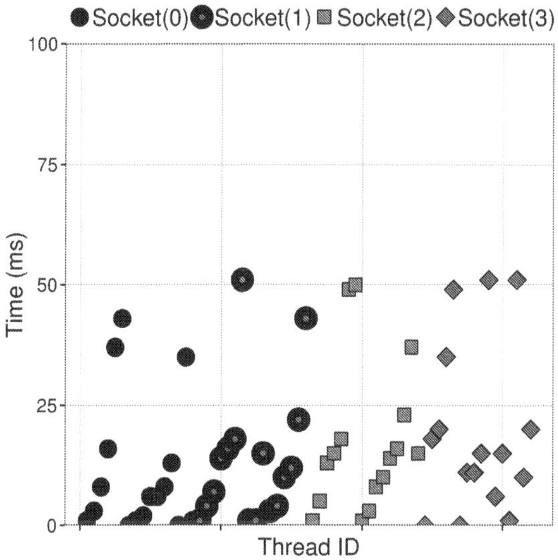

Figure 7: Lock arrival Times of the 64 threads of BT with **Shuffling** across all the four Sockets. DTrace scripts were used to collect the arrival times of 64 threads of BT before acquiring the lock in a 100 milliseconds interval.

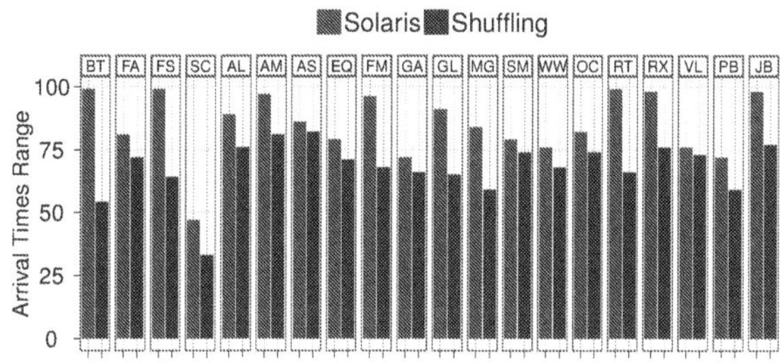

Figure 8: Lock arrival times ranges with Solaris vs. Shuffling.

As shown in Figure 5, for every 500 ms, the Shuffling framework collects lock times using prstat(1) utility with 200 ms sampling interval, constructs thread profile data structures with the lock times and core ids, form groups, and then assigns each of the groups to a set of cores (or Sockets). It repeats this process until completion of the program. Finally, the pset_lwp_bind(2) system call is used for binding a group of threads to a set of cores (called a processor-set in Solaris terminology). A processor-set is a pool of cores such that if we assign a multithreaded application to a processor-set, then during load balancing, the OS restricts the migration of threads across the cores within the processor-set [26].

3.3 Impact of Shuffling on Bodytrack (BT)

We show that shuffling based on thread lock time measurements does have the intended effect, i.e. reduction in variance across arrival times of threads on a given Socket. Unlike the lock arrival times of BT with Solaris (Figure 4 in Section 2), as we can see in Figure 7, the lock arrival times of threads are closely clustered minimizing variance when Shuffling is employed. Moreover, Figure 8 shows that the range over which lock arrival times of threads are distributed reduces significantly when Shuffling is used.

Table 1: BT achieves 54% performance improvement.

	Solaris	Shuffling
T_{max} Lock Transfers	68%	43%
LLC Miss Rate	3.3 MPKI	1.9 MPKI
Lock Time	88%	74%
Avg. Execution Time	113 secs	52 secs

When running BT with 64 threads on 64 cores across 4 Sockets with Shuffling, only around 43% of the time the lock transfers take place between the local Socket and a remote Socket. In other words, T_{max} lock transfers are encountered roughly 2/5th of the time. However, as we described in Section 2, with Solaris, T_{max} lock transfers are encountered roughly 2/3rd of the time. Therefore, Shuffling dramatically reduces high overhead lock transfers and thus, reduces LLC misses on the critical path. While LLC miss rate of BT with Solaris is 3.3 MPKI, LLC miss rate with Shuffling is 1.9 MPKI. Moreover, lock time of BT with Solaris is 88%, lock time with Shuffling is 74%. That is, with Shuffling, there is 42% reduction in LLC miss rate and lock time reduces by 14%. BT achieves a large performance improvement (54%) with Shuffling. Table 1 summarizes these observations.

The large improvement in performance of BT is in part due to additional contributing factors: reduction in coherence traffic and inter-Socket thread migrations. By minimizing coherence traffic, Shuffling reduces latency of LLC miss. Moreover, by keeping threads close to locks, Shuffling reduces lock time; thus, threads go to sleep state far less often with Shuffling compared to Solaris. We observed that when a thread made a transition from sleep state to a ready state, often the core on which it last ran is not available and it is migrated to a core available on another Socket. Therefore, Shuffling encounters far fewer thread migrations between Sockets than Solaris -- we observed that while the inter-Socket thread migration rate with Solaris was 270 migrations per second, it is only 16 migrations per second with Shuffling.

We have explained how Shuffling improves the performance of the BT multithreaded program. In the next section, we present its evaluation with a wide variety of multithreaded programs.

4 Evaluation

We demonstrate the merits of Shuffling via experimental evaluation of the performance of several multithreaded applications. We also provide a detailed explanation of the overheads associated with Shuffling. We seek answers of the following questions using these experiments:

- Does Shuffling achieve better performance for multithreaded programs than modern OS such as Solaris which is oblivious of the lock contention among multiple threads belonging to an application?
- How does Shuffling perform compared to the state-of-the art cache contention management technque [3] and PBind (pinning one thread to core)?
- Is Shuffling effective in running multiple multithreaded programs simultaneously on multisocket systems?

We compare Shuffling with the following:

(i) Solaris -- the default Oracle Solaris 11.

(ii) DINO[3] is a state-of-the-art cache contention management technique. It reduces cache contention (LLC miss rate) by separating memory intensive threads by scheduling them on different sockets of a multicore machine. By combining low memory-intensive threads with high memory-intensive threads, the cache pressure is balanced across sockets and thus overall cache miss-rate is reduced.

(iii) PSets only permits intra-socket migration of threads, i.e. threads can migrate from one core to another on the same Socket. PSets scheduling essentially divides threads into four groups at the beginning of execution and assigns them to four Sockets. That is assigning threads 1 to 16 to Socket(0), threads 17 to 32 to Socket(1), threads 33 to 48 to Socket(2), and threads 49 to 64 to Socket(3). PSets neither changes the groups of threads nor migrate threads between the groups.

(iv) PBind is nothing but the commonly used one-thread-per-core Binding (or pinning) model, i.e. it does not allow any thread migrations. Using pbind(1) utility, we bind 64 threads to 64 cores, one thread per core. The difference between PSets and PBind is that thread migrations are allowed *within the groups (or processors)* with Psets.

4.1 Experimental Setup

Our experimental setup consists of a 64-core machine running Oracle Solaris 11. Figure 2 shows its configuration. We have chosen Solaris OS as its Memory Placement Optimization feature and Chip Multithreading optimization allow to effectively support multicore multiprocessor systems with large number of cores. Specifically, Solaris kernel is aware of the latency topology of the hardware via locality groups that guides scheduling and resource allocation decisions. It provides several effective low-overhead observability tools (e.g., DTrace [8]). Solaris uses next touch memory allocation policy [26]. All programs considered use pthreads and pthreads use adaptive_mutex locks (spin-then-block policy) [21].

Benchmarks. We evaluate Shuffling using a wide variety of 33 multithreaded programs including SPEC jbb2005, PBZIP2, and programs from PARSEC, SPEC OMP2001, and SPLASH2 suites. The implementations of PARSEC programs and SPALSH2 are based upon *pthreads* and we ran them using native inputs (i.e., the largest inputs available). SPEC OMP2001 programs were run on medium sized inputs. SPEC jbb2005 (JBB) with single JVM is used in all our experiments.

We present detailed performance data for 20 programs of Figure 1. These programs have substantial parallelism and high lock times. For the remaining 13 programs (of all the 33 programs) with low lock times (i.e., less than 5%), data is presented to simply show that their performance is unaffected by Shuffling. We also exclude programs with very short running times (< 10 seconds).

Performance Metrics. We ran each experiment 10 times and present average and coefficient of variation (CV) results from the 10 runs. Coefficient of variation is defined as the ratio of the standard deviation to the mean. The performance metrics we use are: *percentage reduction in running time* for all the programs except SPECjbb2005 (*improvement in throughput*). We ran programs with 64 threads to use all four Sockets in all these experiments.

Table 2: Performance improvements relative to Solaris. Shuffling improves performance up to 54% and an average of 13%. Shuffling significantly outperforms DINO, PSets, and Pbind.

	Performance Improvement (%)			
Program	**Shuffling**	**DINO**	**PSets**	**PBind**
BT	54.1	-5.0	-2.0	-3.3
FA	6.0	2.1	7.0	-12.7
FS	12.0	-13.1	1.1	1.0
SC	29.0	6.0	-13.0	-15.0
AM	9.3	-11.0	1.0	-115.0
AS	13.0	-21.0	4.6	-2.3
AL	13.2	-17.0	-1.0	-95.0
EQ	9.0	-6.0	-0.1	-2.3
FM	10.7	-5.8	2.0	1.0
GA	4.0	-9.0	-0.1	2.5
GL	9.1	-5.1	0.1	-4.6
MG	8.8	-8.0	1.0	-11.8
SM	4.7	-5.0	0.1	1.9
WW	5.2	-6.0	-2.0	-17.2
OC	13.4	3.1	4.2	2.1
RT	4.0	-10.8	2.0	-4.0
RX	19.0	5.0	-13.0	-7.4
VL	12.8	-7.0	2.8	-1.0
PB	13.0	11.2	-12.9	-21.0
JB	14.0	-2.0	-1.0	-7.4

4.2 Performance Benefits

As we can see in Table 2, Shuffling significantly outperforms default Solaris as well as all other techniques. Substantial performance improvements (13% on average) are observed over the default Solaris. For the *bodytrack (*BT*)* program the improvement is the highest -- around 54%. The throughput of SPEC jbb2005 (JB) is improved by 14%. The programs that exhibit high lock contention get high performance improvements with Shuffling. PSets is slightly better than DINO and it also outperforms Shuffling for the low memory intensive and low lock contention program, FA. Shuffling achieves low performance improvements for the programs (e.g., SM) with large working sets. This is because of the tradeoff between sacrificed cache locality and improved lock acquisition times.

However, both PSets and DINO give worse performance for several programs even when compared to the default Solaris scheduler. DINO outperforms Solaris for programs with low lock contention -- programs PB, RX, FA, and SC. Compared to Solaris, DINO gives better performance for 25% of the programs and PSets for 40% of the programs. However, the default Solaris scheduler is better on average compared to both DINO and PSets scheduling techniques. Though DINO is effective for a mix of *single threaded* workloads where half of the threads are memory-intensive and other half are CPU-intensive, it may not work well for multithreaded programs with *high lock contention.* One can view Shuffling and DINO as complementary techniques that can be potentially combined to further improve performance -- using DINO for lock contention free, but memory intensive programs.

Figure 9 shows lock times and LLC miss rates of the 20 programs. As we can see, Shuffling reduces both the lock times and LLC miss rates compared to Solaris, and thus improves performance. Moreover, as we can see in Figure 10,

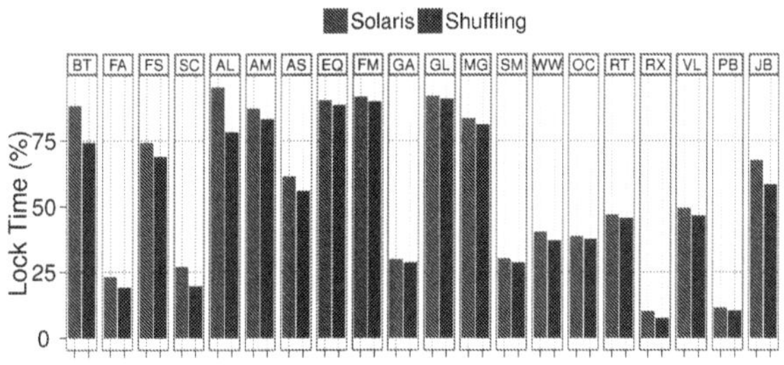

(a) Lock times.

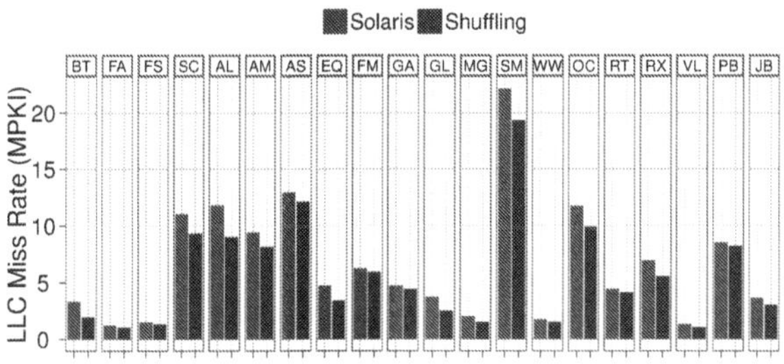

(b) LLC miss rates.

Figure 9: Shuffling reduces both lock times and LLC misses.

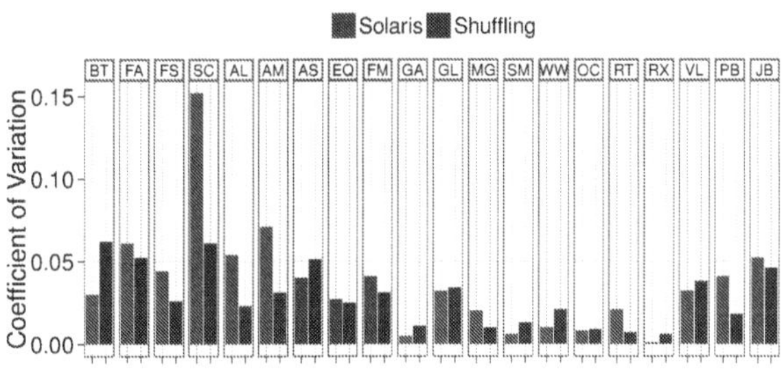

Figure 10: Shuffling reduces performance variation.

the performance variation is low (coefficient of variation $<$ 0.1) for most of the programs with both Solaris and Shuffling.

4.2.1 Why PBind Degrades Performance?

As we can see in Table 2, PBind (pinning one thread per core) significantly degrades performance of several programs compared to the other algorithms. Specifically, PBind gives poor performance for programs with high lock contention on multicore multiprocessor systems with a large number of cores. As the threads of a multithreaded program do not migrate across Sockets of a multicore multiprocessor system with PBind, the frequency of high overhead lock transfers between Sockets increases compared to the default Solaris. This leads to an increase of LLC misses on the critical path of the multithreaded program, which leads to degraded performance [34].

4.2.2 Shuffling the remaining 13 programs.

While the above detailed performance data is for the 20 programs with high lock times, we also applied Shuffling to the remaining 13 programs (of all the 33 programs). We divide these 13 programs into two groups: 1) with low lock times and 2) with very short running times. The programs in the first group have low lock times (less than 5% of the execution time) because the serial part of the execution, executed by the main thread, accounts for 90% to 95% of the execution time -- the programs are blackscholes, dedup, canneal, ferret, x264, vips, and raytrace from PARSEC. The purpose of this experiment was to determine if Shuffling can hurt performance when it is applied to programs where it is not needed. We observed that the change in execution time was insignificant, i.e. less than 0.5%. This is not surprising as, when lock times are small, the cost of Shuffling is simply the cost of monitoring as no thread migrations are triggered. The programs in the second group have very short running times (between 2 secs and 5 secs) -- the programs are barnes, fft, fmm, lu, radiocity, and water from SPLASH2.

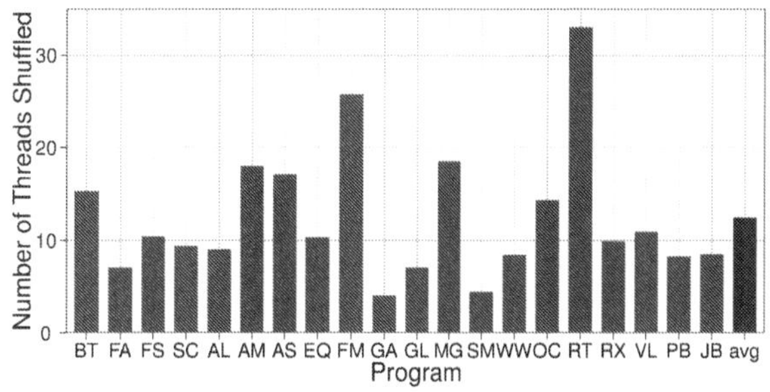

Figure 11: The degree of Shuffling.

4.3 Overhead of Shuffling

Now let us consider the overhead of Shuffling. The cost of monitoring thread lock times is very low – around 1% of the CPU utilization can be attributed to the monitoring task. The cost of migrating threads during shuffling is also small. The bar graph in Figure 11 shows the average number of threads shuffled (across Sockets) in a single shuffle operation for each of the programs. This number ranges from a minimum of 4 threads for GA to a maximum of 32 threads for RT. Across all the programs, the average is 12.4 threads being migrated during each shuffling operation. Since the total number of threads is 64, this represents around 19% of the threads. The system call for changing the binding of a single thread from cores in one CPU to cores in another CPU is around 29 microseconds. Therefore every 500 milliseconds Shuffling spends around 360 microseconds (29×12.4) on changing the binding of migrated threads. Thus, this represents 0.0007% of the execution time. Therefore, the overhead of Shuffling is negligible.

4.4 Time Varying Behavior of Degree of Shuffling

Finally we study the time varying behavior of thread shuffling as observed throughout the executions of the programs. In Figure 12 the number of threads that are shuffled is plotted over the entire execution of the programs. We see several different types of behavior if we examine the behavior following the startup period, i.e. the initial period of execution. For some benchmarks (BT, FA, AM, AS, MG, RT, RX, VL, WW) the execution can be divided into *small number of intervals* such that during each interval the number of threads shuffled *varies within a narrow range*. For a few benchmarks (FS, AL, SC, EQ, GA, GL, SM) the number of threads shuffled *varies rapidly within a narrow range* after the initial execution period. For some programs (PB, JB) the number of threads shuffled *varies rapidly across a wide range*. Finally, for some programs *often no threads are migrated* – (GA, GL, SC, SM).

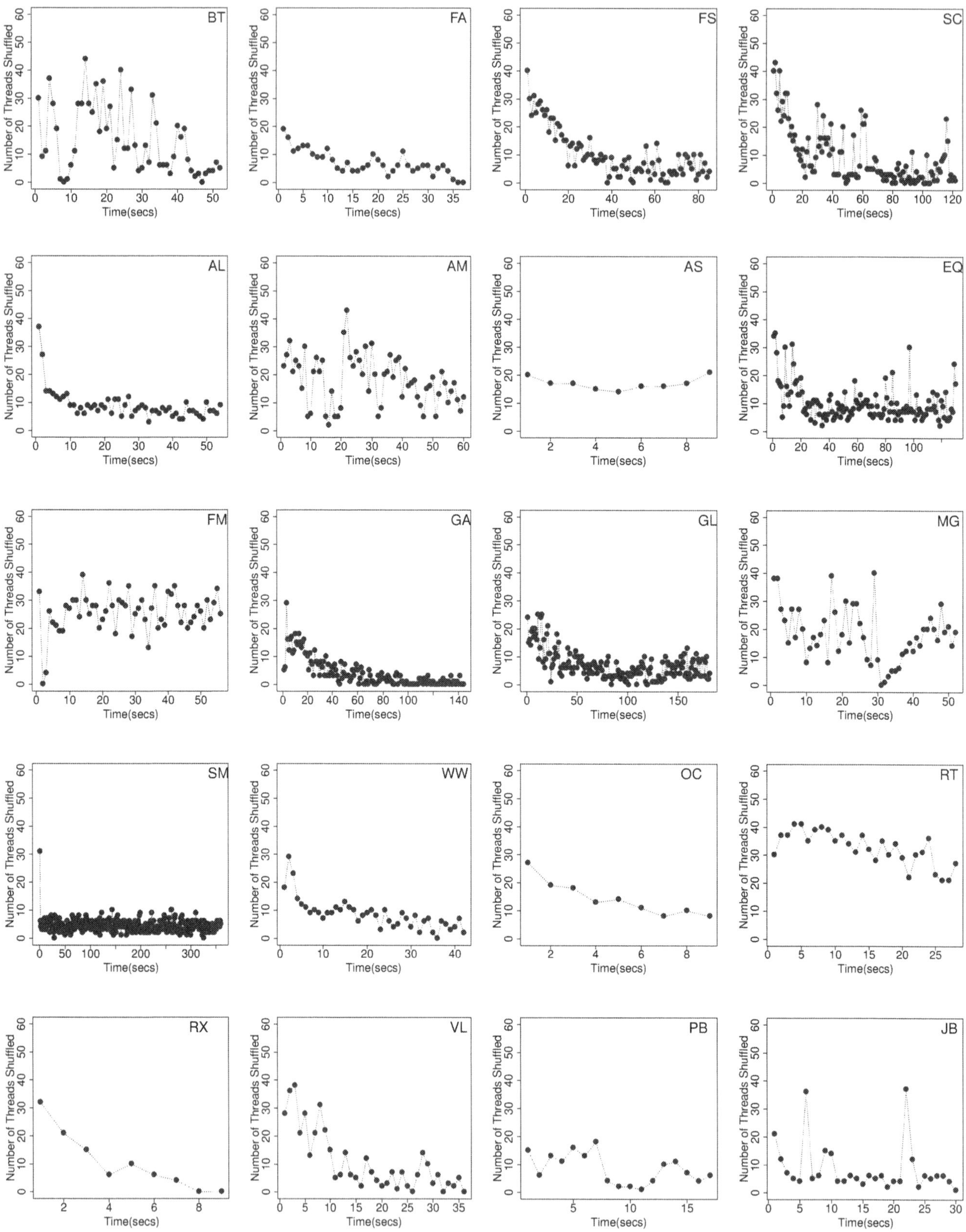

Figure 12: Time varying behaviour of degree of thread shuffling. The number of threads that are shuffled every 500 milliseconds is plotted over the entire execution of the programs.

Table 3: Shuffling multiple applications. Running times of the programs are expressed in seconds (s).

	FS	MG	AL	AM	FS	AL
Solaris	106s	74s	71s	72s	104s	69s
Shuffling	83s	67s	62s	65s	82s	62s
Improvement	21.7%	9.5%	12.7%	9.7%	21.2%	10.1%

4.5 Multiple Applications

So far we have considered performance of a single application being run on the system. In practice multiple multithreaded applications may be run simultaneously on the system. Next we ran pairs of programs, each using all 4 Sockets, to see if Shuffling improves performance of both applications. We ran a pair of compute intensive applications (FS and MG); a pair of memory intensive applications (AL and AM); and a combination of compute (FS) and memory (AL) intensive applications. The results of running these application pairs with Solaris 11 and Shuffling are presented in Table 3 (*s* next to the times indicates seconds). As we can see, in all three cases, both applications benefit from Shuffling and their performance improvements are: 21.7% and 9.5%; 12.7% and 9.7%; and 21.2% and 10.1%. Therefore we conclude that Shuffling is robust because it is beneficial for the multiple applications that are running on each Socket simultaneously.

5 Related Work

There are many aspects of the lock contention problem and thus range of strategies have been proposed to address lock contention. Three specific approaches proposed in prior work include: *thread migration* [19, 40]; *thread clustering* [50]; and *contention management* [50, 21].

5.1 Thread Migration Techniques

The work most closely related to our work is RCL [19] in which authors make the observation that most multithreaded applications do not scale to the number of cores found in modern multicore architectures, and therefore it may be beneficial to dedicate some of the cores to serving critical sections. While this technique works well for some multithreaded applications, it has the drawback that application must be modified -- critical sections must be identified and reengineered [19]. However, Shuffling does not modify application code and can be applied *on-the-fly* to any application that is run on the system. Moreover, it is also effective for scheduling multiple multithreaded applications and its overhead is negligible.

Another work closely related to our work is [40] in which authors make the observation that, in multicore multiprocessor systems, it may be beneficial to employ thread migration to reduce the execution time cost due to acquiring of locks. They propose a migration technique that is incorporated in the OS thread scheduler. While this technique performs well for a few microbenchmarks [40], for majority of SPLASH2 programs the technique frequently yielded large performance degradation. Our Shuffling technique is superior to [40] as it consistently provided performance improvements across a large set of multithreaded programs including SPLASH2 programs. [13] uses an online model to determine how many cores to allocate to lock intensive programs to reduce lock contention in the kernel space. The idea is to separate lock-intensive kernel tasks from lock-free kernel tasks and control kernel lock contention by allocating appropriate number of cores. Shuffling focuses on reducing lock contention in the user space by adaptively migrating threads across sockets of multicore multi-CPU system. Unlike [13], Shuffling is effective for coscheduling multiple applications.

Cache contention aware scheduling techniques also employ thread migration across Sockets. These techniques are guided by the last-level cache miss-rates [3, 52, 1, 22, 24, 25, 44, 45, 29, 46, 51, 31]. While these techniques are highly effective for workloads consisting of multiple single threaded programs, they are not effective in scheduling threads of a multithreaded program on a cache-coherent multicore multiprocessor system. This is because they do not consider lock contention among the threads of a program while making thread scheduling decisions. Unlike the above, we demonstrate that Shuffling significantly outperforms these techniques and also it very effective in scheduling of threads of multiple multithreaded applications. [16, 35] presents load balancing techniques to improve performance of multithreaded programs.

5.2 Thread Clustering Techniques

A number of thread clustering techniques have been developed to improve program performance [50, 47, 43]. Of these, the technique in [50] is aimed at reducing the overhead caused by lock contention. This is achieved by clustering threads that contend for the same lock and then schedule them on the same processor. The number of threads in a cluster can be large, in fact all threads in an application will be in the same cluster if they are synchronizing on a barrier. Thus, load is no longer balanced, and parallelism is sacrificed. The authors state "it is possible that the performance benefit of reducing contention is greater than the performance benefit of higher parallelism". In contrast, our Shuffling framework maintains load balance and thus does not sacrifice parallelism. Finally, while the approach presented in [50] is effective for server workloads, our approach is more relevant for highly parallel applications.

The clustering techniques in [47, 43] have a different objective. In [47] authors examine thread placement algorithms to group threads that share memory regions together onto the same processor so as to maximize cache sharing and reuse. It is assumed that the shared-region information is known a priori, i.e. this information is not ascertained dynamically. In [43], Tam et al. propose a thread clustering technique to detect shared memory regions dynamically. In contrast, we focus on minimizing lock transfers between Sockets, and thus minimizing *critical* LLC misses of applications running on a multicore multiprocessor machine with a large number of cores.

5.3 Contention Management Techniques

Another cause of performance degradation is *lock-holder* thread preemptions as they slow down the progress of thread holding the lock. In [50] a technique is presented for reducing lock holder preemptions. While it is important to avoid lock-holder preemptions, this technique is complementary to our approach. Preventing lock-holder preemptions reduces the duration for which a thread *holds* the lock while our thread shuffling techniques reduce the time it takes for a thread to *acquire* a lock. [21, 33] propose a load control mechanism to decouple load management from lock contention management. This approach uses blocking to control the number of runnable threads and then spinning in response to contention. While above techniques are aimed at contention management, our work is aimed at reducing the overhead of contention that manifests after the management techniques have been applied.

5.4 Other Works

Complementary to our work are improved locking and synchronization algorithms. In [14, 15, 36] authors propose new locking mechanisms. In contrast, our work focuses on adapting the location of threads across the Sockets of a cache-coherent multicore multiprocessor machine to reduce the lock transfers between Sockets and thus critical LLC misses. In [10] NUMA's impact on performance of different barrier synchronization algorithms is studied but no solutions are proposed. Several researchers [7, 23, 11, 48, 38, 12, 27, 18] studied the impact of NUMA on the performance of parallel applications and developed optimizations and adaptive scheduling techniques. Gupta et al. [18] explored the impact of the scheduling strategies on the caching behavior. Chandra et al. [9], evaluate different scheduling and page migration policies on a cache-coherent multiprocessor system. Sasaki et al. [37] developed a scheduling technique for allocating optimal number of cores to multithreaded programs. None of the above works consider lock-access latency and critical section processing times of threads for effective scheduling them on multicore machines.

6 Conclusions

We demonstrated that the performance of a multithreaded application with high lock contention running on a multicore multiprocessor system is very sensitive to the distribution of threads across multiple Sockets. To address this problem, we presented Shuffling that reduces transfer of locks between Sockets by migrating threads of a multithreaded program across Sockets such that threads seeking locks are more likely to find the locks on the same Socket. Migrating threads between Sockets is preferable to moving locks between Sockets. This is because when multiple threads are contending for locks and shared data, they are not doing useful work and hence the thread migration cost is not expected to impact the execution time. However, lock transfer times are on the critical path of execution and hence preventing lock transfers between Sockets reduces execution time. We evaluated Shuffling with a wide variety of multithreaded programs and the experimental results show that Shuffling achieves up to 54% reduction in execution time and an average reduction of 13%. Moreover it has very low overhead and it does not require any changes to the application source code or the OS kernel.

7 Acknowledgments

This work is supported by National Science Foundation grants CCF-1157377, CCF-0963996, CCF-0905509, and CSR-0912850 to the University of California Riverside.

8 References

[1] M. Bhadauria and S. A. McKee. An Approach to Resource-Aware Co-Scheduling for CMPs. In *ICS*, 2010.

[2] C. Bienia, S. Kumar, J.P. Singh, and K. Li. The PARSEC Benchmark Suite: Characterization and Architectural Implications. In *PACT*, 2008.

[3] S. Blagodurov, S. Zhuravlev, M. Dashti, and A. Fedorova. A Case for NUMA-aware Contention Management on Multicore Systems. In *USENIX ATC*, 2011.

[4] S. Boyd-Wickizer, R. Morris, and M. F. Kaashoek. Reinventing Scheduling for Multicore Systems. In *HotOS*, 2009.

[5] S. Boyd-Wickizer, H. Chen, R. Chen, Y.Mao, F. Kaashoek, R.Morris, A. Pesterev, L. Stein,M.Wu, Y. D. Y. Zhang, and Z. Zhang. Corey: An operating system for many cores. In *OSDI*, 2008.

[6] S. Boyd-Wickizer, A. T. Clements, Y. Mao, A. Pesterev, F. Kaashoek, R.Morris, and N. Zeldovich. An Analysis of Linux Scalability to Many Cores. In *OSDI*, 2010.

[7] T. Brecht. On the Importance of Parallel Application Placement in NUMA Multiprocessors. In *SEDMS*, 1993.

[8] B. Cantrill, M. Shapiro, and A. Leventhal. Dynamic instrumentation of production systems. In *USENIX ATC*, 2004.

[9] R. Chandra, S. Devine, B. Verghese, A. Gupta, and M Rosenblum. Scheduling and page migration for multiprocessor compute servers. In *ASPLOS 1994*.

[10] J. Chen, W. Watson, and W. Mao. Multi-Threading Performance on Commodity Multi-core Processors. In *HPC-Asia*, 2007.

[11] J. Corbalan, X. Martorell, and J. Labarta. Evaluation of the Memory Page Migration Influence in the System Performance: the Case of the SGI O2000. In *SC*, 2003.

[12] J. Corbalan, X. Martorell, and J. Labarta. Performance-driven processor allocation. In *OSDI*, 2000.

[13] Y. Cui, Y. Wang, Y. Chen, and Y.Shi. Lock-contention-aware scheduler: A scalable and energy-efficient method for addressing scalability collapse on multicore systems. In *ACM TACO*, 4, Article 44, Jan. 2013.

[14] D. Dice, V. Marathe, and N. Shavit. Flat Combining NUMA Locks. In *SPAA*, 2011.

[15] D. Dice, V. Marathe, and N. Shavit. Lock Cohorting: A General Technique for Designing NUMA Locks. In *PPoPP*, 2012.

[16] X. Ding, K. Wang, P.B. Gibbons, and X. Zhang. BWS: balanced work stealing for time-sharing multicores. In *Eurosys*, 2012.

[17] E. Frachtenberg, D. G. Feitelson, F. Petrini, and J. Fernandez. Adaptive parallel job scheduling with flexible coscheduling. In *IEEE TPDS*, (2005), 16(11).

[18] A. Gupta, A. Tucker, and S. Urushibara. The Impact Of Operating System Scheduling Policies And Synchronization Methods On Performance Of Parallel Applications. In *SIGMETRICS*, 1991.

[19] L. Jean-Pierre, D. Florian, T. Gaël, L. Julia and M. Gilles. Remote core locking: migrating critical-section execution to improve the performance of multithreaded applications. In *USENIX ATC*, 2012.

[20] J. A. Joao, M. A. Suleman, O. Mutlu, and Y. N. Patt. Bottleneck Identification and Scheduling in Multithreaded Applications. In *ASPLOS*, 2012.

[21] R. Johnson, R. Stoica, A. Ailamaki, and T. C. Mowry. Decoupling contention management from scheduling. In *ASPLOS*, 2010.

[22] R. Knauerhase, P. Brett, B. Hohlt, T. Li, and S. Hahn. Using OS Observations to Improve Performance in Multicore Systems. In *IEEE Micro*, 2008

[23] R.P. Larowe, C. S. Ellis, and M. A. Holliday. Evaluation of NUMA Memory Management Through Modeling and Measurements. In *IEEE TPDS*, (1991), 688 -- 701.

[24] Z. Majo and T. R. Gross. Memory management in NUMA multicore systems: Trapped between cache contention and interconnect overhead. In *ISMM*, 2011.

[25] J. Mars, L. Tang, R. Hundt, K. Skadron, and M. L. Soffa. Bubble-up: Increasing utilization in modern warehouse scale computers via sensible co-locations. In *MICRO*, 2011.

[26] R. McDougall and J. Mauro. Solaris Internals. Prentice Hall Publications, Second Edition, 2006.

[27] R. McGregor, C. Antonopoulos, and D. Nikolopoulos. Scheduling algorithms for effective thread pairing on hybrid multiprocessors. In *IPDPS*, 2005.

[28] A. Mendelson and F. Gabbay. 2001. The effect of seance communication on multiprocessing systems. In *ACM Trans. Comput. Syst.* 19, 2 (May 2001), 252-281.

[29] A. Merkel, J. Stoess, and F. Bellosa, Resource-conscious scheduling for energy efficiency on multicore processors. In *Eurosys*, 2010.

[30] PBZIP2. `http://compression.ca/pbzip2/`

[31] K. K. Pusukuri, D. Vengerov, A. Fedorova, and V .Kalogeraki. FACT: a framework for adaptive contention-aware thread migrations. In *CF*, 2011.

[32] K. K. Pusukuri, R. Gupta, L. N. Bhuyan. Thread Reinforcer: Dynamically Determining Number of Threads via OS Level Monitoring. In IISWC, 2011.

[33] K. K. Pusukuri, R. Gupta, L. N. Bhuyan. No More Backstabbing... A Faithful Scheduling Policy for Multithreaded Programs. In *PACT*, 2011.

[34] K.K. Pusukuri and D. Johnson. Has one-thread-per-core binding model become obsolete for multithreaded programs running on multicore systems. In *USENIX HotPar*, 2013.

[35] K. K. Pusukuri, R. Gupta, L. N. Bhuyan. An Effective OS Load Balancing Technique for Multicore Multiprocessor Systems. Technical Report, Sept. 2012. University of California, Riverside.

[36] Z. Radovic and E. Hagersten. RH Lock: A Scalable Hierarchical Spin Lock. In *WMPI*, 2012.

[37] H. Sasaki, T. Tanimoto, K. Inoue, and H. Nakamura. Scalability-based manycore partitioning. In *PACT*, 2012.

[38] C. Severance and R. Enbody. Comparing gang scheduling with dynamic space sharing on symmetric multiprocessors using automatic self-allocating threads. In *IPPS*, 1997.

[39] A. Snavely, D.M. Tullsen, G. Voelker. Symbiotic Job scheduling For A Simultaneous Multithreading Processor. In *ASPLOS*, 2000.

[40] S. Sridharan, B. Keck, R. Murphy, S. Chandra, and P. Kogge. Thread migration to improve synchronization performance. In Workshop on Operating System Interference in High Performance Applications, 2006

[41] SPEC and the benchmark names SPEC OMP2001, SPEC jbb2005 are registered trademarks of the Standard Performance Evaluation Corporation. For more information, see `www.spec.org`.

[42] P. Sweazey and A. J. Smith. A Class of Compatible Cache Consistency Protocols and Their Support by the IEEE Futurebus. In *ISCA*, 1986.

[43] D. Tam, R. Azimi, and M. Stumm. Thread Clustering: Sharing-Aware Scheduling on SMP-CMP-SMT Multiprocessors. In *Eurosys*, 2007.

[44] L. Tang, J. Mars, N. Vachharajani, R. Hundt, and M. L. Soffa. The Impact of Memory Subsystem Resource Sharing on Datacenter Applications.. In *ISCA*, 2011.

[45] L. Tang, J. Mars, and M. L. Soffa. Compiling For Niceness: Mitigating Contention for QOS in Warehouse Scale Computers. In *CGO*, 2012.

[46] L. Tang, J. Mars, X. Zhang, R. Hagmann, R. Hundt, and E. Tune. Optimizing GoogleâĂŹs Warehouse Scale Computers: The NUMA Experience. In *HPCA*, 2013.

[47] R. Thekkath and S. J. Eggers. Impact of Sharing-Based Thread Placement on Multithreaded Architectures. In *ISCA*, 1994.

[48] VMware ESX Server 2 NUMA Support. White paper. `http://www.vmware.com/pdf/esx2_NUMA.pdf.`

[49] S. C. Woo, M. Ohara, E. Torrie, J. P. Singh, and A. Gupta. The SPLASH-2 programs: characterization and methodological considerations. In *ISCA*, 1995.

[50] F. Xian, W. Srisa-an, and H. Jiang. Contention-aware scheduler: unlocking execution parallelism in multithreaded java programs. In *OOPSLA*, 2008.

[51] X. Xiang, B. Bao, C. Ding, K. Shen: Cache Conscious Task Regrouping on Multicore Processors. In *CCGRID*, 2012.

[52] S. Zhuravlev, S. Blagodurov, and A. Fedorova. Addressing Shared Resource Contention in Multicore Processors via Scheduling. In *ASPLOS*, 2010.

Keynote

Domain-Specific Models for Innovation in Analytics

Bob Blainey
Hardware Acceleration Laboratory, IBM Software Group
Markham, Ontario, Canada

Abstract

Big data is a transformational force for businesses and organizations of every stripe. The ability to rapidly and accurately derive insights from massive amounts of data is becoming a critical competitive differentiator so it is driving continuous innovation among business analysts, data scientists, and computer engineers. Two of the most important success factors for analytic techniques are the ability to quickly develop and incrementally evolve them to suit changing business needs and the ability to scale these techniques using parallel computing to process huge collections of data. Unfortunately, these goals are often at odds with each other because innovation at the algorithm and data model level requires a combination of domain knowledge and expertise in data analysis while achieving high scale demands expertise in parallel computing, cloud computing and even hardware acceleration. In this talk, I will examine various approaches to bridging these two goals, with a focus on domain-specific models that simultaneously improve the agility of analytics development and the achievement of efficient parallel scaling.

PACT'14, August 24–27, 2014, Edmonton, AB, Canada.
ACM 978-1-4503-2809-8/14/08.
http://dx.doi.org/10.1145/2628071.2635931 2

ACM Classification:
D.1.0 Software, PROGRAMMING TECHNIQUES: General
J.0 Computer Applications, GENERAL

Author Keywords: Application Development, analytics, domain-specific models, parallel computing, parallel scaling

Bio

Bob Blainey is an IBM Fellow and the technical architect of the Hardware Acceleration Laboratory in IBM's Software Group. Bob has been with IBM for over 20 years, with a consistent focus on deep optimization of software for IBM systems. He spent many years working on compiler-based transformations for parallelism and for high performance on systems, at the microprocessor, node and cluster level. More recently, Bob has had a focus on re-imagining the relationship between software and hardware in the post-scaling world, which includes optimization of IBM systems and software in the short term and the creation of new system structures in the longer term using disruptive technologies.

OpenTuner: An Extensible Framework for Program Autotuning

Jason Ansel Shoaib Kamil Kalyan Veeramachaneni
Jonathan Ragan-Kelley Jeffrey Bosboom
Una-May O'Reilly Saman Amarasinghe
Massachusetts Institute of Technology
Cambridge, MA
{jansel, skamil, kalyan, jrk, jbosboom, unamay, saman}@csail.mit.edu

ABSTRACT

Program autotuning has been shown to achieve better or more portable performance in a number of domains. However, autotuners themselves are rarely portable between projects, for a number of reasons: using a domain-informed search space representation is critical to achieving good results; search spaces can be intractably large and require advanced machine learning techniques; and the landscape of search spaces can vary greatly between different problems, sometimes requiring domain specific search techniques to explore efficiently.

This paper introduces OpenTuner, a new open source framework for building domain-specific multi-objective program autotuners. OpenTuner supports fully-customizable configuration representations, an extensible technique representation to allow for domain-specific techniques, and an easy to use interface for communicating with the program to be autotuned. A key capability inside OpenTuner is the use of ensembles of disparate search techniques simultaneously; techniques that perform well will dynamically be allocated a larger proportion of tests. We demonstrate the efficacy and generality of OpenTuner by building autotuners for 7 distinct projects and 16 total benchmarks, showing speedups over prior techniques of these projects of up to 2.8× with little programmer effort.

1. INTRODUCTION

Program autotuning is increasingly being used in domains such as high performance computing and graphics to optimize programs. Program autotuning augments traditional human-guided optimization by offloading some or all of the search for an optimal program implementation to an automated search technique. Rather than optimizing a program directly, the programmer expresses a search space of possible implementations and optimizations. Autotuning can often make the optimization process more efficient as autotuners are able to search larger spaces than is possible by hand. Autotuning also provides performance portability, as the autotuning process can easily be re-run on new machines which require different sets of optimizations. Finally, multi-objective autotuning can be used to trade off between performance and accuracy, or other criteria such as energy consumption and memory usage, and provide programs which meet given performance or quality of service targets.

While the practice of autotuning has increased in popularity, autotuners themselves often remain relatively simple and project specific. There are three main challenges which make the development of autotuning frameworks difficult.

The first challenge is using the right configuration representation for the problem. Configurations can contain parameters that vary from a single integer for a block size to a much more complex type such as an expression tree representing a set of instructions. The creator of the autotuner must find ways to represent their complex domain-specific data structures and constraints. When these data structures are naively mapped to simpler representations, such as a point in high dimensional space, locality information is lost which makes the search problem much more difficult. Picking the right representation for the search space is critical to having an effective autotuner. To date, all autotuners that have used a representation other than the simplest ones have had custom project-specific representations.

The second challenge is the size of the valid configuration space. While some prior autotuners have worked hard to prune the configuration space, we have found that for many problems excessive search space pruning will miss out on non-intuitive good configurations. We believe providing all the valid configurations of these search spaces is better than artificially constraining search spaces and possibly missing optimal solutions. Search spaces can be very large, up to 10^{3600} possible configurations for one of our benchmarks. Full exhaustive search of such a space will not complete in human lifetimes! Thus, intelligent machine learning techniques are required to seek out a good result with a small number of experiments.

The third challenge is the landscape of the configuration space. If the configuration space is a monotonic function, a search technique biased towards this type of search space

PACT'14, August 24–27, 2014, Edmonton, AB, Canada.

http://dx.doi.org/10.1145/2628071.2628092.

(such as a hill climber) will be able to find the optimal configuration. If the search space is discontinuous and haphazard an evolution algorithm may perform better. However, in practice search spaces are much more complex, with discontinuities, high dimensionality, plateaus, hills with some of the configuration parameters strongly coupled and some others independent from each other. A search technique that is optimal in one type of configuration space may fail to locate an adequate configuration in another. It is difficult to provide a robust system that performs well in a variety of situations. Additionally, many application domains will have domain-specific search techniques (such as scheduling or blocking heuristics) which may be critical to finding an optimal solution efficiently. This has caused most prior autotuners to use customized search techniques tailored to their specific problem. This requires machine learning expertise in addition to the individual domain expertise to build an autotuner for a system. We believe that this is one of the main reasons that, while autotuners are recognized as critical for performance optimization, they have not seen commodity adoption.

In this paper we present OpenTuner, a new framework for building domain-specific program autotuners. OpenTuner features an extensible configuration and technique representation able to support complex and user-defined data types and custom search heuristics. It contains a library of predefined data types and search techniques to make it easy to setup a new project. Thus, OpenTuner solves the custom configuration problem by providing not only a library of data types that will be sufficient for most projects, but also extensible data types that can be used to support more complex domain specific representations when needed.

A core concept in OpenTuner is the use of *ensembles* of search techniques. Many search techniques (both built in and user-defined) are run at the same time, each testing candidate configurations. Techniques which perform well by finding better configurations are allocated larger budgets of tests to run, while techniques which perform poorly are allocated fewer tests or disabled entirely. Techniques are able to share results using a common results database to constructively help each other in finding an optimal solution. algorithms add results from other techniques as new members of their population. To allocate tests between techniques we use an optimal solution to the *multi-armed bandit* problem using area under the curve credit assignment. Ensembles of techniques solve the large and complex search space problem by providing both a robust solutions to many types of large search spaces and a way to seamlessly incorporate domain specific search techniques.

1.1 Contributions

This paper makes the following contributions:

- To the best of our knowledge, OpenTuner is the first to introduce a general framework to describe complex search spaces for program autotuning.
- OpenTuner introduces the concept of ensembles of search techniques to program autotuning, which allow many search techniques to work together to find an optimal solution.
- OpenTuner provides more sophisticated search techniques than typical program autotuners. This enables expanded uses of program autotuning to solve more complex search problems and pushes the state of the art forward in program autotuning in a way that can easily be adopted by other projects.
- We demonstrate the versatility of our framework by building autotuners for 7 distinct projects and demonstrate the effectiveness of the system with 16 total benchmarks, showing speedups over existing techniques of up to 2.8×.
- We show that OpenTuner is able to succeed both in massively large search spaces, exceeding 10^{3600} possible configurations in size, and in smaller search spaces using less than 2% of the tests required for exhaustive search.

2. RELATED WORK

Package	Domain	Search Method
Active Harmony [31]	Runtime System	Nelder-Mead
ATLAS [34]	Dense Linear Algebra	Exhaustive
FFTW [14]	Fast Fourier Transform	Exhaustive/Dynamic Prog.
Insieme [19]	Compiler	Differential Evolution
OSKI [33]	Sparse Linear Algebra	Exhaustive+Heuristic
PATUS [9]	Stencil Computations	Nelder-Mead or Evolutionary
PetaBricks [4]	Programming Language	Bottom-up Evolutionary
Sepya [21]	Stencil Computations	Random-Restart Gradient Ascent
SPIRAL [28]	DSP Algorithms	Pareto Active Learning

Figure 1: Summary of selected related projects using autotuning

A number of offline empirical autotuning frameworks have been developed for building efficient, portable libraries in specific domains; selected projects and techniques used are summarized in Figure 1. ATLAS [34] utilizes empirical autotuning to produce an optimized matrix multiply routine. FFTW [14] uses empirical autotuning to combine solvers for FFTs. Other autotuning systems include SPIRAL [28] for digital signal processing PATUS [9] and Sepya [21] for stencil computations, and OSKI [33] for sparse matrix kernels.

The area of iterative compilation contains many projects that use different machine learning techniques to optimize lower level compiler optimizations [2, 15, 26, 1]. These projects change both the order that compiler passes are applied and the types of passes that are applied.

In the dynamic autotuning space, there have been a number of systems developed [18, 17, 22, 6, 8, 5] that focus on creating applications that can monitor and automatically tune themselves to optimize a particular objective. Many of these systems employ a control systems based autotuner that operates on a linear model of the application being tuned. For example, PowerDial [18] converts static configuration parameters that already exist in a program into dynamic knobs that can be tuned at runtime, with the goal of trading QoS guarantees for meeting performance and power usage goals. The system uses an offline learning stage to construct a linear model of the choice configuration space which can be subsequently tuned using a linear control system. The system employs the heartbeat framework [16] to provide feedback to the control system. A similar technique is employed in [17], where a simpler heuristic-based controller dynamically adjusts the degree of loop perforation performed on a target application to trade QoS for performance.

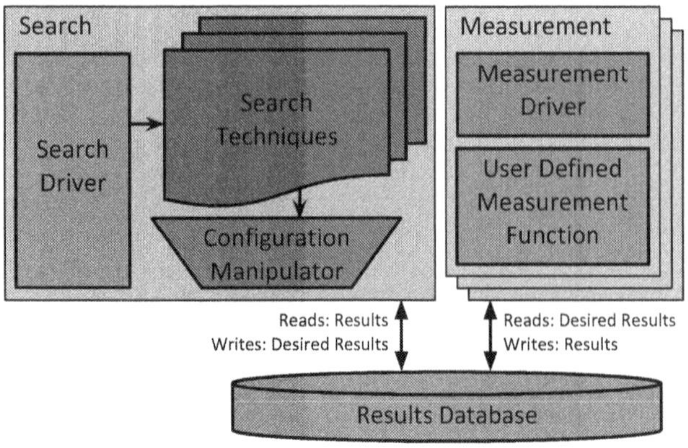

Figure 2: Overview of the major components in the OpenTuner framework.

Related to our Mario benchmark, Murphy [23] presents algorithms for playing NES games based on example human inputs. In contrast, this paper's Mario example has no knowledge of the game except for pixels moved to the right.

3. THE OPENTUNER FRAMEWORK

Our terminology reflects that the autotuning problem is cast as a search problem. The search space is made up of *configurations*, which are concrete assignments of a set of *parameters*. Parameters can be *primitive* such as an integer or *complex* such as a permutation of a list. When the performance, output accuracy, or other metrics of a configuration are measured (typically by running it in a domain-specific way), we call this measurement a *result*. *Search techniques* are methods for exploring the search space and make requests for measurement called *desired results*. Search techniques can change configurations using a user-defined *configuration manipulator*, which also includes *parameters* corresponding directly the parameters in the configuration. Some parameters include *manipulators*, which are opaque functions that make stochastic changes to a specific parameter in a configuration.

Figure 2 provides an overview of the major components in OpenTuner. The *search* process includes techniques, which use the user defined configuration manipulator in order to read and write configurations. The *measurement* processes evaluate candidate configurations using a user defined measurement function. These two components communicate exclusively through a *results database* used to record all results collected during the tuning process, as well as providing ability to perform multiple measurements in parallel.

3.1 OpenTuner Usage

To implement an autotuner with OpenTuner, first, the user must define the search space by creating a *configuration manipulator*. This configuration manipulator includes a set of parameter objects which OpenTuner will search over. Second, the user must define a *run* function which evaluates the fitness of a given configuration in the search space to produce a result. These must be implemented in a small Python program in order to interface with the OpenTuner API.

Figure 3 shows an example of using OpenTuner to search over the space of GCC compiler flags in order to minimize

```
import opentuner
from opentuner import ConfigurationManipulator
from opentuner import EnumParameter
from opentuner import IntegerParameter
from opentuner import MeasurementInterface
from opentuner import Result

GCC_FLAGS = [
  'align-functions', 'align-jumps', 'align-labels',
  'branch-count-reg', 'branch-probabilities',
  # ... (176 total)
]

# (name, min, max)
GCC_PARAMS = [
  ('early-inlining-insns', 0, 1000),
  ('gcse-cost-distance-ratio', 0, 100),
  # ... (145 total)
]

class GccFlagsTuner(MeasurementInterface):

  def manipulator(self):
    """
    Define the search space by creating a
    ConfigurationManipulator
    """
    manipulator = ConfigurationManipulator()
    manipulator.add_parameter(
      IntegerParameter('opt_level', 0, 3))
    for flag in GCC_FLAGS:
      manipulator.add_parameter(
        EnumParameter(flag,
                      ['on', 'off', 'default']))
    for param, min, max in GCC_PARAMS:
      manipulator.add_parameter(
        IntegerParameter(param, min, max))
    return manipulator

  def run(self, desired_result, input, limit):
    """
    Compile and run a given configuration then
    return performance
    """
    cfg = desired_result.configuration.data
    gcc_cmd = 'g++ raytracer.cpp -o ./tmp.bin'
    gcc_cmd += ' -O{0}'.format(cfg['opt_level'])
    for flag in GCC_FLAGS:
      if cfg[flag] == 'on':
        gcc_cmd += ' -f{0}'.format(flag)
      elif cfg[flag] == 'off':
        gcc_cmd += ' -fno-{0}'.format(flag)
    for param, min, max in GCC_PARAMS:
      gcc_cmd += ' --param {0}={1}'.format(
        param, cfg[param])

    compile_result = self.call_program(gcc_cmd)
    assert compile_result['returncode'] == 0
    run_result = self.call_program('./tmp.bin')
    assert run_result['returncode'] == 0
    return Result(time=run_result['time'])

if __name__ == '__main__':
  argparser = opentuner.default_argparser()
  GccFlagsTuner.main(argparser.parse_args())
```

Figure 3: GCC/G++ flags autotuner using OpenTuner.

execution time of the resulting program. In Section 4, we present results on an expanded version of this example which obtains up to 2.8x speedup over `-O3`.

This example tunes three types of flags to GCC. First it chooses between the four optimization levels `-O0`, `-O1`, `-O2`, `-O3`. Second, for 176 flags listed on line 8 it decides between turning the flag on (with `-fFLAG`), off (with `-fno-FLAG`), or omitting the flag to allow the default value to take precedence. Including the default value as a choice is not necessary for completeness, but speeds up convergence and results in shorter command lines. Finally, it assigns a bounded integer value to the 145 parameters on line 15 with the `--param NAME=VALUE` command line option.

The method `manipulator` (line 23), is called once at startup and creates a `ConfigurationManipulator` object which defines the search space of GCC flags. All accesses to configurations by search techniques are done through the configuration manipulator. For optimization level, an `IntegerParameter` between 0 and 3 is created. For each flag, a `EnumParameter` is created which can take the values `on`, `off`, and `default`. Finally, for the remaining bounded GCC parameters, an `IntegerParameter` is created with the appropriate range.

The method `run` (line 40) implements the measurement function for configurations. First, the configuration is realized as a specific command line to `g++`. Next, this `g++` command line is run to produce an executable, `tmp.bin`, which is then run using `call_program`. `call_program` is a convenience function which runs and measures the execution time of the given program. Finally, a `Result` is constructed and returned, which is a database record type containing many other optional fields such as `time`, `accuracy`, and `energy`. By default OpenTuner minimizes the `time` field, but this can be customized.

3.2 Search Techniques

To provide robust search, OpenTuner includes techniques that can handle many types of search spaces and runs a collection of search techniques at the same time. Techniques which perform well are allocated more tests, while techniques which perform poorly are allocated fewer tests. Techniques share results through the results database, so that improvements made by one technique can benefit other techniques. This sharing occurs in technique-specific ways; for example, evolutionary techniques add results found by other techniques as members of their population. OpenTuner techniques are meant to be extended. Users can define custom techniques which implement domain-specific heuristics and add them to *ensembles* of pre-defined techniques.

Ensembles of techniques are created by instantiating a *meta technique*, which is a technique made up of a collection of other techniques. The OpenTuner search driver interacts with a single *root* technique, which is typically a meta technique. When the meta technique gets allocated tests, it incrementally decides how to divide theses tests among its sub-techniques. OpenTuner contains an extensible class hierarchy of techniques and meta techniques, which can be combined together and used in autotuners.

3.2.1 AUC Bandit Meta Technique

In addition to a number of simple meta techniques, such as round robin, OpenTuner's core meta technique used in results is the *multi-armed bandit with sliding window, area under the curve credit assignment* (AUC Bandit) meta technique. A similar technique was used in [25] in the different context of online operator selection. It is based on an optimal solution to the multi-armed bandit problem [12]. The multi-armed bandit problem is the problem of picking levers to pull on a slot machine with many arms each with an unknown payout probability. The sliding window makes the technique only consider a subset of history (the length of the window) when making decisions. This meta-technique encapsulates a fundamental trade-off between *exploitation* (using the best known technique) and *exploration* (estimating the performance of all techniques).

The AUC Bandit meta technique assigns each test to the technique, t, defined by the formula $\arg\max_t(AUC_t + C\sqrt{\frac{2\lg|H|}{H_t}})$ where $|H|$ is the length of the sliding history window, H_t is the number of times the technique has been used in that history window, C is a constant controlling the exploration/exploitation trade-off, and AUC_t is the credit assignment term quantifying the performance of the technique in the sliding window. The second term in the equation is the exploration term which gets smaller the more often a technique is used.

The area under the curve credit assignment mechanism, based on [13], draws a curve by looking at the history for a specific technique and looking only at if a technique yielded a new global best or not. If the technique yielded a new global best, a upward line is drawn, otherwise a flat line is drawn. The area under this curve (scaled to a maximum value of 1) is the total credit attributed to the technique. This credit assignment mechanism can be described more precisely by the formula: $AUC_t = \frac{2}{|V_t|(|V_t|+1)}\sum_{i=1}^{|V_t|} iV_{t,i}$ where V_t is the list of uses of t in the sliding window history. $V_{t,i}$ is 1 if using technique t the ith time in the history resulted in a speedup, otherwise 0.

3.2.2 Other Techniques

OpenTuner includes implementations of the techniques: differential evolution; many variants of Nelder-Mead search and Torczon hillclimbers; a number of evolutionary mutation techniques; pattern search; particle swarm optimization; and random search. OpenTuner also includes a bandit mutation technique which uses the same AUC Bandit method to decide which manipulator function across all parameters to call on the best known configuration. These techniques span a range of strategies and are each biased to perform best in different types of search spaces. They also each contain many settings which can be configured to change their behavior. Each technique has been modified so that with some probability it will use information found by other techniques if other techniques have discovered a better configuration.

The default meta technique, used in results in this paper and meant to be robust, uses an AUC Bandit meta technique to combine greedy mutation, differential evolution, and two hill climber instances.

3.3 Configuration Manipulator

The configuration manipulator provides a layer of abstraction between the search techniques and the raw configuration structure. It is primarily responsible for managing a list of parameter objects, each of which can be

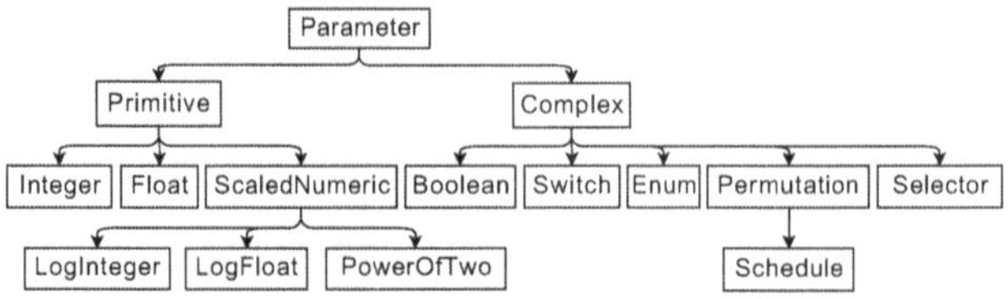

Figure 4: Hierarchy of built in parameter types. User defined types can be added at any point below Primitive or Complex in the tree.

used by search techniques to read and write parts of the underlying configuration.

The default implementation of the configuration manipulator uses a fixed list of parameters and stores the configuration as a dictionary from parameter name to parameter-dependent data type. The configuration manipulator can be extended by the user either to change the underlying data structure used for configurations or to support a dynamic list of parameters that is dependent on the configuration instance.

3.3.1 Parameter Types

OpenTuner has a hierarchy of built-in parameter types. Each parameter type is responsible for interfacing between the raw representation of a parameter in the configuration and the standardized view of that parameter presented to the search techniques. Parameter types can be extended both to change the underlying representation, and to change the abstraction provided to search techniques to cause a parameter to be search in different ways.

From the viewpoint of search techniques there are two main types of parameters, each of which provides a different abstraction to the search techniques:

Primitive parameters present a view to search techniques of a numeric value with an upper and lower bound. These upper and lower bounds can be dependent on the configuration instance.

The built in parameter types `Float` and `LogFloat` (and similarly `Integer` and `LogInteger`) both have identical representations in the configuration, but present a different view of the underlying value to the search techniques. `Float` is presented directly to to search techniques, while `LogFloat` presents a log scaled view of the underlying parameter to search techniques. To a search technique, halving and doubling a log scaled parameter are changes of equal magnitude. Log scaled variants of parameters are often better for parameters such as block sizes where fixed changes in values have diminishing effects the larger the parameter becomes. `PowerOfTwo` is a commonly used special case, similar to `LogInteger`, where the legal values of the parameter are restricted to powers of two.

Complex parameters present a more opaque view to search techniques. Complex parameters have a variable set of manipulation operators (manipulators) which make stochastic changes to the underlying parameter. These manipulators are arbitrary functions defined on the parameter which can make high level type dependent changes. Complex parameters are meant to be easily extended to add domain specific structures to the search space. New complex parameters define custom manipulation operators for use by the configuration manipulators.

The built in parameter types `Boolean`, `Switch`, and `Enum` could theoretically also be represented as primitive parameters, since they each can be translated directly to a small integer representation. However, in the context of search techniques they make more sense as complex parameters. This is because, for primitive parameters, search techniques will attempt to follow gradients. These parameter types are unordered collections of values for which no gradients exist. Thus, the complex parameter abstraction is a more efficient representation to search over.

The `Permutation` parameter type assigns an order to a given list of values and has manipulators which make various types of random changes to the permutation. A `Schedule` parameter is a `Permutation` with a set of dependencies that limit the legal order. Schedules are implemented as a permutation that gets topologically sorted after each change. Finally, a `Selector` parameter is a special type of tree which is used to define a mapping from an integer input to an enumerated value type.

In addition to these primary primitive and complex abstractions for parameter types, there are a number of derived ways that search techniques will interact with parameters in order to more precisely convey intent. These are additional methods on parameter which contain default implementations for both primitive and complex parameter types. These methods can optionally be overridden for specific parameters types to improve search techniques. Parameter types will work without these methods being overridden, but implementing them can improve results.

As an example, a common operation in many search techniques is to add the difference between configuration A and B to configuration C. This is used both in differential evolution and many hill climbers. Complex parameters have a default implementation of this indent which compares the value of the parameter in the 3 configurations: if $A = B$, then there is no difference and the result is C; similarly, if $B = C$, then A is returned; otherwise a change should be made so random manipulators are called. This works in general, but for individual parameter types there are often better interpretations. For example, with permutations one could calculate the positional movement of each item in the list and calculate a new permutation by applying these movements again.

3.4 Objectives

OpenTuner supports multiple user-defined objectives. Result records have fields for `time`, `accuracy`, `energy`, `size`, `confidence`, and user defined data. The default objective is to minimize time. Many other objectives are supported, such as: maximize accuracy; threshold accuracy while minimizing time; and maximize accuracy then minimize size. The user can easily define their own objective by defining comparison operators and display methods on a subclass of `Objective`.

3.5 Search Driver and Measurement

OpenTuner is divided into two submodules, search and measurement. The search driver and measurement driver in each of these modules orchestrate most of the framework of the search process. These two modules communicate only through the results database. The measurement module is minimal by design and is primarily a wrapper around the user defined measurement function which creates results from configurations.

This division between search and measurement is motivated by a number of different factors:

- To allow parallelism between multiple search measurement processes, possibly across different machines. Parallelism is most important in the measurement processes since in most autotuning applications measurement costs dominate. To allow for parallelism the search driver will make multiple requests for desired results without waiting for each request to be fulfilled. If a specific technique is blocked waiting for results, other techniques in the ensemble will used to fill out requests to prevent idle time.
- The separation of the measurement modules is desirable to support online learning and sideline learning. In these setups, autotuning is not done before deployment of an application, but is done online as an application is running or during idle time. Since the measurement module is minimal by design, it can be replaced by an domain specific online learning module which periodically examines the database to decide which configuration to use and records performance back to the database.
- Finally, in many embedded or mobile settings which require constrained measurement environments it is desirable to have a minimal measurement module which can easily be re-implemented in other languages without needing to modify the majority of the OpenTuner framework.

3.6 Results Database

The results database is a fully featured SQL database. All major database types are supported, and SQLite is used if the user has not configured a database type so that no setup is required. It allows different techniques to query and share results in a variety of ways and is useful for introspection about the performance of techniques across large numbers of runs of the autotuner.

4. EXPERIMENTAL RESULTS

Project	Benchmark	Possible Configurations
GCC/G++ Flags	*all*	10^{806}
Halide	Blur	10^{25}
Halide	Wavelet	10^{32}
Halide	Bilateral	10^{176}
HPL	*n/a*	$10^{9.9}$
PetaBricks	Poisson	10^{3657}
PetaBricks	Sort	10^{90}
PetaBricks	Strassen	10^{188}
PetaBricks	TriSolve	10^{1559}
Stencil	*all*	$10^{6.5}$
Unitary	*n/a*	10^{21}
Mario	*n/a*	10^{6328}

Figure 5: Search space sizes in number of possible configurations, as represented in OpenTuner.

We validated OpenTuner by using it to implemented autotuners for seven distinct projects. This section describes these seven projects, the autotuners we implemented, and presents results comparing to prior practices in each project.

Figure 5 lists, for each benchmark, the number of distinct configurations that can be generated by OpenTuner. This measure is not perfect because some configurations may be semantically equivalent and the search space depends on the representation chosen in OpenTuner. It does, however, provide a sense of the relative size of each search space, which is useful as a first approximation of tuning difficulty. For many of these benchmarks, the size of the search space makes exhaustive search intractable. Thus, we compare to the best performance obtained by the benchmark authors when optimality is impossible to quantify.

For each benchmark, we keep the environment as constant as possible, but do not use the same environment for all benchmarks, due to particular requirements for each benchmark, and because one (the stencil benchmark) is based on data from an environment outside our control.

4.1 GCC/G++ Flags

The GCC/G++ flags autotuner is described in detail in Section 3.1. There are a number features that were omitted from the earlier example code for simplicity, which are included in the full version of the autotuner.

First, we added error checking to gracefully handle the compiler or the output program hanging, crashing, running out of memory, or otherwise going wrong. Our tests uncovered a number of bugs in GCC which triggered internal compiler errors and we implemented code to detect, diagnose, and avoid error-causing sets of flags. We are submitting bug reports for these crashes to the GCC developers.

Second, instead of using a fixed list of flags and parameters (which the example does for simplicity), our full autotuner automatically extracts the supported flags from `g++ --help=optimizers`. Parameters and legal ranges are extracted automatically from `params.def` in the GCC source code.

Additionally, there were a number of smaller features such as: time limits to abort slow tests which will not be optimal; use of `LogInteger` parameter types for some values; a `save_final_config` method to output the final flags; and many command line options to control autotuner behavior.

We ran experiments using `gcc 4.7.3-1ubuntu1`, on an 8 total core, 2-socket Xeon E5320. We allowed flags such as `-ffast-math` which can change rounding or NaN behavior of floating-point numbers and have small impacts on program results. We still observe speedups with these flags removed.

For target programs to optimize we used: a fast Fourier transform in C, fft.c, taken from the SPLASH2 [35] benchmark suite; a C++ template matrix multiply, `matrix-multiply.cpp`, written by Xiang Fan [11] (version 3); a C++ ray tracer, `raytracer.cpp`, taken from the scratchpixel website [27]; and a genetic algorithm to solve the traveling salesman program in C++, `tsp_ga.cpp`, by Kristoffer Nordkvist [24], which we modified to run deterministically. These programs were chosen to span a range from highly optimized codes, like `fft.c` which contains cache aware tiling and threading, to less optimized codes, like `matrixmultiply.cpp` which contains only a transpose of one of the inputs.

Figure 6 shows the performance for autotuning GCC flags on these four different sample programs. Final speedups ranged from 1.15× for FFT to 2.82× for matrix multiply.

Figure 7 shows a separate experiment to try to understand which flags contributed the most to the speedups obtained. Full GCC command lines found contained over 250 options

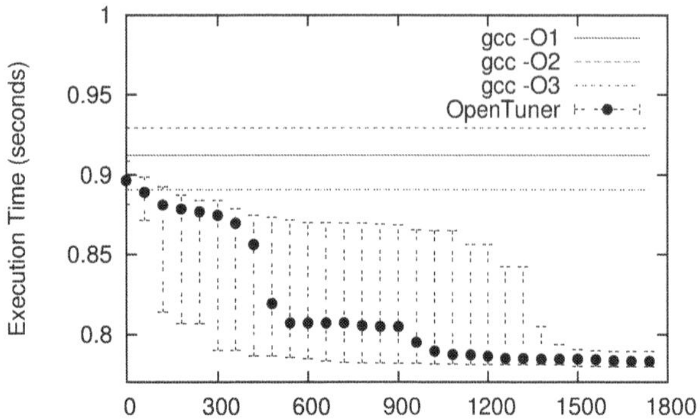

(a) fft.c

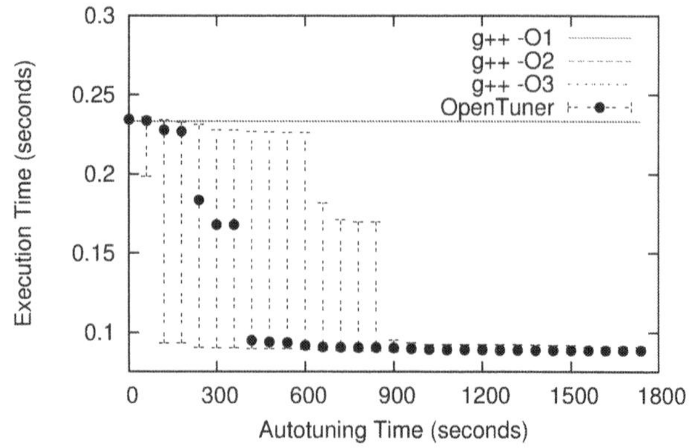

(b) matrixmultiply.cpp

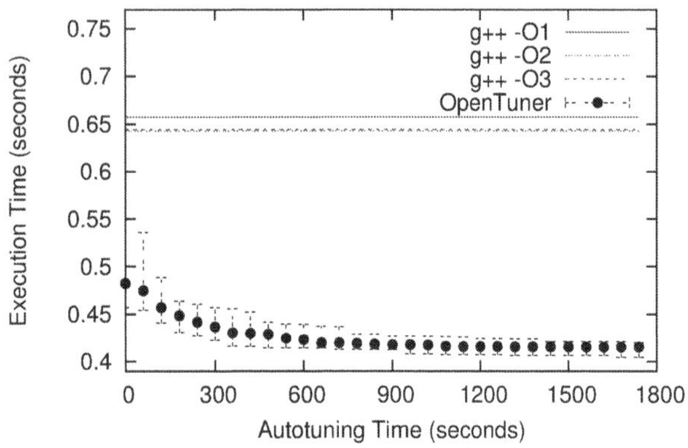

(c) raytracer.cpp

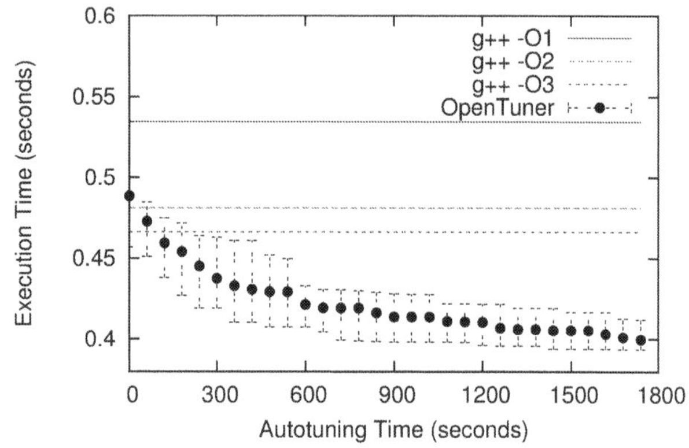

(d) tsp_ga.cpp

Figure 6: **GCC/G++ Flags**: Execution time (lower is better) as a function of autotuning time. Aggregated performance of 30 runs of OpenTuner, error bars indicate median, 20th, and 80th percentiles. Note that in (b) the O1/O2/O3 and in (c) the O2/O3 lines are on top of each other and may be difficult to see.

and are difficult understand by hand. To approximate the importance of each flag, we measured the slowdown resulting from removing it from the autotuned GCC command. We normalize all slowdowns to sum to 100%. This experiment was conducted on a single run of the autotuner. This measurement of importance is imperfect because flags can interact in complex ways and are not independent. We note that the total slowdown from removing each flag independently is larger than the slowdown of removing all flags.

The benchmarks show interesting behavior and varying sets of optimal flags. The matrix multiply benchmark reaches optimal performance through a few large steps, and its speedup is dominated by 3 flags: `-fno-exceptions`, `-fwrapv`, and `-funsafe-math-optimizations`. On the other hand, TSP takes many small, incremental steps and its speedup is spread over a large number of flags with smaller effects. The FFT benchmark is heavily hand optimized and performs more poorly at `-O3` than at `-O2`; the flags found for it are primarily disabling, rather than enabling, various compiler optimizations which interact poorly with its hand-written optimizations. While there are some patterns, each benchmark requires a different set of flags to get the best performance.

4.2 Halide

Halide [29, 30] is a domain-specific language and compiler for image processing and computational photography, specifically targeted towards image processing *pipelines* (graphs) that contain many stages. Halide separates the expression of the kernels and pipeline itself from the pipeline's *schedule*, which defines the order of execution and placement of data by which it is mapped to machine execution. The schedule dictates how the Halide compiler synthesizes code for a given pipeline. This allows expert programmers to easily define and explore the space of complex schedules which result in high performance.

Until today, production uses of Halide have relied on hand-tuned schedules written by experts. The autotuning problem in Halide is to *automatically* synthesize schedules and search for high-performance configurations of a given pipeline on a given architecture. The Halide project previously integrated a custom autotuner to automatically search over the space of schedules, but it was removed because it became too complex to maintain and was difficult to use in practice.[1]

[1]Unfortunately, the original Halide autotuner cannot be used as a baseline to compare against, because the Halide language and compiler have changed too much since its removal to make direct comparison meaningful.

Flag (Importance)	
-fno-tree-vectorize	(25.0%)
-funroll-loops	(6.7%)
-fno-jump-tables	(5.4%)
-fno-inline	(5.0%)
-fno-ipa-pure-const	(4.8%)
-fno-tree-cselim	(4.7%)
-fno-rerun-cse-after-loop	(4.5%)
-fno-tree-forwprop	(4.0%)
-fno-tree-tail-merge	(4.0%)
-fno-cprop-registers	(3.2%)
264 other flags	(32.7%)

(a) fft.c

Flag (Importance)	
-fno-exceptions	(28.5%)
-fwrapv	(27.8%)
-funsafe-math-optimizations	(27.0%)
--param=large-stack-frame=65	(1.1%)
-fschedule-insns2	(1.0%)
-funroll-loops	(0.9%)
-fno-ivopts	(0.8%)
--param=sccvn-max-scc-size=2995	(0.7%)
--param=max-sched-extend-regions-iters=2	(0.6%)
--param=slp-max-insns-in-bb=1786	(0.6%)
272 other flags	(10.9 %)

(b) matrixmultiply.cpp

Flag (Importance)	
-funsafe-math-optimizations	(21.1%)
-ffinite-math-only	(9.4%)
-frename-registers	(3.9%)
-fwhole-program	(2.8%)
--param=selsched-insns-to-rename=2	(2.4%)
-fno-tree-dominator-opts	(2.3%)
--param=min-crossjump-insns=17	(2.2%)
--param=max-crossjump-edges=31	(2.1%)
--param=sched-state-edge-prob-cutoff=17	(2.0%)
--param=sms-loop-average-count-threshold=4	(1.8%)
265 other flags	(49.9 %)

(c) raytracer.cpp

Flag (Importance)	
-freorder-blocks-and-partition	(2.8%)
-funroll-all-loops	(1.9%)
--param=omega-max-geqs=64	(1.8%)
--param=predictable-branch-outcome=2	(1.5%)
--param=min-insn-to-prefetch-ratio=36	(1.5%)
-fno-rename-registers	(1.4%)
--param=max-unswitch-insns=200	(1.4%)
--param=omega-max-keys=2000	(1.4%)
--param=max-delay-slot-live-search=83	(1.3%)
--param=prefetch-latency=50	(1.3%)
279 other flags	(83.7%)

(d) tsp_ga.cpp

Figure 7: Top 10 most important GCC flags for each benchmark. Importance is defined as the slowdown when the flag is removed from the final configuration. Importance is normalized to sum to 100%.

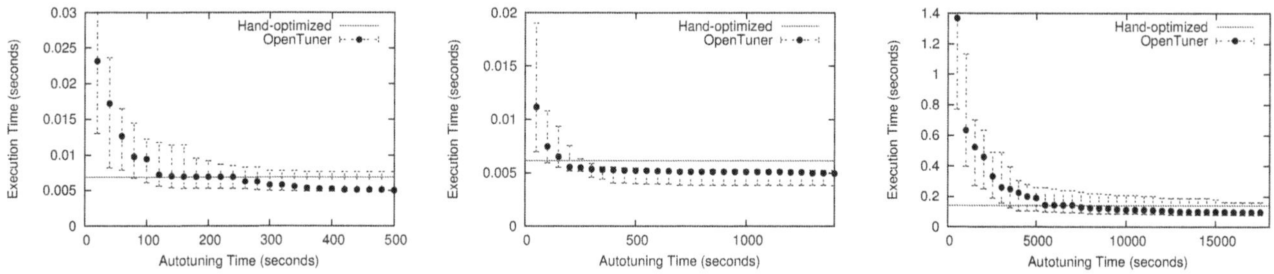

(a) Blur (b) Wavelet (c) Bilateral

Figure 8: **Halide**: Execution time (lower is better) as a function of autotuning time. Aggregated performance of 30 runs of OpenTuner, error bars indicate median, 20th, and 80th percentiles.

Halide's model of schedules is based on defining three things for each function in a pipeline:

1. In what order pixels within the stage should be evaluated.
2. At what granularity pixels should be interleaved between producer and consumer stages.
3. At what granularity pixels should be stored for reuse.

In the Halide language, these choices are specified by applying schedule operators to each function. The composition of potentially many schedule operators for each function together define the organization of computations and data for a whole pipeline.

For example, the best hand-tuned schedule (against which we compare our autotuner) for a two-stage separable blur pipeline is written as follows:

```
blur_y.split(y, y, yi, 8)
      .parallel(y)
      .vectorize(x, 8);
blur_x.store_at(blur_y, y)
      .compute_at(blur_y, yi)
      .vectorize(x, 8);
```

`blur_y(x, y)` and `blur_y(x, y)` are the Halide functions which make up the pipeline. The scheduling operators available to the autotuner are the following:

- `split` introduces a new variable and loop nest by adding a layer of blocking. Recursive splits make the search space theoretically infinite; we limit the number of splits to at most 4 per dimension per function, which is sufficient in practice. We represent each of these splits as a `PowerOfTwoParameter`, where setting the size of the split to 1 corresponds to not using the split operator.

- `parallel`, `vectorize`, and `unroll` cause the loop nest associated with a given variable in the function to be executed in parallel (over multiple threads), vectorized (e.g., with SSE), or unrolled. OpenTuner represents each of these operators as a parameter per variable per function (including variables introduced by splits). The `parallel` operator is a `BooleanParameter`, while `vectorize` and `unroll` are `PowerOfTwoParameters` like splits.

- `reorder` / `reorder_storage` take a list of variables and reorganizes the loop nest order or storage order for those variables. We encode a single `reorder` and a single `reorder_storage` for each function. We represent `reorder_storage` as a `PermutationParameter` over the original (pre-split) variables in the function. The `reorder` operator for each function is a `ScheduleParameter` over all the post-split variables, with the permutation constraint that the split children of a single variable are ordered in a fixed order relative to each other, to remove redundancy in the choice space.

Together, these operators define the order of execution (as a perfectly nested loop) and storage layout *within* the domain of each function, independently. Finally, the granularity of interleaving and storage *between* stages are specified by two more operators:

- `compute_at` specifies the granularity at which a given function should be computed within its consumers.

- `store_at` specifies the granularity at which a given function should be stored for reuse by its consumers.

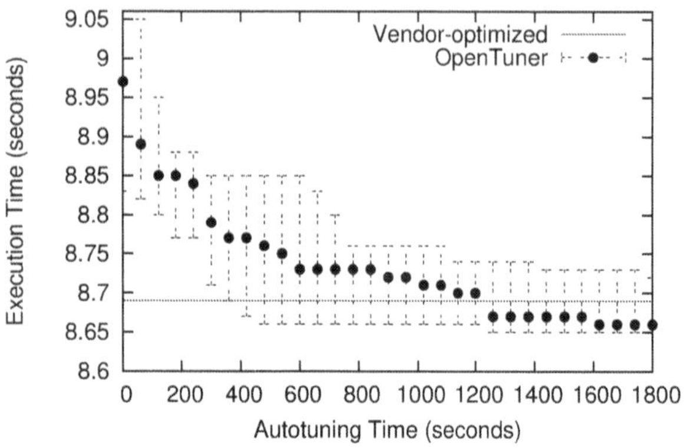

Figure 9: **High Performance Linpack**: Execution time (lower is better) as a function of autotuning time. Aggregated performance of 30 runs of OpenTuner, error bars indicate median, 20th, and 80th percentiles.

Both granularity choices are specified as a level in the loop nest of a downstream function whose scope encloses all uses of the producer. These producer-consumer granularity choices are the most difficult parameters to encode and search, because the valid choices for these parameters are inter-dependent with both granularity and order choices for all other functions in the pipeline. Naïvely encoding these parameters without respecting this interdependence creates numerous invalid schedules—which are meaningless in Halide's schedule language and rejected by the compiler—for each valid schedule.

The result of all these operators is a schedule space that is an exceedingly complex tree; transformations can add or delete subtrees, for example. Searching over such a space is far more difficult when it must be encoded in simple integer parameters, so we take advantage of OpenTuner's ability to encode more complex parameter types. We represented the set of all compute and storage interleaving choices for a whole pipeline as a single instance of a custom, domain-specific parameter type. The parameter extends a `ScheduleParameter`, encoding open and close pairs for each scope in the scheduled pipeline's loop nest, with a correction step which projects any invalid permutations back into the space of meaningful schedules.

Figure 8 presents results for three benchmarks drawn from Halide's standard demo applications: a two-stage blur, an inverse Daubechies wavelet transform, and a fast bilateral filter using the bilateral grid. For all three of these examples OpenTuner is able to create schedules that match or beat the best hand optimized schedules shipping with the Halide source code. Results were collected on three IvyBridge-generation Intel processors[2] using the latest release of Halide.

4.3 High Performance Linpack

The High Performance Linpack benchmark [10] is used to evaluate floating point performance of machines ranging from small multiprocessors to large-scale clusters, and is the evaluation criterion for the Top 500 [32] supercomputer benchmark. The benchmark measures the speed of solving a large random dense linear system of equations using distributed memory. Achieving optimal performance requires tuning about fifteen parameters, including matrix block sizes and algorithmic parameters. To assist in tuning, HPL includes a built in autotuner that uses exhaustive search over user-provided discrete values of the parameters.

We run HPL on a 2.93 GHz Intel Sandy Bridge quad-core machine running Linux kernel 3.2.0, compiled with GCC 4.5 and using the Intel Math Kernel Library (MKL) 11.0 for optimized math operations. For comparison purposes, we evaluate performance relative to Intel's optimized HPL implementation[3]. We encode the input tuning parameters for HPL as naïvely as possible, without using any machine-specific knowledge. For most parameters, we utilize `EnumParameter` or `SwitchParameter`, as they generally represent discrete choices in the algorithm used. The major parameter that controls performance is the blocksize of the matrix; this we represent as an `IntegerParameter` to give as much freedom as possible for the autotuner for searching. Another major parameter controls the distribution of the matrix onto the processors; we represent this by enumerating all 2D decompositions possible for the number of processors on the machine.

Figure 9 shows the results of 30 tuning runs using OpenTuner, compared with the vendor-provided performance. The median performance across runs, after 1200 seconds of autotuning, exceeds the performance of Intel's optimized parameters. Overall, OpenTuner obtains a best performance of 86.5% of theoretical peak performance on this machine, while exploring a miniscule amount of the overall search space. Furthermore, the blocksize chosen is not a power of two, and is generally a value unlikely to be guessed for use in hand-tuning.

4.4 PetaBricks

PetaBricks [3] is an implicitly parallel language and compiler which incorporates the concept of algorithmic choice into the language. The PetaBricks language provides a framework for the programmer to describe multiple ways of solving a problem while allowing the autotuner to determine which combination of ways is best for the user's situation. The search space of PetaBricks programs is both over low level optimizations and over different algorithms. The autotuner is used to synthesize *poly-algorithms* which weave many individual algorithms together by switching dynamically between them at recursive call sites.

The primary components in the search space for PetaBricks programs are *algorithmic selectors* which are used to synthesize instances of poly-algorithms from algorithmic choices in the PetaBricks language. A selector is used to map input sizes to algorithmic choices, and is represented by a list of cutoffs and choices. As an example, the selector [InsertionSort, 500, QuickSort, 1000, MergeSort] would correspond to synthesizing the function:

```
void Sort(List& list) {
  if(list.length < 500)
    InsertionSort(list);
  else if( list.length < 1000)
    QuickSort(list);
  else
    MergeSort(list);
}
```

[2]Blur was tuned on a Core i5-3550, wavelet on a Core i7-3770, and bilateral grid on a 12 cores of a dual-socket Xeon E5-2695 v2 server.

[3]Available at `http://software.intel.com/en-us/articles/intel-math-kernel-library-linpack-download`.

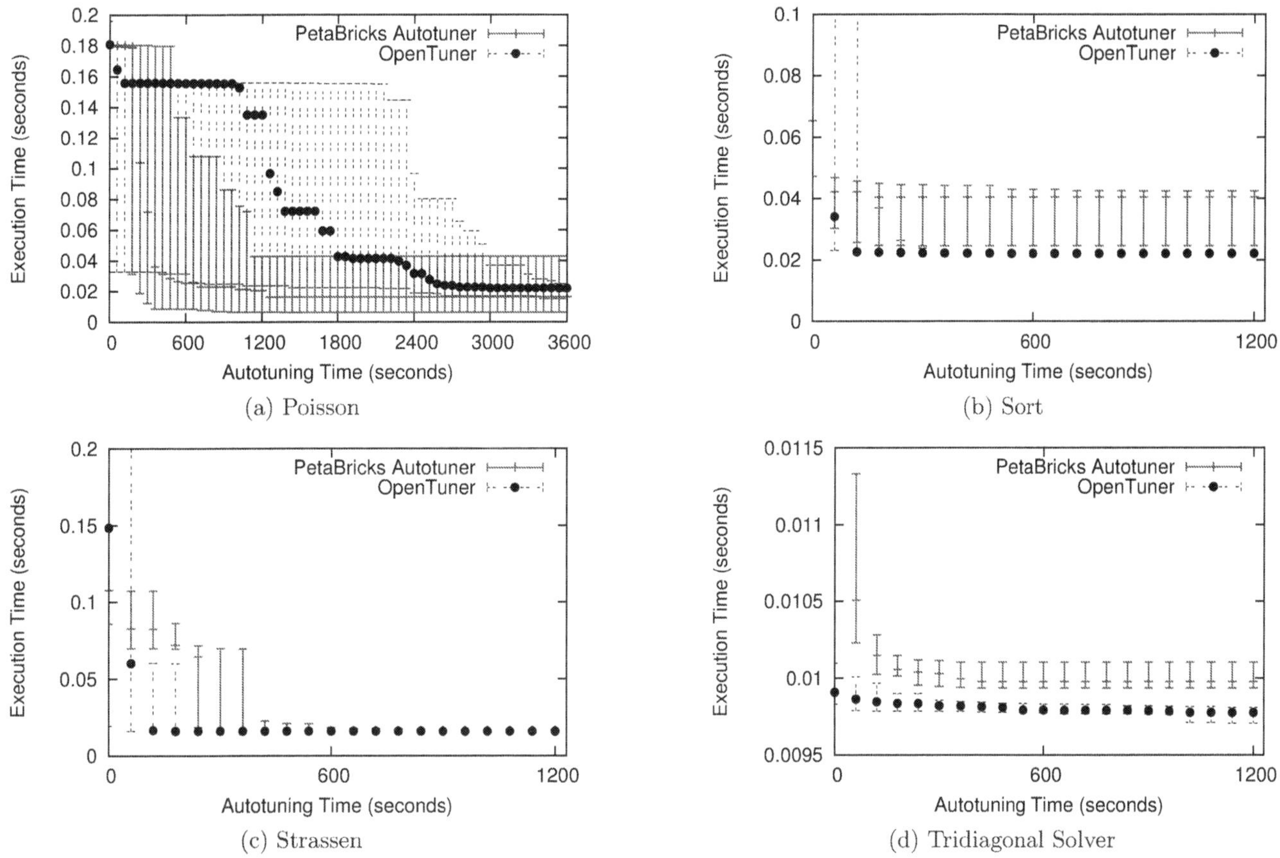

Figure 10: **PetaBricks**: Execution time (lower is better) as a function of autotuning time. Aggregated performance of 30 runs of OpenTuner, error bars indicate median, 20th, and 80th percentiles.

where `QuickSort` and `MergeSort` recursively call `Sort` so the program dynamically switches between sorting methods as recursive calls are made on smaller and smaller lists. We used the general `SelectorParameter` to represent this choice type, which internally keeps track of the order of the algorithmic choices and the cutoffs. PetaBricks programs contain many algorithmic selectors and a large number of other parameter types, such as block sizes, thread counts, iteration counts, and program specific parameters.

Results using OpenTuner compared to the built-in PetaBricks autotuner are shown in Figure 10. The PetaBricks autotuner uses a different strategy that starts with tests on very small problem inputs and incrementally works up to full sized inputs [4]. In all cases, the autotuners arrive at similar solutions, and for Strassen, the exact same solution. For Sort and Tridiagonal Solver, OpenTuner beats the native PetaBricks autotuner, while for Poisson the PetaBricks autotuner arrives at a better solution, but has much higher variance.

The Poisson equation solver (Figure 10a) presents the most difficult search space. The search space for Poisson in PetaBricks is described in detail in [7]. It is a variable accuracy benchmark where the goal of the autotuner is to find a solution that provides 8-digits of accuracy while minimizing time. All points in Figure 10a satisfy the accuracy target, so we do not display accuracy. OpenTuner uses the *ThresholdAccuracyMinimizeTime* objective described in Section 3.4. The Poisson search space selects between direct solvers, iterative solvers, and multigrid solvers where the shape of the multigrid V-cycle/W-cycle is defined by the autotuner. The optimal solution is a poly-algorithm composed of multigrid W-cycles. However, it is difficult to obtain 8 digits of accuracy with randomly generated multigrid cycle shapes, though it is easy with a direct solver (which solves the problem exactly). This creates a large "plateau" which is difficult for the autotuners to improve upon, and is shown near 0.16. The native PetaBricks autotuner is less affected by this plateau because it constructs algorithms incrementally bottom up; however the use of these smaller input sizes causes larger variance as mistakes early on get amplified.

4.5 Stencil

In [20], the authors describe a generalized system for autotuning memory-bound stencil computations on modern multicore machines and GPUs. By composing domain-specific transformations, the authors explore a large space of implementations for each kernel; the original autotuning methodology involves exhaustive search over thousands of implementations for each kernel.

We obtained the raw execution data, courtesy of the authors, and use OpenTuner instead of exhaustive search on the data from a Nehalem-class 2.66 GHz Intel Xeon machine, running Linux 2.6. We compare against the optimal performance obtained by the original autotuning

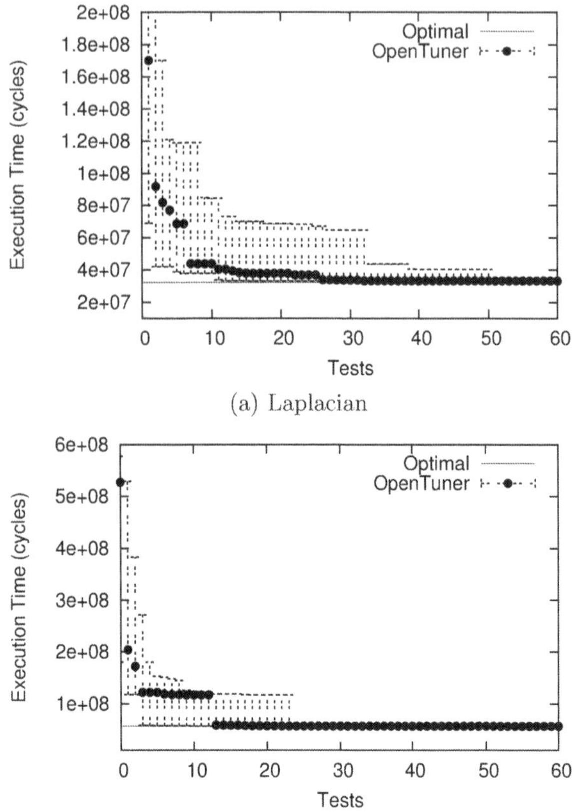

(a) Laplacian

(b) Divergence

Figure 11: **Stencil**: Execution time (lower is better) as a function of tests. Aggregated performance of 30 runs of OpenTuner, error bars indicate median, 20th, and 80th percentiles.

system through exhaustive search. The search space for this problem involves searching for parameters for the parallel decomposition, cache and thread blocking, and loop unrolling for each kernel; to limit the impact of control flow and cache misalignment, these parameters depend on one another (for example, the loop unrolling will be a small integer divisor of the thread blocking). We encode these parameters as `PowerOfTwoParameters` but ensure that invalid combinations are discarded.

Figure 11 shows the results of using OpenTuner for the Laplacian and divergence kernel benchmarks, showing the median performance obtained over 30 trials as a function of the number of tests (results for the gradient kernel are similar, so we omit them for brevity). OpenTuner is able to obtain peak performance on Laplacian after less than 35 tests of candidate implementations and 25 implementations for divergence; thus, using OpenTuner, less than 2% of the search space needs to be explored to reach optimal performance. These results show that even for problems where exhaustive search is tractable (though it may take days), OpenTuner can drastically improve convergence to the optimal performance with little programmer effort.

4.6 Unitary Matrices

As a somewhat different example, we use OpenTuner in an example from physics, namely the quantum control problem of synthesizing unitary matrices in $SU(2)$ in optimal time,

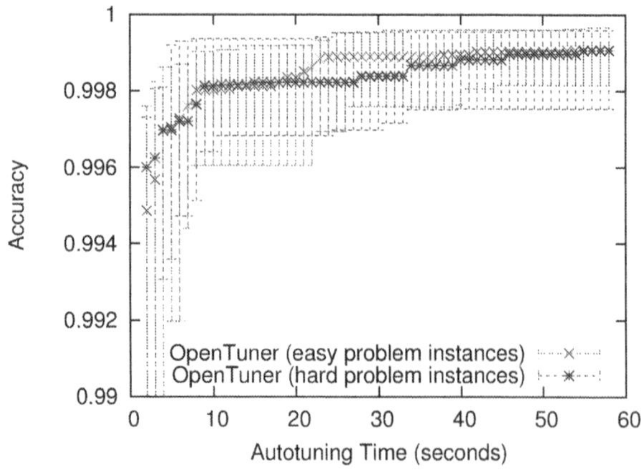

Figure 12: **Unitary**: Accuracy (higher is better) as a function of autotuning time. Aggregated performance of 30 runs of OpenTuner, error bars indicate median, 20th, and 80th percentiles.

using a finite control set composed of rotations around two non-parallel axes. (Such rotations generate the complete space $SU(2)$.)

Unlike other examples, which use OpenTuner as a traditional autotuner to optimize a program, the Unitary example uses OpenTuner to perform a search over the problem space as a subroutine at runtime in a program. The problem has a fixed set of operators (or controls), represented as matrices, and the goal is to find a sequence of operators that, when multiplied together, produce a given target matrix. The objective function is an accuracy value defined as a function of the distance of the product of the sequence to the goal (also called the *trace fidelity*).

Figure 12 shows the performance of the Unitary example on both easy and hard instances of the problem. For both types of problem instance OpenTuner is able to meet the accuracy target within the first few seconds. This is example shows that OpenTuner can be used for more types of search problems than just program autotuning.

4.7 Mario

To demonstrate OpenTuner's versatility, we used the system to learn to play Super Mario Bros., a Nintendo Entertainment System game in which the player, as Mario, runs to the right, jumping over pits and onto enemies' heads to reach the flagpole at the end of each level. We use OpenTuner to search for a sequence of button presses that completes the game's first level. The button presses are written to a file and played back in the NES emulator FCEUX. The emulator is configured to evaluate candidate input sequences faster than real time. OpenTuner evaluates 96 input sequences in parallel in different instances of the emulator. A Lua script running in the emulator detects when Mario dies or reaches the flagpole by monitoring a location in the emulated memory. At that time it reports the number of pixels Mario has moved to the right, which is the objective function OpenTuner tries to maximize. The game is deterministic, so only one trial is necessary to evaluate this function. OpenTuner does not interpret the game's graphics or read the emulated memory; the objective function's value is the only information OpenTuner receives. Horizontal movement is controlled by many `EnumParameters` choosing

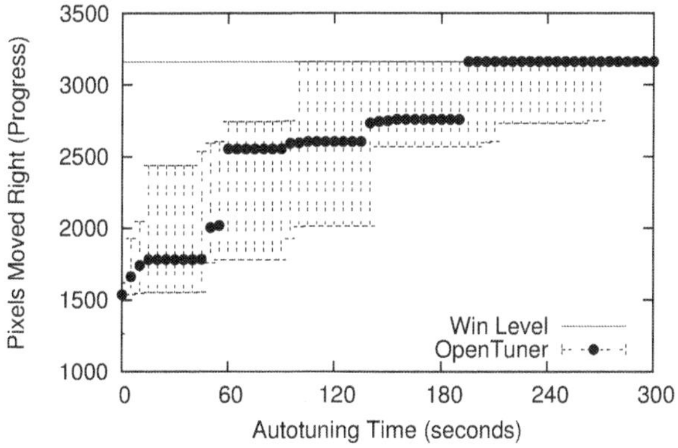

Figure 13: **Mario**: Pixels Mario moves to the right (higher is better) as a function of autotuning time. Reaching pixel 3161 (the flagpole) completes the level. Aggregated performance of 30 runs of OpenTuner, error bars indicate median, 20th, and 80th percentiles.

to run or walk left or right or to not move, each paired with an `IntParameter` specifying the duration of the movement in frames. As the goal is to move right, the search space is given a 3 to 1 right-moving bias. Jumping is controlled by `IntParameters` specifying on which frames to jump and how long to hold the jump button.

Figure 13 shows the performance of the Mario example. OpenTuner rapidly reaches 1500 pixels because many initial (mostly random) configurations will make it that far in the level. The bottlenecks evident in the figure correspond to pits which Mario must jump over, which requires coordinating all four kinds of parameter: Mario must jump on the correct frame for a long enough duration, having built up speed from walking or running right for a long enough duration, and then must not return left into the pit. Performance is aided by a "ratcheting" effect: due to the NES's memory limits, portions of the level that have scrolled off the screen are quickly overwritten with new portions, so the game only allows Mario to move left one screen (up to 256 pixels) from his furthest-right position. The final sequences complete the level after between 3500 and 5000 input actions.

5. CONCLUSIONS

We have shown OpenTuner, a new framework for building domain-specific multi-objective program autotuners. OpenTuner supports fully customizable configuration representations and an extensible technique representation to allow for domain-specific techniques. OpenTuner introduces the concept of ensembles of search techniques in autotuning, which allow many search techniques to work together to find an optimal solution and provides a more robust search than a single technique alone.

While implementing these seven autotuners in OpenTuner, the biggest lesson we learned reinforced a core message of this paper of the need for domain-specific representations and domain-specific search techniques in autotuning. As an example, the initial version of the PetaBricks autotuner we implemented just used a point in high dimensional space as the configuration representation. This generic mapping of the search space did not work at all. It produced final configurations an order of magnitude slower than the results presented from our autotuner that uses selector parameter types. Similarly, Halide's search space strongly motivates domain specific techniques that make large coordinated jumps, for example, swapping scheduling operators on x and y across all functions in the program. We were able to add domain-specific representations and techniques to OpenTuner at a fraction of the time and effort of building a fully custom system for that project. OpenTuner was able to seamlessly integrate the techniques with its ensemble approach.

OpenTuner is free and open source[4] and as the community adds more techniques and representations to this flexible framework, there will be less of a need to create a new representation or techniques for each project and we hope that the system will work out-of-the-box for most creators of autotuners. OpenTuner pushes the state of the art forward in program autotuning in a way that can easily be adopted by other projects. We hope that OpenTuner will be an enabling technology that will allow the expanded use of program autotuning both to more domains and by expanding the role of program autotuning in existing domains.

6. ACKNOWLEDGEMENTS

We would like to thank Clarice Aiello for contributing the Unitary benchmark program. We gratefully acknowledge Connelly Barnes for helpful discussions and bug fixes related to autotuning the Halide project.

This work is partially supported by DOE award DE-SC0005288 and DOD DARPA award HR0011-10-9-0009. This research used resources of the National Energy Research Scientific Computing Center, which is supported by the Office of Science of the U.S. Department of Energy under Contract No. DE-AC02-05CH11231.

7. REFERENCES

[1] F. Agakov, E. Bonilla, J. Cavazos, B. Franke, G. Fursin, M. F. P. O'boyle, J. Thomson, M. Toussaint, and C. K. I. Williams, "Using machine learning to focus iterative optimization," in *CGO'06*, 2006, pp. 295–305.

[2] L. Almagor, K. D. Cooper, A. Grosul, T. J. Harvey, S. W. Reeves, D. Subramanian, L. Torczon, and T. Waterman, "Finding effective compilation sequences." in *LCTES'04*, 2004, pp. 231–239.

[3] J. Ansel, C. Chan, Y. L. Wong, M. Olszewski, Q. Zhao, A. Edelman, and S. Amarasinghe, "PetaBricks: A language and compiler for algorithmic choice," in *PLDI*, Dublin, Ireland, Jun 2009.

[4] J. Ansel, M. Pacula, S. Amarasinghe, and U.-M. O'Reilly, "An efficient evolutionary algorithm for solving bottom up problems," in *Annual Conference on Genetic and Evolutionary Computation*, Dublin, Ireland, July 2011.

[5] W. Baek and T. Chilimbi, "Green: A framework for supporting energy-conscious programming using controlled approximation," in *PLDI*, June 2010.

[6] V. Bhat, M. Parashar, . Hua Liu, M. Khandekar, N. Kandasamy, and S. Abdelwahed, "Enabling self-managing applications using model-based online

[4]Available from `http://opentuner.org/`

control strategies," in *International Conference on Autonomic Computing*, Washington, DC, 2006.

[7] C. Chan, J. Ansel, Y. L. Wong, S. Amarasinghe, and A. Edelman, "Autotuning multigrid with PetaBricks," in *Supercomputing*, Portland, OR, Nov 2009.

[8] F. Chang and V. Karamcheti, "A framework for automatic adaptation of tunable distributed applications," *Cluster Computing*, vol. 4, March 2001.

[9] M. Christen, O. Schenk, and H. Burkhart, "Patus: A code generation and autotuning framework for parallel iterative stencil computations on modern microarchitectures." in *IPDPS*. IEEE, 2011.

[10] J. J. Dongarra, P. Luszczek, and A. Petitet, "The LINPACK Benchmark: past, present and future," *Concurrency and Computation: Practice and Experience*, vol. 15, no. 9, pp. 803–820, 2003.

[11] X. Fan, "Optimize your code: Matrix multiplication," https://tinyurl.com/kuvzbp9, 2009.

[12] A. Fialho, L. Da Costa, M. Schoenauer, and M. Sebag, "Analyzing bandit-based adaptive operator selection mechanisms," *Annals of Mathematics and Artificial Intelligence – Special Issue on Learning and Intelligent Optimization*, 2010.

[13] A. Fialho, R. Ros, M. Schoenauer, and M. Sebag, "Comparison-based adaptive strategy selection with bandits in differential evolution," in *PPSN'10*, ser. LNCS, R. S. et al., Ed., vol. 6238. Springer, September 2010.

[14] M. Frigo and S. G. Johnson, "The design and implementation of FFTW3," *IEEE*, vol. 93, no. 2, February 2005.

[15] G. Fursin, C. Miranda, O. Temam, M. Namolaru, E. Yom-Tov, A. Zaks, B. Mendelson, E. Bonilla, J. Thomson, H. Leather, C. Williams, M. O'Boyle, P. Barnard, E. Ashton, E. Courtois, and F. Bodin, "MILEPOST GCC: machine learning based research compiler," in *Proceedings of the GCC Developers' Summit*, Jul 2008.

[16] H. Hoffmann, J. Eastep, M. D. Santambrogio, J. E. Miller, and A. Agarwal, "Application heartbeats: a generic interface for specifying program performance and goals in autonomous computing environments," in *ICAC*, New York, NY, 2010.

[17] H. Hoffmann, S. Misailovic, S. Sidiroglou, A. Agarwal, and M. Rinard, "Using code perforation to improve performance, reduce energy consumption, and respond to failures," Massachusetts Institute of Technology, Tech. Rep. MIT-CSAIL-TR-2209-042, Sep 2009.

[18] H. Hoffmann, S. Sidiroglou, M. Carbin, S. Misailovic, A. Agarwal, and M. Rinard, "Power-aware computing with dynamic knobs," in *ASPLOS*, 2011.

[19] H. Jordan, P. Thoman, J. J. Durillo, S. Pellegrini, P. Gschwandtner, T. Fahringer, and H. Moritsch, "A multi-objective auto-tuning framework for parallel codes," in *Proceedings of the International Conference on High Performance Computing, Networking, Storage and Analysis*, ser. SC '12, 2012.

[20] S. Kamil, C. Chan, L. Oliker, J. Shalf, and S. Williams, "An auto-tuning framework for parallel multicore stencil computations," in *IPDPS'10*, 2010, pp. 1–12.

[21] S. A. Kamil, "Productive high performance parallel programming with auto-tuned domain-specific embedded languages," Ph.D. dissertation, EECS Department, University of California, Berkeley, Jan 2013.

[22] G. Karsai, A. Ledeczi, J. Sztipanovits, G. Peceli, G. Simon, and T. Kovacshazy, "An approach to self-adaptive software based on supervisory control," in *International Workshop in Self-adaptive software*, 2001.

[23] T. Murphy VII, "The first level of Super Mario Bros. is easy with lexicographic orderings and time travel," April 2013.

[24] K. Nordkvist, "Solving TSP with a genetic algorithm in C++," https://tinyurl.com/lq3uqlh, 2012.

[25] M. Pacula, J. Ansel, S. Amarasinghe, and U.-M. O'Reilly, "Hyperparameter tuning in bandit-based adaptive operator selection," in *European Conference on the Applications of Evolutionary Computation*, Malaga, Spain, Apr 2012.

[26] E. Park, L.-N. Pouche, J. Cavazos, A. Cohen, and P. Sadayappan, "Predictive modeling in a polyhedral optimization space," in *CGO'11*, April 2011, pp. 119 –129.

[27] S. Pixel, "3D Basic Lessons: Writing a simple raytracer," https://tinyurl.com/lp8ncnw, 2012.

[28] M. Püschel, J. M. F. Moura, B. Singer, J. Xiong, J. R. Johnson, D. A. Padua, M. M. Veloso, and R. W. Johnson, "Spiral: A generator for platform-adapted libraries of signal processing alogorithms," *IJHPCA*, vol. 18, no. 1, 2004.

[29] J. Ragan-Kelley, A. Adams, S. Paris, M. Levoy, S. Amarasinghe, and F. Durand, "Decoupling algorithms from schedules for easy optimization of image processing pipelines," *ACM Trans. Graph.*, vol. 31, no. 4, pp. 32:1–32:12, Jul. 2012.

[30] J. Ragan-Kelley, C. Barnes, A. Adams, S. Paris, F. Durand, and S. Amarasinghe, "Halide: a language and compiler for optimizing parallelism, locality, and recomputation in image processing pipelines," in *Proceedings of the 34th ACM SIGPLAN conference on Programming language design and implementation*, ser. PLDI '13. New York, NY, USA: ACM, 2013, pp. 519–530.

[31] C. Tapus, I.-H. Chung, and J. K. Hollingsworth, "Active harmony: Towards automated performance tuning," in *In Proceedings from the Conference on High Performance Networking and Computing*, 2003.

[32] Top500, "Top 500 supercomputer sites," http://www.top500.org/, 2010.

[33] R. Vuduc, J. W. Demmel, and K. A. Yelick, "OSKI: A library of automatically tuned sparse matrix kernels," in *Scientific Discovery through Advanced Computing Conference*, San Francisco, CA, June 2005.

[34] R. C. Whaley and J. J. Dongarra, "Automatically tuned linear algebra software," in *Supercomputing*, Washington, DC, 1998.

[35] S. Woo, M. Ohara, E. Torrie, J. Singh, and A. Gupta, "The SPLASH-2 programs: characterization and methodological considerations," in *Symposium on Computer Architecture News*, June 1995.

Velociraptor: An Embedded Compiler Toolkit for Numerical Programs Targeting CPUs and GPUs

Rahul Garg
School of Computer Science
McGill University
Montreal, Canada
rahul.garg@mail.mcgill.ca

Laurie Hendren
School of Computer Science
McGill University
Montreal, Canada
hendren@cs.mcgill.ca

ABSTRACT

Developing just-in-time (JIT) compilers that that allow scientific programmers to efficiently target both CPUs and GPUs is of increasing interest. However building such compilers requires considerable effort. We present a reusable and embeddable compiler toolkit called Velociraptor that can be used to easily build compilers for numerical programs targeting multicores and GPUs.

Velociraptor provides a new high-level IR called VRIR which has been specifically designed for numeric computations, with rich support for arrays, plus support for high-level parallel and GPU constructs. A compiler developer uses Velociraptor by generating VRIR for key parts of an input program. Velociraptor provides an optimizing compiler toolkit for generating CPU and GPU code and also provides a smart runtime system to manage the GPU.

To demonstrate Velociraptor in action, we present two proof-of-concept case studies: a GPU extension for a JIT implementation of MATLAB language, and a JIT compiler for Python targeting CPUs and GPUs.

Categories and Subject Descriptors

D.3.4 [**Programming Languages**]: Compilers

Keywords

GPU hybrid systems; Compiler framework for Array-Based Language; MATLAB; Python

1. INTRODUCTION

Array-based languages such as MATLAB [13], Python (particularly NumPy [22]) and R [19] have become extremely popular for scientific and technical computing. However, many implementations of such languages were not designed for performance.

Better performance can be achieved in two ways. First, some implementations such as CPython are not even JIT-compiled. In this case, a JIT compiler targeting serial CPU execution needs to be retrofitted to the language implementation. If there is an existing JIT compiler, further performance enhancement will require a good analysis and transformation infrastructure. Second, languages and compilers can be evolved to target modern hardware such as multi-core CPUs and highly parallel co-processors such as GPUs and Xeon Phi. In this case, new compilation infrastructures targeting multi-core CPUs and GPUs need to be written. A GPU runtime will also be required to manage GPU task dispatch, as well as GPU memory and data transfers between CPU and GPU.

Building JIT compilers for numerical programs targeting CPUs and GPUs can require substantial effort. Our goal in this work is to simplify the work of building dynamic compilers for numerical programs targeting CPUs and GPUs. Our suggested solution to simplify the problem of building such compilers is to provide an embeddable, reusable compiler toolkit specialized for compiling numerical array-based programs to CPUs and GPUs. Once the toolkit is built, it can be reused in multiple projects.

We have designed and implemented such a toolkit called Velociraptor that demonstrates the feasibility of this approach. Velociraptor consists of two pieces. The first piece is an optimizing dynamic compiler infrastructure that generates LLVM and OpenCL for CPUs and GPUs respectively. The second piece is a smart and portable GPU runtime, VRRuntime, built on top of OpenCL. Velociraptor is designed to be embedded into a larger compiler, which we call the *containing compiler*. We also provide two case studies of integrating Velociraptor to demonstrate the utility of the approach.

We first examine some criteria that led to our design and then conclude this section with our contributions.

1.1 Design goals

Focus on numerical programs and arrays

We focus on numerical parts of the program. Numerical computations, particularly those utilizing arrays, are the performance critical part of many scientific programs. Numerical computations are also the most likely candidates to benefit from GPUs which are an important motivation behind this work. Array-based languages such as MATLAB and Python expose versatile array datatypes with high-level array and matrix arithmetic operators and flexible indexing schemes. Any proposed infrastructure or solution needs to have an intermediate representation (IR) with a rich array datatype.

PACT'14, August 24–27, 2014, Edmonton, AB, Canada.

ACM 978-1-4503-2809-8/14/08 ...$15.00.
http://dx.doi.org/10.1145/2628071.2628097.

IR support for parallelism and GPUs

We are focusing on languages such as MATLAB and Python, which are popular because they are productive. A typical user of such languages will usually prefer high-level solutions to targeting modern hybrid (CPU/GPU) hardware One example is that a programmer, or an automated tool, might simply specify that a particular computation or loop should be executed in parallel or that a section of code should be executed on the GPU. Such high-level constructs need to be represented in the intermediate representation (IR) of any proposed infrastructure. Compiling these high-level constructs to either parallel CPU code or to GPU kernels, as required by the construct, should be the responsibility of the proposed solution. In addition to code generation, any proposed solution will also need to automatically insert required runtime calls to data transfers, GPU task dispatch and synchronization.

Reusability across languages

Currently, every just-in-time (JIT) compiler project targeting hybrid systems is forced to write their infrastructure from scratch. For example, MATLAB compiler researchers don't benefit from the code written for Python compilers. However, the types of compiler and runtime facilities required for efficient implementation of numerical computations in various array-based languages is qualitatively very similar. Ideally, the same compiler codebase can be reused across multiple language implementations. A shared and reusable infrastructure that is not tied to a single programming language, and that everyone can contribute to, will simplify the work of compiler writers and also encourage sharing of code and algorithms in the community.

Integration with existing language runtimes

Existing implementations face the challenge of maintaining compatibility with existing libraries. For example, many Python libraries have some parts written in C/C++ and depend on the CPython's C/C++ extension API. In such cases, a gradual evolution may be more pragmatic than a complete rewrite of the language implementation. For example, a compiler for numerical subset of Python can be written as an add-on module to the Python interpreter instead of writing a brand-new Python implementation. Tools such as Numba [15] and Cython [23], which have become popular in the Python community, illustrate this approach.

Thus, our design criterion is that our solution needs to integrate with existing internal data structures of each language runtime, particularly the data structure representing arrays in the language. This design criterion immediately rules out certain designs. For example, one may consider implementing a standalone virtual-machine that exposes a bytecode specialized for numerical computations and then simply compile each language to this VM. However, a standalone VM will have its own internal data-structures that will be difficult to interface with existing language runtimes especially if reusability across multiple language implementations is desired. We have chosen an embeddable design with well-defined integration points so that our compiler framework can be easily integrated into existing toolchains while maintaining compatibility.

1.2 Contributions

System design

The first contribution was to define the overall system design. We proposed the design criteria of our work in Section 1.1. The details of our proposed system design are given in Section 2. The system design involved defining the distribution of work and interfacing between Velociraptor and the compiler into which Velociraptor is being embedded such that the compiler writer integrating Velociraptor into a containing compiler needs to do minimal work.

Domain-specific and flexible IR design

The second contribution was defining a domain-specific IR for Velociraptor specialized for numeric computing. As discussed in the design challenges, this IR needs to be flexible enough to model the semantics of multiple numerical programming languages. In particular, the array datatype provided in the IR needs to be rich enough to model various indexing schemes and array operators found in multiple programming languages such as MATLAB and Python/NumPy. Further, this IR needs to be simple to generate from a containing compiler to facilitate easy integration of Velociraptor. Finally, in addition to serial constructs, the IR needs high-level constructs to be able to express parallelism as well as expressing the parts of the program to be offloaded to a GPU. We address these challenges by defining a novel domain-specific IR called VRIR which is discussed in Section 3.

Compiler and runtime contributions

We have implemented an optimizing, multi-pass compiler toolchain that performs many analysis and transformations and produces LLVM for CPUs and OpenCL for GPUs. Our compiler infrastructure is described in Section 4. We also describe a novel memory reuse optimization for library functions such as array addition.

The compiler toolchain needs to be complemented by a GPU runtime. We have built VRRuntime, a GPU runtime that provides a high-level task-graph based API to the code generator. The runtime automatically handles all data transfers and task dispatch to the GPU. VRRuntime is implemented on top of OpenCL and is described in Section 5. VRRuntime provides asynchronous dispatch, automatic CPU-GPU data transfer management and GPU memory management. While similar techniques have been implemented in other runtimes, the implementation in the context of array-based programming languages required solving several subtle issues and is a new contribution.

Demonstrating the utility of Velociraptor

To demonstrate the reusability of Velociraptor, we have used it in two projects described in Section 6. The first case study is an extension of McVM [6], a just-in-time compiler and interpreter for MATLAB language. In this project, we embedded Velociraptor in McVM to enable support for GPUs, while CPU code generation is done by McVM. The second project is a JIT compiler designed as an add-on to the CPython interpreter. It takes as input annotated Python code and generates CPU and GPU Python code using Velociraptor. This demonstrates how a compiler could leverage Velociraptor to do both the CPU and GPU code generation.

We briefly describe our experience in integrating Velociraptor into these two toolchains and then report benchmark results from both these case studies.

2. SYSTEM DESIGN

The first challenge was to specify the services that should be provided by an embedded toolkit and how it would integrate into an existing compilation infrastructure.

Consider a typical just-in-time (JIT) compiler for a dynamic language targeting CPUs shown in Figure 1. Such a compiler takes program source code as input, converts into its intermediate representation, does analysis (such as type inference), possibly does code transformations and finally generates CPU code. Now consider that a JIT compiler developer wants to extend his/her compiler to target hybrid systems by embedding Velociraptor into the compiler. We call the resulting extended compiler as a *containing compiler* while Velociraptor is called the *embedded compiler*.

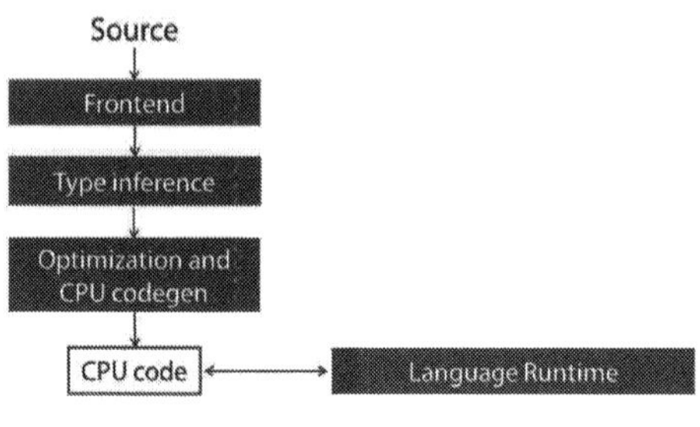

Figure 1: Possible design of a conventional compiler targeting CPUs. You want to extend this compiler to support multicores and GPUs

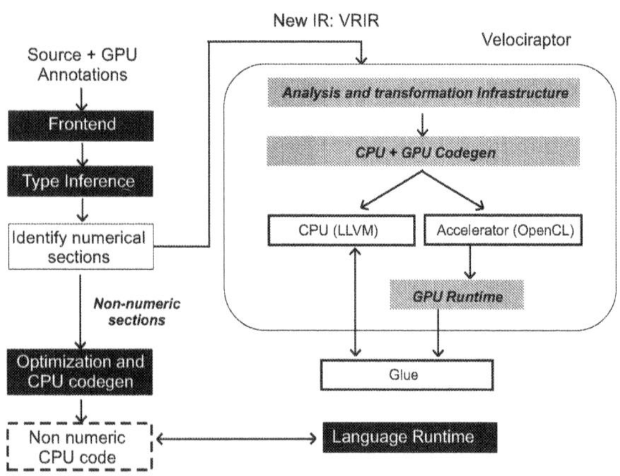

Figure 2: Containing compiler embedding Velociraptor, and showing the parts provided by Velociraptor

We have built the Velociraptor toolkit to simplify the building of containing compilers that want to compile numerical computations to CPUs and GPUs. The key idea is that Velociraptor is embedded inside the containing compiler and it takes over the duties of generating code for numerical sections of the program. Numerical sections of the program may include numerical computations that execute on the CPU, as well as numerical computations that are annotated to be executed on GPUs. Our design goal was to ensure that the containing compiler requires minimal work to integrate Velociraptor.

Figure 2 demonstrates how our approach cleanly integrates with a containing compiler and provides a detailed overview of the entire toolchain including the services provided by Velociraptor. The conventional passes are shown in the dark shaded boxes, while our toolkit, Velociraptor, is shown in the overlay box on the right. The compiler developer who wants to integrate Velociraptor into an existing JIT compiler only needs to add two new components.

First, the compiler developer introduces a new pass in the containing compiler. This new pass identifies numerical parts of the program, such as floating-point computations using arrays including parallel-loops and potential GPU sections, that it wants to handover to Velociraptor. This new pass will be performed after conventional frontend passes and analysis such as type inference performed by many JIT compilers for dynamic languages. The identified numeric sections are outlined into functions and the containing compiler compiles the outlined functions to VRIR functions.

The second addition to be done by the compiler writer is to provide a small amount of glue code to expose the language runtime to Velociraptor. The glue code has several components. Velociraptor needs to know about the representation of array objects in the runtime. The compiler writer provides several typedefs from the existing implementation's array object structure to some typenames Velociraptor implementation uses, and also provides the implementation of macros and functions to access the fields of the array object structure. In addition, the compiler writer provides a representation of the array object structure in LLVM. Finally, Velociraptor defines an abstract API for memory management, such as array object allocations and managing reference counts (if applicable) and the compiler writer provides the implementation of the API. Thus, Velociraptor integrates cleanly into the existing data-structures and does not require invasive changes that might break compatibility with external libraries.

Velociraptor takes over the major responsibility of compiling VRIR to CPU and GPU code and returns a function pointer corresponding to the compiled version of each VRIR function. The containing compiler replaces calls to the outlined function in the original code with calls to the function pointer returned by Velociraptor. Non-numerical parts of the program, such as dealing with file IO, string operations and non-array data structures are handled by the containing compiler in its normal fashion.

Velociraptor provides analysis and transformation infrastructure for VRIR as well as code generation backends for CPUs and GPUs. Portability is a key concern for us and we chose to build our CPU and GPU backends upon portable technologies, LLVM for CPUs, and OpenCL for GPUs. Behind the scenes, Velociraptor also provides a smart runtime system VRRuntime to efficiently manage GPU memory, CPU-GPU synchronization and task dispatch. However, VRRuntime is completely transparent to the containing compiler, and the containing compiler does not need to do any work to use VRRuntime.

3. DESIGN OF VRIR

A key design decision in our approach is that the numeric computations should be separated from from the rest of the program, and that our IR should concentrate on those numerical computations. This decision was motivated by an internal study of thousands of MATLAB programs using an in-house static analysis tool. We have found that typically the core numeric computations in a program use a procedural style and mostly use scalar and array datatypes. We have based the design of VRIR on this study and on our own experiences in dealing with scientific programmers.

VRIR is a high-level, procedural, typed, abstract syntax tree (AST) based program representation. With VRIR, our objective is to cover the common cases of numeric computations. VRIR is designed to be easy to generate from languages like MATLAB or Python and the constructs supported will be familiar to any MATLAB or Python/NumPy programmer. We have defined C++ classes corresponding to each tree node type. We have also defined an XML-based representation of VRIR. Containing compilers can build the XML representation of VRIR and pass that to Velociraptor, or alternatively can use the C++ API directly to build the VRIR trees. Note that VRIR is not meant for representing all parts of the program, such as functions dealing with complex data structures or various I/O devices. The parts of the program that cannot be compiled to VRIR are compiled by the containing compiler in the usual fashion, using the containing compiler's CPU-based code generator, and do not go through Velociraptor.

In the remainder of this section we present the important details of VRIR. A detailed specification and examples are available on our website.[1] The basic structure and constructs of VRIR are introduced in Section 3.1 and supported datatypes are introduced in Section 3.2. VRIR supports a rich array datatype which is flexible enough to model most common uses of arrays in multiple languages such as MATLAB or Python. Array indexing and operators are introduced in Section 3.3. In addition to serial constructs, VRIR supports parallel and GPU constructs in the same IR and these are discussed in Section 3.4. Finally, error handling and memory management are discussed in Section 3.5 and in Section 3.6 respectively.

3.1 Structure of VRIR programs and basic constructs in VRIR

Modules

The top-level construct in VRIR is a *module* and each module consists of one or more functions. Functions in a module can call either the standard library functions provided in VRIR or other functions in the same module, but cannot call functions in other modules.

Modules are self-contained compilation units. This design choice was made because we are targeting OpenCL 1.1, and OpenCL 1.1 requires that the generated OpenCL program should be self-contained. We will be able to remove this restriction once we start targeting OpenCL 1.2, which separates compilation of OpenCL kernels from linking. However, important vendors such as Nvidia currently only provide OpenCL 1.1 implementations.

Functions

Functions have a name, type signature, a list of arguments, a symbol table and a function body. The function body is a statement list.

[1] http://www.sable.mcgill.ca/mclab/gpu

Statements

VRIR supports common statements such as assignments, for-loops, while-loops, conditionals, break and continue statements, return statements, expression statements and statement lists. One of the main goals of VRIR is to provide constructs for parallel and GPU computing through high-level constructs and we describe the supported constructs in Section 3.4.

Expressions

Expression constructs provided include constants, name expressions, scalar and array arithmetic operators, comparison and logical operators, function calls (including standard math library calls), and array indexing operators. All expressions are typed. We have been especially careful in the design of VRIR for arrays and array indexing, in order to ensure that VRIR can faithfully represent arrays from a wide variety of source languages.

3.2 Supported datatypes

Knowing the type of variables and expressions is important for efficient code-generation, particularly for GPUs. Thus, we have made the design decision that all variables and expressions in VRIR are typed. It is the job of the containing compiler to generate the VRIR, and the appropriate types. Velociraptor is aimed at providing code generation and backend optimizations, and is typically called after a type checking or inference pass has already occurred. We have carefully chosen the datatypes in VRIR to be able to represent useful and interesting numerical computations.

Scalar types

VRIR has real and complex datatypes. Basic types include integer (32-bit and 64-bit), floating-point (32-bit and 64-bit) and boolean. For every basic scalar type, we also provide a corresponding complex scalar type. While most languages only provide floating-point complex variables, MATLAB has the concept of integer complex variables as well, and thus we provided complex types for each corresponding basic scalar type.

Array types

Array types consist of three parts: the scalar element-type, the number of dimensions and a layout. The layout must be one of the following three: row-major, column-major or strided-view. For arrays of row- or column-major layouts, indices are converted into addresses using the regular rules for such layouts. The strided-view layout is inspired from the `ndarray` datatype in Python's NumPy library.

We have made a design decision that the value of array sizes and strides are not part of the type system. Thus, while the number of dimensions and element type of a variable are fixed throughout the lifetime of the variable, it may be assigned to arrays of different sizes and shapes at different points in the program. This allows cases such as assigning a variable to an array of different size in different iterations of a loop, such as in some successive reduction algorithms. Further, requiring fixed constant or symbolic array sizes in the type system can also generate complexity. For example, determining the type of operations such as array slicing or array allocation, where the value of the operands determines the size of the resulting array, would be difficult if the array sizes are included in the type system. Thus, we chose to not include array sizes and strides in the type system for flexibility and simplicity.

The number of dimensions of an array variable is fixed in the type system because it allows efficient code-generation and optimizations and only sacrifices small amount of flexibility for most practical cases.

Domain types

Domain types represent multidimensional strided rectangular domains respectively. An n-dimensional domain contains n integer triplets specifying the start, stop and stride in each dimension. This is primarily useful for specifying iteration domains. A one-dimensional specialization of domains is called a range type, and is provided for convenience.

Tuple type

The tuple type is inspired from Python's tuple type and can also be used for one-dimensional cell arrays in MATLAB with some restrictions. A tuple is a composite type, with a fixed number of components of known types. The components can be obtained using constant integer indexes into a tuple.

Void type

The Void type is similar to void type in C. Functions that do not return a value have the void type as return type.

Function types

Function types specify the type signature of a function. VRIR functions have a fixed number of arguments and outputs. The input arguments can be any type (except void). The return type can either be void, or one or more values each of any type excluding void.

3.2.1 Dynamically-typed languages and VRIR

Languages such as MATLAB and Python/NumPy are dynamically typed while we require that the types of all variables be known in VRIR. A good JIT compiler, such as McVM [6], will often perform type inference before code generation. If a compiler is unable to infer types, users are often willing to add a few type hints for performance critical functions to their program such as in the Julia [4] language or the widely used Python compilation tool Cython [23]. Finally, if the containing compiler is unable to infer the types of variables, it can use its regular code generation backend for CPUs as a fallback, instead of using Velociraptor.

3.3 Array indexing and operators

3.3.1 Array indexing

Array indexing semantics vary amongst different programming languages, thus VRIR provides a rich set of array indexing modes to support these various semantics. The indexing behavior depends upon the number and type of index parameters, as well as several optional attributes defined for the array indexing nodes. Consider a n-dimensional array A indexed using d indices. VRIR has the following indexing modes:

Integer indices

If n integer indices are specified, then the address selected is calculated using rules of the layout of the array (row-major, column-major or stride-based). If $d < n$, and all indices are integers, then different languages have different rules and therefore we have provided an attribute called *flattened indexing*. When flattened indexing is true, the behavior is similar to MATLAB where the last $n - d + 1$ dimensions are treated as a single flattened dimension of size $\prod_{k=m}^{d} u_k$ where u_k is the size of the array in the k-th dimension. When flattened indexing is false, the behavior is similar to NumPy and the remaining $d - m$ indices are implicitly filled-in as ranges spanning the size of the corresponding dimension.

Negative indexing

This attribute is inspired from Python's negative indexing and affects both of the above cases. In languages like Java, if the size of the k-th dimension of the array is u_k, then the index in the dimension must be in the set $[0, u_k - 1]$. However, in NumPy, if an index i_k is less than zero, then the index is converted into the actual index $u_k + i_k$. For example, let the index i_k be equal to -1. Then, the index is converted to $u_k + i_k$, or $u_k - 1$, which is the last element in the dimension. We have a boolean attribute in the array index node to distinguish between these two cases.

Enabling/disabling index bounds checks

Array bounds-checks can be enabled/disabled for each individual indexing operation. This allows the containing compiler to pass information about array bounds-checks, obtained through compiler analysis, language semantics or programmer annotations, to Velociraptor.

Row-major, column-major and strided arrays

The layout of the array being indexed determines the arithmetic used for converting the indices to addresses.

Zero or one-based indexing

A global variable, set by the containing compiler, controls whether one-based or zero-based indexing is used for the language.

Slicing arrays - Data sharing or copying

An array can be sliced by supplying a range instead of an integer as an index. Consider an array slicing operation such as $A[m:n]$. Array slicing operations return an array. Some languages like Python have array slicing operators that return a new view over the same data while other languages like MATLAB return a copy of the data. We support both possibilities in VRIR through a boolean attribute of array index nodes.

Using arrays as indices

Arrays can also be indexed using a single integer array (let it be named B) as index. B is interpreted as a set of indices into A corresponding to the integer values contained in B and the operator returns a new array with indexed elements copied into the new array.

3.3.2 Array operators

Array-based languages often support high-level operators that work on entire matrices. Thus, VRIR provides built-in element-wise operation on arrays (such as addition, multiplication, subtraction and division), matrix multiplication and matrix-vector multiplication operators. Unary functions provided include operators for sum and product reduction as well as transcendental and trigonometric functions operating element-wise on arrays.

3.4 Support for parallel and GPU programming

Programmers using languages such as MATLAB and Python are usually domain experts rather than experts in modern hardware architectures and would prefer high-level constructs to expose the hardware. VRIR is meant to be close to the source language. Therefore, we have focused on supporting high-level constructs to take advantage of parallel and hybrid hardware systems. Low-level, machine-specific details such as the number of CPU cores or the GPU memory hierarchy are not exposed in VRIR. The task of mapping VRIR to machine specific hardware is done by Velociraptor. The constructs are as follows:

Parallel-for loops and atomics

Parallel-loops are loops defined over a multi-dimensional domain where each iteration can be executed in parallel. We also support some atomic constructs, such as compare and swap, inside a parallel-for loop.

Implicitly parallel operators

VRIR has a number of implicitly parallel built-in operators such as matrix addition and matrix multiply. Velociraptor takes advantage of parallel libraries for these operators where possible.

Parallel map

Parallel map takes as input a function f and n arrays or scalars as inputs. The function f must be a scalar function that takes n scalars as inputs and returns a scalar. At least one of the arguments to map should be an array, and all the input arrays should have the same size and shape. The operator applies the function f element-wise to each element in the input arrays in parallel, and produces an output array of the same shape.

Reduction sum and product

We support two reduce operators: sum and product of an array either along a given axis or for all elements of the array.

Accelerated sections

Any statement list can be marked as an *accelerated section*, and it is a hint for Velociraptor that the code inside the section should be executed on a GPU, if present. Velociraptor and its GPU runtime (VRRuntime) infer and manage all the required data transfers between the CPU and GPU automatically. At the end of the section, the values of all the variables are synchronized back to the CPU, though some optimizations are performed by Velociraptor and VRRuntime to eliminate unneeded transfers.

In VRIR, accelerated sections can contain multiple statements. Thus, multiple loop-nests or array operators can be inside a single accelerated section. We made this decision because a larger accelerated section can enable the compiler or runtime to perform more optimizations compared to accelerated sections with a single loop-nest.

3.5 Error reporting

We support array out-of-bounds errors in serial CPU code, parallel CPU loops and also in GPU kernels. Previous compilers have only usually supported out-of-bounds errors on CPUs and thus error handling is a distinguishing feature of our system.

In serial CPU code, errors act similar to exceptions and unwind the call stack. However, there is no ability to catch or handle such errors within VRIR code, and all exception handling (if any) must happen outside of VRIR code. In parallel loops or in GPU sections, multiple errors may be thrown in parallel. Further, GPU computation APIs such as OpenCL have very limited support for exception handling, thus the design of VRIR had to find some way of handling errors in a reasonable fashion.

We provide the guarantee that if there is are array out-of-bounds errors in a parallel loop or GPU section, then one of the errors will be reported but we do not specify which one. Further, if one iteration of a parallel-loop, or one statement in a GPU section raises an error, then it may prevent the execution of other iterations of the parallel-for loop or other statements in the GPU section. These guarantees are not as strong as in the serial case, but these still help the programmer in debugging while lowering the execution overhead and simplifying the compiler.

3.6 Memory management

Different containing compiler implementations have different memory management schemes. VRIR and Velociraptor provide automatic cleanup of scalar variables, but for array variables we allow the containing compiler to use the appropriate memory management scheme. Containing compilers can insert explicit instructions in VRIR for array allocation, array deallocation as well as reference counting, as required. Thus we support three models: manual memory management, reference counting, as well as conservative GCs such as Boehm GC. It is up to the containing compiler to select the memory management model.

4. COMPILATION ENGINE

A compiler developer using Velociraptor only needs to concentrate on generating the high-level VRIR, and then Velociraptor provides an optimizing compilation engine that compiles VRIR to LLVM code for CPUs and OpenCL for GPUs. Velociraptor is a multipass compiler with many analysis and optimization phases. The key compilation phases are shown in Velociraptor are shown in Figure 3.

The high-level nature of VRIR was necessary for implementing many of these optimizations. We have implemented some optimizations specific to array-based languages, such as bounds-check elimination and memory reuse optimizations for array operators. These optimizations cannot be implemented in lower-level IRs like LLVM which have no concept of higher-level array constructs that we include in VRIR. Many of the optimizations are common to both CPUs and GPUs and our design decision to have both CPU and GPU sections in the same unified IR (VRIR) makes implementing such optimizations simpler. Finally, VRIR also allows passing some bounds-check information from the host compiler. VRIR allows enabling/disabling bounds-checks on each array subscript separately. Thus, if the host compiler knows that some array references do not need to be bounds-

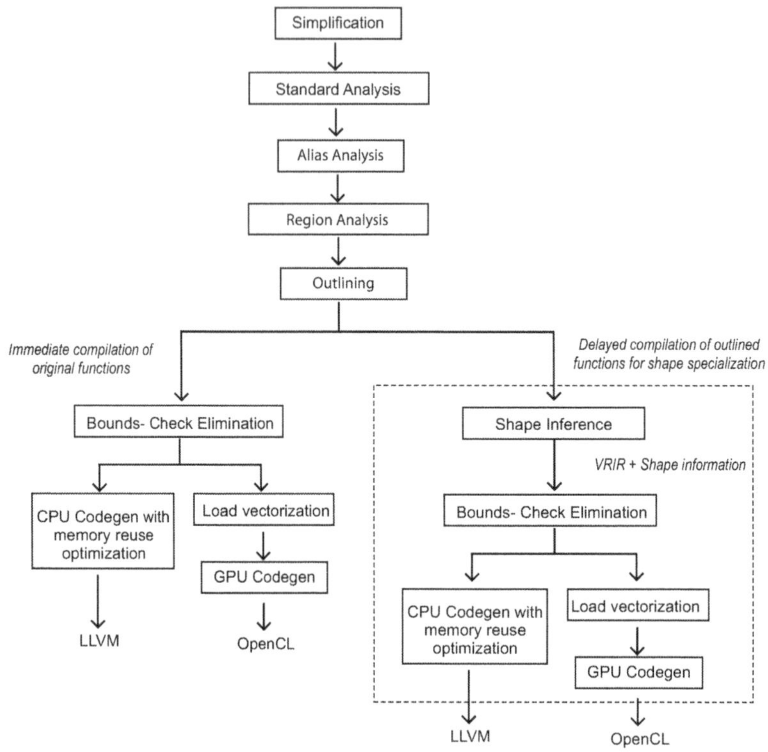

Figure 3: Compiler analysis, transformation and code generation infrastructure provided by Velociraptor

checked, then the host can simply encode this information in the VRIR given to Velociraptor.

Simplification and standard analysis

Velociraptor operates in multiple passes and the overall picture is shown in Figure 3. First, we simplify VRIR into a form similar to three address code. The simplification breaks down complex expressions involving array arithmetic, array indexing and function calls. Expressions which may perform implicit array allocation, such as matrix addition operators which return a new array as the result, are explicitly marked as allocating expressions. The simplifications enable simpler implementation of some flow analysis. Next, we perform some standard analysis such as live variables and reaching definitions analysis.

Alias analysis

We then perform alias analysis. Alias analysis is particularly important for languages like Python, where NumPy arrays may be aliased and having good aliasing information can enable the compiler to do better optimizations. We have implemented a fast, flow-insensitive, context-insensitive algorithm which proceeds in two phases. The algorithm operates upon an undirected graph with array variables and allocation sites as nodes and initially contains no edges. The first phase traverses statements inside the function and inserts edges as follows. We insert an edge between two variables when we encounter a reference array assignment of a variable to another variable. We insert an edge between a variable and an allocation site if the allocation is assigned to the variable. In the second phase, we find connected components in the graph which is a linear time operation in number of nodes and edges. Any two variables in the same connected component may be aliased.

Shape specialization

Many important optimizations depend upon accurate information about shapes in the program, such as sizes and strides of arrays as well as information about loop-bounds. We have implemented a just-in-time shape specialization in Velociraptor where the code is specialized based on shape information gathered at runtime. The analysis first performs *Region Analysis* that finds regions of code that may benefit from shape specialization. The identified regions are outlined into separate functions, and the compilation of these outlined functions is delayed until they are called. When the outlined functions are called, a shape inference pass determines the shape information and is used for code generation. Details of our JIT specialization system can be found elsewhere [9].

Array bounds-check elimination

Many array languages have array bounds-checks which can be a significant overhead, particularly on GPUs. There are many approaches of performing bounds-check elimination. However, Velociraptor is a JIT compiler and thus compilation time is an issue, thus we have chosen to implement two fast, but effective, intra-procedural techniques that are similar to previous work [14].

The first approach is based on elimination of redundant checks. Consider an array A and consider two references $A[expr_0, expr_1]$ and $A[expr_0, expr_2]$ which occur in the stated order inside the loop where $expr_0$, $expr_1$ and $expr_2$ are scalar expressions. If the value of $expr_0$ is the same in both array references, then the bounds-check on the second instance of $expr_0$ can be eliminated.

The second approach is based upon moving some checks outside the loop. Consider a nested loop L. The compiler identifies a set S of array index expressions where each subscript is an affine function of loop variables. For each subscript in S, we generate a corresponding test outside the loop. We generate a new version L' of the loop where the bounds-check for subscripts in S are disabled. If the generated tests pass at runtime, then L' is executed otherwise the original loop L is executed.

Load vectorization

Next, for GPU sections, we perform *load vectorization*, an optimization where we attempt to merge loads into a single packed load. On some GPUs, effective memory read bandwidth for 128-bit loads is better than 64-bit or 32-bit loads. Load vectorization attempts to identify the scalar 32-bit or 64-bit loads that can be combined into wider loads. We perform load vectorization for two array load operations that have a distance of one (i.e. are contiguous), are known to be within bounds and and proven to not have any read-write dependencies in the loop.

CPU Code generation

The compiler compiles CPU code to LLVM. Considerable work was required to generate code for various constructs in VRIR. Some of the constructs that proved particularly challenging include parallel loops, the various flexible indexing schemes in VRIR, handling multiple return values, handling errors such as array out-of-bounds and finally handling library functions. VRIR has many library functions operating on arrays, such as array addition and we provide implementations of these library functions. Our implementation calls the BLAS where possible.

Memory reuse optimization for library functions

We have implemented a new optimization for CPU library functions. Consider the statement: $C = A + B$ where A, B and C are arrays. Language semantics of most array languages are that the expression $A + B$ will allocate a new array. A simple library function implementation will take A and B as inputs, allocate a new array of the right size, perform the computation and return the new array.

However, in some cases, the result array C may have a previous definition and may already be of the required size. In this case, we may be be able to avoid reallocating C. Thus, we have implemented a modified library function that takes C as input in addition to A and B, and checks if C is of the right size. The compiler only calls this optimized library function if C has a previous definition and if the array C is not aliased with other arrays. Overall, this optimization saves unnecessary memory allocations and reduces pressure on the memory allocator and garbage collector.

GPU code generation

Inside GPU sections, library functions as well as parallel loops are offloaded to the GPU. The GPU implementation of library functions is provided by RaijinCL [10] while parallel loops are compiled to OpenCL kernels. Velociraptor generates a task for VRRuntime for each computation to be offloaded to the GPU. Each VRRuntime task requires the specification of data dependences and Velociraptor generates this information. Control flow dependences, such as an if-conditional choosing between two parallel loops, usually need to be evaluated on the CPU. Velociraptor generates explicit synchronization calls to VRRuntime if required by control flow. Inside GPU sections, array allocations and operations such as array slicing are also handled by VRRuntime. Thus, our compiler framework is responsible for generation of correct code while our runtime manages the actual execution of the GPU kernels and management of GPU resources.

5. HIGH-PERFORMANCE RUNTIME

VRRuntime provides a simple GPU runtime API and takes over the responsibility of data transfers and task dispatch to the GPU, greatly simplifying the design of our compiler. VRRuntime provides a task queue to Velociraptor's compiler. Tasks encapsulate an operation such as a call to an OpenCL kernel generated by Velociraptor from a user-defined loop, a call to a library function such as matrix-multiply, or some other operation such as array assignment or slicing. Each task specifies the variables potentially read and written by the task. Based upon the data dependence information specified in the task, as well as actual aliasing information obtained at runtime, VRRuntime automatically determines the data transfers required between the CPU and GPU for completion of the tasks.

In contrast to previous GPU runtime research such as StarPU [2], our system is a higher level solution that is aware of high-level VRIR array operators. Providing the high-level API while providing optimizations such as asynchronous dispatch required solution of issues such as updating shape and alias information and these solutions are discussed in Section 5.2.

5.1 VRRuntime optimizations

VRRuntime has several important optimizations that allow for good performance:

Asynchronous dispatch

Enqueuing a task in VRRuntime is a non-blocking operation. The CPU thread that enqueued the operation can then continue to do other useful work until the result of the enqueued task is required on the CPU. At that point, the enqueuing thread can request the runtime to return a pointer to the required variable and VRRuntime will finish all necessary pending tasks and return the variable. Asynchronous dispatch allows the CPU to enqueue a large number of tasks to the OpenCL GPU queue without waiting for the first GPU task to finish. Inserting multiple kernels in the GPU's hardware job queue can keep it continuously busy, and lower the overheads associated with task dispatch.

Copy-on-write optimizations

Consider the case where variable A is explicitly cloned and assigned to variable B. VRRuntime does not perform the cloning operation until required. For each computation submitted to VRRuntime after the copy, VRRuntime examines the operands read and potentially written in the task using meta-information submitted to VRRuntime by the compiler. If VRRuntime does not encounter any computation that may potentially write A or B after the deep copy, then the deep copy operation is not performed. This is a variation of copy-on-write technique, where we can characterize our technique as copy-on-potential-write. Copy-on-write has been implemented for CPU arrays in systems such as MATLAB [24], and for various CPU data-structures in libraries such as Qt, but we implement it for GPU arrays.

Data transfers in parallel with GPU computation

Consider when two tasks are enqueued to VRRuntime. After the first task is enqueued, instead of waiting for the first task to finish, VRRuntime initiates the data transfer required for the second task, if possible. Thus, the data transfer overheads can be somewhat mitigated by overlapping them with computation. Under the hood VRRuntime maintains two OpenCL queues because some OpenCL implementations require that data transfers be placed in a different OpenCL queue if they are to be performed in parallel with computations.

5.2 Maintaining shape and alias information

Shape information

Our runtime offers a higher level API that is aware of various array and matrix operators such as matrix multiplication and array slicing in VRIR. Thus, in contrast to APIs such as StarPU [2], our API allows the compiler to enqueue operators such as matrix multiplication without specifying any additional details such as the size of the operands.

However, the kernels are dispatched to the OpenCL queue, and OpenCL requires that the user of the API should specify the size of the execution domain of a kernel at the time of enqueuing the kernel. Thus, VRRuntime needs to automatically find out the shape of arrays involved in these higher-level operators at the time of enqueuing the kernel. In a simple CPU library call, the parameters such as array sizes are looked up at runtime from the array data-structure. In our case, due to asynchronous dispatch, the operands of a library call being enqueued may be the result of a previous task that has not yet completed and thus may not have been allocated yet. Further, the operands may never get allocated on the CPU if they are not utilized on the CPU. Thus, we cannot simply query CPU-side array data-structures to dispatch library calls on the GPU.

We solve the issue of shape information by maintaining the information about shapes of array variables in a separate table. The shape information maintained by VRRuntime is the information about shape of the array that would result if all the tasks that have been enqueued are completed. Whenever a task is enqueued, this shape information table is updated. For example, if a matrix multiplication call is enqueued, we update the shape information of the result array based upon shapes of the operands.

Alias and CPU-GPU synchronization information

Aliasing information is required to make correct decisions about mapping of variables to GPU buffers. Consider two arrays A and B. Some tasks may read/write A while some other tasks read/write B. Each array has an address range that it points to. Our strategy is that we want to allocate a unique GPU buffer for each CPU address range potentially accessed inside a kernel. Having a unique GPU copy of each address range ensures correctness when there is a data dependence within or across different kernels. If the arrays are not aliased, then we can simply allocate one GPU buffer corresponding to A, and a separate GPU buffer for B. However, if the arrays are indeed aliased, then we allocate a single GPU buffer that corresponds to the CPU address range encompassing both A and B.

We have chosen a compiler-assisted solution to the problem. Velociraptor analyzes the GPU section and finds all the arrays that may potentially occur inside the region and specifies this list to VRRuntime at the beginning of a GPU section. VRRuntime then constructs and maintains two tables of information. The first table contains information about array variables including the address range of the array, the GPU buffer corresponding to the array, the last task dispatched that might potentially write to the array, whether the CPU and GPU copy are synchronized and if not then whether the CPU or the GPU copy contains the freshest data. The second table has information about GPU buffers such as the CPU address range it corresponds to and the variables pointing to the GPU buffer. These tables are updated whenever a task is enqueued or a synchronization point is reached.

6. TWO CASE-STUDIES

6.1 McVM integration

McVM is a virtual machine for the MATLAB language. McVM is part of the McLAB project, which is a modular toolkit for analysis and transformation of MATLAB and extensions. McVM includes a type specializing just-in-time compiler and performs many analysis such as live variable analysis, reaching definitions analysis and type inference. Prior to this work, McVM generated LLVM code for CPUs only, and did not have any support for parallel loops or GPU computations. We added two language constructs to McVM. First, we added a parallel-for (parfor) loop. We have also provided *gpu_begin*() and *gpu_end*() section markers that indicate to the compiler that the section should be offloaded to the GPU, if possible.

In Section 2, we describe that a compiler writer must provide a pass to identify which sections to compile using Velociraptor, and also needs to provide glue code. We provide both of these pieces for McVM.

In this implementation, the method of choosing suitable numerical sections is to only invoke Velociraptor to compile parallel-for loops and GPU sections. We use McVM's existing code generation facilities for the rest of the program because McVM's LLVM based CPU code generator already implements some optimizations. We made the following modifications to McVM in order to support parfor loops and GPU sections. After McVM has finished type inference, McVM looks for parfor loops and GPU sections and first verifies that the code can be compiled to VRIR. For example, if some of the types were unknown, then they cannot be compiled to VRIR. If the code cannot be compiled to VRIR, then code is converted to serial CPU code and handled by McVM's usual code generator. If the code passes verification, then McVM outlines these new constructs into special functions, compiles them into XML representation of VRIR, then asks Velociraptor to compile and return the function pointers to the outlined code. The original code is then replaced by a call to the outlined function. In MATLAB, arguments are passed into functions by value. However, we have implemented calls to outlined functions as call-by-reference because the side effects in the outlined code need to propagate back to the original function for correctness.

We have also provided glue code for exposing McVM's internal data-structures to Velociraptor. This required providing a McVM-specific implementation of Velociraptor's abstract memory allocation APIs, telling Velociraptor about MATLAB language semantics (such as using one-based indexing), exposing LLVM representation of various array classes and providing macros and functions for field access of array class members.

6.2 Python integration

We have written a proof-of-concept compiler for a numeric subset of Python, including the NumPy library, that integrates with the standard Python [18] interpreter.

As described in Section 2, any implementation needs to identify and outline numerical sections and needs to provide glue code. In our prototype, we require that the programmers outline suitable numerical sections manually. The idea is that only a few numerical functions in a Python program are compiled, while the rest of the program is interpreted by the Python interpreter. As for glue code, we have provided all the glue code necessary to interface Velociraptor with the necessary data structures in CPython and the NumPy library. We have provided glue code in C++ using the Python/C API for exposing NumPy arrays to Velociraptor, for exposing reference counting mechanism of Python interpreter to Velociraptor, and for reporting the out-of-bounds exceptions generated in code compiled by Velociraptor back to the user. We wrote a little glue code in C++ to wrap the function pointers returned by Velociraptor into Python functions.

Now we briefly describe the language constructs handled and extensions provided by our Python compiler. Our compiler can handle scalar numerical datatypes, NumPy arrays and tuples. Many of the commonly used constructs are handled including for-loops, while-loops, conditionals, various array indexing and slicing operators as well as many math library functions for arrays. We currently require that the programmer provides the type signature of the function through a decorator we have defined, and then our compiler infers the type of the local variables. We require that the type of a variable not change within a function. Some of these limitations can be removed if a just-in-time type specializing compiler is implemented. However, this is out of scope of this paper.

We have provided several extensions to the Python language to enable use of multi-cores and GPUs. First, we have defined a parallel-for loop by defining a special function *prange*, and have defined that any for-loop that iterates over a *prange* will run in parallel. Second, we have defined *prange* to return a multi-dimensional domain object rather than a single-dimensional range. Finally, we also provide constructs (*gpu_begin*() and *gpu_end*()) that act as markers to annotate blocks of code to be executed on the GPU.

In this compiler, all the code generation is handled by Velociraptor. The frontend of the compiler is written in Python itself. Python has a standard library module called *ast* which provides functionality to construct an AST from Python source code. Our frontend uses this module to construct untyped ASTs. Then our Python compiler performs type inference on this AST by propagating the types of the function parameters provided by the user into the body of the function. The function is then compiled by our Python compiler to VRIR in a separate pass.

6.3 Development Experience

For Python, where we required the programmer to manually separate the numerical sections, the development experience was very straightforward. For McVM, we found that building the outlining infrastructure was the most challenging aspect of the project. McVM maintains various internal data-structures holding information from various analyses such as live variable analysis. After outlining, all such analysis data-structures need to be updated and doing this correctly required some effort. However, once outlining was done, generating VRIR was straightforward.

Overall, we found that using Velociraptor enabled some saving in the development time of both compilers. As an indirect estimate, we can look at the number of lines of code (LoC) required. For McVM, the integration required about 5000 lines of code and we think that there is further possibility of reduction in LoC through better refactoring. Our Python compiler required only about 4000 lines of C++ and 300 lines of Python which is substantially smaller than Velociraptor. Velociraptor itself is about 11000 lines of code. Further, some of the implementation details of Velociraptor are quite subtle, such as asynchronous dispatch and require effort much beyond what the LoC metric suggests. Code reuse across different compilers really improved the development experience. For example, if a McVM test case failed and was found to be a Velociraptor bug, then fixing the bug often also benefited our Python compiler.

A secondary benefit of our design is that the technique of upfront identification and separation of well-behaved numerical sections from other parts of the program turned out to be very useful. Analysis and optimizations operating on VRIR can be more aggressive in their assumptions and can be simpler and faster to implement compared to an IR designed for representing the entire program. We have been able to very quickly prototype ideas about optimizations in Velociraptor without worrying about the full, and potentially very complicated, semantics of languages like MATLAB.

7. CASE STUDIES: EXPERIMENTAL RESULTS

Although the focus of this paper is the semantics of VRIR and design of the toolkit, we also wanted to see what the potential performance benefits could be. To get a first idea of the performance possibilities, we evaluated the performance of code generated by Velociraptor for both CPUs and GPUs on a variety of Python and McVM benchmarks.

7.1 Machine information

Our experiments were performed on two different machines containing GPUs from two different families. Descriptions of the machines are as follows:

1. Machine M1: Core i7 3820, 2x Radeon 7970, 8GB DDR3, Ubuntu 12.04, Catalyst 13.4
2. Machine M2: Core i7 920, Tesla C2050, GTX 480, 6GB DDR3, Ubuntu 12.04, Nvidia driver version 280.13.

Machine M1 and M2 contain two GPUs each. We used one Radeon 7970 and Tesla C2050 respectively for computation, and reserve the other GPU in each machine for handling display duties. We used CPython v3.2, PyPy 2.1 and MATLAB R2013a 64-bit in tests. Each test was performed ten times and we report the mean.

7.2 McVM performance

For McVM, we looked at benchmarks used by previous projects such as McVM and MEGHA [16] and chose four parallelizable benchmarks and added GPU annotations. The benchmarks in this section make heavy use of implicitly parallel vectorized operators such as vector arithmetic operators. We distinguish three cases here: McVM performance without Velociraptor, multi-core performance with Velociraptor and GPU-accelerated performance with Velociraptor. We used MATLAB as the baseline and report performance in Table 1 as speedups over MATLAB.

All the benchmarks contained GPU sections. For the Velociraptor generated GPU version, we tested under four settings: Velociraptor compiler and runtime optimizations enabled, compiler optimizations disabled but runtime optimizations enabled, compiler optimizations disabled but runtime optimizations disabled and finally both compiler and runtime optimizations disabled.

However, in order to compare McVM and Velociraptor generated CPU code, we also ran the tests where we forced Velociraptor to only generate CPU code. We found that the CPU code generated by Velociraptor was never slower than the code generated by McVM's LLVM-based backend and thus there is no disadvantage in using Velociraptor even for CPU code.

For the GPU version, Velociraptor runtime optimizations provide up to 15% increase in performance. This is primarily due to asynchronous dispatch implemented in the runtime. Asynchronous dispatch allows the CPU to enqueue a large number of tasks without waiting for the GPU to finish. Synchronous dispatch adds overhead for waiting upon completion of kernel calls and this overhead can be significant for small kernels such as vector addition.

7.3 Python performance

We evaluated Python performance on four Python benchmarks. These benchmarks come from a set of Python benchmarks proposed by members of NumPy community. We added type, parallelization and GPU section annotations in these benchmarks.

We tested our compiler on three different versions of each benchmark: a serial CPU version, a parallel CPU version and a GPU version. For the CPU versions, we we tested the code generation in two cases: with Velociraptor optimizations enabled and disabled. For the GPU version, we tested under four settings similar to the ones discussed in previous section. Finally, we measured the the performance of the PyPy 2.1 implementation of Python. PyPy has its own JIT compiler and we found that PyPy was significantly faster than CPython on these benchmarks and thus we use PyPy as a realistic baseline. The results are presented in Table 2 as speedups over PyPy.

We observed that serial unoptimized CPU code generated by Velociraptor is between 3 to 37 times faster than PyPy depending upon the benchmark. Parallel CPU code generated by Velociraptor was generally two to six times faster than serial CPU code generated by Velociraptor. We used quad-core processors and more than four times speedup can be explained by the fact the CPUs are hyper-threaded and run eight threads. Optimized GPU code generated by Velociraptor can be up to seven times faster than generated optimized parallel CPU code provided that the data transfer overhead is not substantial.

Compiler optimizations provided between 1% to 35% performance improvement on CPUs and between 1% and 52% performance improvement on GPUs depending upon the benchmark. We observed that the compiler eliminated between 50 and 100 percent of array bounds-checks in the innermost loop in these benchmarks.

8. RELATED WORK

There has been considerable interest in using GPUs from dynamic array-based languages. The earliest attempts have been to create wrappers around CUDA and OpenCL API that still require the programmer to write the kernel code by hand and exposing a few vendor specific libraries. Such attempts include PyCUDA [11] and PyOpenCL [12]. The current version of MATLAB's proprietary parallel computing toolbox also falls in this category at the time of writing. Our approach does not require writing any GPU code by hand.

There has also been interest in compiling array-based languages to GPUs. Copperhead [5] is a compiler that generates CUDA from annotated Python code. Copperhead does not handle loops, but instead focuses on higher-order functions like map. jit4GPU [8] was a dynamic compiler that compiled annotated Python loops to AMD's deprecated CAL API. Theano [3] is a Python library that compiles expression trees to CUDA. In addition to GPU code generation, it also includes features like symbolic differentiation. Parakeet [21] is a compiler that takes as input annotated Python code and generates CUDA for GPUs and LLVM for CPUs. MEGHA[16] is a static compiler for compiling MATLAB to mixed CPU/GPU system. Their system required no annotations, and discovered sections of code suitable for execution on GPUs through profile-directed feedback. Jacket [17] is a proprietary add-on for MATLAB that exposes a large library of GPU functions, and also has a compiler for generating GPU code for limited cases. Numba [15] is a NumPy-aware JIT compiler for compiling Python to LLVM. The work has some similarities to our work on the CPU side, including support for various array layouts, but it is tied to Python and therefore does not support the indexing schemes not supported by Python. Numba also provides an initial prototype of generating CUDA kernels, given the body of the kernel (equivalent to the body of a parallel loop) in Python. However, it assumes the programmer has some knowledge of CUDA, and exposes some CUDA specific variables (such as thread-block index) to the programmer. Furthermore, unlike our work, it is not a general facility for annotating entire regions of code as GPU-executable and will mostly be useful for converting individual loop-nests to CUDA.

One possible approach to building a multi-language compiler for GPUs is to compile bytecode of high-level VMs to GPUs. This is complementary to our approach and there are two recent examples of this approach. AMD's Aparapi [1] provides a compiler that compiles Java bytecode of a method to an OpenCL kernel body, and the generated kernel can then be applied over a domain. Unlike VRIR, which contains multi-dimensional arrays and high-level array operators, Aparapi is a low-level model where only one-dimensional

Benchmark	Machine	McVM	Velociraptor CPU		GPU accelerated			
Compiler opts		N/A	No	Yes	No	Yes	No	Yes
Runtime opts		N/A	N/A	N/A	No	No	Yes	Yes
clos	M1	0.99	0.99	0.98	3.18	3.22	3.20	3.25
	M2	1.0	0.99	0.99	2.24	2.18	2.24	2.28
nb1d	M1	1.58	1.50	1.61	2.92	2.88	3.04	3.04
	M2	1.30	1.34	1.45	3.40	3.37	3.62	3.61
nb3d	M1	0.2	0.51	0.54	1.64	1.67	1.72	1.72
	M2	0.22	0.72	0.72	2.43	2.40	2.63	2.63
fdtd	M1	0.15	0.47	0.47	1.92	1.90	1.97	1.97
	M2	0.13	0.54	0.53	2.04	2.04	2.12	2.08

Table 1: Speedup of McVM + Velociraptor generated code over MATLAB JIT

Benchmark	Machine	CPU Serial		CPU Parallel		GPU accelerated			
Compiler opts		No	Yes	No	Yes	No	Yes	No	Yes
Runtime opts		N/A	N/A	N/A	N/A	No	No	Yes	Yes
arc-distance	M1	3.36	4.15	9.84	11.64	8.19	9.3	8.33	9.63
	M2	3.12	3.55	10.9	11.91	8.84	9.75	8.59	9.72
julia	M1	34.8	37.0	213.4	214.8	1517	1502	1525	1511.8
	M2	37.0	37.5	170.2	172.2	729.3	775.8	744	756
growcut	M1	13.3	18.5	42.8	60.1	118.1	168.4	116.6	173.4
	M2	11.5	15.4	37.9	49.7	90.3	137.9	93.2	137.7
rosen-der	M1	15.5	18.7	31.1	40.0	32.6	33.8	32.9	34.1
	M2	12.9	15.7	25.0	29.4	25.6	28.0	25.6	28.4

Table 2: Speedup of CPython + Velociraptor generated code over PyPy JIT

arrays are allowed with Java's simple indexing operators. Dandelion [20] is a LINQ style extension to .net that cross-compiles .net bytecode to CUDA. The programming style for LINQ is quite different from the loop and array-operator based approach in our work.

To our knowledge, there has not been prior work on embeddable or reusable compilers for GPUs. The only work in this area that we are aware of is NOVA [7]. NOVA is a static compiler for a domain-specific compiler for a new functional language and it generates CUDA code. Velociraptor and NOVA provide different programming styles (imperative loop and array-based vs functional respectively) and different compilation models (dynamic vs static respectively). Collins et al. claim that NOVA can be used as an embedded domain-specific language but did not show any such embedded uses whereas we integrated our toolkit in two compilers.

To summarize, in contrast to previous research, our toolkit is an embeddable and reusable compiler targeting both CPUs and GPUs and is not limited to one programming language. We have carefully considered the variations of array indexing schemes, array layout semantics and array operators of the programming languages and offer a complete solution for popular scientific computing languages.

However, while we described the differences from previous research, our toolkit is meant to complement and enable, not compete, with other compiler researchers. Had our tools existed earlier, most of the previously mentioned systems could have used it while focusing their time elsewhere. For example, MEGHA's automatic identification of GPU sections, the type inference work of Parakeet or Theano's work on symbolic facilities are all complementary to our work. We believe toolkits such as Velociraptor will free other researchers to work on various open problems in programming language design and implementation rather than spend the time writing backends or design GPU runtimes.

9. CONCLUSIONS AND FUTURE WORK

The development of JIT compilers for array-based languages to produce efficient CPU and GPU code is an important problem. In some cases, compiler writers may be writing entirely new language runtimes. In other cases, language implementors are more interested in evolving current language runtimes for the sake of compatibility and development time.

We first discussed some design goals of our project and how certain designs are ruled out because of constraints such as handling existing language runtimes. Based on our design goals, we proposed a toolkit-based approach to simplify the building of JIT compilers for array-based languages. We have presented an embedded toolkit that can be used by compiler writers inside their own compiler to compile numerical array-based code to both CPU as well as GPU code. The toolkit is reusable across two languages. We discussed a new high-level IR called VRIR to achieve this language portability. VRIR can be used to express a wide variety of core array-based computations and can contain code sections for both CPUs and GPUs. The toolkit is designed to be embedded inside existing language implementations. In order to simplify the evolution of existing codebases, our toolkit does not require rewriting of data-structures such as array representations inside the language runtime.

The toolkit provides optimization and code generation facilities as well as a GPU runtime. Compiler writers can simply generate VRIR for key parts of their input programs, and then use Velociraptor to automatically generate CPU/GPU code for their target architecture. Our compilation engine and runtime library takes care of many issues, including the communication between the CPU and GPU as well as capturing errors. We have implemented many standard analysis and optimizations. While some general optimization techniques are well-known, we faced some challenges in adapting them to our framework. We discuss our solutions to problems such as as asynchronous dispatch of GPU kernels and reusing memory allocations in CPU library functions to our system.

To demonstrate the toolkit, we used it in two very different projects. The first project was using the toolkit to extend a MATLAB JIT, from McVM, to handle GPU computations. The second is a proof-of-concept compiler for Python, which was written as an add-on to the existing CPython implementation, where we used both the CPU and GPU code generation capabilities of Velociraptor.Thus, we showed that Velociraptor can handle the language semantics of two different languages, and that our APIs and implementation are generic enough to be interfaced with two different existing language runtimes.

For our framework, now that the toolkit is established and we have two prototype applications of the toolkit, we are working on refining those prototypes and adding further optimizations and transformations to the generated code as well as adding more backends such as a static CPU backend. We are also working on performance studies with a broad range of CPU-GPU hybrid systems and on a much larger benchmark set.

To summarize, we demonstrated that a toolkit based approach can work for building compilers for array-based languages. A shared, reusable toolkit can be very useful for the community and our presented compiler toolkit is the first such framework. We hope that other researchers will use our toolkit for their own compilers. Most importantly, we view our toolkit as a starting point and we hope that our work will spark the discussion in the community about the need and potential designs of such toolkits.

10. REFERENCES

[1] Advanced Micro Devices Inc. Aparapi. `http://code.google.com/p/aparapi/`.

[2] C. Augonnet, S. Thibault, R. Namyst, and P.-A. Wacrenier. StarPU: A Unified Platform for Task Scheduling on Heterogeneous Multicore Architectures. *Concurrency and Computation: Practice and Experience, Special Issue: Euro-Par 2009*, 23:187–198, Feb. 2011.

[3] J. Bergstra, O. Breuleux, F. Bastien, P. Lamblin, R. Pascanu, G. Desjardins, J. Turian, D. Warde-Farley, and Y. Bengio. Theano: a CPU and GPU math expression compiler. In *SciPy 2010*, June 2010.

[4] J. Bezanson, S. Karpinski, V. B. Shah, and A. Edelman. Julia: A fast dynamic language for technical computing. *CoRR*, abs/1209.5145, 2012.

[5] B. Catanzaro, M. Garland, and K. Keutzer. Copperhead: compiling an embedded data parallel language. In *PPOPP 2011*, pages 47–56, 2011.

[6] M. Chevalier-Boisvert, L. Hendren, and C. Verbrugge. Optimizing MATLAB through just-in-time specialization. In *CC 2010*, pages 46–65, 2010.

[7] A. Collins, D. Grewe, V. Grover, S. Lee, and A. Susnea. NOVA : A functional language for data parallelism. Technical report, Nvidia Research, 2013.

[8] R. Garg and J. N. Amaral. Compiling Python to a hybrid execution environment. In *GPGPU 2010*, pages 19–30, 2010.

[9] R. Garg and L. Hendren. Just-in-time shape inference for array-based languages. In *ARRAY'14 workshop at PLDI 2014*, 2014.

[10] R. Garg and L. Hendren. A portable and high-performance general matrix-multiply (GEMM) library for GPUs and single-chip CPU/GPU systems. In *Proceedings of 22nd Euromicro International Conference on Parallel, Distributed and network-based Processing, Special session on GPU computing*, 2014.

[11] A. Klöckner. PyCUDA. `http://mathema.tician.de/software/pycuda`.

[12] A. Klöckner. PyOpenCL web page. `http://mathema.tician.de/software/pyopencl`.

[13] MathWorks. MATLAB: The Language of Technical Computing.

[14] N. T. V. Nguyen, F. Irigoin, C. Ancourt, and R. Keryell. Efficient intraprocedural array bound checking. Technical report, Ecole des Mines de Paris, 2000.

[15] T. Oliphant. Numba Python bytecode to LLVM translator. In *Proceedings of the Python for Scientific Computing Conference (SciPy)*, June 2012. Oral Presentation.

[16] A. Prasad, J. Anantpur, and R. Govindarajan. Automatic compilation of MATLAB programs for synergistic execution on heterogeneous processors. In *PLDI 2011*, pages 152–163, 2011.

[17] G. Pryor, B. Lucey, S. Maddipatla, C. McClanahan, J. Melonakos, V. Venugopalakrishnan, K. Patel, P. Yalamanchili, and J. Malcolm. High-level GPU computing with Jacket for MATLAB and C/C++. *Proceedings of SPIE (online)*, 8060(806005), 2011.

[18] Python.org. Python Programming Language: Official Website.

[19] R-project.org. The R Project for Statistical Computing.

[20] C. J. Rossbach, Y. Yu, J. Currey, J.-P. Martin, and D. Fetterly. Dandelion: a compiler and runtime for heterogeneous systems. In *SOSP'13: The 24th ACM Symposium on Operating Systems Principles*, 2013.

[21] A. Rubinsteyn, E. Hielscher, N. Weinman, and D. Shasha. Parakeet: A just-in-time parallel accelerator for Python. In *HotPar 12*, 2012.

[22] SciPy.org. NumPy: Scientific Computing Tools for Python.

[23] D. S. Seljebotn. Fast numerical computations with Cython. In G. Varoquaux, S. van der Walt, and J. Millman, editors, *Proceedings of the 8th Python in Science Conference*, pages 15 – 22, Pasadena, CA USA, 2009.

[24] L. Shure. Memory management for functions and variables. `http://blogs.mathworks.com/loren/2006/05/10/memory-management-for-functions-and-variables/`.

Memory Scheduling Towards High-Throughput Cooperative Heterogeneous Computing

Hao Wang[†], Ripudaman Singh[†], Michael J. Schulte[‡], Nam Sung Kim[†]

[†]The University of Wisconsin-Madison, WI, U.S.A. [‡]Advanced Micro Devices, TX, U.S.A.

{hwang223, rsingh27, nskim3}@wisc.edu michael.schulte@amd.com

Abstract

Technology scaling enables the integration of both the CPU and the GPU into a single chip for higher throughput and energy efficiency. In such a single-chip heterogeneous processor (SCHP), its memory bandwidth is the most critically shared resource, requiring judicious management to maximize the throughput. Previous studies on memory scheduling for SCHPs have focused on the scenario where multiple applications are running on the CPU and the GPU respectively, which we denote as a multi-tasking scenario. However, another increasingly important usage scenario for SCHPs is cooperative heterogeneous computing, where a single parallel application is partitioned between the CPU and the GPU such that the overall throughput is maximized.

In previous studies on memory scheduling techniques for chip multi-processors (CMPs) and SCHPs, the first-ready first-come-first-service (FR-FCFS) scheduling policy was used as an inept baseline due to its fairness issue. However, in a cooperative heterogeneous computing scenario, we first demonstrate that FR-FCFS actually offers nearly 10% higher throughput than two recently proposed memory scheduling techniques designed for a multi-tasking scenario. Second, based on our analysis on memory access characteristics in a cooperative heterogeneous computing scenario, we propose various optimization techniques that enhance the row-buffer locality by 10%, reduce the service latency of CPU memory requests by 26%, and improve the overall throughput by up to 8% compared to FR-FCFS.

Categories and Subject Descriptors

C.1.3 [**Processor Architecture**]: Other Architecture Styles – Heterogeneous (hybrid) systems; B.3.2 [**Memory Structures**]: Design Styles – Primary memory

Keywords

Memory scheduling; Heterogeneous processor

1. Introduction

The memory bandwidth has been one of the most critically shared resources for chip multi-processors (CMPs). Neither the off-chip memory speed nor the number of I/O links scales as well as the number of cores per chip, fundamentally limiting the system's performance. Previous studies proposed to exploit application behaviors and characteristics to effectively manage the memory system shared by multiple cores [1,2,3]. Recently, both the GPU and the CPU are integrated into a single chip, such as AMD's accelerated processing unit (APU) [4] and Intel's Ivy Bridge processor [5]. Generally, the CPU is designed for high single-thread performance, but it cannot tolerate long memory access latency. In contrast, the GPU is designed for high throughput and it can often hide long memory access latency with a large number of hardware threads. Yet, it still requires high bandwidth to provide high throughput.

Recent studies proposed novel techniques to manage the limited memory bandwidth resource between the CPU and the GPU. A QoS-aware memory scheduling technique was proposed to dynamically adjust the priority of CPU and GPU requests to ensure that the GPU meets a real-time constraint for graphics applications with a minimum negative impact on CPU performance [6]. A staged memory scheduler (SMS), which decouples the primary functions of a memory controller into three stages, was presented in [7]. It improves fairness and performance by maximizing CPU performance while satisfying certain target GPU performance (e.g., frame rate). Basically, these studies on memory scheduling for SCHPs have focused on a multi-tasking scenario that the GPU and the CPU are running graphics and multiple general-purpose applications, respectively.

However, there exists another increasingly important usage scenario of SCHPs, where a single parallel application is partitioned between and run on both the CPU and the GPU. This cooperative heterogeneous computing approach utilizes both the CPU and the GPU as compute devices to maximize the overall throughput. There have been early studies on programming frameworks that adaptively partition a given application between heterogeneous processors to improve overall throughput and/or energy efficiency [8,9]. Recently, with the introduction of the OpenCL standard, a single parallel application can utilize both the CPU and the GPU within the same execution context, under which OpenCL kernels and memory objects are shared by default [10]. It was reported that a cooperative heterogeneous computing approach using an Intel Core i7-3770K processor provided 2.55× and 1.89× higher throughput than using only the CPU or the GPU for two industry benchmarks, LuxMark [11] and Sandra [12], respectively [13].

Under such a specific yet important computing model, an alternative guideline for designing memory scheduling techniques is needed due to the following two reasons. First, the evaluation metric for cooperative heterogeneous computing is fundamentally different from that for multi-tasking. When multiple applications are running on a processor, fairness is a key concern for developing memory scheduling techniques. Some of the previous studies also attempt to improve overall system performance; however, as explicitly mentioned in [7], it is usually not straightforward to define the system performance in an SCHP

PACT'14, August 24–27, 2014, Edmonton, AB, Canada.

http://dx.doi.org/10.1145/2628071.2628096

running multiple applications. In contrast, when we consider a cooperative heterogeneous computing scenario, the design objective is clearly to maximize overall throughput. Furthermore, we observe that guaranteeing fairness between the CPU and the GPU becomes less meaningful and such an attempt often degrades the overall throughput. For example, if a given application runs more efficient on the GPU than the CPU, more computation will be allocated to the GPU. In this circumstance, enforcing fairness (e.g. minimizing maximum slowdown of the CPU [14,2,7]) can degrade overall throughput. Second, memory-intensive applications are likely to substantially degrade the performance of less memory-intensive applications with application-oblivious memory scheduling policies. This is one of the key challenges that previous studies on memory scheduling attempted to tackle [1,2,3,7]. One of the key principles in previous memory scheduling techniques is to prioritize the requests from non-memory-intensive applications over memory-intensive ones. This intuitively makes sense since prioritizing requests from non-memory-intensive applications substantially improve their performance without a notable negative impact on other memory-intensive ones; non-memory-intensive ones will not consume much bandwidth even with high priority. In contrast, in a cooperative heterogeneous computing scenario, the CPU and the GPU will show relatively similar memory access characteristics, since essentially it is a single application running on both sides. For instance, an application that is inherently memory-intensive will generate intensive memory requests from both sides, although the access patterns and intensities will be different due to the asymmetries in core frequency, the number of hardware threads, and on-chip cache hierarchy. Therefore, the memory controller's awareness of the difference in application characteristics will lose its effectiveness in the context of single-application cooperative heterogeneous computing.

In this paper, we first take two advanced memory scheduling techniques: SMS, and fair queuing memory system (FQMS) [15], which are proposed for multi-tasking SCHPs and CMPs, respectively. Comparing SMS and FQMS against FR-FCFS in the context of cooperative heterogeneous computing, we demonstrate that both SMS and FQMS perform notably worse than FR-FCFS, which has been considered as an undesirable candidate for heterogeneous processors due to serious fairness problem in a multi-tasking scenario.

Second, we perform a comprehensive analysis on the memory access characteristics and patterns in cooperative heterogeneous computing. Then we propose a novel memory scheduler that improves the overall throughput of cooperative heterogeneous computing SCHPs, with various optimization techniques. Considering the CPU is more latency-sensitive, we selectively prioritize CPU requests at both the front-end scheduling and back-end data bus arbitration stages. To adapt the degree of prioritization for CPU requests in a fine-grained manner, we also introduce a parameter that is programmable at runtime to control the fraction of CPU requests to be prioritized. Furthermore, we offer another runtime technique that adaptively locks one or more banks for a certain time period after observing specific regularity in access patterns when a single parallel application is running on an SCHP. This can reduce interferences between the CPU and GPU requests while avoiding introduction of additional latency like a batch scheduling approach [7].

This paper is organized as follows: Section 2 provides backgrounds. Section 3 describes the experimental methodology. Section 4 analyzes the memory access characteristics and patterns of parallel applications running on cooperative heterogeneous computing SCHPs. Section 5 describes our proposed memory scheduler. Section 6 discusses evaluation results. Section 7 summarizes related work. Section 8 concludes our study.

2. Background & Motivation

2.1 Cooperative Heterogeneous Computing

Compared to running a single application on either the CPU or the GPU, running it on both the CPU and the GPU (i.e., cooperative heterogeneous computing) can achieve higher throughput and power efficiency [16,17]. However, one of the key challenges with cooperative heterogeneous computing was lack of programming model and runtime system support for heterogeneous abstraction. The introduction of OpenCL standard makes the first step to allow compute devices (e.g., CPU, GPU, FPGA, etc.) to have an identical look from a high-level software perspective. Figure 1 shows how an OpenCL application can be partitioned between and distributed to the CPU and GPU on a heterogeneous system. The kernel and memory objects created at a context level are shared between the CPU and the GPU. A workload can be partitioned at the granularity of work group, because there is no explicit synchronization between two work groups.

Some key challenges to effectively support true cooperative heterogeneous computing based on the current OpenCL standard and platform include (i) memory space management and (ii) automatic load balancing between the CPU and the GPU [13]. First, the memory objects are shared in the current heterogeneous computing system, but the CPU and the GPU have separate copies of data in separate memory space [18]. A weak consistency model is maintained between the CPU and the GPU, and therefore we observed on a real AMD Trinity system that the CPU and the GPU tend to delay each other if they try to write to the same memory object. However, by using properly-aligned, non-overlapping sub-buffers, the CPU and the GPU can simultaneously write to the same memory buffer [19]. Furthermore, with the industrial trend towards tighter integration of the CPU and the GPU sharing the memory space, such as recently announced AMD's heterogeneous unified memory access (*hUMA*) for their next generation APUs [18], cooperative heterogeneous computing is expected to be increasingly appealing.

Second, as for the load balancing issue, ideally there should have a shared command queue to dynamically schedule the

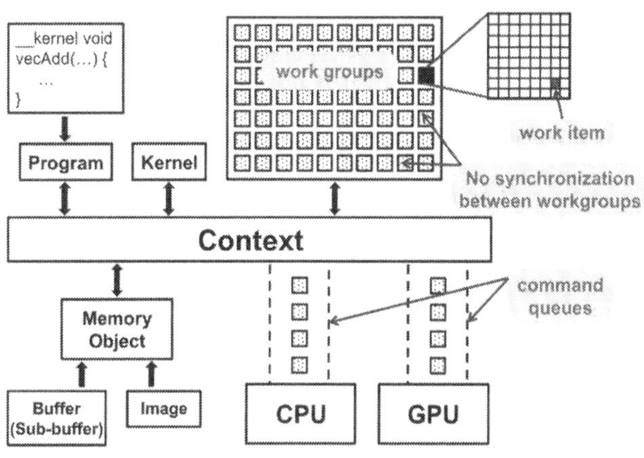

Figure 1. OpenCL application in a heterogeneous system. Workload partitioning happens at the granularity of work group (corresponding to thread block in CUDA terminology).

Table 1. System configurations.

# of CPU cores	8	# of GPU SMs	16	Channels/Ranks/Banks	2 / 2 / 8
CPU Freq	4.0 GHz	GPU Freq	800 MHz	DRAM Freq	800 MHz
CPU core width	4	GPU # of registers per SM	16384	Data bus width	64 bits / channel
CPU IL1 and DL1	32KB-private / 2-way	GPU # of threads per SM	1024	Row buffer size	2 KB
CPU L2 per core	4MB-shared / 16-way	GPU # of CTAs per SM	8	tCAS / tRCD / tRP	13.75 / 13.75 / 13.75 ns
CPU store buffer	16 per core	GPU on-chip RAM per SM	32KB	tRAS / tRC	35 / 48.75 ns

computation and balance the workload between heterogeneous compute devices, instead of having separate command queues for the CPU and the GPU as shown in Figure 1. There are previous studies on load balancing using profiling-based adaptive mapping [9] and predictive modeling-based static partitioning [20]. Recently, Intel demonstrated an OpenCL implementation of an N-Body simulation using an Intel Sandybridge processor comprised of a quad-core CPU and a GPU [21]. It partitions the bodies between the CPU and the GPU, which is enforced by setting the corresponding global work size when enqueuing a kernel to the CPU or GPU command queue. Then it iteratively balances the load according to the runtime statistics from the previous iteration.

2.2 Memory System Organization

The modern main memory system typically has multiple channels operating independently. Each channel connects to one or more memory modules (e.g., dual-inline memory modules (DIMMs)) which, in turn, can be divided into one or more ranks. Each rank consists of multiple banks (e.g., 8 for DDR3) which can be viewed as 2-dimensional arrays of memory cells. In order to access a block of data, the entire row is read into the *row buffer* (i.e., *activate*). Subsequent reads and writes to the same row can be serviced directly from the row buffer, leading to lower access latency. In contrast, an access to a different row will result in additional latency to *precharge* and *activate* the new row.

On the processor side, each channel has a memory controller that interacts with the DIMMs. It typically includes a request buffer, on which the scheduling algorithm is applied. Modern out-of-order schedulers often prioritize row-buffer hit requests to improve overall DRAM throughput [22]. Recent studies proposed to apply application-aware priority schemes to the request buffer for better fairness and performance [1]. The memory controller also keeps track of the state of each bank, takes care of various DRAM timing constraints, and issues DRAM commands accordingly.

3. Experimental Methodology

In this section, we first describe the architectural simulation setup and system configuration parameters. Then we present the benchmarks used for cooperative heterogeneous computing and the simulation approach. Finally, we briefly describe memory scheduling techniques such as FR-FCFS, SMS and FQMS that are compared against our techniques.

3.1 Simulation Framework

We use a cycle-level integrated gem5+GPGPU-Sim simulator [17] to perform our evaluations. gem5 models out-of-order cores and a MOESI cache coherence protocol of the CPU [23]; GPGPU-Sim models the streaming multiprocessors (SMs) and on-chip interconnects of the GPU [24]. A cycle-driven memory controller is developed to service the memory requests from both gem5 and GPGPU-Sim. The memory controller keeps track of the state of each DRAM bank and various timing information based on DDR3-1600 specification [25]. Table 1 summarizes the key configuration parameters of the evaluated system. We aim to model a heterogeneous processor similar to an AMD APU, on which the last-level cache is not shared between the CPU and the GPU.

3.2 Benchmarks

We use ten benchmarks from Rodinia [26], a benchmark suite designed for heterogeneous computing. It covers applications from a wide range of domains, including pattern recognition, graph algorithms, fluid dynamics, medical imaging, physics simulation, data mining, multi-body dynamics, linear algebra, bioinformatics, grid traversal, and image processing. Table 2 summarizes the abbreviation and input data size of each benchmark.

We annotate the parallel portion of each benchmark, which generally dominates the total execution time of these data-parallel applications, as region of interest, and perform the analysis and evaluation only on the parallel portion. We modify the loop boundary or global work size in benchmark source code to partition the work between the CPU and the GPU. The total execution time is the maximum of the execution times of the CPU and the GPU. Generally, most benchmarks execute one or more parallel kernels for many iterations, such as CFD; or the benchmark itself is a kernel that will be executed iteratively in real use, such as LUD. This enables the iterative load balancing and thus we assume the benchmarks can quickly converge to the optimal workload partitioning point [17].

3.3 FR-FCFS, SMS and FQMS

We implemented three existing or recently proposed memory scheduling techniques. FR-FCFS is a conventional scheduling policy that prioritizes requests resulting in row-buffer hit. It maximizes the utilization of memory system, while it does not exploit any application characteristics. As a result, when multiple

Table 2. Benchmarks for heterogeneous computing.

Benchmark	Acronym	Input Data Size
Back Propagation	BP	262,144 input nodes
Breadth-First Search	BFS	1,000,000 nodes
CFD Solver	CFD	200k elements
HotSpot	HS	1024×1024 data points
K-Means	KMN	204,800 points, 34 features
LavaMD	LMD	216 boxes, 100 particles per box
Particle Filter	PTF	10,000 particles
PathFinder	PF	Width = 1,000,000
SRAD	SRAD	2048×2048 data points
Streamcluster	SC	65536 data points

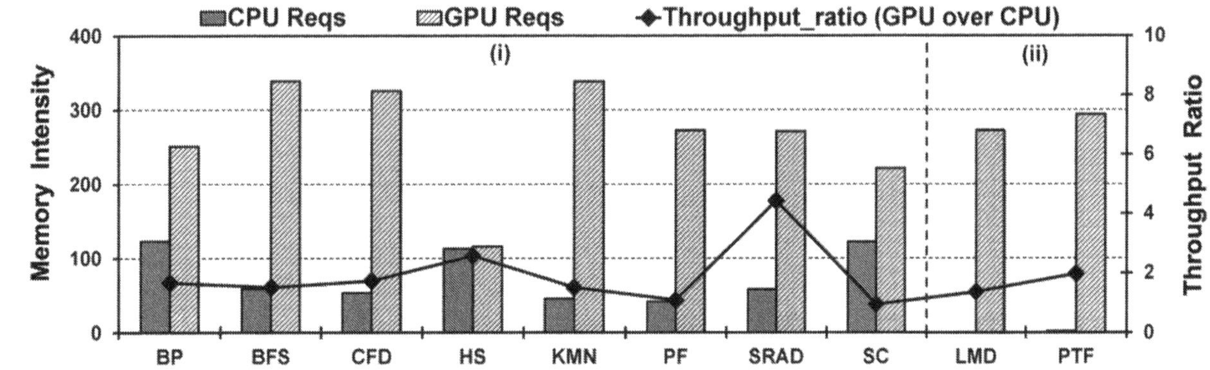

Figure 2. Memory intensity of 10 parallel benchmarks in Table 2 running on the CPU and the GPU, respectively.

applications are running simultaneously, a memory-intensive application with high spatial locality is likely to significantly degrade the performance of non-memory-intensive applications. Furthermore, the integration of a GPU on the same die with a CPU could further worsen the situation since graphics applications typically generate excessive memory requests which exhibit high spatial locality.

Recent studies proposed various memory scheduling techniques to guarantee the fairness and provide QoS to each application running on the shared memory system [7]. SMS refers to staged memory scheduling, which is a novel memory controller design to improve the performance, fairness, and scalability in SCHP systems. It decouples the primary functions of a memory controller into three stages. In the first stage, it groups memory requests into batches per source (CPU core or GPU) FIFO queues to preserve row-buffer locality. The second stage performs batch scheduling across applications to improve fairness. The batch scheduler uses a short-job-first (SJF) policy with a probability of p, and a round-robin policy otherwise. p is a tunable parameter that can be used to adjust the priorities of the CPU and the GPU. We sweep the value of p from 0 to 1 with a step size of 0.1 and take the best result.

Our FQMS implementation adapts a fair queuing memory system for SCHP systems [15]. The basic approach is to guarantee each core/thread receives its allocated share of memory bandwidth, and therefore provide QoS to all threads. Each incoming request is annotated with virtual start and finish times. Virtual times are calculated based on the arrival time, the virtual finish time of a previous request to the same bank, the service time of the request, and the bandwidth share allocated to the thread. They represent the times on a virtual private memory system whose performance is scaled with the allocated bandwidth share. The scheduler prioritizes requests based on the earliest virtual finish time, because it is the deadline to offer QoS of a thread. Similarly, we sweep the bandwidth partitioning point from 0.1 versus 0.9 to 0.9 versus 0.1 at the granularity of 0.1 and take the best result.

4. Memory Characteristics of Cooperative Heterogeneous Computing

We gather the memory access characteristics of the ten benchmarks listed in Table 2 for a cooperative heterogeneous computing scenario. Figure 2 presents the memory request intensities of the CPU and the GPU, when each application is running alone in the system. The throughput ratio of the GPU over the CPU running the same benchmark is also plotted on Figure 2. All ten benchmarks in Figure 2 are categorized into two groups. In group (ii), the CPU generates much fewer requests than the GPU, because a large L2 cache of the CPU filters most CPU memory requests for these benchmarks. However, most benchmarks are categorized in group (i), which exhibit comparable memory intensities (i.e., memory requests per kilo memory cycles) between the CPU and the GPU because fundamentally it is the same application that runs on both the CPU and the GPU. In contrast, in a multi-tasking scenario, one or a mix of SPEC CPU2006 benchmarks may run on the CPU and a graphics or GPGPU application may run on the GPU. In such a case, the memory access characteristics of the CPU and the GPU can be substantially diverse.

In order to depict the distinction between multi-tasking and cooperative heterogeneous computing scenarios in memory characteristics, we show three examples in Figure 3. We gather the memory requests per kilo memory cycles (MPKC), row-buffer locality (RBL) and bank-level parallelism (BLP) for different applications. Figure 3(a) describes a multi-tasking scenario that has one GPGPU application (*Back Propagation*) running on the GPU and multiple SPEC CPU2006 applications running on the

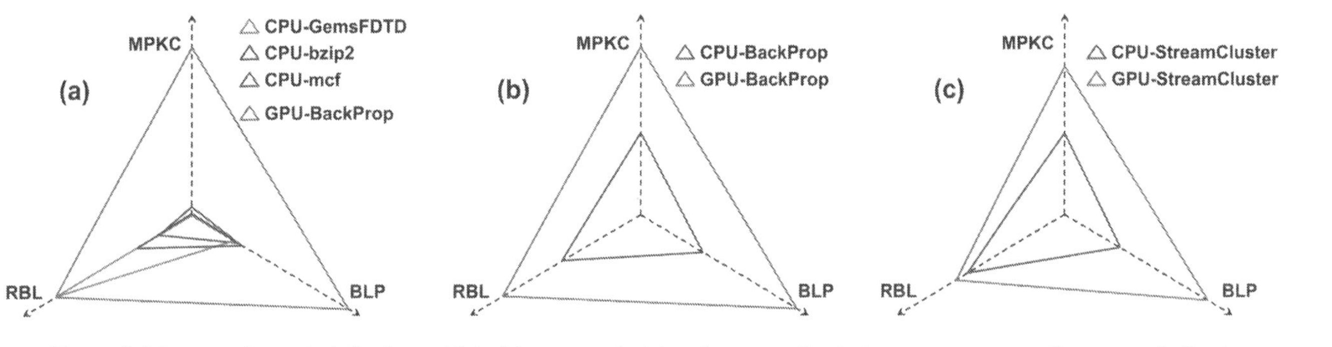

Figure 3. Memory characteristics in multi-tasking scenario (a) and cooperative heterogeneous computing scenario (b, c).

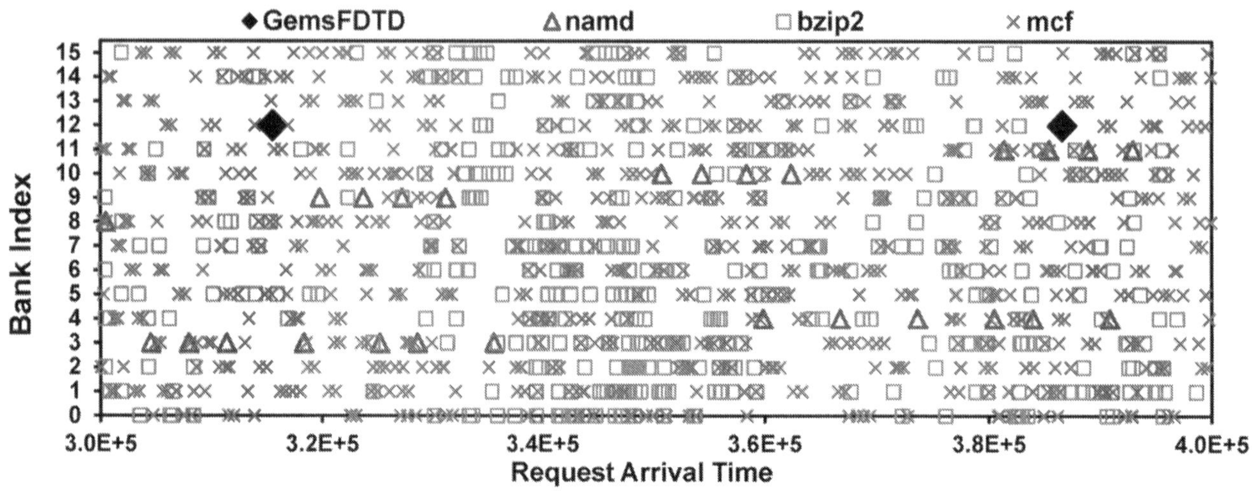

Figure 4. Memory access pattern for a mix of 4 SPEC CPU2006 applications running on a four-core CPU. The x-axis represents the time a request arrives at memory controller; the y-axis represents the bank index of the requests.

CPU. Since essentially the executed applications are dissimilar, there is no correlation in memory characteristics between the GPU and CPU applications. Especially the memory intensity of CPU applications is far lower than the GPU application. In contrast, Figure 3(b) and (c) represent cooperative heterogeneous computing scenarios that have one single parallel application running on both the CPU and the GPU. As we can see, there is a clear similarity between the CPU and the GPU in memory characteristics.

This is one of the key observations that motivate us to re-consider the existing memory scheduling algorithm. Previous studies on application-aware memory schedulers for a multi-tasking scenario attempt to prevent the interference from memory-intensive applications, especially those with high row-buffer locality. The basic approach to tackle this problem is to always prioritize requests from non-memory-intensive applications over memory-intensive ones. The rationale behind this approach is that prioritizing requests from non-memory-intensive applications can substantially improve the performance of these applications, without degrading the performance of memory-intensive applications, because the prioritized (non-memory-intensive) applications only consume trivial bandwidth. Consequently, the effectiveness of such a scheduling principle relies on the substantial distinction in memory characteristics among applications. However, when a single parallel application running on an SCHP, we will see similar memory characteristics between CPU and GPU requests.

Figure 4 presents the access pattern of a mix of four SPEC CPU2006 benchmarks (i.e. multi-tasking scenario) with diverse levels of memory intensities. We track the arrival time of each memory request and sort all the requests based on the bank index that they access in one of the dual memory channels. As we can observe, the memory accesses depicted in Figure 4 are fairly random, especially for *namd* and *bzip2*. Therefore, the useful information we can obtain from the access pattern is very limited. In contrast, Figure 5 plots the access pattern of a parallel benchmark, *Back Propagation*, running on an SCHP system. The access pattern shown in Figure 5 clearly exhibits regularity. The requests appear as separate periodical strips for the CPU and the GPU. Due to the dissimilarity in core frequency and the number of hardware threads, the recurrent CPU strips have a different period and slope from the GPU strips, leading to periodic overlaps with each other, indicating the CPU and the GPU are accessing the same bank in the same period of time. As introduced in Section 2.2, this is where the interference happens and the potential row-buffer conflict penalty is paid. Previous studies

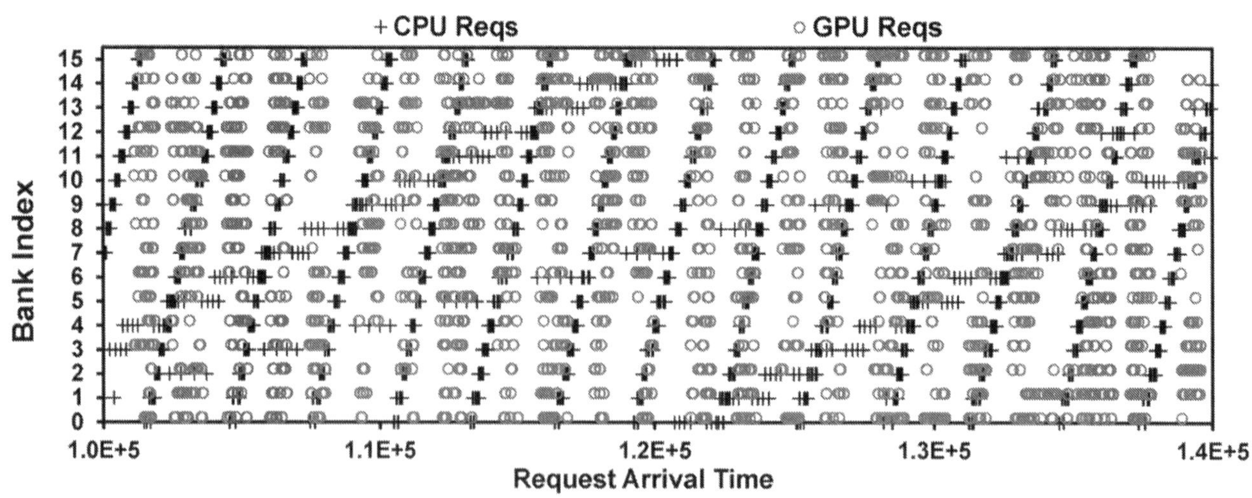

Figure 5. Memory access pattern for *Back Propagation* running on both the CPU and the GPU.

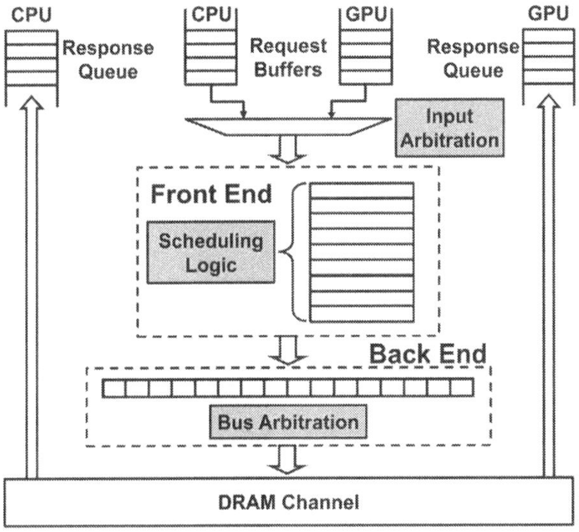

Figure 6. Memory controller organization.

proposed to (i) group requests into batches based on the requesting application and the accessing row, and (ii) schedule the batches of requests based on row-buffer locality [7]. However, the batch formation introduces additional latency which can be undesirable for high-throughput computing. Instead, we can exploit the regularity in access patterns of these data-parallel applications, and thus apply specific optimizations. More specifically, memory requests from the CPU to a certain bank are fairly concentrated since the CPU maintains much fewer active hardware threads than the GPU. Further, the bank access sequences are highly predictable. Therefore, we can simply apply a lock on the bank that the CPU is accessing for a short period of time to preserve the row-buffer locality.

5. Memory Scheduling for High-Throughput Cooperative Heterogeneous Computing

5.1 Memory Controller Organization

Figure 6 illustrates a typical design of a memory controller. First, the CPU and the GPU have its own in-order request buffer. An input arbitration is performed every cycle to determine which side will push a request into the front-end scheduling buffer, to which a scheduling algorithm is applied. This front-end scheduling buffer is fairly small since it is impractical to have a large buffer with sophisticated out-of-order scheduling logic enforced [7]. When a request is scheduled for a service, it is popped up from the front-end buffer, and pushed into the back-end per-bank command queue. At the back-end, it tracks the state of each DRAM bank, and manages various timing constraints. Note that the back-end command queue only has one entry per bank, in order to provide simple and straightforward information to the front-end scheduling logic. Finally, bus arbitration is performed among the banks to choose a ready command to be issued to a DRAM channel.

5.2 Scheduling Techniques

The key concept of our proposed scheduling techniques consider two aspects: (i) since the CPU is more latency-sensitive, we attempt to reduce the average service latency of CPU requests as much as possible by giving the CPU requests high priority, yet without explicitly constraining GPU requests; (ii) we need a parameter that can adjust the degree of prioritization in a fine-grained manner to accommodate various workload partitioning points and thus different relative importance between the CPU and the GPU.

Prioritization of CPU requests: First, we enable the prioritization of CPU requests at various stages in the memory controller depicted in Figure 6. At the input arbitration stage, requests from the CPU buffer can be prioritized; at the front-end scheduling queue, beyond the commonly used FR-FCFS policy [22], the CPU requests can be prioritized such that an old CPU request receives higher priority than a ready GPU request; at the back-end stage, the bus arbitration can also prioritize CPU requests over GPU requests that are arbitrated in a round-robin fashion.

Fine-grained adjustment of prioritization: As mentioned earlier, the relative importance of CPU and GPU performance depends on how given workload is partitioned between the CPU and the GPU. For example, assume that 80% of the workload is assigned to the GPU. Even if CPU performance is significantly degraded, it may still not be desirable to highly prioritize CPU requests. This is because the GPU may contribute more to the overall throughput while giving unnecessarily high priority to CPU requests often hurts GPU performance. Considering the workload partitioning point varies across benchmarks and architectures of the CPU and the GPU, it is desirable to have a parameter that can adjust the degree of prioritization in a fine-grained manner. Therefore, we introduce a prioritization threshold value (P_{th}) that decides the fraction of CPU requests that are prioritized. When a CPU request enters a memory controller, we attach one bit to the request to indicate whether or not the request is prioritized. The scheduling logic will only enforce the aforementioned prioritization techniques when the CPU request is tagged as a prioritized one.

Adjusting P_{th} at runtime: Previous studies have been using software-programmable configuration parameters to dynamically adjust the priority at runtime [7,15]. Nevertheless, such an adjustment at runtime is always challenging, because the optimal parameters depend on the characteristics and performance requirement of a given application at runtime. Especially in a multi-tasking scenario, it may require the system to determine which application is unexpectedly slowed down by the system itself, which may further require either an off-line profiling or predicting technique. However, in the context of cooperative heterogeneous computing, determining such parameters can be simple and straightforward. As mentioned earlier, these data-parallel applications generally have many iterations (e.g., 2000 iterations for CFD by default in original code). The runtime system can gather the performance statistics (i.e. kernel execution time) after each iteration, and then it can iteratively search for better performance. As an example, we can start from $P_{th} = 0$; then after each iteration, we increase the P_{th} by 0.1 to see if we obtain a better result (i.e. shorter execution time of one iteration). Therefore, within no more than ten iterations, we can find the optimal P_{th} parameter. Algorithm 1 presents the runtime tuning algorithm to obtain optimal P_{th}.

Adaptive bank lock: While exploring our prioritization technique, we observe that simply prioritizing CPU requests at the front-end scheduling buffer is not effective enough. For example, when a CPU request arrives at a memory controller, ideally it is expected to be serviced immediately considering its high priority. However, another GPU request to the same bank may have been already scheduled before the CPU request actually enters the scheduling buffer. Consequently, the CPU request has to wait for *tRAS* even it has a high priority. Further, we discover that such a

Algorithm 1. Runtime algorithm to adjust P_{th}.

```
Initialize:
    Pth = 0;                                  // init. Pth to 0
    Is_Stop = FALSE;
[TCPU; TGPU] = get_exe_time(Pth);             // first kernel launch; get exe. time of CPU & GPU
TOverall = Max(TCPU, TGPU);                   // assuming automatic load balancing, TCPU ≈ TGPU
while (!Is_Stop && Pth <= 1.0) {              // repeat until greedy search is completed
    Pth = Pth + 0.1;                          // increment Pth by 0.1
    [TCPU; TGPU] = get_exe_time(Pth);         // next kernel iteration; get exe. Time
    T = Max(TCPU, TGPU);
    if (T < TOverall)                         // if better, continue search
        TOverall = T;
    else                                      // if worse, stop searching & roll back Pth
        Is_Stop = True; Pth = Pth - 0.1;
}
Opt_Pth = Pth;
```

case occurs frequently due to the high memory intensity and bank-level parallelism of GPU requests, as indicated in Figure 3 and Figure 5. Therefore, we propose to lock a bank in advance, which prevents any GPU requests from being scheduled to the corresponding bank. Consequently, the bank stays idle even with pending GPU requests to the bank in buffer, and thus the bank is ready to service a CPU request as soon as the CPU request arrives. To support such a lock technique, we maintain one counter, which serves as a lock, for each bank at the front-end stage. If the counter of a certain bank has a non-zero value, the scheduling logic will not schedule a GPU request to that bank. Let's say the current counter value is zero and a CPU request is issued to the corresponding bank. This sets the counter value to a lock cycle value (N_{LC}). Afterwards the counter value is decremented every cycle, indicating that the lock will be effective for the next N_{LC} cycles.

Adjusting N_{LC} at runtime: We need to ensure that the lock lasts long enough to cover subsequent CPU requests to the same bank while minimizing the negative impact on GPU throughput. This requires us to adapt N_{LC} dynamically at runtime, because memory access characteristics and patterns vary from one application to another, as well as from one interval to another and from one partitioning point to another for a given application. We have another counter for each bank to periodically track the time interval between the first and last requests to certain bank within a time window (e.g., 200 memory cycles), which becomes the basis to determine the N_{LC} value for the next interval and is denoted as the expected N_{LC} value (N_{LC_EXP}). We update N_{LC} by taking the average of current N_{LC} and N_{LC_EXP} values for better stability when adjusting the N_{LC} value at runtime; we will further discuss this in Section 6. We also apply an upper limit on N_{LC} to prevent unexpectedly long lock cycles.

6. Experimental Results

6.1 Effectiveness of Bank Lock Scheme

Figure 7 presents the effectiveness of the adaptive bank lock scheme described above in Section 5.2. In order to demonstrate the effectiveness of dynamically adjusting a lock cycle value (N_{LC}), we measure the percentage of CPU requests that are covered by bank locks (i.e., bank lock coverage). As a static oracle case, we sweep the N_{LC} value over multiple runs and choose the best result. On average, the bank lock with the optimal fixed N_{LC} value covers 80% of the CPU requests. In comparison, our adaptive technique that adjust the N_{LC} value dynamically at runtime achieves on average 76% coverage, indicating our adaptive bank lock technique can effectively cover a large fraction of the CPU requests.

Our simulation results also suggest that the CPU requests, which are covered by bank locks, demonstrates significant queuing latency reduction at the front-end stage (on average 51%) compared to the case that only high priority is applied to CPU requests for scheduling memory requests. In contrast, the GPU throughput degradation introduced by bank lock is only 3% on average, as shown in Figure 7.

6.2 Row-Buffer Locality and Latency Analysis

Figure 8 shows the row-buffer locality of memory requests for the CPU and the GPU, respectively. First, SMS has lower row-buffer

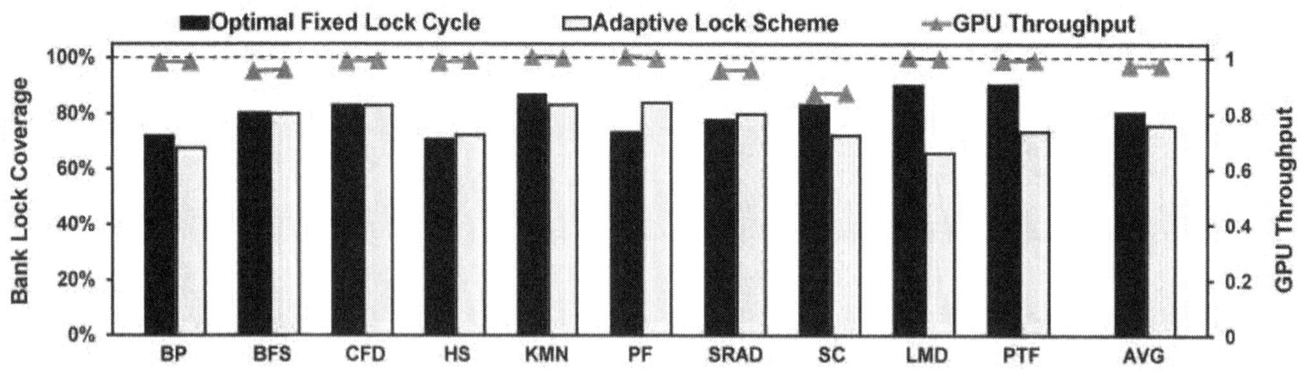

Figure 7. Effectiveness of our adaptive bank lock technique, and the impact on GPU throughput. "Bank Lock Coverage" represents the percentage of CPU requests covered by applying bank locks; GPU throughput is normalized to the baseline FR-FCFS case. "Optimal Fixed Lock Cycle" sweeps N_{LC} and chooses the best result; "Adaptive Lock Scheme" uses the runtime technique to decide N_{LC} as described in Section 5.2.

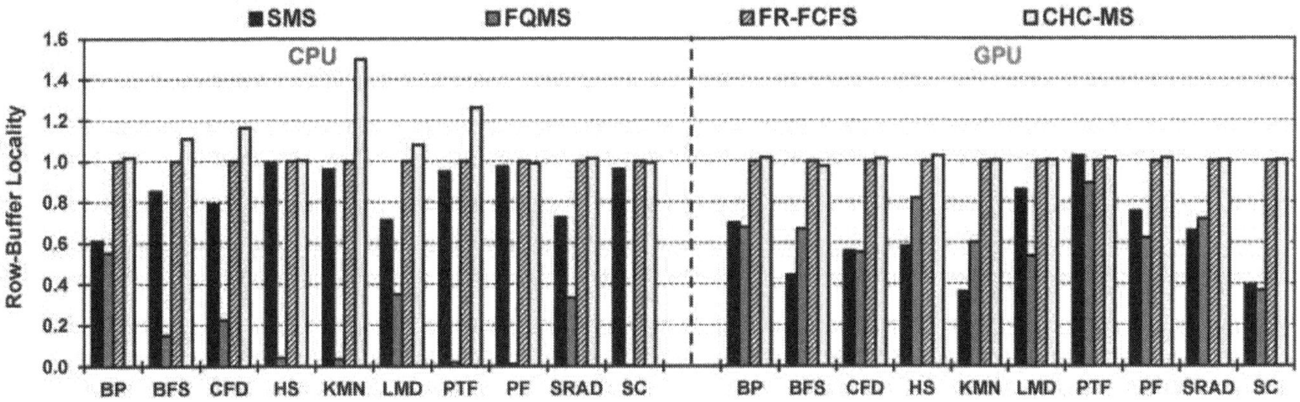

Figure 8. Row-buffer locality of (a) CPU requests and (b) GPU requests for SMS, FQMS, FR-FCFS and CHC-MS. Row-buffer locality values are measured by the fraction of accesses that hit in the row buffer, and are normalized to FR-FCFS case.

locality on both the CPU and the GPU. The reason is that although it uses batch scheduling to preserve the locality, its in-order scheduling imposes a fundamental limit on the available locality. Second, FQMS performs poorly in terms of row-buffer locality, especially for the CPU. This is related to its original design target. FQMS is designed to provide QoS for all threads. Therefore, it schedules the requests strictly based on their virtual finish time such that it can even hurt the inherent locality. Finally, our proposed scheme targeting cooperative heterogeneous computing (*CHC-MS*) improves the row-buffer locality of CPU requests by 10% on average, indicating the effectiveness of our bank lock technique. In addition, the row-buffer locality of GPU requests is also slightly higher than FR-FCFS, because our bank lock technique helps to reduce the interference between CPU and GPU requests.

Figure 9 shows the average latency of memory requests for the CPU and the GPU, respectively. First, SMS has higher average latency than FR-FCFS on both the CPU and the GPU. SMS has a stage of batch formation, where an incoming request has to wait in the buffer until the subsequent requests from the same source to form a batch. While this method helps to preserve the row-buffer locality, it also inevitably introduces additional queuing latency. Second, compared to FR-FCFS, FQMS shows lower latency for CPU requests, but relatively much higher latency for GPU requests. This matches the design objective of FQMS. CPU requests are probably delayed in FR-FCFS, while FQMS attempts to guarantee the fairness and provide QoS to both the CPU and the GPU. As a result, GPU performance is sacrificed to improve CPU performance. However, in fact, the GPU performance is more important as it contributes more to the overall throughput. Finally, our CHC-MS reduces the latency of CPU requests by 26% while only increasing the latency of GPU requests by 7%.

6.3 Throughput Analysis

Figure 10 presents the throughput with different degrees of prioritization for the CPU and the GPU, respectively. The P_{th} parameter decides the percentage of prioritized CPU requests. As we prioritize more CPU requests, the throughput of CPU increases significantly, while GPU throughput is inevitably degraded, yet at a lower rate than the improvement of the CPU. This is because (i) the GPU is able to hide the memory latency to certain extent while the CPU is very sensitive to the long latency and thus the prioritization of CPU requests will help the CPU more and hurt the GPU less; and (ii) the bank lock scheme we use only rejects GPU requests (i.e. lock the bank for the CPU) for a short period of time as indicated by Figure 5, and hence it minimize the negative impact on GPU performance while preserve the row-buffer locality of CPU requests. However, it may not be desirable to always prioritize CPU requests since the GPU may contribute more to the overall throughput depending on the optimal workload partitioning pint. Therefore, tunable P_{th} enables a large optimization space to accommodate different workload partitioning points and hence the varying relative importance of the CPU and the GPU.

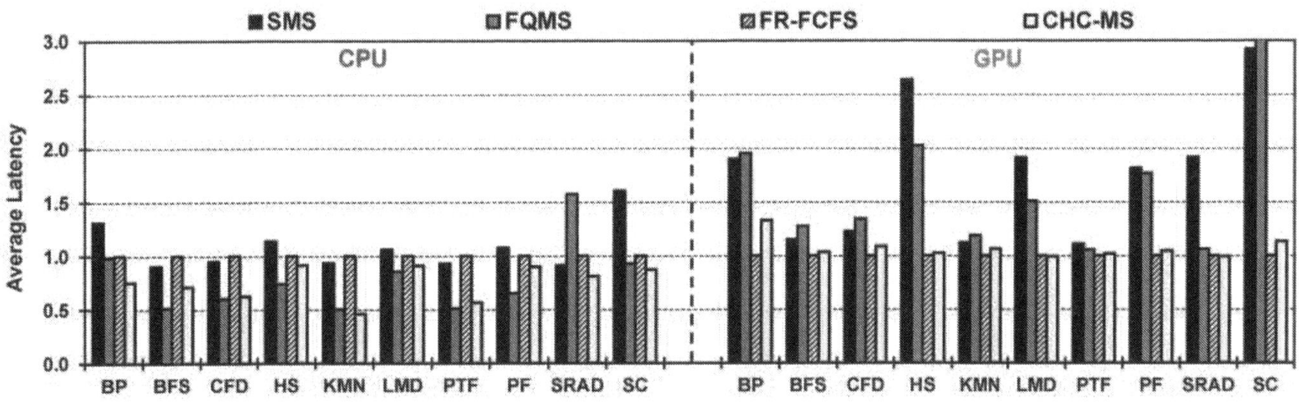

Figure 9. Average Latency of CPU requests (left) and GPU requests (right) for SMS, FQMS, FR-FCFS and CHC-MS. CAS latency and service latency are excluded since they are constant. Latency values are normalized to FR-FCFS case.

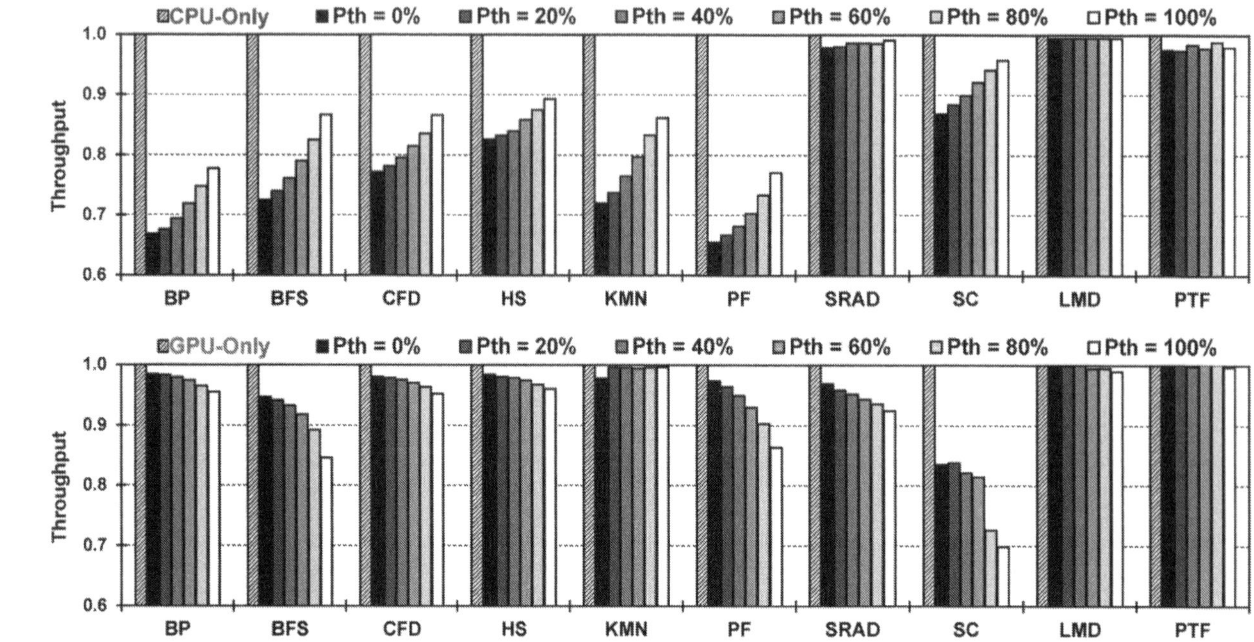

Figure 10. Throughput of the CPU (up) and the GPU (down) with different prioritization threshold (P_{th}). Throughput values of the CPU and the GPU are normalized to CPU-only and GPU-only case, respectively.

Figure 11 presents the overall throughput of SMS, FQMS, FR-FCFS, and CHC-MS. All throughput values are normalized to FR-FCFS case. We also plot the optimal degree of prioritization (P_{th}) that gives the best result for CHC-MS. First of all, we find that conventional FR-FCFS policy, which has been criticized for use in CMPs or SCHPs, actually performs better than SMS and FQMS by 10% and 6%, respectively. An intuitive explanation is that it is one single application running on both the CPU and the GPU, which is similar to the conventional uniprocessor case, and therefore FR-FCFS is preferred due to its capability to provide high bus utilization. Finally, our scheme (CHC-MS) achieves up to 8% and on average 3% additional throughput improvement over FR-FCFS, which is 13% higher than SMS and 10% higher than FQMS.

7. Related Work

7.1 Memory Scheduling on CMPs

There have been many studies focused on memory scheduling for CPU-only systems. Rixner introduced the well-known FR-FCFS scheduling policy that prioritizes row-buffer hits to achieve higher DRAM throughput and bus utilization [22]. FR-FCFS has been readily accepted for unicore processors; however, it does not provide any fairness guarantees when used in chip multiprocessors, since FR-FCFS tends to favor applications with high row locality. Recently proposed policies that attempt to make memory controller aware of characteristics of different applications running in the system, and provide QoS to all applications. Parallelism-aware batch scheduling (PAR-BS) scheme issues requests in batches to provide fairness and tries to maintain original bank level parallelism of an application [1]. Adaptive per-thread least-attained-servic scheuler (ATLAS) tries to prioritize requests from applications that have recieved least memory service [2]. Finally, thread cluster memory scheduling (TCM) attempts to improve both system throughput and fairness by dividing applications into two clusters (i.e., latency-sensitve and bandwidth-sensitive clusters) based on bank level parallelism, row-buffer locality and memory intensity of the applications

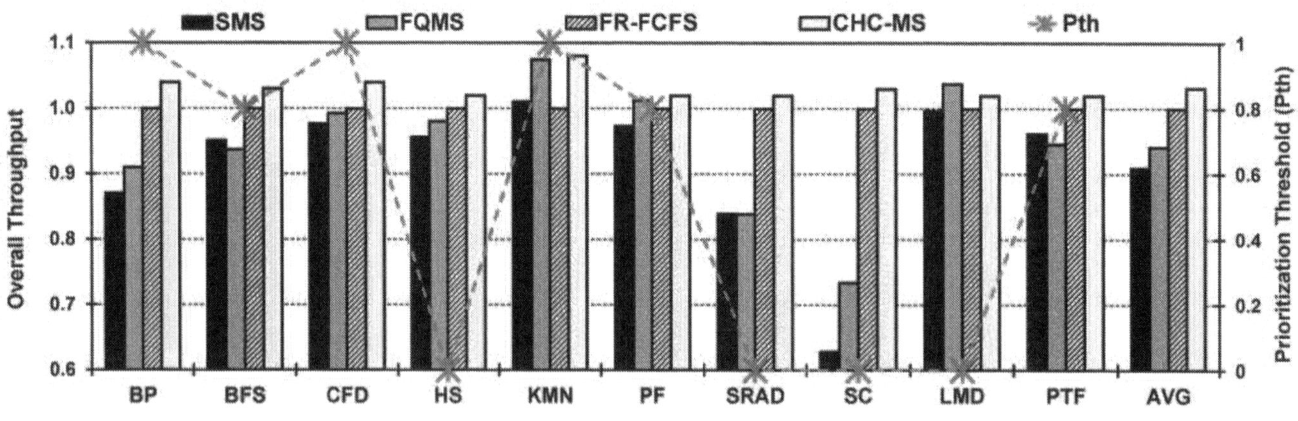

Figure 11. Overall throughput of SMS, FQMS, FR-FCFS and CHC-MS, and the optimal P_{th} giving the best result for CHC-MS. Throughput values are normalized to SMS.

running in the system; it always prioritize requests from the latency-sensitive cluster [3].

As described in [7], these scheduling schemes do not perform well in a heterogeneous system due to the difference in memory access behavior of CPU and GPU applications. FR-FCFS will favor GPU because of its higher row locality. ATLAS tends to degrade GPU while TCM tends to classify memory-intensive CPU applications into latency-sensitive cluster because of large difference between memory intensities of CPU and GPU applications.

7.2 Memory Scheduling on SCHPs

As mentioned earlier, previous studies on memory scheduling for heterogeneous processors have focused on multi-tasking scenario where the CPU and the GPU run general-purpose and graphics applications, respectively. QoS-aware memory controller [6] monitors the progress of rendering process of the graphics application, and dynamically adjusts the priority of CPU and GPU memory requests. The scheduling algorithm maintains CPU priority when possible, but increases the priority of GPU when it is likely to miss the real-time deadline for target frame rate, based on the progress tracking result. However, this approach is specific to the scenario described in their paper. Considering the scenario that we focus on (i.e. single-application cooperative heterogeneous computing), there is not a real-time deadline to catch and thus it undermines the basic idea of tracking the progress of GPU applications and adjusting scheduling strategy dynamically.

SMS [7] is described earlier and evaluated in this paper. In addition to the analysis performed above, intuitively the fundamental differences include (i) the system throughput metric does not have a straightforward definition in their context; (ii) the featured fairness metric is less meaningful in our context while overall throughput measured in terms of total execution time is our key concern.

8. Conclusion

In this paper, we first analyze various memory scheduling techniques on SCHPs in the context of cooperative heterogeneous computing, where a single parallel application is partitioned between and concurrently runs on the CPU and the GPU to maximize overall throughput. We demonstrate that existing memory scheduling techniques proposed for a multi-tasking scenario are not efficient for cooperative heterogeneous computing. Our analysis indicates that (i) previous scheduling techniques optimized for a multi-tasking scenario consider fairness among applications as the key concern, which in fact hurts the overall throughput in cooperative heterogeneous computing running a single parallel application; and (ii) the memory access characteristics and patterns of a single parallel application running on an SCHP are dissimilar from those of multiple applications. We discover that the conventional FR-FCFS policy, which is believed to be inept in multi-core era, is actually very competent for high-throughput cooperative heterogeneous computing. Finally, based on our analysis on memory access characteristics and patterns, we propose a new memory scheduling technique (CHC-MS) optimized for cooperative heterogeneous computing. CHC-MS considerably enhances row-buffer locality, reduces service latency of CPU memory requests, and improves overall throughput compared to FR-FCFS, SMS, and FQMS in the context of cooperative heterogeneous computing scenario.

Acknowledgement

This work was supported in part by generous grants from AMD and NSF (CNS-1217102). Nam Sung Kim has a financial interest in AMD and Samsung Electronics.

Reference

[1] Onur Mutlu and Thomas Moscibroda, "Parallelism-aware batch scheduling: enhancing both performance and fairness of shared DRAM systems," in *ISCA-35*, 2008.

[2] Yoongu Kim, Onur Mutlu, Mor Harchol-Balter, and Dongsu Han, "ATLAS: A scalable and high-performance scheduling algorithm for multiple memory controllers," in *HPCA-16*, 2010.

[3] Yoongu Kim, Michael Papamichael, Onur Mutlu, and Mor Harchol-Balter, "Thread cluster memory scheduling: exploiting differences in memory access behavior," in *MICRO-43*, 2010.

[4] Alexander Branover, Denis Foley, and Maurice Steinman, "AMD Fusion APU: Llano," *IEEE Micro*, vol. 32, no. 2, pp. 28-37, 2012.

[5] Satish Damaraju et al., "A 22nm IA multi-CPU and GPU System-on-Chip," in *ISSCC*, 2012.

[6] Min Kyu Jeong, Mattan Erez, Chander Sudanthi, and Nigel Paver, "A QoS-aware memory controller for dynamically balancing GPU and CPU bandwidth use in an MPSoC," in *DAC-49*, 2012.

[7] Rachata Ausavarungnirun, Kevin Kai-Wei Chang, Lavanya Subramanian, Gabriel H. Loh, and Onur Mutlu, "Staged memory scheduling: achieving high performance and scalability in heterogeneous systems," in *ISCA-39*, 2012.

[8] Michael D. Linderman, Jamison D. Collins, Hong Wang, and Teresa H. Meng, "Merge: a programming model for heterogeneous multi-core systems," in *ASPLOS-13*, 2008.

[9] Chi-Keung Luk, Sunpyo Hong, and Hyesoon Kim, "Qilin: Exploiting parallelism on heterogeneous multiprocessors with adaptive mapping," in *MICRO-42*, 2009.

[10] John E. Stone, David Gohara, and Guochun Shi, "OpenCL: A parallel programming standard for heterogeneous computing systems," *Computing in Science and Engineering*, vol. 12, no. 3, pp. 66-73, 2010.

[11] LuxMark. [Online]. http://www.luxrender.net/wiki/LuxMark

[12] SiSoftware. [Online]. http://www.sisoftware.net/

[13] Maxim Shevtsov, "OpenCL: the advantages of heterogeneous approach," , March 2013. [Online]. http://software.intel.com/en-us/articles/opencl-the-advantages-of-heterogeneous-approach

[14] Hans Vandierendonck and Andre Seznec, "Fairness metrics for multi-threaded processors," *IEEE Computer Architecture Letters*, vol. 10, no. 1, pp. 4-7, 2011.

[15] Kyle J. Nesbit, Nidhi Aggarwal, James Laudon, and Smith E. James, "Fair Queuing Memory Systems," in *Proceedings of the 39th Annual IEEE/ACM International Symposium on Microarchitecture (MICRO 39)*, 2006.

[16] Rakesh Kumar, Dean M. Tullsen, Norman P. Jouppi, and Parthasarathy Ranganathan, "Heterogeneous chip multiprocessors," *IEEE Computer*, vol. 38, no. 11, pp. 32-38, 2005.

[17] Hao Wang, Vijay Sathish, Ripudaman Singh, Michael J. Schulte, and Nam Sung Kim, "Workload and power budget partitioning for single-chip heterogeneous processors," in *PACT-21*, 2012.

[18] AMD hUMA introduced: Heterogeneous Unified Memory Access. [Online]. http://www.bit-tech.net/news/hardware/2013/04/30/amd-huma-heterogeneous-unified-memory-acces/

[19] Writing to a Shared Resource (Intel). [Online]. http://software.intel.com/sites/landingpage/opencl/optimization-guide/Writing_to_a_Shared_Resource.htm

[20] Dominik Grewe and Michael F.P. O'Boyle, "A Static Task Partitioning Approach for Heterogeneous Systems Using OpenCL," *Compiler Construction*, pp. 286-305, 2011.

[21] Maxim Shevtsov, Boaz Ouriel, and Ayal Zaks, "OpenCL sample for heterogeneous N-Body simulation," in *HiPEAC Computing Systems Week*, 2013.

[22] Scott Rixner, William J. Dally, Ujval J. Kapasi, Peter Mattson, and John D. Owens, "Memory access scheduling," in *ISCA-27*, 2000.

[23] Nathan Binkert et al., "The gem5 simulator," *ACM SIGARCH Computer Architecture News*, vol. 39, no. 2, pp. 1-7, 2011.

[24] Ali Bakhoda, George L. Yuan, Wilson W. L. Fung, Henry Wong, and Tor M. Aamodt, "Analyzing CUDA workloads using a detailed GPU simulator," in *ISPASS*, 2009.

[25] Samsung, "4Gb B-die DDR3 SDRAM," Rev. 1.2, 2011.

[26] Shuai Che et al., "Rodinia: A benchmark suite for heterogeneous computing," in *IISWC*, 2009.

Bounded Memory Scheduling of Dynamic Task Graphs

Dragoş Sbîrlea
Rice University
dragos@rice.edu

Zoran Budimlić
Rice University
zoran@rice.edu

Vivek Sarkar
Rice University
vsarkar@rice.edu

ABSTRACT

It is now widely recognized that increased levels of parallelism is a necessary condition for improved application performance on multicore computers. However, as the number of cores increases, the memory-per-core ratio is expected to further decrease, making per-core memory efficiency of parallel programs an even more important concern in future systems. For many parallel applications, the memory requirements can be significantly larger than for their sequential counterparts and, more importantly, their memory utilization depends critically on the schedule used when running them.

To address this problem we propose *bounded memory scheduling* (BMS) for parallel programs expressed as dynamic task graphs, in which an upper bound is imposed on the program's peak memory. Using the inspector/executor model, BMS tailors the set of allowable schedules to either guarantee that the program can be executed within the given memory bound, or throw an error during the inspector phase without running the computation if no feasible schedule can be found.

Since solving BMS is NP-hard, we propose an approach in which we first use our heuristic algorithm, and if it fails we fall back on a more expensive optimal approach which is sped up by the best-effort result of the heuristic.

Through evaluation on seven benchmarks, we show that BMS gracefully spans the spectrum between fully parallel and serial execution with decreasing memory bounds. Comparison with OpenMP shows that BMS-CnC can execute in 53% of the memory required by OpenMP while running at 90% (or more) of OpenMP's performance.

Keywords

task graphs; task scheduling; inspector/executor

1. INTRODUCTION

Multicore, with its increasing levels of parallelism, has arrived at a time when memory capacity has already stopped scaling [26]. Currently, memory per core is decreasing by 30% every two years [27] and projections state that it will soon drop to megabytes in extreme scale systems [29]. As expressed by IBM, this is an important challenge to overcome for exascale computing, since "our ability to sense, collect, generate and calculate on data is growing faster than our ability to to access, manage and even store that data." [43]. But this problem is not only an obstacle for future supercomputers; for the embedded multicore processors, memory is already at a premium today.

Unfortunately, parallel execution is known to increase memory requirements compared to a serial baseline [8]. The community has been aware of this problem since the 1990s: "The amount of memory required by a parallel program may be spectacularly larger than the memory required by an equivalent sequential program .... parallel memory requirements may vary from run to run, even with the same data" [11]. Without mitigation techniques, the increased memory consumption can lead to an increased occurrence of out-of-memory errors [16].

Modern programming systems for parallel applications are not aware of and do not control the peak memory footprint, making it difficult for programmers to ensure their program will not run out of memory[1]. We believe this lack of control over peak memory usage stems from a more in-depth challenge: programming systems do not have access to the dependence structure (task communication and creation relationships) of a program.

In light of these problems, we propose a programming system that targets the *bounded memory scheduling* (BMS) problem: *Given a parallel program P with input I and a memory bound M, can P complete execution in the memory bound M?*

We propose an inspector/executor [35] based model that enables dynamic program analysis, transformation and optimization based on the computation task graph at runtime, but before running the application. To the best of our knowledge, this work is the first to consider the BMS problem in the context of dynamic task scheduling. This problem is a more general case of the register sufficiency problem [20], which has been well studied due to its importance in compiler code generation. In the context of task scheduling, additional difficulty arises from the fact that, in most programming systems, there is insufficient information at the point when a task is created to decide if it should be de-

[1] In contrast, embedded applications tend to be memory-aware but usually offer little flexibility in scheduling and mapping of individual components.

PACT'14, August 24–27, 2014, Edmonton, AB, Canada.
Copyright 2014 ACM 978-1-4503-2809-8/14/08 ...$15.00.
http://dx.doi.org/10.1145/2628071.2628090.

ferred or handed to the scheduler directly in order to maintain the memory usage within the desired bound. Without an oracle to answer this question, the BMS problem becomes intractable. We propose a scheduling approach in which the role of the oracle is performed by the inspector phase of an inspector/executor [35] system. Our parallel programming model (see Section 3) enables the inspector to build the computation graph of compliant applications without running the internals of computation steps in the application, thereby revealing both the parent-child relationships for tasks and the reader-writer relationships for data. With this knowledge, the inspector can identify scheduling restrictions that lead to bounded-memory execution. These restrictions are then enforced by the executor stage, when the application runs on a load-balancing work-stealing scheduler. The result is a hybrid scheduling approach which obeys a memory bound but retains the advantages of dynamic scheduling.

The main contributions of this paper are:

- *a heuristic algorithm for BMS based on the inspector/executor model* for identifying a set of schedules that fit a desired memory bound. The BMS algorithm is run in the inspector phase and works by imposing restrictions on the executor phase.
- *an optimal algorithm for bounded memory scheduling* based on integer linear programming; as opposed to the heuristic algorithm, it is optimal in that it ensures finding a schedule that fits the memory bound if one such schedule exists. By proposing an efficient ILP formulation and by using the result of the heuristic BMS to hot-start the optimal algorithm, our formulation works on graphs that are an order of magnitude larger than those reported in previous work on ILP-based register scheduling.
- *a schedule reuse technique* to amortize the cost of the BMS inspector across multiple executions by matching new runs to previously computed schedules. This technique works whenever the runs have the same dynamic computation graph, even if their inputs differ and, to the best of our knowledge, is the first to reuse inspector-executor results across application runs.
- *experimental evaluation on several benchmarks* showing that the range of memory bounds and parallel performance delivered by BMS gracefully spans the spectrum from serial to fully parallel execution.

2. BACKGROUND: THE CONCURRENT COLLECTIONS PROGRAMMING MODEL

The programming model used in this work is an extension of the Concurrent Collections (CnC) [10] model. CnC applications consist of tasks (called *steps*), uniquely identified by a *step collection* specifying the code that the task will run, and a tuple called the *step tag* identifying a specific instance of a step. Tasks communicate through dynamic single assignment variables called *items*. Items are grouped together into *item collections* which contain logically related items and are uniquely identified by tuples called *keys*.

Once a step is spawned, it can read items by calling the `item_collection.get(key)` function which returns the item value. `Get` calls block until some other step produces the item with that key, which is performed through `item_collection.put(key, value)`. As long as the dynamic single assignment rule is respected and since `gets` are blocking [2], there are no data-races on items. Once steps read their input items, they perform computation and then may produce items (through `put` operations) and/or start new steps through `step_collection.spawn`.

Since items are accessed using tuples as keys (rather than pointer-based references), it is generally not possible to automatically identify which items are dead and should be collected. Instead, the number of expected read operations (called the *get-count* of the item) is specified as an additional parameter to item `put` calls [37].

3. BMS-CNC: AN INSPECTOR/EXECUTOR PARALLEL PROGRAMMING MODEL

Many analyses of task-parallel programs (such as data race detection) require understanding the task-parallel structure of the computation, which is usually unknown at compile time. As a result, many of these analyses build the task graph dynamically, while the application is running. Unfortunately, this is too late for certain optimizations, such as bounding the memory consumption of the program.

We propose the use of an inspector/executor programming model in which an analysis (inspector) phase is performed before any tasks start executing. The inspector uncovers the task creation and data communication patterns of the application without running the internals of computation steps; the information it uncovers can be used for program transformations. As soon as the transformation completes, the executor starts running the transformed program.

Specifically, we introduce BMS-CnC, a CnC variant that adds programmer-written *graph expansion functions*, associated with each step collection. These functions enable the inspector to query the input and output items and spawned steps of each step, without performing a complete step execution. The set of keys corresponding to items read by the step with tag `t` is returned by the programmer-written `get_inputs(t)` function. Similarly, `get_outputs(t)` and `get_spawns(t)` return the keys of items produced by the step and the tags of steps spawned by it. [3]

An additional expansion function deals with those items that are the output of the whole CnC computation. Before spawning the first step, programmer needs to identify items `k` that are read by the environment after all CnC steps have finished, through calls to `declare_get(k)`.

BMS-CnC uses a CnC runtime in which tasks do not start executing until all input items are available (known as strict preconditions [38]), which means that tasks have only two states before termination: *prescribed* (expressed to the runtime by a spawn call) and *running*. In the prescribed state, tasks consume memory consisting of a function pointer and the tag tuple; during execution, they also use the stack. Because they never block, there are only as many task stacks

[2]With the BMS variant of CnC in Section 3, the logic behind gets remains the same, but since the task does not start until all input items are available, blocking is not needed anymore.

[3]Note that tasks can make conditional `puts` and `gets` in BMS-CnC, the only requirement is that these must also be expressed in the corresponding graph expansion function, so any such condition has to be a pure function of the step tag. See subsection 3.2 for a discussion.

as there are workers. Since task stacks are fixed-size[4], the stack memory consumption is constant during execution.

3.1 Programming model characteristics useful for BMS

Several features make CnC an ideal candidate for BMS:

- CnC makes it easy to separate data and computation, simplifying the implementation of the inspector-executor approach and reducing the inspector overhead.
- Assuming there are no data-races, CnC programs are deterministic [10], enabling BMS schedule reuse across multiple runs (Section 7).
- CnC tasks only wait on items, before running [38]. This minimizes the number of task states, making the memory accounting easier than in other models.
- CnC steps finish without waiting for their spawned children to finish and do not use stack variables to communicate with other tasks. This behavior is different from spawn-sync models where parent stack cannot be reclaimed until all children have finished. In BMS-CnC, there will only be as many task stacks as there are worker threads (a constant amount of memory).
- The dynamic single assignment property implies that there are no anti and output dependences between steps, which increases parallelism and gives BMS the maximum flexibility in reordering tasks.
- CnC items are usually tiles, and steps are medium-grained ("macro-dataflow") keeping the graph of the computation at a manageable size and decreasing the overhead of the inspector phase.

3.2 Independent control and data as a requirement for BMS

Since BMS-CnC relies on the programmer to separate the computation graph from the internals of the computation through expansion functions, an important question arises: *Is it always possible to separate the computation structure from the computation itself?* In general, the answer is *no*.

The problem can be illustrated with `step_collection.get_inputs(t)` in the case when the step reads two items. If the key of the second item depends on the value of the first item (not only on the tag of the step) then it is impossible to obtain the key of this second item without actually executing the step that produces the first item. This example is an instance of an application pattern called "data-dependent `gets`". A related pattern is that of "conditional `gets`'," in which the read operation on an item is conditional on the value of a previously read item and leads to the same issue. Similar issues happen for `puts` and can be worked-around by putting empty items instead of doing conditional `puts`.

If the keys of items read and written and tags of steps spawned are only a function of the current step tag, then the application has *independent control and data*, which is needed to accurately model an application using BMS. If the keys and tags depend on the values of items, we say that the application has *coupled control and data*.

When faced with an application with coupled control and data, one possible solution is to include more of the computation itself in the graph expansion functions. In the extreme case, by including all the computation in the expansion functions, we would be able to obtain an accurate dynamic task graph. Unfortunately, in the worst case, the computation would be performed twice, once for the expansion and once for the actual execution. However, our experience is that many application contain independent control and data, thereby supporting the BMS approach. For case studies and a discussion on the problems and benefits of independent control and data, see Sbîrlea et al. [38].

[4]We allocate fixed-size stacks for each task. If more stack space is needed for activation frames, the task can create additional child tasks; if it needs more space for stack data, it can create CnC items instead.

4. BUILDING THE COMPUTATION GRAPH

This section describes the computation graph used by the algorithm; Section 5 describes our heuristic BMS algorithm and Section 6 presents the optimal approach. Section 7 describes the technique for reusing the schedules.

The inspector builds a dynamic computation graph: items and tasks are nodes and the producer-consumer relationships are edges. Because of the dynamic single assignment nature of items, item nodes can only have a single producer, but may have multiple consumer tasks. Tasks can also spawn (prescribe) other tasks and each task has a unique parent.

The graph construction process starts from the node that models interactions with the parts of the program that are outside of CnC. The *environment-in* node produces initial items and spawns initial steps. After the computation completes, the *environment-out* node reads the outputs.

The tasks spawned by the *environment-in* node are added to a worklist of tasks that are expanded serially, by calling the graph expansion functions. For a single task, the process consists of the following steps:

- Call `get_inputs(t)` and add edges from the node of each consumed item to the task node.
- Call `get_outputs(t)` and add edges from the task node to each output item node.
- Call `get_spawns(t)` and add edges from the current task to the child tasks. Add children to the worklist.

The process finishes when all tasks have been expanded[5]. The *environment-out* node is added and connected to the output items of the computation (declared by using the function `item_collection.declare_get(k)`) As an example, the computation graph obtained for Cholesky factorization, is shown in Figure 1.

5. THE HEURISTIC BMS ALGORITHM

After generating the computation graph, the inspector attempts to find bounded memory schedules using the heuristic BMS algorithm, which takes as input the computation graph and a memory bound M. BMS outputs an augmented partial order of tasks such that if a schedule respects the partial order, it will use at most M memory.

[5]During the expansion process, nodes are created when they are referenced for the first time.

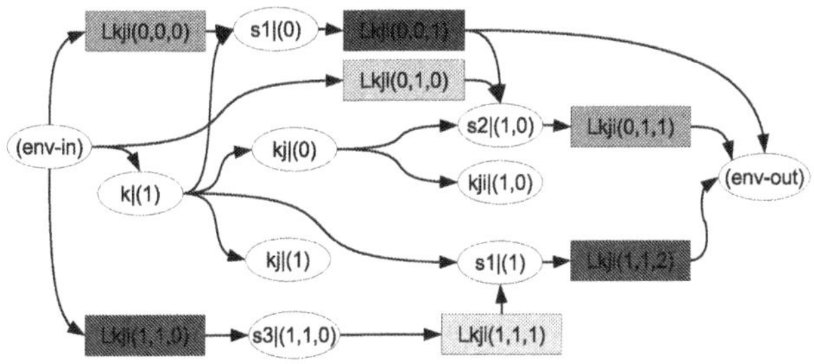

Figure 1: The BMS-CnC computation graph for Cholesky factorization tiled 2×2. Data items are represented as rectangles and Circles represent steps. Nodes are labeled with the collection name followed by the key or tag. Item colors are assigned by the BMS algorithm (Section 5).

Even with substantial simplification, the BMS problem is NP-hard, since the register sufficiency problem [20] which is well-known to be NP-Complete can be reduced to BMS[6]. Furthermore, the size of the computation graph is an order of magnitude larger than the basic block length (which determines the graph size in local register sufficiency). Thus, trying to find a heuristic solution before attempting a more expensive solution is essential. We propose a best effort approach in which, if a set of schedules that execute in less than M memory is found, the program is executed following a dynamically chosen schedule from the set. This leads to the following approximation of the BMS problem: *Given a parallel program P with input I and a computing system with memory size M, find an additional partial task ordering TO such that any schedule of P that also respects TO uses at most M peak memory.* If no schedule is found, BMS returns *false* (even though such a schedule may still exist).

In this initial description *items are assumed to be of a fixed size* and task memory is ignored. Section 8 extends the algorithm to address these simplifications.

Intuitively, given a serial schedule S (i.e., a total order) of the task graph, the BMS algorithm can test if it respects the memory bound by dividing the memory into item-sized slots (called *colors*) and checking that the number of available colors is larger than the maximum number of items live in the sequential schedule. The task graph can then be run in parallel if items assigned to the same color have non-overlapping lifetimes (to ensure that the memory bound is respected). This is enforced by adding ordering edges between the consumers of the item previously assigned to a color and the producer of the next item assigned to that color. To ensure adding ordering edges does not introduce deadlocks, we only add ordering edges that follow the same sequence of creation and collection as in the serial schedule S (since S is a valid topological sort of the graph, this cannot cause cycles).

The pseudocode, shown in Algorithm 1, follows the general list scheduling pattern. It picks a serial ordering of tasks

Algorithm 1 The BMS Algorithm.

```
1: function BMS(G, M, α)
2:                                         ▷ G is the computation graph
3:                                     ▷ M is the desired memory bound
4:                 ▷ α affects the task priority queue (see Section 5.1)
5:   noColors ← M/G.itemsize
6:   freeColors ← INITIALIZESET(noColors)
7:   freeTasks ← PRIORITYQUEUE(α)
8:   PUSH(freeTasks, G.env)
9:   while freeTasks ≠ ∅ do
10:    crtTask ← POP(freeTasks)
11:    for all crtItem ∈ PRODUCEDITEMS(crtTask) do
12:      MARKASPRODUCED(crtItem)
13:      color ← POP(freeColors, crtItem)
14:      if color = null then
15:        return false                 ▷ Failed to find BMS schedule
16:      else
17:        prevItem ← GETSTOREDITEM(color)
18:        for prev ∈ CONSUMERSOF(prevItem) do
19:          ADDEDGE(prev, crtTask)
20:        for all cTask ∈ CONSUMERSOF(prevItem) do
21:          MARKINPUTAVAILABLE(cTask, crtItem)
22:          if READYTORUN(cTask) then
23:            PUSH(freeTasks, cTask)
24:        SETSTOREDITEM(color, crtItem)
25:    for all crtItem ∈ CONSUMEDITEMS(crtTask) do
26:      if UNEXECUTEDCONSUMERS(crtItem) == 0 then
27:        availableColor ← COLOROF(crtItem)
28:        freeColors ← freeColors ∪ availableColor
29:    for all spawn ∈ SPAWNEDTASKS(crtTask) do
30:      MARKPRESCRIBED(spawn)
31:  return true                          ▷ Found BMS schedule
32: end function
```

in the main loop, lines 9 - 30 (by default we use a breadth-first schedule). In each iteration, it extracts one task from the priority queue of "ready to run" tasks (line 10), which is initialized with the only task ready to run at the start: the input environment node (line 8).

We propose two techniques that help the algorithm cope with the different requirements of the bounded memory scheduling problem. These techniques are: successive relaxation of schedules and color assignment for minimum serialization. They are discussed in the next sections.

5.1 Successive relaxation of schedules

If the desired memory bound is small, it is possible that the serial schedule chosen by BMS will not fit the memory bound. It is essential to find a heuristic that enables us to identify a schedule which fits the memory bound and the approach must also be fast, since the executor cannot start before the inspector finishes. Our approach, called *successive relaxation of schedules*, is to sample schedules in a way that trades parallelism for lower memory requirements. We do this by varying the ranking function used to prioritize ready to run tasks in the BMS algorithm. The ranking function varies from the breadth-first (default) to depth first, since we found that breadth-first schedules usually lead to more parallelism/more memory, while depth-first leads to less parallelism/less memory. [7] This choice of different schedules is done by varying α (line 7) from 1 (breath-first) to 0 (depth-

[6]The BMS problem has additional constraints not found in the register sufficiency problem that increase its complexity, such as items of different sizes, tasks that produce multiple items, the fact that inputs and outputs of a task (instruction in the register sufficiency case) are live at the same time.

[7] Depth-first and breath-first ordering of tasks are done on a graph where items are treated as direct edges from producer to consumer. The breadth-first ranking of a node is one larger than its lowest ranking predecessor node. For depth-first, a queue of ready tasks is maintained and nodes

first) which is then used by the priority queue comparison function (lines 12-16) in which the available tasks are stored. If the depth first schedule ($\alpha = 0$) does not fit the bound, we abort the scheduling operation (line 8).

Algorithm 2 Successive relaxation of schedules.

```
1: function SCHEDULE(G, M)
2:   α ← 1
3:   while α ≠ 0 do
4:     success ← BMS(G, M, α)
5:     if success then
6:       return true
7:     α ← α − Δα
8:   return false
9: end function
10:
11:                                   ▷ Used for the task priority queue:
12: function PRIORITYQUEUE.COMPARE( task1, task2)
13:   rank1 ← α × RANKBF(task1) + (1 − α) × RANKDF(task1)
14:   rank2 ← α × RANKBF(task2) + (1 − α) × RANKDF(task2)
15:   return rank1 − rank2
16: end function
```

5.2 Color assignment

The color assignment is important because it drives the insertion of serialization edges, which in turn can affect performance: inserting too many edges increases overhead and bad placement can decrease parallelism. Moreover, a slow coloring heuristic delays the start of the executor stage slowing down the completion of the execution.

Since many steps are already ordered by producer-consumer and step spawning relationships, not all edges inserted by BMS in line 19 of Algorithm 1 actually restrict parallelism. We call these edges *transitive edges*, whereas those that restrict the parallelism are *serialization edges* and need to be enforced during execution. As described below, this distinction is also important for color assignment.

How can one quantify the parallelism decrease caused by coloring? Remember that the resulting schedule runs on a dynamic work stealing scheduler with provable performance guarantees [40] as long as the parallel slack assumption holds. This assumption holds as long as the critical path is not increased too much, so we attempt to insert serialization edges in such a way as to not increase the critical path.

THEOREM 5.1. *Assuming unit-length tasks and a breadth-first schedule, BMS will increase the critical path length with at most the number of serialization edges it inserts.*

PROOF. Since tasks are processed in breadth-first order and the tail of serialization edges is a task that has already been allocated, a serialization edge whose head task is at level k, must start at level $k - i$, with $i \geq 0$ thereby the edge can increase the critical path with at most one. □

Algorithm 3 shows our greedy minimum-serialization heuristic: for each item, we pick the color that leads to the insertion of the fewest serialization edges from steps with breadth first level smaller than the current task. Only if no such edges exist we consider serialization edges that start from the current breadth-first level, since that increases the critical path. If the source of an edge that would be added by BMS is already a predecessor of the destination, then the edge is transitive and is not counted as a serialization.

are numbered in the order in which they are removed from this queue. Nodes are added to the queue when their predecessors have been numbered.

Variable Name	Meaning
issue[task_id]	In which cycle is task *task* issued?
death[item]	In which cycle can item *item* be collected?
color[item]	To which color is item *item* assigned?
indicators	Auxiliary binary variables for disjunction support. At most $5 \times NO\_ITEMS^2$ variables

Table 1: Variables used in the ILP formulation.

Constraint name	Maximum number of constraints
1. Define time of item death	*NO_GETS*
2. Data dependence	*NO_GETS*
3. Color assignment	$5 \times NO\_ITEMS^2$
4. Max_bandwidth	*NO_ITEMS*
5. Earliest start time	*NO_TASKS*
6. Latest start time	*NO_TASKS*

Table 2: Constraints used in the ILP formulation.

Algorithm 3 Assigns item colors.

```
function POP(freeColors, crtItem)
  producer ← GETPRODUCER(crtItem)
  minColor ← null
  minEdges ← MAX_INT
  for color ∈ freeColors do
    prevItem ← GETSTOREDITEM(color)
    edges ← 0
    for consum ∈ ConsumersOf(prevItem) do
      if !ISPREDECESSOR(consum, producer) then
        if BFRANK(prod) ≥ BFRANK(consum) then
          edges ← edges + CONSUMERSCOUNT(prevItem)
        edges ← edges + 1
    if edges < minEdges then
      minEdges ← edges
      minColor ← color
  return minColor
end function
```

6. OPTIMAL BMS THROUGH INTEGER LINEAR PROGRAMMING

Heuristic BMS is fast, but offers no guarantees regarding how much memory reduction it can achieve. If it fails to find a schedule that fits the desired memory bound, we apply an integer linear programming formulation that guarantees finding a schedule for any input memory bound if such a schedule exists. The challenge in using integer linear programming is to formulate the problem in a time and memory-efficient way, so that it can be used for large computation graphs. The formulation and optimizations are described in Section 6.1. Section 6.2 proposes specific lower bounds used to speed up optimal BMS. An additional performance benefit is obtained by using the results of heuristic BMS to speed-up the optimal BMS, as shown in Section 6.3.

For space reasons, we only describe here the optimizations for the ILP formulation of the problem that lead to increased scalability. More details about the formulation can be found in the technical report version [36] of this paper. We propose a disjunctive formulation with variables and constraints shown in Tables 1 and 2.

ILP formulation attempts to find a schedule with the minimum memory bound by minimizing the number of colors used, but interrupts the search as soon as it finds a solution that fits the user-specified memory bound. As shown in Section 9, we are able to solve graphs that are an order of magnitude larger than those in previously published results for the problem of minimum register scheduling.

6.1 Optimization of color assignment constraints

We focused our optimization effort on color assignment constraints because they represent a large majority of the total number of constraints. Color assignment constraints enforce that two items assigned to the same color cannot be live at the same time and could be expressed naively, as the following if-statement:

```
if color[item1] == color[item2] then
   issue[producer[item1]]>death[item2] or
   issue[producer[item2]]>death[item1]
```

The integer linear programming encoding of this if-statement is done by replacing the if-condition with two disjuncts:

```
color[item1] < color[item2] or
    color[item1] > color[item2]
```

We then transform the if statement `if A then B` into a disjunction $\bar{A}$ *or* B.

Then, we apply the technique of using boolean indicator variables (named *a*,*b*.*c*,*d*) and an additional constraint to represent disjunctions [46], obtaining the following equations, in which M and N are big constants:

$$\begin{cases} color[item1] - color[item2] + M \times a \leq M - 1 \\ color[item2] - color[item1] + M \times b \leq M - 1 \\ death[item1] - issue[producer[item2]] + N \times c \leq N - 1 \\ death[item2] - issue[producer[item1]] + N \times d \leq N - 1 \\ a + b + c + d \geq 1 \end{cases}$$

This set of constraints is correct, but inefficient, adding 4 variables and 5 constraints for each pair of items. Decreasing the number of constraints and variables added is essential for efficient execution. To do this, we analyze the possible relations of the lifetime of items as shown in Figure 2. For items that must-overlap, we can elide the third and fourth constraints and corresponding variables. For items that may-overlap we elide either the third or fourth constraints if there is a path as in Figure 2c. For items that cannot overlap, we elide all constraints and associated indicator variables.

Another constraint that can be optimized is the one that defines the time of death (constraint number 2). These constraints restrict the time of death of each item to happen after all the consumers of that item have been issued. In some cases, consumers of the item are ordered by other data dependence edges, so we can omit the time of death constraints corresponding to all but the last consumer.

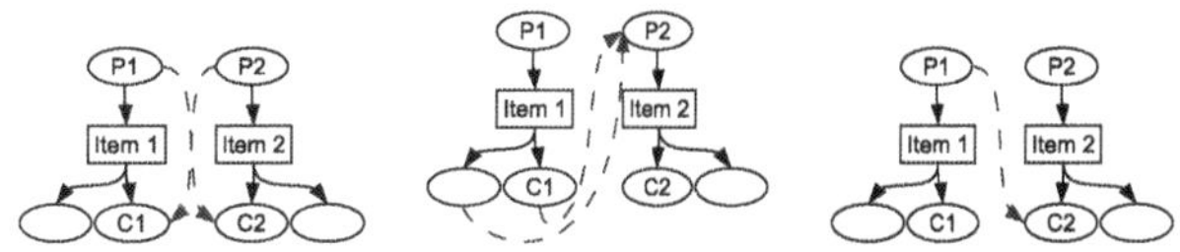

(a) Item lifetimes must overlap. (b) Item lifetimes cannot overlap. (c) Item lifetimes may overlap, but one item must be created first.

Figure 2: Several item patterns enable more efficient encoding of the color assignment constraint. The dotted edges are paths in the graph that enforce the must-overlap, cannot-overlap and may-overlap relations.

6.2 Tight lower bounds to speed up ILP BMS

Often, the tightest possible schedule is found by heuristic BMS, but the ILP solver takes a long time to prove its optimality since it needs to search through many schedules for a possibly better solution. Adding tight lower bounds on the minimum memory possible is important, since the search stops if the heuristic BMS solution equals the lower bound. We propose using two lower bounds, each of which works best for a different type of graphs.

The first lower bound is the memory requirement of the step with the largest number of inputs and outputs. In some cases, this step is the environment-out node and we can improve the bound further by using the following observation: after all but one of the output items are produced, in order to produce the last item, the inputs from which this last item is computed must also be live, and included in the lower bound. For Cholesky factorization, for example, this bound is equal to the minimum memory footprint of the application.

The second bound we propose is useful for applications where, even though each step requires a modest amount of memory, the total footprint is large. This pattern occurs, for example, in divide-and-conquer applications where the memory pressure is proportional to the height of the graph. To handle these cases, we build a tree that is subsumed by the computation graph (the tree identification is done by ignoring all but one of the edges that connect an item to its consumers), and use the Strahler number[8] of the tree as a lower bound. For applications such as merge sort, this happens to be the minimum memory footprint of the application.

6.3 Hot start ILP: Using heuristic BMS to speed up ILP BMS

To decrease the time and memory costs associated with ILP, we combine linear programming with the heuristic approach presented in Section 5. Since the optimal approach is only used when the heuristic algorithm does not find a schedule that fits the desired memory bound, this means that the minimum footprint schedule found by the heuristic can be used as initial solution for the the ILP solver. If the heuristic already found the minimum footprint possible, but the desired footprint is smaller, the ILP will need to confirm the lack of better solutions by solving the linear pro-

[8]The Strahler number [18] is the minimum number of registers required to evaluate an expression tree and can be computed in linear time.

gramming relaxation and checking that the objective value matches the one provided by the heuristic. In this case, using the initial solution, the solver will finish early with the optimal solution being the heuristic one.

7. SCHEDULE REUSE

Traditional inspector/executor systems amortize the inspection cost by reusing the inspector results, for example by executing multiple times a loop that has been inspected once. Since the BMS executor runs only once, we amortize the inspector cost across multiple executions of the application by caching the inspector results. To the best of our knowledge, our approach is the first to reuse inspector-executor results across different runs of an application. The proposed approach can be applied for even if the input parameters differ between runs with the same desired memory bound, as long as the computation graph structure remains unchanged. This requirement is mitigated our model's ability to express applications as serial sequences of parallel kernels that are modeled independently as separate BMS problems. Because schedule reuse is performed at the kernel granularity instead of the application granularity, as long as any kernel has the same computation graph, then that kernel's schedule can be reused.

To determine if the BMS schedule of a previous run fits the current one, one option is to generate the computation graph and compare it with the graph of the previous executions; this can be costly in both time and memory. Instead, we use only a small root set of graph edges and vertices that uniquely identifies the graph[9]. This root set contains two types of edges. First, it contains the edges whose tail vertex is the *environment-in* node. These edges lead to item keys produced by the environment and the tags of the tasks spawned by the environment which uniquely characterize all the items and tasks that will be spawned during the computation. Second, the root set also includes edges whose tail is the *environment-out* node. The tail of these edges are the keys of items read after the computation completes (i.e. the application result); they affect the minimum footprint of the execution because, for the same computation graph, more output items lead to larger minimum memory requirements.

The schedule reuse works as follows. First, we identify the root set. If it does not match with the root set of a previous execution, we expand the whole computation graph, run the BMS algorithm and save the resulting (*serialization edges*, *root set*) pair on disk, in a schedule library, along with a MD5 hash of the root set. For subsequent runs of the application, the inspector will compare the MD5 hashes of the current root set with the root sets from the schedule library. If it finds a matching root set, the inspector loads the serialization edges, avoiding the graph expansion and BMS computation. If there is no match, the only additional work performed is the hashing, since the root set expansion is done anyway during the graph expansion.

Because the root set consists of keys and tags only (no data), matching the root set to the root set of a previous program is fast. The schedule loading consists of reading the set of serialization edges from the schedule library.

[9]This assumes the determinacy of the control flow (step tags) in the program, since BMS-CnC can only express this kind of programs.

As an example, take Cholesky factorization, whose 2×2 tiling is shown in Figure 1. The root set consists of seven edges (four starting from the *env-in* node and three ending in the *env-out* node). In general, for Cholesky factorization tiled $k \times k$, the root set will have an order of $k^2/2$ edges. Since each vertex is identified by 3 integers, the whole root set will have $3 \times k^2$ integers. This is much smaller than the input matrix which is also read from disk. Since the computation graph depends on the matrix size and tile size only and the tile size is usually tuned for the machine the serialization edges can be reused for any input matrix of the same size. Similarly, for image processing applications, the input is usually the same size and the schedules should be reusable all the time.

In applications with irregular graphs, such as the sparse Cholesky factorization as implemented in HSL [24], the root set consists of the keys of non-zero tiles, which is still smaller than the sparse input matrix. The schedule cache consists of the corresponding serialization edges, whose number is inversely proportional to the memory bound.

To conclude, the schedule reuse approach relies on the combination of root sets, hashing and the intrinsic compactness of serialization edges to amortize the inspector overhead across multiple runs of an application.

8. BMS EXTENSIONS

In this section we describe two extensions to the BMS algorithm: the first one adds support for different item sizes and the second one accounts for memory used by waiting and executing tasks.

8.1 Supporting multiple item sizes

To support items of different sizes, one can use the approach of allowing items to be allocated at any memory location. This results in memory fragmentation that requires a global compaction phase to reclaim the free space. The compaction can introduce a barrier during execution of the parallel program, thereby increasing the computation's critical path.

Instead, we observe that applications often have only a few *classes of items*, where all items in a class have the same size (for example the size of the input matrix, the size of a tile)[10]. Memory is initially divided into slots the size of the largest items, each of which can be split into multiple sub-slots suitable for smaller items. When all sub-slots become unused, they are merged into a larger slot. We refer to the colors used for items of the largest size as *root colors*.

Algorithm 4 shows how colors are assigned to items of different sizes. The `Pop(freeColors)` function from the BMS algorithm is replaced by a `PopFromClass(freeColors, crtItem)` function which takes the item that needs space as an additional parameter. The `freeColors` parameter now contains only free root colors. The `PopFromClass` first identifies the class (size) of the item (line 3) and looks for an available color in the list of free colors that is specific to that item class (line 5). If a color is available, we return it (line 21); otherwise, we have to split a root color `freeColors` into sub-colors of size that matches the current item. The number of new colors is determined in line 12 and they are

[10]A similar approach is used by memory allocators of operating systems which have pools of memory objects of different sizes.

added to the list of free colors for that class (line 12). Note that, for each new color, we need to find (line 11) and propagate (line 16) the correct consumers for the item which was last stored in it — this information is needed when inserting ordering edges.

To prevent fragmentation, BMS reassembles sub-colors into root colors. This happens when all sub-colors that are splinters of a root color become available again; we use the function ADDFREECOLORTOCLASS (line 24), which replaces the union operation on line 28 in the BMS algorithm. When allocating a new item to a reclaimed root color, we need to ensure that the lifetimes of the items previously stored in the sub-colors do not overlap with the item later assigned to the root color. This is done by adding ordering edges, but the previously stored items must be recorded by the SETSTOREDITEM and GETSTOREDITEM functions which work with sets of items instead of single items.

Algorithm 4 BMS Extension for items of different sizes.

```
1:            ▷ This function assigns a (sub)color for item crtItem
2: function PopFromClass(freeColors, crtItem)
3:   crtClass ← GetClass(crtItem)
4:   freeSubcolors ← GetFreeColors(crtClass)
5:   color ← Pop(freeSubcolors, crtItem)
6:   if color = null then
7:            ▷ Call Pop function from the BMS algorithm
8:     pageColor ← Pop(freeColors, crtItem)
9:     if pageColor ≠ null then
10:      prevIt ← GetStoredItem(pageColor)
11:      prevConsumers ← ConsumersOf(prevItem)
12:      noSubcolors ← rootSize/class.itemSize
13:      for i = 1 → noSubcolors do
14:        newColor ← newCOLOR()
15:        PushToClass(freeSubcolors, newColor)
16:        SetStoredItem(newColor, crtItem)
17:      color ← Pop(G, freeColorsInClass, crtItem)
18:  if color ≠ null then
19:    rootColor ← GetRootColor(color)
20:    rootColor.uses ← rootColor.uses + 1
21:  return color
22: end function
23:            ▷ This function reclaims a (sub)color
24: function AddFreeColorToClass(
        freeColors, itemColor)
25:  crtClass ← GetClass(itemColor)
26:  rootColor ← GetRootColor(color)
27:  rootColor.uses ← rootColor.uses − 1
28:  if rootColor.uses = 0 then
29:    AddFreeColor(freeColors, rootColor)
30:    itemsSet ← SubColorsOf(rootColor)
31:    SetStoredItem(rootColor, itemsSet)
32: end function
```

8.2 Bounding task memory

In BMS-CnC, tasks have two states: prescribed or executing. This section looks at the memory taken up by tasks. *Executing tasks* use the stacks of the worker threads executing them, so they do not consume additional memory beyond the worker stack space allocated at the start of program execution. BMS can consider worker thread memory starting with a memory bound parameter M_1 that is lower than the total memory M in the system: $M_1 = M - no\_workers * worker\_stack\_size$. Note that since BMS-CnC tasks have fixed-size stacks, large levels of recursion can only be performed by spawning new tasks.

Prescribed tasks are the tasks that have been `spawned` but have not yet started running. In our implementation, these waiting tasks consist only of the task tag and the task function pointer, so their size can be computed by the BMS scheduler. This memory is needed from the moment tasks are created by a `spawn` operation to the moment the task finishes so they are similar to items whose lifetime extends between the moment they are `put` up to the moment their last consumer task finishes execution. The same mechanism used to handle items of different sizes (described in Section 8.1) also handles prescribed tasks.

9. EVALUATION

9.1 Implementation and experimental setup

The BMS-CnC system was implemented on top of Qt-CnC [38], an open-source CnC implementation[11] based on the Qthreads task library [44]. The evaluation was performed on an Intel Xeon E7330 system with 32GB RAM and 16 cores. We instrumented the runtime to keep track of the item memory allocations and item deallocations performed. Because CnC is implicitly parallel and there is no separate CnC serial implementation, we obtain serial execution times by using Qt-CnC (not BMS-CnC) with a single worker thread.

For each application, we present the BMS executor time as a function of the memory bound (see Figure 3). To evaluate the performance of BMS, we note that the minimum memory bound for which BMS finds a schedule should at least match the serial execution memory. When the bound is large enough to fit a normal (CnC) parallel execution, BMS should not lead to performance degradation.

An analysis of the actual memory footprint incurred at each memory bound, is included in the technical report [36] and omitted here due to space limitations.

9.2 Benchmarks

Applications are usually implemented as sequences of parallel computation kernels invoked with different parameters. To maximize the benefits of schedule reuse for such applications, it makes sense to model each parallel kernel independently as a BMS problem, since this enables schedule reuse at the kernel granularity instead of the application granularity. For this reason the evaluation includes several computational kernels instead of fewer large applications. By themselves, the kernels reach footprints which can be satisfied without BMS on today's machines; they will require BMS when used in the context of larger applications containing multiple kernels as well as on future many-core systems with smaller amounts of available memory per core. Table 3 contains a short summary of the benchmarks, their input parameters, computation graph size and conditions for schedule reuse.

Smith-Waterman is a dense linear algebra kernel from the Intel CnC distribution. The results in Figure 3a show that BMS gracefully spans the range between large memory-high performance to low memory with lower performance.

The results for **Blackscholes** (in Figure 3b) show that BMS-CnC is able to control the peak memory from the largest values obtained with CnC parallel execution, to the smallest (serial execution).

[11] `https://code.google.com/p/qthreads/wiki/qtCnC`

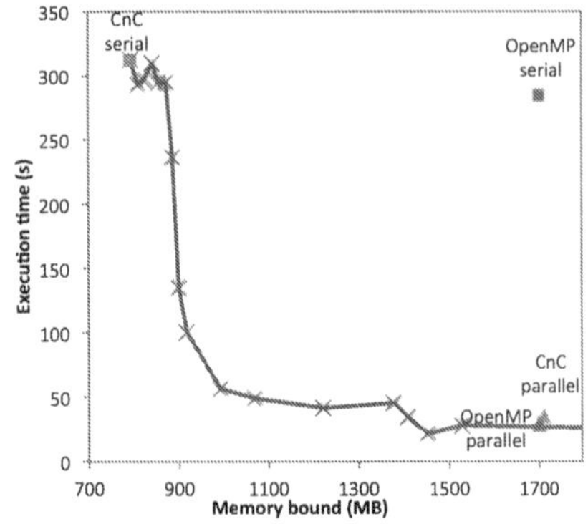

(a) Smith Waterman

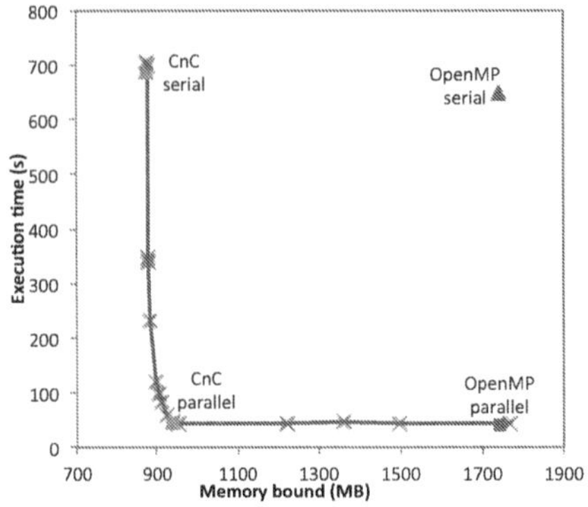

(b) Blackscholes

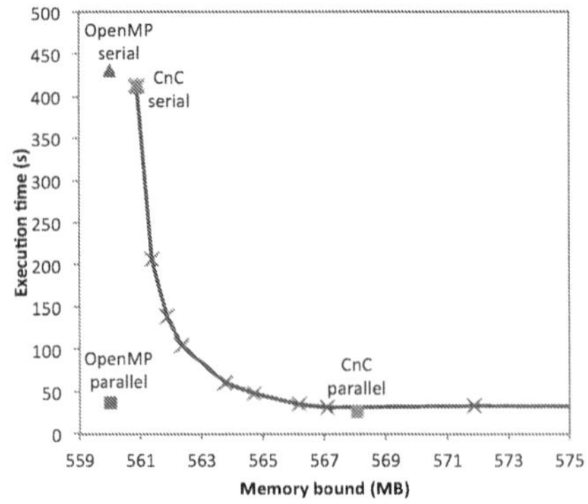

(c) Cholesky

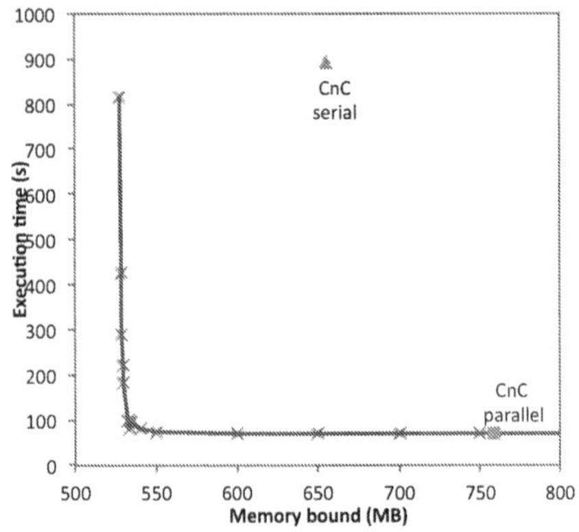

(d) Gauss-Jordan

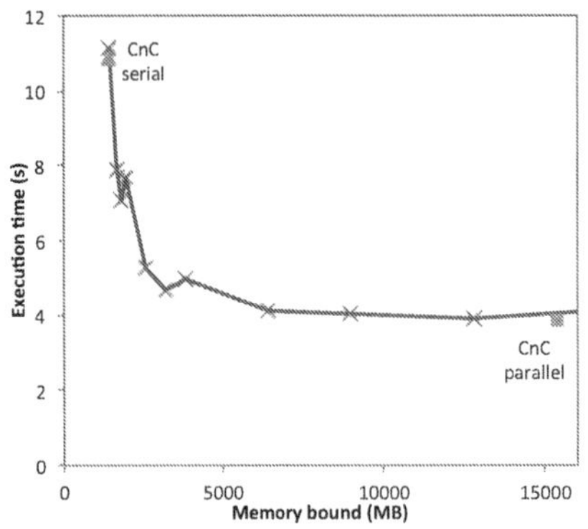

(e) Merge Sort

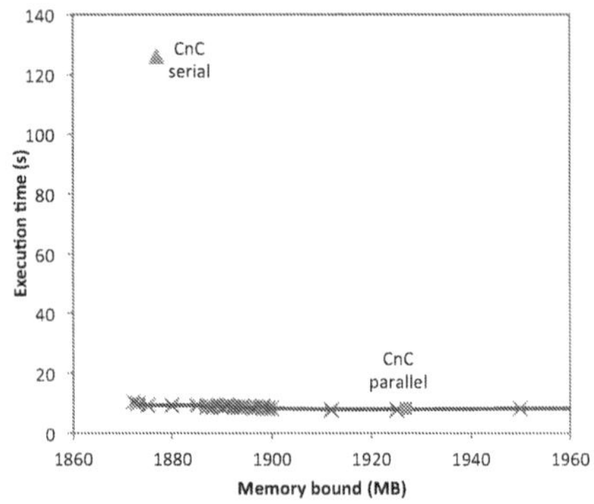

(f) Standard Task Graph (STG) 59

Figure 3: BMS-CnC executor run-time (the red line) as a function of memory bound for each of the benchmarks. BMS-CnC is able to enforce memory bounds down to the serial execution and even lower for Gauss-Jordan and STG 59. OpenMP results included where available.

Benchmark		Type	Graph vertices	Source	Input parameters	Schedule reuse conditions
Smith Waterman		biomedical	5002	in-house	2 sequences of 70000 length and tile size (2000 × 2000)	identical tile sizes identical sequence sizes
Blackscholes		financial	6730	Intel CnC [25] Parsec [5]	number of options (25.6M) and option data	identical number of options
Cholesky		dense algebra	41558	Intel CnC [25] Buttari [12]	input matrix (12000 × 12000) and tile size (125 × 125)	identical tile sizes identical matrix sizes
Gauss-Jordan		dense algebra	8450	Intel CnC [25]	input matrix (4096 × 4096) and tile size (256 × 256)	identical tile sizes identical matrix sizes
Merge Sort		recursive	3582	in-house	vector data (2^{25} integers)	identical input array sizes
STG	sparse	task graph	198	STG [41]	graph shape	identical graph shape
	fpppp	task graph	647	STG [41]	graph shape	identical graph shape
	58, 59	task graph	5402	STG [41]	graph shape	identical graph shape

Table 3: Benchmarks, their inputs, computation graph sizes and the schedule reuse conditions. The corresponding results are shown in Figure 3.

Benchmark	BMS-CnC memory (%) when Speedup is		
	90%	50%	10%
Smith-Waterman	48.8	10.6	0.0
Blackscholes	93.2	10.8	1.4
Cholesky	84.6	46.2	0.0
Gauss-Jordan	0.0	0.0	0.0
Merge Sort	12.0	0.9	0.0
STG 58	12.0	0.0	0.0
STG 59	22.2	0.0	0.0

Table 4: Memory consumption for BMS-CnC when it has 90%, 50% and 10% of the parallel CnC speedup. Values are percentages of the additional memory required by parallel execution - 0% means no increase in footprint, 100 % means maximum increase (same footprint as parallel execution).

The **Cholesky factorization** (Figure 3c) shows BMS enables a trade-off similar to the one in Smith-Waterman, between large memory consumption and high performance.

For **Gauss-Jordan elimination** (see Figure 3d), BMS-CnC is able to enforce a footprint 18% lower than the serial footprint of CnC, with minimal loss of parallelism. This is the result of the abundant parallelism, as well as good coloring heuristics.

For **MergeSort** (Figure 3e) we notice an unusual trend when the desired memory bound is larger than 15MB - the execution time of BMS-CnC in these cases becomes smaller than the CnC parallel execution, even though the actual program footprint is the same. We believe that the performance benefit comes from improved cache locality in the BMS schedules.

The **Standard Task Graph (STG) Set** [41] provides a set of random task graphs from which we picked the largest (STG 59), shown in Figure 3f. Since STG graphs do not contain any work, we used a fixed amount of computation for each task and a fixed size for each item. In both cases, there is sufficient parallelism to hide the BMS constraints up to the boundary condition where BMS cannot find a valid schedule. There is no loss of performance from using BMS with the tightest memory bound, which is lower than serial execution memory. For these graphs, BMS is able to offer the best of both worlds - the footprint of serial execution with the performance of parallel execution.

In summary, BMS shows the ability to control the trade-off between parallelism and memory usage. Furthermore, this trade-off is not linear — there is a "sweet spot" in the memory bound space where BMS enables most of the performance of the unbounded memory parallel execution with only a small increase in memory relative to the serial execution. To further illustrate this, Table 4, shows the memory requirements of BMS-CnC when its speedup is 90%, 50% and 10% of the parallel CnC speedup. The values are percentages of the memory difference between parallel and serial executions. For example, 0% means the BMS-CnC program does not require more memory than serial execution, while 100% would mean that the memory use matches the memory utilization of parallel execution (maximum memory increase).

9.3 OpenMP comparison

OpenMP results have been included in Figure 3 where external implementations of the same benchmarks were available. One interesting pattern is that the OpenMP memory footprint does not vary between the serial and parallel executions because OpenMP encourages programmers to parallelize computation loops while the memory allocation and de-allocation are usually performed outside parallel regions. In BMS-CnC, item lifetime is minimized by allocating items only when needed and by automatically collecting them after their last use.For Smith-Waterman and Blackscholes, BMS-CnC offers similar performance with OpenMP while enabling considerable memory savings. For Blackscholes, for example, OpenMP has a performance advantage of under 10%, but requires twice the memory of CnC, since it pre-allocates all the memory to reduce overhead.

Because the OpenMP implementation of Cholesky exploits less parallelism (barrier style versus dataflow) so so it has a lower memory footprint and lower performance than CnC.

9.4 Minimum memory evaluation

To identify how close the BMS heuristic approach can be to the absolute minimum memory footprint possible, we fed the ILP formulation of the problem to the commercial Gurobi solver which finds find the minimum possible footprint. The results are shown in Table 5. For small and medium problem sizes, both the ILP and BMS approaches can enforce the minimum memory footprint possible, but there are some examples, such as Gauss Jordan, where ILP can obtain a better bound that heuristic BMS.

On larger graphs, the ILP solver may run out of memory or not finish before the 5 hour cutoff. This happens in cases where the two lower bounds are much smaller than the actual feasible minimum memory. We analytically discovered that in 3 out of 4 cases when this happened, the ILP had already found the minimum memory schedule, but had not proved its optimality before running out of time. BMS is capable of finding a schedule with minimum bound in all but 4 out of the 18 cases.

9.5 Runtime comparison of ILP and heuristic BMS

Table 6 shows the run time of the BMS inspector. The ILP approach can handle graphs of up to tens of thousands of vertices, but there are some examples where it either runs out of memory or reaches the 5 hour timeout. However, the hot start optimization in which we provide the heuristic BMS schedule as initial solution for the ILP solver along with the ILP formulation, leads to a considerable speedup and in some cases, such as Blackscholes for medium and large inputs, this avoids a timeout. Heuristic BMS is fast for all graph sizes, but for tight bounds may need to be followed by the hot ILP execution if it cannot find a suitable schedule.

The most closely related previously published results are for finding the minimum numbers of registers needed to execute instruction graphs whose size is in general much smaller than the computation graph sizes. The only public graph and ILP solving time we could find is from the work of Chang et al. [14] and has only 12 vertices. On this graph, their ILP formulation takes one minute (on their 1997 machine), while both the heuristic BMS and ILP BMS finish in under a second (on our system).

Bench	Input	Graph Nodes	Min. mem. (MB) BMS	Min. mem. (MB) ILP	Bounds (MB) Strahler	Bounds (MB) Local
Smith Water-man	small	52	26.6	26.6	15.2	15.2
	med	100	34.2	*34.2	19.0	15.2
	large	2452	141.0	*141.0	22.8	15.2
Cholesky	small	315	0.6	0.6	0.1	0.6
	med	1907	8.2	8.2	0.2	8.2
	large	4555	403.8	NA	1.4	403.8
Black scholes	small	402	63.2	63.2	1.1	63.2
	med	802	125.6	125.6	1.2	125.6
	large	1602	250.4	250.4	1.2	250.4
Gauss Jordan	small	22	62.5	62.5	25.0	62.5
	med	65	150.0	125.0	37.5	125.0
	large	146	250.0	*225.0	50.0	212.5
Merge Sort	small	222	0.9	0.9	0.9	0.4
	med	7166	1.5	1.5	1.5	0.4
	large	14334	1.6	1.6	1.6	0.4
STG	sparse	198	17.6	14.9	1.2	14.9
	fpppp	647	57.4	*57.4	1.2	24.9
	59	5406	468.0	NA	1.8	83.8

Table 5: The minimum memory with heuristic BMS and with ILP and the lower bounds fed to ILP. Cells are marked with * when ILP timeouts.

9.6 Inspector phase time evaluation

The inspector phase consists of building the computation graph and running the BMS algorithm. Schedule caching removes the overhead associated with both these stages and adds some overhead of its own (for hashing the schedules and loading them from disk). Table 7 shows the execution time of the inspector relative to the serial execution. For the BMS runtime we include the smallest and largest time encountered. The reason for this variation is that BMS may take more time for tighter bounds, since the first schedules attempted will fail to observe the memory bound. From the table, we see that graph construction can take up to 20% of execution time and the maximum time needed to run the BMS algorithm can be 3× larger than the serial execution time. Schedule caching is therefore valuable in amortizing the potentially large overhead of the inspector.

9.7 Large memory experiment

For systems without support for paging to disk, BMS enables the execution of programs that would otherwise crash attempting to use more than the available memory, but how does the paging mechanism affect the BMS results?

We analyze application behavior on workloads that require disk paging by using a larger input size for the Smith Waterman application. The results in Figure 4 include the BMS performance for 270, 280 and 310 tiles of the same size, and the graphs show interesting changes relative to Figure 3a. For very tight memory bounds, the BMS-CnC performance is close to serial, because sequential execution is needed to reach the desired memory bounds. As the bound gets larger, performance increases due to more parallelism, until it reaches a performance sweet-spot. This sweet-spot is generally close to the physical memory size (32GB), but its exact location depends on how close the enforced maximum memory bound matches the actual memory used at run-time.

Bench	Input	Graph nodes	Time (s) BMS	Time (s) ILP	Time (s) hot ILP
Smith Waterman	small	52	0.2	1.0	3.6
	med	100	0.7	148	189.51
	large	2452	3.59	NA	NA
Cholesky	small	315	0.0	0.7	0.4
	med	1907	0.1	7920	281
	large	4555	3.6	NA	NA
Blackscholes	small	402	0.1	5403	5
	med	802	0.1	NA	16
	large	1602	250.4	NA	1189
Gauss Jordan	small	22	0.0	0.0	0.0
	med	65	0.1	155	44
	large	146	0.1	NA	NA
Merge Sort	small	222	0.1	40	10
	med	7166	4.1	336	18.61
	large	14334	8.7	NA	28.22
STG	sparse	198	1.1	200	37
	fppp	647	2.5	NA	NA
	59	5406	69.4	NA	NA

Table 6: Performance evaluation of heuristic BMS and ILP with and without hot start. Even with hot start, the ILP approach cannot handle large graphs.

Benchmark	Graph creation(%)	BMS Algorithm Min(%)	BMS Algorithm Max(%)
Smith-Waterman	0.5	17.8	98.1
Blackscholes	3.3	2.1	29.0
Cholesky	2.9	3.8	99.4
Gauss Jordan	20.3	6.6	94.0
Merge Sort	19.8	20.0	310.2
STG 58	0.5	1.0	109.2
STG 59	0.1	0.7	42.5

Table 7: Timing results for the inspector (graph creation and BMS scheduling), as percentages of the serial execution time.

Increasing the memory bound even more leads to a performance degradation because disk swapping starts being used. The last part of the graph shows constant time because the program has already reached its parallel footprint and giving a larger bound does not affect the schedule any more. The sweet-spot enabled by BMS leads to 39% faster execution compared to parallel CnC, showing that BMS can increase performance and lower the memory footprint of applications with large memory requirements.

Comparing the results for the three runs which use inputs of increasingly large sizes (270, 280 and 310 input tiles), we notice that all three have similar curves. Interestingly, the fraction of memory saved by using the BMS sweet-spot instead of parallel execution increases with the input size. The memory savings reach 34% for 310 tiles.

10. RELATED WORK

To the best of our knowledge, this work is the first to tackle the problem of scheduling with a fixed memory bound in the context of dynamic task scheduling, but there is re-

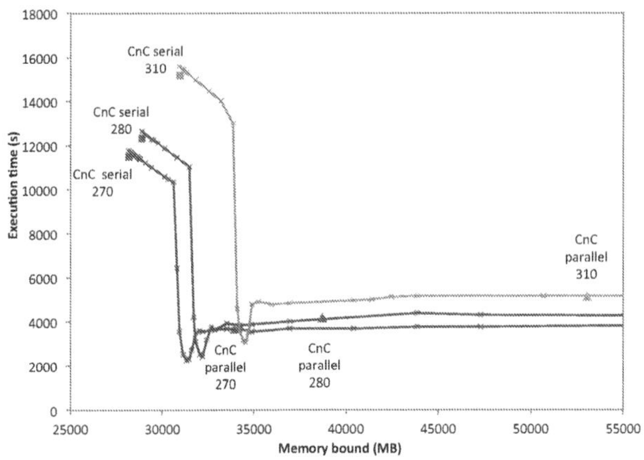

Figure 4: Smith-Waterman results on large inputs (270, 280 and 310 tiles). BMS enables the use of a sweet-spot with good performance and low footprint at the same time because it avoids swapping. The physical memory size is 32 GB and the computation graph for 310 input tiles has 192,202 nodes.

lated work on amortized analysis of memory consumption for parallel programs. Burton [11] was the first to propose bounds on the memory complexity of dynamically scheduled parallel computations. Simpson and Warren [39] present a survey of work in this area. Blelloch et al. [7], Narlikar and Blelloch [32], Blelloch et al. [6] and Fatourou [17] identified increasingly better bounds. The best memory bounds obtained are directly proportional to the memory consumption of a particular serial schedule and include at least an additive factor proportional to the critical path of the computation. In contrast to these approaches in which bounds are dependent on the memory consumption of the particular serial order of tasks and on the number of processors available, BMS-CnC considers the maximum footprint a hard upper bound for execution. Compared to on-the-fly schedulers with asymptotic memory bounds, we can impose fixed memory bounds and work around the on-the-fly restriction by using the inspector-executor model. This enables us to use the whole computation graph in scheduling, effectively turning the scheduling "offline". Because of this, BMS can handle even the worst case (adversary picks worst task spawn ordering in the input program), that could lead these schedulers to unnecessarily large footprints. Also, the performance of BMS is independent of the order of task spawning in the programmer-written schedule. On the other hand, they can offer performance guarantees and have wider applicability because of their less restrictive programming model, on-the-fly approach and no inspector overhead. Other projects [22, 9] analyze the memory consumption of serial programs. Other projects [22, 9, 23, 13] analyze the memory consumption of serial programs, but this is a difficult problem to solve accurately with only static information. The techniques are expensive, based on linear programming, but only need to be computed once per application, compared to the inspector/executor based approach where the valid schedules to be computed once for each computation graph encountered.

BMS is a novel application of the inspector/executor system proposed by Salz [35] who used it to efficiently parallelize irregular computations. Based on inspector/executor, Fu and Yang propose the RAPID system for distributed computation [19] which bounds the memory assigned to copies of memory on each node, but does not bound the footprint of the program.

The BMS problem is related to the widely-studied problems of register sufficiency and combined instruction scheduling and register allocation. Barany and Krall [1] propose a type of code motion to decrease spills by using integer programming to identify the schedules that reduce overlapping lifetimes. Pinter [34] identified the fact that some variables in the program must have overlapping lifetimes while some don't need to which is an opservation that e used in our ILP optimizations; he builds a parallelizable interference graph including "may overlap" edges to ensure that his register allocation does not restrict schedules. In the same context of register allocation and instruction scheduling, Norris and Polloc [33] use the parallelizable interference graph and add data-dependence graph edges (similar to our serialization edges) to remove possible interference. loops. The CRISP project [31] introduced an analytical cost model for balancing register pressure and instruction parallelism goals in a list scheduler which influenced the schedule relaxation technique we propose.

Govindarajan et al. [21] perform scheduling to minimize the number of registers used by a register DDG, an approach called minimum register instruction sequence (MRIS). BMS and MRIS have considerable differences:

- *different scalability requirements:* MRIS has been targeted to basic block DDGs consisting of tens of nodes, whereas BMS must support tens of thousands of nodes, so the BMS heuristics trade accuracy for performance.
- *different reuse models:* Because BMS works on memory instead of registers, the input and output data of a task cannot share the same memory slot, so lineages cannot be formed.
- *different objectives:* While MRIS simply minimizes the number of registers, BMS the best schedule for a given memory bound. The MRIS minimization objective leads to sacrifices of parallelism that are unnecessary for BMS. For example, value chains are created by inserting sequencing edges that force a particular consumer to execute last; BMS avoids this restriction of parallelism by using multiple serialization edges.

The URSA project [4] compares various approaches for combined register allocation. Touati [42] proposes the use of serialization arcs to decrease the number of required registers.There are multiple related projects that apply optimal techniques [45, 2, 28, 3, 30]) for scheduling or register allocation, but a direct comparison is difficult since the objective and constraints differ.

BMS-CnC is the first system that enables the reuse of inspector/executor results across application runs, but there is related work in the idea of schedule memoization [15]. When ensuring program correctness through symbolic execution, the principle of schedule memoization is the following: because the schedule space is very large, it may be untractable to test all schedules for correctness. Instead, a few schedules can be sampled, checked for correctness, memoized and then subsequent executions can be forced to follow one of them.

11. CONCLUSIONS

This paper proposes a new scheduling technique to find memory-efficient parallel schedules for programs expressed as dynamic task graphs. Our technique, called bounded memory scheduling, enforces user-specified memory bounds by restricting schedules and trading off parallelism when necessary. The evaluation on several benchmarks illustrates its ability to accurately control the memory footprint while exploiting the parallelism allowed by the memory bound.

To make use of an inspector/executor approach in the context of dynamic task scheduling, we presented an efficient schedule reuse mechanism. This technique amortizes the inspector overhead by reusing schedules across executions of the application that exhibit the same computation graph — even when the input parameters change.

References

[1] Gergö Barany and Andreas Krall. "Optimal and heuristic global code motion for minimal spilling". In: CC. 2013.

[2] Andrzej Bednarski and Christoph Kessler. "VLIW Code Generation with Integer Programming". In: EuroPar '06.

[3] Peter van Beek and Kent D. Wilken. "Fast Optimal Instruction Scheduling for Single-Issue Processors with Arbitrary Latencies". In: CP '01, pp. 625–639. ISBN: 3-540-42863-1.

[4] David A. Berson et al. "Integrated Instruction Scheduling and Register Allocation Techniques". In: LCPC. 1999.

[5] Christian Bienia. "Benchmarking Modern Multiprocessors". PhD thesis. Princeton University, Jan. 2011.

[6] Guy E. Blelloch, Phillip B. Gibbons, and Yossi Matias. "Provably Efficient Scheduling for Languages with Fine-grained Parallelism". In: *J. ACM* (1999).

[7] Guy Blelloch et al. "Space-efficient scheduling of parallelism with synchronization variables". In: SPAA '97.

[8] Robert D. Blumofe and Charles E. Leiserson. "Scheduling multithreaded computations by work stealing". In: *J. ACM* (1999).

[9] Víctor Braberman et al. "Parametric prediction of heap memory requirements". In: ISMM '08. 2008.

[10] Zoran Budimlić et al. "Concurrent Collections". In: *Scientific Programming* (2010).

[11] F. Warren Burton. "Guaranteeing Good Memory Bounds for Parallel Programs". In: *IEEE Trans. Softw. Eng.* (1996).

[12] Alfredo Buttari et al. "A Class of Parallel Tiled Linear Algebra Algorithms for Multicore Architectures". In: *Parallel Comput.* 35.1 (Jan. 2009), pp. 38–53. ISSN: 0167-8191.

[13] Brian Campbell. "Amortised Memory Analysis Using the Depth of Data Structures". In: ESOP '09.

[14] Chia-Ming Chang et al. "Using ILP for instruction scheduling and register allocation in multi-issue processors". In: *Computers and Mathematics with Applications* 34.9 (1997).

[15] Heming Cui et al. "Stable Deterministic Multithreading Through Schedule Memoization". In: OSDI'10.

[16] I. Dooley et al. "A study of memory-aware scheduling in message driven parallel programs". In: HiPC. 2010.

[17] Panagiota Fatourou. "Low-contention depth-first scheduling of parallel computations with write-once synchronization variables". In: SPAA '01.

[18] P. Flajolet, J.C. Raoult, and J. Vuillemin. "The number of registers required for evaluating arithmetic expressions". In: *Theoretical Computer Science* 9.1 (1979).

[19] Cong Fu and Tao Yang. "Run-time compilation for parallel sparse matrix computations". In: ICS '96.

[20] Michael R. Garey and David S. Johnson. *Computers and Intractability: A Guide to the Theory of NP-Completeness*. 1979. ISBN: 0716710447.

[21] R. Govindarajan et al. "Minimum Register Instruction Sequencing to Reduce Register Spills in Out-of-Order Issue Superscalar Architectures". In: *IEEE Transactions on Computers* (2003).

[22] Martin Hofmann and Steffen Jost. "Static prediction of heap usage for first-order functional programs". In: POPL. 2003.

[23] Martin Hofmann and Dulma Rodriguez. "Efficient type-checking for amortised heap-space analysis". In: CSL'09 / EACSL'09. 2009.

[24] *The HSL Library. A collection of Fortran codes for large scale scientific computation.* URL: http://www.hsl.rl.ac.uk (visited on 06/25/2014).

[25] *Intel Concurrent Collections.* URL: http://software.intel.com/en-us/articles/intel-concurrent-collections-for-cc (visited on 06/25/2014).

[26] Randy Isaac. "Influence of Technology Directions on System Architecture". In: PACT 2001 Keynote.

[27] Kevin Lim et al. "Disaggregated Memory for Expansion and Sharing in Blade Servers". In: ISCA '09.

[28] Castañeda Lozano et al. "Constraint-Based Register Allocation and Instruction Scheduling". In: CP'12.

[29] Yin Lu et al. "Memory-conscious Collective I/O for Extreme Scale HPC Systems". In: ROSS '13.

[30] Abid M. Malik, Jim Mcinnes, and Peter van Beek. "Optimal basic block instruction scheduling for multiple-issue processors using constraint programming". In: *IJAITS* (2008).

[31] Rajeev Motwani et al. *Combining Register Allocation and Instruction Scheduling.* Tech. rep. Stanford, CA, USA, 1995.

[32] Girija J. Narlikar and Guy E. Blelloch. "Space-efficient scheduling of nested parallelism". In: *TOPLAS* (1999).

[33] C. Norris and L.L. Pollock. "A scheduler-sensitive global register allocator". In: SC. 1993.

[34] Shlomit S. Pinter. "Register allocation with instruction scheduling". In: PLDI. 1993.

[35] Joel H. Salz et al. "Run-Time Parallelization and Scheduling of Loops". In: *IEEE Trans. Comput.* (1991).

[36] Dragoş Sbîrlea, Zoran Budimlić, and Vivek Sarkar. *BMS-CnC: Bounded memory scheduling of dynamic task graphs.* Tech. rep. Rice University, Oct. 2013.

[37] Dragoş Sbîrlea, Kathleen Knobe, and Vivek Sarkar. "Folding of tagged single assignment values for memory-efficient parallelism". In: Euro-Par'12.

[38] Dragoş Sbîrlea et al. "The Flexible Preconditions model for Macro-Dataflow Execution". In: *DFM.* 2013.

[39] David J. Simpson and F. Warren Burton. "Space Efficient Execution of Deterministic Parallel Programs". In: *IEEE Trans. Softw. Eng.* (1999).

[40] Daniel Spoonhower et al. "Tight Bounds on Work-stealing Overheads for Parallel Futures". In: SPAA '09.

[41] Takao Tobita and Hironori Kasahara. "A standard task graph set for fair evaluation of multiprocessor scheduling algorithms". In: *Journal of Scheduling* (2002).

[42] Sid Ahmed Ali Touati. "Register Saturation in Superscalar and VLIW Codes". In: CC '01.

[43] David Turek. "The Strategic Future: The Push to Exascale". In: *IBM Science and Innovation Summit.* 2009.

[44] Kyle Wheeler et al. "Qthreads: An API for programming with millions of lightweight threads". In: IPDPS. 2008.

[45] Kent Wilken et al. "Optimal Instruction Scheduling Using Integer Programming". In: PLDI '00.

[46] H.P. Williams. *Model Building in Mathematical Programming.* Wiley, 2013. ISBN: 9781118506189.

Trading Cache Hit Rate for Memory Performance

Wei Ding, Mahmut Kandemir, Diana Guttman, Adwait Jog, Chita R. Das, Praveen Yedlapalli
Department of Computer Science and Engineering
The Pennsylvania State University
University Park, Pennsylvania, USA
{wzd109, kandemir, drg217, adwait, das, praveen}@cse.psu.edu

ABSTRACT

Most of the prior compiler based data locality optimization works target exclusively cache locality optimization, and row-buffer locality in DRAM banks received much less attention. In particular, to the best of our knowledge, there is no single compiler based approach that can improve row-buffer locality in executing irregular applications. This presents a critical problem considering the fact that executing irregular applications in a power and performance efficient manner will be a key requirement to extract maximum benefits from emerging multicore machines and exascale systems. Motivated by these observations, this paper makes the following contributions. First, it presents a compiler-runtime cooperative data layout optimization approach that takes as input an irregular program that has already been optimized for cache locality and generates an output code with the same cache performance but better row-buffer locality (lower number of row-buffer misses). Second, it discusses a more aggressive strategy that sacrifices some cache performance in order to further improve row-buffer performance (i.e., it trades cache performance for memory system performance). The ultimate goal of this strategy is to find the right tradeoff point between cache performance and row-buffer performance so that the overall application performance is improved. Third, the paper performs a detailed evaluation of these two approaches using both an AMD Opteron based multicore system and a multicore simulator. The experimental results, collected using five real-world irregular applications, show that (i) conventional cache optimizations do not improve row-buffer locality significantly; (ii) our first approach achieves about 9.8% execution time improvement by keeping the number of cache misses the same as a cache-optimized code but reducing the number of row-buffer misses; and (iii) our second approach achieves even higher execution time improvements (13.8% on average) by sacrificing cache performance for additional memory performance.

PACT'14, August 24–27, 2014, Edmonton, AB, Canada.

http://dx.doi.org/10.1145/2628071.2628082.

Categories and Subject Descriptors

D.3.4 [**Programming Languages**]: Processors—*Compilers, Optimization*

Keywords

Data locality; compiler; irregular application; cache; row buffer

1. INTRODUCTION

Many data intensive applications are irregular in their data access patterns, inter-thread communication, control flow and storage accesses. Unfortunately, compared to the vast literature we have for dense computations, irregular computations received much less attention from academia and industry. This is partly because optimizing irregular applications is much more challenging than optimizing dense computations as their behavior is significantly more complex and does not lend itself well to static analysis. This presents a critical problem considering the fact that executing irregular applications in a power and performance efficient manner will be a key requirement to extract maximum benefits from emerging multicore machines and future exascale systems.

The most active research areas in the context of irregular applications have been parallelism optimization (i.e., minimizing inter-thread communication [22, 31, 11]) and data locality optimization [13, 15]. It is interesting to note that all prior data locality optimizations targeting irregular programs considered exclusively *cache locality*. However, in modern multicore systems, cache locality is not the only type of locality that matters. For example, current commercial multicores do not only move memory controller on-chip but a majority of them also support multiple memory controllers. Each of these controllers orchestrates data flow into/from multiple memory banks. Row-buffer is a buffer in front of a bank (in DRAM) that holds the most recently-accessed memory row. To keep costs low, the buffering circuitry in DRAM devices is amortized among large rows of cells, resulting in the employment of large (2KB-8KB) buffers in current systems.

While one may think of a row-buffer as another level in the cache hierarchy, it requires special attention because of the following reasons. First, the row-buffer is a single buffer whose "entire contents" are replaced in a row-buffer miss. Therefore, even one intervening access to another row in the same bank can destroy the whole row-buffer locality. Second, a row-buffer serves only for memory accesses issued to the bank it is attached to. This needs to be kept in mind

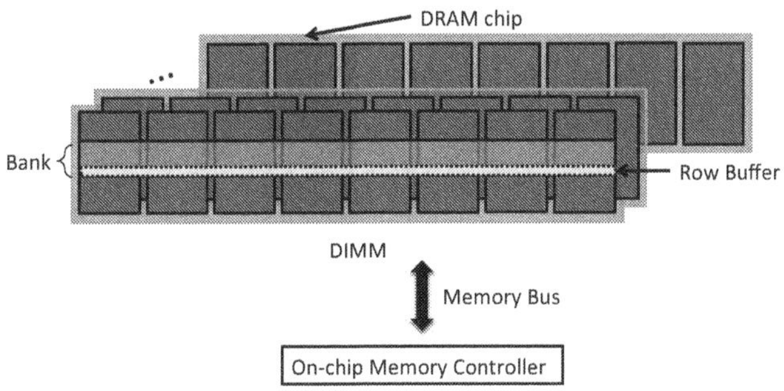

Figure 1: High-level organization of main memory (DRAM).

when optimizing for it. Third, an application that has already been optimized for cache locality may not necessarily exhibit good row buffer locality, and similarly, optimizing exclusively for row-buffer locality may not necessarily improve cache behavior. We are not aware of any prior compiler work that optimizes row-buffer locality of irregular applications. Motivated by this, we make the following contributions in this paper:

- We present a compiler-runtime cooperative data layout optimization approach that takes as input an irregular program that has already been optimized for cache locality and generates an output code with the same cache performance but better row-buffer locality (lower number of row-buffer misses).
- We present an alternate strategy which sacrifices some cache performance in order to further improve row-buffer performance (i.e., it trades cache performance for memory system performance). By carefully determining the amount of cache locality to sacrifice, this strategy improves the overall application performance.
- We perform a detailed, inspector/executor paradigm-based evaluation of these approaches using both an AMD Opteron based multicore system and a multicore simulator. The experimental results, collected using five real-world irregular applications, show that (i) conventional cache optimizations do not improve row-buffer locality significantly; (ii) our first approach achieves about 9.8% execution time improvement by keeping the number of cache misses the same as a cache-optimized code but reducing the number of row-buffer misses; (iii) our second approach achieves even higher execution time improvements (13.8% on average) by sacrificing cache performance for additional memory performance; We also provide experimental evaluation under different values of important architectural parameters such as the number of memory controllers, number of cores, row-buffer size and last level cache capacity, as well as different memory request scheduling algorithms.

2. BACKGROUND

2.1 On-Chip Caches

The cache is a small memory that stores data from frequently used main memory locations. Data is stored in chunks of several words at contiguous addresses called cache lines (or cache blocks). When new data is returned from a request and needs to be stored in the cache, some data already present in the cache may have to be evicted to make room. In a k-way *set-associative* cache, a memory block can be mapped to any of k different cache blocks. The cache replacement policy determines which of the k lines will be evicted and replaced. The state-of-the-art on-chip caches employ various policies such as Random Replacement [16], LRU (Least Recently Used) [16], SLRU [21], Round-robin [3], and PLRU [2]. Each of these policies has its own advantages and disadvantages. Further, except Random Replacement, these policies determine the cache block/line to be replaced by looking at the past references history. LRU is the most commonly used policy where the next cache block to be evicted is the one that has been least recently used. It requires several bits to track when each cache block is accessed. The number of these bits increases as the set-associativity increases. In this work, we focus on the on-chip caches that employ the LRU-like cache replacement policies.

Since accesses to words not currently present in the cache, called cache misses, take much longer to service than cache hits (where the data is present), varies approaches are proposed to try to minimize the number of cache misses by keeping useful data in the cache as much as possible. One way to achieve this is called *data reordering* or *layout reorganization*, which changes the positions of data elements stored in the memory. This technique can be used to put the data that will be used at around the same time on the same cache line; that way, most accesses to that data will hit in the cache.

2.2 Row-Buffers

The main memory consists of several DRAM chips logically organized into banks that are one row wide (which is usually equal to the page size). Each memory bank is accessed one row at a time, and the entire row must be copied into a small buffer called the row-buffer. In a DRAM, upon a read or write request, the data content of the requested row is read by sense ampliers and latched in the row-buffer. Many banks can be accessed in parallel since they each have their own row-buffer. If the memory uses an *open page policy*, the same row is kept in the row buffer after the initial request, allowing multiple accesses to the same row. The data in the row-buffer only changes if a different row is requested. Memory accesses that find their row already in the row buffer are called "row buffer hits" and can be significantly faster than "row buffer misses", which must wait for the row to be copied into the buffer. A row buffer miss can be even slower in the case of a conflict (when another row is already in the row buffer) because the previous row must be copied back before the new row can be brought in. One important factor affecting the row buffer hit rate is the hardware (memory request) scheduling policy [19] used by the memory controller to send requests into the channel. Row-buffer hit rates can also be affected by the data layout, in a similar way to caches. *Row-buffer locality* refers to the reuse of a memory row while its contents are in the row buffer. If two cache lines are frequently accessed together, their row-buffer locality will be better if they are placed in the same memory row (in order to improve row-buffer locality). Otherwise, they will experience row buffer conflicts. As compared to the vast literature on caches, there are only a few prior works [34, 14] on improving row-buffer locality from the compiler perspective, and none of them handles applications with irregular data accesses.

```
Real X(num_nodes), Y(num_edges);
Integer IA(num_edges, 2);
for (t = 1, t < T, t++) {
    for (i = 0, i < num_edges; i++) {
        X(IA(i, 1)) = X(IA(i, 1)) + Y(i);
        X(IA(i, 2)) = X(IA(i, 2)) - Y(i);
    }
}
```

Figure 2: Irregular code example.

2.3 Irregular Applications

In this work, our focus is on irregular application programs, in which a large fraction of data access has the form of $X(IA(f(\cdots)))$, where X and IA are two arrays called *host array* and *index array* [13], respectively, and $f(\cdots)$ is a function of enclosing loop indices and loop-independent constants. In these applications, the value of $IA(f(\cdots))$ is typically *not* known until run-time. Figure 2 illustrates the code structure of a sample irregular application. In this example, *IA(num_edges, 2)* lists the two nodes associated with each edge in a graph. The loop iterates over the edges of the graph and in each iteration, the values related to the two nodes of each edge will be updated accordingly. Traversing this index array will give us a sequence of data elements that will be accessed by the program. Due to the unknown value of index array IA at compile time, the accesses to the host array X are irregular, which makes the irregular code difficult to utilize caches efficiently.

There exist a number of work on improving the performance of irregular applications. One category is called *data reordering* [13, 15], which can be performed directly by rearranging elements in the host arrays. These work include, but not limited to, consecutive packing (CPACK) [13], Reverse Cuthill-McKee (RCM) [24], space filling curves (SFC) [25], recursive coordinate bisection (RCB) [9], multilevel graph partitioning (METIS) [18], and hierarchical clustering algorithm (GPART) [15]. The basic strategy adopted by these work is to relocate the elements such that the elements that tend to be accessed together in a short period of time become close in memory space. To implement this, the inspector-executor module [12, 13, 15] is often used. The inspector preprocesses the memory/data accesses, e.g., obtain the data access sequence of the program by traversing the index array; and the executor simply performs the optimization based on the information obtained by the inspector. There also exist several works on automatically generating inspectors and executors [15]. Figure 3 shows the structure of the inspector module used to implement the data reordering, where $Trans(X, Y)$ is the inspector inserted after each update of the index array. For different data reordering algorithms, the differences are mainly in $Trans(X, Y)$.

```
/* Executor*/
Real X(num_nodes), Y(num_edges);
Real X'(num_nodes), Y'(num_edges);
Integer IA(num_edges, 2);
for (t = 1, t < T, t++) {
  /*If it is time to update the
     interaction list */
  X', Y' = Trans(X, Y);
  for (i = 0, i < num_edges; i++) {
     X'(IA(i, 1)) = X'(IA(i, 1)) + Y'(i);
     X'(IA(i, 2)) = X'(IA(i, 2)) - Y'(i);
  }
}
```

```
/* Inspector*/
Trans(X, Y)
  for (i = 0, i < num_edges; i++) {
    /*data reordering
       algorithms*/
  }
return (X', Y')
```

Figure 3: Using the inspector module module for data reordering.

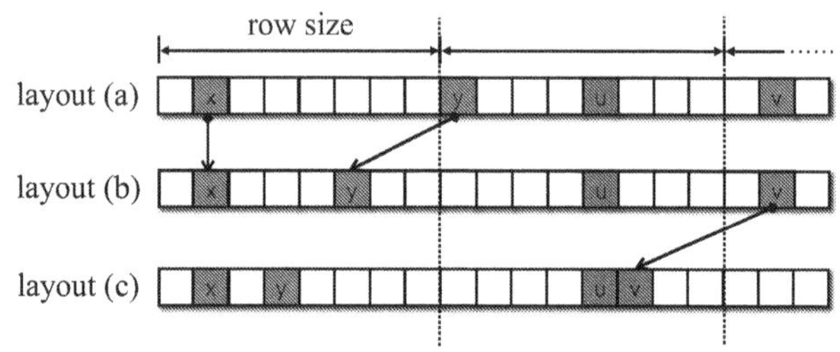

Figure 4: Motivational example. The grey boxes represent the data elements to which the accesses incur last level cache misses. Note that these figures show the layouts (not accesses), and each element shown here may be accessed multiple times during execution.

3. MOTIVATION

To our knowledge, all prior work that target irregular/sparse applications exclusively focus on improving cache locality, and they do not do anything special for row-buffer locality. To put cache locality and row-buffer locality into perspective, let us consider typical miss latencies of the corresponding components. A last level cache (L3) hit in our target AMD based architecture takes 28 clock cycles. A last level cache miss that hits in the row-buffer takes about 90 clock cycles, whereas a row-buffer miss costs more than 350 cycles. Therefore, eliminating one row-buffer miss is expected to bring much more benefits than eliminating a cache miss that would hit in the row buffer. That is to say, the overall performance of an application is not dictated only by the cache performance, but is also influenced by the row-buffer locality.

Figure 4 illustrates a motivational example. It contains three layouts for the same set of data elements. For simplicity, let us assume that, in the original layout (a), all the accesses to the highlighted data elements (grey boxes), x, y, u and v, incur last level cache misses.[1] In this layout, x and y are mapped to different rows. Therefore, if an access to x and an access to y incur successive cache misses (x is accessed first), then the access to y will also incur a row-buffer miss. In contrast, if we can generate a layout such that x and y are mapped to the same row[2], as shown in layout (b), then the access to y will incur a row-buffer hit. Further, if

[1]Unless specified, in the rest of our discussion, when we say "cache misses", we mean the "last level cache misses".

[2]When we say "placing two data elements into the same row", we mean "placing these two data elements into the memory blocks that will be mapped to the same row". Since the row size is usually equal to a page size, from the compiler perspective, this can be achieved by ensuring these two data elements have the same virtual page address. That is to say, we only care whether two data elements reside in the same page or not. As a result, we do not need to take the virtual-to-physical mapping into account.

this layout does not cause any additional cache misses, then the memory access latencies as well as the overall application execution time can be shorten. The layout generated in this way is called *conservative layout*. Compared to the original layout, the conservative layout has the same number of cache misses but fewer row-buffer misses.

Next, let us assume that there exist many accesses to u and v that incur successive cache misses (similar to the case of x and y in the above example), but layout (b) does not place u and v into the same row because doing so will cause additional cache misses. Can we take advantage of this data access pattern to generate a better layout than (b)? Recall that, normally the latency of a row-buffer miss is much higher than the latency of a cache miss. If we can generate a layout such that the overall increased cache miss latency is less than the overall reduced row-buffer miss latency, then the resulting memory access latency will be less than the original one. In other words, we sacrifice some cache performance in order to further improve row-buffer performance. For example, when we change the layout from (b) to (c), if only few accesses to v (which originally incur cache hits) turn into cache misses, and many accesses to v turn to row buffer hits (due to placing u and v into the same row), then with this new layout, the overall memory access latency can still be reduced. A layout generated in this way is called the *fine-grain layout* in this paper. Compared to the original layout, the fine-grain layout usually has more cache misses but fewer row-buffer misses.

The main contribution of this work includes two data layout reorganization (data reordering) approaches that derive conservative layout and fine-grain layout for irregular applications. The *input layout* of our framework could be the original layout or a layout obtained from prior data reuse optimizations that target minimizing cache misses (e.g., [15]). In other words, our starting/original layout can be one that has already been optimized for cache performance.

4. PRELIMINARIES

To simplify our explanation, we introduce the following notation:

- *Seq*: the sequence of data elements obtained by traversing the index array (based on the innermost loop(s)).
- α_x: the *access* to a particular data element x in *Seq*.
- $time(\alpha_x)$: the "logical time stamp" of α_x in *Seq*.
- β_x: the memory block where data element x resides.
- α_x^-: the "most recent access" to β_x before α_x.
- $Caches(\beta_x)$: the set of cache blocks to which β_x can be mapped in a k-way set-associative cache.

DEFINITION 4.1. ***Block Distance.*** *Given* $Caches(\beta_x) = Caches(\beta_y)$*, the block distance between* α_x *and* α_y*, denoted as* $\Delta(\alpha_y, \alpha_x)$*,*[3] *is the number of "distinct" memory blocks that are mapped to* $Caches(\beta_x)$ *and accessed during the time period between* $time(\alpha_x)$ *and* $time(\alpha_y)$.

[3]Note that, here we do not distinguish the appearance order of α_x and α_y in $\Delta(\alpha_y, \alpha_x)$, i.e., $\Delta(\alpha_y, \alpha_x) = \Delta(\alpha_x, \alpha_y)$.

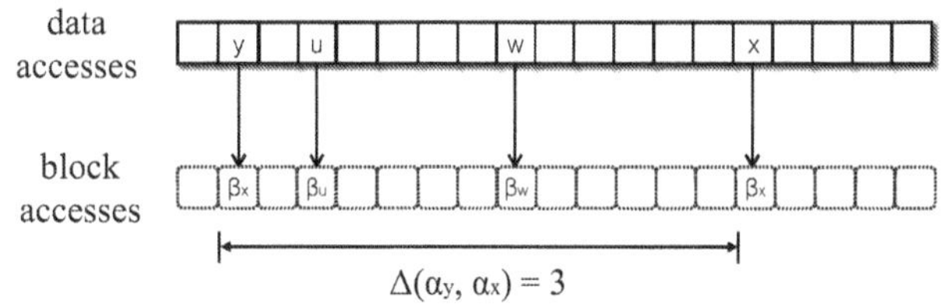

(a) Block distance.

Figure 5: An example that illustrates the block distance concept.

As a special case, when $\alpha_y = \alpha_x^-$, $\Delta(\alpha_x^-, \alpha_x)$ is referred to as the *block reuse distance* of a_x. If $\beta_x = \beta_y$ and α_x is the first access (or α_y is the last access) to the memory block β_x in *Seq*, we define $\Delta(\alpha_y, \alpha_x)$ as ∞. Figure 5 gives an example of the block distance of α_x, where x and y reside in the same memory block ($\beta_x = \beta_y$), and the three memory blocks, β_x, β_u, and β_w, are mapped to the same set of caches ($Caches(\beta_x) = Caches(\beta_u) = Caches(\beta_w)$).

The block distance concept can be used to *determine whether a memory block can be reused or not in the cache.* Given a k-way set associative cache, if $\Delta(\alpha_y, \alpha_x) \leq k$ and $\beta_x = \beta_y$, then α_y ensures that β_x is in the cache at time $time(\alpha_x)$, and consequently, α_x will incur a cache "hit". Note that this conclusion holds true for most LRU-like cache replacement policies, as long as the victim cache block is selected among the k different cache blocks.

5. CONSERVATIVE LAYOUT

DEFINITION 5.1. ***Locality Set.*** *A set of data elements, denoted by* Ω*, forms a* locality set*, if and only if:*

1. $\forall\ x \in \Omega,\ \forall\ y \in \Omega,\ \beta_x = \beta_y$
2. $\forall\ x \in \Omega,\ \exists\ y \in \Omega,\ \exists\ \alpha_x,\ \exists\ \alpha_y\text{:}\ \Delta(\alpha_y, \alpha_x) \leq k$
3. $\forall\ x \notin \Omega,\ \forall\ y \in \Omega,\ \forall\ \alpha_x,\ \forall\ \alpha_y\text{:}\ \Delta(\alpha_y, \alpha_x) > k$

LEMMA 5.2. ***Non-increased Cache Misses:*** *Moving* Ω *from* β_x *to* β_y *will not increase the total number of cache misses in Seq if* $Caches(\beta_y) = Caches(\beta_x)$.

PROOF. Let α_i denote an arbitrary access in *Seq* that originally incurs a cache hit, i.e., $\Delta(\alpha_i^-, \alpha_i) \leq k$. Clearly, if $Caches(\beta_i) \neq Caches(\beta_x)$, then performing the above movement will not change $\Delta(\alpha_i^-, \alpha_i)$. If $Caches(\beta_i) = Caches(\beta_x)$, then after moving G from β_x to β_y, none of the distinct memory blocks in $Caches(\beta_x)$ that are accessed during time period $[time(\alpha_i^-), time(\alpha_i)]$ would change except that β_x will be replaced by β_y. Therefore, in this case, $\Delta(\alpha_i^-, \alpha_i)$ will not be increased, either. As a result, for any access in *Seq* that originally incurs a cache hit, the stated move operation will not change its block reuse distance, i.e., it will still incur a cache hit after this movement. □

To generate the conservative layout, the key is to ensure that the total number of cache misses is *not* increased. We found that, based on Lemma 5.2, this can be achieved by performing the data reordering at a locality set granularity. Specifically, our scheme consists of the following three steps, and the pseudo-code is given in Algorithm 1.

Algorithm 1 Conservative Layout Generation.

/*Identifying locality sets*/
for every access α_x in *Seq* **do**
  if $list_{Caches(\beta_x)}$ is not full or $(\forall \alpha_y \in list_{Caches(\beta_x)} : \beta_x \neq \beta_y)$ **then**
    place α_x into $list_{Caches(\beta_x)}$
  else if $\exists \alpha_y \in list_{Caches(\beta_x)} : \beta_x = \beta_y$ **then**
    replace α_y with α_x in $list_{Caches(\beta_x)}$
    place x and y into the same locality set
  end if
end for
/*Constructing the interference graph*/
for every access α_x in *Seq* **do**
  if $\Delta(\alpha_x^-, \alpha_x) > k \wedge y == \emptyset$ **then**
    $y \leftarrow x$
  else if $\Delta(\alpha_x^-, \alpha_x) > k \wedge y \neq \emptyset \wedge bank(x) = bank(y)$ **then**
    /* assume that $x \in \Omega_1$ and $y \in \Omega_2$ */
    set up edge $e_{1,2}$ between Ω_1 and Ω_2
    $weight(e_{1,2})$ ++
  end if
end for
/*Assigning pages/rows and memory blocks*/
sort edges in non-increasing order based on their weights: $e_1, e_2, \cdots e_p$
for every each pair of locality sets Ω_1 and Ω_2 on e_i **do**
  assign $row(\Omega_1)$ and $row(\Omega_2)$ to the same row.
  assign $block(\Omega_1)$ and $block(\Omega_2)$ to the memory blocks based on Lemma 5.2
end for

Step 1: Identifying the Locality Sets. We identify all the locality sets by traversing the index array (based on the innermost loop(s)). For each cache set, we maintain a list that stores the most recent accesses to k different memory blocks that are mapped to this cache set. In this way, the block distance between the current access α_x and any other access α_y on the list is never greater than k. Therefore, during this index array traversal, only when $\beta_x = \beta_y$ holds, we place x and y into the same locality set.

Step 2: Constructing the Interference Graph. Once the locality sets have been identified, our second step is to construct an *interference graph*, in which each node represents a locality set. If α_x and α_y are the two accesses that incur successive cache misses on *Seq*, and x and y are located in different pages/rows (in the original memory layout), then we set up an edge between the locality sets of x and y. The weight on this edge represents the total number of such α_x and α_y pairs. We construct this graph by making another pass over the index array. Each time when two accesses, α_x and α_y, incur successive cache misses, i.e., $\Delta(\alpha_x^-, \alpha_x) > k$ and $\Delta(\alpha_y^-, \alpha_y) > k$,[4] and x and y reside in different pages/rows, we increase the weight of the edge between the locality sets of x and y by 1. Overall, the weights on the edges of the interference graph evaluate how frequently the accesses to the data elements in two locality sets are missed successively.

Step 3: Assigning Pages/Rows and Memory Blocks. We first sort the edges in the interference graph in a non-increasing order of their weights. This is because, larger the weight of an edge that connects two locality sets, a higher fraction of row-buffer misses can be eliminated by placing these two locality sets into the same page/row. Next, we assign the same row to the locality sets connected by the edge with the largest weight. At this point, we also need to assign the memory blocks to the locality sets within that row. This is carried out by following the rule specified in Lemma 5.2. Once this assignment is finished, we update the available memory positions in this row, and then assign the row to the locality sets connected by the edge with the second largest weight, and so on. If the assignment fails due to the limited memory positions in a row, we simply skip this edge and proceed with the next one.

[4]We use the algorithm similar to Algorithm 1 to calculate $\Delta(\alpha_x^-, \alpha_x)$ and $\Delta(a_y^-, \alpha_y)$.

6. FINE-GRAIN LAYOUT

DEFINITION 6.1. ***Partition.*** *Given $x \in \Omega$, a partition for x is defined as a subset of Ω, denoted as P_x, where $x \in P_x$.*

To generate the fine-grain layout, our basic idea is that, whenever the accesses to two data elements (denoted as x and y) incur successive cache misses and x and y reside in different pages/rows, we try to find two *partitions* for x and y, denoted as P_x and P_y, respectively, such that, when placing P_x and P_y into the same page/row, the increased cache miss latency is less than the reduced row-buffer miss latency.

Our proposed data reordering scheme for generating the fine-grain layout consists of the following steps, and the corresponding pseudo-code is given in Algorithm 2.

Step 1: Constructing the Interference Graph. This step is slightly different from Step 2 described in Section 5. Now, each node in the interference graph represents a data element, instead of a locality set. If α_x and α_y are two accesses that incur successive cache misses on *Seq*, and x and y are located in different pages/rows, then we set up an edge between x and y. The weight on this edge represents the total number of such α_x and α_y pairs, which is also the number of row buffer misses that can be eliminated by placing x and y into the same row.

Step 2: Constructing the Locality Graph. Each locality set Ω corresponds to a locality graph, where each node represents a data element in Ω. We first identify all the locality sets using the strategy given in Algorithm 1, and then construct the locality graph for each locality set as follows. For any access α_u whose block reuse distance is exactly k, if there exist α_x and α_y within time slot $[time(\alpha_u^-), time(\alpha_u)]$, such that x, y and u belong to the same locality set, then we increase the weight of the edge between x and y by 1. As a result, *if we move all the elements in a partition for x, denoted as P_x, to another memory block β'_x, such that $Caches(\beta'_x) = Caches(\beta_x)$, then the number of increased cache misses is at most equal to the sum of the weights of the edges connected to x in the locality graph.* Since each newly-increased cache miss can potentially lead to a row-buffer miss as well, this weight also represents the maximum number of increase in the row-buffer misses. Constructing all these locality graphs requires one additional pass over the index array.

Step 4: Finding Partitions. We first sort the edges in the interference graph in a non-increasing order of their weights, and then process the data elements on each edge in this order. Specifically, given x and y on an edge with

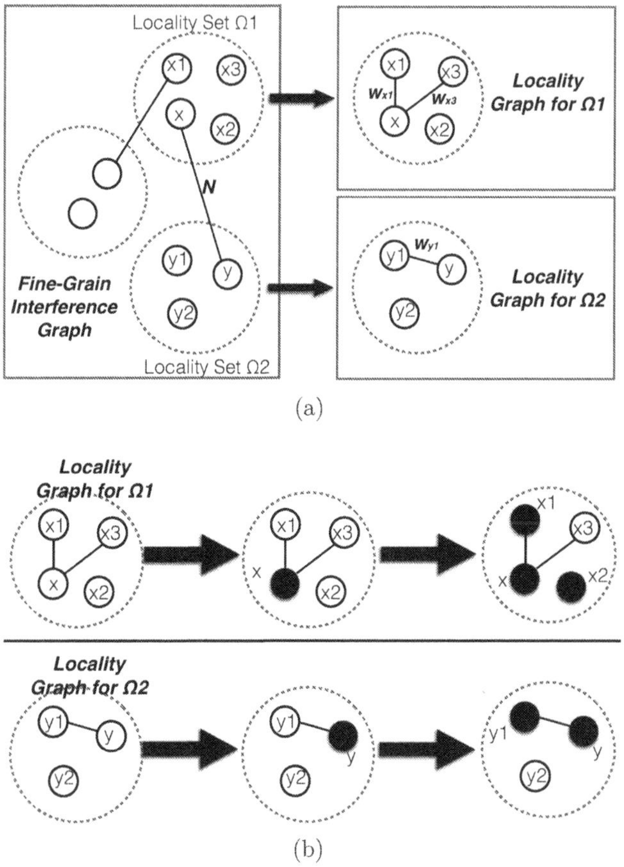

Figure 6: Example of finding the partitions that satisfy Condition (1). In each locality set, the black nodes are considered to be in the same partition (for each locality graph).

weight N, which represents the number of row-buffer misses that can be eliminated by placing x and y into the same row, we first consider isolating x and y from their locality sets, i.e., placing only x into P_x, and only y into P_y. Let N_{ch} and N_{rb} denote the total number of cache misses and row-buffer misses that could be increased by placing P_x and P_y into the memory blocks β'_x and β'_y, respectively, where $Caches(\beta'_x) = Caches(\beta_x)$ and $Caches(\beta'_y) = Caches(\beta_y)$, and δ_{ch} and δ_{rb} denote the miss latencies in the cache and row-buffer, respectively; then if these two partitions causes less overall access latency than the original, we should have:

$$(N - N_{rb}) * \delta_{rb} > N_{ch} * \delta_{ch}. \qquad (1)$$

If Condition (1) is not satisfied, we then consider placing the data elements connected to x (in the locality graph), together with x, into P_x, and the data elements connected to y, together with y, into P_y. We repeat this process until Condition (1) is satisfied.[5] In the worst case when no such partitions can be found, we have $N_{ch} = N_{rb} = 0$, which makes Condition (1) still hold. At this point, the remaining question is how to determine N_{ch} and N_{rb}. Assuming

[5]We are not trying to obtain the optimal solution w.r.t Condition (1). Instead, our point is that, as long as this condition is satisfied, the generated layout will be "better" than the original one.

Algorithm 2 Fine-Grain Layout Generation.

/*Constructing the interference graph*/
for every access α_u in Seq **do**
  if $\Delta(\alpha_u^-, \alpha_u) = k$, $u \in \Omega$ **then**
    for each access in $[time(\alpha_u^-), time(\alpha_u)]$ **do**
      α_x= current_access
      if $Caches(\beta_x) = Caches(\beta_u)$ **then**
        /* $tmp(\beta_x)$ records the previous access */
        if $tmp(\beta_x) = \emptyset$ **then**
          $tmp(\beta_x) = x$
        else
          $y = tmp(\beta_x)$
          set up edge $e_{x,y}$ between x and y
        end if
      end if
    end for
  end if
end for
/* Assigning rows and memory blocks*/
sort edges in non-increasing order based on their weights: $e_1, e_2, \cdots e_p$
for every each pair of x and y on e_i **do**
  $P_x \leftarrow \{x\}$
  $P_y \leftarrow \{y\}$
  $N \leftarrow w(e_{x,y})$
  while $(N - N_{rb}) * \delta_{rb} > N_{ch} * \delta_{ch}$ **do**
    $P_x \leftarrow P_x \cup$ all neighbors of x in the locality graph
    $P_y \leftarrow P_y \cup$ all neighbors of y in the locality graph
  end while
  assign $row(P_x)$ and $row(P_y)$ to the same row.
  assign $block(P_x)$ and $block(P_y)$ to the memory blocks based on Lemma 5.2
end for

that, in the locality graph, x is connected to $x_1, x_2, \cdots, x_m$, with the weights $w_{x_1}, w_{x_2}, \cdots, w_{x_m}$; and y is connected to $y_1, y_2, \cdots, y_n$, with the weights $w_{y_1}, w_{y_2}, \cdots, w_{y_n}$; then we have $N_{ch} = \sum_{i=1}^{m} w_{x_i} + \sum_{i=1}^{n} w_{y_i}$. Since N_{ch} is the upper limit for N_{rb}, in our current implementation, we conservatively have $N_{rb} = N_{ch}$.

Figure 6 illustrates an example for finding the partitions that satisfy Condition (1). In this example, we assume that, in the fine-grain interference graph, the edge between x and y has the highest weight N, and denote the locality sets of x and y as Ω_1 and Ω_2. In order to find the partitions for x and y, we first let $P_x \leftarrow x$ and $P_y \leftarrow y$, i.e., the initial partitions for x and y only contain themselves. At this point, we have $N_{ch} = w_{x_1} + w_{x_3} + w_{y_1}$. Assuming that Condition (1) cannot be satisfied based on this value, then we place all the neighbors of x and y into their partitions, i.e., $P_x = \{x, x_1, x_3\}$ and $P_y = \{y, y_1\}$. Now we have $N_{ch} = 0$, and therefore Condition (1) is satisfied, and the partitions of x and y are found.

Step 4: Assigning Rows and Memory Blocks. Once this process completes, we assign the rows and memory blocks to the partitions (or locality sets in the worst case) of x and y as described in Lemma 5.2.

7. DISCUSSION

Sequential code vs. parallel code: So far our discussion is based on the assumption that the sequence of data accessed by the program, *Seq*, is equal to the sequence of data visited by traversing the index array. Although in a single-threaded application, these two orders are expected to be the same, in a multi-threaded application, the unpredictable interferences across threads make these two orders usually different. However, we want to point out that, assuming these orders equal may be a reasonable approximation. This is because, the foundation of our proposed schemes is the relationship between the block reuse distance of each access and the value of k. That is to say, we only need to know whether this block distance is greater than k or not, and do not need to know its exact value. Therefore, they have certain tolerance to the mismatch between the "assumed" and "actual" data access orders. For example, when determining $\Delta(\alpha_x, \alpha_y)$ (assuming that $\beta_x = \beta_y$), we do not need to figure out the exact position of a_y in the actual data access order, instead, we only need to know if a_y appears in the most-recent k accesses before a_x or vice versa. Therefore, the "assumed" data access order can be considered as a reasonable approximation of "the actual" data access order that will be observed at run time. There also several existing works on how to predict the data access sequence of a multithreaded application more accurately [10, 33], which could be our future research direction.

Complexity analysis: Next we compare the algorithmic complexities of our data ordering scheme with existing schemes that target optimizing cache behavior of irregular applications. We assume that the number of data elements in the data access sequence is N, the length of the index array is E, and the cache size is C. For typical graphs, we have $N >> C$ and $N > E$. The consecutive packing (CPACK) has a cost of $O(E)$, since it rearranges the data elements based on their "first-touch" order and requires one pass through the data access sequence. *GPART* has a cost of $O(E * g(C))$, where $g(C)$ is a constant function greater than 1, since the number of clustering passes is dependent on the cache size, *not* the input data size. As a result, GPART is only a small constant factor more expensive than CPACK. RCB has the complexity of $O(N(log_2N)^2)$, and METIS has the cost $O(2Nlog_2N) + O(E)$ [15]. In comparison, assuming that the inference graph has E' edges, as can be observed in Algorithms 1, conservative layout has the complexity of $O(N) + O(E_1)$ since each of the first two steps requires one pass over the index array ($O(N)$), and the last step requires one traversal of the inference graph ($O(E')$). For the fine-grain layout, let us assume that the inference graph has E_1 edges and the locality graph has E_2 edges and V nodes. Similar to the conservative layout, each of the first two steps requires one pass over the index array ($O(N)$), and the last step has a cost of $O(E_1(V + E_2))$. Therefore, the total cost of generating fine-grain layout is $O(N) + O(E_1(V + E_2))$, which is higher than the cost of generating the conservative layout, and both of our two data reordering schemes have lower complexities than RCB and METIS, but higher complexities than CPACK and GPART.

Implementation overheads: The inspectors are expensive, but their "one-time" cost can be amortized over a long execution time. For example, the inspectors can be inserted outside the loop, and then, execute once before the computation begins, benefiting computations throughout the whole loop. When access patterns change, the inspectors may be invoked, but they need not to be rerun each time the access patterns change. Without rerunning the inspectors, the cache performance may degrade, but the application code still generates correct results. Similar to the prior work, we only modify the implementation of the inspector to embed our data reordering strategies.

Data reordering itself also introduces overheads during the execution (runtime), which mainly comes from two sources. The first is the overhead of the data reordering itself, which can be reduced by adjusting the number of edges in the inference graph and locality graph that need to be traversed. The compiler needs to ensure that this cost does not outweigh any performance gain by data reordering. The second overhead comes from the data redirection after data reordering, which maps the old memory location (before data reordering) to the new memory location (after data reordering). Since each access to a transformed array needs to be redirected to the access to the new memory location, this overhead can be quite expensive. Discussion about how to reduce this type of overhead can be found in [13].

Table 1: Benchmark codes used in our evaluation.

Name	Input Size	L3 Miss Rate	Row-Buffer Miss Rate	Execution Time
PSTT	427.6MB	18.1%	29.6%	9.6sec
PaSTiX	511.6MB	24.3%	41.7%	8.8sec
SSIF	129.3MB	13.7%	24.4%	4.3sec
PPS	738.2MB	21.4%	33.1%	11.1sec
REACT	1.2GB	28.6%	46.9%	13.7sec

Table 2: Architecture specification.

CPU	48 cores; 4 sockets (12 cores/socket); 4 memory controllers/socket (with FR-FCFS scheduling policy); 2.6GHz AMD Opteron cores;
Cache Hierarchy	64KB 2-way associative per core L1 (3 cycles); 512KB 16-way associative per core L2 (12 cycles); 12MB per socket 6-way associative shared L3 (28 cycles)
Memory System	DDR3 1,866MHz DRAM; 8 banks per channel; 8KB row-buffers;

8. EXPERIMENTAL EVALUATION

8.1 Implementation, Benchmarks and Setup

We implement our proposed schemes using the Open64 compiler [4]. In our implementation, the compiler generates run-time library calls to the *inspector module* to process memory access patterns at run-time and identify non-local data needed by each processor, and determines when the inspectors must be rerun if the memory access patterns change in the program code. Specifically, the compiler first makes a pass through the program to identify the index array. Then it finds appropriate locations where inspectors can be inserted. To do this, a top-down traversal of the AST is performed to identify the topmost blocks that contain the writes to the index arrays, but do not contain corresponding irregular array computations. The inspectors will be inserted in these blocks. When the inspector is executed at run-time, it rearranges the contents of the host arrays to generate the desired data reordering by using Algorithms 1 and 2 presented earlier. Later, the executor (the original loop body) will access these reordered data, which helps us to exploit the cache and row-buffer locality.

For each application code in our experimental suite, we tested four different versions: *Original* (the original code without any modification, compiled using the default -O2 compiler flag), *Cache-Optimized* (a version which is optimized using a previously-proposed cache locality enhancement technique (GPART [15]), followed by all data locality optimizations turned on using the -O3 compiler flag – these optimizations include loop permutation as well as tiling among others), *Conservative* (our conservative layout optimization strategy explained in Section 5), and *Fine-Grain* (our fine-grain layout optimization strategy explained in Section 6). We want to point out that, other algorithms such METIS [18] and RCB [9], as mention in Section 7, have significantly higher runtime overheads than GPART and CPACK, and they are quite expensive when used for cache optimizations [15]. Therefore, in a scenario like ours where the layout needs to be modified during the course execution, there is a motivation for reordering-based techniques. In addition, GPART performs better than METIS for most cases [15]. And, since our preliminary experiments also indicated the same, we chose GPART for comparison. However, METIS and similar partitioning tools have a very important role in sparse/irregular application codes. For example, in a cluster-environment, the target-graph can be partitioned using METIS to minimize inter-node communication, and then the local-portion of each node can be laid out in memory using our approach. In that case, METIS and our approach each addresses different aspects of locality: one across nodes (minimizing communication in distributed-memory-space), and the other across cores in a node (cache locality as well as row-buffer locality). In addition, we did not turn on hardware-prefetching in our experiments presented below as it does not bring much benefit in irregular-applications. The experiments with our approach with hardware-prefetching turned-on did not change our savings much (it reduced the additional benefits brought by our approach by less than 1%). Note also that, if the prefetching-algorithm is exposed to our approach, we can adapt our approach by fine-tuning the block-distance-calculation.

For our experimental evaluations, we used five applications: PSTT (parallel sparse FFT) [5], PaSTiX (a high performance parallel solver for very large sparse linear systems based on direct methods) [6], SSIF (sparse symmetric indefinite factorization) [26], PPS (a persistent, pervasive surveillance code), and REACT (Jacobian based combustion modeling code). The last two applications are written by us. We want to emphasize that the first three of these applications are quite large programs (each having more than 5,000 lines excluding library calls). Further, all five applications are memory-intensive and operate on large data structures, creating a high volume of off-chip data traffic. Table 1 gives the salient features of these applications; the last three columns show, respectively, the last level cache miss rate, the row-buffer miss rate, and parallel execution time on our 12 cores (1 socket of) AMD based system (explained below). It is important to note that, as far as row-buffer misses are concerned, these applications exhibit a variety (ranging between 24.4% and 46.9%). Overall, however, these row-buffer miss rates are quite high, and indicate poor row-buffer locality. There are three main reasons for this. First, irregular application inherently have poor locality within memory rows. Second, techniques such as cache block interleaving (i.e., distributing physical memory across controllers at a cache block granularity), while good for memory level parallelism, hurt row-buffer locality as consecutive cache blocks go to different banks, reducing the amount of row buffer reuse. Third, running an irregular application in a multithreaded fashion further spreads data access across the memory space, and this in turn also has a negative impact on row-buffer locality.

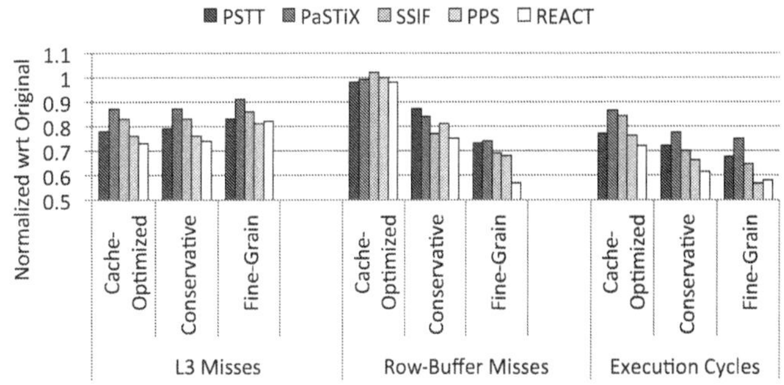

Figure 7: Results with AMD based multicore system.

In this work, we performed two types of evaluations. First, we measured the impact of our optimizations on an AMD Opteron based multicore with 8 cores, 2.6GHz core speed and a total of 12MB L3 last-level cache. The relevant important characteristics of this system are given in Table 2. All the cache and row-buffer statistics reported in this table as well as those presented in the remainder of this section for this AMD based machine are collected by monitoring the Opteron CPU and memory controller performance counters. Second, we also simulated our approach on GEM5 multicore simulator [1]. The reason for the simulation based experiments is this: while the AMD multicore experiments clearly show the impact of our proposed row-buffer optimization, it is not possible in a real hardware to change different parameters and test how our approach would perform, for instance, when we increase the number of memory controllers, change the row-buffer size, bank count, etc. To carry out all these sensitivity studies, we also conducted a simulation-based evaluation.

8.2 Results with AMD Opteron

Figure 7 gives the results collected on one socket (12 cores) of our AMD Opteron based system (multi-socket results will be presented later). The y-axis in this plot represents normalized value (L3 miss rates, row-buffer miss rates, and execution cycles) with respect to Original (the absolute values of these metrics with Original are listed in Table 1). It can be seen that all three optimized versions (Cache-Optimized, Conservative and Fine-Grain) improve – except in two cases –over Original in all metrics quantified. More specifically, Cache-Optimized improves cache performance (with a geometric average of 20.6%) but does not bring much benefit as far as row-buffer locality is concerned, indicating that *conventional cache optimizations may not be very effective when it comes to row-buffers.* This version brings an average of 20.8% reduction in execution cycles compared to Original. Conservative on the other hand exhibits a different behavior. While maintaining the same cache performance as Cache-Optimized (difference between their cache performance is around 1% in some applications), it cuts the row-

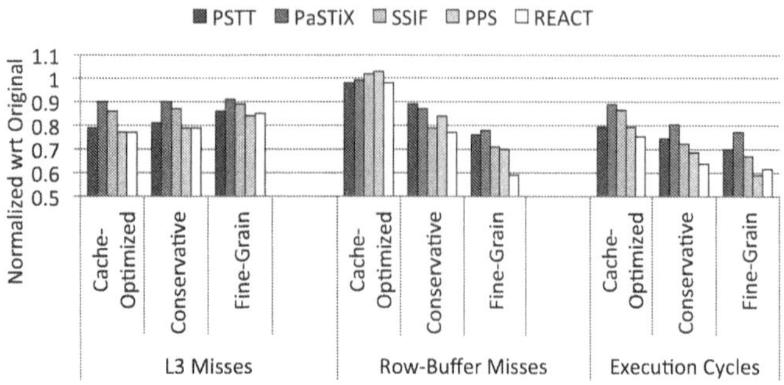

Figure 8: Simulation results.

buffer misses significantly (an average of 19.2% reduction over Original). Finally, Fine-Grain sacrifices some cache performance but in return achieves an average row-buffer miss reduction of 31.8%. At the end, Conservative and Fine-Grain improve 30.6% and 35.6%, respectively, over Original, in terms of execution time. These results demonstrate that *Fine-Grain is very successful in trading cache performance for better overall memory performance*, and selecting the right tradeoff point (which our approach tries to do) can result in significant improvements in execution time as well.

8.3 Simulation Results

We also evaluate the sensitivity of proposed scheme to different important architectural parameters and used a simulator (Gem5 [1]) for that. Specifically, there are four main parameters we wanted to study in detail: row-buffer size, number of memory controllers, number of cores, and L3 capacity. To carry out this study, we first modeled our AMD machine in the simulator as accurately as we can (using the values in the AMD system for all major parameters, the same compiler and the same thread mapping) and tried to replicate the results collected in the real system. The results presented in Figure 8 are a bit different from those in Figure 7 – as far as absolute values are concerned – but the general trends are similar.

In the remainder of this subsection, we present results for only one of our applications (PPS) since the general observations/trends with the others were similar. Figure 9(a) presents the sensitivity of our approach to row-buffer size. Remember that our default buffer size was 8KB (see Table 2). We see that our approaches (Conservative and Fine-Grain) perform better with larger row-buffer sizes. This is because a larger row-buffer size give more flexibility to our approach in reorganizing data elements. While Cache-Optimized also takes advantage of a larger row-buffer size, its improvement is far below than those of Conservative and Fine-Grain, and quickly saturates. Next, we report in Figure 9(b) the impact of varying the number of memory controllers, per socket. Again (and as would be expected), Conservative and Fine-Grain take much better advantage of the increased number of memory controllers. This is mainly because a larger number of controllers means that accesses are spread more in the memory space and this presents more scope to our approaches for optimization. We observe a similar trend when the number of cores per socket is increased (Figure 9(c)) for a similar reason – wider distribution of data accesses in the memory space with increased number

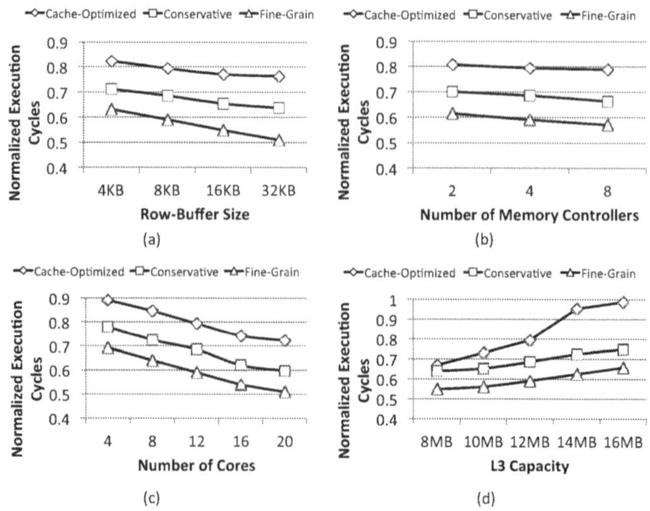

Figure 9: Results of sensitivity analysis (normalized w.r.t original).

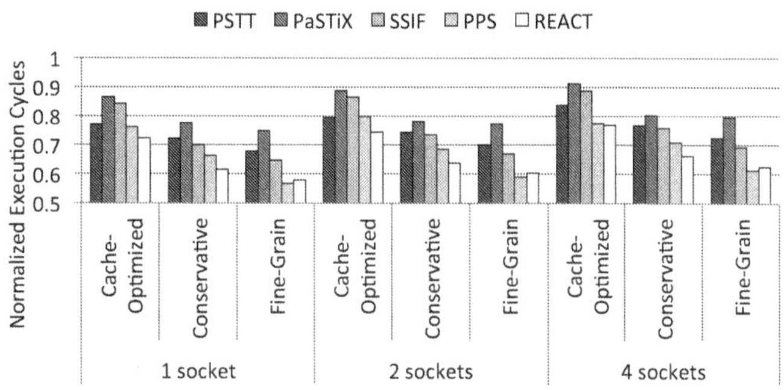

Figure 10: Multi-socket evaluation on AMD (normalized w.r.t original).

of cores. Our last sensitivity study involves changing L3 capacity (from its default value of 12MB). The results plotted in Figure 9(d) show that as cache capacity per core gets reduced, we can expect better savings from our layout optimization approaches.

An important conclusion from these sensitivity experiments is that our approach performs better with larger number of cores, larger number of memory controllers, increased row-buffer sizes and reduced last level cache space per core (not the cumulative LLC size), all of which are current trends in computer architecture. In other words, we can expect our optimizations to continue to be effective in the long run.

8.4 Multi-Socket Evaluation in Opteron

Recall that in our evaluation on the AMD based machine presented above, we used a single socket. Figure 10 plots normalized execution time (with respect to Original) with 2 sockets and 4 sockets as well. In the 2 socket case, each application is parallelized over 24 cores and in the case of 48 cores. The results indicate that, while savings achieved by our approaches, Conservative and Fine-Grain, get a bit reduced with increased socket count, overall they still achieve signifi-

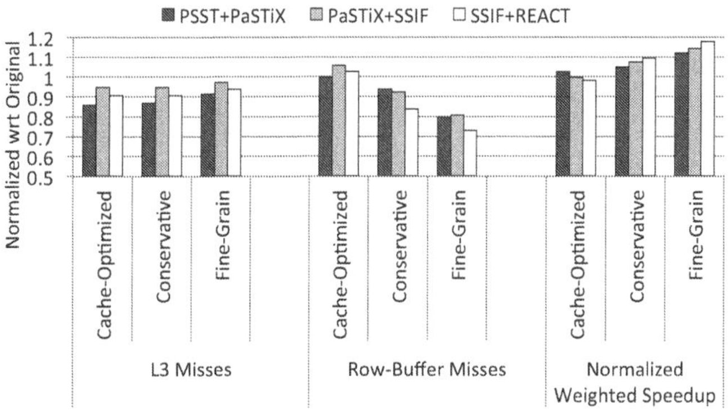

Figure 11: Multiprogrammed workload evaluation on AMD.

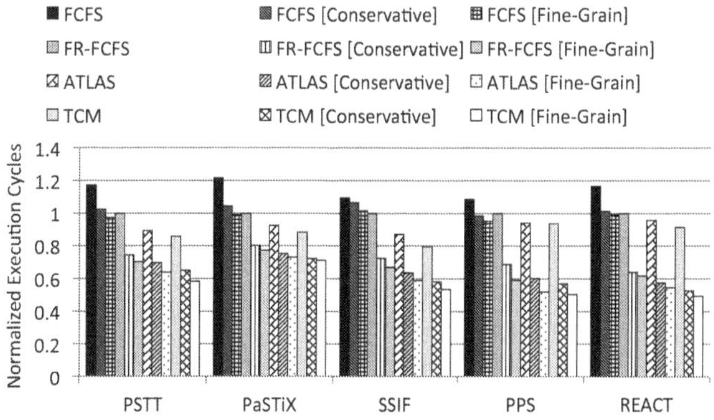

Figure 12: Results with different memory scheduling algorithms (normalized w.r.t FR-FCFS (with original)).

cant savings (the geometric mean of execution improvement is 28.3% and 33.3% in the 2-socket case, and 26.1% and 31.2% in the 4-socket case). The slight reduction when using 2/4 sockets is probably due to non-local accesses (those going from one socket to another) playing a major role in shaping the overall memory performance, and reducing the effectiveness of improved row-buffer behavior.

8.5 Multiprogrammed Workload Evaluation in Opteron

Our last set of experiments focus on the execution of a multiprogrammed workload of multithreaded applications. In this experiment, we formed three workloads, each consisting of two applications executing on 6 cores of a socket. That is, two applications share the cores in a socket equally. It should be noted that we can expect the effectiveness of our approaches to reduce in this case, primarily because both applications in a workload will share the same 4 memory controllers (hence same set of row-buffers) in the socket, and this will cause extra row-buffer conflicts/misses for each application (due to interference). The metric we use to represent performance is "combined speedup", which is basically the average speedup the two applications achieve over their Original versions. The results plotted in Figure 11 show that, when averaged over all three workloads, Conservative and Fine-Grain achieve 7.3% and 14.7% performance improvement. Therefore, it can be concluded that our approach is very effective even if multiple applications share the same set of memory controllers.

8.6 Results with Different Memory Schedulings

DRAM is a major resource shared among cores in a multicore machine, and memory requests from different threads can interfere with each other when accessing this shared resource. Motivated by this, there is a plethora of hardware-based memory request scheduling algorithms oriented towards reducing this potential interference and increase the overall throughput of the memory system. As stated in Table 2, the default memory scheduling we used so far (and the dominant scheduling algorithm in commercial chips) is FR-FCFS, which works by implementing first-come, first-served (FCFS) strategy in serving the memory requests, except when there are memory requests in the queue that target the current memory row in the row-buffer. That is, FR-FCFS give priority to requests that can reuse the row-buffer contents; when no such request can be found in the queue, it resorts to FCFS. Recent years have witnessed more sophisticated memory scheduling policies that are very aggressive in prioritizing memory requests and coordinating memory controllers to further improve memory throughput. Two such schemes are ATLAS [19] and TCM [20]. While ATLAS periodically orders the threads based on the service they have attained from the memory controllers so far, and prioritize those threads that have attained the least service over others in each period, TCM divides the threads into two separate clusters and employ different memory request scheduling policies in each cluster. Using GEM5, we evaluated our conservative and fine-grain layout optimization strategies under pure FCFS (without any prioritization), ATLAS and TCM, and plot results in Figure 12. Note that the bar marked as "FR-FCFS" indicates the execution of Original benchmark under the FR-FCFS policy, and represents the base case that we have used so far. Several interesting observations can be made from this plot. First, the performance of FCFS powered with our layout optimization algorithms are competitive with FR-FCFS with the original codes. Given the fact that going from FCFS to FR-FCFS in hardware requires a lot of additional cost and complexity (as one need to check all the entries in the memory queue to see whether they access the row currently in the row-buffer), we believe that our software based strategy provides a cost effective alternative to hardware optimization. Second, we see that using our approach with FR-FCFS generates better results than using the original codes with ATLAS or TCM. Third, our layout reorganization strategy improves the performance of ATLAS and TCM significantly, and in fact, the highest performance improvement is achieved by TCM (Fine-Grain). In principle, these savings can be further increased by making our approach aware of the underlying memory scheduling algorithm; we postpone the investigation of this problem to a future study.

9. RELATED WORK

There exist many work related to row buffer locality [19, 20, 32, 39, 29, 17, 7, 43]. Lee et. al. [23] tries to reduce interference between reads and writes in the memory channel. They take advantage of row buffer hits by scheduling write backs that will hit in the row buffer before they are evicted from the cache. Awasthi et al. [8] proposed an Access Based Predictor, which keeps a history of the number of accesses to each DRAM page in order to predict how long the row buffer should remain open when that page is present. Yoon et al. [38] avoid the high cost of phase-change memory (PCM) row buffer misses in hybrid memories by moving memory blocks that frequently miss in the row buffer into DRAM. Their scheme also considers row buffer locality as a factor in deciding which blocks to move. Meza et al. [27] study the benefits of smaller row buffer sizes for non-volatile memory. Zhang et al. [41] described causes of row buffer conflicts when using a page interleaving policy. Their work improved row buffer hit rates using permutations that preserve data locality while distributing pages to reduce conflicts. Similarly, [36] tried to improve row buffer hit rates by decreasing the OS page size and moving frequently accessed pages into the same row. Most of these prior works concerning the row buffer locality target hardware, while our work uses compiler optimizations. There have not been as many compiler schemes for row buffer locality. One work [34] uses loop transformations to improve spatial locality of pages and therefore row buffer reuse. Unlike our approach, their optimization relies on dependences between data elements. Also, they target single-thread locality rather than taking into account the row buffer locality of the entire application. Another compiler scheme [14] targeted the row buffer locality of regular applications with affine loops. In contrast, we target irregular applications and try to improve row-buffer locality by trading cache performance for the overall memory performance.

Optimizations for irregular applications often target data layout. Data clustering is an NP-hard problem, as shown in early work by Thabit [37]. Furthermore, Petrank and Rawitz [30] demonstrated that data placement to minimize cache misses is an inapproximable optimization problem. Zhong et al. [42] introduce a metric of the closeness of data accesses based on LRU stack distance called reference affinity. Zhang et al. [40] looked at reference affinity from both a theoretical and a practical perspective. Our concept of a locality set differs from the affinity group described by these papers in that locality set describes a set of elements in the cache with good locality, while an affinity group is built based on the reference affinity metric. More practical approaches to the problem of irregular accesses include [13, 15, 25, 28, 35]. However, all these studies either try to improve parallelism, or reduce runtime overheads, or improve cache performance. None of them addresses row-buffer locality. [15] proposed a hierarchical graph clustering algorithm (GPART) to improve cache locality.

10. CONCLUSIONS

In a system that employs open page policy, exploiting row-buffer locality can be critical. The novel contribution of this paper is a compiler-directed data layout reorganization scheme with the goal of improving row-buffer locality of large, irregular applications. In particular, we propose, implement and test two alternate layout reorganization schemes, the first trying to improve row-buffer hits without negatively affecting the cache locality (hit/miss statistics) of a cache-optimized code, whereas the second one trading off cache hits to further improve the row-buffer hits, and eventually the overall application performance.

Acknowledgment

This research is supported in part by NSF grants #0963839, #1302557, #1213052, #1017882, and #1205618, a grant from INTEL an a grant from MICROSOFT.

11. REFERENCES

[1] "Gem5," *http://gem5.org.*

[2] "Intel pentium 4 and intel xeon processor optimization, reference manual," *http://developer.intel.com.*

[3] "Intel Xscale core, developer's manual," *http://developer.intel.com.*

[4] "Open64," *http://www.open64.net.*

[5] "Spiral: Software/hardware generation for dsp algorithms," *http://www.spiral.net/.*

[6] "The PaSTiX Library," *http://pastix.gforge.inria.fr/.*

[7] R. Ausavarungnirun, K. Kai-wei, C. Lavanya, S. Gabriel, H. Loh, and O. Mutlu, "Staged memory scheduling: achieving high performance and scalability in heterogeneous systems," *In Proceedings of the International Symposium on Computer Architecture*, 2012.

[8] M. Awasthi, D. W. Nellans, R. Balasubramonian, and A. Davis, "Prediction based DRAM row-buffer management in the many-core era," *In Proceedings of the International Conference on Parallel Architectures and Compilation Techniques*, 2011.

[9] M. Berger and S. Bokhari, "A partitioning strategy for non-uniform problems on multiprocessors," *IEEE Trans. Computers*, 1987.

[10] P. Boonserm, B. Wang, S. See, and T. Achalakul, "Improving data processing time with access sequence prediction," in *Proceedings of the International Conference on Parallel and Distributed Systems*, 2012.

[11] P. Carribault, S. Zuckerman, A. Cohen, and W. Jalby, "Deep jam: Conversion of coarse-grain parallelism to instruction-level and vector parallelism for irregular applications," *In Proceedings of the International Conference on Parallel Architectures and Compilation Techniques*, 2005.

[12] R. Das, M. Uysal, J. Saltz, and Y. shin Hwang, "Communication optimizations for irregular scientific computations on distributed memory architectures," *Journal of Parallel and Distributed Computing*, 1993.

[13] C. Ding and K. Kennedy, "Improving cache performance in dynamic applications through data and computation reorganization at run time," *In Proceedings of the Conference on Programming Language Design and Implementation*, 1999.

[14] W. Ding, J. Liu, K. Mahmut, and M. J. Irwin, "Reshaping cache misses to improve row-buffer locality in multicore systems," *In Proceedings of the International Conference on Parallel Architectures and Compilation Techniques*, 2013.

[15] H. Han and C.-W. Tseng, "Exploiting locality for irregular scientific codes," *IEEE Trans. Parallel Distrib. Syst.*, 2006.

[16] J. L. Hennessy and D. Patterson, *Computer Architecture: A Quantitative Approach.* Morgan Kaufmann, 2003.

[17] E. Ipek, O. Mutlu, J. F. Martínez, and R. Caruana, "Self-optimizing memory controllers: A reinforcement learning approach," *In Proceedings of the International Symposium on Computer Architecture*, 2008.

[18] G. Karypis and V. Kumar, "A fast and high quality multilevel scheme for partitioning irregular graphs," *SIAM Journal on Scientific Computing*, 1998.

[19] Y. Kim, D. Han, O. Mutlu, and M. Harchol-balter, "ATLAS: A scalable and high-performance scheduling algorithm for multiple memory controllers," *In Proceedings of the International Symposium On High Performance Computer Architecture*, 2010.

[20] Y. Kim, M. Papamichael, O. Mutlu, and M. Harchol-balter, "Thread cluster memory scheduling: Exploiting differences in memory access behavior," *In Proceedings of the International Symposium on Microarchitecture*, 2010.

[21] D. Kroft, "Lockup-free instruction fetch/prefetch cache organization," *Computer Architecture*, 1981.

[22] M. Kulkarni, M. Burtscher, R. Inkulu, K. Pingali, and C. Casçaval, "How much parallelism is there in irregular applications?" *In Proceedings of the ACM SIGPLAN symposium on Principles and practice of parallel programming*, pp. 3–14, 2009.

[23] C. J. Lee, V. Narasiman, E. Ebrahimi, O. Mutlu, and Y. N. Patt, "Dram-aware last-level cache writeback: Reducing write-caused interference in memory systems," *HPS Technical Report*, 2010.

[24] W. Liu and A. Sherman, "Comparative analysis of the cuthill-mckee and the reverse cuthill-mckee ordering algorithms for sparse matrices," *SIAM Journal on Numerical Analysis*, 1976.

[25] J. Mellor-Crummey, D. Whalley, and K. Kennedy, "Improving memory hierarchy performance for irregular applications," *In Proceedings of the International Conference on Supercomputing*, 1999.

[26] O. Meshar, D. Irony, and S. Toledo, "An out-of-core sparse symmetric-indefinite factorization method," *ACM Trans. Math. Softw.*, 2006.

[27] J. Meza, J. Li, and O. Mutlu, "Evaluating row buffer locality in future non-volatile main memories," *SAFARI Technical Report*, 2012.

[28] N. Mitchell, L. Carter, and J. Ferrante, "Localizing non-affine array references," *In Proceedings of the International Conference on Parallel Architectures and Compilation Techniques*, 1999.

[29] O. Mutlu and T. Moscibroda, "Stall-time fair memory access scheduling for chip multiprocessors," *In Proceedings of the International Symposium on Microarchitecture*, 2007.

[30] E. Petrank and D. Rawitz, "The hardness of cache conscious data placement," *In Proceedings of the Conference on Principles of Programming Languages*, 2002.

[31] K. Pingali, D. Nguyen, M. Kulkarni, M. Burtscher, M. A. Hassaan, R. Kaleem, T.-H. Lee, A. Lenharth, R. Manevich, M. Méndez-Lojo, D. Prountzos, and X. Sui, "The tao of parallelism in algorithms," *In Proceedings of the Conference on Programming Language Design and Implementation.*, 2011.

[32] S. Rixner, W. J. Dally, U. J. Kapasi, P. Mattson, and J. D. Owens, "Memory access scheduling," *In Proceedings of the International Symposium on Computer Architecture*, 2000.

[33] M. F. Sakr, S. P. Levitan, D. M. Chiarulli, B. G. Horne, and C. L. Giles, "Predicting multiprocessor memory access patterns with learning models," *In Proceedings of the International Conference on Machine Learning*, 1997.

[34] J. Shin, J. Chame, and M. W. Hall, "A compiler algorithm for exploiting pagemode memory access in embeddeddram devices," *In Proceedings of the Workshop on Media Streaming Process*, 2002.

[35] M. M. Strout, L. Carter, and J. Ferrante, "Compile-time composition of run-time data and iteration reorderings," *In Proceedings of the Conference on Programming Language Design and Implementation*, 2003.

[36] K. Sudan, N. Chatterjee, D. Nellans, M. Awasthi, R. Balasubramonian, and A. Davis, "Micro-pages: increasing dram efficiency with locality-aware data placement," *In Proceedings of the International Conference on Architectural Support for Programming Languages and Operating Systems*, 2010.

[37] K. Thabit, "Cache management by the compiler," Ph.D. dissertation, Rice University, Houston, TX, USA, 1982.

[38] H. Yoon, J. Meza, R. Ausavarungnirun, R. Harding, and O. Mutlu, "Row buffer locality-aware data placement in hybrid memories," *SAFARI Technical Report*, 2011.

[39] G. L. Yuan, A. Bakhoda, and T. M. Aamodt, "Complexity effective memory access scheduling for many-core accelerator architectures," *In Proceedings of the International Symposium on Microarchitecture*, 2009.

[40] C. Zhang, C. Ding, M. Ogihara, Y. Zhong, and Y. Wu, "A hierarchical model of data locality," *In Proceedings of the Conference on Principles of Programming Languages*, 2006.

[41] Z. Zhang, Z. Zhu, and X. Zhang, "A permutation-based page interleaving scheme to reduce row-buffer conflicts and exploit data locality," *In Proceedings of the International Symposium on Microarchitecture*, 2000.

[42] Y. Zhong, M. Orlovich, X. Shen, and C. Ding, "Array regrouping and structure splitting using whole-program reference affinity," *In Proceedings of the Conference on Programming Language Design and Implementation*, 2004.

[43] Z. Zhu and Z. Zhang, "A performance comparison of dram memory system optimizations for SMT processors," *In Proceedings of the International Symposium on High-Performance Computer Architecture*, 2005.

Compiler Support for Selective Page Migration in NUMA Architectures

Guilherme Piccoli
Unicamp
guilherme.piccoli@students.ic.unicamp.br

Henrique N. Santos
UFMG
hnsantos@dcc.ufmg.br

Raphael E. Rodrigues
UFMG
raphael@dcc.ufmg.br

Christiane Pousa
ETH Zürich
pousa@id.ethz.ch

Edson Borin
Unicamp
edson@ic.unicamp.br

Fernando Magno Quintão Pereira
UFMG
fernando@dcc.ufmg.br

ABSTRACT

Current high-performance multicore processors provide users with a non-uniform memory access model (NUMA). These systems perform better when threads access data on memory banks next to the core where they run. However, ensuring data locality is difficult. In this paper, we propose compiler analyses and code generation methods to support a lightweight runtime system that dynamically migrates memory pages to improve data locality. Our technique combines static and dynamic analyses and is capable of identifying the most promising pages to migrate. Statically, we infer the size of arrays, plus the amount of reuse of each memory access instruction in a program. These estimates rely on a simple, yet accurate, trip count predictor of our own design. This knowledge let's us build templates of dynamic checks, to be filled with values known only at runtime. These checks determine when it is profitable to migrate data closer to the processors where this data is used. Our static analyses are quadratic on the number of variables in a program, and the dynamic checks are $O(1)$ in practice. Our technique does not require any form of user intervention, neither the support of a third-party middleware, nor modifications in the operating system's kernel. We have applied our technique on several parallel algorithms, which are completely oblivious to the asymmetric memory topology, and have observed speedups of up to 4x, compared to static heuristics. We compare our approach against Minas, a middleware that supports NUMA-aware data allocation, and show that we can outperform it by up to 50% in some cases.

Categories and Subject Descriptors

D.3.4 [**Software**]: Programming Languages—*Compilers*

PACT'14, August 24–27, 2014, Edmonton, AB, Canada.
Copyright 2014 ACM 978-1-4503-2809-8/14/08 ...$15.00.
http://dx.doi.org/10.1145/2628071.2628077 .

General Terms

Languages

Keywords

NUMA, static analysis, data placement, memory topology

1. INTRODUCTION

There exist two basic ways to connect processors to memory in a multi-core architecture. The simplest alternative consists in connecting each processor equally to the memory bank. Such architectures are also known as *Symmetric Multiprocessing* (SMP) systems. The other approach is asymmetric: each processor is directly connected to local memory banks and a forwarding mechanism is used to read or write data in remote memory banks. This kind of architecture, known as *Non-Uniform Memory Access*, or NUMA for short, is not a new idea - early designs were already enjoying commercial success in the late 70's. As an example, the Burroughs's B6800 processor, of 1977, is a NUMA architecture. Although the NUMA model used to be mostly common in high performance computing systems, nowadays, we find non-uniform memory layouts in several general-purpose multi-core processors such as the Tilera Tile64, Intel E8870, HP sx2000, and the AMD Opteron. This tendency is likely to remain in vogue, given that the number of cores per chip is predicted to increase even more in the coming years [2, Sec.2.2]. The attractiveness of the NUMA design comes from the fact that it enables parallel data accesses on multiple memory banks; thus reducing memory access conflicts. The ever-increasing speed of processing units is contributing to boost the importance of this advantage.

The performance of memory systems, in general, suffers in face of access conflicts. Such conflicts happen whenever different threads try to read or write data in the same memory bank simultaneously. NUMA machines mitigate this problem by allowing the placement of data in separate memory banks. Therefore, in these architectures, data allocation plays a central role in performance. Ideally, a thread should access data placed in memory located at the core that executes it. We call this memory a local bank, and we call these accesses *local.* Whenever a thread reads or writes data in a remote (non-local) memory bank, the data is copied from a remote location to a local cache - an expensive operation that we call a *remote access*. Yet, the main drawback of remote accesses is not their long traffic time: these accesses are prone to generate access conflicts, leading to resource contention between threads [27].

There have been several different proposals to improve data allocation on NUMA machines. Many of these techniques were published in the late 2000's. Some of these methods are implemented at the operating system level [2, 4, 17, 23], at the hardware level [10, 15, 28], or at the middleware level [6, 8, 19, 24]. These approaches extract information from a program's runtime behavior, but do not take its coding structure into consideration. Other approaches rely on library calls, which give the programmer the opportunity to move memory pages around [5, 14, 26, 29]. These techniques, in our point of view, have a shortcoming: they require the intervention of the programmer. Data placement libraries, for instance, provide developers with ways to determine the allocation of data before a program starts running, or let them migrate memory pages during the program's execution. To benefit from this support, users must be familiar with the underlying memory architecture and with the application's code.

In this paper we have designed and implemented a compiler assisted technique that solves these shortcomings. We introduce a suite of compiler analyses that determine when it is beneficial to move data once a program starts executing. We also use our analyses to generate dynamic checks, which we insert into the program's code. These checks are built as templates that once filled with runtime values - mostly the limits of loops - decide if the operating system should migrate physical memory pages to the cores where they are frequently accessed. The proposed approach is very granular: it can treat data used in different parts of the program in different ways, selectively moving only the memory pages whose migration pays off. Our solution does not demand any extra hardware support. Furthermore, it requires minimal support from the operating system. More specifically, we need the ability to move pages around and some limited form of introspection to find the size of the cache. This support is already present in standard distributions of popular operating systems. Most importantly, our approach does not require any form of user intervention in the application code.

We have implemented our technique using the LLVM [21] compiler, and have tested it on a number of parallel benchmarks, which we ship together with our tool. These benchmarks have been coded using C POSIX Threads and are completely oblivious to the topology of the memory hierarchy. Our results show that programs instrumented with our code transformations outperform the original parallel programs by up to four times, on a 64-core NUMA machine. Furthermore, we compare our approach against Minas [26], a middleware that optimizes data allocation and placement in non-uniform memory access architectures. Minas provides developers with an API which gives them (i) information about the topology of the machine and (ii) mechanisms to determine the initial allocation and placement of data into memory banks. The programs that we generate automatically tend to outperform the programs hand-coded to use the Minas library. These results are encouraging, because our approach does not require any form of intervention from the programmer, whereas Minas is used as a library, which must be manipulated directly by the developer.

2. BACKGROUND

In order to take more benefit from the ever-increasing core count, computer architects have been shifting their designs from the SMP (Symmetric Multiprocessing) model towards the NUMA (Non-Uniform Memory Access) design [20]. Similar to the SMP approach, NUMA architectures allow code running in any core to access any memory word in the system. However, in the NUMA model, the memory banks are distributed among multiple controllers and the data access latency varies accordingly to the memory bank and the core position. Figure 1 shows the topology of a NUMA architecture with four processing cores and four memory controllers. Each memory controller is connected to a memory bank, to a computing core, and to the other memory controllers through the interconnecting bus.

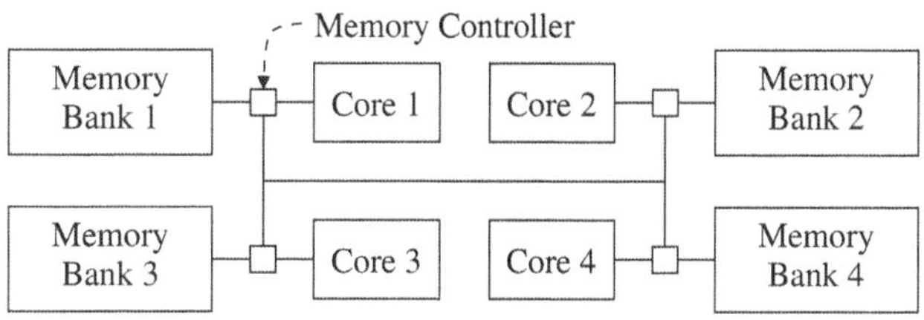

Figure 1: Non-Uniform Memory Access system.

On a NUMA machine, threads running on different cores can access data on different memory banks. However, to develop applications that take full benefit from this capacity, it is important to distribute data on memory banks located next to the cores where the threads that access them are executed. In order to induce this locality, modern operating systems try to allocate pages on memory banks next to the cores that are executing the threads that triggered the page allocation. This is known as "first-touch" policy. However, in many programs, the key data structures are allocated in the main thread, which runs before parallel computation takes place. This setup causes all the data to be allocated on a single memory bank. Unfortunately, in this scenario, all the cores will compete for the same memory controller, as in the SMP approach. The "first-touch" curve in Figure 2 shows the scalability of a parallel program that performs the Cholesky decomposition on several matrices that were initially allocated in the main thread.

A common optimization used in this environment consists in allocating or moving memory pages to memory banks next to the cores executing the threads that tend to use these pages more often [2, 20]. Figure 2 illustrates the remarkable benefits of this technique. The Linux kernel provides system calls to migrate memory pages between memory banks. After migrating the pages, the system updates the page tables to map the virtual page addresses to the new physical page addresses. However, migrating the page may be an expensive operation, and the optimization may only pay off if the data in the page is frequently retrieved from main memory [17]. In this work, we leverage static compiler optimizations and runtime support to improve performance via selective page migration. The gains in Figure 2 were obtained via manual intervention in the source code. We want to derive such gains automatically, via transformations implemented at the compiler level.

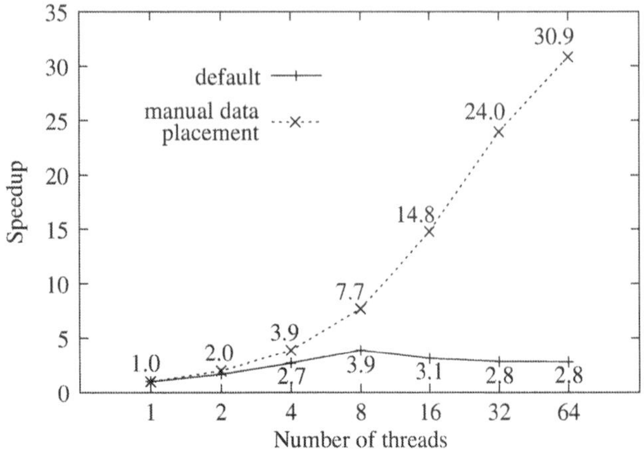

Figure 2: Scalability of a parallel program with first-touch and manual page placement on a 64-core NUMA system. Numbers give speedup compared to a single-threaded application.

(a)
```
1  for (i = Tid × R; i < (Tid + 1) × R + P; i++) {
2    A[i] = 0;
3    for (j0 = i + 1; j0 < N2; j0 += 4) {
4      B[i×N2 + j0] = 0;
5      for (k = j0; k > i; k -= 1) {
6        B[i×N2 + j0] = B[i×N2 + j0] + C[i×N2×N3 + j0×N3 + k];
7      }
8    }
9    for (j1 = i + 1; j1 < N2; j1 += 4) {
10     A[i] = A[i] + B[i×N2 + j1];
11   }
12 }
```

(b)
```
if ((Tid + 1) × R + P > Tid × R) {
  (ArraySt_A, ArrayEd_A) = calc_size_exp_A(N1)
  (ArraySt_B, ArrayEd_B) = calc_size_exp_B(N1, N2)
  (ArraySt_C, ArrayEd_C) = calc_size_exp_A(N1, N2, N3)

  ArrayReuse_A = calc_reuse_exp_A(N1)
  ArrayReuse_B = calc_reuse_exp_B(N1, N2)
  ArrayReuse_C = calc_reuse_exp_C(N1, N2, N3)

  PageReuse_A = ArrayReuse_A / ArraySize_A × PageSize
  PageReuse_B = ArrayReuse_B / ArraySize_B × PageSize
  PageReuse_C = ArrayReuse_C / ArraySize_C × PageSize

  try_migrate(A, ArraySt_A, ArrayEd_A, PageReuse_A)
  try_migrate(B, ArraySt_B, ArrayEd_B, PageReuse_B)
  try_migrate(C, ArraySt_C, ArrayEd_C, PageReuse_C)
}
1  for (i = Tid × R; i < (Tid + 1) × R + P; i++) {
...   ...
12 }
release_migrated_pages(A, ArraySt_A, ArrayEd_A)
release_migrated_pages(A, ArraySt_A, ArrayEd_A)
release_migrated_pages(A, ArraySt_A, ArrayEd_A)
```

Figure 3: (a) Our core example. (b) Instrumented program.

3. SELECTIVE PAGE MIGRATION

Our approach consists in moving pages that we predict to be frequently reused (hot pages) to local memory banks. Most of the page accesses occur inside program loops; hence, our compiler inserts checks before loops that contain array accesses. Such checks determine if it is profitable to migrate the page before the program's flow of execution enters these loops.

Figure 3 illustrates our approach. Throughout the rest of this section, we will use the program in Figure 3 (a), an artificial code that exercises all the facets of the technique proposed here, as our running example. The pattern of loops and array accesses in this program will let us illustrate the main features of our static analyses. We will represent every array access as $a[e]$, where a is a base pointer, and e is an indexing expression. In other words, we linearize every array access. If a is an $N \times M$ matrix, then we write $a[i, j]$ as $a[i \times M + j]$. This notation puts us closer to the internal representation of arrays in our compiler infrastructure. In this example, `Tid` is a special variable, which represents the thread identifier. Figure 3 (b) shows the instrumentation that we insert. We always try to insert code surrounding outermost loops. The conditional test $(\texttt{Tid} + 1) \times R + P > \texttt{Tid} \times R$ in Figure 3 (b) guards us against scenarios where the outermost loop, at line 1, executes zero iterations. With this, we avoid burdening applications that would not benefit from page migration with an unnecessary overhead.

We consider that a block of data should be transferred to a local memory bank if: (i) its memory footprint is larger than the processor's last level cache, and (ii) it is accessed several times by the local thread. We take item (i) - cache size - into consideration because if the data fits in the cache, then it will be naturally copied while accessed. Item (ii) - reuse - is important because the cost of moving a page over is roughly equivalent to the cost of accessing each of its elements once. Thus, we do not save memory accesses by migrating a page whose data is only read or written a few times. We take care of item (i) by determining the size of the arrays that the program manipulates. To determine (ii), we discover the number of times that each array is accessed within a loop. We call such metric the *reuse of the array*. As the reader will notice in Figure 3 (b), we ultimately consider reuse as an estimate of how often the same page is accessed (see the assignment to `PageReuse_A`, for instance). This happens because our unit of data migration is the size of the operating system's virtual page.

In the rest of this section, we describe the static analyses that we use to obtain all the information that our heuristics require. Figure 4 summarizes them. In Section 3.2 we show how to compute symbolic expressions denoting the least and maximum addresses that an array can assume. In order to build these expressions we need one key information: the ranges, i.e., minimum and maximum symbolic values that the variables used to index arrays can assume. We obtain this information via the induction variable analysis that we describe in Section 3.1. In Section 3.4 we discuss how we build symbolic expressions representing the reuse of arrays. To this end, we need to construct symbolic expressions that

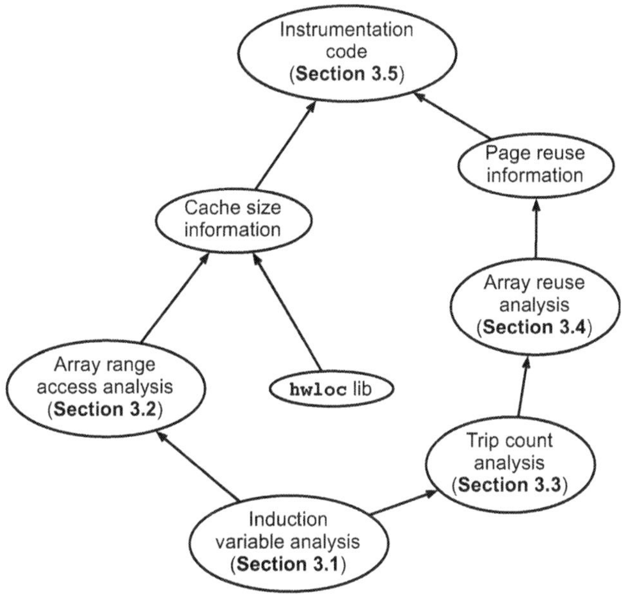

Figure 4: A bird's-eye view of our approach.

describe how many times a nest of loops will execute; we accomplish this task through the analysis discussed in Section 3.3. These symbolic expressions give us the subsidies to instrument the code to perform dynamic tests, as we describe in Section 3.5. These tests require information concerning the topology of the underlying memory architecture, which we obtain via the Portable Hardware Locality (`hwloc`) library [7], again, without any intervention of the programmer.

Loop Jargon. Let S be a subset of nodes of a control flow graph G. S contains a special node H, which we shall call *header* or *entry point*. Following Appel and Palsberg [1, pp.376], we say that S is a *natural loop* if and only if it presents the following three properties:

1. there exists a path from any node in S to H;
2. there exists a path from H to any node in S;
3. there is no path from any node of G to any node of S that does not go across H.

The last property defines S as a *single-entry* region, following Ferrante's nomenclature [16]. An edge between any node in S to H is called a *back-edge*. We adopt Wolfe's definition of *trip count* [31, pp.200]: the number of times any back-edge of a natural loop has been traversed by the program flow within a single execution of the loop.

We call a node $L \in S$ a *latch* or *exit point* if there exists an edge from L to a node N, $N \in G$, $N \notin S$. We say that L is a *natural latch* if one of these two conditions applies:

- $L = H$. In this case we have a *while loop*;
- $L \neq H$, and, for any edge e that starts at L, either e leaves S, or e goes to H. In this case we have a *repeat loop*.

If S contains only one latch, then we call it *single exit*. In this work we consider multiple exit loops featuring only one natural latch. Code generated from typical programming language constructs, i.e., `for`, `while` and `repeat` has this property, as long as the command `goto` is not used.

Symbolic Kernels. In this work we have designed static analyses that associate variables and program labels with *symbols*. We define the *symbolic kernel* of a loop S with header H as the set of variables *alive* at H that are not defined inside S plus the constants (known at compilation time) that are used in the body of S. We adopt the standard definition of *liveness*, i.e., we say that a variable v is alive at a node n of a control flow graph if:

- there exists a path from a point n_d, where v is defined, to a point n_u, where v is used, that goes across n;
- no other definition of v exists between n_d and n.

As an example, variables `Tid`, R, P, N_2, and N_3 constitute the symbolic kernel of the natural loop that starts in line 1 of Figure 3 (a). Similarly, variables `Tid`, R, P, N_2, N_3, i and j_0 are the symbolic kernel of the loop at line 5 in the same figure. We say that E is an *expression* if and only if E is defined by the grammar below. In this definition, s is a symbol, i.e., an element in the symbolic kernel and $n \in \mathbb{N}$:

$$E \ ::= \ n \mid s \mid \min(E,E) \mid \max(E,E) \mid E - E \mid E + E \mid E \times E \mid E/E$$

The techniques that we describe in this paper consist in generating - statically - expressions representing the size and reuse of arrays. We solve these expressions dynamically, once we replace symbols with their runtime values.

3.1 Induction Variable Analysis

The induction variable analysis associates each loop induction variable v with a triple $Ind(v) = (l, u, s)$. The element l is a symbolic expression representing the minimum value that v might assume during the execution of the loop. The parameter u represents the maximum value that v may assume, and $s \in \mathbb{N}$ represents the step of change of v. In this work we restrict our analyses to loops that are controlled by *linearly monotonic induction variables*. The variable `i` is a linear induction variable in a loop if the only definitions of `i` within that loop are of the form `i` = `i` + `c` or `i` = `i` − `c`, where `c` is loop invariant. We call `c` the *step* of `i`. If every redefinition of `i` uses invariants with the same signal, then we say that `i` is monotonic. Any latch contains a *stop condition*: a boolean expression whose evaluation either keeps the program flow in S or leads away from it. If the stop condition uses an induction variable `i`, then we say that the loop is controlled by `i`. For instance, the loop `for(k = j0; k > i; k -= 1)`, at line 5 of Figure 3 (a), has a stop condition `k > i`, which is controlled by variables `i` and `k`. The step of induction variable `k` is one in this example.

To discover the minimum and maximum values that linear monotonic induction variables can assume, we look at the code that initializes them and at the code that limits them. If we have a sequence of nested loops $L_0 \ldots L_n$, where L_i is nested within L_{i-1}, then we run our analysis in L_{i-1} before visiting L_i. With this, we try to build the limits of the induction variable used in L_i as a function of the limits of the induction variables used in L_{i-1}. Figure 5 illustrates our analysis. In this example, first we analyze the loop at line 1 of the example program. This gives us limits for i, the only induction variable used in that loop. Once we find symbolic bounds of i, we move on to discover the limits of

```
1  for (i = Tid × R; i < (Tid + 1) × R + P; i++) {
2    A[i] = 0;
3    for (j0 = i + 1; j0 < N2; j0 += 4) {
4      B[i×N2 + j0] = 0;
5      for (k = j0; k > i; k -= 1) {
6        B[i×N2 + j0] = B[i×N2 + j0] + C[i×N2×N3 + j0×N3 + k];
7      }
8    }
9    for (j1 = i + 1; j1 < N2; j1 += 4) {
10     A[i] = A[i] + B[i×N2 + j1];
11   }
12 }
```

```
Ind(i) = (Tid × R,
          (Tid + 1) × R + P − 1, 1)

Ind(j0) = (i + 1, N2 − 1; 4)
        = (Tid × R + 1, N2 − 1)

Ind(k) = (i + 1, j0, 1)
       = (Tid × R + 1, i + 1, 1)
       = (Tid × R + 1, (Tid + 1) × R + P, 1)

Ind(j1) = (i + 1, N2 − 1, 4)
        = (Tid × R + 1, N2 − 1)
```

Figure 5: Induction variable analysis applied on the program seen in Figure 3 (a).

j_0 and j_1. These variables control the loops at lines 3 and 9, which are nested within the loop on line 1. Therefore, the limits of these two induction variables are built as functions of the limits of i. Finally, we place bounds on k. These bounds are built as functions of the bounds of j_0 and i. To simplify the formulas that we build in such fashion, we use the SymPy library [18] of symbolic manipulation. SymPy uses cylindrical algebraic decomposition [3] to solve the symbolic equations that we feed to it.

Dealing with Multi-Path Induction Variables. An induction variable can be incremented with different steps on the same loop. This happens, for instance, in the program that we show in Figure 6 (Left). In this paper we are interested in the minimum trip count of a loop. In other words, we want to estimate this quantity conservatively. Therefore, we shall be considering the maximum increment over all paths through which an induction variable can be incremented. We can compute this number via Dijkstra's algorithm, which solves the single-source shortest path problem for a graph with non-negative edge path costs [13]. We apply the algorithm on the program's dependence graph, a data structure due to Ferrante *et al.* [16]. In our case, the cost of each edge is the increment that the induction variable can suffer along that path.

Figure 6 (Right) shows the program dependence graph of our example. We use Static Single Assignment form (SSA) [11] to represent programs. In this representation, each variable of a program has only one definition site. Therefore, each redefinition of variable i in Figure 6 (Left) has a new name in the graph in Figure 6 (Right). The ϕ-functions in Figure 6 (Right) join different definitions of variables. As an example, the increment at line 9 can be applied on three different definitions of i. These definitions reach line 9 coming from lines 4, 6, and 8. All these definitions are unified into i_5, which is then incremented; thus producing a new name i_6.

Dijkstra gives us, in this example, the heaviest path $(+4, +1) = +5$, where the weight of a path is the sum of all the increments that the induction variable can suffer along it. We cannot deal with *oscillating* induction variables, i.e., variables that can suffer positive or negative increments through an iteration of a loop. Nevertheless, this situation is rather uncommon, and we have not observed it in a suite of hundreds of benchmarks, as we will discuss in Section 4.

```
1  i = 0
2  while (i < N) {
3    if (DEF_INT_32)
4      i += 4;
5    else if (DEF_INT_16)
6      i += 2;
7    else
8      i += 1;
9    i++;
10 }
```

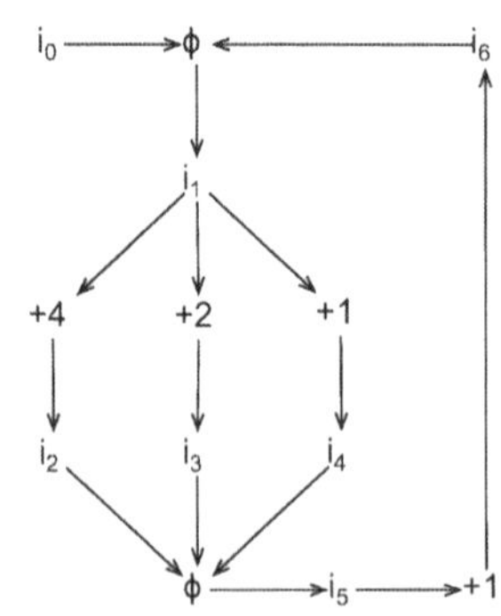

Figure 6: Example with multiple paths in a single loop.

3.2 Array Range Access Analysis

If $a[e]$ is an array access, then we say that the *access range* of $a[e]$ is the minimum and the maximum values that e might assume. We find these two values, i.e., the symbolic minimum and maximum of e, in a two steps approach:

1. we replace every induction variable v used in e by the interval $[l, u]$, where l and u are given by $Ind(v) = (l, u, s)$. Let the resulting symbolic expression be denoted by e_i.
2. we solve e_i using a simple algebra of symbolic intervals, which is defined by the expressions below:
   - $[l_0, u_0] + [l_1, u_1] = [l_0 + l_1, u_0 + u_1]$
   - $[l_0, u_0] - [l_1, u_1] = [\min(l_0 - l_1, u_0 - u_1), \max(l_0 - l_1, u_0 - u_1)]$
   - $[l_0, u_0] \times [l_1, u_1] = [\min(T), \max(T)]$, where $T = \{l_0 \times l_1, l_0 \times u_1, u_0 \times l_1, u_0 \times u_1\}$
   - $[l_0, u_0]/[l_1, u_1] = [\min(T), \max(T)]$, where $T = \{l_0/l_1, l_0/u_1, u_0/l_1, u_0/u_1\}$, if $0 \notin [l_1, u_1]$, otherwise $[-\infty, +\infty]$

Continuing with our example, Figure 7 shows the results of this analysis for three of the array accesses seen in the program of Figure 3 (a). Once we solve the interval expression e_i, for an array access $a[e]$, we bind this access to a symbolic interval $[l, u]$. The syntax $A[i]$ denotes the accesses at lines 2 and 10 of Figure 3. $B[i \times N_2 + j_0]$ denotes the accesses at lines 4 and 6. The access on C happens at line 6 of Figure 3. Notice that internally we use the static single assignment form. Thus, each induction variable has a unique name. Consequently, if a program contains two accesses using the same expression, e.g., $A[e]$ and $B[e]$, then these accesses will give us the same ranges. Also notice that our interval algebra admits several simplifications, mostly concerning products between intervals. For instance, the product $[l, u] \times n, n \in \mathbb{N}, n > 0$ is given by $[n \times l, n \times u]$. As in Section 3.1, we rely on SymPy to perform algebraic simplifications on symbolic expressions.

$$A[i] \begin{cases} min = \texttt{Tid} \times R \\ max = \texttt{Tid} \times R + P - 1 \end{cases}$$

$$B[i \times N_2 + j_0] \begin{cases} min = \texttt{Tid} \times R \times N_2 + 1 \\ max = (\texttt{Tid} \times R + P) \times N_2 - 1 \end{cases}$$

$$C[i \times N_2 \times N_3 + j_0 \times N_3 + k] \begin{cases} min = \texttt{Tid} \times R \times N_2 \times N_3 + \\ \qquad (\texttt{Tid} \times R + 1) \times (N_3 + 1) \\ max = (((\texttt{Tid} + 1) \times R + P) \times N_2 - 1) \\ \qquad \times N_3 + N_2 - 1 \end{cases}$$

Figure 7: Results of the symbolic array range access analysis.

From ranges to sizes. The array range access analysis gives us a way to determine the lowest and highest addressable offsets in an array. Its lowest addressable offset is the minimum between all the lower ranges inferred for it. Naturally, its highest addressable offset is the maximum between all the upper ranges inferred for it. We estimate the size of an array as the difference between its highest and lowest addressable offsets. In Figure 3 (b), this number, for array A, is given by $\texttt{ArrayEd}_\texttt{A} - \texttt{ArraySt}_\texttt{A}$.

3.3 Trip Count Analysis

The reuse of an array a in a loop L is the number of times that a is accessed within L. Therefore, to estimate the reuse of an array a, we must estimate the number of iterations of every loop that contains accesses to a. We perform such estimates via trip count analysis. This analysis associates each loop L in the program with a summation, which gives us the number of times that L executes in relation to its immediate parent loop. If L is not nested within any other loop, then this summation gives us the number of times L executes in the parent function. If L is controlled by an induction variable v, then this summation is given by the expression:

$$\mathit{Trip}(L_v) = \sum_{i=l}^{u} \frac{1}{s}, \text{ where } \mathit{Ind}(v) = (l, u, s)$$

The number of times a loop L_n executes in relation to its parent loops (outermost to innermost) $L_1, L_2, \cdots, L_{n-1}$ is given by sequential application of each loop summation:

$$\sum_{i_1=l_1}^{u_1} \left(\frac{1}{s_1} \times \sum_{i_2=l_2}^{u_2} \left(\frac{1}{s_2} \times \cdots \left(\frac{1}{s_{n-1}} \times \sum_{i_n=l_n}^{u_n} \frac{1}{s_n} \right) \cdots \right) \right)$$

Figure 8 shows the results of our trip count analysis when applied on three loops of the program first seen in Figure 3 (a). All the summations are built as functions of the symbolic kernels of their respective loops. Our summations admit closed formulas, which we determine as successive applications of the identity:

$$\sum_{i=l}^{u} \frac{1}{s} = \frac{u + 1 - l}{s}$$

We obtain such formulas through the **SymPy** library. The three symbolic expressions seen in Figure 8 were produced

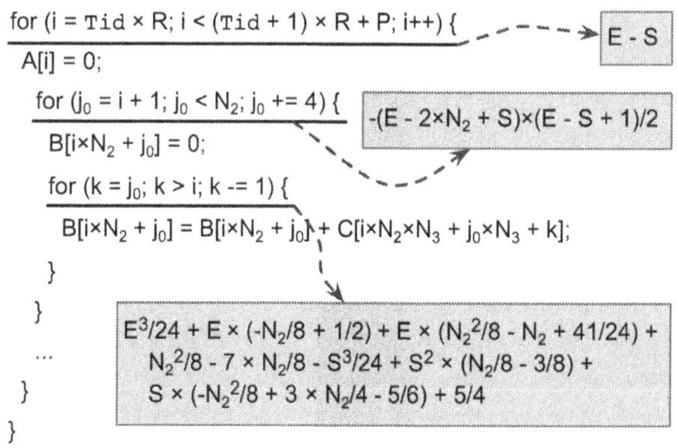

Figure 8: Results of the trip count analysis. We let $S = \texttt{Tid} \times R$, and $E = (\texttt{Tid} + 1) \times R + P$.

in this way. Although they seem complicated, much of their complexity will be optimized away, once we run them through the compiler's standard optimization passes.

3.4 Array Reuse Analysis

Once we have the trip count of every loop L_i, we proceed to determine the reuse of each array. If a program contains an array access $a[e]$, then we say that this access is *immediately within* loop L_i if: (i) the instructions that implement $a[e]$ are inside L_i; and (ii) for every other loop L_j that contains $a[e]$, L_j contains L_i. For each array access, we say that the reuse of that access is the number of times that the access will be executed. We estimate the number of executions of an access as the trip count of its immediate loop. Given an array a, its reuse is the sum of the reuse of all its accesses in a loop nest. For instance, the reuse of array B in our example of Figure 3 is $\mathit{Trip}(L_3) + 2 \times \mathit{Trip}(L_5) + \mathit{Trip}(L_9)$, where L_i is the loop at line i in the figure. We use this formulate because array B is used once immediately within loops L_3 (line 4) and L_9 (line 10), and twice within loop L_5 (line 6). When generating final formulas for reuse estimation, we multiply the reuse of each array access by the page size, as this is the granularity of data that we can migrate.

3.5 Instrumentation Code

Figure 9 shows the final expressions that we insert in the original example to implement our heuristics. The minimum and maximum indexable offsets of the array are computed as the minimum among all the lower bounds and the maximum among all the upper bounds that the range access analysis finds. In the figure, we call these values **ArraySt_A** and **ArrayEd_A** respectively. As mentioned before, the array reuse is the sum of the reuse computed for each use of the array within the loop. In Figure 9 we show the closed formulas that we use to calculate the reuse of array A.

An important question that we must address is: where to place the instrumentation code? Ideally we would like to remove instrumentation checks from inner loops, to decrease the overhead on the target program. Therefore, we place these checks at the earliest program point where all the variables used in the symbolic kernel of a loop are alive. In the example of Figure 3 (a), this point is right before line

```
if ((Tid + 1) × R + P > Tid × R) {
  (ArraySt_A, ArrayEd_A) = (Tid × R, (Tid + 1) × R + P − 1))
  (ArraySt_B, ArrayEd_B) = ...
  (ArraySt_C, ArrayEd_C) = ...

  ArrayReuse_A = (2 × N2 − 2 × Tid × R + R + P) × 2 × (R + P + 1)
  ArrayReuse_B = ...
  ArrayReuse_C = ...

  PageReuse_A = ArrayReuse_A / ArraySize_A × PageSize
  PageReuse_B = ...
  PageReuse_C = ...

  try_migrate(A, ArraySt_A, ArrayEd_A, PageReuse_A)
  ...
}
```

Figure 9: Final expressions used to estimate the size and reuse of array A, seen in Figure 3.

```
(a) try_migrate (Array, Start, End, PageReuse) {
      if (End - Start > CacheSize && PageReuse > Threshold ) {
        PageStart = (Array + Start) / PAGE_SIZE;
        PageEnd   = (Array + End) / PAGE_SIZE;
        (MinMigratablePageStart, MaxMigratablePageEnd) =
                            pin_pages(gettid(), PageStart, PageEnd);
        if (MaxMigratablePageEnd - MinMigratablePageStart > 0) {
          migrate (PageStart, PageEnd);
        }
      }
    }

(b) release_migrated_pages (Array, Start, End) {
      PageStart = (Array + Start) / PAGE_SIZE;
      PageEnd   = (Array + End) / PAGE_SIZE;
      unpin_pages (PageStart, PageEnd);
    }
```

Figure 10: Functions used to implement page migration.

1 of the program. Notice that there exists always a point where we can place the dynamic checks: immediately before the header of the loop, because, by definition, all the variables in the symbolic kernel of the loop are alive at that point.

Dealing with disputes among threads. We implement page migration through two functions: `try_migrate` and `release_migrated_pages`. We show a high-level implementation of these functions at Figure 10. We define a *pinned page* as a page that has been migrated by a call to `try_migrate`. While a page remains in this state, we do not allow further migration of it. With this, we prevent threads from *disputing* a page. We say that two threads dispute a page if: (i) these threads run in different cores; and (ii) these threads try to migrate the same page. If threads were allowed to dispute pages, then the excessive copy of data between memory banks would impose a burden on our system.

Every memory page is initially *unpinned*. During the execution of the program, the state of a page can alternate between unpinned and *pinned*. If a thread touches a page p and successfully migrates it, then it marks p as pinned. Once the thread exits the loop where p is used, it turns that page's state back into unpinned. Our compiler inserts instrumentation code to operate these changes. In Figure 3 (b), page states can change at two points in the code of the instrumented program. Pages can be pinned by one of the three calls of `try_migrate`, right before the loop. In the opposite direction, pages might be unpinned by the three calls of `release_migrated_pages`, which occur right after the loop.

To discover which pages are pinned, we use a binary tree of interval ranges. Each node in this tree represents an interval of virtual memory addresses, which is associated with a thread identifier. The `try_migrate` function attempts to perform the migration of a contiguous range of pages, which is specified by the interval `PageStart - PageEnd`. It is possible that some of the pages in this range are pinned. In this case, the auxiliary function `pin_pages` scans our interval tree, and returns the first contiguous sequence of unpinned pages. Notice that we do not return a maximal sequence of unpinned pages, nor we return multiple intervals of unpinned pages, in case they exist. We use a best effort strategy because we have realized experimentally that this approach yields a good tradeoff between the precision of our heuristic and its efficiency.

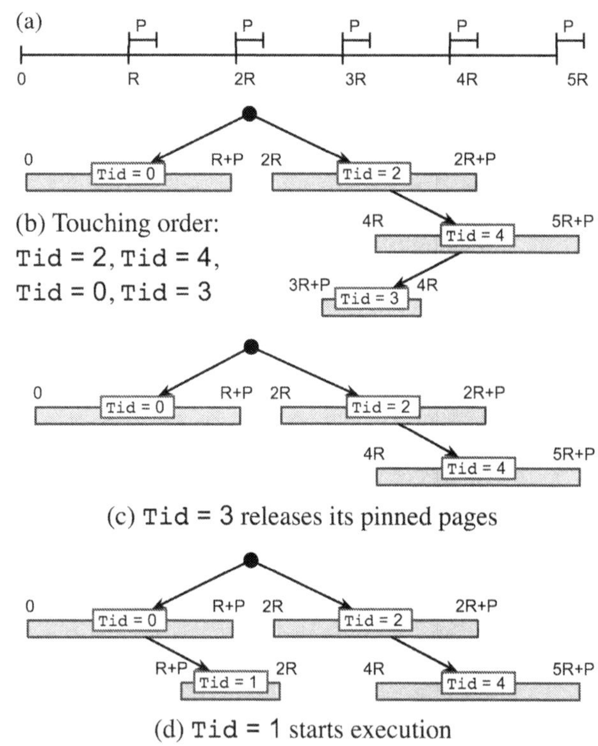

Figure 11: (a) The memory layout and data distribution after an initial round of execution of the program in Figure 3 (a). (b-d) Interval tree showing how pinned pages are organized at different moments of the program execution.

Figure 11 shows how we organize the pinning of pages during a round of execution of our running example, seen in

Figure 3 (a). In this example, threads of identifier `Tid` and `Tid + 1` access overlapping memory regions through $A[i]$ in lines 2 and 10 of Figure 3 (a). Thus, it is possible that one thread will try to migrate a memory page that has been copied by another thread. To avoid this situation, before performing this copy, a thread t must search for the range of data to be copied in our interval tree. If the tree does not contain this range, then t is allowed to perform the migration, and a new entry is added to the tree. On the other hand, if the tree contains part of the range, then a partial migration might take place. As an example, Figure 11 (d) shows the configuration of the interval tree once thread `Tid = 1` attempts to copy pages over. Part of the requested range has been pinned by threads `Tid = 0` and `Tid = 2`. Therefore, thread `1` will be allowed to migrate a range of pages that is smaller than its original request.

4. EXPERIMENTAL RESULTS

The primary goal of this section is to demonstrate that our technique is able to speedup code without human intervention. Most of our techniques rely on our ability to predict the trip count of loops. Thus, a secondary goal of this section is to show that we can perform such predictions reliably. We start the section by diving into this second goal and leave the latter for Section 4.2. Given these two distinct goals, Sections 4.1 and 4.2 use two different benchmark suites. In Section 4.1 we measure the precision of our trip count predictor in the programs of the SPEC CPU 2006 benchmark suite. We use SPEC because this benchmark gives us an extensive number of loops, which we can analyze statically, and measure dynamically. In Section 4.2 we use a suite of parallel benchmarks, which is distributed with our extension of the LLVM compiler. Even though our technique is applicable to sequential code - for example reducing memory access latencies bringing data from remote memory closer to the core where it is needed - the parallel benchmarks give us more opportunities to exercise all the features of our technique.

4.1 Trip Count Prediction

Actual loops have simple topology. Table 1 shows structural characteristics of the loops that we found in SPEC CPU 2006. SPEC gave us a total of 21,336 loops, out of which we could instrument 11,850, i.e., 55.54%. We fail to instrument a loop when we do not find its induction variable. This failure might happen for three main reasons: (i) the loop is controlled by an oscillating induction variable; (ii) it is controlled by a function call; or (iii) it is controlled by data located in memory. We have not found examples of (i) in SPEC. Situation (ii) happens in loops like `while(f());` an example of (iii) is `for (p = a; *p != '0'; p++)`.

Table 1 also shows the number of Strongly Connected Components (SCC) formed by the different induction variables that we found in the loops. This number is usually larger than the number of loops, because some of them might be controlled by more than one induction variable. We have found a few linear monotonic variables that might be incremented through different paths during the execution of the loop. Nevertheless, this number is rather small: 16% of the induction variables present this characteristic.

Hit rate of the predictor. We have developed a profiler that measures the actual trip count of loops. The result of our profiler lets us observe how accurate our heuristic estimates of Section 3.3 are. We have split our accuracy results into seven categories according to the actual number N of iterations:

Program	L	IL	%IL/L	SCC	SP
milc	426	391	91.78%	426	409
namd	623	469	75.28%	781	604
dealII	6,526	3,535	54.17%	7,249	6,077
soplex	742	422	56.87%	807	683
lbm	23	23	100.00%	24	23
bzip2	238	186	78.15%	244	171
gcc	4,614	1,798	38.97%	5,121	4,513
mcf	50	7	14.00%	54	40
gobmk	1,288	1,040	80.75%	1,555	1,283
hmmer	881	664	75.37%	946	825
sjeng	267	106	39.70%	276	221
libquantum	98	77	78.57%	123	100
h264ref	1,870	1,411	75.45%	1,946	1,841
omnetpp	465	238	51.18%	470	379
astar	119	80	67.23%	138	118
xalancbmk	3,106	1,403	45.17%	3,024	2,486
Total	21,336	11,850	55.54%	23,184	19,773

Table 1: L: number of loops. IL: number of loops that we could instrument. SCC: number of induction variables. SP: induction variables having a unique increment.

- $[0, \sqrt{N}]$: Occurs when the estimated trip count is less than or equal to the square root of the actual trip count. For example, if we estimate that a loop will iterate 2 times and it iterates 10 times during its execution, this loop will be classified into this category.
- $]\sqrt{N}, N/2]$: Occurs when the estimated trip count lies between the square root of the actual trip count and half its value. This case happens, for instance, if we estimate that a loop will iterate 4 times, but it actually iterates 10 times.
- $]N/2, N[$: Occurs when the estimated trip count lies between halve the actual trip count and the trip count itself. For example, if we estimate that a loop will iterate 8 times and it iterates 10 times during the actual execution, this loop will be classified into this category.
- $[N, N]$: Occurs when the estimated trip count equals the actual trip count.
- $]N, 2*N]$: Occurs when the estimated trip count is greater than the actual trip count, but is less than or equal to twice its true value. For example, if we estimate that a loop will iterate 16 times, but it actually iterates 10 times, this instance of the loop execution will fall into this category.
- $]2*N, N^2]$: Occurs when the estimated trip count is greater than twice the actual trip count, but is less than or equal to the square of the actual trip count. This case happens, for instance, if we estimate that a loop will iterate 32 times and it iterates 10 times in fact.

Program	$[0, \sqrt{N}]$	$]\sqrt{N}, N/2]$	$]N/2, N[$	$[N, N]$	$]N, 2N]$	$]2N, N^2]$	$]N^2, +\infty]$
SPEC	15,914,068	1,113	2,877,992	955,866,120	44,786,968	6,026,735	37,227,397
Subtotal (%)	1.50%	0.00%	0.27%	89.95%	4.21%	0.57%	3.50%
LLVM	25,525,142	2,078	2,922,080	4,134,074,825	163,974,403	11,363,892	400,209,181
Total (%)	0.54%	0.00%	0.06%	87.25%	3.46%	0.24%	8.45%

Table 2: Precision of the trip count analysis of Section 3.3.

- $]N^2, +\infty]$: Occurs when the estimated trip count is greater than the square of the actual trip count. For example, if we estimate that a loop will iterate 128 times, but it actually iterates 10 times, this run will fall into this category.

Table 2 shows the comparison between the estimated trip count and the actual trip count collected via profiling. "SPEC" summarizes the results for the SPEC CPU benchmarks, while "LLVM" also includes more than 430 benchmarks distributed with the LLVM test suite. While running the programs, each time a loop stops, we collect the actual trip count and compare it with the estimated trip count. Thus, the numbers that we present gives us the quantity of *dynamic instances* of loops during runtime, instead of the number of natural loops in the code. We did this because we may predict correctly the trip count of some executions of a loop, but may predict wrongly the trip count of other instances of the same loop.

4.2 Performance Analysis

In this section we compare the relative performance of four different page allocation policies:

1. **Selective Page Migration**: the technique that we propose.

2. **Minas**: a middleware plus a library that has been developed for NUMA aware architectures [25, Ch.5]. Minas replaces the memory allocation calls of the C standard library with an API of its own [26]. Thus, it decides, at runtime, where memory pages will be placed, based on two policies: first-touch and round robin. Threads are pinned to the cores where they start running. Once a thread asks for memory, it is given space on its local NUMA node. If this node already contains a certain number of active memory pages, then the next requests are scattered around remote memory banks, in round-robin fashion, to decrease memory contention. Minas performs page placement whenever a thread asks for memory, but it does not migrate a page after its creation.

3. **Premature migration**: a policy in which pages are always migrated to the cores in which they are accessed. This migration happens regardless of reuse rate or array size.

4. **Baseline**: a policy that never migrates pages. Once allocated, a page remains in its original memory bank until either it is evicted due to usual page thrashing, or the program terminates. The page allocation policy is first-touch.

We run experiments in a 64-core ccNUMA computer featuring four 16-core AMD Opteron 6282 SE processors. This machine has 8 nodes/memory controllers, each one connected to a memory bank with 16GB of memory. Cores inside a processor are organized in eight pairs. The two cores inside a compute unit share a 64KB L1 instruction cache, a 2MB L2 cache, a floating-point unit (FPU), and a fetch/decode unit. Each core has its own 16KB L1 data cache and integer execution pipeline. The compute units share a 6MB L3 cache. All the performance experiments that we show in this section use all the 64 available cores. Our operating system is Ubuntu 12.04.1 LTS, kernel 3.2.0-23 x86_64.

In order to compare these different page allocation policies we apply them onto six different parallel benchmarks. To ensure reproducibility, these six benchmarks are shipped together with our distribution of the LLVM compiler and are freely available in our repository. The benchmarks were designed and implemented in a way that is oblivious to the memory allocation policy. All these programs implement typical parallel algorithms using C POSIX Threads. Four of our benchmarks are linear algebra applications: matrix multiplication, Cholesky decomposition, LU decomposition, and matrix addition. A fifth benchmark is an implementation of the K-Nearest Neighbors (KNN) data-mining algorithm. Our last benchmark is the parallel bucket sort algorithm. Figure 12 shows our runtime results for these programs.

We first notice that in the case of matrix addition, selective migration always beats premature migration. The reuse rate of each array access is small, since each element is only accessed once. Our heuristic never migrates any page, and thus, it is only slightly worse than the original implementation of the algorithm (baseline), due to its runtime overhead. Nevertheless, a quick inspection of Chart (e), in Figure 12, reveals that this overhead is barely noticeable, as we have been able to hoist the dynamic check to outside the outermost loop in the code. On the average, selective migration is 3% slower than the original algorithm. On the other hand, premature migration always sends pages over, paying the full price of a data transfer, to communicate values that will be read only once. Minas also always beats the premature migration policy; however, its overhead is considerably larger than our technique.

Premature and selective migration yield similar results when applied on LU decomposition, Cholesky decomposition and matrix multiplication, given large inputs. In this case, both approaches migrate the two arrays that are accessed more often. Nevertheless, our heuristic is better than the premature approach for small matrices. This happens because it does not pay off to migrate arrays that are too small, as they fit entirely in cache. Hence, the main memory is only accessed a few times. For very large matrices, our technique yields smaller speedups than premature mi-

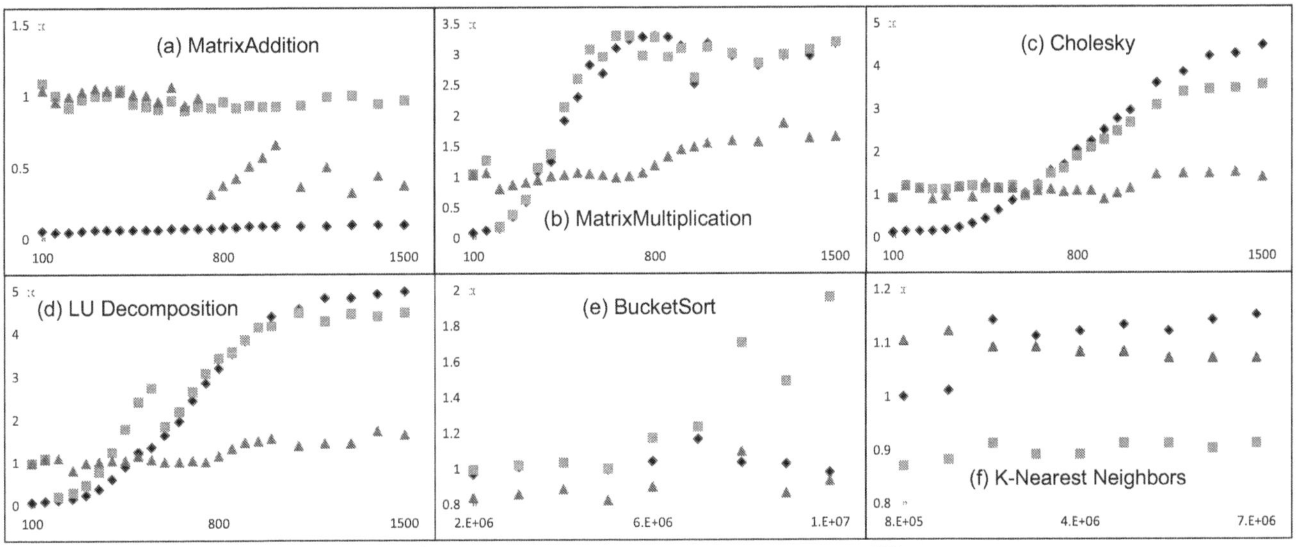

X Axis: size of the input.
Y Axis: speedup relative to baseline.
◆ **Premature migration**: migrate pages to the core where they are used.
1. **Baseline**: do not perform page migration.
■ **Selective Page Migration**: this paper.
▲ **Minas**: middleware approach.

Figure 12: Relative performance between four different page allocation policies. Input size for: (a-d) side of square matrix; (e) size of array to be sorted; (f) size of array of 2D points that constitutes the search space of K-Means.

gration. We believe that this happens due to the overhead of keeping a large number of pages in the interval tree.

Parallel bucket sort gives us a promising result: our heuristic is always better than premature migration. This algorithm has four steps. First it sets up an array of initially empty buckets. Second, it scatters the elements to be sorted into buckets, in such a way that the elements of the first bucket are smaller than the elements of the second bucket, and so on. Third, it sorts the elements of each bucket in parallel. Finally, it merges the elements of the buckets to obtain the complete list of sorted elements. The premature migration policy attempts to migrate pages during all the four phases of the algorithm, whereas we can recognize the small reuse rate of array accesses in all the phases but the third. Thus, in this case we migrate data only when this operation is beneficial to our algorithm.

Finally, our last chart, seen in Figure 12 (f), shows a situation when our heuristic should migrate a page, but it does not - in this case, we deem the amount of array reuse in the K-Nearest Neighbors algorithm too small to justify the page transfer. However, premature migration reveals that this conservative behavior is a mistake in this scenario, given that it delivers gains of up to 15%. Our overhead causes, one the average, a 10% slowdown in the application. This overhead is larger than in the case of matrix addition, shown in Figure 12 (a), because we have not been able to hoist the dynamic test completely outside the outermost loop of KNN.

5. RELATED WORK

To the best of our knowledge, the analyses and optimizations that we describe in Section 3 are novel. However, we are aware of the seminal work of Wolf and Lam [30], which laid the foundations of much of the practice and science of loop analyses. In our work, we preferred to approach loop analysis using symbolic techniques, because we had to generate formulas describing trip counts and array sizes. It is not clear if such formulas could be produced using Wolf and Lam's methods. A work more similar to ours is due to Chatterjee *et al.* [9], which generates exact formulas to bound array regions. Our technique can be refined with more precise models; after all, our formulas give us only estimates, not exact numbers. However, we emphasize that our algorithms are very efficient. Whereas Chatterjee's relational analysis is exponential on the number of bounds, our method is quadratic.

There are techniques to optimize data placement in NUMA aware architectures. These methods speedup programs by reallocating memory pages and mapping threads to cores. Reallocation and mapping reduce load balancing issues, memory contention and remote accesses on NUMA machines [15, 6, 26]. In this section we group the most well known techniques into different categories, depending on which level of the runtime environment they are implemented: hardware, operating system, middleware and libraries.

Hardware. Tikir and Hollingsworth [28] have introduced a profile-driven mechanism based on hardware counters to monitor the memory access behavior of an application. The profile is used to decide whether memory pages should be migrated or not. Cruz *et al.* [10] have proposed a mechanism to detect the communication pattern between threads. Their technique exploits the Translation Lookaside Buffer to obtain the necessary information to map threads to cores. The resulting mapping reduces the communication latency by providing data locality to threads. The work of Dykema *et al.* [15] has introduced a mechanism that implements synchronization for data transfers between two machines with independent memory controllers. Dykema *et al.*'s goal is to use the communication link between the nodes to synchronize memory and to reduce the overhead of data transference. In contrast to these works, we focus on a general solution that does not rely on a specific feature of a target architecture. In other words, this paper proposes a way to speedup applications that does not require modifications in the current NUMA architectures to be effective.

Operating System. Awasthi *et al.* [2] have proposed modifications in the operating system memory allocator to take into account the NUMA design. Their modifications improve virtual-to-physical mappings for every page fault by reducing memory access delays. Migration is performed during runtime and on spare cycles. Löf and Holmgren [23] have introduced a new memory policy named affinity-on-next-touch for the Solaris operating system. This policy allows data migration when threads touch pages on the next time. Thus, the threads can have their data in the same node, allowing more local accesses. Blagodurov *et al.* [4] have introduced a contention-aware scheduling algorithm for NUMA systems. Their work shows how contention-aware algorithms designed for UMA architectures hurt the performance of NUMA multicore systems. Based on these findings, the authors propose an algorithm that minimizes both thread and data migration, while keeping data locality. The proposal has been implemented as a user-level scheduler for the Linux operating system. Diener *et al.* [12] have presented a mechanism to dynamically map threads to machine cores. This technique detects the communication pattern of the application by monitoring a table that logs page accesses. Using such information, their approach migrates threads in order to keep closer the threads that communicate directly. This solution has been implemented inside the Linux kernel. Closer to our work, Li *et al.* [22] have used compiler analyses to determine data placement. Memory allocation, in their case, uses a customized implementation of the `malloc` function, and requires system support: an extra field in memory pages is used to determine its owner. Contrary to these previous work, our solution does not depend on a specific operating system. Even though we have implemented it in Linux, with the `hwloc` library, it will work in any system that gives us: (i) information about the topology of the underlying architecture and (ii) a way to migrate pages.

Middleware. Broquedis *et al.* [6] have proposed a runtime system for OpenMP. This runtime system, called ForestGOMP, groups threads by affinity and performs data migration to reduce NUMA impact on OpenMP applications. Thread grouping and data migration decision is based on hints provided by the OpenMP directives of the application. The developer does not have to modify the application source code, however, the approach only works for OpenMP applications. Castro *et al.* [8] have proposed a machine learning based approach that finds an efficient thread mapping for NUMA systems. This approach takes into account both application and platform characteristics. It relies on software transactional memory to hide from the application developer all mapping decisions. Pilla *et al.* [24] have proposed a load balancing algorithm that migrates tasks over NUMA domains. It equalizes load and guarantees memory affinity by getting runtime information from the application. The algorithm is implemented inside the Charm++ parallel runtime system [19] and does not require code modification. Our solution differs from these previous works because it does not require a target runtime system. Additionally, our technique is more aware of the specific structure of the target program, as it is implemented at the compiler level. Even though we have not compared our approach against all these systems, we believe that our overhead is lower, because we perform most of our computations statically, leaving only fast runtime checks to be executed dynamically.

Library. Library solutions are closely related to the *middleware* category, which we have described previously, but, contrary to it, in this case programmers must change their code using particular APIs. Ribeiro *et al.* [26] presented an API and a runtime environment to allocate and place data over the NUMA machine. This API abstracts to the developer the topology of the architecture and offers mechanisms to determine the initial allocation and placement of application data. Wittmann and Hager [29] presented a software layer that reduces adverse effects of task distribution on ccNUMA systems by sorting tasks into locality queues. Each of these queues is preferably processed by threads that belong to the same locality domain, or node. Dupros *et al.* [14] optimized a parallel seismic wave propagation software for NUMA machines. This optimization was performed via direct modifications of the application to be aware of data allocation and placement. The overall performance of the application has been improved significantly due to the programmer's intervention. Borin and Devloo [5] have discussed the issues of implementing parallel finite elements methods on multicore NUMA machines. Both Dupros *et al.* [14] and Borin and Devloo [5] have modified their application to explicitly manage data and thread placement. Such management has been done via the `numactl` tool and the `libnuma` API. They also have achieved very expressive speedups. Contrary to these previous works, our solution does not require any modification in the source code of the application. Furthermore, our method is not program specific and can be applied to different ranges of applications.

6. CONCLUSION

We have presented a compiler-based technique to improve page placement in NUMA machines. Our approach joins static and dynamic analyses in an effective way to allow parallel benchmarks to benefit from non-uniform memory architectures. We have shown that it is possible to speed software's performance up to four times without programmer's intervention. We are not aware of other solutions that are completely restricted to the compiler: we did not have to modify the operating system nor the memory allocation API used in the C standard library.

Limitations and Future Work. Our implementation currently does not handle OpenMP directives, as they have a particular semantics that we have not yet encoded in our framework. At this time, we only analyze the syntax and semantics that is standard in the intermediate representation of LLVM, our baseline compiler infrastructure. Given the vast amount of benchmarks written in OpenMP, we intend to incorporate its semantics in our analyses.

Software. All the techniques that we have implemented in this paper, plus the benchmarks that we have used in Section 4.2 are publicly available at `http://code.google.com/p/selective-page-migration-ccnuma`.

7. ACKNOWLEDGMENTS

We thank the PACT referees for their very constructive comments. The Unicamp researchers are supported by CAPES,

CNPq, FAPESP and Petrobras. The UFMG researchers are supported by FAPEMIG, CAPES and CNPq. Raphael was partially supported by Intel. We thank the LabMeC (Laboratório de Mecânica Computacional) team for providing us with the machine used in the experiments.

8. REFERENCES

[1] A. W. Appel and J. Palsberg, *Modern Compiler Implementation in Java*, 2nd ed. Cambridge University Press, 2002.

[2] M. Awasthi, D. W. Nellans, K. Sudan, R. Balasubramonian, and A. Davis, "Handling the problems and opportunities posed by multiple on-chip memory controllers," in *PACT*. ACM, 2010, pp. 319–330.

[3] S. Basu, R. Pollack, and M.-F. Roy, *Algorithms in Real Algebraic Geometry*. Springer, 2006.

[4] S. Blagodurov, S. Zhuravlev, A. Fedorova, and A. Kamali, "A case for NUMA-aware contention management on multicore systems," in *PACT*. ACM, 2010, pp. 557–558.

[5] E. Borin and P. Devloo, "Programming finite element methods for ccNUMA processors," in *Int. Conference on Parallel, Distributed, Grid and Cloud Computing for Engineering*. Civil-Comp Press, 2013.

[6] F. Broquedis, N. Furmento, B. Goglin, P.-A. Wacrenier, and R. Namyst, "ForestGOMP: An efficient OpenMP environment for NUMA architectures," *Inter. J. Parallel Programming*, vol. 38, no. 5-6, pp. 418–439, 2010.

[7] F. Broquedis, J. Clet-Ortega, S. Moreaud, N. Furmento, B. Goglin, G. Mercier, S. Thibault, and R. Namyst, "hwloc: A generic framework for managing hardware affinities in HPC applications," in *PDP*. IEEE, 2010, pp. 180–186.

[8] M. Castro, L. F. W. Góes, C. P. Ribeiro, M. Cole, M. Cintra, and J.-F. Méhaut, "A machine learning-based approach for thread mapping on transactional memory applications," in *High Performance Computing Conference (HiPC)*. Bangalore, India: IEEE, 2011, pp. 1–10.

[9] S. Chatterjee, E. Parker, P. J. Hanlon, and A. R. Lebeck, "Exact analysis of the cache behavior of nested loops," in *PLDI*. ACM, 2001, pp. 286–297.

[10] E. Cruz, M. Diener, and P. Navaux, "Using the translation lookaside buffer to map threads in parallel applications based on shared memory," in *IPDPS*, 2012, pp. 532–543.

[11] R. Cytron, J. Ferrante, B. K. Rosen, M. N. Wegman, and F. K. Zadeck, "Efficiently computing static single assignment form and the control dependence graph," *TOPLAS*, vol. 13, no. 4, pp. 451–490, 1991.

[12] M. Diener, E. Cruz, and P. Navaux, "Communication-based mapping using shared pages," in *IPDPS*, 2013, pp. 700–711.

[13] E. W. Dijkstra, "A note on two problems in connexion with graphs," *Numerische Mathematik*, vol. 1, pp. 269–271, 1959.

[14] F. Dupros, C. P. Ribeiro, A. Carissimi, and J.-F. Méhaut, "Parallel simulations of seismic wave propagation on NUMA architectures," in *PARCO*. IOS, 2009, pp. 67–74.

[15] G. L. Dykema, D. H. Bassett, and J. L. Lach, "Mechanisms for synchronizing data transfers between non-uniform memory architecture computers," 2012, US Patent 8,244,930.

[16] J. Ferrante, J. Ottenstein, and D. Warren, "The program dependence graph and its use in optimization," *TOPLAS*, vol. 9, no. 3, pp. 319–349, 1987.

[17] B. Goglin and N. Furmento, "Enabling high-performance memory-migration in Linux for multithreaded applications," in *MTAAP*. IEEE, 2009.

[18] D. Joyner, O. Čertík, A. Meurer, and B. E. Granger, "Open source computer algebra systems: SymPy," *ACM Commun. Comput. Algebra*, vol. 45, no. 3/4, pp. 225–234, 2012.

[19] L. V. Kale and A. Bhatele, Eds., *Parallel Science and Engineering Applications: The Charm++ Approach*. Taylor & Francis Group, CRC Press, Nov. 2013.

[20] C. Lameter, "An overview of non-uniform memory access," *Commun. ACM*, vol. 56, no. 9, pp. 59–54, 2013.

[21] C. Lattner and V. S. Adve, "LLVM: A compilation framework for lifelong program analysis & transformation," in *CGO*. IEEE, 2004, pp. 75–88.

[22] Y. Li, R. Melhem, A. Abousamra, and A. Jones, "Compiler-assisted data distribution for chip multiprocessors," in *PACT*. ACM, 2010, pp. 501–512.

[23] H. Löf and S. Holmgren, "affinity-on-next-touch: increasing the performance of an industrial PDE solver on a cc-NUMA system," in *ICS*. ACM, 2005, pp. 387–392.

[24] L. L. Pilla, C. P. Ribeiro, P. Coucheney, F. Broquedis, B. Gaujal, P. O. Navaux, and J.-F. Méhaut, "A topology-aware load balancing algorithm for clustered hierarchical multi-core machines," *Future Generation Computer Systems*, vol. 30, no. 0, pp. 191 – 201, 2014.

[25] C. P. Ribeiro, "Contributions on memory affinity management for hierarchical shared memory multi-core platforms," Ph.D. dissertation, University of Grenoble, 2011.

[26] C. P. Ribeiro, J.-F. Méhaut, and A. Carissimi, "Memory affinity management for numerical scientific applications over multi-core multiprocessors with hierarchical memory," in *IPDPS Workshops*. IEEE, 2010, pp. 1–4.

[27] L. Tang, J. Mars, X. Zhang, R. Hagmann, R. Hundt, and E. Tune, "Optimizing Google's warehouse scale computers: The NUMA experience," in *HPCA*. IEEE, 2013.

[28] M. M. Tikir and J. K. Hollingsworth, "Using hardware counters to automatically improve memory performance," in *Supercomputing*. IEEE, 2004, pp. 46–46.

[29] M. Wittmann and G. Hager, "Optimizing ccNUMA locality for task-parallel execution under OpenMP and TBB on multicore-based systems," 2011.

[30] M. E. Wolf and M. S. Lam, "A data locality optimizing algorithm," in *PLDI*. ACM, 1991, pp. 30–44.

[31] M. Wolfe, *High Performance Compilers for Parallel Computing*, 1st ed. Adison-Wesley, 1996.

COLORIS: A Dynamic Cache Partitioning System Using Page Coloring

Ying Ye, Richard West, Zhuoqun Cheng, and Ye Li
Computer Science Department, Boston University
Boston, MA, USA
yingy@cs.bu.edu, richwest@cs.bu.edu, czq@cs.bu.edu, liye@cs.bu.edu

ABSTRACT

Shared caches in multicore processors are subject to contention from co-running threads. The resultant interference can lead to highly-variable performance for individual applications. This is particularly problematic for real-time applications, requiring predictable timing guarantees. Previous work has applied page coloring techniques to partition a shared cache, so that conflict misses are minimized amongst co-running workloads. However, prior page coloring techniques have not addressed the problem of partitioning a cache on over-committed processors where there are more executable threads than cores. Similarly, page coloring techniques have not proven efficient at adapting the cache partition sizes for threads with varying memory demands.

This paper presents a memory management framework called COLORIS, which provides support for both static and dynamic cache partitioning using page coloring. COLORIS supports novel policies to reconfigure the assignment of page colors amongst application threads in over-committed systems. For quality-of-service (QoS), COLORIS monitors the cache miss rates of running applications and triggers re-partitioning of the cache to prevent miss rates exceeding applications-specific ranges. This paper presents the design and evaluation of COLORIS as applied to Linux. We show the efficiency and effectiveness of COLORIS to color memory pages for a set of SPEC CPU2006 workloads, thereby enhancing performance isolation over existing page coloring techniques.

Categories and Subject Descriptors

D.4.2 [**Storage Management**]: Main memory

Keywords

Cache and memory management; dynamic page coloring; multicore; performance isolation

PACT'14, August 24–27, 2014, Edmonton, AB, Canada.

ACM 978-1-4503-2809-8/14/08 ...$15.00.
http://dx.doi.org/10.1145/2628071.2628104.

1. INTRODUCTION

Multicore platforms are gaining popularity these days, both in general computing and embedded domains. They have the ability to support concurrent workloads with less circuit area, lower power consumption and lower cost. Tightly-coupled on-chip resources allow faster data sharing between processing cores, at the same time, suffering from potentially heavy resource contention. Modern processors often devote the largest fraction of on-chip transistors to caches, mostly the shared last-level cache (LLC), the performance of which is crucial for the overall processing capability of processors, especially for running memory-bound applications. Yet, in most commercial off-the-shelf (COTS) systems, only best effort service is provided for accessing the shared LLC. Multiple processes run simultaneously on those systems, interfering with one another on cache accesses. Data stored in a cache line with strong access locality from one process may be evicted at an arbitrary time due to another process's access to different data mapped to the same cache line. Interleaving cache accesses can potentially ruin program locality, the fundamental assumption hardware caches are built upon. Depending on the workload, the degree of interference on application performance can vary significantly [13]. Thus, QoS cannot be guaranteed in such systems.

For safety-critical real-time systems, cache-related performance variations can lead to task timing violations, and potential life-threatening situations. Therefore, performance isolation is desirable in these systems. Although private caches eliminate cache contention for threads mapped to different caches, they offer a smaller storage capacity than a single shared cache, and additionally require coherency protocols to maintain consistency of shared data. Alternatively, shared caches can be used in conjunction with techniques that minimize cache interference, such as page coloring, cache-aware scheduling or hardware cache partitioning.

One of the first uses of page coloring was in virtual address translation in the MIPS system [31]. It was later adopted by operating system memory subsystems [3, 12] and compilers [4], to reduce application cache self-conflicts. Recent work [14, 29, 35] applied page coloring on multicore systems to partition shared caches, and demonstrated enhanced isolation amongst applications. However, the result of previous work has also revealed some open issues related with page coloring, especially with respect to dynamic recoloring and, hence, re-partitioning.

First of all, knowing when to perform re-partitioning is non-trivial. Dynamic phase changing behaviors [1] of applications lead to fluctuating resource demands, which may cause poor cache utilization under static partitioning. To re-partition the shared cache, we want to clearly capture program phase transitions on-the-fly. Even without phase changes, when an application is just started, it is hard to determine its best cache partition size without a-priori knowledge. Existing page coloring techniques either do not adaptively adjust partitions, at least not efficiently, or they fail to identify application phase transitions.

Secondly, finding the optimal partition size to minimize cache misses for a given workload is difficult. If the goal is fairness or QoS, proper performance metrics have to be defined to guide dynamic re-partitioning. For example, some researchers have attempted to construct cache utility curves, which capture the miss rates for applications at different cache occupancies [19, 26, 30, 33, 37], but this is typically expensive to do in a working system.

Another issue with page coloring is the significant overhead with re-partitioning, also called recoloring. Recoloring is cumbersome. It involves allocating new page frames, copying memory between pages and freeing old page frames as necessary. To make the matter worse, naive page selection during recoloring may cause inefficient use of newly allocated cache space. Altogether, the benefit of dynamic partitioning can be undermined.

Lastly, in over-committed systems, excessive recoloring operations may result from the interleaved execution of multiple processes. A simple example would be a 2-core, 6-page-color system with two running processes (P1, P2) and one ready process (P3). The page colors allocated to these three processes might be $\{1, 2, 3\}, \{4, 5, 6\}$ and $\{1, 2, 3\}$, respectively. If a scheduler suspends P2 and dispatches P3 to co-run with P1, two processes will be contending for the same three page colors. This may result in significant contention on a subset of the entire cache space. At this point, either recoloring has to be performed or performance isolation is compromised.

Our work tries to solve the problems associated with implementing dynamic page coloring in production systems. Specifically, this paper describes the implementation of an efficient page recoloring framework in the Linux kernel, called "COLORIS" (COLOR ISolation). COLORIS attempts to isolate cache accesses of different applications, thereby reducing their conflict misses compared to a scheme that lacks cache partitioning. We propose two recoloring policies and compare their performance, while considering factors such as when to trigger recoloring and which processes should be affected. Using the SPEC CPU2006 benchmark, we show the performance of COLORIS on an over-committed multicore platform, where there are more schedulable threads than cores.

The rest of this paper is organized as follows: Section 2 introduces basic page coloring concepts. Section 3 describes the design of the COLORIS framework, with focus on the proposed recoloring mechanism. An evaluation of COLORIS in provided in Section 4. Related work is then described in Section 5, followed by conclusions and future work.

[1]Phase changes might be due to switching between localities such as function loops and procedures within a running program.

2. BACKGROUND

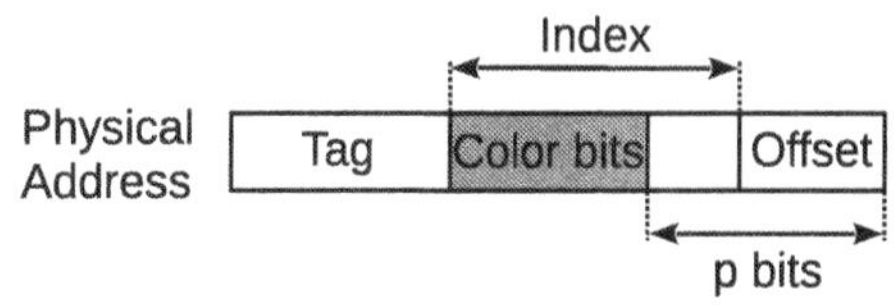

Figure 1: Page Color Bits

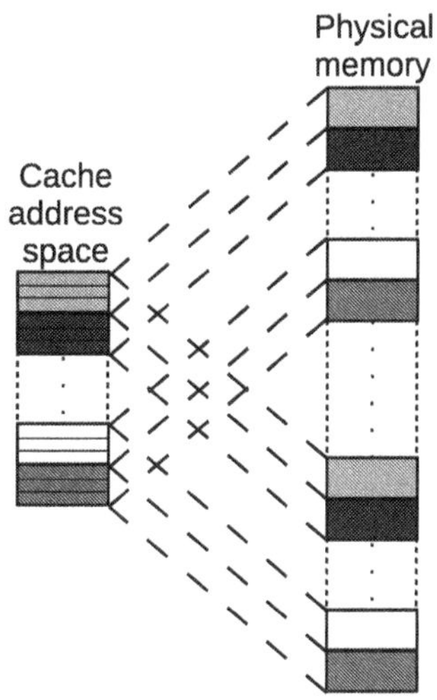

Figure 2: Mapping Between Memory Pages and Cache Space

On most modern architectures, a shared LLC is physically indexed and set associative. When a physical address is used in a cache lookup operation, it is divided into a *Tag*, an *Index* and an *Offset* as shown in Figure 1. The *Offset* bits are used to specify the byte offset location of the desired data within a specific cache line. *Index* bits select a cache set. *Tag* bits are checked against the current cache line to determine a cache hit or miss. Operating systems that manage memory at page granularity use the least significant p bits of a physical address as a byte offset within a page of memory. These p bits typically overlap with the least-significant *Index* bits, leaving the most significant indexing bits to form the *Color* bits (as shown in the shaded area of Figure 1). Two or more pages of physical memory addressed with different color bits are guaranteed *not* to map to the same set of cache lines.

Using color bits, it is possible for an operating system to implement a color-aware memory allocator to control the mapping of physical pages to sets of cache lines. This is illustrated by Figure 2. Pages mapped to the same set of cache lines are said to have the same *page color*. The total number of page colors is derived from the following equation:

$$number\ of\ colors = \frac{cache\ size}{number\ of\ ways \times page\ size}$$

Limitations. Some recent architectures have now introduced *cache slices* [36]. This new cache arrangement imposes a challenge for page coloring techniques since the mapping between memory and cache slices is made opaque. If the hash function for mapping physical addresses to cache sets inside a slice remains the same as above, then it may be possible to treat each slice as though it were a separate cache.

That way, the problem is equivalent to page coloring on N separate caches each of size M, where M is the size of a slice and $N \cdot M$ is the full capacity of the original cache. We will show in later experiments that COLORIS is able to effectively partition caches on architectures featuring slices.

3. COLORIS ARCHITECTURE

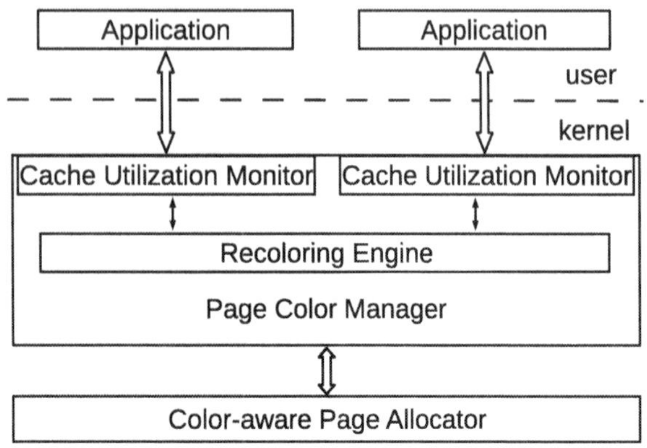

Figure 3: COLORIS Architecture Overview

COLORIS is comprised of two major components: a Page Color Manager and a Color-aware Page Allocator. The Color-aware Page Allocator is capable of allocating page frames of specific colors. The Page Color Manager is responsible for assigning initial page colors to processes, monitoring process cache usage metrics, and performing color assignment adjustment according to system specific objectives (e.g. fairness, QoS, or performance). An architectural overview of COLORIS is shown in Figure 3.

Though the design of COLORIS is system-agnostic, we implemented a prototype version inside the Linux kernel to utilize existing applications and benchmarks for evaluation purposes.

3.1 Color-aware Page Allocator

The Linux kernel allocates single page frames from the per-CPU page frame cache. The page frame cache maintains a list of free pages [2] allocated from the Buddy System. Tam et al [29] made the Linux page frame cache color-aware by splitting the single free list into multiple lists, each corresponding to one particular page color. To refill a list with a specific color, the Buddy System has to be called repeatedly until a page of the correct color is returned. This approach can potentially add significant overhead and compromise the benefit of page coloring.

Instead of using the existing Linux memory allocation framework, we decided to replace it with our own efficient color-aware allocator. In COLORIS, a memory pool is used to serve all page requests. Inside the pool, free pages of the same colors are linked together to form multiple lists. Figure 4 shows the structure of our new page allocator.

In order to reduce the engineering complexity, we decided to keep the original Linux Buddy System interface in COLORIS. This is achieved by maintaining per-process color assignments in the Page Color Manager. Upon receiving an allocation request, the Color-aware Page Allocator communicates with the Page Color Manager to determine the colors already assigned to the requesting process. The allocator then picks one of these colors in a round-robin manner, and returns a page with that color from the memory pool. If that color does not exist, the allocator attempts to pick another color assigned to the process. If all currently assigned colors are unavailable, then the allocator calls the Buddy System to populate the memory pool with new pages of arbitrary colors. By keeping the memory pool large enough, communication with the Buddy System is minimized. When a page is freed, we first try to place it back into the memory pool and only return it to the Linux page frame cache if the corresponding list is full.

[2]Strictly speaking, two lists are used for performance optimization.

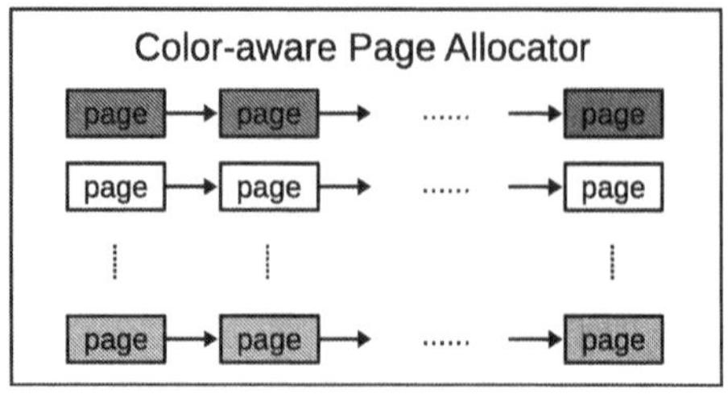

Figure 4: Page Allocator

Additionally, instead of managing only data pages [24], COLORIS also supports page coloring of program code pages. This increases cache isolation between processes, except for cases where code is shared. However, we believe shared code should be avoided as much as possible, as a trade off between memory utilization and maximum isolation. For certain libraries, such as *libc*, we acknowledge this is not always practical. For cases where sharing is practically unavoidable, COLORIS randomly selects page colors upon request. An alternative to this is to reserve a dedicated set of page colors for shared memory usage.

3.2 Page Color Manager

The Page Color Manager manages page color resources amongst application processes according to specific policies. In the simplest form, the Page Color Manager statically partitions hardware caches according to various color assignment schemes. The most intuitive approach is to strictly assign different page colors to different processes so that they land on different parts of the shared cache. While this provides the maximum degree of isolation, it also limits the maximum number of processes supported. Consider, for example, a system with 4 cores, 64 page colors and 16 MB memory per color – at most 64 processes can be supported with 1 color each, with the memory footprint of every process limited to no more than 16 MB. Additionally, cache utilization is as low as 6.25% in the worst case when all cores are active.

To mitigate the problem of cache utilization, we want to make optimal color assignments for application processes according to their cache demands. However, this requires a-priori knowledge that is difficult to acquire for most applications. Consequently, we decided to adopt a more flexible color assignment scheme that does not require offline profiling when optimal assignments are not provided.

In this new scheme, the cache is divided into N sections of contiguous page colors on a platform of N processing cores.

Each section is then assigned to a specific core, which we call the local core of all the colors within this section. All the other cores will be referred to as remote cores. When a new process is created, COLORIS searches for a core with the lightest workload and assigns the whole cache section of the core to the process. As a result, in a system with a total of C page colors, every process will be assigned $\frac{C}{N}$ colors. This means that N co-running processes can fully utilize the cache.

For load balancing, process migration can be invoked and the entire address space needs to be recolored. Migration may also be applied to reduce memory bus contention, by placing memory intensive processes to the same cores. However, since migration incurs prohibitive overhead, it should be avoided when possible.

Though the previous static partitioning scheme is simple, it can still potentially lead to low cache utilization for an under utilized system and when there are dynamic program phase changes. A more practical way would be to assign a default-sized partition first, and then gradually approach the best size through re-partitioning (i.e. recoloring). Thus, for a page coloring technique to be truly useful in production systems, dynamic partitioning is essential.

In COLORIS, we extended the Page Color Manager with dynamic partitioning capabilities, by introducing a comprehensive recoloring mechanism. Our primary design focus of this recoloring mechanism is to make it effective and efficient even in over-committed systems.

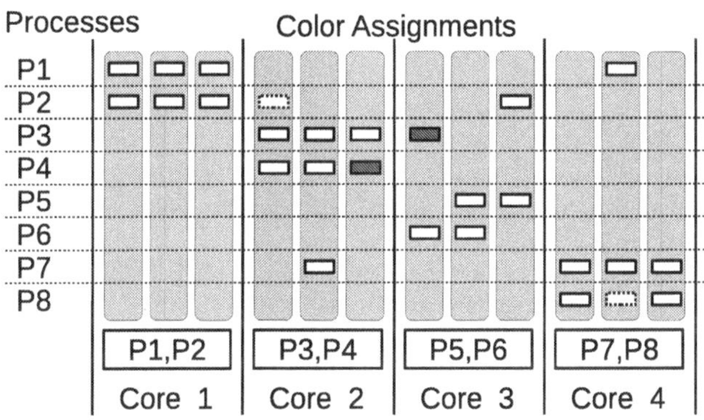

Figure 5: COLORIS Page Coloring Scheme

Starting with the initial color assignments described earlier, the Page Color Manager attempts to make online color assignment changes based on dynamic application behaviors. For applications that do not require the entire local cache section, some colors can be reclaimed; for applications that demand more cache space, colors from other sections can be shared. An example is illustrated in Figure 5. In this example, the twelve columns represent twelve different page colors. Every block within a column is an ownership token denoting that the process having this token (in the same row) is assigned the corresponding color.

Since the local cache section can now be shared, limited cache interference between processes may happen. In this case, a global coordination amongst schedulers on each core is useful. By sharing the information on page color usages and scheduling processes accordingly, the likelihood of cache contention is reduced. While a cache-aware scheduler is not implemented in COLORIS, we leave it as future work.

We have also considered an alternative design for color assignment. Instead of re-partitioning at the granularity of processes, we can adjust the size of a cache section for each core. Before doing that, we need a mechanism for online application classification in terms of cache demands. We want to move applications of the same class to the same core in order to maintain high cache utilization. For online classification, there are several useful areas of study [11, 19, 32, 33, 34].

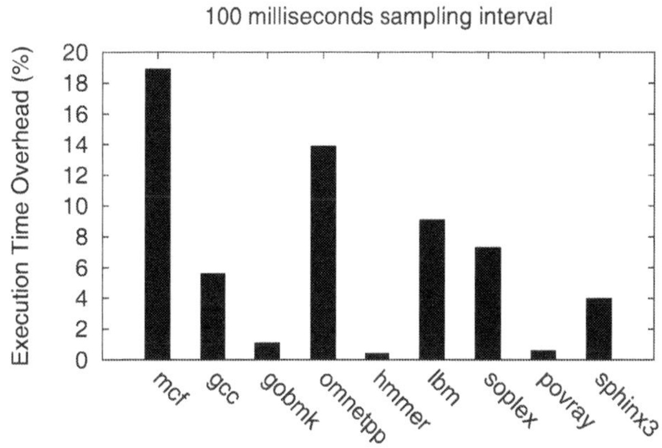

Figure 6: Overhead of Hot Page Identification

Cache Utilization Monitor. The Cache Utilization Monitor is responsible for measuring the cache usage of individual applications, and making decisions about partition adjustments. To start with, we need to introduce the concept of *hotness*, which is the key for partition adjustment. In previous work, page color hotness is defined as the aggregate access frequency of page frames with the same color [35]. It was used to help reduce the cost of cache re-partitioning by only recoloring pages of hot colors. However, hotness identification requires expensive periodic page table scans, which may result in worse performance than if hot page identification is not used at all. We conducted a preliminary experiment on the proposed approach from this work with SPEC CPU2006. The results from Figure 6 clearly support our argument.

Based on this observation, we decided upon a new definition of hotness. One approach is to define it as a function of the number of free pages in the target color. A second approach, which is more appropriate and has been adopted in COLORIS, is to use the number of processes sharing the same color as the definition of hotness. This information can be used to avoid heavy cache contention by assigning cold colors to newly created processes. Due to its simplicity, we believe this to be a suitable metric in practical systems.

Following the re-definition of hotness, we now describe the two recoloring approaches in COLORIS. In the first approach, ALLOC_COLORS(*UNIT*) is invoked to add *UNIT* colors to a process, whenever it runs out of memory with its pre-existing colors. Here, *UNIT* is a configurable number of colors. The second approach triggers recoloring when a process's cache demand exceeds its current assignment. This is determined by monitoring the cache miss rate for a given process, defined as cache misses with respect to total

Algorithm 1 Cache Utilization Monitor

```
procedure MONITOR(cmr)
    assignment = assignment_of(current)
    if cmr > HighThreshold then
        if isCold = False then
            isHot ← True
            return
        end if
        new = ALLOC_COLORS(UNIT)
        /* triggers Recoloring Engine */
        assignment+ = new
        isCold ← False
    else if cmr < LowThreshold then
        if isHot = True then
            isHot ← False
            isCold ← True
            victims = PICK_VICTIMS(UNIT)
            /* triggers Recoloring Engine */
            assignment− = victims
        end if
    end if
end procedure

procedure ALLOC_COLORS(num)
    new ← φ
    while num > 0 do
        if needRemote() then
            new+ = pick_coldest_remote()
        else
            new+ = pick_coldest_local()
        end if
        num ← num − 1
    end while
    return new
end procedure

procedure PICK_VICTIMS(num)
    victims ← φ
    while num > 0 do
        if hasRemote() then
            victims+ = pick_hottest_remote()
        else
            victims+ = pick_hottest_local()
        end if
        num ← num − 1
    end while
    return victims
end procedure
```

accesses over a sample period, using hardware performance counters commonly available on modern processors.

We set up two global cache miss rate thresholds when the system starts up, *HighThreshold* and *LowThreshold*. Applications with miss rates higher than *HighThreshold* are the ones needing more cache space; others with miss rates below *LowThreshold* are willing to provide vacant cache space for re-partitioning. Procedure *MONITOR* in Algorithm 1 is used to trigger recoloring. It takes the cache miss rate (*cmr*) of the current process (*current*) over a period of time (*PERIOD*) as input. The *needRemote()* function returns *True* if *current* has already been using the entire local cache section. The *hasRemote()* function returns *True* if *current* owns colors from remote cache sections. The boolean variable *isHot* is used to indicate when the cache miss rate of a process goes above a specific threshold. It acts as a signal to indicate that a process needs more page colors. Conversely, *isCold* is set when extra page colors are available. Both variables are global to all processes.

Functions *pick_coldest_remote()* and *pick_hottest_remote()* choose a color in a remote cache section belonging to the *current* process, with the smallest or largest global hotness value, respectively. Similarly, *pick_coldest_local()* and *pick_hottest_local()* return a color from the local cache section, owned by *current*, with the smallest or largest remote hotness value, respectively. Here, we define global hotness as the number of owners of a color running on all cores, while remote hotness is the number of owners of a color running on remote cores. We also define a local color to be any color within a local cache section.

The key insight of using remote hotness is that, when adding or taking away a local color to/from a process, we do not care about other processes running on the same core. Since they cannot run simultaneously with one another, there is no cache interference amongst them for sharing colors. In Figure 5, we show all four cases where the four functions above are called respectively. The figure illustrates a state transition during recoloring. Solid white blocks indicate the process owns the corresponding color before and after recoloring. Dashed white blocks indicate the process has the color before recoloring. Similarly, dark blocks indicate the process is assigned the color after recoloring.

Despite the global thresholds, we also allow individual applications to provide their private threshold pair as part of QoS specification. When QoS specification is not available, global thresholds are used.

While dynamic partitioning can benefit from the information provided by cache utility curves, such information is not easily obtainable in a running system. Without this information, COLORIS' objective is to enhance QoS by attempting to maintain application miss rates below *HighThreshold*, given sufficient capacity. Sufficient capacity here means there are some other applications, with miss rates lower than *LowThreshold*, that are able to provide enough free colors. If there exists a cache partitioning scheme that guarantees no application's miss rate exceeds *HighThreshold*, COLORIS attempts to achieve such guarantee.

Notice that the Cache Utilization Monitor takes into account both cache miss rates and the number of cache references. When the number of references is small, miss rate for a process is set to zero, to indicate the cache is not being used significantly. Likewise, in situations where frequent page recoloring is not beneficial to overall performance, it is possible to disable recoloring for individual processes.

Recoloring Engine. The Recoloring Engine performs two tasks: (1) shrinkage of color assignments, and (2)expansion of color assignments. Lazy recoloring [14] is adopted for shrinking a color assignment. Basically, we look for pages of specific colors that are going to be taken away and clear the present bits of their page table entries. At the same time, an unused bit of every page table entry whose present bit is cleared is set to identify the page as needing recoloring. However, we do not set a target color for each page to be recolored. In the page fault handler, we allocate a new page from the page allocator and copy the content of the old page to it. Since round-robin is used in page allocation, as described in Section 3.1, pages to be recolored are eventually spread out uniformly across the cache partition assigned to the process.

Assignment expansion is more complicated than shrinkage. The major reason being that it is difficult to figure out which pages should be moved to the new colors. Ideally, we want memory accesses to be redistributed evenly across the new cache partition. In COLORIS, we currently consider two selection policies.

1) *Selective Moving* – In this policy, we take the set associativity of the cache into consideration. Assuming an n-way set associative cache, we know that one page color of the cache can hold up to n pages at the same time. We therefore scan the whole page table of the current process and recolor one in every $n + 1$ pages of the same color, trying to minimize cache evictions when big data structures with contiguous memory are being accessed. These pages will be immediately moved to the newly assigned colors in a round-robin manner.

2) *Redistribution* – When the expansion is triggered, we first go through the entire page table of the current process and clear the access bit of every entry. The access bit is a special bit in page table entry on x86 platforms; whenever the page in that entry is accessed, this bit is automatically set by hardware. After a fixed time window *WIN*, we scan the page table again and find all entries with the access bit set. Pages in those entries have all been accessed during the time window. Since it is hard to re-balance the cache hotness by moving selected pages, we let the process itself perform the redistribution. That is, all accessed pages are recolored using lazy recoloring as mentioned above.

Comparing these two policies, *Selective Moving* is simpler and more light-weight. However, *Redistribution* is likely to be more powerful for re-balancing cache hotness. Their effectiveness is evaluated in the next section.

4. EVALUATION

We conducted a series of experiments to evaluate the performance and effectiveness of the COLORIS page coloring framework. We implemented a prototype system for a 32-bit Ubuntu 12.04 Linux OS with kernel version 3.8.8. All the experiments except the last one in Section 4.5 were conducted using the SPEC CPU2006 benchmark suite on a Dell PowerEdge T410 machine with a quad-core Intel Xeon E5506 2.13GHz processor and 8GB of RAM. A total of 4MB 16-way set-associative L3 cache was shared amongst the 4 cores of the processor. As a result, there were 64 page colors available in the system with 4KB page size. Since we set the size of the memory pool in our Color-aware Page Allocator to be 1GB, each color provided up to 16MB of memory for application use.

4.1 Allocator Implementation Overhead

In the first experiment, we compared the performance of the original Linux memory allocator with COLORIS's page allocator to evaluate the efficiency of our implementation. In Linux, we ran each SPEC benchmark alone in the system without co-runners and recorded their execution times. In COLORIS, we assigned all colors, effectively the entire cache, to every program and ran them with the same configuration. In the latter case, COLORIS picked page colors in round-robin manner for each application page request. Table 1 shows that our page allocator achieved similar performance as the original Linux Buddy System.

	Linux (sec)	COLORIS (sec)
gobmk	736	738
gcc	507	495
libquantum	773	778
bzip2	961	956
sphinx3	864	866
omnetpp	476	480
povray	366	367
hmmer	849	850
h264ref	1131	1128
mcf	450	444
soplex	429	428
leslie3d	797	799
gromacs	1386	1384
namd	790	792
milc	671	679
gamess	1503	1510
zeusmp	842	841
soplex	429	428
tonto	977	977
wrf	1328	1323
calculix	1517	1512
sjeng	871	868
astar	777	773
perlbench	569	569
cactusADM	1796	1788
GemsFDTD	725	728
lbm	533	535

Table 1: Allocator Implementation Overhead

4.2 Effectiveness of Page Coloring

The benefit of page coloring is the performance isolation between running processes. In the following experiments, we tried to evaluate the effectiveness of page coloring for applications of different characteristics. We first selected three groups of benchmarks: {*sphinx3, leslie3d, libquantum*}, {*leslie3d, h264ref, gromacs*}, and {*povray, h264ref, gromacs*}. According to their memory access intensity, we call them the heavy background workload (H), the medium background workload (M) and the light background workload (L), respectively. Three foreground benchmarks were then selected: *omnetpp*, *gobmk* and *hmmer*. *omnetpp* has a very large memory footprint and is memory-intensive. *gobmk*, with a small footprint, is less memory-intensive but cache-sensitive. *hmmer* is similar to *gobmk* except for cache-sensitivity, due to its small working set.

For every experiment, we chose one foreground workload and one background workload. The three background programs were started first, each pinned to a different core. The foreground workload started execution after a delay of one second on the fourth core. The background workload remained executing during the entire life of the foreground workload. We denote experiments with page coloring as P experiments, and experiments with heavy, medium, and light background workloads as H, M, and L experiments, respectively. For example, an experiment running foreground and heavy background workloads together with page coloring is labeled as H + P. In any experiment with page coloring, every workload was assigned 16 page colors.

We also had two control groups: the first group, S, ran only the foreground workloads, with page coloring limiting

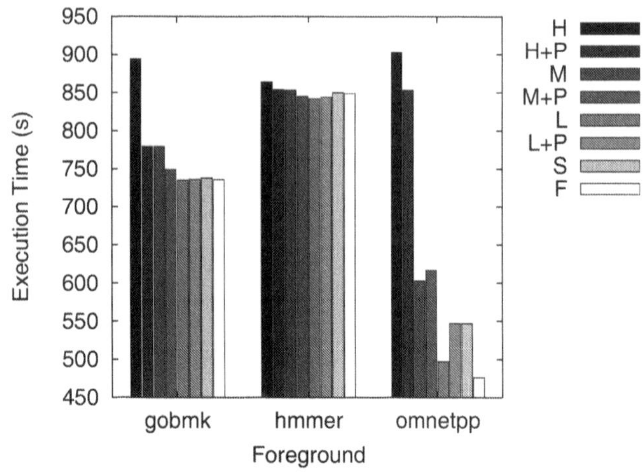

Figure 7: Execution Time of Foreground Workload

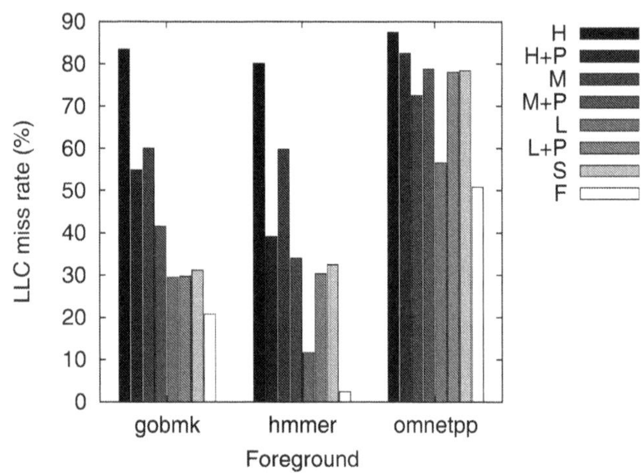

Figure 8: Cache Miss Rate of Foreground Workload

access to a quarter of the last-level cache; the second group, F, also ran only the foreground workloads but without page coloring, thereby allowing access to the full cache. We conducted all experiments three times and recorded the average execution times and LLC miss rates of each foreground workload. The results are shown in Figure 7 and Figure 8.

As can be seen in Figure 7 (H and H + P), the cache-sensitive workload *gobmk* experienced a performance gain of as much as 13% under the interference of a heavy background workload with page coloring. For non-cache-sensitive workload *hmmer*, page coloring was less effective.

With ideal performance isolation, given the same cache partition size, a foreground workload running with background workload should exhibit the same behavior as when it is running alone in the system (which is represented by the control group S). As Figure 7 shows, with the presence of interference, COLORIS was able to constrain the performance variations of *gobmk*, *hmmer* and *omnetpp* to within 5%, 0.5% and 55% respectively, as compared to S. Without page coloring, the variations can be as much as 21%, 2% and 90%, as compared to F. For *omnetpp*, a 39% reduction in variation was achieved.

Notice that *omnetpp* suffered higher miss rate when page coloring was enabled (comparing L and L+P). This is mainly caused by the high self-conflict from limiting its memory accesses to just $\frac{1}{4}$ of the entire cache (as shown in Figure 8).

4.3 Recoloring Evaluation

Configurations	LowThreshold (%)	HighThreshold (%)
C1	30	65
C2	30	75
C3	0	100
C4	(40, 0, 30, 40)	(80, 60, 65, 80)
C5	-	-
C6	30	75

Table 2: Experimental Configurations

To demonstrate the benefit of recoloring, we designed a set of experiments with four benchmarks, *povray*, *tonto*, *omnetpp* and *gamess*. Amongst them, only *omnetpp* is memory-intensive and cache-hungry, meaning the more cache space there is, the lower its cache miss rate will be. If the other three benchmarks are similar to *omnetpp* in terms of cache demand, then there will be no possibility for re-partitioning. Configurations for different experiments are listed in Table 2. In all the configurations *WIN* was set to 3ms (except for C6), *UNIT* to 4, and *PERIOD* to 5 seconds. (40, 0, 30, 40) in C4 means assigning these four *LowThresholds* to *povray*, *tonto*, *omnetpp* and *gamess*, respectively, instead of using global *LowThreshold*. Note that the thresholds of configuration C3 prevent page recoloring altogether. Configuration C5 was used for the special case in which every benchmark ran alone with full cache space access.

All the experiments were carried out by fixing each benchmark to a different core. The four benchmarks were started at the same time, each with 16 non-overlapping page colors. Each experiment was run for more than an hour. After the first minute, we set up the performance counters to collect LLC miss rates and the numbers of instructions retired from user-level (to exclude kernel overhead) over a measured *60 minutes* interval. At the same time, the Cache Utilization Monitor was also enabled. For these experiments, the LLC was fully utilized, which meant colors needed to be removed from one application before they could be re-assigned to another. The final result was produced by repeating the same experiments three times and taking the average, which is shown in Figure 9, Table 3 and Table 4.

With static cache partitioning (C3), the miss rate of *omnetpp* reached 77.8%. With the help of recoloring (C1 and C2), the miss rate was successfully limited to below *HighThreshold* thus meeting the system default QoS requirement. By comparing miss rates of *omnetpp* between C1 and C2, we can tell that the degree of improvement for cache-hungry applications depends on how we set up the thresholds. As shown in Table 3, despite the recoloring overhead, *omnetpp* had received 3.3% – 9.4% performance gain, proving that our approaches are practical. *povray* managed to keep the same miss rate with fewer cache lines since its working set is small enough to fit into private L2 cache. Although the other two benchmarks, *tonto* and *gamess*, were negatively affected by reduced cache sizes, the system overall performance remained roughly the same.

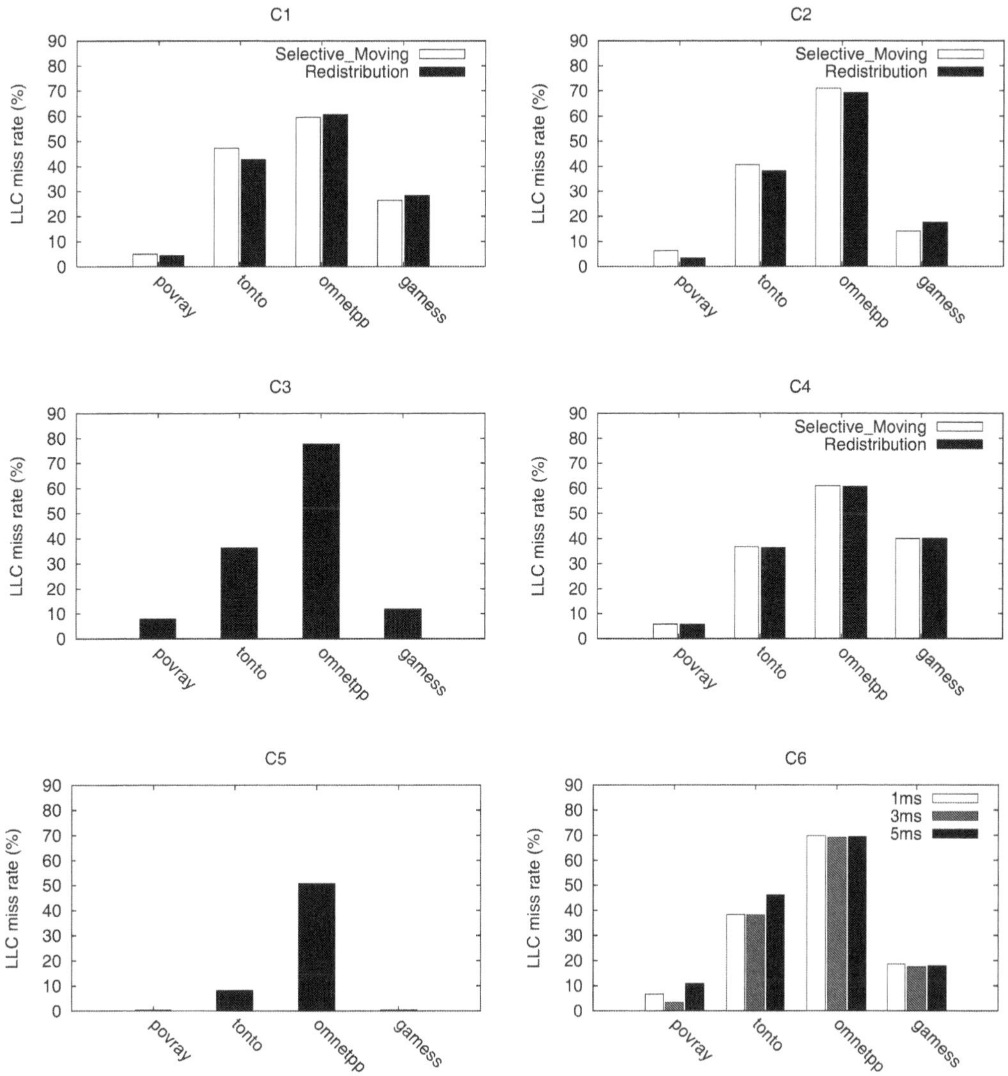

Figure 9: LLC Miss Rates

		C1	C2(C6.WIN=3)	C3	C4	C6.WIN=1	C6.WIN=5
Selective Moving	**povray**	100.1	101.8	102.2	100.7	-	-
	tonto	88.9	90.7	91.6	91.4	-	-
	omnetpp	46.2	43.6	42.2	45.8	-	-
	gamess	120.9	122.8	123.1	119.2	-	-
	total	356.1	358.9	359.1	357.1	-	-
Redistribution	**povray**	100.2	101.7	-	100.7	101.7	101.8
	tonto	90.0	91.4	-	91.4	91.2	89.9
	omnetpp	46.0	44.1	-	46.0	43.9	43.8
	gamess	121.1	122.3	-	119.3	121.3	122.5
	total	357.3	359.5	-	357.4	358.1	358.0

Table 3: Instructions Retired in One Hour $(\times 10^{11})$

Instead of using system default QoS specification, reasonable individual specifications can also be satisfied by the COLORIS framework as shown in C4. By setting *LowThreshold* to 0 for *tonto*, we avoided decreasing its cache space, and limited its miss rate to below 40%. The result shows that recoloring is effective for guaranteeing QoS requirements of individual applications.

Table 4 lists the total number of pages recolored in all the experiments. It can be seen that *Redistribution* incurred higher overhead as compared to *Selective Moving*. How-

	C1	C2(C6.WIN=3)	C4	C6.WIN=1	C6.WIN=5
Selective Moving	10746	3845	8791	-	-
Redistribution	32749	22243	33547	6476	30174

Table 4: Recoloring Overhead (Total # Pages Recolored)

ever, *Redistribution* achieved a slightly better overall system performance if we look at the total instructions retired in Table 3. The result indicates that *Redistribution* is more effective in utilizing newly assigned cache space.

Following this observation, we then evaluated the impact of window size *WIN* on the effectiveness of the *Redistribution* policy in C6. *omnetpp* was the only application that received an expanded cache space during the experiment. Its performance under different window sizes stayed the same, which suggests that larger window size may not help improve performance, as recoloring overhead will increase as well.

Finally, Table 5 shows the stable color assignments for each repetition of the above experiments. Within each 4-element tuple, the numbers are the sizes of color assignments for *povray*, *tonto*, *omnetpp* and *gamess* respectively. Across multiple repetitions of the same experiment, stable-state color assignments are fairly consistent. This indicates the COLORIS recoloring mechanism is stable.

4.4 Performance in Over-Committed Systems

In these experiments, we tried to evaluate the design of COLORIS for over-committed systems. We first created four groups of SPEC benchmarks (G1, G2, G3, G4): {*gobmk*, *sphinx3*}, {*gromacs*, *leslie3d*}, {*h264ref*, *omnetpp*}, {*povray*, *gamess*}. Programs were started with ten seconds interval in the following order: *gobmk*, *gromacs*, *h264ref*, *povray*, *sphinx3*, *leslie3d*, *omnetpp*, *gamess*. One minute after the last benchmark program was started, we enabled hardware performance counters and the Cache Utilization Monitor (if used). All experiments were then run for an hour, at the end of which results were collected.

When running experiments in COLORIS, benchmark programs received their initial color assignments in a round-robin fashion, since all colors had zero hotness at the beginning. According to their launching order, programs in group Gx were assigned the cache section belonging to core x. After assignment, they were pinned automatically to those cores. For experiments in Linux, we pinned each group onto the same core similar to the COLORIS experiments. By doing this, we eliminated the difference of memory bus contention between the two sets of experiments. The same experiments were carried out with three different configurations, C7, C8 and C9. In C7, recoloring used the *Redistribution* policy, *WIN* = 3ms, UNIT = 4, PERIOD = 5s and system-wide thresholds were set to (*LowThreshold*, *HighThreshold*) = (20%, 75%). An individual QoS specification (0%, 100%) was also provided to *leslie3d*, which essentially disabled recoloring. The reason being *leslie3d* is an LLC-thrashing [11] application that does not benefit from assignment expansion (known through offline profiling). In C8, a static partitioning scheme was used. For C9, applications were run in Linux without page coloring. Results from Figure 10 show that COLORIS performs no worse than Linux in heavy over-committed cases, while at the same time guaranteeing QoS for applications.

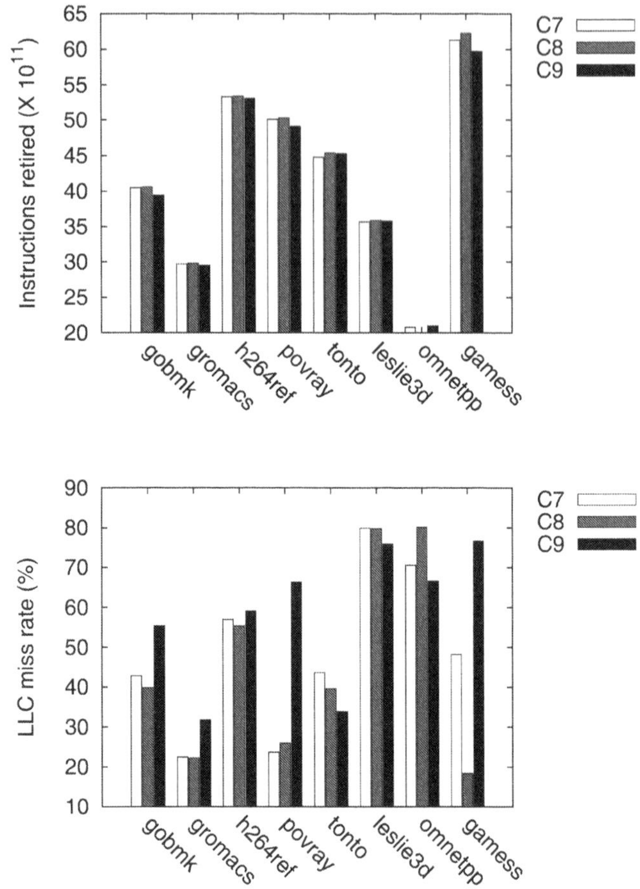

Figure 10: Over-Committed System Performance

4.5 Page Coloring on Cache Slices

In order to prove that page coloring can work with the latest cache-slice architecture, we conducted another set of experiments similar to the ones in Section 4.2, but on an Intel Core i3-2100 Sandy Bridge dual-core processor. It has two 1.5MB, 12-way set-associative L3 cache slices. The system also features 4GB DDR3 RAM. The three background workloads were: H = {*libquantum*}, M = {*h264ref*}, L = {*povray*}. The results are shown in Figure 11. Note that for *omnetpp* with a light background workload (case L), the execution time is exactly 350 seconds. The performance with a heavy background workload clearly demonstrates the isolation provided by page coloring.

5. RELATED WORK

5.1 Software Cache Partitioning

Page coloring [31] was first introduced as a way to manage shared caches on multicore processors in [23]. Cho and

		C1	C2(C6.WIN=3)	C4	C6.WIN=1	C6.WIN=5
Selective Moving	EXP(1)	(4,8,44,8)	(8,16,28,12)	(4,16,40,4)	-	-
	EXP(2)	(4,12,40,8)	(16,12,24,12)	(4,16,40,4)	-	-
	EXP(3)	(4,8,44,8)	(12,12,28,12)	(4,16,40,4)	-	-
Redistribution	EXP(1)	(4,12,40,8)	(12,16,28,8)	(4,16,40,4)	(8,12,28,16)	(16,8,28,12)
	EXP(2)	(4,12,40,8)	(8,16,28,12)	(4,16,40,4)	(12,16,28,8)	(16,12,28,8)
	EXP(3)	(4,12,40,8)	(12,12,28,12)	(4,16,40,4)	(16,16,28,4)	(12,12,28,12)

Table 5: Stable-State Color Assignments (povray, tonto, omnetpp, gamess)

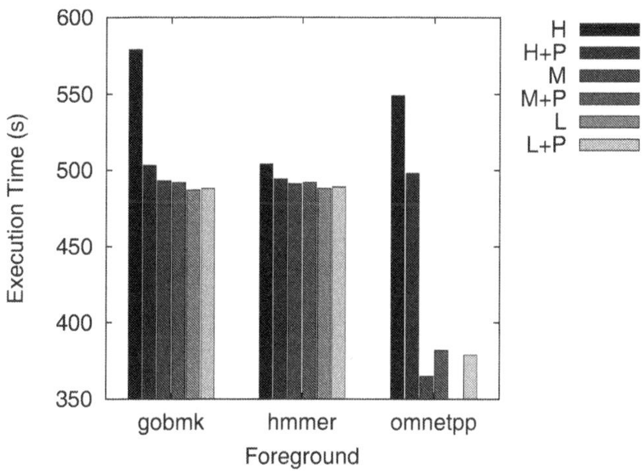

Figure 11: Page Coloring with Cache Slices

Jin [6] applied page coloring to a multicore system with a distributed shared cache, with the goal to place data in cache slices that are closer to the CPU running the target application. Tam et al [29] implemented static page coloring in a prototype Linux system.

Lin et al [14] later investigated recoloring policies for fully committed systems, having the same number of co-running workloads as cores. While these policies can be applied to a 2-core platform, their complexity grows exponentially as the number of cores increases. Moreover, page hotness [35] is ignored when picking pages for recoloring, leading to inefficient use of newly assigned colors when all recolored pages are barely accessed. Using hot pages can effectively reduce the number of pages to be recolored, but it pays additional overhead from hotness identification.

Recent cache management work has attempted to divide the cache into different usages. Soares et al [24] determined cache-unfriendly pages via online profiling and mapped them to a pollute buffer, which is a small portion of the cache. Lu et al [16] let a user-level allocator cooperate with a kernel page allocator to provide object-level cache partitioning, in which the partitions are decided offline. The basic idea is to force user-level data structures with weak locality to use a reserved part of the cache, while other data structures use the rest.

Another interesting work proposed an SRM-Buffer [7], which reduces cache interference from kernel address space. In systems like Linux, the page cache usually occupies a significant amount of memory – one burst of accesses to it may incur large-scale cache evictions, hurting application performance. To address this problem, the authors limited the range of page colors that can be used by the Linux page cache during a file IO burst.

5.2 Hardware Cache Partitioning

Unlike software partitioning, which divides a shared cache among applications, hardware partitioning usually assigns different sections of cache to different cores. Way partitioning [5, 21, 28] and block partitioning [27] are the two common approaches for partitioning a shared cache. Way partitioning restricts cache replacement for a core to a specific set of ways in an n-way set-associative cache. Block partitioning enforces partitions within individual sets. Rafique et al [20] developed a loose form of block partitioning, which only limits the total number of cache lines each core can occupy. Others [10, 22] partitioned cache blocks statistically, allowing minor interference while retaining cache occupancies. A hybrid approach was proposed by Mancuso et al [17], which combines page coloring with way partitioning, effectively turning a shared LLC into scratchpad memory [1] for a fixed set of hot data. Srikantaiah et al [25] argued that cache partitions should be assigned to CPU sets instead of individual CPUs, facilitating constructive sharing for multi-threaded applications. Current trends also favor the design of configurable or hybrid (private/shared) caches [2, 8, 9, 15, 18, 36], which assign cache slices for different uses.

5.3 Cache Utility Curves

Cache utility curves provide a rich set of information to determine the optimal-sized cache partitions. Zhou et al [37] described a software approach to generate miss-rate curves (MRCs) online. The approach maintains an LRU page list for each address space. Page accesses are determined by either periodically scanning page table entries or clearing present bits of entries and causing page faults. Tam et al [30] built RapidMRC by using a sampled data address register (SDAR) available on the PowerPC to record all addresses of memory requests over sampled periods. In other work on cache-aware fair and efficient scheduling (CAFÉ [33]), utility curves were generated through online cache occupancy modeling.

Finally, there has been work focused on the development of new hardware to construct utility curves. Suh et al [26] proposed way counters and set counters for computing the marginal reduction in cache misses as cache space shrinks. However, their approach requires an application to run on its own, with access to the entire cache, in order to accumulate utility data. To overcome this limitation, Qureshi and Patt [19] implemented the UMON monitoring circuit, which acts like a copy of the cache. UMON collects complete utility data when only a portion of the cache is allowed for access, regardless of contention from other cores.

6. CONCLUSIONS AND FUTURE WORK

On multicore platforms, processes compete for a shared last-level cache, causing conflict misses and performance variations. COLORIS addresses this problem by extending traditional OSes with static and dynamic cache partitioning capabilities. In the static scheme, COLORIS exclusively assigns different page colors to processes on different cores. In the dynamic scheme, a Cache Utilization Monitor measures application cache usage online and triggers re-partitioning to satisfy QoS demands of individual applications. To achieve efficient re-partitioning, two page selection policies are described: *Selective Moving* and *Redistribution*. When applied to over-committed systems, COLORIS tries to maintain good cache isolation amongst processes, attempting to minimize cache interference, by carefully managing page colors in a Page Color Manager. Our experimental results show that COLORIS is able to reduce the performance variation due to co-running workload interference by up to 39%, and successfully provides QoS for memory-bound applications.

COLORIS supports dynamic partitioning in systems that are over-committed. In such cases, COLORIS allows a limited amount of sharing of page colors with application processes on remote cores. The performance of COLORIS is at least as good as vanilla Linux implementations for heavily over-committed situations, while significantly outperforming vanilla Linux for cases where the system is less loaded.

Future work will investigate cache-aware scheduling algorithms that cooperate with COLORIS, as we attempt to eliminate cache conflict misses by different workloads altogether. In particular, we will investigate ways to provide hard guarantees on the isolation between workloads, which is important for real-time applications with deadlines. In addition to cache contention, we will also consider factors such as shared memory buses and NUMA interconnects on multi-socket and manycore architectures [3].

7. ACKNOWLEDGMENTS

This material is based upon work supported by the National Science Foundation under Grant No. 1117025. Any opinions, findings, and conclusions or recommendations expressed in this material are those of the author(s) and do not necessarily reflect the views of the National Science Foundation.

8. REFERENCES

[1] R. Banakar, S. Steinke, B.-S. Lee, M. Balakrishnan, and P. Marwedel. Scratchpad memory: Design alternative for cache on-chip memory in embedded systems. In *Proceedings of the 10th International Symposium on Hardware/Software Codesign*, CODES '02, pages 73–78, New York, NY, USA, 2002.

[2] N. Beckmann and D. Sanchez. Jigsaw: Scalable software-defined caches. In *Proceedings of the 22nd International Conference on Parallel Architectures and Compilation Techniques*, pages 213–224, Piscataway, NJ, USA, 2013.

[3] B. K. Bray, W. L. Lunch, and M. J. Flynn. Page allocation to reduce access time of physical caches. Technical report, Stanford, CA, USA, 1990.

[3]COLORIS source code is available upon request.

[4] E. Bugnion, J. M. Anderson, T. C. Mowry, M. Rosenblum, and M. S. Lam. Compiler-directed page coloring for multiprocessors. In *Proceedings of the 7th International Conference on Architectural Support for Programming Languages and Operating Systems*, pages 244–255, New York, NY, USA, 1996.

[5] D. Chiou, P. Jain, L. Rudolph, and S. Devadas. Application-specific memory management for embedded systems using software-controlled caches. In *Proceedings of the 37th Annual Design Automation Conference*, pages 416–419, New York, NY, USA, 2000.

[6] S. Cho and L. Jin. Managing distributed, shared L2 caches through OS-level page allocation. In *Proceedings of the 39th Annual IEEE/ACM International Symposium on Microarchitecture*, pages 455–468, Washington, DC, USA, 2006.

[7] X. Ding, K. Wang, and X. Zhang. SRM-buffer: an OS buffer management technique to prevent last level cache from thrashing in multicores. In *Proceedings of the 6th ACM European Conference on Computer Systems*, pages 243–256, New York, NY, USA, 2011.

[8] H. Dybdahl and P. Stenstrom. An adaptive shared/private NUCA cache partitioning scheme for chip multiprocessors. In *Proceedings of the 13th International Symposium on High-Performance Computer Architecture*, pages 2–12, Washington, DC, USA, 2007.

[9] J. Huh, C. Kim, H. Shafi, L. Zhang, D. Burger, and S. W. Keckler. A NUCA substrate for flexible CMP cache sharing. In *Proceedings of the 19th Annual International Conference on Supercomputing*, pages 31–40, New York, NY, USA, 2005.

[10] R. Iyer. CQoS: A framework for enabling QoS in shared caches of CMP platforms. In *Proceedings of the 18th Annual International Conference on Supercomputing*, pages 257–266, New York, NY, USA, 2004.

[11] A. Jaleel, H. H. Najaf-abadi, S. Subramaniam, S. C. Steely, and J. Emer. CRUISE: cache replacement and utility-aware scheduling. In *Proceedings of the 17th International Conference on Architectural Support for Programming Languages and Operating Systems*, pages 249–260, New York, NY, USA, 2012.

[12] R. E. Kessler and M. D. Hill. Page placement algorithms for large real-indexed caches. *ACM Trans. Comput. Syst.*, 10(4):338–359, Nov. 1992.

[13] S. Kim, D. Chandra, and Y. Solihin. Fair cache sharing and partitioning in a chip multiprocessor architecture. In *Proceedings of the 13th International Conference on Parallel Architectures and Compilation Techniques*, October 2004.

[14] J. Lin, Q. Lu, X. Ding, Z. Zhang, X. Zhang, and P. Sadayappan. Gaining insights into multicore cache partitioning: Bridging the gap between simulation and real systems. In *Proceedings of the 14th International Symposium on High-Performance Computer Architecture*, pages 367–378, 2008.

[15] C. Liu, A. Sivasubramaniam, and M. Kandemir. Organizing the last line of defense before hitting the memory wall for CMPs. In *Proceedings of the 10th*

International Symposium on High-Performance Computer Architecture, pages 176–185, 2004.

[16] Q. Lu, J. Lin, X. Ding, Z. Zhang, X. Zhang, and P. Sadayappan. Soft-OLP: Improving hardware cache performance through software-controlled object-level partitioning. In *Proceedings of the 18th International Conference on Parallel Architectures and Compilation Techniques*, pages 246–257, 2009.

[17] R. Mancuso, R. Dudko, E. Betti, M. Cesati, M. Caccamo, and R. Pellizzoni. Real-time cache management framework for multi-core architectures. In *Proceedings of the 19th Real-Time and Embedded Technology and Applications Symposium*, pages 45–54, 2013.

[18] R. Manikantan, K. Rajan, and R. Govindarajan. Nucache: An efficient multicore cache organization based on next-use distance. In *Proceedings of the 17th International Symposium on High-Performance Computer Architecture*, pages 243–253, Feb 2011.

[19] M. K. Qureshi and Y. N. Patt. Utility-based cache partitioning: A low-overhead, high-performance, runtime mechanism to partition shared caches. In *Proceedings of the 39th Annual IEEE/ACM International Symposium on Microarchitecture*, pages 423–432, Washington, DC, USA, 2006.

[20] N. Rafique, W.-T. Lim, and M. Thottethodi. Architectural support for operating system-driven CMP cache management. In *Proceedings of the 15th International Conference on Parallel Architectures and Compilation Techniques*, pages 2–12, New York, NY, USA, 2006.

[21] P. Ranganathan, S. Adve, and N. P. Jouppi. Reconfigurable caches and their application to media processing. In *Proceedings of the 27th Annual International Symposium on Computer Architecture*, pages 214–224, New York, NY, USA, 2000.

[22] D. Sanchez and C. Kozyrakis. Vantage: Scalable and efficient fine-grain cache partitioning. In *Proceedings of the 38th Annual International Symposium on Computer Architecture*, pages 57–68, New York, NY, USA, 2011.

[23] T. Sherwood, B. Calder, and J. Emer. Reducing cache misses using hardware and software page placement. In *Proceedings of the 13th International Conference on Supercomputing*, pages 155–164, New York, NY, USA, 1999.

[24] L. Soares, D. Tam, and M. Stumm. Reducing the harmful effects of last-level cache polluters with an OS-level, software-only pollute buffer. In *Proceedings of the 41st annual IEEE/ACM International Symposium on Microarchitecture*, pages 258–269, Washington, DC, USA, 2008.

[25] S. Srikantaiah, R. Das, A. K. Mishra, C. R. Das, and M. Kandemir. A case for integrated processor-cache partitioning in chip multiprocessors. In *Proceedings of the Conference on High-Performance Computing Networking, Storage and Analysis*, pages 6:1–6:12, New York, NY, USA, 2009.

[26] G. E. Suh, S. Devadas, and L. Rudolph. A new memory monitoring scheme for memory-aware scheduling and partitioning. In *Proceedings of the 8th International Symposium on High-Performance Computer Architecture*, pages 117–128, 2002.

[27] G. E. Suh, L. Rudolph, and S. Devadas. Dynamic cache partitioning for simultaneous multithreading systems. In *Proceedings of the IASTED International Conference on Parallel and Distributed Computing and Systems*, pages 116–127, 2001.

[28] G. E. Suh, L. Rudolph, and S. Devadas. Dynamic partitioning of shared cache memory. *J. Supercomput.*, 28(1):7–26, Apr. 2004.

[29] D. Tam, R. Azimi, L. Soares, and M. Stumm. Managing shared L2 caches on multicore systems in software. In *Proceedings of the Workshop on the Interaction between Operating Systems and Computer Architecture*, 2007.

[30] D. K. Tam, R. Azimi, L. B. Soares, and M. Stumm. RapidMRC: Approximating L2 miss rate curves on commodity systems for online optimizations. In *Proceedings of the 14th International Conference on Architectural Support for Programming Languages and Operating Systems*, pages 121–132, New York, NY, USA, 2009.

[31] G. Taylor, P. Davies, and M. Farmwald. The TLB slice–a low-cost high-speed address translation mechanism. In *Proceedings of the 17th Annual International Symposium on Computer Architecture*, pages 355–363, New York, NY, USA, 1990.

[32] R. West, P. Zaroo, C. A. Waldspurger, and X. Zhang. Online cache modeling for commodity multicore processors. *SIGOPS Oper. Syst. Rev.*, 44(4):19–29, Dec. 2010.

[33] R. West, P. Zaroo, C. A. Waldspurger, and X. Zhang. CAFÉ: Cache-aware fair and efficient scheduling for CMPs. In *Multicore Technology: Architecture, Reconfiguration and Modeling*. CRC Press, 2013.

[34] Y. Xie and G. Loh. Dynamic classification of program memory behaviors in CMPs. In *the 2nd Workshop on Chip Multiprocessor Memory Systems and Interconnects*, 2008.

[35] X. Zhang, S. Dwarkadas, and K. Shen. Towards practical page coloring-based multicore cache management. In *Proceedings of the 4th ACM European Conference on Computer Systems*, pages 89–102, New York, NY, USA, 2009.

[36] L. Zhao, R. Iyer, M. Upton, and D. Newell. Towards hybrid last level caches for chip-multiprocessors. *SIGARCH Comput. Archit. News*, 36(2):56–63, May 2008.

[37] P. Zhou, V. Pandey, J. Sundaresan, A. Raghuraman, Y. Zhou, and S. Kumar. Dynamic tracking of page miss ratio curve for memory management. In *Proceedings of the 11th International Conference on Architectural Support for Programming Languages and Operating Systems*, pages 177–188, New York, NY, USA, 2004.

PEMOGEN: Automatic Adaptive Performance Modeling during Program Runtime

Arnamoy Bhattacharyya
ETH Zurich
arnamoy.bhattacharyya@inf.ethz.ch

Torsten Hoefler
ETH Zurich
htor@inf.ethz.ch

ABSTRACT

Traditional means of gathering performance data are tracing, which is limited by the available storage, and profiling, which has limited accuracy. Performance modeling is often used to interpret the tracing data and generate performance predictions. We aim to complement the traditional data collection mechanisms with online performance modeling, a method that generates performance models while the application is running. This allows us to greatly reduce the storage overhead while still producing accurate predictions. We present PEMOGEN, our compilation and modeling framework that automatically instruments applications to generate performance models during program execution. We demonstrate the ability of PEMOGEN to both reduce storage cost and improve the prediction accuracy compared to traditional techniques such as least squares fitting. With our tool, we automatically detect 3,370 kernels from fifteen NAS and Mantevo applications and model their execution time with a median coefficient of variation ($\bar{R}^2$) of 0.81. These automatically generated performance models can be used to quickly assess the scaling and potential bottlenecks with regards to any input parameter and the number of processes of a parallel application.

1. INTRODUCTION

Performance analysis is the bread and butter of performance engineers. The optimization process can often be divided into performance data collection, interpretation to find bottlenecks, and code changes to overcome those bottlenecks. The first step, data collection, typically utilizes application tracing or profiling. The collected data is then analyzed with the help of performance tools. Performance engineers derive mental models at various complexities ranging from back-of-the-envelope to highly complex performance models to represent application performance. Those models then guide the tuning of the target application code, for example, algorithmic optimizations, architecture optimization, middleware and runtime optimization, or policy optimization.

Various offline machine-learning techniques such as Neural networks or Support Vector Machines (SVM) have been used to build predictor models that can be used to extrapolate or interpolate application performance and scaling based on trace data [26]. However, most of the machine learning predictor models used so far are complex functions consisting of many model parameters, making the models hard to interpret. The generation of machine learning models needs sufficiently much training data. The gathering of the huge amount of training data comes with two costs: (1) a series of training runs has to be performed that might not be feasible for long-running HPC application, and (2) the storage space of the profiling data can be potentially huge.

Only a small number of tools support performance modeling to help the user to guide decisions and predict bottlenecks outside the executed configurations [7]. Semi-empirical performance modeling [19] is used to generate interpretable performance models that can be presented to users so that they can estimate how the program's performance changes with the change in values of the input parameters. Optimizing compilers can also use the generated models to guide decisions. Empirical or semi-empirical performance models work in a similar fashion to the machine-learning techniques in the sense that the performance models of the kernels are built after collecting the training data offline [7] and therefore also suffer from storage cost.

In this work, we propose to automatically *learn* performance models during normal application execution to eliminate storage costs and reduce runtime overheads. We develop a tool that automatically instruments applications for modeling and a runtime library for performance modeling based on advances in online statistical learning methods. Our generated binaries are completely self-contained and fully equipped for automatic model generation. The data collection and generation can be controlled by the user and is stopped once the models reach a specified quality. An overview of our tool-chain is shown in Figure 1. We now briefly discuss LASSO, a statistical technique that can be used to generate interpretable models.

Least absolute shrinkage and selection operator (LASSO).

is a statistical technique to generate interpretable regression models by eliminating parameters that are not significant in the model construction. Recently, Garrigues et al. [14] proposed a homotopy algorithm to use LASSO in an

PACT'14, August 24–27, 2014, Edmonton, AB, Canada.

ACM 978-1-4503-2809-8/14/08 ...$15.00.
http://dx.doi.org/10.1145/2628071.2628100 .

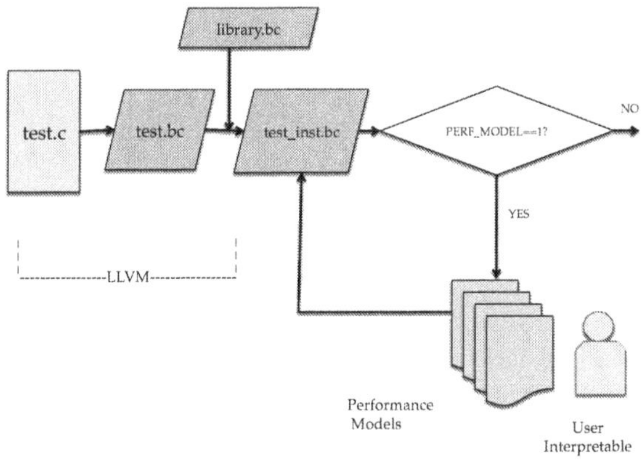

Figure 1: Work-flow of PEMOGEN. The code is compiled and instrumented using LLVM [25]. Based on the value of an environment variable PERF_MODEL, the instrumented code generates the performance models for kernels. The generated models can again be read by the code for model update and/or prediction.

online setting so that the model update can be performed as new data arrives one at a time. We show how to use their algorithm to build an application performance model automatically and transparently from the user. The user has to only supply the names of the input parameters that influence the execution time of a program and the desired threshold for goodness of fit of the generated model(s). A subset of the program input parameters become the parameters of the generated model. These two information are required because identifying the model parameters require knowledge from the domain expert and it's impossible to predict the accuracy of the performance model required by the user.

Research Contribution.

Our contributions to the state of the art are as follows:

- We propose a new static representation of the program called the Loop-Call Graph (LCG) that helps to automatically identify the *kernels* in the application.
- We propose a methodology for adaptive model generation so that the profiling and model update can be turned on and off automatically based on the goodness of fit (adjusted R^2) of the generated performance model on new data.
- We combine these two techniques into PEMOGEN, an automatic tool to generate interpretable performance models dynamically and transparently from the user.
- We present the results of model generation for the kernels in the NAS and Mantevo benchmarks.

2. METHODOLOGY

Automatically generating human-understandable performance models for codes involves several steps: (1) kernel identification, (2) identifying critical input parameters, (3) collect performance data, and (4) select and parameterize model hypotheses. Those steps are similar to but not identical to the manual steps proposed in earlier research [18,19]. We will now describe each of these steps in detail.

2.1 Automatic Identification of Kernels

The first step before building a performance model automatically is to determine the portions in the program for which the performance models have to be generated. These program portions are called *kernels*. The cumulative performance of all the *kernels* gives an estimate of the performance of the program for a set of program parameter values.

For the identification of *kernels*, we consider well defined program structures: natural *loops* and *functions*. We define a new static graph representation of the program called a *Loop-Call Graph (LCG)*. If a program P has a set of functions $F = (f_1, f_2, \ldots, f_{n_1})$ and a set of loops $L = (l_1, l_2, \ldots, l_{n_2})$, then the LCG is a directed graph that can be formally defined as:

DEFINITION 1. *An LCG is a graph* $G = \langle V, E\rangle$ *where*

- $V = F \cup L$
- $E = (e_1, e_2, \ldots, e_{n_3})$ *where* $e_i = (v_1, v_2) \wedge v_1, v_2 \in V$

Where (v_1, v_2) means that control flows from v_1 to v_2. We use the LCG to aid the dynamic construction of *kernels* for different call sites and contexts. We define kernel as:

DEFINITION 2. *A kernel* k *is a sub-graph* $G' = \langle V', E'\rangle$ *of the LCG* G *where*

- $V' \subseteq V$
- $E' \subseteq E \wedge ((v_1, v_2) \in E' \Rightarrow v_1, v_2 \in V')$

Each *kernel* is constructed from the dynamic call-chain starting from the entry point of the program. A kernel is composed of a subset of nodes of the LCG that are connected by a dynamic calling relation, denoted as $\rightarrow$, in the program.

To illustrate how we construct the LCG, consider the following pseudocode:

```
int my_func() {
        for(...) S1;
}
int main() {
        for(...) my_func();
        for(...) S2;
        my_func();
}
```

S1 and S2 are arbitrary sets of statements that do not contain additional loops. Figure 2 shows the LCG of this code.

This program has a set of functions $F = (a, b)$, and a set of loops $L = (a_1, a_2, b_1)$. Where 'a' and 'b' represent 'main' and 'my_func', respectively, and a_i denotes the ith loop in function a. A specific execution of our example program may lead to the following set of kernels at runtime: $K = \{(a), (a \rightarrow a_1), (a \rightarrow a_1 \rightarrow b), (a \rightarrow a_1 \rightarrow b \rightarrow b_1), (a \rightarrow b), (a \rightarrow b \rightarrow b_1), (a \rightarrow a_2)\}$.

2.2 Values of Model Parameters

After all kernels have been identified, the next step is to identify the input parameters that should be used to build a performance model for a specific kernel. The first task is to assemble a list of all input parameters that influence the

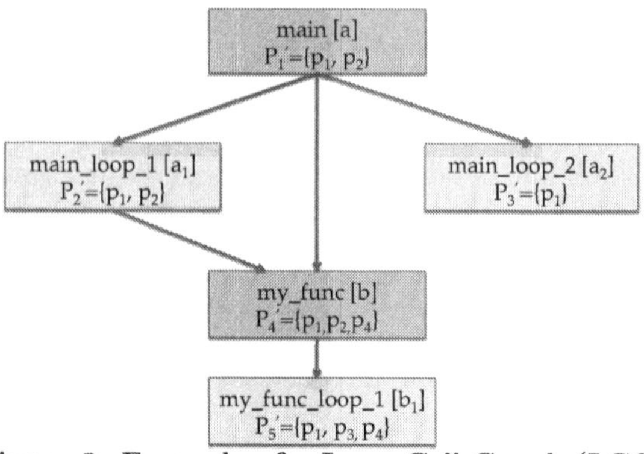

Figure 2: Example of a Loop Call Graph (LCG).

runtime of the application. We call such parameters *critical (input) parameters* [19].

Critical parameters should be scalar values such as sizes of dimensions or number of iterations. If the execution time of the program is determined by an input file or a vector, then it should be condensed into the smallest number of scalar critical parameters (e.g., if the input file is a sparse matrix, the critical parameter could be the number of non-zero elements in the matrix). A domain expert has to determine the complete set of parameters and supply them to PEMOGEN. We identify the set of parameters as $P = (p_1, p_2, \dots, p_n)$.

Not all parameters may influence each kernel. Thus, PEMOGEN relates the specified parameters to the source code and uses static analysis to determine the parameters $P_i' \subseteq P$ that influence the runtime of each specific kernel k_i. PEMOGEN performs pointer analysis to construct use-def chains [3] from all statements in each function and loop in V and checks which critical parameters are used. It conservatively adds the parameter to the parameter set P_i' for may-dependencies. Finally, we use the following maps from each kernel to its parameter set during runtime to collect the profile $f_i : k_i \leftarrow P_i'$, $0 < i < |K|$.

The profiled dynamic value of the input parameters and the static mapping information between the kernels and their parameter sets are used in the construction of performance models of kernels.

2.3 Target Metrics

Our tool can generate kernel models for various metrics such as hardware performance counters, the number of messages communicated, the size of messages communicated, and the execution time. Without loss of generality, We choose to present the absolute execution time [16]. It is often the noisiest metric and thus the most challenging one for any modeling algorithm. The absolute execution time is the time elapsed for the execution of instructions that are parts of nested kernel. For example, in Figure 2, while calculating the absolute execution time of the kernel $a \to b$, we do not include the execution time of the kernel $a \to b \to b_1$ though they are nested.

2.4 Dynamic Construction of Performance Models

Shrinkage is a method in statistics where a penalty is applied to the coefficients of the regression predictor model and thus the coefficients values are shrunk to bring them close to zero. Shrinkage techniques are useful in cases where there is high correlation between the model parameters or in cases where some parameters cause the model to overfit. By selecting the parameter that best describe the model, these shrinkage methods often result in better prediction accuracy. Ridge regression technique [22] adds a L_2 penalty to the coefficients and thus shrunk the coefficients of models close to '0' but does not shrink any coefficient to '0' and therefore cannot eliminate any parameter. Therefore, although the ridge regression technique builds model with better prediction accuracy, the generated models are not different from the ordinary least square regression in terms of user interpretability.

By adding a L_1-penalty to the regression coefficients, the *Least absolute shrinkage and selection operator* (LASSO) technique [36] bridges the gap between user interpretability and prediction accuracy of the generated models. Due to the ability of LASSO in the generation of interpretable models, the LASSO method generated significant interest in statistics [9, 36], signal processing [10, 13] and machine learning [17, 31] communities.

We utilize the recently developed online version of the Least Absolute Shrinkage and Selection Operator (LASSO) method. We call this method oLASSO in the remainder of this paper.

First, we describe the regular (offline) LASSO briefly: LASSO assigns an L_1 penalty to the coefficients of input parameters (predictors) which leads to sparse solutions and thus achieves results that are easier to interpret. LASSO accepts n training examples or observations $(y_i, x_{ij}) \in \mathbb{R} \times \mathbb{R}^m$, $i = (1, 2, \dots, n)$ and $j = (1, 2, \dots, m)$. We assume we have m input parameters for the model. Here y is the performance metric we want to model and x is the set of input parameters. We wish to fit a linear model to predict the response y_i as a function of x_{ij} and a feature vector $\theta \in \mathbb{R}^m, y_i = x_i^T\theta + v_i$, where v_i represents the noise in the observation. The LASSO optimization problem is given by

$$\min_{\theta} \frac{1}{2} \sum_{i=1}^{n} (x_i^T\theta - y_i)^2 + \mu_n \|\theta\|_1 \tag{1}$$

where μ_n is a regularization parameter. The solution of Equation 1 is typically sparse, i.e. the solution θ has few entries that are non-zero, and therefore identifies which dimensions in x_i are useful to predict the response y_i. The original LASSO proposal [36] did not have the additional $\frac{1}{2}$ multiplied with the first term of Equation (1). It was later shown that the LASSO problem is equivalent to the Basis Pursuit Denoising (BPDN) optimization problem which needs the multiplier $\frac{1}{2}$. Also BPDN representation of LASSO makes it algorithmically easier to solve. LASSO is particularly useful in our case because LASSO is used in cases where the number of observations is less than the number of predictor variables and it generates a model that is more interpretable than Ordinary Least Square Regression [8] or Ridge Regression [22].

The offline LASSO algorithm works on a set of precomputed observations (training data). To use LASSO in an online fashion, we choose a homotopy algorithm proposed by Garrigues et al. [14]. Following this algorithm, the model is updated as dynamic training data $(y_i, x_{ij})_{i=1,\dots,n}$ arrive one at a time. Let $\theta^{(n)}$ be the solution of the LASSO after observing n training examples and $\theta^{(n+1)}$ the solution after observing a new dynamic data point $(y_{n+1}, x_{n+1,j}) \in \mathbb{R} \times \mathbb{R}^m$.

Let $X \in \mathbb{R}^{n \times m}$ be a matrix whose i^{th} row is equal to x_i^T and $y = (y_1, \ldots, y_n)^T$, they introduce the following optimization problem that allows them to compute a homotopy from θ^n to θ^{n+1}:

$$\theta(t, \mu) = \underset{\theta}{\operatorname{argmin}} \frac{1}{2} \left\| \begin{pmatrix} X \\ tx_{n+1}^T \end{pmatrix} \theta - \begin{pmatrix} y \\ ty_{n+1} \end{pmatrix} \right\|_2^2 + \mu \|\theta\|_1 \quad (2)$$

The algorithm computes a path from $\theta^{(n)}$ to $\theta^{(n+1)}$ in two steps where $\theta^{(n)} = \theta(0, \mu_n)$ and $\theta^{(n+1)} = \theta(1, \mu_{n+1})$.

1. Vary the regularization parameter from μ_n to μ_{n+1} with $t = 0$. This amounts to computing a piecewise linear regularization path between μ_n to μ_{n+1} [11, 29, 32].

2. Vary the parameter t from 0 to 1 with $\mu_n = \mu_{n+1}$.

The solution of the LASSO problem can be computed once the active set (the indices in θ that have non-zero coefficients) and signs of the coefficients are known [14]. Therefore the intuition behind the two-step algorithm is to discover the active set and signs of the coefficients for computing $\theta^{(n+1)}$ at $t = 1$. For achieving this, the algorithm starts with the active set and signs available at $t = 0$, which is essentially calculated using LARS (step 1). Then the algorithm continues until a 'transition point' (value of t where the active set changes). At this point, the necessary updates to the active set and signs of the coefficients are met. These procedure iteratively continues until $t = 1$. Next the solution $\theta^{(n+1)}$ can be computed using the final active set and signs of the coefficients at $t = 1$.

2.5 Selection of the regularization parameter

The amount of regularization depends indeed on the variance of the noise present in the data which is not known a priori. It is therefore not obvious how to determine the amount of regularization. We use Garrigues' algorithm for choosing the best regularization parameter as new data arrives [14]. The algorithm uses $\mu_n = n\lambda_n$ such that λ_n is the weighting factor between the average mean squared error and the l_1-norm. The algorithm selects λ_n in a data-driven manner. The problem with n observations is given by:

$$\theta(\lambda) = \underset{\theta}{\operatorname{argmin}} \frac{1}{2n} \sum_{i=1}^{n} (x_i^T \theta - y_i)^2 + \lambda \|\theta\|^2 \quad (3)$$

As $\theta(\lambda)$ is piecewise linear, therefore its gradient can be computed unless λ is a transition point. If $err(\lambda) = (x_{n+1}^T \theta(\lambda) - y_{n+1})^2$ is the error on the new observation. they update to select λ_{n+1} is as follows:

$$\log \lambda_{n+1} = \log \lambda_n - \eta \frac{\partial err}{\partial \log \lambda}(\lambda_n) \quad (4)$$

$$\Rightarrow \lambda_{n+1} = \lambda_n \times \exp\left\{2n\eta x_{n+1,1}^T (X_1^T X_1)^{-1} v_1 (x_{n+1}^T \theta_1 - y_{n+1})\right\} \quad (5)$$

where the solution after n observations corresponding to the regularization parameter λ_n is given by and $v_1 = sign(\theta_1)$. Therefore the new observation is used as a test set, which allows the update of the regularization parameter before introducing the new observation by varying t from 0 to 1. The update is performed in the *log* domain to ensure that λ_n is always positive.

3. IMPLEMENTATION

PEMOGEN is implemented using LLVM [25] for performing the LCG construction and instrumentation. Figure 1 describes the execution flow of a program instrumented by PEMOGEN. The user can enable or disable the model generation by setting an environment variable. The model generation works transparently during the program runtime and the generated models for kernels are stored in a file that can be consulted by either the user or a performance monitoring and optimization system. In addition, following executions of the instrumented binary can also read the file to refine the model further.

3.1 Kernel Identification and Instrumentation

PEMOGEN uses the middle end of LLVM to analyze the intermediate representation (IR) of the program to build the LCG. Natural loops and functions are well-formed structures in the LLVM IR. After the identification of LCG nodes, PEMOGEN instruments the IR to prepare the IR for data collection of the intended metric. We implement the data collection functionality in a library that is automatically linked to the generated program executable.

Optionally, PEMOGEN can output the LCG in the dot graph language for visualization. If the program is compiled with debug information, the generated LCG contains code information such as source code file name and line number. This is particularly useful to map the kernels to the source code to identify specific latent performance problems.

3.2 Parameter Specification

The scalar model parameters have to be supplied by a domain expert. An LLVM pass instruments the source code so that the values of the model parameters are captured dynamically. The parameters can be of different types:

- **A member of a structure**: In this case, the parameter name has to be supplied along with the structure name.

- **A local variable in a function**: In this case, the parameter name has to be supplied along with the function name.

- **A global variable or a macro**: In this case, the parameter name is sufficient.

We use the following EBNF for the parameter file:

$$\begin{array}{rcl} \langle\text{file}\rangle & \models & \langle\text{line}\rangle\ \langle\text{newline}\rangle \mid \langle\text{line}\rangle \\ \langle\text{line}\rangle & \models & \langle\text{word}\rangle\ \langle\text{space}\rangle\ \langle\text{flag}\rangle\ \langle\text{space}\rangle\ \langle\text{word}\rangle \\ \langle\text{flag}\rangle & \models & \langle 0\rangle \mid \langle 1\rangle \mid \langle 2\rangle \mid \langle 3\rangle \\ \langle\text{word}\rangle & \models & \langle\text{wchar}\rangle\ \langle\text{word}\rangle \mid \langle\text{wchar}\rangle \\ \langle\text{wchar}\rangle & \models & \langle\text{cchar}\rangle \mid \langle\text{ichar}\rangle \\ \langle\text{cchar}\rangle & \models & \text{A}\ldots\text{Z} \mid \text{a}\ldots\text{z} \mid 0\ldots 9 \\ \langle\text{ichar}\rangle & \models & \_ \end{array}$$

Each line contains three tokens: The first token is the parameter name as in the source code, the second token indicates the type of parameters ('0' for parameter inside structure, '1' for parameter inside function, '2' for global parameter, and '3' for parameter declared as macro), and the third token specifies the context (function name or struct name).

3.3 Mapping of Parameters to Kernels

We now discuss how we determine the set P_i' for each kernel k_i. We assume that the value of critical parameters does not change during program execution. For each specified critical parameter, PEMOGEN finds the statement in the IR that first accesses it. Then it performs a pointer analysis with all the access instructions in the body of each LCG node (a function or a natural loop) to find which kernels use the critical parameter. In the case where the pointer analysis reports a *may point-to* relation, PEMOGEN conservatively adds the name of the parameter in the parameter list of the kernel. PEMOGEN maps parameters to LCG nodes statically during compile time and then uses the static information to aggregate parameter lists for each kernel during runtime.

For parameters defined as macros, the tool conservatively adds them to the parameter list of all LCG nodes.

3.4 Constructing the oLASSO

PEMOGEN uses a reference implementation of the oLASSO algorithm [29] for constructing the online performance model. It selects the best predictor model from a pool of *model hypotheses*. We extended the Performance Model Normal Form (PMNF) as described by Calotoiu et al. [7] to use it with more than one parameter. Our Extended PMNF (EPMNF) for a parameter set P is given as:

$$f(P) = \sum_{i=1}^{|P|} \sum_{k=1}^{n} c_i . p_i^{j_{ik}} \log_2^{l_{ik}}(p_i) \tag{6}$$

This representation is, of course, not exhaustive, but proved practical in most scenarios since it is a consequence of how most computer algorithms are designed. A possible assignment of all c_{ik}, j_{ik} and l_{ik} in an EPMNF expression is called a *model hypothesis*.

The oLASSO method calculates the coefficients for each candidate model hypothesis. In this way, a number of coefficient vectors, one for each model hypothesis is generated. When a new measured value arrives, each model is tested using their goodness of fit on new values. If the goodness of fit of more than one model falls within an acceptable range (the acceptable fitting range, ϵ, has to be specified by the user), the model with fewer parameters is selected and the other models are discarded. If the selected model's fit goes above the acceptable range, we start building the whole set of model hypothesis again and continue updating them until we find a model whose fit falls within the specified ϵ.

3.5 Reducing the Overhead of Model Generation

There can be significant overhead for updating the models for *loops* and *functions* that are called a number of times from a call site. Because in that case, the instrumented code has to call the model update function every time a new data point is generated. This can potentially be a problem for inner loops that may have thousands of iterations.

To have a balance between the collection of data for a metric and model update, we call the model generating function on batches of data points.

3.6 Model Confidence

The model update is enabled or disabled based on the fitting of the generated model on new data and the user-supplied acceptable fitting range ϵ.

We also sample the test data for measuring the fitting. As mentioned in the previous step, the model is updated for a batch of x observations at once instead of calling the model update function each time a new observation is received. The next x data points are used as *test* data and the adjusted R-square (ARS) of the predictions by the model is calculated on the test data:

$$\mathrm{R}^2 \equiv 1 - \frac{\sum_{i=1}^{x}(y_i - f_i)^2}{\sum_{i=1}^{x}(y_i - \bar{y})^2} \tag{7}$$

$$\mathrm{ARS} = \mathrm{R}^2 - (1 - \mathrm{R}^2)\frac{m}{x - m - 1} \tag{8}$$

Where x and m are the test data batch size and number of parameters respectively. If for a program, we can't collect a batch of data points, we keep the metric data temporarily until we have a batch. Still this method has much less storage overhead than other online methods mainly the storage overhead from HPC applications come from *kernels* that run a large number of times, either in parallel or in a loop. But in our technique, that is a favourable case because we do not have to store temporary data for a large number of batches.

We use the state machine shown in Figure 3 to evaluate the confidence of a model hypothesis. We assign counters to each model hypothesis. When the model is built for the first time, the confidence value (counter) is initiated to '0'. With each successful prediction (if ARS $< \epsilon$, where ϵ is supplied by user) the confidence of the model in incremented by one. If the model's fit is above the user defined range, the models confidence in decremented by one. The three states of the

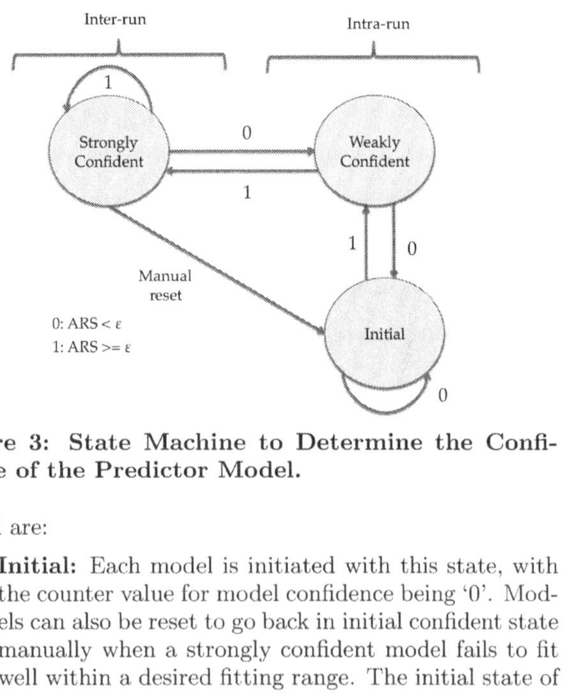

Figure 3: State Machine to Determine the Confidence of the Predictor Model.

model are:

- **Initial:** Each model is initiated with this state, with the counter value for model confidence being '0'. Models can also be reset to go back in initial confident state manually when a strongly confident model fails to fit well within a desired fitting range. The initial state of the model is updated each time a new test data batch arrives within an application run or across application runs (for kernels whose training batch does not reach value x within an application run).

Table 1: Applications from NAS [30] and Mantevo Benchmarks [1] and their input parameters.

Code	Description	Parameters (some abbreviated from original long names)
BT	Block tri-diagonal solver	grid_points(1), grid_points(2), grid_points(3), niter, dt
CG	Conjugate gradient, irregular memory access	na, nonzer, niter, shift
DC	Create data cube views	input_tuples, attrnum, memoryLimit, dim, mnum
EP	Embarrassingly parallel random number generator	m, mk, mm, nn, nk, nq, epsilon, a, s
FT	discrete 3D fast Fourier transform	nx, ny, nz, maxdim, niter_default, ntotal, nxp, nyp, ntotalp
IS	Bucket sorting	{total_keys,max_key,num_buckets}_log_2, max_iters, test_array_size
LU	Lower-upper Gauss-Seidel solver	ipr, inorm, nitmax, dt, omega, tolnwt(1, 2, 3, 4, 5), nx, ny, nz
MG	Multi-grid on a sequence of meshes	lt, nit, nx, ny, nz
SP	Scalar penta-diagonal solver	nx, ny, nz, niter, dt_default
UA	Unstructured adaptive mesh	lelt, lmor, refine_max, fre, niter, nmxh, alpha
Cloverleaf	Compressible Euler solver on a Cartesian grid	states(energy, density, svel, yvel), end_time, end_step, x_cells, y_cells, {x,y}min, {x,y}max, {initial, max}_timestep, timestep_rise
CoMD	Typical computations in molecular dynamics	n{x,y,z}, {x,y,z}proc, nsteps, time_step, initial_{temp,delta}
FE	Proxy application for unstructured finite element codes	nx, ny, nz
MiniGhost	Difference stencil in three dimensional domain	nx, ny, nz, stencil, num_vars, perc_sum, num_sp, error_tol, rep_diff
HPCCG	Approximation of unstructured implicit finite element	nx, ny, nz

- **Weakly Confident:** A initial state of a model hypothesis can become weakly confident when the model hypothesis' counter reaches the value '5'. We have found this value gives a good balance between model hypothesis updation overhead and keeping the ARS of the model within the user defined range for the set of benchmarks used. This state is also used within an application run to determine the confidence within a run.
- **Strongly confident:** In this state, the model updation as well as data collection for the *kernel* is turned off. Using this state gives us a change to optimize the data collection and model update overhead. We show the effect of this optimization in Section 4.6. The strongly confident state is an inter-run measure of confidence and therefore we keep a separate counter for the strongly confident state information. After the execution of the program with a certain set of parameter values, the strongly confidence counter of all the model hypotheses in weakly confident state is incremented by one. Once the strong confidence counter reaches the value '10', the model hypothesis goes to strongly confident state, where both the data collection and update is turned off. Of course using this method, the *kernels* whose behaviour largely varies according to different input parameter values can't be modeled. But while determining the performance of a program, the performance model of these *kernels* can be assumed to have any value for estimation.

There is another well known metric for determining model confidence, which is called root mean squared error (RMSE). But we did not use RMSE because by using ARS, we had an interpretable fit of the model on new data and could determine how good the built model is. As the kernels that have largely fluctuating behaviour for different parameter values are not targeted by our technique, the ARS on new data gives an estimate of the generated model's confidence in predicting the performance of non-fluctuating kernels.

4. EXPERIMENTAL EVALUATION

We applied PEMOGEN to the NAS parallel benchmarks [30] and the Mantevo benchmarks [1]. Table 1 provides an overview of all test programs and their critical parameters. The instrumented versions of these two benchmarks were run on a Cray XC30 (Piz Daint) supercomputer. Each node has eight Intel SandyBridge CPU cores with 32 GiB memories and one NVIDIA Tesla K20X GPU. All nodes are connected with Cray's Aries network in a Dragonfly topology.

We used the *dragonegg* plugin of LLVM-3.3 to compile Fortran codes. The benchmarks are instrumented using the LLVM compiler and then the binary was generated from the bitcode using the LLVM assembler and the GCC-4.8.2 linker with '-O3' optimization.

For constructing the set of candidate model hypotheses from the EPMNF as described in Section 3.4, we used the following values of $j_{ik} = \{-1, 0, \frac{1}{3}, \frac{1}{2}, 2, \frac{3}{2}, 3\}$ and $l_{ik} = \{0, 1, 2\}$. Using other values for i_k and j_k only increased the model generation overhead but did not increase the prediction accuracy in our benchmarks significantly. For example, if a kernel has two parameters p_1 and p_2 in its parameter set, we would start with the following set of hypothesis functions: $(p_1 + p_2)$, $(\sqrt{p_1} + \sqrt{p_2})$, $\left(\sqrt{p_1^3} + \sqrt{p_2^3}\right)$, $\left(\sqrt{p_2^3}\log^2 p_1 + \sqrt{p_2^3}\log^2 p_2\right), \cdots$, $(\log^2 p_1 + \log^2 p_2)$. Each model hypothesis is a linear combination of the input parameters and we did not consider interaction terms (e.g., p_1/p_2, p_1p_3). This set of candidate pools is not exhaustive for representation of kernels. Again if we had to consider the linear combination of all possible permutations of model hypotheses, the candidate model space for each kernel would become $21m$ where m is the number of parameters. This might cause a huge overhead in model generation in an online setting. Therefore we added one candidate kernel that is formed by the linear combination of the above 21 hypothesis. This gave us to find some interesting terms in the generated models and also took care of the overhead

4.1 Kernel Detection

Table 2 summarizes various application characteristics. It shows the number of statically identified functions and loops and the number of dynamically detected kernels. The context-sensitive kernel detection may lead to a large number of kernels if loops or functions are called from many different contexts. However, our results show that for the benchmarks considered, the maximum number of kernels discovered is 664 for the application UA from the NAS benchmarks, indicating a lesser number of different call sites for functions that contain a large number of loops. Theoretically, the number of kernels could vary depending on the input. We did not observe any such variation in our experiments.

Table 2: Number of functions ("Func"), loops, kernels ("Ker"), and parameters ("Par") for all benchmarks. Column "Zero" shows how many parameters were shrunk to zero (on average) by oLASSO and "Trace" shows the required storage in GiB for offline model generation.

Code	Func	Loops	Ker	Par	Zero	Trace
BT	28	181	211	6	1	25
CG	16	47	30	5	0	3.4
DC	79	104	178	6	1	12.45
EP	10	9	12	10	3	.75
FT	21	42	39	10	2	14.5
IS	5	16	12	6	3	1.2
LU	27	172	165	14	3	15.6
MG	24	77	98	6	2	14.5
SP	29	250	229	6	2	23.3
UA	75	473	664	8	2	28
Cloverleaf	88	634	645	16	2	25.4
CoMD	135	118	210	11	1	11
FE	546	130	610	6	4	20
MiniGhost	33	114	137	10	5	11
HPCCG	114	28	130	4	0	8

4.2 Experimental Design

We perform two experiments for each code: First, we collect the data during the execution to perform ordinary least squares (OLS) and the standard (offline) LASSO, called fLASSO in the following. In the second run, we utilize PEMOGEN to compute the parameters using oLASSO during the application run. For OLS and fLASSO, we used the `lm` [8] and `glmnet` [12] functions implemented in GNU R, respectively.

For obtaining the results of Sections 4.3, 4.4, 4.5, and 4.6, the benchmarks were run with the ten different sets of input parameter values for each of the three regression techniques to generate the performance models. Then, for calculating ARS, we ran the benchmarks with five new sets of parameter values, different from the values used in the training run. All parameters were either chosen from the different classes of NAS benchmarks or by varying the parameters in the input file of Mantevo benchmarks.

We also report the time overhead of running the three regression methods. Results show that the optimization using the state confidence machine as described is Section 3.6 reduced the profiling overhead of oLASSO as compared to the two other methods by halting the execution of kernels whose ARS became greater than user supplied 'ϵ' (we chose the value to be .85).

4.3 Goodness of fit of Performance Models

The LASSO method not only simplifies the generated performance model by shrinking some parameter coefficients to zero, but also it achieves better prediction accuracy than ordinary least square regression (OLS). The lower accuracy of OLS could be due to overfitting if there are correlations between the model parameters or some parameters do not influence the runtime. Especially the second is likely because we include parameters conservatively (cf. Section 3.2).

Figure 4 shows the ARS for all benchmarks and all three methods. We see that oLASSO has always the same or lower ARS than OLS, meaning the models generated by online LASSO have better prediction accuracy. The ARS pattern for both OLS and online LASSO agrees for the kernels in the application. The most significant difference between OLS and online LASSO can be seen in the MiniGhost and EP benchmarks indicating the existence of correlated parameters and and their elimination using LASSO. The ARS of oLASSO is generally very close to that of fLASSO with oLASSO being slightly worse in the general case.

4.4 Parameter Selection

To give an idea about the ability of oLASSO in generating interpretable models, we report the average number of model parameters whose coefficients were shrunk to 0. Table 2 shows the total number of parameters of the applications and the average number of zero-coefficient parameters (column "Zero") in the NAS and Mantevo benchmarks.

There can be various reasons why a parameter's coefficient is shrunk to zero. Either the parameter has high correlation with another parameter or the parameter is not *important* in the generation of the performance model. In the later case OLS will try to still use the parameter and suffer from overfitting. These parameters appear in the parameter set of a kernel because of our conservative approach of adding parameters to the parameter list when either the pointer analysis is unsure of a points-to relation (*may* points-to case) or there is no scope of pointer analysis (macro definitions). Comparing the results in Table 2 and Figure 4, we can see that the average number of parameters whose coefficients are shrunk to zero has a contribution towards the better prediction accuracy of online LASSO in case of benchmarks like EP, IS, FT, and MiniGhost.

4.5 Storage Cost Elimination

A major advantage of an online model generation technique comes from its ability to eliminate the temporary storage cost that is needed to store the profile information for a number of training runs. As the model generation process continues in an incremental fashion as data arrive one at a time, there is no need to keep the data for the previous training runs and then feeding the data to a model generation technique as in the case of regular regression.

The online model generation also eliminates the cost of running the application a number of times to train the generated model with the profile data. The more training runs with different values of the model parameters, the merrier. But it is impossible to explore the whole space of possible values of the model parameters for the generation of a model with a 100% accuracy. Therefore in most cases the training runs are stopped after a desired prediction accuracy of the generated model has been reached. In other words, if the model's ARS is within an acceptable range, the training runs stopped and the application continues to execute without modeling. We chose an ARS range of .85 as an acceptable value for fitting.

In this section we report the required storage cost and the time necessary for training runs for the offline regression techniques (fLASSO and OLS) for the NAS and the Mantevo benchmarks. The storage cost is reported for the ten different sets of parameter values as were used in the previous experiments.

As the number of kernels grows in the program, the storage cost of the profiles also grows. For example, in Table 2,

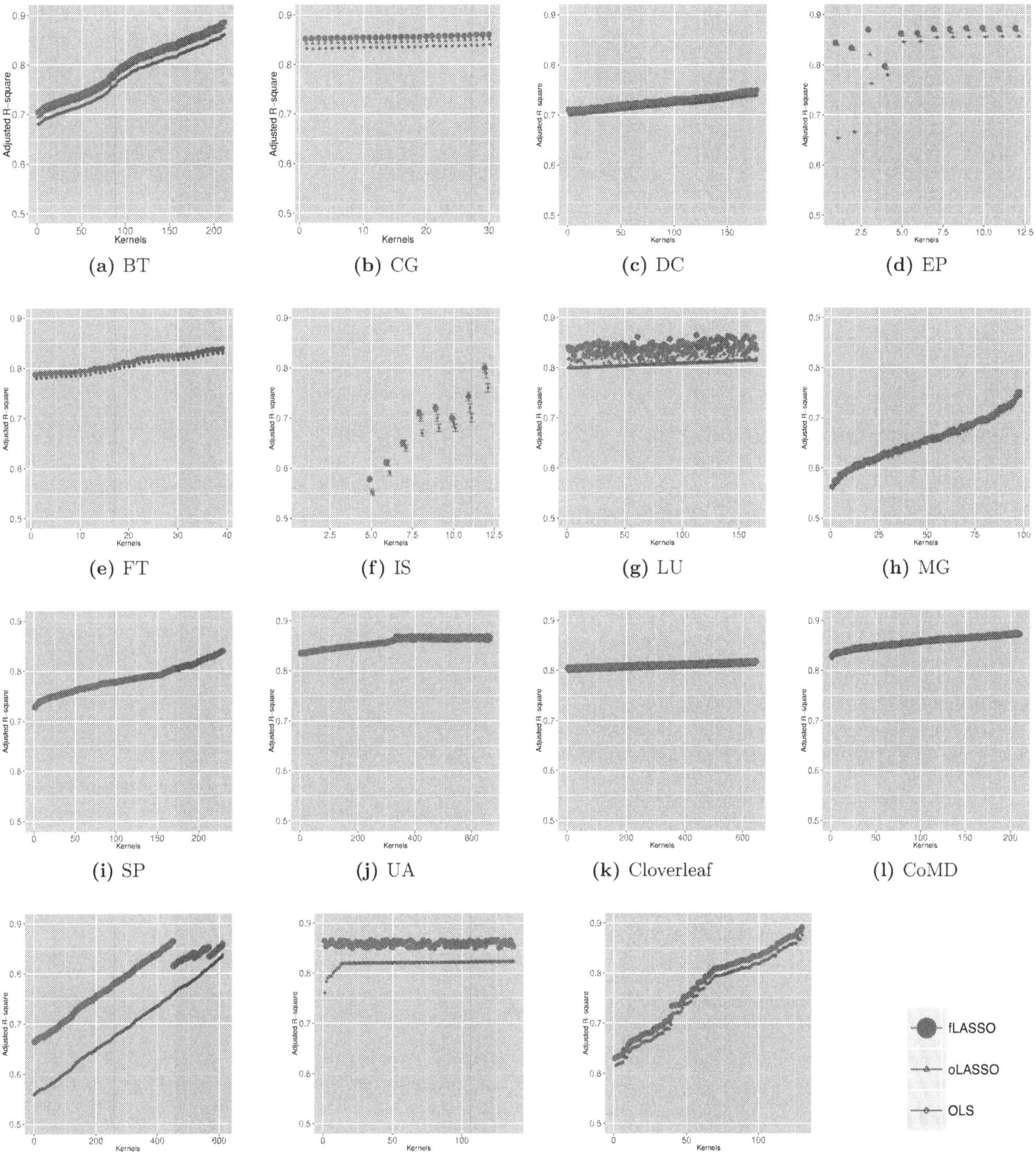

(a) BT (b) CG (c) DC (d) EP

(e) FT (f) IS (g) LU (h) MG

(i) SP (j) UA (k) Cloverleaf (l) CoMD

(m) FE (n) MiniGhost (o) HPCCG

Figure 4: Comparison of predicting performance of oLASSO with OLS and Regular offline LASSO (fLASSO) in terms of their fit on new test data. The 95% confidence interval for the ARS is also included in the figure. The ARS values can range from '0' to '1' and higher is better. The *kernels* are sorted as per the ARS values of OLS along the x-axis.

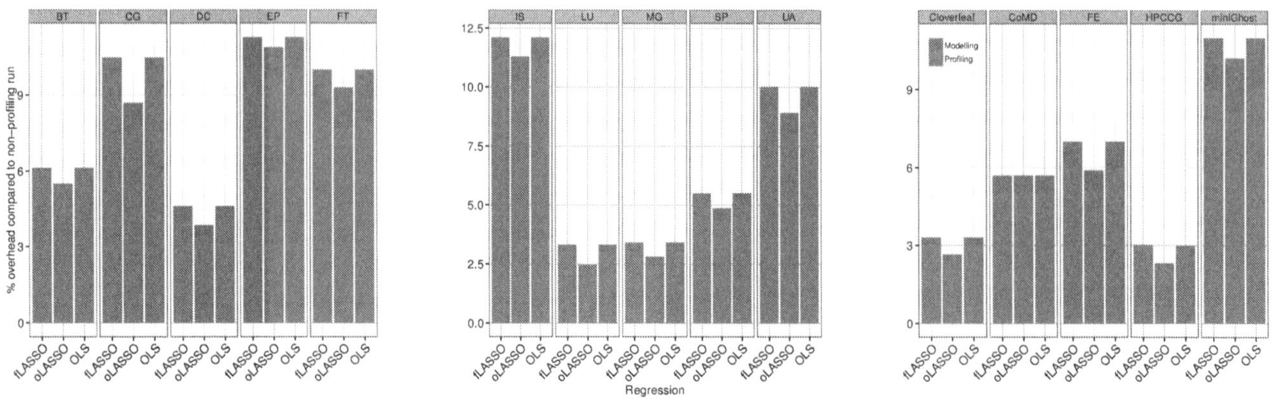

Figure 5: Time Overhead of three LASSO methods. The profiling and model generation time has been shown separately.

UA, *BT*, *Cloverleaf* benchmarks have a huge storage overhead due to the presence of the highest number of kernels. In general, all our offline experiments required between several hundreds of Megabytes and several Gigabytes storage. The oLASSO algorithm requires to store a maximum of $36 \times m$ floating point values and is therefore well suited for online model learning.

4.6 Overheads of Online and Offline Modeling

In this section, we describe the overhead of running the three different regression techniques for model generation. The overhead comes from both profiling and model generation (OLS, fLASSO, oLASSO) and model update (oLASSO). As seen in Figure 5, profiling constitutes a significant portion of the overhead in all the three techniques. The data collection overhead depends both on the number of kernels and the number of times they are executed in the program. The data collection overhead for oLASSO is less than that of the offline techniques due to the use of the confidence-state machine as described in Section 3.6. This optimization allows the overhead of oLASSO being smaller than fLASSO though the model generation overhead of fLASSO sometimes is less than the model generation and update overhead of oLASSO. The computational complexity of oLASSO is $O(d^2)$ where d is the number of active parameters (whose coefficients are non zero) at a step [29]. For the fLASSO, the computational complexity is $O(Nm)$ where N data points are present for m number of input parameters [12]. As the cardinality of the input parameter set is not very high in our case, the model generation overhead for fLASSO did not have a significant advantage over oLASSO.

5. CASE STUDIES

We now present two different case studies, one from NAS and one from the Mantevo benchmarks to illustrate our method in detail.

5.1 IS

IS is a NAS benchmark that implements the bucket sort algorithm. We randomly chose the main iteration loop of the NAS IS benchmark. IS has the following input parameters: `total_keys_log_2` (p_1), `max_key_log_2` (p_2), `num_buckets_log_2` (p_3), `max_iterations` (p_4), `test_array_size` (p_5), and `num_procs` (p_6). First for building the prediction model using oLASSO, we run the benchmarks 25 times with different random combinations of the sets parameter values as follows: p_1=(16, 20, 23, 25), p_2=(10, 16, 19, 21), p_3=(8, 10, 12), p_4=(5, 10, 15, 20), p_5=(15, 20, 22, 25, 28), p_6=(16, 20, 32, 64, 80). The runtime model generated from the 25 runs had the `max_key_log_2` parameter eliminated:

$$T = .004p_1 - 1.01p_3 + 0.04p_4 + 1.107p_5 \log p_5 + \frac{330.45}{p_6} \quad (9)$$

Using the model of Equation (9), we plotted the predictions and the actual execution times using a new set of parameter values: p_1=12, p_3=9, p_4=25, p_5=8 with changing p_6 and p_1=22, p_3=6, p_4=35, p_6=32 with changing p_5. We kept all the parameter values fixed but changed one parameter to observe the predicted and actual trends in the execution times with change in values of that one parameter. We repeat this experiment for the two paramters: number of processors and the `test_array_size`. From Figure 6, the oLASSO generated model was able to predict the performance trend with changing values of both number of processes and `test_array_size`.

5.2 HPCCG

HPCCG is a simple conjugate gradient benchmark that has 4 input parameters: `nx` (p_1), `ny` (p_2), `nz` (p_3), `num_procs` (p_4). For training the model, we ran the benchmark 25 times using random combinations from the following sets of input parameter values: p_1=(16, 32, 64, 100, 110, 120, 800, 1000), p_2=(16, 32, 64, 100, 110, 120, 800, 1000), p_3=(16, 32, 64, 100, 110, 120, 800, 1000), p_4=(8, 16, 32, 64, 128, 256). The generated model for the `ddot` kernel of the HPCCG benchmark in *weak scaling* mode was:

$$T = 0.79p_1 + 0.02p_3 + 1.11\sqrt{p_4}\log p_4 \quad (10)$$

The absence of parameter `ny` can be explained by the fact that function `ddot` works on the current row of the 3-D stencil. The points in the current row of the stencil are skipped in either `nx` or `ny` based on their values. The skipped points in the y-direction accounts for the removal of `ny` from the model. Also as the function operates on rows, the relation with `nz` is much less than that with `nx`.

We used the same method as IS to find out how well the model fits for new data using different sets of input parameter values as are used in training. The values used were p_1=80, p_2=40, p_3=55, with changing p_4 and p_2=14, p_3=125, p_4=32, with changing p_1. For plotting, we kept all the parameter values fixed but varied one parameter at a time. We chose the nx and num_procs parameters for evaluating the model predictions for the HPCCG benchmark. Figure 6 shows the results.

As can be seen from Figure 6, the model was able to successfully fit in the performance trend of the kernel.

6. RELATED WORK

Model-based Simulation is a simulation technique where not each hardware detail is investigated but abstract models are used to determine the runtime or resource consumption. The simulation time can be less than the execution time leading to a "simulation speedup" of several orders of magnitude [21, 37, 41] while still accurately capturing important details of the execution. This technique has been used to discover important performance effects [20], however, it often fails to provide the required insight to understand the root cause of such effects. It is a complex task to execute such simulations in practice such that simulation tools are often only used by computer scientists and not by application developers. Nevertheless, model-based simulation is a very accurate practical and accurate technique to predict large-scale performance.

The use of performance modeling manually has been explored before. Hoefler et al. aimed to popularize performance modeling by defining a simple six-step process to create application performance models [19]. Bauer, Gottlieb, and Hoefler show how to model performance variations using simple statistical tools [5]. They also describe how to measure the influence of certain system parameters such as the network topology.

There are approaches that focus on models generated for a very specific purpose but less on human-readable general-purpose models. For example, Ipek et al. propose multi-layer artificial neural networks to learn application performance [24] and Lee et al. compare different schemes for automated machine-based performance learning and prediction [26]. Zhai, Chen, and Zheng extrapolate single-node performance to complex parallel machines [40]. Wu and Muller [39] extrapolate traces to larger process counts and can thus predict communication operations.

There is also ample research in building performance tools that can hint optimization opportunities. The authors of the Statistical Stall Breakdown [4] describe a mechanism that samples hardware counters and dynamically multiplexes hardware counters to compute a breakdown model for a PowerPC based microprocessor.

The work presented in [23] focuses on automating the process for parallel performance experimentation, analysis and problem diagnosis. Such mechanism is built on top of the PerfExplorer performance data mining system combined with the OpenUH [27] compiler infrastructure. The usage of PerfExplorer is useful for easy comparison of several experiments using the same application, and the selective instrumentation of TAU [34] helps avoid excessive overhead during the execution and gives the opportunity to provide optimization suggestions to the user.

The PerfExpert [6] tool employs the HPCToolkit [35] measurement system to execute a structured sequence of performance counter measurements to detect probable core, socket and node-level performance bottlenecks in important procedures and loops of an application.

The work described in [33] characterizes the memory behavior, including memory footprint, memory bandwidth and cache efficiency of several scientific applications. Based on the analysis of the executions of such applications they also estimate the impact of the memory system on the amount of the instruction stalls and on the real computation performance. Their results are shown per application execution, summing up all the information from the different tasks.

There are other performance tools that exploit processor hardware counters and that have integrated sampling capabilities into their analyses. Tools like TAU, Scalasca [38], HPC-Toolkit, use sampling in addition to instrumentation, their sampling capabilities are mainly focused on assigning time consumption to source code lines instead of providing finer details on the hardware counters.

Approaches exist to reduce the cost of storage and time of offline modeling. For example, the database of stored profiles are analyzed to discover parts of an application that represent the whole program execution and the performance of only that portion of the program is observed instead of the whole execution [34]. There are approaches to filter out profile data of program parts that take negligible time [15]. There are proposals of using statistical techniques (e.g. PCA, F-Ratio analysis) to reduce the dimensionality of huge collected profile data so that the analysis techniques can scale [2].

Gonzalez et al. presents a tool that automatically characterizes the different computation regions of the program [15]. They use density based clustering algorithms to performance counters to find similar code regions (that belong to the same counter). Their clustering is based on two hardware metric combination: Processor cycle combined with IPC and Completed Instructions, L1 and L2 Cache misses [15]..

Servat et al. detects clusters based on IPC and number of instructions committed and then detects the change of performance counters like cache misses inside the clusters [28]. They modify the code manually for optimization based on the detected phase changes (slope of hardware counters w.r.t time) to get performance improvement.

But none of these above methods gave a solution to build the performance models in an online setting that would greatly reduce the storage cost. Also none of the above methods talked about the interpretability of the generated model. To our knowledge, our research is the first method of using oLASSO to generate interpretable performance models in an online fashion.

7. CONCLUSION

We demonstrated PEMOGEN, an automatic tool that can generate dynamic and adaptive, interpretable performance models using the Least Absolute Shrinkage and Selection Operator (LASSO) technique in an online fashion. PEMOGEN can be downloaded from http://spcl.inf.ethz.ch/Research/Performance/PEMOGEN/

We showed that the Coefficient of Variation (adjusted R^2) of online LASSO (oLASSO) is significantly better than ordinary least square regression (OLS) and very close to that of the offline LASSO (fLASSO). Based on our results, we argue

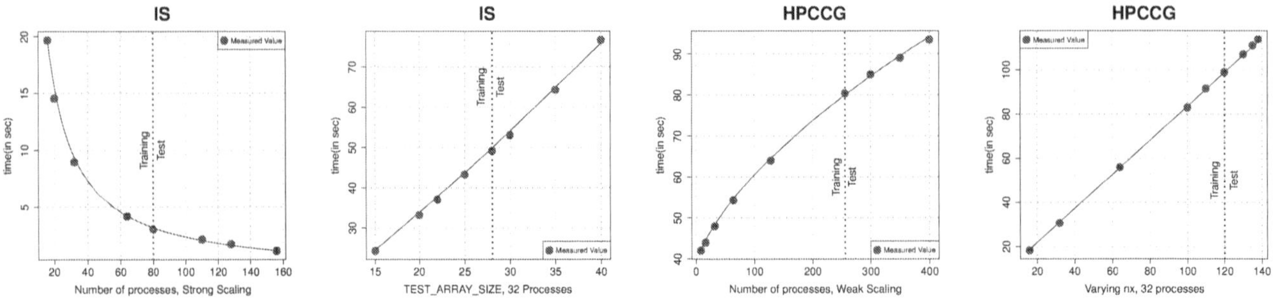

(a) Varying num_procs (b) Varying TEST_ARRAY_SIZE (c) Varying num_procs (d) Varying nx

Figure 6: The predicted and actual performance trends of IS and HPCCG kernels with varying the values of one parameter, while keeping the other parameter values fixed.

that using online LASSO is a better choice for the generation of performance models in HPC applications not only because the model generation and update can run transparently as the application runs and can automatically be turned on and off based on some confidence value of the model, but also the online technique greatly reduces the storage cost of training data. We also showed the effectiveness of using a confidence state machine in reducing the profiling overhead in online LASSO.

We expect that our technique to generate self-modeling applications will rapidly become state-of-the-art in high-performance programming.

8. REFERENCES

[1] Mantevo Project. http://mantevo.org.

[2] D. H. Ahn and J. S. Vetter. Scalable analysis techniques for microprocessor performance counter metrics. In *SC'02: Proceedings of the 2002 ACM/IEEE conference on Supercomputing*, pages 1–16, 2002.

[3] A. V. Aho, J. E. Hopcroft, and J. D. Ullman. *The Design and Analysis of Computer Algorithms.* Addison-Wesley Publishing Company, 1974.

[4] R. Azimi, M. Stumm, and R. Wisniewski. Online performance analysis by statistical sampling of microprocessor performance counters. In *ICS'05:Proceedings of the 19th Annual International Conference on Supercomputing*, pages 101–110, 2005.

[5] G. Bauer, S. Gottlieb, and T. Hoefler. Performance modeling and comparative analysis of the MILC lattice QCD application su3 rmd. In *Proc. of CCGrid*, 2012.

[6] M. Burtscher, B.-D. Kim, J. M. J. Diamond, L. Koesterke, and J. Browne. PerfExpert: an easy-to-use performance diagnosis tool for HPC applications. In *Proceedings of the 2010 ACM/IEEE International Conference for High Performance Computing, Networking, Storage and Analysis*, pages 1–11, 2010.

[7] A. Calotoiu, T. Hoefler, M. Poke, and F. Wolf. Using Automated Performance Modeling to Find Scalability Bugs in Complex Codes. In *Proceedings of SC13: International Conference for High Performance Computing, Networking, Storage and Analysis*, SC '13, pages 45:1–45:12, 2013.

[8] J. M. Chambers. *Linear models, Chapter 4 of Statistical models in S.* Wadsworth & Brooks/Cole, 1992.

[9] Y. Dodge. *Statistical Data Analysis Based on the L1-Norm and Related Methods.* Birkhauser, 2002.

[10] D. Donoho. Compressed sensing. *Information Theory, IEEE Transactions on*, 52(4):1289–1306, April 2006.

[11] B. Efron, T. Hastie, I. Johnstone, and R. Tibshirani. Least angle regression. *Annals of Statistics*, 32:407–499, 2004.

[12] J. Friedman, T. Hastie, and R. Tibshirani. Regularization Paths for Generalized Linear Models via Coordinate Descent. *Journal of Statistical Software*, 33(1):1–22, 2010.

[13] J.-J. Fuchs. On sparse representations in arbitrary redundant bases. *Information Theory, IEEE Transactions on*, 50(6):1341–1344, June 2004.

[14] P. Garrigues and L. El Ghaoui. An homotopy algorithm for the Lasso with online observations. In *Neural Information Processing Systems (NIPS)*, volume 21, 2008.

[15] J. Gonzalez, J. Gimenez, and J. Labarta. Automatic detection of parallel applications computation phases. In *IPDPS*, pages 1–11, 2009.

[16] S. L. Graham, P. B. Kessler, and M. K. Mckusick. Gprof: A Call Graph Execution Profiler. In *Proceedings of the 1982 SIGPLAN Symposium on Compiler Construction*, SIGPLAN '82, pages 120–126, 1982.

[17] I. Guyon and A. Elisseeff. An Introduction to Variable and Feature Selection. *J. Mach. Learn. Res.*, 3:1157–1182, Mar. 2003.

[18] T. Hoefler. Bridging Performance Analysis Tools and Analytic Performance Modeling for HPC. In *Proceedings of Workshop on Productivity and Performance (PROPER 2010).* Springer, Dec. 2010.

[19] T. Hoefler, W. Gropp, W. Kramer, and M. Snir. Performance Modeling for Systematic Performance Tuning. SC '11, pages 6:1–6:12, 2011.

[20] T. Hoefler, T. Schneider, and A. Lumsdaine. Characterizing the Influence of System Noise on Large-Scale Applications by Simulation. In *Proceedings of the 2010 ACM/IEEE International Conference for High Performance Computing, Networking, Storage and Analysis*, SC '10, pages 1–11, 2010.

[21] T. Hoefler, T. Schneider, and A. Lumsdaine. LogGOPSim - Simulating Large-Scale Applications in the LogGOPS Model. In *Proceedings of the 19th ACM International Symposium on High Performance Distributed Computing*, pages 597–604. ACM, Jun. 2010.

[22] A. E. Hoerl and R. W. Kennard. Ridge Regression: Biased Estimation for Nonorthogonal Problems. *Technometrics*, 12(1):55–67, 1970.

[23] K. Huck, O. Hernandez, V. Bui, S. Chandrasekaran, B. Chapman, A. Malony, L. McInnes, and B. Norris. Capturing performance knowledge for automated analysis. In *Proceedings of the 2008 ACM/IEEE Conference on Supercomputing, SC'08*, pages 49:1–49:10, 2008.

[24] E. Ipek, B. R. de Supinski, M. Schulz, and S. A. McKee. An approach to performance prediction for parallel applications. In *Proc. of the 11th Intl. Euro-Par Conference*, pages 196–205, 2005.

[25] C. Lattner and V. Adve. LLVM: A Compilation Framework for Lifelong Program Analysis & Transformation. In *Proceedings of the 2004 International Symposium on Code Generation and Optimization (CGO'04)*, Palo Alto, California, Mar 2004.

[26] B. C. Lee, D. M. Brooks, B. R. de Supinski, M. Schulz, K. Singh, and S. A. McKee. Methods of inference and learning for performance modeling of parallel applications. In *Proc. of the 12th ACM SIGPLAN Symposium on Principles and Practice of Parallel Programming, (PPoPP'07)*, pages 249–258, 2007.

[27] C. Liao, O. Hernandez, B. Chapman, W. Chen, and W. Zheng. OpenUH: an optimizing, portable OpenMP compiler. In *12th Workshop on Compilers for Parallel Computers*, 2006.

[28] G. Llort, J. Gonzalez, H. Servat, J. Gimenez, and J. Labarta. On-line detection of large-scale parallel application's structure. In *Parallel Distributed Processing (IPDPS), 2010 IEEE International Symposium on*, pages 1–10, 2010.

[29] D. Malioutov, M. Cetin, and A. Willsky. Homotopy continuation for sparse signal representation. In *Acoustics, Speech, and Signal Processing, 2005. Proceedings. (ICASSP '05). IEEE International Conference on*, volume 5, pages v/733–v/736 Vol. 5, March 2005.

[30] NASA. NAS Parallel Benchmarks. https://www.nas.nasa.gov/publications/npb.html.

[31] A. Y. Ng. Feature Selection, L1 vs. L2 Regularization, and Rotational Invariance. In *Proceedings of the Twenty-first International Conference on Machine Learning*, ICML '04, pages 78–, 2004.

[32] M. R. Osborne. An effective method for computing regression quantiles. *IMA Journal of Numerical Analysis*, 12(2), 1992.

[33] M. Pavlovic, Y. Etsion, and A. Ramirez. Analysis of memory system requirements for scientific computing. In *IEEE International Symposium on Workload Characterization*, 2009.

[34] S. Shende and A. Malony. The TAU parallel performance system. *International Journal of High Performance Computer Applications*, 20:287–311, 2006.

[35] N. Tallent, J. Mellor-Crummey, L. Adhianto, M. Fagan, and M. Krentel. HPCToolkit: performance tools for scientific computing. *Journal of Physics: Conference Series*, 012088, 2008.

[36] R. Tibshirani. Regression Shrinkage and Selection Via the Lasso. *Journal of the Royal Statistical Society, Series B*, 58:267–288, 1994.

[37] M. Tikir, M. Laurenzano, L. Carrington, and A. Snavely. PSINS: An open source event tracer and execution simulator. In *DoD High Performance Computing Modernization Program Users Group Conference (HPCMP-UGC), 2009*, pages 444–449, June 2009.

[38] F. Wolf, B. Wylie, E. Abraham, D. Becker, W. Frings, K. Furlinger, M. Geimer, M.-A. Hermanns, B. Mohr, S. Moore, M. Pfeifer, and Z. Szebenyi. Usage of the SCALASCA for scalable performance analysis of large-scale parallel applications. In *Tools for High Performance Computing*, pages 157–167, 2008.

[39] X. Wu and F. Muller. Scalaextrap: Trace-based communication extrapolation for SPMD programs. *ACM Transactions on Programming Languages and Systems*, 34(1), 2012.

[40] J. Zhai, W. Chen, and W. Zheng. Phantom: predicting performance of parallel applications on large-scale parallel machines using a single node. *SIGPLAN Notices*, 45(5):305–314, 2010.

[41] G. Zheng, G. Gupta, E. Bohm, I. Dooley, and L. Kale. Simulating Large Scale Parallel Applications Using Statistical Models for Sequential Execution Blocks. In *Parallel and Distributed Systems (ICPADS), 2010 IEEE 16th International Conference on*, pages 221–228, Dec 2010.

ArrayTool: A Lightweight Profiler to Guide Array Regrouping

Xu Liu, Kamal Sharma, John Mellor-Crummey
Department of Computer Science, Rice University
Houston, TX, USA
{xl10, kgs1, johnmc}@rice.edu

ABSTRACT

Memory hierarchies in modern computer systems are complex; often, they include multi-level caches and multiple memory controllers on the same chip. Without careful design, programs suffer from unnecessary data movement between caches and memory, degrading performance and increasing energy consumption. Array regrouping can significantly improve data locality by improving spatial reuse of data and reducing cache contention. However, existing techniques for identifying opportunities for array regrouping are lacking in three ways. First, they provide inadequate information to guide regrouping. Second, the cost of monitoring employed by prior tools to identify regrouping opportunities limits the use of these methods in practice. Third, existing metrics for quantifying the benefits of array regrouping can lead to inappropriate transformations that hurt performance. In this paper, we describe ArrayTool — a lightweight profiler that guides array regrouping. ArrayTool has three unique capabilities. First, it focuses attention on arrays with significant access latency. Second, it identifies the feasibility and quantifies the benefits of regrouping arrays with lightweight array-centric profiling. Third, it works on both shared-memory and distributed-memory parallel programs. To illustrate the utility of ArrayTool, we employ it to analyze three benchmarks. Using the guidance it provides, we regroup program arrays, improving performance from 25% to a factor of two.

Keywords

Array-centric profiling, array regrouping, data locality.

1. INTRODUCTION

Modern processors employ a hierarchy of caches to reduce the average data access latency to memory. Usually, caches farther from CPU have higher access latency and lower data transfer bandwidth. To use the memory hierarchy well, one needs to maintain good data locality in caches, avoid cache contention, and prefetch data effectively.

PACT'14, August 24–27, 2014, Edmonton, AB, Canada.

ACM 978-1-4503-2809-8/14/08 ...$15.00.
http://dx.doi.org/10.1145/2628071.2628102.

```
for (i = 0; i < N; i++)
    B[i] = A1[i] + A2[i] + ... + An[i];
```

The original code uses independent arrays A_1, A_2 ... A_n in a loop.

```
for (i = 0; i < N; i++)
    B[i] = Arr[i].A1 + Arr[i].A2 + ... + Arr[i].An;
```

The optimized code regroups arrays A_1, A_2 ... A_n into Arr. $Arr[i].A_m$ represents $A_m[i]$ $(1 \leq m \leq n)$.

Figure 1: The code and data structures before and after array regrouping.

Memory accesses that stage data into the fastest caches and access it thoroughly before it is evicted are said to have excellent data locality. There are two types of data locality: *spatial* and *temporal*. An access pattern exploits *spatial* locality when it accesses a memory location and then accesses nearby locations soon afterward. Typically, spatial locality goes unexploited when accessing data with a large stride or indirection. An access pattern exhibits *temporal* locality when it accesses a memory location multiple times.

Access patterns with poor spatial locality cause useless data to be loaded into cache. Such access patterns squander much of a processors's memory bandwidth loading values from main memory that will never be used before being evicted. Access patterns are prefetch friendly if they are regular or can be handled easily by software or hardware prefetchers. For example, hardware stream prefetchers only manage a limited number of streams.

Array regrouping is a technique that can enhance data spatial locality [4], avoid poor memory bandwidth usage [5], and improve data prefetching [22]. Figure 1 illustrates a basic array regrouping transformation. Before regrouping, each iteration may load as many as n cache lines into cache as it reads an element of each of n distinct arrays. If n is large, each iteration accesses many cache lines that may conflict with one another and cause conflict misses. After regrouping, all words are compressed into one or a few contiguous cache lines, which improves spatial locality and reduces cache contention. Moreover, compacting accesses to a few cache lines in each iteration can also reduce bandwidth requests. Finally, the regrouping reduces the number of prefetch streams from n to one. If n is larger than the number of streams that a prefetcher can handle, array regrouping can make the access pattern more prefetch friendly [22].

Array regrouping has been studied for over a decade [4, 5, 11, 24, 28]. To the best of our knowledge, all existing methods compute a metric known as *array affinity* to guide array regrouping. To identify regrouping opportunities, one considers all arrays, evaluates their access patterns to build an affinity graph, and partitions the graph by clustering arrays with high affinities. Ideally, regrouping arrays in the same partition leads to better performance.

However, this method falls short in several respects. First, real programs often use a large number of arrays. Evaluating computing affinities between all pairs of arrays is unnecessary and impractical. Regrouping arrays whose accesses don't impact performance will yield little benefit. Second, prior tools have identified candidates for array regrouping by using code instrumentation to gather information about access patterns. The high overhead of this approach can make it impractical to use on long-running applications. One tool [24] employs lightweight profiling and compiler-based static analysis in an effort to reduce the overhead of identifying candidates for regrouping. However, their lightweight profiling adds more than 100% overhead and static analysis is not effective for irregular loops and indirect memory accesses. Finally, existing tools mainly focus on sequential and threaded programs and have not been designed for use on distributed-memory programs, such as those based on MPI.

To address these limitations, we developed ArrayTool. ArrayTool employs a lightweight array-centric profiling method that efficiently evaluates the feasibility and benefits of array regrouping by computing a novel affinity metric. To reduce the cost of affinity analysis, ArrayTool filters out arrays whose accesses have an insignificant impact on performance from the list of regrouping candidates. ArrayTool is designed to analyze parallel programs: it can gather and analyze data from one or more multi-threaded processes running on one or more nodes of a parallel system.

ArrayTool is compiler-independent. It works on dynamically linked, optimized executables without the need for recompilation. More importantly, one does not need *a priori* knowledge of programs to analyze them with ArrayTool. ArrayTool provides guidance to users about how to regroup program arrays. To illustrate the effectiveness of ArrayTool's analysis and regrouping suggestions, we use ArrayTool to analyze three parallel programs. Experiments show that with the guidance by ArrayTool, we can easily identify opportunities for array regrouping. Applying the suggested regrouping optimizations to the programs we studied improved their performance from 25% to a factor of two.

The next section discusses the challenges of identifying array regrouping opportunities in real parallel programs. Section 3 describes hardware support for address sampling, which provides the foundation for ArrayTool's lightweight profiling. Section 4 describes how ArrayTool uses address sampling to identify regrouping opportunities in parallel programs. Section 5 presents case studies with three parallel benchmarks to illustrate the utility of ArrayTool. Section 6 discusses related work. Section 7 presents our conclusions and outlines our plans for future work.

2. MOTIVATION

One faces several challenges when attempting to identify opportunities for array regrouping in large applications and to exploit them. The rest of this section describes three challenges for applying regrouping to real parallel programs.

2.1 Challenges of complex programs

Unlike benchmarks, scientific programs often use hundreds of arrays. The declarations and uses of arrays can be spread across dozens of files, hundreds of functions, and thousands of source code lines. Examining every combination of arrays for regrouping is time consuming and often impractical. Many array regrouping opportunities are pointless to explore. First, not every array pair can be regrouped legally. Second, regrouping two infrequently accessed arrays yields little benefit. Third, regrouping two arrays may not be always beneficial due to their access patterns. Besides these challenges, complex array structures and data flows, such as multi-dimensional arrays and aliases in a program add additional difficulties in choosing regrouping strategies and applying regrouping. A practical tool for analyzing array regrouping opportunities should filter out arrays unimportant to performance and those that cannot be regrouped.

2.2 Limitations of existing analysis methods

Prior work builds affinity array graphs [28] to decide which arrays should be regrouped for better performance. Each node in the graph represents an array in the program; a weighted edge connecting two nodes denotes how frequently the arrays are accessed together. We refer to this existing approach as frequency-based affinity graph.

There are two main drawbacks to the frequency-based affinity graph technique. First, building graphs involves either compiler support or heavyweight memory access instrumentation. On one hand, static analysis cannot accurately analyze irregular loops, indirect memory references, and complex dataflows with aliases. On the other hand, the online profiling method instruments memory accesses or loops, which incurs large overhead. The state-of-the-art lightweight profiler for computing array affinities adds more than 100% runtime overhead [24].

Second, frequency-based affinity graphs use the access frequency to compute the affinity between two arrays. However, the frequency cannot reflect the true affinity between two arrays. For example, two arrays might be accessed together in a loop 1,000 times causing 3,000 cycles access latency. However, these two arrays might also be accessed separately in different loops 100 times, causing 30,000 cycles latency. According to the frequency-based affinity computation, these two arrays are referenced together most of the time, so they have a strong affinity for regrouping. However, regrouping them may hurt performance because the two arrays are not referenced together for their most significant accesses. Consequently, traditional frequency-based affinity graphs are inadequate to guide array regrouping for real applications. We need to redefine affinities between arrays and compute them with other metrics.

2.3 Challenges of parallelism

For threaded programs, one needs to compute array affinities inside a thread or across threads [11]. For parallel programs coded with distributed memory models, like MPI, computing array affinities needs to evaluate access patterns of these arrays in different process ranks. Since processes have separate address spaces, the same array may be allocated with a different address range in each process. Computing affinity for distributed-memory programs requires analysis of accesses across all processes. Finally, a parallel program's arrays may have different access latency characteristics when the program is run sequentially. For that reason, we develop a method to analyze parallel program executions.

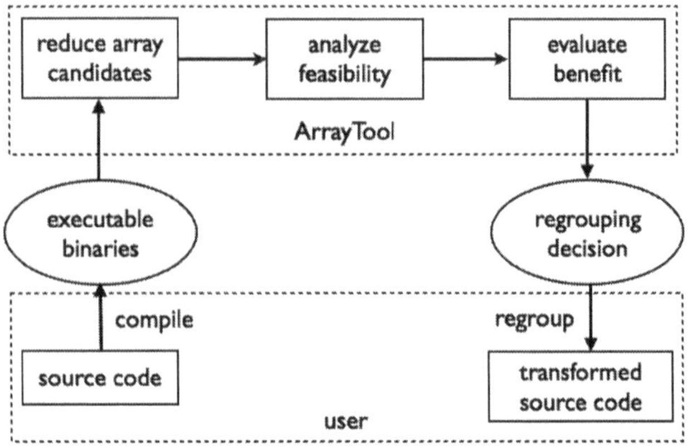

Figure 2: The workflow of array regrouping. ArrayTool collects performance profiles during program execution and analyzes these profiles to provide performance insights. ArrayTool also recommends a set of methods for users to derive regrouping decisions from these insights. Users need manual effort to use regrouping decisions to optimize source code.

3. ADDRESS SAMPLING

Address sampling forms the basis of array-centric profiling in ArrayTool. ArrayTool's address sampling requires three hardware features: (1) support for sampling memory accesses, (2) support for capturing latency of sampled memory accesses, and (3) support to record a precise instruction pointer and an effective data address for a sampled access.

Three modern processor architectures provide the support we need for address sampling: AMD Opteron (family 10h and successors), Intel Nehalem, and Intel Itanium2. These processors support address sampling with different hardware mechanisms. AMD Opteron processors provide support for address sampling with their mechanism for instruction-based sampling (IBS) [6]. IBS records detailed information about an instruction during its execution in the pipeline, including the effective address for a load/store, details about the memory hierarchy response (e.g., cache and TLB miss or misalignment), and various latency measures. In contrast, Intel Nehalem processors and their successors provide the necessary support through (PEBS) [8] and Intel Itanium2 provides the necessary support with its Data Event Address Registers (DEAR) [9]. Neither IBM POWER nor ARM have sufficient support for address sampling. IBM POWER can sample addresses but cannot associate access latency with samples; ARM processors do not have any of the required support.

ArrayTool leverages mechanisms for address sampling to support array-centric profiling, which collects performance data with low overhead to guide array regrouping. The case studies in Section 5 were performed on an AMD Opteron; however, ArrayTool supports the Intel architectures as well.

4. ARRAYTOOL

ArrayTool is based on the address sampling techniques described in the previous section. Figure 2 shows ArrayTool's role in the overall workflow of array regrouping. ArrayTool takes an unmodified, fully optimized binary as input and monitors its execution on real hardware. Then based on the performance data, ArrayTool recommends three kinds of analysis methods, and provides regrouping decisions. Finally, the programer refactors the source code according to ArrayTool's regrouping guidance. In the following sections, we describe how ArrayTool monitors data access patterns, assesses their impact on program performance, and uses this information to identify regrouping opportunities. Section 4.1 shows how we eliminate insignificant arrays from consideration for regrouping optimization. Section 4.2 describes how we identify the feasibility of regrouping two arrays. Section 4.3 discusses the metric we use to assess the benefit of regrouping. Section 4.4 highlights the challenges we address for parallel programs.

4.1 Filtering out insignificant arrays

ArrayTool employs array-centric profiling to identify significant arrays as candidates for regrouping. Array-centric profiling first identifies arrays used in the program. Then, it evaluates the contribution of each array to the overall program's performance. To identify arrays, we monitor the memory allocation for each array. Such memory can be allocated in static data, a thread's stack, or a process's heap. We do not monitor arrays allocated on the stack directly. One may change stack arrays into static or heap arrays for examination.

Arrays allocated in the static data section of a load module are static arrays. Each static array has a named entry in the symbol table that identifies the memory range for the variable with an offset from the beginning of the load module. The life cycle of static arrays begins when the enclosing load module, i.e., executable or shared library, is loaded into memory and ends when the load module is unloaded. The profiler tracks the loading and unloading of load modules. When a load module is loaded into memory, ArrayTool reads the load module's symbol table to extract information about the memory range for each of its static arrays. ArrayTool inserts these memory ranges into a map for future use. All load modules in use are linked in a list for easy traversal. If a load module is unloaded, the load module together with its map of static arrays is removed from the list.

Arrays in the heap are allocated dynamically during execution by one of the *malloc* family of functions (malloc, calloc, realloc). Since heap-allocated arrays may be known by different aliases, e.g., function parameters, at different points in an execution, ArrayTool uses the full call path of the allocation point for a heap-allocated array to uniquely identify it throughout its lifetime. To associate a heap-allocated array with its allocation call path, ArrayTool wraps memory allocation and free operations in a monitored execution. At each monitored allocation, ArrayTool enters into a map an association between the address range of an array and its allocation point. At each monitored free, ArrayTool deletes an association from the map. Thus, if the same memory range is reallocated to another variable, ArrayTool can distinguish the new variable from the old one.

After identifying arrays used in the program, ArrayTool then monitors data accesses and attributes performance information to each array accessed. ArrayTool systematically samples the data addresses accessed during a program execution. Upon each sample, ArrayTool associates this sample with the array that includes the effective data address. Hardware mechanisms for address sampling report memory latency for data accesses. ArrayTool attributes latency for data accesses to the array accessed (if any). Arrays associated with large access latency are the ones worth considering for regrouping. In contrast, arrays with few or no access latency associated are insignificant and should be eliminated from the regrouping candidate list. This array-centric profiling helps ArrayTool to focus its regrouping analysis only on significant arrays.

4.2 Assessing regrouping feasibility

Regrouping arbitrary arrays is not always feasible. We describe three conditions that prevent regrouping and describe methods used by ArrayTool to identify these conditions using data collected using address sampling.

4.2.1 *Memory layout limit*

Two arrays with different layouts cannot be regrouped. Two arrays have the same memory layout *iff* they have the same number of dimensions and size for each dimension. To identify the memory layout of an array, we examine its allocation site, where the memory layout is determined. Static arrays are allocated at their declaration points. We use the array name and declaration location obtained from the debugging information generated by the compiler to uniquely identify a static array's allocation site. We identify allocation sites of heap allocated arrays by determining their allocation call paths. ArrayTool maps these call paths to source code with the help of debugging information. From the allocation site in the source code, one can determine the layout (dimension, size, and data type) of any static or heap-allocated array.

4.2.2 *Lifetime limit*

Each array has a lifetime. A static array's lifetime begins when the module containing it is loaded and ends when the module is unloaded. A heap-allocated array lives between its allocation and when it is freed. We consider two arrays for regrouping only if their lifetimes overlap. To determine the lifetime of each array, we record timestamps when the array is allocated and freed.

4.2.3 *Location limit*

Arrays can live in different load modules. Usually, arrays allocated in different load modules cannot be regrouped, which we call a location limit. A static array cannot be regrouped with a heap-allocated array, because they live in different parts of the address space. We developed a method to associate static and heap allocated arrays with load modules. Because memory ranges of static arrays fall into address ranges of load modules, we associate the memory ranges allocated for static arrays with the load modules as their locations. Memory allocated for arrays in the heap is distinct from the static data of load modules, so we identify the location of each heap allocation by its call path.

4.3 Predicting regrouping benefits

After filtering out insignificant and infeasible arrays for regrouping, ArrayTool needs to identify arrays for which regrouping would be beneficial. As we describe in the following sections, ArrayTool considers two factors that affect regrouping benefit: (1) array affinities and (2) array access patterns.

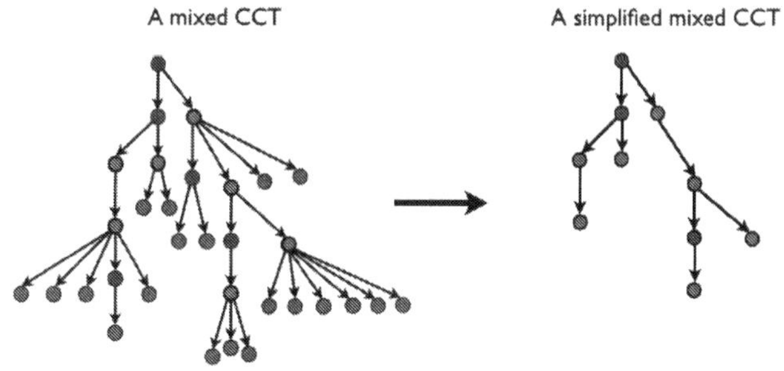

Figure 3: An example of a mixed CCT and its simplified tree which remains the paths to loop nests and eliminate leaf nodes unless they are loop nests. In a mixed CCT, the blue nodes are functions; green nodes are loops; and red nodes are instructions where samples occur.

4.3.1 *Array affinities*

Two arrays have high affinity if they are always accessed together. Section 2 describes how prior work determines array affinities based on access frequencies. Here, we describe a novel method used by ArrayTool to compute affinities with high accuracy and low overhead.

First, ArrayTool profiles the program with code-centric analysis in addition to the array-centric analysis described in Section 4.1. Each address sample is attributed not only to the array accessed, but also to the full calling context using call stack unwinding [19]. The full call path reaching the sampled instruction consists of a sequence of return addresses. A return address can be enclosed in zero or more loop nests at various levels in the call chain. To identify loops surrounding each memory access, we parse the machine code for a program, build a control flow graph (CFG) for each procedure, and then use interval analysis [7] to identify loops in each procedure's CFG. With information about loops for each procedure in addition to the call path, we can identify all the loops in which a memory access is dynamically nested. We refer to call paths augmented with loop information as *mixed call paths*, which provide the foundation for our affinity analysis.

Second, we create mixed calling context trees (CCT) from mixed call paths. A CCT [1] is a compact data structure to maintain call paths. It merges common prefixes of call paths to reduce the storage overhead. Similarly, a mixed calling context tree is a union of mixed call paths with common prefixes merged. Figure 3 shows an example of a mixed calling context tree. Interior nodes in blue or green in the tree denote call sites and loops respectively, while leaf nodes in red denote sampled memory access instructions. For each monitored array, we create a mixed CCT for its accesses, annotated with performance metrics such as access latency.

Finally, we compute array affinities from mixed CCTs. For any two arrays that are significant enough and feasible for regrouping, we compare their mixed CCTs. We compute array affinities from two aspects: co-references and weights. Co-reference of two arrays measure how often two arrays are accessed together in the same loop nest. A weight quantifies the significance of accesses in each loop nest. To compute the co-references R_c between two arrays, we simplify their mixed CCTs by pruning call paths to convert all leaf nodes as loops, as shown in Figure 3, and quantify the similarity of the two simplified mixed CCTs with Equation 1. In this equation, P_{common} is the number of common paths in the two simplified mixed CCTs associated with the two arrays. P_1 and P_2 are the numbers of paths in the simplified mixed CCTs for the two arrays, respectively. Their union counts the total unique paths in the two trees. Ideally, if the co-reference value of two arrays is 1, meaning all paths are common to the two trees, the two arrays are referenced together and better candidates for regrouping.

$$R_c = \frac{P_{common}}{P_1 \bigcup P_2} \tag{1}$$

We can improve the utility of R_c with R_{cw} by considering access latency in each loop nest context. The reason this is useful is that loop nests have varying levels of significance. Consider the case where two arrays are accessed together in 90% loop nests which are insignificant, while accessed separately in other 10% loop nests which are significant. In this case, regrouping two arrays with an R_c as high as 0.9 computed using Equation 1 may hurt performance.

To improve analysis accuracy, we use a weight metric to quantify the significance of loop nests. Weight is defined as the array access latency captured by the address sampling technique. Equation 2 shows a weighted revision of Equation 1. In this equation, $W_{uncommon}$ is the sum of the weights of uncommon loop nests between the two arrays under analysis; W_{total} is the sum of the total weights of all loop nests in which both arrays are accessed.

$$R_{cw} = 1 - \frac{W_{uncommon}}{W_{total}} \tag{2}$$

If the total weights of uncommon loop nests are large, even if two arrays are accessed together in 90% of the loop nests, R_{cw} would be small, suggesting that the arrays should not be grouped together

4.3.2 Array access patterns

The affinity computation in the previous section only considers aggregate accesses of arrays at the loop level. However, a high R_{cw} value cannot guarantee a performance benefit after grouping the two arrays. Formally, we define four access pattern conflicts that cancel the performance benefit from array regrouping. These four conflicts can occur between arrays which have high R_{cw}.

- Space conflict: accessing different sections of two arrays. For example, the first loop in Figure 4 accesses the first half of `A` but the second half of `B`.
- Time conflict: no time overlap for referencing two arrays. For example, the second loop in Figure 4 accesses `A` in the first half of the loop iterations, but accesses `B` in the other half of the loop iterations.
- Order conflict: different orders in accessing elements of two arrays. For example, the third loop in Figure 4 accesses `A` in an ascending order but accesses `B` in descending order.
- Type conflict: accesses to one array are reads but accesses to another array are writes. Regrouping arrays with type conflicts may cause unnecessary data transfer in the memory hierarchy due to the write policy.

```
for (i = 0; i < N/2; i++) {
    C[i] = A[i];
    D[i] = B[i+N/2];
}
```

Different parts of `A` and `B` are accessed together in the loop.

```
for (i = 0; i < N; i++) {
    if (i < N/2) C[i] = A[i];
    else D[i] = B[i];
}
```

`A` and `B` are accessed in different halves of the loop.

```
for (i = 0; i < N; i++) {
    C[i] = A[i];
    D[i] = B[N-i-1];
}
```

`A` and `B` have different access orders.

Figure 4: Arrays accessed in the same loop of high R_{cw} but have different access patterns. regrouping `A` and `B` leads to no benefit. Regrouping `A` and `C`.

For example, one should not expect performance improvement by regrouping `A` and `C` in Figure 4.

To identify these four access pattern conflicts with low overhead, ArrayTool employs address sampling as described in Section 3. ArrayTool analyzes access patterns using address-centric and time-centric methods. Consider a memory access sample m to an array `V`. For this sample, our address-centric analysis computes the addresses that form the lower and upper bounds of the range accessed by m and update the lower and upper bounds of `V` accessed for each procedure and loop along the mixed call path to m. For the same sample, our time-centric analysis records the access timestamp that forms the lower and upper bounds of time range for accessing `V`. Like our address-centric analysis, our time-centric analysis also computes the lower and upper time bounds of `V` accesses for each procedure and loop along the mixed call path to m.

From address- and time-centric analysis, ArrayTool generates an address interval and a time interval for array accesses for each context, i.e., instruction, loop, function, and whole program. ArrayTool uses these two intervals to identify pattern conflicts. If address intervals of two arrays have no/little logical overlap, i.e., they refer to different parts of their respective arrays, these two arrays have a space conflict, e.g., `A` and `B` in the first loop in Figure 4. If time intervals of two arrays have no/little overlap, these two arrays have a time conflict, e.g., `A` and `B` in the second loop in Figure 4. If referencing the boundaries of two arrays' address intervals in a reverse order, these two arrays have order conflict, e.g., `A` and `B` in the third loop in Figure 4. Finally, for type conflict, ArrayTool leverages address sampling techniques to identify whether a sampled memory access is a read or a write.

Consequently, ArrayTool suggests two arrays with high R_{cw} and without access pattern conflict are final regrouping candidates.

4.4 Parallel challenges

ArrayTool faces unique challenges profiling parallel programs to identify array regrouping opportunities. There are two kinds of parallelism: shared memory parallelism and distributed memory parallelism. For threaded programs, we need to evaluate an array's access pattern across threads. As ArrayTool already computes the address and time intervals for array accesses in each thread, ArrayTool plots these intervals according to thread IDs to show access patterns across threads. Only arrays with the same access pattern across threads are worth regrouping.

Moreover, distributed memory parallel programs allocate arrays in different address spaces, which complicates identification of array regrouping opportunities. As far as we know, there is no prior work that considers array regrouping problems in distributed memory programs. We describe the difficulties of analyzing such programs and how ArrayTool addresses them. First, the number of arrays allocated increases according to the program scale. To enable scalable analysis, we aggregate the analysis of arrays allocated in different address spaces if they have the same name (for static arrays) or allocation call path (for dynamic arrays). Second, we add another condition to identify regrouping feasibility. If two arrays are allocated in different address space (i.e., in different MPI processes), they cannot be regrouped. To identify this case, we record the process ID that allocates arrays. Each array has a vector to record these process IDs. Only two arrays with the same vector can be regrouped. Third, accesses to an array can be dispersed in different MPI processes. ArrayTool aggregates all of these accesses to construct the simplified mixed CCT across processes for R_{cw} calculation. Finally, like computing access patterns across threads, ArrayTool computes access patterns across processes by plotting address and time intervals collected from all processes. Two arrays with the same patterns are suitable for regrouping.

Finally, for hybrid programming models such as MPI+threads, ArrayTool combines the analysis methods for shared and distributed memory programs. The only unique challenge for hybrid programs is large scalability. There can be thousands to millions of processes/threads used in a distributed-memory system. Showing all address and time intervals for access pattern analysis from such large scale execution is impractical. To solve this problem, ArrayTool can sample a fraction of processes/threads for analysis. In the next section, we will show how ArrayTool effectively identifies array regrouping opportunities.

5. CASE STUDIES

Our test platform is a single node server with four AMD Magny-Cours processors, known as a non-uniform memory access (NUMA) system. This machine has 48 cores and 128 GB memory. On this platform, we used AMD's instruction-based sampling as the foundation for address sampling by ArrayTool's profiler. To demonstrate ArrayTool's utility, we studied the following three memory-bound benchmarks for our case studies. We ran these benchmarks using either a shared or distributed memory programming model.

- LULESH [13], an application benchmark developed by Lawrence Livermore National Laboratory (LLNL), is an Arbitrary Lagrangian Eulerian code that solves the Sedov blast wave problem for one material in 3D. In this paper, we study a highly-tuned LULESH implementation written in C++ with OpenMP. We run LULESH with 48 threads on a $90 \times 90 \times 90$ three-dimensional mesh.

app	native execution time	ArrayTool's overhead
LULESH	296s	+22%
IRS	73s	+14%
SRAD	34s	+17.6%

Table 1: ArrayTool's measurement overhead for the three benchmarks.

- IRS, a LLNL Sequoia benchmark [14], is an implicit radiation solver. It solves a diffusion equation on a three-dimensional, block structured mesh. IRS is important for LLNL because the style of *for* loops and array indexing used in IRS is very representative of the coding style that is used widely in production applications at LLNL. IRS, with careful optimization by LLNL's code team, is written in C and parallelized with hybrid MPI and OpenMP. We run IRS with 4 MPI processes and 12 OpenMP threads in each process. The input for IRS is a $60 \times 60 \times 60$ 3-dimensional matrix.
- SRAD (Speckle Reducing Anisotropic Diffusion) [26] , one of Rodinia benchmarks [2], is a diffusion method for ultrasonic and radar imaging applications based on partial differential equations. It is parallelized with OpenMP. In the experiment, we ran it with 48 threads. The input size is a 10240×10240 domain with 50 iterations.

These benchmarks have been already optimized for NUMA architectures . We use `numactl` [12] to balance the memory allocation across NUMA domains to avoid bandwidth contention. We first evaluate the overhead generated by ArrayTool's profiler. We profile all of these benchmarks with a sampling period of 64K instructions. To reduce the overhead, we only sample memory accesses, ignoring arithmetic and other instructions. We use *gcc* to compile all of the three benchmarks with `-g -O2` options. Table 1 shows ArrayTool's profiling overhead, which is less than 18% on average. Because ArrayTool's overhead is very small, one can apply it for large-scale production code executions. In the following sections, we first study each benchmark individually with ArrayTool and then summarize our analysis to understand why array regrouping leads to better performance.

5.1 LULESH

Figure 5 shows ArrayTool's GUI that identifies significant arrays as regrouping candidates. The GUI consists of three panes. The top pane shows the source code of the monitored program; the bottom left pane shows the array-centric profiling results that list either array names or array allocation sites, which can be mapped to the source code; the bottom right pane shows the metrics that are associated with each array. In our experiment, we use memory access latency (in CPU cycles) to measure the significance of arrays. We only highlight six arrays with their names on the left of their allocation sites, which account for more than 4% of total latency each. Besides these six arrays, there are also other arrays can be regrouped for better performance. However, these six arrays have the highest priority for regrouping.

From the top pane of Figure 5, we can see these six arrays have the same dimension and size. They are all allocated at the beginning of the program and freed at the end. Both

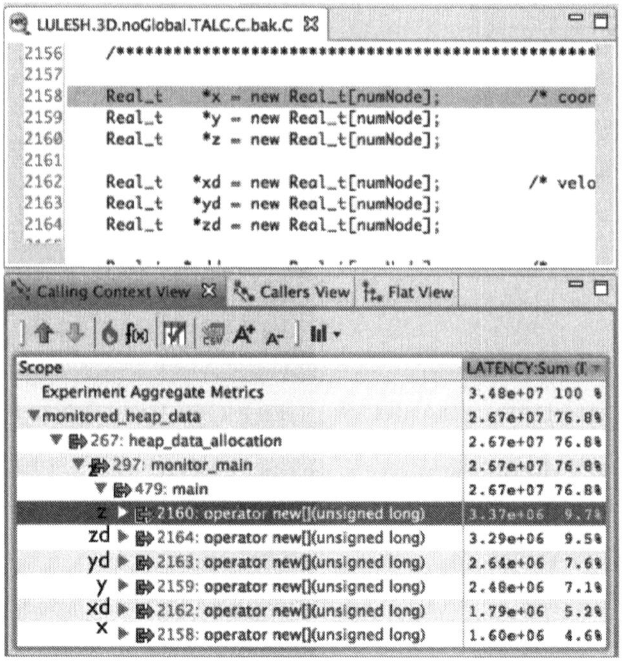

Figure 5: ArrayTool's profiling results that identify significant arrays in LULESH. Array names are on the left of their allocation sites.

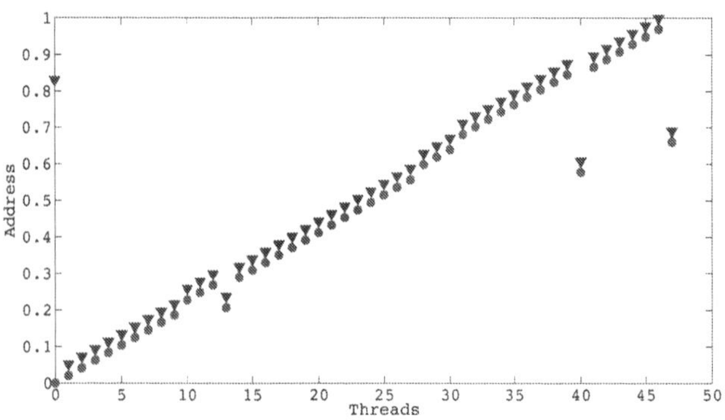

Figure 6: The access pattern of array z. The horizontal axis is the threads. The vertical axis shows a variable's address range in [0, 1] accessed by each thread: triangles are upper bounds and circles are lower bounds. This regular access pattern shows that each thread works on a subsection of array z in an ascending order, except three outliers. The occurrence of outliers is because of the thread migration. All other significant arrays used in LULESH have a similar access pattern as z's.

time and space overlap analysis shows these arrays are feasible for regrouping. ArrayTool first analyzes the access patterns of these six arrays. Figure 6 shows that all these arrays have a common access patterns across threads. This regular pattern in the figure means all loops access these arrays in an ascending order. Therefore, access pattern analysis does not show any objection to regrouping these arrays.

Next, we examine the simplified mixed CCT of these six arrays. We only show the analysis of three representative

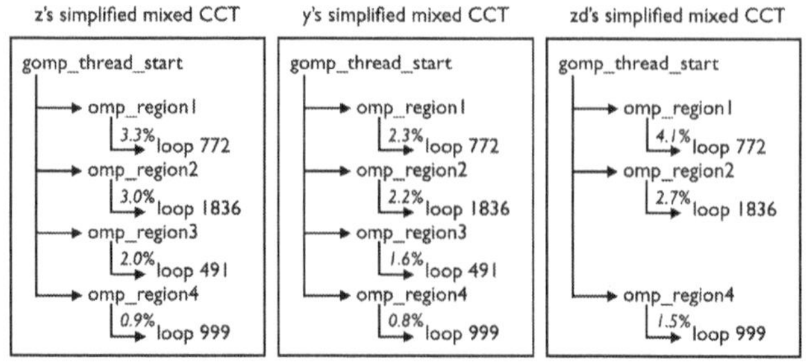

Figure 7: Simplified mixed CCTs for array z, y, and zd. This figure shows the abstraction of CCT structures from ArrayTool's outputs: omp_region denotes a OpenMP parallel region on the call path; loop with a number denotes the loop detected by ArrayTool at that line number; the percentage on the arrow denotes the percentage of access latency to the variable in that loop over the aggregate memory access latency in the whole program.

R_{cw}	x	y	z	xd	yd	zd
x	1	1	1	0.9	0.9	0.9
y	-	1	1	0.9	0.9	0.9
z	-	-	1	0.9	0.9	0.9
xd	-	-	-	1	1	1
yd	-	-	-	-	1	1
zd	-	-	-	-	-	1

Table 2: ArrayTool computes R_{cw} between any two of the examined six arrays. An array has R_{cw} as 1 with itself.

arrays: z, y, and zd. Figure 7 shows these arrays' simplified mixed CCTs. From Figure 7, we can see that both array z and y's simplified mixed CCTs consist of four loops. According to our affinity calculation equation, z and y have an affinity R_{cw} of 1 because their paths are all common, regardless the difference of weights of access latency in each loop. Therefore, y and z should be regrouped without any consideration. On the other hand, zd has a different simplified mixed CCT from z's. Based on Equation 2, we compute the affinity R_{cw} between z and zd as 0.9. It means that although z and zd are not always accessed together, loops in which they are accessed separately are insignificant. Therefore, z and zd should be regrouped.

Table 2 shows R_{cw} computed between any two of these six arrays with similar ArrayTool's analysis. There are two cluster of arrays with R_{cw} of 1: (1) x, y, z, and (2) xd, yd, zd. Affinities between arrays of these two clusters are around 0.9, which is high enough to deem all six arrays as one cluster. Consequently, ArrayTool gives the decision that x, y, z, xd, yd, and zd should be regrouped. Regrouping them leads to a speedup of 1.16× for the whole LULESH program.

Besides these six arrays that ArrayTool already examined, ArrayTool also identifies another group of nine arrays used in LULESH for regrouping. Each of these nine arrays accounts for more than 1% of total memory access latency. Regrouping all of these 15 arrays into two groups suggested by ArrayTool yields a 1.25× speedup for the whole LULESH program.

```
matrix.cbl = MALLOT(double, size) ;
matrix.cbc = MALLOT(double, size) ;
...
matrix.dfc = MALLOT(double, size) ;
matrix.dfr = MALLOT(double, size) ;
```

Figure 8: Significant arrays that are used in IRS, reported by ArrayTool. These arrays form the structure of the matrix used in IRS. This matrix of the same structure is allocated and freed four times in different contexts.

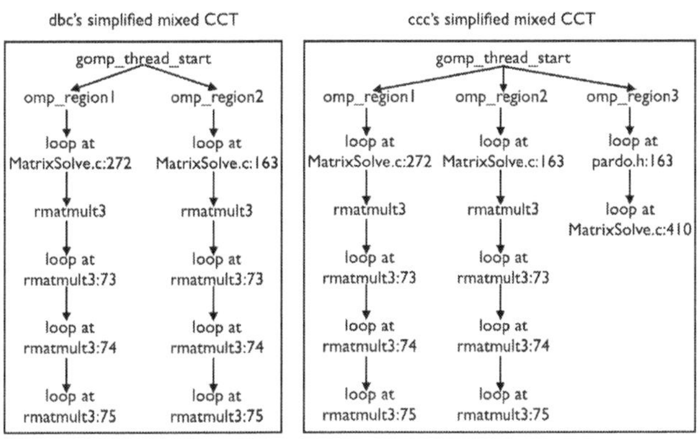

Figure 9: Simplified mixed CCTs for the two of most significant arrays dbc and ccc used in IRS. This figure shows the abstraction of the CCTs from the output of ArrayTool.

5.2 IRS

Figure 8 shows the allocation sites of significant arrays used in IRS, reported by ArrayTool. As shown in the figure, there are 14 arrays allocated in a call path that forms a 3-dimensional matrix. From the profiling result, we know that the matrix is allocated and freed four times with the same memory layout, while the figure only shows one instance. All of these arrays are one-dimensional of the same size. Moreover, these arrays have the same live space and range.

Figure 9 shows the simplified mixed CCTs of the two most significant arrays `dbc` and `ccc`. The two arrays have two common mixed call paths and `ccc` has a unique one. The affinity between `dbc` and `ccc` R_{cw} is 0.88. This means that the unique call path of `ccc` is insignificant.

Figure 10 shows the access patterns of `dbc` and `ccc`. From the figure, we can see that only eight out of ten threads access `dbc` and `ccc` in each MPI rank. Both `dbc` and `ccc` have such pattern because they are referenced together in a parallel loop that only distributes work to eight threads. Moreover, each of those eight threads in each MPI rank accesses the whole range of the two arrays due to the access pattern interval in the figure. From the source code of loops (on line 73-75) in the simplified mixed CCTs from Figure 9, we find that `dbc` and `ccc` are both accessed with unit stride in ascending order. Consequently, we draw the decision that `dbc` and `ccc` should be regrouped to reduce the number of prefetch streams from two to one.

Further analysis of these 14 significant arrays by ArrayTool shows that R_{cw} is larger than 0.85 between any two arrays. The arrays do not have any access pattern conflict with any other. Therefore ArrayTool suggests that all of these 14 arrays should be grouped. Regrouping these arrays achieves a 2.09× speedup for the kernel loop nests in IRS.

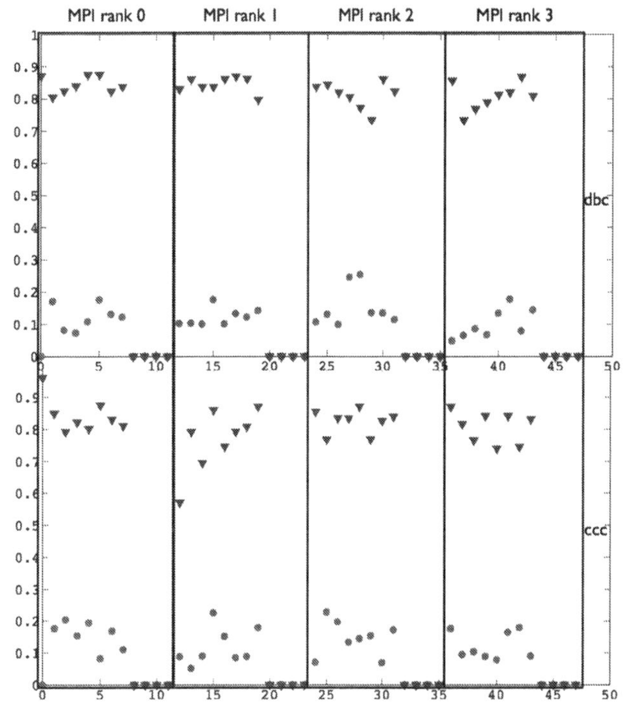

Figure 10: Access patterns of array dbc and ccc across 48 threads.

```
0.0%  I = (float *)malloc( size_I * sizeof(float) );
12.4% J = (float *)malloc( size_I * sizeof(float) );
4.9%  c = (float *)malloc(sizeof(float)* size_I) ;

0.0%  iN = (int *)malloc(sizeof(unsigned int*) * rows) ;
0.0%  iS = (int *)malloc(sizeof(unsigned int*) * rows) ;
0.1%  jW = (int *)malloc(sizeof(unsigned int*) * cols) ;
1.5%  jE = (int *)malloc(sizeof(unsigned int*) * cols) ;

2.7%  dN = (float *)malloc(sizeof(float)* size_I) ;
3.8%  dS = (float *)malloc(sizeof(float)* size_I) ;
5.1%  dW = (float *)malloc(sizeof(float)* size_I) ;
5.6%  dE = (float *)malloc(sizeof(float)* size_I) ;
```

Figure 11: ArrayTool identifies arrays used in SRAD. From the feasibility analysis, these arrays can be divided into two groups. One group of arrays allocated inside the rectangle of dash lines, while the other consists of arrays allocated inside the rectangle of solid lines. The percentages on the left of array allocation sites are the access latency ratio over the aggregate sampled accesses in the whole program.

5.3 SRAD

SRAD mainly uses 11 arrays which can be regrouped into two clusters according to ArrayTool's feasibility analysis. From ArrayTool's profiling in Figure 11, `iN`, `iS`, `jW`, and `jE` are insignificant, so we do not consider regrouping these four arrays. Moreover, array `I` only accounts for 0.1% of total sampled memory accesses. ArrayTool shows that although

HW Perf. Counter	Base	Regrouped	Base/Regrouped
L1_DCM	179.45×10^7	29.53×10^7	6.07
L2_DCM	25.42×10^7	11.03×10^7	2.31
TLB_DM	3.39×10^6	3.01×10^6	1.12
L2REQUESTS : HW_PREFETCH_FROM_DC	3.55×10^6	221.43×10^6	0.016
L2REQUESTS : ALL	3.30×10^9	1.59×10^9	2.08
L2 HW DC REQUEST%*	0.10	13.91	-
MEMORY_CONTROLLER_REQUESTS : PREFETCH_REQUESTS	85.31×10^6	72.58×10^6	1.18
MEMORY_CONTROLLER_REQUESTS : ALL	2.40×10^9	2.20×10^9	1.09

*L2 HW DC REQUEST % = (L2REQUESTS : HW_PREFETCH_FROM_DC / L2REQUESTS : ALL)%

Table 3: Hardware Performance Counter measurements for IRS's computation kernel on AMD Platform.

```
#pragma omp parallel for
for(int i=0; i<rows; i++) {
  for(int j=0; j<cols; j++) {
      k = i*cols+j;
      cN = c[k];
      cS = c[iS[i]*cols+j];
      cW = c[k];
      cE = c[i*cols+jE[j]];
      D = cN*dN[k]+cS*dS[k]+cW*dW[k]+cE*dE[k];
      J[k] = J[k]+0.25*lambda*D;
  }
}
```

Figure 12: The kernel parallel loop nest in SRAD accesses significant arrays.

these four arrays have large R_{cw}, regrouping them cannot significantly improve the whole program performance. To prove ArrayTool's analysis, we regrouped iN, iS, jW, and jE and obtained less than a 1.02× speedup in running time compared with the original version..

Then, we analyze simplified mixed CCTs and access patterns from ArrayTool to show that arrays J, c, dN, dS, dW, and dE should be regrouped for better performance. ArrayTool collects access pattern across threads of all these six arrays. All of these arrays have a common access pattern that is of the similar regular shape as shown in Figure 6. Moreover, These arrays have the same simplified mixed CCT, leading R_{cw} between any two arrays to be 1. Therefore, ArrayTool suggests that all of these six arrays should be regrouped. The regrouping result shows 1.89× speedup in running time for the whole SRAD benchmark.

It is worth of noting that profiling-based access pattern analysis outperforms compiler-based static analysis used in previous work [24, 11] in this case study. Figure 12 shows the key OpenMP loop in SRAD that accesses c using indirect indices. Without analyzing access patterns at runtime, we cannot know c has a regular access patterns as other arrays that are referenced with a direct index k. Without regrouping c with other arrays, we only obtained 1.47× speedup in running time.

5.4 Analysis of array regrouping

In this section, we show that the reason program performance improves with array regrouping is that array grouping improves locality and prefetching on our test machine.

Table 3 shows the hardware performance counter measurements for IRS's computation kernel on our AMD test system. Experimentation with the other two benchmarks showed similar changes. Results show 6.07× improvement for L1 Cache Misses and 2.31× for L2 Cache Misses. These results prove that regrouping significantly improves the locality behavior of an application. Merging the array references improves spatial locality across the data cache levels. TLB misses improved 1.12× compared to the base version. The relative reduction in TLB misses was less than those for the data caches. We speculate that the TLB was large enough to hold a data page for each of the distinct arrays accessed in IRS. For efficient prefetching, AMD Opterons have two kinds of hardware prefetchers: DC (Data Cache) prefetch and MC (Memory Controller) prefetch [22]. From the table, L2REQUESTS:HW_PREFETCH_FROM_DC refers to DC prefetches initiated at the L2 cache level and MEMORY_CONTROLLER_REQUESTS: PREFETCH_REQUESTS refers to Memory Controller prefetch requests. Array regrouping significantly improves the DC prefetching as seen in these results. In the base version, we find that only about 0.10% of all the L2 requests are due to DC prefetching. However, for the regrouped version, this value improves to 13.91%. The improvement is the result of fewer prefetch streams after grouping arrays. In the base case, there are 27 different array references that need to be prefetched simultaneously. In contrast, after regrouping only a single prefetch stream is needed for each group of arrays. This effect causes the prefetch stream bandwidth to improve significantly compared to the base version, thereby improving the overall execution time.

From the results, we see that there was no significant difference in the MC prefetches. We speculate that this effect is due to the better management of DC prefetches. IRS benchmark's computation kernel prefetching pattern has stride access of one cache line which is detected by DC logic. MC prefetching would be more useful beyond the single strided access patterns. Improving the performance of MC prefetching would be an interesting future topic.

Overall, our analysis shows why array regrouping improves program performance: it enhances data locality and prefetching.

6. RELATED WORK

In this section, we focus on distinguishing ArrayTool from existing work of both array regrouping in Section 6.1 and other data transformation methods for data locality improvement for parallel programs in Section 6.2.

6.1 Array regrouping

Ding and Kennedy [4] introduced a compiler-aided array regrouping method. Their method is conservative and does not consider the weight of data accesses. Moreover, their method uses a research compiler that supported only Fortran 77. Another compiler-based approach [3] abstracts the array regrouping problem to a graph partitioning problem and formalizes it with a mathematical framework.

Zhong et al [28] defined a profiling-based method to compute array affinities for regrouping. Their profiling method generates better regrouping decisions than static analysis. Their affinity computation gathers information by monitoring each memory access to compute reuse distance histogram, so it is several orders of magnitude slower than a native program execution. According to the latest work [25] from their group, their reuse distance method slows down the program execution by 153× on average. Moreover, they filtered out accesses with short reuse distances and only focused on access with long reuse distances. However, such reuse distance metric only assesses cache capacity misses. ArrayTool's latency metric considers not only capacity misses, but also conflict misses and poor prefetching patterns.

Shen et al [24] proposed a method to compute frequency-based affinities between arrays. They either used static estimation or lightweight profiling with code instrumentation to assess each loop's trip count that is used for affinity computation. Moreover, They used compiler analysis to extract data layout and access patterns. Later, Jiang et al [11] extended this approach to work for multi-threaded programs. However, their static estimation only works for loops with regular structure and it is unclear how they handle array aliasing. Furthermore, their lightweight instrumentation still adds more than 100% runtime overhead.

Jeon et al. [10] encoded memory accesses with regular expressions. They applied pool allocation and exploit data layout transformation according to field affinities. Like Shen's approach, their affinity estimation is also based on static analysis.

Marin et al. [22] regrouped arrays for efficient memory prefetching. They used a simulation method to identify prefetch streams in loop nests and regrouped these streams if they exceed the number of streams that can be handled by hardware perfetcher. However, their approach does not analyze the feasibility of array regrouping. Moreover, the simulation method incurs more than 60x slowdown compared to native execution.

Shortcomings of the aforementioned approaches for identifying regrouping opportunities are as follows. First, they are compiler dependent, which prohibits them from wide application. Second, their affinity computation method is either inaccurate (for static analysis) or has high overhead (for profiling). Third, all of these approaches need to monitor all the arrays used in the program, which does not take the array significance into consideration. Fourth, the frequency-based affinity metric, known as the state-of-the-art approach, is misleading as described in Section 2.2. Fifth, no existing profiling-based approach handles programs parallelized with MPI. As our contribution, ArrayTool addresses all of these shortcomings.

6.2 Data layout for parallel programs

Liu and Mellor-Crummey [15, 19] developed a data-centric profiler that can identify problematic arrays and their access patterns with poor locality in MPI and threaded programs. Unlike ArrayTool, their approach focused on measurement rather than analysis. Based on this data-centric profiler, they developed methods to provide guidance to improve temporal locality via enhancing data reuse [17], and optimize NUMA locality via co-locating data with computation [16]. However, they cannot provide optimization suggestion for regrouping arrays.

ThreadSpotter [23] analyzes memory accesses for parallel programs and provides optimization guidance. Unlike ArrayTool, ThreadSpotter uses binary instrumentation to monitor memory accesses. Moreover, it does not provide any array regrouping analysis.

Zhang et al [27] introduced a data layout framework that improves on-chip cache locality by observing data patterns across threads. Lu et al [20] also proposed a simulation-based data layout optimization method, targeting non-uniform cache access architectures. Both approaches simulate cache hierarchies and runs all experiments in the simulator not the real machine. Moreover, Their optimization works within single arrays not across multiple arrays.

Lu et al. developed Soft-OLP [21], a framework improving the performance of last level caches. Soft-OLP monitors memory accesses via binary instrumentation and computes per-object reuse distance to estimate the usage of L2 caches for arrays. Soft-OLP's memory profiler incurs 50× – 80×, which only applies to programs with small input sets.

To the best of our knowledge, ArrayTool is the first framework that provides both low-overhead measurement and effective analysis to identify array regrouping opportunities in parallel programs.

7. CONCLUSIONS AND FUTURE WORK

This paper describes the design and implementation of ArrayTool, a sampling-based, lightweight profiling tool that can guide locality optimization by identifying arrays that should be regrouped. ArrayTools quantifies affinities between arrays and analyzes their access patterns to provide necessary data to identify regrouping opportunities. With three case studies, we show that ArrayTool guides effective array regrouping optimization. In the context of our case studies, the suggested regroupings significantly improve performance.

Our future work on ArrayTool is four-fold. First, as shown in Figure 2, ArrayTool does not fully automate the workflow of array regrouping. Users still need to transform the code manually to apply regrouping decisions. We plan to develop a compiler technique to regroup arrays automatically. Second, we plan to construct the full calling contexts of OpenMP parallel regions using the lightweight method described in literature [18]. As show in Figure 7 and 9, all OpenMP parallel regions do not have the full context due to the thread pool used by the OpenMP runtime. With full contexts of OpenMP parallel regions, we can give more accurate analysis for array affinities. Third, ArrayTool currently uses R_{cw} to quantify the benefit of array regrouping. However, R_{cw} is not intuitive because one cannot assess the performance improvement after regrouping. In the future, we plan to derive a new quantitative metric to directly evaluate regrouping benefits. Fourth, ArrayTool suggests array regroupings that are beneficial, but is not always optimal. We found that there can be multiple potential regroupings that would be useful. For example, in LULESH, we can regroup all `x`, `y`, `z`, `xd`, `yd`, and `zd` together as an array; or regroup `x`, `y` and `z` into an array, `xd`, `yd`, and `zd` into another array. We plan to extend ArrayTool to automatically identify and suggest optimal regroupings in the future.

Acknowledgements

We thank Rice HPCToolkit team who provide the foundational support for ArrayTool. We are grateful to Prof. Vivek Sarkar and Rice Habanero team for valuable inputs and motivation during the course of this work.

8. REFERENCES

[1] M. Arnold and P. F. Sweeney. Approximating the calling context tree via sampling. Technical Report 21789, IBM, 1999.

[2] S. Che et al. Rodinia: A benchmark suite for heterogeneous computing. In *Proc. of the 2009 IEEE Intl. Symp. on Workload Characterization (IISWC)*, pages 44–54, Washington, DC, USA, 2009.

[3] V. De La Luz and M. Kandemir. Array regrouping and its use in compiling data-intensive embedded applications. *IEEE Trans. Comput.*, 53(1):1–19, Jan. 2004.

[4] C. Ding and K. Kennedy. Inter-array data regrouping. In *In Proceedings of The 12th International Workshop on Languages and Compilers for Parallel Computing*, 1999.

[5] C. Ding and K. Kennedy. Improving effective bandwidth through compiler enhancement of global cache reuse. *Journal of Parallel and Distributed Computing*, 64(1), 2004.

[6] P. J. Drongowski. Instruction-based sampling: A new performance analysis technique for AMD family 10h processors. `http://developer.amd.com/Assets/AMD_IBS_paper_EN.pdf`, November 2007.

[7] P. Havlak. Nesting of reducible and irreducible loops. *ACM TOPLAS*, 19(4):557–567, 1997.

[8] Intel Corporation. Intel 64 and IA-32 architectures software developer's manual, Volume 3B: System programming guide, Part 2, Number 253669-032US. `http://www.intel.com/Assets/PDF/manual/253669.pdf`, June 2010.

[9] Intel Corporation. Intel Itanium Processor 9300 series reference manual for software development and optimization. `http://www.intel.com/Assets/PDF/manual/323602.pdf`, March 2010.

[10] J. Jeon, K. Shin, and H. Han. Abstracting access patterns of dynamic memory using regular expressions. *ACM TACO*, 5(4):18:1–18:28, Mar. 2009.

[11] Y. Jiang, E. Z. Zhang, X. Shen, Y. Gao, and R. Archambault. Array regrouping on cmp with non-uniform cache sharing. In *Proceedings of the 23rd International Conference on Languages and Compilers for Parallel Computing*, LCPC'10, pages 92–105, Berlin, Heidelberg, 2011. Springer-Verlag.

[12] A. Kleen. numactl – Linux man page. `http://linux.die.net/man/8/numactl`, 2005.

[13] Lawrence Livermore National Laboratory. Livermore Unstructured Lagrangian Explicit Shock Hydrodynamics (LULESH). `https://codesign.llnl.gov/lulesh.php`.

[14] Lawrence Livermore National Laboratory. LLNL Sequoia Benchmarks. `https://asc.llnl.gov/sequoia/benchmarks`.

[15] X. Liu and J. Mellor-Crummey. Pinpointing data locality problems using data-centric analysis. In *Proc. of CGO'11*, pages 171–180, Washington, DC, 2011.

[16] X. Liu and J. Mellor-Crummey. A tool to analyze the performance of multithreaded programs on NUMA architectures. In *Proceedings of the 19th ACM SIGPLAN Symposium on Principles and Practice of Parallel Programming*, PPoPP '14, pages 259–272, New York, NY, USA, 2014. ACM.

[17] X. Liu and J. Mellor-Crummey. Pinpointing data locality bottlenecks with low overheads. In *Proc. of ISPASS 2013*, Austin, TX, USA, April 21-23, 2013.

[18] X. Liu, J. Mellor-Crummey, and M. Fagan. A new approach for performance analysis of OpenMP programs. In *Proceedings of the 27th International ACM Conference on International Conference on Supercomputing*, ICS '13, pages 69–80, Eugene, Oregon, USA, 2013. ACM.

[19] X. Liu and J. M. Mellor-Crummey. A data-centric profiler for parallel programs. In *Proc. of the 2013 ACM/IEEE Conference on Supercomputing*, Denver, CO, USA, 2013.

[20] Q. Lu et al. Data layout transformation for enhancing data locality on nuca chip multiprocessors. In *Proc. of the* 18th *Intl. Conference on Parallel Architectures and Compilation Techniques*, pages 348–357, Sept 2009.

[21] Q. Lu et al. Soft-OLP: Improving hardware cache performance through software-controlled object-level partitioning. In *Proc. of the* 18th *Intl. Conf. on Parallel Architectures and Compilation Techniques*, PACT '09, pages 246–257, Washington, DC, USA, 2009. IEEE Computer Society.

[22] G. Marin, C. McCurdy, and J. S. Vetter. Diagnosis and optimization of application prefetching performance. In *Proc. of the* 27th *ACM Intl. Conference on Supercomputing*, ICS '13, pages 303–312, New York, NY, USA, 2013. ACM.

[23] Rogue Wave Software. ThreadSpotter manual, version 2012.1. `http://www.roguewave.com/documents.aspx?EntryId=1492`, August 2012.

[24] X. Shen, Y. Gao, C. Ding, and R. Archambault. Lightweight reference affinity analysis. In *Proc. of the* 19th *Annual Intl. Conf. on Supercomputing*, pages 131–140, New York, NY, USA, 2005. ACM.

[25] X. Xiang, C. Ding, H. Luo, and B. Bao. Hotl: A higher order theory of locality. In *Proceedings of the Eighteenth International Conference on Architectural Support for Programming Languages and Operating Systems*, ASPLOS '13, pages 343–356, New York, NY, USA, 2013. ACM.

[26] Y. Yu and S. T. Acton. Speckle reducing anisotropic diffusion. *IEEE Transactions on Image Processing*, 11(11), 2002.

[27] Y. Zhang, W. Ding, J. Liu, and M. Kandemir. Optimizing data layouts for parallel computation on multicores. In *Proc. of the 2011 Intl. Conf. on Parallel Architectures and Compilation Techniques*, pages 143–154, Oct 2011.

[28] Y. Zhong, M. Orlovich, X. Shen, and C. Ding. Array regrouping and structure splitting using whole-program reference affinity. In *Proc. of the ACM SIGPLAN 2004 Conf. on Programming Language Design and Implementation*, PLDI '04, pages 255–266, New York, NY, USA, 2004. ACM.

Design for Scalability in Enterprise SSDs

Arash Tavakkol[†], Mohammad Arjomand[†], and Hamid Sarbazi-Azad[†‡]
[†]HPCAN Lab, Computer Engineering Department, Sharif University of Technology, Tehran, Iran
[‡]School of Computer Science, Institute for Research in Fundamental Sciences (IPM), Tehran, Iran
{tavakkol,arjomand}@ce.sharif.edu, azad@{sharif.edu,ipm.ir}

ABSTRACT

Solid State Drives (SSDs) have recently emerged as a high speed random access alternative to classical magnetic disks. To date, SSD designs have been largely based on multi-channel bus architecture that confronts serious scalability problems in high-end enterprise SSDs with dozens of flash memory chips and a gigabyte host interface. This forces the community to rapidly change the bus-based inter-flash standards to respond to ever increasing application demands. In this paper, we first give a deep look at how different flash parameters and SSD internal designs affect the actual performance and scalability of the conventional architecture. Our experiments show that SSD performance improvement through either enhancing intra-chip parallelism or increasing the number of flash units is limited by frequent contentions occurred on the shared channels. Our discussion will be followed up by presenting and evaluating a network-based protocol adopted for flash communications in SSDs that addresses design constraints of the multi-channel bus architecture. This protocol leverages the properties of interconnection networks to attain a high performance SSD. Further, we will show and discuss that using this communication paradigm not only helps to obtain better SSD backend latency and throughput, but also to lower the variance of response time compared to the conventional designs. In addition, greater number of flash chips can be added with much less concerns on board-level signal integrity challenges including channels' maximum capacitive load, output drivers' slew rate, and impedance control.

Categories and Subject Descriptors

B.3.2 [**Memory Structures**]: Design Styles—*mass storage*; D.4.2 [**Operating Systems**]: Storage Management—*secondary storage*; B.4.3 [**Input/Output and Data Communications**]: Interconnections—*topology*

PACT'14, August 24–27, 2014, Edmonton, AB, Canada.

http://dx.doi.org/10.1145/2628071.2628098 .

Keywords

NAND flash memory; I/O Interface; Solid State Drive; Interconnection Network

1. INTRODUCTION

Enterprise applications are among the most costly workloads today in terms of IT infrastructure and resources, due to the complexities involved in running these systems and their huge storage requirements. An enterprise storage must meet capacity, performance, and reliability requirements, while minimizing the cost. Therefore, today's storage systems are steadily marching towards using Solid State Drives (SSDs), mainly because of their higher performance and lower power consumption compared to magnetic disks.

To enhance the overall performance and capacity, SSDs employ a multi-chip architecture where tens of flash memory chips are used. For generic SSDs, the overall bandwidth is usually bounded by the host interface, e.g., SCSI, PATA and SATA. Thus, multiple flash chips in the SSD usually share channels or buses to connect to the controller where channels are arranged in a way that their collective bandwidth matches the host interface bandwidth [8, 30, 48]. High-end SSDs in enterprise servers, on the other side, have a gigabyte host interface [48]. A straightforward approach to gain this bandwidth in the backend is to design for maximum parallelism by using dedicated channels for each flash chip [31, 44]. This increases the complexity of flash controller and needs to utilize hardware accelerators [26] or hierarchal controllers [26] for high performance design. Hence, current enterprise SSDs tend to use more channels (yet relatively moderate values), e.g., 8 to 32 channels in PMC NVMe controllers [41, 42, 43], 8 channels in Marvell 88NV9145 family [35] and SandForce SF-2000 family [45].

In this paper, we focus on scalability analysis of the enterprise SSDs. Scalability in enterprise systems is usually achieved by adding more flash memory chips to a channel and render multiple chips busy by exploiting striping allocation [34, 48]. Despite its advantages, the scalability of this design is in jeopardy: although the bus concept is well understood and is easy to employ, it quickly becomes a communication bottleneck in a heavily-loaded channel. Therefore, electrical properties like slew rate and duty cycle distortion does not allow attaching more than a few chips to a channel, for example ONFI 3.2 allows to attach up to 8 flash units working at at maximum bandwidth of 533 MB/s [7]. As more flash chips are attached to the channel, the power usage and latency per communication event grow due to the larger collective capacitive load. Thus, scalability becomes an important concern in today's SSDs and flash standardization work groups are steadily seeking for solutions to enhance the properties of bus-based communication for more and more available bandwidth. This way, from 2008, we have seen successive introduction of the communication standards to enhance 50 MB/s bandwidth in conventional SDR to 533 MB/s in NV-DDR2 or Toggle DDR [5, 7]. This transfer rate cannot be achieved easily and designers must follow specific rules to keep good behavior in signal integrity such as On-Die Termination (ODT), differential clocks, and short channel wires [20, 49].

To cope with this issue, Tavakkol *et al.* [50] suggested to leverage a network-based controller-to-flash communication structure. Their proposal, named as Network-on-SSD (NoSSD), gives higher performance, larger bandwidth, more scalability, and better reliability with least concern about signal distribution problems. In other words, NoSSD is an interconnection network between flashes and the controller that pipelines the global wires, so that their electrical properties are improved and well controlled. These controlled electrical parameters, finally, enable the use of signaling circuits that can largely reduce communication propagation latency and increase the working frequency with much less concerns on the signal integrity. More importantly, sharing communication resources among many I/O requests makes more efficient use of the resources: when one set of flash memory chips are idle, others can continue using network resources. Unfortunately, Tavakkol's study suffers form lack of key design considerations, especially those related to the implementation details of network routers and a realistic messaging protocol for a practical model of NoSSD. In this paper and after our detailed scalability analysis, we will go over the proper choices for NoSSD routers' configuration along with details of the messaging protocol to conduct flash command execution using underlying network infrastructure.

To summarize, this paper has two novel contributions: 1) we extensively analyze the opportunities to scale SSD storage subsystem by examining effects of different flash parameters/structures and multi-channel architecture of SSDs. To the best of our knowledge, such a study is not accomplished in the past and our results will highlight the inefficiency sources of SSD scalability. 2) The proper configuration of the NoSSD routers is described based on board-level inter-flash communication requirements. Different NoSSD design rules, including packet prioritization policy, packet injection policy for controller, and controller to network communication placement are investigated to help achieving higher performance results. Finally, a messaging protocol is proposed to efficiently conduct NAND flash command execution through NoSSD. We hope that our findings help the academic and industrial communities to revise inter-flash communications when thinking about high performance enterprise SSDs.

2. BACKGROUND

In this section, we describe the internal architecture of a standard enterprise SSD and summarize the structural characteristics of NAND flash as storage medium.

2.1 The NAND Flash: Organization and Operation

In a NAND flash, the unit of read and program (write) operations is one page of data but latency asymmetry is observed when a page is read or programmed; we can read any page in a NAND flash, but we must perform an erase operation before programming data to a page. The erase operation is performed at the granularity of a block consisting multiple adjacent pages. Regarding bit density of a cell, single level cell (SLC) and multi level cell (MLC) are two types of NAND flash. The capacity of MLC flash doubles that of SLC type, but SLC flash enjoys lower operational latency and higher endurance.

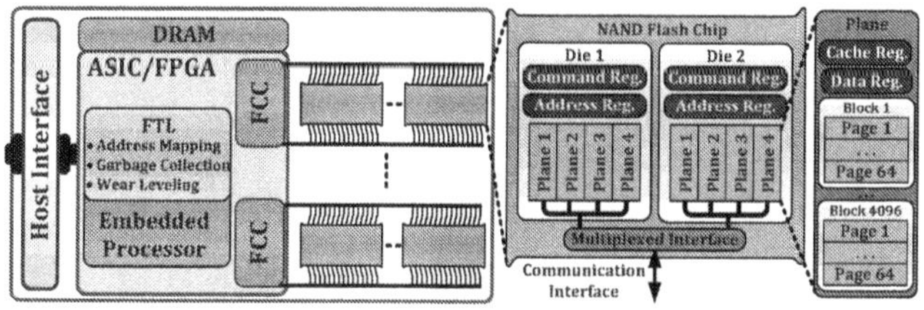

Figure 1: The internal architecture of enterprise SSDs and the structure of NAND flash memory chips.

Figure 1 shows the general organization of a flash memory chip. Within a chip, one or more dies share a single multiplexed interface. Each die can be selected individually and execute a command independent of others, which improves the overall throughput. Using a shared interface by all dies leads to a reduction in I/O bus complexity, but increases contention between requests. A die is typically composed of two or more planes, the smallest units to serve an I/O request. In fact, each plane has a separate wordline for accessing the flash memory pages, which results in an important consequence that multiple requests can be served simultaneously in different planes. However, to this end, the requests must adhere to the rules of multi-plane commands: the pages executing a multi-plane read/program operation must have the same die, block and page addresses; and the blocks executing a multi-plane erase operation must have the same die and block addresses. In addition to multi-plane commands, most of NAND flash memory chips provide other types of advanced commands to support die interleaving and copy-back execution. Interleaved commands provide parallelism within a chip, and copy-back commands enable a page to be copied within a plane without utilizing communication channels.

2.2 Enterprise SSD Internals

Our discussion is based on the architecture of standard enterprise SSDs, widely used in similar studies [17, 18, 38, 44, 48]. Variations of this architecture have been adopted in modern high-end enterprise SSDs, e.g., Fusion-io ioDrive2 Duo [18] and Intel910 series [26]. In enterprise SSDs, PCI Express is usually used as the host interface, where links provide a total bandwidth of 3.2-4 GB/s to exploit tens of flash chips in parallel [17, 48].

The high-level view of a multi-channel enterprise SSD is shown in Figure 1. The SSD uses a FPGA or ASIC between the PCI Express interface and flash channels to implement flash translation layer (FTL) and flash channel controllers (FCCs). FCCs are independently integrated into the FPGA/ASIC for each channel to maximize parallelism. Each FCC consists of a control logic, two independent buffers for read and write, and a NAND interface. There are usually tens of flash memory chips on the board and the controller is equipped with a large amount of RAM to keep FTL mapping information or behave as a cache buffer. FTL is responsible for following tasks:

Address mapping. To emulate disk functionalities, FTL translates the host logical page addresses to internal physical page addresses through an address mapping policy.

Garbage collection (GC). The erase-before-write property and block-level erasure hinder in-place update of the page data, and hence the SSD controller uses a page invalidation mechanism in conjunction with an out-of-place update policy. This policy necessitates erase operation when device runs out of clean pages. A process called garbage collector is then triggered which selects a candidate block and rewrites its valid page into a free block and finally erases it. The garbage collection is very costly due to the required program/erase operations. To remedy this problem, FTL tries to keep user-visible capacity to a fraction of total physical pages, called over-provisioning, below which garbage collection is performed aggressively. The over-provisioning is typically expressed in terms of *spare factor* which is the ratio of added space to the total storage space [54]. Beside this mechanism, modern FTLs may trigger garbage collection process sooner, when SSD is idle and the number of free pages in a flash chip is low (known as background GC).

Wear leveling. Wear-out is one of the most oft-cited concerns about flash memory which causes physical damages to the cells and is not reversible. The datasheet of a flash chip reports a number of 1–100K erase cycles a block can undergo before it becomes unreliable. To this end, FTLs usually use caching, rescheduling, and uniformly distributing the writes to mitigate quick wear-out [11, 12].

3. EXPERIMENTAL METHODOLOGY

We perform discrete-event trace-driven simulation of enterprise SSDs with different communication models using SSDsim [24] augmented with Xmulator [4] interconnection network simulator. Although there are few famous SSD simulators, such as Microsoft SSD model for DiskSim [9], none of them provide a reasonable implementation of the controller-to-flash-chips communication model. However, SSDSim precisely implements ONFI signaling model and its accuracy has been verified using hardware prototyping [24]. Figure 2 depicts a logical view of our simulation methodology. SSDsim gets disk traces as the input workload and is capable of simulating all components shown in Figure 1, including FTL functionsalities and buffer management algorithms at FCC. Once a request is scheduled at a FCC, Xmulator is invoked. Xmulator is a parameterized interconnection network simulator that reports network latency and throughput estimations. Finally, the estimated communication latency and operation latency are sent back to SSDsim for future scheduling.

Enterprise SSD System. We model 1–2 TB enterprise SSDs detailed in Table 1, each with a spare factor of 30% [1]. As a high-end storage system, the configurations considered here have 8 or 4 independent channels each supporting 8 or 16 flash chips, respectively.

Controller Model. The simulated SSD controller runs a fully dynamic page level FTL [19], where a logical page address is not translated to a pre-determined plane by default.

[1]In lifetime-critical enterprise applications, higher spare factor limits are desired. For instance, Intel 910 series has a raw capacity of 1792 GB and user visible capacity of 800 GB (55% spare factor).

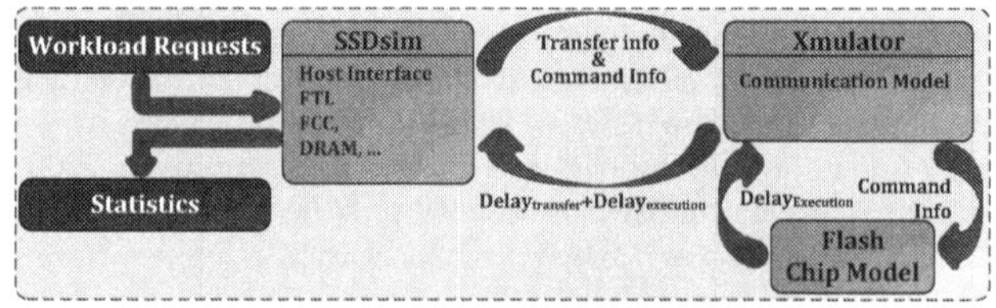

Figure 2: Simulation methodology.

Table 1: Main characteristics of simulated SSDs.

Multi channel SSD
8 Channels, 8 Flash Chips per Channel, Channel Width = 8 bit, NAND Interface Transfer Delay = 5 ns (ONFI NV-DDR), Page Allocation Strategy = Dynamic, Spare Factor = 30%
NAND flash (Micron [37])
Page Size = 4 kB, Metadata Size = 224 B, Block Size = 128 pages, 2 Planes per Die, 8 Dies per Flash Chip, Flash Chip Capacity = 32 GB, Read Latency = 35 µs, Program Latency=350 µs, Erase Latency=1.5 ms

Instead, FTL assigns a logical page to any free physical page of the entire SSD in a round-robin fashion, balancing the load and better exploiting the parallelism of the SSD architecture. A dynamic mapping strategy provides superior performance improvement in comparison with static mapping strategies [51]. Besides, FTL triggers the background GC process when the ratio of free pages within a plane drops below 40%. For the flash chips, we use the timing and organization characteristics of a real 256 Gbit (32 GB) SLC NAND product [37], summarized in Table 1.

Shared Channel Model. To exactly model the timing and strength of the NAND drivers located at FCCs of the shared channels, we use the nominal resistance and capacitance options of the considered flash product (given in [37]).

Workloads. Table 2 shows the selected real workloads from standard benchmark suits, reflecting high-end enterprise environments. TPCC [52] and TPCE [53] workloads are two groups of benchmark programs reflecting On-Line Transaction Processing (OLTP) applications, collected by Microsoft [1]. Two other OLTP traces, namely Financial1 and Financial2, were collected at two large financial institutions [3]. Exchange workload was collected on a Microsoft Exchange 2007 SP1 mail server for 5000 corporate users [1]. MSN traces were collected on an enterprise file server [2]. MSRC workloads were collected at Microsoft Research Cambridge data center servers previously characterized in [39]. WebSearch was collected from a popular internet search engine [3]. We also use a set of synthetic traces created by DiskSim's trace generator [9], to provide better understanding of the proposed communication infrastructure, .

Metrics. Our main performance metrics for the enterprise SSD evaluations are *average response time* and *maximum IOPS*. The response time is defined as the time elapsed from the arrival of a host I/O request until the response is sent back via SSD's host interface. For maximum IOPS calculation, we count the number of accomplished I/O operations in the unit of time when SSD is under full stress condition. To reach this condition, we ignore the inter-arrival time of I/O events and successively service them when there is at least one free slot in the host interface queue.

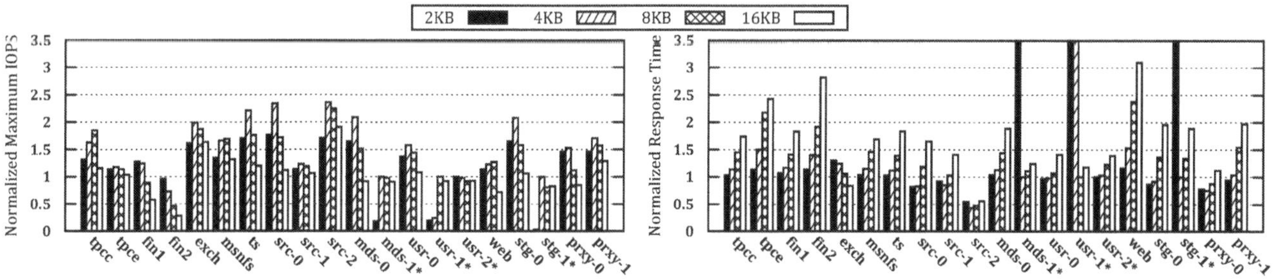

Figure 3: SSD performance vs. page size for different workloads. The results are normalized to those of 1 kB page size, except for workloads tagged with star (*) that saturate SSD in small page sizes because of their high rate of I/O requests (cf. Table 2). The figure shows how the employment of page size larger than 4 kB degrades the overall performance of SSD.

Table 2: Characteristics of the evaluated I/O workloads.

Trace	Read Ratio	Req. Size[a] Mean/Mode	Inter Arrv.[b]	Workload Description
tpcc	0.67	8.2 / 8	0.29	Microsoft TPC-C (OLTP)
tpce	0.94	8.1 / 8	0.45	Microsoft TPC-E (OLTP)
fin1	0.23	3.4 / 3	8.19	Financial1 (OLTP)
fin2	0.82	2.4 / 0.5	11.08	Financial2 (OLTP)
exch	0.28	15.9 / 8	1.05	Microsoft Exchange server
msnfs	0.67	10.1 / 8	0.51	MSN storage file sever
ts	0.18	9 / 4	387.95	Terminal server at MSRC
src-0	0.11	7.2 / 4	448.63	Source control 2-0 at MSRC
src-1	0.98	59.3 / 64	1044.68	Source control 2-1 at MSRC
src-2	0.3	56.3 / 64	547.66	Source control 2-2 at MSRC
mds-0	0.12	9.2 / 4	499.41	Media server 0 at MSRC
mds-1	0.93	56.8 / 64	366.46	Media server 1 at MSRC
usr-0	0.4	22.7 / 4	270.25	User home dirs 0 at MSRC
usr-1	0.91	49.5 / 64	13.36	User home dirs 1 at MSRC
usr-2	0.81	43.8 / 64	57.22	User home dirs 2 at MSRC
web	0.99	15.2 / 8	2.99	WebSearch
stg-0	0.64	40.8 / 64	297.79	Web staging 0 at MSRC
stg-1	0.15	11.6 / 4	275.27	Web staging 1 at MSRC
prxy-0	0.03	4.8 / 1	48.16	Web proxy 0 at MSRC
prxy-1	0.65	12.6 / 8	3.58	Web proxy 1 at MSRC,
synth	0,0.5,1.0	0.5 to 1024	1.00	Synthetic, from DiskSim

[a] Kilobytes [b] Milliseconds

4. MULTI-CHANNEL SSD SCALABILITY

During last two decades, the improvements in flash memory technology have led to different effects on storage devices: bit density increases, but other important features including performance, lifetime, and energy are drastically reduced. On the other hand, the SSD vendors strive to provide higher capacity products while keeping their performance at a reasonable level [20, 49]. Accordingly, scaling the SSD capacity necessitates proper scaling of I/O performance to keep flash memory utilization at the highest level. SSD scalability is always a matter of debate and recently attracted interests in academic and industry [14, 20, 21, 49].

The SSD storage hierarchy consists of four levels: 1) plane, 2) die, 3) chip, and 4) channel, and any attempt to scale SSD should target increasing capacity at one or more of them. In this section, we discuss SSD scalability behavior with respect to increasing storage capacity at each level. To elucidate how much performance improvement is due to the higher capacity or parallelism and how much is the contribution of process technology, we assume a fixed feature size (20 nm) and focus on SSD scalability.

4.1 Increasing Plane Capacity

The finest way to increase plane capacity is page size expansion by embedding more memory cells or increasing bit storage density of each cell. NAND flash is subject to wear-out failure and requires some types of ECCs to achieve a certain level of reliability. Thus, as the page size increases, a strong ECC is required that imposes considerable latency overheads to read and program operations. On the other side, increasing bit density to two or more bits per cell significantly reduces read/program performance because of slow circuit-level mechanisms required for correct detection/adjustment of memory cell's voltage level. For instance, Grupp *et al.* showed that density increase from 1 to 3 bits/cell will result in a performance degradation factor of 3–10 for I/O requests [21].

At architecture level, page size expansion has advantages and disadvantages. Larger page size results in lower number of executed operations, as on each access a large amount of data chunks are brought in or out. However, this performance enhancement is saturating and will be increased up to a point that the unit of host I/O requests equals the NAND flash memory page size. Increasing page size beyond this threshold is not beneficial and even can result in declined performance due to the partially-updated pages. Partial updates require read-modify-write operations (reading the stored page content, transferring to the controller, and merging with the updated data) and increase the chip-waiting time as the controller should wait for a busy chip to become idle in order to read a page. In addition to the above disadvantage, the transfer time of page data increases proportional to the page size. For read operations, this is extremely challenging since transfer time is close to the command execution time and this overhead may diminish the savings in number of executed commands [49].

Figure 3 illustrates the effects of page size on the performance of a SSD with configuration mentioned in Section 3. The results are normalized to those of 1 kB page size, except for the workloads where internal SSD traffic load saturates for small page sizes; in these cases (marked with *), the smallest page size (>1 kB) with unsaturated results is used for normalization. In general, the maximum SSD IOPS stops increasing at 4 kB page size and then starts decreasing owing to higher transfer time of a huge page and frequent partial updates. To have a better understanding, Table 3 reports the *ratio of partial updates*, *average read/program operation count per I/O request* and *average internal transfer size* for different pages sizes. The results confirm the increasing/decreasing trend of IOPS in Figure 3. We see that ratio of partial updates and resultant average transfer size sharply increase as page size exceeds 4 kB. So, the per-

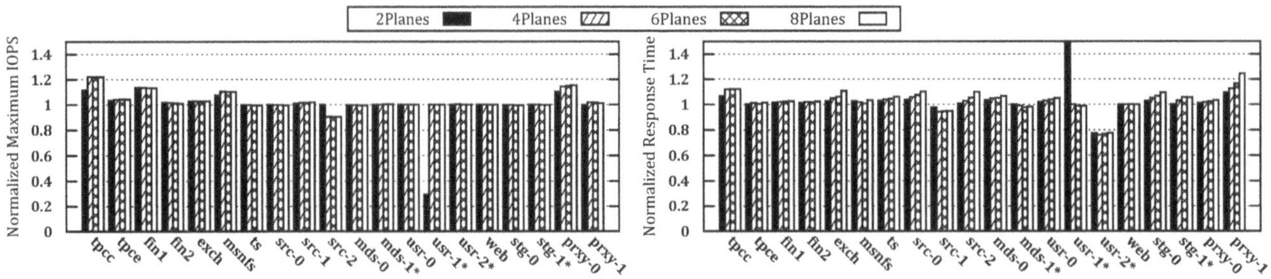

Figure 4: SSD performance vs. number of planes per die for different workloads. While the IOPS of target SSD remains roughly constant, response time increases in 6 or 8 planes per die.

formance improvement due to reduction in the number of I/O operations is not large enough to mitigate the performance loss of the increased partial updates and transfer size. We observed a similar behavior for SSD's response time, and depending on the application, the response time steadily increases from 2 kB page size to 4 kB, 8 kB or 16 kB. In sum, scaling SSD's capacity at finest granularity (page size) seems to result in lower I/O traffic, but significantly suffers from partial update and transfer size overheads.

We can also enlarge plane size by embedding more data pages. As a plane is the smallest unit to process a page request and has no means for internal parallelism, adding pages to a plane gives no performance gain if it does not increase bit-line latency. Therefore, this approach does not brings better capacity and performance for scalable design.

4.2 Increasing Die Capacity

We can increase SSD capacity by adding more planes to a die and expect that plane-level parallelism helps us to stripe requests for better performance. In theory this is correct, but extreme use of plane-level parallelism confronts serious limitations in practice: 1) As described in Section 2, plane-level commands have to be applied at the same page address of planes within a die. Then, finding requests in the controller queues that can be handled at same addresses of planes in a die is not always successful; 2) The allocation scheme has significant impact on the chance of finding multi-plane commands. Hu *et al.* [25] showed that the static allocation with channels/dies striping in priority and the dynamic allocation give best performance results for current SSDs. However, both schemes reduce the chance of executing multi-plane commands. Indeed, they empirically showed that when dynamic allocation scheme is employed in a multi-channel SSD, multi-plane commands are not required since the exploration of channel-level and chip-level parallelism alone can deal with majority of the requests. Then, reordering, rescheduling and classification algorithms, like PAQ [27] or the proposed schemes in [10, 40], have a very low chance to find multi-plane commands.

To explore the effect of plane-level parallelism on SSD performance, we assumed a maximum of 8 planes per die and conducted simulations for a SSD with configuration in Section 3. The experiments are for dynamic allocation scheme [25] and PAQ scheduling [27]. Figure 4 demonstrates the maximum IOPS and average response time for evaluated workloads normalized to the configuration with 1 plane per die. The results confirm that adding planes to a die may improve IOPS since the average number of executed operations per die can be increased through multi-plane commands.

Table 3: The effect of pages size increase on the executed commands in SSD evaluated in Figure 3.

Page Size (kB)	1	2	4	8	16
Partial Update Ratio	0.02	0.06	0.09	0.21	0.30
ReadOp/Req.[a]	16.1	8.4	4.4	2.7	2.1
ProgramOp/Req.[a]	21.6	11.1	5.8	3.3	2.4
Xfer/Req. (kB)[b]	37.7	39.0	40.8	48.0	72.0

[a] Read/program operation count per I/O request
[b] Internal transfer size per I/O request (kB)

Nevertheless, the improvement rate is almost negligible for half of the workloads and it usually remains unchanged for the die size of $\geq$ 4 planes. Figure 4 also shows that improving plane-level parallelism generally increases the average response time. Even though there are exceptions, this trend can be justified by the interactions between dynamic page allocation scheme and multi-plane command execution [25]. We conclude that having 2 or 4 planes per die is the most proper design choice for majority of workloads, beyond which performance can be degraded substantially.

Based on the above discussions on capacity increment at plane-level and die-level, we should say that intra-die scaling approaches are all limited by performance requirements of enterprise SSDs. Accordingly, the inevitable solution is to employ more dies or chips to increase capacity while fulfilling performance demands through die interleaving, flash chip pipelining, and channel striping by proper page allocation strategies [28, 49]. State-of-the-art enterprise SSD products follow the same approach to achieve true scalability [18, 26].

4.3 Increasing Flash Chip Capacity

One may consider increasing chip capacity by adding more dies and hence improving the chance for interleaving command execution to concurrently read, program, and erase pages and blocks of different dies. Moreover, interleaving provides an opportunity to overlap data transfer to a die with command execution of other dies within the same chip. Figure 5 shows this fact by giving the percentage of time that a flash chip spends in either of the following four states:

1. Exclusive transfer: one die is transferring data while others are waiting for data transfer or are idle.
2. Overlapped transfer and command execution: some dies are executing command and some are transferring data. The remaining dies are idle.
3. Exclusive command execution: one or multiple dies are executing commands while others (if any) are idle.
4. Idle: all dies are idle.

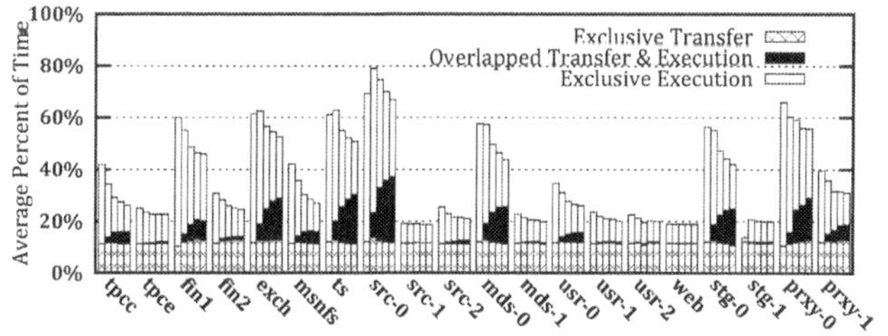

Figure 5: Average percent of time that each flash chip spends in data transfer or execution states. For each workload, number of dies per chip is set to 1, 2, 4, 6, and 8 from left to right.

In this experiment, we use the SSD configuration in Table 3 and varying number of dies per flash chip from 1 to 8. The figure shows that the time percentage that a flash chip exclusively transfers data to/from a die remains nearly constant regardless of the number of dies and workload. This is because of the technique used to conduct die interleaved commands which issues a command when all dies within the flash chip are idle [25]. In addition, data or command information transfer is triggered at the same time but in a sequential order. Data transfer and command execution of multiple dies within a flash chip can be more overlapped as die-level parallelism increases. Nevertheless, it stops after some level of parallelism above which it is not practically possible to improve chance of overlapping. The reason is that dies within a chip maximally utilize the available bandwidth for the chip and percentage of time, in which at least one die is transferring data, becomes nearly fixed (exclusive transfer + overlapped transfer and command execution in Figure 5).

Therefore the overall disk throughput is expected to improve as the die-level parallelism increases, but it stops improving after a certain level of parallelism. Figure 6 reports the maximum IOPS and average response time for different number of dies per flash chip. The results are given for 2 dies to 8 dies per chip configurations, normalized to the results for the configuration with 1 die. We remark that dynamic allocation strategy prefers to execute interleaved commands for higher die utilization, leading to higher throughput but in cost of worse response time [25]. Then, increasing flash chip capacity by means of excessive die interleaving is not a proper solution and is inherently limited by the channel bandwidth.

4.4 Increasing Number of Flash Chips

The primary option to increase SSD's capacity is to employ more flash memory chips. Today's state-of-the-art enterprise SSDs consist of more than 30 flash memory chips arranged on single-layer or multi-layer boards [18, 23, 26]. In a multi-channel configuration, more flash memory chips can be added either by enhancing channel-level parallelism (i.e., more shared channels) or by increasing chip-level parallelism (more flash chips sharing a channel). Increasing channel-level parallelism can be used to maximize independent connections to the controller, thereby minimizing the total cost of data and command transfer, performancewise. As stated in Section 2.2, FCCs of enterprise SSDs are usually dedicated to channels and are all embedded into the same FPGA/ASIC controller chip. Therefore, adding more channels necessitates rethinking of the controller logic and pin assignment that is costly. This is why 8-channel controller is a common configuration in many current products [35, 45] and adding more channels requires some hardware accelerators or special design techniques to drive huge number of resources [42, 43].

Added flash chips can be assigned to channels and expect that chip-level parallelism helps us to freely distribute read/program operations. The greater the number of connected flash chips to a shared channel, the higher capacitive load on the bus and lower performance. So, SSD standards like ONFI are always putting strict constraints on maximum load of a channel in order to deliver highest bandwidth. For example, ONFI 3.2 [7] allows maximum capacitance of 32.7 pF for I/O pins to guarantee 533 MB/s transfer rate when 8 flash chips are connected to a channel.

4.5 Summary

Despite the fact that increasing the number of functional units (chips or dies) is an inevitable approach to achieve capacity scaling, our analysis in last two subsections indicate that the limited bandwidth of channels is a potential showstopper to attain scalability goals. To this end, researchers and manufacturers look for flexible and high performance ways to cope with this problem. Some vendors such as Intel [26] and Fusion-io [18] use a high-level solution in which a set of small-sized SSD modules in conjunction with a front-end request distributor are used to produce a high-capacity product. The front-end chip may be a RAID controller or just a simple bridge. The 800 GB version of Intel 910 Series is a well-known example in this line which constitutes an on-chip PCIe-to-SAS bridge together with four 200 GB SSD modules each containing its own ASIC controller [26]. Even though such solution keeps the flash channel interface unchanged, it dramatically increases the cost of SSD controller due to the additional front-end logic and per module controller. Moreover, the number of failure points are increased in SSD and a single failure of a small-sized module brings the whole array down. Some vendors pay the extra cost and capacity penalties of RAID1 or RAID5 to alleviate this problem while others provide each module as an independent disk, i.e., there is no a single disk and customer must relay on software RAID techniques to achieve a single volume.

On the contrary, changing the flash communication interface may be a reasonable solution to alleviate bandwidth constraints of multi-channel bus structure. Using a shared and segmented network communication structure is a straightforward and promising alternative. For instance, HLNAND introduced a fully-packetized command and address format to enable connecting flash chips to the controller through a daisy-ring topology [46] or hierarchical ring topology [20]. Recently, Tavakkol *et al.* proposed a more generic and regular network-based design paradigm, namely Network-on-SSD (NoSSD) [50], which showed significant performance over conventional designs. In a similar manner, we suggest to use such a network-based solution and extend the preliminary NoSSD model for building large-scale SSDs. In the next section, we go over the details of NoSSD architecture and support it with messaging and communication protocols for inter-flash SSD communications.

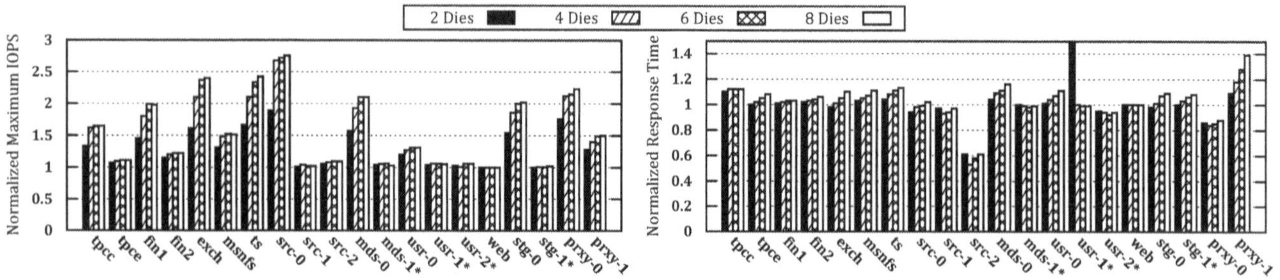

Figure 6: SSD performance vs. number of dies per flash chip for different workloads. While the IOPS remains a constant at highly-loaded channels, response time drastically increases (between 10% to 40% for various configurations).

5. INTER-FLASH NETWORKING

Network-on-SSD consists of routing nodes and communication links to connect adjacent flash chips following some specific topology. NoSSD is inspired by the proven concepts and techniques from on-chip and off-chip interconnection networks in multiprocessors [15]. NoSSD is different from layered communication abstraction models and is orthogonal to flash-related command execution and communication decoupling techniques. In this section, we first present a component-based view of NoSSD and introduce the basic building blocks of a typical NoSSD. Then, we look at system-level architectural issues relevant to NoSSD design and enterprise storage.

5.1 A Simple NoSSD Example

Figure 7 shows a sample NoSSD structured as a grid supporting controller-to-flash-chips communications. Instead of the shared and dedicated channels, a more general scheme is adopted, employing a grid of routing elements spread out among flash memory chips, interconnected by communication links. At the first glance, a tree-like network seems great due to higher traffic rate at the controller side. However, this topology provides less inter-node route parallelism compared to grid topology in addition to other design constraints that lead us to use grid topology: 1) in dynamic page mapping, where a logical page address has the highest freedom to be mapped at any flash chip/die/plane, garbage collection needs page movement between flash chips. The grid topology greatly helps in this issue by providing some direct paths between chips that does not necessarily pass through FCC; 2) special FCC to network connection methods (see Section 5.4), that decrease the average FCC to flash chips distance, best suite the grid topology; 3) FCC can use higher number of regularly-patterned connections to the network since the pin-out/logic complexity of NoSSD is greatly simplified in grid network compared to bus and tree.

We adopt a simplified perspective where NoSSD contains the following fundamental components.

Flash memory network adapters. They implement the interface by which a flash memory chip connects to NoSSD. Due to structural differences between network transmission unit (i.e., packet) and NAND flash memory command execution data (i.e., page or command), the network adapter should manipulate and arrange data for both sides. A good network adapter must provide a low latency path to the network while incurring no cost to commodity NAND flash.

Routers. They route data based on a chosen protocol and flow control scheme. Details of the input-buffered router element alongside flash memory logic are shown in Figure 7. We suggest to use 4 injection/ejection channels per router to reduce waiting time of the sent/arrived packets.

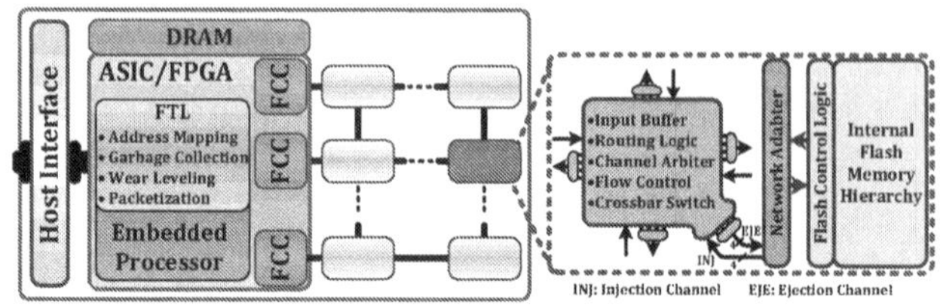

Figure 7: Topological illustration of NoSSD.

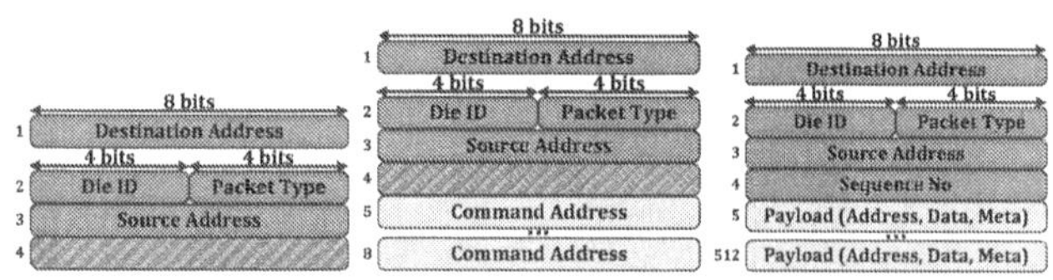

(a) 4 flits (b) 8 flits (c) 512 flits

Figure 8: Packet format for different packet types in Table 4.

Links. They connect the routers and flash controller and provide the raw bandwidth. To maintain the wiring costs low and alleviate pin-out constraint, links are bidirectional.

FCC (redesigned). Shared-buffer interfaces are used to connect SSD controller to NoSSD. These interfaces are tuned to the messaging protocol and flow control scheme. In fact, FCC simply emulates network adapter functionalities.

Figure 7 shows a high-level view of the NoSSD. To realize NoSSD, detailed *messaging protocol, flow control and routing mechanism* and *controller placement* must be considered.

5.2 Packet Format and Messaging Protocol

As described above, the network adapter decouples the flash chip and the controller from NoSSD. In other words, network adapter handles encapsulation of NAND flash messages, generated by either the controller or flash chips, for the routing strategy. A NAND flash message consists of command, data, and metadata that is broken into packets for transmission over NoSSD. At the lowest transmission level (i.e., link), the basic datagram are flits (atomic flow control units forming a packet). In NoSSD, we assume that flit is the minimum size of datagram that can be transmitted in one link transaction; it is set to 8 bits for our NoSSD model in Section 6.

Figure 8 shows the packet formats of NoSSD consisting of

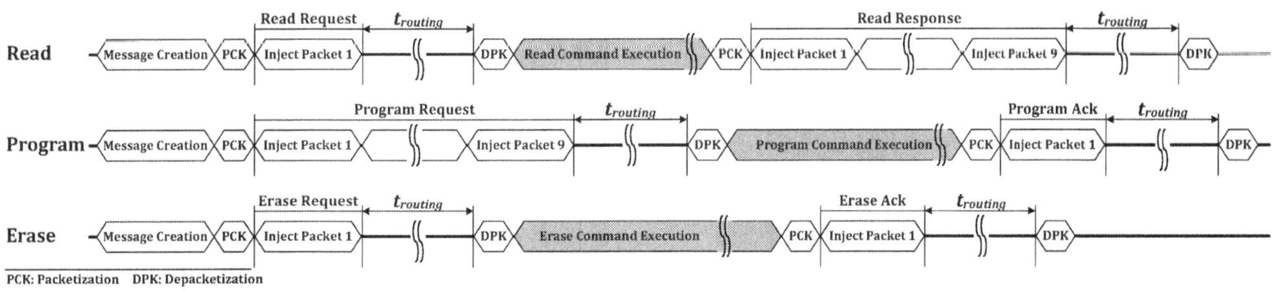

Figure 9: NoSSD messaging protocol for basic NAND flash operations.

Table 4: Binary encoding and length of packet types. The reserved binary codes are for advanced commands.

Type	Code	Len.	Type	Code	Len.
Read Req.	0000	8	Erase Req.	0100	8
Read Resp.	0001	512	Erase Ack.	0101	4
Program Req.	0010	512	Reserved	1xxx	x
Program Ack.	0011	4			

header flits followed by payloads. The header part includes source and destination addresses and packet sequence number. Two additional 4-bit units are used to identify the type of a packet and ID number of the target die. The binary encoding of the packet types is presented in Table 4 based on which packet length is also determined. Each packet belonging to the same message has the same ID number to differentiate it from other packets, when it reaches the controller or flash chips. Upon receiving packets at the destination, the network adapter uses packet sequence number to depacketize the received command or data.

Figure 9 illustrates the messaging protocol to conduct basic command execution of the flash chip. To initiate a read operation, the controller encapsulates the command and target page address into a message which is then packetized to a single 8-flit *Read Request* packet (Figure 8b). Having the read command executed, the flash chip produces a message containing the data and metadata of the read page. Assuming 4 kB page and 224 B metadata, as considered in Section 3, this message is sent to the controller through nine 512-flit *Read Response* packets (Figure 8c). To issue a program operation, on the other hand, the controller generates a message, containing the page address, data, and metadata, that is broken into nine 512-flit *Program Request* packets. Upon finishing program command execution, the target flash chip generates a short 4-flit *Program Ack* acknowledge packet (Figure 8a). A similar mechanism is used during erase operation by a pair of *Erase Request* and *Erase Ack* packets.

5.3 Router Organization and Functionalities

In this section, we describe the router organization of NoSSD and its corresponding functionalities.

NoSSD Router. Figure 7 clearly specifies the major components of a router in NoSSD including buffers, crossbar switch, routing and arbitration unit, and link controller. The switch connects the input buffers to output ports, while routing and arbitration unit implements the algorithm dictating these connections. Moreover, the routing logic is separately implemented for each input port; so, it can simultaneously forward maximum number of flits per input/output switching pairs to reduce routing delay and enhance communication bandwidth. Based on this model, NoSSD routers use a pipelined synchronous architecture while intra-router data transfer is handled asynchronously using the link controller.

Wormhole NoSSD. In this work, NoSSD utilizes wormhole switching mechanism merely for transport of data, and the routing mechanism for determining the path of data transport. NoSSD guarantees lossless packet delivery using wormhole switching which prevents buffer overflow at input/output ports [15]. Wormhole combines packet switching with the data streaming quality of channel pipeline communication to attain a minimal packet latency. At each hop, router looks at the header to determine the proper outpot port and immediately forwards it; subsequent flits are forwarded as they arrive. This causes the packet to experience an extremely reduced amount of network transfer latency and, as a consequence, the overall NoSSD performance is improved. When the path is determined, ahead of crossbar switch, each flit has to wait for availability of free slots in the next hop buffer and then preempts output channel via arbitration. At last, flits are transmitted over physical links. When header reaches the destination, the local ejection port is allocated for flit-by-flit delivery of the packet to network adapter.

ON/OFF Flow Control in NoSSD Routers. To ensure a correct and lossless operation, NoSSD utilizes ON/OFF wormhole flow control mechanism where each downstream router uses a status signal to inform the upstream side about the availability of free buffer slots. While status signal is ON and there are flits waiting for dispatch, the upstream router keeps on flit transmission. However, it stops sending flits upon status turn off since buffer slot shortage will cause flit loss on the downstream side. In practice, this signal is turned off when the number of free slots falls below a predetermined threshold value. This value should be chosen to guarantee storage of on-the-fly flits while signal is propagated back to the upstream side. Consequently, there is a lower limit for the minimum buffer size of each input port that must be considered during NoSSD design. Regarding the router model in Section 6, the minimum buffer size is 10 flits based on the rules given in [15].

NoSSD uses bidirectional channels to alleviate pin-out constraints on both sides of FCC and flash chips. A channel demands two ON/OFF signals for each direction and a token signal, namely Transfer Token, is shared between adjacent routers to manage channel accesses and avoid contentions. One side is allowed to transfer when the token signal is low while other side sends flits when Transfer Token is high. Upon finishing flit transmission, the sender inverts the token value to grant access permission to the opposite side.

The ON/OFF flow control and wormhole switching guarantee in-order delivery of flits within a packet. However, multi-path and prioritized routing, described in section 5.4, may cause out-of-order delivery of the packets within a message. Nonetheless, the packet sequence number can be simply used for accurate recovery of the original message.

5.4 NoSSD Design Rules for High Performance SSDs

Priority-based Transmission. Performance of NoSSD may suffer from long transmission latency of *Read Response* and *Write Request* packets. In fact, in wormhole switching, a stalled long packet may cause serious side effects on the transmission latency of other packets due to blocking propagation.

To mitigate this shortcoming, NoSSD routers exploit a packet prioritization scheme for arbitration on the accesses to output channels. To this end, router micro-architecture is slightly modified in order to alter the normal FIFO arbitration policy and give higher priority to some packets (based on some rules). To explain these rules, we classify packets into two groups: small packets including *Read Request*, *Program Ack*, *Erase Request* and *Erase Ack*, and large packets including *Read Response* and *Program Request* packets.

Rule 1. ***Small packets are always handled first.*** *Following this policy, transfer delay of small packets is reduced but waiting time of large packets is increased. We expect that the performance improvement achieved by accelerating the transmission of small packets is large enough to compensate for the latency loss of large packets. This rule does not result in starvation for large packets since generation of small packets always depends on NAND flash operation execution; hence, generation rate of a burst of small packets is predictably low.*

Rule 2. ***Transmitting a sequence of large packets are prioritized.*** *When NoSSD uses XY routing, Read Response or Program Request packets of the same message are always routed on the same path. Therefore, if a large packet is granted to use a channel, we can keep it for another upcoming packet (that will be received at the same port and with same die ID) to be transmitted immediately. Therefore, read/program data will be always transmitted in chunks that improve response time. This approach generally differs from circuit switching since large packets may stall at intermediate routers when there are many requests in the network.*

Traffic-Aware Packet Injection. On write transactions, FTL triggers an allocation process to choose free pages for data storage. Static allocation tries to uniformly distribute page writes among flash chips following a predetermined mapping rule; that is target flash chip, die, and plane address is determined based on logical page address. Dynamic allocation, on the other hand, assigns pages dynamically by considering different factors such as idle/busy state of the channels and flash chips and priority order of parallelism. At the first step, FTL searches for a free physical channel based on round-robin approach. Next, within the allocated channel, it assigns a free flash chip and then allocates die and plane using the same round-robin method. Although dynamic allocation provides better performance, it suffers from degraded random read latency [24]. Actually,

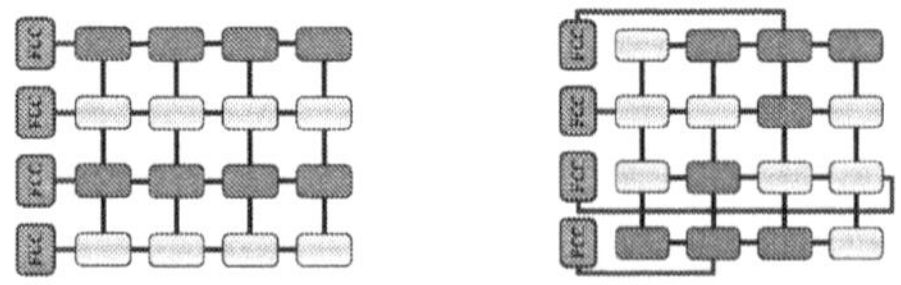

(a) One Sided (b) All Sided

Figure 10: One- vs. all-sided FCC-to-NoSSD connections.

allocations considering write performance and cell wearout result in a non-uniform distribution of read operations that may not be tolerable. To relieve read latency degradation, the controller in the ultimate NoSSD design, is augmented with a simple traffic-aware injection mechanism. Each FCC has a counter referring to the number of packets waiting to be sent. Depending on the counter values, controller chooses the less-stressed FCC for packet injection.

Controller Placement. The NoSSD design in Figure 7 uses a grid topology and has FCCs positioned near to the left side of network. However, keeping NoSSD regularity in mind, there are multiple other ways to connect FCCs to NoSSD routers. These different configurations of the FCC-to-NoSSD connection can have a dramatic impact on the latency and bandwidth characteristics of the network, especially for grid topology which is not edge symmetric. Furthermore, by reducing the variance in the number of hops per request as well as packet latency and channel load, NoSSD's performance seems to be less sensitive to the flash chip on which a page is mapped. In the ultimate NoSSD design that is evaluated in Section 6, we examine one-sided and all-sided FCC placement policies, as shown in Figure 10. In all-sided configuration, we try to provide better and predictable latency and bandwidth characteristics by evenly distributing FCCs in all sides of NoSSD (middle of each side). Please note that the longer wires of all-sided placement still have lower latency with respect to the multi-channel bus wires since each output driver, either at FCC or NoSSD side, sees much lower capacitive load.

5.5 Implementation Issues

In a conventional multi-channel architecture, a flash controller consists of two parts: 1) a unit responsible for controlling the sequence of micro-operations required for NAND flash functionalities and error correction schemes, and 2) a signaling mechanism for transmitting controller commands to flash chips. In NoSSD controller, on the other hand, managing read/write requests are accomplished by the flash chips themselves. Thus, controller's functionality is limited to be the interface logic between the front-end processor and network substrate. This simplifies controller logic which is highly desirable in modern SSDs[2].

In a NoSSD flash chip, the network adapter, buffer storage, crossbar switch, channel arbiters, and router logic are the newly added parts. Among the mentioned elements, buffers occupy most of the router's area. To mitigate signal propagation delay and fully utilize channel bandwidth, we assume buffer depth of 512 flits per input channel which means a 4 kB buffer space per router. To estimate the area

[2]Many companies try to embed some memory-related functions (like error correction) into the NAND flashes so that the controller cost is reduced; an example is Managed NAND by Micron [36].

Table 5: Characteristics of the simulated NoSSD model.

NoSSD
Channel Width = 8 bit, Inter-router Propagation Delay = 5 ns, Pipeline Stages = 3, Pipeline Stage Delay = 5 ns, Input Buffer Size = 512 flit, Routing Algorithm = XY

overhead of the router, we used Orion 2 [29]. We set process technology to 32 nm, as it is the smallest available choice in Orion 2 that matches ever shrinking feature size of NAND flash memory. The results show that the buffer and crossbar area is about 0.17 mm^2 and 0.03 mm^2, respectively, while the arbitration and routing logics just occupy 0.002 mm^2. Next, we use NVSim [16] to achieve an estimation for the area of a typical 4 GB NAND flash die with the properties mentioned in Table 1. The results show that the die area is about 72 mm^2 and thus a set of 4/8 dies within a 16/32 GB flash chip occupy 288/576 mm^2. In other words, the area overhead of a NoSSD router is less than 0.1% of the flash storage area. Please note that due to model limitations, we ignored some components in each part, i.e., the NAND peripheral and command control circuits for memory and the network adapter for NoSSD.

Regarding signaling requirements, NoSSD also simplifies FCC implementation logic since each communication channel is managed via 3 control signals regardless of the number of flash chips. Indeed, FCC in a multi-channel architecture has to drive tens of control signals that is proportional to the number of dies sharing a channel [25]. In addition, as mentioned in the NAND flash chip standards [5, 6], SSD designers should care about capacitive and resistive load of a bus channel for reliable and high-performance transfers [6]. NoSSD, nevertheless, can remove these electrical constraints since each channel is just shared between two adjacent routers and the global wiring is provided by (semi-)regular topologies, e.g., mesh (grid) and torus.

6. EVALUATION

To compare NoSSD's performance against a baseline multi-channel SSD design, we use the simulation methodology and flash chip model described in Section 3. For NoSSD, the flash chips are organized as a grid topology with XY routing [15]. As an abbreviation, we simply use $m{\times}n$ notation for a grid configuration of m rows and n columns. The multi-channel SSD structure with same size, m channels and n flash chips per channel, is denoted with $mCnP$. The NoSSD router is the same as model introduced by Dally and Towles [15] without virtual channel multiplexing. The router pipeline consists of three stages each with 5 ns latency: 1) buffer write and route computation for header flits, 2) switch allocation, and 3) switch traversal, followed by link traversal. Table 5 summarizes the evaluated router configuration. Please note that, the default packet injection policy in the FCC is round-robin.

6.1 NoSSD vs Multi-Channel SSD Performance

Figure 11 presents the normalized maximum IOPS and average response time of real workload traces in 4×16 and 8×8 NoSSD configurations with respect to the same-sized multi-channel SSD. We see that NoSSD enhances the maximum IOPS by 37%–180% (100%, on average) whereas it reduces the average and worst-case response time by 22% and 8%, respectively. In addition, Figure 12 illustrates the

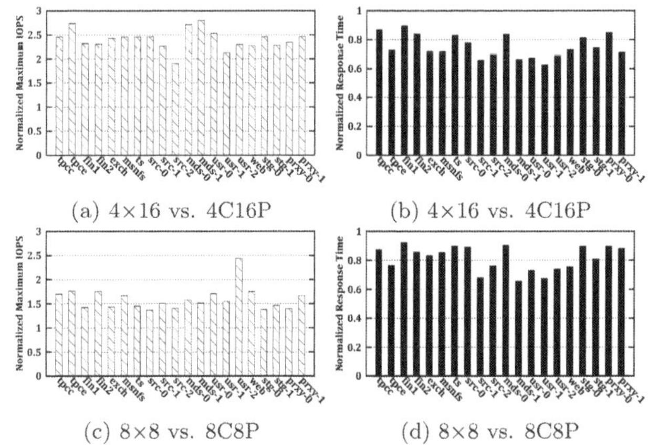

(a) 4×16 vs. 4C16P (b) 4×16 vs. 4C16P

(c) 8×8 vs. 8C8P (d) 8×8 vs. 8C8P

Figure 11: Normalized average response time and maximum IOPS of NoSSD to the multi-channel baseline. MC stands for multi-channel SSD.

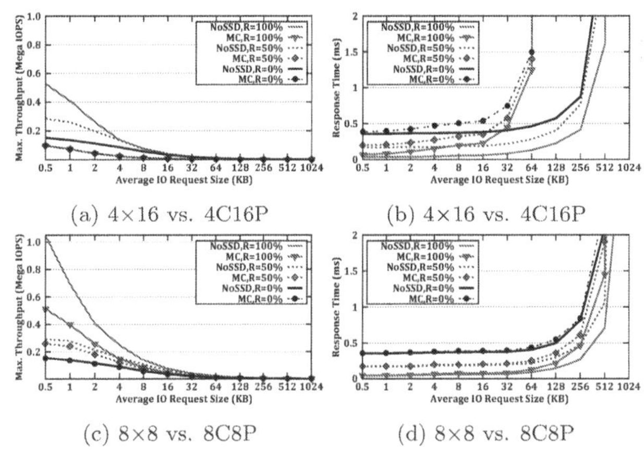

(a) 4×16 vs. 4C16P (b) 4×16 vs. 4C16P

(c) 8×8 vs. 8C8P (d) 8×8 vs. 8C8P

Figure 12: Response time and maximum IOPS of NoSSD and multi-channel baseline under synthetic workloads.

maximum achievable IOPS and average response time of the NoSSD and multi-channel SSD designs for different request sizes in synthetic workloads. Regarding the results of both real and synthetic workloads, we can make the following conclusions:

- NoSSD achieves much more performance improvement (compared to the conventional design) when channel-level parallelism is low. This is primarily due to better utilization of resources in NoSSD by pipelining/parallelizing requests among routers, while path diversity and round-robin packet injection collectively provide a substrate to balance load in the network.
- As the ratio of read requests increases in the workload, NoSSD achieves higher performance improvement. In fact, read-oriented workloads are more sensitive to the communication delays, since the execution time of a read operation is comparable with controller-to-flash communication delay.
- NoSSD provides great response time gains when workload request size is large. Contrarily, the greatest IOPS improvement is seen for smaller request sizes.
- By scaling SSD capacity via increasing channel-level par-

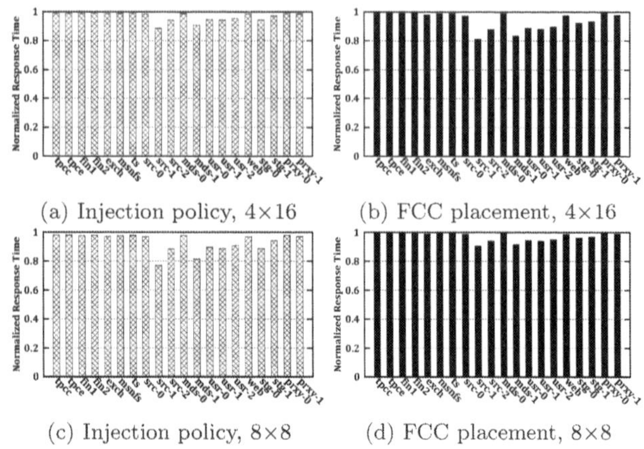

(a) Injection policy, 4×16 (b) FCC placement, 4×16

(c) Injection policy, 8×8 (d) FCC placement, 8×8

Figure 13: The effect of enhancing FCC to NoSSD communication (a),(c) via traffic-aware injection policy and (b),(d) via FCC placement.

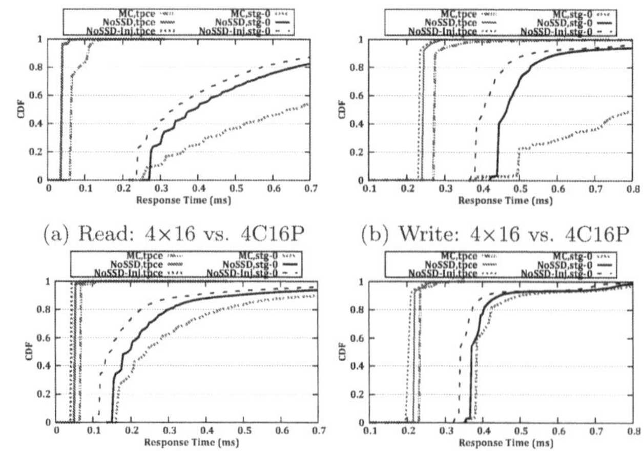

(a) Read: 4×16 vs. 4C16P (b) Write: 4×16 vs. 4C16P

(c) Read: 8×8 vs. 8C8P (d) Write: 8×8 vs. 8C8P

Figure 14: Cumulative distribution function (CDF) of the read and write response time of the two representative workloads, i.e., `tpce` and `stg-0`, for NoSSD with normal injection (NoSSD), NoSSD with traffic-aware injection (NoSSD-Inj) and multi-channel SSD (MC).

allelism, the overall performance gain of using NoSSD decreases (higher response time and lower IOPS values). Comparing results of 4×16 and 8×8 in terms of response time shows that maximum increase in overall response time is about 10% for `prxy-1`. In all other applications, however, response time increase of high channel-level parallelism is very small (4%, on average). For maximum IOPS results, the reason for larger throughput improvement in 4×16 NoSSD compared to 8×8 NoSSD is two-sided. First, the dynamic allocation scheme well uses higher channel-level parallelism in *8C8P* baseline and hence NoSSD has less chance to improve performance. Second, the 4×16 configuration roughly doubles the chip-level parallelism and NoSSD can better pipeline flash operation execution over adjacent flash chips.

6.2 Performance of Packet Injection Policy and FCC Placement

So far, we have shown performance improvement results for NoSSD, **without** considering design considerations of packet injection and FCC placement. For the sake of completeness, Figure 13a and Figure 13c illustrate the response time of NoSSD with the traffic-aware packet injection policy, normalized to that of the same size NoSSD with the normal (round-robin) injection policy. As can be seen, the maximum performance improvement using this policy is 23% (in case of `src-1` in 8×8 NoSSD) while it is negligible in most of the other workloads. On the average, injection policy gives an aggregate response time improvement of 7% and 4% for 8×8 and 4×16 NoSSDs, respectively. Nevertheless, we deduce that traffic-aware packet injection policy achieves better response time improvement for workloads with large average request sizes (`src-1`, `src-2`, `mds-1`, `usr-0`, `usr-1`, `usr-2`). The reason is that such workloads considerably benefit from the path diversity provided by the traffic-aware injection policy.

Figure 13b and Figure 13d show the response time of 8×8 and 4×16 NoSSDs with all-sided FCC placement, normalized to the same-sized NoSSD with one-sided placement. As the results show, all-sided FCC placement can reduce response time by up to 19% (and 5%, on average) for the evaluated configurations. Again, we can see that NoSSD performance is sensitive to the FCC placement when the average request size of the workload is large.

6.3 Response Time Variation

One of the major challenges with current multi-channel SSD architectures is their large variance of response time. This variability is specially harmful for streaming and time-critical applications where a deterministic response time must be guaranteed. To mitigate this variation, current enterprise SSDs rely on buffering methods and reconfigurable SSD controllers that result in more complex controller design. Figure 14 compares the response time variation of NoSSD and conventional SSDs by plotting the cumulative distribution function (CDF) of response time values. To increase readability, we just selected two representative applications with small request size (`tpce`) and large request size (`stg-0`). We see that the CDF curve of NoSSD sharply rises for `stg-0` (large request sizes better use resource sharing in NoSSD) and shows a considerable response-time predictability thanks to its path diversity and pipelined routing. For `tpce`, with small requests, the improvement is marginal.

7. RELATED WORK

Improving SSD performance and scalability for enterprise systems has been extensively explored in recent years. The main discussion is that since most of read requests are processed synchronously by OLTP and database system, even a single stall, caused by either slow programs, limited parallelism, or path latency of the controller, may considerably limit the overall SSD throughput [32, 33]. There are many studies trying to address this issue in high-throughput enterprise systems:

Enhancing channel-level parallelism. Enterprise SSD vendors improve capacity and I/O throughput by increasing the number of channels and employing suitable page allocation strategies [24, 34]. Although highly parallel channels relax resource contention, they substantially increase the cost of controller [31, 44, 48].

Utilizing intra-flash chip parallelism. Alongside channel level parallelism, FTL management policies can be designed to fully exploit parallelism provided at other levels of the SSD architecture [8, 10, 13, 22, 27, 40]. However, such solutions greatly suffer from additional latency and controller complexity required to attain their goals.
Design customization for enterprise workloads. An alternative strategy is to customize SSD architecture for efficient service of the requests in transactional workloads [26, 47, 48]. Similar to other solutions, architecture customization generally increases cost complexity of the controller. Recently, HLNAND proposed a scalable architecture which is built upon a unique daisy-ring architecture [46] or hierarchical ring topology [20]. In comparison with NoSSD, HLNAND products provide much less path diversity and their performance is still restricted by a single FCC at the controller side while NoSSD shares FCCs to get better performance/reliability. There are other examples of enterprise SSDs supporting a large number of flash chips at the backend. In contrast to NoSSD, these designs rely on hierarchal controllers (e.g. Intel 910 [26]) or hardware accelerators (e.g. PMC NVEMC [43]) at the cost of increased complexity and decreased reliability.

8. CONCLUSION

In this paper, we concentrated on the scalability challenges of the common enterprise SSD designs based on multichannel communication architecture. Based on our evaluation, the intra-die scaling approaches are all prohibited by the performance requirements of enterprise SSDs. Therefore, the inevitable solution is to employ more dies in the design and exploit high-level (i.e., channel and flash chip) parallelism and request striping to enhance the overall SSD performance. However, simulation results show that higher level solutions are also limited by controller complexity and bus characteristics. Motivated by these observations, we proposed protocol and configurations for realizing a network-based communication structure (i.e., NoSSD), to achieve a high-performance SSD interconnect that is highly scalable and enjoys design regularity. The simulation results for NoSSD and its design considerations reveal higher performance, larger bandwidth, and more scalability when compared to the conventional design. We believe this paper is just an initial step in influencing SSD's scalability using architectural and interconnect enhancements. Considering the effect of different functionalities (e.g., garbage collection) and exploring different network topologies are of future research activities in this line.

9. REFERENCES

[1] Microsoft enterprise traces. `http://iotta.snia.org/traces/list/BlockIO`.

[2] Microsoft production server traces. `http://iotta.snia.org/traces/list/BlockIO`.

[3] UMass trace repository. `http://traces.cs.umass.edu`.

[4] Xmulator simulator. Ver. 6.0. `http://www.xmulator.com/`.

[5] JEDEC standard, NAND flash interface interoperability, Oct 2012.

[6] Open NAND flash interface specification 3.1, Sep 2012.

[7] Open NAND flash interface specification 3.2, Jun 2013.

[8] N. Agrawal et al. Design tradeoffs for SSD performance. In *USENIX ATC'08*, pages 57–70, Jun 2008.

[9] J. S. Bucy et al. The DiskSim Simulation Environment Version 4.0 Reference Manual. Technical Report CMU-PDL-08-101, Parallel Data Laboratory, Carnegie Mellon University, May 2008.

[10] A. M. Caulfield et al. Gordon: using flash memory to build fast, power-efficient clusters for data-intensive applications. In *ASPLOS XIV*, pages 217–228, Mar 2009.

[11] L.-P. Chang. On efficient wear leveling for large-scale flash-memory storage systems. In *SAC'07*, pages 1126–1130, Mar 2007.

[12] Y.-H. Chang et al. Endurance enhancement of flash-memory storage systems: an efficient static wear leveling design. In *DAC'07*, pages 212–217, Jun 2007.

[13] F. Chen et al. Essential roles of exploiting internal parallelism of flash memory based solid state drives in high-speed data processing. In *HPCA'11*, pages 266–277, Feb 2011.

[14] B. Collins. SAS SSDs - building blocks for high-performance enterprise storage. In *Flash Memory Summit*, Aug 2011.

[15] W. Dally and B. Towles. *Principles and Practices of Interconnection Networks*. Morgan Kaufmann Publishers Inc., San Francisco, CA, USA, 2003.

[16] X. Dong et al. Nvsim: A circuit-level performance, energy, and area model for emerging nonvolatile memory. *IEEE TCAD*, 31(7):994–1007, Jul 2012.

[17] K. Eshghi and R. Micheloni. SSD architecture and PCI Express interface. In *Inside Solid State Drives (SSDs)*, volume 37 of *Springer in Advanced Microelectronics*, pages 19–45. 2013.

[18] Fusion-io, Inc. ioDriveIIDuo data sheet, 2013.

[19] E. Gal and S. Toledo. Algorithms and data structures for flash memories. *ACM Comput. Surv.*, 37(2):138–163, Jun 2005.

[20] P. Gillingham et al. 800 MB/s DDR NAND flash memory multi-chip package with source-synchronous interface for point-to-point ring topology. *IEEE Access*, 1:811–816, 2013.

[21] L. Grupp et al. The bleak future of NAND flash memory. In *FAST'12*, pages 17–24, Feb 2012.

[22] L. M. Grupp et al. The harey tortoise: Managing heterogeneous write performance in SSDs. In *USENIX ATC'13*, pages 79–90, Jun 2013.

[23] HGST, a Western Digital company. Ultrastar SSD800MM, enterprise solid state drives, 2013.

[24] Y. Hu et al. Performance impact and interplay of SSD parallelism through advanced commands, allocation strategy and data granularity. In *ICS'11*, pages 96–107, May-Jun 2011.

[25] Y. Hu et al. Exploring and exploiting the multilevel parallelism inside SSDs for improved performance and endurance. *IEEE TC*, 62(6):1141–1155, Jun 2013.

[26] Intel Corporation. Intel solid-state drive 910 series, product specification, 2013.

[27] M. Jung et al. Physically addressed queueing (PAQ):

improving parallelism in solid state disks. In *ISCA'12*, pages 404–415, Jun 2012.

[28] M. Jung and M. Kandemir. An evaluation of different page allocation strategies on high-speed SSDs. In *HotStorage'12*, Jun 2012.

[29] A. Kahng et al. Orion 2.0: A fast and accurate noc power and area model for early-stage design space exploration. In *DATE '09*, pages 423–428, Feb 2009.

[30] J.-U. Kang et al. A multi-channel architecture for high-performance NAND flash-based storage system. *J. Systems Architecture*, 53(9):644–658, Sep 2007.

[31] D. Lavenier et al. Seed-based genomic sequence comparison using a FPGA/FLASH accelerator. In *FPGA'06*, pages 41–48, Dec 2006.

[32] S.-W. Lee et al. A case for flash memory SSD in enterprise database applications. In *SIGMOD'08*, pages 1075–1086, Jun 2008.

[33] S.-W. Lee et al. Advances in flash memory SSD technology for enterprise database applications. In *SIGMOD'09*, pages 863–870, Jun 2009.

[34] S. Liang. Algorithms designs and implementations for page allocation in SSD firmware and SSD caching in storage systems. Master's thesis, Computer Science and Engineering, The Ohio State University, 2010.

[35] Marvell. Marvell 88NV9145: Native PCIe gen 2.0 x 1 NAND flash controller, 2011.

[36] Micron Technology, Inc. Managed NAND.

[37] Micron Technology, Inc. MT29F256G08AECCB NAND flash memory, 2010.

[38] Micron Technology, Inc. Micron P420m PCIe SSD product brief, May 2013.

[39] D. Narayanan et al. Write off-loading: Practical power management for enterprise storage. *ACM Trans. Storage*, 4(3):10:1–10:23, Nov 2008.

[40] C. Park et al. Exploiting internal parallelism of flash-based SSDs. *IEEE CAL*, 9(1):9–12, Jan 2010.

[41] PMC-Sierra. 89HF08P08CG3 8-Channel x8 PCIe Gen3 enterprise NV-DRAM controller, May 2013.

[42] PMC-Sierra. 89HF16P04CG3 16-Channel x4 PCIe Gen3 enterprise flash controller, May 2013.

[43] PMC-Sierra. 89HF32P08CG3 32-Channel x8 PCIe Gen3 enterprise flash controller, May 2013.

[44] R. Rivera. Distributed data acquisition and storage architecture for the SuperNova acceleration probe. *IEEE Trans. Nuc. Sci.*, 55(1):246–250, Feb 2008.

[45] SandForce. SandForce SF-2000 flash storage processors, Apr 2013.

[46] R. Schuetz et al. Hyperlink nand flash architecture for mass storage applications. In *NVSMW'07*, Aug 2007.

[47] Y. J. Seong et al. Hydra: A block-mapped parallel flash memory solid-state disk architecture. *IEEE TC*, 59(7):905–921, Jul 2010.

[48] J.-Y. Shin et al. FTL design exploration in reconfigurable high-performance SSD for server applications. In *ICS'09*, pages 338–349, Jun 2009.

[49] A. Silvagni. NAND DDR interface. In *Inside NAND Flash Memories*, pages 161–196. Springer Netherlands, 2010.

[50] A. Tavakkol et al. Network-on-SSD: A scalable and high-performance communication design paradigm for SSDs. *IEEE CAL*, 12(1):5–8, Jan 2013.

[51] A. Tavakkol et al. Unleashing the potentials of dynamism for page allocation strategies in SSDs. In *SIGMETRICS '14*, pages 551–552, Jun 2014.

[52] Transaction Processing Performance Council (TPC). TPC benchmark^{TM} C, standard specification, Feb 2010.

[53] Transaction Processing Performance Council (TPC). TPC benchmark^{TM} E, standard specification, 2010.

[54] B. Van Houdt. A mean field model for a class of garbage collection algorithms in flash-based solid state drives. In *SIGMETRICS'13*, Jun 2013.

D^{2}MA: Accelerating Coarse-Grained Data Transfer for GPUs

D. Anoushe Jamshidi, Mehrzad Samadi, and Scott Mahlke
Advanced Computer Architecture Laboratory
University of Michigan - Ann Arbor, MI
{ajamshid, mehrzads, mahlke}@umich.edu

ABSTRACT

To achieve high performance on many-core architectures like GPUs, it is crucial to efficiently utilize the available memory bandwidth. Currently, it is common to use fast, on-chip scratchpad memories, like the shared memory available on GPUs' shader cores, to buffer data for computation. This buffering, however, has some sources of inefficiency that hinder it from most efficiently utilizing the available memory resources. These issues stem from shader resources being used for repeated, regular address calculations, a need to shuffle data multiple times between a physically unified on-chip memory, and forcing all threads to synchronize to ensure RAW consistency based on the speed of the slowest threads. To address these inefficiencies, we propose Data-Parallel DMA, or D^{2}MA. D^{2}MA is a reimagination of traditional DMA that addresses the challenges of extending DMA to thousands of concurrently executing threads. D^{2}MA decouples address generation from the shader's computational resources, provides a more direct and efficient path for data in global memory to travel into the shared memory, and introduces a novel dynamic synchronization scheme that is transparent to the programmer. These advancements allow D^{2}MA to achieve speedups as high as 2.29x, and reduces the average time to buffer data by 81% on average.

Categories and Subject Descriptors

C.1.2 [**Processor Architectures**]: Multiple Data Stream Architectures (Multiprocessors)—Single-instruction-stream, multiple-data-stream processors (SIMD)

Keywords

GPUs; DMA; Software-managed Caches; Shared Memory; Dynamic Management; Throughput Processing

1. INTRODUCTION

In modern computing systems, *graphics processing units (GPUs)* have become ubiquitous. While GPUs traditionally have been used to efficiently render graphics, over the last decade major GPU vendors have unlocked the potential of their high-throughput, many-core products to be used for more general purpose, albeit massively data-parallel computations. Systems ranging from smartphones [25] to supercomputers [26] can now use GPUs to accelerate applications in domains such as multimedia processing, machine learning, financial modeling, linear algebra, and scientific computing. Using programming models like CUDA [22] or OpenCL [17], software developers can leverage the computational efficiency of many-core GPUs with their data-parallel code across a broad spectrum of devices.

Many-core architectures like GPUs typically achieve high performance when provided thousands of threads to concurrently execute. Problems arise, however, when trying to deliver enough data to these threads for them to compute upon. There is a long latency when loading data from a GPU's off-chip memory, possibly greater than 400 cycles on NVIDIA architectures [22]. Ideally, when threads stall due to such long latency operations, there will be many other threads that are schedulable for execution. While this may be the case for applications that perform a great deal of computation compared to memory transfers, in practice there are many memory-intensive applications that have low compute-to-memory characteristics. In such scenarios, most threads may be requesting data from memory simultaneously, creating high contention for memory resources. These applications will not have enough threads ready for execution, causing their performance to suffer, and simply adding more threads will not necessarily improve this performance.

Simply expanding and improving the existing memory subsystem in GPUs may not necessarily improve memory-intensive application performance either. According to GPU device specifications, there should be ample bandwidth to quickly move data between off-chip memory and the core. After all, most medium- to high-end GPUs are provisioned with 100-300+ GB/s of memory bandwidth to their off-chip global memories [24]. However, when memory-intensive applications attempt to fully utilize the GPU's cores, they can easily saturate the memory resources between the cores and off-chip memory, such as buffers between core load/store units and the memory interconnect or miss status holding registers (MSHRs) in caches. Simply providing more bandwidth or expanding existing memory resources are both too costly and will not necessarily ameliorate this problem [16, 28]. To demonstrate this, a model of the NVIDIA GTX480 was augmented to have infinite memory resources (that is, MSHRs and all buffers between shaders and DRAM), and 28 benchmarks from the NVIDIA SDK were simulated us-

PACT'14, August 24–27, 2014, Edmonton, AB, Canada.
Copyright 2014 ACM 978-1-4503-2809-8/14/08 ...$15.00.
http://dx.doi.org/10.1145/2628071.2628072 .

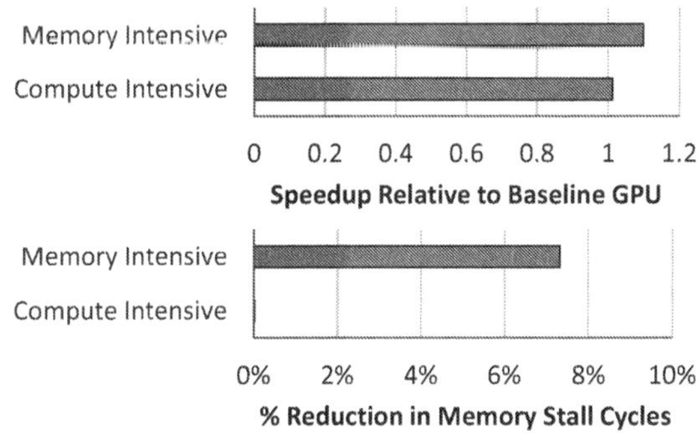

Figure 1: A balanced increase in the amount of memory resources does not guarantee improved performance and bandwidth utilization.

ing this model. Figure 1 shows that the mean speedups and memory stall cycle reductions that this theoretical device achieves for memory intensive applications are limited to roughly 10%, while computationally intensive benchmarks see marginal gains from such costly hardware over-provisioning. Even with infinite memory resources, neither compute- nor memory-bound applications see great improvements in their performance as the number of cycles they stall for memory transfers are only slightly impacted. Thus, even with a vast array of computational and memory hardware provisions, a GPU's performance can still suffer as it struggles to efficiently fetch data from off-chip memory for processing. Other approaches should be considered to better utilize the existing memory resources.

Numerous techniques have been introduced that help improve bandwidth utilization. One commonly used technique is to buffer tiles or blocks of data from global memory in a fast, on-chip shared memory [22]. Once the tile is in shared memory, computation can continue quickly and many delays associated with the GPU's memory subsystem can be greatly reduced. While this paradigm can easily be deployed in software and works with modern GPUs, there are software and microarchitectural inefficiencies that may hamper the performance of applications using this scheme. These include overheads from generating addresses for each load and store instruction, redundancy of data as buffered data will occupy space in both the L1 cache and the shared memory when both memories are in fact unified, coarse-grained synchronization penalties in order to guarantee read-after-write data consistency, and unnecessary register file usage to move data from the global to the shared memory.

Other software techniques like CudaDMA [4] and Sponge [11] attempt to improve this idea by using some GPU computation resources to help manage the buffering. They achieve this by specializing threads to handle transfer of data from global to shared memory, but by doing so they consume computational hardware to generate addresses and perform these transfers and limit the number of threads able to concurrently perform computation. Furthermore, these works do little to address the inefficiencies of the current buffering paradigm on modern GPUs.

Other works have introduced novel GPU prefetching hardware [19, 31] to help applications that do not have enough threads to hide memory latency. Prefetching schemes however are speculative and can potentially degrade bandwidth utilization due to inaccurate data prefetches. An alternative to prefetching is to decouple some memory accesses from a processor's datapath with some additional hardware support. Direct memory access (DMA) controllers arc one such example of this. Some single- and multi-core architectures, like the IBM Cell BE [8], use direct memory access (DMA) to move data between peripherals and memories asynchronously with respect to the CPU. By doing so, the CPU avoids consuming execution resources to calculate memory addresses and can reduce stalling when waiting for data by overlapping computation with transfer. However, as DMA was not envisioned for architectures that execute on thousands of threads simultaneously, difficult challenges prevent the direct adoption of DMA for GPUs. Such challenges include selecting which threads should begin a DMA transaction, how to concurrently interleave transactions for many threads, and how to inform threads that their transfer is complete on a non-interruptible architecture. This work addresses these challenges to bring the benefits of decoupled memory accesses provided by traditional DMA-enabled devices to many-core, heavily multi-threaded GPUs.

To improve bandwidth utilization as well as application performance, we propose a decoupled memory access scheme for GPUs called Data-Parallel DMA, or D^2MA. D^2MA provides an efficient path for tiles of data to travel from off-chip global memory to fast access, on-chip shared memory, while decoupling bulk address generation for these transfers from the rest of the core's pipeline. To accomplish this, a new DMA engine is added to each shader core that is capable of rapidly generating coalesced memory requests given a single base address and the size of a buffer for each resident concurrent thread array (CTA)[1]. The engine is also capable of generating special addressing patterns that are frequently found in data-parallel code, including tiles with a surrounding halo and blank column insertion to avoid bank conflicts in shared memory. When buffer transfers complete, threads waiting for their data tile need to be signaled to continue execution. We introduce a novel waiting scheme that is managed in hardware and maintains read-after-write consistency while being entirely transparent to the programmer. Finally, to minimize the burden of using D^2MA in GPU code, a few simple API calls are introduced that allow the programmer to provide the DMA engine with the necessary information to buffer a tile of data in the shared memory.

Our results show that by decoupling coarse-grained memory buffering from the rest of the shader's pipeline, D^2MA is able to drastically reduce the number of cycles where all resident CTAs on a shader are stalled waiting for a memory transfer to less than 1%. On average, the duration of a transfer of a tile of data from global to shared memory was reduced by 81%. The geometric mean speedup accomplished by reducing these stalls and transfer times was around 36%.

In summary, the main contributions of this work are:

- A simple new functional unit, the DMA engine, that can rapidly generate coalesced memory requests to global memory in bulk without using the shader's computational execution units.
- Support for specialized address generation for data with halos and for shared memory bank conflict avoidance.

[1]In this paper, we will frequently use NVIDIA/CUDA terminology to describe GPU hardware and programming. A CUDA thread block is a collection of threads that maps to a GPU CTA [27].

- An efficient path for responses from global memory to flow to the shared memory that reduces data redundancy and register usage.
- A novel hardware scheme that enforces read-after-write consistency, is transparent to the programmer, and obviates the need for coarse-grained synchronization.

2. BACKGROUND AND MOTIVATION

This section describes the ways that GPUs hide the memory access latencies and the inefficiencies of buffering data into shared memory, and discusses the challenges of addressing them when using DMA, a tried-and-true solution to such issues for CPUs, on multi-threaded GPUs.

2.1 Hiding GPU Memory Access Latency

One of the most important characteristics of data-parallel programs that target GPUs is that they expose enough thread level parallelism to hide the long latencies of global memory accesses and some arithmetic operations. When the shader core's execution units are waiting for a long latency operation to complete, the shader's warp[2] scheduler will attempt to find another warp that is ready for execution to run in the meantime. When running applications with enough threads and high compute-to-memory ratios, swapping warps may be able to hide most long latency operations, but when an application does not have enough threads or is too memory intensive the scheduler may not have enough ready warps to issue, thus stalling the shader core.

To prevent poor performance for such memory intensive applications, many applications take advantage of low-latency on-chip shared memory by buffering tiles of data from off-chip global memory into it. Each shader core has a limited amount of shared memory available – NVIDIA architectures provide a maximum of 48KB per core, compared to gigabytes of off-chip memory. The scope of data sharing is limited to the threads within a CTA, and the amount of space allocated to a CTA is limited by the number of CTAs that are simultaneously issued to a shader.[3] The programmer must carefully account for this when utilizing shared memory, as the amount of data buffered into shared memory will directly impact how many CTAs can be launched concurrently per shader core. While this may seem restrictive, the shared memory is located so close to a shader's functional units that frequent random accesses to the tile are feasible provided that care is taken to avoid bank conflicts. The same random accesses of the data in global memory would incur coalescing penalties and long round trip latencies to transfer each segment of data [22]. When shared memory buffering is applied, it can greatly improve performance by reducing the cycles during which the shader stalls for global memory accesses.

2.2 Inefficiencies when Buffering into Shared Memory

While buffering data using shared memory can positively impact application performance and off-chip bandwidth utilization, there are inefficiencies in this process for modern GPU hardware [4]. Figure 2 details the many steps required to perform each transfer of data from global into shared memory. Before any transfer can begin, the addresses of the source data and the destination must be calculated. These instructions are fetched, decoded and issued to ALUs for computation (❶), and the results of execution are written back to the register file (❷). While the ALUs are calculating these addresses, the instructions that load from global memory are fetched and decoded and are waiting at issue for the scoreboard to indicate that the addresses are ready as shown by ❸. Once the scoreboard permits their issue, the loads use the memory unit to generate coalesced memory requests. These requests first probe the L1 data cache, where compulsory misses are very likely as each buffer transfer is fetching a new and unique tile of data from global memory. After missing in the L1 cache, the request is sent to the L2 cache and global memory through the interconnect (❹). Meanwhile, the instructions that will store the fetched data into shared memory have progressed to the issue stage, awaiting the results of the loads (❺). After a few hundred shader cycles, the memory responses for these loads will return to the shader. When this happens (❻), the data updates the shader's L1 data cache (as shown by the cross-hatched box) and are written back to the register file. Finally, ❼ shows that the store instructions are issued to the memory unit, and the results of the global loads in the register file are stored into the shared memory. This process repeats until the entire tile is transferred, that is, until all warps involved have completed their stores to shared memory.

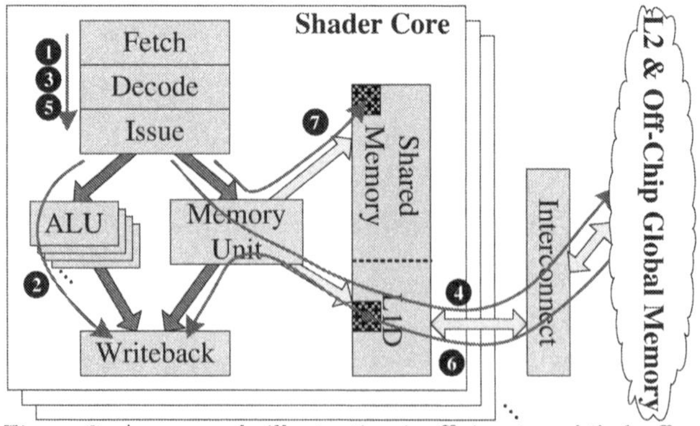

Figure 2: An example illustrating inefficiencies while buffering data into the shared memory.

Close examination of the example in Figure 2 reveals a few key sources of inefficiency during the transfer of a tile from global to shared memory. The first occurs at the ISA level. Each transfer is composed of numerous instructions to generate addresses, launch loads from global memory, and store results to shared memory. The hardware must issue a batch of these instructions for each cache block (128B) of data to be transferred, and since applications buffering into shared memory are likely to be memory-intensive, many instruction batches must be issued. However, the shape of the data being transferred is typically very regular, e.g. data packed in a 2-D matrix. With the existing ISA, there is no way to exploit the regularity of this data without executing all these instructions. The second inefficiency compounds the first with structural hardware limitations – to calculate the base addresses for the loads and stores, the shader's ALUs are consumed to perform additions and multiplications and cannot be used by other warps to perform computations.

[2]In modern NVIDIA GPUs, a warp is a collection of 32 threads that execute the same instructions in lockstep on a shader core [22].

[3]The NVIDIA Fermi architecture allows eight CTAs to be simultaneously resident on a shader core, while Kepler permits sixteen [23].

A third major inefficiency is caused by the microarchitectural layout of the shared memory and L1 data cache. In the NVIDIA Fermi architecture[4], these two memories are actually unified and coexist in the same memory [10, 21]. As shown by ❻, when the response from global memory returns to the shader the L1 is updated, and later when the store to shared memory occurs (❼) the data is again written to a different partition of the same, unified memory. This produces redundant data existing in this unified shader memory, and can pollute the L1 data cache as the recently transferred tile of data is unlikely to be reused by other global memory operations or future tile transfers. Furthermore, because there is no direct path for the load's memory response to go to shared memory, it's journey is lengthened by writing the fetched data to the register file so that a future store instruction can write this data into the shared memory.

One thing that is not pictured in Figure 2 is the synchronization required to prevent read-after-write consistency errors. As each warp is responsible for transferring a part of each tile, some warps may finish their transfer before others. If these warps attempt to continue execution and try to access data in shared memory that is still being buffered by other warps, they will not be computing on the desired tile of data, but rather some stale or otherwise incorrect data. To prevent this, the programmer must insert a barrier after this transfer (i.e. *__syncthreads*() in CUDA) which prevents warps from continuing forward until all warps reach this synchronization point. However, this implies that the slowest warp determines the end time of the transfer, and can prevent other warps that may be computing on data independent of the transferred tile from continuing.

All these sources of inefficiency indicates that there is some room for optimization in the GPU's ISA and microarchitecture. To improve upon the modern state-of-the-art of GPUs, we focus on adopting ideas from a well-established feature of CPUs, Direct Memory Access.

2.3 Traditional DMA on CPUs

The problem of gathering data for computation in a timely manner and without excessively consuming processing resources has been a concern for architects since time immemorial. In the early 1980s, Direct Memory Access (DMA) was pioneered by IBM to decouple long duration data transfers between peripheral devices and main memory from the CPU's datapath. Before DMA, if a program requested data from a peripheral, e.g. a floppy drive, it would either (a) poll the device to determine when the transfer completes, forcing the CPU to sit idle until the program can resume, or (b) let the operating system schedule other tasks until an interrupt signals that the data is ready. Both schemes incur high overheads when reading large amounts of data from devices as the CPU was spending a great deal of time calculating new addresses, issuing commands to move the data from a peripheral to memory, and performing bookkeeping to track the transfer's progress. With DMA, the program simply commands a DMA controller, a small hardware addition next to the CPU, to start copying a certain number of bytes between a specified memory address and a selected device. The DMA controller is responsible for generating addresses for data to be transferred to/from, issuing commands to the two endpoints, and arbitrating for the data bus, freeing the CPU's computation resources for other uses. Once a transfer completes, the DMA controller interrupts the CPU to indicate that the program's data is ready in memory, and the program continues execution [12, 27].

Many of the inefficiencies of GPU buffer transfers described in Section 2.2 seem like they could be solved using DMA-style transfers. However, reusing existing DMA designs and ideas for the GPU is not straightforward. As DMA was originally created for systems with very few threads executing simultaneously, DMA requires a reimagining when applied to a GPU capable of executing thousands of threads at the same time. This poses a few major challenges, listed below:

- Which CTA's warps should command a DMA controller to start a transaction?
- How can transactions from many warps be interleaved to occur concurrently?
- How does the DMA engine keep track of such pending transfers with reasonable overheads?

Furthermore, GPUs are not interruptible devices. If a memory transfer is offloaded to a DMA controller, it needs some way to inform the program that its transfer is complete. All of these challenges necessitate a rethinking of DMA before it can be applied to a GPU architecture.

3. D²MA OVERVIEW

As discussed in Section 2, a number of inefficiencies in modern GPUs are exposed when buffering global memory data in a shader's shared memory, which can prevent memory-intensive applications that employ such buffering from achieving their potential performance. The goal of this work is to address these bottlenecks by overlapping computation and buffer transfers, creating a slipstream effect that permits future computations to occur sooner than with the current buffering paradigm. In order to accomplish this, this work proposes a new direct memory access scheme that has been reimagined for GPUs called Data-Parallel DMA, or D^{2}MA. D^{2}MA accomplishes this by: *a)* decoupling address generation and memory accesses for data within the tile being buffered from the ALUs and memory units of the shaders by utilizing a new functional unit: the DMA engine; *b)* providing a direct path for data to travel from the off-chip global memory to the on-chip shared memory; *c)* ensuring that a pipelined stream of successive memory requests are issued to the global memory in a timely manner; and *d)* permitting warps to execute up to the point where an instruction attempts to load data from in-progress buffer transfer before forcing the warp to stop execution and wait for the completion of the transfer. In this section, we will discuss these improvements. Their implementation details will be explored in Section 4.

The current paradigm accomplishes data buffering into the shared memory by performing many address calculations and memory operations that consume the shader's primary functional units, depicted in Figure 2. To free these units for other computation, D^{2}MA decouples almost all buffering operations from the shader pipeline by adding a DMA engine to each shader core as shown in Figure 3. As multiple

[4]The programmer can set the partition size so that 48KB is dedicated to shared memory and 16 to the L1 or vice versa. NVIDIA's Kepler architecture appears to have the same unified shared & L1 data cache with an added 32KB shared/32KB L1 configuration [23].

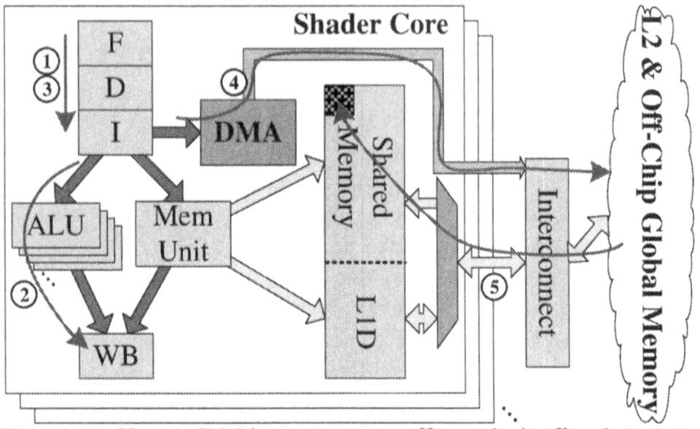

Figure 3: How a DMA engine can efficiently buffer data into the shared memory.

CTAs can be resident in a shader, each shader can be responsible for at least one buffer transfer occurring for each CTA. D^2MA's engine is capable of tracking not just one transfer per CTA, but can also permit multiple transfers to occur simultaneously for each CTA. Although DMA accesses are decoupled from the shader's pipeline, the DMA engine still requires the shader's ALUs to calculate two base addresses per tile transfer for each CTA, one for the source and one for the destination (①, ②). Once these two addresses are computed, however, the shader's functional units are never used again to facilitate the buffer transfer for a CTA. Instead, the DMA engine is passed configuration parameters, including the two base addresses, the size of each element and the number of elements in the buffer, and information describing the memory layout of the data being copied (i.e. the access stride for 1D data, or the order and leading dimension of matrix data). These configuration commands are implemented as two new instructions which are fetched, decoded, and wait for their operands (the aforementioned parameters) to be ready at the issue stage (③) like any other warp instruction.

Once a CTA has configured the DMA engine, the engine begins generating global memory addresses to load data from in a pipelined fashion and wholly independent of the shader's ALUs. As the shape of the data being buffered is very regular and is expected to be densely packed, at least until it encounters a stride boundary, the addresses of successive elements will naturally occur in a coalesced manner, obviating extra coalescing logic that exists in the shader's memory unit for general global memory accesses. When addresses are ready, memory requests are directly issued to the global memory through a shared memory port to the interconnect (④). As this memory request goes directly to the L2 and global memories, it bypasses probing the L1 data cache entirely, where it is likely to miss for reasons described in Section 2.2, and avoids modifying state in the L1.

During global address generation, the DMA engine concurrently computes the shared memory addresses associated with global addresses, and requests for data are sent to the global memory. Once responses to DMA requests start returning to the shader core (⑤), D^2MA stores each responses' data directly to the shared memory using the generated addresses. By selectively forwarding DMA responses to the shared memory, the data will only exist once in this physically unified L1 and shared memory space. Furthermore, the L1 will not be polluted with buffer data that should only persist until the next tile is transferred.

In order to prevent read-after-write consistency errors during buffering while remaining decoupled from the shader's pipeline, D^2MA replaces the coarse-grained synchronization instructions used in the current paradigm with a unique warp waiting scheme that is entirely managed in hardware and is transparent to the programmer. This scheme allows warps to continue execution until an instruction attempts to read data in shared memory that is currently being buffered. When such an event occurs, the load from shared memory gets squashed and its warp's next PC is rolled back to that of the squashed instruction. The warp gets marked as waiting for DMA, allowing the warp scheduler to issue a different warp that is ready for execution to the shader's functional units. As many warps in a CTA may be waiting for a DMA transfer to continue, the DMA engine tracks the waiting warps per CTA, and when the transfer completes it informs the scheduler that these warps may continue execution. When these warps are reissued, their next PC was rewound, allowing the load from shared memory to re-execute, thus preserving program correctness while preventing the shared memory from being read before a buffered tile was ready.

4. IMPLEMENTATION AND DESIGN

In this section, we detail the hardware modifications and additions to the shader core that are necessary to implement D^2MA. At the heart of this work is the DMA engine, as seen in Figure 3 and detailed in Figure 4. The DMA engine manages the buffering operations for all CTAs issued to a shader. Its key components include: an array of DMA controllers which contain all necessary configuration and bookkeeping metadata for buffer transfers (Section 4.1); a specialized address generation unit capable of creating one memory request for global data per cycle while concurrently generating each datum's associated shared memory address (Section 4.2); and a mechanism to prevent RAW consistency violations caused by attempted accesses to an incomplete transfer's data (Section 4.3). Section 4.4 details D^2MA's programming model.

4.1 DMA Controllers

The DMA engine contains one DMA controller per resident CTA, empowering D^2MA to manage simultaneous buffering operations for all the CTAs on a shader. Each controller contains all the configuration and bookkeeping metadata necessary to facilitate a buffer transfer in a table called the buffer management table. The tables are provisioned with four entries, allowing each CTA to launch up to four buffering operations at the same time.

When a DMA configuration instruction is issued to the engine, it populates this metadata into entries in the buffer management table, shown in Figure 4, associated with the instruction's CTA and the buffer specified by the instruction. Once configured, the table entry will contain the global and shared base addresses of the tile (64b and 16b, respectively), the number of elements to transfer (16b), the byte size of an element (encoded into 2b[5]), the stride of the data (16b), and flags that indicate the dimensionality of the data (1b[6]) and if a special addressing mode is enabled (2b). There are two supported special addressing modes, detailed in Section 4.2.1. One of the addressing modes creates a halo around the tile of data for stencil applications. This requires extra configuration data as each buffer must know the number of halo rows (16b) and columns (16b) that surround the

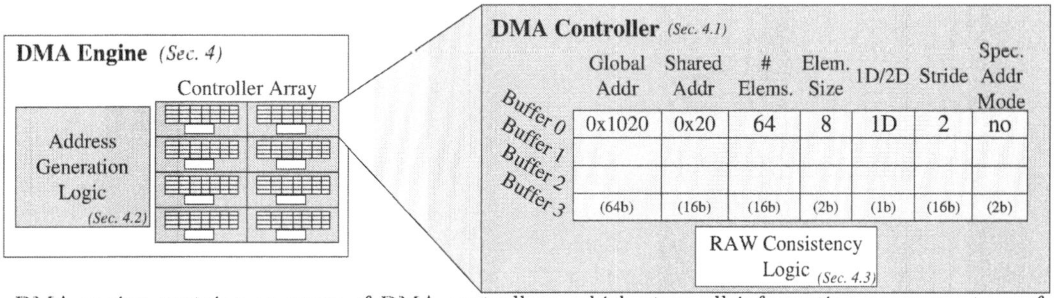

Figure 4: A DMA engine contains an array of DMA controllers, which store all information necessary to perform a buffer transfer, and specialized address generation logic.

tile, an indicator as to the position of the tile relative to the entire data (8b), as well as a constant to be stored in this halo region around the tile's data (16b). The other addressing mode is used to prevent shared memory bank conflicts, and shares these configuration bits with the halo addressing mode to store the number of elements that get stored in a shared memory bank. In total, each DMA controller requires 692 bits (173 bits per buffer) of metadata to configure and track a DMA transfer.

As all warps within a CTA execute the same configuration instructions, once a particular CTA's buffer is fully configured, the engine will not modify the buffer's table entry again and will commit all future configuration instructions.[7] When configured, the controller informs the DMA engine that a buffer transfer is ready for ignition, and the engine can commence this transfer.

4.2 DMA Memory Transaction Handling

When a transfer is ready, the DMA engine uses its address generation logic to efficiently generate memory requests to move this tile of data from global into shared memory. The requests are sent through the shader's existing memory subsystem to the global memory, and when responses are received, data is directly stored to the shared memory without modifying the L1D or requiring any writeback to registers.

Once a CTA's buffer is marked as ready for ignition and the specialized address generation (AGEN) logic is available, the DMA engine routes the buffer's metadata from the associated controller's buffer management table to the address generation logic. The AGEN logic is controlled by a byte counter (Figure 5a) that tracks if all addresses for this transfer have been generated. The total size is calculated by shifting the number of elements by the encoded size of each element and is stored in a register. The counter is incremented depending on whether the buffer's metadata indicates the data stored in global memory is unit-strided, or has a non-unit stride.

When data has a unit stride (Figure 5b), every element is packed contiguously in global memory, so the AGEN logic can easily generate global addresses based on segment boundaries.[8] In this case, the engine's AGEN logic can issue one request for a segment of data per cycle. For the non-unit stride case, data is still contiguous in global memory but is not densely packed. The data that is of interest will exist with distance equal to the stride between each element.

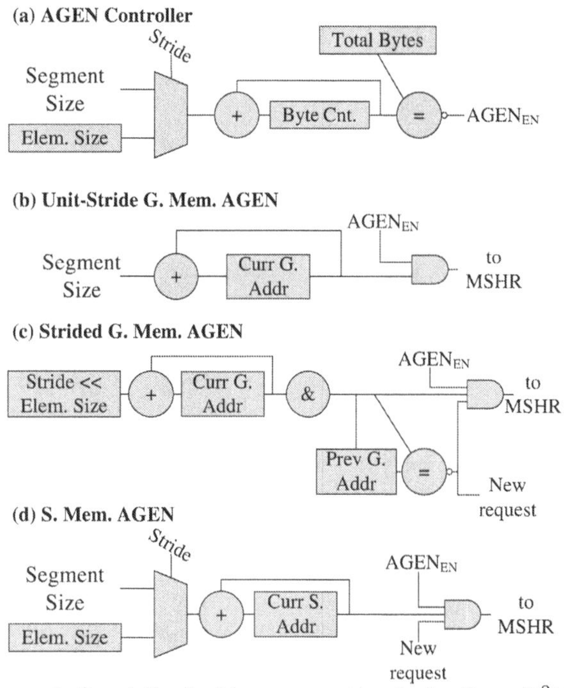

Figure 5: Specialized address generation logic allows D^2MA to rapidly issue memory requests and decouples all address generation from the shader's computational resources.

Because of this, some contiguous segments will not contain data of interest, so the AGEN logic only sends requests for those that do. As shown in Figure 5c, the address of the current element is stored in a register. To extract the segment address from this, the lower seven bits are masked off (&). Then, this segment address is compared to the one generated in the previous cycle. If they are not equal, this element is in a new segment and a new global memory request is ready to be issued. Because of this, it is possible that it will take multiple cycles to generate a strided memory request for each segment. As global addresses are generated, the AGEN logic also generates the shared memory addresses associated with each global segment (Figure 5d). If no special addressing mode is specified, data is expected to be contiguous and densely packed in shared memory. If the global addresses are strided, then the shared memory AGEN logic only issues a new shared memory address if the strided AGEN circuit signals that it created a new request.

As discussed in Section 3, D^2MA will write a response's data directly to shared memory and not to the L1D. In order

[5] Two bits are needed to represent all data type sizes: 1B, 2B, 4B and 8B.

[6] D^2MA currently supports 1D and 2D tile transfers.

[7] Configuration instructions can later change the buffer management table entries once a buffer transfer has completed.

[8] Segments can be 32, 64 or 128B wide for NVIDIA architectures [22].

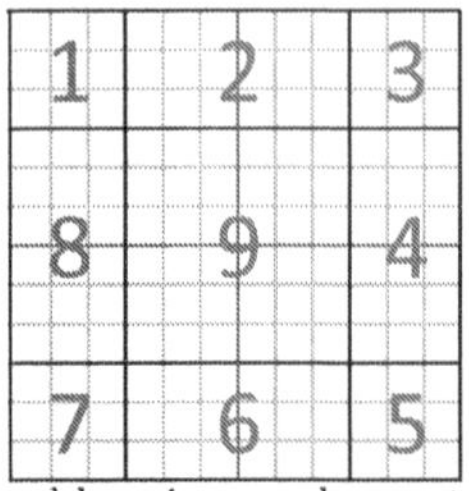

Figure 6: The halo addressing mode must track which region of the entire matrix a tile is coming from to determine what data is stored in the halo. There are nine possible regions.

to accomplish this, the MSHRs in the L1D are shared between the DMA engine and memory unit, and each MSHR has been provisioned with a 16b shared address field. When both the global request and its associated shared memory address(es) are generated by the AGEN logic, they are directly sent to the MSHR table, where the global and shared addresses are written if an entry is available. If the global address of a response from memory matches an MSHR entry that also contains a shared memory address (identifying a DMA response), the data gets stored to that location in the shared memory rather than the in the L1D.

To avoid complications of adding more nodes to the interconnect, the shader's memory port to the on-chip interconnect is shared between the DMA engine and the shader's memory unit. In case of contention between the engine and memory unit, all memory unit requests are given priority to ensure that computation is given priority over DMA operation.

4.2.1 Special Addressing Modes

D^2MA supports two special addressing modes. The first, called bank conflict resolution, spaces data stored to shared memory out so that when multiple threads access the buffer, they do not all attempt to read from the same bank at the same time. When shared memory addresses are generated, the AGEN logic only permits n elements to be stored per memory bank, as specified by buffer's metadata.

The second addressing mode creates a halo surrounding the buffered tile in shared memory. This is commonly used in image processing and physics simulations to include neighboring data when computing on a tile. This halo is either filled with data from neighboring tiles or with a constant value if that tile is on the border of the entire data. Figure 6 shows that every tile resides in a region that determines what data needs to be stored in its halo in shared memory. Interior tiles (region nine) will have halos that contain data from neighboring tiles. Exterior tiles (regions one through eight) have some rows and/or columns that will contain a neighboring tile's data and others that will contain the halo constant. When a halo is applied to a tile, the AGEN logic needs to know the region from which this tile belongs. The programmer supplies the current tile's region when configuring a new tile transfer. The size of the halo, the halo constant, and the current tile's region are loaded from the buffer's metadata for use by the AGEN logic. Based on the region the tile is in and the number of halo rows and columns for the tile, the AGEN logic will generate global and shared memory addresses for the transfer. For the exterior regions where some of the halo data is constant, the DMA engine will store the halo constant to the exterior halo parts of these tiles in shared memory while the global memory requests are in flight.

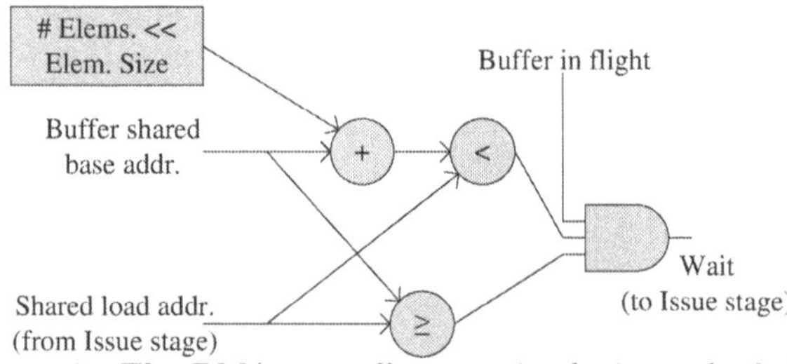

Figure 7: The DMA controller contains logic to check if a read-after-write consistency violation will occur if a shared load is issued that conflicts with an in progress DMA transfer.

4.3 Dynamic Synchronization Support

One of the goals of this work is to obviate the need for all warps to wait for a CTA's transfer to complete. To accomplish this, D^2MA dynamically monitors all instructions that load from shared memory while DMA transfers are in progress, and if loads are found to alias with a buffer in transit, their warps are forced to wait until the buffer transfer completes. This allows work independent of the buffered data to continue to execute in these warps past a point where a programmer would normally have forced a coarse-grained synchronization to occur.

Dynamic synchronization is achieved by collaboration between the DMA engine and the warp scheduler. If transfers are in progress and a load from shared memory instruction is encountered at the issue stage, the source address of the load is forwarded to the DMA engine. The DMA engine routes this address to all of its DMA controllers, where Read-After-Write (RAW) Consistency Logic (Figure 4) compares the address to the ranges of possible shared memory addresses for all in-flight buffers. The logic displayed in Figure 7 is used to perform this checking. To determine buffer address ranges, the total number of bytes transferred by a buffer is added to that buffer's shared base address. Two digital comparators then check to see if the shared load's address is within this range. If both comparators return true, and the associated buffer's table entry was fully configured, this indicates that a RAW consistency violation has occurred. In this case, a signal is sent back to the issue stage, informing the scheduler that this load's warp needs to wait. Upon receipt of such a wait signal, the scheduler will mark this instruction's warp as waiting for a DMA transfer to complete, allowing a different warp to be issued, and the scheduler will rewind the next PC of the shared load instruction's warp so that the load can re-execute when the warp is allowed to continue.

When a DMA transfer for a CTA has completed, the DMA engine passes the CTA ID to the warp scheduler so that it may release all warps within the CTA that may have been waiting. Each DMA controller will contain one of the circuits shown in Figure 7 per buffer entry, for a total of four RAW consistency checking circuits per controller. Implementing this functionality in hardware allows a guarantee of consistency while remaining transparent to the programmer.

4.4 D^2MA Programming Model

To simplify the process of programming using D^2MA, we extend intrinsics that map directly to DMA engine configu-

```
1  __global__ void
2  sgemv_DMA(int n, int m, int n1, float alpha,
3            float *A, int lda, float *x, float *y)
4  {
5    __shared__ float buff[VEC_ELMTS];
6    dma_set_datatype_float();
7    dma_configure_flat_unit_stride(buff,
8                                   x,
9                                   VEC_ELMTS);
10
11   int ind = blockIdx.x * num_threads
12                       + threadIdx.x;
13   A += ind;
14   float res = 0.f;
15   int k = 0;
16   for(int i=0; i<n1; i += VEC_ELMTS)
17   {
18     for(int j=0; j < VEC_ELMTS; j++)
19     {
20       res+=A[0]*buff[j];
21       A+=lda;
22     }
23     k += VEC_ELMTS;
24     if (k < n1)
25       dma_execute(buff, x+k, 0);
26   }
27
28   if (ind<n)
29     y[ind] = alpha * res;
30 }
```

Figure 8: A sgemv kernel written using D^2MA.

ration instructions. Figure 8 shows a sgemv kernel written using these intrinsics to enable DMA operation. Lines 6-9 show the initial configuration, where the buffer is configured for source data which is a flat, unit-stride, 1D vector comprised of *VEC_ELMTS* number of floats. The *dma_set_datatype_float*() intrinsic sets the data type of this buffer, while the *dma_configure_flat_unit_stride*() sets the global and shared base addresses and the size of the buffer. After configuration, the DMA engine will start this transfer, and the kernel's execution will continue. Lines 10-19 are independent of the transfer in progress and can execute without waiting, and if the transfer is still in progress at line 20, the DMA engine will stall the warp attempting to execute this load from the shared buffer. By using D^2MA, the programmer does not need to worry about placing *__syncthreads*() in their code. At the end of the outer loop, the *dma_execute*() on line 25 begins the transferring the next tile of data into *buff*. Shown here are only a subset of the available intrinsics, other intrinsics permit configuring 2D matrices and strided accesses, setting the data type to be any possible data type, including packed floats, and enabling the special addressing modes.

5. EXPERIMENTAL EVALUATION

We model D^2MA's engine and all necessary microarchitectural modifications in GPGPU-Sim version 3.2.1 [3, 1]. Our baseline GPU is similar to the NVIDIA GTX480 [21] architecture, and the configuration parameters passed to GPGPU-Sim can be seen in Table 1. To evaluate D^2MA, we selected all benchmarks from the NVIDIA CUDA SDK [2] and the Rodinia benchmark suite [6, 7] that contained kernels utilizing the current paradigm of buffering highly regular tiles of data into shared memory, and we created D^2MA-optimized versions of these kernels instrumented using D^2MA's intrinsics discussed in Section 4.4. A list of the benchmarks is shown in Table 2. Overall speedups achieved by using D^2MA are surveyed in Section 5.1. In Section 5.2, we analyze the improvement in the duration of a buffer transfer when using D^2MA. We explore a breakdown of how D^2MA optimizes buffering with a case study in Section 5.3, and compare D^2MA to a software DMA scheme in Section 5.4. Finally, we discuss the implementation overhead of D^2MA in Section 5.5.

Number of shaders	15
Threads per shader	1536
Threads per warp	32
SIMD lane width	32
CTAs per shader	8
Registers per shader	32768
Shared memory per shader	48KB
DMA engines per shader	1
Warp scheduling policy	Greedy-then-oldest
L1 cache (size/assoc/block size)	16KB/4-way/128B
L2 cache (size/assoc/block size)	768KB/16-way/128B
Number of memory channels	8
Memory bandwidth	179.2 GB/s
Memory controller	Out-of-order (FR-FCFS)

Table 1: GPGPU-Sim configuration

Abbr.	Description	Ref.
DCT	Discrete cosine transform	[2]
MM	Matrix multiplication	[2]
DWT	1D Haar wavelet transform	[2]
TRANS1	Matrix transpose (coalesced)	[2]
TRANS2	Matrix transpose (diagonal)	[2]
FW	Fast Walsh transform	[2]
GAUSS	Gaussian filter	[2]
MEAN	Mean filter	[2]
SOBEL	Sobel filter	[2]
PATH	Shortest path finding	[6, 7]
SGEMV	Matrix-vector mult.	[4]
LUD1	LU decomposition (internal)	[6, 7]
LUD2	LU decomposition (diagonal)	[6, 7]

Table 2: Benchmarks used to evaluate D^2MA

5.1 Overall Performance

Figure 9 shows the overall speedup achieved when using D^2MA to optimize the transfer of data from off-chip global memory to on-chip shared memory. By efficiently generating memory requests and forwarding responses directly to the shared memory, D^2MA is able to achieve up to 2.29x and on average 1.36x speedup over kernels using the current buffering paradigm on modern GPU hardware. All but one D^2MA-enabled kernels see some degree of speedup. As D^2MA automatically generates addresses and issues memory requests, the shader's ALUs are not used for this task, reducing the number of dynamic instructions executed as shown by Figure 10. On average, D^2MA reduces the number of instructions executed by 7%.

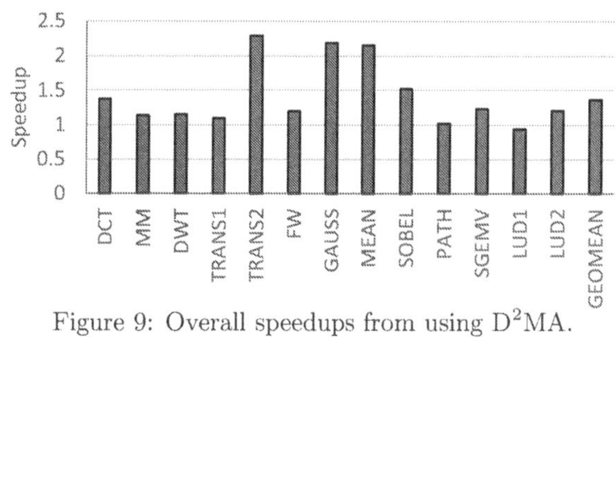

Figure 9: Overall speedups from using D^2MA.

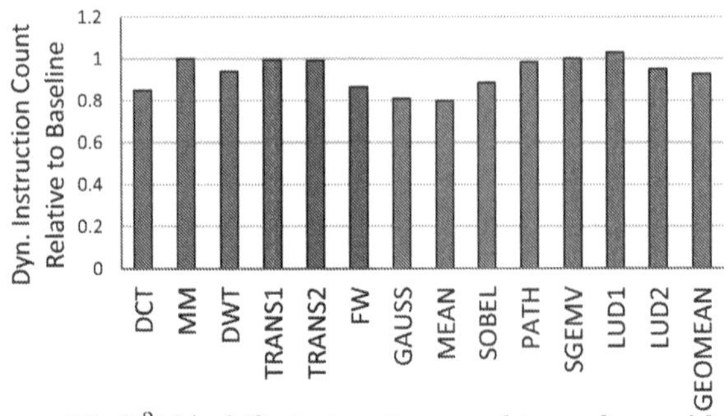

Figure 10: D^{2}MA shifts instructions used to perform address generation and memory transactions to dedicated hardware, reducing the number of dynamic instructions executed when performing a buffering operation.

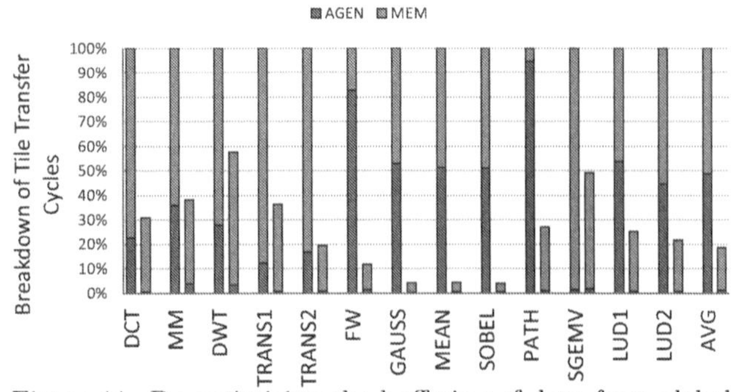

Figure 11: By optimizing the buffering of data from global into shared memory, D^{2}MA on average more than halves the cycles to transfer a tile of data. For each benchmark, the left bar represents baseline results, and the right bar shows D^{2}MA results relative to the baseline. (Lower is better.)

The *GAUSS*, *MEAN*, and *SOBEL* kernels show major benefits as these kernels utilize D^{2}MA's special halo addressing mode. The original code required conditional logic to determine whether the threads needed to store a constant or a neighboring tile's data to the halo surrounding the current tile being buffered. By allowing the DMA engine's specialized address generation logic to handle this computation, the optimized kernels achieve 2.19x, 2.15x, and 1.52x speedups, respectively. These speedups correlate closely with their large reduction in the number of dynamic instructions, which are reduced by up to 20%.

PATH shows a case that gets very little speedup (1.02x). In this case, the buffering operation in *PATH*'s kernel accounts for a very small fraction of its total execution time, so the speedup achieved by optimizing buffering is small. *MM* and *DWT* also exhibit a similar compute-to-memory characteristic as *PATH* and thus get limited speedups of 1.14x and 1.15x, respectively.

*LUD*1 is the only kernel that experiences slight loss in performance. The code footprint of the baseline kernel is very small, and only one transfer is performed per kernel call. Every time the D^{2}MA kernel is called, it must configure the DMA engine, which causes 3% more instructions to be executed compared to the baseline kernel. These factors account for this kernel's 7% performance degradation.

In order to analyze the performance of the remaining benchmarks, we turn to a more detailed study of D^{2}MA's improved buffer transfer performance.

5.2 Analyzing Buffering Performance

When analyzing the buffer transfers within kernels, we found that D^{2}MA is on average able to reduce the transfer time by 81% when compared to the current buffering paradigm. Figure 11 shows the breakdown of tile transfer cycles into address generation (AGEN) and memory transaction (MEM) cycles. It also shows the average improvement in overall transfer time for the D^{2}MA-enabled kernels normalized to that of the baseline kernels.

The significant improvements observed in both address generation and memory transfer cycles are primarily due to the decoupling of a buffering operation from dependencies upon other instructions and the shader's functional units. D^{2}MA's dedicated address generation logic accounts for a 98% reduction in AGEN cycles. As the baseline scheme requires each warp to transfer a part of a tile to shared memory, a transfer's performance becomes dependent on the warp scheduler allowing every warp to fetch their portion of the tile. On the contrary, once a DMA engine is configured, D^{2}MA generates segment addresses and issues them to memory wholly independent of the warp scheduler. This accounts for the average reduction in MEM cycles of 66%.

Generally, all D^{2}MA-optimized kernels see significant reductions in transfer duration due to buffering. For some benchmarks (*MM*, *DWT*, *PATH*), this did not necessarily translate into an overall speedup in execution time. Although *SGEMV* shows an improvement in transfer time comparable to that of *DWT* and *PATH*, *SGEMV* performs much simpler computation compared to these kernels, allowing it to achieve a better overall speedup of 1.23x.

As discussed in Section 5.1, the three filters (*GAUSS*, *MEAN*, and *SOBEL*) achieve very high speedups by allowing the DMA engine to handle generation of their tile's halo addresses. Figure 10 supports these findings as it shows that the baseline kernels spent a significant number of cycles performing address generation. By allowing dedicated logic to generate these special halo addresses and streamlining the issuing of their memory requests, D^{2}MA greatly reduces each of these kernel's address generation cycles by 99%. Combined with the timely issue of memory requests described in Section 5.1, these benchmarks see an average transfer duration reduction of 96%.

The *TRANS*1 kernel performs a transpose of a large matrix in a sequential, tile-by-tile fashion, while the *TRANS*2 kernel performs the transpose reordered along diagonal strips of the original matrix. While both kernels have similar code, they are buffering tiles in different orders. The baseline sequential kernel (*TRANS*1) suffers from high miss rates (about 50%) in the L2 cache, lengthening its transfer duration. The D^{2}MA version of this kernel achieves limited improvement for this kernel because D^{2}MA's optimizations are not meant to improve L2 caching performance. *TRANS*2's diagonal tile access pattern results in far fewer misses in the L2 with a miss rate of just 4%, and this allows D^{2}MA to improve the reduction in this kernel's transfer time by 17% over that of *TRANS*1. The reduction in transfer time accounts for the major overall speedup of the *TRANS*2 kernel. For similar tile ordering reasons, the access patterns of the two *LUD* kernels similarly account for one kernel performing slightly better than the other.

We also examine how frequently the shader is forced to stall due to memory operations in a buffer transfer compared to the kernel's whole execution time. Shaders are forced to stall during a transfer when all threads amongst the CTAs assigned to the shader are waiting for memory transactions to complete. On average, the baseline benchmarks spend about 7% of their cycles stalled due to buffering inefficiencies. By decoupling the buffering operation from the shader's ALUs and memory unit and more efficiently moving data between the global and shared memories, D^2MA nearly eliminates these stall cycles. The D^2MA-enabled kernels, on average, stall for less than 1% of their total execution cycles.

5.3 Case Study: Breaking Down Transfer Times

To present a breakdown of transfer and compute times, we examine the execution of *SAXPY*, a scaled vector addition benchmark from [4]. We run a version of the kernel that buffers both vectors to be added into shared memory as our baseline, and optimized this kernel using the D^2MA intrinsics. *SAXPY* contains fairly simple computations, as each tile will contain two vectors that get added together. This makes the buffering operation's transfer time critical when achieving good overall performance. The timelines presented in Figure 12 are from simulated executions of the two versions of the *SAXPY* kernel, both running two CTAs (b_0 and b_1) on a single shader. Times are broken down into cycles when address generation (*agen*), memory transfer (*mem*), and computation (*comp*) occur.

In Figure 12a, we see the baseline's execution timeline. Each buffering operation has some overhead for address generation before a memory transfer can begin. Because all threads in the CTA will be involved in the transferring of each vector, the two transfers are serialized. Only after all threads involved in the transfer complete can the baseline kernel perform the actual vector addition. If we compare this to the D^2MA-optimized kernel's execution, displayed in Figure 12b, address generation is compressed by greater than 2/3, allowing memory transfers to occur sooner. Furthermore, both vectors are buffered simultaneously as each CTA utilizes two of their DMA controller's four available buffers. By improving address generation and overlapping these transfers, two periods of computation occur before cycle 2000, compared to just one for the baseline. Also, the computation in the DMA kernel is able to start slightly earlier than the baseline version, as D^2MA's dynamic synchronization does not force all threads to wait when some are ready to continue.

5.4 Case Study: Comparing with CudaDMA

CudaDMA [4] is a software solution that provides DMA-like emulation for CUDA kernels. Using fine-grained synchronization, CudaDMA allows the majority of warps to focus on computation on data while a few warps are tasked with buffering tiles of data from global into shared memory.

To compare D^2MA with CudaDMA, we optimized a matrix-vector multiplication (*SGEMV*) kernel for D^2MA and ran it along with kernels optimized using CudaDMA and the baseline software buffering approach. All three kernels transferred the subsections of the vector into shared memory using a single buffer. While the CudaDMA-optimized code achieved a 1.10x speedup over the baseline, D^2MA surpassed CudaDMA, achieving a 1.23x speedup over the baseline kernel. CudaDMA's warp specialization decouples memory access instructions from those performing computation, allowing for its gains over the baseline. As described in Section 5.1, D^2MA's dedicated hardware DMA engine obviates the need for these memory instructions and handles all address generation and issuing of memory requests in a manner that is almost entirely decoupled from the shader's existing functional units and warp scheduling.

Controller Array	45169.4 µm²	2.40 mW
AGEN Logic	2246.6 µm²	0.16 mW
RAW Consistency Logic	1493.8 µm²	0.29 mW
Total per shader	54604.3 µm²	3.72 mW

Table 3: DMA Engine Hardware Overhead

5.5 Implementation Overhead

Each shader is provisioned with one DMA engine, and all of its controllers require a total of 692 bytes of storage space to track buffering operations. Each of the shader's shared memory and L1D cache's 32 MSHRs are provisioned with 16 bits to track which shared memory address is associated with a memory response's global address, requiring 64 bytes of space. Compared to each shader's 32768 32-bit registers and 64KB shared memory/L1 data cache [21], the storage overhead of D^2MA is miniscule.

To estimate the total area overhead of the DMA engine, we created a Verilog model and synthesized it using Synopsis Design Compiler with a commercial 45 nm cell library. Table 3 shows the area and power overheads of a single DMA engine reported by the synthesis of our model. When each of the GTX480's 15 shaders is augmented with a DMA engine, D^2MA only requires about 0.016% of the total chip area and increases power consumption by only 0.022%.[9]

6. RELATED WORK

There are several works that attempt to improve the GPU performance by overlapping computation and memory accesses [4, 11]. Bauer et al [4] propose a software managed approach to overlap compute with memory access. They divide warps into computation and memory warps, where the latter retrieves data for the former. Hormati et al [11] use a high level abstraction to launch helper threads which bring data from global memory to shared memory and overlap computation. While these works improve upon the baseline buffering paradigm in [22], they require some of the shader's computational resources to be used to buffer data, whereas D^2MA decouples almost all operations related to buffering using a new functional unit, the DMA engine.

Memory prefetching is another way of improving memory accesses for GPUs [19, 31]. MT [19] provides hardware and software prefetching mechanisms designed for GPUs which exploit the existence of common memory access behavior among fine-grained threads. APOGEE [31] is another hardware prefetching mechanism which adapts to the memory access patterns found in graphics and scientific applications. Jog et al [13] propose a prefetch-aware scheduling scheme that enables a simple prefetcher to be effective in tolerating memory latencies. D^2MA differs from these works in that it is not predictive and relies on explicit instructions to fetch data. Due to this, D^2MA does not suffer from inaccuracy and only fetches data when instructed.

Different warp schedulers have also been introduced to improve the utilization of GPU memory systems [18, 9, 15, 20, 30, 14]. Lakshminarayana and Kim et al [18] evaluated various scheduling techniques for DRAM optimization. For systems with no hardware-managed caches, they proposed a scheduler which is fair to all warps. Gebhart et al [9] proposed a two-level scheduling technique to improve

[9]The NVIDIA GTX480 architecture has a 529 mm² die size and a TDP of 250 W [5].

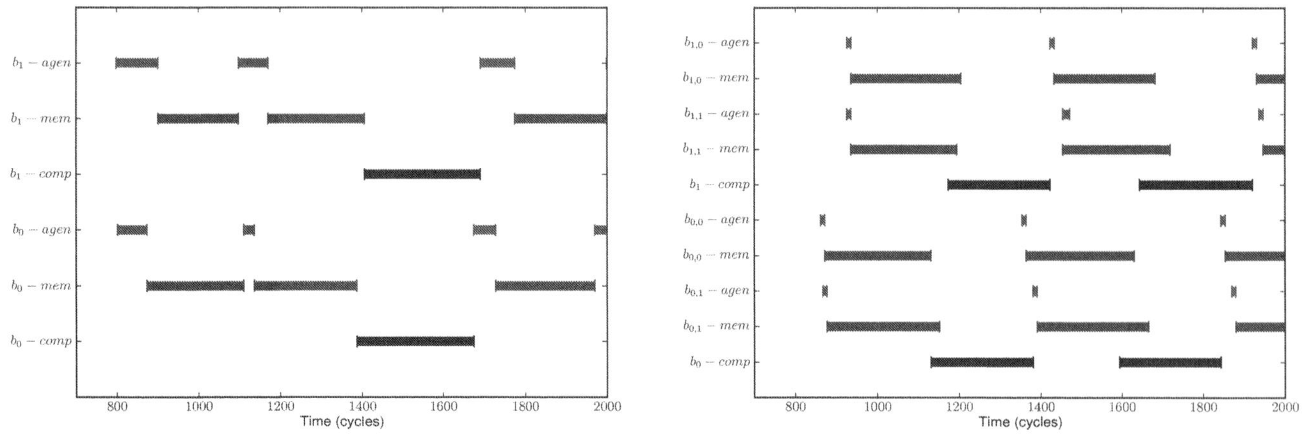

(a) Baseline

(b) D²MA

Figure 12: When two CTAs of $SAXPY$ are run with DMA support (12b), its transfer times are significantly reduced, allowing more computation to occur in the same time frame when compared to the baseline (12a). $b_{X,Y}$ indicates the CTA ID (X) and buffer number (Y).

register file energy efficiency. Kayiran et al [15] reduced the saturation of the memory subsystem by throttling the number of CTAs that are active on a SM. Narasiman et al [20] proposed a two-level warp scheduler which divided warps into fetch groups, and first scheduled within the fetch groups and then switched groups when all warps within a fetch group were stalled. Rogers et al [30] have shown similar results for a two-level scheduler. Jog et al [14] proposed a CTA-aware Locality BLP scheduler which reduced cache contention and used memory-bank level parallelism to improve performance. D²MA currently improves energy performance independent of the warp scheduler, however new scheduling schemes to further improve memory transaction overlapping will be considered in future work.

Rogers et al [30] proposed a cache-conscious scheduling mechanism which used locality detection hardware in the cache to moderate the number of warps that accessed the cache and controlled cache thrashing. Gebhart et al [10] proposed a unified scratchpad, register file and data cache to better distribute the on-chip resources depending on the application. LAMAR [29] introduced a locality-aware memory hierarchy which provides the ability to tune the memory access granularity. LAMAR used a hardware predictor to predict when fine-grained accesses occurred, and optimized bandwidth utilization for such accesses. Unlike LAMAR, D²MA's goal is to improve the memory utilization for coarse-grained accesses.

7. CONCLUSION

In order to achieve high performance on GPUs, effectively utilizing memory bandwidth is critical. One common technique to improve the memory utilization is have the programmer explicitly buffer tiles of data from off-chip memory into a fast on-chip memory for computation. Although this technique improves the performance of memory-bound applications, there is more room for improvement by reducing the overhead of generating addresses for each load and store instruction, and eliminating the redundancy of data as buffered data will occupy space in both the L1 cache and the shared memory when both memories are in fact unified.

In this work, we propose D²MA to provide an efficient way to buffer tiles of data from global memory into fast access shared memory. This engine decouples the bulk address generation required to transfer tiles from the rest of the shader pipeline. This way, shaders can continue execution while DMA is transferring data from the global memory. It also supports different special addressing modes that are common in various GPU applications. D²MA is also equipped with a novel waiting scheme that is managed in hardware and maintains read-after-write consistency while being entirely transparent to the programmer. Across 13 different kernels, D²MA yields an average of 36% performance improvement while reducing the duration of a transfer of a tile of data from global to shared memory by 81%.

Acknowledgements

We would like to thank the anonymous reviewers whose excellent feedback helped shaped the final draft of this work, as well as Janghaeng Lee, Ankit Sethia, and Prateek Tandon for their insights and comments. This research was supported by the National Science Foundation under grant CNS-0964478.

8. REFERENCES

[1] "GPGPU-Sim," http://gpgpu-sim.org.

[2] "NVIDIA GPU Computing SDK," http://developer.nvidia.com/gpu-computing-sdk.

[3] A. Bakhoda, G. L. Yuan, W. W. L. Fung, H. Wong, and T. M. Aamodt, "Analyzing CUDA workloads using a detailed GPU simulator," in *Proc. of the 2009 IEEE Symposium on Performance Analysis of Systems and Software*, Apr. 2009, pp. 163–174.

[4] M. Bauer, H. Cook, and B. Khailany, "CudaDMA: Optimizing gpu memory bandwidth via warp specialization," in *Proceedings of 2011 International Conference for High Performance Computing, Networking, Storage and Analysis*, 2011, pp. 12:1–12:11.

[5] J. S. Brunhaver, K. Fatahalian, and P. Hanrahan, "Hardware implementation of micropolygon

rasterization with motion and defocus blur," in *Proceedings of the 2010 Conference on High Performance Graphics*, 2010, pp. 1–9.

[6] S. Che, M. Boyer, J. Meng, D. Tarjan, J. W. Sheaffer, S.-H. Lee, and K. Skadron, "Rodinia: A benchmark suite for heterogeneous computing," in *Proc. of the IEEE Symposium on Workload Characterization*, 2009, pp. 44–54.

[7] S. Che, J. W. Sheaffer, M. Boyer, L. G. Szafaryn, L. Wang, and K. Skadron, "A characterization of the rodinia benchmark suite with comparison to contemporary cmp workloads," in *Proc. of the IEEE Symposium on Workload Characterization*, 2010, pp. 1–11.

[8] T. Chen, R. Raghavan, J. N. Dale, and E. Iwata, "Cell broadband engine architecture and its first implementation: A performance view," *IBM J. Res. Dev.*, vol. 51, no. 5, pp. 559 – 572, Sept 2007.

[9] M. Gebhart, D. R. Johnson, D. Tarjan, S. W. Keckler, W. J. Dally, E. Lindholm, and K. Skadron, "Energy-efficient mechanisms for managing thread context in throughput processors," in *Proc. of the 38th Annual International Symposium on Computer Architecture*, 2011, pp. 235–246.

[10] M. Gebhart, S. W. Keckler, B. Khailany, R. Krashinsky, and W. J. Dally, "Unifying primary cache, scratch, and register file memories in a throughput processor," ser. Proc. of the 45th Annual International Symposium on Microarchitecture, 2012, pp. 96–106.

[11] A. H. Hormati, M. Samadi, M. Woh, T. Mudge, and S. Mahlke, "Sponge: portable stream programming on graphics engines," in *16th International Conference on Architectural Support for Programming Languages and Operating Systems*, 2011, pp. 381–392.

[12] P. Horowitz and W. Hill, *The Art of Electronics, Second Edition.* Cambridge University Press, 1991.

[13] A. Jog, O. Kayiran, A. K. Mishra, M. T. Kandemir, O. Mutlu, R. Iyer, and C. R. Das, "Orchestrated scheduling and prefetching for GPGPUs," in *Proceedings of the 40th Annual International Symposium on Computer Architecture*, 2013, pp. 332–343.

[14] A. Jog, O. Kayiran, C. Nachiappan, A. K. Mishra, M. T. Kandemir, O. Mutlu, R. Iyer, and C. R. Das, "OWL: cooperative thread array aware scheduling techniques for improving GPGPU performance," ser. 18th International Conference on Architectural Support for Programming Languages and Operating Systems, 2013, pp. 395–406.

[15] O. Kayiran, A. Jog, M. T. Kandemir, and C. R. Das, "Neither more nor less: Optimizing thread-level parallelism for gpgpus," in *Proceedings of the 22nd International Conference on Parallel Architectures and Compilation Techniques*, 2013, pp. 157–166.

[16] S. W. Keckler, W. J. Dally, B. Khailany, M. Garland, and D. Glasco, "GPUs and the Future of Parallel Computing," *IEEE Micro*, vol. 31, no. 5, pp. 7–17, 2011.

[17] KHRONOS Group, "OpenCL - the open standard for parallel programming of heterogeneous systems," 2013. [Online]. Available: http://www.khronos.org

[18] N. B. Lakshminarayana, J. Lee, H. Kim, and J. Shin, "Dram scheduling policy for GPGPU architectures based on a potential function," *Computer Architecture Letters*, vol. 11, no. 2, pp. 33–36, 2012.

[19] J. Lee, N. Lakshminarayana, H. Kim, and R. Vuduc, "Many-thread aware prefetching mechanisms for GPGPU applications," in *Proc. of the 43rd Annual International Symposium on Microarchitecture*, 2010, pp. 213–224.

[20] V. Narasiman, M. Shebanow, C. J. Lee, R. Miftakhutdinov, O. Mutlu, and Y. N. Patt, "Improving GPU performance via large warps and two-level warp scheduling," in *Proceedings of the 44th Annual IEEE/ACM International Symposium on Microarchitecture*, 2011, pp. 308–317.

[21] NVIDIA, "Fermi: Nvidia's next generation CUDA compute architecture," 2009, http://www.nvidia.com/content/PDF/ fermi_white_papers/NVIDIA_Fermi_Compute_Architect - ure_Whitepaper.pdf.

[22] *CUDA C Programming Guide*, NVIDIA, Oct. 2012.

[23] NVIDIA, "NVIDIA's next generation CUDA compute architecture: Kepler GK110," 2012, www.nvidia.com/content/PDF/NVIDIA_Kepler_GK110 _Architecture_Whitepaper.pdf.

[24] ——, "Whitepaper: NVIDIA geforce GTX 680," 2012, http://www.geforce.com/Active/en_US/en_US/pdf/ GeForce-GTX-680-Whitepaper-FINAL.pdf.

[25] ——, "NVIDIA Tegra K1: A new era in mobile computing," 2014, http://www.nvidia.com/content/ PDF/tegra_white_papers/tegra-K1-whitepaper.pdf.

[26] Oak Ridge Leadership Computing Facility, "Titan: Built for science," 2012, http://www.olcf.ornl.gov/wp-content/themes/olcf/titan/Titan_BuiltForScience.pdf.

[27] D. A. Patterson and J. L. Hennessy, *Computer Organization and Design: The Hardware/Software Interface, Fourth Edition.* Elsevier, 2012.

[28] J. Power, A. Basu, J. Gu, S. Puthoor, B. M. Beckmann, M. D. Hill, S. K. Reinhardt, and D. A. Wood, "Heterogeneous system coherence for integrated CPU-GPU systems," in *Proc. of the 46th Annual International Symposium on Microarchitecture*, 2013, pp. 457–467.

[29] M. Rhu, M. Sullivan, J. Leng, and M. Erez, "A locality-aware memory hierarchy for energy-efficient GPU architectures," in *Proc. of the 46th Annual International Symposium on Microarchitecture*, 2013, pp. 86–98.

[30] T. G. Rogers, M. O'Connor, and T. M. Aamodt, "Cache-conscious wavefront scheduling," ser. Proc. of the 45th Annual International Symposium on Microarchitecture, 2012, pp. 72–83.

[31] A. Sethia, G. Dasika, M. Samadi, and S. Mahlke, "APOGEE: Adaptive prefetching on GPUs for energy efficiency," in *Proc. of the 22nd International Conference on Parallel Architectures and Compilation Techniques*, 2013, pp. 73–82.

VAST: The Illusion of a Large Memory Space for GPUs

Janghaeng Lee, Mehrzad Samadi, and Scott Mahlke

Advanced Computer Architecture Laboratory
University of Michigan - Ann Arbor, MI, USA
{jhaeng, mehrzads, mahlke}@umich.edu

ABSTRACT

Heterogeneous systems equipped with traditional processors (CPUs) and graphics processing units (GPUs) have enabled processing large data sets. With new programming models, such as OpenCL and CUDA, programmers are encouraged to offload data parallel workloads to GPUs as much as possible in order to fully utilize the available resources. Unfortunately, offloading work is strictly limited by the size of the physical memory on a specific GPU. In this paper, we present Virtual Address Space for Throughput processors (VAST), an automatic GPU memory management system that provides an OpenCL program with the illusion of a virtual memory space . Based on the available physical memory on the target GPU, VAST does the following: automatically partitions the data parallel workload into chunks; efficiently extracts the precise working set required for the divided workload; rearranges the working set in contiguous memory space; and, transforms the kernel to operate on the reorganized working set. With VAST, the programmer is responsible for developing a data parallel kernel in OpenCL without concern for physical memory space limitations of individual GPUs. VAST transparently handles code generation dealing with the constraints of the actual physical memory and improves the retargetability of the OpenCL with moderate overhead. Experiments demonstrate that a real GPU, NVIDIA GTX 760 with 2 GB of memory, can compute any size of data without program changes achieving 2.6x speedup over CPU exeuction, which is a realistic alternative for large data computation.

Categories and Subject Descriptors

D.3.4 [**Programming Languages**]: Processors—*Run-time environments; Code generation*

General Terms

Design, Experimentation, Performance

Keywords

Virtual memory, GPU, Optimization

PACT'14, August 24–27, 2014, Edmonton, AB, Canada.

http://dx.doi.org/10.1145/2628071.2628075.

1. INTRODUCTION

Graphics processing units (GPUs) have emerged as the computational workhorse of throughput oriented applications because of their low cost, high performance, and wide availability [11]. Modern GPUs achieve several TFLOPS of peak performance while costing a few hundred dollars. The advent of new programming models, such as OpenCL [7] and CUDA [5], makes it possible to utilize GPUs for processing massive data in parallel for general purpose applications. By leveraging these programming models, programmers can develop data parallel kernels for GPUs that achieve speedups of 4-100x over traditional processors (CPUs) [24].

Unfortunately, discrete GPUs have a critical limitation: the entire data to process *must* reside in GPU memory before execution. When the data size exceeds the physical memory of the GPU, the user must fall back to the CPU which supports nearly arbitrary data sizes through virtual addressing. Smart programmers can overcome this restriction by applying a *divide-and-conquer* approach. In this case, the programmer explicitly divides the workload into smaller chunks and executes a series of kernels each processing a subset of the data. This approach is not a panacea, however. Even in the simple case where the kernel operates on contiguous data chunks, explicit data management is tedious, requiring explicit buffer allocations and data transfer to/from the host. For non-contiguous data, divide-and-conquer is more complex. Lastly, partitioning decisions change across GPUs with differing amounts of physical memory.

A natural question is why do GPUs not support virtual addressing to eliminate this problem as CPUs have done for many decades [26, 10]. Through a combination of hardware (e.g., translation lookaside buffers) and operating system support (e.g., page tables), CPUs provide the appearance of a nearly infinite address space to facilitate processing large data sets. However, virtualizing the address space of discrete GPUs is difficult for the following reasons:

- Discrete GPUs have separate memories that use different address spaces, and each transaction between the host and GPU is expensive.
- GPUs do not interact with the operating systems for memory management, but instead directly access their physical memory.
- Execution on GPUs is non-preemptive, therefore all data must be present in the physical memory before execution.

The combination of these factors makes it difficult to execute kernels on GPUs whose total memory footprint exceeds the physical memory size on the GPU without programmer intervention. As the size of data to process keeps increasing, this limitation will become more significant.

To tackle these challenges, we present *Virtual Address Space for Throughput processors* (VAST), a run-time software system that provides the programmer with the illusion of a virtual memory space for commodity OpenCL devices. VAST transparently divides and transfers working sets based on the available physical memory space on the target GPU and automatically merges partial outputs. To virtualize the memory space, VAST adopts a *look-ahead page table (LPT)*, a new type of page table that contains a list of virtual pages that will be accessed by specific ranges of the OpenCL workload. LPT differs from conventional page tables used in operating systems in that the LPT is filled up before the pages are actually accessed. With LPT, VAST decomposes the working set into individual *page frames* for execution of the partial workload. Page frames are packed into a contiguous buffer (*frame buffer*) that will reside in the GPU's physical memory and LPT represents the mapping of an OpenCL buffer from the CPU's virtual space into the GPU's physical space (the frame buffer). Instead of transferring the entire data to the GPU, VAST transfers the LPT and frame buffer for each partial workload. At the same time, VAST transforms the kernel to access memory through the LPT (e.g., software address translation).

The VAST runtime system significantly improves GPU portability as it can utilize any GPU for larger sized workloads. The challenges of VAST are four fold: dividing an arbitrary workload based on the available physical memory size, efficiently generating the LPT and frame buffer, transforming the kernel to use the relocated and packed data, and avoiding replicated transfers due to reuse of data across partial workloads. To address these issues, this paper makes following contributions:

- A code transformation methodology that quickly inspects memory access locations of an OpenCL kernel in order to generate LPTs.
- A novel technique that partitions an OpenCL workload into partial workloads based on the physical memory constraints of a GPU and packs the corresponding data into a frame buffer using LPTs.
- Kernel transformation techniques to access data out of the frame buffer using LPTs.
- A technique to avoid replicated data transfers to the GPU.
- A comprehensive performance evaluation of VAST on real hardware consisting of an Intel Core i7 CPU and an NVIDIA GTX 760 GPU.

The rest of the paper is organized as follows. Section 2 discusses the OpenCL execution model and opportunities for virtualizing GPU memory space. Section 3 explains the overview of VAST, and then the implementation is discussed in Section 4. The experimental results of using VAST for various OpenCL applications are presented in Section 5. Section 6 discusses the related work in this area. And finally, we conclude in Section 7.

2. BACKGROUND AND OPPORTUNITIES

This section briefly describes the OpenCL execution model and discusses memory consistency of OpenCL to understand the semantics of executing partial workloads of an OpenCL kernel.

2.1 OpenCL Execution Model

In OpenCL, the basic unit of execution is a single *work-item* which corresponds to a thread. A group of work-items executing the same code are weaved together to form a *work-group*. These work-groups are combined to form a unit of execution called *NDRange, N-Dimensional Range*, where each NDRange is scheduled by a command queue. For the execution, the OpenCL program assumes that the underlying devices consist of a number of compute units (CUs) which are further split into processing elements (PEs). When executing a kernel, work-groups are mapped to CUs, and work-items are assigned to PEs. In order to launch a kernel, a programmer must define the number of work-groups in NDRange, and the number of work-items in a work-group. In real hardware, since the number of actual cores are limited, CUs and PEs are virtualized by the hardware scheduler or OpenCL drivers.

```
__kernel void
matrixMul(__global float* C,
          __global float* A, __global float* B,
          int wA, int wB,
          int range_from, int range_to)
{
    int gid_x   = get_group_id(0);
    int gid_y   = get_group_id(1);
    int size_x  = get_num_groups(0);
    int flat_id = gid_x + gid_y * size_x;
    // check whether to execute
    if (flat_id < range_from || flat_id > range_to)
      return;

    int idx = get_global_id(0);
    int idy = get_global_id(1);

    float value = 0;
    for (int k = 0; k < wA; ++k) {
      value += A[idy * wA + k] * B[k * wB + idx];
    }
    C[idy * wA + idx] = value;
}
```

Figure 1: The code transformation for partial execution of an OpenCL kernel. The kernel takes two additional arguments for the work-group range to execute, and grey backgrounded code is also inserted at the beginning of the kernel to check if the work-group is to be executed. The work-groups out of the range will terminate the execution immediately.

2.2 Memory Consistency and Partial Execution

OpenCL uses a relaxed memory consistency model for *local* memory within a work-group and for *global* memory within a kernel's workspace, NDRange. Each work-item (thread) in the same work-group sees the same view of local memory only at a synchronization point where a *barrier* appears. Similarly, every work-group in the same kernel is guaranteed to see the same view of the global memory only at the end of kernel execution, which is another synchronization point. This means that the ordering of execution does not have to be guaranteed across work-groups in a kernel, but guaranteed only across synchronization points [20].

Based on this memory consistency model, an OpenCL kernel can be executed in parallel at a work-group granularity without concern of the execution order. If a kernel executes a subset of work-groups instead of the entire NDRange, the result at the end of kernel execution would be incomplete. However, if the rest of the work-groups are later executed, it would correctly complete. This feature enables splitting workloads without concern for write-conflicts among work-groups [20]. By simply assigning a subset of work-groups for execution exclusively, partial results would appear interleaved in the memory space. Correct final results are completed when every work-group finishes the execution.

Through the code transformation, the host program can control the number of executed work-groups as shown in Figure 1. By inserting checking code at the beginning of the kernel, every work-item checks if the work-group it belongs to is supposed to execute. If it should not, the work-group terminates the execution immediately and the GPU will schedule it out. In this way, we can limit the total amount of memory accessed by those work-groups to a predefined amount (the GPU's physical memory size). This memory is reorganized into page frames and packed into a frame buffer by VAST. A look-ahead page table (LPT) is then used to map between the original CPU address to the page frame address for the GPU. We refer to this model as *partial execution* and the goal of VAST is to automate the decomposition and to restrict the kernel as necessary to realize software-managed paging.

While splitting data-parallel workloads at a work-group granularity, two important factors are *global barriers* and *atomic operations* because the execution of work-groups should be ordered at those points. Usually, these global synchronization points are handled by either hardware or software. In a hardware approach, the hardware scheduler will save the context to the memory and swap out the entire work-group until all work-groups reach the synchronization point. On the other hand, in a software approach, the entire kernel is broken down into multiple kernels at the global synchronization point, then the split kernels are executed in order. VAST can make use of this software approach, but in this paper, we do not evaluate applications with these semantics.

3. VAST SYSTEM OVERVIEW

VAST is an abstraction layer located between an application and the OpenCL library. The VAST layer overloads all OpenCL APIs including device-querying functions. By overloading device-querying APIs, VAST provides the application with the illusion of a virtual GPU device that has very large amount of memory. With the virtual device, programmers can allocate buffers as much as they need without concern for the physical memory size.

In order to virtualize address space of OpenCL kernels, actual data must be rearranged into page frames with the look-ahead page table (LPT), which is filled with a list of pointers to the corresponding page frames that will be accessed during the execution. In addition, the OpenCL kernel must access data through the LPT and frame buffer (address translation), as similar to the conventional program accessing data through TLBs and the operating system's page table. After kernel execution, the output buffer for the LPT and page frames must be recovered to original memory space on the host.

The rest of this section describes execution flow of VAST system and illustrates timeline of VAST execution.

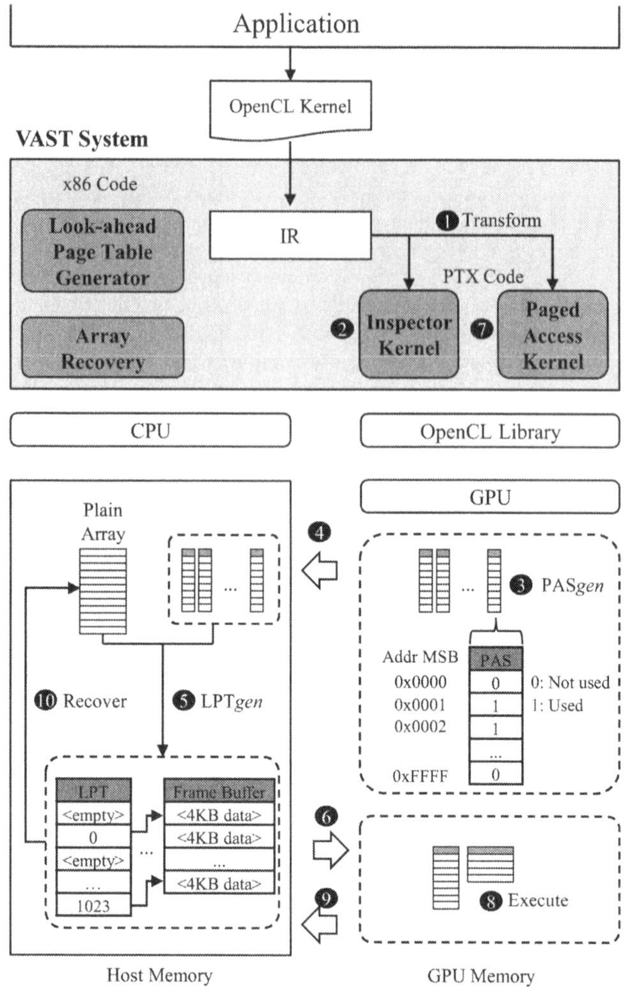

Figure 2: The VAST system located between applications and OpenCL library. VAST takes an OpenCL kernel and transforms it into the inspector kernel and the paged access kernel. At kernel launch, the GPU generates PASs ($PASgen$) by launching the inspector kernel, then transfers them to the host to create LPT and frame buffer ($LPTgen$). Next, LPT and frame buffer are transferred to the GPU in order to execute the paged access kernel.

3.1 VAST System Execution Flow

Figure 2 illustrates sequences of VAST system operations. First, VAST compiles an OpenCL kernel into intermediate representations (IRs), and then generates a GPU binary (PTX) for the ***Inspector Kernel***, and the ***Paged Access Kernel*** as shown in Figure 2 ❶.

After a compilation request, the application will request the kernel launch. On this request, VAST first launches the *Inspector Kernel* ❷ that only inspects usage of global arguments (arguments with `__global` keyword) and fills up the *Page Accessed Sets* (PASs) ❸. PAS contains boolean values that represent whether a work-group has accessed each page. Note that each work-group has its own PAS for each global argument of the kernel, and the size of PAS is fixed as $Ceil(\frac{AllocSize}{PageSize})$ where $AllocSize$ is actual OpenCL buffer allocation size from the application. For example, 4GB of OpenCL buffer will require 1MB of PAS with 4KB pages. In order to reduce the number of PASs, one PAS can be shared among several work-groups. In this case, one PAS represents the pages accessed by a subset of work-groups.

Next, VAST transfers PASs from the GPU to the host ❹, and then the host fills up the LPT and frame buffers using the PASs until the size of frame buffer reaches the available GPU memory size ❺. After that, VAST allocates the actual buffers for the LPT and frame buffer on the GPU, and transfers them to the GPU device ❻. At this point, VAST knows how many work-groups should be executed as it has generated the LPT and frame buffer for the specific range of work-groups. In order to execute specific range of work-groups of the kernel, the *Paged Access Kernel* also takes additional parameters for the ranges of work-groups to execute as discussed in Section 2.2. Once VAST finishes the transfer, it launches the *Paged Access Kernel* ❼, which accesses the memory through the LPT.

During execution, the frame buffer in the device memory will be updated ❽, and after the execution, VAST will transfer them back to the host memory space ❾. Finally, VAST recovers arrays using the LPT and modified frame buffer ❿, and repeats the steps from LPT generation ❺ to recovery ❿ until all work-groups finish their execution.

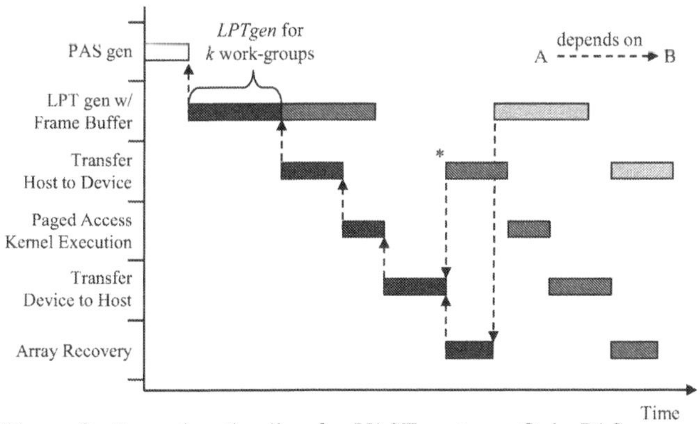

Figure 3: Execution timeline for VAST system. Only PAS generation and the first LPT generation cost is exposed. Other LPT generations and array recoveries are overlapped from data transfer and kernel execution. With double buffering, the second LPT generation starts immediately after the first LPT generation.

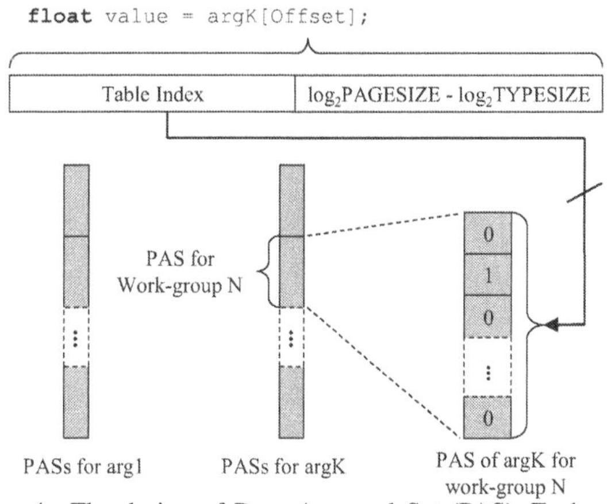

Figure 4: The design of Page Accessed Set (PAS). Each work-group has its own PAS for each global argument. Each entry of PAS has a boolean value that represents whether corresponding page has been accessed by the work-group.

3.2 VAST Execution Timeline

Figure 3 visualizes the timeline of VAST execution. As shown, the cost of generating LPTs and frame buffers can be hidden by overlapping them with data transfer and kernel execution. Thus, the only exposed cost is PAS generation and the first LPT generation. Mind that VAST allocates LPTs and frame buffers twice on the host for double buffering. With double buffering, the next LPT generation can proceed right after the previous LPT generation, as shown in Figure 3.

One important point from Figure 3 is that transferring the second working set to the GPU (marked as *) starts after retrieving the first partial result back to the host, not after the kernel execution. The main reason is that some pages written in the first partial execution can also be written by the work-groups in the second partial execution. Similar to data forwarding in a CPU pipeline datapath, VAST forwards only written pages from the previous execution to the next execution. Details of forwarding shared pages will be discussed in Section 4.4.

Another feature of VAST is that it avoids duplicated data transfer. To illustrate, if page frames of a global argument during the partial execution are identical to that of the next execution, VAST skips LPT and frame buffer generation as well as buffer transfer for the next execution.

4. IMPLEMENTATION

This section discusses the implementation of VAST system including design of PAS, kernel transformations, and how to create LPT and frame buffers using PASs. Also, the ways to handle shared pages and to avoid duplicated data transfers are discussed.

4.1 The Design of Page Accessed Set

As described in Section 3.1, the first step for VAST is launching the inspector kernel on the GPU in order to generate *Page Accessed Sets* (PASs). PAS represents a list of pages accessed by a set of work-groups during execution. Therefore, each entry of PAS contains a boolean value as shown in Figure 4. Later, these PASs will be used on the host to generate *Look-ahead Page Table* (LPT), which contains pointers to the page frames.

The inspector kernel is able to execute on the GPU without transferring the working set because most OpenCL kernels use a combination of work-item index and scalar variables as the index of global array access. Upon this property, VAST passes only scalar and `__constant` arguments to the inspector kernel along with the NDRange information (size of work-groups and work-items) for PAS generation. If global array access depends on the value of a global argument, (e.g. indirect memory access), the inspector code is leveraged on the host, and the host generates PASs directly.

As shown in Figure 4, VAST makes use of single level paging because it minimizes both PAS generation time for the inspector kernel and address translation time for the paged access kernel. As a result, with 4KB pages, 4 GB of data can be fit into 1 MB of PAS if each entry uses 1 byte to store a boolean value. However, if PASs are maintained per work-group per global argument, the size of overall PASs can become significant if the kernel is launched with a large number of work-groups. For this reason, VAST makes a set of consecutive work-groups to share one PAS depending on the number of work-groups. The number of work-groups per PAS is determined statically using the equation below.

$$WORKGROUP\_PER\_PAS = Ceil\left(\frac{\frac{MEMSIZE}{32}}{\frac{AllocSize}{TOTAL\_WORKGROUP}}\right) \quad (1)$$

The assumption behind this equation is that one work-group accesses the space of $\frac{AllocSize}{TOTAL\_WORKGROUP}$. With this assumption, VAST computes the number of work-groups not to exceed $\frac{MEMSIZE}{32}$ accesses. This is a rough estimation, and if it appears that the number is too small or large, VAST adjust the number dynamically.

When several work-groups try to modify the shared PAS, atomic operation is not necessary because according to NVIDIA's programming guide [5], if a non-atomic instruction executed by more than one thread writes to the same location in global memory, only one thread performs a write and which thread does it is undefined. Thus, it is safe to share one PAS among several work-groups and work-items because every work-item will try to write the same boolean value (`TRUE`).

4.2 OpenCL Kernel Transformation

As shown in Figure 2 - ❶, VAST transforms each OpenCL kernel into an inspector kernel and paged access kernel. Both kernel transformations only focus on usages of global arguments, but the difference is that the inspector kernel replace entire memory operations with the new stores, while the paged access kernel replaces only the bases and offsets of memory operations as shown in Figure 5.

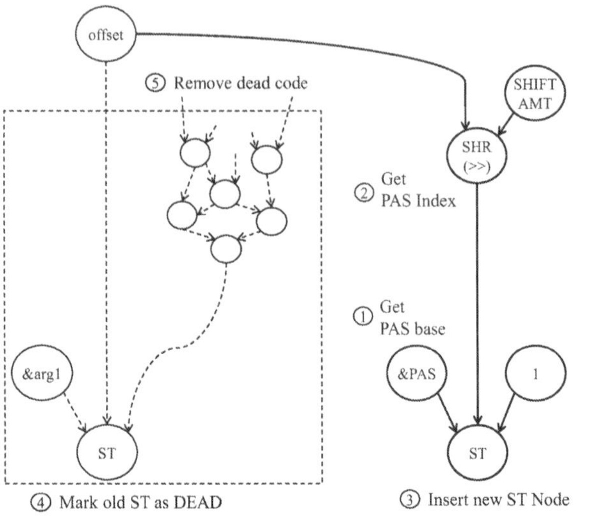

(a) DFG for the inspector kernel

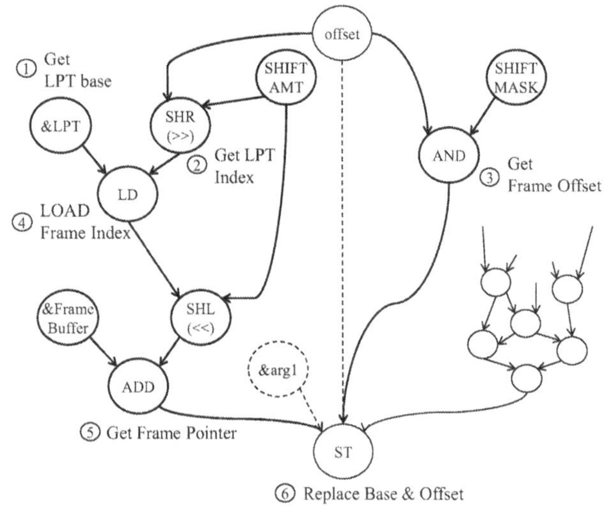

(b) DFG for the paged access kernel

Figure 5: Data flow graphs for the kernel transformation. In the inspector kernel (a), all computational code are removed by dead code elimination. In paged access kernel (b), the base and the offset are replaced with new nodes for address translation.

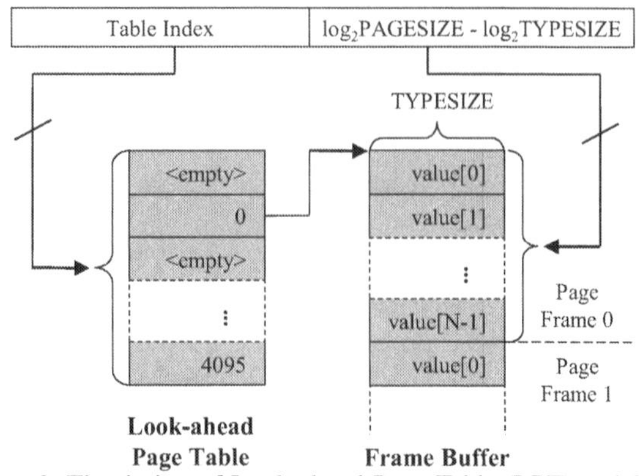

Figure 6: The design of Look-ahead Page Table (LPT) and frame buffer. One pair of LPT and frame buffer corresponds to one global argument.

In detail, the first step for the inspector kernel transformation is to inline function calls in the kernel in order to avoid expensive inter-procedural analysis. In general, every function call can be inlined since the OpenCL programming model prohibits recursive calls as it adopts SIMT execution model that does not allow threads to execute different instructions at a time [20]. Next, VAST adds arguments for PASs to the kernel, each of which corresponds to the respective global arguments. Besides, the arguments for each PAS's size are added to the inspector kernel because each work-group finds out their own PAS base by offsetting the PAS argument by $flat\_work\_group\_id \times PAS\_SIZE$ as shown in Figure 4. Note that the size of PAS differs by global argument because it depends on the actual OpenCL buffer allocation size from the application.

Once the kernel arguments are setup, VAST performs several steps to transform the kernel as illustrated in Figure 5(a). First, VAST finds out load (LD) or store (ST) instruction that accesses global argument using Def-Use (DU) chains. Next, it matches the base of LD/ST to the base of the PAS. After VAST gets the corresponding PAS base, it inserts a node that computes the PAS index using the offset of the LD/ST instruction. The amount of shifting the offset is determined statically by looking at the type of base pointer and the page size as shown below.

$$SHIFT\_AMT = log_2 PAGESIZE - Ceil(log_2 TYPESIZE) \quad (2)$$

For example, the offset of **`float`** type array will be shifted right 10 bits if the page size is 4,096 bytes for the index of PAS. VAST also supports a custom type such as `struct`, but in the page frame, those array elements will be aligned to the order of magnitude through $Ceil()$ function in the equation. The next step is to insert a new store instruction with the PAS base, and PAS index as shown in Figure 5(a). Finally, VAST proceeds with *dead code elimination* (DCE) using the mark-sweep algorithm [28] in order to remove all the computation code as well as the dead control flows. Because computation code and unrelated control flows are removed by DCE, the inspector kernel completes PAS generation very quickly, which is evaluated in Section 5.

In the meantime, VAST also generates the *Paged Access Kernel*. Similar to the inspector kernel, VAST also adds additional arguments for *LPT* and *frame buffer* for each global argument to the paged access kernel. In addition, it inserts two additional arguments for the range of work-groups to execute as well as checking code at the beginning of the kernel for the *partial execution* as discussed in Section 2.2.

After setting up the kernel arguments, VAST only inspects uses of global array access using DU chains as the same as the initial step for the inspector kernel. For each use of global arguments, VAST inserts nodes for *address translation* based on the design of LPT and frame buffer as shown in Figure 6. As shown in the figure, an additional `LOAD` is used for querying the target frame index. The `LOAD` address of LPT is likely to be the same among work-items, because OpenCL programmers are encouraged to write the kernel to access the memory coalesced between work-items to fully utilize memory parallelism. Once the nodes for the frame pointer and the frame offset are added, VAST replaces the original base and offset operands of memory access with the frame pointer and the frame offset respectively as shown in Figure 5(b).

Pointer Aliasing is also handled in VAST during kernel transformations. As OpenCL kernels can use a local pointer variable, aliased global pointers also must be considered for both the inspector kernel and the paged access kernel. An important property of an OpenCL program is that the `__global` keyword implicitly in-

Algorithm 1 PAS Reduction

```
1: k = 1
2: RangeFrom = 1
3: ReducedPAS[1..NumArgs][1..PAS_SIZE] = 0
4: MemFull_PAS[1..N][1..NumArgs][1..PAS_SIZE] = 0
5: for i = 1 to PAS_CNT do
6:     TotalMemUsed = 0
7:     for j = 1 to NUM_ARGS do
8:         MemFull_PAS[k][j] = ReducedPAS[j]
9:         ReducedPAS[j] = OR_REDUCE(ReducedPAS[j], PAS[j][i])
10:        MemUsed = SUM_REDUCE(ReducedPAS[j])×PAGE_SIZE
11:        TotalMemUsed = TotalMemUsed + MemUsed
12:    end for
13:    if TotalMemUsed > MEM_SIZE then
14:        i = i - 1                              ▷ Roll-back one step
15:        k = k + 1
16:        StoreRange(RangeFrom, i)               ▷ Store partial execution range
17:        RangeFrom = i + 1
18:        ReducedPAS[1..NumArgs][1..PAS_SIZE] = 0          ▷ Reset
19:    end if
20: end for
21: StoreRange(RangeFrom, PAS_CNT)                ▷ Store the last range
22: return MemFull_PAS[1..k]                      ▷ return reduced PASs
```

cludes `restrict` keyword, thus global arguments will not alias each other (*No-Alias*). In other words, any pointer variable that will alias to a global argument must be declared with the `__global` keyword. As a results, the aliasing of all global pointers can be determined as either *No-Alias* or *Must-Alias* through basic alias analysis. With this alias result, VAST can keep track of aliased pointers by offsetting the base. If an aliased global pointer uses different type (typecast), VAST uses different $SHIFT\_AMT$ for the aliased pointer during transformation.

4.3 Look-ahead Page Table Generation

Once PASs are generated by launching the inspector kernel, those are transferred to the host in order to generate *Look-ahead Page Table* (LPT) and frame buffer. As shown in Figure 4 and 6, LPT differs from PAS in that the entry of LPT contains a frame pointer (4 bytes), while PAS contains a boolean variable (1 byte). Moreover, LPT stands for one global argument, while PAS is maintained per global argument per work-groups as discussed in previous sections. LPT can be produced multiple times for one global argument because one LPT is for a single sequence of partial execution, which executes for the working set that fits into GPU memory as shown in Figure 3.

In order to generate LPT using PASs, VAST follows several steps. Considering that each PAS stores the list of pages accessed by a set of work-groups, the first step is to reduce several PASs, which will contain the list of pages accessed by *multiple* sets of work-groups. This reduction process is done until the accessed page size in the reduced PASs for all global arguments does not exceed the physical memory size. Algorithm 1 illustrates how VAST reduces the PASs. As illustrated in the algorithm, the outermost loop (line 5-20) iterates over the sets of work-groups, and the PAS used by a set of work-groups are OR-reduced to the PAS used by the next set of work-groups for each global argument (at line 9). As a result, OR-reduced PASs will contain the pages accessed by the multiple sets of work-groups. After OR-reduction, VAST checks the number of accessed pages by executing SUM-reduce on reduced PAS (line 10-11). If the total page size of the reduced PAS exceeds the GPU memory, it stores the range for *partial execution* (line 13-19), and continue reduction until PASs for all the work-groups are processed.

The time complexity of this algorithm is $O(kNM)$, where k is the number of global arguments, N is the number of work-groups, and M is the number of PAS entry count. In general, k is a very small number (<5) and N can be reduced by letting several work-groups to share one PAS. Furthermore, reduction operation, which takes $O(M)$, can be further optimized by utilizing SIMD instructions as reducing two entries is independent from reducing other entries. In other words, 16 entries can be reduced at once with the 128-bit SIMD instruction as each PAS entry consists of a single byte. As a result, the entire PAS reduction produce negligible overhead, which is evaluated in Section 5.

Once reduced PASs were computed, VAST keeps reduced PASs and the ranges of work-groups for the partial execution. Each reduced PAS that corresponds to the range will represent a list of pages that will be accessed by the range of work-groups to be executed.

With reduced PASs, the next step is to allocate the frame buffer for each global argument on the host. At this point, VAST knows how much memory space is required for the frame buffer by multiplying the page size by the number of valid (`TRUE`) entries in the reduced PAS. Finally, VAST starts to fill up the LPT and the frame buffers by iterating entries of the reduced PASs. If the entry value of PAS is `TRUE`, it copies the corresponding page of the plain array to the contiguous memory space, the *frame buffer*. At the same time, the location (index) of the page frame in the frame buffer is stored to the entry of LPT as shown in Figure 6. One intelligent feature is that if the corresponding argument is a *Write-Only* argument, VAST fills up the frame buffer only for the shared pages, which will be discussed in detail in the next section.

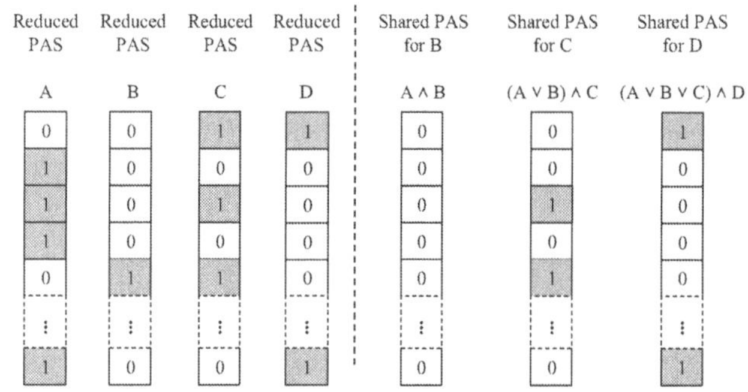

Figure 7: PAS generation for shared pages (shared PAS). Each reduced PAS is used for a single sequence of partial execution. As the sequence of partial execution increases, the number of logical operations increase for shared PAS as VAST should check pages used in the previous sequences.

4.4 Forwarding Shared Pages

As discussed in Section 2, the OpenCL uses a relaxed memory consistency model for *global* memory within NDRange. Thus, any order of work-group execution will produce the same result without concerning write-conflicts among work-groups. However, in VAST, the granularity of memory transaction between the host and the GPU is a page frame, which is much larger than usual memory write. As a result, *false sharing* of a page may occur among the work-groups with regards to a *writable* frame buffer because more than one work-group can change the same page even though they write different location within the page. Sharing the same pages between work-groups within the same sequence of partial execution is safe because there is no write-conflict within a page as discussed. However, if a page was shared among work-groups in different sequences of partial execution, VAST must transfer up-to-date page frames for each partial execution due to *Write-After-Write* (WAW) dependencies. One option is that VAST waits for the partial output to be arrived from the previous partial execution, and also waits for the partial output to be recovered to the plain array. After that, VAST proceeds with LPT and frame buffer generation in order to transfer up-to-date page frames for the next partial execution.

Obviously, this option brings a serious serialization of the execution, because LPT and frame buffer generation could be overlapped from the kernel execution and transferring data back and forth between the host and the GPU as shown in Figure 3. In order to avoid serialization, VAST precomputes shared pages among each sequence of partial execution, and selectively copies the shared pages by looking at the list of shared pages (*Shared PAS*). A shared PAS for partial execution can be precomputed using reduced PASs shown in Figure 7. The example in the figure illustrate that there are four reduced PASs, which means the entire kernel execution was decomposed into four sequences of partial execution. At each sequence, every accessed page in the PAS must be compared with the same page in previous sequences of PAS. For example, at the fourth sequence D, VAST performs *OR-reduce* PASs for all previous sequences, A to C, which represents all the pages accessed by the previous sequences of partial execution. After that, VAST *AND-reduce* it with the PAS of the fourth sequence. VAST also keeps these shared PASs only for the *write* arguments, and selectively copies the frame buffer when the partial results are transferred back to the host.

4.5 Transfer Optimization

While VAST performs several sequences of partial execution, the working set between consecutive sequences can be exactly same. In this case, VAST does not have to regenerate the LPT and frame buffer for the next sequence, since those are already present in the GPU memory from the previous sequence. In order to remove duplicated transfer between partial executions, VAST also compares the reduced PAS with the previous reduced PAS before generating LPT and frame buffer. The comparison is done using XOR-reduction between two PASs. If all the entries of XOR-reduced PAS are filled with `TRUE`, it means the pages required by the next partial execution is exactly the same as the previous one. With this optimization, VAST can further improve performance, and this optimization is evaluated in Section 5.4.

5. EVALUATION

Implementation: VAST was prototyped using Clang [1] for OpenCL front-end, and Low-Level Virtual Machine (LLVM) 3.3 [19] for the back-end. Once Clang parses the OpenCL kernel and generates the IRs, LLVM transforms it to the inspector kernel and the paged access kernel. After transformation is done, it lowers IRs to PTX binary to launch the kernels in the GPU. In order to evaluate an OpenCL kernel with indirect memory accesses, VAST also transforms the kernel into inspector code in x86 for PAS generation in the CPU.

Baseline: For the experiments, we used a real machine configured as shown in Table 1. We used the OpenCL execution on the CPU device as our baseline under the assumption that OpenCL kernels are fallen back to the CPU device (OpenCL's logical device) when the working set size exceeds the GPU's memory. This is possible because the CPU device, which shares the address space with the host, has 32 GB of memory, and thus it can execute on a large working set. For the CPU execution, we used the Intel OpenCL library [2], which fully utilizes all cores with simultaneous multi threading (SMT) and SIMD instructions (SSE and AVX). In addition, the Intel OpenCL library allows a kernel to access the host's memory directly if the buffer was created with the `CL_MEM_USE_HOST_PTR` flag. Therefore, our baseline does not include data transfer time.

Device	Intel Core i7 - 3770	NVIDIA GTX 760 (Kepler)
# of Cores	4 (8 Threads)	336
Clock Freq.	3.2 GHz	1.62 GHz
Memory (B/W)	32 GB DDR3 (12.8 GB/s)	2 GB GDDR5 (192 GB/s)
Peak Perf.	435.2 GFlops [4]	2,258 GFlops
OpenCL Ver.	Intel SDK 2013 [2]	CUDA SDK 5.5 [5]
PCIe (B/W)	3.0 x16 (15.76 GB/s)	
OS	Ubuntu Linux 12.04 LTS	

Table 1: Experimental Setup

Also, we measured wall clock time on VAST system that includes PAS, LPT, and frame buffer generation as well as buffer transfer, paged access kernel execution, and array recovery.

Benchmarks: For the evaluation, we used the benchmarks from NVIDIA Computing SDK [3]. We bailed out very simple benchmarks such as *BandwidthTest*, *InlinePTX*, *VectorAdd*, etc, but we added *sparse vector matrix multiplication* (SpMV) from our implementation in order to evaluate the kernel with indirect memory accesses. Because the benchmark suite is for evaluating NVIDIA GPUs, some benchmarks are unable to take large inputs. For these benchmarks, we only modified them to take large inputs. The list of applications, execution parameters, and working set size are shown in Table 2. To evaluate the scalability of the GPU, we used a working set size of more than GPU memory size (2 GB).

GPU with infinite memory (InfGPU): We also estimated the performance of a hypothetical GPU which is assumed to have infinite physical memory. In order to estimate kernel execution time on InfGPU, we measured the baseline (**CPU**) kernel execution time for a workload of 2 GB, which is the limit of the real GPU memory. Next, we compare this execution time with the baseline execution time for the an actual size of workload as defined in Table 2. By comparing these two execution times, we computed *scaling factor* of kernel execution time. After that, we ran 2 GB of workload on the real GPU, and multiplied the kernel execution time by the scaling factor. Meanwhile, in order to estimate the transfer time for actual workload, we also measured the time for 2 GB of data transfer to the real GPU, and then extrapolated it to the actual size as shown in Table 2.

5.1 Results

First, we evaluated the speedup of VAST system over Intel OpenCL execution varying page size as shown in Figure 8. As shown in the figure, VAST performs better on every benchmark, geometric mean of 2.6x speedup with 4KB page frame, even though it involves the time for LPT generation, buffer transfer time, and array recovery. In general, as shown in the figure, reducing the page frame size brings slowdown on both PAS and LPT generation due to increased number of PAS entries. However, having too large a page frame size (8KB) may also have a negative effect as it may increase internal fragmentation, the ratio of unused data in a page frame. More internal fragmentation produces unnecessary data copy between plain array to the frame buffer, and thus additional buffer transfer between the host and the GPU.

In Figure 8, most benchmarks showed a performance gap between VAST and InfGPU. The gap generally comes from the exposed cost of generating the first LPT and frame buffer as well as the last array recovery (prolog and epilog of pipelined execution), which is not necessary for InfGPU. On the contrary, for compute-intensive benchmarks, such as MatrixMul and NBody, VAST performs as good as InfGPU. The main reason is that these compute-intensive kernels have smaller working sets, which makes the exposed cost negligible.

Application	Execution Parameters	OpenCL Kernel	Buffer Size			# of Work-groups	# of Work-groups / PAS
			Input	Output	Total		
BlackScholes	256 million options	BlackScholes	3.0 GB	2.0 GB	5.0 GB	1,024	16
FDTD3d	3D dimsize=1024, Radius=2	FiniteDifferences	4.0 GB	4.0 GB	8.0 GB	4,096	32
MatrixMul	20,480×20,480 matrices	MatrixMul	3.1 GB	1.6 GB	4.7 GB	409,600	8,192
MedianFilter	30,720×17,820 PPM image	ckMedian	2.0 GB	2.0 GB	4.0 GB	8,294,400	131,072
MersenneTwister	1.15 billion numbers	MersenneTwister	1 MB	4.3 GB	4.3 GB	512	8
		BoxMuller	4.3 GB	4.3 GB	8.6 GB	512	8
Nbody	41 million particles	IntegrateBodies_MT	1.3 GB	1.3 GB	2.6 GB	81,920	32,768
Reduction	940 million numbers	Reduce6	3.5 GB	64 KB	3.5 GB	16,384	512
SobelFilter	30,720×17,820 PPM image	ckSobel	2.0 GB	2.0 GB	4.0 GB	8,294,400	131,072
SpMV	8 M x 64 matrix, 4 M vector	SparseMV_ELL	4.0 GB	32 MB	4.0 GB	8,192	128

Table 2: Benchmark Specification

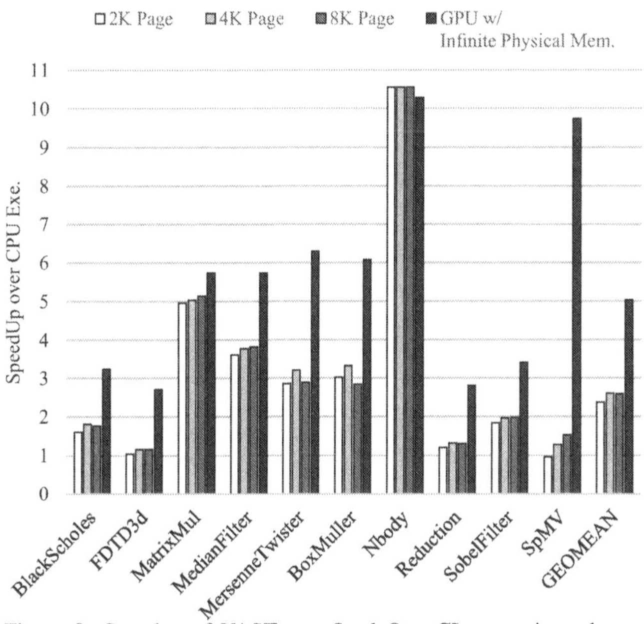

Figure 8: Speedup of VAST over Intel OpenCL execution when varying the page frame size. The performance of InfGPU was estimated by extrapolating the performance on a small workload.

Specially, VAST outperforms InfGPU on NBody as shown in Figure 8. According to the implementation of NBody in NVIDIA Computing SDK, the entire input data is accessed by every work-item, but the start locations of global memory accesses among work-items are different in order to avoid all multiprocessors trying to read the same memory locations at once. This implementation can cause scattered accesses. For example, the working set for the last work-group starts to access the tail of the array, and then accesses the head of the array. In VAST, scattered memory locations are gathered into contiguous page frames, resulting in speedup from more memory level parallelism. The overhead and benefit of paged accesses are discussed in detail in Section 5.3.

On the other hand, SpMV shows a huge performance gap between VAST and InfGPU as shown in Figure 8. The reason is that PAS generation is performed on the CPU due to indirect memory accesses. Nevertheless, VAST shows better performance than the baseline on SpMV, which is the realistic performance. Considering that indirect memory accesses are rare in OpenCL kernel, VAST achieves 63% of the InfGPU performance on average excluding SpMV. Detailed behaviors of each benchmark including PAS generation will be discussed in Section 5.2.

Another point from Figure 8 is that speedup of SpMV increases as the size of the frame grows. The main reason is that PASs are generated using the CPU due to indirect memory accesses, while the performance of generating PASs in the CPU are heavily dependent on the size of PASs due to cache size of the CPU. In detail, the sparse matrix is originally an 8M×4M dense matrix and it is converted to an 8M×64 sparse matrix, with another 8M×64 matrix that contains non-zero column indices (index matrix). For 64 columns of the index matrix, we put random numbers among 8 millions, which is the actual width of the dense matrix. During PAS generation, PASs for input vector will be accessed very frequently among work-groups. Because non-zero column index values are randomly used within 8 million, having small PAS will have higher probability of fitting into lower level cache. To illustrate, for 4GB input matrices as shown in Table 2, 2KB page frame size results in 2 MB of PAS, while 8KB page frame size requires only 512KB of PAS.

5.2 Execution Time Breakdown

In order to analyze detailed behaviors of VAST for each benchmark, we measured the time for each stage of VAST system from PAS generation to array recovery as discussed in Section 3 and 4. Figure 9 illustrates the timeline of VAST execution for each benchmark using 4KB page frame size. In the figure, each color corresponds to a sequence of partial execution. To explain the result, *PAS gen* includes the time spent in the inspector kernel to generate PASs and also involves the time for transferring PASs to the host. *PAS reduction* shows the time to compute reduced PASs for partial execution. Through this step, PASs for all sequences of partial executions are ready. Next, *PAS/Frame gen* illustrates the time to generate LPT using PASs and copying the working set from the plain array to frame buffers. While the first LPT and frame buffer are generated, shared PASs for the next partial execution are computed in background. *HostToDev* is the time spent in transferring LPTs and frame buffers of the input arguments to the GPU, but also includes the time for forwarding shared page frames of the output arguments from the previous partial execution. Last, *Kernel Exe.* represents paged kernel execution time, and *Recovery* is for the time to copy page frames to the output array in the host.

As shown in the figure, *PAS gen* and *PAS reduction*, the initial cost, takes a small amounts of time out of the entire execution, except for SpMV. The reason why SpMV shows large overhead on *PAS gen* is that PASs are generated using the CPU due to indirect memory accesses. Even though PAS generation was parallelized using multiple threads on the CPU, the cost of *PAS gen* overwhelms other parts of execution. However, VAST still outperforms CPU execution on SpMV as shown in Figure 8.

While SpMV indirectly accesses the real arrays by simply loading the index from the index array, there could be a case where

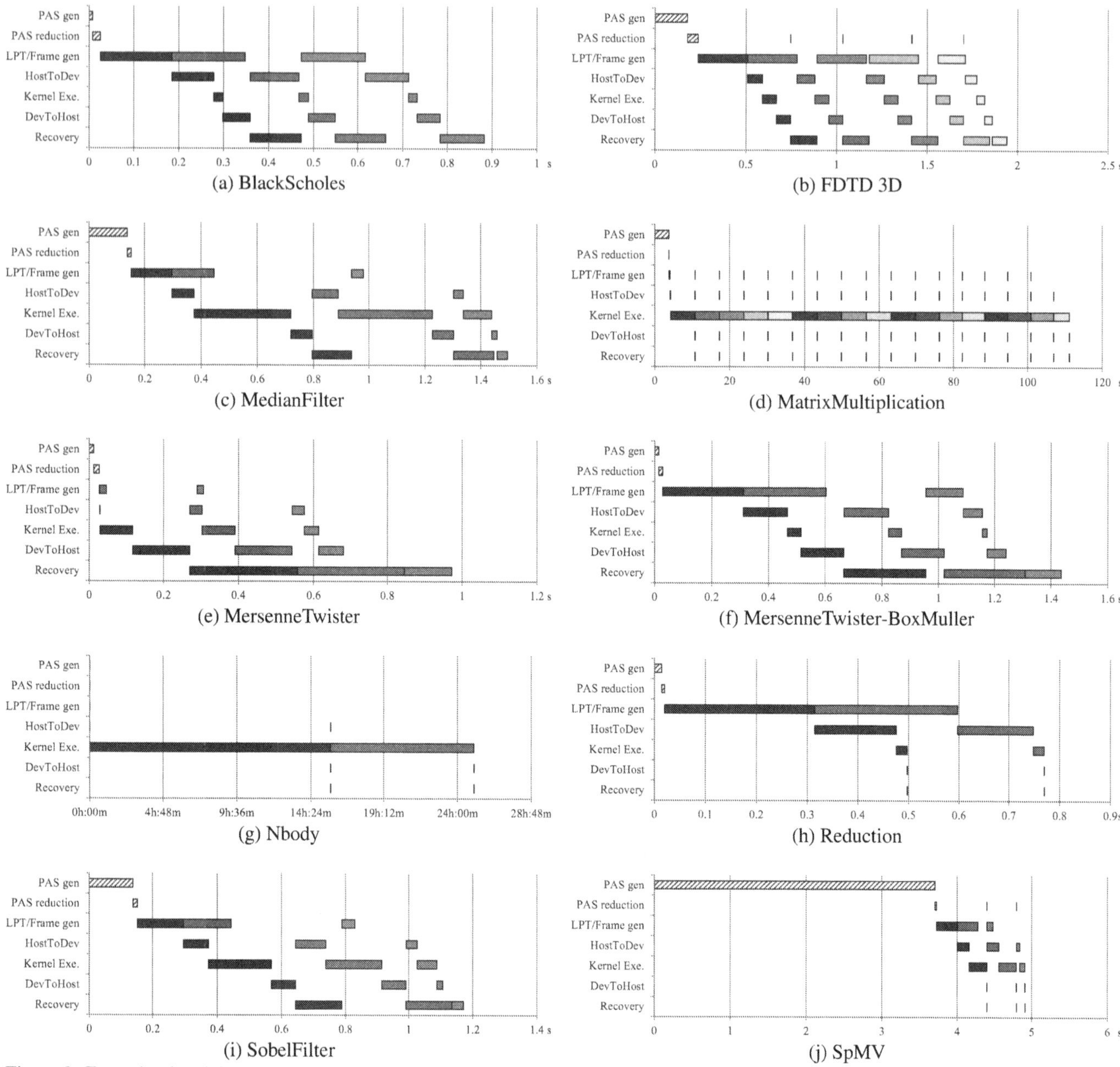

Figure 9: Execution breakdown of VAST for each benchmark with a 4KB page frame size. Each color corresponds to a sequence of partial execution. The time for LPT/Frame gen includes the time for forwarding shared page frames of the output buffer.

the computation of the index is complex. In this case, VAST still forces the CPU to generate PASs even if actual computations are simple. As a result, most of the execution time is spent in PAS generation on the CPU. Therefore, if this pattern is detected, it is more desirable to revert the entire computation back to the CPU.

On the other hand, the execution time of compute-intensive benchmarks, such as MedianFilter, MatrixMul, and Nbody, is heavily dependent on the kernel execution time. Especially for MatrixMul and Nbody, the initial cost of generating LPT and the cost of transferring data are almost invisible from the entire execution time. The reason why MatrixMul performs lots of partial executions is that a small number of work-groups require the maximum number of physical memory space (2 GB). The detailed behavior of MatrixMul is discussed in Section 5.4.

Other than SpMV and compute-intensive benchmarks, every benchmark shows that there is no critical bottleneck during partial executions, as transferring partial working set from the host to the GPU (*HostToDev*) starts right after getting partial results back from the GPU (*DevToHost*). In some benchmarks, however, *HostToDev* waits for *LPT/Frame gen* in the later sequences of partial execution. The reason why *LPT/Frame gen* and *Recovery* takes considerable amount of time is mainly due to copying frame buffer within the host memory, which has less bandwidth compared to others. This latency will decrease in the future as DRAM bandwidth increases (e.g. DDR 4). Meanwhile, this delay can be also hidden if VAST uses triple-buffering for the LPT and the frame buffers, which would require more preserved memory space in the host.

In Figure 9(e) for MersenneTwister, one thing to notice is that *LPT/Frame gen* takes some time only for the second and third par-

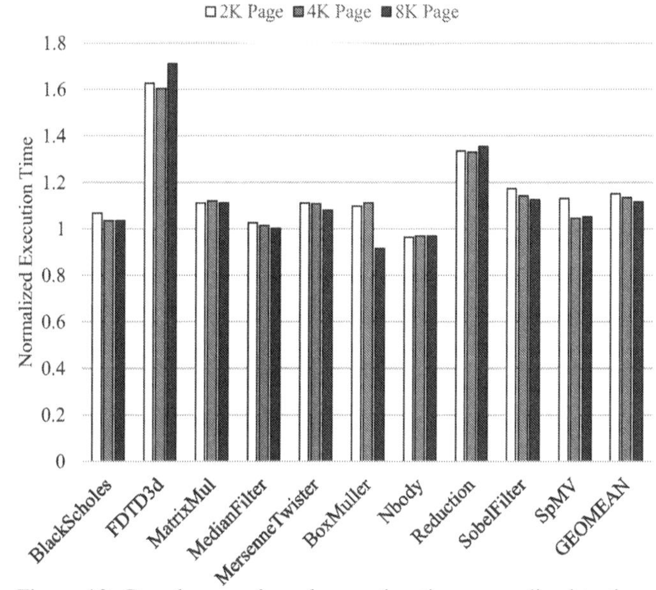

Figure 10: Paged access kernel execution time normalized to the original kernel execution time. Working set size for each benchmark is approximately 1.6GB which does not exceed the physical memory size. This illustrates page lookup overhead during kernel executions.

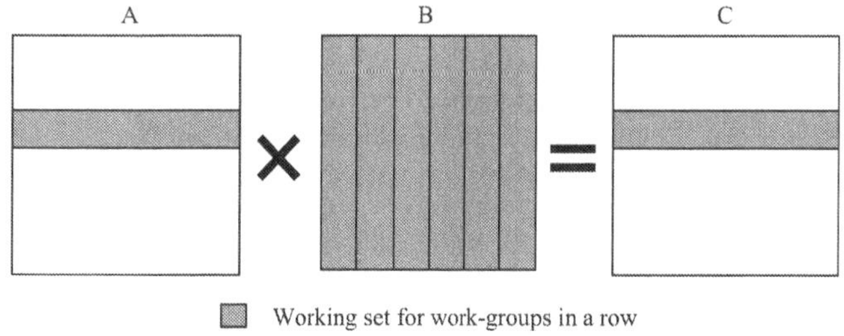

(a) Dividing the workload of matrix multiplication

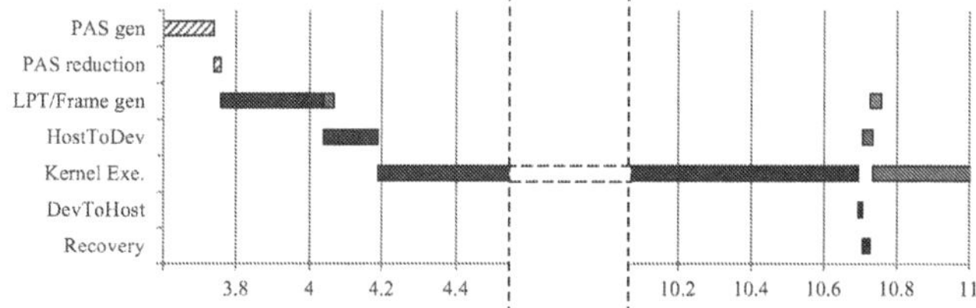

(b) Zoomed-in time line of VAST execution

Figure 11: Details of Matrix Multiplication. (a) shows that the entire matrix B is required for generating an output row. (b) illustrates VAST that does not transfer matrix B (HostToDev) again for the second partial execution.

tial executions. MersenneTwister is a random number generator, which takes seeds as an input (few bytes of data), while the outputs are a huge number of random numbers. The reason why VAST takes some time for *LPT/Frame gen* in spite of small sized input is that the time includes shared PAS computation for the partial outputs.

5.3 Page Lookup Overhead

As discussed in Section 3 and 4, if the working set size exceeds GPU's memory size, VAST transforms the OpenCL kernels to make them access the data through LPT. As a result, one additional memory access occurs for each global memory access for page lookups. In the worst case, VAST could experience 2x slowdown due to doubled memory accesses for looking up pages. However, a realistic lookup overhead will not be significant because the size of LPT is small enough to fit in the GPU's cache and all the work-items in a work-group have a higher probability of looking up the same page, taking advantage of memory level parallelism. In order to evaluate accurate page lookup overhead, we forced VAST to execute paged access kernels on a small working set, and compared the time spent in the GPU for the kernel execution. For the overhead estimation, we chose our working set size as approximately 1.6GB to not exceed the physical memory size on the GPU.

Figure 10 illustrates paged access kernel execution time, normalized to normal kernel execution time. As shown in the figure, page lookups bring 13.4% overhead on average with 4KB page size. A majority of the benchmarks shows less than 10% page lookup overhead, but FDTD3d shows considerable overhead. FDTD3d is a 3-dimensional stencil benchmark in which 3-dimensional adjacent input elements must be accessed to compute one output element. In this case, working sets of adjacent work-items are not contiguous in linear array space, thus VAST cannot benefit from reorganized page frames, causing noticeable overhead. In the meantime, VAST shows better performance on NBody by taking advantage of the memory level parallelism from gathered pages as discussed in Section 5.1.

Similarly, VAST performs better on BoxMuller with an 8KB page size as shown in Figure 10. The reason why BoxMuller shows a considerable performance difference upon varied page sizes is due to the memory access patterns of each work-item. BoxMuller was implemented to have each work-item access two memory locations with the distance of 128KB. With 4KB page size, two page lookups are necessary because the distance between two pages in the LPT is 32 elements (128 bytes). On the other hand, with an 8KB page size, the distance is reduced to 16 elements, thus two page frame indices can be brought into 128 bytes of a cache line at once. In addition to this cache effect, speedup on BoxMuller also comes from rearranging data in the contiguous page frames.

5.4 Case Study

In this section, we further investigate the performance of Matrix Multiplication (*MatrixMul*) on VAST since it is often used to measure the practical performance in GFlops for the system. We also discuss the case where the kernel has complicated indirect memory accesses.

In the implementation of MatrixMul from NVIDIA SDK, each work-item is in charge of generating one element of output matrix (matrix C). To generate one element, each work-item must access the entire row of source matrix A and the column of source matrix B. As a result, work-groups that are in charge of generating a set of output rows will require a set of rows of matrix A and the entire matrix B as shown in Figure 11(a). Based on this property, an expert programmer can manually modify the application to handle large matrix sizes that exceed GPU memory by following several steps. First, the program starts by getting the physical memory size of the GPU, and then checks if matrix B fits into the GPU memory. If it fits into the memory, the programmer makes it transfer matrix B to the GPU only once. After subtracting the size of matrix B from available memory size, the programmer calculates working set size for one work-group in order to get the number of rows per iteration based on the size of rest GPU memory. Once the number of rows for each iteration is calculated, the program executes the matrix multiplication kernel within a loop, and offset the matrix A and C to copy sub matrices (rectangular matrices) to the GPU device.

VAST automatically follows the exact same procedures above since it avoids duplicated data transfer as discussed in Section 4.5. Figure 11(b) illustrates the subset of the time frame in Figure 9(d). As shown in the figure, only the first transfer time (*HostToDev*) takes approximately 0.15 seconds, while next transfer time takes less than 0.03 seconds. This is because the entire matrix B is transferred to the GPU only once at the first transfer, while working set for matrix A and C are decomposed into partial rows and the partial rows are transferred to the GPU during rest of executions. Including every cost of VAST system, VAST achieves 155 GFlops for 20,480×20,480 matrices, while hand-modified code reached 171 GFlops. Nonetheless, the most significant advantage of VAST is that it can provide support for arbitrary type of OpenCL kernel, even with indirect memory accesses as described in the previous section.

6. RELATED WORK

A variety of research has been done to virtualize OpenCL devices as OpenCL programming models expose hardware details, such as the number of processing elements, the number of registers, and the physical memory size in each level of the hierarchy.

While a series of previous works tried to virtualize GPU hardwares in order to alleviate the efforts in optimizing performance [12, 29, 25], other types of researches focus on virtualizing multiple GPUs to distribute the workload automatically [21, 16, 17, 20, 18]. Although they split data parallel workloads into several parts to distribute them over multiple computing devices, they either limit the data parallel kernels to have specific memory access patterns [16, 17, 21, 18], or distribute the entire data to each device assuming the entire working set fits into each GPU memory [20]. On the contrary, VAST fully virtualizes the GPU memory that also supports kernels with indirect memory access pattern.

In the mean time, numerous works have proposed automatic CPU-GPU communication in order to remove explicit memory management [14, 13]. CGCM [14] uses compile-time type-inference to statically determine the types of data structures and transfer them between CPU and GPU memories, DyManD [13] employs runtime libraries to allocate data-structures in CPU and GPU memories. However, they only manage communications between kernels in cyclic patterns, assuming the entire working set fits into GPU memory. Larger data sets require explicit programmer management. More recently, OpenACC [6] and OpenHMPP [8] proposed new programming standards that consist of a set of compiler directives at a higher level, which hides hardware details from programmers. Despite these efforts, programmers must explicitly mange buffer transfer due to physical memory size on the GPU.

Inspector-executor (IE) model, which is applied to VAST, has been also adopted in the field of distributed systems [9, 22, 27]. In their works, the inspector code is used for identifying precise loop-carried dependencies for irregular access pattern in order to distribute loop iterations over multiple nodes. Although some of their works perform data compaction to reduce communication cost between nodes, the target system extracts the compacted data assuming that the target node has a plenty of memory space supported by virtual address space. On the other hand, VAST makes use of the inspector to generate LPT in order to provide virtual memory space on GPUs, while the executer is transformed from the original code to access through LPT.

Recently, there has been research projects to virtualize GPU memory [15, 23]. RSVM [15] is a region based virtual memory running on both CPU and GPU. In this work, programmers must define regions as the basic data unit abstractions. Then, RSVM manages these regions and transfers them if necessary. However, VAST does not need the programmer to think about access patterns of threads and divide the memory manually, thus, VAST is fully automatic and transparent. Pichai et al. [23] explored address translations on GPUs by putting translation look-aside buffers (TLBs) in the shader cores. Their work allows a unified virtual/physical memory space among CPUs and GPUs. However, they only target integrated CPU/GPU systems that share physical memory while VAST handles systems with descrete GPUs.

7. CONCLUSION

In this paper, we presented the VAST system that provides the programmer with an illusion of large memory space for OpenCL devices. Virtualizing memory space for the GPU is done by automatically partitioning the OpenCL's NDRange into subsets of work-groups, and efficiently splitting the working set into several chunks required by a subset of work-groups based on available physical memory on the GPU. With the subsets of work-groups and divided working set, VAST performs partial execution multiple times consecutively.

To support these procedures, we introduced a new type of page table, LPT, which has addresses of page frames that will be accessed by a subset of work-groups on the GPU, and we introduced code transformation techniques to generate LPT efficiently and to make OpenCL kernels access memories through LPT.

Our experiments showed that NVIDIA GTX 760 GPU with 2 GB of memory successfully executed for more than 2 GB of working set regardless of memory access pattern. In addition, VAST achieved 2.6x speedup over CPU execution, which is a realistic alternative for large data computation.

8. ACKNOWLEDGEMENT

We thank the anonymous referees who provided excellent feedback. This research was supported by National Science Foundation grants CNS-0964478 and SHF-1217917, and the Defense Advanced Research Projects Agency (DARPA) under the Power Efficiency Revolution for Embedded Computing Technologies (PERFECT) program.

9. REFERENCES

[1] Clang: A C language family frontend for LLVM. http://clang.llvm.org.

[2] Intel(R) SDK for OpenCL Applications 2013. http://software.intel.com/en-us/vcsource/tools/opencl-sdk.

[3] NVIDIA GPU Computing SDK. http://developer.nvidia.com/gpu-computing-sdk.

[4] Intel(R) Core i7-3700 Desktop Processor Series, 2012. http://download.intel.com/support/processors/corei7/sb/core_i7-3700_d.pdf.

[5] *CUDA C Programming Guide*, 2014. http://docs.nvidia.com/cuda.

[6] OpenACC, directives for accelerators, 2014. http://www.openacc.org.

[7] OpenCL - the open standard for parallel programming of heterogeneous systems, 2014.

[8] OpenHMPP, Hybrid Multicore Parallel Programming, 2014. http://www.openhmpp.org.

[9] A. Basumallik and R. Eigenmann. Optimizing irregular shared-memory applications for distributed-memory systems. In *Proc. of the 11th ACM SIGPLAN Symposium on Principles and Practice of Parallel Programming*, pages 119–128, 2006.

[10] A. Bensoussan, C. T. Clingen, and R. C. Daley. The Multics virtual memory: concepts and design. *Communications of the ACM*, 15(5):308–318, May 1972.

[11] J. Canny and H. Zhao. Big Data Analytics with Small Footprint: Squaring the Cloud. In *Proc. of the 19th International Conference on Knowledge Discovery and Data Mining*, pages 95–103, 2013.

[12] A. H. Hormati, M. Samadi, M. Woh, T. Mudge, and S. Mahlke. Sponge: portable stream programming on graphics engines. In *16th International Conference on Architectural Support for Programming Languages and Operating Systems*, pages 381–392, 2011.

[13] T. B. Jablin, J. A. Jablin, P. Prabhu, F. Liu, and D. I. August. Dynamically managed data for CPU-GPU architectures. In *Proc. of the 2012 International Symposium on Code Generation and Optimization*, pages 165–174, 2012.

[14] T. B. Jablin, P. Prabhu, J. A. Jablin, N. P. Johnson, S. R. Beard, and D. I. August. Automatic CPU-GPU communication management and optimization. In *Proc. of the '11 Conference on Programming Language Design and Implementation*, pages 142–151, 2011.

[15] F. Ji, H. Lin, and X. Ma. RSVM: A region-based software virtual memory for GPU. In *Proc. of the 22nd International Conference on Parallel Architectures and Compilation Techniques*, pages 269–278, 2013.

[16] J. Kim, H. Kim, J. H. Lee, and J. Lee. Achieving a single compute device image in OpenCL for multiple GPUs. In *Proc. of the 16th ACM SIGPLAN Symposium on Principles and Practice of Parallel Programming*, pages 277–288, 2011.

[17] J. Kim, S. Seo, J. Lee, J. Nah, G. Jo, and J. Lee. SnuCL: an OpenCL framework for heterogeneous CPU/GPU clusters. In *Proc. of the 2012 International Conference on Supercomputing*, pages 341–352, 2012.

[18] K. Kofler, I. Grasso, B. Cosenza, and T. Fahringer. An Automatic Input-sensitive Approach for Heterogeneous Task Partitioning. In *Proc. of the 2013 International Conference on Supercomputing*, pages 149–160, 2013.

[19] C. Lattner and V. Adve. LLVM: A compilation framework for lifelong program analysis & transformation. In *Proc. of the 2004 International Symposium on Code Generation and Optimization*, pages 75–86, 2004.

[20] J. Lee, M. Samadi, Y. Park, and S. Mahlke. Transparent CPU-GPU collaboration for data parallel kernels on heterogeneous systems. In *Proc. of the 22nd International Conference on Parallel Architectures and Compilation Techniques*, pages 245–256, 2013.

[21] C.-K. Luk, S. Hong, and H. Kim. Qilin: exploiting parallelism on heterogeneous multiprocessors with adaptive mapping. In *Proc. of the 42nd Annual International Symposium on Microarchitecture*, pages 45–55, 2009.

[22] S.-J. Min and R. Eigenmann. Optimizing irregular shared-memory applications for clusters. In *Proc. of the 2008 International Conference on Supercomputing*, pages 256–265, 2008.

[23] B. Pichai, L. Hsu, and A. Bhattacharjee. Architectural Support for Address Translation on GPUs: Designing Memory Management Units for CPU/GPUs with Unified Address Spaces. In *19th International Conference on Architectural Support for Programming Languages and Operating Systems*, pages 743–758, 2014.

[24] S. Ryoo, C. I. Rodrigues, S. S. Baghsorkhi, S. S. Stone, D. B. Kirk, and W. mei W. Hwu. Optimization principles and application performance evaluation of a multithreaded GPU using CUDA. In *Proc. of the 13th ACM SIGPLAN Symposium on Principles and Practice of Parallel Programming*, pages 73–82, 2008.

[25] M. Samadi, A. Hormati, M. Mehrara, J. Lee, and S. Mahlke. Adaptive input-aware compilation for graphics engines. In *Proc. of the '12 Conference on Programming Language Design and Implementation*, pages 13–22, 2012.

[26] D. Sayre. Is automatic "folding" of programs efficient enough to displace manual? *Communications of the ACM*, 12(12):656–660, Dec. 1969.

[27] S. Sharma, R. Ponnusamy, B. Moon, H. Yuan-Shin, R. Das, and J. Saltz. Run-time and compile-time support for adaptive irregular problems. pages 97–106, 1994.

[28] L. Torczon and K. Cooper. *Engineering A Compiler*. Morgan Kaufmann Publishers Inc., 2nd edition, 2011.

[29] Y. Yang, P. Xiang, J. Kong, and H. Zhou. A GPGPU compiler for memory optimization and parallelism management. In *Proc. of the '10 Conference on Programming Language Design and Implementation*, pages 86–97, 2010.

Automatic Optimization of Thread-Coarsening for Graphics Processors

Alberto Magni
School of Informatics
University of Edinburgh
United Kingdom
a.magni@sms.ed.ac.uk

Christophe Dubach
School of Informatics
University of Edinburgh
United Kingdom
christophe.dubach@ed.ac.uk

Michael O'Boyle
School of Informatics
University of Edinburgh
United Kingdom
mob@inf.ed.ac.uk

ABSTRACT

OpenCL has been designed to achieve functional portability across multi-core devices from different vendors. However, the lack of a single cross-target optimizing compiler severely limits performance portability of OpenCL programs. Programmers need to manually tune applications for each specific device, preventing effective portability. We target a compiler transformation specific for data-parallel languages: *thread-coarsening* and show it can improve performance across different GPU devices. We then address the problem of selecting the best value for the coarsening factor parameter, *i.e.*, deciding how many threads to merge together. We experimentally show that this is a hard problem to solve: good configurations are difficult to find and naive coarsening in fact leads to substantial slowdowns. We propose a solution based on a machine-learning model that predicts the best coarsening factor using kernel-function static features. The model automatically specializes to the different architectures considered. We evaluate our approach on 17 benchmarks on four devices: two Nvidia GPUs and two different generations of AMD GPUs. Using our technique, we achieve speedups between 1.11× and 1.33× on average.

1. INTRODUCTION

Graphical Processing Units (GPUs) are widely used for high performance computing. They provide cost-effective parallelism for a wide range of applications. The success of these devices has lead to the introduction of a diverse range of architectures from many hardware manufacturers. This has created the need for a common programming language to harness the available parallelism in a portable way. OpenCL is an industry-standard language for GPUs that offers program portability across accelerators of different vendors: a single piece of OpenCL code is guaranteed to be executable on many diverse devices.

A uniform language specification, however, still requires programmers to manually optimize kernel code to improve performance on each target architecture. This is a tedious process, which requires knowledge of hardware behavior, and must be repeated each time the hardware is updated. This problem is particularly acute for GPUs which undergo rapid hardware evolution.

The solution to this problem is a cross-architectural optimizer capable of achieving performance portability. Current proposals for cross-architectural compiler support [21, 34] all involve working on source-to-source transformations. Compiler intermediate representations [6] and ISAs [5] that span across devices of different vendors have still to reach full support.

This paper studies the issue of performance portability focusing on the optimization of the *thread-coarsening* compiler transformation. Thread coarsening [21, 30, 31] merges together two or more parallel threads, increasing the amount of work performed by a single thread, and reducing the total number of threads instantiated. Selecting the best coarsening factor, *i.e.*, the number of threads to merge together, is a trade-off between exploiting thread-level parallelism and avoiding execution of redundant instructions. Making the correct choice leads to significant speedups on all our platforms. Our data show that picking the optimal coarsening factor is difficult since most configurations lead to performance downgrade and only careful selection of the coarsening factor gives improvements. Selecting the best parameter requires knowledge of the particular hardware platform, *i.e.*, different GPUs have different optimal factors

In this work we select the coarsening factor using an automated machine learning technique. We build our model based on a cascade of neural networks that decide whether it is beneficial to apply coarsening. The inputs to the model are static code features extracted from the parallel OpenCL code. These features include, among the others, branch divergence and instruction mix information. The technique is applied to four GPU architectures: *Fermi* and *Kepler* from Nvidia and *Cypress* and *Tahiti* from AMD. While naive coarsening misses optimization opportunities, our approach gives an average performance improvement of 1.16x, 1.11x, 1.33x, 1.30x respectively.

In summary the paper makes the following contributions:

- We provide a characterization of the optimization space across four architectures.
- We develop a machine learning technique based on a neural network to predict coarsening.
- We show significant performance improvements across 17 benchmarks

PACT'14, August 24–27, 2014, Edmonton, AB, Canada.

http://dx.doi.org/10.1145/2628071.2628087.

The remainder of the paper is organized as follows. Section 2.1 provides a brief overview of OpenCL and describes the thread coarsening transformation. A motivating example for the problem is provided in section 3. Section 4 describes the experimental setup and the compiler infrastructure. Section 5 presents a characterization of the optimization space. Section 6 describes the machine the machine learning model. The results are presented in Section 7. Section 8 presents the related work and section 9 concludes the paper.

2. BACKGROUND

2.1 OpenCL

OpenCL is a cross-vendor programming language used for massively parallel multi-core graphic processors. OpenCL kernel functions define the operations carried out by each data-parallel hardware-thread. Kernels are compiled at runtime on the *host* (a standard CPU) and sent to execution onto the *device* (in our case a GPU). It is the programmer's responsibility to decide how many threads to instantiate and how to arrange them into *work-groups*, defining the so-called *NDRange* of *thread-ids*. Each *thread-id* corresponds to thread executing within a work-group. Work-items in a work-group are guaranteed to be scheduled onto a single core and can share data in local memory and synchronize using barriers.

OpenCL programmers, usually, instantiate as many threads as they have data element to process. This results in hundreds of thousands of threads being scheduled on the target device, maximizing the degree of parallelism. However, there is no guarantee that this policy is the best for each possible target device. Consider for instance the presence of thread-invariant instructions [18, 33] which produces the same results independently from the thread executing them. Maximizing the number of threads might increase the total number of redundant operations executed by the GPU.

2.2 Thread Coarsening

One way to prevent the problems associated with having too fine-grained parallelism is to merge threads together. This reduces the redundancy in the number of integer operations and branches performed per floating point operation. This transformation, known as *thread coarsening* [21, 30, 31], works by fusing multiple work items together increasing the amount of work performed by a single thread and reducing the overall number of launched threads. While it appears to be an easy task for the programmer, it is preferable to apply this transformation automatically using a compiler for two reasons: (1) the merging is done by replicating instructions inside the kernel, which is error-prone to do by hand; (2) the *Coarsening Factor* (*i.e.*, the number of times the body of the thread is replicated) which gives the best performance depends on the program and on the hardware.

The coarsening transformation we implemented increases the amount of work performed by the kernel by replicating the instructions in its body. Leveraging divergence analysis [9, 15, 18] only instructions that depend on the *thread-id* (divergent instructions) are replicated. This reduces the overhead of executing uniform instructions across multiple threads. Divergent instructions are replicated and inserted right after the original ones updating the *thread-id* to work on the correct data elements. Finally, the number of instantiated thread is reduced at runtime.

```
kernel void square(global float* in, out) {
  int gid = get_global_id(0);
  out[gid] = in[gid]*in[gid]; }
```

(a) Original code

```
1 kernel void square2x(global float* in, out) {
2   int gid = get_global_id(0);
3   int tid0 = 2*gid+0;
4   int tid1 = 2*gid+1;
5   out[tid0] = in[tid0]*in[tid0];
6   out[tid1] = in[tid1]*in[tid1]; }
```

(b) After coarsening with factor 2

Figure 1. Vector square example in OpenCL. In the original code each thread takes the square of one element of the input array a. When coarsened by a factor two b , each thread now processes two elements of the input array.

Figure 1 shows a kernel that calculates the square of the element of the input array. In the original code, each thread is responsible for squaring one element of the input array. After coarsening has been applied with factor two, each thread processes two element of the input array. As can be see on lines 3–4 of figure 1b, the index in the input array are calculated from the original thread iteration space as returned by the OpenCL *get_global_id(0)* function. Prior work on this compiler transformation ([21]) presents how to effectively manage branches and loops.

3. MOTIVATION

This section motivates the work explaining the importance of determining whether to coarsen, and by how much. Figure 2 shows the speedup given by thread-coarsening over the baseline (no coarsening) as a function of the corsening factor for two benchmarks on different GPUs.

The first figure 2a shows the performance of *NBody* on two AMD architectures: *Cypress* and *Tahiti*. Even though these two devices are from the same vendor, they have significant architectural differences [3]. Cypress cores are VLIW while Tahiti cores have processing elements working in SIMD fashion. Such differences are reflected in the different reactions shown by the benchmark to the coarsening transformation. The higher degree of ILP made available by coarsening in the *NBody* benchmark is successfully exploited by the VLIW cores of *Cypress* ensuring a significant speedup. The same does not apply to *Tahiti* where no improvement can be obtained and we record a significant slowdown for higher factors.

Differences across architectures also emerge for *BinarySearch*. Here, we make a comparison between the AMD *Tahiti* and the Nvidia *Fermi* architectures. On the first device *BinarySearch* ensures an improvement of 2.3x over the default for coarsening factor 8. On Nvidia, however, no improvement can be obtained.

From these simple examples it is clear that optimizing the coarsening pass is an important problem. In addition, the coarsening factor must be determined on a per-program and per-platform basis. Classical hand-written heuristics

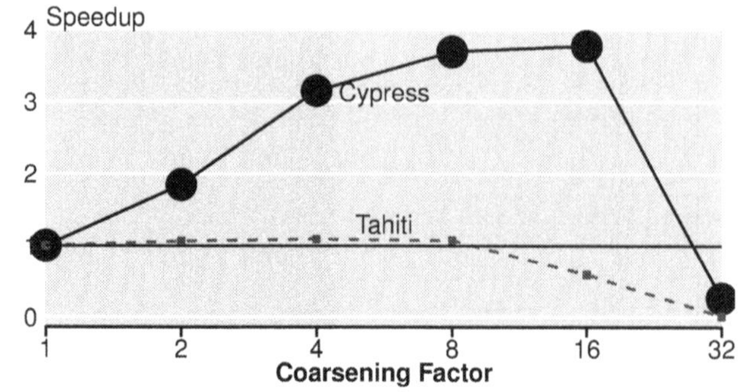

(a) *NBody* run on *Cypress* and *Tahiti*

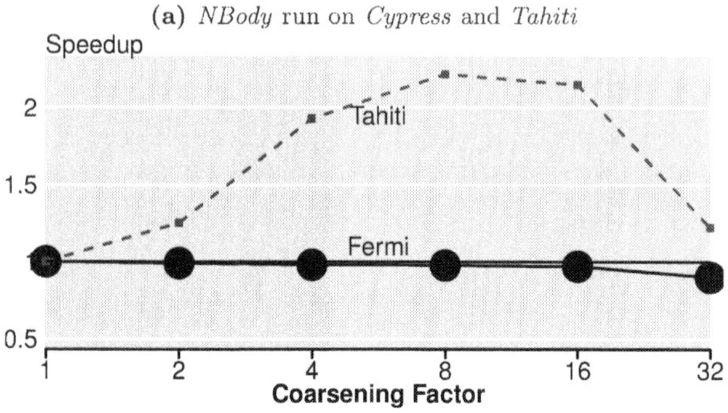

(b) *BinarySearch* run on *Fermi* and *Tahiti*

Figure 2. Speedup achieved with thread coarsening as a function of the coarsening factor for *NBody* and *Binary-Search*

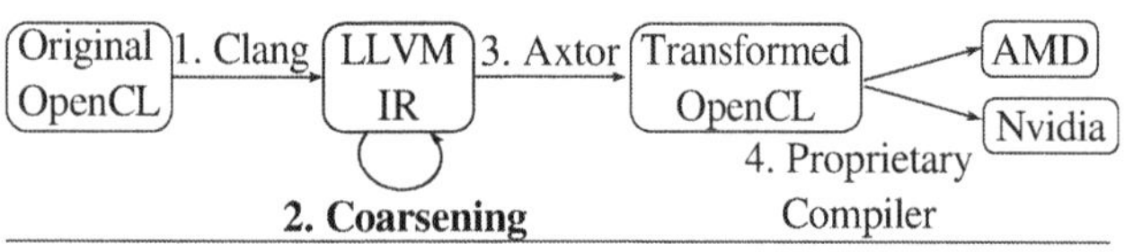

Figure 3. Compiler toolchain

are not only complex to develop, but are likely to fail due to the variety of programs and ever-changing OpenCL devices available.

4. EXPERIMENTAL SETUP

This section describes the compiler toolchain (4.1), the coarsening stride (4.2), the benchmarks (4.3) and the devices used in the experiments (4.4).

4.1 Compiler Toolchain

One way to automatically evaluate a compiler transformation in OpenCL on multiple devices is to use a source-to-source compiler. It avoids the need to have access to potentially properietary compiler internals. Alternative approaches based on SPIR [6] could also be used in the future, when it is going to reach wide adoption. Figure 3 shows our compilation infrastructure. The OpenCL C code of the target kernel is translated to LLVM bitcode using the *clang* open-source front-end (stage 1). The coarsening transformation is applied at the LLVM bitcode level (stage 2). The transformed LLVM program is then translated back to OpenCL C using the *axtor* [24] LLVM OpenCL-backend (stage 3). The transformed OpenCL program is then fed into the hardware vendor proprietary compiler (stage 4) for code generation.

	Program name	Source	Num. Threads
1)	binarySearch	AMD SDK	268M
2)	blackscholes	Nvidia SDK	16M
3)	convolution	AMD SDK	6K
4)	dwtHaar1D	AMD SDK	2M
5)	fastWalsh	AMD SDK	33M
6)	floydWarshall	AMD SDK	(8K x 8K)
7)	mriQ	Parboil	524K
8)	mt	AMD SDK	(4K x 4K)
9)	mtLocal	AMD SDK	(4K x 4K)
10)	mvCoal	Nvidia SDK	16K
11)	mvUncoal	Nvidia SDK	16K
12)	nbody	AMD SDK	131K
13)	reduce	AMD SDK	67M
14)	sgemm	Parboil	(3K x 3K)
15)	sobel	AMD SDK	(1K x 1K)
16)	spmv	Parboil	262K
17)	stencil	Parboil	(3K x 510 x 62)

Table 1. OpenCL applications with the reference number of threads.

4.2 Coarsening Factor

In this work we address the tuning of the *coarsening factor* parameter. The first one controls how many threads to merge together. For our experiments we allowed this parameter to have the following values: $[1, 2, 4, 8, 16, 32]$. Where coarsening factor of 1 corresponds to the original program. We limited our evaluations to powers of two since these are the most widely applicable parameter values, given the reference input sizes for the considered benchmarks. The tuning technique in the next chapters can be easily extended to support non powers of two.

4.3 Benchmarks

We have used 17 benchmarks from various sources as shown in table 1. In the case of the *Parboil* benchmarks we used the *opencl_base* version. The table also shows the global size (total number of threads) used. The baseline performance reported in the results section is that of the best work group size as opposed to the default one chose by the programmer. This is necessary to give a fair comparison across platforms when the original benchmark is written specifically for one platform. Each experiment has been repeated 50 times aggregating the results using the median. Previous work ([22]) has shown that the choice for the optimal coarsening factor is consistent across input sizes. For this reason we restricted our analysis to the input size (*i.e.*, total number of threads running) for the uncoarsened kernel listed in table 1.

4.4 Devices

For our experiments we used four devices from two vendors. From Nvidia we used GTX480 and Tesla K20c. The first one is based on the Fermi architecture [2] with 15 streaming multiprocessors (SM) and 32 CUDA cores for each. The Tesla K20c has the latest Kepler architecture [4]. K20c has 13 SMs each with 192 CUDA cores.

From AMD we used the Radeon HD 5900 and Tahiti 7970. The first one, codenamed Cypress, has 20 SIMD cores each with 16 thread processors, a 5-way VLIW core. The Graphics Core Next architecture in Tahiti 7970 is a radical change

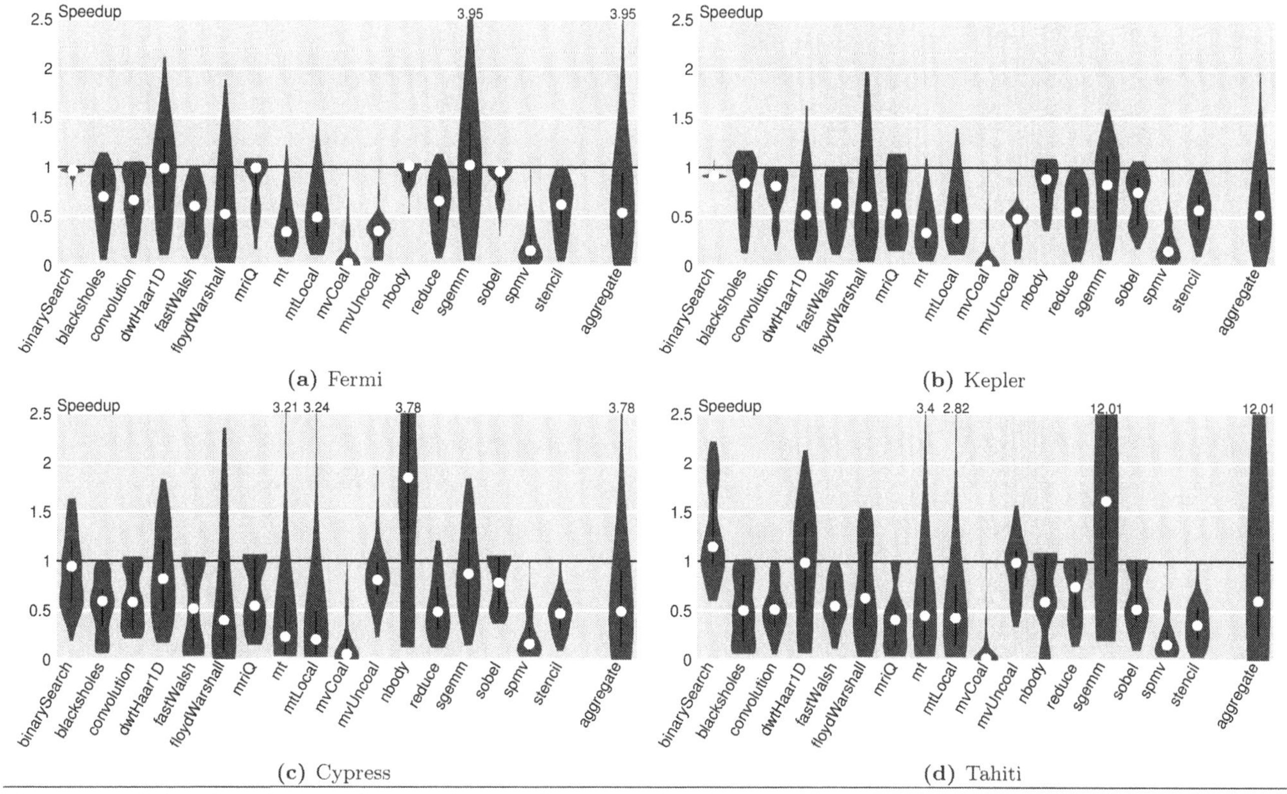

Figure 4. Violin plots showing the distribution of speedups for all the benchmarks on the four devices. The shape of the violin corresponds to the speedup distribution. They indicate on how hard it is to tune a program. The thick black line shows where 50% of the data lies. The white dot is the position of the median.

Name	Model	GPU Driver	OpenCL version	Linux kernel
Fermi	Nvidia GTX 480	304.54	1.1 CUDA 5.0.1	3.2.0
Kepler	Nvidia K20c	331.20	1.1 CUDA 5.0.1	3.7.10
Cypress	AMD HD5900	1124.2	1.2 SDK 1124.2	3.1.10
Tahiti	AMD HD7970	1084.4	1.2 SDK 1084.4	3.1.10

Table 2. OpenCL devices used for our experiments.

for AMD. Each of the 32 computing cores contains 4 vector units (of 16 lanes each) operating in SIMD mode. This exploits the advantages of dynamic scheduling as opposed to the static scheduling needed by VLIW cores.

5. OPTIMIZATION SPACE CHARACTERISTICS

In the motivating example, in figure 2, we showed that different applications behave differently with respect to coarsening on different devices. In this section we expand on this topic and present the overall optimization space.

5.1 Distribution of Speedup

The violin plots in figure 4 show the distribution of the speedups (over no coarsening) achievable by changing the coarsening factor and the local work group size. The width of each violin corresponds to the proportions of configurations with a certain speedup. The white dot denotes the median speedup, while the thick black line shows where 50% of the data lies. These plots are effective in highlighting differences and similarities in spaces of different applications. Intuitively, violins with a pointy top correspond to benchmarks difficult to optimize: configurations giving the maximum performance are few. For example consider *mt* and *mtLocal* (matrix multiplication and matrix multiplication with local memory). These two program show similar shapes among the two Nvidia and AMD devices. On the other hand *nbody* shows different shapes among the four architectures: a large improvement is available on *Cypress* while no performance gain can be obtained on the other three devices. Interesting cases for analysis are benchmarks such as *mvCoal* and *spmv*. They have an extremely pointy top with the whole violin lying below 1, meaning no performance improvement is possible on these benchmarks with coarsening. Consider now the aggregate violin in the final column of each subfigure. This shows the distribution of speedups across all programs. In all the four cases the white dots lies well below the 1, near 0.5 in most cases. This means that on average, the coarsening transformation will slow programs down. This fact coupled with the different optimization distributions shows how difficult choosing the right coarsening factor is. This is probably the reason why there is little prior work in determining the right coarsening factor. The model presented in section 6 tackles this problem of selecting an appropriate factor for each program.

5.2 Coarsening Factor Characterization

The objective of this work is the determination of the best thread-coarsening factor. In this section we quantify how

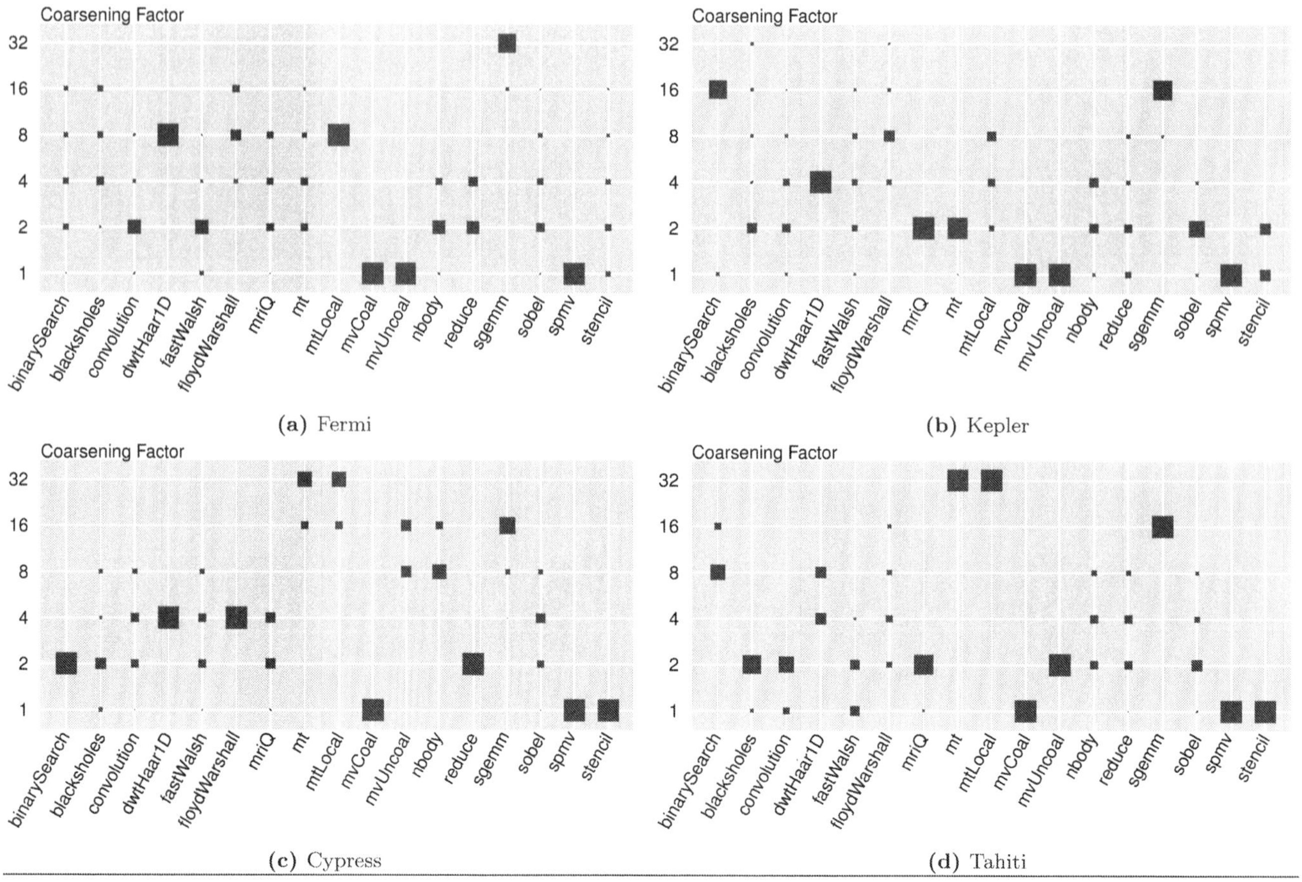

(a) Fermi (b) Kepler (c) Cypress (d) Tahiti

Figure 5. Hinton diagram showing the percentage of configurations with the given coarsening factor in the performing top 5% configurations. Intuitively, the larger the square is the more likely it is for the given coarsening factor to perform close to the optimum.

this parameter varies across program and platform. Figure 5 shows a Hinton diagram for each target device. For each benchmark and coarsening factor it plots a square. The size of the square is proportional to the percentage of configurations having the given coarsening factor among the top 5% performing ones. Intuitively: the larger the square is, the more likely it is that the corresponding coarsening factor will perform well. From these plots it is immediately clear that no single factor can give good performance for all the programs. On the two Nvidia devices (*Fermi* and *Kepler*) the optimal coarsening factor tends to be among 1, 2, or 4, with few exceptions. On the two AMD architectures (*Tahiti* and *Cypress*) instead the best coarsening factor are often larger (4 or 8).

In section 7 we provide an evaluation of the improvement that can be obtained using a single coarsening factor for all the programs. We compare our prediction model against this baseline.

5.3 Cross-architecture optimization portability

In this section we investigate if the knowledge of the best coarsening factor for one architecture can be successfully exploited to a new platform. This study fulfills two purposes: (1) it characterizes the diversity of the devices that are evaluated in this work, (2) it studies how successful would an optimizer tuned for a given platform be when ported to another one. For this task we explored all coarsening factors on all the kernel and devices selecting the best for each. Given two devices A and B we then evaluate for each kernel the performance of the best coarsening factor of A (*Search-Device*) on B (*Target-Device*). Figure 6 reports the results of this analysis for all combinations of A and B.

From these plots we can see, for example, that performance transfers effectively from *Kepler* to *Fermi* (where we reach 77% of the maximum speedup) but, interestingly, the contrary is not true (where only 47% is attainable). Its important to notice that porting performance across Nvidia and AMD leads to bad performance on average. For example the best configurations from *Fermi* and *Kepler* give 28% and 41% of the maximum on *Cypress*. Similarly bad performance is given when porting from *Cypress* and *Tahiti* to *Kepler*.

Consider that these results represent the upper bound of how an optimizer specialized for one architecture would behave when applied to another one. Any realistic compiler heuristic when applied to an unseen program, would perform considerably worse than this. This shows that performance portability is not guaranteed when going across vendors, even if we have optimized the same program on a previous device This justifies the need to specialize the choice of the coarsening configuration on a per-platform basis relying on a flexible optimizer.

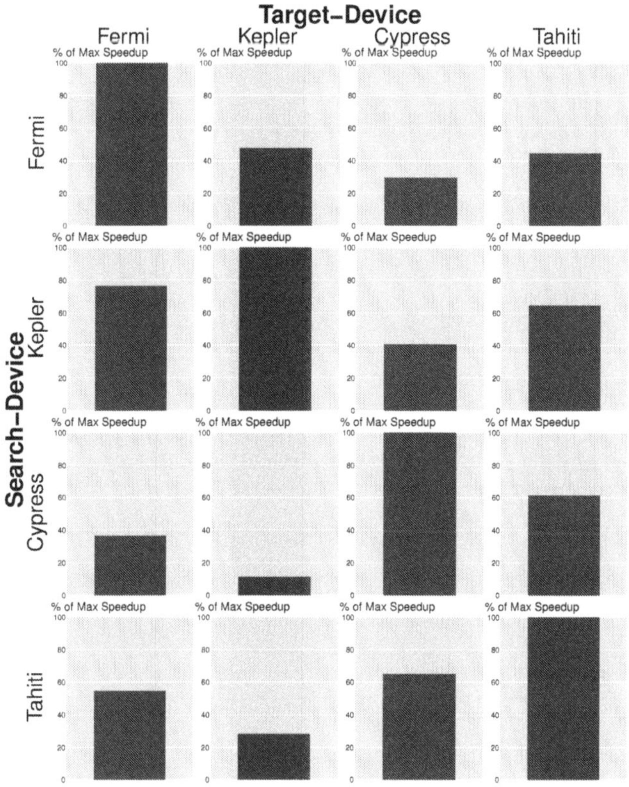

Figure 6. Each barplot reports the percentage of the maximum performance of *Target-Device* (columns) is obtained when evaluating the best configuration found searching on *Search-Device* (rows). When *Target-Device* and *Search-Device* are the same the bar reached 100% by construction. For example, the *Fermi-Cypress* subplot (on the top-left) shows that 37% of the maximum performance of *Cypress* is achievable when using the best configuration coming from *Fermi*.

6. PREDICTIVE MODEL

The goal of the model is to decide the optimal coarsening factor for each kernel on a specific architecture. The model works using static program features extracted at compile time. Relying on these features, the model makes a binary decision on whether to coarsen or not. By iteratively querying the model we can decide when to stop coarsening. We train a new model for each architecture: four in total.

6.1 Training

This section describes how we generate training data.

We use Leave One Out Cross Validation. This standard machine learning technique works selecting one benchmark for testing and using the remaining ones for training. This means we train our model on 16 benchmarks and apply it to the testing program. We repeat this process 17 times, one for each test case.

Figure 7 gives a visual representation of the training process. OpenCL kernels from the training set are compiled and run with the six different coarsening factors. During the compilation step (Phase 1) a compiler-analysis pass collects static features of each different version of the code. The full list of these features is given in section 6.3. In Phase 2 we run all the different versions of the program arranging the results

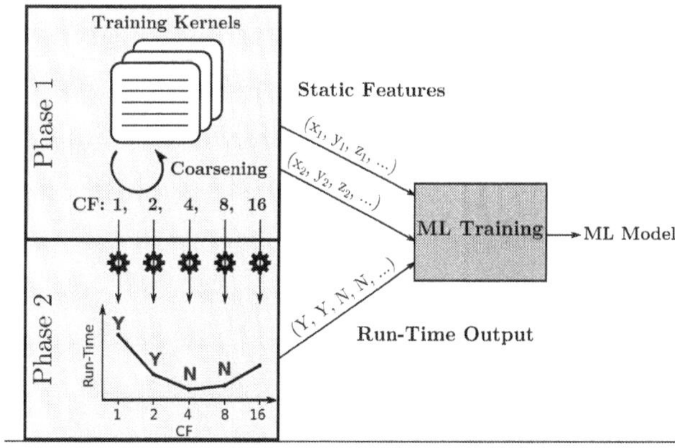

Figure 7. Model training overview. In Phase 1) we collect static features of the kernel functions. In Phase 2) we run the testing programs collecting the binary output variables.

by increasing coarsening factor. The binary training output variable is computed answering the following question: *Is further coarsening going to improve the performance of the current version?* Asking this question on each version of the kernel function will generate a tuple of binary values. Then, for each kernel the 5 sets of features and the 5-tuple of binary variables are used for training the machine learning model. This process is repeated for each target architecture.

6.2 Cascade NN Model

Our model is built using Neural Networks for classification. Neural Networks [7] are a supervised learning algorithm that classify data-points assigning to each of them the expected probability to belong to a given class.

Given a previously unseen program the model determines whether coarsening should be applied or not. If the answer is yes, the model is applied again to the coarsened version of the program to determine if we should keep going or stop coarsening. In the latter case, the model is called a third time deciding if the program should be coarsened one more time and so on. Figure 8 gives an overview of how the model is applied. Such model relies on the peculiar shape of the coarsening performance curve, which shows improvement up until the optimal coarsening factor.

Further coarsening leads to performance degradation. This common behavior is shown with figure 2. Note that no actual recompilation of the program is needed. The values of the features for the coarsened versions can be statically computed from the values of the uncoarsened version. This it true because the coarsening transformation, from the source-code point of view, behaves in a predictable manner. The model simply takes as input the static features of the original OpenCL kernel and gives as output the predicted coarsening factor. This makes extremely easy to integrate such model in a real optimizer compiler.

We choose the cascading predictor to implement a conservative approach. By iteratively querying the model in multiple intermediate steps we make sure to limit the application of thread coarsening only to those applications which truly benefit from it. This is a beneficial property, since large coarsening factors are rarely optimal (consider the Hinton diagrams in figure 5).

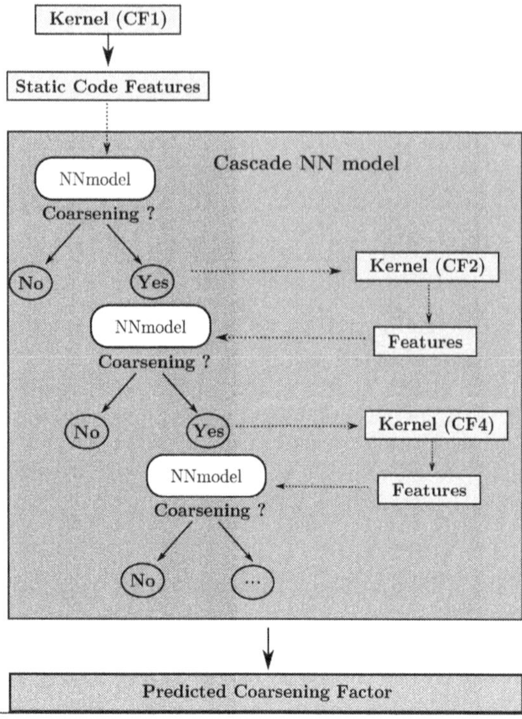

Figure 8. High-level view the use of our Neural Network cascade model. Static source code features of the program are extracted from the original kernel code and fed into the model which decides whether to coarsen or not. If yes, new features are computed and the model is queried again. From a high level point of view the model simply computes the best coarsening factor from static program characteristics. At the end of the process the program is compiled using the predicted factor.

6.3 Program Features

This section describes the static feature selection process. The model is based exclusively on static characteristics of the target OpenCL kernel function. These characteristics, called features, are extracted using a function pass working on the LLVM intermediate representation. Note that, since our goal is to develop a *portable* optimizer, we don't use any architecture-specific feature. We apply our function analysis at the LLVM-bitcode level because this is the lowest level of abstraction that is portable across architectures. In particular, we do not collect any information after instruction scheduling or register allocation, since these are target-specific phases. We first describe the candidate features. This is followed by the process used to reduce these to a smaller useful subset.

6.3.1 *Candidate Feature*

The full list of candidate features is given in table 3. We selected these based on the results of previous work [21]; where we analyzed which hardware performance counters are affected by the coarsening transformation. These are the number of executed branches, memory utilization (in terms of load and cache utilization) and instruction level parallelism (ILP). We approximate these *dynamic* counters using *static* code characteristics counterparts, such as the total number of kernel instructions, static number of branches and divergent regions and static ILP. There are 17 candidate static features that approximate the six most important dynamic counters.

Feature Name	Description
BasicBlocks	Number of Basic Blocks
Branches	Number of Branches
DivInsts	Number of Divergent Instructions
DivRegionInsts	Number of Instructions in Divergent Regions
DivRegionInstsRatio	Ratio between the Number of instructions inside Divergent Regions and the Total number of instructions
DivRegions	Number of Divergent Regions
TotInsts	Number of Instructions
FPInsts	Number of Floating point Instructions
ILP	Average ILP per Basic Block
Int/FP Inst Ratio	Ration between Integer and Floating Point Instructions
IntInsts	Number of Integer Instructions
MathFunctions	Number of Math Builtin Functions
MLP	Average MLP per Basic Block
Loads	Number of Loads
Stores	Number of Stores
UniformLoads	Number of Loads that do not depend on the Coarsening Direction
Barriers	Number of Barriers

Table 3. Candidate static features used by the machine learning model.

Absolute Features.

Divergent control flow has a strong impact on performance for graphics processors because it forces the serialization of instructions that would normally be executed concurrently on the different lanes of a warp [1]. The degree of a kernel thread divergence is measured using the results of *divergence analysis*. We count the total number of divergent instructions (instructions that depend on the *thread-id*, *i.e.*, the position of the work-item in the NDRange space), the total number of divergent regions (CFG regions controlled by a divergent branch) and their relative size with respect to the overall number of instructions in the kernel. Other counters related to the complexity of the control flow of the kernel are the total number of blocks. Finally we also compute the average per-block theoretical ILP and Memory Level Parallelism (MLP) at the LLVM instruction level. To compute the static ILP and MLP we followed the methodology presented in prior work [27].

Relative Features.

As described in section 2.2 the effects of thread coarsening on the shape of the code are highly predictable. Thanks to this property we can statically compute the value that features will assume after the application of the coarsening transformation. This information is used during training and prediction. In particular, for each feature, we also calculate its relative increase caused by thread coarsening. This value is computed according to the following formula:

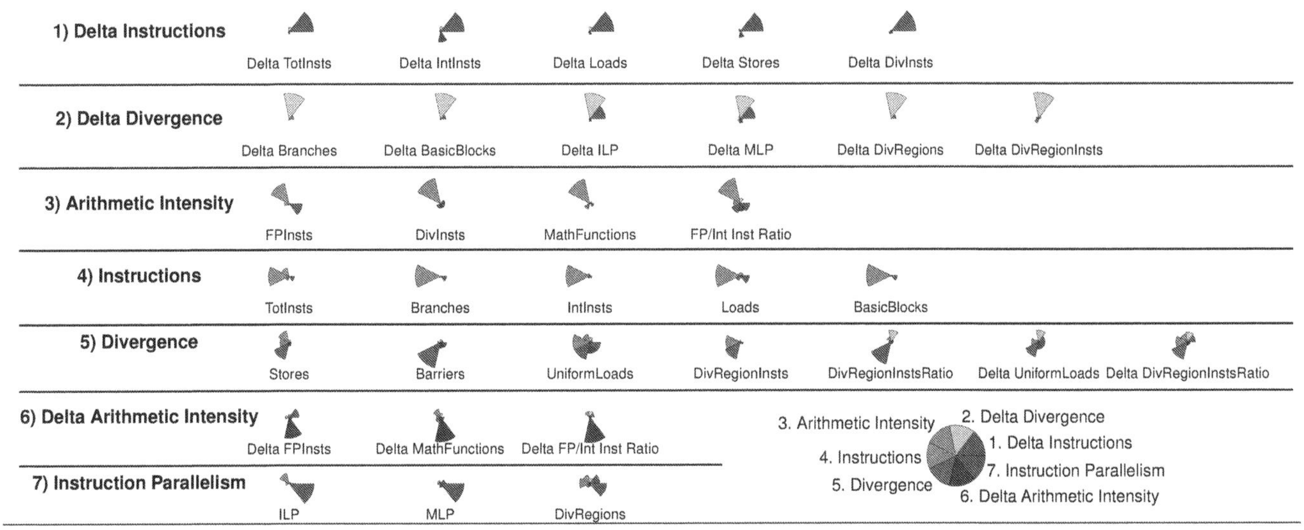

Figure 9. Result of the PCA analysis with Varimax rotation. The seven resulting components are labeled on the left and sorted according to their relative importance (the amount of variance of the feature space covered by each of them). On the right-end side segment-plots depicts the contribution of each original feature to a given output principal component. Features are laid out in rows according to the component they contribute to.

1) Delta instructions
2) Delta divergence
3) Arithmetic Intensity
4) Instructions
5) Divergence
6) Delta Arithmetic Intensity
7) Instruction Parallelism

Table 4. Final features selected after the application of Principal Component Analysis.

$\frac{(feature_{After} - feature_{Before})}{feature_{Before}}$, where $feature_{Before}$ and $feature_{After}$ are the values of the feature before and after coarsening. In the remainder of the paper delta features are identified by *Delta* added to the feature name.

6.3.2 *Feature Selection*

This section describes how we select features starting from the candidate ones.

Principal Component Analysis.

The large number of features (absolute plus deltas) is automatically reduced using the standard technique of Principal Component Analysis.

It is important to notice that we use the same set of features in table 3 for all devices without manual intervention. Principal Components Analysis minimizes the cross-correlation of the input features by linearly aggregating those features that are highly correlated and therefore redundant. After application of PCA we have the 7 final selected features in table 4 which describe 95% of the variance of the original space.

With the goal of providing an understanding of the importance of each feature we applied to the results of naive PCA a space transformation called Varimax rotation [23]. This transformation makes sure that each feature of the original space contributes either very strongly or very weakly to each new principal component. Such a property makes easier to interpret the output of PCA and allows one to label each principal component with a meaningful name based on the features that contribute to it. A similar approach to PCA has been followed by Kerr *et al.* [16] for prediction of execution time of parallel applications in heterogeneous environments.

Figure 9 shows the result of the PCA with Varimax rotation when reducing the space from 34 candidate features to the 7 components. The new principal components are organized by rows and labeled on the left. Each segment plot shows which component a given original feature contributes to. Components are sorted by rows according to their relative importance: how much of the feature variance they cover. So the most important component is labeled *Delta Instructions*. This component groups together features describing by how much the number of instructions in the kernel body increases while coarsening.

The second most important component (*Delta Divergence*) describes the increase in the amount of divergence. It is interesting to notice that the two most important components describe the *difference* of characteristics in the feature space rather then their absolute value. Absolute features account for a smaller amount of variance of the feature space. Section 7.4 describes how two representative features of the first two components are related to the results of the coarsening transformation and how they are used for prediction.

7. RESULTS

This section presents the evaluation of our machine learning predictor. All the speedups reported in this section are relative to the execution time of the original application executed without applying the coarsening transformation, *i.e.,* coarsening factor 1.

7.1 Unique Factor Model Description

To offer a rigorous evaluation of our machine learning model we compare its performance against a simple heuristic. Given a set of training programs with the corresponding

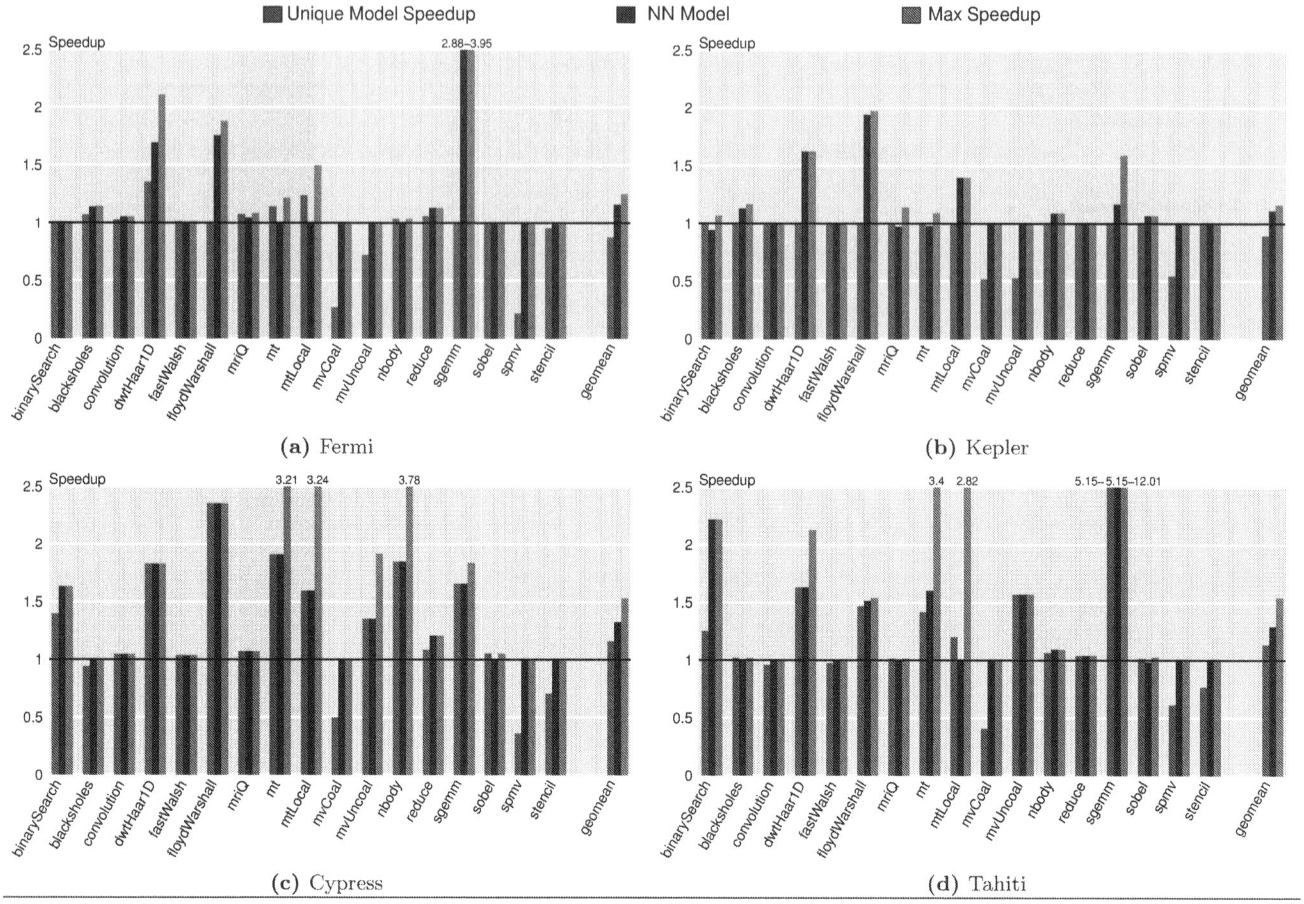

Figure 10. Bar-plots summarizing the results. The first bar (■) represents the speedup given by *Unique Model*. The second bar (■) is the speedup given by the *NN Model*. The third bar (■) is the maximum speedup attainable with thread coarsening.

speedups for each coarsening factor we compute the single best factor on average for that platform. The chosen value will then subsequently be applied on the testing program (not present in the original training set). This optimization policy makes the assumption (often wrong) that programs behave similarly to one-another and, therefore, similar optimization parameters give comparable performance. We employed this simple average-based policy because of lack of similar previous work against which to compare our model. In the following sections we call this simple model *Unique Model*. Our machine learning based predictor is called *NN Model*.

7.2 Performance Evaluation

Figure 10 shows the results of our experiments for the four target devices. We report three bars: one for the performance of *Unique Model*, the second one for *NN Model* and the final one shows the maximum speedup attainable with coarsening.

Performance of Unique Model.

We first observe that *Unique Model* performs poorly on all the devices. On the two Nvidia it results in a slowdown on average, while on AMD its gives an improvement over the baseline but it is far from the optimal. This difference of *Unique Model* across the two vendors can be explained considering that on Nvidia the performance profile is quite irregular. Either a benchmark greatly benefit from coarsening, such as *sgemm* and *floydWarshall* or it does not at all, as in the case of *spmv* and *stencil*. These two types of behavior make hard to estimate performance based on the average trend without considering the inherent properties of each benchmark. On AMD, *Unique Model* records a speedup since coarsening given on average higher improvements (1.53x and 1.54x) and a larger number of kernels benefit from it.

Divergent Kernels.

Applications such as *mvCoal*, *spmv* and *stencil* are penalized by coarsening on all the devices, *i.e.*, the best factor is 1. The reason for this lies in the divergent behavior of these applications. These kernels are enclosed into divergent regions checking for the bounds of the iteration space. Such a pattern is particular detrimental to the baseline performance on GPUs and coarsening makes this problem worse. *Unique Model* leads to significant slowdowns on these kernels since they deviate from the norm. The features *DivRegions* and *DivRegionInsts* model the degree of divergence in the kernel body. Leveraging this information *NN Model* successfully predicts coarsening factor 1 for all the benchmarks for which *Unique Model* leads to slowdowns. This positive result is a consequence of the conservative design policy of our cascade model (section 6.2).

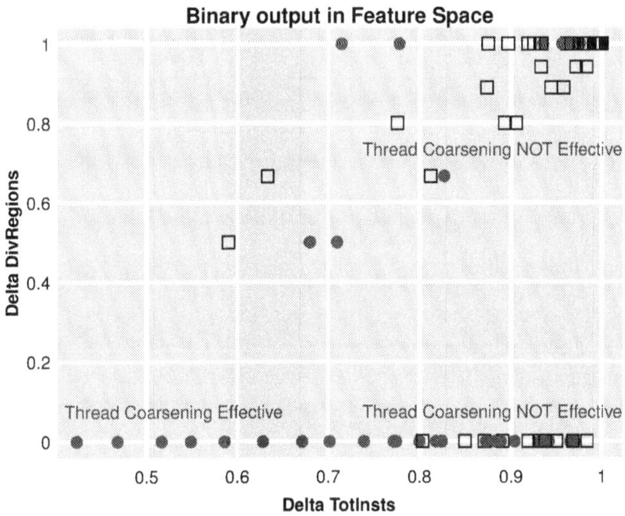

Figure 11. All our training data-points laid out according to two of the most relevant features: *Delta TotInsts* and *Delta DivRegions*. A dot identifies that coarsening is successful, a square that is not. The red labels highlights different regions of the feature space.

Uniform Kernels.

On the other hand *NN Model* enables coarsening effectively for benchmarks such as *sgemm* and *floydWarshall* on all architectures. These two applications show high speedups with coarsening. This is because they benefit from the reduction in redundant memory operations that coarsening ensures. Such a characteristic is expressed in the feature *UniformLoads*. In [21] we propose an explanation for this behavior.

The two applications for which *NN Model* fails to achieve significant improvements are *mt* and *mtLocal*. On AMD in particular these two kernels benefit from coarsening but the model does not take advantage of the possible gain. The reason lies in the particular shape of the code of these two programs. They contain few instructions, just loads and stores. Thus coarsening leads to the replication of all the instructions in the function body. Consequently this makes the feature *Delta TotInst* and *Delta Divergent Insts* have high values. Usually this signifies that coarsening should be disabled.

In summary, *NN Model* gives an average performance improvement of 1.16x, 1.11x, 1.33x, 1.30x on *Fermi*, *Kepler*, *Cypress* and *Tahiti* respectively. Our model never spoils performance significantly in any of the 68 cases. The largest performance penalty happens on *binarySearch* run on *Kepler* and it is about 5%.

7.3 Accuracy of prediction

Table 5 shows the predicted coarsening factor against the optimal one for all programs and devices. From this table we confirm the diversity of the best optimization factor as described by the Hinton diagrams in figure 5. We also see that *NN Model* seldom overshoots the factor and always predicts *no coarsening* (*i.e.*, factor 1) when the optimal is one.

7.4 Model Analysis

This section provides an understanding of how the *NN Model* predicts the coarsening factor relying on the distribution of the training points in the feature space. Figure 11 shows all the points in our data set, *i.e.*, all kernels for all the coarsening factors, arranged in the two dimensional space of *Delta TotInsts* and *Delta DivRegions* for AMD *Cypress*. The plot shows a dot for each benchmark for which coarsening is effective and a square when it is not, these are our training data. From this plot we clearly see that *Delta DivRegions* (on the y-axis) splits the data points in two clusters: one for which its value is 0 and one for which its value is positive. For the first cluster other features will discriminate these points in a higher-dimensional space. In the first cluster fall kernels such as *mt*, *sgemm* or *mri-q* which do not have any divergent region. The second cluster instead contains *mvCoal*, *stencil*, *spmv*, kernels whose body is enclosed by divergent branches. The feature on the x-axis instead represent the overall difference in instructions in the kernel body before and after coarsening.

From the distribution of dots and square we notice the following trends. (1) Configurations at the bottom of the graph (with low *Delta DivRegions*) tend to benefit from coarsening. Not having divergent regions in the original code means that coarsening is likely to be effective. The opposite also holds, since configurations in the top half of the plot usually do not benefit from the transformation. (2) Configurations on the right-hand side of the plot are likely not to benefit from coarsening. A sharp increase in the instruction number signifies a high level of divergence leading to poor performance.

8. RELATED WORK

Thread coarsening.

Volkov *et al.* [31] were the first to introduce thread coarsening as a compiler transformation for GPGPU computation, they focused on linear algebra applications. Unkule *et al.* [30] proposed an evaluation of coarsening as a compiler pass. Coarsening has only been applied by hand to a limited set of CUDA applications. Experiments have been deployed only on only one device with no explanation of the performance results. Coarsening is one of transformations used by Yang *et al.* [34] in their cross-architectural compiler for OpenCL. Their source-to-source transformations have been implemented in the Cetus compiler working on the AST. This limits the applicability of their methodology to simple linear algebra programs, thus missing the possibility of studying the effects of transformations on complex benchmarks. None of the mentioned works proposed a heuristic or a model to automatically determine the coarsening factor, they are mere evaluations of the attainable performance.

GPU optimizations.

The search for the maximum performance on graphics processors has lead to the development of application-specific auto-tuners. Examples of these are [8] and [10]. Much research has been put also in more widely applicable transformations for GPUs. Ryoo *et al.* [25] have been the first to propose compiler transformations for GPGPU computing. They address memory-related optimizations with the goal of improving access patterns. Liu *et al.* [19] perform

Kernel	Fermi		Kepler		Cypress		Tahiti	
	Predicted	Best	Predicted	Best	Predicted	Best	Predicted	Best
binarySearch	1	1	4	16	2	2	8	8
blackscholes	4	8	2	4	1	1	1	2
convolution	4	4	1	1	4	4	1	1
dwtHaar1D	4	8	4	4	4	4	2	4
fastWalsh	1	2	1	1	8	4	1	1
floydWarshall	4	16	4	8	4	4	4	16
mriQ	8	4	4	2	4	4	1	2
mt	1	8	4	2	4	32	4	32
mtLocal	1	8	4	4	4	32	1	32
mvCoal	1	1	1	1	1	1	1	1
mvUncoal	1	1	1	1	4	8	2	2
nbody	1	2	2	2	2	16	4	4
reduce	4	4	1	1	2	2	2	4
sgemm	8	32	2	16	4	8	2	16
sobel	1	1	2	2	1	4	8	4
spmv	1	1	1	1	1	1	1	1
stencil	1	8	1	1	1	1	1	1

Table 5. The table reports the best coarsening factors compared against the ones predicted by *NN Model* for all programs and devices.

an analysis of input sensitivity of CUDA programs choosing the best local work size according the input size. Zhang *et al.* [35] propose a dynamic thread remapping policy to reduce the impact on performance of branch divergence and non-coalesced accesses. High level program tuning for GPUs has been the target of extensive research too. Sponge [13] is a compiler toolchain for the optimization of streaming programs for GPUs. Dubach *et al.* [12] propose a set of compiler optimizations to improve performance of OpenCL programs generated by the Lime Java compiler.

Compiler-transformation tuning using machine learning.

Much research as been focused on the tuning of compiler transformations using machine learning. Stephenson *et al.* [28] have introduced two classification models to determine the best unrolling factor the loops of the SPEC 2000 benchmarks. In [20], a nearest neigbour model is used to select a set of optimizations for numerical Java programs. In [11] Dubach *et al.* predict the performance of an optimized version of a program given static features and profile runs of different versions of the same single-threaded program using a Neural Network for modelling. Sanchez *et al.* [26] employ Support Vector Machines to improve compilation time and start-up performance of Just-In-Time compilation. SVMs are also used in [32] to map streaming programs to multi-cores. Machine learning has been used by Stock *et al.* [29] use an ensemble of various machine learning models for tuning the parameters of automatic loop vectorization for application-specific polyhedral programs. More recently Jia *et al.* have employed regression trees to explore the space of algorithmic and hardware parameters for OpenCL GPU applications [14]. Finally, Lee *et al.* [17] employ a variety of machine learning methods for performance prediction of parallel applications.

9. CONCLUSION

This paper addresses the problem of performance portability for general purpose computing on GPUs by optimizing the coarsening factor for the thread-coarsening transformation pass. We first presented an evaluation of the complexity of the problem characterizing the optimization space. On top of the insights gained with this analysis we built a machine learning model based on a Neural Network to determine the best coarsening factor on four GPUs from two different vendors. The proposed technique achieves a average performance improvement of 1.16x, 1.11x, 1.33x, 1.30x on *Fermi*, *Kepler*, *Cypress* and *Tahiti* respectively, without penalizing performance.

10. REFERENCES

[1] Nvidia Corporation *The Cuda specification.*

[2] Nvidia's Next Generation CUDA Compute Architecture: Fermi `http://www.nvidia.com/content/PDF/fermi_white_papers/NVIDIA_Fermi_Compute_Architecture_Whitepaper.pdf`, 2009.

[3] *AMD Accelerated parallel processing OpenCL*, 2012.

[4] Nvidia's Next Generation CUDA Compute Architecture: Kepler `http://www.nvidia.com/content/PDF/kepler/NVIDIA-Kepler-GK110-Architecture-Whitepaper.pdf`, 2012.

[5] HSA Programmer's Reference Manual: HSAIL Virtual ISA and Programming Model, Compiler Writer's Guide, and Object Format (BRIG), 2013.

[6] The SPIR Specification, Standard Portable Intermediate Representation, Version 1.2, Jan. 2014.

[7] C. M. Bishop. *Neural Networks for Pattern Recognition.* Oxford University Press, Inc., New York, NY, USA, 1995.

[8] J. W. Choi, A. Singh, and R. W. Vuduc. Model-driven autotuning of sparse matrix-vector multiply on gpus.

PPoPP '10, pages 115–126, New York, NY, USA, 2010. ACM.
[9] B. Coutinho, D. Sampaio, F. Pereira, and W. Meira. Divergence analysis and optimizations. PACT, pages 320 –329, oct. 2011.
[10] Y. Dotsenko, S. S. Baghsorkhi, B. Lloyd, and N. K. Govindaraju. Auto-tuning of fast fourier transform on graphics processors. *SIGPLAN Not.*, 46(8):257–266, Feb. 2011.
[11] C. Dubach, J. Cavazos, B. Franke, G. Fursin, M. F. O'Boyle, and O. Temam. Fast compiler optimisation evaluation using code-feature based performance prediction. CF '07, pages 131–142, New York, NY, USA, 2007. ACM.
[12] C. Dubach, P. Cheng, R. M. Rabbah, D. F. Bacon, and S. J. Fink. Compiling a high-level language for gpus: (via language support for architectures and compilers). In *PLDI*, pages 1–12, 2012.
[13] A. H. Hormati, M. Samadi, M. Woh, T. Mudge, and S. Mahlke. Sponge: portable stream programming on graphics engines. ASPLOS '11, pages 381–392, New York, NY, USA, 2011. ACM.
[14] W. Jia, K. Shaw, and M. Martonosi. Starchart: Hardware and software optimization using recursive partitioning regression trees. PACT '13, 2013.
[15] R. Karrenberg and S. Hack. Improving performance of opencl on cpus. CC, pages 1–20, 2012.
[16] A. Kerr, G. Diamos, and S. Yalamanchili. Modeling gpu-cpu workloads and systems. GPGPU '10, pages 31–42, New York, NY, USA, 2010. ACM.
[17] B. C. Lee, D. M. Brooks, B. R. de Supinski, M. Schulz, K. Singh, and S. A. McKee. Methods of inference and learning for performance modeling of parallel applications. PPoPP '07, pages 249–258, New York, NY, USA, 2007. ACM.
[18] Y. Lee, R. Krashinsky, V. Grover, S. W. Keckler, and K. AsanoviÄĞ. Convergence and scalarization for data-parallel architectures, 2013.
[19] Y. Liu, E. Zhang, and X. Shen. A cross-input adaptive framework for gpu program optimizations. IPDPS '09, pages 1 –10, may 2009.
[20] S. Long and M. F. O'Boyle. Adptive java optimisation using instance-based learning. ICS, pages 237–246, 2004.
[21] A. Magni, C. Dubach, and M. F. O'Boyle. A large-scale cross-architecture evaluation of thread-coarsening. SC '13. ACM, 2013.
[22] A. Magni, C. Dubach, and M. F. P. O'Boyle. Exploiting gpu hardware saturation for fast compiler optimization. GPGPU-7, 2014.
[23] B. Manly. *Multivariate Statistical Methods: A Primer, Third Edition.* Taylor & Francis, 2004.
[24] S. Moll. Decompilation of LLVM IR, 2011.
[25] S. Ryoo, C. I. Rodrigues, S. S. Baghsorkhi, S. S. Stone, D. B. Kirk, and W.-m. W. Hwu. Optimization principles and application performance evaluation of a multithreaded gpu using cuda. PPoPP '08, pages 73–82, New York, NY, USA, 2008. ACM.
[26] R. Sanchez, J. Amaral, D. Szafron, M. Pirvu, and M. Stoodley. Using machines to learn method-specific compilation strategies. CGO '11, pages 257 –266, april 2011.
[27] J. Sim, A. Dasgupta, H. Kim, and R. Vuduc. A performance analysis framework for identifying potential benefits in gpgpu applications. PPoPP '12, pages 11–22, New York, NY, USA, 2012. ACM.
[28] M. Stephenson and S. Amarasinghe. Predicting unroll factors using supervised classification. CGO '05, pages 123–134, Washington, DC, USA, 2005. IEEE Computer Society.
[29] K. Stock, L.-N. Pouchet, and P. Sadayappan. Using machine learning to improve automatic vectorization. *ACM Trans. Archit. Code Optim.*, 8(4):50:1–50:23, Jan. 2012.
[30] S. Unkule, C. Shaltz, and A. Qasem. Automatic restructuring of gpu kernels for exploiting inter-thread data locality. CC, pages 21–40, 2012.
[31] V. Volkov and J. W. Demmel. Benchmarking gpus to tune dense linear algebra. SC '08, pages 31:1–31:11, Piscataway, NJ, USA, 2008. IEEE Press.
[32] Z. Wang and M. F. O'Boyle. Partitioning streaming parallelism for multi-cores: A machine learning based approach. PACT, 2010.
[33] P. Xiang, Y. Yang, M. Mantor, N. Rubin, L. R. Hsu, and H. Zhou. Exploiting uniform vector instructions for gpgpu performance, energy efficiency, and opportunistic reliability enhancement. ICS '13, pages 433–442, New York, NY, USA, 2013. ACM.
[34] Y. Yang, P. Xiang, J. Kong, M. Mantor, and H. Zhou. A unified optimizing compiler framework for different gpgpu architectures. *TACO*, 9(2):9, 2012.
[35] E. Z. Zhang, Y. Jiang, Z. Guo, K. Tian, and X. Shen. On-the-fly elimination of dynamic irregularities for gpu computing. ASPLOS '11, pages 369–380, New York, NY, USA, 2011. ACM.

Automatic Execution of Single-GPU Computations across Multiple GPUs

[Extended Abstract]

Javier Cabezas§, Lluís Vilanova§, Isaac Gelado⌀, Thomas B. Jablin*
Nacho Navarro§‡, Wen-mei Hwu*
§Barcelona Supercomputing Center, ⌀NVIDIA Corporation, *University of Illinois,
‡Universitat Politècnica de Catalunya
{first.last}@bsc.es, isaac@nvidia.com, nacho@ac.upc.edu, {jablin,w-hwu}@illinois.edu

ABSTRACT

We present AMGE, a programming framework and runtime system to decompose data and GPU kernels and execute them on multiple GPUs concurrently. AMGE exploits the remote memory access capability of recent GPUs to guarantee data accessibility regardless of its physical location, thus allowing AMGE to safely decompose and distribute arrays across GPU memories. AMGE also includes a compiler analysis to detect array access patterns in GPU kernels. The runtime uses this information to automatically choose the best computation and data distribution configuration. Through effective use of GPU caches, AMGE achieves good scalability in spite of the limited interconnect bandwidth between GPUs. Results show 1.95× and 3.73× execution speedups for 2 and 4 GPUs for a wide range of dense computations compared to the original versions on a single GPU.

Categories and Subject Descriptors

C.1.4 [**Processor Architectures**]: Parallel Architectures; D.1.3 [**Programming Techniques**]: Parallel Programming

Keywords

Multi-GPU programming; NUMA

1. AMGE OVERVIEW

AMGE is a C++ programming framework to distribute data and GPU kernels to be collaboratively executed on all the GPUs in the system. This greatly simplifies the task of programming multi-GPU systems.

Figure 1 shows the components in AMGE and how they interact with the hardware. AMGE aggregates the GPU resources in the system and exposes them as a *single virtual GPU*. Thus, programmers are relieved from the burden of decomposing the problem and managing several GPUs.

PACT'14, August 24–27, 2014, Edmonton, AB, Canada.
ACM 978-1-4503-2809-8/14/08.
http://dx.doi.org/10.1145/2628071.2628109.

The AMGE compiler is a source-to-source compiler, based on the LLVM framework, that analyzes all CUDA kernels, detects all array access patterns and stores this information in the program executable. Array information is key for the compiler pass to produce meaningful information. However, C/C++ forces programmers to flatten dynamically-allocated multi-dimensional arrays into 1D arrays. This harms code readability and makes almost impossible for static analysis to extract the dimensionality and the array access patterns information. Thus, AMGE provides a new data type for multi-dimensional arrays that is used by the compiler analysis.

A key feature in AMGE is the utilization of *remote memory accesses* between GPUs [1]. On each reference to the array, the underlying implementation determines whether the element being referenced is hosted in the memory local to the GPU or on a different GPU. References from a GPU to parts of the array stored in different GPU memories are handled using remote memory accesses. While this is a costly operation, GPUs' latency tolerance gives AMGE limited ability to absorb its overhead. This approach ensures that computation can always be decomposed and executed across multiple GPUs regardless the chosen data distribution. Moreover, this removes the requirement for the compiler analysis to precisely determine the bounds of the memory ranges accessed by a computation partition, and only provide information about the detected array memory access patterns in each GPU kernel.

On each kernel call, *the AMGE runtime* transparently determines the best computation grid and array decompositions using the compiler-provided access pattern information and distributes them across all GPUs.

Memory model: Arrays are decomposed and/or replicated before each kernel call. Input arrays can be safely replicated, but replication of output arrays requires special handling. After a kernel call, partial modifications in each copy need to be merged to provide a consistent view of the array, before using it in another kernel or in the host code. Previous solutions [4, 5] transfer all copies back to the CPU memory for a merge step, which imposes a large performance overhead in many workloads. We avoid this problem by not allowing output arrays to be replicated. Instead, output arrays are always distributed across GPU memories, and accessed through remote memory accesses if necessary.

AMGE implements the Asymmetric Distributed Shared Memory (ADSM [3]) model to allow arrays to be used both

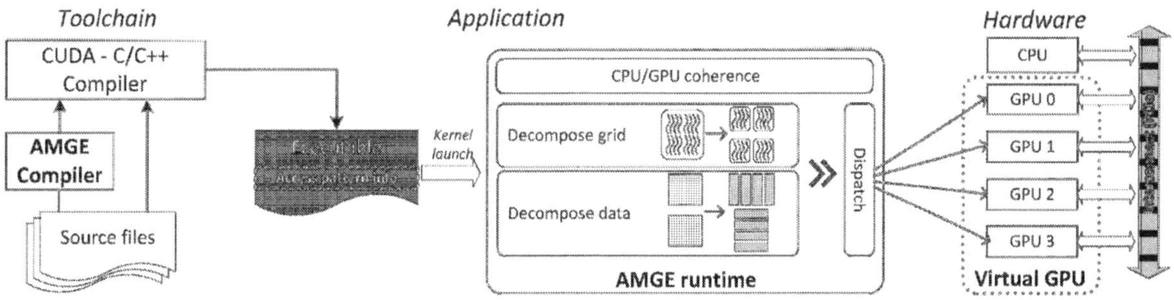

Figure 1: Overview of AMGE components. The compiler extracts array access pattern information and stores it in the program binary. The runtime system uses this information to decompose and distribute computation and data across the GPUs in the system.

```
1   void sgemm(ndarray<float, 2, storage::cmo> C, ndarray<float, 2, storage::cmo> A,
2              ndarray<float, 2> B)
3   {
4     float partial[SGEMM_TILE_N];
5     __shared__ float b_tile_sh[SGEMM_TILE_HEIGHT][SGEMM_TILE_N];
6     for (int i = 0; i < SGEMM_TILE_N; i++) partial[i] = 0.0f;
7
8     int mid = threadIdx.y * blockDim.x + threadIdx.x;
9     int row = blockIdx.x * (SGEMM_TILE_N * SGEMM_TILE_HEIGHT) + mid;
10    int col = blockIdx.y *  SGEMM_TILE_N + threadIdx.x;
11
12    for (int i = 0; i < A.get_dim(1); i += SGEMM_TILE_HEIGHT) {
13      b_tile_sh[threadIdx.y][threadIdx.x] = B(i + threadIdx.y, col);
14      __syncthreads();
15      for (int j = 0; j < SGEMM_TILE_HEIGHT; ++j) {
16        float a = A(row, i + j);
17        for (int k = 0; k < SGEMM_TILE_N; ++k)
18          partial[k] += a * b_tile_sh[j][k];
19      }
20      __syncthreads();
21    }
22    for (int i = 0; i < SGEMM_TILE_N; i++)
23      C(row, i + by * SGEMM_TILE_N) = partial[i];
24  }
```

Listing 1: sgemm CUDA code using AMGE.

```
1   // Initialize A and B in the host code
2   ndarray<float, 2, storage::cmo> A;
3   ndarray<float, 2>               B;
4
5   read_array("A.dat", A);
6   read_array("B.dat", B);
7
8   ndarray<float, 2, storage::cmo> C(A.get_dim(1), B.get_dim(0));
9   // Computation grid size
10  dim3 block(MATRIXMUL_TILE_N, SGEMM_TILE_HEIGHT);
11  dim3 grid(C.get_dim(1)/(SGEMM_TILE_N * SGEMM_TILE_HEIGHT),
12            C.get_dim(0)/SGEMM_TILE_N);
13  // Kernel launch. A, B and C are used in the GPU code
14  sgemm<<<grid, block>>>(C, A, B);
15  // Write results for C into a file
16  write_array("C.dat", C);
```

Listing 2: sgemm host code using AMGE.

by host and GPU code. ADSM assumes a release consistency model in which allocations belong to the CPU code by default and are implicitly acquired/released by the GPU on kernel call boundaries. The runtime transparently transfers arrays between CPU and GPU memories as needed.

2. EXAMPLE: MATRIX MULTIPLICATION

Kernel code written for a single GPU requires only minor modifications to use AMGE. Listing 1 shows the GPU code of a single-precision floating point matrix-matrix multiplication (i.e., sgemm) computation using AMGE. This kernel is based on an efficient algorithm by Volkov and Demmel [2] that requires A and C matrices to be stored in *column major* order, and B in *row major* order. The grey background highlights the modifications to the original code. The only requirement for the kernel to be automatically decomposed is the utilization of the array data type (lines 1-2), and its associated indexing routines (lines 12, 13, 16 and 23). The data type is implemented by the `ndarray<T, Dims, Storage>` C++ class template, where `T` is the type of the elements, `Dims` is the number of dimensions of the array, and `Storage` is an optional parameter that defines the storage type (*row major* by default). Indexing routines removes the need for index linearization on array accesses, resulting a more readable and compiler analysis friendly source code. The kernel uses a 2D computation grid, in which each thread block computes a 2D tile of C by traversing A and B on their X and Y dimensions, respectively. The compiler detects this pattern and stores it in the program executable so that it is accessible later by the runtime.

Listing 2 shows the CPU code of the `sgemm` computation. Input matrices `A` and `B` are declared in lines 2 and 3. Objects created from the `ndarray` template can be passed both to CPU and GPU routines. For example, they are passed by reference to the `read_array` routine (lines 5 and 6) to be initialized with the contents of a file. The `C` output matrix is declared and initialized using the sizes of the read matrices (line 8). These very same objects (i.e., matrices) are passed to the kernel call function. The AMGE runtime intercepts the kernel call, decomposes the computation grid and matrices using the information registered by the compiler, and distributes both computation and data across all the GPUs in the system. Finally, `C` is passed to the `write_array` routine by reference to be written to a file. It is worth noting that there are no explicit data transfers between host and GPU memories. The runtime transparently detects when data is used and needs to be transferred between them.

3. REFERENCES

[1] NVIDIA GPUDirect. https://developer.nvidia.com/gpudirect, 2012.

[2] M. Garland, S. Le Grand, J. Nickolls, J. Anderson, J. Hardwick, S. Morton, E. Phillips, Y. Zhang, and V. Volkov. Parallel computing experiences with CUDA. *IEEE Micro*, 28(4), July 2008.

[3] I. Gelado, J. E. Stone, J. Cabezas, S. Patel, N. Navarro, and W. W. Hwu. An asymmetric distributed shared memory model for heterogeneous parallel systems. ASPLOS XV, 2010.

[4] J. Kim, H. Kim, J. H. Lee, and J. Lee. Achieving a single compute device image in OpenCL for multiple GPUs. PPoPP '11, 2011.

[5] J. Lee, M. Samadi, Y. Park, and S. Mahlke. Transparent CPU-GPU collaboration for data-parallel kernels on heterogeneous systems. PACT '13, 2013.

LCA: A Memory Link and Cache-Aware Co-Scheduling Approach for CMPs

Alexandros-Herodotos Haritatos
School of ECE
NTUA
aharit@cslab.ece.ntua.gr

Georgios Goumas
School of ECE
NTUA
goumas@cslab.ece.ntua.gr

Nikos Anastopoulos
School of ECE
NTUA
anastop@cslab.ece.ntua.gr

Konstantinos Nikas
School of ECE
NTUA
knikas@cslab.ece.ntua.gr

Kornilios Kourtis
Dept. of Computer Science
ETH
kkourt@inf.ethz.ch

Nectarios Koziris
School of ECE
NTUA
nkoziris@cslab.ece.ntua.gr

ABSTRACT

This paper presents LCA, a memory Link and Cache-Aware co-scheduling approach for CMPs. It is based on a novel application classification scheme that monitors resource utilization across the entire memory hierarchy from main memory down to CPU cores. This enables us to predict application interference accurately and support a co-scheduling algorithm that outperforms state-of-the-art scheduling policies both in terms of throughput and fairness. As LCA depends on information collected at runtime by existing monitoring mechanisms of modern processors, it can be easily incorporated in real-life co-scheduling scenarios with various application features and platform configurations.

Keywords

LCA; scheduling; contention aware

1. INTRODUCTION

Chip multiprocessors (CMPs) execute concurrently a large number of threads, which share hardware resources such as caches, memory links and memory controllers, This sharing can create resource contention, which can impact a thread's performance compared to isolated execution. Contention-aware *co-scheduling* attempts to mitigate the effects of co-execution and meet a mix of objectives including system throughput, fairness, QoS, or energy consumption.

Proposed contention-aware scheduling frameworks rely on an application classification scheme that predicts application interference under a co-execution scenario [5,7,8,11,12]. Our classification approach has the following novel objectives: (a) detect contention on both the shared memory link and LLC; (b) rely only on information that can be collected at runtime by existing monitoring mechanisms of modern processors; and (c) require no additional hardware support. LCA decreases average application interference and distributes co-execution penalties between applications in a much fairer way compared to state-of-the-art schedulers, such as the Linux scheduler or prior contention-aware schemes balancing LLC misses (LLC_MRB) [3,4] or memory link bandwidth (LBB) [3,10].

PACT'14, August 24–27, 2014, Edmonton, AB, Canada.
ACM 978-1-4503-2809-8/14/08.
http://dx.doi.org/10.1145/2628071.2628123.

2. CLASSIFICATION SCHEME

We focus on contention situations that can occur on the memory link, the shared LLC or both. We identify the following four application classes:

- *N*: Applications that restrict their activity to their private part of the memory hierarchy or within the core. They create no contention to the shared resources and therefore no interference.
- *C*: Applications with heavy activity on the shared LLC. The impact of Cs co-execution is difficult to predict. Cache organization and replacement policies are expected to handle high activity from different applications on the LLC efficiently. However, if these exhibit similar data access patterns, contention will be high.
- *LC*: Applications with significant activity on both the LLC and the memory link. These cause some interefence and thus slowdowns to C applications. On the other hand, competition between multiple LCs is not high.
- *L*: Memory link intensive applications. Due to their streaming nature, they thrash the LLC which is catastrophic for C applications. When co-executing with an LC, the L will suffer some interference due to the LC's medium demands for memory link bandwidth, while the LC is expected to suffer higher slowdown due to both memory bandwidth shortage and cache thrashing by the L application. Finally, multiple Ls compete for the memory link and a slowdown is expected.

Our classification method is implemented as a decision tree. First we look at the memory link utilization to distinguish L from LC applications. When this is too low, we discern C from N applications using cache link utilization, reuse location and memory uops to total uops ratio. All data are collected at runtime by performance counters utilities.

3. SCHEDULING ALGORITHM

The interference pattern between the four classes imposes a prioritization in the formation of application pairs. Co-execution of $L - C$, $L - L$ and $L - LC$ needs to be avoided as much as possible. Our algorithm is a greedy one with $O(n)$ complexity that forms pairs in a predefined order. It starts by working on N applications and co-schedules them first with all the Ls (that impose the greatest harm), then with Cs (that suffer the greatest harm) and finally with LCs. Remaining Cs are first matched with LCs and if needed with Cs, and then remaining LCs are matched first with Ls and if needed with LCs. Finaly pairs are created from any remaining L applications.

4. EVALUATION

Evaluation is performed on an Intel® Xeon® CPU E5-4620 with 8 cores, private L1 and L2, 16MB 16-way shared L3 and 64GB memory. The platform runs Debian with kernel 3.7.10. All the schedulers are implemented in userspace.

Each class is populated with four benchmarks from a variety of suites [1,2,9]. All applications run with four threads and exhibit a single execution phase. To evaluate the performance of the system at full load, we define a time window, in which every application that terminates starts again.

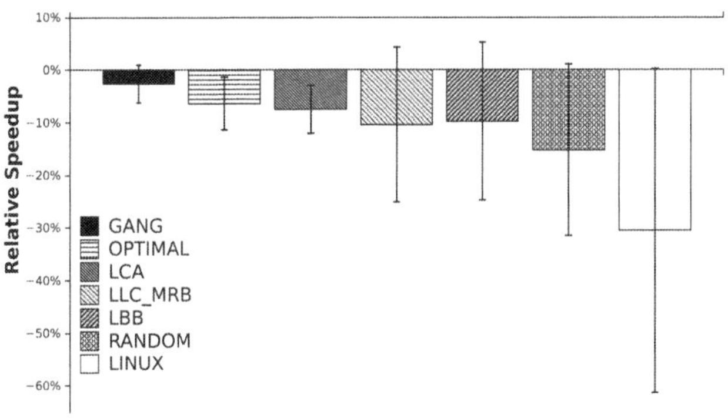

Figure 1: Average slowdown over standalone execution

Figure 1 illustrates the average speedups across all applications. Error bars indicate standard deviation. LCA exhibits similar performance to the optimal scheduler [6], which demonstrates the efficiency of our classification approach. More importantly, LCA exhibits significantly lower deviation than LLC_MRB, LBB and random and even optimal in some cases. This indicates that LCA is much fairer, as it manages to distribute co-execution penalties more uniformly across applications.

5. CONCLUSIONS AND FUTURE WORK

We have proposed a novel application classification scheme that inspects data traffic and resource utilization across the entire memory hierarchy. Based on this, we devised the LCA scheduling algorithm which alleviates the effects of resource contention. LCA outperforms all other schedulers both in terms of average application throughput, achieving performance levels that vary by $\pm 2\%$ with respect to optimal performance, and in terms of fairness as it distributes overheads across applications in a more uniform way.

As future work, we intend to extend this work in the following directions: a) handle more complex scheduling scenarios such as varying number of co-runners and I/O-bound applications, and b) incorporate our proposed scheduler in large-scale cloud environments for scheduling cloud workloads and managing data-centre resources efficiently.

6. ACKNOWLEDGEMENT

This research was funded by project I-PARTS: "Integrating Parallel Run-Time Systems for Efficient Resource Allocation in Multicore Systems" (code 2504) of Action ARISTEIA, co-financed by the European Union (European Social Fund) and Hellenic national funds through the Operational Program "Education and Lifelong Learning" (NSRF 2007-2013).

7. REFERENCES

[1] pChase benchmark. https://github.com/maleadt/pChase.

[2] D. H. Bailey, E. Barszcz, J. T. Barton, D. S. Browning, R. L. Carter, L. Dagum, R. A. Fatoohi, P. O. Frederickson, T. A. Lasinski, R. S. Schreiber, H. D. Simon, V. Venkatakrishnan, and S. K. Weeratunga. The NAS parallel benchmarks - Summary and preliminary results. In *SC '91*, New York, NY, USA, 1991. ACM.

[3] Major Bhadauria and Sally A. McKee. An approach to resource-aware co-scheduling for CMPs. In *ICS '10*, pages 189–199, New York, NY, USA, 2010. ACM.

[4] Sergey Blagodurov, Sergey Zhuravlev, and Alexandra Fedorova. Contention-aware scheduling on multicore systems. *ACM Trans. Comput. Syst.*, 28(4):8:1–8:45, December 2010.

[5] Dhruba Chandra, Fei Guo, Seongbeom Kim, and Yan Solihin. Predicting inter-thread cache contention on a chip multi-processor architecture. In *HPCA '05*, 2005.

[6] Yunlian Jiang, Xipeng Shen, Jie Chen, and Rahul Tripathi. Analysis and approximation of optimal co-scheduling on chip multiprocessors. In *PACT '08*, New York, USA, 2008. ACM.

[7] Evangelos Koukis and Nectarios Koziris. Memory bandwidth aware scheduling for SMP cluster nodes. In *PDP '05*. IEEE, 2005.

[8] Jiang Lin, Qingda Lu, Xiaoning Ding, Zhao Zhang, Xiaodong Zhang, and P. Sadayappan. Gaining insights into multicore cache partitioning: Bridging the gap between simulation and real systems. In *HPCA '08*, 2008.

[9] John D. McCalpin. Memory bandwidth and machine balance in current high performance computers. *IEEE Computer Society Technical Committee on Computer Architecture (TCCA) Newsletter*, pages 19–25, December 1995.

[10] Andreas Merkel, Jan Stoess, and Frank Bellosa. Resource-conscious scheduling for energy efficiency on multicore processors. In *EuroSys '10*, USA, 2010. ACM.

[11] Lingjia Tang, Jason Mars, and Mary Lou Soffa. Contentiousness vs. sensitivity: improving contention aware runtime systems on multicore architectures. In *EXADAPT '11*, USA, 2011. ACM.

[12] Yuejian Xie and Gabriel Loh. Dynamic classification of program memory behaviors in CMPs. In *CMP-MSI '08*, China, 2008.

A Run-Time Power Manager Exploiting Software Parallelism

Simon Holmbacka
Turku Centre for Computer Science - TUCS
Turku, FIN
sholmbac@abo.fi

Sébastien Lafond
Department of Information Technologies
Åbo Akademi University
Turku, FIN
slafond@abo.fi

Johan Lilius
Department of Information Technologies
Åbo Akademi University
Turku, FIN
jolilius@abo.fi

ABSTRACT

In this paper we unify the existing power saving techniques: DVFS and DPM (sleep states) and show how an optimized balance between dynamic and static power leads to minimal energy consumption.

1. INTRODUCTION

Parallelism in software has not only been an argument for performance but also for energy efficiency [3]. The literature demonstrates how applications are implemented for multi-threaded execution, and with lower clock frequency achieve the same performance as their single-threaded versions with less energy consumed. However, this approach is only valid as long as the increase in static power when enabling cores is less than the decrease in dynamic power when reducing the clock frequency. As manufacturing technologies shrink and the cores increase in number, the static power in the transistors increases and starts to dominate the total power dissipation [1]. This means that parallelization of applications reaches a limit beyond which energy efficiency is no longer increasing. Power managers currently lack capabilities for controlling static power and the optimal point of parallelization.

This work presents an approach to include both static and dynamic power in the power management system. We extend applications with the possibility to express parallelism as a *P-value* which describes the level of scalability for the selected hardware. We present a model-based power optimizer capable of intercepting the meta data expressed in the applications and we demonstrate how power and performance can be modeled as a practical non-linear optimization problem with this information. By expressing the parallelism, the optimizer can find the most power efficient balance between clock frequency and active cores leading to minimal energy consumption.

2. RUN-TIME POWER MANAGER

PACT'14, August 24–27, 2014, Edmonton, AB, Canada.
ACM 978-1-4503-2809-8/14/08.
http://dx.doi.org/10.1145/2628071.2628116.

Current power managers, such as the frequency governors in Linux, base the resource allocation purely on system workload levels. This means that the power management has no information of the program behavior such as its parallelism. The structure of our power manager supports P-value injection and QoS declaration in the applications by using a function call to the provided power management library. Figure 1 shows the information flow from application to actuator:

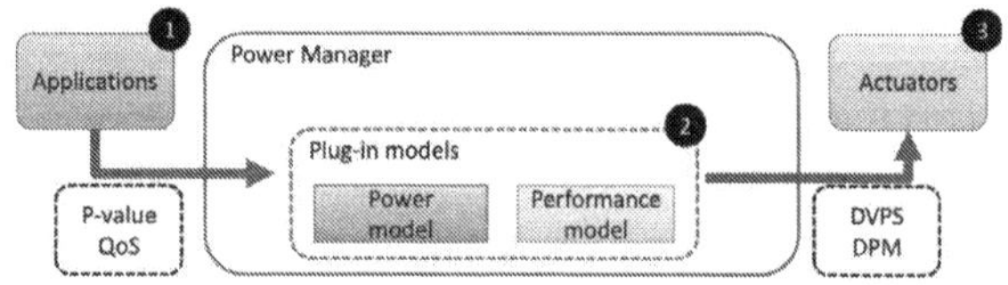

Figure 1: Information flow from application to actuator

1) Applications are user space programs connected to the optimizer and are capable of expressing QoS and P-value(s)
2) The Optimizer determines the optimal combination of DVFS and DPM based on the QoS and P-value inputs from the Applications and the mathematical cost models
3) Actuators are power saving techniques (DVFS and DPM), with a degree of utilization determined by the Optimizer

Power model The actuator utilization is dependent on a power and a performance model used for defining an optimization problem. We trained the power model of the chosen chip by increasing the frequency and the number of active cores step-wise while fully loading the system. As workload we ran the `stress` benchmark under Linux on four threads during all tests, which stressed all active cores on the CPU to their maximum performance. The dissipated power was measured for each point and is shown Figure 2. The goal

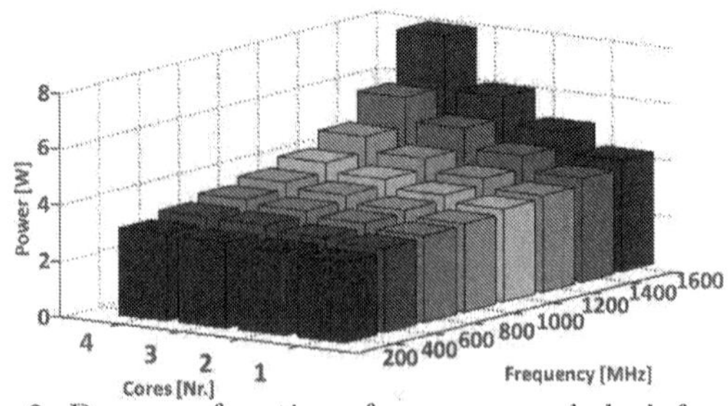

Figure 2: Power as function of nr. cores and clock frequency

is to define a surface as close as possible to the data values in Figure 2, which includes the control variables. The third degree polynomial

$$P(q,c) = p_{00} + p_{10}q + p_{01}c + p_{20}q^2 + p_{11}qc + p_{30}q^3 + p_{21}q^2c \quad (1)$$

where p_{xx} are coefficients was used to define the surface. We used Levenberg-Marquardt's curve fitting algorithm to find the optimal coefficients which minimize the square error.

Performance model The performance model was divided into two parts: DVFS and DPM. We modeled DVFS performance as a linear combination of clock frequency q as: $\text{Perf}(\text{App}_n, q) = K_q \cdot q$ where K_q is a constant, which means that 2x increase in clock frequency models double speed-up.

In contrast to the rather easy relation between performance and clock frequency, modeling the performance as a function of nr. of cores is more difficult since the result depends highly on the inherited parallelism and scalability in the program. The performance model used was based on Amdahl's law:

$\text{Perf}(\text{App}_n, c) = K_c \cdot \frac{1}{(1-P)+\frac{P}{c}}$ where K_c is a constant, P is application parallelism and c is the number of cores. This models a higher performance increase as long as the nr. of cores is low but decreases as the nr. of cores increase.

Definition of optimization problem The objective of the solver is to determine an actuator configuration which minimizes the power while still providing sufficient resources to all applications. The required resources are given as a *setpoint* S, and the actual performance is monitored and sent to the power manager. The lack of resources in the applications is calculated as the difference between actual performance and the setpoint and appears as a positive error value E in the optimizer. The application can request more resources by setting a lower bound *QoS limit* Q, which indicates the lowest tolerable performance. We defined the power optimization problem as:

$$\text{Minimize}\{\text{Power}(q,c)\}\text{Subject to:} \\ \forall n \in \text{Applications}: E_n - (q+c) < S_n - Q_n \quad (2)$$

where the variables: q and c are the actuators. S_n is the setpoint, E_n is the error value and Q_n is the lower QoS limit. The optimization rule states to minimize power while eliminating enough errors to reach at least the lower bound QoS limit. This is achieved by setting the actuators (q, c) to a level sufficiently high for each application n.

3. EXPERIMENTAL RESULTS

The first evaluations were run on a many-core simulator implemented in TrueTime and was capable of measuring energy for different levels of task parallelism. We simulated a video player playing one HD and one SD video. In the HD case, the energy consumption is highest around $P = 0.8$ and decreases in both directions. This is, firstly, because a lower scalability prohibits the system from using a sufficient amount of cores and idle resources are shut down to save power. The cost of disabling resources is a degradation in QoS which might or might not be acceptable to the user. Secondly, increasing the scalability allows the system to activate more cores and hence reduce the clock frequency. The static power P_s increased by activating the cores is significantly lower than the dynamic power P_d saved when decreasing the clock frequency, which results in energy savings. However, the energy consumption reaches, in both cases, an energy plateau at certain points (roughly at $P = 0.91$ for the HD case and $P = 0.7$ for the SD case). At this point

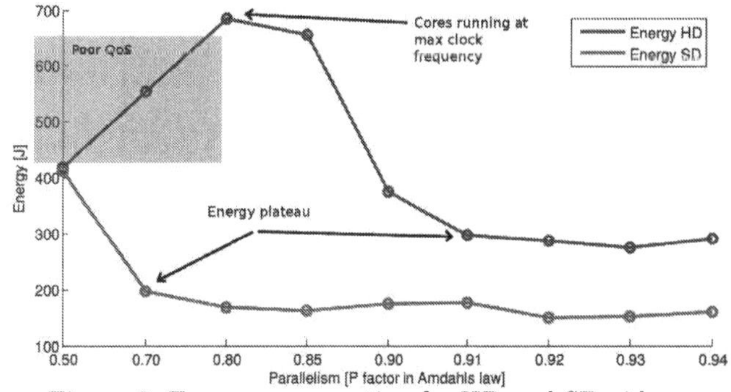

Figure 3: Energy consumption for HD and SD video

the scalability of the application is not strongly worth improving – from an energy point of view – since mapping the application onto even more cores will only result in a static power increase approximately equal to the related dynamic power decrease i.e. $\Delta P_s \approx \Delta P_d$.

The second evaluations were run on a quad-core ARM platform using `mplayer` video decoding threads. We furthermore we stressed the system with background load with different utilization factors. The `mplayer` threads were fixed to `-lavdopts threads=4`, i.e. four `mplayer` threads, and we generated two background threads each with the load level in the range [10% - 90%] using Spurg-Bench [2]. The Spurg-Bench threads were run on a lower priority to not degrade the video playback, and the threads executed a fixed number of operations during the video playback. We decoded a 720p video during the background loads in the range [10% - 60%] and a 480p video during loads in the range [70% - 90%] to not overload the system. The results are shown in Figure 4 for a run in both hot (+20°C) and cold (−20°C) temperature.

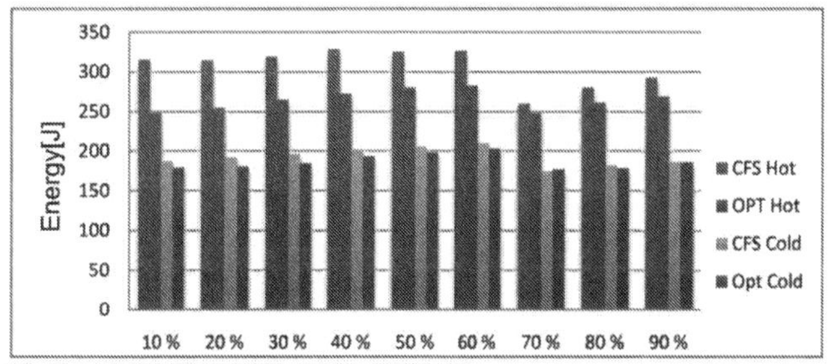

Figure 4: Mplayer benchmark in combination with background loads, x-axis is the load level of the background task

Since our optimizer relies on both DVFS and DPM it manages the power usage more efficiently and has an edge over the default power management (CFS).

4. REFERENCES

[1] R. Jejurikar, C. Pereira, and R. Gupta. Leakage aware dynamic voltage scaling for real-time embedded systems. In *Proceedings of the 41st annual DAC*, pages 275–280. ACM, 2004.

[2] W. Lund. Spurg-bench: Q&d microbenchmark software. `https://github.com/ESLab/spurg-bench`, May 2013.

[3] I. Takouna, W. Dawoud, and C. Meinel. Accurate mutlicore processor power models for power-aware resource management. In *DASC, 2011 IEEE Ninth International Conference on*, pages 419–426, 2011.

Graph-based Performance Accounting for Chip Multiprocessor Memory Systems

Magnus Jahre
Norwegian University of Science and Technology (NTNU)
NO-7491 Trondheim, Norway
magnus.jahre@idi.ntnu.no

ABSTRACT

Chip Multiprocessor (CMP) memory systems share memory system resources between processor cores. While this sharing enables good resource utilization and fast inter-processor communication, it also makes the performance of an application depend on its co-runners. This breaks the system software assumption that a process has the same rate of progress regardless of the co-schedule, potentially leading to priority inversion, missed deadlines, unpredictable interactive performance and non-compliance with service level agreements. In this work, we present a novel graph-based technique that accurately estimates the performance an application would experience without memory system interference. Dynamic interference-free performance estimates can enable scheduling algorithms and management policies that optimize directly for system performance metrics.

Categories and Subject Descriptors

C.1 [**Processor Architectures**]: Multiple Data Stream Architectures (Multiprocessors)

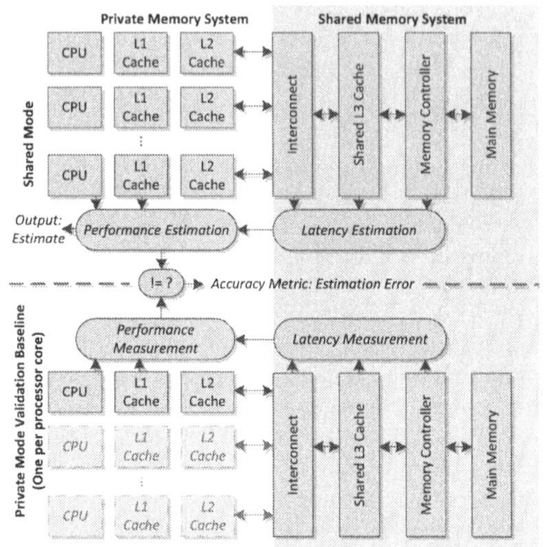

Figure 1: Performance Accounting Overview

1. INTRODUCTION

Chip Multi-Processors (CMPs) share memory system resources to improve resource utilization and enable low latency inter-processor communication. Unfortunately, shared resources make destructive interference possible, and application performance may be significantly reduced due to co-runner behavior. In addition, system software scheduling policies commonly assume that the progress made by each process is proportional to the length of its time slice. Destructive interference breaks this assumption and may result in priority inversion, unpredictable interactive performance and not complying with service level agreements [2].

Recent research has identified two main ways of managing destructive interference. First, system software scheduling policies can be made interference aware (e.g. [5, 2]). These schemes commonly increase the time slices of the interference victims. Second, shared memory system resources like the shared cache (e.g. [8, 7]) or off-chip memory bus (e.g. [6]) can be made thread-aware. In this case, dynamic interference management policies are implemented in hardware. These policies commonly make their allocations based on performance estimates [8] or locally available performance related metrics like shared cache miss rates [7].

Figure 1 illustrates the main operation of a dynamic performance accounting technique. The key requirement is to estimate the performance a process would experience with exclusive access to all shared resources [3, 6, 4]. To validate the estimation accuracy, the *shared mode estimates* (top half of Figure 1) are compared *private mode measurements* (bottom half of Figure 1). The private mode is equivalent to the process running alone in one processor core of the CMP with all other cores disabled and is only used to provide measurements for off-line validation. The purpose of a dynamic performance accounting technique is to provide accurate *shared mode estimates of private mode performance* to a resource management scheme or OS scheduler at regular intervals.

Previous research has provided techniques for estimating the memory latency impact of interference [2, 4]. In the memory bus and on-chip interconnect, the cost of interference is the additional latency due to requests waiting in queues while requests from other processors are serviced. In the shared cache, the cost of interference is the miss penalty of cache misses that are private mode hits. How-

PACT'14, August 24–27, 2014, Edmonton, AB, Canada.
ACM 978-1-4503-2809-8/14/08.
http://dx.doi.org/10.1145/2628071.2628111.

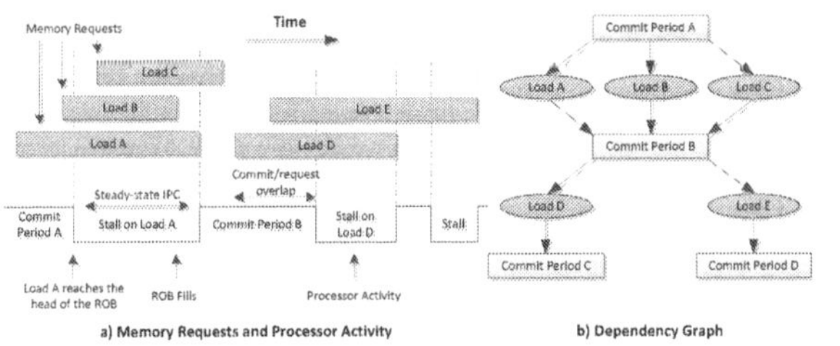

Figure 2: Memory Request Example

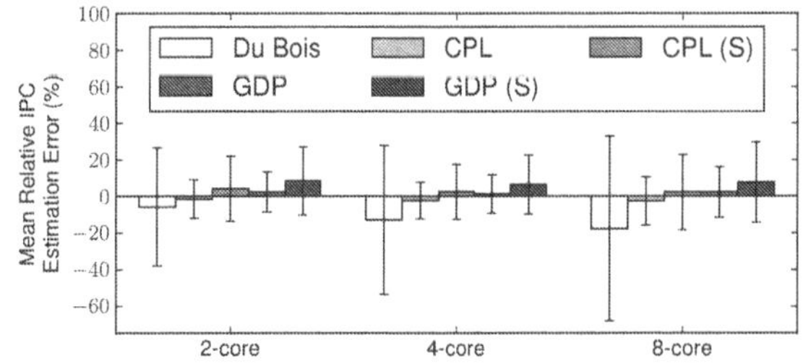

Figure 3: IPC Estimation Error (S=Sampled)

ever, the relationship between latency and performance is complex due to the variety of latency hiding mechanisms implemented in modern processors (out-of-order execution, non-blocking caches, etc.). Thus, private mode latency estimates are only a first step towards performance-targeted resource management schemes. Our *Graph-based Dynamic Performance (GDP)* estimation technique uses the private mode latency estimates of the *Dynamic Interference Estimation Framework (DIEF)* [4] to provide accurate private mode performance estimates.

2. GRAPH-BASED ACCOUNTING

The key observation that led to this work is that a private mode performance estimation technique should be constructed using a property that is very similar in the shared and private modes. Since the only difference between the two modes is the latency of memory requests, it follows that such properties should be latency independent. In other words, we build our scheme on the similarities between the shared and private modes while previous research has focused on detecting the differences [2, 5].

This insight is exploited in the design of GDP. GDP explicitly accounts for the two main effects that contribute to memory latency hiding. The first effect is due to the processor's ability to service multiple memory requests concurrently (i.e. *Memory Level Parallelism (MLP)*). GDP dynamically builds a graph that records the dependencies between memory requests and periods where the processor commits instructions. GDP also accounts for the second latency hiding effect which is the overlap cycles where the memory latency is concealed by out-of-order execution.

The dependency graph represents the relationship between memory requests and forward progress in program execution. This graph is constructed with two rules: (1) The parent of a memory request is the commit period that started closest in time before the request was issued. (2) The child of a memory request is the commit period that finished closest in time after the request completed.

Figure 2 illustrates the dependency graph construction. *Loads A, B and C* are children of *Commit A* since they were issued after *Commit A* started and parents of *Commit B* because they completed before *Commit B* completed. *Load D and E* are the parents of *Commit C and D*, respectively. Since memory requests are serviced in parallel, the *Critical Path Length (CPL)* of the dependency graph determines the number of non-overlapped memory operations necessary to execute the program. Thus, the private mode stall cycles can be estimated by multiplying the average private mode latency estimate by the CPL.

We use the system call emulation mode of the M5 simulator [1] for our experiments. Figure 3 shows the mean and standard deviation of the IPC estimation errors for the estimates using only the CPL and the full GDP technique (CPL and overlap). We present the results for our techniques with and without sampled Auxiliary Tag Directories (ATDs), and compare to Du Bois et al. [2] with full-map ATDs. Figure 3 shows that GDP without sampling is very accurate. With sampling, DIEF underestimates the private mode latency which cause both CPL and GDP to overestimate private mode performance.

3. CONCLUSION AND FURTHER WORK

Shared memory system resources lead to destructive interference between co-scheduled applications and reduced performance predictability. In this work, we have presented the GDP estimation technique that uses a dependency graph to relate memory latency to processor stall cycles. Our next steps are to first thoroughly evaluate GDP and then use it to develop model-based, performance-targeted resource management schemes.

4. REFERENCES

[1] N. L. Binkert et al. The M5 Simulator: Modeling Networked Systems. *IEEE Micro*, 26(4):52–60, 2006.

[2] K. Du Bois, S. Eyerman, and L. Eeckhout. Per-thread Cycle Accounting in Multicore Processors. *ACM Trans. Archit. Code Optim.*, 9(4), 2013.

[3] S. Eyerman and L. Eeckhout. System-Level Performance Metrics for Multiprogram Workloads. *IEEE Micro*, 28(3), 2008.

[4] M. Jahre et al. DIEF: An Accurate Interference Feedback Mechanism for Chip Multiprocessor Memory Systems. In *Int. Conf. on High-Performance Embedded Architectures and Compilers (HiPEAC)*, 2010.

[5] C. Luque et al. CPU Accounting for Multicore Processors. *IEEE Trans. on Computers*, 61(2), 2012.

[6] O. Mutlu and T. Moscibroda. Parallelism-Aware Batch Scheduling: Enhancing both Performance and Fairness of Shared DRAM Systems. In *Proc. of the 35th An. Int. Symp. on Comp. Arch. (ISCA)*, 2008.

[7] M. K. Qureshi and Y. N. Patt. Utility-Based Cache Partitioning: A Low-Overhead, High-Performance, Runtime Mechanism to Partition Shared Caches. In *Proc. of the Int. Symp. on Microarch. (MICRO)*, 2006.

[8] X. Zhou, W. Chen, and W. Zheng. Cache Sharing Management for Performance Fairness in Chip Multiprocessors. In *Proc. of the Int. Conf. on Parallel Arch. and Compilation Techniques (PACT)*, 2009.

SQRL: Hardware Accelerator for Collecting Software Data Structures

Snehasish Kumar, Arrvindh Shriraman
School of Computing Science
Simon Fraser University
{ska124,ashriram}@cs.sfu.ca

Vijayalakshmi Srinivasan
IBM Research
viji@us.ibm.com

Dan Lin, Jordon Phillips
School of Computing Science
Simon Fraser University
{lindanl,jjp14}@cs.sfu.ca

ABSTRACT

Software data structures are a critical aspect of emerging data-centric applications which makes it imperative to improve the energy efficiency of data delivery. We propose SQRL, a hardware accelerator that integrates with the last-level-cache (LLC) and enables energy-efficient iterative computation on data structures. SQRL integrates a data structure-specific LLC refill engine (Collector) with a compute array of lightweight processing elements (PEs). The collector exploits knowledge of the compute kernel to i) run ahead of the PEs in a decoupled fashion to gather data objects and ii) throttle fetch rate and adaptively tile the dataset based on the locality characteristics. The collector exploits data structure knowledge to find the memory level parallelism and eliminate data structure instructions.

1. Introduction

Emerging applications in a diverse set of fields depend on iterative computation over large data structures [4]. Interestingly, the main benefits of parallelizing such applications come from fetching multiple data objects simultaneously and hiding long memory latencies. Unfortunately, the load/store interface of general-purpose processors do not scale to exploit the available memory bandwidth.

We propose *SQRL*, an accelerator that integrates with the last-level-cache and enables energy-efficient iterative computation on data structures. Supporting iterative computation requires *SQRL* to adapt to the locality requirements of the compute kernel and effectively supply data as the kernel streams over the entire dataset. Inspired by the decoupled access-execute paradigm [6], *SQRL* partitions iterative computation on data structures into two regions: the data collection and the compute kernel. *SQRL* employs a data structure-specific controller (called the Collector) that traverses the data structure, fetching the elements and staging the corresponding cache lines in the LLC until the array of Processing Elements (PEs) consume them. The PEs operate on the data objects implicitly supplied by the collector. *SQRL* is aware of the compute iterations and appropriately tiles the data to fit in the LLC to prevent thrashing. Similarly, the collector is aware of the organization of the data structure and runs ahead of the compute kernel so as to prefetch the objects to hide memory latency. The collector stalls if the LLC starts getting filled with locked lines to ensure the LLC does not evict data which has not been consumed by the compute kernel.

PACT'14, August 24–27, 2014, Edmonton, AB, Canada.
Copyright 2014 ACM 978-1-4503-2809-8/14/08 ...$15.00.
http://dx.doi.org/10.1145/2628071.2628118.

2. *SQRL*: Hardware accelerator for collecting software data structures

To assist the acceleration of iterative computation on data structures, we have developed a software runtime to construct a load slice and store slice which include information on the type of data structures, the location of the data structure and the object indices needed within an iteration. Our benchmarks are implemented using C++ STL (Standard Template Library) and use templated iterators. We replace the iterators with calls to the SQRL's C++ runtime environment. We illustrate SQRL's operation using Vector Collectors for the Blackscholes benchmark. Each iteration in Blackscholes (Figure 1) reads 5 vector elements of type float, one vector of type char and writes into a float vector. The load slice of Blackscholes consists of the following vectors, spot[],strike[],rate[],volatility[], time[] and type[] and the store slice consists of price[]; all vectors employ a unit stride.

In *Blackscholes*, each of the vectors are accessed with a unit stride i.e., in the ith iteration the ith element is accessed. The `Keys/Iter` is a single entry with offset 0. The descriptor limits the number of vectors accessed per-loop iteration (8 in this paper). The descriptor for spot[] in *Blackscholes* would be: <LD,&spot[0], FLOAT (4 bytes), nOptions (length of vector), [0] (unit stride access) >.

The loop is unrolled with each PE executing a single iteration of the compute kernel; PEs sync up after each iteration. Each iteration requires space for 4×5 (floats) + 1 (char) + 4 (float) = 25 bytes. The 1 KB *OBJ-$* can thus hold data for 40 iterations of the *Blackscholes* kernel (a loop tile). As shown in Figure 1, the Collector issues an asynchronous request for data (❸). Once the data is filled into the LLC, the Ref. Counter is set (❹) to ensure that the data is not evicted prior to consumption by the PEs. The collector pushes the required data into the *OBJ-$* (❶) and starts a wavefront (set of iterations) to commence execution (❷). Each wavefront consists of 8 concurrent iterations (as *SQRL* has 8 PEs). For *Blackscholes*, there 5 wavefronts are executed until all the data in the *OBJ-$* is consumed and a refill (❶) is required. The dirty data in the *OBJ-$* is written back to the LLC and the Ref. Counter is unset (❺).

3. Evaluation

We evaluate SQRL using a detailed cycle-accurate x86 simulator and the parameters are summarized in Table 1. We use Macsim [1] to model the out-of-order core(footnote), GEMS [2] to model the cache hierarchy, and DRAMsim2 [5] to model the main memory of the system. We added support for SQRL's cores into Macsim, and model the state machine of SQRL's collectors. We model core and

```
begin blackscholes
   // Initialize collectors
   c_spot = new coll(LD,&spot,FP,#length,0,VEC)
   ...
   c_time = new coll (LD,&time,FP,#length,0,VEC)
   // Run collectors in step.
   group.add (c_spot...c_time);

  // Unroll to # of PEs. Tile based on Obj.$ size.
  start(kernel(),#iterations)
end
```

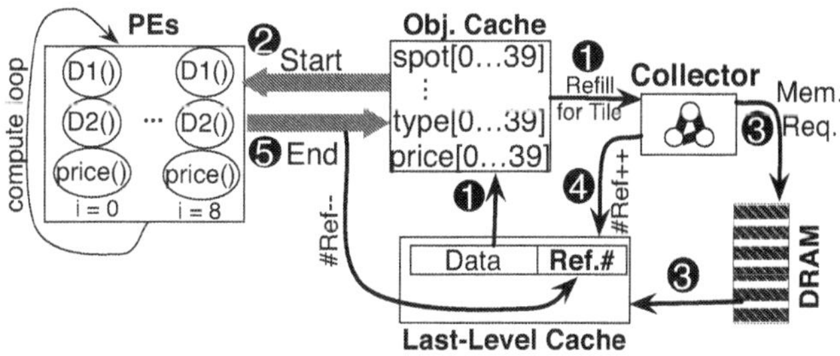

Left: Blackscholes kernel modified to work with *SQRL*. ❶ Loop tile refill from LLC triggered every 40 iterations as *OBJ-$* can hold 40 iterations worth of data. ❷ Execution proceeds in tiles. In Blackscholes a tile of 40 iterations executed on the PE as 8 unrolled iterations at a time. ❸ Memory request issued by collector to fetch the cache blocks corresponding to the data structure. LLC refills from memory. ❹ collector locks line by setting Ref.# to number of elements needed in the iteration. ❺ When the compute iteration completes, the PE decrements the reference count to release the cache lines. Ref.#: 6bit field.

Figure 1: Blackscholes Execution on *SQRL*.

PE energy using McPAT using 45nm technology, and use CACTI [3] to model energy of the caches. The energy consumption of SQRL components are modeled with the templates for the register files, buffers, and ALUs from the Niagara 1 pipeline.

We evaluate the efficacy of *SQRL* on a set of 6 benchmarks, *Blackscholes, Datacube, BTree, HashTable, TextSearch, Recommender*. The workloads include multiple iterative regions and we profile the entire run apart from the initialization phase.

Table 1: System parameters

Cores	2 GHz, 4-way OOO, 96 entry ROB, 6 ALU, 2 FPU
L1	64K 4-way D-Cache, 3 cycles
LLC	4M shared 16 way, 4 Banks, 20 cycles Directory-based MESI
Energy Params	L1 (100pJ Hit). LLC (230pJ hit) L1-LLC link (6.8pJ/byte), LLC-DRAM (62.5 pJ per byte)
***SQRL* Components**	
	2GHz. 8 PEs, 4 stages in-order at 2 Ghz, 1 FPU and 1 ALU (per PE) Instruction buffer (1KB, 256 entries) INT RF: 32 entries, FP RF: 32 entries
	Obj-$ (1KB fully-assoc. sector cache, 32 tags). 1 cycle
***SQRL* Area Overhead** (at 45nm using McPAT)	
SQRL	24.099mm^2 (8 PEs)
SQRL w/o FPU	5.46mm^2

3.1 *SQRL* vs. OOO Baseline

Result 1: *SQRL* improves performance of the kernel by 18× compared to a general purpose processor. Maximum speedup (BTree): 111×. Minimum speedup (Blackscholes): 7×.
Result 2: *SQRL* is able to reduce energy in the PEs relative to the OOO core by 8× on average.
Result 3: On-chip network energy is reduced on average by 2× by eliminating L1-LLC transfers.
Result 4: *SQRL*'s shallow memory hierarchy helps reduce on-chip cache access energy by 21×.
Result 5: *SQRL* is able to attain on average a 13× increase in off-chip DRAM bandwidth. Max: 102×(BTree)

4. Summary

We have focused on exploiting data structure information to provide compute accelerators and kilo-instruction processors with energy-efficient interfaces to the memory hierarchy. We developed *SQRL*, a hardware accelerator that integrates with the LLC and supports

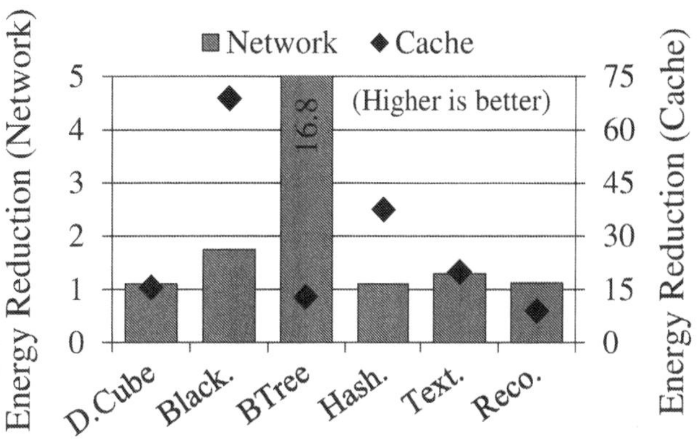

Figure 2: Energy reduction (Unit: × Times). *SQRL* vs OOO. Left Y-axis: Network energy. Right Y-axis: Cache energy.

energy efficient iterative computation on software data structures. SQRL exploits information about the computation kernel and actively manages the space in the LLC to ensure that no data fetch is wasted. SQRL deploys cache refill engines that are customized for software data structures which increases the memory level parallelism, eliminates the penalty of transfers through the cache hierarchy, and removes data structure instructions.

5. References

[1] Macsim : Simulator for heterogeneous architecture - https://code.google.com/p/macsim/.

[2] M. M. K. Martin, D. J. Sorin, B. M. Beckmann, M. R. Marty, M. Xu, A. R. Alameldeen, K. E. Moore, M. D. Hill, and D. A. Wood. Multifacet's general execution-driven multiprocessor simulator (gems) toolset. *SIGARCH Comput. Archit. News*, 33(4):92–99, Nov. 2005.

[3] N. Muralimanohar, R. Balasubramonian, and N. Jouppi. Optimizing NUCA Organizations and Wiring Alternatives for Large Caches with CACTI 6.0. In *PROC of the 40th MICRO*, 2007.

[4] P. Ranganathan. From Micro-processors to Nanostores: Rethinking Data-Centric Systems. *Computer*, 44(January):39–48, 2011.

[5] P. Rosenfeld, E. Cooper-Balis, and B. Jacob. Dramsim2: A cycle accurate memory system simulator. *Computer Architecture Letters*, 10(1):16 –19, jan.-june 2011.

[6] J. E. Smith. Decoupled access/execute computer architectures. In *25 years of the international symposia on computer architecture (selected papers)*, 1998.

Optimizing Stencil Code via Locality of Computation*

[Extended Abstract]

Yulong Luo Guangming Tan
State Key Laboratory of Computer Architecture
Institute of Computing Technology, Chinese Academy of Sciences
Beijing, China
{luoyulong,tgm}@ncic.ac.cn

ABSTRACT

Stencil computation is a performance critical kernel used in scientific and engineering applications. We define a term of locality of computation to guide stencil optimization by either architecture or compiler. Being analogous to locality of reference, computational behavior is also classified into spatial locality and temporal locality. This paper develops equivalent computation elimination (ECE) approach in multi-level loop for exploiting temporal locality of computation. The strength of ECE lies on an intermediate-based searching algorithm to eliminate inter-iteration computational redundancies of all possible combination and a multiple dimensions replacement algorithm to replace redundant computation across loops of multiple dimensions. We implemented ECE in ROSE compiler infrastructure. The experiment shows that ECE improves performance by 20% on average due to the consciousness of temporal locality.

Categories and Subject Descriptors

D.3.4 [**Programming Languages**]: Processors—*optimization, compilers*

General Terms

Theory,Algorithms

Keywords

Stencil ; locality of computation ; equivalent computation elimination ; ROSE

1. INTRODUCTION

Stencil is an important computing pattern in scientific and engineering areas such as heat diffusion, electromagnetic, and fluid dynamics. Due to the importance of stencil computation, there have been amount of work related to stencil optimization [5]. In summary, these work can be classified into memory optimization and computation optimization. People put most of their efforts on memory optimization for attacking the memory wall problem such as cache blocking, loop unrolling. Another complementary performance improvement comes from computation optimization. In fact, for some high order stencil computation, the floating-point operations contribute a considerable part of execution time.

In this paper, we propose a novel principle that reveals some particular computation phenomenons of stencil: locality of computation, and we develop an equivalent computation elimination (ECE) to exploit such locality of computation. Unlike the previous techniques that only address the inner-loop locality (or redundancy) [1–4], our algorithm can detect inter-loop locality and eliminate the computation redundancy across loops with multiple dimensions.

2. LOCALITY OF COMPUTATION

Locality of reference is a phenomenon that the same value or values in a small area are accessed frequently in the runtime of program, it reveals the behavior of some specific programs, which guides us to optimize program more effectively. Basically, the term of locality of computation borrows from locality of reference. In spatial locality of reference, a small area of data are be accessed frequently during a short time. In temporal locality of reference, a reference to memory address is accessed multiple times during the course of program life time.

As a 27-point stencil computation that illustrated in the figure 1, the same computations are repeated computed frequently or the computation are executed continuous in a short duration time, which lets us found locality is also common for computation in some specific program during the runtime. Like the concept in locality of reference, spatial locality of computation reflects the continuity of computational behaviors in spatial dimension, while the temporal locality of computation reflects the similarity of computational behaviors in temporal dimension.

3. EQUIVALENT COMPUTATION ELIMINATION

The spatial locality of computation falls into SIMD optimization while temporal locality of computation is involved with elimination of computational redundancy. Obviously, common subexpression is one type of redundancy. The chal-

*(Produces the permission block, and copyright information). For use with SIG-ALTERNATE.CLS. Supported by ACM.

PACT'14, August 24–27, 2014, Edmonton, AB, Canada.
ACM 978-1-4503-2809-8/14/08.
http://dx.doi.org/10.1145/2628071.2628121 .

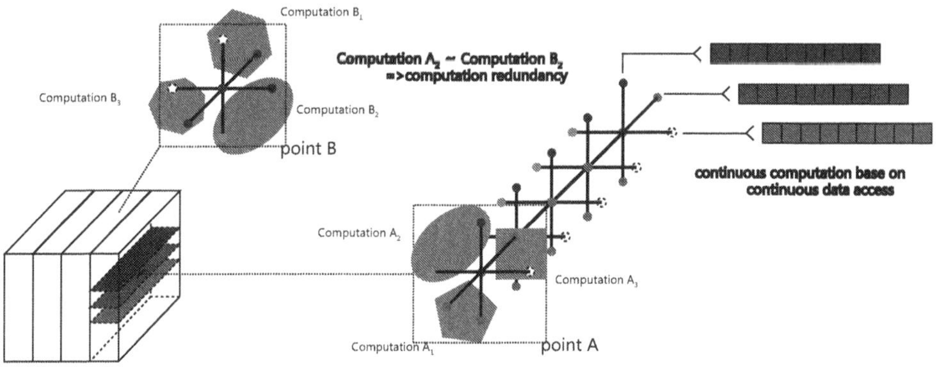

Figure 1: An illustration of spatial locality of computation and temporal locality of computation

lenge to be addressed by Equivalent Computation Elimination (ECE) is to detect and eliminate the inter-iterations computational redundancies in multiple level loops even two redundancies cross in multiple dimension.

Table 1: Computation redundancy elimination algorithms

	method	arithmetic operation	inner loop	mutiple loop
CSE	value numbering	√	X	X
CSR	data dependence analysis +scalar replacement	X	√	X
ESR+	value numbering + CSR	√	√	X
ECE	Intermediate-based search + Multi-dimension replacement	√	√	√

Table 1 summarizes technical features of our ECE and other existing redundancy elimination like techniques. Two remarkable techniques in ECE include the intermediate-based searching in full problem space and multiple dimensions replacement with coordination transformation. The most significant difference is that ECE breaks the barrier of redundancy elimination in the inner loop.

We implemented ECE in ROSE compiler infrastructure. Firstly, a stencil code is transformed into an abstract syntax tree of target code to a more inclusive representation and generates all the possible redundant expressions based on the origin expressions. Secondly, an intermediate-based search is performed on these redundant expressions. It finds the redundancy relationship of these expressions among multiple dimensions, produces candidates of equivalent computation expression pairs. Finally, an optimization solution is selected based on these candidates according the number of register files in target machine, transform the source code.

4. EXPERIMENT

We use the locality of computation principle to guide optimization of four stencil kernels: perform SIMDization through view of spatial locality of computation and ECE through view of temporal locality of computation. The average improvement of benchmarks is about 167%, 147% contributed by spatial locality and 20% contributed by temporal locality.

5. CONCLUSIONS

We define locality of computation that comprises compiler optimization techniques including both spatial locality

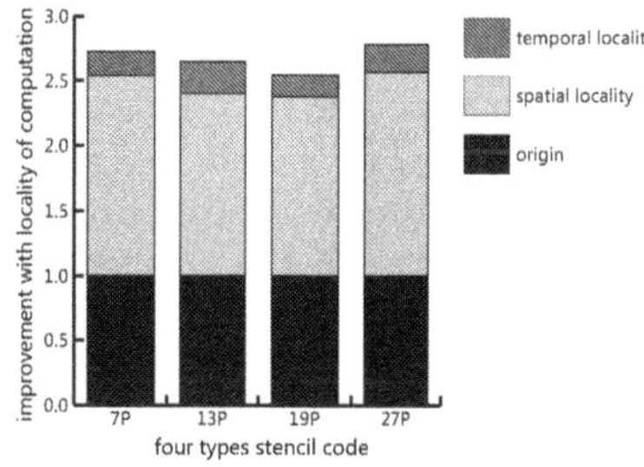

Figure 2: An illustration of spatial locality of computation and temporal locality of computation

(SIMDization) and temporal locality (redundancy elimination). We further design and implement a redundant computation elimination algorithm (ECE) in ROSE compiler to exploit temporal locality of computation.

6. REFERENCES

[1] S. Carr and K. Kennedy, "Scalar replacement in the presence of conditional control flow," *Software: Practice And Experience*, 1994.

[2] K. Cooper, J. Eckhardt, and K. Kennedy, "Redundancy elimination revisited," *Proceedings of the 17th international conference on Parallel architectures and compilation techniques - PACT '08*, p. 12, 2008.

[3] S. C. K. K. David Callahan, "Improving Register Allocation for Subscripted Variables," in *PLDI*, 1990.

[4] S. J. Deitz, B. L. Chamberlain, and L. Snyder, "Eliminating redundancies in sum-of-product array computations," in *Proceedings of the 15th international conference on Supercomputing*. ACM, 2001, pp. 65–77.

[5] G. Jin and J. Mellor, "Increasing temporal locality with skewing and recursive blocking," *Crummey*.

ADHA: Automatic Data layout framework for Heterogeneous Architectures

Deepak Majeti,
Kuldeep S. Meel
Rice University
{deepak, kuldeep}@rice.edu

Rajkishore Barik
Intel Labs
rajkishore.barik@intel.com

Vivek Sarkar
Rice University
vsarkar@rice.edu

ABSTRACT

Data layouts play a crucial role in determining the performance of a given application running on a given architecture. Existing parallel programming frameworks for both multicore and heterogeneous systems leave the onus of selecting a data layout to the programmer. Therefore, shifting the burden of data layout selection to optimizing compilers can greatly enhance programmer productivity and application performance. In this work, we introduce ADHA: a two-level hierarchal formulation of the data layout problem for modern heterogeneous architectures. We have created a reference implementation of ADHA in the Heterogeneous Habanero-C (H2C) parallel programming system. ADHA shows significant performance benefits of up to 6.92× compared to manually specified layouts for two benchmark programs running on a CPU+GPU heterogeneous platform.

Categories and Subject Descriptors

D.3.4 [**Software**]: PROGRAMMING LANGUAGES—*Processors, Compilers*

Keywords

Compilers, Data Layout, Heterogeneous Architectures

1. INTRODUCTION

In recent years, the end of Dennard scaling has brought about significant changes in the fundamental processor design. We are now entering an era of heterogeneous and specialized processors, and this trend is expected to continue in the future. One dominant heterogeneous architecture found in many systems today is a CPU+GPU system. The processor architecture, the memory hierarchy and cache structures are significantly different on the CPU and GPU sides. With such diverse characteristics, it not only hard to program these systems in a portable manner, but also quite challenging to optimize them.

One major factor which impacts performance is the data layout [4, 5]. The choice of a good data layout depends on several factors including target machine parallelism, memory hierarchy, data access patterns, and input size. An application program with multiple data-parallel kernels can map each kernel onto any of the heterogeneous processors. It is hard for the programmer to determine if a single layout is best for all the kernels or if a better choice is to select different data layouts for different kernels with data remapping operations performed in between kernels. Also, the programmer has to manually re-write the code for each data layout combination even to just evaluate the best data layout. The number of combinations increase exponentially with the number of kernels and the number of fields accessed by each kernel increase.

To overcome this limitation, we design ADHA: a two-level compiler based automatic data layout framework and a reference implementation of the same in the Heterogeneous Habanero-C [2] (H2C) programming system. The lower level formulation deals with the data layout problem for a parallel code region, and provides a greedy algorithm that uses an *affinity graph* to obtain approximate solutions. The higher level formulation targets data layouts for the entire program, for which we provide a graph-based shortest path algorithm that uses the data layouts for the code regions computed in the lower level. In this work, we consider only *AoS (Array of structure)* and *SoA (Structure of Array)* layouts.

2. OVERALL FRAMEWORK

We denote a data/task-parallel operation that is executed either on the CPU or on the GPU as a section. A H2C program may consist of several forasync parallel loop constructs, each of which constitutes a section of it's own.

Our automatic data layout framework, ADHA, consists of two steps. The first step consists of a greedy strategy with the goal of determining the "optimal data-layout of a section" or simply ODS. The key idea is to construct an affinity graph for a H2C program where the "nodes" of the affinity graph represent the fields (and arrays) being accessed in the section and the "edges" represent the affinity between two fields. The affinity weight of an edge is computed based on the number of common occurrences between the two nodes involving the edge. Once the affinity graph is constructed, we employ a greedy clustering algorithm to cluster the fields. The cluster size is determined based on the underlying architecture (e.g., cache size and memory hierarchy). The result of the clustering algorithm is used to combine the fields in structures.

The next step involves finding the best data-layout for the entire H2C program (denoted as "program data-layout"

PACT'14, August 24–27, 2014, Edmonton, AB, Canada.
ACM 978-1-4503-2809-8/14/08.
http://dx.doi.org/10.1145/2628071.2628122.

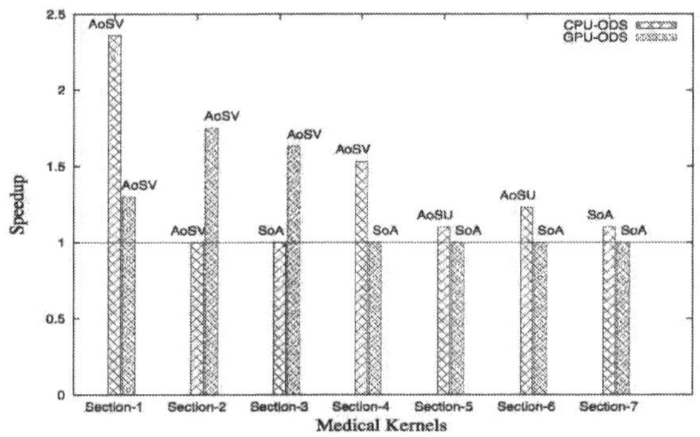

Figure 1: Speedup of the Medical sections

or simply PDL) from the computed best data layouts for each section. First, we construct a control flow graph for each section (denoted as SCFG). We then construct a rooted directed acyclic graph with the first section as the root. Each pair of sections either share two edges, namely the combine edge and the remap edge, or none. The edge weight of the combine edge represents the loss in performance due to combining the two sections involving the edge and assigning an intermediate data layout. The data layout of the combined sections is obtained running the ODS pass on the merged section.

The remap edge weight is the cost of remapping from the parent section to the child section , which is computed based on the number of common fields in the two sections. We then employ the shortest path algorithm to determine the best data layout for the entire program. For the PDL pass, we provide a tuning profile of the execution times of both the CPU and GPU (since we do not perform the mapping automatically). The output of the PDL pass gives us the best data layout along with the mapping to the CPU or the GPU.

Our implementation of ADHA automatically compiles forasync loops down to OpenCL with the corresponding data layout output by the ODS + PDL pass. ADHA can be employed to efficiently run a H2C program on modern CPU+GPU platforms that support OpenCL.

3. EXPERIMENTAL EVALUATION

We evaluated our implementation of ADHA with two benchmarks arising from different domains as summarized in Table 1. **#S** denotes the number of sections and **#F** denotes the number of fields in the entire program. **Medical** is from the CDSC benchmark suite [1] and **K-Means** is from the Rodinia suite [3].

Description	#S	#F	Input
`Medical` Image Registration	7	6	256×256×256
`K-Means` Clustering Algorithm	2	32	8388608

Table 1: Benchmarks Description

The experiments were conducted on a Intel-X5660 CPU with 6 cores running at 2.8GHz and a NVIDIA Tesla-M2050 GPU with 8 SMs running at 575 MHz. We use gcc version 4.4.6 with O2 optimization level. For each of the benchmarks, we executed the OpenCL code with the original data layout and with the automatically generated layout from ADHA on both the CPU and GPU.

Medical image registration consists of 7 sections. Sections(1-3) have heavy control flow and do not vectorize while sections(4-7) are vectorizable. Table 2 shows the fields accessed by all the sections and the different data layouts generated by the ODS pass for each of the sections. For instance, *AoSU* lays out fields $V1$,$V2$,$V3$,S,T and *interpT* as individual arrays using SoA layout and interleaves the fields $U1$,$U2$,$U3$ using an AoS layout. Figure 1 shows the speedup from the data

Data Layout	Description
SoA	V1,V2,V3,U1,U2,U3,S,T,interpT
AoSU	V1,V2,V3,{U1,U2,U3},S,T,interpT
AoSV	{V1,V2,V3},U1,U2,U3,S,T,interpT

Table 2: Medical Imaging ODS Data Layouts

layout generated by the ODS pass compared to the original SoA layout by executing the seven sections on CPU and GPU. ODS pass performs better for most of the sections on the CPU. On the GPU, the SoA layout performs the best for sections-(4-7) due to memory coalescing. The GPU benefits from cache locality for sections-(1-3).

Platform	Layout Description	Speedup
CPU-ODS	32 Fields belong to SoA	5.5
GPU-ODS	4 AoS of size 8 each	1

Table 3: KMeans Section-1 ODS and Speedup

The benchmark *K-Means* consists of two sections: the first section is a data parallel loop while the second section performs reduction on all the features. The second section is executed sequentially in the original implementation, owing to the difficulty of implementing reduction over varying number of variables using OpenCL. The original data layout for both these sections is SoA. The first section CPU-ODS is an AoS layout and the GPU-ODS is SoA layout and are shown along with their speedups in Table 3. The AoS layout which is the output from the ODS pass for the second section improves its performance by a factor of 8×. This is because the second section suffers a lot of cache misses due to the SoA layout.

Table 4 provides the speedup obtained by the overall data-layout from the PDL pass. As stated before, the PDL pass gives the mapping onto CPU or GPU along with the data-layout. For the Medical benchmark, sections-(1-3) are mapped onto the CPU with *AOSV* layout and then a remap operation is performed to *SOA* layout with sections-(4-7) mapped to the GPU. *K-Means* sections-(1-2) are both mapped onto the CPU with a combined AoS layout.

Benchmark	section Mapping SCFG	Speedup
Medical	CPU-ODS(1-3) remap GPU-ODS(4-7)	1.34
K-Means	CPU-ODS combine CPU-ODS	6.92

Table 4: PDL Speedup for Medical and K-Means

4. REFERENCES

[1] "CDSC Research Applications." [Online]. Available: http://www.cdsc.ucla.edu/research/

[2] "Heterogeneous Habanero-C." [Online]. Available: http://habanero.rice.edu/Heterogeneous+Habanero-C

[3] Che *et al.*, "Rodinia: A benchmark suite for heterogeneous computing," ser. ISWC'09, Oct 2009.

[4] D. Majeti *et al.*, "Compiler Driven Data Layout Transformation for Heterogeneous Platforms," in *Proc. HeteroPar*, 2013.

[5] I.-J. Sung *et al.*, "Data layout transformation exploiting memory-level parallelism in structured grid many-core applications," in *Proc. of PACT*, 2010.

Active Learning Accelerated Automatic Heuristic Construction for Parallel Program Mapping

William F. Ogilvie
University of Edinburgh
s0198982@inf.ed.ac.uk

Pavlos Petoumenos
University of Edinburgh
ppetoume@inf.ed.ac.uk

Zheng Wang
Lancaster University
z.wang@lancaster.ac.uk

Hugh Leather
University of Edinburgh
hleather@inf.ed.ac.uk

ABSTRACT

Building effective optimization heuristics is a challenging task which often takes developers several months if not years to complete. Predictive modelling has recently emerged as a promising solution, automatically constructing heuristics from training data, however, obtaining this data can take months per platform. This is becoming an ever more critical problem as the pace of change in architecture increases. Indeed, if no solution is found we shall be left with out of date heuristics which cannot extract the best performance from modern machines.

In this work, we present a low-cost predictive modelling approach for automatic heuristic construction which significantly reduces this training overhead. Typically in supervised learning the training instances are randomly selected to evaluate regardless of how much useful information they carry, but this wastes effort on parts of the space that contribute little to the quality of the produced heuristic. Our approach, on the other hand, uses active learning to select and only focus on the most useful training examples and thus reduces the training overhead.

We demonstrate this technique by automatically creating a model to determine on which device to execute four parallel programs at differing problem dimensions for a representative CPU–GPU based system. Our methodology is remarkably simple and yet effective, making it a strong candidate for wide adoption. At high levels of classification accuracy the average learning speed-up is 3x, as compared to the state-of-the-art.

Categories and Subject Descriptors

D.3.4 [**Programming Languages**]: Processors—*compilers, optimization*

Keywords

Active Learning; Machine Learning; Compilers

PACT'14, August 24–27, 2014, Edmonton, AB, Canada.
ACM 978-1-4503-2809-8/14/08.
http://dx.doi.org/10.1145/2628071.2628128.

1. INTRODUCTION

Creating analytical models on which optimization heuristics can be based has become harder as processor complexity has increased. Compiler developers often have to spend months if not years to get a model perfected for a single target architecture, and since modern compilers often support a wide range of disparate platforms most have been found to be out of date [2].

Machine Learning based predictive modelling has rapidly emerged as a viable means of automating heuristic construction [1, 3]; by running example programs (optimized in different ways) and observing how the variations affect program run-time a machine learning tool can predict good settings with which to compile new, as yet unseen, programs. This new research area is promising, having the potential to fundamentally change the way compiler heuristics are designed, but suffers from a number of issues. One major concern is the cost of collecting training examples. While machine learning allows us to automatically construct heuristics with little human involvement, the cost of generating training examples (that allow a learning algorithm to accumulate knowledge) is often very expensive.

In this work we present a novel, low-cost predictive modelling approach that can significantly reduce the overhead of collecting training examples for parallel program mapping without sacrificing prediction accuracy. The usual procedure in supervised learning is to passively collect training examples at random, regardless of how useful they might be to the learner. We propose using *active learning* instead, which is a method by which the learning algorithm itself is able to iteratively choose the training instances it believes carry the greatest information based upon whatever knowledge it has already accumulated. Specifically, we use active learning to automatically construct a heuristic to determine which processor will give the better performance on a CPU–GPU based heterogeneous system at differing problem sizes for a given program. We evaluate our system by comparing it with the typical random sampling methodology, used in the bulk of prior work. The experimental results show that our technique accelerates training by a factor of 3x on average.

2. OUR APPROACH

We use a heterogeneous Query-by-Committee (QBC) implementation of active learning, which is so-named because it requires that a number of different models be generated us-

Benchmark	Dim	Min	Max	Step	Size	Cand
HotSpot	2	1	128	1	$16,384$	10,000
MatMul	3	1	256	1	$1.6x10^7$	10,000
Pathfinder	2	2	1024	1	$1.0x10^6$	10,000
SRAD	2	128	1024	16	$3,136$	2,636

Table 1: The sizes of the input spaces for each benchmark. *Dim* indicates the number of dimensions – each dimension is then treated in the same way for our case study. *Min* gives the minimum value of each dimension. *Max* gives the maximum value of each dimension. *Step* gives the step value on each dimension. *Size* is the total number of points in the input space. *Cand* is the number of points in the candidate set for each benchmark.

ing distinct member algorithms. The idea is that each QBC member is given random training examples or instances. Since every member is different they form unique models from this information. To choose the next instance to learn from each algorithm in turn attempts to guess the classification (CPU or GPU) of pre-selected random unlabelled points. A subset is formed from these candidates comprising those instances for which the committee is in most disagreement. Finally, a single instance is chosen randomly from this group, it is then labelled and added to the training set of each classifier. This process repeats until some completion criterion are met.

3. EXPERIMENTAL SETUP

We evaluated our approach on a heterogeneous platform comprised of an Intel Core i7 4770 (3.4 GHz) CPU and NVIDIA GeForce GTX Titan (6GB) GPU. The benchmarks we used were taken from the Rodinia suite, namely `HotSpot`, `PathFinder`, and `SRAD`. We also included a simple matrix multiplication application. Each benchmark was chosen because it has equivalent OPENMP and OPENCL implementations and a multidimensional problem space.

QBC *Algorithms.*

Our committee comprised 12 unique machine learning algorithms, taken from the Weka tool-kit. They are `Logistic`, `MultilayerPerceptron`, `IB1`, `IBk`, `KStar`, `RandomForest`, `LogitBoost`, `MultiClassClassifier`, `RandomCommittee`, `NNge`, `ADTree`, and `RandomTree`: all configured with default parameters. These 12 were specifically selected for their capability of producing a binary predictor from numeric inputs and the fact that they have been widely used in prior work.

Program Input space.

The sizes of the input spaces for each benchmark were chosen to give realistic inputs to learn over. Table 1 describes the number of dimensions and their range for each benchmark. That table also gives the total number of inputs for each benchmark.

Initial Training Set and Candidate Set Sizes.

For all benchmarks the minimum initial training set size of one was used. The candidate set size (shown in Table 1) was chosen to be 10,000 examples, or the largest number possible under the problem size constraints.

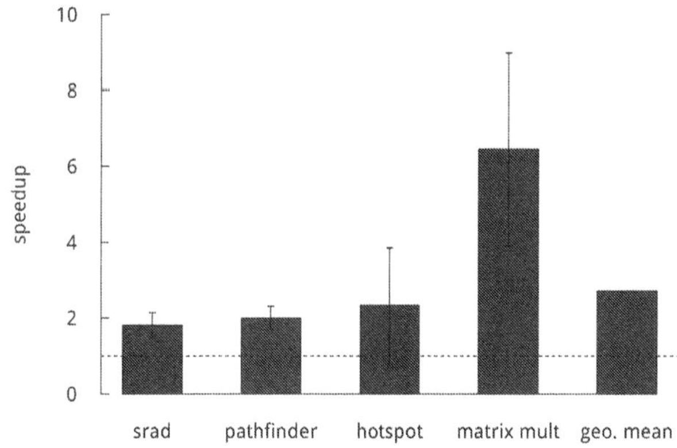

Figure 1: On average our approach requires 3x fewer training examples to create a high quality heuristic than a random sampling technique. These speed-up values are defined as the number of training instances required for the accuracy of a heuristic to plateau using the random technique divided by that for our QBC implementation.

Termination Criterion.

In all cases, the active learning iterations were halted at 200 steps. This value was selected because for all benchmarks the learning improvement had plateaued by that time.

Run-time Measurement and Device Comparison.

To determine if a benchmark is better suited to the CPU or GPU for a given input it was run on each processor at least 10 times, and at most 200 times. We employed a number of statistical techniques to ensure our data was as accurate as possible, including Welch's t-test, equivalence testing, and interquartile-range outlier removal.

Testing.

For testing, a set of 500 inputs were excluded from any training sets. Both our active and passive learning experiments were run 10 times and the arithmetic mean of the accuracy was taken, where the accuracy of each experiment was the average accuracy of all 12 models.

4. RESULTS

Figure 1 shows the average learning speed-up of our approach over the classical random sampling technique. The actual values are based on the number of training examples required to produce a heuristic which is at least 90% accurate. Overall, we are able to accelerate training by 3x on average. In real terms, this translates to a saving of weeks of compute time.

5. REFERENCES

[1] D. Grewe, Z. Wang, and M. O'Boyle. Portable mapping of data parallel programs to opencl for heterogeneous systems. In *CGO '13*.

[2] S. Kulkarni and J. Cavazos. Mitigating the compiler optimization phase-ordering problem using machine learning. In *OOPSLA '12*.

[3] Z. Wang and M. F. O'Boyle. Partitioning streaming parallelism for multi-cores: A machine learning based approach. In *PACT '10*.

Preemptive Thread Block Scheduling with Online Structural Runtime Prediction for Concurrent GPGPU Kernels

Sreepathi Pai
The University of Texas at Austin
Austin, Texas
sreepai@ices.utexas.edu

R. Govindarajan
Indian Institute of Science
Bangalore, India
govind@serc.iisc.in

Matthew J. Thazhuthaveetil
Indian Institute of Science
Bangalore, India
mjt@serc.iisc.in

ABSTRACT

Recent NVIDIA Graphics Processing Units (GPUs) can execute multiple kernels concurrently. On these GPUs, the thread block scheduler (TBS) currently uses the FIFO policy to schedule thread blocks of concurrent kernels. We show that the FIFO policy leaves performance to chance, resulting in significant loss of performance and fairness. To improve performance and fairness, we propose use of the preemptive Shortest Remaining Time First (SRTF) policy instead. Although SRTF requires an estimate of runtime of GPU kernels, we show that such an estimate of the runtime can be easily obtained using online profiling and exploiting a simple observation on GPU kernels' grid structure. Specifically, we propose a novel Structural Runtime Predictor. Using a simple Staircase model of GPU kernel execution, we show that the runtime of a kernel can be predicted by profiling only the first few thread blocks. We evaluate an online predictor based on this model on benchmarks from ERCBench, and find that it can estimate the actual runtime reasonably well after the execution of only a single thread block. Next, we design a thread block scheduler that is both concurrent kernel-aware and uses this predictor. We implement the Shortest Remaining Time First (SRTF) policy and evaluate it on two-program workloads from ERCBench. SRTF improves STP by 1.18x and ANTT by 2.25x over FIFO. When compared to MPMax, a state-of-the-art resource allocation policy for concurrent kernels, SRTF improves STP by 1.16x and ANTT by 1.3x. To improve fairness, we also propose SRTF/Adaptive which controls resource usage of concurrently executing kernels to maximize fairness. SRTF/Adaptive improves STP by 1.12x, ANTT by 2.23x and Fairness by 2.95x compared to FIFO. Overall, our implementation of SRTF achieves system throughput to within 12.64% of Shortest Job First (SJF, an oracle optimal scheduling policy), bridging 49% of the gap between FIFO and SJF.

PACT'14, August 24–27, 2014, Edmonton, AB, Canada.
ACM 978-1-4503-2809-8/14/08.
http://dx.doi.org/10.1145/2628071.2628117.

Categories and Subject Descriptors

D.3.3 [**Programming Languages**]: Language Constructs and Features; C.1.2 [**Processor Architectures**]: Multiple Data Stream Architectures (Multiprocessors)

1. INTRODUCTION

Concurrent kernel execution in Graphics Processing Units (GPUs), such as the NVIDIA Fermi and Kepler families, exploits task-level parallelism among independent GPU kernels primarily by *space-sharing*. Each GPU kernel exclusively occupies the resources (i.e. registers, thread contexts, shared memory) it needs and concurrent execution is only achieved if there are enough resources left over to accommodate any concurrent kernel. Therefore, NVIDIA positions concurrent kernel execution as allowing "programs that execute a number of small kernels to utilize the whole GPU".

Programs whose kernels already utilize the whole GPU ("large kernels") – most kernels in Rodinia, Parboil2, etc. – do not benefit from concurrent kernel execution and execute serially. However, since every GPU kernel is organized as a hierarchy, a *grid* of *thread blocks* and executes at thread block granularity, recent works on concurrent GPU kernel execution have been able to achieve concurrent execution for large kernels. However, on current GPU hardware, concurrent kernels are executed in arrival order (i.e. FIFO). We show that FIFO is a poor choice and that preemptive scheduling policies such as those presented herein improve throughput and turnaround time.

This work focuses on the *Thread Block Scheduler* (TBS), the first-level hardware scheduler in GPUs. In particular, we propose two thread block scheduling policies – Shortest Remaining Time First (SRTF) and SRTF/Adaptive – for concurrent GPGPU workloads. These policies use estimates of kernel runtime to determine their scheduling decisions when executing concurrent workloads, we propose a novel online runtime predictor for GPU grids to provide these estimates of runtime. Our predictor is based on an observation that the GPU kernel execution time is approximated by a simple linear function of the durations of its thread blocks, and therefore online profiling of the first few thread blocks suffices to estimate the kernel execution time for scheduling.

2. STRUCTURAL RUNTIME PREDICTION

Our principle of *Structural Prediction* on which our online predictor is based essentially views the execution of a grid's N thread blocks (all of which have the same code) as N repeated executions of the same program. So profiling the first few thread blocks of a grid lets us predict the behaviour of the remaining thread blocks. In this work, the runtime of a thread block is used to predict the runtime of the whole kernel. We call this *Structural Runtime Prediction*.

Assuming that all thread blocks take the same time to complete, our *Staircase model* approximates runtime using the following equation for runtime $T = (\lceil N/R \rceil)\, t \quad (1)$.

Here, $N = B/N_{SM}$ where the original B thread blocks are assumed to be evenly distributed across N_{SM} streaming multiprocessors (SMs). The grid's maximum residency, R, can be determined at launch time. The value of t can be obtained by sampling, possibly as soon as a single thread block finishes execution. However, for timely predictions, the grid must execute more than R blocks per SM.

To evaluate the Staircase model, we instrumented major kernels in the Parboil2 and the ERCBench suites to record the start and end time of each thread block and the SM it executed on and ran them on a Fermi-based NVIDIA Tesla C2070, with a quad-core Intel Xeon W3550 CPU, 16GB RAM and running Debian Linux 6.0 (64-bit) with CUDA driver 295.41 and CUDA runtime 4.2.

Using these recorded end times, linear regression resulted in normalized predictions between 0.99x to 1.11x of actual runtime for ERCBench and 0.87x to 1.13x for Parboil2. This strongly supports our hypothesis that GPU kernel runtime is a linear function. For the Staircase model, predictions normalized to actual runtime lie between 0.54x to 1.18x for ERCBench and 0.39x to 1.49x for Parboil2. If we exclude outliers, normalized predictions are between 0.66x and 1.18x for ERCBench and 0.6x and 1.2x for Parboil2.

The major causes for inaccuracy for the Staircase model are (i) non-Staircase model behaviour precipitated by the the first R blocks each ending at different times leading to staggering in the starting times of subsequent blocks; (ii) differing work per thread block because thread block durations depended on *value* of their inputs, e.g. `render` in RayTrace; (iii) poor static load-balancing across SMs. Concurrent execution affected throughput due to changes in residencies and hence changed t and total runtime. Co-running kernels and the exact resource split between them also affected t.

3. SCHEDULER AND POLICIES

The Simple Slicing (SS) runtime predictor is an online, concurrent-kernel aware predictor based on Equation 1 that tries to correct for systematic inaccuracies. Its prediction of runtime is an estimate of how much time a kernel would take to complete if it was running from now (i.e. the time at which the prediction is made) to completion, under the current conditions (t, residency and co-runners).

Since t can change as the kernel executes, we split the execution into multiple *slices*. Currently, each slice is demarcated by kernel launches and kernel endings. We assume that t is constant within a slice when predicting timings for blocks in that slice. Finally, as each SM can vary in behaviour, our predictor predicts runtimes for each kernel on a per-SM basis.

$$Pred\_Cycles = Active\_Kernel\_Cycles + \frac{(Total\_Blocks - Done\_Blocks) \times t}{Resident\_Blocks} \quad (2)$$

Total_Blocks and *Done_Blocks* count the number of thread blocks assigned to and completed on a SM respectively. The actual runtime of a kernel so far, *Active_Kernel_Cycles*, is used to correct predictor drift. For ERCBench, the SS predictor is accurate to between 0.48x to 1.08x of actual runtime after observing t for only one thread block.

Scheduler	STP	ANTT	Fairness
FIFO	1.35	3.66	0.19
MPMAX	1.37	2.15	0.36
SRTF	1.59	1.63	0.52
SRTF/ADAPTIVE	1.51	1.64	0.56
SJF	1.82	1.13	0.80

Table 1: Geomean STP, ANTT and Fairness for various scheduling policies. Note that ANTT is a lower-is-better metric.

We evaluate four policies: *Shortest Remaining Time First (SRTF)* which executes a single kernel at a time pre-empting the running kernel if newly arrived kernels are deemed to finish faster (using a sampling run); *SRTF/Adaptive* which statically shares resources between running kernels if it deems SRTF unfair; *Just-in-time MPMax*, a resource-allocation policy; and *FIFO* based on the NVIDIA Fermi Thread Block Scheduler. SRTF and SRTF/Adaptive use estimates of runtime provided by the Simple Slicing predictor to guide their scheduling decisions.

4. EVALUATION

The primary metrics evaluated are are system throughput (STP), average normalized turnaround time (ANTT)and the StrictF metric for fairness. StrictF is defined as the ratio of minimum slowdown to maximum slowdown, with a value of 1 indicating high fairness.

We use all possible 28 2-program workloads from the ERCBench suite running them on GPGPU-Sim simulator (3.2.0) modified to support execution of concurrent kernels. A zero sampling (ZS) experiment provides accurate runtimes to the SRTF to evaluate sensitivity to predictor accuracy. The results are summarized in Table 1 with full discussion in [1].

SRTF is very tolerant of errors in the simple slicing predictor. Zero-sampling improves STP by only 3% to 1.64 and ANTT by 22% to 1.33, thus we find that the inability to preempt running thread blocks is the major performance limiter for GPU scheduling.

5. CONCLUSION

We presented a novel online runtime predictor for GPU kernels that exploited the structure of kernel grids to obtain runtime predictions by observing thread block durations. We used it to build a thread block scheduler with runtime aware policies, SRTF and SRTF/Adaptive, that were found superior to the other realizable policies in terms of system throughput, turnaround time and fairness. Compared to FIFO, SRTF improved STP by 1.18x and ANTT by 2.25x. SRTF also outperformed MPMax with improvements of 1.16x in STP and 1.3x in ANTT. Our SRTF/Adaptive policy achieved the highest fairness among all the realizable policies, 2.95x better than FIFO. Finally, SRTF bridged 49% of the gap between FIFO and SJF, approaching to within 12.64% of SJF's throughput.

6. REFERENCES

[1] S. Pai, R. Govindarajan, and M. J. Thazhuthaveetil, "Preemptive Thread Block Scheduling with Online Structural Runtime Prediction for Concurrent GPGPU Kernels," in *CoRR* abs/1406.6037, 2014.

Using STT-RAM to Enable Energy-Efficient Near-Threshold Chip Multiprocessors*

Xiang Pan
Computer Science and Engineering
The Ohio State University
panxi@cse.ohio-state.edu

Radu Teodorescu
Computer Science and Engineering
The Ohio State University
teodores@cse.ohio-state.edu

ABSTRACT

Near-threshold computing is gaining traction as an energy-efficient solution for power-constrained systems. This paper proposes a novel near-threshold chip multiprocessor design that uses non-volatile spin-transfer torque random access memory (STT-RAM) technology to implement all on-chip caches. This technology has several advantages over SRAM that are particularly useful in near-threshold designs. Primarily, STT-RAM has very low leakage, saving a substantial fraction of the power consumed by near-threshold chips. In addition, the STT-RAM components run at a higher supply voltage to speed up write operations. This has the effect of making cache reads very fast to the point where L1 caches can be shared by several cores, improving performance. Overall, the proposed design saves 11–33% energy compared to an SRAM-based near-threshold system.

1. INTRODUCTION

Power consumption is now a first-class constraint in microprocessor design. Agressive supply voltage (V_{dd}) reduction to close to (or even below) the transistor threshold voltage (V_{th}) has been investigated as an energy-efficient solution for driving future processors with hundreds of cores [2]. Near-threshold operation lowers power consumption by about 100× at a cost of 10× lower operating frequency, potentially improving energy efficiency by an order of magnitude. However, near-threshold operation faces several challenges including decreased reliability, increased sensitivity to process variation, and high relative leakage power.

While dynamic power scales quadratically with supply voltage and linearly with frequency, leakage power only scales linearly with V_{dd}. As a result, leakage power dominates power consumption at low voltages. Most of that leakage is dissipated by on-chip caches, which can account for 20–40% of the total power depending on size.

We present a novel near-threshold chip multiprocessor design that uses non-volatile spin-transfer torque memory (STT-RAM) technology to implement all on-chip caches. This technology has several advantages over SRAM that are particularly useful in near-threshold designs such as low leakage, high density, and high endurance. A drawback of STT-RAM is its higher write latency and energy compared to SRAM. The proposed design runs the STT-RAM components of the chip at a higher supply voltage to speed up write operations. This has the effect of making cache reads very fast to the point where L1 caches can be shared by several cores within a cluster. This eliminates the need for within-cluster cache coherence improving latency and energy. We leverage the shared cache design in our CMP to help mitigate the effects of variation in core frequency.

Evaluation using parallel benchmarks from SPLASH2 and PARSEC shows average energy savings of 11–33% (depending on cache size) and performance improvement of 17% relative to the baseline near-threshold system.

*This work was supported in part by the Defense Advanced Research Projects Agency under the PERFECT (DARPA-BAA-12-24) program and the National Science Foundation under grants CCF-1117799 and CCF-1253933.

PACT'14, August 24–27, 2014, Edmonton, AB, Canada.
ACM 978-1-4503-2809-8/14/08.
http://dx.doi.org/10.1145/2628071.2628132 .

2. NT CMP WITH STT-RAM CACHES

We design an NT CMP processor that replaces SRAM caches with STT-RAM versions. The CMP is organized in clusters that share a last-level cache (L3). The CMP has two externally regulated voltage domains. One domain, which contains most of the cores' logic is set at low NT V_{dd}. The second domain, which includes the entire STT-RAM cache hierarchy and a few logic units, runs at high (nominal) V_{dd}. The main reason for running the STT-RAM domain at nominal V_{dd} is to improve write speed. Since cores will generally run at lower frequencies at NTV, the write latency is relatively smaller (about 3 cycles for a core running at 500MHz).

Shared Cache Hierarchy: The nominal voltage STT-RAM cache has very fast read speeds, on the order of 0.4ns for a 256K L1 cache. This is much faster than needed for single-cycle cache reads at the lower NT frequencies (250MHz-1.25GHz). We exploit this property by sharing a single L1 instruction and an L1 data cache, as well as an L2 cache between all the cores in each cluster. This is achieved by running the shared L1 caches at high frequency (2.5GHz in our experiments - to match the 0.4ns access time) and time-multiplexing requests from the cores in each cluster. This greatly reduces the latency cost of sharing data between threads executing on different cores. It also reduces implementation complexity and energy cost.

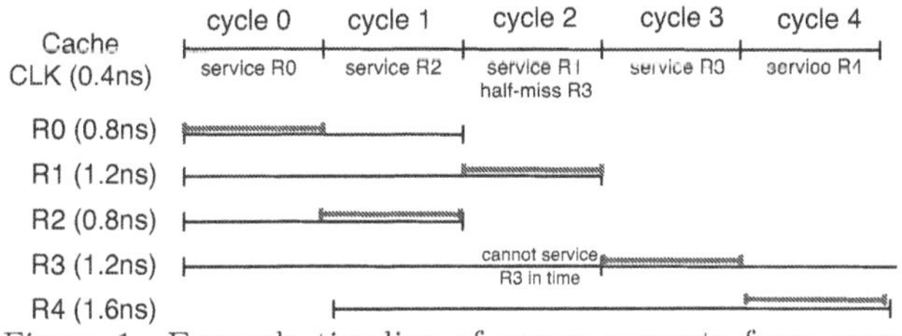

Figure 1: Example timeline of access requests from cores running at different frequencies to a fast shared cache.

Since our design allows cores in the same cluster to run at different frequencies, arbitrating access to the shared cache has to account for the different latency tolerances of each core. To simplify the implementation, the shared cache and all cores run at a frequencies corresponding to integer multipliers of a base clock period. As a result, all cache accesses align at cycle boundaries with the high frequency cache.

Figure 1 shows an example timeline illustrating how multiple access requests (R0-R4) from cores running with different clock periods (0.8ns-1.6ns) are served by the cache. In cycle 0 the cache receives requests R0-R3 from four different cores. For each request the figure includes a line segment that represents the cycle time of the core issuing that request. For instance, R1 comes from a core running at 833MHz (1.2ns clock cycle time). To ensure that, in the event of a hit, the cache responds within a single core clock cycle, the cache must send the data by the end of cache cycle 2.

In cycle 0 we have four new requests out of which the cache can only service one. In this example request R0 is the most urgent, so it will be serviced first, followed by request R2 in cycle 1. In cycle 2 both requests R1 and R3 are expiring but only one can be serviced. The controller chooses to serve R1; for R3 a "half-miss" event will be sent to the processor to indicate that the request could not be fulfilled in a single cycle, but this is not necessarily an L1 miss. Request R3 will be rescheduled to the following cycle.

Mitigating Frequency Variation: The shared cache design significantly reduces thread migration overhead. We leverage this benefit to reduce the effects of core-to-core frequency variation on application performance. In this design we allow cores to run at their best frequency, resulting in heterogeneous performance. To deal with this heterogeneity, we periodically migrate applications between fast and slow cores. The goal is to ensure multiple threads of parallel applications make roughly equal progress even though they are running on cores with different frequencies.

3. EVALUATION

Methodology: We modeled a 64-core CMP with a range of cluster sizes from 4 to 32 cores. Most experiments were conducted with a cluster size of 16 cores, which we found to be optimal. We also experimented with three cache sizes: small, medium, and large. Each core is a dual-issue out-of-order architecture. We used SESC to perform all our simulations and NVSim [1] to get STT-RAM latency and energy. We ran SPLASH-2 and PARSEC.

Power Analysis: Figure 2 shows the reduction in power consumption from the proposed architecture without thread migration (SH-STT-NoMig). We show results for three cache configurations: small, medium, and large. The medium size cache is the most typical one, with about 1MB/core of total cache capacity. We compare to a baseline that uses SRAM

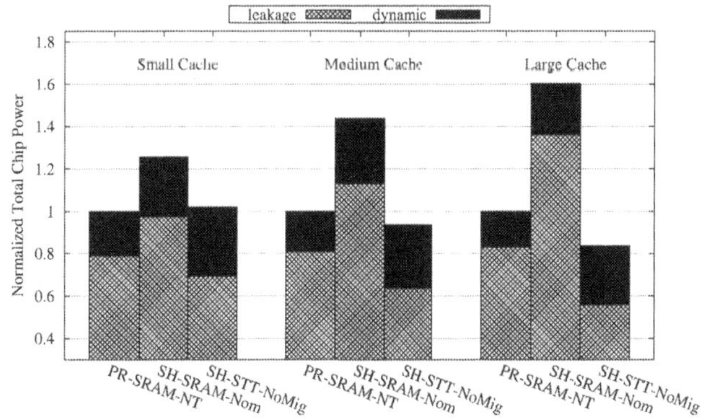

Figure 2: Power reduction of proposed design for three L2/L3 cache sizes: small, medium, and large.

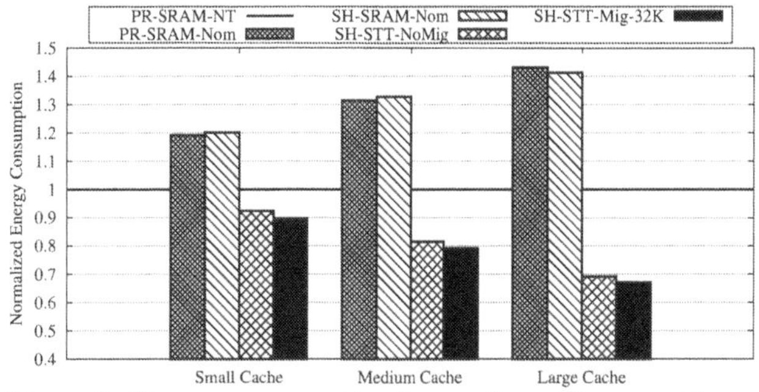

Figure 3: Energy consumption for small, medium, and large L2 and L3 cache configurations.

caches running at NT voltages in a traditional private cache hierarchy (PR-SRAM-NT).

We can see that power is lower for SH-STT-NoMig compared to the baseline in all configurations except for the small cache one. The reduction in total power comes from lower leakage power at the cost of slightly increased dynamic power. For the medium and large configurations the power savings are significant, at 6.4% and 16.3% respectively.

For reference, we also compare to a SRAM design with shared cache running at nominal voltage (SH-SRAM-Nom). SH-SRAM-Nom uses between 20% and 100% more power than SH-STT-NoMig for the three cache sizes. This is due to the much higher leakage power consumed by SRAM.

Energy Analysis: Our proposed design lowers power consumption and reduces execution time. This results in important energy savings. Figure 3 shows that SH-STT-NoMig has 8% to 30% lower energy than the SRAM baseline depending on the cache size configuration. As expected we see much larger energy savings for the large cache configurations. We also show that the PR-SRAM-Nom configuration which uses SRAM caches at nominal V_{dd} uses 20-40% more energy than the NT SRAM baseline (PR-SRAM-NT).

4. REFERENCES

[1] X. Dong, C. Xu, Y. Xie, and N. P. Jouppi, "NVSim: A Circuit-Level Performance, Energy, and Area Model for Emerging Nonvolatile Memory," *IEEE Transactions on Computer-Aided Design of Integrated Circuits and Systems*, vol. 31, no. 7, pp. 994–1007, July 2012.

[2] R. Dreslinski, M. Wieckowski, D. Blaauw, D. Sylvester, and T. Mudge, "Near-Threshold Computing: Reclaiming Moore's Law Through Energy Efficient Integrated Circuits," *Proceedings of the IEEE*, vol. 98, no. 2, pp. 253–266, February 2010.

Protection and Utilization in Shared Cache Through Rationing *

Raj Parihar Jacob Brock† Chen Ding† Michael C. Huang
Dept. of Electrical & Computer Engineering †Dept. of Computer Science
University of Rochester, Rochester, NY 14627, USA
{parihar@ece. jbrock@cs. cding@cs. michael.huang@}rochester.edu

ABSTRACT

Shared cache is generally optimized for overall throughput, fairness, or both. Increasingly in shared environments, *e.g.*, compute clouds, users are unrelated to one another. In such circumstances, an overall gain in throughput does not justify an individual loss. This paper explores a new strategy for conservative sharing, which protects the cache occupancy for individual programs, but still enables full cache sharing whenever there is unused space.

Keywords

Cache management, Protection, Rationing

1. INTRODUCTION

We present a new hardware based mechanism called *cache rationing*. In cache rationing, each core/program is assigned a portion of the shared cache as its ration. Hardware support protects each program's ration from eviction by a peer program, but allows any program to utilize unused cache space in another's ration. Accounting is done using some hardware support: an *access bit* in each cache line tracks whether that line has been used recently, and each core tracks its cache usage using a *ration counter*.

The rationing support also allows hardware-software collaborative caching [6]. In particular, we can add a single "hint bit" to indicate a special memory load and store. A special operation marks the cached data as "evict-me" by clearing the access bit upon the special access. This interface allows collaborative caching and can further improve the performance of rationed cache.

2. CACHE RATIONING

A ration for a CPU core/program is the guaranteed effective size of space in the shared cache that is allocated to the core/program. The ration can be specified by software, *e.g.*, through privileged instructions. Here we show how cache rationing is designed to meet its objectives of protection and utilization at the same time.

Ration Counter.

To implement our rationing mechanism, we require the storage of a *ration counter* for each core. Each cache line needs to store a reference to the ration counter of its owner. The ration counter stores two integer values: its owner's *ration size*, and its owner's *cache usage* (the number of blocks in the cache that it loaded).

The maintenance logic is shown in the pseudo-code as follows. There are three cases: a cache load (upon a miss), an eviction, and a normal access (a hit). At a cache load, we set the owner record to point to the ration counter of the loader and increment it. At an eviction, we decrement the owner's ration counter. The code for a normal access accounts for data sharing by assigning ownership of the accessed block to its most recent user.

```
fetch_at_miss( blk, p )
  blk.owner's_counter = p.ration_counter
  blk.owner's_counter ++
evict( blk )
  blk.owner's_counter --
access_at_hit( blk, p )
  if blk.owner's_counter != p.ration_counter
    blk.owner's_counter --
    blk.owner's_counter = p.ration_counter
    blk.owner's_counter ++
```

Access Bit.

The second hardware extension is the *access bit* for detecting an unused ration. Each block has an access bit, which is set whenever the block is referenced. Periodically, all access bits are reset. A rationed cache block is deemed unused if either it is not owned or the access bit is zero.

Rationing Control.

On a miss to a completely occupied cache, the following algorithm chooses which block to evict:

```
miss( blk, p1 )
  if repl exist s.t. !repl.owned or !repl.accessed
    replace repl with blk
  elsif p1.at_or_over_ration?
    replace LRU block of p1
  else  # p2 over ration
    replace LRU block of p2
```

2.1 Example Illustration and Comparison

Rationing has two goals: cache resource protection, and cache resource utilization. In Figure 1, we show an example for each. Assume we have two cores, each accessing a

*This work is supported by NSF CAREER award CCF-0747324, CCF-1116104, an IBM Fellowship, and by NSFC under the grant 61328201.

PACT'14, August 24–27, 2014, Edmonton, AB, Canada.
ACM 978-1-4503-2809-8/14/08.
http://dx.doi.org/10.1145/2628071.2628120 .

Figure 1: *Top:* Rationing performs as well as partitioning and better than sharing because it protects core 1 against interference by core 2. *Bottom:* Rationing performs as well as sharing and better than partitioning because core 2 is allowed to utilize core 1's ration. Non-compulsory misses are shaded.

separate set of data, and an evenly rationed cache with two blocks for each core.

Figure 1 shows the access trace for each core on the left hand side. It also shows the content of access bits (one for each block) and ration counters (one for each core). In the interleaved execution, if two requests come at the same time, we arbitrarily assume that the cache sees the request from core 1 first. The two examples demonstrate that cache rationing can combine the advantages of cache partitioning and sharing while avoiding their problems.

Protection.

The top example in Figure 1 shows resource protection. In this case, core 1 uses 2 blocks, which it can hold entirely within its ration. In free-for-all sharing, data from core 2 can evict data used by core 1. In contrast, the partitioned cache and the rationed cache do not permit core 2 to intrude on the ration of core 1. Due to the lack of protection, the free-for-all policy causes the most misses. Partitioning and rationing perform equally well by providing resource protection. However, the mechanisms are different. As the next example shows, rationing permits sharing.

Utilization.

The bottom example in Figure 1 shows cache utilization. If core 1 uses just 1 block, and core 2 uses 3, fixed partitioning would under-utilize the space partitioned for core 1. Free-for-all sharing and rationing, in contrast, can fully utilize the 4 cache blocks for the 4 program blocks. In Figure 2, we show the comparison of partitioning, free-for-all and rationing for *eon* co-run with SPEC 2000 applications. It is evident that rationing never slows down *eon* and often achieves good speed up for the co-running program. In contrast, partitioning never achieves any speed up and free-for-all speeds up programs at the cost of slowing down *eon*. Detailed results are included in the technical report [4].

2.2 Interaction with Other Optimizations

In this section, we discuss the ease of integration of rationing with some of the other designs. A number of processors provide special load/store instructions that a program can use to influence hardware cache management [2, 5, 6, 7]. Such cache hints can be used to mark accesses whose data will have no chance of reuse before eviction (this can be done using compiler analysis [1, 6]). Taking the hints, the hardware can choose not to cache those data.

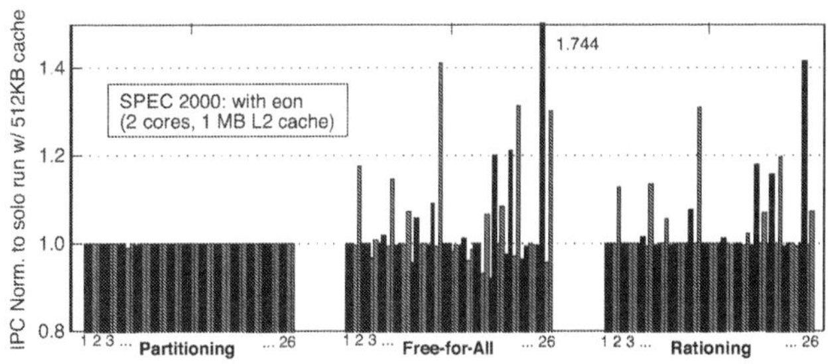

Figure 2: SPEC 2000 benchmarks co-run with the *eon* benchmark. The first bar in each pair represents *eon*. While free-for-all sharing maximizes utilization, it punishes *eon* by allowing its peer to hog the cache.

Regardless of what the software does, it needs the hardware instruction in order to mark a data block and tell the hardware to replace it before replacing other blocks. Such an instruction can be readily supported by cache rationing by zeroing the access bit when a hint bit suggests that a block should not be kept in cache.

As an example, consider two cores sharing a 4-block cache. Let the access traces be **xyzxyz...** for one core and **abcabc...** for the other. With equal rationing, neither core has enough cache to obtain any reuse. However, with cache hints, the software can free up cache space by zeroing every other access bit. In this case, the non-compulsory miss ratio can be shown to be reduced from 1 to 1/2. In [3], it is shown that a hint-based solution can achieve optimal caching.

3. SUMMARY

This paper presents rationing for shared-cache management that protects the ration of each program while at the same time finds and utilizes unused ration among the co-run programs. The new support can be added on top of existing cache architecture with minimal additional hardware. When an application does not use all its ration, rationing achieves good utilization similar to free-for-all cache sharing. When a program exerts strong interference, rationing provides good protection similar to cache partitioning. In addition, rationing provides an integrated design for cache sharing and software-hardware collaboration.

4. REFERENCES

[1] K. Beyls and E. H. D'Hollander. Generating cache hints for improved program efficiency. *Journal of Systems Architecture*, 51(4):223–250, 2005.

[2] J. Brock, X. Gu, B. Bao, and C. Ding. Pacman: Program-assisted cache management. In *Proceedings of ISMM*, 2013.

[3] X. Gu, T. Bai, Y. Gao, C. Zhang, R. Archambault, and C. Ding. P-OPT: Program-directed optimal cache management. In *Proceedings of the LCPC Workshop*, pages 217–231, 2008.

[4] R. Parihar, J. Brock, C. Ding, and M. C. Huang. Protection, utilization and collaboration in shared cache through rationing. Technical Report TR-995, University of Rochester, Nov 2013.

[5] S. Rus, R. Ashok, and D. X. Li. Automated locality optimization based on the reuse distance of string operations. In *Proceedings of CGO*, pages 181–190, 2011.

[6] Z. Wang, K. S. McKinley, A. L.Rosenberg, and C. C. Weems. Using the compiler to improve cache replacement decisions. In *Proceedings of PACT*, Charlottesville, Virginia, 2002.

[7] X. Yang, S. M. Blackburn, D. Frampton, J. B. Sartor, and K. S. McKinley. Why nothing matters: the impact of zeroing. In *Proceedings of OOPSLA*, pages 307–324, 2011.

Automatic Parallelism through Macro Dataflow in High-level Array Languages

Pushkar Ratnalikar
pratnali@cs.indiana.edu

Arun Chauhan*
achauhan@cs.indiana.edu

School of Informatics and Computing
Indiana University
Bloomington, IN

ABSTRACT

Dataflow computation is a powerful paradigm for parallel computing that is especially attractive on modern machines with multiple avenues for parallelism. However, adopting this model has been challenging as neither hardware- nor language-based approaches have been successful, except, in specialized contexts. We argue that general-purpose array languages, such as MATLAB, are good candidates for automatic translation to *macro* dataflow-style execution, where each array operation naturally maps to a *macro* dataflow operation and the model can be efficiently executed on contemporary multicore architecture. We support our argument with a fully automatic compilation technique to translate MATLAB programs to dynamic dataflow graphs that are capable of handling unbounded structured control flow. These graphs can be executed on multicore machines in an event driven fashion with the help of a runtime system built on top of Intel's Threading Building Blocks (TBB). By letting each task itself be data parallel, we are able to leverage existing data-parallel libraries and utilize parallelism at multiple levels. Our experiments on a set of benchmarks show speedups of up to 18x using our approach, over the original data-parallel code on a machine with two 16-core processors.

Categories and Subject Descriptors

D.3.4 [**Programming Languages**]: Processor—*compilers, Run-time environments*

Keywords

MATLAB, task-parallelism, dataflow computation

1. INTRODUCTION

Exploiting parallelism at multiple levels afforded by modern computers continues to be a challenge. A substantial amount of research effort has been directed at this challenge in the past. One possible solution is the use of dataflow paradigm of programming [2]. Unfortunately, neither specialized hardware nor programming languages have gained much popularity.

MATLAB provides a natural syntax for writing code that closely corresponds to the underlying mathematical formulations. Array syntax in MATLAB helps in highlighting fine-grained data parallelism in the program through vector statements. Indeed, MATLAB ships with multi-threaded libraries that optimize several types of vector operations. However, parallelism across statements is not expolited.

Imperative languages, such as MATLAB, operate in the realm of Von Neumann model. Dataflow-style execution provides a compelling alternative that needs to only respect the partial ordering imposed by data and control dependencies. This means parallelism across program statements can be exploited. The challenge is to implement this on mainstream hardware. This translates to two main problems:

1) Partitioning the program into macro operations, or tasks, that maximize parallelism while minimizing the overhead per task; and
2) Scheduling the tasks so that all the control- and data-dependencies in the original program are satisfied.

We present a heuristic solution for the first problem by treating array statements as anchors and replicating the required scalar statements (involving only simple scalar computations) to satisfy data dependencies. The approach is practicable in typical MATLAB programs due to the large majority of array statements that constitute the overwhelming bulk of the computation. The second problem is solved by creating a carefully orchestrated set of tasks that dynamically spawn new tasks, as needed, based on the control dependencies in original program. This makes it possible to handle loops with unbounded iteration counts (while loops). Individual tasks are free to utilize the underlying data-parallel libraries.

2. APPROACH

We have prototyped our strategy for MATLAB. Our compiler automatically translates MATLAB to task-parallel C++ code that uses a runtime system built on top of TBB for dataflow-style execution and Armadillo C++, a data-parallel linear algebra library.

The compiler uses type inference to identify array statements and scalar statements. Scalar statements are replicated around array statements, as needed. The loops are canonicalized by inserting counters to track iteration counts.

*Currently at Google Inc.

PACT'14, August 24–27, 2014, Edmonton, AB, Canada.
ACM 978-1-4503-2809-8/14/08.
http://dx.doi.org/10.1145/2628071.2628131.

Since the statements updating the counters are scalar they also get replicated with the tasks formed out of array statements in the loop body.

The flow of data between statements across control flow join points needs to be predicated on the control-flow conditions in the original program. These conditions, computed using a control dependence graph, usually get replicated (since these are usually scalar expressions) with the relevant tasks. Thus, we do not need any special *gate tasks* to control the flow of data, which is an important difference between our strategy and the past approaches [3, 4, 1].

Strict adherence to dataflow model using *single assignment* semantics eliminates all but true dependencies. While that can improve parallelism in principle, it can introduce unacceptably high data copying costs for arrays. We use a hybrid approach where the scalar variables are passed by value and the array variables are passed by reference, dramatically reducing data copying at the cost of reduced parallelism across tasks.

Our runtime system is built on top of Intel TBB. Its primary job is to enable dataflow style execution of code and garbage collection. It keeps track of inputs to tasks and triggers their execution when all the inputs are available. It also maintains a *reference count* for each array and garbage collects it when the count drops to zero.

3. EXPERIMENTAL EVALUATION

We evaluated our approach on four beanchmarks, including `Wave Cross Covariance`, a DSP kernel; `QR`, a QR decomposition kernel; `NBody 1D`, which performs n-body simulation; and `ComputeNew`, which is a kernel in a molecular dynamics application. Experiments were run in MATLAB version 2013a on a dual 16-core AMD Opteron 6380 (2.5 GHz, 64 GB DDR3 memory,16 MB L3 cache).

In Figure 1 "Task-Parallel" indicates the speedups achieved using our approach over baseline MATLAB code run in multi-threaded data-parallel mode, for increasing input sizes. In order to isolate the gains from translating to C++ we ran the code with a single task, represented by "Data-Parallel", so that only intra-task data-parallelism is utilized, as in the original MATLAB code. Our hybrid approach triumphs over the code where only data-parallelism is leveraged and also multi-threaded MATLAB code. Some of the gain comes from translation to C++, as the "Data-Parallel" line indicates. However, in case of `ComputeNew`, an irregular computation involving operations with logical indexing, MATLAB performs better than "Data-Parallel" C++ code. This is due to the inefficient implementation of logical indexing in Armadillo C++. Figure 2 gives the number of concurrently executing tasks for each of the selected benchmarks. Lower sub-plot magnifies the portion of upper sub-plot between red verticle lines. The number of concurrently executing tasks is consistently high and is indicative of latent parallelism between program statements, which our approach is able to leverage.

4. CONCLUSION AND FUTURE WORK

In this paper we have shown a fully automatic method of translating imperative programs written in MATLAB to utilize the latent task-parallelism within the applications, in addition to the data parallelism that is obvious in the array statements. We have shown that this approach can be implemented using dataflow-style execution using existing

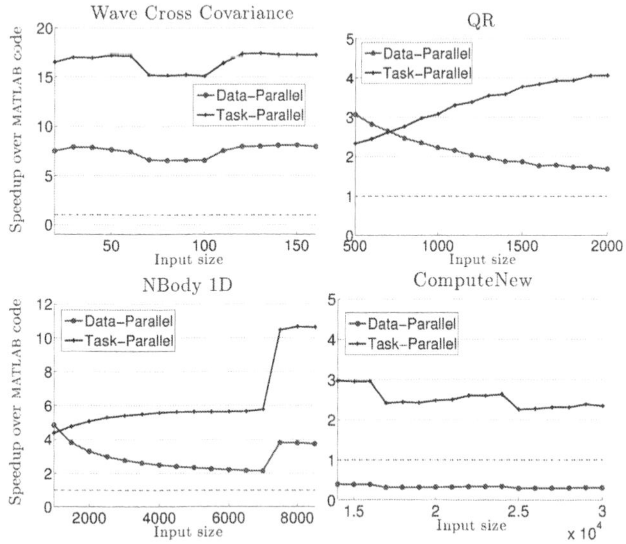

Figure 1: Performance against input sizes of 4 selected benchmarks on a 32-core machine.

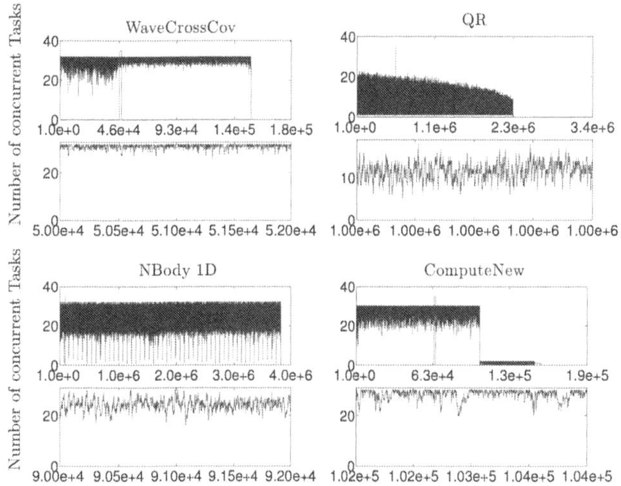

Figure 2: Concurrently Executing Tasks

task libraries. Possible future work includes more sophisticated algorithms to identify tasks and extending the execution model to heterogeneous environments such as GPUs.

5. REFERENCES

[1] M. Beck, R. Johnson, and K. Pingali. From control flow to dataflow. *Journal for Parallel and Distributed Computing*, 1991.

[2] W. M. Johnston, J. R. P. Hanna, and R. J. Millar. Advances in dataflow programming languages. *ACM Comput. Surv.*, 36(1):1–34, Mar. 2004.

[3] K. J. Ottenstein, R. A. Ballance, and A. B. MacCabe. The program dependence web: A representation supporting control-, data-, and demand-driven interpretation of imperative languages. *SIGPLAN Not.*, 25(6):257–271, June 1990.

[4] P. Tu and D. Padua. Gated SSA-based demand-driven symbolic analysis for parallelizing compilers. In *Proceedings of the 9th International Conference on Supercomputing*, ICS '95, pages 414–423, New York, NY, USA, 1995. ACM.

A Runtime Support Mechanism for Fast Mode Switching of a Self-Morphing Core for Power Efficiency

Sudarshan Srinivasan, Nithesh Kurella,
Israel Koren, Sandip Kundu
ECE Department,
University of Massachusetts Amherst,
MA, USA
{ssrinivasan, kurellalaks, koren,
kundu}@ecs.umass.edu

Rance Rodrigues
NVIDIA
Beaverton, Oregon, USA
rance.rodrigues@gmail.com

ABSTRACT

Asymmetric multicore processors (AMPs) consist of cores executing the same ISA, but differing in microarchitectural resources, performance, and power consumption. As the computational bottleneck of a workload shifts from one resource to the next, during its course of execution, reassigning it to the core where it runs most efficiently can improve the overall energy efficiency. Simulation studies show that the performance bottlenecks can shift frequently, often within a few thousands cycles. With frequent core hooping, the overhead of thread migration becomes significant. To mitigate this overhead, we propose a morphable core that can assume one of four possible configurations to address the dominant performance bottlenecks, while retaining the same cache and registers. This way the architectural state remains intact while the morphable core is reconfigured in resources and frequency. We then implement a runtime scheme to decide the best configuration to run on and switch configuration as necessary. Simulation results indicate that on the average, the proposed scheme results in performance/watt improvement of 41%.

Categories and Subject Descriptors

C.1.3 [**Processor Architectures**]: Adaptable architectures

Keywords

Asymmetric multi-core processors; Hardware Performance Counters; Core Morphing

1. INTRODUCTION

Previous research on Asymmetric Multi-core Processors (AMPs) has identified multiple opportunities for exploiting the processors' asymmetry. A key to AMP efficiency is having a mix of core types with different power and performance characteristics so that a program phase of an application is mapped to a core which achieves the best energy efficiency. [2].

Most AMP design references feature a high performance Out-of Order (OOO) core combined with a smaller low performance and energy efficient In-Order (InO) core. ARM's big.Little^{TM}is an example of such a design [1]. However, a workload's performance on a particular core type depends on larger set of processor resources since workloads are diverse in nature. Thus, a larger set of diverse cores that could address the shifting resource needs during various program phases of an application is needed.

Navada *et al.* explored non-monotonic AMP cores that are specifically designed to address bottlenecks that result in poor performance [4]. Their set of AMP cores consist of a narrow core which suits application with low ILP, a large window core for application phases which have window bottlenecks (reorder buffer, issue queue), a wider core for phases that have width bottlenecks (fetch and issue width) and finally, a normal super-scalar OOO core to target most common scenarios. Core configurations similar to these four core types form the base for our work in this paper.

Recent research has shown that power savings opportunities can often be found in much shorter time scales, typically measured in thousands of instructions[3]. To support such fine grain switching, self-morphing core architectures where an OOO core dynamically morphs into an InO core during run time have been proposed [3]. Morphing was considered only between two extreme architectures, i.e., a wide issue OOO core and an InO core. However, as discussed previously, the resource bottlenecks or excesses can be quite diverse thus missing out on important power performance optimization opportunities. In this paper we present a novel morphing architecture in which the core dynamically switches between four OOO core execution modes of varying fetch and issue width, buffer sizes (IQ, LSQ, ROB) and clock frequency.

2. SELF MORPHING ARCHITECTURE

Our self morphing architecture consist of a single core whose resources are banked; they can be turned on or off and the frequency can be raised or lowered to configure the core to each of the four core modes shown in Table I. Our baseline execution mode is an average OOO core (AC) that will be dynamically morphed into one out of the other three modes, namely, wider core (WC), narrow core(NC) and larger window core (LW) during run time. The four modes have dif-

PACT'14, August 24–27, 2014, Edmonton, AB, Canada.
ACM 978-1-4503-2809-8/14/08 .
http://dx.doi.org/10.1145/2628071.2628124

Table 1: Architecture parameters of the four core modes.

CoreType	ClockPeriod(ns)	Buffer size (IQ,LSQ,ROB)	Width (fetch,issue)
AC	0.6	32,128,128	3,4
NC	0.5	32,64,64	2,2
LW	0.7	48,128,384	4,4
WC	0.7	32,128,128	6,6

ferent buffer sizes, varying fetch and issue widths and also run at different frequencies. Decoding units are also subsequently powered on/off when fetch and issue width are resized. Still, all four modes have the same cache sizes with I-cache size of 64KB, D-cache size of 64KB and the L2 cache size of 2MB. This allows us to resize resources dynamically leaving the content of the cache intact, which in turn allows fine grain switching.

3. RUNTIME SUPPORT FOR SELF MORPHING

The computational resource requirements of an application change during its execution and are not available beforehand. Hence, an online mechanism that is computationally fast and reasonably accurate, is required in guiding the application to the right core configuration at run time. The decision to select the most appropriate core configuration for the current application phase is made by computing the throughput/watt for each of the configurations and selecting the one that provides the highest throughput/watt (measured in IPS^2/Watt). To calculate the throughput/watt, we use a hardware performance counters based linear regression model to estimate the power and performance on each of the different configurations. The counters used in this work consist of IPC, Cache activity, Branch activity, Instructions committed and Buffer-full stalls. Our results indicate that we can predit power and performance in each of the core modes with reasonable accurancy with average errors of 15% and 8% for predicitng power and IPC, respectively.

4. MORPHING OVERHEAD

Switching between one morph core to another is based on the IPS^2/Watt metric. The decision to morph from one core mode to another is taken if the IPS^2/Watt computed for one of the other three core modes is greater by at least 5% than that for the currently used core mode. When a core mode switch happens, we drain the core pipeline and resize the core buffers and frequency (depending on the core we are morphing into) and start executing instructions in the newly morphed core. Fine grain DVFS with on-chip regulator is employed to switch voltage/frequency at fine granularity with an overhead of 200 cycles. The overhead of banking for ROB, IQ and LSQ is taken to be 10 cycles to power off a particular bank. Once the bank to be turned off is selected, we wait until the existing instructions in this bank has committed before switching off that bank. On average, this morphing overhead has been estimated to be 500 cycles.

5. RESULTS

In this section we evaluate our proposed self morphing scheme. The core parameters considered are listed in Table

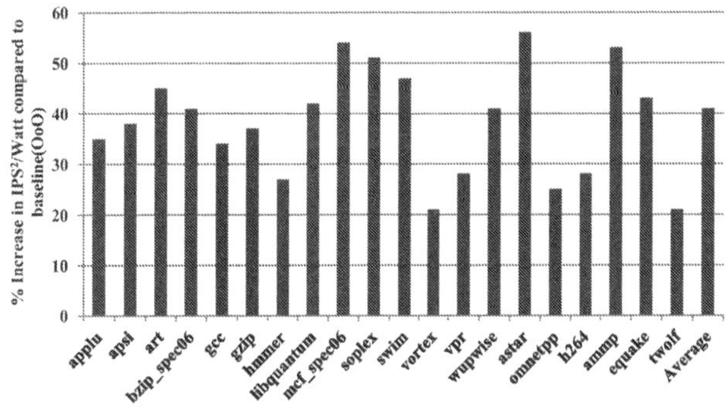

Figure 1: % Improvement in IPS^2/Watt of proposed self-morphing scheme with 4 modes

I. We use gem5 as our cycle accurate simulator with integrated McPAT modeling framework to compute the power of the cores and caches. We evaluate our proposed scheme using the SPEC benchmark suite. The benchmarks were compiled using gcc for Alpha ISA with -O2 optimization. All our evaluations were carried out by running each benchmark for 2 billion instructions after skipping the first 2 billion.

The percentage improvement in IPS^2/Watt of our proposed self-morphing scheme with four core types when compared to the baseline where applications are run completely on the Average core type (AC) is shown in Figure 1. On average we achieve IPS^2/Watt benefits of 41% and performance improvement of 10% compared to the baseline.

6. CONCLUSION

In this paper, we presented a self-morphing core that can morph into one of four different core types. The selected core types are suited to address most common performance bottlenecks found in SPEC benchmarks. Based on a small number of performance counters, a novel co-designed runtime system predicts the performance and power across all core modes based on statistics obtained from the current core type (whichever it may be) and uses this information to morph into the core type that offers the best energy efficiency. Our results indicate that we can achieve an average throughput/watt gain of 41% over executing on a standard core.

7. REFERENCES

[1] P. Greenhalgh. Big.little processing with arm cortex-a15 and cortex-a7.

[2] R. Kumar et al. Single-isa heterogeneous multi-core architectures: The potential for processor power reduction. In *Microarchitecture, 2003. MICRO-36. Proceedings. 36th Annual IEEE/ACM International Symposium on*, pages 81–92. IEEE, 2003.

[3] A. Lukefahr et al. Composite cores: Pushing heterogeneity into a core. In *Proceedings of the 2012 45th Annual IEEE/ACM International Symposium on Microarchitecture*. IEEE Computer Society, 2012.

[4] S. Navada et al. A unified view of non-monotonic core selection and application steering in heterogeneous chip multiprocessors. In *Proceedings of the 22nd international conference on Parallel architectures and compilation techniques*, pages 133–144. IEEE Press, 2013.

Rollback-Free Value Prediction with Approximate Loads

Bradley Thwaites Gennady Pekhimenko§ Amir Yazdanbakhsh Jongse Park Girish Mururu
Hadi Esmaeilzadeh Onur Mutlu§ Todd Mowry§
Georgia Institute of Technology §Carnegie Mellon University

{bthwaites,a.yazdanbakhsh,jspark,girishmururu}@gatech.edu gpekhime@cs.cmu.edu
hadi@cc.gatech.edu onur@cmu.edu tcm@cs.cmu.edu

ABSTRACT

This paper demonstrates how to utilize the inherent error resilience of a wide range of applications to mitigate the memory wall—the discrepancy between core and memory speed. We define a new microarchitecturally-triggered approximation technique called rollback-free value prediction. This technique predicts the value of safe-to-approximate loads when they miss in the cache without tracking mispredictions or requiring costly recovery from misspeculations. This technique mitigates the memory wall by allowing the core to continue computation without stalling for long-latency memory accesses. Our detailed study of the quality trade-offs shows that with a modern out-of-order processor, average 8% (up to 19%) performance improvement is possible with 0.8% (up to 1.8%) average quality loss on an approximable subset of SPEC CPU 2000/2006.

1 Introduction

Due to diminishing gains from CMOS scaling and the overwhelming growth of data, a growing body of recent work [6, 9, 11, 1, 10, 4, 8, 13, 3, 15] investigates approximation techniques in general-purpose computing that trade *Quality of Result* (QoR) for gains in performance and efficiency. These techniques exploit the inherent error resiliency of a wide range of applications including web search, data analytics, image processing, cyber-physical systems, recognition, and optimization to improve performance and efficiency through approximation. Instances of these approximation techniques include (i) voltage over-scaling [9, 4]; (ii) loop perforation [15]; (iii) loop early termination [3]; (iv) computation substitution [11, 8, 2, 1, 3]; (v) limited fault recovery [6]; and (vi) approximate storage design [10, 13]. We define a new technique, rollback-free value prediction, which operates at the fine granularity of a single load instruction. We exclusively focus on mitigating the effects of cache misses through exploiting application error-tolerance. A unique characteristic of our technique is its trigger. Microarchitectural events, namely cache misses, invoke the approximation rather than explicit software invocation as in other techniques. Despite these differences, our technique may be effectively combined with prior work on approximation due to its concentrated and limited use of approximation. Rollback-free value prediction speculates on the value of an *approximate load* that misses in the cache, allowing computation to continue with speculative values without rollback from mispredictions[1]. We define approximate loads as instructions that with low probability may return values other than what is stored in the memory. Thus, due to the approximate load semantics, tracking mispredictions and costly rollback from misspeculations is avoided. However, our design principle for rollback-free value prediction is to restrain the effects of approximation to low levels and only utilize approximation when it is most beneficial.

Following this design principle, we have identified the following three challenges that must be addressed in order to effectively realize the rollback-free value prediction approximation technique.

(i) Targeting performance-critical and safe loads. A framework needs to be developed that only employs rollback-free value prediction on performance-critical loads. To this end, we develop a profile-driven approach that identifies a limited set of performance-critical loads as candidates for rollback-free prediction. The profiling pass identifies which loads cause the majority of cache misses, and which ones may be approximated at low quality cost. We then utilize explicit programmer oversight to only approximate loads whose approximation will never lead to program crashes (Section 2).

(ii) Utilizing fast-learning load value predictors. Due to the single-load granularity of our technique, the prediction mechanisms should be light weight and fast learning. We investigate using two-delta [7] and stride [14] predictors and show that two-delta provides significant performance gains with very low quality degradation.

(iii) Integrating the rollback-free prediction in the architecture. Both low-overhead microarchitectural and architectural extensions are needed to intercept cache misses for approximate loads and continue execution. Section 3 provides details about our design.

2 Profile-Directed Approximation

Providing safety guarantees. Any viable approximation technique needs to provide strict guarantees that the program will only experience graceful quality degradation without catastrophic failure. We define a safety violation as an execution which, due to approximation, leads to a catastrophic failure such as segmentation fault, invalid jump address, memory out of bounds error, or infinite loop. As other approximation techniques [9, 3, 13, 12], the programmer is responsible for identifying the safe-to-approximate loads through programming language constructs. However, to reduce programmer effort, our profiling pass presents an initial set of performance-critical loads to the programmer as described below.

Targeting performance-critical loads. To limit the undesirable effects of approximation to the lowest level, we develop an automated compile-time profiling pass that consists of two stages. The first stage determines the set of load instructions which account for the largest portion of cache misses. As prior work has shown [5] and our own experiments corroborate, a few load instructions tend to produce a large majority of cache misses. Since our prediction hardware has limited resources, we select as candidates only those loads which can provide significant benefit with approximation, typically 15-20 of them. The second profiling pass further prunes this subset by examining whether individually approximating these candidate loads will lead to significant quality degradation or increase in runtime. The profiler observes the resulting output quality and eliminates any candidate load which significantly degrades quality or causes an increase in runtime relative to a fully precise baseline.

[1]The work in [16] explores recovery-free value prediction for prefetch generation, but the speculative values never affect the microarchitectural state as in our technique.

PACT'14, August 24–27, 2014, Edmonton, AB, Canada.
ACM 978-1-4503-2809-8/14/08.
http://dx.doi.org/10.1145/2628071.2628110 .

3 Rollback Free Value Prediction

While profiling identifies approximate loads at compile time, the architecture support enables rollback-free prediction at runtime.

ISA support and semantics. To avoid exposing memory subsystem or value prediction details to the compiler, we define a probabilistic semantic for approximate loads and provide a simple hardware/software interface. For all load instructions in the ISA, we introduce a dual *approximate* variant. A bit in the opcode identifies whether the load is precise or approximate. Semantically, executing the load.approx Reg<id>, MEMORY<address> instruction will assign Reg<id> the exact value stored in MEMORY<address> with probability p, and an arbitrary value with probability $1 - p$. In practice, p is usually high with our approximation technique for two reasons. First, our technique is only triggered by cache misses. Loads which hit in the cache will always return the correct value, a common case for modern architectures with high cache hit rate. Second, even when a cache miss happens, the value predictor can predict the correct value or at least a reasonably close value. These effects inherently limit the undesirable effects of approximation.

Microarchitecture integration. When an approximate load misses in the cache, the value predictor intercepts the event and generates a prediction value. The predictor writes this value to the physical register, then sends a broadcast message to the reservation stations. The approximate load then commits normally. However, the data request is still sent to the memory.[2] When the data for an approximate load arrives, the core updates the prediction tables without checking the status of the approximate load that generated the request.

Predictor design. We examine both two-delta [7] and stride value predictors [14]. Two-delta is an extension of the stride predictor in which the stride value is only updated when the same stride is observed twice or more in a row. Although we used these predictors, our technique is independent of the specific prediction mechanism. Since our profiling pass produces a small number of load instructions for approximation, we use a prediction table with only 256 entries (6 KB overhead). The table index is a hash of the load PC.

4 Methodology and Results

We use an approximable subset of SPEC CPU 2000/2006 to evaluate our technique. Similar to [15], we define a quantitative metric to understand the quality degradation. For each SPEC benchmark, we compare the relevant numerical outputs and compute the normalized root mean square error. For profiling and quality evaluations, we use Valgrind with Cachegrind. For performance evaluations, we use the Marssx86 cycle-accurate simulator. The core is modeled after the Nehalem microarchitecture. The baseline memory system includes a 32 KB L1 cache and a 2 MB L2 with a 200-cycle memory latency. In modern processors, the LLC cache size is usually 2 MB × number of cores. Thus, a 2 MB LLC is used for our single core experiments. We sweep LLC size and issue width to investigate how our technique performs under increased memory pressure. We use Simpoint to identify the representative application phases.

Figure 1 shows how different value prediction mechanisms, in particular stride [14] and two-delta prediction, affect quality of results. With stride prediction, the average quality loss is 10.8%, but with two-delta prediction, the average loss is reduced to 0.8%. Figure 2 shows the application speedup for each configuration studied. We observe that rollback-free value prediction improves application performance with the default system (first bar) by as much as 19.2% (geometric mean: 8.1%). As expected, the observed benefits are inversely correlated with the degree of memory pressure (e.g., the smaller the cache and/or the larger the width, the higher the benefits). The highest average improvement is 15.2% (for 512KB and 4-wide configuration), up to a maximum of 40.1%.

[2]Our current scheme merely targets reducing effective memory latency. However, we are exploring designs that drop a certain fraction of the requests to reduce memory bandwidth requirements.

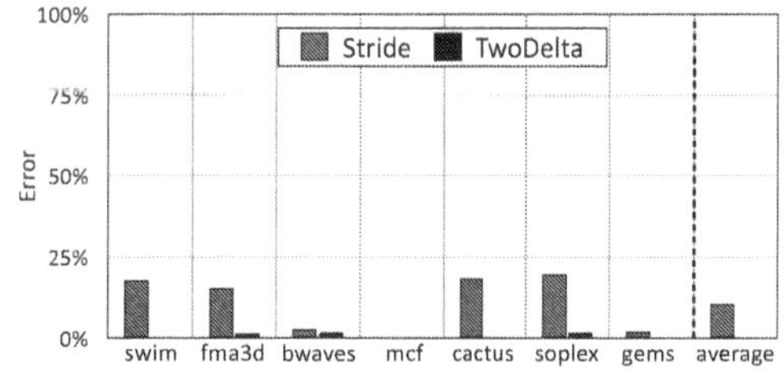

Figure 1: Error with stride and two-delta predictors.

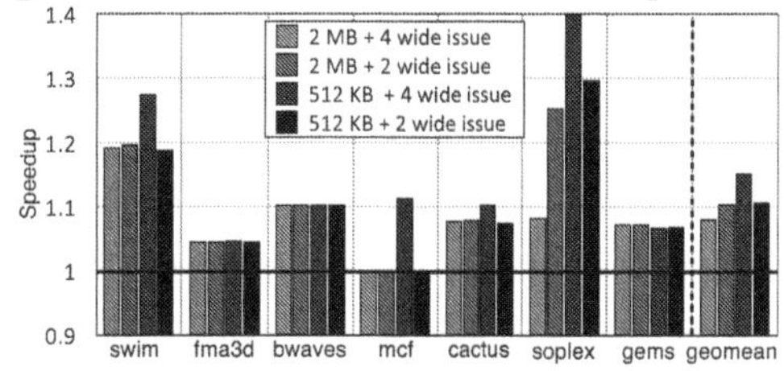

Figure 2: Speedup for different configurations with two-delta prediction (baseline: no value prediction).

5 Conclusions

In the emerging landscape of computing in which mobile and cloud services aim to provide a more personalized experience for users, applications with error resiliency are becoming dominant. Leveraging this error resiliency, we introduce a new rollback-free value prediction technique to mitigate the memory wall. Our technique represents a new class of approximation techniques that are triggered by microarchitectural events, e.g., cache misses. The microarchitectural trigger and our profiling technique limit the undesirable effects of approximation to small levels, while delivering significant gains in performance. Our sensitivity studies confirmed that when the memory subsystem is under pressure, even greater benefits are possible. These results suggest that our technique will be even more effective as we enter the era of processing overwhelming amounts of data that put more pressure on the memory subsystem.

References

[1] C. Alvarez *et al.*, "Fuzzy memoization for floating-point multimedia applications," *IEEE Trans. Comput.*, 2005.

[2] R. S. Amant *et al.*, "General-purpose code acceleration with limited-precision analog computation," in *ISCA*, 2014.

[3] W. Baek and T. M. Chilimbi, "Green: A framework for supporting energy-conscious programming using controlled approximation," in *PLDI*, 2010.

[4] L. N. Chakrapani *et al.*, "Ultra-efficient (embedded) SOC architectures based on probabilistic CMOS (PCMOS) technology," in *DATE*, 2006.

[5] J. D. Collins *et al.*, "Speculative precomputation: Long-range prefetching of delinquent loads," in *ISCA*, 2001.

[6] M. de Kruijf *et al.*, "Relax: An architectural framework for software recovery of hardware faults," in *ISCA*, 2010.

[7] R. J. Eickemeyer and S. Vassiliadis, "A load-instruction unit for pipelined processors," *IBM JRD*, 1993.

[8] H. Esmaeilzadeh *et al.*, "Neural acceleration for general-purpose approximate programs," in *MICRO*, 2012.

[9] H. Esmaeilzadeh *et al.*, "Architecture support for disciplined approximate programming," in *ASPLOS*, 2012.

[10] S. Liu *et al.*, "Flikker: Saving refresh-power in mobile devices through critical data partitioning," in *ASPLOS*, 2011.

[11] M. Samadi *et al.*, "Sage: self-tuning approximation for graphics engines," in *MICRO*, 2013.

[12] A. Sampson *et al.*, "EnerJ: Approximate data types for safe and general low-power computation," in *PLDI*, 2011.

[13] A. Sampson *et al.*, "Approximate storage in solid-state memories," in *MICRO*, 2013.

[14] Y. Sazeides and J. E. Smith, "The predictability of data values," in *MICRO*, 1997.

[15] S. Sidiroglou-Douskos *et al.*, "Managing performance vs. accuracy trade-offs with loop perforation," in *FSE*, 2011.

[16] H. Zhou and T. M. Conte, "Enhancing memory level parallelism via recovery-free value prediction," in *ICS*, 2003.

This work was supported in part by a gift from Google.

Measuring Flexibility in Single-ISA Heterogeneous Processors

Erik Tomusk Christophe Dubach Michael O'Boyle
University of Edinburgh, UK
{E.Tomusk, christophe.dubach, mob} @ed.ac.uk

ABSTRACT

Single-ISA heterogeneous processors are a promising method for enabling runtime power flexibility. Low-priority programs run on low-power cores, and high-priority programs run on high-power cores. In recent years, a number of methods for heterogeneous design space exploration have emerged. These methods search the design space for Pareto frontiers of cores that are optimal for power and speed. We demonstrate that a heterogeneous processor cannot be composed by simply selecting some cores from a Pareto-optimal set; the selection must give even coverage of the design space. We then define a metric—*clumpiness*—for measuring how well selected heterogeneous cores cover the design space.

Categories and Subject Descriptors

C.4 [**Performance of Systems**]: Performance attributes, Design studies

Keywords

Clumpiness; heterogeneous design space exploration; single-ISA; Pareto-optimal

1. INTRODUCTION

Single-ISA heterogeneous processors are already available in the consumer space [4], and their design is the topic of ongoing research. A common method of design space exploration is to find a set of cores that is Pareto-optimal for power and speed [5, 8]. These methods do not offer guidance on which cores should be selected; they expect the designer to select cores from the Pareto-optimal set using external criteria. In section 2, we demonstrate that simply selecting some cores from a Pareto-optimal set will not guarantee that the selection makes effective use of heterogeneity. Then in section 3, we propose a metric for *clumpiness* to quantify the intuitive notion that a good selection of heterogeneous cores will provide uniform coverage of the design space.

2. MOTIVATING EXAMPLE

Given two different selections of heterogeneous cores, it should be possible to determine which is better. Consider

PACT'14, August 24–27, 2014, Edmonton, AB, Canada.
ACM 978-1-4503-2809-8/14/08.
http://dx.doi.org/10.1145/2628071.2628125.

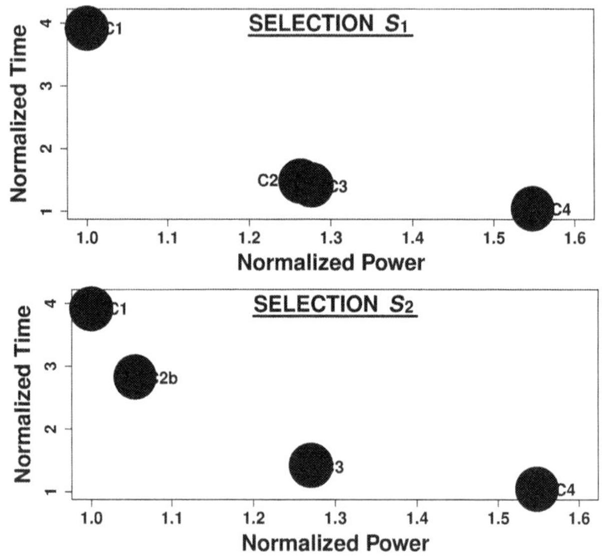

Figure 1: Two possibilities for selecting four Pareto-optimal cores for *AES*. The axes are normalized—1 on the time axis is fastest, 4 is four times slower, etc. Selection S_1 shows two cores clumped together.

figure 1. Two possible ways of selecting four Pareto-optimal cores are shown. Both selection S_1 (top) and selection S_2 (bottom) contain cores *C1*, *C3*, and *C4*. S_1 also contains *C2a*, while S_2 contains *C2b*. All five cores are Pareto-optimal for power and execution time, but S_2 is intuitively better for two reasons: First, S_2 provides the end user with ***graceful performance degradation*** (flexibility) in a power-constrained environment. If there is insufficient power to run on, e.g., *C3*, execution will be on *C2b* with a moderate speed reduction. In contrast, the gap between *C1* and *C2a* in S_1 is so large that if execution cannot take place on *C2a*, the user will experience a significant slowdown when execution moves to *C1*. Second, S_1 also has the opposite problem: the gap between *C2a* and *C3* is so small that the two cores are homogeneous for all practical purposes. There is no justification for the ***engineering effort*** required to design both, despite the fact that both are Pareto-optimal. In the following paragraphs, we first note the source of the data in figure 1. We then show that quantifying the intuitive difference between the two selections is non-trivial.

Data source We use gem5 [1] and McPAT [6] to simulate the *AES* encryption benchmark from EEMBC DENBench (digital entertainment benchmark) on 3000 out-of-order cores sampled from a large design space. The design space includes 19 microarchitectural parameters controlling L1 cache, queues, the branch predictor, etc. We find the Pareto frontier of cores that are optimal for power and execution time. From the 76 cores on the frontier, we make two selections of four cores each (figure 1).

Average waste metric As noted above, time is wasted when running on a lower-power core. We can quantify average wasted time, TW, with equation 1. N is the number of intervals between cores, ΔP_r is the difference between the highest- and lowest-power core in the set, ΔP_i is the difference between the highest- and lowest-power core in interval i, $\max(T_i)$ is execution time on the slowest core in interval i, and $\overline{T_i}$ is an estimate for average time in interval i. $\overline{T_i}$ is derived from all cores in the Pareto-optimal set.

$$TW = \sum_{i=1}^{N} \frac{\Delta P_i}{\Delta P_r} \left(\frac{\max(T_i) - \overline{T_i}}{\overline{T_i}} \right) \tag{1}$$

Even though differences between selection $\mathcal{S}_1$ and $\mathcal{S}_2$ are intuitively significant, their average wasted time differs by only 5% (table 1). This is because the large gap between *C1* and *C2a* is averaged away by the minuscule gap between *C2a* and *C3*—the two problems with $\mathcal{S}_1$ cancel each other out. We can conclude that a metric based on an average fails to capture worst-case behavior and cannot effectively differentiate between a good and bad selection of cores.

Worst-case waste metric An alternative approach would be to measure worst-case behavior—the selection that minimizes the maximum gap between cores is considered best. This approach introduces a masking problem: two selections could have very similar worst-case gaps between cores, with the rest of the cores distributed completely differently (not pictured). Any metric that uses a local feature of a selection to evaluate the entire selection will inevitably make erroneous comparisons.

3. A METRIC FOR CLUMPINESS

We propose the *clumpiness* metric for differentiating between selections of heterogeneous cores. Clumpiness measures the same intuitive concept as entropy-based diversity [3], but while diversity is difficult to normalize and depends on a user-selected density function, clumpiness is normalized and does not require tuning. Clumpiness is related to ϵ-coverage and δ-uniformity [7], and Δ-nonuniformity [2].

Clumpiness is represented with כ (*kaph*) and is defined in equation 2 for a 1-dimensional distribution. כ is calculated over the range $[r_1, r_2]$ for N number of ordered points x. The first term in the numerator of equation 2 measures the distance from the beginning of the range to the first point. The second term measures the distance from the last point to the end of the range. The third term measures the distance from each intermediate point to the halfway mark between its two neighboring points. כ ranges from 0 (even distribution) to 1 (one tight cluster of points).

$$\text{כ} = \frac{(x_1 - r_1) + (r_2 - x_N) + \sum_{i=2}^{N-1} d_i}{r_2 - r_1} \tag{2}$$

$$d_i = \left| x_i - \frac{x_{i-1} + x_{i+1}}{2} \right|$$

Clumpiness takes all points into account, but measures point density locally. Local features cannot be averaged away, but neither can they dominate the metric. Equation 2 can be readily extended to more dimensions, but since we are considering points that lie on a curve, a 1-dimensional version of כ is sufficient.

	Selection $\mathcal{S}_1$	Selection $\mathcal{S}_2$
Avg. Waste (TW)	24%	19%
Clumpiness (כ)	47%	22%

Table 1: Clumpiness more accurately quantifies the intuition that selection $\mathcal{S}_2$ is significantly better

To measure the clumpiness of selections $\mathcal{S}_1$ and $\mathcal{S}_2$, we flatten the points in 2-dimensional, normalized power-time space to one dimension using the Euclidean distance between points. E.g., for selection $\mathcal{S}_1$, *C1* is at the origin. *C2a* is at 2.45, as this is the Euclidean distance to *C1*. *C3* is at 2.51, since the Euclidean distance to *C2a* is only 0.06. r_1 and r_2 are set to the coordinates of *C1* and *C4*, respectively.

The כ-values for the two flattened selections are in table 1. Clumpiness expresses what is intuitively obvious—that selection $\mathcal{S}_1$ is much more clustered (more than 2×), and that selection $\mathcal{S}_2$ gives more even coverage of the space.

4. CONCLUSION

Considerable effort has been invested into methods of design spaces exploration for power- and speed-optimal cores. The problem of selecting cores from Pareto-optimal sets has seen much less attention. We have defined clumpiness (כ) to quantify the intuition that some selections of cores are better than others. Selections with a high כ-value waste engineering effort on nearly identical cores while also leaving large performance gaps between cores. A small כ, on the other hand, indicates that a set of cores maximizes runtime flexibility. Unlike related metrics, כ evaluates both the spread and uniformity of points without the need to be tuned to the specific problem. Clumpiness provides a simple way for evaluating future work on heterogeneous core selection.

5. REFERENCES

[1] N. Binkert et al. The gem5 simulator. *SIGARCH Computer Architure News*, 39(2), Aug 2011.

[2] K. Deb et al. A fast and elitist multiobjective genetic algorithm: NSGA-II. *IEEE Trans. on Evolutionary Computation*, 6(2), Apr 2002.

[3] A. Farhang-Mehr and S. Azarm. Diversity assessment of Pareto optimal solution sets: An entropy approach. In *CEC*, May 2002.

[4] P. Greenhalgh. Big.little processing with ARM Cortex-A15 & Cortex-A7. White paper, ARM Ltd., 2011.

[5] B. C. Lee and D. M. Brooks. Illustrative design space studies with microarchitectural regression models. In *HPCA*, 2007.

[6] S. Li et al. McPAT: An integrated power, area, and timing modeling framework for multicore and manycore architectures. In *MICRO*, 2009.

[7] S. Sayın. Measuring the quality of discrete representations of efficient sets in multiple objective mathematical programming. *Mathematical Programming*, 87(3), 2000.

[8] Y. Turakhia et al. HaDeS: Architectural synthesis for heterogeneous dark silicon chip multi-processors. In *DAC*, 2013.

SM-Centric Transformation: Circumventing Hardware Restrictions for Flexible GPU Scheduling

Bo Wu*, Guoyang Chen*, Dong Li+, Xipeng Shen*, Jeffrey S. Vetter+
*The College of William and Mary, Virginia, USA
+Oak Ridge National Laboratory, Tennessee, USA
*{bwu,gchen01,xshen}@cs.wm.edu, +{lid1,vetter}@ornl.gov

ABSTRACT

To circumvent the limitation from the hardware scheduler on GPU, we create an SM-centric transformation technique. This technique enables complete control of the mapping between tasks and streaming multi-processors (SMs), and enables controlling the number of active thread blocks on each SM. Results show that our approach achieves better speedup than previous ones with kernel co-run cases.

Categories and Subject Descriptors: D.3.4 [Programming Languages]: Processors—*optimization, compilers*

General Terms: Performance, Experimentation.

Keywords: GPGPU, Scheduling, Program Co-Run

1. INTRODUCTION

GPU's high throughput relies on its massive parallelism: A GPU application typically generates tens of thousands of threads with hundreds of them remaining active during any execution point. Scheduling, which determines when and where a task is processed, is critical for tapping into the full power of GPU. However, unlike scheduling on CPU which is controllable at software levels, GPU's scheduler is implemented in a hardware component. This situation makes GPU scheduling out of reach of compilers and runtime; also, the fact that how the hardware-based GPU scheduling mechanism works is undisclosed makes the situation even worse. As a result, some important optimizations based on scheduling are difficult to apply to GPU.

Persistent threads [2] is a technique to circumvent the limitation of hardware scheduler. Its central idea is to generate only a small number of thread blocks which remain active until all tasks have been processed. *Persistent threads* flexibly determines the total number of active thread blocks and the execution order of tasks. However, it has two limitations. The first limitation comes from the randomness in the hardware scheduler. Our experiments showed that the scheduling is not round-robin, contrary to common perception, and does not guarantee an even distribution of thread blocks, even if the number of thread blocks is small. Hence, *persistent threads* may underutilize hardware resource if some SMs obtain less thread blocks than others. Second, *persistent threads* has no support for deciding on which SM a task should run, which is important for some optimizations of locality enhancement.

This work proposes SM-centric transformation, a pure software technique to enable complete control of task scheduling on GPU. It solves the limitation of *persistent threads*. Its two key components, SM-centric task selection and a filling-retreating scheme, work hand in hand to allow flexible control of the number of active thread blocks on each SM and the mapping between tasks and SMs. It opens up new optimization opportunities.

2. SM-CENTRIC TRANSFORMATION

In this section, we first describe the idea of SM-centric task selection and its correctness problem induced by the hardware scheduler. Then, we explain how the filling-retreating scheme solves the problem and also enables flexible parallelism control on each SM.

2.1 SM-Centric Task Selection

The GPU threads are grouped into thread blocks (the workers), each processing a job. Usually, the programmer builds the mapping between jobs and workers, as shown in Figure 1 (a). Since the workers are arbitrarily scheduled to SMs, the mapping between jobs and SMs is also arbitrary. *Persistent threads*, as illustrated in Figure 1 (b), maintains a global job queue. The workers grab jobs from the queue once they are idle. As such, *persistent threads* can map jobs to workers. However, the thread block's placement on SM is controlled by hardware, so is the binding between tasks and SMs.

The SM-centric task selection breaks the binding between workers and jobs, but maps jobs to SMs instead. As shown in Figure 1 (c), before the kernel launches, a job queue is created for each SM. When a worker begins execution, it first checks the SM it runs on and processes the next job in the job queue associated with the host SM. Note that different from *persistent threads*, a worker only processes one job. Therefore, for this idea to work, the number of workers scheduled by an SM should be at least the same as the number of jobs in the associated job queue. This property, however, does not hold due to the randomness in the hardware scheduler, and create a program correctness problem.

2.2 Filling-Retreating Scheme

To solve the correctness problem of SM-centric task selection, we design a filling-retreating scheme, shown in Fig-

PACT'14, August 24–27, 2014, Edmonton, AB, Canada.
ACM 978-1-4503-2809-8/14/08.
http://dx.doi.org/10.1145/2628071.2628130.

```
kernel_org()
  jobID = f (workerID);
  processJob (jobID);
```

(a) original kernel

```
createJobQ4workers(); // on CPU

kernel_persist()
  while (jobID = JobQ[workerID].next() != null)
    processJob (jobID);
```

(b) with persistent thread

```
createJobQ4sms(); // on CPU

kernel_smc()
  smID = getSMID();
  jobID = JobQ[smID].next();
  if (jobID != null)
    processJob (jobID);
```

(c) with SM-centric task selection

Figure 1: Conceptual relations among jobs, workers, and SMs.

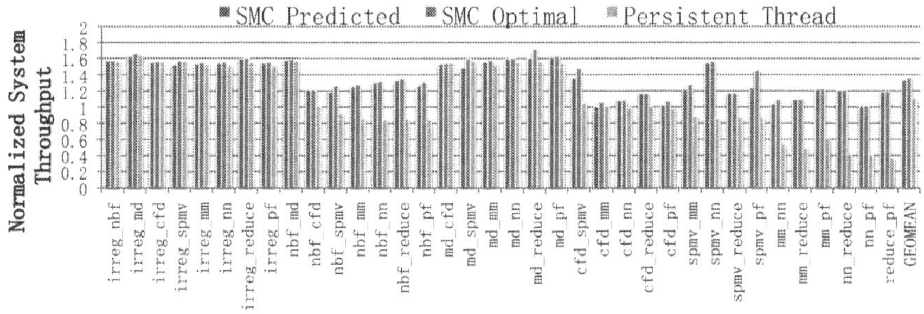

Figure 3: Improvement on system throughput.

```
createJobQ4sms(); // on CPU

kernel_smc()
  smID = getSMID();
  workers = workerCounters[smID]++; // atomic
  if (workers > wantedNumPerSM)
    return;
  while (jobID = JobQ[smID].next() != null)
    processJob (jobID);
```

Figure 2: Pseudo code of a GPU kernel in a *filling-retreating* scheme.

ure 2. The basic idea is to maintain a fixed number (usually small) of workers on each SM, which process all jobs in the corresponding queue. By analyzing and characterizing the GPU kernel at runtime, we determine the maximum number of active thread blocks on each SM, denoted as M. Given N SMs, we generate $M \times N$ workers. We found that the hardware scheduler always distributes all workers to SMs, as long as the hardware resources are enough to accommodate that many. This process is called *filling*. Afterwards, to control the number of active workers per SM (i.e., $wantedNumPerSM$, and $wantedNumPerSM < M$), the extra workers ($M - wantedNumPerSM$) exit immediately. This process is called *retreating*. Based on these two processes, we can control which jobs should be processed by which SM and how many workers per SM.

3. PRELIMINARY RESULTS

Previous studies [3] report that some GPU applications show sub-linear speedups with the increase of SMs. To more efficiently use hardware resource, SM partitioning [1] was evaluated in simulation to support kernel co-runs. But due to the hardware scheduler limitation, the partitioning has never been able to be evaluated on real hardware. SM-centric transformation, through precise control of the mapping between tasks and SMs, enables SM partitioning on real GPUs.

We evaluate SM-centric transformation with the cases of co-runs of two kernels on an NVIDIA Tesla M2075 GPU card. For each co-run case, we must decide the number of SMs allocated to each kernel and the number of active thread blocks on each SM. For this purpose, we design an online sampling and search algorithm to make the configuration decision based on a runtime performance model.

Figure 3 shows the performance results for the co-run of each pair of nine kernels. "SMC Predicted" and "SMC Optimal" represent performance improvement because of SM-centric transformation with the configurations predicted by the online model and with the best configuration through exhaustive offline search. We observe that *persistent threads* produces 11% performance improvement over the original kernels, but it slows down some co-runs (e.g., nn and pf) by as much as 60% because of the lack of enough parallelism. SM-centric transformation yields on average 37% performance gain, and hence is a much better choice.

4. CONCLUSIONS

We present SM-centric transformation, a method to map tasks to SMs and enable parallelism control on GPU. Our exploration on optimizing kernel co-runs show a lot of promises with this new optimization method.

Acknowledgment This material is based upon work supported by NSF Grants (1320796 and CAREER) and DOE Early Career Award.

5. REFERENCES

[1] J. T. Adriaens, K. Compton, N. S. Kim, and M. J. Schulte. The Case for GPGPU Spatial Multitasking. In *International Symposium on High Performance Computer Architecture*, 2012.

[2] K. Gupta, J. A. Stuart, and J. D. Owens. A study of persistent threads style gpu programming for gpgpu workloads. In *Innovative Parallel Computing*, 2012.

[3] S. Hong and H. Kim. An integrated gpu power and performance model. In *Proceedings of the 37th Annual International Symposium on Computer Architecture*, ISCA '10, 2010.

Author Index

www.ingramcontent.com/pod-product-compliance
Ingram Content Group UK Ltd.
Pitfield, Milton Keynes, MK11 3LW, UK
UKHW051415290926
15471UKWH00009B/1609

9 781450 332620